MOON

W9-DAY-908

VIRGINIA & MARYLAND

MICHAELA RIVA GAASERUD

Contents

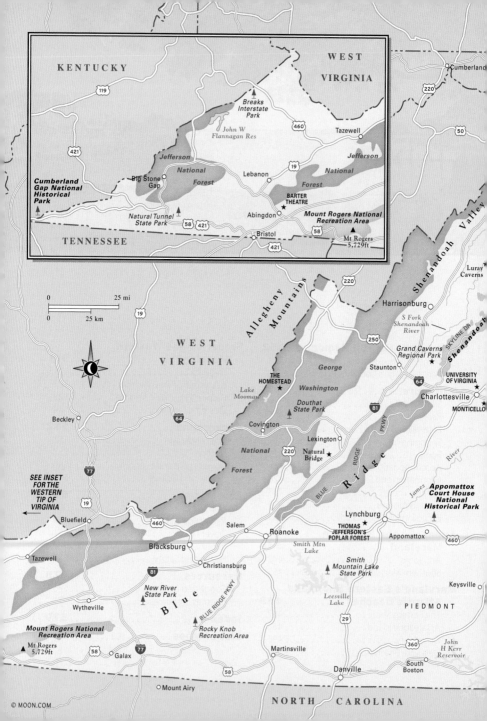

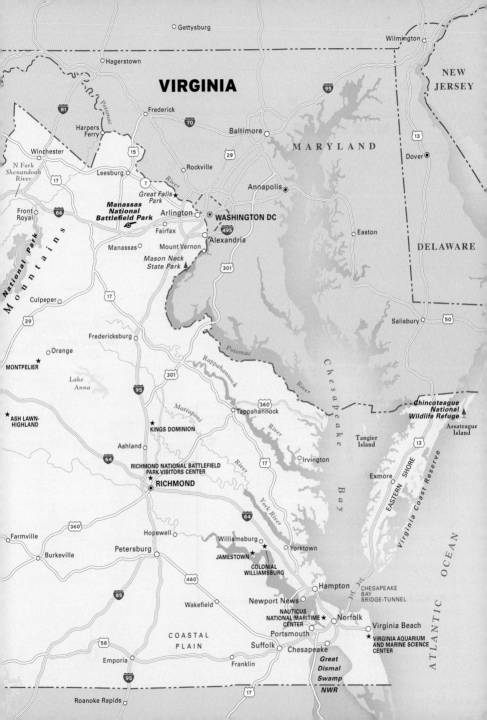

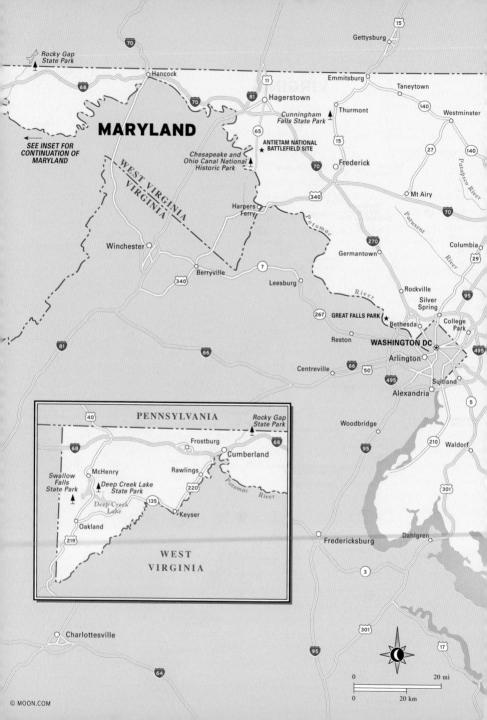

DISCOVER

Virginia & Maryland

In Virginia and Maryland, history comes alive. Follow in the footsteps of Thomas Jefferson at stately Monticello. Raise a glass at George Washington's favorite tavern in Colonial Williamsburg. Tread hallowed ground at Civil War battlefields such as Manassas and Antietam.

Alongside monuments, historic sites, and museums, Washington DC offers urban pursuits like fine dining and buzzing nightlife. And don't overlook Baltimore, which refracts big-city charms through its own quirky lens.

Not far from these thriving metropolitan areas you'll find sleepy mountain towns, quaint fishing villages, and an abundance of natural beauty. Wander through glowing fall foliage along the Blue Ridge Parkway. Summit the peak of Old Rag Mountain in Shenandoah National Park. Sail on the Chesapeake Bay before cracking a claw at a waterfront crab house in Annapolis. Stroll the bustling Ocean City Boardwalk. Relax on the quiet beaches of Assateague and Chincoteague Islands, where wild ponies roam free.

Welcome to Virginia and Maryland, where there's always something new to discover.

Clockwise from top left: wild pony on Assateague Island; downtown Annapolis; historic marker at Fell's Point; visitors on the grounds of the Virginia Museum of Fine Arts; Luray Caverns; Mather Gorge, Great Falls Park

11 TOP
EXPERIENCES

1 **Set Sail:** Home to the **U.S. Naval Academy,** the historic seaport of **Annapolis** boasts that it's the sailing capital of the world (page 445). It's a great place to take to the water yourself and explore the Chesapeake Bay (page 448).

2 **Take a Road Trip on Skyline Drive:** This stunning 105-mile route runs along the mountain ridges of **Shenandoah National Park** (page 242).

3 **Go Back in Time in Colonial Williamsburg:** Immerse yourself in colonial life at the largest living history museum in the world (page 176).

4 **Visit Presidential Homes:** Get unique insights into the lives of the founding fathers at George Washington's **Mount Vernon** (page 130) and Thomas Jefferson's **Monticello** (pictured, page 301).

5 **Tour Civil War Battlefields:** More major battles in the Civil War took place in Virginia than in any other state. Today, history buffs can walk in the footprints of the soldiers who fought there (page 26).

6 **Stroll Baltimore's Inner Harbor:** Spend the day—or several days—exploring the museums, shops, and restaurants along the waterfront promenade, with stops at the **National Aquarium** (pictured, page 391) and the unique collection of **historic ships** (page 393).

7 **Hit the Atlantic Beaches:** Explore the bustling boardwalk of **Ocean City** (page 491), the historic charm of **Lewes** (page 508), or find a happy medium in **Rehoboth Beach** (page 504).

<<<

8 **Retreat to Deep Creek Lake:** Countless recreation opportunities and abundant wildlife make the largest lake in Maryland a popular vacation spot (page 547).

>>>

9 **Feast on Crab:** No trip would be complete without sampling the local crustacean cuisine (page 29).

<<<

10 **Walk the National Mall:** The two-mile stretch from the **Lincoln Memorial** (pictured) to the **U.S. Capitol** has some of the country's most iconic monuments, including the **Washington Monument** and the **Vietnam Veterans Memorial** (page 42).

11 **Learn Something New at the Smithsonian:** Its museums and galleries – 11 on the National Mall and an additional 6 in the DC area – make it the largest museum in the world (page 46).

>>>

Planning Your Trip

Where to Go

Washington DC

Washington DC is nestled between Virginia and Maryland on the banks of the Potomac River. Best known for politics, government, and **monuments and museums,** the city is also home to universities, nightlife, art, theater, and sports. One of the largest (and cleanest) cities in the country, Washington DC offers trendy neighborhoods, **upscale shopping,** the **National Cathedral,** the **National Zoo,** and professional sports arenas. The nation's capital is easy to navigate, especially with the help of landmarks such as the **Washington Monument** and the **U.S. Capitol.**

Northern Virginia

From the busy halls of the **Pentagon** in **Arlington** and the trendy streets of historic **Old Town Alexandria** to the quaint alleyways of **Middleburg,** Northern Virginia is a cornucopia of culture, history, business, outdoor recreation, culinary delights, and shopping. It is a central corridor for the technology industry, yet houses key attractions such as **Mount Vernon,** the plantation home of **George Washington.** Northern Virginia's residents make up roughly one-third of the entire state population.

Coastal Virginia

Visiting Coastal Virginia is a great way to take a break from everyday stresses and learn about history or relax on the beach. **Colonial Williamsburg,** a living museum that vividly displays what life in colonial times was like, is one of the most popular historical attractions in the country. Just a short drive away are the resort area of **Virginia Beach** and the sleepy seaside communities on **Virginia's Eastern Shore.** The

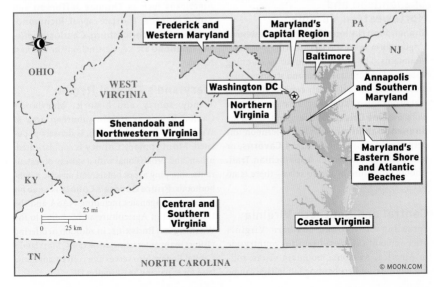

Dark Hollow Falls in Shenandoah National Park

region offers port towns, battleships, and beautiful, clean beaches all within a short drive of one another.

Shenandoah and Northwestern Virginia

Shenandoah National Park and Northwestern Virginia form a very special part of the Blue Ridge Mountains. The area is known for its stunning vistas, and picturesque rivers and streams crisscross the region and loosely connect the towns that sit on the park's doorstep. Take a scenic drive along **Skyline Drive,** white-water raft down the **Shenandoah River,** spend an afternoon underground in mysterious **Luray Caverns,** or take a hike on the famous **Appalachian Trail.** Choose adventure or opt to relax—there is no wrong answer.

Central and Southern Virginia

Sprawling Central and Southern Virginia offer some of the most beautiful countryside in America. Awesome mountain vistas, rolling foothills, and enchanting fall foliage can be found in this region, especially along the **Blue Ridge Parkway.** The site of many colleges and universities including the **University of Virginia,** the region was also home to famous Americans such as **Thomas Jefferson** and **James Monroe.** The state capital, **Richmond,** and historic **Fredericksburg, Charlottesville,** and **Roanoke** are key destinations in this vast region.

Maryland's Capital Region

Trendy, sporty, and historic, Maryland's Capital Region is a main suburban area of Washington DC and, as such, is densely populated. **Montgomery County** is sophisticated, urban, and professional with a variety of restaurants, shopping areas, hotels, and upscale neighborhoods. **Prince George's County** is a hub for government agencies including NASA and the Department of Agriculture and is home to the **Washington Redskins.** In addition to offering visitors many interesting attractions, Maryland's Capital Region also serves as a convenient home base for exploring Washington DC.

Baltimore

The city of Baltimore, once a rough industrial port, has undergone a series of urban renewal plans over the past few decades. As a result, it has blossomed into a major tourist destination that offers many **fascinating museums, entertainment venues,** professional sporting events such as the **Preakness Stakes,** and the famous **Inner Harbor.** Side trips include **Westminster,** which hosted both Union and Confederate troops during the Civil War, and lovely **Havre de Grace,** sitting at the head of the Chesapeake Bay.

Annapolis and Southern Maryland

The nation's sailing capital, **Annapolis,** is the top destination on the mainland banks of the Chesapeake Bay due to its waterfront location, charming historic district, and trendy boutiques and taverns. A busy recreational harbor, the city features an endless supply of blue crabs, oysters, and other delectable seafood. It is also home to the **U.S. Naval Academy.** Scenic Southern Maryland offers a slower, relaxed pace in its idyllic seaside towns such as **Solomons Island** and **Chesapeake Beach** and historic cities such as **St. Mary's City.**

Maryland's Eastern Shore and Atlantic Beaches

Picturesque fishing towns, blue crabs, and sunsets—these are all traits of Maryland's Eastern Shore. **Chestertown, St. Michaels,** and **Tilghman Island** offer alluring charm and a window into life along the Chesapeake Bay. Maryland's Atlantic beaches are a symphony of contrasts. **Assateague Island** calms your spirits as you share the beaches with wild ponies. **Ocean City** offers an exciting boardwalk and active nightlife. Three neighboring beach communities on the Delaware shore—**Bethany Beach, Rehoboth Beach,** and **Lewes**—are popular vacation spots.

Frederick and Western Maryland

Frederick offers old-town charm, antiques shopping, and terrific food. Some of the region's finest

kayaker at Fell's Point

Frederick County, Maryland

restaurants are tucked into the appealing historic downtown. Western Maryland is the "mountain side" of the state, where the railroad used to rule and the scenery is tranquil and pretty. **Deep Creek Lake,** with its 65 miles of shoreline, is a popular getaway spot for Washingtonians. Whether your idea of vacation is visiting **Civil War sites,** boating, or riding a steam engine through the mountains, you can find it all in Western Maryland.

When to Go

If you have the luxury of choosing your time to visit, **late spring** (May and June) and **fall** (September and October) are usually the **best times** to explore Virginia and Maryland. The weather is most pleasant, and there are fewer tourists to compete with. Although **summer** is the **prime tourist season,** unless your plans involve some beach time or a stay in a mountain retreat, the humidity can be a bit overwhelming.

The fall foliage in the region is some of the most spectacular in the country. A drive through the Blue Ridge Mountains in October can lead to some of the most stunning scenery in the East. If your focus is on historical sites and museums, the **winter** months (with the exception of the holiday season) can mean **short or no wait times** for popular attractions. Just be prepared for some sites to be closed or to have shorter hours.

The Best of Virginia and Maryland

Virginia and Maryland encompass a large amount of land. It can take six hours to drive from Washington DC to the southern end of Virginia and nearly four hours to drive from Western Maryland to the Eastern Shore. A 12-day trip provides the opportunity to hit most of the highlights of the region and get a good feel for both states.

Washington DC makes a good starting point for exploration of Virginia and Maryland. It is centrally located and convenient for air, train, bus, and car travel. Spend a couple of days at the beginning of your trip exploring this marvelous city.

Frederick and Western Maryland
DAY 1
From Washington DC, drive three hours northwest to the far reaches of Maryland to enjoy the mountain air at **Deep Creek Lake.** On your way, stop in **Frederick** for lunch in the historic downtown area. Overnight in one of the lovely cabins at **The Lodges at Sunset Village** at Deep Creek Lake.

DAY 2
Spend the day at **Deep Creek Lake State Park,** enjoying the outdoors. Swim, fish, or canoe on the beautiful lake or take a hike on one of the many trails on Meadow Mountain. Spend the night in another local inn or pitch a tent at the **Meadow Mountain Campground.**

Shenandoah and Northwestern Virginia
DAY 3
Drive 2.25 hours southeast into Virginia and have lunch in charming **Winchester** at the **Union**

Colonial Williamsburg

downtown Frederick

Jack Pub and Restaurant. Then spend a little time touring this lovely town and visit the **Museum of the Shenandoah Valley** before continuing 30 minutes south to **Front Royal,** the gateway to Shenandoah National Park. Visit a stunning subterranean world at **Skyline Caverns,** then spend the night in Front Royal.

DAY 4

Make this day all about **Shenandoah National Park.** Drive **Skyline Drive** and stop along the way to take in breathtaking vistas or to do a short hike. End your day by driving to Lexington and spending the night in this historic town.

Central Virginia

DAY 5

Spend the morning in **Lexington** seeing the sights. Take a carriage tour or visit the **Virginia Military Institute** and the **George C. Marshall Museum.** Then make the scenic one-hour drive east to **Charlottesville** and visit a vineyard before treating yourself to a night at either the **The Clifton** or **Keswick Hall.**

DAY 6

Visit Thomas Jefferson's **Monticello** in the morning and then have lunch on the hip downtown mall in Charlottesville. After lunch, drive southeast about an hour to the state capital of **Richmond.** Orient yourself in this busy city and, if time allows, take in the **Science Museum of Virginia.** Overnight in Richmond. For a splurge, spend the night in the historic **Jefferson Hotel.**

Coastal Virginia

DAY 7

Visit **Capitol Square** in Richmond before heading southeast for a one-hour drive to **Colonial Williamsburg.** Dine in **Merchants Square** and spend the night in one of several hotels run by the **Colonial Williamsburg Foundation.**

DAY 8

Lose yourself in U.S. history by dedicating the day to exploring Colonial Williamsburg. Visit the **museums,** shop in the authentic **colonial shops,** grab a sweet potato muffin at the **Raleigh Tavern Bakery,** talk to the costumed interpreters, and drink and dine in the local **taverns.** Spend another night in Williamsburg.

DAY 9

Make the 1.25-hour drive to **Virginia Beach** early so you can enjoy a day on the Atlantic. Visit the **Virginia Aquarium & Marine Science Center** and walk the famous boardwalk. Enjoy fresh seafood at one of the local restaurants and spend the night in a hotel right on the ocean.

Maryland's Eastern Shore and Atlantic Beaches

DAY 10

Drive northeast three hours through the famous **Chesapeake Bay Bridge-Tunnel** and continue up the scenic Eastern Shore to **Ocean City.** Soak in the activity on the busy boardwalk and be sure to eat some **Thrasher's French Fries.** Spend the rest of your day at the beach.

DAY 11

Drive two hours northwest to the charming Eastern Shore town of **St. Michaels.** The sharp contrast to Ocean City will be readily noticeable as you stroll through the historic downtown area full of restaurants and boutiques or perhaps take a cruise from the waterfront. Spend the night in St. Michaels in one of the waterfront inns.

Annapolis

DAY 12

On your last day, drive about an hour northwest over the **Chesapeake Bay Bridge** to Maryland's capital city, **Annapolis.** This beautiful and historic waterfront city on the Chesapeake Bay is the perfect place to end your trip. Visit the **Annapolis City Dock,** the **U.S. Naval Academy,** and the **Maryland State House.** Be sure to dine on local blue crabs if you're a seafood lover.

The Mariners' Museum in Newport News

Best Scenic Drives

Skyline Drive

FALL FOLIAGE
Skyline Drive (page 242)
Starting point: Front Royal, VA
Ending point: Waynesboro, VA
105 miles; 3 hours

Virginia is known for having one of the most spectacular leaf displays in the country, and Skyline Drive in Shenandoah National Park showcases the best of the best.

Blue Ridge Parkway (page 311)
Starting point: Waynesboro, VA
Ending point: Cherokee, NC
469 miles total, 217 in Virginia; 6 hours in Virginia

The Blue Ridge Parkway begins where Skyline Drive ends. The most scenic portion is the 114 miles between Waynesboro and Roanoke.

HISTORICAL ROOTS
Antietam Campaign Scenic Byway (page 534)
Starting point: White's Ferry, MD
Ending point: Sharpsburg, MD
126 miles; 4 hours

This route begins where Robert E. Lee and his army crossed the Potomac River into Maryland and ends at Antietam National Battlefield, where Lee's forces retreated back into West Virginia.

Colonial Parkway (page 175)
Starting point: Yorktown, VA
Ending point: Jamestown, VA
23 miles; 35 minutes

This parkway was designed to unify the "Historic Triangle" of Williamsburg, Jamestown, and Yorktown, while preserving the area's scenery and wildlife.

SALTY AIR
Chesapeake Bay Bridge-Tunnel (page 219)
Starting point: South Hampton Roads, VA
Ending point: Eastern Shore, VA
20 miles; 30 minutes

This engineering masterpiece, which spans the mouth of the Chesapeake Bay, takes vehicles over a series of bridges and through two-mile-long tunnels.

MOUNTAIN TOWNS
Virginia's Western Highlands (page 264)
Starting point: Monterey, VA
Ending point: Covington, VA
55 miles; 1.25 hours

Take scenic Route 220 through iconic mountain towns such as Warm Springs and Hot Springs, where the famed Omni Homestead Resort is located.

Battles and Brews

Virginia and Maryland have a colorful history. More Civil War battles were fought in Virginia than in any other state, but the region is also known for its Revolutionary War past, colonial history, and, of course, the development of our nation's government and capital. This six-day itinerary starts in Yorktown, Virginia, and ends in Gettysburg, Pennsylvania. The 400-mile trip covers some of the most significant historical cities in the region and includes refreshing stops in some of the best local pubs.

Day 1

Start in Yorktown, Virginia, and take in the **Yorktown Battlefield,** where the last major battle of the Revolutionary War was fought. The battlefield is part of the **Colonial National Historical Park.** Stop in the **Yorktown Pub** for a beer, oysters, and hush puppies. Spend the night in Yorktown at the **Hornsby House Inn.**

Day 2

Drive two hours north to Fredericksburg and spend the day touring the **Fredericksburg & Spotsylvania National Military Park.** Spend a relaxing evening at the **Kenmore Inn** and have a drink in its historic pub.

Day 3

Drive one hour north to **Manassas National Battlefield Park** and explore the site of two major Civil War battles. Continue on to the old town area of Manassas and have a beer and a cheesesteak at the **Philadelphia Tavern.** Spend the night in Manassas.

Day 4

Drive 1.5 hours southwest to the **New Market Battlefield,** where Union troops were forced out of the Shenandoah Valley. Then head to scenic Luray for dinner and delightful beverages at

Yorktown Victory Monument in Colonial National Historical Park

Civil War Battlefields

historic Chatham Manor, part of Fredericksburg & Spotsylvania National Military Park

Virginia hosted more major Civil War battles than any other state and more than 2,000 "military events" during the war. This was due in part to the relocation of the Confederate Capital near the beginning of the war from Montgomery, Alabama, to Richmond. As such, only a mere 150 miles separated Washington DC and Richmond, and Virginia often found itself in the center of conflict. By the time General Lee surrendered in 1865, a large portion of Virginia had been scarred or destroyed by war.

Many of the battlefields in Virginia are now protected as national historical sites and parks, and visitors from across the nation come to pay tribute, participate in battle reenactments, and see firsthand the land that played such an important role in shaping our country's history. Many beautiful and haunting monuments, statues, and exhibits now stand on these hallowed grounds to help both interpret the history of each battle and to serve as reminders of the many young lives lost there. Key Civil War battlefields in Virginia include:

- **Fredericksburg & Spotsylvania National Military Park (1862-1862):** the second-largest military park in the world and the site of four Civil War battles (page 271)

- **Manassas National Battlefield Park (July 21, 1861 and August 28-30, 1862):** the site of the First Battle of Bull Run, the first major land battle in the war, and the Second Battle of Bull Run, the biggest simultaneous mass assault of the Civil War (page 142)

- **Petersburg National Battlefield (June 1864-April 1865):** the site of the longest single Civil War military event, lasting more than nine months and producing 70,000 casualties (page 296)

- **Richmond National Battlefield Park (1861-1865):** a collection of 12 individual sites that preserve more than 1,900 acres of Civil War history (page 285)

- **New Market Battlefield State Historical Park (May 15, 1864):** the site of the only occasion in American history when college cadets were responsible for victory in combat, forcing Union troops out of the Shenandoah Valley (page 254)

Moonshadows Restaurant. Spend the night in Luray.

Day 5

Drive 1.75 hours north to **Antietam National Battlefield** in Sharpsburg, Maryland, to visit the site of the bloodiest single-day battle during the Civil War. Continue on to historic Frederick and stop in **Flying Dog Brewery** for a tour and tasting. Spend the night in Frederick.

Day 6

Drive 45 minutes north to downtown Gettysburg, Pennsylvania, where the famous **Battle of Gettysburg** spilled onto the streets, and then tour the **Gettysburg National Military Park.** End your day at **Garryowen Irish Pub** for some Guinness and a Reuben sandwich. Spend the night in Gettysburg.

If You're Looking For...

Virginia and Maryland offer more than history, culture, and a beautiful landscape. There are outdoor activities galore for the active traveler. You could spend a lifetime here and still not experience all the recreation available in the region, but the following are a good start.

Hiking

- Hike some of the legendary **Appalachian Trail** in **Harpers Ferry.**
- Challenge yourself on the famous **Old Rag Mountain** hike in **Shenandoah National Park.**
- Hike through beautiful **Swallow Falls State Park** and past **Muddy Creek Falls,** the highest waterfall in Maryland.
- Hikers of all abilities can enjoy the popular **Billy Goat Trail** between the historic **C&O Canal** and the **Potomac River** in **Montgomery County.**

Biking

- Bike to historic **Harpers Ferry** on the **C&O Canal Towpath.**
- Cycle five miles of gravel trails through scenic **Great Falls Park.**
- Mountain bike part of the **Cross County Trail** system in **Wakefield Park.**

Sailing Cruises

- Take a two-hour sailing cruise on a stunning wooden schooner in **Annapolis.**
- Climb aboard the schooner *Sultana,* a British Royal Navy Ship replica in **Chestertown Harbor.**
- Take a romantic sunset sail on the schooner *Alliance* or a pirate cruise on its sister *Serenity* in historic **Yorktown.**

Rafting

- Take a guided rafting trip on the **Shenandoah River** or **Potomac River** near Harpers Ferry.
- Enjoy a family rafting adventure with **Wisp Resort** near **Deep Creek Lake.**

Kayaking

- Experienced white-water kayakers can take on the highly challenging **Potomac River** near Great Falls, while calmer waters can be found downstream at **Mason Neck State Park.**
- Two regional lakes, **Triadelphia Reservoir** and **Rocky Gorge Reservoir,** offer wonderful kayaking in **Montgomery County.**
- Paddle with bottlenose dolphins with **Chesapean Outdoors** at the north end of **Virginia Beach.**

Seven Days on the Eastern Shore

Virginia and Maryland share a rare commodity in the Eastern Shore. This coastal area is a 180-mile-long peninsula that sits east of the Chesapeake Bay and west of the Atlantic Ocean. It is sparsely populated in both states and contains one-third of Maryland's land area but only 8 percent of its population. A trip to the Eastern Shore is like stepping back in time. Historic towns, charming fishing villages, vast natural areas, and abundant seafood make this a prime recreation destination.

Day 1

Begin your trip in the northern part of the region in **Chestertown,** Maryland. This historic colonial waterfront town sits on the banks of the Chester River and is a wonderful place to stroll, eat, and just relax. You can also take an educational course on the schooner *Sultana.* Stay the night in a local inn.

Day 2

Drive south for an hour to the charming waterfront town of **St. Michaels** in Maryland. This is one of the loveliest spots on the Eastern Shore and where many Washingtonians have second homes. The town has fine restaurants, shopping, a good museum, and a lot of character. Spend the night in St. Michaels in one of the fine inns or a local bed-and-breakfast.

Day 3

Step back in time by taking a ferry from Crisfield, Maryland, to **Tangier Island** in Virginia. Crisfield is a two-hour drive south of St. Michaels, and the ferry is a 1.25-hour ride. The isolated island sits in the middle of the Chesapeake Bay and is rapidly sinking into the bay (it should hang on while you visit). There are almost no cars on the island, but you can rent a golf cart. The people

biking in Loudoun County

Best Places to Eat Crab

Tim's Rivershore Restaurant & Crabhouse

The slogan *"Maryland Is for Crabs"* is meant to be taken literally. The blue crab is the designated Maryland state crustacean, and people in this region know how and where to crack a claw.

VIRGINIA

- **Tim's Rivershore Restaurant & Crabhouse** (page 145) in Dumfries offers a beachy atmosphere and waterfront dining on the Potomac River. This supercasual crab house is a party spot in the summer with live music and a boating crowd.

- **The Crazy Crab Restaurant** (page 174) in the Reedville Marina is a small, family-owned restaurant on the waterfront. The seafood can't get any fresher, as you can literally see the owner walk outside and harvest it.

- The **Crab Shack** (page 200) sits on the James River in Newport News and has great views throughout its window-lined dining room and deck. It offers fresh seafood and a casual atmosphere.

- The folks at **AW Shucks Raw Bar & Grill** (page 209) in Norfolk believe that any meal can include seafood. They are famous for burgers topped with lump crab, and the portions are huge.

- **Four Brothers Crab House & Ice Cream Deck** (page 226) is out on Tangier Island, the "Soft Crab Capital of the World." A trip to this isolated island in the middle of the Chesapeake Bay requires a 12-mile ferry ride.

MARYLAND

- The original Crab Bomb, with 10 ounces of jumbo lump crabmeat, can be found at **Jerry's Seafood** (page 381) in Bowie.

- Quarter-pound crab cakes with no filler, seasoned to perfection, are the calling card of a local Annapolis favorite called **Chick & Ruth's Delly** (page 451). Just a block from the State House, this sandwich shop opened in 1965 under owners Chick and Ruth Levitt, and it has been growing ever since.

- A traditional crab house with huge notoriety in the Annapolis area is **Cantler's Riverside Inn** (page 452). It is situated on a cove right on the water and sells local steamed crabs by the dozen (in all sizes).

- **Buddy's Crabs and Ribs** (page 452) is a lively icon on Main Street in Annapolis. Steamed crab is the entrée of choice at Buddy's, but the homemade crab cakes are also famous.

- For more suggestions on where to crack a claw in Maryland, see page 452.

are friendly, the seafood is fantastic, and there is a nice quiet beach that will make you feel miles away from civilization (which you actually are). If you don't mind the solitude, stay the night on the island, or else head back to the Eastern Shore the same day on the ferry.

Day 4

Continue south from Crisfield (1.25 hours) to the charming village of **Onancock,** Virginia. Rent a kayak, have lunch, and take a leisure day exploring the town. Spend the night in Onancock.

Day 5

Drive about an hour northeast to the Atlantic side of the Eastern Shore to **Chincoteague Island** in Virginia. Explore the **Chincoteague National Wildlife Refuge** and look for signs of the wild ponies that live there. Take a short hike to the **Assateague Island Lighthouse,** and spend the night on the island.

Day 6

Leave the calm of nature behind and drive 1.25 hours north to bustling **Ocean City,** Maryland. This beach town is crazy-busy in the summer and offers a wide, active boardwalk, nightlife, and many amusements. Eat some french fries on the boardwalk, ride a Ferris wheel, and then rent a beach umbrella for some downtime on the sand.

Day 7

End your trip with a drive one hour north to the harborfront community of **Lewes,** Delaware. Enjoy a sightseeing cruise from the harbor, spend the afternoon at **Cape Henlopen State Park,** or stroll the enchanting streets of the historic town.

World War II observation tower at Cape Henlopen State Park

History Comes Alive

musicians at the Maryland Renaissance Festival

Virginia and Maryland offer several unique opportunities to become part of history.

VIRGINIA

- **Colonial Williamsburg** (page 176) in Williamsburg, Virginia, is the largest living-history museum in the country at 301 acres. It revives a real colonial American city and draws visitors into the action as part of the town. Costumed interpreters work and dress as those from colonial times did and provide genuine goods and services to tourists. Visitors can sleep in restored inns, dine in authentic taverns, and have conversations with actors portraying 18th-century Americans.

- A few miles from Williamsburg is another living-history museum called the **Jamestown Settlement** (page 186). This museum features a Powhatan Village, a settlers' fortress, and the ships the town's inhabitants arrived on. The interpretive guides are very well informed, interesting, and good-humored.

MARYLAND

- Civil War buffs will enjoy the many annual battle reenactments that take place throughout the region. One of the most popular is the **Gettysburg National Civil War Battle Reenactment** (page 527) that is held each July. It includes three exciting battles, field demonstrations, live mortar fire demonstrations, living-history programs, and all-day activities.

- Visitors can step even further back in time and completely away from U.S. history by attending the **Maryland Renaissance Festival** (page 449) near Annapolis. This outstanding annual event spans 19 weekend days in August, September, and October and draws thousands of costumed and plainclothes patrons. Step through the front gate into a 16th-century English village and instantly become part of the show.

Washington DC

Awe-inspiring Washington DC, nestled between
Virginia and Maryland on the banks of the Potomac River, is best known for government, politics, and museums. Stunning marble monuments dominate the landscape and are a constant reminder of our country's powerful beginnings, while stately government buildings act as the working engine guiding our nation.

One of the largest cities in the nation, Washington is also home to several universities, trendy neighborhoods, professional sports arenas, and attractions such as the National Zoo. The city boasts tremendous nightlife, art, theater, and upscale shopping. On average, around 21 million visitors come to DC annually.

Although much of the city is historic and upscale, there are also parts

Highlights

Look for ★ to find recommended sights, activities, dining, and lodging.

★ **Washington Monument:** This 555-foot-tall monument is a tribute to America's first president and a focal point of the National Mall (page 42).

★ **Lincoln Memorial:** This stunning Doric-style monument sitting on the banks of the Potomac River is a grand memorial to President Abraham Lincoln (page 42).

★ **Vietnam Veterans Memorial:** This moving memorial honors those who fought and died or went missing in action during the Vietnam War (page 43).

★ **National Museum of African American History and Culture:** The only national museum dedicated to African American history and culture, this popular museum is the 19th and most recent Smithsonian Institution Museum (page 46).

★ **National Museum of Natural History:** The most visited natural history museum in the world, this treasure features more than 126 million specimens in 325,000 square feet of exhibit space (page 47).

★ **National Air and Space Museum:** It features the largest collection of air- and space-craft in the world (page 49).

★ **White House:** Tour the home and work-place of the president of the United States (page 50).

★ **Jefferson Memorial:** Sitting on the shore of the famous Tidal Basin is this stunning

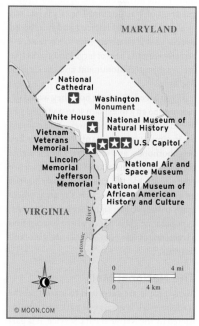

memorial to the author of the Declaration of Independence (page 51).

★ **U.S. Capitol:** The grand neoclassical-style Capitol Building is the official meeting site for the U.S. Congress (page 55).

★ **National Cathedral:** This massive Gothic cathedral in Upper Northwest DC is the sixth-largest cathedral in the world (page 66).

of Washington DC that are impoverished, comprising mostly minority demographics. Many of these residents face homelessness and unemployment. These areas exist side by side with the affluent and wealthy. In a strange way, Washington DC does truly represent the country, even if its residents don't have voting representation in Congress.

ORIENTATION

The city is divided into four quadrants, with the U.S. Capitol sitting in all four. The Capitol Building, however, doesn't sit in the center of the city, which means that the quadrants are not equal in terms of square mileage. The majority of the city and the lion's share of the attractions are in the northwest quadrant of Washington. The city is laid out in a grid pattern of lettered and numbered streets, so it is relatively easy to navigate, especially with the help of large landmarks like the Washington Monument and the Capitol Building.

If you asked 10 people how they would divide up the city to explain it to a visitor, you would get 10 different answers. Some would do it simply by quadrants, others by key neighborhoods, and still others by the sights themselves. For the sake of this guide, we are going to divide the city by popular tourist areas so that we can include key areas where many of the popular sights are located, as well as popular neighborhoods where you can find a tremendous selection of food, nightlife, and festivals.

The National Mall

Many people are surprised to learn that the National Mall is a national park and administered by the National Park Service. It is part of an area known as the National Mall and Memorial Parks unit. The exact boundaries of the mall have always been difficult to define, but according to the National Park Service, it is "the area encompassed by Constitution and Pennsylvania Avenues NW on the north, 1st Street on the east, Independence and Maryland Avenues on the south, and 14th Street on the west." It may be easier to visualize by saying that the Mall is basically the entire three-mile stretch between the Lincoln Memorial at the west end and the U.S. Capitol at the east end. The Washington Monument is a focal point of the Mall and sits just to the west of its center. Often, many areas just outside the Mall's official boundaries are still considered to be "on the Mall."

A plan for the National Mall originally designed in 1791 by Pierre L'Enfant laid out a "Grand Avenue," but it was never carried out. The Mall served several other purposes prior to reaching its current state. During the Civil War, the land was utilized primarily for military purposes—drilling troops, the production of arms, and even slaughtering cattle. Permission was even given to the railroad in the late 1800s to lay tracks across part of the Mall.

The National Mall is the primary tourist area in Washington DC, and visitors should plan on spending a significant amount of time here. Simply put, it is packed with monuments and lined with museums. (Some are even underground.) The Department of Agriculture is also on the Mall. When you set out to explore, wear comfortable walking shoes and be sure your camera is charged.

Capitol Hill

Capitol Hill is the political center of the country. It is home to the U.S. Congress and also the largest historical residential neighborhood in the city. Geographically, Capitol Hill is literally a hill that rises as you approach the Capitol from the west. The U.S. Capitol is on the crest of the hill.

Capitol Hill sits in both the southeast and northeast quadrants of the city. To the north is the H Street Corridor, to the south is the Washington Navy Yard, to the east is

---

Previous: the tidal basin near the Jefferson Memorial; Vietnam War Memorial; the White House

Washington DC

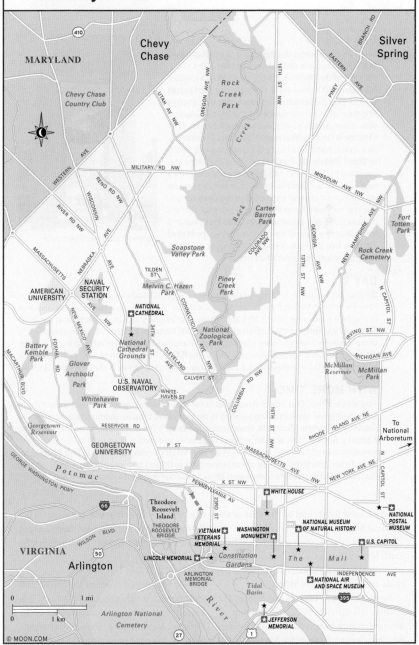

MARYLAND

Chevy Chase

Silver Spring

410

BRANCH RD

EASTERN AVE

PINEY

Chevy Chase Country Club

Rock Creek Park

16TH ST NW

UTAH AVE NW

OREGON AVE NW

Creek

MILITARY RD NW

MISSOURI AVE NW

WESTERN AVE

RENO RD NW

RIVER RD NW

WISCONSIN AVE

NEBRASKA AVE

Rock

Carter Barron Park

COLORADO AVE NW

GEORGIA AVE NW

NEW HAMPSHIRE AVE

Fort Totten Park

MASSACHUSETTS

Soapstone Valley Park

Rock Creek Cemetery

N CAPITOL ST

AMERICAN UNIVERSITY

NAVAL SECURITY STATION

TILDEN ST

Melvin C. Hazen Park

Piney Creek Park

13TH ST NW

NEW MEXICO AVE NW

NATIONAL CATHEDRAL

34TH ST

CONNECTICUT AVE NW

IRVING ST NW

MACARTHUR BLVD

FOXHALL RD

National Cathedral Grounds

CLEVELAND AVE

National Zoological Park

MICHIGAN AVE

Battery Kemble Park

Glover Archbold Park

U.S. NAVAL OBSERVATORY

CALVERT ST

McMillan Reservoir

McMillan Park

Whitehaven Park

WHITE-HAVEN ST

COLUMBIA RD NW

16TH ST NW

Georgetown Reservoir

RESERVOIR RD

GEORGETOWN UNIVERSITY

P ST

RHODE ISLAND AVE NE

N CAPITOL ST

To National Arboretum

Potomac

MASSACHUSETTS AVE NW

NEW YORK AVE NE

GEORGE WASHINGTON PKWY

K ST NW

PENNSYLVANIA AV

WHITE HOUSE

66

Theodore Roosevelt Island

23RD ST

NATIONAL MUSEUM OF NATURAL HISTORY

NATIONAL POSTAL MUSEUM

THEODORE ROOSEVELT BRIDGE

VIETNAM VETERANS MEMORIAL

WASHINGTON MONUMENT

U.S. CAPITOL

VIRGINIA

WILSON BLVD

LINCOLN MEMORIAL

Constitution Gardens

The Mall

Arlington

50

ARLINGTON MEMORIAL BRIDGE

INDEPENDENCE AVE

NATIONAL AIR AND SPACE MUSEUM

395

Tidal Basin

0   1 mi

0   1 km

River

JEFFERSON MEMORIAL

Arlington National Cemetery

27

1

© MOON.COM

DAY 1

Begin your trip with a day dedicated to the **National Mall.** Put on your walking shoes and start with a bird's-eye view of the city from the top of the **Washington Monument,** then walk through the **National World War II Memorial** on your way to the **Lincoln Memorial.** Choose several of the many beautiful **war memorials** to visit, such as the **Korean War Memorial** and the **Vietnam Veterans Memorial.** Pick up lunch at a local food truck and find a nice bench in **West Potomac Park** to rest your feet. Ride Metrorail up to Capitol Hill and spend the afternoon on a tour of the **U.S. Capitol.** When your feet can take no more, catch a cab or car service to Dupont Circle for dinner, and then walk east on M Street to enjoy some of the city's nightlife at the rooftop bar at **Ozio Restaurant and Lounge.** Spend the night in the nearby **Hotel Tabard Inn** or, if you feel like splurging, at the **Hay-Adams,** overlooking the White House.

National World War II Memorial

DAY 2

On your second day in DC, plan to visit some of the **Smithsonian Institution** museums. After breakfast at the inn, if you're feeling spry, walk the 10 or so blocks down to the National Mall or else take a cab or car service. Pick and choose your favorites such as the **National Air and Space Museum** and the **National Museum of Natural History.** Grab lunch inside one of the museums when you need a break, or sample another one of DC's great food trucks outside. When you've overloaded on museums, walk to the **P.O.V. Roof Terrace and Lounge** at the W Washington D.C. Hotel and have a cocktail, then go for a late dinner at the **Old Ebbitt Grill.**

WITH MORE TIME

Take Metrorail into **Old Town Alexandria** for a day in one of the country's oldest port cities. Stroll the historic streets to window-shop in the many **boutiques** and then take a tour of the **Gadsby's Tavern Museum.** Have lunch at **Gadsby's Tavern** and then visit the **Torpedo Factory Art Center,** with three floors of galleries and studios. If you still have energy, take a walking tour of Old Town and then get off your feet for a relaxing dinner at **The Majestic.** After dinner, take Metrorail, cab, or car service back to DC and take a **nighttime tour of the National Mall** to see the monuments lit up. Spend one last night in the nation's capital.

the Anacostia River, and to the west is the National Mall.

Many politicians, their staff, journalists, and lobbyists live on Capitol Hill. Residential streets are lined with homes from different periods, many of which are historic.

Pennsylvania Avenue is the hub of the commercial district on Capitol Hill and offers restaurants, bars, and shops. The oldest continually running fresh-food market in the

city, called **Eastern Market,** is just east of the Capitol Building. This popular shopping spot is housed in a 19th-century brick building.

District Wharf

The District Wharf is one of the newest and most popular neighborhoods in the city. It is a trendy, mile-long area located south of the National Mall on the Potomac River waterfront. At the time of writing, the first phase

The Capitol Architect: Pierre L'Enfant

Washington DC owes a great portion of its inspiring design to Pierre Charles L'Enfant (1754-1825), a French-born American architect and civil engineer. L'Enfant came to America to fight in the Revolutionary War and later became George Washington's number one city planner. L'Enfant designed Washington DC from scratch. He dreamed up a city that was to rise out of a mix of hills, forests, marshes, and plantation land into an extravagant capital city with wide avenues, beautiful buildings, and public squares.

L'Enfant's city included a grand "public walk," which is seen today in the National Mall. His city plan was based on European models, but incorporated American ideals. The design was created from the idea that every citizen is equally important. This is shown in the Mall design, since it is open in all corners.

of the wharf was completed and the neighborhood was already fully established and thriving with dining, shopping, residential and commercial real estate, live music venues, and many events and festivals. Parking can be tricky in this area, with just a few parking garages.

Downtown

"Downtown" may sound a bit broad, but the term actually refers to the central business district in Northwest Washington DC. Geographically, the area is difficult to clearly define, but it is generally accepted as being bordered by P Street NW to the north, Constitution Avenue NW to the south, 4th Street NW to the east, and 15th Street NW to the west.

Some notable areas included in the downtown district are the **K Street Corridor,** which used to be known as the Power Lobbying Corridor and still houses many law firms and businesses (although most of the lobbying firms have relocated to other parts of the city); **Federal Triangle** (bordered by 15th Street NW, Constitution Avenue NW, Pennsylvania Avenue NW, and E Street NW), a triangular area that is home to 10 large federal and city buildings; and **Judiciary Square** (bounded by H Street NW to the north, Pennsylvania Avenue to the south, the I-395 access tunnel to the east, and 6th Street NW to the west), a small neighborhood housing federal and municipal courthouses and offices.

The area also includes the **Penn Quarter** neighborhood, which extends roughly between F and H Streets NW and between 5th and 10th Streets. The name "Penn Quarter" is relatively new. This once sketchy area had new life breathed into it with the opening of the **Capital One Arena** (7th and F Streets) in 1997, which was originally called the MCI Center (and later the Verizon Center) and is home to the **Washington Capitals** professional hockey team and the **Washington Wizards** and **Washington Mystics** professional basketball teams. Now the area is a bustling arts and entertainment district with galleries, museums, restaurants, hotels, and shopping.

At its northern boundaries, Penn Quarter overlaps with the small historic neighborhood of **Chinatown.** Chinatown runs along H and I Streets NW between 5th and 8th Streets NW. It has roughly 20 authentic Asian restaurants and small businesses and is known for its annual Chinese New Year celebration as well as its signature Friendship Arch built over H Street at 7th Street.

Dupont Circle

Dupont Circle is a historic district in Northwest Washington DC. It is technically also the traffic circle at the intersection of Massachusetts Avenue NW, Connecticut Avenue NW, New Hampshire Avenue NW, P Street NW, and 19th Street NW, as well as a park and a neighborhood.

Choosing the Location of the Nation's Capital

Prior to 1800, the newly formed Congress met in several locations in the mid-Atlantic region. Where to establish the permanent federal government became a highly contested topic that went unresolved for many years. Finally, on July 16, 1790, President George Washington was officially put in charge of selecting a location for the permanent capital and appointing three commissioners to oversee its birth. Washington chose a 10-square-mile piece of land from property in both Virginia and Maryland sitting on both sides of the Potomac River.

The old myth is that DC was built on a swamp. This isn't exactly true. The area was a tidal plain but encompassed tobacco fields, cornfields, woods, waterside bluffs, and wetlands along the river. Washington DC is rich with waterways (the Potomac River, Anacostia River, Rock Creek, and others), but most of the land designated for the city was not marshy.

Congress met in the new location for the first time on November 17, 1800, and the move was completed in 1801. In 1846, land that formerly belonged to Virginia (on what is now the Virginia side of the Potomac River) was returned to Virginia. It is said that George Washington never felt comfortable calling the capital Washington, so instead he referred to it as "The Federal City."

The neighborhood of Dupont Circle lies roughly between Florida Avenue NW to the north, M Street NW to the south, 16th Street NW to the east, and 22nd Street NW to the west.

Dupont Circle is often considered the center of Washington DC's nightlife. It is home to many people in their 20s and also a popular neighborhood among the gay and lesbian community. There are many multilevel apartment buildings and row houses that have been split into apartments here.

Northwest of Dupont Circle along Massachusetts Avenue is an area of the city where many foreign embassies are located. This is commonly referred to as **Embassy Row.** Although less than half of the more than 175 embassies in DC are in this area, it has one of the largest concentrations (most are between Scott Circle and Wisconsin Avenue). Many of the embassies were formerly the homes of wealthy families who made their fortunes from the railroad, mining, banking and publishing industries and even politics in the late 1800s. You'll recognize the embassies by the country flags flying out front.

Georgetown

Georgetown has long been known as a trendy yet historic neighborhood with excellent shopping, food, and nightlife. It sits on the Potomac River in Northwest DC, west of downtown and upriver from the National Mall. The area can be loosely defined as being bordered by the Potomac River to the south, Glover Park to the north, Rock Creek to the east, and Georgetown University to the west.

The intersection of M Street and Wisconsin Avenue is the hub of the commercial area, where high-end stores, top-notch restaurants, bars, and The Shops at Georgetown Park are located. Washington Harbor is also a popular area of Georgetown and offers waterfront dining on K Street, between 30th and 31st Streets. The historic Chesapeake & Ohio Canal (C&O Canal) runs between M and K Streets.

Georgetown is home to many politicians and lobbyists and is traditionally one of the most affluent neighborhoods in Washington. Famous people who have lived here include Thomas Jefferson, Francis Scott Key, Alexander Graham Bell, John F. Kennedy, John Kerry, Bob Woodward, and Madeleine Albright.

Many movies have also been filmed in the neighborhood. One of the most notable was the 1973 horror flick *The Exorcist,* which was set here and filmed here in part. Other films include *St. Elmo's Fire* (1985), *No Way Out* (1987), *True Lies* (1994), *Enemy of the State*

(1998), *Minority Report* (2002), *The Girl Next Door* (2004), *Wedding Crashers* (2005), and *Transformers* (2007).

Georgetown is not directly accessible by the Metrorail, Washington DC's subway system, but the local DC Circulator bus runs from 19th Street and N Street at the Dupont Metrorail station (on the Dupont-Georgetown-Rosslyn route) to the Rosslyn Metrorail station in Arlington, and it stops along M Street in Georgetown. The Union Station-Georgetown route also stops in Georgetown as it runs from Union Station to Georgetown along K Street. It also has stops on M Street.

Adams Morgan

Adams Morgan is a lively neighborhood in Northwest DC centered on the intersection of 18th Street and Columbia Road. This culturally diverse neighborhood is north of Dupont Circle, south of Mt. Pleasant, east of Kalorama, and west of Columbia Heights. It is considered to be the center of the city's Hispanic community.

Adams Morgan is known for its thriving nightlife. It has more than 40 bars, a great selection of restaurants, nightclubs, coffeehouses, galleries, and shops (most are located along 18th Street). Cuisine from all parts of the globe can be found, from Ethiopian to Caribbean.

Adams Morgan is a popular neighborhood for young professionals and has many 19th- and early 20th-century apartment buildings and row houses.

Upper Northwest

Some of the country's wealthiest people live in the Upper Northwest section of Washington DC. It is a very pretty part of the city that is largely residential with many suburban-looking tree-lined streets. Although the sights are somewhat spread out, many are accessible by Metrorail.

Just a half mile north of Georgetown is **Glover Park,** a neighborhood of apartment buildings and row houses that were built in the 1920s and '30s. Much of the area's nightlife is found in Glover Park, although compared to neighboring Georgetown, it caters to a slightly older clientele and is less crowded. Glover Park is also slightly west of the **U.S. Naval Observatory** (home to the nation's **Master Clock**) and the vice president's mansion (1 Observatory Circle).

Northeast of Glover Park is **Woodley Park,** which has some key attractions such as the **National Cathedral** and the **National Zoo.** Farther north are **Cleveland Park, Van Ness,** and **Tenleytown,** along Wisconsin and Connecticut Avenues. Each has its own local restaurants, bars, and shopping. To the west is **American University.**

Southwest of American University is a lesser-known neighborhood called the **Palisades,** on the western border of the city along the Potomac River and C&O Canal. This is an elite neighborhood with a few good, high-end restaurants.

Farther north and right on the Maryland state line is **Friendship Heights,** which is technically part of **Chevy Chase.** Friendship Heights has notable wealth and is known for its upscale stores along Wisconsin Avenue and a mall called the **Chevy Chase Pavilion.**

Metrorail's Red Line operates throughout Upper Northwest. The stops are easy to navigate because the stations are named after neighborhoods and sights. The National Cathedral, Glover Park, and the Palisades do not have Metrorail service.

U Street Corridor

The U Street Corridor is a residential and commercial neighborhood in Northwest Washington DC that extends for nine blocks along U Street between 9th and 18th Streets. In the 1920s, this part of the city was known as "Black Broadway" and was one of the largest African American communities in the country. Several famous jazz musicians lived in the neighborhood, including Duke Ellington and Jelly Roll Morton. Others frequented the area's jazz clubs.

Today the U Street Corridor is home to

The National Mall

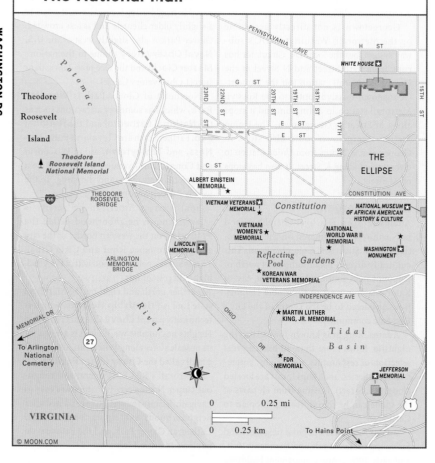

restaurants, nightclubs, music venues, and shops. The intersection of 9th and U Streets is known as "Little Ethiopia" for its concentration of Ethiopian businesses and restaurants.

PLANNING YOUR TIME

Washington DC encompasses approximately 68 square miles, so it is easy to get from one attraction to the next. The truth is, Washington DC has so much to offer, it could take weeks to feel that you've exhausted your opportunities for exploration. That's why it is best to focus on a few key areas when familiarizing

yourself with the city and to come prepared with a plan of action or at least a list of the top sights you'd like to see.

The National Mall and Memorial Parks are where most of the key monuments and museums are located. This is an area most first-time visitors focus on to see known landmarks such as the Washington Monument, Lincoln and Jefferson Memorials, and several Smithsonian museums. This area can be explored in a long weekend, but allow more time if you want to visit each of the museums.

Most people spend their first trip to

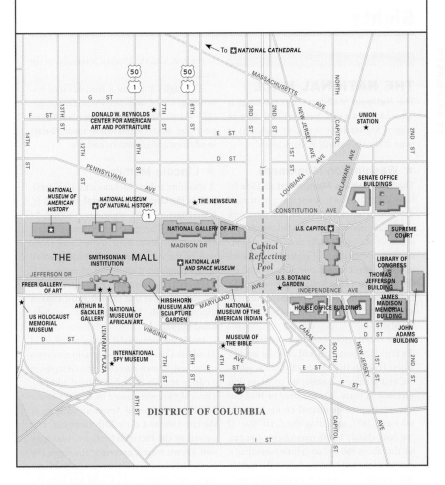

The following appears within the map image:

To ✦ NATIONAL CATHEDRAL

50 / 1   50 / 1

G ST

MASSACHUSETTS   AVE

UNION STATION ★

F ST   13TH ST   DONALD W. REYNOLDS CENTER FOR AMERICAN ART AND PORTRAITURE ★   7TH ST   6TH ST   3RD ST   2ND ST   NEW JERSEY AVE   NORTH CAPITOL   2ND ST

14TH ST   12TH ST   9TH ST   E ST   ST   ST   1ST ST   LOUISIANA AVE   DELAWARE AVE

PENNSYLVANIA   AVE   D ST   SENATE OFFICE BUILDINGS

NATIONAL MUSEUM OF AMERICAN HISTORY   ✦ NATIONAL MUSEUM OF NATURAL HISTORY   ★ THE NEWSEUM   CONSTITUTION   AVE

1   NATIONAL GALLERY OF ART   U.S. CAPITOL ✦   SUPREME COURT

MADISON DR   Capitol Reflecting Pool

THE   SMITHSONIAN INSTITUTION   MALL   ✦ NATIONAL AIR AND SPACE MUSEUM   LIBRARY OF CONGRESS

JEFFERSON DR   U.S. BOTANIC GARDEN ★   THOMAS JEFFERSON BUILDING

FREER GALLERY OF ART   AVE   INDEPENDENCE   AVE

★   ARTHUR M. SACKLER GALLERY   NATIONAL MUSEUM OF AFRICAN ART   HIRSHHORN MUSEUM AND SCULPTURE GARDEN   MARYLAND   NATIONAL MUSEUM OF THE AMERICAN INDIAN   HOUSE OFFICE BUILDINGS   JAMES MADISON MEMORIAL BUILDING

US HOLOCAUST MEMORIAL MUSEUM   VIRGINIA   C ST   JOHN ADAMS BUILDING

D ST   MUSEUM OF ★ THE BIBLE   D ST

L'ENFANT PLAZA   INTERNATIONAL SPY MUSEUM   7TH ST   6TH ST   4TH ST   AVE   E ST   E ST   1ST ST   2ND ST

CANAL ST   SOUTH   NEW JERSEY   F ST

9TH ST   **DISTRICT OF COLUMBIA**   CAPITOL ST   AVE

I ST

Washington DC exploring the National Mall and visiting the government buildings on Capitol Hill. Repeat visitors, or those with ample time, then branch out to explore some of the wonderful neighborhoods in Northwest DC, spending time in Georgetown, Dupont Circle, Adams Morgan, and other key locations to get more of the flavor of the city and to take in the zoo or National Cathedral.

Above all, be realistic about what you and

any travel companions can take in during a day. Three or four top sights a day can be more than enough if they include walking through museums and taking tours.

If you are planning to stay in Washington DC and not stray far from the city limits, there is no need to have a car during your visit. Many of the sights, restaurants, and hotels are accessible by public transportation or a short cab or car-service ride, and parking can be expensive and sometimes difficult to find.

Sights

TOP EXPERIENCE

THE NATIONAL MALL

The National Mall (www.nps.gov/nacc) is open 24 hours a day. National Park Service rangers are available to answer questions at most of the sights daily 9:30am-10pm.

★ Washington Monument

The **Washington Monument** (2 15th St. NW, 202/426-6841, www.nps.gov/wamo, daily except July 4 and Dec. 25, 9am-5pm with longer summer hours, free but ticket required) is one of the most easily recognized landmarks in the country. This slender, 555-foot-tall stone structure is centrally located on the Mall (east of the Reflecting Pool and the Lincoln Memorial) and is a great landmark with which to orient yourself when touring the Mall.

The Washington Monument is a tribute to the first U.S. president and also the world's tallest true obelisk. Made of marble, granite, and bluestone gneiss, its construction spanned 36 years. Work started in 1848 but was interrupted by several events between 1854 and 1877, including the Civil War. If you look closely at the monument, you can tell that about 150 feet up (a little more than a quarter of the way) the shading of the marble differs slightly. This was due to the long break in construction. The capstone was finally set in 1884, and the monument was dedicated in early 1885. It opened to the public in 1888.

The Washington Monument, upon its completion, was the world's tallest structure. It only held this distinction for one year, however: The Eiffel Tower took over the honor after it was completed in Paris, France.

Visitors can take an elevator to the top of the monument to enjoy stunning views of the city. From the viewing windows, the White House can be seen to the north, the Jefferson Memorial to the south, the Capitol Building to the east, and the Lincoln Memorial to the west.

Although admission is free, advance reservations can be made at www.recreation.gov (877-444-6777) with a reservation fee of $1.00 per ticket. Reservations can be made 90 days in advance and are non-refundable.

★ Lincoln Memorial

A stunning tribute to America's 16th president is the **Lincoln Memorial** (off 23rd St. NW, 202/426-6841, www.nps.gov/linc, 24 hours, free). This grand limestone and marble monument was built in the Greek Doric style on the western end of the National Mall across from the Washington Monument. It has 36 exterior columns, which represent the number of states that existed at the time of Lincoln's death. The monument was dedicated in 1922.

Inside the memorial is a huge sculpture of Abraham Lincoln and inscriptions from two of his best-known speeches (the Gettysburg Address and his second inaugural address). The sculpture was created by Daniel Chester French, an acclaimed American sculptor of the late 19th and early 20th centuries, and carved by the Piccirilli brothers, who were well-known marble carvers at the time. The memorial is one of the most recognized landmarks in Washington DC and has been the site of many famous speeches, including Martin Luther King Jr.'s "I Have a Dream" speech.

Albert Einstein Memorial

Where else but on the National Mall can you sit with one of the greatest scientific minds of all time? Just north of the Lincoln Memorial is the bronze **Albert Einstein Memorial** statue sculpted by Robert Berks. It is set in a group of trees on the southwest side of the grounds of the **National Academy of Sciences** (2101 Constitution Ave. NW). Einstein is seated and

Secrets of the Lincoln Memorial

the Lincoln Memorial under construction in 1920

Many myths surround the Lincoln Memorial. Some say Abraham Lincoln is buried under the monument or entombed inside it, but this is false (Lincoln is buried in Springfield, Illinois). Others think the 57 steps leading up to the statue chamber represent Lincoln's age when he died, but in reality, he was only 56.

One question that is repeatedly asked throughout the local community is what, if anything, lies underneath the memorial? Given that the structure was built on tidal marsh from the Potomac River that was once actually under water, it might make sense that nothing could be under it, but the rumor that something exists there is actually true.

Underneath the Lincoln Memorial is a cavernous area with dirt floors and concrete walls. Hanging from the ceiling beneath where Lincoln sits are hundreds of stalactite formations. The stalactites are long, slender, and pale in color, and they are growing in this artificial cave as the result of water slowly dripping through the monument, which started when it was built.

Other interesting features in the underbelly of the monument are cartoon drawings that were sketched on several support columns by the workers who built the monument. One of the drawings depicts characters from the old *Mutt and Jeff* cartoon, which started running in 1907 and was the first daily newspaper comic strip.

Tours of the cavernous area ceased after 9/11, but this author can vouch for its existence, since in the 1970s and '80s, local children were treated to a tour on elementary school field trips.

has papers with mathematical equations in his lap symbolizing his scientific achievements.

War Memorials
★ VIETNAM VETERANS MEMORIAL

One of the most visited war memorials is the **Vietnam Veterans Memorial** (Constitution Ave. between 21st St. and 23rd St., 202/426-6841, www.nps.gov/vive, www.thewall-usa. com, 24 hours, free). This moving memorial honors U.S. service members who fought and died in the Vietnam War and also those who are missing in action. There are three parts to the memorial: the **Three Soldiers Statue,** the **Vietnam Women's Memorial,** and the **Vietnam Veterans Memorial Wall.**

The focal point of the memorial is the Vietnam Veterans Memorial Wall. Completed in 1982, it is actually two 246-foot-long walls that are sunken into the ground and have the names of more than 58,000 service members who died in the war etched into them in chronological order. (The exact number changes each year as names are added.) When visitors look at the wall, they can see their reflections next to the etched names, symbolically linking the past and present. There is a path along the base of the wall so visitors can walk along it, read names, and, if desired, make pencil rubbings of a particular name.

The memorial is at the west end of the National Mall, adjacent to the Lincoln Memorial in West Potomac Park. It is open to the public 24 hours a day, and park staff conduct free daily interpretive programs throughout the day and are available to answer questions between 9:30am and 10pm daily.

NATIONAL WORLD WAR II MEMORIAL

The **National World War II Memorial** (17th St. between Constitution Ave. and Independence Ave., 800/639-4992, www.wwiimemorial.com, www.nps.gov/nwwm, 24 hours, free) honors the more than 400,000 people who died in World War II, the 16 million people who served the United States during the war in the armed forces, and the millions of people who provided support from home. The memorial contains 56 pillars and two triumphal arches arranged in a semicircle around a fountain and plaza. A Freedom Wall sits on the west side of the memorial bearing more than 4,000 gold stars on it, each representing 100 Americans who lost their lives in the war. An inscription in front of the wall reads, "Here we mark the price of freedom." The memorial opened to the public in 2004 and is administered by the National Park Service. It is on the east end of the Reflecting Pool, between the Washington Monument and the Lincoln Memorial.

KOREAN WAR VETERANS MEMORIAL

The beautiful and haunting **Korean War Veterans Memorial** (17th St. SW, 202/426-6841, www.nps.gov/kwvm, 24 hours, free) is also in West Potomac Park, southeast of the Lincoln Memorial. Erected in 1995, it is dedicated to service members who served in the Korean War. The memorial was designed in the shape of a triangle intersecting a circle with walls depicting images of land, sea, and air troops who supported the war. The focal point, however, is 19 larger than life-size stainless steel statues designed by Frank Gaylord within the walled triangle. The seven-foot-tall figures represent a patrol squad with members from each branch of the armed forces making their way through the harsh Korean terrain, represented by strips of granite and bushes. The figures are dressed in full combat gear and look incredibly lifelike. The memorial is lit up at night, and when the figures are reflected on the surrounding wall, there appear to be 38 soldiers, which represents the 38th parallel dividing the two Koreas.

National Gallery of Art

The **National Gallery of Art** (4th St. and Constitution Ave. NW, 202/737-4215, www.nga.gov, Mon.-Sat. 10am-5pm, Sun. 11am-6pm, free) first opened in 1937 when Andrew W. Mellon donated funding and a large art collection from multiple collectors for the enjoyment of the people of the United States. The gallery traces the development of Western art from the Middle Ages to current times through paintings, prints, drawings, sculpture, photographs, and other media. The only portrait in the Western Hemisphere painted by Leonardo da Vinci is housed in this museum. The gallery is a campus that includes the original museum building (the West Building), which features sculpture galleries with over 900 works or art; the newer East

1: Vietnam Women's Memorial designed by Glenna Goodacre 2: the East Building of the National Gallery of Art 3: Washington Monument and the Capitol behind the Reflecting Pool

Building, which contains a collection of modern paintings, drawings, prints, offices, and research centers; and a 6.1-acre outdoor sculpture garden (open year-round) that offers an ice-skating rink from mid-November through mid-March.

Smithsonian Institution Museums

Washington DC is known for its incredible museums. The most noted are those that are part of the **Smithsonian Institution** (www. si.edu), the largest museum and research complex in the world. The Smithsonian Institution was founded in 1846 and is administered by the U.S. government.

Oddly, the founding donor of the institution was British chemist and mineralogist James Smithson, who had never even been to the United States. An amateur scientist, Smithson inherited a large estate and in turn had no heirs to leave it to. His will stipulated that his estate would be donated to the founding of an educational institute in Washington DC.

The Smithsonian Institution was established as a trust, and it functions as a body of the U.S. government, although separate from the legislative, executive, and judicial branches. Funding for the museums comes from contributions, the institution's own endowment, memberships, government support, and retail and concession revenues. The Smithsonian employs approximately 6,300 people.

The majority of the Smithsonian museums, 19 in fact, are in DC, and many of them are architectural and historical landmarks. Nine research centers and the National Zoological Park are also part of the Smithsonian collection in Washington DC. Most of the Smithsonian facilities are open to the public daily except for December 25, with free admission.

The Smithsonian family also stretches to other parts of the country, including Virginia,

Maryland, New York City, and Arizona. There are also many other museums that are affiliated with the organization.

First-timers to Washington DC will want to visit at least one of the major Smithsonian museums, but will most likely fill their dance card with several of the "biggies" on the National Mall (of which there are 11). Visitors should be aware that most of the museums on the National Mall do not offer dedicated parking facilities and require visitors to pass through security screenings upon entry.

SMITHSONIAN CASTLE

Information on the Smithsonian can be found on the south side of the Mall at its headquarters, called the **Smithsonian Castle** (1000 Jefferson Dr. SW, 202/633-1000, www.si.edu, daily 8:30am-5:30pm, free). This sandstone building, which opened in 1855, looks like something out of a fairy tale and houses an exhibit hall, administrative offices, and Smithson's remains (which were laid to rest in a crypt under the castle).

★ NATIONAL MUSEUM OF AFRICAN AMERICAN HISTORY AND CULTURE

The much anticipated **National Museum of African American History and Culture** (1400 Constitution Ave. NW, 844/750-3012, www.nmaahc.si.edu, daily 10am-5:30pm, free, timed-entry pass required) opened to rave reviews and throngs of visitors in 2016 and has been going strong ever since. As the only national museum dedicated to African American history and culture, this incredible museum houses more than 37,000 artifacts and is the 19th Smithsonian Institution museum. The 350,000-square-foot building itself is an architectural masterpiece and has sustainable features in its construction and operation. It features five aboveground stories and three below ground. Powerful and poignant exhibits explore all facets of the African American experience and illustrate the nation's journey from slavery through segregation and the Civil Rights movement, right up to the current day. There are countless exhibits, both permanent and temporary, with items such as Nat Turner's bible, artwork from Charles Alston and Henry O. Tanner, Michael Jackson's fedora, and a Southern plantation cabin. Many special tours and events are offered at the museum (check their website for the latest). Due to the museum's popularity, timed-entry passes during peak times are required.

The museum is also home to the popular **Sweet Home Café** (daily 10am-5pm), which offers authentic selections that showcase African American culture and current food traditions with a focus on locally sourced ingredients.

NATIONAL MUSEUM OF AMERICAN HISTORY

The **National Museum of American History** (Constitution Ave. NW, between 12th St. and 14th St., 202/633-1000, www.americanhistory.si.edu, daily 10am-5:30pm, free) is devoted to exhibits explaining the cultural, social, scientific, technological, military, and political development of the United States. The museum has three floors housing more than three million artifacts. Wings on each floor represent a different theme, each of which is represented by a large, significant, landmark object. Some examples include the 1865 Vassar Telescope in the west wing of the first floor, which is focused on science and innovation; a Civil War draft wheel in the east wing of the third floor, which is focused on political history; and a statue of George Washington in the west wing of the second floor, which focuses on American lives.

Some museum highlights include the Star-Spangled Banner, George Washington's uniform, Thomas Jefferson's lap desk, Archie Bunker's chair from the TV series *All in the Family,* Dorothy's ruby slippers from *The Wizard of Oz,* and the inaugural dresses worn by all the first ladies. The museum also houses the Warner Bros. Theater, which features films, lectures, and concerts.

The one-hour guided tours offered are a good way to see the highlights quickly if you have a full docket of sights to get to on the same day. There is no public parking at the museum. Visitors riding Metrorail can use either the Smithsonian Mall or Federal Triangle stop.

★ NATIONAL MUSEUM OF NATURAL HISTORY

Another favorite Smithsonian creation is the **National Museum of Natural History** (10th St. and Constitution Ave. NW, 202/633-1000, www.mnh.si.edu, daily 10am-5:30pm, free). It first opened its doors in 1910 and is said to be the most visited natural history museum worldwide. The main building encloses 325,000 square feet of exhibit space and is overall the size of 18 football fields. The museum collections include more than 126 million specimens.

Visitors can expect to see plants, animals, fossils, rocks, meteorites, and cultural artifacts including "Henry," the iconic 13-plus-foot-tall African elephant (the largest ever killed by humans), the jaws of a giant prehistoric shark, the stunning Hope Diamond (which is 45.52 carats), and David H. Koch Hall of Fossils (dinosaur hall). There's also a live butterfly pavilion (adults $7.50, children 2-12 $6.50, seniors 65 and over $7). The museum is also home to the largest group of scientists (approximately 185) dedicated to studying the history of the world. Visitor concierges are available to answer questions throughout the museum and can be identified by their green vests. There is no public parking at the museum. Visitors riding Metrorail should exit at the Smithsonian station (Mall exit) on the Blue and Orange Lines.

NATIONAL MUSEUM OF THE AMERICAN INDIAN

The **National Museum of the American Indian** (4th St. and Independence Ave. SW, 202/633-1000, www.americanindian.si.edu, daily 10am-5:30pm, free) opened in 2004 and is the first national museum focused exclusively on Native Americans. The five-story,

250,000-square-foot limestone building sits on more than four acres of what is made to look like wetlands. The museum features approximately 825,000 items that represent more than 12,000 years of history and 1,200 indigenous American cultures. It also offers exhibits, film screenings, public programs, cultural presentations, and school programs.

★ NATIONAL AIR AND SPACE MUSEUM

An overwhelming favorite in the Smithsonian family of museums is the **National Air and Space Museum** (Independence Ave. SW at 6th St. SW, 202/633-2214, IMAX 866/868-7774, www.airandspace.si.edu, daily 10am-5:30pm, free, IMAX and planetarium entry extra). This incredible museum features the largest collection of air- and spacecraft in the world and is also a center for research on historic aviation, spaceflight, planetary science, geophysics, and terrestrial geology. The exhibit space of 21 galleries and more than 160,000 square feet of floor space opened in 1976. Most of the hundreds of aircraft, spacecraft, rockets, missiles, and other aviation artifacts on display are originals.

Some highlights you can expect to see include the *Spirit of St. Louis,* the Apollo Lunar Module, a DC-3 airplane, a real lunar rock, and the *Star Trek* starship *Enterprise* studio model.

Another great attraction located inside the National Air and Space Museum is the **Albert Einstein Planetarium** (adults $9, youth 2-12 $7.50, military and seniors 60 and over $8). Several shows are offered daily and take visitors through the night sky with a first-of-its-kind SkyVision dual digital projection system and digital surround sound.

Other favorite attractions in the museum include the **Lockheed Martin IMAX Theater** (IMAX shows adults $9, youth 2-12 $7.50, military and seniors 60 and over $8,

feature films adults $15, youth 2-12 $13.50, military and seniors 60 and over $14), flight simulators, and an observatory (located on the southeast terrace). One of the best museum shops is also here, and dining facilities are offered on-site.

Free 90-minute museum tours are offered daily at 10:30am and 1pm. There is no public parking at the museum, but several public pay lots are nearby. Metrorail riders should use the L'Enfant Plaza stop and exit at Maryland Avenue.

HIRSHHORN MUSEUM

Many people think the **Hirshhorn Museum and Sculpture Garden** (700 Independence Ave. SW, 202/633-1000, www.hirshhorn.si.edu, daily 10am-5:30pm, free) looks like a giant spaceship parked near the Mall. The design is an open concrete cylinder (231 feet in diameter) standing on four large supports. The idea behind this structure was for it to provide a sharp contrast to everything else around it. It succeeded. This modern art museum, which opened in the 1960s, houses one of the premier collections of contemporary paintings and sculptures in the country focusing on the post-World War II era. A sculpture garden is located outside the museum.

NATIONAL MUSEUM OF AFRICAN ART

The **National Museum of African Art** (950 Independence Ave. SW, 202/633-4600, www.africa.si.edu, daily 10am-5:30pm, free) is part of a quadrangle complex behind the Smithsonian Castle. The building is mostly underground and contains the largest public collection of African art in the nation with approximately 9,000 artifacts. Pieces include sculpture, jewelry, musical instruments, maps, films, and photographs.

FREER GALLERY OF ART AND ARTHUR M. SACKLER GALLERY

The **Freer Gallery of Art** and the subterranean **Arthur M. Sackler Gallery** (1050 Independence Ave. SW, 202/633-1000, www.

1: Smithsonian Castle 2: National Museum of African American History and Culture 3: "Henry" the Elephant at the National Museum of Natural History 4: National Air and Space Museum

freersackler.si.edu, daily 10am-5:30pm, free) together form the national collections of Asian art. They contain the largest Asian art research library in the country (inside the Sackler Gallery) as well as art from all parts of Asia. Their collection of American art includes pieces by well-known artists such as Winslow Homer, Augustus Saint-Gaudens, and John Singer Sargent.

The Freer Gallery features Asian collections spanning 6,000 years that date back to the Neolithic era. Specific collections include stone sculptures from ancient Egypt, Chinese paintings, Persian manuscripts, and Korean pottery.

The Freer's most famous exhibit is the **Peacock Room in Blue and White,** which was the dining room of a mansion in London owned by Frederick Leyland in the late 1800s. The room was designed for display of Leyland's blue and white Chinese porcelain. Artist James McNeill Whistler consulted on the room's colors in 1876 and 1877 and painted intricate patterns of blue and gold that looked similar to peacock plumage. Charles Lang Freer bought the room in 1904, shipped it to his home in Detroit, Michigan, and began filling the shelves with ceramics from Japan, Korea, China, Iran, and Syria. Today, blue and white Chinese porcelains dating back to the Kangxi period (1662-1722) are again displayed in the Peacock Room, as they were in the 1870s.

The Sackler Gallery contains a founding collection of approximately 1,000 items that were donated by American psychiatrist, entrepreneur, and philanthropist Arthur M. Sackler. The collection has both ancient and contemporary items including South and Southeast Asian sculpture, Chinese jade, and Middle Eastern ceramics. The museums are on the south side of the Mall.

MALL CAROUSEL

It may come as a surprise that the Smithsonian operates the **Mall Carousel** (12th St. and Jefferson Dr. SW, 202/633-1000, www.nationalcarousel.com, daily 10am-5:30pm, $3.50). This favorite children's thrill ride with the blue and yellow awning is in front of the Smithsonian Castle. It offers three minutes of fun on faded painted ponies that were built in the 1940s. The carousel was originally at the Gwynn Oak Amusement Park in Maryland prior to coming to the Mall.

WHITE HOUSE AREA
★ White House

Not technically part of the National Mall, the **White House** (1600 Pennsylvania Ave. NW, 202/456-1111, www.whitehouse.gov, free) sits nearby on Pennsylvania Avenue and can be seen from Constitution Avenue. The White House is easily the most recognized residence in the country as the home and workplace of the president of the United States.

The site for the White House was chosen by George Washington in 1791, but John Adams was the first president to live there in 1800. (Mrs. Adams is said to have hung their wash in the East Room.) The house suffered a fire set by the British during the War of 1812, but it was rebuilt and has undergone several renovations since then. The White House currently has 6 levels, 132 rooms, and 35 bathrooms.

It is possible to take a self-guided tour of the White House (the only presidential home in the world that is open to the public), but requests must be made through your member of Congress. Tours are available Tuesday-Thursday 7:30am-11:30am and Friday-Saturday 7:30am-1:30pm. Requests can be made up to three months in advance but must be made at least three weeks in advance. There is no charge for the tour, but it is advised to make a reservation early since space is limited. Citizens of foreign countries may request a tour through their individual embassies in Washington DC. All visitors are required to present current government-issued photo identification or a passport.

The **White House Visitor Center** (1450 Pennsylvania Ave. NW, www.nps.gov, daily 7:30am-4pm, free) is in the Commerce Building. It offers an information booth, exhibits, restrooms, drinking fountains, and a first-aid area.

Presidential Firsts

- **Andrew Jackson** was the first president to ride in a train.
- **James Polk** was the first president to have his photograph taken.
- **Millard Fillmore** was the first president to have a bathtub with running water.
- **Rutherford B. Hayes** was the first president to have a telephone in the White House.
- **Benjamin Harrison** was the first president to have a Christmas tree in the White House.
- **Theodore Roosevelt** was the first president to ride in a car. He was also the first to travel outside the country while in office.
- **Calvin Coolidge** was the first president to be heard over radio.
- **Franklin D. Roosevelt** was the first president to fly in an airplane and the first to appear on television.

Lafayette Square

Lafayette Square (H St. between 15th St. and 17th St. NW, www.nps.gov, 24 hours, free) is a seven-acre park across Pennsylvania Avenue from the White House (it is also known as **Lafayette Park**). The park was designed as part of the White House grounds—and was originally named President's Park—but was separated when Pennsylvania Avenue was built in 1804. Lafayette Square has a checkered past. It has been home to a racetrack, a slave market, a graveyard, and a soldier encampment during the War of 1812. It's no wonder the park is said to be the most haunted location in the city. Today, the park offers green grass and five large statues: an equestrian statue of President Andrew Jackson and four of Revolutionary War heroes. The closest Metrorail stop is McPherson Square. The park is maintained by the National Park Service.

President's Park South

President's Park South, which is more commonly referred to as **The Ellipse,** is a 52-acre park that sits just south of the White House. Technically, the Ellipse is the name of the street that runs the circumference of the park. The park is a large grassy circle that is open to the public and is the site of various events. If you hear locals say they are at or on the Ellipse, they mean they are in the park bordered by Ellipse Road.

TIDAL BASIN AREA
The Tidal Basin

The Tidal Basin is a 107-acre reservoir in **West Potomac Park** that sits between the Potomac River and the Washington Channel (a two-mile-long channel that empties into the Anacostia River). Several major memorials are adjacent to the Tidal Basin, including the Jefferson Memorial, the Martin Luther King Jr. Memorial, and the Franklin Delano Roosevelt Memorial. The Tidal Basin is best known as the center of the National Cherry Blossom Festival; it is lined with many Japanese cherry trees.

★ Jefferson Memorial

Although it was only built in 1942, the **Thomas Jefferson Memorial** (16 E. Basin Dr. SW, 202/426-6841, www.nps.gov/thje, 24 hours, free), which sits on the south shore of the Tidal Basin in West Potomac Park, is one of the most recognized memorials in DC. This neoclassical building dedicated to our third president is built on land that once served as a popular bathing beach along the Potomac River.

The memorial building is made up of circular marble steps, a portico, a circular colonnade, and a shallow dome open to the elements. Inside stands a 19-foot-high bronze statue of Thomas Jefferson designed by Rudolph Evans, looking north toward his former residence, the White House. The statue was added to the memorial four years after its dedication. Many of Jefferson's writings are inscribed on the memorial.

The site of the Jefferson Memorial is adorned with many Japanese cherry trees, which were a gift from Japan in 1912. The trees are world famous for their beautiful spring blossoms and are the centerpiece for the annual National Cherry Blossom Festival.

Martin Luther King, Jr. Memorial

One of the newest memorials is the **Martin Luther King, Jr. Memorial** (1850 West Basin Dr. SW, 202/426-6841, www.nps.gov/mlkm, 24 hours, free) in West Potomac Park southwest of the National Mall. The memorial sits on four acres and was unveiled in 2011.

The design of the memorial is based on a line from King's "I Have a Dream" speech: "Out of a mountain of despair, a stone of hope." A 30-foot-high relief of the civil rights leader is called the *Stone of Hope,* sculpted by Lei Yixin, and stands just past two pieces of granite symbolizing the "mountain of despair." Additionally, a 450-foot-long wall includes inscriptions of excerpts from many of King's speeches. Martin Luther King Jr. is the first African American to be honored with a memorial near the National Mall. He is also only the fourth person to be memorialized who was not a U.S. president.

Franklin Delano Roosevelt Memorial

The **Franklin Delano Roosevelt Memorial** (400 West Basin Dr. SW, 202/485-9880, www.

nps.gov/frde, 24 hours, free) sits on more than seven acres and consists of four outdoor rooms, one for each of FDR's office terms. Running water is an important component of the memorial, as are sculptures depicting scenes with FDR. Each of the rooms contains a waterfall, and the sculptures become larger and more detailed in consecutive rooms. The intention was to show the increasing complexities faced by FDR during his presidency as related to the Depression and war. This is the only memorial to include a depiction of a first lady: Eleanor Roosevelt is depicted in a bronze statue standing before the United Nations emblem.

There is, in fact, another FDR Memorial. FDR was said to have told his trusted friend and Supreme Court justice Felix Frankfurter, "If they are to put up any memorial to me, I should like it to be placed in the center of that green plot in front of the Archives Building. I should like it to consist of a block about the size [of this desk]." Because of this, the first FDR memorial was erected in the 1960s on the corner of 9th Street and Pennsylvania Avenue. It is a simple memorial that met his wishes and consists of a small block of stone that reads, "In Memory of Franklin Delano Roosevelt 1882-1945."

U.S. Holocaust Memorial Museum

The **U.S. Holocaust Memorial Museum** (100 Raoul Wallenberg Pl. SW, 202/488-0400, www.ushmm.org, daily 10am-5:30pm, free) is dedicated to the interpretation of Holocaust history. Its goal is to help leaders and citizens "confront hatred, prevent genocide, and promote human dignity." This museum, perhaps more than most, is of international interest: Visitors from more than 100 countries have walked through its doors since it first opened in 1993. The museum houses more than 12,750 artifacts including prisoner uniforms, a casting of a gas chamber door, and religious articles. Its collections include 1,000 hours of archival footage and 80,000 photographs. It

---

1: Marin Luther King, Jr. Memorial carved by sculptor Lei Yixin **2:** statue of First Lady Eleanor Roosevelt sculpted by Neil Estern

also has information on 200,000 registered survivors, a library, and archives.

Permanent exhibits that show a chronological history of the Holocaust can be accessed on the first floor. A free pass must be obtained for the permanent exhibits March-August but not during the rest of the year. The passes are available at the museum on the day of your visit or can be reserved online. Entrance to other exhibits and memorial spaces is from the first, second, and concourse levels. There is a café on the 15th Street side of the building. This museum can be overwhelming for young children and is best for teenagers and adults.

Bureau of Engraving and Printing

As its web address indicates, the **Bureau of Engraving and Printing** (14th St. and C St. SW, 202/874-2330, www.moneyfactory.gov, Mon.-Fri. 8:30am-6pm, free) is a huge money factory. It produces U.S. currency notes and literally prints billions of dollars each year. Fresh money is delivered to the Federal Reserve System (the nation's central bank). Visitors can take guided tours or walk along the gallery to view the production floor where millions of dollars are being printed. The free 40-minute tour includes a film and explanation of the production process. No ticket is required for tours September-February. Tours run every 15 minutes between 9am and 10:45am and between 12:30pm and 2pm. During peak season (Mar.-Aug.), free tickets are required for tours. Tickets can be obtained at the ticket booth on-site (which opens at 8am) and are for the same day only. Plan to be in line between 6:30am and 7am for the best chance of getting tickets. One person may get up to four tickets.

SOUTH OF THE NATIONAL MALL
International Spy Museum

Enter the world of espionage at the only public museum in the country dedicated to professional spies. The **International Spy Museum** (700 L'Enfant Plaza SW,

Who is Featured on U.S. Paper Currency

- $1 bill: George Washington (1st U.S. president)

- $2 bill: Thomas Jefferson (3rd U.S. president)

- $5 bill: Abraham Lincoln (16th U.S. president)

- $10 bill: Alexander Hamilton (1st secretary of the treasury)

- $20 bill: Currently Andrew Jackson (7th U.S. president)

- $50 bill: Ulysses S. Grant (18th U.S. president)

- $100 bill: Ben Franklin (statesman)

202/393-7798, www.spymuseum.org, Sun.-Thurs. 9am-7pm, Fri.-Sat. 9am-8pm, adults $24.95, youth 7-12 $14.95, children 6 and under free, seniors/military/law enforcement/intelligence community/college students $19.95) is a fantastic and intriguing museum that enjoyed a vast expansion when it moved in 2019 from its former location in Penn Quarter to L'Enfant Plaza between the National Mall and District Wharf. This remarkable museum houses the largest collection of international artifacts geared toward the secret world of spies. Exhibits focus on some of the most secretive missions across the globe and strive to educate the public about their role in historic events.

The museum features artifacts created specifically for intelligence services (think lipstick pistols, disguises, and Enigma cipher machines) and first-person accounts from distinguished intelligence professionals. It brings an elusive world to life through state-of-the-art interactive exhibits designed to challenge visitors and doesn't shy away from the darker side of the profession. Their

Undercover Mission even tests visitors' spy skills as they go on a mission through the museum and tracks their performance on interactives. The end result is a "debrief" and access to a special website for further engagement. Plan on spending a minimum of two hours here.

Museum of the Bible

The **Museum of the Bible** (400 4th St. SW, 866/430-6682, www.museumofthebible.org, daily 10am-5pm, adults $24.99, children 7-17 $14.99, children 6 and under free, seniors/military/first responders/students $19.99) opened its doors in 2017 in a massive 430,000-square-foot building just south of the National Mall. The museum uses advanced technology to engage visitors of all ages in a personal experience with the Bible and features both permanent and temporary exhibits. Artifacts span 3,500 years of history, and the museum is also focused on education and research. The sixth floor is home to **Manna** (daily 11am-4pm, $6-18), a "fast casual" restaurant featuring Mediterranean dishes made from seasonal ingredients.

CAPITOL HILL
★ U.S. Capitol

The centerpiece of Capitol Hill is none other than the grand neoclassical-style **U.S. Capitol** (1st St. and E. Capitol St., 202/226-8000, www.visitthecapitol.gov, Mon.-Sat. 8:30am-4:30pm, free) itself, which sits on 274 acres at the east end of the National Mall. The Capitol Building is the official meeting location of the U.S. Congress. First-time visitors to the city should take the time to tour this national icon and view our elected officials hard at work.

The Capitol Building comprises a central dome towering above a rotunda, flanked by two wings. The building technically has two fronts, one on the east side and one on the west side. The north wing houses the U.S. Senate chamber and the south wing is for the U.S. House of Representatives chamber. Public galleries sit above each so visitors can watch the proceedings. Each of the many rooms in the Capitol is designated with either an "S" for those on the Senate side of the rotunda or "H" for those on the House side.

George Washington laid the cornerstone of the Capitol in 1793. The Senate wing was completed in 1800 (Congress held its first session there the same year), and the House wing was completed in 1811. Since its original construction, the building has undergone many expansions, renovations, and even a rebuilding after it was partially burned by the British during the War of 1812. The Capitol, in its early days, was used for other purposes in addition to government functions. In fact, church services were held there on Sundays until after the Civil War.

Underground tunnels and a private subway connect the Capitol Building with the Congressional office buildings. The Senate office buildings are located to the north on Constitution Avenue, and the House office buildings are located to the south on Independence Avenue. The public may only ride the subway when escorted by a staff member with appropriate identification.

Visitors to the Capitol enter through the three-level underground **U.S. Capitol Visitor Center** (beneath the east front plaza at 1st St. and E. Capitol St., 202/226-8000). The center is a security checkpoint, and visitors should be prepared to wait in line for screening before entering. The center also offers educational exhibits, restrooms, and a food court. The visitors center is open Monday-Saturday 8:30am-4:30pm, but the Capitol Building itself can only be visited on an official tour. Tours are free and can be arranged in advance through the Advance Reservation System (www.visitthecapitol.gov) or through the office of a senator or representative. Tours are given Monday-Saturday 8:40am-3:20pm and last one hour. They include the **Crypt, Rotunda,** and **National Statuary Hall**. Those wishing to watch the House or Senate in session must obtain a pass from their senator or representative's office. International visitors can obtain a ticket at

Capitol Hill

NATIONAL
POSTAL MUSEUM ★

F ST NE

F ST NE

UNION
STATION ■

E ST NE

E ST NE

395

MASSACHUSETTS AVE NW

D ST NE

D ST NE

3RD ST NE

5TH ST NE

6TH ST NE

MARYLAND AVE NE

LOUISIANA AVE NE

DELAWARE AVE NE

C ST NE

C ST NE

C ST NE

MASSACHUSETTS AVE NW

C ST NE

MARYLAND AVE NE

CONSTITUTION AVE NE

12TH ST NE

PENNSYLVANIA AVE NW

U.S. SUPREME
COURT ★

A ST NE

4TH ST NE

5TH ST NE

6TH ST NE

7TH ST NE

8TH ST NE

9TH ST NE

10TH ST NE

E CAPITOL ST

1ST ST NE

2ND ST NE

★ U.S. CAPITOL

EAST CAPITOL ST NE

E CAPITOL ST

THOMAS ★
JEFFERSON
BUILDING

★
JOHN ADAMS
BUILDING

A ST SE

11TH ST NE

MARYLAND
AVE SW

★
U.S.
BOTANIC
GARDEN

INDEPENDENCE AVE SW

INDEPENDENCE AVE SE

NORTH CAROLINA AVE SE

1ST ST SE

JAMES ★
MADISON
MEMORIAL
BUILDING

■ CAPITOL HILL
HOTEL

PENNSYLVANIA AVE SE

EASTERN
MARKET

1ST ST SE

2ND ST SE

C ST SE

C ST SE

7TH ST SE

8TH ST SE

C ST SE

NEW JERSEY AVE SE

C ST SW

D ST SE

695

WASHINGTON AVE SW

D ST SE

D ST SE

395

E ST SE

E ST SE

▼ BELGA
CAFE

3RD ST SE

4TH ST SE

5TH ST SE

6TH ST SE

7TH ST SE

8TH ST SE

9TH ST SE

10TH ST SE

11TH ST SE

12TH ST SE

G ST SE

0   200 yds

0   200 m

VIRGINIA AVE SE

I ST SE

695

© MOON.COM

the Capitol with valid photo identification. Plan to arrive 45 minutes before a scheduled tour to allow enough time to get through security.

Summerhouse

The **Summerhouse** (on the west front lawn of the U.S. Capitol Building on the Senate side, www.aoc.gov, 24 hours, free) is a little oasis hidden in a group of trees. This small, decorative, hexagonal brick building offers a cool

place for visitors to rest. It was constructed around 1880 and is anchored by a fountain that once offered spring water. There are nice benches here with seating for 22 that are covered by a tile roof.

U.S. Supreme Court

Behind the U.S. Capitol Building on 1st Street (between E. Capitol St. and Maryland

1: U.S. Botanic Garden 2: U.S. Capitol

DC's Skyline: Onward and Upward?

Unlike most large cities in the country, Washington DC has a low skyline. When the first skyscrapers were going up in the late 1800s elsewhere in the world, DC residents became concerned that if tall buildings were constructed in the city, Washington would lose its European feel. So in 1899, Congress passed the Heights of Buildings Act, which limited the vertical reach of buildings in the nation's capital to no more than 130 feet. This act was later amended (in 1910) to allow buildings to be 20 feet higher than the width of the adjacent street. The only exception is on Pennsylvania Avenue between 1st and 15th Streets. More than 100 years later, the act is now being reviewed for possible revision because the inability to expand the skyline upward has limited the city's tax base and potential for growth.

Ave.) is the **Supreme Court of the United States** (1 1st St. NE, 202/479-3000, www.supremecourt.gov, Mon.-Fri. 9am-4:30pm, free). The Supreme Court is the highest court in the nation, and the current building was completed in 1935 (court was previously held in the Capitol Building). The main entrance faces the Capitol Building and welcomes visitors with a 252-foot-wide oval plaza. Fountains, benches, and flagpoles are on either side of the plaza. Marble columns support the pediment on the Corinthian-style building.

The court building is open to the public during the week, and visitors are encouraged to listen to a variety of courtroom lectures when the Supreme Court is not sitting. Lectures are scheduled every hour on the half hour and begin at 9:30am. The final lecture of the day starts at 3:30pm. A calendar is online with the daily lecture schedule. Visitors can also take in exhibits focused on the work of the Supreme Court, the justices' lives, and the architecture of the Supreme Court building. When the court is sitting, visitors are welcome to see our justice system in action by attending oral arguments. Seating, which is limited and granted on a first-come, first-served basis, is available for an entire argument or for a three-minute viewing. Prior to the beginning of a session, two lines form in front of the courthouse outside on the plaza. One line is for those wishing to sit in on the entire argument, and the other is for those wishing to witness a three-minute sample.

All visitors are required to pass through a security screening that includes X-raying personal items and walking through metal detectors.

Library of Congress

It's hard to imagine that the original collection of books held by the **Library of Congress** (www.loc.gov) went up in flames during the War of 1812 when the British set fire to the Capitol Building where the collection was kept. Fortunately, Thomas Jefferson had a rather substantial collection of personal books with more than 6,500 volumes that he agreed to sell to Congress to rebuild the collection.

Today the Library of Congress, which is a research library and the country's oldest federal cultural institution, is contained in three government buildings on Capitol Hill and one building in Virginia. It is also the largest library in the world. Its collections include upward of 32 million cataloged books, 61 million manuscripts, more than one million U.S. government publications, one million newspapers from all over the world, and more than 120,000 comic books. Its publications are printed in 470 languages.

The main library building is the beautiful **Thomas Jefferson Building** (10 1st St. SE, between Independence Ave. and E. Capitol St., 202/707-8000). This is the oldest building in the complex, having opened in 1897. This building is a feast for the eyes with its murals, mosaics, sculptures, and impressive main reading room containing 236 desks sitting under a 160-foot dome. A visitor center is located at the west front entrance (Mon.-Sat. 8:30am-4:30pm). Free one-hour guided tours are available, during which visitors can learn about the building's architecture and symbolic art. Tours are given Monday-Friday 10:30am-3:30pm and Saturday 10:30am-2:30pm.

The other two library buildings on Capitol Hill are the nearby **John Adams Building** (2nd St. SE, between Independence Ave. and E. Capitol St.) and the **James Madison Memorial Building** (Independence Ave. SE, between 1st St. and 2nd St.). The latter is home to the **Mary Pickford Theater,** which is the "motion picture and television reading room" of the library.

The library primarily exists as a research tool for answering inquiries from members of Congress through the Congressional Research Service. The library is open to the public, but only library employees, members of Congress, and other top-level government officials can actually check books out.

U.S. Botanic Garden

A lovely contrast to memorials, office buildings, and monuments, the **U.S. Botanic Garden** (100 Maryland Ave. SW, 202/225-8333, www.usbg.gov, daily 10am-5pm, free) is the oldest continuously operating garden of its type in the country. Just southwest of the Capitol, this national greenhouse opened in 1850 and has been in its current location since 1933. Major attractions at the garden include a rose garden, butterfly garden, the First Ladies' Water Garden, the Lawn Terrace, and an outdoor amphitheater. The garden houses nearly 10,000 living specimens; the oldest are more than 165 years old.

Smithsonian National Postal Museum

A lesser-known Smithsonian Institution museum is the **National Postal Museum** (2 Massachusetts Ave. NE, 202/633-5555, www.postalmuseum.si.edu, daily 10am-5:30pm, free). Located near Union Station, the museum contains exhibits of stamps and philatelic items, mail-delivery vehicles, and historical artifacts from America's postal system.

DOWNTOWN
National Archives

Only in Washington DC can you see the original Declaration of Independence, the Constitution, and the Bill of Rights. These powerful documents live in the Rotunda for the Charters of Freedom at the **National Archives Building** (700 Pennsylvania Ave. NW, visitors' entrance on Constitution Ave. between 7th St. and 9th St. NW, 866/272-6272, www.archives.gov, daily 10am-5:30pm, extended summer hours, free). They can be viewed by the public daily, but are then lowered into the vault for safekeeping after hours.

Also known as Archives I, the National Archives Building is the headquarters for the National Archives and Records Administration, an independent agency of the U.S. government that is responsible for preserving historical records. Countless additional documents are on permanent exhibit in the public vaults, including treaties, photographs, telegrams, maps, and films. Interactive exhibits allow visitors to get close to some of the most interesting documents.

Reynolds Center

The revitalized Penn Quarter area of downtown gets more and more hip each year as space is renovated and new attractions move in. A prime example is the Smithsonian's **Reynolds Center** (8th St. and F St. NW, 202/633-1000, www.americanart.si.edu, daily 11:30am-7pm, free), which covers an entire block in the Chinatown neighborhood in what was one of the first patent office buildings. The Reynolds Center is officially named the **Donald W. Reynolds Center for American Art and Portraiture,** and it consists of two Smithsonian museums, the **Smithsonian American Art Museum** and the **National Portrait Gallery.** The massive Greek Revival building dates back to 1836 and originally

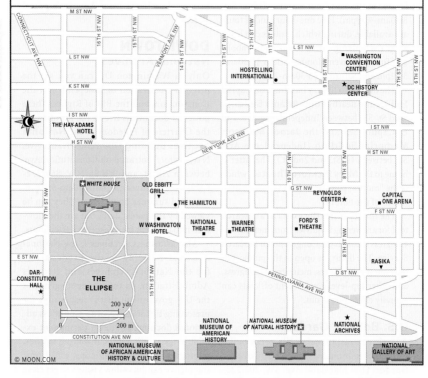

Downtown DC

took 31 years to construct. The Smithsonian American Art Museum features a wide variety of American art and houses works by significant artists such Georgia O'Keeffe, Albert Bierstadt, and Nam June Paik. The National Portrait Gallery contains images of many famous Americans. The museums are above the Gallery Place-Chinatown Metrorail station on the Red, Yellow, and Green Lines.

National Building Museum

If architecture, building, and design intrigue you, the **National Building Museum** (401 F St. NW, 202/272-2448, www.nbm.org, Mon.-Sat. 10am-5pm, Sun. 11am-5pm, adults $16, youth 3-17/students/seniors 60 and over $13) is a must-see. As the country's leading cultural institution committed to interpreting the impact and history of the built environment, this

family-friendly museum offers exhibits, public programs, and festivals. The museum itself is a spectacular building with an impressive Great Hall that contains 75-foot Corinthian columns and a 1,200-foot terra-cotta frieze. Exhibits include *House & Home,* which provides a tour of familiar and surprising homes, and *Play Work Build,* an exploration exhibit that allows children and adults to fill an exhibition wall with virtual blocks and then knock them down.

DC History Center

The **DC History Center** (801 K St. NW, 202/516-1363, www.dchistory.org, Tues.-Sat. 10am-5pm, Sun. noon-5pm, free), located in the Carnegie Library on Mount Vernon Square, opened in 2019 and features exhibits on the history of Washington DC. It is run

Dupont Circle

by the Historical Society of Washington, D.C. and includes three exhibit areas, the Kiplinger Research Library, and the DC History Center Store. The city's flagship Apple store is also in the building.

Ford's Theatre

Still a thriving theatrical venue, the famous **Ford's Theatre** (511 10th St. NW, 202/347-4833, www.fords.org, daily 9am-4:30pm, $3) is the site where President Lincoln was assassinated on April 14, 1865. It is also a historical site with a museum focusing on Abraham Lincoln's presidency, assassination, and legacy. Artifacts featured in the museum include the contents of Lincoln's pockets on the day he died, the single-shot .44-caliber derringer that John Wilkes Booth used to kill Lincoln, and two life masks. The **Petersen House** (516 10th St, NW, 202/347-4833, daily 9:30am-5:30pm), where Lincoln died, is located across the street and can also be visited with a Ford's Theatre ticket. The **Center for Education and Leadership** (514 10th St., 202/347-4833, daily 9:30am-5:30pm) is adjacent to the Petersen House and can only be entered through the house. It can also be visited with a Ford's Theatre historic site ticket. It has a 34-foot tower full of books on Lincoln, accessible by a winding staircase. The books in the tower are made from aluminum and represent 205 real titles on Lincoln. This unusual work of art symbolizes that the last word about Lincoln will never be written. There are also exhibits that teach about the hunt for John Wilkes Booth and Lincoln's funeral train. A theatrical audio tour of the theater is available for $5. Ford's Theatre is located in the Penn Quarter area.

DUPONT CIRCLE
Dupont Circle Park

Maintained by the National Park Service, **Dupont Circle Park** has been the location of many political rallies, and it is also a gathering place for chess players to challenge one another on permanent stone chessboards. The central double-tiered white marble fountain, installed in 1920, offers seating; it replaced a memorial statue of Samuel Francis Du Pont, a rear admiral during the Civil War, that was placed there in 1884. The fountain was designed by the cocreators of the Lincoln Memorial and represents the sea, stars, and wind.

The Phillips Collection

The Dupont Circle neighborhood is home to the original late 19th-century Renoir painting *Luncheon of the Boating Party*. It lives at **The Phillips Collection** (1600 21st St. NW, 202/387-2151, www.phillipscollection.org, Tues.-Sat. 10am-5pm, Sun. noon-6:30pm, adults $12, 18 and under free, students/seniors 62 and over $10), an intimate impressionist and modern art museum founded in 1921 by Duncan Phillips. The museum includes the founder's former home and extensive new galleries. Other featured works (there are more than 3,000) include pieces by Vincent van

---

I Got You Babe

Just southwest of Dupont Circle on New Hampshire Avenue is a small, triangular wedge of land that memorializes pop star and politician **Sonny Bono**. Officially called Sonny Bono Park, the patch of grass has benches and a plaque (that draws a striking resemblance to a manhole cover) honoring the late statesman, who died in a ski accident in 1998.

Gogh, Claude Monet, Pablo Picasso, Georgia O'Keeffe, and Winslow Homer.

GEORGETOWN
Dumbarton Oaks

The **Dumbarton Oaks Research Library and Collection** (1703 32nd St. NW, 202/339-6400, www.doaks.org, museum Tues.-Sun. 11:30am-5:30pm, free, gardens Tues.-Sun. Nov. 1-Mar. 14 2pm-5pm, free, Mar. 15-Oct. 31 2pm-6pm, adults $10, children 2-12 $5, seniors 60 and over and military $8) is a gorgeous, historic, and romantic estate museum and garden. It was a private estate for many years before being donated to Harvard University in 1940. The estate was the site of a series of important diplomatic meetings in 1944 that laid the foundation for the development of the United Nations. Today the museum offers exhibitions of Byzantine and pre-Columbian art (including more than 12,000 Byzantine coins); Asian, European, and American art; and European furnishings. The 10-acre park boasts a fine example of a European-style formal garden, with more than 1,000 rosebushes, an herb garden, and stone fountains.

Georgetown University

Georgetown is anchored by the 104-acre campus of **Georgetown University** (37th St. and

---

1: Ford's Theatre 2: people relaxing around the Dupont Circle fountain 3: shops along M Street in Georgetown

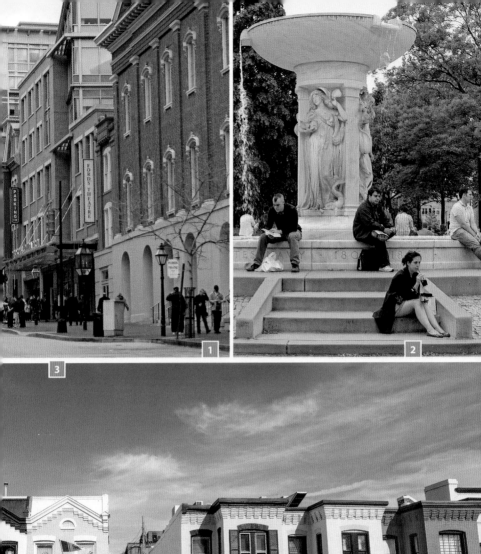

Georgetown

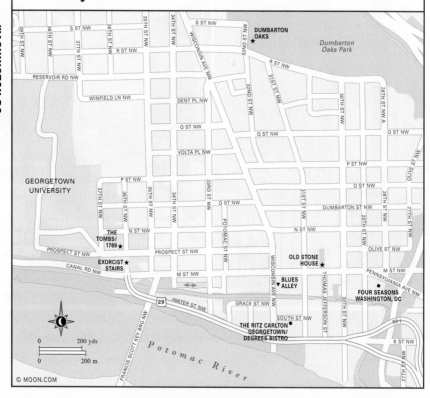

O St. NW, 202/687-0100, www.georgetown. edu). Noted for its law school in particular, this private research university offers nine graduate and undergraduate schools with a total enrollment of around 17,000 students. Georgetown was established in 1789 and is the oldest Catholic and Jesuit university in the country. Notable alumni include President Bill Clinton, actor Bradley Cooper, and the late U.S. Supreme Court justice Antonin Scalia.

Old Stone House

The oldest standing building in DC, and also the city's last pre-Revolutionary colonial building still on its original foundation, was built in 1765 and is simply called the **Old Stone House** (3051 M St. NW, 202/426-6851, www.nps.gov, Wed.-Sun. noon-5pm, free). This excellent example of vernacular architecture was constructed in three phases and served many purposes throughout the years including being a hat shop, tailor's shop, locksmith shop, and even a used-car dealership. The house was renovated in the 1950s and turned into a museum by the National Park Service. Today, visitors can learn the history of the house from park rangers and view the home's kitchen, bedrooms, and parlor, all authentically furnished to reflect the daily lives of average Americans in the 18th century. The Old Stone House is said to be haunted by countless spirits.

Adams Morgan and Upper Northwest

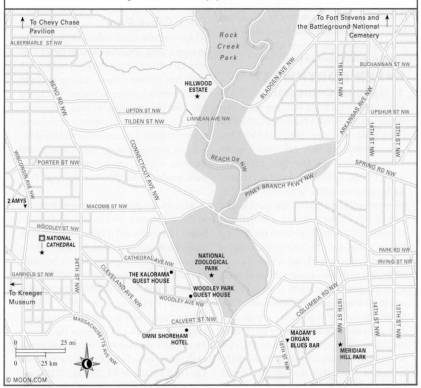

To Chevy Chase Pavilion

ALBERMARLE ST NW

Rock Creek Park

To Fort Stevens and the Battleground National Cemetery

BUCHANNAN ST NW

16TH ST NW

BLADGEN AVE NW

ARKANSAS AVE NW

UPSHUR ST NW

14TH ST NW

13TH ST NW

HILLWOOD ESTATE ★

RENO RD NW

UPTON ST NW

TILDEN ST NW

LINNEAN AVE NW

CONNECTICUT AVE NW

BEACH DR NW

PORTER ST NW

SPRING RD NW

PINEY BRANCH PKWY NW

WISCONSIN AVE NW

2 AMYS ▼

MACOMB ST NW

PARK RD NW

IRVING ST NW

WOODLEY ST NW

★ NATIONAL CATHEDRAL ★

CATHEDRAL AVE NW

NATIONAL ZOOLOGICAL PARK ★

COLUMBIA RD NW

16TH ST NW

14TH ST NW

13TH ST NW

34TH ST NW

GARFIELD ST NW

CLEVELAND AVE NW

THE KALORAMA GUEST HOUSE ●

WOODLEY PARK GUEST HOUSE ●

To Kreeger Museum

WOODLEY AVE NW

MASSACHUSETTS AVE NW

CALVERT ST NW

0   25 mi

0   25 km

OMNI SHOREHAM HOTEL

MADAM'S ▼ ORGAN BLUES BAR

18TH ST NW

★ MERIDIAN HILL PARK

© MOON.COM

Exorcist Stairs

One of the most notable movie scenes filmed in Georgetown was the climactic scene in *The Exorcist,* where the priest hurls himself out the window of a house and down a steep staircase to his death to rid himself of the devil. The famed staircase is still part of the Georgetown landscape and has 75 steps that connect Prospect Street with M Street. There are three landings on the staircase, and the entire length of the stairs is equal to the height of a five-story building. For filming purposes, a fake front was constructed on the house located at the top of the steps to make it appear that the bedroom in the movie overlooked the staircase. In real life, the home is set back a healthy distance from the top of the stairs. It

is not uncommon to see Georgetown students running the stairs. Hoya athletes are known to run it 10 or more times. The steps are located at the end of 36th Street.

ADAMS MORGAN
Meridian Hill Park

Meridian Hill Park (15th, 16th, W, and Euclid Sts. NW, free) is a 12-acre urban park maintained by the National Park Service. It is near Adams Morgan in the Columbia Heights neighborhood. The park was built in the early 1900s and sits on a hillside. It is well landscaped and includes dramatic staircases, benches, and concrete walkways. The focal point of the park is a 13-basin cascading waterfall fountain in a formal garden. There are also a number of statues in the park. This is a popular place to steal some relaxation in the summer, and many people take advantage of this secret little garden in the city. Drummers form circles on Sunday afternoons in the summertime, but people come to spread a blanket and play catch nearly all year.

UPPER NORTHWEST
★ National Cathedral

Many visitors are filled with awe when they see the beautiful Gothic **National Cathedral** (3101 Wisconsin Ave. NW, 202/537-6200, www.cathedral.org, Mon.-Fri. 10am-5pm, Sat. 10am-4pm, Sun. 12:45pm-4pm, adults $12, youth 5-17 $8, children under 5 free, seniors/students/active military/veterans $8). This imposing edifice, which is the sixth-largest cathedral in the world, is hard to miss. It took 83 years (1907 to 1990) to carve the 150,000 tons of stone, and this impressive building has a few tricks up its sleeve. A tour is a must (they offer more than a dozen different ones), since the great docents will provide you access to the towers and crypt, which are off limits should you try to go there on your own. Although the regular tours are impressive, the behind-the-scenes tour (adults $27, children 11 and up/seniors/military/students $23) is the best. You'll walk through hidden hallways, get a close look at the stunning stained glass windows, and learn the cathedral's secrets (like how Darth Vader lives high on the northwest tower in the form of a grotesque that was sculpted after a public competition was held to suggest designs for grotesques and gargoyles). You'll also get a grand view from the cathedral's roof. Be ready for stair climbing, heights, and close quarters. Participants must be at least 11 years old. Reservations can be made online.

Organ demonstrations are given on most Mondays and Wednesdays at 12:30pm. They are impressive and loud. Regular Episcopal worship services are held at the cathedral; a schedule is posted on the website. A café (Mon.-Fri. 7am-6pm, Sat.-Sun. 8am-6pm) is located in the Old Baptistry building next to the cathedral, where the public can purchase light fare such as sandwiches, coffee, and pastries. Parking is available under the cathedral.

Rock Creek Park

It's hard to believe that with all DC has to offer in such a small area, there's room for a 1,754-acre park. **Rock Creek Park** (202/895-6000, www.nps.gov/rocr, open during daylight hours, free) is a prime recreation area in the city that offers running, walking, equestrian, and cycling trails, a golf course, a professional tennis stadium, a nature center and planetarium, an outdoor concert venue, playground facilities, wildlife, and cultural exhibits. The park is administered by the National Park Service.

Visitors can enjoy a real sense of outdoors in this urban park, which consists of woods, fields, and creeks and is home to wildflowers and wildlife such as coyotes, beavers, and fox. The park borders Upper Northwest DC to the east and has long stretches of roads (including Rock Creek Pkwy. and Beach Dr.) that are closed to cars on weekends. Fifteen miles of hiking trails, a bike path that runs the entire length of the park and connects the Lincoln Memorial to the Maryland border, and horseback riding from **Rock Creek Park Horse Center** (5100 Glover Rd., 202/362-0117, www.rockcreekhorsecenter.com, lessons starting $55 per hour, one-hour trail rides $45) are just some of the activities available to visitors. The park's **Nature Center** (5200 Glover Rd., 202/895-6070, Wed.-Sun. 9am-5pm) is a good place to start your exploration. Another attraction is the **Peirce Mill** (2401 Tilden St. NW, at Beach Dr., 202/895-6070, Apr.-Oct. Fri.-Sun. 10am-4pm, Nov.-Feb. Sat.-Sun. noon-4pm, Mar. Sat.-Sun. 10am-4pm, free). It is the only existing water-powered gristmill in DC.

The park is relatively safe for a city park, but it is still advisable to enjoy it with a friend. Leashed dogs are allowed in the park. It is good to keep in mind that on weekdays

1: National Cathedral 2: the 22 Corinthian sandstone columns in the National Arboretum

Rock Creek Parkway is one-way going south 6:45am-9:30am and one-way going north 3:45pm-6:30pm.

National Zoological Park

The Smithsonian's **National Zoological Park** (3001 Connecticut Ave. NW, 202/633-4888, www.nationalzoo.si.edu, daily Oct. 1-Mar. 14, grounds 8am-5pm, visitor center and exhibit buildings 9am-4pm, daily Mar. 15-Sept. 30, grounds 8am-7pm, visitor center and exhibit buildings 9am-6pm, free), commonly called the National Zoo, is one of the oldest zoos in the country. The 163-acre park is near the Woodley Park Metrorail station on the edge of Rock Creek Park. The zoo, founded in 1889, is constantly undergoing updates and renovations. Hundreds of animals are tucked into habitats along hillsides, in the woods, and in specially built temperature-controlled animal houses. Since entrance to the park is free, many local residents use the several miles of nicely paved pathways on their regular walking or running routes.

Well-known residents include giant pandas from China, great apes, elephants, Komodo dragons, and much more. Many of the species at the zoo are endangered. Unique exhibits include the Elephant Walk, where Asian elephants can take daily treks for exercise, and a skywalk for orangutans, where a series of high cables and towers allow them to move between two buildings and over spectators below. Another favorite is the American Trail, which features sea lions, wolves, eagles, and other animals native to North America. The zoo also features a Think Tank, where visitors can learn how animals think through a series of interactive displays that are available to the zoo's orangutans at their leisure. The best time to visit the zoo is on weekday mornings when there are fewer crowds and the animals are more active. Although it is free to enter the zoo, there is a parking fee of $25.

Hillwood Estate, Museum & Gardens

Those in the know are fans of the wonderful **Hillwood Estate, Museum & Gardens** (4155 Linnean Ave. NW, 202/686-5807, www.hillwoodmuseum.org, Tues.-Sun. 10am-5pm, suggested donation adults $18, college students $10, children 6-18 $5, seniors $15, children under 6 free), the former home of prominent businesswoman, philanthropist, and heiress to the Post Cereal fortune Marjorie Merriweather Post. This stately and luxurious home with a Georgian-style facade was purchased by Post in 1955 and used for entertaining and to house her abundant collections of French and Russian art, including an extraordinary collection of Fabergé eggs. The artwork is rivaled by the exquisite French- and Japanese-style gardens, where visitors can relax after taking a tour. One-hour guided tours and self-guided tours are available with the suggested donation. A café and gift shop are on-site.

Kreeger Museum

The **Kreeger Museum** (2401 Foxhall Rd. NW, 202/337-3050, www.kreegermuseum.org, Tues.-Sat. 10am-4pm, suggested donation adults $10, students/seniors/military $8) is a private museum that often passes under the radar of tourists due to its Foxhall neighborhood location and small size. This little gem of an attraction features 19th- and 20th-century sculptures and paintings by many world-renowned artists such as Monet, Picasso, Rodin, and van Gogh. It also offers works by local artists and traditional African art. The building is the former home of David and Carmen Kreeger and sits on more than five acres of sculpture gardens and woods.

Battleground National Cemetery

One of the smallest national cemeteries in the nation is the **Battleground National Cemetery** (6625 Georgia Ave., 202/895-6000, www.nps.gov, daily dawn-dusk, free). It is the burial ground for 41 Union soldiers who died in the 1864 Battle of Fort Stevens, the sole Civil War battle to take place in DC. The engagement marked the end of a Confederate effort to act offensively against the national capital. The battle is the only one in Civil War history during which the U.S. president (Abraham Lincoln) came under direct fire. Lincoln rode out to observe the fight and was fired on briefly by sharpshooters (he was then ordered to take cover). After the battle, a one-acre plot of farmland was seized and used to bury the dead. That night, Lincoln came to the site and dedicated it as a national cemetery. Visitors can see grave markers, four monuments to the units that fought in the battle, and a marble rostrum that has eight Doric columns. The rostrum is the site of the annual Memorial Day services at the cemetery. The National Park Service manages the cemetery.

Nearby **Fort Stevens** (1339 Fort Stevens Dr., www.nps.gov, daily dawn-dusk, free), the actual site of the battle, is partially restored and is also maintained by the National Park Service. It was part of a series of fortifications constructed around Washington DC during the Civil War. Visitors can see much of the fort still intact, including the cannons (now facing urban streets). You can even stand on the spot where then future Supreme Court justice Oliver Wendell Holmes is said to have shouted at President Lincoln, "Get down, you fool!" when he was shot at.

NORTHEAST DC
National Arboretum

Northeast of Capitol Hill (2.2 miles from the Capitol Building) is a little-recognized attraction that first opened in 1927: the **National Arboretum** (3501 New York Ave. NE, 202/245-2726, www.usna.usda.gov, daily 8am-5pm, free). This lovely 446-acre campus has more than nine miles of roads that connect many gardens and plant collections where there is always something in bloom. Seventy-six staff members and more than 140 volunteers oversee the arboretum, which was created to "serve the public need for scientific research, education, and gardens that conserve and showcase plants to enhance the environment." Parking areas are available near many of the major collections, and bike racks

are also on hand. The original 22 columns from the east side of the Capitol Building found a home here when the Capitol was enlarged in the 1950s; they now sit on display in a field. The **National Bonsai & Penjing Museum** (daily 10am-4pm, free) is also located on the arboretum grounds, as is a gift shop. Leashed pets are welcome, and there are public restrooms in the administrative building.

TOURS

A great way to see the city is to take an organized tour. There is a wide variety to choose from, including trolley tours, boat tours, and walking tours.

Trolley, Bus, and Boat Tours

One of the most popular motorized tours in the city is given by **Old Town Trolley** (844/356-2603, www.trolleytours.com, daily 9am-5pm, $45). This lively narrated tour covers more than 100 points of interest and offers a "hop on-hop off" format where guests can get off at 17 stops and pick up another trolley (which stops at each location every 30 minutes) at their leisure. Sights include the Lincoln Memorial, the White House, Smithsonian Institution museums, and many more. No reservations are required, and visitors can board and reboard all day. Tickets can be purchased online or at the sales desk in **Union Station** (50 Massachusetts Ave. NE, stop #4) and at the **Washington Welcome Center** (1005 E St. NW, stop #1).

Old Town Trolley also offers a 2.5-hour **Monuments by Moonlight** tour ($40.50) that allows visitors to see the illuminated monuments and memorials. Stops include the FDR Memorial, Iwo Jima Memorial (in Arlington, Virginia), the Lincoln Memorial, and Vietnam Veterans Memorial. This narrated tour includes some fun ghost stories as well. The tour leaves nightly from Union Station.

Another popular tour is the **DC Ducks Tour** (855/969-0828, www.dcducks.com, adults $45, children 12 and under $33).

Guests explore the city on both land and water in a "Duck," a unique vehicle that is part bus, part boat. Ninety-minute trips start at Union Station (50 Massachusetts Ave. NE), drive to the National Mall, and end with a cruise along the Potomac River. The tours are narrated by "wise-quacking" captains who offer a wealth of historical facts and corny jokes.

Another "hop on-hop off" tour is the **Open Top Big Bus Tour** (877/332-8689, www.bigbustours.com, daily 9am-5pm, one-day pass adults $50, children 5-15 $40, 2-day pass adults $60, children 5-15 $50). Guests can take in two routes around the city from a double-decker bus with an open-air top deck. Tickets can be purchased online and on any of their buses.

For a view from the water, sign up for a cruise with **Potomac Riverboat Company** (703/684-0580, www.potomacriverboatco.com). They offer several sightseeing tours leaving from different locations around the region, including their 60-minute "Monument Tour from the Wharf" (950 Wharf St., adults from $20, children from $14).

Walking Tours

Free guided walking tours of DC's monuments are available through **DC by Foot** (202/370-1830, www.freetoursbyfoot.com/dc, free but tips appreciated). These unique tours feature animated, energetic tour guides who work purely on tips. Because of this, they do their best to entertain you while providing unique stories about Washington's most famous residents. Private tours are also available.

Ghost tours are a good way to get in touch with the spirits of the city. Several tour operators offer walking tours around some of the most haunted sites in the city. **Washington Walks** (202/484-1565, www.washingtonwalks.com) offers **Most Haunted Houses** tours (Oct. Fri.-Sat. at 7:30pm, $20). Two-hour walking tours begin at the corner of New York Avenue and 18th Street NW. This is just one of many walking tours they offer throughout the year.

Recreation

SPECTATOR SPORTS

The nation's capital is home to many professional sports teams and hosts countless sporting events throughout the year.

The **Washington Nationals** baseball team, which came to DC in 2005, plays at **Nationals Park** (1500 S. Capitol St. SE, 202/675-6287, www.mlb.com). The stadium sits on the banks of the Anacostia River in the Navy Yard neighborhood and seats approximately 41,500 people. The Washington Monument and Capitol Building can be seen from the upper stands.

The **Capital One Arena** (601 F St. NW, 202/628-3200, www.capitalonearena.com) in Penn Quarter is home to the city's professional hockey team (the NHL's **Washington Capitals**), two pro basketball teams (the NBA's **Washington Wizards** and the WNBA's **Washington Mystics**), and Georgetown University's men's basketball team (the Georgetown Hoyas).

DC's professional soccer team, the **D.C. United,** received a brand-new home in 2018 at **Audi Field** (100 Potomac Ave. SW, www.audifieldddc.com), two miles south of the U.S. Capitol. The **Washington Redskins** (www.redskins.com) NFL football team plays at **FedExField** in Landover, Maryland.

Other professional sporting events make their way annually to DC. The **Citi Open** (www.citiopentennis.com) tennis tournament is part of the U.S. Open Series. Professional players from around the globe compete for

1: Josh Gibson statue, designed by sculptor Omri Amrany, outside of Nationals Park 2: paddleboarding on the Potomac River near Key Bridge, Georgetown

Run DC

Runners and triathletes make their way to Washington DC regularly to partake in many annual races. These are just a few of the numerous events scheduled throughout the year.

- **Rock 'n' Roll DC Marathon & Half Marathon** (Mar., www.runrocknroll.com)
- **Credit Union Cherry Blossom Ten Mile Run** (Apr., www.cherryblossom.org)
- **Capitol Hill Classic 10K** (May, www.capitolhillclassic.com)
- **Komen Global Race for the Cure 5K** (Sept., www.info-komen.org)
- **Army 10-Miler** (Oct., www.armytenmiler.com)
- **Marine Corps Marathon** (Oct., www.marinemarathon.com)

more than $1.8 million in this world-class event. The nine-day tournament is held at the tennis center in Rock Creek Park at the end of July and beginning of August.

The **Washington International Horse Show** (www.wihs.org) is a yearly championship event held at Capital One Arena at the end of October. Approximately 600 horses and riders compete for more than $400,000 in prize money and titles. The event includes show jumping, dressage, equitation, hunters, barrel racing, and terrier races.

CANOEING AND KAYAKING

Those interested in paddling a canoe or kayak on the Potomac River are in for a treat. Viewing the city from the calm of the river puts it in a whole new perspective. Rentals are available at several locations, including the **Key Bridge Boathouse** (3500 Water St. NW, 202/337-9642, http://boatingindc.com) and **Thompson Boat Center** (2900 Virginia Ave. NW, 202/333-9543, http://boatingindc.com). Rentals are $16 per hour for a single and $22 per hour for a double kayak. Canoes are $25 per hour.

BIKING

Another great option for getting around the city on two wheels is joining **Capital Bikeshare** (www.capitalbikeshare.com) for a day, three days, a month, or a year.

Members gain access to more than 1,800 bikes in 350 locations throughout the city (including Arlington and Alexandria in Virginia). Twenty-four-hour memberships are $8. Passes can be purchased at kiosks at each bike station.

An 11-mile rail-to-trail route called the **Capital Crescent Trail** starts in Georgetown on K Street. The trail runs parallel to the C&O Canal Towpath for the first three miles but then goes through upscale neighborhoods in Northwest DC. The initial seven miles between Georgetown and Bethesda, Maryland, are paved, but an additional four miles of unpaved trail (mostly crushed stone) can be ridden to Silver Spring, Maryland. The two trails are connected by a tunnel under downtown Bethesda.

Bike Tours

Year-round daily bike tours around Washington DC are offered by **Fat Tire Tours** (502 23rd St. NW, 202/626-0017, www.fattiretours.com, starting at $42). Comfortable beach cruisers are used in the tours, and riders can expect to see sights such as the Lincoln Memorial, White House, Vietnam Veterans Memorial, and the Capitol Building.

Another popular bike tour company is **Bike and Roll Washington DC** (202/842-2453, www.bikeandrollldc.com). They offer seasonal guided tours by bike (three hours, adults $44, children 12 and under $34) and Segway (2.5 hours, $64) from their National Mall location (955 L'Enfant Plaza SW) and year-round tours from their Union Station location (50 Massachusetts Ave. NE, 202/962-0206).

ICE-SKATING

A great way to impress a date on a cold winter night is by going ice-skating at the **National Gallery of Art Sculpture Garden and Ice Skating Rink** (700 Constitution Ave. NW, 202/216-9397). Skate in the shadows of some of the city's most well-known buildings and in view of many of the garden's wonderful sculptures. This enchanting rink is especially romantic at night.

PLAYGROUND

For the coolest playground in town, visit **Turtle Park** (Friendship Park, 4500 Van Ness St. NW, 202/282-2198) in Upper Northwest. The focal point is a huge sandbox with turtle sculptures for climbing on and a "sprayground" for cleaning off the sand and cooling off. There are also ball fields in the park and a recreation center.

Entertainment and Events

THEATER

The premier theater in Washington DC is the **John F. Kennedy Center for the Performing Arts** (2700 F St. NW, 202/467-4600, www.kennedy-center.org). This incredible venue is a landmark on the banks of the Potomac River and first opened in 1971. It hosts more annual performances than any other facility in the country, with approximately 2,000 theater, dance, musical, and multimedia performances each year. There are three primary theaters within the center. The **Concert Hall** seats approximately 2,400 guests and is the largest performance space in the center. It features seven Hadeland crystal chandeliers (courtesy of Norway) and a 4,144-pipe organ (a gift from the Filene Foundation of Boston). The Concert Hall is also home to the **National Symphony Orchestra.** The **Opera House,** with its unique red and gold silk curtain (a gift from Japan), seats approximately 2,300 guests and features a Lobmeyr crystal chandelier (courtesy of Austria). It is the primary venue for opera, ballet, and large-scale musical performances and home to the **Washington National Opera,** the **Suzanne Farrell Ballet,** and the yearly **Kennedy Center Honors.** The **Eisenhower Theater** seats approximately 1,163 guests and hosts smaller-scale operas, plays, and musicals. In addition, **The REACH** was unveiled in 2019 as an open-stage living theater and immersive learning center. It complements the Kennedy Center's mission and vision of an inclusive, interactive, and accessible modern arts center.

The historic **National Theatre** (1321 Pennsylvania Ave. NW, 202/628-6161, www.thenationaldc.com) playhouse is the oldest theater venue in DC. It is three blocks from the White House and has entertained many presidents since its founding in 1835. In fact, Abraham Lincoln's son Tad was attending a production of *Aladdin and the Wonderful Lamp* at the National Theatre at the time his father was assassinated in Ford's Theatre. Today the theater is known for hosting mostly Broadway musicals.

Originally built as a movie palace in 1924, the **Warner Theatre** (513 13th St. NW, 202/783-4000, www.warnertheatredc.com) was then called the Earle Theatre and hosted live vaudeville and silent movies. During the 1940s the theater showed movies exclusively and was renamed for its owner, Harry Warner of Warner Bros. fame. The theater suffered in the 1970s, but was revived shortly after as a concert venue. After major renovations between 1989 and 1992, the theater reopened with theatrical, dance, and musical productions and has since hosted great performers such as Frank Sinatra. It is a landmark in the Penn Quarter neighborhood.

Nearby, **Ford's Theatre** (511 10th St. NW, 202/347-4833, www.fords.org) is most famous as the location of the assassination of President Lincoln in 1865. Following his death, the theater closed. After a long stint as a warehouse and an office building, it finally reopened more than 100 years later in 1968 and again began to host performances. Today it is an active venue with a full schedule of plays and musicals.

A well-known regional theater company in DC is the **Shakespeare Theatre Company** (202/547-1122, www.shakespearetheatre.org). This highly regarded company presents primarily Shakespearean productions but also offers works by other classic playwrights. The company manages the **Harman Center for the Arts,** which consists of two venues in Penn Quarter: the **Landsburgh Theatre** (450 7th St. NW) and **Sidney Harman Hall** (610 F St. NW).

For more-experimental, cutting-edge performances, catch a production by the **Woolly Mammoth Theatre Company** (641 D St. NW, 202/393-3939, www.woollymammoth. net). They develop and produce new plays and pride themselves on being "Washington's most daring theatre company."

In Southwest DC, **Arena Stage at the Mead Center for American Theater** (1101 6th St. SW, 202/488-3300, www.arenastage. org) takes the title of being the largest not-for-profit theater in the city. It features a broad range of performances, including the classics and new-play premiers as well as educational programs.

A unique performance venue is the **Carter Barron Amphitheatre** (4850 Colorado Ave. NW, 202/426-0486, www.nps. gov/rocr) in Rock Creek Park. The beautiful, 4,200-seat outdoor amphitheater is operated by the National Park Service and offers a range of performances including concerts, theater, and dance. Many are provided at no charge.

The historic **AMC Uptown 1** (3426 Connecticut Ave. NW, www.amctheatres. com) is a single-screen movie theater in the Cleveland Park neighborhood run by AMC Theatres. The theater first opened in 1936 and has been the site for many Hollywood movie premieres. The curved, 70-foot-long and 40-foot-high screen is considered to be the best in the DC area, and the theater can seat 850 people.

ARENAS AND HALLS

There are several large performance arenas in the city. **Capital One Arena** (601 F St. NW, 202/628-3200, www.capitalonearena. com) was formerly the Verizon Center and anchors the Penn Quarter neighborhood. It is home to several professional sports teams (Washington Capitals, Washington Wizards, and Washington Mystics) but also hosts numerous concerts and other large-scale performances. **Audi Field** (100 Potomac Ave. SW, www.audifieldddc.com) opened in 2018 as the home field for the D.C. United professional soccer team. This state-of-the-art arena is located southeast of the District Wharf. **Robert F. Kennedy Memorial Stadium (RFK)** (2400 E. Capitol St. SE, 202/587-5000, www.eventsdc.com) is the former home of the Washington Redskins and now hosts concerts, conventions, and other events.

Historic **DAR Constitution Hall** (1776 D St. NW, 202/628-1776, www.dar.org), near the White House, was built in 1929 by the Daughters of the American Revolution as a venue for their annual convention. This 3,200-seat hall, which formerly only hosted classical shows and opera, is now a concert venue for rock, pop, hip-hop, and soul.

The 2.3 million-square-foot **Walter E. Washington Convention Center** (801 Mt. Vernon Pl, NW, 202/249-3000, www. dcconvention.com) offers 703,000 square feet of event space, 77 meeting rooms, and the largest ballroom in the city. It hosts countless events throughout the year in the downtown area.

MUSIC VENUES

The most recent addition to the DC music scene is **The Anthem** (901 Wharf St. SW, 202/888-0020, www.theathemdc.com), on the District Wharf. This gorgeous, 6,000-seat concert venue hosts well-known rockers, hip-hop artists, and other stars in its acoustically optimized environment. Food and drinks are available in the arena (no cash), and shows sell out early. Recent shows include The Raconteurs, Jenny Lewis, and Tame Impala. A much more intimate music space (150 seats) and also on the Wharf is **Pearl Street Warehouse** (33 Pearl St. SW, 202/380-9620, www.pearlstreetwarehouse.com). They feature everything from rock to bluegrass music.

The **U Street Corridor** can be called the center of the music scene in Washington DC. Once the haunt of legends such as Duke Ellington, the area carries on his legacy through venues such as **Twins Jazz** (1344 U St. NW, top floor, 202/234-0072, www.twinsjazz.com), which offers live jazz five to six nights a week. This unassuming club with red interior walls looks like someone's home on the outside. It also features Ethiopian, Caribbean, and American food.

The **U Street Music Hall** (1115 U St. NW, 202/588-1889, www.ustreetmusichall.com) is a live-music and DJ dance club. It features a cork-cushioned, 1,200-square-foot dance floor.

For a broader range of music options, the popular **9:30 Club** (815 V St. NW, 202/265-0930, www.930.com) hosts everyone from Echo and the Bunnymen to Corey Smith. This unassuming venue is on the corner of 9th and V Streets. Shows are general admission and standing room only. They have four full bars and a coffee bar and also serve food.

The **Black Cat** (1811 14th St. NW, 202/667-4490, www.blackcatdc.com) hosts a variety of local, national, and international independent and alternative bands. They offer two stages and are a cash-only establishment.

Two small venues that highlight primarily local bands are the **Velvet Lounge** (915 U St. NW, 202/462-3213, www.velvetloungedc.com) and **DC9** (1940 9th St. NW, 202/483-5000, www.dc9.club).

Other areas of the city host great musical artists as well. An intimate venue for hearing live jazz is **Blues Alley** (1073 Wisconsin Ave. NW, 202/337-4141, www.bluesalley.com) in Georgetown. This local landmark consistently delivers quality jazz and a fun atmosphere. They serve food, but the main attraction is the music.

Two blocks from the White House, **The Hamilton** (600 14th St. NW, 202/787-1000, www.thehamiltondc.com) hosts visionary musical performers in an intimate setting.

NIGHTLIFE
Downtown

For the chance to rub elbows with celebrities, professional athletes, and young, hip Washingtonians, grab a drink at the downtown **P.O.V. Roof Terrace and Lounge** (515 15th St. NW, 202/661-2437, www.povrooftop.com, Sun.-Thurs. 11am-midnight, Fri.-Sat. 11am-2am) at the W Washington D.C. Hotel. This rooftop bar and terrace is one of the top hot spots in DC and has phenomenal views of the city through 12-foot-tall windows. They serve premium-brand liquor and a tapas menu. No sneakers or athletic wear is permitted; collared shirts are preferred. Expect a wait to get in on weekends.

Perfect martinis and a more relaxed atmosphere can be found across from the White House at the **Off the Record Bar** (800 16th St. NW, 202/638-6600, www.hayadams.com, Sun.-Thurs. 11:30am-midnight, Fri.-Sat. 11:30am-12:30am) at the Hay-Adams hotel.

Just a little west of downtown and a little south of Dupont Circle on M Street is **Ozio Restaurant and Lounge** (1813 M St. NW, 202/822-6000, www.oziodc.com, Tues.-Thurs. 5pm-2am, Fri. 5pm-3am, Sat. 6pm-3am, Sun. noon-2am). This huge, multilevel club is somewhat upscale and often has a business crowd. They have great martinis, cigars, and a lively rooftop lounge.

Dupont Circle

One of the most exclusive nightlife spots in the city is the **Eighteenth Street Lounge** (1212 18th St. NW, 202/466-3922, www.18thstlounge.com, Tues.-Thurs. 5pm-2am, Fri. 5pm-3am, Sat. 9pm-3am, Sun. 9pm-2am), in the former home of Teddy Roosevelt. This restored row house mansion is classy, and you must be dressed appropriately to enter. There are high ceilings, a dance floor, retro decor, and multiple rooms, each with its own theme and bar.

The **Bar Rouge** (1315 16th St. NW, 202/232-8000, www.rougehotel.com, daily 5pm-10pm) in the Kimpton Rouge is a popular choice for happy hour and evening cocktails. This sleek, modern lounge has good happy hour specials on weekdays. They also serve food.

A lively Latin American scene can be found at **Café Citron** (1343 Connecticut Ave. NW, 202/530-8844, www.cafecitrondc.com, Mon.-Tues. 7pm-2am, Wed.-Thurs. 5pm-2am, Fri.-Sat. 5pm-3am), a two-level lounge that features salsa and other international music. This place can get rowdy on weekends, and they are known for having outstanding mojitos.

Georgetown

A sophisticated place to grab a drink at pretty much any time is the **Degrees Bistro** (3100 S St. NW, 202/912-4100, www.ritzcarlton.com, daily 5pm-midnight), in the Ritz-Carlton Georgetown. This relaxing lounge brings a bit of New York City to the nation's capital with its chic decor, dependable drinks, and great potential for people watching.

A Georgetown favorite since 1962, **The Tombs** (1226 36th St. NW, 202/337-6668, www.tombs.com, Mon.-Thurs. 11:30am-1:30am, Fri. 11:30am-2:30am, Sat. 11am-2:30am, Sun. 9:30am-1:30am) is a casual bar and local hangout for students at Georgetown University. This place served as the inspiration for the setting of *St. Elmo's Fire*. Owned by the Clyde's family of restaurants, it is located in the basement of upscale restaurant 1789. If you're in the mood for good burgers, beer, and a college crowd, or if you're just a fan of *St. Elmo's Fire*, this is the place for you.

If you're looking for live music and an inviting bar scene, check out **Gypsy Sally's** (3401 K St. NW, 202/333-7700, www.gypsysallys.com, Vinyl Lounge Tues. 6pm-midnight, Wed.-Sat. 6pm-2am, Sun.-Mon. if there is a show in the Music Room; Music Room open on show nights only). Not quite your typical nightlife spot, it's located in a renovated old building below the Whitehurst Freeway where K Street gives way to a recreation trail. Folk bands draw a casual,

Best Rooftop Bars

There may be no better way to soak up the vibe of the city than by grabbing a cool drink on a summer evening at a rooftop bar. Following are some of the most popular DC bars and lounges with a bird's-eye view:

- The **DNV Rooftop Bar** (1155 14th St. NW, 202/379-4366, www.viceroyhotelsandresorts.com) is in The Donovan hotel in Thomas Circle at the intersection of Massachusetts Avenue, Vermont Avenue, 14th Street, and M Street NW. This lively poolside lounge offers chaise lounges, a full-service bar, small plates, brunch, panoramic views, and great martinis.

- For stunning views of the Potomac River and the District Wharf, stop in **Whiskey Charlie** (975 7th St. SW, 202/488-2500, www.whiskeycharliewharf.com). This trendy rooftop bar sits atop the Canopy by Hilton Washington, DC hotel. They offer full bar service and food.

- Take in views of Embassy Row and the Dupont Circle neighborhood from the **Sky Bar** at the **Beacon Bar and Grill** (1615 Rhode Island Ave. NW, 202/872-1126, www.bbgwdc.com). They offer full bar service and light fare.

- A lively rooftop bar located in a Mexican restaurant in the U Street Corridor is **El Centro D.F.** (1819 14th St. NW, 202/328-3131, www.eatelcentro.com). Their two-level rooftop has two bars and 200 types of tequila.

- Another U Street neighborhood favorite is **Marvin** (2007 14th St. NW, 202/797-7171, www.marvindc.com). Their rooftop beer garden offers more than 30 Belgian ales and blondes.

- The largest open-air seating area in Adams Morgan is at **Perry's Restaurant** (1811 Columbia Rd. NW, 202/234-6218, www.perrysam.com). They have good happy hour specials, views of the city, and a fun rooftop atmosphere.

- One of "the" places to go in DC is the **P.O.V. Roof Terrace and Lounge** (515 15th St. NW, 202/661-2437, www.povrooftop.com) at the W Washington D.C. Hotel. This rooftop bar and terrace is one of the top hot spots in DC and has phenomenal views of the city through 12-foot-tall windows.

down-to-earth crowd that isn't afraid to have a few drinks and dance. When a show is going on, you must have tickets to visit the Music Room, but the Vinyl Lounge upstairs (with views of the Potomac River) is open for dinner and drinks.

Adams Morgan

Adams Morgan is known as one of the city's top nightlife areas. It has the largest concentration of bars, restaurants, and nightclubs of any neighborhood in the city. Be aware that on weekend nights, the streets can be so packed with people that it is hard to move around.

One of the best-known bars is **Madam's Organ Blues Bar** (2461 18th St. NW, 202/667-5370, www.madamsorgan.com, Sun.-Thurs. 5pm-2am, Fri.-Sat. 5pm-3am), which offers a diverse crowd, nightly live music, and

dancing. This is a dive-type bar with a slightly older crowd than the frequent college or just-out-of-college patrons that inhabit many of the establishments in Adams Morgan.

Club Heaven and Hell (2327 18th St. NW, 202/667-4355, www.clubheavenandhelldc.com, Sun.-Thurs. 5pm-1:30am, Fri.-Sat. 5pm-3am) has the largest dance floor in Adams Morgan. They have three floors—Heaven, Purgatory, and Hell—with DJs spinning top 40, hip-hop, and retro music.

Bossa Bistro and Lounge (2463 18th St. NW, 202/667-0088, www.bossadc.com, Tues.-Thurs. 5:30pm-2am, Fri.-Sat. 5:30pm-3am, Sun. 5:30pm-2am) is a cozy neighborhood restaurant that serves Brazilian food and offers live music (such as jazz and international) four nights a week and DJs on other nights. In contrast to many options in

Adams Morgan, this is an intimate place to relax in a low-key, dimly lit interior with food and atmosphere.

Habana Village (1834 Columbia Rd. NW, 202/462-6310, www.habanavillage.com, Tues.-Wed. 5pm-11pm, Thurs. 5pm-midnight, Fri.-Sat. 5pm-3am, Sun. 5pm-10pm) is a Cuban restaurant and dance club offering live music and dance lessons.

Upper Northwest

Although Upper Northwest is not the most happening nightlife spot in the city, it does offer some friendly, comfortable options for those not looking to see or be seen.

Atomic Billiards (3427 Connecticut Ave. NW, 202/363-7665, www.atomicbilliards.com, Sun.-Thurs. 4pm-2am, Fri.-Sat. 4pm-3am), in the Cleveland Park neighborhood, is a funky, futuristic-looking pool hall. They also have shuffleboard and darts. They serve good beer on tap but don't have a kitchen. They are located in the basement.

Another basement bar with pool, table tennis, shuffleboard, beer, and sandwiches is **Breadsoda** (2233 Wisconsin Ave. NW, 202/333-7445, www.breadsoda.com, Sun.-Thurs. noon-2am, Fri.-Sat. noon-3am). Tuesdays are tacos-and-ping pong night in this cozy, 1970s-style subterranean bar.

U Street Corridor

Made-to-order drinks are created at **The Gibson** (2009 14th St. NW, 202/232-2156, www.thegibsondc.com, Mon.-Sat. from 6pm), just off U Street. This interesting establishment could be called a modern-day speakeasy. Call ahead and make a reservation at the bar or at one of their booths or tables, then ring the bell when you arrive at the nondescript, tenement-style building. A professional mixologist will concoct something special for you, or you can order a drink off the small menu. Don't expect to eat (they don't serve food), and above all, don't stay longer than your allotted two hours—there's sure to be someone waiting to take your spot.

EVENTS

The nation's capital hosts countless events year-round. Whether it's a festival, athletic event, or holiday celebration, there is something going on nearly every day of the year.

Restaurant Week (www.ramw.org, lunch $22, dinner $35) happens twice a year, in January and August. Two hundred of the most popular restaurants in DC offer prix fixe lunch and dinner menus. The event is sponsored by the Restaurant Association of Metropolitan Washington. Reservations are recommended.

Chinese dragon dances, live music, and a parade are just some of the festivities during the 15-day annual **Chinese New Year Celebration** (H St. NW between 5th St. and 9th St.) in the Chinatown area of downtown DC. Beginning with the new moon on the first day of the Chinese New Year and ending with the full moon, this late-January or early February celebration brings the area's culture to life with a bang of fireworks. The Gallery Place-Chinatown Metrorail stop will put you in the right place for this free event.

The yearly **Washington Auto Show** (www.washingtonautoshow.com, $5-42) is a large event that brings more than 600 new vehicles from both domestic and overseas automakers to the Washington Convention Center. The show is held for 10 days in April and draws hundreds of thousands of visitors.

The coming of the Easter Bunny brings the annual **White House Easter Egg Roll** (www.whitehouse.gov), a tradition that started back in 1878 when President Rutherford B. Hayes opened the White House grounds to local children for egg rolling on the Monday after Easter. Successive presidents have continued this long-standing event, which takes place on the South Lawn.

Washington's signature event is the annual **National Cherry Blossom Festival** (www.nationalcherryblossomfestival.org). This three-week event coincides (ideally) with the blooming of the hundreds of Japanese cherry trees that were given to the United States in 1912 by Japan. The trees are planted all around the Tidal Basin and, when blooming, are a spectacular sight to see. Unfortunately, this huge event means gridlock on the highways and congestion on the sidewalks, but it is a great time to photograph the city. There's a parade, a kite festival, concerts, a 10-mile footrace, and much more. The festival is held late March–mid-April.

Memorial Day is big in Washington DC as thousands descend on the city for a day of remembrance. Many family-friendly events are held throughout the city, and the free **National Memorial Day Concert** (www.pbs.org) is held on the West Lawn of the U.S. Capitol. The concert features patriotic themes to honor Americans who have served our country during times of conflict. Other events include the **National Memorial Day Parade** (www.americanveteranscenter.org).

June brings the annual **Capital Pride** (www.capitalpride.org) event celebrating the gay, lesbian, bisexual, and transgender communities. There are more than 50 educational and entertainment events including a street festival and parade.

The **DC Jazz Festival** (www.dcjazzfest.org) is also held in June and features more than 100 jazz performances throughout the city. Major jazz artists from around the globe participate in this 12-day celebration. Venues include clubs, museums, hotels, and restaurants.

The **Smithsonian Folklife Festival** (www.festival.si.edu) takes place annually during the last week in June and the first week

in July. It is held outdoors on the National Mall. The festival is a living-heritage exposition with music, crafts, and artistry. The festival is free to attend.

There's no better place to celebrate the Fourth of July than the National Mall. **America's Independence Day Celebrations** include a parade along Constitution Avenue (www.july4thparade.com), concerts, and a spectacular fireworks display over the Washington Monument.

The premier running event in DC is the annual **Marine Corps Marathon** (www.marinemarathon.com). Known as "The People's Marathon," this 26.2-mile race was first held in 1975 and now has 30,000 participants each October.

Another completely different type of race is the annual **High Heel Race** in Dupont Circle. Each Tuesday before Halloween at 9pm, nearly 100 drag queens sporting elaborate outfits sprint down 17th Street NW over the three blocks between R and Church Streets. The event has been held for more than 30 years and draws thousands of spectators.

During the first week in December, the **National Christmas Tree Lighting** (www.thenationaltree.org) is a special event that takes place on the Ellipse. The president attends the lighting, which is surrounded by additional highlights such as military band concerts and performances by celebrities. A separate event is held annually for the lighting of the national menorah (www.afldc.org).

Shopping

Washington DC has great neighborhood shopping with unique stores and boutiques. Some of the stores are geared toward high-end consumers, but there are also many "finds" if you know where to look.

CAPITOL HILL

Traditional retail shopping can be found on Capitol Hill at **Union Station** (50

Massachusetts Ave. NE, www.unionstationdc.com), which has more than 65 stores, including national retailers such as Ann Taylor, The Body Shop, Jos. A. Bank Clothiers, and Victoria's Secret. A handful of specialty boutiques are also represented, such as **Lost City Art** (202/289-6977), which offers Indonesian statues, masks, murals, jewelry, and household items.

Eastern Market (225 7th St. SE, www. easternmarket-dc.org) is a prime destination in DC for fresh food and handmade arts and crafts. Since 1873, the market has been a community hub on Capitol Hill. It offers several shopping spaces: The **South Hall Market** (Tues.-Fri. 7am-7pm, Sat. 7am-6pm, Sun. 9am-5pm) is an indoor space featuring 13 merchants offering a large variety of food, such as produce, baked goods, meat, and dairy products. The **Weekend Farmers' Line** is an open-air space that is open on weekends and offers fresh local produce and snacks. Those searching for local crafts and antiques can find them at the **Weekend Outdoor Market.** Vendors in this area carry ethno-specific handcrafts, vintage goods, and arts and crafts. There is also a farmers market on Tuesdays.

DISTRICT WHARF

The development of District Wharf includes an ever-growing selection of national retail shops and trendy boutiques. The list is evolving and can be found at: www.wharfdc.com/shops.

A Beautiful Closet (20 District Square SW, 202/488-1809, Mon.-Tues. 11am-6pm, Wed. 11am-7pm, Thur.-Fri. 11am-8pm, Sat. 11am-9pm, Sun. 11am-7pm) is a boutique that sells clothing, jewelry, home décor, and fair trade goods from around the world.

Politics and Prose Bookstore (70 District Square SW, 202/488-3867, Daily 10am-10pm) is an independent bookstore featuring a large variety of books, gifts, and stationary. They also host book signings and other events.

DOWNTOWN

The revitalized Penn Quarter area features more than just museums, the Capital One Arena, and cool new restaurants. The neighborhood has plenty of shopping and features some of the best-known national retailers, such as Pottery Barn and Urban Outfitters.

A selection of trendy individual shops is also here, such as **Fahrney's Pens** (1317 F St. NW, 202/628-9525, www.fahrneyspens.com, Mon.-Fri. 9:30am-6pm, Sat. 10am-5pm), a pen store with a long DC tradition, and **Pua Naturally** (400 7th St. NW, 202/347-4543, www.puanaturally.com, by appointment only: Tues.-Fri. 1pm-6pm, Sat. 1pm-5pm, closed Sun.-Mon.), a retail clothing studio that works with a cooperative of master tailors, block printers, and seamstresses in Nepal and India.

DUPONT CIRCLE

Lively Dupont Circle features an eclectic choice of gift shops, clothing stores, bookstores, and art galleries. If you're looking for a quirky gift, one-of-a-kind handcrafts, greeting cards, or chocolate, stop in **The Chocolate Moose** (1743 L St. NW, 202/463-0992, www.chocolatemoosedc.com). Serious antiques lovers will be intrigued by the offerings at **Geoffrey Diner Gallery** (1730 21st St. NW, 202/904-5005, www.dinergallery.com). They have items from the 19th and 20th centuries, contemporary fine art, European and American crafts, and Tiffany lamps.

GEORGETOWN

Everyone from first ladies to celebrities has made their way down M Street looking for a special find. Georgetown offers great antiques, cool clothing, and unique local boutiques. Most of the stores can be found along M Street and Wisconsin Avenue. The famous mall **Georgetown Park** (3222 M St., www.georgetownpark.com) has been transformed from an enclosed mall to one where tenants front M Street and Wisconsin Avenue. It offers a mix of retail and restaurant space.

UPPER NORTHWEST

The best shopping in Upper Northwest is in the Friendship Heights neighborhood, along the Maryland state border. **Chevy Chase Pavilion** (5335 Wisconsin Ave. NW, www.chevychasepavilion.com, Mon.-Sat. 7am-11pm, Sun. 7am-9pm) is a shopping mall

---

1: people shopping for art **2:** the National Cherry Blossom Festival drawing visitors to the Tidal Basin

that features national chains such as J. Crew, World Market, and Old Navy. It is across Wisconsin Avenue from another small, upscale mall, **Mazza Gallerie** (5300 Wisconsin Ave. NW, www.mazzagallerie.com, Mon.-Fri. 10am-8pm, Sat. 10am-7pm, Sun. noon-6pm).

Mazza Gallerie features stores such as Neiman Marcus and Saks Fifth Avenue. There is also a movie theater at the mall and a parking garage. The shopping district is accessible by Metrorail on the Red Line at the Friendship Heights stop.

Food

THE NATIONAL MALL
Asian Fusion
For a trendy night out, dine at **The Source** (575 Pennsylvania Ave. NW, 202/637-6100, www.wolfgangpuck.com, Tues.-Thurs. 11:30am-2:30pm and 5:30pm-10pm, Fri. 11:30am-2:30pm and 5:30pm-11pm, and Sat. 11:30am-3pm and 5:30pm-11pm, $31-60). This popular Wolfgang Puck restaurant is adjacent to the Newseum and was a date-night choice for Michelle and Barack Obama. The Source offers a seven-course tasting menu for $135, and the lower-level lounge offers small plates and a dim sum brunch on Saturday. The modern dining room on the second floor offers a contemporary Asian menu. Floor-to-ceiling windows and a polished tile floor give the space an inviting atmosphere, and there is plush leather seating. A beautiful wine wall with more than 2,000 bottles is a focal point. A seasonal patio is available for outdoor dining.

CAPITOL HILL
American
A Capitol Hill classic is the **Tune Inn** (331 Pennsylvania Ave. SE, 202/543-2725, Mon.-Fri. 8am-2am, Sat.-Sun. 8am-3:30am, $5-13). This historic burger-and-beer bar is quirky: The decor is a symphony in taxidermy (complete with a deer rump and a beer-drinking black bear), but the beer is cheap (by DC standards) and the burgers are tasty.

For delicious, Southern-inspired cooking, dine at **Art and Soul** (415 New Jersey Ave. NW, 202/393-7777, www.artandsouldc.com, Mon.-Fri. 7am-10:30am, 11:30am-3:30pm,

and 5:30 pm-10pm, Sat.-Sun. 7am-3pm and 5:30 pm-10pm, $24-44). They are known for their fried chicken sandwich, and they have a lovely, dog-friendly patio for nice weather.

Belgian
The intimate **Belga Café** (514 8th St. SE, 202/544-0100, www.belgacafe.com, lunch Mon.-Fri. 11am-4pm, brunch Sat.-Sun. 9am-4pm, dinner Mon.-Thurs. 4pm-10pm, Fri.-Sat. 4pm-11pm, and Sun. 4pm-9:30pm, $15-38) serves waffles (with savory or sweet toppings) that will make your knees weak, and their dinner entrées are delicious renditions of items such as mussels (flecked with bacon and steamed in red ale), truffle macaroni and cheese, and Flemish beef stew. They also have a nice beer list. The place is small (the first floor of a row house), and there is exposed brick inside with an open kitchen (read: the noise level is high). There is usually a wait, but the staff is friendly (even to children), and on nice days there is added seating outside.

DISTRICT WHARF
Asian
Go on a funky culinary journey through Southeast Asia at **Kaliwa** (751 Wharf St. SW., 202/516-4739, www.kaliwadc.com, daily lunch from 11:30am, dinner from 5:30pm, $15-24). This visually appealing, waterfront restaurant offers selections from Korea, Thailand, and the Philippines, all described in their native language (a glossary is available for translations). Dishes are meant to be shared and are served when ready. They recommend patrons

order 2-3 items per person. The decor features soaring ceilings, wooden tables, and exotic chandeliers.

Seafood

A taste of coastal Spain can be enjoyed at **Del Mar** (791 Wharf St. SW, 202/525-1402, www.delmardc.com, Sun.-Thurs. 5pm-10pm, Fri.-Sat. 5pm-10:30pm, $30-75), courtesy of DC culinary legends Fabio and Maria Trabocchi. Throw in a dramatic water view and delightful cocktails and you have a reason to celebrate (bring on the paella!). Authentic seafood dishes from Mallorca headline the menu with tapas, stews, and grilled fish. Their dress code is upscale casual.

Hank's Oyster Bar (701 Wharf St. SW, 202/817-3055, www.hanksoysterbar.com, Mon.-Thurs. 11:30am-10pm, Fri. 11:30am-11pm, Sat. 11am-11pm, Sun. 11am-10pm, $14-32) is located on the waterfront and offers indoor and outdoor seating. They are known for their happy hour specials at the bar, but they also offer a good variety of "New England Beach fare" (mostly seafood) dishes. They seem to have a knack for hiring friendly staff. If you like lobster, try the lobster deviled eggs or the lobster roll. They have several other locations around DC and in Old Town Alexandria.

DOWNTOWN
American

It's hard to pass up an opportunity to dine at **Old Ebbitt Grill** (675 15th St. NW, 202/347-4800, www.ebbitt.com, Mon.-Fri. 7:30am-1am, Sat.-Sun. 8:30am-1am, $9-37), the oldest saloon in Washington DC. This historic restaurant is near the White House and was frequented by presidents such as Grant, Cleveland, and Theodore Roosevelt. Currently part of the Clyde's restaurant group, this old favorite is always bustling with political personalities, journalists, and theater patrons. It's a casual, fun place but shows its long history through marble bars and mahogany booths outfitted in velvet. They have an oyster bar and a menu of

burgers, pasta, steak, and seafood. They also serve breakfast during the week and brunch on weekends.

Indian

Upscale Indian cuisine can be found at ★ **Rasika** (633 D St. NW, 202/637-1222, www.rasikarestaurant.com, lunch Mon.-Fri. 11:30am-2:30pm, dinner Mon.-Thurs. 5:30pm-10:30pm and Fri.-Sat. 5pm-11pm, $19-36) in Penn Quarter. This fabulous restaurant is one of the best in the area for modern Indian cuisine. A personal favorite for an entrée is the lamb Roganjosh (although the black cod is also spectacular). They also offer a four-course tasting menu for $60, a six-course tasting menu for $75, and a pre-theater three-course menu before 6:30pm for $37. This restaurant is red hot on the popularity list, and a reservation is highly recommended. They have a second location at 1190 New Hampshire Avenue NW.

Italian

The vintage-style pizzeria bistro **Matchbox** (750 E St. NW, 202/289-4441, www.matchboxrestaurants.com, Mon.-Thurs. 11am-10:30pm, Fri. 11am-1am, Sat. 10am-1am, Sun. 10am-10:30pm, $10-35) is a favorite in the Penn Quarter neighborhood for pregaming before an event at Capital One Arena. They are known for their incredible pizza and also for their mini-burger appetizers topped with onion straws, but they also offer a full menu of sandwiches and entrées. The atmosphere in this multilevel hot spot is fun, lively, and slightly funky. There are 11 other locations throughout the DC area (in DC, Virginia, and Maryland).

Spanish/Portuguese

The toughest reservation in town and a meal that will blow you away (first when you taste the food and again when you see the bill) is ★ **Minibar by José Andrés** (855 E St. NW, 202/393-0812, www.minibarbyjoseandres.com, Tues.-Sat. seatings at 6pm, 6:30pm, 8:30pm, and 9pm, $275). This "culinary

Food Truck Culture

food trucks on the National Mall

Food trucks have always been part of the lunch scene in Washington DC, but today their quality and diversity have elevated them to noteworthy status.

Dangerously Delicious Pies (www.pieshopdc.com) was the first truck to spawn a brick-and-mortar eatery (at 1339 H St. NE), although the majority of the trucks are stand-alone businesses. Dangerously Delicious Pies serves both sweet and savory pie slices out of its bright red truck. **Himalayan Soul Food** made a name for itself with delicious, generously stuffed dumplings, while the **BBQ Bus** (www.bbqbusdc.com) serves up tender ribs and pulled pork. Even more specialized is **Ball or Nothing,** (www.ballornothingdc.com), which serves meatballs and boldly states, "our balls are for everyone." This local favorite offers traditional meatballs, veggie meatballs, wild boar meatballs, and interesting sides such as mascarpone polenta and roasted peach and spinach salad.

So how do you find these rolling treasures? These meals on wheels can be found on many major roads in the business and tourist areas of the city. Some have their own websites that give their location schedule and others use Twitter to provide their up-to-the-minute whereabouts. Many can also be found on **Food Truck Fiesta** (www.foodtruckfiesta.com), a website geared toward tracking the trucks. When in doubt, try the truck with the longest line. It doesn't take long for word to spread about a great food truck find.

journey" of molecular gastronomy comprises a preset 20-plus-course tasting menu (1-2 bites each) that is a combination of art and science. There is no menu; you simply eat what is served that evening (examples include beech mushroom risotto with truffle, pillow of PB&J, grilled lobster with peanut butter and honey, and apple meringue "pigs" with bacon ice cream).

Seatings are small, just six guests at each of four seatings a night. Guests move through different rooms during the meal. The serving team walks guests through each course (plan on staying about 2-3 hours) and shares the beauty of the ingredients that were selected for each and the technique behind their creation. The $275 price tag does not include drinks, tax, or gratuity. Optional drink pairings are available. Reservations open in two-month periods starting one month prior and can be made online. This is truly a once-in-a-lifetime dining experience.

Turkish/Greek

Another creation of chef José Andrés is the very popular **Zaytinya** (701 9th St. NW, 202/638-0800, www.zaytinya.com, Sun.-Mon. 11am-10pm, Tues.-Thurs. 11am-11pm, Fri.-Sat. 11am-midnight, small plates $7-20). They serve a large and delicious menu of tapas in a casual setting. This is a good choice for both vegetarians and meat eaters. Menu examples include pan-roasted dorado, Turkish-style *pastirma* (cured beef), and knisa lamb chops. They also offer a chef's experience for $65. There is a bar overlooking the dining room for people watching. This is a good place to try some of the creations of one of DC's most famous chefs.

DUPONT CIRCLE
Asian

A tiny restaurant with a big following. That's **Little Serow** (1511 17th St. NW, www.littleserow.com, Tues.-Thurs. 5:30pm-10pm, Fri.-Sat. 5:30pm-10:30pm, $54), a quirky, highly regarded, northern Thailand-inspired restaurant with very limited seating (no parties larger than four). No need to ponder over the menu—the only choice is a family-style fixed-priced menu that changes every Tuesday and normally includes pork, seafood, and nuts (with no substitutions). The food is spicy, flavorful, and notably different from other local Thai restaurants. Come ready to wait. Patrons line up at the door as early as 4:30 (there are no reservations). If there's a wait when you arrive, the friendly staff will text you when your table is ready. The restaurant is hard to find because there is no visible sign outside.

For fast-casual food that's part Chinese and part Korean, stop at **Chiko** (2029 P St. NW, 202/331-3040, www.chikodc.com, Sun.-Thurs. 11am-10pm, Fri.-Sat. 11am-11pm, $15-18). Try their well-known Orange-ish Chicken, Smashed Salmon, or the delightful Pork and Kimchi pot stickers. Service is first-come, first-served, but reservations are available at their small Kitchen Counter that include interaction with their cooks, multiple courses of their well-known dishes, and a front-row seat to their open kitchen ($50 per person, excluding beverages, tax, and tips).

Greek

Tucked inside a normal-looking row house is one of the best culinary outposts in the city. ★ **Komi** (1509 17th St. NW, 202/332-9200, www.komirestaurant.com, Tues.-Sat. 5:30pm-9:30pm, $165) serves a preset multicourse dinner for $165 per person. The experience starts with several light dishes and progresses to hearty fare and finally dessert. Wine pairing is offered as an option for an additional $85. They do not even have a printed menu. This intimate eatery is steered by a young chef named Johnny Monis, who prepares incredible Greek dishes inspired by family recipes. The menu is different every night, making this the perfect find for foodies—foodies with deep pockets, that is.

GEORGETOWN
American

Timeless quality can be found at **1789** (1226 36th St. NW, 202/965-1789, www.1789restaurant.com, Mon.-Thurs. 5pm-10pm, Fri.-Sat. 5pm-11pm, Sun. 5pm-10pm, $32-59, five-course tasting menu $105), open since 1962. Part of the Clyde's family of restaurants, 1789 is tried-and-true with starched linen tablecloths and candlelight. The restaurant has three floors and six rooms for dining, each with a unique name, ambience, and a common theme of antiques and equestrian decor. Jackets used to be required but are now preferred. The restaurant serves a diverse menu of seafood, steak, pork, duck, and a few vegetarian selections. The food is high quality and consistent, and the service is impeccable. This is a lovely spot for a date or a business dinner.

Just east of Georgetown on M Street, the **Blue Duck Tavern** (1201 24th St. NW, 202/419-6755, www.blueducktavern.com, Mon.-Thurs. 6:30am-10:30am, 11:30am-2:30pm, and 5:30pm-10:30pm, Fri. 6:30am-10:30am, 11:30am-2:30pm, and 5:30pm-11pm,

Sat. 6:30am-10:30am, 11am-2:30pm, and 5:30pm-11pm, Sun. 6:30am-10:30am, 11am-2:30pm, and 5:30pm-10:30pm, $26-52) is a traditional American restaurant that is known for hosting power players from DC's political scene. It also prides itself on using simple, flavor-enhancing cooking methods such as smoking, braising, and roasting. The restaurant is known for both its food and its lovely atmosphere. Handmade wood furnishings and an open kitchen help give it a warm, gathering-place-type feel, although with a contemporary flair. The food sounds simple, with selections such as beef ribs, organic chicken, and halibut, but the dishes are elegantly prepared and beautifully served.

Farmers Fishers Bakers (3000 K St. NW, Washington Harbor, 202/298-8783, www.farmersfishersbakers.com, Mon.-Wed. 7:30am-10:30am and 11am-10pm, Thurs. 7:30am-10:30am and 11am-11pm, Fri. 7:30am-10:30am and 11am-midnight, Sat. 9am-midnight, Sun. 9am-10pm, $12-34) is part of the Farmers Restaurant Group and is a modern, upscale, casual option in Washington Harbor. The restaurant group supports American family farmers and sources regionally and seasonally when possible. Farmers Fishers Bakers offer an in-house bakery, full bar with 24 beer taps, a sushi counter, and a patio with views of the water. Guests are greeted outside in winter with a fire pit, and the inside decor features several different themes for varying dining experiences. The menu is large and includes pizza, sandwiches, salads, and seafood. Their burger with blue cheese and a side of potato salad is a good choice on any day.

Bakery

Many people have heard of **Georgetown Cupcake** (3301 M St. NW, 202/333-8448, www.georgetowncupcake.com, Mon.-Sat. 10am-9pm, Sun. 10am-8pm, under $10), made famous by the reality television series *DC Cupcakes,* but they may not know about a nearby gem called **Baked & Wired** (1052 Thomas Jefferson St. NW, 703/663-8727,

www.bakedandwired.com, Mon.-Thurs. 7am-8pm, Fri. 7am-9pm, Sat. 8am-9pm, Sun. 8am-8pm, under $10), south of the C&O Canal between 30th and 31st Streets. This little independent bakery sells great coffee and a large variety of freshly made bakery items including more than 20 types of cupcakes with names such as Chocolate Cupcake of Doom and Pretty Bitchin'. They turn out amazing baked goods amid a fun, inviting atmosphere. Look for the pink bicycle outside, and don't forget to take home some Hippie Crack (homemade granola) for later.

Italian

The place to celebrity-spot in Georgetown is **Café Milano** (3251 Prospect St. NW, 202/333-6183, www.cafemilano.com, Mon.-Tues. 11:30am-11pm, Wed.-Sat. 11:30am-midnight, Sun. 11am-11pm, $17-75). Political VIPs and visiting Hollywood stars frequent this upscale Italian restaurant, as do local Georgetown socialites. The southern coastal Italian cuisine is consistently good, but diners come more to people watch and enjoy the pleasant atmosphere afforded by the floor-to-ceiling windows and open sidewalk patio. There is normally a sophisticated crowd, and good wine is flowing.

Another great choice for Italian is **Filomena Ristorante** (1063 Wisconsin Ave. NW, 202/338-8800, www.filomena.com, daily 11:30am-11pm, $15-47). This well-known restaurant opened in 1983 and serves authentic, delicious Italian cuisine. You can even see the pasta being made on the way in. Many celebrities and dignitaries have dined here, including Bono from U2 and President Clinton. Seating is a little close together, but the excellent food will make you overlook this. Portions are large, and the service is friendly and attentive. Personal favorites include the Linguini Cardinale and Gnocchi Della Mamma.

ADAMS MORGAN
American
Mintwood Place (1813 Columbia Rd. NW, 202/234-6732, www.mintwoodplace.

com, Tues.-Thurs. 5:30pm-10pm, Fri. 5:30pm-10:30pm, Sat. 10:30am-2:30pm and 5:30pm-10:30pm, Sun. 10:30am-2:30pm and 5:30pm-9pm, $17-34) has a pleasant, modern-farmhouse ambience and a lovely patio. They offer a unique menu of American food with some French influence (such as trout, chicken liver mousse, and a cheeseburger) with lovely presentation. This is a great place to try something new and maybe impress a date. The restaurant is small, and some of the tables are close together, but it has a casual, neighborhood feel despite its chunky price tag.

Italian
Al Volo Osteria (1790 Columbia Rd. NW, 202/758-0759, www.cucina-alvolo.com, Sun.-Thurs. 5pm-10pm, Fri.-Sat. 5pm-11pm, $9-20) is a popular Italian restaurant in a somewhat funky neighborhood. If you're a fan of good, house-made pasta, this is the place to go. The pasta is incredibly fresh, and diners have an open view to the kitchen. The menu is familiar (pick a pasta, pick a sauce, or order pizza and salad), but with some fresh healthy choices (red beet fusilli, cherry tomato sauce, etc.). This is a casual place where the focus is on the food.

Vegetarian
A vegetarian hot spot that the rest of us can also enjoy, the **Amsterdam Falafelshop** (2425 18th St. NW, 202/234-1969, www.falafelshop.com, Sun.-Mon. 11am-midnight, Tues.-Wed. 11am-2:30am, Thurs. 11am-3am, Fri.-Sat. 11am-4am, under $5-15) is known for its perfectly crisp, yet soft, balls of fried chickpeas placed inside pita bread or in a bowl. The concept is simple: You order your falafel, they make it for you in under five minutes, and then you decide which of the 21 toppings and sauces you want from the garnish bar. The shop is open late and also offers sides and desserts.

UPPER NORTHWEST
American
A traditional greasy-spoon breakfast joint

is **Steak 'n Egg** (4700 Wisconsin Ave. NW, 202/686-1201, www.osmanandjoes.com, 24 hours, $7-18). It offers all the wonderful eggs, sausages, hash browns, and biscuits you could ask for, with ultracasual 24-hour-diner charm. As the name implies, they also have steak, as well as burgers, sandwiches, shakes, and good coffee.

Going to the zoo? Even if you are not, stop at ★ **Duke's Counter** (3000 Connecticut Ave. NW, 202/733-4808, www.dukesgrocery.com, Mon.-Thurs. 11am-10pm, Fri. 11am-midnight, Sat. 10am-midnight, Sun. 10am-10pm, $8-15), a wonderful, British-inspired gastropub located across the street from the National Zoo entrance in Woodley Park. They serve scrumptious, overstuffed sandwiches with names such as Fired Up Chicken and Italian Stallion, alongside items such as hummus, curry poutine, and avocado toast. The menu was put together with great care and includes seasonal cocktails. They have a cool, copper-topped bar (open late) and a seasonal patio.

German
Take it from a German girl who has eaten her way through the Old Country: Some of the best traditional German fare in the entire DC area is served at **Old Europe** (2434 Wisconsin Ave. NW, 202/333-7600, www.old-europe.com, Wed.-Thurs. 11:30am-2:30pm and 5pm-9pm, Fri.-Sat. 11:30am-2:30pm and 5pm-10pm, Sun. noon-3:30pm and 4pm-8pm, $15-27). They have all the favorites including schnitzel, sauerbraten, and brats, all served in a lively, homeland atmosphere. The menu is wide-ranging and includes a good selection of traditional side dishes (potato pancakes, red cabbage, potato dumplings). They also have German wine, beer, and spirits (have you ever seen Jägermeister on a printed menu?).

Italian
DC's most popular pizzeria is easily ★ **2 Amys** (3715 Macomb St. NW, 202/885-5700, www.2amyspizza.com, Mon. 5pm-10pm, Tues.-Thurs. 11am-10pm, Fri.-Sat.

11am-11pm, Sun. noon-10pm, $7-15). This gourmet Italian restaurant specializes in authentic Neapolitan pizza. The incredible smell alone will make your mouth water when you walk into this hopping, noisy establishment. The cute bar area is a great place to wait for your table. Although they make other menu items just as well, the focus here is really on the pizza, which lives up to the hype. It is actually one of the few restaurants in the country certified by the D.O.C. (Denominazione di Origine Controllata), an Italian entity that specifies the legally permitted ingredients and preparation methods required to make authentic Neapolitan pizza.

Japanese

It's hard to imagine that good sushi can be found in DC at a decent price, but **Kotobuki** (4822 MacArthur Blvd. NW, 202/625-9080, www.kotobukidc.com, Tues.-Thurs. noon-2:30pm and 5pm-9:30pm, Fri.-Sat. noon-2:30pm and 5pm-10:30pm, Sun. 5pm-9:30pm, $12-30) is that needle in a haystack. It is a tiny restaurant (above another one owned by the same people), and there is usually a line for a table, but the prices are good, the fish is fresh, and the sushi is authentic.

Seafood

In the Palisades neighborhood is **BlackSalt Fish Market & Restaurant** (4883 MacArthur Blvd. NW, 202/342-9101, www.blacksaltrestaurant.com, Mon.-Thurs. 11:30am-2:30pm and 5:30pm-9:30pm, Fri. 11:30am-2:30pm and 5:30pm-10pm, Sat. 11:30am-2:30pm and 5pm-10pm, Sun. 11am-2pm and 5pm-9pm, $17-69), a well-known spot serving New American seafood. The seafood is extremely fresh, and they offer innovative combinations such as Thai Coconut & Galangal Seafood Stew, Cumin Spiced Tuna, and Tempura Fried Dungeness Crab Salad. They also offer a five-course tasting menu for $90 and a seven-course tasting menu for $120. Wine pairings are $50 and $70. There's an adjoining seafood market that sells some of the best fish in the city.

U STREET CORRIDOR
American

A long-standing tradition on U Street is ★ **Ben's Chili Bowl** (1213 U St. NW, 202/667-0909, www.benschilibowl.com, Mon.-Thurs. 6am-2am, Fri. 6am-4am, Sat. 7am-4am, Sun. 11am-midnight, under $10). This historic eatery opened in 1958 and has seen a lot of changes through its windows. It has weathered the rise, fall, and rebirth of the U Street Corridor and could well be the only business on this stretch of street that survived both the riots of 1968 following the assassination of Martin Luther King Jr. and the construction of the Metrorail Green Line. Ben's is "Home of the Famous Chili Dog," which is what has drawn people (including Barack Obama and the Travel Channel's Anthony Bourdain) through its doors and to its red barstools for decades. They serve breakfast and a "main menu" the rest of the day, but chili dogs are available anytime they're open. The staff is smiling and friendly, and celebrities and regular folks are all treated equally.

Busboys and Poets (2021 14th St. NW, 202/387-7638, www.busboysandpoets.com, Mon.-Thurs. 7am-midnight, Fri. 7am-1am, Sat. 8am-1am, Sun. 8am-midnight, $7-26) is a local gathering place and restaurant with a loyal following. It now has seven locations. It is known as a progressive establishment and also as a community resource for artists, activists, and writers. The 14th Street location is large and serves breakfast daily until 11am. The rest of the day they offer soup, sandwiches, panini, pizza, and entrées (after 5pm) with a Southern flair (think catfish, shrimp and grits, and pasta). They offer vegetarian, vegan, and gluten-free selections as well, and there is a progressive bookstore on-site.

Greek

Fantastic gyros are what all the hype is about at **The Greek Spot** (2017 11th St. NW, 202/265-3118, www.greekspotdc.com, Mon.-Fri. 11am-10:30pm, Sat. noon-10:30pm,

$7-18). This is a very casual "fast-food" restaurant that makes tasty Greek meals in a hurry. They serve lamb and beef gyros, vegetarian gyros (made with soy steak strips), chicken souvlaki, and other sandwiches and burgers. The food is tender and inexpensive and has developed quite the local following. They also prepare and deliver takeout orders.

Accommodations

Where you book a room in Washington DC will likely depend on your itinerary. If you are primarily touring museums and monuments, then make a reservation near the National Mall, Capitol Hill, or in the downtown area. If you prefer new accommodations with a water view, then the District Wharf is a good choice. If you desire the charm of the historic neighborhoods this city has to offer, then a room near Dupont Circle, in Upper Northwest, or in Georgetown could be a good option.

Accommodations in Washington DC run the gamut in price range. However, choice hotels near the popular attractions are pricey year-round, and some are downright outrageous. An alternative for booking a room is to stay across the Potomac River in nearby Arlington or Alexandria, Virginia. It can be less expensive, yet still convenient to the city's major attractions by car, bus, or Metrorail.

THE NATIONAL MALL
Under $100

Reservations for a hostel stay can be made months in advance with **Hostelling International-Washington DC** (1009 11th St. NW, 202/737-2333, www.hiusa.org, $30-119). Accommodations are close to the National Mall, Metrorail, and many of the popular DC attractions. This former hotel has 250 beds and offers shared, dorm-style lodging and some semiprivate rooms. Bathrooms are shared, and there is a kitchen and laundry facility on-site. There is also high-speed Internet.

CAPITOL HILL
$100-200

If you want to stay on Capitol Hill, the **Capitol Hill Hotel** (200 C St. SE., 202/543-6000, www.capitolhillhotel-dc.com, $134-262) offers lovely boutique accommodations in a residential neighborhood. This is the closest hotel to the Capitol Building and is about one block from the Capitol South Metrorail stop. All 153 rooms are suites with kitchenettes or kitchens. Continental breakfast is included, as well as bike rentals. They also have wine and cookies in the afternoon on weekdays. Valet parking ($50) is available, and the hotel is pet friendly ($150). Their decor appropriately includes vintage political-cartoon art and cherry blossom designs. This hotel is a great value for the location.

DISTRICT WHARF
$200-300

A good hotel choice right on the wharf is the **Hyatt House Washington DC/The Wharf** (725 Wharf St. SW, 202/554-1234, www.hyatt.com, $215-660). This new hotel is in the center of the District Wharf neighborhood and offers terrific river views. It is one mile from the National Mall and about a 10-minute walk to the L'Enfant Plaza Metrorail station. The hotel has 237 guest rooms, a fitness center, and outdoor pool. Free breakfast is included, and the hotel is pet friendly. Another hotel located right on the Wharf is the **InterContinental Washington DC/The Wharf** (801 Wharf St. SW, 202/800-0844, www.wharfintercontinentaldc.com, $265-442). This modern, luxury hotel boasts great waterfront views of the Potomac River in the heart of the Wharf neighborhood. During the summer, the majority of the rooms are around $300.

DOWNTOWN

$100-200

One of the best values in the city is the ★ **Hotel Tabard Inn** (1739 N St. NW, 202/785-1277, www.tabardinn.com, $125-325), five blocks from the White House on a pretty, tree-lined street. The hotel has 35 uniquely designed rooms in three town houses. The houses were built between 1880 and 1890. Rates vary depending on the size of the room and whether it has a shared or private bathroom. Reservations are taken for specific price categories, not for specific rooms. There are no televisions in the guest rooms.

All rates include a guest pass to the Washington Sports Club gym and a $15 food and beverage credit. Free wireless Internet is also available throughout the inn. The inn is known for having live jazz. Valet parking is $39 per day.

Over $300

For a presidential stay in DC, book a room at the ★ **Hay-Adams** (800 16th St. NW, 202/638-6600, www.hayadams.com, $289-2,039) at 16th and H Streets NW. This beautiful downtown hotel has 145 guest rooms and 21 luxury suites. Some of the rooms offer stunning views of local landmarks such as the White House and Lafayette Square. The Hay-Adams was built in 1928 in the Italian Renaissance style and has the appearance of a large private mansion. It sits on the land where the homes of Secretary of State John Hay and historian Henry Adams (author and relative of John Adams and John Quincy Adams) once stood.

The hotel has hosted many important political figures and was the choice for President Obama and his family in the weeks leading up to his first inauguration in 2008.

Visitors taking in the National Mall sights will enjoy the convenient location of this hotel, situated near the White House, downtown attractions, and the Metrorail. The hotel features beautiful, traditionally decorated rooms with molded ceilings, quality furnishings, ample space, comfortable beds, and wonderful amenities such as fluffy bathrobes. The food at the hotel is also excellent.

The service at the Hay-Adams is outstanding, and from the moment you walk through the front door, it is obvious you will be well taken care of. The hotel's slogan is, "Where nothing is overlooked but the White House," and they mean it.

If you're traveling to DC for the full historical experience and you'd like to indulge in famous accommodations, then the ★ **Willard InterContinental Hotel** (1401 Pennsylvania Ave. NW, 202/628-9100, www.ihg.com, $189-3,989) is a good choice. The Willard is more than 150 years old and is considered to be one of the most prestigious hotels in the city. It is one block from the White House and has been called the "Residence of Presidents" because it has hosted nearly every U.S. president since Franklin Pierce stayed there in 1853. Other famous guests include Martin Luther King Jr. (who stayed there during the time he delivered his famous "I Have a Dream" speech), Charles Dickens, Mark Twain, and Buffalo Bill. The hotel even has its own little museum.

The Willard is beautifully restored and has a grand lobby, comfortable rooms, and outstanding service. The hotel has 12 floors, 335 guest rooms, and 41 suites. It also has a wonderful on-site restaurant.

Another beautifully restored historic hotel is **The Jefferson** (1200 16th St. NW, 202/448-2300, www.jeffersondc.com, $300-594), located roughly halfway between the White House and Dupont Circle. Built as a luxury apartment building in 1923, the beaux arts building was converted to a hotel in 1955 and underwent major renovations in 2009, which included incorporating modern-day features (such as a chef's kitchen and spa) into the original framework. The hotel maintains a large collection of antiques, artwork, and original signed documents. It has 95 guest rooms and suites and

---

1: Ben's Chili Bowl 2: Willard InterContinental Hotel 3: restaurants and specialty shops in Union Station

three on-site restaurants. They also have an Executive Canine Officer (ECO) named Lord Monticello (Monti)—a rescue dog that lives at the hotel. The hotel is dog friendly ($50 fee) and provides dog beds, bowls, treats, and a map of nearby dog-friendly establishments and walking routes.

Off Lafayette Park near the White House is the lovely **Sofitel Washington DC Lafayette Square** (806 15th St. NW, 202/730-8800, www.sofitel.accorhotels.com, $206-618). This sophisticated hotel is art deco with a modern flair. The rooms are beautifully appointed and feature soft lighting and fluffy linens. There is also a comfortable lounge area for guests and an on-site restaurant. The location is perfect for touring the city since it is near the National Mall, downtown attractions, and the Metrorail. Ask for a room facing south or east (or simply ask to face the White House).

DUPONT CIRCLE
$100-200

A trendy boutique hotel in the Dupont Circle neighborhood is the 137-room **Kimpton Rouge** (1315 16th St. NW, 202/232-8000, www.rougehotel.com, $103-236). This popular Kimpton hotel has a modern design, a fitness room, good amenities, and is pet friendly. Red is their signature color, which seems to be worked in everywhere. Their rooms are well outfitted with stocked minibars, high-speed Internet, 37-inch plasma televisions, Aveda bath products, and voicemail. Ten rooms feature kitchenettes and entertainment areas. There is a great bar on-site, and approximately 75 restaurants are within walking distance. They also have a state-of-the-art fitness center. The staff is exceptional. Pets are welcome.

$200-300

A wonderful Kimpton hotel in the Dupont Circle neighborhood is the ★ **Kimpton Carlyle Hotel** (1731 New Hampshire Ave. NW, 202/234-3200, www.carlylehoteldc. com, $122-675). This art deco hotel has 170 rooms with ample space, sitting areas, fully equipped kitchens, and Tempur-Pedic beds. The eight-story offering is on a residential street, three blocks from the Dupont Circle fountain. There is a restaurant on-site, a fitness center, free bike use, Tesla and universal charging stations, a daily wine hour, and valet parking ($48). The hotel is pet friendly.

Over $300

The most imaginative hotel in the city is **The Mansion on O Street** (2020 O St. NW, 202/496-2000, www.omansion.com, $375-25,000), just southwest of Dupont Circle. This one-of-a-kind boutique hotel consists of four 1892 townhomes linked to form a luxury inn complex containing guest rooms, a ballroom, multiple dining rooms, conference rooms, and many surprises. Each accommodation has its specialty: It could be a rainforest shower, pirate's tub, tanning room, a shower made from an English telephone booth, extensive gardens with fountains and a barbecue, an aquarium, or a bathroom that's so incredible that legendary jazz musician Miles Davis decided to have dinner in it. That's just the tip of the iceberg at this ultracreative mansion. There's a museum on-site that is equally creative and changes displays daily. There are more than 100 rooms, 70 secret doors, and hidden passageways to explore. Everything in the mansion is for sale, so if you really like something, for a price, it can be yours. Many famous people have stayed in this eclectic world of fantasy, including Kim Basinger, Hillary Clinton, and Sylvester Stallone. Reservations are only taken online.

GEORGETOWN
$200-300

Charming inn accommodations can be found at **The Avery Georgetown** (2616 P St. NW, 202/827-4390, www.averygeorgetown.com, $159-364). This beautiful neighborhood inn offers 15 colorful yet elegant guest rooms with modern furnishings. Amenities include pillow-top mattresses, Netflix, Hulu, and minibars stocked with complimentary refreshments.

Over $300

For a five-star stay in Georgetown, make a reservation at the **Four Seasons Washington, DC** (2800 Pennsylvania Ave. NW, 202/342-0444, www.fourseasons.com, $680-1,925). This high-end hotel is known for its spacious rooms and suites. It is also the only five-star, five-diamond luxury hotel in the city. The Four Seasons is a contemporary hotel with a warm and welcoming ambience. The professional staff is truly exceptional and tends to every guest personally. There is a fitness center, a pool, steam rooms, a sauna, and an aerobics studio on-site. Babysitting is also available. This is a very busy hotel when special events are going on in the city, yet even when the hotel is full, it never feels crowded, and the service is spot-on. The hotel is in a romantic Georgetown neighborhood, yet is convenient to the National Mall and all the city attractions.

UPPER NORTHWEST
$100-200

The **Kalorama Guest House** (2700 Cathedral Ave. NW, 202/588-8188, www.kaloramaguesthouse.com, $109-239) is actually two Victorian town houses—the main house and a nice brick town house—in Upper Northwest with 10 guest rooms total. Located in a cute neighborhood less than a block from the National Zoo, it is a good bargain for the area. Don't expect many amenities in the rooms (no telephone and no television). Some of the rooms have shared bathrooms, but you can fall asleep listening to the sound of monkeys howling in the distance at the zoo and wake to a freshly made continental breakfast in the main house.

$200-300

★ **Woodley Park Guest House** (2647 Woodley Rd. NW, 202/667-0218, www.dcinns.com, $220-292) is one of the nicest bed-and-breakfasts in DC. In a historic neighborhood in Upper Northwest, they offer 15 comfortable and quiet guest rooms and exceptional service. The owners are truly service-oriented, and they help make the city feel personal and accessible. This is a wonderful choice in a quiet location for both business and leisure travel. The rooms have free wireless Internet, and a delicious, fresh continental breakfast is served daily.

The **Omni Shoreham Hotel** (2500 Calvert St. NW, 202/234-0700, www.omnihotels.com, $224-1,353) is a luxurious landmark built in 1930. It has 836 guest rooms, some of which have wonderful views of Rock Creek Park. This historic hotel hosted its first inaugural ball in 1933 (for Franklin D. Roosevelt) and has hosted inaugural balls for each president that followed during the 20th century (Bill Clinton even played his saxophone there during his ball in 1993). At one time, it was the number one choice for accommodations for dignitaries and the rich and famous and has housed such notables as the Beatles and emperors. The hotel offers rooms and suites of varying sizes and prices, with the lower-end rooms being quite affordable and the upper-end suites being very expensive. An elegant restaurant is located in the hotel. The rooms have free wireless Internet, and there is an outdoor heated pool, a fitness center, and more than 100,000 square feet of meeting space.

The Ghost Suite

It's no secret that the **Omni Shoreham Hotel** (2500 Calvert St. NW, 202/234-0700, www. omnihotels.com, $224-1,353) in Upper Northwest DC has some pretty peculiar things going on in Suite 870. The grand and historic hotel, which was built in 1930, originally had an extravagant apartment on the eighth floor where a minor shareholder in the property lived with his family and housekeeper. Shortly after they moved into the apartment, the housekeeper was found dead in her bed in the apartment. Not long after, the family's adopted daughter (the only child in the family) also died mysteriously in the apartment amid rumors of suicide or a possible drug overdose.

The family remained in the apartment for 40 years and finally moved out in 1973. The once extravagant apartment was in shambles when they left and was closed off to the rest of the hotel and abandoned. Once the apartment was empty, guests in neighboring rooms began reporting disturbances. Televisions and lights would go on and off, doors would slam shut, people would feel breezes as if someone had walked by, and many reports of loud noises (including someone playing the piano) were reported coming from the apartment. Many of the strange sounds were reported to be coming from Room 864, which was the housekeeper's bedroom.

In 1997 the hotel decided to renovate the apartment and turn it into a presidential suite. During construction, a worker fell from the balcony to his death. Upon completion of the suite's restoration, the hotel appropriately named it "The Ghost Suite."

It is reported that to this day many guests claim seeing a little girl running through the halls and an older woman in a long dress roaming around alone.

Information and Services

VISITORS INFORMATION

Additional information on Washington DC can be found at www.washington.org or by stopping by the **Washington Welcome Center** (1005 E St. NW, 202/347-6609, daily 9am-8pm).

MEDIA

The most widely circulated daily newspaper in Washington DC is the *Washington Post* (www.washingtonpost.com), featuring world and local news and with an emphasis on national politics. The *Washington Times* (www.washingtontimes.com) is another daily newspaper that has a wide following.

Weekly and specialty newspapers include the *Washington City Paper* (www. washingtoncitypaper.com), an alternative weekly newspaper, and the *Washington Informer* (www.washingtoninformer.com), a weekly newspaper serving the DC area's African American population.

EMERGENCY SERVICES

In the event of an emergency, call 911.

The **Metropolitan Police Department** (202/727-9099, www.mpdc.dc.gov) is the municipal law-enforcement agency in Washington DC. It is one of the 10 largest police forces in the country.

There are no fewer than 10 hospitals in the city. Some of the ones ranked highest nationally include **MedStar Washington Hospital Center** (110 Irving St. NW, 202/877-7000, www.whcenter.org), **MedStar Georgetown University Hospital** (3800 Reservoir Rd. NW, 202/444-2000, www. medstargeorgetown.org), and **George Washington University Hospital** (900 23rd St. NW, 202/715-4000, www. gwhospital.com).

Getting There

AIR

Three major airports serve Washington DC. **Ronald Reagan Washington National Airport (DCA)** (703/417-8000, www.flyreagan.com), just outside the city in Arlington, Virginia, is serviced by the Blue and Yellow Lines of the Metrorail. Taxi service is available at the Arrivals curb outside the baggage claim area of each terminal. Rental cars are also available on the first floor in parking garage A. A shuttle operates outside each baggage claim area to the rental car counter. It is a 15-minute drive to downtown Washington DC from the airport.

Washington Dulles International Airport (IAD) (703/572-2700, www.flydulles.com), 27 miles west of the city in Dulles, Virginia, is a 35-minute drive from downtown Washington DC. Bus service between Dulles Airport and the Metrorail at the Wiehle Avenue Station in Reston (Silver Line) is available through the **Silver Line Express Bus Service** (703/572-7661, $5 one-way, children under 2 free). Tickets can be purchased at the ticket counter in the main terminal at Arrivals door 4. Buses depart approximately every 15-20 minutes. Passengers going from the Wiehle Avenue Metrorail station should exit at the north side of the station to board the bus. Tickets can be purchased from the bus driver. **Metrobus** (202/637-7000, www.wmata.com) operates an express bus (Route 5A) between Dulles Airport and the L'Enfant Plaza Metrorail station in Washington DC. Passengers can board the bus at the airport at the Ground Transportation curb (on the Arrivals level) at curb location 2E. Car services such as Uber and Lyft are also available. An extension of Metrorail's Silver Line is planned and will provide a one-seat ride to downtown Washington DC from Dulles Airport in the future.

Baltimore/Washington International Thurgood Marshall Airport (BWI) (410/859-7111, www.bwiairport.com), 32 miles from Washington DC near Baltimore, Maryland, is approximately 50 minutes by car to Washington DC. It is serviced on weekdays by MARC commuter trains at the BWI Marshall rail station. Free shuttles are available from the station to the airport terminal. Shuttle stops can be found on the lower-level terminal road. Metrobus service is available between BWI and the Greenbelt Metrorail station (Green Line) on the **BWI Express Metro.** Bus service is available seven days a week with buses running every 40 minutes.

Washington Dulles Taxi and Sedan (703/554-3509, www.washingtondullestaxisedan.com) provides taxi and sedan service for passengers at all three airports. Shuttle service is also available from all three airports through **SuperShuttle** (800/258-3826, www.supershuttle.com).

CAR

Arriving in Washington DC by car is fairly common. Several major highways lead into the city, such as I-395 from the south in Virginia, I-66 from the southwest in Virginia, and I-295 from the northeast in Maryland. US 50 is the only primary road that runs through the city (on the eastern side) and connects Virginia and Maryland. Most hotels have some provision for parking, although it may come at a significant cost. There is also public parking on some streets and at many public garages throughout the city.

TRAIN

Amtrak (800/872-7245, www.amtrak.com) provides service to Washington DC through beautiful **Union Station** (50 Massachusetts Ave. NE, www.unionstationdc.com) on Capitol Hill. Amtrak connects with the **Maryland Area Rail Commuter (MARC)** system (410/539-5000, www.mta.maryland. gov), a service that runs Monday-Friday and connects Union Station with the Baltimore area, southern Maryland, and northeastern West Virginia; and with **Virginia Railway Express** (703/684-1001, www.vre.org), a service that runs weekdays only between Fredericksburg, Virginia, and Union Station and Manassas, Virginia, and Union Station.

BUS

A **Greyhound** (202/289-5141, www. greyhound.com) bus station is located at Union Station (50 Massachusetts Ave. NE). There is a second station in Dupont Circle at 1610 Connecticut Avenue NW.

Getting Around

METRORAIL

Washington DC and the surrounding area has a clean, reliable, and generally safe subway system called the **Metrorail** (202/637-7000, www.wmata.com) that is run by the **Washington Metropolitan Area Transit Authority (WMATA).** The Metrorail system is commonly known as "The Metro" and provides service to more than 600,000 customers a day. The system is number two in the country in terms of ticket sales and serves more than 90 stations throughout DC, Virginia, and Maryland. Visit the WMATA website for current delays and alerts.

There are six color-coded rail lines: Red, Orange, Blue, Yellow, Green, and Silver. The system layout is easy to understand (most stations are named for the neighborhood they serve), and getting from one station to another normally requires no more than a single transfer. Metrorail stations are marked with large "M" signs at the entrance that have colored stripes around them to show which line they serve. A complete list of fares and a map of each train line can be found on the website (fares are $2.25-6 during peak hours). Metrorail opens at 5am on weekdays, 7am on Saturdays, and 8am on Sundays. It closes at 11:30pm Monday-Thursday, 1am Friday-Saturday, and 11pm on Sunday. Bicycles are permitted during nonpeak hours. It is important to note that doors on each train do not operate like an elevator door and will not reopen if you stick your arm or hand in them as they close. Never stand in the way of a closing door.

Permanent, rechargeable farecards called **SmarTrip** cards can be purchased online and at Metrorail stations. Riders can recharge their cards online. SmarTrip holders receive a discount on Metrorail and Metrobus service (the cards can be used for both).

METROBUS

WMATA also runs **Metrobus** (202/637-7000, www.wmata.com, $2-4.25) service from Metrorail stops and throughout the city. They operate 325 routes to 11,500 bus stops in Washington DC, Virginia, and Maryland. For a complete listing, visit the website. Bicycle racks are provided on Metrobuses and can accommodate two bikes. Permanent, rechargeable farecards called **SmarTrip** cards can be purchased online and at Metrorail stations. Riders can recharge their cards online. Metrobus accepts SmarTrip or cash.

The **DC Circulator** (202/671-2020, www. dccirculator.com, hours vary by route, free) is a free local bus service with six bus routes to key areas in the city. Some of the areas it serves include Georgetown, Dupont Circle, Rosslyn (in Arlington, Virginia), Union Station, the Navy Yard Metrorail stop, Adams Morgan, and the Potomac Avenue Metrorail stop.

TAXIS AND PRIVATE TRANSPORT

Some neighborhoods in the city, such as Georgetown and Adams Morgan, are not serviced by Metrorail, so traveling by taxi or car service can be an easy way to reach these areas and is also a good alternative for direct transport between two locations. Fares are charged on a meter on a distance-traveled basis. There are many taxi services throughout the city. Sixteen companies can be booked through **DC Taxi Online** (www.dctaxionline. com). Standard taxi fares in Washington DC are $3.50 for the first eighth of a mile, with each additional mile costing $2.16. Hourly wait rates are $25.

Uber (www.uber.com) and **Lyft** (www. lyft.com) are hugely popular and easily accessible throughout Washington DC and are hailed over the Internet. Charges for the services are made directly to your credit card for a quick and easy transaction. These are fast, cost-effective, and easy ways to travel around the city. Rates are quoted on their websites.

Northern Virginia

Just across the Potomac River from the nation's capital, Northern Virginia is a cornucopia of culture, history, outdoor recreation, culinary delights, and shopping. While most of Northern Virginia is shaped by its proximity to Washington DC, the region also includes rolling hunt country, vineyards, and palatial estates in its western reaches, as well as beautiful views of the Blue Ridge Mountains.

Northern Virginia includes four counties (Arlington, Fairfax, Loudoun, and Prince William) as well as the independent cities of Alexandria, Fairfax, Falls Church, Manassas, and Manassas Park. The regional population comprises roughly one-third of the entire population of Virginia. As a central corridor for government contractors and the technology industry, the area tends to be upscale.

Highlights

Look for ★ to find recommended sights, activities, dining, and lodging.

★ **Arlington National Cemetery:** More than 300,000 plain white headstones stand in neat rows as a somber tribute to those who have served our nation. This is also the site of the Tomb of the Unknowns and the eternal flame at John F. Kennedy's grave site (page 102).

★ **Torpedo Factory Art Center:** This 82-studio art center in Old Town Alexandria hosts three floors of galleries in a former torpedo factory (page 113).

★ **Great Falls Park:** A 77-foot waterfall drops into Mather Gorge on the Potomac River, acting as an impressive backdrop to a park full of outdoor activities (page 127).

★ **National Air and Space Museum Steven F. Udvar-Hazy Center:** This Smithsonian Institution museum features an awe-inspiring aviation hangar that displays historic aircraft on three levels (page 128).

★ **George Washington's Mount Vernon:** Get a window into Washington's private life and the world of an 18th-century plantation (page 130).

★ **Wolf Trap National Park for the Performing Arts:** This unique venue is the nation's only national park created for the performing arts (page 135).

★ **Manassas National Battlefield Park:** This site of two major American Civil War battles is a great place for die-hard historians. The park

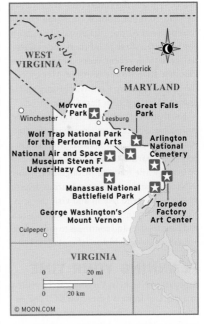

encompasses more than 5,000 acres of fields, woods, and streams (page 142).

★ **Morven Park:** Once home to Virginia governor Westmoreland Davis, this historic estate features the original mansion, two museums, an equestrian center, historic gardens, sports fields, and hiking trails (page 152).

The densely populated areas of Arlington and Alexandria abut Washington DC and border the Potomac River. Arlington is known for its national landmarks, military memorials, and trendy restaurants and shopping areas, while Alexandria is best known for its historic Old Town area, which supports a diversity of shops, excellent restaurants, and perhaps the ghosts of our country's founding fathers, who once walked the city's streets and gathered in its taverns.

Fairfax is the most populous jurisdiction in Virginia, but Loudoun has been growing steadily over the past few decades as new neighborhoods and business parks slowly take over what used to be mostly rolling hills and horse farms.

The second-largest county in Virginia, Prince William, is 35 miles from Washington DC and 20 miles from Washington Dulles International Airport. Its proximity to both has spurred a surge in business and residential growth in recent years. Bordering the Potomac River to the south of Alexandria, the county is rich in Civil War history and is home to Marine Corps Base Quantico.

Northern Virginia attracts entrepreneurs, politicians, advocates, artists, environmentalists, immigrants, and nomads from all corners of the earth. A variety of languages can be heard while walking through nearly any public area, and neighborhoods are as diverse as the people who live in and visit the area. Northern Virginia combines cosmopolitan and countryside, and continues to grow while preserving its deep historical roots.

PLANNING YOUR TIME

Any part of Northern Virginia can be visited in a day trip from Washington DC. The entire area can be covered in a busy few days, but four or five days will give you time to get a real feel for all it offers.

If you plan to stay in Virginia, where you sleep will depend on your priorities. Sights are spread throughout Northern Virginia, so it's best to pick your accommodations based on the atmosphere you like. If you want to stay where restaurants and shopping are within walking distance, consider Old Town Alexandria. If a cozy bed-and-breakfast is more your style, make a reservation in hunt country in Middleburg. Whatever you choose, the biggest consideration for your schedule will be traffic. The Washington DC area is notorious for highway congestion, and this is true year-round.

To avoid the heaviest traffic, don't travel during rush hour, which unfortunately can span many hours each weekday. The best time to travel on weekdays, especially if you are driving I-495 (the Beltway) or I-66, is between 10am and 3pm. Also, if you plan on arriving in the area or leaving the area on a Friday, avoid major arteries (I-495, I-66, and I-95) after 3pm. Friday-afternoon traffic will taint your view of the area. Another thing to be mindful of is high-occupancy/toll (HOT) lane restrictions. These require a minimum of two or three people to be in the car to use the roadway or specific lanes or you must pay a toll during specific times of day (and the toll amount will depend on the volume of traffic). Several major arteries such as I-66, I-395, I-95, and the Dulles Toll Road have these restrictions during prime commuting hours; for a listing of restrictions, visit www.virginiadot.org. The good news is that drivers around Northern Virginia are generally courteous.

Some public transportation is available in Northern Virginia through the **Washington Metropolitan Area Transit Authority (WMATA)** (www.wmata.com), which operates **Metrobus** and **Metrorail** service, although coverage isn't extensive in all parts of Northern Virginia. It is often more convenient to move around by car if that is an option.

Limited county bus transportation is also available in Arlington County, Alexandria, Fairfax County, and Loudoun County,

---

Previous: George Washington's Mount Vernon; Civil War cannons at Manassas National Battlefield Park; Great Falls Park

Northern Virginia

© MOON.COM

5 mi

5 km

MARYLAND

WEST VIRGINIA

WASHINGTON DC

MARYLAND

Silver Spring

Rockville

Potomac River

GREAT FALLS PARK

Great Falls

Riverbend Park

McLean

Tysons Corner

Vienna

WOLF TRAP NATIONAL PARK FOR THE PERFORMING ARTS

Falls Church

Fairfax

Arlington

ARLINGTON

FORT WARD

ARLINGTON NATIONAL CEMETERY

RONALD REAGAN WASHINGTON NATIONAL AIRPORT

TORPEDO FACTORY ART CENTER

GEORGE WASHINGTON'S MOUNT VERNON

Alexandria

Huntley Meadows Park

WOODLAWN AND POPE-LEIGHEY HOUSE

Springfield

SEE "ARLINGTON COUNTY AND VICINITY" MAP

FAIRFAX

Fountainhead Regional Park

Occoquan River

Occoquan Reservoir

Bull Run Regional Park

Bull Run Creek

Manassas

PRINCE WILLIAM

Gainesville

Haymarket

Ball's Bluff Battlefield Regional Park and Ball's Bluff National Cemetery

WHITE'S FERRY

MORVEN PARK

Leesburg

Herndon

DULLES GREENWAY

WASHINGTON-DULLES INTERNATIONAL AIRPORT

NATIONAL AIR AND SPACE MUSEUM STEVEN F. UDVAR-HAZY CENTER

MANASSAS NATIONAL BATTLEFIELD PARK

OATLANDS HISTORIC HOUSE AND GARDENS

LOUDOUN

Lovettsville

Waterford

Hamilton

Hillsboro

Purcellville

Bluemont

Glenwood Park

Middleburg

The Plains

Upperville

Harpers Ferry National Historical Park

Berryville

CLARKE

Shenandoah River

Blue Ridge Mountains

Sky Meadows State Park

To Front Royal and I-81

FAUQUIER

Warrenton

RAPPAHANNOCK

through the Arlington Transit (ART), Alexandria Transit Company (DASH), Fairfax Connector, and Loudoun County Transit, respectively. These services are geared toward commuters; so again, driving is usually the quickest and easiest way to see the sights.

Two major airports service the Northern Virginia area. The first is **Ronald Reagan Washington National Airport** (703/417-8000, www.flyreagan.com) in Arlington. Metrorail's Blue and Yellow Lines connect to this airport. The second is **Washington Dulles International Airport** (703/572-2700, www.flydulles.com) in Dulles, Virginia.

The **Leesburg Executive Airport (JYO)** (1001 Sycolin Rd., Leesburg, 703/737-7125, www.leesburgva.gov), owned and operated by the city of Leesburg, is one of the two busiest general aviation (GA) airports in Virginia. This airport is 35 miles from Washington DC and is a reliever airport for Washington Dulles International Airport.

Arlington

Arlington is the closest Virginia suburb to Washington DC. Just across the Potomac River from the capital, Arlington encompasses 26 square miles, is easily accessed from DC by four bridges and by public transportation (11 Metrorail stops and bus service), and has more than 234,000 residents.

Because of its proximity to the nation's capital, Arlington supports many federal buildings, national agencies, and memorials. Between this and the numerous businesses that call Arlington home, it sometimes seems like an extension of Washington DC rather than part of Virginia. Arlington contains more office space than downtown Los Angeles. Business centers in Arlington include the areas of Ballston, Clarendon, and Crystal City (where Amazon's East Coast headquarters will be located), but hotels, restaurants, and attractions are spread out all over Arlington County.

Arlington is a highly diverse community. Approximately 27 percent of the county's residents speak a language besides English at home. This contributes to a wonderful array of authentic food establishments from around the globe.

Originally slated to be part of Washington DC, Arlington was trimmed from the city plan in 1847 when it was established as Alexandria County. In 1920, the name was changed to Arlington, after the George Washington Parke Custis estate honoring the earl of Arlington.

Arlington is a place you will want to step in and out of during a visit to the nation's capital, but unless you are attending a specific event or coming for work, you don't need to plan an entire week there. It is so easily accessible that you can pick and choose your activities and see the highlights in a day or two.

SIGHTS
★ Arlington National Cemetery

The most famous cemetery in the nation is **Arlington National Cemetery** (1 Memorial Dr., 877/907-8585, www.arlingtoncemetery. mil, Apr.-Sept. daily 8am-7pm, Oct.-Mar. daily 8am-5pm, free). The cemetery is a sprawling 624-acre site where more than 400,000 soldiers from every U.S. military conflict are buried. The uniform white tombstones form an orderly quilt across the rolling green fields of the cemetery and are meticulously maintained. Called "Our Nation's Most Sacred Shrine," as the resting place for many generations of our nation's heroes, the cemetery grows daily: On average, more than two dozen funerals are held each weekday. In 1948, a group of women formed the Arlington Ladies, a volunteer group whose members attend services for all veterans and ensure that

Arlington County and Vicinity

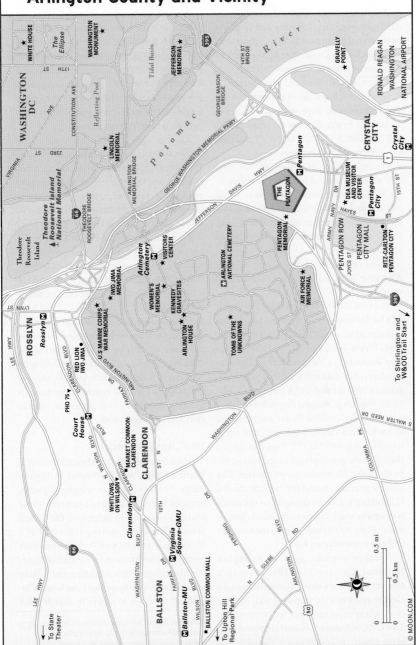

© MOON.COM

no member of the armed forces is ever buried alone.

A welcome center marks the entrance to Arlington National Cemetery and is always open when the cemetery is. Maps, grave locations, guidebooks, and other information on the cemetery can be obtained at the center, and there are restrooms and a bookstore.

Interpretive bus tours of the cemetery depart continuously from the welcome center. Tickets can be purchased at the center (adults $15, children 3-11 $7.25, senior 65 and over $11, uniformed military free).

Private cars are not allowed in the cemetery except by special permission, but parking is available off Memorial Drive in a paid parking garage, and there is a dedicated stop for the cemetery on the Metrorail Blue Line. Please remember that this is not a park but an active cemetery.

There are several key sights within Arlington National Cemetery that are well worth a visit.

The first and the best known is the **Tomb of the Unknowns.** The tomb houses the remains of unidentified American soldiers from World Wars I and II and the Korean War. Remains of a Vietnam War soldier were also housed in the tomb until they were identified in 1998 through DNA testing and relocated. That crypt remains empty but serves as a symbol. The Medal of Honor was presented to each of the interred soldiers, and these medals, along with the U.S. flags that draped their caskets, are displayed to the rear of the tomb in the Memorial Amphitheater. The tomb is guarded around the clock by the 3rd U.S. Infantry, and the changing of the guard is a popular tourist attraction. Guard changes occur every 30 minutes during the summer and every hour during winter.

Another popular sight at Arlington National Cemetery is the **Women's Memorial** (www.womensmemorial.org), an elegant semicircular retaining wall built of stone at the main entrance to the cemetery. This is the only major national memorial honoring American servicewomen. The memorial is open to the public every day (8am-5pm) except Christmas Day.

A short walk uphill from the Women's Memorial is the eternal flame and burial site of **John F. Kennedy.** This is one of the most-visited graves in the cemetery. **Jacqueline Kennedy Onassis** is buried next to him, and **Robert F. Kennedy** was laid to rest nearby in a grave marked (at his request) with only a single white wooden cross and excerpts from two of his civil rights speeches.

Another sight to visit while in Arlington National Cemetery is the **Arlington House, The Robert E. Lee Memorial** (321 Sherman Dr., Fort Myer, 703/235-1530, www.nps.gov/arho, daily 10am-4pm, free). This former home of George Washington Parke Custis, whose daughter married Robert E. Lee, is actually a national park and maintained by the National Park Service. The Greek revival-style mansion, which underwent a major renovation in 2019, sits on land that was once part of a 1,100-acre plantation where the Lee family lived for three decades before the Civil War. Expect to see period furnishings inside the home and to learn the interesting story of how the home was lost by the family during the Civil War. The site is the highest in Arlington National Cemetery and offers terrific views of Washington DC. The house is open for self-guided tours and is a 10-minute walk from the cemetery welcome center.

Iwo Jima Memorial

The **Iwo Jima Memorial,** also called the **U.S. Marine Corps War Memorial** (Arlington Ridge, 703/289-2500, www.nps.gov/gwmp, open 24 hours, free) stands to honor those Marines who died in defense of the United States. This awe-inspiring memorial is a 32-foot-tall granite and bronze sculpture created in the likeness of a Pulitzer Prize-winning photograph depicting the raising of the American flag on Iwo Jima (a small island off the coast of Japan) in March 1945,

1: headstones at Arlington National Cemetery **2:** Iwo Jim Memorial designed by sculptor Felix de Weldon and architect Horace W. Peaslee

near the end of World War II. The sculpture illustrates the U.S. flag being raised by five Marines and a Navy hospital corpsman. The detail in the memorial is stunning, and its enormous size adds to its inspirational appeal. This off-the-beaten-path memorial is definitely worth seeking out. It's a half-mile walk from the Rosslyn Metrorail station and slightly farther from the Arlington Cemetery Metrorail station.

National 9/11 Pentagon Memorial

The **National 9/11 Pentagon Memorial** (1 N. Rotary Rd., Pentagon, 301/740-3388, www. pentagonmemorial.org, open 24 hours, free) is a haunting, thought-provoking memorial dedicated to the 184 people who lost their lives at the Pentagon in the terrorist attacks of September 11, 2001. This two-acre memorial is just outside the Pentagon and is made up of 184 benches, one for each of the men and women who died on the plane that hit the building or inside the building. Illuminated fountains run beneath each bench. If you look at the side of the Pentagon building, it is easy to tell where the plane crashed: The stone replaced in the repair is slightly different in color from the rest of the building. The memorial is open all the time and can be accessed from the Pentagon stop on the Yellow or Blue Line on the Metrorail. Restrooms are available daily 7am-10pm.

Air Force Memorial

The **Air Force Memorial** (1 Air Force Memorial Dr., 703/979-0674, www.afdw. af.mil, daily 8am-8pm, free) is a sight that's visible from a considerable distance. Its three elegant, stainless steel and concrete spires stretch 270 feet toward the sky, honoring the service and lives of the men and women of the U.S. Air Force.

Drug Enforcement Administration Museum and Visitors Center

The **Drug Enforcement Administration Museum and Visitors Center** (700 Army Navy Dr., 202/307-3463, www.deamuseum. org, Tues.-Sat. 10am-4pm, free) is a learning center dedicated to educating the public about drugs, addiction, law enforcement, and the history of drugs in the United States. It does so through a series of displays that discuss the impact of federal law enforcement on the evolving nature of licit and illicit drug use in the country.

RECREATION
Trails

There are many paved bike trails throughout Northern Virginia, and several go through Arlington. The 18-mile **Mount Vernon Trail** runs between Theodore Roosevelt Island (an 88-acre island and national park that sits in the Potomac River near the Roosevelt Bridge) and George Washington's Mount Vernon. The trail runs along the George Washington Memorial Parkway and passes by Gravelly Point Park and Ronald Reagan Washington National Airport and goes into Old Town Alexandria.

The **Four Mile Run Trail** is a 6.2-mile paved path that begins at **Bluemont Junction Park** (744 N. Emerson St.) and runs toward the Mount Vernon Trail and Ronald Reagan Washington National Airport. The **Washington & Old Dominion Trail** also begins in Arlington in the Shirlington area and runs west 45 miles to Purcellville, Virginia. One offshoot of the trail is the **Martha Custis Trail,** which intersects the Washington & Old Dominion Trail at mile marker 4. The Martha Custis Trail heads directly into Washington DC through Arlington on a four-mile paved path parallel to Route 66. There are a handful of climbs and some winding turns, but nothing too difficult. For a detailed map visit www. bikewashington.org.

Trail runners will enjoy the **Potomac Heritage Trail.** It begins on the west side of Theodore Roosevelt Island at the parking lot and runs 10 miles to the west end of the I-495 bridge. It passes through woods along the river, crosses small cliff tops, and spans a few streams. It is blazed in blue.

Hiking in Washington & Old Dominion Railroad Regional Park

The **Washington & Old Dominion Trail** (www. wodfriends.org) is known as Virginia's skinniest park. It's hard to believe that a regional park can be 45 miles long and just 100 feet wide, but this popular trail is exactly that. It begins at the intersection of Shirlington Road and Four Mile Run Drive in Arlington (just two blocks north of I-395) and follows an old rail route west through Falls Church (crossing over State Route 7) and into Vienna. A bridle path parallels the trail starting in Vienna, and the two paths continue through Reston, Herndon, Ashburn, and Leesburg before ending in the cute town of Purcellville on 21st Street.

Trains followed this route for more than 100 years (1859-1968), but today it is widely used for biking, running, walking, and inline skating. The asphalt trail is predominantly rolling, although there are many nice flat sections. There are few true hills, but the trail does gain in overall elevation heading west.

Washington & Old Dominion Trail

Proper trail etiquette includes staying to the right side of the path as you travel and making yourself known to slower traffic as you pass on the left. A simple "Passing left" callout is enough to warn people when you are going around them on the trail.

There are several rest areas. The largest is the Smiths Switch Station in Ashburn. This stop offers two portable toilets, a covered rest area, and vending machines. Another unofficial but extremely popular stop is at the Ashburn Road crossing at the **Carolina Brothers Pit Barbeque** restaurant and shop (20702 Ashburn Rd., 703/729-7070, www.carolinabrothers.com, Mon.-Thurs. 10:30am-7pm, Fri.-Sat. 10:30am-8pm, Sun. 10:30am-7pm, $6-20). It's hard to ignore the smell of their barbecue cooking, and they have a wonderful outdoor area with tables and umbrellas and numerous bike racks. They also sell drinks and snacks. There are several more porta-potty stops along the trail, including in Reston and Leesburg. As the trail passes through Vienna, it borders a Whole Foods Market where many people like to stop as well. There's also a community center in Vienna with public bathrooms.

For additional information and trail maps, visit **NOVA Parks** (www.novaparks.com) or the **Arlington County Department of Parks and Recreation** (703/228-4747, www. parks.arlingtonva.us).

Parks

Gravelly Point Park (George Washington Pkwy., daily dawn to dusk, free) is a very popular spot for plane-watching. Its proximity to the runways at Ronald Reagan Washington National Airport offers spectacular close-up views of planes as they approach and depart from the airport. The park sits directly on the Potomac River and offers a boat launch, picnic tables, and plenty of open spaces on which to throw down a blanket. A bike path also runs around the park. There's a three-hour limit on parking (which is enforced), so set your cell phone alarm if you plan to nap. This is also a great spot for watching the fireworks on the National Mall on the Fourth of July, but you'll have to get here early to find parking. The entrance to the park is only available from the northbound lanes of the parkway.

Upton Hill Regional Park (6060 Wilson Blvd., 703/534-3437, www.novaparks.com) is a popular family recreation area with a large outdoor water park, a playground, a miniature golf course, and batting cages for both baseball and softball. There is a basic snack bar with reasonable prices. Each activity in the park has its own hours of operation, so it's best to consult the website.

Theodore Roosevelt Island (703/289-2500, www.nps.gov/this) is a beautiful island in the Potomac River accessed off the northbound lanes of the George Washington Memorial Parkway. There are wooded trails and a 47-foot-tall monument to Roosevelt. Ranger tours are available to learn about the local wildlife. The views are beautiful if you can ignore the noise from the planes taking off and landing at Ronald Reagan Washington National Airport.

Another family recreation area is **Bluemont Park** (601 N. Manchester St., 703/228-6525, www.parks.arlingtonva.us). This 70-acre park offers many family activities including picnicking, horseshoes, fishing, a playground, a basketball court, a baseball field, tennis, volleyball, a playground, and disc golf.

For a complete list of Arlington County parks, visit www.parks.arlingtonva.us.

Canoeing and Kayaking

There are two good launch areas on the Potomac River in Arlington. The first is **Columbia Island Marina** (202/347-0173, www.boatingindc.com) off the George Washington Parkway, and the second is **Gravelly Point Park** (George Washington Pkwy.).

Four-hour guided "D.C. Monument Tour" kayak trips on the Potomac River are available through **Potomac Paddlesports** (301/881-2628, www.potomacpaddlesports.com, $95). Trips leave from Columbia Island Marina in Arlington.

ENTERTAINMENT AND EVENTS
Theater

The **Signature Theatre** (4200 Campbell Ave., 703/820-9771, www.sigtheatre.org), in the shopping area of Shirlington, is a professional nonprofit theater company that features contemporary performances. Although it runs many traditional productions, it is widely known for its musical theater and inventive twists on lesser-known works. A top regional theater with an interesting design, set among a great selection of restaurants and shopping, the Signature Theatre has become a popular destination for the entire metropolitan area. Tickets are reasonably priced but can be difficult to obtain at the last minute.

The State Theatre in nearby Falls Church (220 N. Washington St., Falls Church, 703/237-0300, www.thestatetheatre.com) used to be an old-time movie theater, complete with balcony seating. In recent years, the theater has been renovated as a prime venue for concerts and comedy. There are several levels of seating and standing areas (including the balcony). Food and beverages are served, and table seating can be reserved. This is a fun venue with first-rate entertainment. Parking can be difficult, so plan to arrive early.

After seeing a performance at the **Synetic Theater** (1800 S. Bell St., 703/824-8060, www.synetictheater.org) you may reevaluate the whole theater experience. The goal of this award-winning company is to be the premier American physical theater—in short, this means they perform without speaking. Known for their Shakespeare productions, the theater uses movement, acrobatics, dance, music, and a number of other communication forms to create a very distinct form of theater, telling classic stories in an untraditional way.

Nightlife

The **Arlington Cinema & Drafthouse** (2903 Columbia Pike, 703/486-2345, http://acdh.arlingtondrafthouse.com) is a tradition in Northern Virginia. It opened its doors in 1985 and has served up dinner and a movie (with a full bar) ever since. The theater also offers live entertainment and broadcasts sporting events. This venue is also available for rent for private parties.

A local institution on Wilson Boulevard

is **Whitlows on Wilson** (2854 Wilson Blvd., 703/276-9693, www.whitlows.com, Mon.-Fri. 11am-2am, Sat.-Sun. 9am-2am). This historic venue, which was originally located in Washington DC (in 1946), features rock, reggae, hip-hop, dance, and blues shows many nights. They have food and drink specials throughout the week. Be sure to look around for reclaimed items such as the bowling lane bar top, booths from St. Patrick's Catholic Church, and chairs from the old Arlington County courthouse.

Another local favorite on Wilson Boulevard is **Galaxy Hut** (2711 Wilson Blvd., 703/525-8646, www.galaxyhut.com, daily 5pm-2am). This funky dive bar opened in 1990 as Arlington's first craft beer bar. They have 28 taps and live music Sundays and Mondays ($5).

Drinks and board games. That's really all you need to know about **The Board Room** (925 N. Garfield St., 703/248-9439, www.theboardroomva.com, Mon.-Fri. 4pm-2am, Sat.-Sun. 11am-2am). This unique, mostly 21-and-over venue offers dozens of board games to play ($2 or you can bring your own), an extensive bar menu, and food. This is a fun place with many special events (wine tasting, happy hour, trivia, etc.). The entrance is around the corner from the street address. This venue also houses the intimate **Ms. Peacock's Champagne Lounge** (929 N. Garfield St., www.mspeacockschampagne.com, Wed.-Thurs. 6pm-midnight, Fri.-Sat. 6pm-1am), a speakeasy-style lounge with an upscale feel and extensive champagne and cocktail list.

Festivals

There are a number of annual festivals held in Arlington. One of the most popular is the **Ballston Quarterfest** (www.quarterfestballston.org), a food, drink, and entertainment festival held each May along Wilson Boulevard. Admission to this lively street festival is free, but tickets must be purchased for the street pub and restaurant crawl. The **Feel the Heritage** event in February at the **Charles Drew Community Center** (3500 23rd St. S, www.parks.arlingtonva.us) celebrates African American culture with live music, vendors, children's activities, food, and a hall of history.

The **Arlington County Fair** (www.arlingtoncountyfair.us) is also popular. It is one of the largest free annual events on the East Coast and draws over 50,000 people each August. The fair is held at the **Thomas Jefferson Community Center** (3501 S. 2nd St.). Shuttle service is available from nearby Metro stations.

SHOPPING

There are six primary shopping areas in Arlington. **Ballston Quarter** (4238 Wilson Blvd., www.ballstonquarter.com) is a four-level enclosed mall at the corner of Glebe Road and Wilson Boulevard. The mall includes national stores such as Macy's, a movie theater, a health club, and many smaller shops. The **Market Common Clarendon** (2800 Clarendon Blvd., www.marketcommonclarendon.com) is at the Clarendon Orange Line Metrorail stop. It is primarily an outdoor shopping mall (with garage parking) that has national name-brand retailers such as Crate & Barrel, Barnes & Noble, and Ann Taylor along with local boutiques. There is also a Whole Foods Market in the shopping center.

Fashion Centre at Pentagon City (1100 S. Hayes St., www.simon.com) is a large mall with many national retailers such as Apple, Macy's, Nordstrom, and Banana Republic. **Pentagon Row** (1201 S. Joyce Street, www.pentagonrow.com) also offers shopping and restaurants in a central plaza with outdoor cafés and ice-skating in winter. It is off I-395 (a parking garage is available) near the Pentagon City Metro station on the Yellow and Blue Lines.

The **Village at Shirlington** (2700 S. Quincy St., www.villageatshirlington.com) has become a popular gathering place because of its great choices of restaurants and small shops. It is an outdoor mall, but garage parking is available. If you are in the Crystal City area, there are plenty of restaurants and shops between 12th and 23rd Streets near the Crystal City Metro stop in an area known as the **Crystal City Shops** (1750 Crystal Dr. and 2100 Crystal Dr., www.thecrystalcityshops.com). Many retailers and restaurants are located below ground along a unique network of walkways.

FOOD

Arlington is known for its diversity of wonderful food. Many eateries serve authentic fare from around the globe and do so at a reasonable price.

American

★ **The Lost Dog Café** (5876 Washington Blvd., 703/237-1552, www.lostdogcafe.com, Mon.-Sat. 11am-11pm, Sun. 11am-10pm, $7-26) is a local favorite for three reasons: great food, great beer, and its ties to the Lost Dog & Cat Rescue Foundation (founded by the restaurant owners). The restaurant is a lively, friendly, and casual café and gourmet pizza deli that serves a creative and delicious assortment of specialty pizzas, sandwiches, salads, and pasta. Menu items have names such as Kujo Pie (tomato sauce with pesto, artichoke hearts, grilled chicken, fresh tomatoes, mozzarella, and basil) and Dog Collars (onion rings). The bar stocks more than 200 types of beer, and the staff is knowledgeable and helpful. The decor is completely done in "dog"—although due to health regulations, no dogs are allowed inside. A portion of the proceeds goes to the foundation, but the food alone is reason to come. Consult the website for additional locations.

For classic diner food, try **Metro 29 Diner** (4711 Lee Hwy., 703/528-2464, www.metro29diner.com, daily 6am-midnight, $5-30). This local institution was featured on the TV show *Diners, Drive-ins and Dives*. They provide a monster menu of delicious homemade food and serve it up fresh in their 12,000-square-foot restaurant. All food is made from scratch; they even make their gravy in house and fresh challah bread for their French toast. They serve breakfast, lunch, and dinner, and they're open late. The service is friendly, and the place has a true diner feel.

Asian

A good Thai option is **Thai Square** (3217 Columbia Pike, 703/685-7040, www.thaisquarerestaurant.com, Mon.-Thurs. 11:30am-10pm, Fri. 11:30am-10:30pm, Sat. noon-10:30pm, Sun. noon-10pm, $9-18). This plain, no-frills restaurant built a reputation on its food. Street parking can be tough, but the service is good and the specials delicious. If you like spicy Thai food, this is an especially good choice.

Some of the most flavorful and creative Chinese food in the area is made at the legendary ★ **Peking Gourmet** (6029 Leesburg Pike, Falls Church, 703/671-8088, www.pekinggourmet.com, Sun.-Thurs. 11am-10:30pm, Fri.-Sat. 11am-11pm, $12-50) in nearby Falls Church. The gallery of celebrity photos hanging on the wall speaks volumes regarding the clientele at the restaurant, and it's not unusual to have VIPs in house. The signature dish is the Peking duck, which is nothing short of amazing. It arrives whole and is expertly carved tableside. Other must-try dishes include the chicken and garlic shoots (when available) and the crispy beef. Hands down, this is *the* best Chinese restaurant in Northern Virginia, and as such, it is crowded—so be sure to make a reservation.

If you're craving pho and only pho, stop by **Pho 75** (1721 Wilson Blvd., 703/525-7355, daily 10am-9pm, under $10). It is one of the original pho restaurants in the area, and they know pho. The soup is hot, delicious, and reasonably priced.

French

If you're feeling the itch for French food, try **La Cote d'Or Café** (6876 Lee Hwy., 703/538-3033, www.lacotedorarlington.com, lunch Mon.-Fri. 11:30am-3pm, brunch Sat.-Sun. 11am-3pm, dinner Sun.-Thurs. 5pm-9pm,

Fri.-Sat. 5pm-10pm, $23-38), a family-owned restaurant that is named after the Burgundy region in France. They serve delicious bistro-style French food—crepes, filet, and sea-food—and a carefully selected wine list. The service is friendly and attentive, and you can expect an overall pleasant dining experience in a comfortable, French-country atmosphere.

Italian

As the name suggests, **The Italian Store** (3123 Lee Hwy., 703/528-6266, www.italianstore.com, Mon.-Fri. 10am-9pm, Sat. 10am-8pm, Sun. 11am-6pm, $7-25) is a casual authentic takeout pizzeria and sandwich store combined with an Italian market. Simply put, this place is fabulous. Fresh ingredients, homemade pasta, and Italian wines are just part of the recipe for success. This is a very popular carryout restaurant and is geared toward that, so if you come during peak lunch hours, be prepared to wait. There's a second location at 5837 Washington Boulevard.

Middle Eastern

For a quick meal or to curb a late-night appetite, stop in **Kabob Palace** (2315 S. Eads St., 703/486-3535, open 24 hours, $9-20) in Crystal City. The kabobs are tender and flavorful (the lamb is especially juicy), and the sides are authentic and delicious. Their rice is tasty and fluffy, and their mango lassi is refreshing. The clientele is diverse and lively, and the service is usually good.

Turkish

Yayla Bistro (2201 N. Westmoreland St., 703/533-5600, www.yaylabistro.com, Sun.-Thurs. 11am-9pm, Fri.-Sat. 11am-10pm, $10-25) has a dedicated following. They serve authentic, Turkish food in an elegant and relaxed setting. The menu includes spreads, salads, flatbreads, and delicious grilled meat (such as filet mignon, lamb, and salmon). They also offer a nice selection of Turkish wine.

Treats and Coffee

After trying the **Best Buns Bread Company** (4010 Campbell Ave. 703/578-1500, www.greatamericanrestaurants.com, Mon. 6am-7pm, Tues.-Fri. 6am-8pm, Sat. 7am-8pm, Sun. 7am-7pm, under $15) in Shirlington, you will look for an excuse to come back, maybe even the same day. Whether you're craving sweets, bread, or a sandwich, this is the place to go. They are part of the Great American Restaurants group, which includes **Carlyle Grand Café** (4000 Campbell Ave., 703/931-0777, www.greatamericanrestaurants.com, Mon.-Thurs. 11:30am-10:30pm, Fri. 11:30am-11:30pm, Sat. 10:30am-11:30pm, Sun. 9:30am-10:30pm, $13-28) next door. Carlyle Grand serves flavorful American food such as salads, sandwiches, and seafood in a lively environment. They also have a wonderful brunch menu on weekends.

For a good cup of joe, try the **Java Shack** (2507 N. Franklin Rd., 703/527-9556, Mon.-Sat. 7am-7pm, Sun. 8am-7pm, under $10), just off of Wilson Boulevard. It's pet friendly, people friendly, casual, a little quirky, and best of all, it serves good coffee and tea. The atmosphere is very relaxing, which is rare to find in the hubbub of Northern Virginia. The porch is especially pleasant for catching up with friends on a nice day.

Farmers Markets

Arlington has many wonderful farmers markets, and some are year-round. For a list of markets and locations, visit www.arlingtonva.us.

Arlington has several good farmers markets: the **Arlington County Farmers Market** (2100 Clarendon Blvd., Sat. May-Dec. 8am-noon, Jan.-Apr. 9am-noon), the **Clarendon Farmers Market** (3140 Wilson Blvd, 703/812-8881, Apr.-Dec., Wed. 3pm-7pm), the **Columbia Pike Farmers Market** (corner of S. Walter Reed Drive and Columbia Pike, www.columbia-pike.org/fm/, year-round Sun. 9am-1pm), and the **Crystal City Farmers Market** (Crystal City Drive between 18th and 20th Streets, www.crystalcity.org, Mid-May-Oct. Tues. 3pm-7pm).

ACCOMMODATIONS

Spending the night in Arlington can often be a less expensive alternative to staying in Washington DC. There are mostly large chain hotels in Arlington, but there are a few lesser-known alternatives that shouldn't be overlooked.

$100-200

There are few reliable hotels priced under $200 a night in peak tourist season in Arlington. The **Red Lion Hotel Rosslyn Iwo Jima** (1501 Arlington Blvd., 703/524-5000, www.redlion.com, $99-108) is a consistent option. The hotel is reasonably priced, especially for its location: It's minutes from the Iwo Jima Memorial, a short drive to Ronald Reagan Washington National Airport, and walking distance to the Rosslyn Metro stop. It is also convenient to many Washington DC attractions. There are 141 rooms, and they have complimentary bike rentals. The rooms are older and aren't fancy, but they are comfortable and have free wireless Internet. There is also on-site parking.

The ★ **Hilton Garden Inn Arlington/Shirlington** (4271 Campbell Ave., 703/820-0440, www.hiltongardeninn3.hilton.com, $133-193) is nicely located in a neighborhood of shops, restaurants, and theaters. It is also convenient to Washington DC. The rooms are amply sized and have comfortable beds. The service is friendly and professional. There are 142 rooms, and standard amenities come with each, including free high-speed Internet, a fitness center, a business center, and a swimming pool. The hotel also offers complimentary shuttle service to Ronald Reagan Washington National Airport and the Pentagon City Metrorail stop.

$200-300

The **Residence Inn Arlington Courthouse** (1401 N. Adams St., 703/312-2100, www.marriott.com, $121-409) is a modern, ecofriendly, 176-room hotel in Courthouse Village by the Courthouse Metrorail stop on the Orange Line. Many shops and restaurants are within easy walking distance, and pizza delivery is available to your room. Suites are pleasantly decorated and include wireless Internet and full kitchens. There is also a fitness center and a beautiful indoor pool with a lifeguard. Breakfast is included. There is on-site parking and the hotel allows pets, both for an additional fee.

If you need to stay near Ronald Reagan Washington National Airport, the 161-room **Hampton Inn & Suites Reagan National Airport** (2000 Richmond Hwy., 703/418-8181, www.hamptoninn3.com, $140-308) is a good option. They offer quick shuttle service to the airport and are close to the Metro. Rooms are spacious and include amenities such as free wireless Internet, flat-screen televisions, microwaves, and refrigerators. The beds are comfortable and the bathrooms are modern. Parking is available for $25 per day.

Le Meridien Arlington (1121 19th St. N., 703/351-9170, www.lemeridienva.com, $87-369) is a boutique hotel in the Rosslyn area of Arlington. It has 154 guest rooms and is nicely appointed with comfortable modern furniture. The staff is friendly, and the hotel is convenient to the Rosslyn Metrorail stop and a short walk to Georgetown. The on-site gym is above normal hotel standards, and there is a parking garage available. Book a room with a view of Georgetown across the Potomac River, and take advantage of happy hour on the large patio. The lobby is located on the 4th floor of the building, which can be a little confusing when checking in. There is also a charge for in-room wireless Internet. Le Meridien is a Marriott hotel.

Over $300

The **Ritz-Carlton, Pentagon City** (1250 S. Hayes St., 703/415-5000, www.ritzcarlton.com, $202-5000) is minutes from the Pentagon City Metrorail station. This hotel is consistent in offering a comfortable stay with great beds and attentive service, and they are top-notch for hosting conferences. The location itself is a draw, just minutes from downtown Washington DC and steps from shopping and restaurants. There are 366 guest rooms, and the hotel is pet friendly (for an additional fee).

INFORMATION AND SERVICES

For additional information on Arlington, contact the **Arlington Convention and Visitors Service** (1100 N. Glebe Rd., 800/677-6267, www.stayarlington.com, Mon.-Fri. 8am-5pm).

GETTING THERE AND AROUND

Arlington is just southwest of Washington DC on the other side of the Potomac River. It is a short drive across the Potomac River via the Memorial, Roosevelt, Francis Scott Key, and 14th Street Bridges or a short ride on **Metrorail** (202/637-7000, www.wmata.com).

If you plan to stay in Arlington and tour DC, Metrorail is a great way to get there. Service between Washington DC and Arlington is provided via the Orange, Blue, and Yellow Lines. Key stops in Arlington include Ronald Reagan Washington National Airport (Blue and Yellow), Pentagon City (Blue and Yellow), and Clarendon (Orange).

Regional **Metrobus** (202/637-7000, www.wmata.com) service is available in Arlington and also connects Arlington with DC. A list of the routes serving Arlington can be found at www.arlingtontransit.com. **Arlington Transit (ART)** (703/228-7433, www.arlingtontransit.com, $2) provides supplemental bus service to the regional Metrobus system by covering neighborhoods within Arlington County not served by Metrobus.

Ronald Reagan Washington National Airport (703/417-8000, www.flyreagan.com) is in Arlington and is the primary arrival and departure point for air travel to Washington DC.

Old Town Alexandria and Vicinity

One of the country's oldest port cities, Old Town Alexandria has a long and vibrant history. Founded in 1749, the town sits on the banks of the Potomac River and offers scenic views of Washington DC and National Harbor.

Old Town Alexandria was an important shipping port because it was the last good anchorage on the river before the falls upstream. Homes, taverns, shipyards, and public warehouses quickly sprang up along the waterfront, and many of our country's founding fathers walked its streets, frequented its taverns, and worshiped in its churches. Teams of horses and oxen rolled hogsheads (large wooden barrels) of tobacco, the primary export at the time, down the streets of Old Town to the waterfront. Soon hemp and wheat joined it in the export trade to England.

The town is well preserved through

meticulous restoration efforts and looks much the same as it did when George Washington and Robert E. Lee walked its cobblestone streets. More than 4,000 buildings from the 18th and 19th centuries still stand today, giving the city an authentic colonial feel. Other famous residents have included Jim Morrison and Mama Cass. Stroll along the waterfront on a summer evening and enjoy live music or dine in one of the many unique restaurants. This is an area you can see in one day, but you may choose to return again and again.

SIGHTS
★ Torpedo Factory Art Center
The **Torpedo Factory Art Center** (105 N. Union St., 703/746-4570, www.torpedofactory.org, daily 10am-6pm and Thurs. until 9pm, free) contains three floors of galleries and studios where visitors can see artists at work and

purchase original artwork. The center has 82 studios, seven galleries, an art school, and a museum that provides a unique window into Alexandria's history called the **Alexandria Archaeology Museum** (3rd fl., 703/746-4399, www.alexandriava.gov, Tues.-Fri. 10am-3pm, Sat. 10am-5pm, Sun. 1pm-5pm, free). The art center is on the Old Town waterfront, in a former factory that actually produced torpedoes (U.S. Naval Torpedo Station) after World War I. A torpedo that was made in the factory is displayed in the main hall of the building. Today, more than 165 visual artists practice their trade here and encourage visitors to observe them at work. Two workshops are also located inside the Torpedo Factory.

Carlyle House

The beautiful **Carlyle House Historic Park** (121 N. Fairfax St., 703/549-2997, www.novaparks.com, Tues.-Sat. 10am-4pm, Sun. noon-4pm, adults $5, children 6-12 $3, children under 6 free) is the historic home of British merchant John Carlyle. It was built in 1753 and quickly became the focal point of the political and social circles in Alexandria. One of the first private homes built in Old Town, it is the only 18th-century Palladian home built of stone. Tours of the

house provide a good window into life in Alexandria prior to the Revolutionary War. Many special events are held at the house throughout the year.

Gadsby's Tavern Museum

The **Gadsby's Tavern Museum** (134 N. Royal St., 703/746-4242, www.alexandriava. gov, Nov.-Mar. Wed.-Sat. 11am-4pm, Sun. 1pm-4pm, Apr.-Oct. Tues.-Sat. 10am-5pm, Sun.-Mon. 1pm-5pm, adults $5, children 5-12 $3, children under 5 free) includes two 18th-century brick buildings named after John Gadsby: a tavern (circa 1785) and a hotel (built in 1792). Just after the development of Alexandria in the late 1700s, the Gadsby buildings became the center of life and business in Alexandria. Prominent people who visited the establishment included George Washington, Thomas Jefferson, John Adams, James Madison, James Monroe, and the Marquis de Lafayette. The tavern and hotel were restored as a museum that now serves to educate visitors on the history, architecture, and social customs of the colonial period. The short, informative tours are truly fascinating and really give visitors a sense of the history of the period and the people who walked the tavern's halls.

Old Town Alexandria

Old Town Alexandria

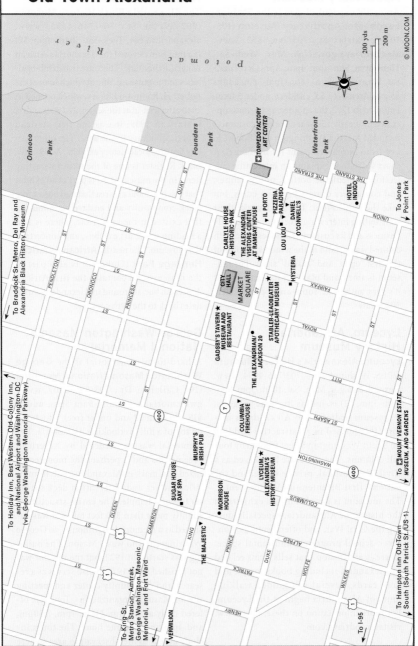

Potomac River

Orinoco Park

Founders Park

Waterfront Park

200 yds
200 m

© MOON.COM

TORPEDO FACTORY ART CENTER

CARLYLE HOUSE HISTORIC PARK ★

THE ALEXANDRIA VISITORS CENTER AT RAMSAY HOUSE

IL PORTO ▸

PIZZERIA PARADISO ▸

LOU LOU ▸

DANIEL O'CONNELL'S

HOTEL INDIGO ●

To Jones Point Park ▸

HYSTERIA ■

STABLER-LEADBEATER APOTHECARY MUSEUM ■

CITY HALL

MARKET SQUARE ★

GADSBY'S TAVERN MUSEUM AND RESTAURANT ★

THE ALEXANDRIAN/ ● JACKSON 20

COLUMBIA FIREHOUSE ▸

MURPHY'S ▸ IRISH PUB

SUGAR HOUSE ■ DAY SPA

MORRISON ● HOUSE

LYCEUM, ALEXANDRIA'S ★ HISTORY MUSEUM

THE MAJESTIC ▸

VERMILION ▸

QUAY ST

PENDLETON ST

ORONOCO ST

PRINCESS ST

QUEEN ST

CAMERON ST

KING ST

PRINCE ST

DUKE ST

WOLFE ST

WILKES ST

PATRICK ST

HENRY ST

ALFRED ST

COLUMBUS ST

WASHINGTON ST

ST ASAPH ST

PITT ST

ROYAL ST

FAIRFAX ST

LEE ST

UNION ST

THE STRAND

400

7

400

1

1

1

1

To Braddock St. Metro, Del Ray and Alexandria Black History Museum ▸

To Holiday Inn, Best Western Old Colony Inn, and National Airport and Washington DC (via George Washington Memorial Parkway) ▴

To King St. Metro Station, Amtrak, George Washington Masonic Memorial, and Fort Ward ▾

To I-95 ▾

To Hampton Inn Old-Town South (South Patrick St./US 1) ▸

To MOUNT VERNON ESTATE, MUSEUM, AND GARDENS ▸

Stabler-Leadbeater Apothecary Museum

An easily overlooked gem is the **Stabler-Leadbeater Apothecary Museum** (105-107 S. Fairfax St., 703/746-3852, www.alexandriava.gov, Nov.-Mar. Wed.-Sat. 11am-4pm, Sun. 1pm-4pm, Apr.-Oct. Tues.-Sat. 10am-5pm, Sun.-Mon. 1pm-5pm, adults $5, children 5-12 $3, children under 5 free). Founded in 1792, the apothecary business operated for nearly 150 years; famous customers included Martha Washington and Robert E. Lee (who purchased paint for his home). A short video tour explains an interesting collection of medicine bottles, pill machines, and containers of native-grown cures, but take the guided tour. The guides take their time telling interesting stories of this family business and its customers. Globes filled with colored water stand in the window as some of the first "open" and "closed" signs. The museum is small and plain on the outside, but it's very authentic. Tours are approximately 30 minutes.

Lyceum, Alexandria's History Museum

Lyceum, Alexandria's History Museum (201 S. Washington St., 703/746-4994, www.alexandriava.gov, Mon.-Sat. 10am-5pm, Sun. 1pm-5pm, $2) is, just as its name suggests, a museum dedicated to Alexandria's history. It is housed in an attractive building on South Washington Street fronted by four tall columns. The structure has served as a Civil War hospital, private home, and the nation's first Bicentennial Visitor Center. The museum is simple but has exhibits on the history of Alexandria, especially during the Civil War, and offers lectures, concerts, school programs, and rental space. There is a gift shop that sells items related to Alexandria including books, maps, and note cards. Several self-guided walking tours of Alexandria begin at the Lyceum. For more information on these, visit www.visitalexandriava.com.

Alexandria Black History Museum

The **Alexandria Black History Museum** (902 Wythe St., 703/746-4356, www.alexandriava.gov, Tues.-Sat. 10am-4pm, $2) is a museum devoted to Alexandria's African American heritage. There are two exhibit galleries in the museum, one of which houses the Robert H. Robinson Library, which opened in 1940 after a sit-in at the segregated Alexandria Library in 1939; it was the first African American library in the area. The other gallery features local history exhibits. A 1797 Free Black Register is one of the most interesting items in the museum and is part of an exhibit that teaches about an area that had both a free black community and enslaved community that existed at the same time. There is also a reading room, art exhibits, and concerts at the museum. The nearby **African American Heritage Park** (Duke St.) is also part of the museum and contains the first African American burial ground in Alexandria, which dates back to the 19th century.

George Washington Masonic National Memorial

A hard-to-miss memorial is the **George Washington Masonic National Memorial** (101 Callahan Dr., 703/683-2007, www.gwmemorial.org, daily 9am-5pm, adults $18, children 12 and under free), which sits on top of a hill overlooking Alexandria. The memorial was constructed by American Freemasons and is perhaps the most recognized landmark in Alexandria, with its multifloor tower and observation deck sitting on top of a temple. The entire structure is slightly more than 330 feet tall and was designed as a memorial "lighthouse" to George Washington, who was a Mason. The building was started in 1922, but the interior was not finished until 1970. It also serves as a research and community center and meeting site for Masonic organizations. Tours are offered daily at 9:30am, 11am, 1pm, 2:30pm, and 4pm and last one hour. The tours include access to the observation area (where there is a panoramic view of Alexandria), so a tour is recommended. The museum is a bit dark inside but displays some of George Washington's personal belongings. The memorial is approximately four blocks from the King Street Metrorail station.

Fort Ward Park and Museum

A great place to relax on a nice day and learn a little history is the **Fort Ward Park and Museum** (4301 W. Braddock Rd., 703/746-4848, www.alexandriava.gov, museum Tues.-Sat. 10am-5pm, Sun. noon-5pm, park daily 9am-sunset, free). This fort was constructed during the Civil War by Union troops to protect Washington DC from Confederate forces. It is the best-preserved fort of the system of Union forts and batteries built for that purpose. Since approximately 90 percent of the fort's original walls are intact and much of the fort was restored to its original form, it is easy to see the design. There is a small museum with Civil War collectibles and exhibits and a nice open park with picnic spots and walking paths.

Tours

There are many guided tours available in Old Town. Some of the most popular tours are walking nighttime ghost tours, such as those hosted by **Footsteps to the Past** (703/683-3451, www.visitalexandriava.com, Mar.-Nov, $15) and **Alexandria Colonial Tours** (703/519-1749, www.alexcolonialtours.com, $10-15), where tour guides dressed in period costumes tell chilling historical stories and legends. There are also guided and self-guided bike tours from **Bike and Roll DC** (202/842-2453, www.bikeandrolldc.com, starting at $34) and seasonal sightseeing cruises with **The Potomac Riverboat Company** (703/684-0580, www.potomacriverboatco.com, starting at $20). Foodies will embrace the three-hour food-focused walking tours offered by **DC Metro Food Tours** (202/851-2268, www.dcmetrofoodtours.com, $65).

RECREATION
TopGolf

If you're looking for something different to do, try **TopGolf Alexandria** (6625 S. Van Dorn St., 703/924-2600, www.topgolf.com, starting at $25). TopGolf is a golf entertainment complex where guests can play different point-scoring golf games using personalized microchipped golf balls. The games are similar to bowling and darts but use golf balls and clubs. No golf experience is necessary.

Parks
CAMERON RUN REGIONAL PARK

Cameron Run Regional Park (4001 Eisenhower Ave., 703/960-0767, www.novaparks.com, fees vary per activity) may be showing its age, but it's still a fun place to take the kids for a day of water fun (wave pool and waterslides), minigolf, and batting cages.

FORT HUNT PARK

Located near the Potomac River, **Fort Hunt Park** (8999 Fort Hunt Park, 202/439-7325, www.nps.gov/gwmp) once belonged to George Washington's estate (Mount Vernon), and batteries in the park defended the river during the Spanish-American War. Today, the park is a favorite for family and corporate picnics, offering lovely open fields and hardwood trees. There is a paved loop that is friendly to cyclists, walkers, and runners, and a pavilion hosts summer concerts.

HUNTLEY MEADOWS PARK

Wildlife-watching is possible in the middle of suburban Northern Virginia at **Huntley Meadows Park** (3701 Lockheed Blvd., 703/768-2525, www.fairfaxcounty.gov, free). This 1,425-acre park offers great wetland wildlife-viewing from its half-mile boardwalk trail and observation tower. The park is a noted birding area, with more than 200 species, and also supports beavers, frogs, and dragonflies. A visitors center has exhibits, and there are two miles of hiking trails.

RIVER FARM

The headquarters of the American Horticultural Society (AHS) is at **River Farm** (7931 E. Boulevard Dr., 703/768-5700, www.ahsgardening.org, free). River Farm was one of George Washington's five farms. The 25-acre site is beautifully landscaped and includes a circa 1757 home that now houses the AHS. The largest specimen of an Osage orange tree in the country is at River Farm; it is said to have been a gift to the Washington family from Thomas Jefferson (Jefferson received Osage orange seedlings from the Lewis and Clark expedition of 1804-1806). There is no charge for admission to the farm and the house, but donations are appreciated.

Boating

You can launch a boat or kayak from **Belle Haven Marina** (1201 Belle Haven Rd., 703/768-0018, www.saildc.com) or learn to sail at their sailing school. Located on the Potomac River, their sailing school was founded in 1975, and they run the largest full-time sailing program on the Potomac. Boats are available for rent.

Biking

Old Town Alexandria is a very bike-friendly area. There are many bike-friendly businesses that encourage employees and guests to ride bikes to their facilities. The 18-mile **Mount Vernon Trail** runs between Theodore Roosevelt Island (an 88-acre island and national park that sits in the Potomac River near the Roosevelt Bridge) and George Washington's Mount Vernon. The trail passes right through Old Town Alexandria but can be a little tricky since it runs along the street. For a map of the trail, visit www.bikewashington.org. Bikes can be rented from **Big Wheel Bikes** (2 Prince St., 703/739-2300, www.bigwheelbikes.com, $7 per hour or $35 per day).

Golf

The **Greendale Golf Course** (6700 Telegraph Rd., 703/971-6170, www.fairfaxcounty.gov, open year-round, $31-40) is an 18-hole regulation golf course covering 148 acres. The terrain is rolling with asphalt cart paths. The course was designed to be challenging with water hazards and tight fairways. The facility includes a putting green, clubhouse with food service, club rentals, cart rentals, and golfing supplies. Golf lessons are also available.

The nine-hole, par-35 **Pinecrest Golf Course** (6600 Little River Tpke., 703/941-1061, www.fairfaxcounty.gov, open year-round, $20-23) is a challenging executive golf course. The course is narrow and includes hills and ponds. It is geared toward both novice golfers and serious players.

Day Spas

Old Town has many salons and day spas. If you are looking for a massage or any number of professional spa services, visit the **Sugar House Day Spa & Salon** (111 N. Alfred St., 703/549-9940, www.sugarhousedayspa.com). They are in a cute row house on North Alfred Street and offer a warm, professional atmosphere with high-quality (female only) massage therapists. Another good option is **Fountains Day Spa** (422 S. Washington St., 703/549-1990, www.fountainsdayspa.com), in a yellow house on Washington Street and offering high-quality massages and a large variety of other spa services. For waxing and other specialty salon services, **Aida Spa** (1309 King St., 2nd Fl., 703/535-7875, www.aidaspaoldtown.com) is the place to go. The owner specializes in skin care, face-and-body treatments, and makeup.

ENTERTAINMENT AND EVENTS
Music and Theater

The Birchmere (3701 Mount Vernon Ave., 703/549-7500, www.birchmere.com, $20-115) is a legendary concert hall seating approximately 500 people that hosts nationally known bands in many genres including folk, jazz, bluegrass, country, and rock. There is table seating at the main stage with food service.

The bandstand includes a dance area. The theater offers a casual, intimate atmosphere with decent food. Parking is a little tricky, so consult the website for directions.

Other good choices for an evening of live music are **Basin Street Lounge** (219 King St., 703/549-1141, www.219restaurant.com), a sophisticated and intimate establishment above the 219 Restaurant that hosts live jazz and blues nightly, and **Murphy's A Grand Irish Pub** (713 King St., 703/548-1717, www.murphyspub.com). Murphy's serves traditional Irish food, has a good selection of beers on tap, and has live music most nights. It has a lively pub atmosphere and friendly patrons and servers.

The Little Theatre of Alexandria (600 Wolfe St., 703/683-0496, www.thelittletheatre.com) was founded in 1934 and is one of just a handful of community theaters in the United States with its own building. Many famous people have sat in its audience including President Harry S. Truman, Lady Bird Johnson, and President George W. Bush. The theater hosts a seven-show season.

Festivals and Events

Old Town hosts numerous festivals and events throughout the year. Following are just some of the fun experiences visitors can participate in. Visit www.visitalexandriava.com for a full list of events.

The **Alexandria Film Festival** (www.alexfilmfest.com) is an annual tradition in November that celebrates the work of both established and emerging filmmakers from around the world. Dozens of films, including independents, shorts, documentaries, animation, and features, are shown in multiple locations around Alexandria.

Those fortunate enough to be in Old Town Alexandria during **Alexandria Restaurant Week** (www.visitalexandriava.com) are in for a treat. For 10 days in August, more than 70 area restaurants offer special menus at discounted prices. It's a great time for visitors to sample the variety of cuisine available in Old Town and for residents to try new establishments.

The **Alexandria King Street Art Festival** (www.artfestival.com) is an annual street festival that takes place on King Street in September. Voted one of the top 100 art festivals in the United States by *Sunshine Artist Magazine,* the juried festival features pieces from artists selected for the quality and originality of their work. Paintings, sculpture, jewelry, photography, and ceramics are just some of the types of art visitors can expect to see. The show stretches down several blocks of King Street to the waterfront.

SHOPPING

Old Town Alexandria is a shopaholic's dream. Block after block of award-winning boutiques, national-brand stores, and specialty shops can exhaust even the most fit shopper. Whether you're looking for clothes, souvenirs, antiques, artwork, or something unusual and funky, you can participate in a tradition of buying and sharing bounty that started back in colonial times. The primary shopping area stretches 11 blocks from the Potomac River up King Street.

Imagine Artwear (1124 King St., 703/548-1461, www.imagineartwear.com) has been a fixture in the community since 1988. They sell contemporary crafts, clothing, jewelry, and other accessories created by American artists. This store is a local favorite, as is **Lou Lou** (132 King St., 703/299-9505, www.loulouboutiques.com). Lou Lou sells jewelry and accessories at reasonable prices. They offer a wide variety of colors and designs.

For the little ones and moms to be, **529 Kids Consign** (122 S. Royal St., 703/567-4518, www.529kidsconsign.com) is a consignment boutique that specializes in high quality kids and maternity wear for "hip moms and cool kids."

To search for a particular type of store, visit www.visitalexandriava.com.

Bring Fido

Old Town Alexandria is extremely dog friendly. Specialty shops cater specifically to our canine friends, and many others put out water bowls and treats in front of their doorways.

HOTELS

Many hotels in Old Town allow dogs in their rooms. The Kimpton hotels, in particular, have a history of being pet friendly and include added amenities for dogs such as honor bars stocked with pet treats, pet bedding, and pet bowls. Some dog-friendly hotels include:

- **Morrison House—A Kimpton Hotel** (116 S. Alfred St., 703/838-8000, www.morrisonhouse.com)

- **Hotel Indigo** (220 S. Union St., 703/721-3800, www.hotelindigooldtownalexandria.com)

- **Residence Inn by Marriott Alexandria Old Town South at Carlyle** (2345 Mill Rd., 703/549-1155, www.marriott.com)

- **Westin Alexandria** (400 Courthouse Sq., 703/253-8600, www.westinalexandria.com)

- **The Alexandrian Old Town Alexandria** (480 King St., 703/549-6080, www.marriott.com)

- **Holiday Inn & Suites Alexandria-Historic District** (625 1st St., 703/548-6300, www.ihg.com)

- **Lorien Hotel & Spa—A Kimpton Hotel** (1600 King St., 703/894-3434, www.lorienhotelandspa.com)

- **Sheraton Suites Alexandria** (801 N. Saint Asaph St., 703/836-4700, www.sheratonsuitesalexandria.com)

DINING

Dog-friendly dining is also fairly common in Old Town Alexandria. By law, pets are not permitted inside restaurants, but many dining spots have seasonal seating outdoors where well-behaved dogs are permitted to join their owners. Following are examples of dog-friendly restaurants, but others can be found by looking for outdoor cafés where other dogs are sitting or establishments that have water bowls outside their doors. If you are uncertain, be sure to ask the host or hostess about the restaurant's policy.

FOOD

American

★ **The Majestic** (911 King St., 703/837-9117, www.themajesticva.com, Mon.-Thurs. 11:30am-midnight, Fri. 11:30am-1am, Sat. 10am-1am, Sun. 10am-midnight, $16-30) is a small gem of a restaurant right in the heart of Old Town. It serves American comfort food and has a history dating back to 1932. The decor is modern and inviting and makes for a fun place to gather with friends, family, or business associates. Step off the street right into the bar and grab a drink while you wait for a table. It is obvious that great care goes into designing each menu item, so don't hesitate to ask your server for more details. Seafood is a specialty here, but you may find it prepared with a new twist such as with an unusual spice or paired with a nontraditional side. The seared scallops are a personal favorite, or the Majestic Burger with its delightful bacon jam. No matter what you choose save room for dessert. If you're lucky to see their coconut cake on the menu, be sure to order it. It is fresh, moist, and just plain out of this world.

- Doggie Happy Hour is a regular event at **Jackson 20** (480 King St., adjacent to the Alexandrian Hotel, 703/549-6080). It is held seasonally on Tuesdays (5pm-8pm) and is a popular Old Town tradition.

- **Vola's Dockside Grill** (101 N. Unions St., 703/935-8890) is known for their dog-friendly atmosphere and has a menu just for furry patrons with three selections that actually sound pretty good (including a 5 oz. sirloin).

- Other restaurants that allow furry friends on their outdoor patios include **Haute Dogs and Fries** (610 Montgomery St., 703/548-3891) and **The Dairy Godmother** (2310 Mount Vernon Ave., 703/683-7767), where they offer puppy pops.

PET-SUPPLY STORES

There are several specialty pet-supply stores in Old Town Alexandria and the vicinity where you can purchase gourmet treats, toys, food, and other supplies:

- **The Dog Park** (705 King St., 703/888-2818, www.thedogparkva.biz)

- **The Olde Towne School for Dogs** (529 Oronoco St., 703/836-7643, www.otsfd.com)

- **Nature's Nibbles** (2601 Mount Vernon Ave., 703/931-5241, www.naturesnibbles.com)

OLD TOWN ATTRACTIONS

Several Old Town Alexandria attractions allow dogs to accompany their owners:

- **Potomac Riverboat Company** (105 N. Unions St., 703/684-0580, www.potomacriverboatco.com) offers 45-minute canine harbor cruises on Saturdays from June to mid-September. Tickets are $24.99 for adults and $15.75 for children 2-11. Children under 2 and dogs ride free.

- The **Torpedo Factory Art Center** (105 N. Union St., 703/746-4570, www.torpedofactory.org) allows well-behaved dogs on leashes.

- **Footsteps to the Past** (724/272-8433, www.visitalexandriava.com) offers dog-friendly guided walking tours of Alexandria.

- The **Alexandria Visitors Center at Ramsay House** (221 King St., 703/746-3301) allows dogs to visit with their owners.

Virtue Feed & Grain (106 S. Union St., 571/970-3669, www.virtuefeedgrain.com, Mon.-Sat. 11:30am-1am, Sun. 10am-1am, $9-32) is housed in a historic brick building on South Union Street that was used as a feed house on the waterfront in the 1800s. They serve a casual menu of burgers, tacos, and entrees such as salmon, shrimp and grits, and steak. The interior is a symphony in reclaimed materials such as wood, brick, and the original concrete floors, with large newly added windows. The two-level space is lively and includes a unique porch with wraparound windows on the second level for private parties. Save room for dessert—they have a scrumptious peanut butter pie.

Gadsby's Tavern (138 N. Royal St., 703/548-1288, www.gadsbystavernrestaurant.com, brunch Sun. 11am-3pm, lunch Mon.-Sat. 11:30am-3pm, dinner daily 5:30pm-10pm, $22-30) offers a rare historical dining experience and one that's unique to Old Town Alexandria. Situated next door to Gadsby's Museum, the tavern has served patrons since the late 1700s. Dine in a space once frequented by George Washington, Thomas

Jefferson, John Adams, James Madison, and James Monroe. The attentive staff is dressed in period attire, and the cozy, candlelit decor depicts the colonial period, but this is not a theater. Great attention is given to both the menu and the dining experience. There is a nice selection of steaks, chops, and seafood, including George Washington's Favorite, which is grilled breast of duck with scalloped potatoes, corn pudding, *rhotekraut* (red cabbage), and a port wine orange glaze.

Another one-of-a-kind dining experience can be had at the **Columbia Firehouse** (109 S. Saint Asaph St., 703/683-1776, www.columbiafirehouse.com, brunch Sat.-Sun. 11am-3pm, lunch Tues.-Fri. 11:30am-3pm, dinner Mon. 5:30pm-9pm, Tues.-Thurs. 5:30pm-10pm, Fri.-Sat. 5:30pm-11pm, Sun. 4:30pm-9pm, $15-39). The restaurant was once a firehouse (built in 1883) and is now a historical, well-preserved eatery in the heart of Old Town. This modern American brasserie and bar still shows its firehouse roots with original exposed brickwork. There is a varied menu of pub food and more-intricate dishes that includes a raw bar, salads, sandwiches, steak, and daily specials. If you're a fan of mussels, the Firehouse serves them three delicious ways. Perfect for foodies, families, and friends, this is an upbeat establishment with a comfortable feel.

It would be difficult to suggest restaurants in Old Town without including **Vermilion Restaurant** (1120 King St., 703/684-9669, www.vermilionrestaurant.com, brunch Sat.-Sun. 10:30am-2:30pm, lunch Mon. and Wed.-Fri. 11:30am-3pm, dinner Mon.-Thurs. 5:30pm-10pm, Fri.-Sat. 5:30pm-11pm, Sun. 5pm-9pm, $19-32). They serve contemporary American food at its finest for lunch and dinner, with entrées such as wild halibut, crusted lamb, and ricotta gnocchi. The menu is small but done well. They also offer a four-course tasting menu for $72. The restaurant is committed to locally grown goods.

French

BRABO Brasserie (1600 King St., 703/894-3440, www.braborestaurant.com, brunch Sunday 11am-2:30pm, dinner Mon.-Thurs. 5pm-10pm, Fri.-Sat. 5pm-11pm, Sun. 5pm-9pm, $23-44), adjacent to the Lorien Hotel & Spa, initially attracts guests with its warm but elegant atmosphere, but keeps them coming back for the exquisite cuisine. Pan-seared sea bass, lamb shank, and Shrimp Boudin Blanc are just some of the entrées created by the award-winning chef. The service is

Virtue Feed & Grain

impeccable, and there's even a communal table for those wishing to mingle. There's also a tasting room and market.

★ **Le Refuge Restaurant** (127 N. Washington St., 703/548-4661, www. lerefugealexandria.com, lunch Mon.-Sat. 11:30am-2:30pm, dinner Mon.-Sat. 5:30pm-10pm, $25-40) is one of the best-kept secrets in Alexandria. This small, family-owned French country bistro feels more like Paris than Virginia. The menu includes favorites such as beef Wellington, bouillabaisse, and rack of lamb as well as daily specials. The setting is cozy and even a bit snug, but the food and service are excellent. They also offer a three-course prix fixe lunch for $22 and a three-course prix fixe dinner for $35.

Irish

What could be more Irish than a restaurant called **Daniel O'Connell's** (112 King St., 703/739-1124, www.danieloconnells.com, daily 11am-1am, $10-17)? This lively spot on King Street serves up traditional Irish fare with a few interesting modifications. Try an Irish Egg Roll or the Dublin Nachos to start your meal. Follow with some classic fish-and-chips, a Guinness burger, or corned beef and cabbage. The menu changes regularly, which is refreshing for an Irish pub, and everything is served with a wide Irish smile. The old brick building gives the restaurant an authentic Old Town feel, and after one too many Guinness stouts, it can be difficult to find your way through the maze of rooms and staircases to the restroom. If you're lucky enough to score a rooftop patio seat overlooking King Street on a nice evening, plan to stay for a while—you won't want to give up your table.

Another fun Irish pub is **Murphy's Irish Pub** (713 King St., 703/548-1717, www. murphyspub.com, Mon.-Sat. 11am-2am, Sun. 10am-2am, $10-15). They offer warm pub fare and entertainment nightly.

Italian

Made-from-scratch Italian cooking can be found at **Il Porto Italian Ristorante** (121 King St., 703/836-8833, www. ilportoristorante.com, Mon.-Thurs. 11am-10pm, Fri.-Sat. 11am-11pm, Sun. 11am-10pm, $19-30). This Old Town classic opened in 1973 and has a steady following. Traditional pasta dishes are flavorful and filling, as are other Italian staples such as chicken parmigiana and fresh seafood selections.

If you're in the mood for pizza, try **Pizzeria Paradiso** (124 King St., 703/837-1245, www.eatyourpizza.com, Mon.-Thurs. 11:30am-10pm, Fri.-Sat. 11:30am-11pm, Sun. noon-10pm, $12-21), the King Street outlet of a small local chain. The pizza is some of the best in the area and is made with fresh ingredients. The beer list is impressive, and the staff is very friendly and attentive. There is a long list of available toppings, including some less traditional options such as roast lamb, potatoes, hot cherry peppers, and capers.

Treats

One cupcake bakery that does a particularly good job is **Lavender Moon Cupcakery** (116 S. Royal St., 703/683-0588, Sun.-Thurs. 11am-8pm, Fri.-Sat. 11am-9pm, under $10). The selections vary daily, but some sample flavors include s'mores, flourless chocolate, lemon, passion fruit, and blood orange Dreamsicle.

Farmers Markets

There are several farmers markets in Old Town Alexandria and the vicinity. Some are seasonal and some are held year-round. The **Old Town Farmers' Market** (301 King St., Sat. 7am-noon, year-round) is the oldest farmers market in the nation held continuously at the same location. George Washington sent produce grown at Mount Vernon to this market. Other farmers markets include: **Del Ray Farmers Market** (corner of East Oxford Ave. and Mount Vernon Ave., Sat. 8am-noon, year-round); **Four Mile Run Farmers & Artisans Market** (4109 Mount Vernon Ave., Apr.-Oct. Sun. 9am-1pm,); and **West End Farmers Market** (Ben Brenman Park, 4800 Brenman Park Dr., May-Oct. Sun. 8:30am-1pm).

Sidetrip: A Taste for Del Ray

Just northwest of Old Town Alexandria, along Mount Vernon Avenue, is Del Ray, a hip little neighborhood full of coffee shops, art galleries, specialty food stores, and cafés. This trendy little pocket of Northern Virginia has a population of mostly young families, working couples, and singles who can be seen walking the streets with their dogs or strollers or working on their laptops behind café windows.

This pleasant neighborhood didn't always have a laid-back vibe; in fact, not long ago (during the early aughts), it was a place you may have only heard about on the nightly news. In recent years, Del Ray has blossomed into a friendly, funky place to live where eateries now dominate the main thoroughfare and real estate prices have skyrocketed. Also a great place to visit, Del Ray has many good options to satisfy the palate.

One of the most well-known eateries in Del Ray is **The Evening Star Café** (2000 Mount Vernon Ave., 703/549-5051, www.eveningstarcafe.net, brunch Sat.-Sun. 10am-2:30pm, dinner daily from 5:30pm, $14-26). They offer a modern twist on classic Southern cooking. Try their chicken and succotash, flat iron streak, or chicken-fried oysters.

Just off Mount Vernon Avenue, **Del Ray Café** (205 E. Howell Ave., 703/717-9151, www.delraycafe.com, Sun.-Thurs. 8am-2:30pm and 5pm-9pm, Fri.-Sat 8am-2:30pm and 5pm-10pm, $21-32) is a farm-to-table French-American café serving breakfast, lunch, and dinner in a cute house with a red-roofed porch. This is an especially good choice for breakfast—try the crab eggs Benedict or one of the organic omelets.

If you're craving food from south of the border, **Los Tios Grill** (2615 Mount Vernon Ave., 703/299-9290, www.lostiosgrill.com, Sun.-Thurs. 11am-10pm, Fri.-Sat.11am-11pm, $7-25), a Tex-Mex and Salvadoran restaurant, and **Taqueria Poblano** (2400-B Mount Vernon Ave., 703/548-8226, www.taqueriapoblano.com, Mon. and Wed.-Fri. 11am-3pm and 5pm-10pm, Sat. 11am-10pm, Sun. 10am-9pm, $4-18), a Mexican restaurant, are both known for their good food and margaritas.

For a good Philly cheesesteak, try **Al's Steakhouse** (1504 Mount Vernon Ave., 703/836-9443, www.alssteak.com, Mon.-Wed. 10am-8pm, Thurs.-Sat. 7am-8pm, Sun. 7am-4pm, $6-20). The plain brick exterior is easy to miss, but locals know this is the best place for a Philly fix.

Cheese lovers won't want to miss **Cheesetique** (2411 Mount Vernon Ave., 703/706-5300, www.cheesetique.com, Mon.-Fri. 11am-10pm, Sat.-Sun. 10am-10pm, $6-11), an artisan cheese shop with a wine and cheese bar. Sample cheese, take home cheese, or order from a menu of cheese-influenced selections.

For dessert try the **Dairy Godmother** (2310 Mount Vernon Ave., 703/683-7767, www.thedairygodmother.com, Sun.-Mon. noon-9pm, Wed.-Sat. noon-10pm, under $10). This funky frozen-custard shop was made famous when the Obama family stopped in for dessert back in 2009.

ACCOMMODATIONS

As with most of Northern Virginia, accommodations in Old Town Alexandria consist mostly of chain hotels. However, there are a few good boutique hotels that offer unique lodgings right in Old Town.

$100-200

Reasonably priced accommodations near Old Town Alexandria can be found at the **Holiday Inn Express & Suites Alexandria-Fort Belvoir** (6055 Richmond Hwy., 571/257-9555, www.alexandriafortbelvoirhotel.com,

$113-128). This hotel offers 144 spacious rooms and friendly service. Rooms have large flat-screen televisions and comfortable beds. There is a small indoor pool and fitness center. Breakfast is included, as is high-speed Internet, and there is free shuttle service to the Huntington Metrorail station as well as free on-site parking.

If you don't have a car and you want to be convenient to the Metrorail and have easy access to shops and restaurants, try the **Hampton Inn Alexandria-Old Town/King Street Metro** (1616 King St., 703/299-9900,

www.hamptoninn3.hilton.com, $123-189).
This 80-room hotel one block from the King
Street Metrorail station offers comfortable
rooms, free Internet, complimentary breakfast, a fitness center, and an outdoor pool. The
local trolley stops right outside the door, so
guests can easily go shopping and dine at local
restaurants. Parking is available for a fee, but
it is not the most convenient.

$200-300

The Alexandrian (480 King St., 703/549-
6080, www.thealexandrian.com, $155-366)
is part of Marriott's Autograph Collection.
This stunning red brick hotel has a fantastic location on King Street. It offers 241 guest
rooms and luxury suites. Rooms are spacious,
and the staff is gracious and accommodating. There is a 24-hour fitness center and indoor heated pool. The hotel is dog friendly,
and they host doggie happy hours during the
summer. Self-parking ($32) and valet park-
ing ($38) are both available for a nightly fee.

The modern ★ **Hotel Indigo** (220
S. Union St., 703/721-3800, www.hotel
indigooldtownalexandria.com, $122-354) is
a delightful, InterContinental Hotels Group
boutique hotel with a water view. During
construction of the hotel, opened in 2017, a
50-foot ship from the 18th century was discovered during excavation. The hotel is conveniently located near King Street and the water
taxi (perfect for those taking in a Nats game).
It features a fitness center, outdoor patio, and
is pet friendly. The rooms are simple but well
appointed and feature Aveda products. The
staff is terrific. Opt for an eastern-facing (waterfront) room toward the south side of the
building. Self-parking is available across the
street for $25 and valet for $34. There is an on-
site restaurant overlooking the river.

The **Morrison House** (116 S. Alfred
St., 703/838-8000, www.morrisonhouse.
com, $203-334) is another lovely hotel in
Marriott's Autograph Collection in Old
Town Alexandria. This hotel is decorated
with federal-style reproduction furnishings
such as four-poster beds and is housed in a

stately brick building near King Street. The
hotel underwent a multimillion-dollar facelift
in 2016. The 45 guest rooms and three suites
are comfortable, and the common areas have
a nice open feel. The staff is very friendly and
accommodating, and guests are made to feel
welcome. The hotel is pet friendly, and valet
parking is available for $38 per night.

The **Residence Inn Alexandria Old
Town** (1456 Duke St., 703/548-5474, www.
marriott.com, $136-440) delivers consistently
high-quality service and 240 comfortable
guest suites. The hotel is geared toward extended stays: All suites offer a full kitchen and
separate living and dining areas. It is approximately two blocks to the King Street Metrorail
station and within walking distance of many
Old Town attractions. Shuttle service is available to the Metro and waterfront. A plentiful
breakfast is included, and there is an indoor
pool and fitness center. Two-bedroom suites
are available, and parking is available for a
fee. Last-minute weekend deals are sometimes available on the website. The hotel is
pet friendly.

A Kimpton hotel, the **Lorien Hotel &
Spa** (1600 King St., 703/894-3434, www.
lorienhotelandspa.com, $170-305) is less than
two blocks from the Metrorail. This modern,
well-appointed boutique hotel offers a friendly
atmosphere and 107 very comfortable guest
rooms. This award-winning establishment offers many extras, such as a welcome glass of
wine, and first-class service. As the name implies, there's a full-service spa on-site (the only
hotel spa in Old Town). Book a corner room if
you like a lot of windows. This is a quiet hotel
within walking distance of the waterfront. It
is also pet friendly.

INFORMATION AND SERVICES

A good place to begin your explora-
tion of Old Town Alexandria is at **The
Alexandria Visitors Center at Ramsay
House** (221 King St., 703/746-3301, www.
visitalexandriava.com, Sun.-Wed. 10am-6pm,
Thurs.-Sat. 10am-8pm). They offer maps and

brochures and sell tickets to some local attractions and tours. If you plan to visit multiple sights, consider purchasing the **Alexandria Key to the City** museum pass ($15). This visitor pass provides admission to nine historic sites and includes dozens of discounts at area shops, restaurants, and attractions (including 40 percent off admission to Mount Vernon).

GETTING THERE

Old Town Alexandria is approximately seven miles south of Washington DC on the opposite side of the Potomac River. It is accessible by the George Washington Memorial Parkway and I-495 (Beltway).

Old Town is accessible by **Metrorail** (202/637-7000, www.wmata.com). The Yellow and Blue Lines both stop at the **King Street Metro station,** which is on King Street near the George Washington Masonic Memorial.

Amtrak (800/872-7245, www.amtrak.com) has a train station in Alexandria at 110 Callahan Drive.

GETTING AROUND

The Alexandria Transit Company's **DASH** (703/746-3274, www.dashbus.com, $1.75)

bus system provides reliable service in Alexandria and offers service between Metrobus stops, Metrorail, and the Virginia Railway Express. There is service from the King Street Metro stop down King Street to Market Square every 15 minutes or so. The fare is $1.75, and exact change is required. A detailed schedule and route map are available on the website.

The free **King Street Trolley** (www.visitalexandriava.com) is another good way to get around Old Town. This fleet of hybrid trolleys runs every 15 minutes between North Union Street and the King Street Metro station (daily 10am-10:15pm) with 20 stops along Old Town's main shopping and restaurant district.

Round-trip water taxis are also available through **The Potomac Riverboat Company** (211 N. Union St., 703/684-0580, www.potomacriverboatco.com, unlimited daily pass adults $30, children $17) between Old Town Alexandria, the Gaylord National Hotel in National Harbor, Maryland, The Wharf in DC, and directly to Washington Nationals baseball games in DC.

Fairfax County

Fairfax County encompasses 395 square miles and is the largest county in Virginia by population, with more than 1.1 million residents. Nearly a quarter of the jobs in the county are technology related, giving it the largest concentration of technology jobs in the country. It is also a very diverse county, with approximately one-half of the residents speaking a language other than English at home. Fairfax County is a suburban area of Washington DC with a large population of commuters. As the popularity of telecommuting grows, more and more people are able to work from home, but don't let that fool you into thinking the phenomenon has lessened highway congestion during rush hour.

Fairfax County contains half of the DC area's Fortune 500 companies and is also home to many government intelligence agencies, including the Central Intelligence Agency, National Reconnaissance Office, and the National Counterterrorism Center.

Visitors will find a densely populated area with pleasant neighborhoods, parks, and many strip malls. There are countless good restaurants, excellent shopping, and a diversity of outdoor recreation opportunities in Fairfax County. Depending on your focus, Fairfax County can be explored in a day or two and is easily accessible from Washington DC for dining and events.

SIGHTS
Near the Beltway

I-495 is a 64-mile highway that runs around Washington DC and through Virginia and Maryland; it is commonly known as the **Capital Beltway** or just the **Beltway**. It runs through much of the eastern portion of Fairfax County.

OLD TOWN FAIRFAX

Although the city of Fairfax formally includes just a six-square-mile area, many of the surrounding neighborhoods share a Fairfax address and are within Fairfax County. Established in 1742, the city of Fairfax was the site of several Civil War events and then remained mostly a residential community of farms and homes until the 1950s and '60s. At that time it experienced a rapid population growth that leveled off some in the 1970s but has since resumed. **Old Town Fairfax** is a good starting point for exploration, with its quaint shops and restaurants. The **Civil War Interpretive Center at Historic Blenheim** (3610 Old Lee Hwy., 703/591-0560, www.fairfaxva.gov, Tues.-Sat. 10am-3pm, free) is a 12-acre attraction with an interpretive center and several historic buildings, including the Blenheim farmhouse, built in 1859. The house contains the largest and best-preserved Civil War inscription examples in the country, which were left on a wall by more than 100 Union soldiers while they occupied the Fairfax Courthouse in 1862 and 1863. The inscriptions include art and poetry and provide good insight into the lives of the soldiers during the war. The interpretive center features an illustrated timeline of events that took place during the Civil War in Fairfax. There is also a lecture hall and gift shop. Guided tours are offered at 1pm Tuesday through Saturday.

The **Fairfax Station Railroad Museum** (11200 Fairfax Station Rd., Fairfax Station, 703/425-9225, www.fairfax-station.org, Sun. 1pm-4pm, adults $4, children 5-15 $2, children 4 and under free), in nearby Fairfax Station, is a rebuilt train depot and museum that preserves a time in Civil War history when wounded soldiers were transported from the depot to hospitals in Washington DC and Alexandria. It later became a hub for commerce in the county and a center for social activity. The station remained open until 1973. Numerous items were donated to the museum, including a refurbished caboose and a railroad-crossing gate from Norfolk Southern.

The **National Firearms Museum** (11250 Waples Mill Rd., Fairfax, 703/267-1600, www.nramuseum.org, daily 9:30am-5pm, free), a National Rifle Association institution, contains a diverse collection of civilian and military firearms and accessories.

MEADOWLARK BOTANICAL GARDENS

Meadowlark Botanical Gardens (9750 Meadowlark Gardens Ct., Vienna, 703/255-3631, www.novaparks.com, June-Aug. daily 10am-8pm, Apr. and Sept. daily 10am-7pm, Mar. and Oct. daily 10am-6pm, May daily 10am-7:30pm, Nov.-Dec. daily 10am-4:30pm, Jan.-Feb. daily 10am-5pm, adults $6, children 6-17 and seniors 55 and over $3, children under 6 free) is a 95-acre property with large ornamental garden displays and unusual native plant collections. A network of walking trails provides access. There are three gazebos at the gardens that can be reserved for private use. A beautiful glass atrium looks out over the park and can be rented for weddings and receptions. During the holidays, they offer a brilliant light display that can be enjoyed along the walking trails.

Western Fairfax County

Western Fairfax County borders Loudoun County to the west and Prince William County to the south.

★ GREAT FALLS PARK

Great Falls Park (9200 Old Dominion Dr., Great Falls, www.nps.gov/grfa, daily 7am-dark, individual fee for entering on foot, horse, or bicycle $7, children under 15 free, vehicle fee for one vehicle and all passengers

$15) is one of Northern Virginia's prime outdoor destinations. In this 800-acre national park, the Potomac River plunges 77 feet into Mather Gorge over a series of jagged rocks. The falls are impressive to say the least and especially so after heavy rain. Three well-placed and -maintained overlooks provide spectacular views of the falls. There is a visitors center (daily 10am-4pm), plenty of picnic areas, and wooded trails for hiking, mountain biking, and horseback riding. Great Falls Park is also a popular area for rock climbing and whitewater kayaking. Admission pass is good for seven consecutive days.

COLVIN RUN MILL

A leisurely afternoon can be spent at **Colvin Run Mill** (10017 Colvin Run Rd., Great Falls, 703/759-2771, www.fairfaxcounty.gov, Wed.-Mon. 11am-4pm, parking and grounds free, tours adults $8, students 16 and over with ID $7, children and seniors $6). This historic mill and general store harkens back to a time when things were a bit simpler. Take a tour of the restored mill that was built in 1811 and learn about the large waterwheel and how grain was ground. Visit the general store and purchase stone-ground cornmeal, grits, penny candy, and books. This is a lovely park with plenty of picnic space and interesting seasonal activities.

★ NATIONAL AIR AND SPACE MUSEUM STEVEN F. UDVAR-HAZY CENTER

The **National Air and Space Museum Steven F. Udvar-Hazy Center** (14390 Air and Space Museum Pkwy., Chantilly, 703/572-4118, www.airandspace.si.edu, daily 10am-5:30pm, free, $15 parking before 4pm) is owned by the Smithsonian Institution and is the companion museum to the Air and Space Museum on the National Mall. The two sites together are the crown jewel of the Smithsonian and display the largest collection of space and aviation artifacts in the world. The awe-inspiring aviation hangar building allows for the display of aircraft on three

levels. Thousands of artifacts may be viewed on the hangar floor and from elevated skywalks and include helicopters, experimental aircraft, and retired spacecraft and airplanes. The soaring ceilings and open design of the hangar allow visitors to fully appreciate the size and significance of the items. Exhibits include the Lockheed SR-71 Blackbird (the fastest jet in the world), the *Enola Gay,* the de Havilland Chipmunk aerobatic airplane, and the space shuttle *Discovery.* Visitors can also watch planes take off and land at Washington Dulles International Airport from the Donald D. Engen Tower, which provides a 360-degree view of the airport. The Udvar-Hazy Center is less crowded than the Air and Space Museum in DC but can still pack in the people on summer weekends. Other features in the museum include an IMAX theater and gift shop. The only dining option inside the center is a McDonald's and McCafé, so if this doesn't suit your palate, make plans to eat at a local restaurant. All visitors must go through security screening when entering.

SULLY HISTORIC SITE

Also in Chantilly is the **Sully Historic Site** (3650 Historic Sully Way, Chantilly, 703/437-1794, www.fairfaxcounty.gov, Mar.-Dec. Wed.-Mon. 11am-4pm, Jan.-Feb. Wed.-Mon. 11am-3pm, tours for adults $8, students 16 and over with ID $7, children 5-15 and seniors 65 and over $6), which is in the National Register of Historic Places. The main house was built in 1799 by Robert E. Lee's uncle Richard Bland Lee, a politician who served in the Virginia House of Delegates and was the first Northern Virginia representative in the U.S. House of Representatives. The home is a combination of Georgian and federal architecture, and the historic grounds also include original outbuildings. Guided tours are given on the hour and focus on the early life of the Richard Bland Lee family. On-site programs

1: Great Falls Park **2:** National Air and Space Museum Steven F. Udvar-Hazy Center **3:** George Washington's whiskey distillery and gristmill **4:** George Washington's Mount Vernon

reflect Fairfax County history through the 20th century. There is a gift shop.

Southern Fairfax County

★ GEORGE WASHINGTON'S MOUNT VERNON

George Washington's Mount Vernon (3200 Mount Vernon Memorial Hwy., Alexandria, 703/780-2000, www.mountvernon.org, Apr.-Oct. daily 9am-5pm, Nov.-Mar., daily 9am-4pm, adults $20, youth 6-11 $12, children 5 and under free) is one of the premier attractions in Northern Virginia and is the most popular historic estate in the country. Sitting on the banks of the Potomac River eight miles south of Old Town Alexandria, this picturesque manor was George Washington's plantation house.

The land surrounding Mount Vernon became the property of the Washington family in 1674. George Washington built his mansion in stages between 1757 and 1778. Prior to its construction, a smaller house built for Washington's half-brother Lawrence, who died in 1752, occupied the site. George Washington became the sole owner of the estate in 1761 and intended to be primarily a tobacco farmer (although his military career ended up substantially interfering with this plan). The plantation started out with tobacco as the staple crop, but later grew wheat, grain, and corn.

Visiting Mount Vernon: Once you purchase your ticket to Mount Vernon, you enter through the orientation center, where a bronze statue of George, Martha, and two of George's step-grandchildren immediately greets you. Be sure to pick up a brochure and map of the estate and then watch the orientation movie in one of the two adjacent theaters. From the orientation center, you will take a walkway that continues to the idyllic Bowling Green, the expansive lawn that surrounds the mansion and outbuildings. Plan on a minimum of three hours for your visit.

The home is constructed of wood and underwent several renovations during Washington's lifetime. The style is loosely considered to be part Georgian and British Palladian, although with classical influences. The house is somewhat modest as far as historic estates go. It has a five-part Palladian design that features a central mansion connected by two curved colonnades to the servants' hall and kitchen. The riverfront facade has a commanding view of the Potomac, and its exterior pine boards were beveled and then coated with layers of white paint and sand to make the house appear to be made of brick. The stunning red roof and its large cupola are distinguishing features.

Mount Vernon's interior has been meticulously restored to appear as it did in 1799, during the final year of George Washington's life. As such, the rooms are painted in their original vibrant colors, including some in bright shades of blue and green. The interior, as with the exterior, is rather modest but is adorned with original pieces.

The estate is a great place to learn about George Washington's life and times. Tours are self-guided, but spirited costumed interpreters are on hand to reveal stories behind every room in the mansion including how and where George Washington died and who his houseguests were (such as the famous French nobleman the Marquis de Lafayette).

In addition to the mansion with original furnishings, the nearly 50-acre estate (which at one time was over 8,000 acres) includes a dozen original structures and Washington's tomb (where he and Martha Washington are buried).

George Washington designed the outbuildings, gardens, and lanes running through the estate to be both practical and aesthetically pleasing. The outbuildings supported the work of the plantation, and more than a dozen are open to the public, including the kitchen, smokehouse, slave quarters, stable, outhouses, and a blacksmith shop. The estate is still a working farm, much as it was when Washington lived here. Costumed interpreters are featured in many of the buildings and give live demonstrations of the work performed in them. Three miles south of Mount Vernon on Route 235 is George Washington's **whiskey distillery and gristmill** (Apr.-Oct. daily 10am-5pm, included with general admission). They are still functioning today as they did in the 18th century and produce authentic products.

Four gardens on six enclosed acres can be visited at Mount Vernon. Staff test new plant varieties and provide beautiful flowers for display. **Gardens and groves** walking tours ($10 in addition to general admission) are offered daily and last approximately 60 minutes.

If you are in town in May or October, partake in the **Mount Vernon Wine Festival & Sunset Tour.** This twice-yearly event celebrates wine history in Virginia with exclusive evening tours of the mansion and cellar. Live jazz is played on the east lawn, and don't be surprised if George and Martha make a special appearance. Tickets sell out quickly and are $42-52.

Getting There: Mount Vernon is accessible by Metrorail and bus. Those arriving by **Metrorail** (202/637-7000, www.wmata.com) can take the Yellow Line to the Huntington Station and then exit onto Huntington Avenue on the lower level. From there, take the **Fairfax Connector** (703/339-7200, www.fairfaxcounty.gov) bus 101 on the Fort Hunt Line to Mount Vernon.

If arriving by **car,** take the George Washington Memorial Parkway all the way to its southern terminus. **Bicycle** is another great way to arrive. Cyclists can take the scenic Mount Vernon Trail, which runs near the western bank of the Potomac River and offers great views of the water, to the estate.

Another fun option is to arrive by boat through **The Potomac Riverboat Company** (703/548-7655, www.potomacriverboatco.com, round-trip adults $50, children $39, including admission to Mount Vernon). Boat trips depart from Old Town Alexandria, Virginia, and National Harbor, Maryland.

WOODLAWN AND POPE-LEIGHEY HOUSE

The **Woodlawn Estate** and the **Pope-Leighey House** (9000 Richmond Hwy., Alexandria, 703/570-6902, www.woodlawnpopeleighey.org, Fri.-Mon. 11am-4pm, combined tickets for adults $20, students K-12 $11, seniors 62 and over and active military $18) are two historic homes that share a National Trust for Historic Preservation site. **Woodlawn Estate** (individual tickets for adults $10, students K-12 $6, seniors 62 and over and active military $8) is a historic plantation home that was originally part of George Washington's Mount Vernon Estate. It is located three miles west of Mount Vernon. The home was built between 1800 and 1805 for George Washington's nephew, Lawrence Lewis, and his bride, Martha Washington's granddaughter, Nelly Parke Custis, as a wedding gift. The main mansion is made of brick and has sandstone trim. It has 86 windows (many that are larger than four feet wide by eight feet tall) and looks imposing with its formal facade. The 126-acre estate originally contained 2,000 acres. The home has since had several owners, including playwright Paul Kester, who moved in with his 60 cats. Take a tour of this beautiful residence and be sure to ask your docent a lot of questions. Guides are very knowledgeable about the estate, and participant interaction can really enhance the experience.

The **Pope-Leighey House** (individual tickets for adults $15, students K-12 $7.50, seniors 62 and over and active military $12), a modest house with an exterior made of cypress, is a Frank Lloyd Wright home that was originally built in Falls Church, Virginia, in 1939. When a highway expansion threatened the home, it was given to the National Trust for Historic Preservation and moved to the Woodlawn grounds. The home now resides permanently on the grounds and can be toured. The two homes are a bit of an odd combination, but both are beautiful. Areas of the estate can be rented for special events, and the site also houses a nonprofit farm called the Arcadia Center for Sustainable Food & Agriculture.

GUNSTON HALL

Another popular historic plantation is **Gunston Hall** (10709 Gunston Rd., Mason Neck, 703/550-9220, www.gunstonhall.org, daily 9:30am-5pm, grounds open until 6pm, adults $10, children 6-18 $5, seniors 60 and over $8), former home of George Mason. The statesman authored the Virginia Declaration of Rights and was one of his era's most influential figures. He was one of the first people to call for American liberties such as religious tolerance and freedom of the press. Although Mason helped frame the U.S. Constitution, he declined to sign the document because it did not abolish slavery and lacked a bill of rights. Mason's home was built between 1755 and 1759 and originally sat on 5,500 acres. It was a tobacco and corn plantation. It is famous for its intricate Georgian architecture and extraordinary interior that represents Gothic, French modern, Chinese, Palladian, and classical styles. Many details, such as the carvings in its Palladian Room, were created by an indentured servant named William Bernard Sears, whom Mason brought from London to work on Gunston Hall. The estate now includes 550 acres of surrounding land on the Potomac River and has reconstructed outbuildings, a 250-year-old boxwood-lined walkway, and hiking trails down to the water. Guided tours are offered daily every half hour 9:30am-4:30pm.

RECREATION
Parks
MASON NECK STATE PARK

Mason Neck State Park (7301 High Point Rd., Lorton, 703/339-2385, www.dcr.virginia.gov, $10) is in southern Fairfax County approximately 20 miles from Washington DC. This 1,825-acre park sits on a peninsula and is bordered by Pohick Bay to the north, Belmont Bay to the south, and the Potomac River to the east. The park offers endless opportunities for outdoor recreation, including more than four miles of unpaved hiking and biking trails and three miles of paved trails and elevated walkways above marsh areas for wildlife-watching. Fresh- and brackish-water fishing is accessible in the park (with a valid Virginia or Maryland fishing license), and cartop boat-launch facilities are available. Kayaks and canoes can be rented on-site. The park is also a bird-watcher's paradise. It has resident bald eagles and migratory tundra swans and ducks. A visitors center offers exhibits, a gift shop, and a meeting room. The entrance to the park is off Gunston Road and is shared by the 2,277-acre **Elizabeth Hartwell Mason Neck National Wildlife Refuge** (703/490-4979, www.fws.gov, free), which was the first national wildlife refuge specifically established for the protection of bald eagles and also features one of the East Coast's largest heronries.

ALGONKIAN REGIONAL PARK

Algonkian Regional Park (47001 Fairway Dr., Sterling, 703/450-4655, www.novaparks.com, free admission, activities have individual charges) sits on the banks of the Potomac River and offers trails, a boat launch, picnic facilities, cabin rentals, fishing, ball fields, a large water-park complex, miniature golf, and an 18-hole, par-72 golf course. Kayak tours and other scheduled events take place during the summer months.

BULL RUN REGIONAL PARK

Bull Run Regional Park (7700 Bull Run Dr., Centreville, 703/631-0550, www.novaparks.com, $8) is a spacious, scenic park with open fields, woodland trails, a water park, and a public shooting center. The park hosts festivals and special events throughout the year and can accommodate thousands of people at a time.

LAKE FAIRFAX

Lake Fairfax (1400 Lake Fairfax Dr., Reston, 703/471-5414, www.fairfaxcounty.gov, free for county residents, otherwise $10) is a 476-acre park featuring an 18-acre lake, a water park (The Water Mine), campgrounds, ball fields, mountain biking trails, picnic areas, seasonal fishing, boating, a carousel, and a playground. Nominal fees are charged for the water park, carousel, boating, and camping.

FRYING PAN FARM PARK
Frying Pan Farm Park (2709 W. Ox Rd., Herndon, 703/437-9101, www.fairfaxcounty. gov, free) is a living-history farm (Kidwell Farm) with animals, wagon rides, horse-show facilities, and a country store. Visitors can view farm animals such as cows, goats, pigs, rabbits, and horses and learn about what Virginia farm life was like in the early to mid-20th century. Beginner horseback riding lessons are also offered.

Mountain Biking
Wakefield Park (8100 Braddock Rd., 703/321-7080, www.fairfaxcounty.gov, free) has some of the best mountain biking trails in Northern Virginia. They are great for beginner and intermediate riders with some more challenging sections. The trails are part of a larger network of county trails, including the **Cross County Trail** system. There's also a skate park at Wakefield where they hold skateboarding and BMX classes. Wakefield Park also offers night riding from dusk to 10:30pm year-round on Monday, Tuesday, and Thursday nights. Otherwise the park is open dawn to dusk.

Another premier mountain biking park is **Fountainhead Regional Park** (10875 Hampton Rd., Fairfax Station, 703/250-9124, www.novaparks.com, free). Miles of trails were developed in this park along the Occoquan Reservoir by mountain bikers for mountain bikers. These are technical trails, full of tight turns, steep climbs, stream crossings, and log hops. It's one of the best mountain biking areas in the Washington DC region. Call ahead for trail conditions.

Great Falls Park (9200 Old Dominion Dr., Great Falls, www.nps.gov/grfa, individual fee for entering on foot, horse, or bicycle $7, children under age 15 free, vehicle fee for one vehicle and all passengers $15) also offers

nice nontechnical mountain biking with great views of the Potomac River. Nature lovers looking for a moderate ride can pedal to the right (when looking at the river) to pick up a few miles of dirt carriage roads and trails. There are some steep climbs, loose gravel, and rocks but nothing too technical. There are also single-track trails in the park if you head to the left of the parking lot. These trails lead to Riverbend Park and offer some hills. Obtain a trail map from the visitors center before you head out.

Many Fairfax County parks allow mountain biking on their trails. Additional information on the following trails can be obtained from the **Fairfax County Park Authority** (www.fairfaxcounty.gov). **Clarks Crossing** (9850 Clarks Crossing Rd., Vienna) offers 3.2 miles of natural trails connecting to the W&OD Trail. The **Colvin Run Stream Valley** trail (Hunter Mill Rd. and Rte. 7, Reston) is a lovely, 3-mile natural trail that runs between Hunter Mill Road and Route 7. The **Fred Crabtree** park trail (2801 Fox Mill Rd., Herndon) offers 2 miles of wooded trails. **Lake Fairfax Park** offers a challenging network of wooded trails in Reston.

Trails
There are many hiking, running, and walking trails in Fairfax County. Most parks in the area offer some kind of recreational trails. To download trail maps in Fairfax County, visit www.fairfaxcounty.gov.

Golf
The premier public golf course in Fairfax County is **Westfields Golf Club** (13940 Balmoral Greens Ave., Clifton, 703/631-3300, www.westfieldsgolf.com, $89-109). This award-winning, nationally recognized course was designed by Fred Couples and is considered enjoyable for novices yet challenging for experienced players. The course incorporates natural wetlands, beech and oak trees, and rolling hills. The atmosphere is inviting and professional, and the service is outstanding. The complex includes a clubhouse, pro shop,

driving range, putting green, fitting studio, and restaurant.

Another great course is the **Laurel Hill Golf Club** (8701 Laurel Crest Dr., Lorton, 703/493-8849, www.fairfaxcounty.gov, $39-99). This is an exciting 18-hole course that was built on land that once housed the DC Department of Corrections facility at Lorton. This course, run by the Fairfax County Park Authority, was ranked in the top 10 municipal courses nationwide and has hosted several notable tournaments.

Pleasant Valley Golfers' Club (4715 Pleasant Valley Rd., Chantilly, 703/222-7900, www.pleasantvalleygc.com, $40-88) is another Fairfax County Park Authority course, but it is managed independently and is considered higher-end. The well-respected 18-hole course also offers a driving range.

The **Reston National Golf Course** (11875 Sunrise Valley Dr., 703/620-9333, www.restonnationalgc.com, $29-84) is one of Northern Virginia's classic golf courses. It was designed by Ed Ault and is home to the Nike Golf Learning Center, a leading golf-instruction program. Reston National offers a driving range and putting and chipping greens. Unsubstantiated legend says that the land the course was built on was once owned by Hugh Hefner. Whether or not this is true, an aerial view of the course does strike a stunning resemblance to the Playboy bunny symbol.

An older course with a lot of character is the **Algonkian Regional Park Golf Course** (47001 Fairway Dr., Sterling, 703/450-4655, www.novaparks.com, $29.50-48). This 18-hole, par-72 course offers long, straight, flat, tree-lined fairways on the front nine and hills and water holes on the back nine. Electric and pull carts are available. No metal spikes are allowed.

Rock Climbing

Great Falls Park (9200 Old Dominion Dr., Great Falls, www.nps.gov/grfa) is a rock climber's paradise with more than 200 climbing routes on the Virginia side of the river. Most climbs are around 50 feet and overhanging. Trad climbing is not recommended, so bring plenty of rope for toprope anchors. The fall is the best time to climb; the water is low, and the climbs offer sun until late in the day.

Canoeing and Kayaking

There are several good launch sites for private canoes and kayaks in Fairfax County. **Algonkian Regional Park** (47001 Fairway Dr., Sterling, 703/450-4655, www.novaparks.com, shore launch $6, ramp $7) has a nice boat ramp on the Potomac River. Paddlers should paddle upstream. **Mason Neck State Park** (Gunston Rd., Mount Vernon, 703/339-2385, www.dcr.virginia.gov, $7 admission, $5 launch) is another good spot to launch and offers paddlers several places to paddle, including Pohick Bay, Belmont Bay, and the Potomac River. Canoe and kayak rentals are available on-site and a cartop launch is provided. **Fountainhead Regional Park** (10875 Hampton Rd., Fairfax Station, 703/250-9124, www.novaparks.com, free) offers a launch site on the Occoquan Reservoir (shore launch $6, ramp $7), kayak rentals ($13 per hour), and canoe rentals ($11 per hour).

Fishing

Burke Lake Park (7315 Ox Rd., Fairfax Station, 703/323-6600, www.fairfaxcounty.gov) has a 218-acre lake with wonderful largemouth bass fishing, making it a popular spot. The park offers shoreline fishing, four fishing bulkheads, a fishing pier, bait and tackle sales, rowboat rentals, and a boat launch.

Lake Fairfax Park (1400 Lake Fairfax Dr., Reston, 703/471-5414, www.fairfaxcountry.gov) offers spring trout fishing in its 18-acre lake and year-round fishing for catfish, bass, sunfish, black crappie, bluegill, and bullhead. Other good fishing spots include **Fountainhead Regional Park** (703/250-9124, www.novaparks.com) and **Riverbend Park** (8700 Potomac Hills St., Great Falls, 703/759-9018, www.fairfaxcounty.gov).

ENTERTAINMENT AND EVENTS

Music and Theater

★ WOLF TRAP NATIONAL PARK FOR THE PERFORMING ARTS

There are few performance venues in the country that compare to the **Filene Center** at **Wolf Trap National Park for the Performing Arts** (1645 Trap Rd., Vienna, 703/255-1868, www.wolftrap.org). This beautiful, indoor/outdoor amphitheater is set on 130 acres of rolling hills and woods, just 20 miles from Washington DC and 3 miles from the Beltway. It is the country's only national park dedicated to the performing arts. It offers a full lineup of concerts, musicals, dance, and other types of performances through the summer from well-known artists and performance companies. Bring a picnic and eat on the lawn before or during the show (many lawn seats are available), or enjoy one of the on-site eateries (reservations are required). October-May, **The Barns at Wolf Trap,** two 18th-century barns that were relocated from upstate New York, offer indoor performances, making this an interesting and inspiring year-round venue. Free parking is available at the park for performances, and the **Wolf Trap Express Shuttle** offers round-trip service

($5) from the West Falls Church Metrorail station to the Filene Center for most performances. Shuttle service begins two hours prior to showtime and runs every 20 minutes. Return shuttle service leaves 20 minutes after the end of each show but no later than 11pm.

EAGLEBANK ARENA

The **EagleBank Arena** (4500 Patriot Circle, Fairfax, 703/993-3000, www.eaglebankarena. com) is on the campus of George Mason University in Fairfax. In addition to hosting campus events, the center features sporting events, concerts, and family performances. Legends such as Bruce Springsteen, Bob Dylan, and the Harlem Globetrotters have performed there.

JAMMIN JAVA

Approximately 15 miles west of Washington DC, in Vienna, Virginia, is **Jammin Java** (227 Maple Ave., 703/255-1566, www. jamminjava.com), a small but important venue in the metropolitan music community. They have live music every night and also hold children's concerts on many mornings. They feature well-known artists such as Ingrid Michaelson, Citizen Cope, and Bon Iver as well as Washington DC favorites such as Bill

Filene Center at Wolf Trap National Park for the Performing Arts

Kirchen and Eddie from Ohio. All concerts are general admission. Tickets can be purchased online.

Festivals and Events

There are many festivals and events that fill the calendar in Fairfax County. One popular venue is the **Reston Town Center** (11900 Market St., www.restontowncenter.com), which hosts festivals throughout the year, including the **Northern Virginia Fine Arts Festival, Pet Fiesta, Taste of Reston,** and **Concerts on the Town** music series held on Saturday nights in the summer. Visit the website for a full schedule and details.

The **Workhouse Arts Center** (9518 Workhouse Way, Lorton, 703/584-2900, www. workhousearts.org) is a vibrant arts center that is housed in a former prison in Lorton. The center is recognized both regionally and nationally for innovative collaborations of visual and performing arts, community engagement, education, and history. The center has galleries, a theater, and six buildings that house artist studios. It supports more than 100 artists, and visitors are encouraged to interact with them. The center hosts many events throughout the year, such as the **Workhouse Brewfest** (Sept.) and the popular **Haunted Trail** (Oct.), and offers more than 800 classes and workshops.

One of the premier festivals in Northern Virginia is the annual **Vintage Virginia Wine Festival** (Bull Run Regional Park, Chantilly, www.vintagevirginia.com, $45), which is held in early June in Centreville. A 20-minute drive from Washington DC, the festival offers wine tasting, local winemakers, more than 100 vendors, food, and entertainment.

Celebrate Fairfax (12000 Government Center Pkwy., Fairfax, 703/324-3247, www. celebratefairfax.com, $10-20) is another popular annual event. It began as the Fairfax Fair and is now the county's largest annual community celebration, entertaining tens of thousands of people during three days in mid-June. The celebration is held on 25 acres and

has more than 300 exhibitors sharing food, crafts, and activities. There are also carnival rides, nightly fireworks, and seven stages of live concerts including several big-name bands. Entertainment in the past has included well-known artists such as Third Eye Blind, The Bangles, Rusted Root, and Pat Benatar.

Civil War buffs won't want to miss the **Civil War Encampment Weekend** (3650 Historic Sully Way, 703/437-1794, www.fairfaxcounty. gov, $7-9) at the Sully Historic Site. For two days in August, visitors can watch Civil War reenactors re-create daily life during that era. Daily skirmishes include infantry, artillery, and cavalry. Live music and a fashion show are also part of the festivities.

The **Bull Run Festival of Lights** (Bull Run Regional Park, Chantilly, 703/631-0550, www.bullrunfestivaloflights.com, Mon.-Thurs. $20 per car, Fri.-Sun. $25 per car) is a highlight of the holiday season for thousands of visitors. This six-week festival is a winter wonderland of light displays that can be explored from the comfort of your car. More than 130,000 spectators drive through this 2.5-mile-long holiday wonderland each season.

SHOPPING

You don't have to look far to find shopping in Fairfax County. Strip malls are everywhere, and just about every national chain store imaginable can be found. There are several large malls that are very popular with both visitors and residents.

The most well-known shopping mall in Northern Virginia is **Tysons Corner Center** (1961 Chain Bridge Rd., Tysons Corner, www. tysonscornercenter.com). With more than 300 stores and restaurants, this is a premier destination for serious shoppers. The upscale sister mall to Tysons Corner Center is **Tysons Galleria** (2001 International Dr., McLean, www.tysonsgalleria.com).

The **Reston Town Center** (11900 Market St., Reston, 703/579-6720, www. restontowncenter.com) is a mini city in itself. Many national-brand shops line its streets, and festivals and concerts are scheduled in its center throughout much of the year.

The **Mosaic District** (2910 District Ave., Fairfax, www.mosaicdistrict.com) is an outdoor, upscale shopping and dining district with independent boutiques, upscale national chains, health-minded grocery shopping, and a cinema.

FOOD
Near the Beltway
INDIAN

There are two standout restaurants in the area for Indian food. The first is ★ **Jaipur Royal Indian Cuisine** (9401 Lee Hwy., Fairfax, 703/766-1111, www.jaipurcuisine.com, daily 11:30am-2:30pm and 5:30pm-10pm, $11-20). This very popular restaurant features a delicious and well-priced lunch buffet (weekdays $11.95, weekends $14.95) with plentiful selections that include a variety of vegetarian dishes. Dinner brings a large selection of delightful entrées made from spices that are prepared fresh each day for each individual dish. The decor is authentic and cheerful, and the staff is friendly and helpful with suggestions. Personal favorites include the Mango Prawn Curry, the Malai Kofta, and the Murgh Tikka Masala. If you like your dish hot, be sure to ask for "American hot" unless you're positive you can endure "Indian hot," which is a whole new level of hot. Reservations are a must on weekends.

The second is **Haandi** (1222 W. Broad St., Falls Church, 703/533-3501, www.haandi.com, Sun.-Thurs. 11:30am-2:30pm and 5pm-10pm, Fri.-Sat. 11:30am-2:30pm and 5pm-10:30pm, $12-23). This award-winning restaurant perfects the art of authentic Indian cooking. Although the names of the dishes may sound familiar, the range of flavors, the kitchen's skill with using spices, and the attention to detail are unrivaled. Start with an order of samosas and tantalize your taste buds as you look through the extensive menu of entrées. There are no wrong choices. When in doubt, ask your server for help; they are knowledgeable and eager to help. Reservations are highly recommended.

ITALIAN

Some of the best Italian food in Fairfax is at **Dolce Vita** (10824 Fairfax Blvd., Fairfax, 703/385-1530, www.dolcevitaitaliankitchenandwinebar.com, Mon.-Thurs. 11:30am-9:30pm, Fri.-Sat. 11:30am-10:30pm, Sun. 5pm-9:30pm, $13-41). This cozy little restaurant pairs delicious Italian cuisine with a comfortable, friendly atmosphere. The large, wood-burning brick oven is a focal point in the small dining area, which is decorated with scenes from the Tuscan countryside. The food is mostly traditional Italian fare with an emphasis on fresh ingredients. They also prepare slightly lighter sauces and manage to do so without sacrificing any taste. The restaurant has a huge following with locals and those in the know and can be crowded during peak hours. They also have a wine bar next door with a daily happy hour, wine tastings, and dinner pairings.

MEXICAN

If you're in the mood for Mexican food, try the **Coyote Grille and Cantina** (10266 Main St., Fairfax, 703/591-0006, www.coyotegrille.com, Mon.-Thurs. 11am-9:30pm, Fri.-Sat. 11am-10pm, Sun. 11am-9pm, $8-18) in Fairfax. They offer authentic recipes and a menu refreshingly different from the usual chain fare. The atmosphere is lively, and they have a loyal local client base. Their Southwestern-style entrées include traditional items such as burritos and fajitas and some unexpected twists such as the addition of sweet potatoes in their Fiesta Salad and their Coyote Burger with chipotle dressing. Their heated year-round patio has a margarita bar where they make more than a dozen varieties of scrumptious margaritas. They also have delicious desserts that go beyond fried ice cream and flan (such as a brownie sundae) and full brunch on Sunday.

PERSIAN

Outstanding Persian food is served at **Shamshiry** (8607 Westwood Center Dr., Vienna, 703/448-8883, www.shamshiry.com, Sun.-Thurs. 11:30am-11pm, Fri.-Sat. 11:30am-1am, $6-21), in the Tysons Corner

Local Brews

Even self-proclaimed beer snobs will find something to rave about in Northern Virginia's local beer scene. In recent years, a growing number of new brewers have come onto the radar to compete with the more established breweries. The result is a good selection of locally made beer spread out across much of Northern Virginia.

Founded by former employees of local craft beer pioneer Old Dominion Brewing, the **Lost Rhino Brewing Company** (21730 Red Rum Dr. #142, Ashburn, 571/291-2083, www.lostrhino.com, Tues. 4pm-9pm, Wed.-Thurs. 11:30am-9pm, Fri.-Sat. 11:30am-10pm, Sun. noon-5pm) is a leader in the local brew scene. Named after the surfing term "rhino chaser," which means "someone out to find the best waves, biggest waves, an adventurer," they offer a fantastic selection of artfully crafted beers that just plain taste great. The brewery and tasting room is tucked away in a warehouse in Ashburn, but it's a fun place for a tasting and draws quite a crowd on the weekends. They also have a larger restaurant with space for events in nearby Brambleton called **Lost**

Lost Rhino Retreat

Rhino Retreat (22885 Brambleton Plaza, Ashburn, 703/327-0311, www.lostrhinoretreat.com, Mon.-Thurs. 11:30am-10pm, Fri.-Sat. 11:30am-11pm, Sun. 11:30am-9pm). Try their delicious Barrel-Aged Stout and order a giant Bavarian-style pretzel on the side.

Another brewery with Old Dominion ties is **Old Ox Brewery** (44652 Guilford Dr., Ashburn, 703/729-8375, www.oldoxbrewery.com, Tues.-Thurs. 4pm-9pm, Fri. 2:30pm-10pm, Sat. 11am-10pm, Sun. 11am-7pm), which has a 30-barrel brewhouse. They partner with a local food truck or food vendor to provide a varying menu. The brewery is easily accessible from the Washington & Old Dominion Trail between mile markers 25 and 25.5.

Caboose Brewing Company (www.caboosebrewing.com) entered the market with their cozy **Caboose Tavern** located just off the Washington & Old Dominion Trail in Vienna (520 Mill St. NW, Vienna, 703/865-8580, Mon.-Thurs. 4pm-11pm, Fri. noon-midnight, Sat. 11am-midnight, Sun. 11am-10pm). In addition to brewing great beer, their focus is on health and the environment, and it shows with their community atmosphere and innovative menu, made from mostly sustainably sourced ingredients. Immediate success led to a second, larger location in the Mosaic District of Fairfax called **Caboose Commons** (2918 Eskridge Rd., Fairfax, 703/663-8833, Sun.-Thurs. 7am-11pm, Fri.-Sat. 7am-1pm). Caboose Commons is also a coffeehouse.

The oldest packaging brewery in the area can be found in Alexandria at **Port City Brewing Company** (3950 Wheeler Ave., Alexandria, 703/797-2739, www.portcitybrewing.com, Mon.-Wed. 4pm-9pm, Thurs. 4pm-10pm, Fri. 3pm-10pm, Sat. noon-10pm, Sun. noon-8pm). All of their beers are unfiltered, and you can find their top-notch Port City Porter along with other favorites at distributors throughout the mid-Atlantic. They have food-truck service at their tasting room.

A perfect day in the Virginia countryside might include a visit to **Vanish Farmwoods Brewery** (42245 Black Hops Ln., Leesburg, 703/779-7407, www.vanishbeer.com. Mon.-Wed. noon-9pm, Thurs.-Fri. noon-10pm, Sat. 11am-10pm, Sun. 11am-9pm). This beautiful brewery has one of the best beer menus in the area with more than 20 taps. They also have great pizza and barbeque. If you're into sour ales, try their Juicy Tangerine. Other top picks include their Milk Stout and house IPA (Ghost Fleet). Bring the dog and the kids.

Another great bet for a day outing is **Dirt Farm Brewing** (18701 Foggy Bottom Rd., Bluemont, 540/554-2337, www.dirtfarmbrewing.com, Sat.-Thurs. noon-7pm, Fri. noon-9pm). They pour small-batch, hand-crafted beer produced from ingredients grown on their farm and complement it with a stunning view of the Loudoun Valley. A fresh, seasonal menu is also available.

area. If you're not sure which succulent kabob dish to order, try their specialty Chelo Kabob Shamshiry, a combination of *kubideh* (ground beef) and *barg* (steak). The portions are large and the restaurant is very popular, so go early or plan to wait for a table. They also offer takeout.

VIETNAMESE

Four Sisters Vietnamese Restaurant (8190 Strawberry Ln., Falls Church, 703/539-8566, www.foursistersrestaurant.com, daily 11am-9:45pm, $10-28) is all about delicious food, beautiful ambience, and reasonable prices. This award-winning restaurant offers an extensive and well-planned menu of light and flavorful Vietnamese food. If you aren't sure what to order, they offer dinners for 2, 4, 6, and 10 diners. The selections are wonderful and offer a good sampling of the chef's talents. They also offer a gluten-free menu. Reservations are highly recommended on weekends. Be sure to take note of the flower arrangements in the restaurant—they are made from real, fresh flowers, and they are spectacular.

Western Fairfax County
AMERICAN

One of the Reston Town Center's most noted restaurants is **Passion Fish** (11960 Democracy Dr., Reston, 703/230-3474, www.passionfishreston.com, Mon.-Thurs. 11:30am-10:30pm, Fri. 11:30am-11:30pm, Sat. 4pm-11:30pm, Sun. 10:30am-9pm, $23-48). Elegant, open, and airy, the atmosphere alone (which mimics a classic ocean liner) draws diners looking to enjoy seafood. The menu is primarily seafood, with some interesting twists. Selections from the raw bar, sushi, salads, and succulent entrées sit alongside sweet potato fries, mac and cheese, and jasmine rice with red Thai curry. Steak is also available. A favorite venue for business lunches and dinners, the restaurant also has a sophisticated bar menu and seasonal outdoor seating.

For something leisurely or romantic, try the **Vinifera Wine Bar Bistro** (11750 Sunrise Valley Dr., Reston, 703/234-3550, daily 6:30am-10pm, $19-32), in the Westin Hotel in Reston. It is a great place to bring a date or relax while traveling on business. The trendy spot offers great wine and equally tasty cuisine. Order multiple small plates to accompany wine by the glass, or order a full-size entrée for a bigger commitment. Weather permitting, sit on the patio by a fire pit. There is little noise or street activity, making this a delightful rare find in the area. Even if you aren't on vacation, it will feel like it. They serve breakfast, lunch, and dinner.

Bazin's on Church (111 Church St., Vienna, 703/255-7212, www.bazinsonchurch. com, brunch Sun. 11am-2pm, lunch Tues.-Fri. 11:30am-2pm, dinner Tues.-Thurs. 5pm-10pm, Fri.-Sat. 5pm-10:30pm, Sun. 5pm-9:30pm, $19-38) in Vienna is a contemporary American restaurant specializing in items made from organic and seasonal ingredients. There is also a wine bar with more than 500 selections from around the world. Wine-tasting is available. Dinner entrées include seafood, pasta, and steak, all prepared with unique and delicious recipes. The brunch offers mouthwatering options such as bananas foster French toast and filet sliders. The atmosphere is inviting with large windows, low lighting, and exposed brick walls. This small section of Vienna has a great contemporary feel to it, yet is easy to get to and has free parking. They also offer an extensive gluten-free menu.

If you're looking for a great sandwich or a slice of New York-style pizza, **Santini's** (11804 Baron Cameron Ave., Reston, 703/481-3333, www.mysantinis.com, Mon.-Sat. 9am-10pm, Sun. 9am-9pm, $6-15) in Reston is the place to go. This family-owned New York-style deli is the best sandwich joint in the area. The food is fresh, made to order, and simply delicious. A great place for families and team gatherings, it's also a comfortable spot to grab a beer and watch the game. Santini's offers reasonable prices, fresh food, and friendly, personal service. They also have locations in Sterling, Ashburn, Oakton, McLean, Fairfax, and Chantilly.

Mookie's BBQ (1141 Walker Rd., Great Falls, 703/759-2386, www.mookiesbbq.com, Tues.-Thurs. 11am-9pm, Fri.-Sat. 11am-10pm, Sun. 10am-9pm, $10-36) grew out of a competition barbecue and catering company. They serve outstanding barbecue pork, chicken, ribs, and salads.

FRENCH

For a special celebration or a romantic dinner, it is hard to top ★ **L'Auberge Chez François** (332 Springvale Rd., Great Falls, 703/759-3800, www.laubergechezfrancois. com, Tues.-Fri. 11:30am-1:30pm and 5pm-9pm, Sat. 11:30am-1:30pm and 4:30pm-9:30pm, Sun. noon-7:30pm, $75-85). This family-owned restaurant began back in 1954 in Washington DC and relocated to Great Falls in 1975, where it has been a destination in itself ever since. The food and service are simply first-rate, with exceptional attention paid to every detail. But what makes this place special is that regardless of who the famous person may be at the next table, or how many couples are getting engaged that night, the atmosphere is always relaxed and comfortable. Dinner is a six-course prix fixe menu with entrée selections that include seafood, filet, lamb, and their signature chateaubriand for two. Lunch is a four-course prix fixe menu for $45. Reservations are a must and usually are required weeks in advance for prime times, but walk-ins are accepted on the beautiful terrace when the weather is nice. A scaled-down version of the menu is offered on the lower level of the restaurant in the **Jacques' Brasserie and Jacques' Bar Rouge** (Tues.-Fri. 11:30am-1:30pm and 5pm-9pm, Sat. 11:30am-1:30pm and 4:30pm-9:30pm, Sun. noon-7:30pm).

IRISH

The Old Brogue (760C Walker Rd., Great Falls, 703/759-3309, www.oldbrogue.com, Mon.-Thurs. 11am-midnight, Fri.-Sat. 11am-2am, Sun. 10am-10pm, $8-27) is *the* place to go in Great Falls. It's a family-owned institution that began on St. Patrick's Day in 1981. This cozy pub welcomes everyone with an international bar menu, fresh food, traditional Irish fare, and live entertainment. Start with Irish potato skins or some ginger fried calamari. Follow that up with cottage pie or the savory blackened-salmon salad. They also serve Sunday brunch. Everyone is family at the Old Brogue, and it's one of the few places in this fast-paced area where people relax and chat with strangers at the next table.

ITALIAN AND MEDITERRANEAN

If you need a quick, delicious meal for dine in or takeout, stop by **Cafesano** (11130 South Lakes Dr., Reston, 571/257-0854, www. cafesano.com, daily 11am-9pm, $8-18). They offer a wide variety of yummy salads, pasta, kabobs, paninis, wraps, and brick oven pizza with many healthy choices. They also have the best prices in the area for beer and wine. Order at the counter and take your drink and number to your seat. They'll find you when your food is ready. When you're done, take your dishes to the trash and dish bins. There's a second location in Dulles (21305 Windmill Parc Dr., 571/748-7077).

VEGETARIAN

You don't have to be a vegetarian to enjoy **Sunflower Vegetarian Restaurant** (2531 Chain Bridge Rd., Vienna, 703/319-3888, www.crystalsunflower.com, Mon.-Sat. 11:30am-10pm, Sun. noon-10pm, $9-13). In fact, chances are you would never know it was vegetarian just by tasting the food: The tasty Asian-influenced entrées at Sunflower actually mimic meat in texture and taste. The flavors are delicious. First-timers can't go wrong with the local favorite, General Tso's Surprise. The surprise is that there really isn't meat in it, which you'd never guess.

Southern Fairfax County
AMERICAN

★ **Trummer's on Main** (7134 Main St., Clifton, 703/266-1623, www. trummersonmain.com, brunch Sun. 11am-2pm, lunch Sat. noon-2:30pm, dinner

Tues.-Thurs. 5:30pm-9pm, Fri.-Sat. 5pm-10pm, Sun. 5pm-8pm, $19-58) is the hot spot in Clifton. The chef and owner was named one of *Food & Wine Magazine*'s Best New Chefs shortly after Trummer's opened back in 2010, and happy patrons have been coming ever since. Trummer's offers creative American cuisine and handcrafted cocktails (including their signature drink, the Titanic, which is too good to be missed). The ever-changing main plates include seafood, beef, chicken, pork, and vegetarian selections. The chef also offers a daily five-course tasting menu that can be ordered when making your reservation ($86, wine pairing an additional $62). It's imperative to save room for dessert: The pastry chef is nothing short of amazing. The atmosphere is hip and relaxing with high ceilings and many windows. The food presentation is exquisite. The cozy bar with its interesting stone pillars is a great place to meet friends, sample drinks, and try the bar menu.

ACCOMMODATIONS
$100-200

The majority of accommodations in Fairfax County are in national chain hotels. One exception is the **Stafford House** (3746 Chain Bridge Rd., 703/385-9024, www.staffordhouse.net, $129-199) bed-and-breakfast. This comfortable, friendly establishment is a nice change of pace in a convenient location. Each of its two rooms has a private entrance and parking. Breakfast is delivered to your room each morning, and rooms are equipped with many amenities including a fireplace. The owners are very friendly and helpful and contribute to an enjoyable stay.

$200-300

Many hotels in the county are geared toward business travelers and, as such, offer discounted rates on the weekends. The **Residence Inn Tysons Corner Mall** (8400 Old Courthouse Rd., Vienna, 703/917-0800, www.marriott.com, $96-279) is a six-floor, 121-room hotel near Tysons Corner. They offer a free American breakfast daily. This is an older hotel, but it has been renovated and the staff is friendly and attentive. It is also pet friendly ($75 fee).

The **Hilton McLean Tysons Corner** (7920 Jones Branch Dr., McLean, 703/847-5000, www3.hilton.com, $104-831) is another good option in Tysons Corner. It is convenient to shopping and has modern, attractive decor. There are 458 guest rooms.

One hotel that stands out from the crowd in Fairfax County is the **Westin Reston Heights** (11750 Sunrise Valley Dr., Reston, 703/391-9000, www.westinreston.com, $94-274). It is a modern hotel with 191 guest rooms and a quiet location. There is also a wonderful wine bar on-site.

Another stand out is the **Hyatt Regency Reston** (1800 Presidents St., Reston, 703/709-1234, www.hyatt.com, $113-409), in the beautiful Reston Town Center. It has 518 rooms and anchors the upscale outdoor mall. The interior has modern decor, and free shuttle service is available to and from Washington Dulles International Airport.

Over $300

The **Ritz-Carlton, Tysons Corner** (1700 Tysons Blvd., McLean, 703/506-4300, www.ritzcarlton.com, $169-819) is a high-end option in Tysons Corner with 398 guest rooms, direct access to shopping, and a better-than-average fitness room.

Camping

Camping is limited in Fairfax County, but there are a few parks with nice campgrounds. The first is **Lake Fairfax Park** (1400 Lake Fairfax Dr., Reston, 703/471-5414, www.fairfaxcounty.gov, $28-50) in Reston. Tent and RV camping are available. There are 136 campsites (54 with electrical hookups), a bathhouse, a dump station, picnic tables, grills, and public telephones. Reservations are required, and the campground is open year-round.

The second is the campground at **Burke Lake Park** (7315 Ox Rd., Fairfax Station, 703/323-6600, www.fairfaxcounty.gov,

$28-31). There are 100 wooded campsites (no electric or water hookups), a bathhouse, a dump station, camp store, ice, picnic tables, grills, fire rings, and public telephones. The campground is open mid-April through late October.

Another is **Bull Run Regional Park** (7700 Bull Run Dr., Centreville, 703/631-0550, www. novapark.com, $29-47), which offers RV sites with electric-only service, full-service RV sites, tent sites, group camping areas, and rustic cabins. There are two bathhouses and a camp store. All sites include charcoal grills, picnic tables, and fire rings.

INFORMATION AND SERVICES

The **Fairfax Museum & Visitors Center** (10209 Main St., 703/385-8414, www. fairfaxva.gov, daily 9am-5pm) is in the historic former Fairfax Elementary School, built in 1873. Visitors can pick up information on special events, transportation, restaurants, and lodging. The museum offers exhibits on the history of Fairfax City and walking tours of Old Town Fairfax in the spring and fall. Additional information on the entire county can be found at www.fxva.com.

GETTING THERE AND AROUND

Fairfax County is accessible in some areas by **Metrorail** and **Metrobus** (www.wmata. com), but visitors will greatly benefit from having access to a car.

The city of Fairfax offers the **CUE Bus System** (703/385-7859, www.fairfaxva.gov, Mon.-Fri. 6am-11pm, Sat. 8:30am-8:30pm, Sun. 9:30am-6pm, $1.75) for public transportation around town. Buses accept exact change and SmarTrip cards. Students and seniors can receive discounts. A bus schedule is available on the website.

Additional bus service in the county is provided by the **Fairfax Connector** (703/339-7200, www.fairfaxcounty.gov, $2). This service is countywide. Please consult the website for routes and schedules.

Prince William County

Prince William County is approximately 35 miles southwest of Washington DC. It stretches from the foothills of the Appalachian Mountains to the banks of the Potomac River and contains primarily suburban commuter communities but with a bit more rural feel than neighboring Fairfax County. The county has a number of historical landmarks, including the famous Manassas battlefield. It also offers outdoor recreation along the river and in several large parks.

For many years, the population in Prince William County was focused in Manassas, which was a large railroad junction, and Woodbridge, near the Potomac River. In recent decades the population has expanded significantly throughout the county, making it one of the most populated counties in the state.

SIGHTS
★ Manassas National Battlefield Park

The premier attraction in Prince William County is **Manassas National Battlefield Park** (6511 Sudley Rd., Manassas, 703/361-1339, www.nps.gov/mana, daily dawn to dusk, free, donations accepted). This historic battlefield was established as a national park in 1940 to preserve the site of two well-known Civil War battles: the First Battle of Bull Run (July 21, 1861), which was the first major land battle in the war; and the Second Battle of Bull Run (August 28-30, 1862), which was the biggest simultaneous mass assault of the Civil War and signaled the height of the Confederate army's

1: Civil War cannons at Manassas National Battlefield Park **2:** National Museum of the Marine Corps

power. The battles are also referred to as the First and Second Battles of Manassas. The reason there are two names for each battle is because the North usually named a battle after a nearby body of water (creek, river, or stream) and the South named battles after towns and railroads. So the Confederate army named the battles after Manassas Junction and the Union army named them after the Bull Run stream. It was at this site that Confederate general Thomas J. Jackson was nicknamed "Stonewall" Jackson.

The park encompasses more than 5,000 acres of meadows, woods, and streams. When visiting the battlefield, you can see the site where the battles took place and also visit three buildings: the **Henry Hill Visitor Center,** the **Brawner Farm Interpretive Center,** and the **Stone House.**

The **Henry Hill Visitor Center** (daily 8:30am-5pm) is on Sudley Road near the southern park entrance. It houses exhibits and information on the First Battle of Bull Run that include uniforms from the era, weapons, and field gear. It also offers an electronic battle map that visitors can interact with for a quick lesson in field strategy and tactics. Take the time to watch the 45-minute orientation film offered at the center; it is interesting and informative. It is shown on the hour. There is also a bookstore.

The **Brawner Farm Interpretive Center** (daily 9am-5pm) is the location of the opening phase of the Second Battle of Bull Run. There are exhibits and audiovisual programs that give a detailed overview of the second battle. There is a parking lot off of Pageland Lane on the western side of the park.

The **Stone House** (weekends only 10am-4:30pm) is a two-story brick house that was built in 1848 and served as a hospital during both battles at Bull Run. It is near the intersection of Sudley Road and Lee Highway.

Other attractions in the park include the **Stone Bridge,** which the Union army retreated across after both battles; **Battery Heights,** where Confederate batteries fired on the attacking Union troops at the Brawner Farm; **Matthews Hill,** the site of the opening phase of the first battle; and **Groveton,** the remains of a Civil War-era village. There are many other points of interest in the park as well. A great way to see many of them is by taking a self-guided walking tour of the one-mile **Henry Hill Loop Trail** that begins at the Henry Hill Visitor Center.

More than 900,000 people visit the battlefield yearly. Guided tours running 30 to 45 minutes are available from the Henry Hill Visitor Center.

National Museum of the Marine Corps

The **National Museum of the Marine Corps** (18900 Richmond Hwy., Triangle, 877/635-1775, www.usmcmuseum.com, daily 9am-5pm, free) is in Triangle, adjacent to the **Marine Corps Base Quantico.** The museum was built to serve as an ongoing tribute to U.S. Marines of the past, present, and future. The beautiful, soaring 210-foot design can be seen from I-95, and it is reminiscent of the famous Iwo Jima flag-raising image from World War II. The museum opened in 2006 and continues to expand. It houses interactive exhibits using innovative technology and shows visitors what it is like to be a marine. An example of this is the Legacy Walk, which uses lifelike cast figures of individual marines, photographs, maps, and artifacts to illustrate the evolution of the Marine Corps. Artifacts on display in the museum include aircraft, vehicles, weapons, uniforms, and personal items. A small fee is charged to experience the flight simulator.

Ben Lomond Historic Site

Those looking for a historical site with a new twist will enjoy the **Ben Lomond Historic Site** (10321 Sudley Manor Dr., Manassas, 703/367-7872, www.pwcgov.org, house hours May-Oct. Thurs.-Mon. 11am-4pm, grounds open daily dawn-dusk, adults $5, children under 6 free, active military $3). This is a hands-on historical experience with a focus on medicine. The federal-style manor house, built in 1837, is within five miles of Manassas National Battlefield Park, and it served as both a Confederate and Union hospital during the Civil War. The site includes the main house (where visitors can learn about medical techniques used during the Civil War and even see fake blood), slave quarters, and a smokehouse. Original graffiti written by Union soldiers in 1862 can still be seen on the walls. There is also an heirloom rose garden on the property with rare and antique plants. The garden is one of the largest public rose gardens in the country, with approximately 160 different cultivars. This is a great museum for kids and teenagers. Tours are given on the hour.

Occoquan Waterfront

More than 50 shops and restaurants line the quaint streets along the Occoquan River on the historic **Occoquan Waterfront** (www. occoquanwaterfront.com). The town began as a site for public tobacco warehouses as early as 1734, and its name means "at the end of the water." With a mostly industrial past due to its water access, the town has transformed into a residential community served by small businesses. Antiques stores, galleries, gift shops, and boutiques are just some of the shops visitors will find. Many festivals and events are held throughout the year on the streets and even in the water. Check out the website to see what is happening when you're in town.

RECREATION
Splashdown Water Park

Splashdown Water Park (7500 Ben Lomond Park Dr., Manassas, 703/792-8204, www.splashdownwaterpark.com, 48 inches or taller $16, under 48 inches $12.25, seniors 60 and over $9.50, spectators $9.50) is the largest water park in Northern Virginia. It features five unique water areas and a variety of food options. Some of the fun activities it offers include waterslides, a lazy river, a 25-meter lap pool, bubblers, fountains, cannonball slides, and a beach. They also offer swimming lessons.

Prince William Forest Park

Prince William Forest Park (18170 Park Entrance Rd., Triangle, 703/221-7181, www. nps.gov/prwi, $15 per vehicle for a 7-day pass) is a 15,000-acre all-season destination. It offers hiking, mountain biking, fishing, bird-watching, and cross-country skiing. There are 37 miles of hiking trails (the most extensive hiking network in Northern Virginia) and 21 miles of mountain biking roads and trails. Road biking on a 12-mile scenic stretch of road is also permitted, and the path has light traffic and great natural scenery. The visitors center is open daily March-October 9am-5pm, November-February 8am-4pm.

Leesylvania State Park

Leesylvania State Park (2001 Daniel K. Ludwig Dr., Woodbridge, 703/730-8205, www. dcr.virginia.gov, $10) is in southeast Prince William County, approximately 25 miles from Washington DC. The park is the site of the former Leesylvania Plantation, where General Robert E. Lee's father, Henry Lee III (aka Light Horse Harry), was born. Created in 1992, the park encompasses 542 acres on a peninsula bordered by the Potomac River, Neabsco Creek, and Powells Creek. The park has five hiking trails, including a segment of the **Potomac Heritage National Scenic Trail.** There are also many scenic overlooks to the Potomac River, and the one at Freestone Point is on the remains of a gun battery used by the Confederates in the Civil War. Fishing and boating are popular sports in the park. There is a boat ramp, a cartop launch for canoes and kayaks, and a 300-foot fishing pier. There is a large visitors center with nature displays, information on the history of the park, and a gift shop. Canoe tours, nature walks, guided hikes, and children's fishing tournaments are available. Picnic shelters are also available for rent.

A fun kayaking option is to launch from the park and paddle south on the Potomac River a short way to **Tim's Rivershore Restaurant & Crabhouse** (1510 Cherry Hill Rd., Dumfries, 703/441-1375, www.

timsrivershore.com, $10-31) for a seafood lunch on their deck. The restaurant is visible from the cartop launch, and there's a beach at Tim's to land your kayaks. A short paddle north to Neabsco Creek will take you past a shoreline of cute houses by the railroad tracks.

Largemouth bass are plentiful in the Potomac River near Leesylvania State Park. Other sport fish include catfish, perch, and striped bass. Overnight boating and fishing pier usage are allowed March-October.

Northwest Federal Field at Pfitzner Stadium

The **Northwest Federal Field at Pfitzner Stadium** (7 County Complex Ct., Woodbridge, 703/590-2311) is a minor league baseball stadium and the home field of the Potomac Nationals, a Class A affiliate of the Washington Nationals. The stadium holds 6,000 spectators.

Golf

The **Old Hickory Golf Club** (11921 Chanceford Dr., Woodbridge, 703/580-9000, www.golfoldhickory.com, $57-75) is an upscale golf and banquet facility in Woodbridge. The 18-hole, par-72 course was designed by Tim Freeland and is the sister course to Raspberry Falls in Leesburg. It is a well-maintained course with fast greens.

There are three public golf courses run by the **Prince William County Park Authority.** The first is the **Prince William Golf Course** (14631 Vint Hill Rd., Nokesville, 703/754-7111, www.princewilliamgolf.com, $20-44) in Nokesville. This course was built in the 1960s by local farmers. It is an 18-hole, par-70 course geared toward beginner and intermediate golfers and offers wide fairways and gentle knolls. There is also a driving range, a large putting and chipping green, a practice bunker, and PGA instruction.

The second, **Forest Greens Golf Club** (4500 Poa Annua Ln., Triangle, 703/221-0123, www.forestgreens.com, $25-59) in Triangle, offers resort amenities. This 18-hole, par-72 course was given four stars by *Golf Digest* and

features gently rolling terrain, tree-lined fairways, and protected greens. Designed by architect Clyde Johnston, the course offers an interesting layout with elevated tees, large landing areas, and few blind shots. This facility also includes a driving range, a pro shop, a putting and chipping green, PGA instruction, and a beverage cart on the course.

The third golf course is the 9-hole, par-3 **Lake Ridge Park Golf Course** (12350 Cotton Mill Dr., Woodbridge, 703/494-5564, www.lakeridgegc.com, $12) in Woodbridge. This course is an affordable novice course designed to help improve players' short games.

Bird-Watching

There are two prime birding locations in Prince William County. The first is the **Manassas National Battlefield Park** (6511 Sudley Rd., Manassas, 703/361-1339, www. nps.gov/mana, free, donations accepted), which was named an Audubon Important Bird Area. Park residents include the eastern meadowlark, barn owl, northern harrier, Savannah sparrow, and grasshopper sparrow.

The second is the **Prince William Forest Park** (18170 Park Entrance Rd., Triangle, 703/221-7181, www.nps.gov/prwi, $15 for a 7-day pass), a 15,000-acre national park in Triangle. The park is known as one of the premier birding habitats in Northern Virginia and has residents such as cedar waxwings, warblers, and kingfishers.

ENTERTAINMENT AND EVENTS
Jiffy Lube Live

A bustling venue for summer outdoor concerts is **Jiffy Lube Live** (7800 Cellar Door Dr., Bristow, 703/754-6400, www.livenation. com). This 25,000-capacity pavilion hosts many big-name bands, artists, and other performers. Reserved seating is underneath an overhang and protected from weather, while general admission is out on the lawn. Past performances include the Dave Matthews Band, The Who, Aerosmith, Jimmy Buffett, and Kelly Clarkson. Traffic entering and exiting the pavilion is notorious for being very slow, so plan accordingly.

Hylton Performing Arts Center

The **Hylton Performing Arts Center** (10960 George Mason Circle, Manassas, 703/993-7550, www.hyltoncenter.org) is a modern performing arts center at the Prince William Campus of George Mason University. The center includes 85,000 square feet of performance space including an elegant opera house, a family theater, and an art gallery. Performances include concerts, theater, comedy, dance, and other performing arts. Visit the website for a list of upcoming events.

Fairs and Festivals

The **Occoquan Arts and Craft Show** (www.visitpwc.com) is an annual event held in early June on the streets of historic downtown Occoquan. The show is hosted by the town of Occoquan and has been in existence for more than 50 years. Vendors include local merchants, crafters, and food, and there is live music. During the event, the roads are closed to traffic to make room for vendors and visitors. Information on parking and shuttle service can be found on the website.

The annual **Manassas Heritage Railway Festival** (9201 Center St., Manassas, 703/361-6599, www.visitmanassas.org, $5-6) takes place in June and draws more than 30,000 visitors each year. Enjoy a day of train-oriented activities, including train rides, model train displays, music, train memorabilia vendors, and other performances.

Another popular festival held in Manassas in June is the **Manassas Jazz Festival** (9101 Prince William St., 703/361-6599, www.visitmanassas.org, $25-130). This festival is held on Father's Day on the Manassas Museum Lawn in Old Town Manassas.

SHOPPING

Keeping in step with the rest of Northern Virginia, Prince William County offers a multitude of strip malls with many national retailers. The most well-known shopping area, however, is **Potomac Mills** (2700 Potomac Mills Circle, Woodbridge, 703/496-9330, www.simon.com, Mon.-Sat. 10am-9pm, Sun. 11am-6pm), right on I-95 near Woodbridge. Potomac Mills is the largest outlet mall in Virginia, with more than 200 stores. It is an indoor mall and also offers 25 food retailers and movie theaters.

Manassas Mall (8300 Sudley Rd., Manassas, 703/368-0181, www.manassasmall. com) is a traditional mall with more than 100 stores.

FOOD
American

The ★ **Philadelphia Tavern** (9413 Main St., Manassas, 703/393-1776, www. thephiladelphiatavern.com, daily 11am-2am, $6-16) is the place in Manassas to go for cheesesteaks, brews, and a little bit of everything else. The signature "Build Your Own Original Cheesesteak" is a local favorite. Try it with American cheese and Cheese Whiz. With daily specials like Tuesday's Virginia Beer and Burger Night and Wing Wednesday, every day is a little different at the tavern. Located in the historic district, the building was constructed in 1940 and was formerly a liquor store and storehouse. It was converted to the tavern in the 1990s as a replica of the common corner bar found in Philadelphia neighborhoods.

For casual seafood in a lovely setting, try **Madigans Waterfront** (201 Mill St., Occoquan, 703/494-6373, www. madiganswaterfront.com, daily 11am-10pm, $9-36). Madigans is right on the waterfront in historic Occoquan and offers a large deck with a tiki bar, many seafood selections, steak, pasta, and oysters year-round. They also have a sandwich menu with favorites such as shrimp salad, crab cakes, and an assortment of wraps. If you're looking for a relaxing waterfront setting, Madigans is a good choice.

French
The ★ **Bistro L'Hermitage** (12724 Occoquan

Rd., Woodbridge, 703/499-9550, www.bistrolhermitage.com, Tues.-Wed. 5pm-10pm, Thurs. 11:30am-2:30pm and 5pm-10pm, Fri. 11:30am-2:30pm and 5pm-11pm, Sat. 11:30am-2:30pm and 5pm-11pm, Sun. 11:30am-2:30pm and 5pm-10pm, $26-36) is a cozy French bistro located in Woodbridge but near the charming and historic Occoquan Waterfront. They serve fine French cuisine for brunch, lunch, and dinner. Dinner entrées include many seafood dishes as well as roasted duck, steak, roasted chicken, and veal liver. The restaurant offers delicious, well-presented food, good ambience, and friendly service.

Greek

For great Greek food go to **Katerina's Greek Cuisine** (9212 Center St., Manassas, 703/361-4976, www.katerinasgreekcuisine.com, Sun.-Thurs. 11am-9pm, Fri.-Sat. 11am-10pm, $7-22) in Manassas. This impressive little restaurant combines family recipes with fresh ingredients. If you're not sure what to order, try the Taste of Greece combination dinner or a traditional gyro platter. If someone in your party isn't keen on Greek food, they also offer burgers.

Mexican

Wonderful authentic Mexican food can be found in Haymarket at **El Vaquero West** (14910 Washington St., Haymarket, 703/753-0801, Mon.-Thurs. 11am-10pm, Fri. 11am-11pm, Sat. 11am-10pm, Sun. 11am-9pm, $7-20). People travel from all parts of Northern Virginia to enjoy the white queso and the dozens of freshly prepared menu items (most from family recipes). The chips and salsa are average, but the rest of the food will keep you coming back. The huge burritos are a favorite and come in all varieties. The restaurant is small and very family friendly. The wait staff is extremely nice, and both staff and patrons are lively and always seem to enjoy themselves. Try a Texas-style margarita, which comes in three sizes, and then order your entrée by the menu item number. Don't be thrown by the numbering system;

there really isn't one. You'll understand when you see the menu. The portions are big, the food is consistent, and the prices are very reasonable. This is easily one of the best Mexican restaurants in the region.

Farmers Markets

Haymarket's Farmers Market (Town Hall parking lot, 15000 Washington St., 703/753-2600, www.townofhaymarket.org, Apr.-Oct. Sat. 8am-2pm) is a Virginia-producer-only weekly market featuring fresh produce, specialty items, and baked goods.

ACCOMMODATIONS
$100-200

The **Hampton Inn Manassas** (7295 Williamson Blvd., Manassas, 703/369-1100, www.hamptoninn3.hilton.com, $132-193) is a reasonably priced hotel near I-66. It is approximately 20 minutes from Washington Dulles International Airport. The hotel offers 125 pleasant, clean rooms, a fitness center, and free Internet. Complimentary breakfast is available each morning.

The **Holiday Inn Manassas Battlefield** (10424 Balls Ford Rd., 571/292-5400, www.ihg.com, $128) is convenient to I-66 and the Manassas Battlefield. This modern hotel offers visitors 104 spacious guest rooms with a few extra touches such as nice hair products in the bathrooms and an attentive staff. Breakfast is included each morning with your stay. A pleasant indoor pool and hot tub and small fitness room are also on-site.

The **SpringHill Suites Potomac Mills** (14325 Crossing Pl., Woodbridge, 703/576-9000, www.marriott.com, $103-146) in Woodbridge is conveniently located off exit 158 of I-95 near the Potomac Mills shopping area. There are 98 spacious guest rooms. The hotel is modern, and the staff goes out of its way to make guests comfortable. Breakfast is included, and there is a pool, fitness center, and a free laundry facility on-site. Free high-speed Internet and parking are included.

A good value near I-95 is the **Country Inn & Suites by Radisson, Potomac Mills** (2621

Prince William Pkwy., Woodbridge, 703/492-6868, www.radissonhotels.com, $79-103). This hotel offers 100 nice guest rooms, complimentary coffee, tea, hot chocolate, and friendly service. The rooms have comfortable beds, microwaves, and refrigerators. Breakfast is included. There is also an indoor pool. The hotel is convenient for Potomac Mills shopping.

Camping

Prince William Forest Park (18170 Park Entrance Rd., Triangle, 703/221-7181, www.nps.gov/prwi, $26-80 plus $15 entrance fee) has two campgrounds (some sites can accommodate up to 40 people) and backcountry camping. One campground is open all year. Cabin camping is available in five cabins, four of which were built during the Great Depression and are now listed in the National Register of Historic Places. Cabin rentals are available May-October and can accommodate between 4 and 10 people ($40-60).

INFORMATION AND SERVICES

The **Historic Manassas Visitor Center** (9431 West St., Manassas, 703/361-6599, daily 9am-5pm) is housed in an early 20th-century train depot in the center of town. Another good resource for Manassas information is www.visitmanassas.org.

For additional information on Prince William County in general, visit www.visitpwc.com.

GETTING AROUND

The **OmniRide** (703/730-6664, www.omniride.com, times vary by location, $1.55) is a local bus service in Prince William County. The service is unique because buses are able to alter their routes to accommodate additional service locations when there is available time in their schedules.

Loudoun County

It is hard to believe that at one time Loudoun County was considered the northwestern frontier of Virginia. Loudoun became a county in 1757 during the French and Indian War. It was named after John Campbell, the fourth earl of Loudoun (of Ayrshire, Scotland), who was the commander in chief of the British and colonial troops. Leesburg became the county seat around 1760. When the British invaded Washington DC during the War of 1812, the county clerk in Loudoun hid the Constitution and the Declaration of Independence in a family vault in a home just southeast of Leesburg.

President James Monroe had a home in Loudoun County called Oak Hill. Located in Aldie (13 miles south of Leesburg), it was there that he wrote the Monroe Doctrine in 1823. Oak Hill is currently a private residence and not open to the public.

Loudoun was a divided county during the Civil War. Sitting on the border between the North and the South, it became a thoroughfare of sorts for both Union and Confederate troops. Communities in Loudoun were often stripped of their horses and resources as the troops came through, leaving many residents in dire straits. Some residents began to fight back as members of John Singleton Mosby's partisan rangers, and Mosby became known as the "Gray Ghost of the Confederacy" after experiencing success with his hit-and-run strategy.

After the war, the railroad expanded west through Loudoun and new communities sprang up. The county saw the development of many farms and summer homes for Washingtonians. In the 1960s, the county began to blossom into a full-fledged suburb of Washington DC and experienced a population growth of 600 percent during a 40-year span. Today substantial growth continues,

NORTHERN VIRGINIA
LOUDOUN COUNTY

and many homes and businesses are built in the county yearly, making it one of the wealthiest and most populous counties in the state.

Visitors to Loudoun County will find large housing developments and strip malls, but despite incredible growth, the area is also known as "Virginia hunt country" for its history of foxhunting, and many wineries grace its rolling terrain. The historic towns of Leesburg and Middleburg have maintained their charm and should be high on the list of places to visit.

GETTING THERE AND AROUND

Loudoun County Transit (703/771-5665, www.loudoun.gov) provides commuter bus service from Loudoun County to Washington DC, the Pentagon, Crystal City, and Rosslyn (Arlington) for $11 one-way and to the Wiehle-Reston Metrorail station for $1.50 one-way. Service begins at multiple park-and-ride lots throughout Loudoun County. For a map of parking lot locations, visit www.loudoun.gov.

LEESBURG

Leesburg is a historic town 45 miles west of Washington DC and 15 minutes from Washington Dulles International Airport. Its roots stretch back more than 250 years, but this bustling town has seen tremendous growth over the past two decades as suburban sprawl found its way into Loudoun County and then continued to explode. Spend a day or a weekend exploring historic downtown Leesburg, watch a point-to-point horse race sponsored by the Loudoun Hunt, or spend an afternoon shopping at the Leesburg Outlets.

Sights
HISTORIC DOWNTOWN LEESBURG

Leesburg was established in 1758 and is the seat of Loudoun County. At the outbreak of the Civil War, the town was prospering and had approximately 1,700 residents. Leesburg is just two miles south of the Potomac River, which at the time divided the North and South. During the war, the town suffered

frequent raids and fighting in its streets, and it changed hands nearly 150 times. Following the war, Leesburg's proximity to Washington DC helped it recover economically, and it eventually became a primary stop for the railroad. Today, visitors to **Historic Downtown Leesburg** (www.visitloudoun.org) can see beautiful 18th- and 19th-century architecture, walk its brick sidewalks, visit many unique shops, eat in trendy restaurants, and partake in special events and festivals. Blue tourist information signs direct the way to the **visitors center** (112-G South St., 703/771-2617, daily 9am-5pm), which is a great place to begin exploration.

OATLANDS HISTORIC HOUSE AND GARDENS

A National Trust Historic Site and National Historic Landmark, **Oatlands Historic House and Gardens** (20850 Oatlands Plantation Ln., 703/777-3174, www.oatlands.org, mid-Apr.-Dec. daily 10am-5pm, guided tours Thurs.-Sun., house $15, active military $12, gardens only $10) is a lovely example of a Virginia plantation. Just six miles south of downtown Leesburg, Oatlands was built in the early 19th century and was a thriving 3,408-acre wheat plantation. It was owned by George Carter, a descendant of one of Virginia's most well-known families. A large federal-style mansion was started near the southern border of the property but ended up being finished in the 1820s in the Greek revival style. Many outbuildings were added, including a smokehouse, greenhouse, and barn. The plantation prospered until the time of the Civil War, but the family's wealth declined after the war and the plantation became a girls' school and boardinghouse.

In 1897, the mansion and 60 acres were sold to *Washington Post* founder Stilson Hutchins, although he never actually lived there. In 1903, the property was purchased by William and Edith Eustis, who were avid outdoors lovers and saw the potential for restoring the

1: Oatlands Historic House **2:** Morven Park

home and neglected gardens and using the property for foxhunting. In 1964, after Edith's passing, her daughters donated the mansion (furnished) and 261 acres to the National Trust for Historic Preservation.

Oatlands is now open to the public April-December. Forty-minute interpretive guided tours of the first floor are available, and self-guided tours of the second floor are encouraged. They also feature the Smokehouse exhibit, which teaches about the lives of the enslaved individuals who are part of the estate's history.

The formal terraced Oatlands Gardens and grounds are open to visitors. These 200-year-old gardens were designed in the Tidewater Virginia style and have multiple terraces carved into a hillside. Box hedges, trees, vegetables, shrubs, and flowers are part of the plantings, and the beautiful stonework was quarried locally. There are also many sculptures in the gardens (thanks to the Eustises' son-in-law, who was the first director of the National Gallery of Art). Be sure to take in the wonderful view of Bull Run Mountain.

Many events are held at Oatlands throughout the year; check their website for information. There's a gift shop on-site but no food facilities. However, there are plenty of places to enjoy a relaxing picnic on the grounds.

★ MORVEN PARK

Morven Park (17195 Southern Planter Ln., 703/777-2414, www.morvenpark.org, grounds open daily 8am-5pm, free) is a special place in Loudoun County. This 1,200-acre estate was home to Virginia governor Westmoreland Davis, who served as governor 1918-1922, for 40 years. The site now offers the original mansion (Governor's Residence), two museums, an equestrian center, historic gardens, sports fields, hiking trails, and beautiful country scenery. Many public events are held at Morven Park throughout the year including Civil War reenactments, equestrian competitions, and festivals. It is also the "forever home" to pardoned White House turkeys.

The Governor's Residence is worth a trip itself. It evolved from a fieldstone farmhouse built in 1781 into a beautiful turn-of-the-20th-century mansion. The stately home with its white exterior and columned facade sits on a rise surrounded by a blanket of pristine lawn. It supports an unusual mix of architectural styles that includes a Greek Revival portico, a Jacobean dining room, French drawing room, and a renaissance great hall. The furnishings are also an eclectic mix that includes 16th-century Belgian tapestries and pieces from the Renaissance and neo-Renaissance. A terraced, formal garden sits just behind the house and can be toured at leisure with admission to the Governor's Residence.

Other museums on-site include the Carriage Museum, which houses an assortment of antique vehicles, and the Museum of Hounds & Hunting (inside the Governor's Residence), which preserves art and memorabilia of foxhunting in Virginia. All-inclusive tours of the Mansion and Carriage Museum are available (Thurs.-Mon. noon-5pm, adults $10, children 6-12 $5, children 5 and under free). No ticket is needed for the Museum of Hounds & Hunting.

Other points of interest include information on Morven Park during the Civil War (offered on the grounds through permanent historical markers and periodic living-history programs, free) and the beautiful parklike grounds surrounding the mansion (free).

The equestrian center at Morven Park (41580 Tutt Ln.) hosts local, regional, national, and international equestrian events including horse trials, schooling shows, trail rides, clinics, polo events, races, and dressage events. It includes indoor and outdoor arenas, a series of stunning cross-country courses, and sporting fields. Morven Park is two miles north of downtown Leesburg.

LOUDOUN MUSEUM

The Loudoun Museum (16 Loudoun St. SW, 703/777-7427, www.loudounmuseum. org, Fri.-Sun. 10am-4pm, free) is dedicated to Loudoun County's rich and diverse heritage.

It offers educational exhibits that are a little different from other museums since the artifacts displayed are authentic items formerly owned by county residents. The museum's goal is to tell the stories of the people from the county. Exhibits include original documents, photographs, maps, furniture, and toys. There are also exhibits geared specifically toward kids.

GEORGE C. MARSHALL HOUSE

The **George C. Marshall House** (312 E. Market St., 703/777-1301, www. georgecmarshall.org, Sat. 10am-5pm, Sun. 1pm-5pm, adults $15, seniors $10, students $5, active military free) was the home of General George C. Marshall, Chief of Staff of the Army, Special Envoy to China, Secretary of State, Secretary of Defense, and President of the American Red Cross. He was also a Nobel Peace Prize winner in 1953. The home sits on nearly four acres in the Historic District and is a National Historic Landmark. The Marshalls lived in the home between 1941 and 1959, and 90 percent of the belongings in the home were owned by them.

LEESBURG ANIMAL PARK

A fun place to take the kids is the **Leesburg Animal Park** (19270 James Monroe Hwy., 703/433-0002, www.leesburganimalpark. com, Tues.-Sun. 10am-5pm, adults $14.95, children and seniors $10.95, children under 2 free), a 21-acre family petting zoo. It offers an animal-petting and -feeding area with residents such as llamas, bunnies, deer, lambs, pigs, and camels and exotic animal exhibits with animals such as lemurs, gibbons, zebras, porcupines, and tortoises. Kids of all ages can participate in many park activities. They offer pony and camel rides, wagon rides, and other activities, too. The favorite event of the year at the park is their **Pumpkin Village** (www.pumpkinfestleesburg.com), which is open daily between late September and early November. Visitors can enjoy a kids' hay maze, slides, an obstacle course, face and pumpkin painting, and many more seasonal activities.

THOMAS BALCH LIBRARY

The **Thomas Balch Library** (208 W. Market St., 703/737-7195, www.leesburgva.gov, hours vary daily) features collections on Loudoun County, Virginia history, genealogy, military history, and the American Civil War. The library is operated by the town of Leesburg. The library is also a designated Underground Railroad research site.

BALL'S BLUFF BATTLEFIELD REGIONAL PARK

Ball's Bluff Battlefield Regional Park (Ball's Bluff Rd., 703/737-7800, www. novaparks.com, daily dawn-dusk, free) preserves the site where the first Civil War engagement in Loudoun County took place, the Battle of Ball's Bluff, in October 1861. Visitors can enjoy seven miles of marked hiking trails and read interpretive signs that describe the battle. The park surrounds **Ball's Bluff National Cemetery,** the third-smallest national cemetery in the country. A small monument dedicated to a Confederate soldier who was killed in the battle, Clinton Hatcher, may be found in the cemetery. A second memorial is dedicated to the memory of a Union colonel, Edward D. Baker, who was also killed in the battle. Baker was a U.S. Senator at the time he was killed. Efforts are underway to restore the battlefield to its original appearance. Guided tours are available by appointment.

WINERIES

With more than 40 wineries, Loudoun County boasts more wineries than any other county in Virginia. More information can be found at www.visitloudoun.org and the county's Wine Growers Association website (www. loudounwine.com). **Point to Point Winery & Vineyard Tours** are also available through **Point to Point Limousine** (703/771-8100, www.pointtopointlimo.com, from $40 per person).

Stone Tower Winery (19925 Hogback Mountain Rd, 703/777-2797, www. stonetowerwinery.com, Thurs.-Mon. 11am-6pm, tastings $20) is a stunningly beautiful and large winery that sits on over 200 acres. The property consists of multiple buildings including two tasting rooms (one is family friendly and the other is 21 and over). There is also an upscale picnic area. The wines are delicious and the staff delightful. Specialty tours and tastings are offered, and this is a great place to plan an event or bring a group (groups of nine or more require a reservation). A tip from this white-wine lover: Try the sauvignon blanc.

Red-wine lovers shouldn't miss a tasting at **Fabbioli Cellars** (15669 Limestone School Rd., 703/771-1197, www.fabbioliwines.com, daily 11am-5pm, tastings $15). This small, family-owned boutique vineyard and winery grows and makes high-quality red wines (and only red wines). Tastings include a food pairing (chocolate or savory). The staff is very knowledgeable and goes out of its way to make everyone feel welcome. This is an ideal outing for a small group. Groups with more than eight people should make a reservation.

Recreation

GOLF

The **Raspberry Falls Golf and Hunt Club** (41601 Raspberry Dr., 703/779-2555, www.raspberryfalls.com, $35-95) is a beautiful and challenging 18-hole, par-72 course that is open to the public. The award-winning course was designed by Gary Player to evoke the feeling of the British Isles. This is evident in the rolling terrain, stone walls, rambling streams, and bunkers. The course has elevated tee boxes and lush bent grass greens. The course is set against the backdrop of the Catoctin Mountains, and holes 3 and 18 have particularly nice views. This is one of the most popular daily-fee courses in Northern Virginia.

PARKS

If you're looking for a nice short hike with good views of the Potomac River, visit **Red Rock Wilderness Overlook Regional Park** (43098 Edwards Ferry Rd., 703/779-9372, www.novaparks.com, free). This 67-acre park is four miles east of downtown Leesburg

and offers a two-mile loop trail through the woods and over hills to a panoramic view of the river. Trail terrain varies from moderate to strenuous in some places. Dogs are allowed on leashes, and there are no restroom facilities in the park.

Entertainment and Events

The **Loudoun Hunt Point to Point Races** are held annually in mid-April at the historic **Oatlands Historic House and Gardens** (20850 Oatlands Plantation Ln., 703/728-0545, www.loudounhunt.com, $40 per car). The races were first held in 1966 and are known for featuring challenging timber and hurdle courses that test the abilities of the local and global competitors.

Classic-car enthusiasts won't want to miss the annual **Leesburg Classic Car Show** (www.leesburgva.gov, free). This event is usually held in May and takes place in downtown Leesburg. More than 200 classic cars are on display, including street rods and muscle cars. The event is free to spectators.

Music lovers will enjoy the free **Acoustic on the Green** (Town Hall Green, 25 W. Market St., www.leesburgva.gov) summer concert series in downtown Leesburg. Concerts are held on Saturday evenings 7pm-8:30pm June-August.

The **Leesburg Air Show** (1000 Sycolin Rd., www.leesburgairshow.com, free) is a much-anticipated free annual air show that is held at the **Leesburg Executive Airport** at the end of September. The show features many types of planes, including experimental aircraft and warbirds from World War II. The show has air performances and tarmac attractions, and food is available for purchase.

Shopping

Historic Downtown Leesburg offers antiques stores, art galleries, and other specialty shops. The primary shopping area is on Market, Loudoun, and King Streets.

Since 1998, the **Black Shutter Antique Center** (1 Loudoun St., SE, 703/443-9579, www.blackshutterantiques.com, Mon.-Sat.,

10:30am-5:30pm, Sun., 12pm-5pm) has offered 20 rooms of antique merchandise in a historic 19th century home. They feature art, furniture, maps, clothing, and books.

In recent years, Leesburg has become synonymous with outlets. People travel from all over the region to shop at the **Leesburg Corner Premium Outlets** (241 Fort Evans Rd., 703/737-3071, www.premiumoutlets. com). The mall houses 110 outlets including stores for designer fashion, shoes, children's clothes, leather, jewelry, housewares, and gifts. There is also a food court, and other national chain restaurants are nearby.

The **Village at Leesburg** (1602 Village Market Blvd., 571/291-2288, www. villageatleesburg.com) is a modern, 57-acre open-air shopping plaza with upscale retailers and restaurants. The anchor store is **Wegmans** food market.

The **Dulles Town Center** (21100 Dulles Town Circle, Dulles, 703/404-7120, www. shopdullestowncenter.com) offers many national-brand stores and restaurants with ample free parking. It is located at the intersection of Route 7 and Route 28, 10 miles east of Leesburg.

Food
AMERICAN
One part wine-tasting, one part farm-to-table experience, **The Wine Kitchen** (7 S. King St., 703/777-9463, www.thewinekitchen.com, Tues.-Thurs. 11:30am-9pm, Fri.-Sat. 11:30am-10:30pm, Sun. 11:30am-9pm, $10-37) is a small, cozy restaurant with a modern vibe. Wine is served with clever and humorous description cards, and the food selection is interesting and beautifully presented. The staff is very knowledgeable about the wine and food and makes excellent recommendations. If you are unsure what to order, try a wine flight.

Tuscarora Mill (203 Harrison St., 703/771-9300, www.tuskies.com, Mon.-Thurs. 11am-10pm, Fri.-Sat. 11am-midnight, Sun. 10am-9pm, $20-48) is a local institution in Leesburg. The food is consistent and delicious, and the warm, historic ambience is inviting.

The owners of this establishment really care about the food and guests at their restaurants (they own another great restaurant in nearby Purcellville called **Magnolias at the Mill,** which is equally wonderful). There's an informal bar area to grab a casual drink (they have a great wine list), and the dining area is good for groups. This is a good place for a date or to visit with friends. Tuscarora Mill is also known for their beer- and wine-pairing dinners. They are fantastic. The chef goes out of his way to prepare delicious and unexpected combinations. Check the website for a schedule.

Lightfoot Restaurant (11 N. King St., 703/771-2233, www.lightfootrestaurant. com, Mon.-Thurs. 11:30am-11pm, Fri.-Sat. 11:30am-midnight, Sun. 11am-9pm, $15-33) serves contemporary food in a great atmosphere. The building is a restored turn-of-the-20th-century bank building with many interesting and original architectural features and artifacts as well as original French posters from the 1920s. There are two bars, one with a grand piano, and an open kitchen with a chef's table. If you are unsure what to order, the onion-and-field-mushroom soup, fried green tomatoes with shrimp, crab cakes, and filet are all excellent choices. There is a private parking lot in back of the restaurant and street parking out front.

ITALIAN
The popular **Fireworks Pizza** (201 Harrison St., 703/779-8400, www.fireworkspizza.com, opens daily at 11am, $10-19) restaurant housed in the former Leesburg Freight Depot has fantastic pizza (try the Smokey Blue Pizza) and a great beer selection. The sandwiches are good too. The ambience is warm and friendly, and on nice days, the porch adds much-needed seating. If you come on the weekend, expect a wait. Great food, a fun vibe, and reasonable prices make this place a gem in the heart of historic Leesburg. Their patio is dog friendly.

TREATS
When your sweet tooth is acting up, stop in **Mom's Apple Pie** (220 Loudoun St. SE,

703/771-8590, www.momsapplepieco.com, Mon.-Fri. 7:30am-6:30pm, Sat. 8am-6pm, Sun. 10am-5pm), at the fork in the road between Loudoun Street and Market Street. As the name implies, they have fantastic pie, cookies, cupcakes, bread, and other baked goods. A Leesburg tradition, this establishment is known for baking natural, preservative-free pies. They even grow much of their own fruit.

FARMERS MARKETS
Leesburg hosts several great farmers markets featuring local producers such as **Shenandoah Seasonal** (www.shenandoahseasonal.com) from Boyce, Virginia.

The **Leesburg Saturday Farmers Market** (Virginia Village Shopping Center on Catoctin Circle SE, 540/454-8089, www.loudounfarmersmarkets.org, Nov.-Apr. 9am-noon, May-Oct. 8am-noon) is open year-round. There is also a seasonal Wednesday market in the same location (May-mid-Sept. 4pm-7pm).

The **One Loudoun Farmers Market** (Atwater Dr., Ashburn, www.eatloco.org) is also open year-round, Saturdays 9am-1pm.

The **Brambleton Market** (Brambleton Plaza, Brambleton, www.eatloco.org) is held seasonally on Sundays 9am-1pm.

Accommodations
There is a wide assortment of national chain hotels in Leesburg. Many are on the newer side as part of the rapid growth in Loudoun County in recent decades. If you're looking for someplace unique, there are several good options.

$100-200
The Country Comfort Bed and Breakfast (19724 Evergreen Mills Rd., 703/926-6994, www.countrycomfortbedandbreakfast.com, $175-200) offers two suites near downtown Leesburg that are more like apartments. Guests are treated to a scrumptious home-cooked breakfast of their choice delivered each morning. Refrigerators are stocked with sodas, water, juice, and snacks, which are available throughout the stay. The suites have king beds, private bathrooms, a work area, high-speed Internet, and a living/dining area. The Evergreen Suite also has a private deck.

$200-300
The beautiful **Stone Gables Bed and Breakfast** (19077 Loudoun Orchard Rd., 703/303-6364, www.stonegables-bb.com, $225-250) offers four luxurious guest rooms in a rare, fully renovated, stone gabled barn. The property includes 10 acres, a pool, and close proximity to the W&OD Bike Trail. A full hot breakfast is included.

Lansdowne Resort (44050 Woodridge Pkwy., 703/729-8400, www.lansdowneresort.com, $163-699) has 305 guest rooms in the Potomac River valley, approximately four miles east of Leesburg. Amenities at the resort include a golf course, spa, health club, tennis courts, indoor and outdoor pools, and on-site restaurants. This resort offers beautiful grounds, a great view, and a quiet atmosphere. It is a popular location for business conferences.

Information and Services
Visitor information on Leesburg can be found at www.leesburgva.gov and www.visitloudoun.org, or visit the **Loudoun County Visitors Center** (112-G South St., 703/771-2617, www.visitloudoun.org, daily 9am-5pm).

MIDDLEBURG
Middleburg is an oasis in Northern Virginia just 42 miles west of Washington DC. Its stunning landscape, rich Civil War history, and beautifully restored buildings make it a very special place for visitors to explore. The area truly has the look of the English countryside: ribbons of low stone walls wind across lush pastures, and acres and acres of pristine

---

1: downtown Leesburg **2:** Lightfoot Restaurant
3: Mom's Apple Pie

The Gray Ghost

Throughout American Civil War history, the operatives of one man in particular continue to fascinate scholars and history buffs alike. Colonel John Singleton Mosby, known as "the Gray Ghost," was a free-thinking man whose dislike for routine military life eventually led him to develop an independent guerrilla group that made forays throughout Loudoun County.

An attorney by profession and a graduate of the University of Virginia, Mosby joined his local militia unit as a private soldier in 1861. With the outbreak of the Civil War, his cavalry unit joined the Confederate forces. Mosby's strength was in scouting and patrolling duties, and he became a member of J. E. B. Stuart's personal staff.

In 1863, with nine men from his regiment, Mosby began guerrilla attacks on isolated Union posts in Northern Virginia and Maryland. Mosby led lightning-quick cavalry strikes aimed at disrupting supply lines and communication.

Mosby's men swelled in numbers and soon became known as "Mosby's Rangers." Many of Mosby's Rangers were volunteers who had never had any formal military training. Many brought their own uniforms and weapons. Their two most important items were their pistols and their horses. They often assembled near a blacksmith's shop so their horses' feet could be tended to.

When things became dangerous, the Rangers would melt into the night. They'd stay with friends or family, or simply camp out in the hills. Loudoun became known as Mosby's Confederacy, and Union commanders were furious with his success. Because of their guerrilla tactics and tendency to keep their spoils, the Rangers were often viewed by Federal officials as criminals rather than soldiers.

On March 9, 1863, Mosby led 29 Rangers through Federal lines at the Fairfax Courthouse and captured General Edwin Stoughton, 33 men, and 58 horses. A sack of gold and silver coins worth $350,000 was also taken, but Mosby was forced to bury it when chased by Union troops. Allegedly, he was never able to recover the loot, and it is still said to be buried between two tall pine trees in a shallow hole between Haymarket and New Baltimore.

By April 1865, Mosby had been promoted to colonel, had been wounded seven times, and was in command of eight companies. His last raid was on April 10, the day after Robert E. Lee surrendered at Appomattox. At that time, he had more than 700 men in his command.

After the war, Mosby continued to practice law in Warrenton. Mosby wrote two books while serving terms as U.S. consul to Hong Kong and assistant attorney in the Justice Department. They are titled *Mosby's War Reminiscences and Stuart's Cavalry Campaigns (1887)* and *Stuart's Cavalry in the Gettysburg Campaign (1908)*. He died on May 30, 1916, in Washington DC.

farmland blanket the foothills of the Blue Ridge Mountains. Middleburg has over 160 historic buildings, and nearly every one has a unique story. Some housed troops during the Civil War, others were shot at, and some hid well-known figures such as John Singleton Mosby (aka the Gray Ghost) and his band of raiders.

Middleburg is horse and hunt country. Many of its residents have family histories in equine sports competitions, and many U.S. Olympic riders live and train in the Middleburg area. As such, equine events and festivals attract visitors from all over the country.

Sights
THE VILLAGE OF MIDDLEBURG

Middleburg was developed in the mid-1700s and was later named for its location midway between Alexandria and Winchester. The town (with a local population of around 850 people) was established in 1787 and has many Civil War roots. It is beautifully preserved as a quaint, colonial island in an otherwise busy Northern Virginia. The main attraction is the village of Middleburg itself. This charming, historic section is lined with family-owned shops, inns, and restaurants and is well worth a day trip from Washington DC or other parts of Virginia and Maryland. Take a stroll down

Washington Street, and you'll feel miles and possibly centuries away from the busy nation's capital, as you become part of the historic landscape. The people are friendly, the pace is relaxed, and the merchandise is often rare and unusual.

NATIONAL SPORTING LIBRARY & MUSEUM

The **National Sporting Library & Museum** (102 The Plains Rd., 540/687-6542, www. nationalsporting.org, Wed.-Sun. 10am-5pm, library free, museum adults $10, youth 13-18 $8, children 12 and under free, seniors 65 and over $8) is a beautiful site dedicated to preserving equestrian, angling, and field sports literature, art, and culture. It is a research facility and art museum (located in two buildings) with more than 24,000 books and pieces of art. Be sure to look closely at the beautiful, haunting horse statue in front of the library. It is a memorial to the horses who lost their lives in the Civil War.

MOUNT DEFIANCE CIDERY & DISTILLERY

Mount Defiance Cidery & Distillery (207 W. Washington St., 540/687-8100, www. mtdefiance.com, Tues.-Sun. noon-6pm, tastings $10-15) is located right on West Washington Street. They create small-batch, handcrafted, classic hard cider and spirits. Their cidery produces farmhouse blends and a single-variety cider but is also known for unique infused and co-fermented ciders (honey, five-pepper, blueberry, etc.). The distillery focuses on classic spirits from both colonial America and Europe, such as apple brandy, apple liqueur, rum, and absinthe. They have a second location called the **Mount Defiance Cider Barn** (495 E. Washington St.).

ALDIE MILL HISTORIC PARK

The **Aldie Mill Historic Park** (39401 John Mosby Hwy., Aldie, 703/327-9777, www. novaparks.com, mid-Apr.-mid-Nov. Sat.-Sun. noon-5pm, free), just east of Middleburg, is a

fully operational restored gristmill that dates back to 1807. Visitors can witness live grinding demonstrations, and tours of the mill are available. The mill is a popular location for weddings and events.

WINERIES AND VINEYARDS

Middleburg is on the edge of Virginia wine country and home to a number of outstanding wineries, vineyards, and tasting rooms that are worth visiting for their relaxing atmosphere and, of course, wine.

The beautiful **Boxwood Winery** (2042 Burrland Ln., 540/687-8778, www. boxwoodwinery.com, Nov.-Apr. Fri.-Sun. 11am-6pm, May-Oct. Thurs.-Sun. 11am-6pm) is owned by former Washington Redskins owner John Kent Cooke. They produce red and white wine in the Bordeaux tradition. Tastings by the glass or flight are available by appointment at the winery in Middleburg, but they also have several tasting rooms throughout the Washington DC area (consult their website for current locations).

Chrysalis Vineyards (39025 John Mosby Hwy., Middleburg, 540/687-8222, www. chrysaliswine.com, Mon-Thurs. noon-6pm, Fri.-Sat. noon-8pm, Sun. noon-7pm, tastings $15 for 10 wines) is located just west of Aldie on Route 50 in the Ag District Center. They specialize in unusual French and Spanish grape varietals and also in the native Virginia Norton grape.

Greenhill Winery and Vineyards (23595 Winery Ln., 540/687-6968, www. greenhillvineyards.com, May-Sept. Mon.-Thurs. noon-6pm, Fri-Sun. noon-7pm, Oct.-Apr. daily noon-6pm, tastings $14) is a beautiful destination winery. They offer a tasting room, club house, and farm store. This is an adults-only winery.

Recreation
HORSEBACK RIDING

It seems like everyone in Middleburg owns a pair of riding boots. Most of the farms are privately owned and don't offer riding to the public, but if you are interested in giving it

The War Horse

There is something beautiful and haunting about the three-quarters life-size bronze sculpture that stands in the courtyard of the National Sporting Library & Museum in Middleburg. It depicts a thin, exhausted, war-weary Civil War horse wearing authentic Civil War-style tack.

This sculpture was created in the mind of Paul Mellon, a well-known American philanthropist, Thoroughbred racehorse breeder, and coheir to the Mellon Bank fortune who lived in nearby Upperville. Mellon was profoundly moved by Robert F. O'Neill Jr.'s book *The Cavalry Battles of Aldie, Middleburg and Upperville, June 10-27, 1863,* which told of human and horse bloodshed during a 17-day period in the American Civil War. After reading the book, Mellon felt compelled to do something for all the horses that died during the war.

To that point no monuments had been erected to honor the war's tremendous equine losses. The idea of a memorial came up one day while Mellon was speaking with the director and others at the National Sporting Library. The idea grew into a vision for an extraordinary bronze sculpture to honor all mules and horses from both the Union and Confederate armies.

Extensive research was conducted on the number of equine fatalities and also on the type of leather tack and gear they wore during battle. Mellon then took the idea to sculptor Tessa Pullan from Rutland, England, whom he had worked with earlier on a statue of his 1993 Kentucky Derby winner, Sea Hero.

A tremendous amount of time was spent consulting with many sources to create a design that was completely authentic. An example is the horse's stance, with his back leg bent, which is how horses stand when they are tired. Another is the scabbard worn by the horse. It is shown without a sword to indicate that the horse's rider was lost in battle. Care was also taken to fit the horse with gear that could have been from either the Union or Confederate side.

More extensive research showed that a realistic estimate of equine losses during the war was between 1,350,000 and 1,500,000, an astonishing and unsettling number. This number is reflected in the inscription at the bottom of the statue.

The library's Civil War horse was completed in 1997 and is now one of the most visited landmarks in the area. Local residents feel a personal attachment to the statue and often place horse blankets over it when the weather is cold.

a try, **Foxrock Stables** (37744 Featherbed Farm Ln., 703/346-4029, www.foxrockstables.com) offers lessons and summer camps.

BIKING

Road cycling and mountain biking are very popular in Middleburg. The beautiful and rolling country roads draw bikers from all over Northern Virginia, and the incredible scenery keeps them coming back. This has caused some friction between the local residents and visiting cyclists. The roads in Middleburg do not have bike lanes, so traffic is shared between bikes and cars. Although there is little traffic compared to the rest of the region, the hairpin turns and low shoulders can create a dangerous situation for both drivers and cyclists. Use extreme caution when biking in Middleburg and be sensitive to traffic. A good resource for finding bike routes in the area is www.mapmyride.com.

HOT-AIR BALLOONING

For high-flying adventure, try a hot-air balloon ride with **Balloons Unlimited** (23217 Meetinghouse Ln., Aldie, 703/327-0444, www.balloonsunlimited.com, adults $225, children 12 and under $125). Rides begin in several locations depending on the weather. Two flights are scheduled daily.

Entertainment and Events

CHRISTMAS IN MIDDLEBURG

One of Loudoun County's largest annual events is **Christmas in Middleburg** (Washington St., 571/278-5658, www.christmasinmiddleburg.org), held annually on the first Saturday in December. This day-long celebration in horse country includes a unique parade with more than 700 horses, llamas, alpacas, and hounds. An assortment of troops, bands, and floats also join the march down Washington Street along with fire trucks and, of course, Santa in a horse-drawn coach. The final phase of the celebration is a wine crawl where adults can enjoy samples from area vineyards and food in local restaurants.

HUNT COUNTRY STABLE TOUR

The **Hunt Country Stable Tour** (www.trinityupperville.org/hunt-country-stable-tour, $30-35, children under 10 free) is a 60-plus-year tradition in Middleburg and neighboring Upperville. This self-driven stable tour takes visitors through some of the most impressive private horse stables in the region. The tour is held over Memorial Day weekend and includes Thoroughbred breeding farms, foxhunting barns, and show hunter barns. A remarkable experience for horse lovers and nonequestrians alike, this is a great way to spend a day in the beautiful Virginia countryside.

UPPERVILLE COLT & HORSE SHOW

The **Upperville Colt & Horse Show** (Upperville Show Grounds, on Rte. 50 between Middleburg and Upperville, 540/687-5740, www.upperville.com, parking $45 for the week) is the longest-running horse show in the country. It was founded in 1853 and is held each year at the **Upperville Show Grounds.** More than 2,000 horses and riders compete each year over seven days at the beginning of June under towering oak trees in a beautiful storybook setting. Young riders on ponies and Olympic and World Cup riders and horses are all part of this well-known event.

THE MIDDLEBURG SPRING RACES AND THE VIRGINIA FALL RACES

The **Middleburg Spring Races** (www.middleburgspringraces.com) and **The Virginia Fall Races** (www.vafallraces.com) are two annual point-to-point (steeplechase) horse races with a long tradition in Middleburg. Both are held at **Glenwood Park** (36800 Glenwood Park Ln.), less than two miles north of downtown Middleburg. The spring races are in April, and the fall races are in October.

VIRGINIA GOLD CUP RACES

The premier event at the premier equestrian venue in Northern Virginia is the **Virginia Gold Cup Races** (540/347-2612, www.vagoldcup.com) at Great Meadows. This event is held eight miles south of downtown Middleburg in a nearby village called The Plains. The grand point-to-point race is held the first Saturday in May (rain or shine) and brings out the best gourmet tailgates in town. The day of racing dates back to 1922, and now more than 50,000 spectators from all over the Washington DC area descend on hunt country to enjoy this festive eating, drinking, people-watching, and yes, horse-watching event. The race itself is extremely demanding, with horses running more than four miles and jumping over four- to five-foot solid rail fences. The **International Gold Cup Races** are held at the same venue in October. Tickets to both events must be purchased well in advance.

Shopping

The village of Middleburg is an elegant and

historic shopping area right on Route 50 (John S. Mosby Highway). Unique boutiques housed in beautiful old buildings line the streets and offer goods from all over the world. Most stores are individually owned and operated specialty shops with hand-selected merchandise. It is obvious the owners take great pride in these establishments.

Food

AMERICAN

The Red Fox Inn and Tavern (2 E. Washington St., 540/687-6301, www.redfox. com, Mon.-Fri. 8am-10am and 5pm-9pm, Sat. 11am-2pm and 5pm-9pm, Sun. 11am-2pm and 5pm-8pm, $14-60) is a historic tavern in the heart of Middleburg that serves traditional Virginia-style food using cooking techniques such as roasting, smoking, and braising. Hearty breakfasts, relaxing brunch, and cozy candlelight dinners draw people to the tavern from all over the region. The stone fireplace and handcrafted furnishings are a good complement to the seasonal menus featuring traditional Southern and Virginia ingredients. If you've never tried peanut soup, this is the place to order it. The wine list includes both imported and domestic wines and includes many local Virginia wines. The restaurant offers great ambience, consistently good food, and friendly service. There are several additional dining spaces on the property, including the **Night Fox Pub.**

If you're looking for breakfast, a gourmet sandwich, or a picnic to take with you to a winery, or you need to purchase gourmet ingredients, the **Market Salamander** (200 W. Washington St., 540/687-9720, www. marketsalamander.com, Wed.-Thurs. 8am-2pm, Fri.-Sun. 8am-4pm, $8-21) is the place to visit. It is a chef's market, complete with an in-house café, custom cake bakery, and catering services. The market sells produce, prime aged meat, seafood, artisanal cheese, house-baked bread, pastries, wine, and a variety of imported packaged goods. The focal point in the market is the open display kitchen where the chef's daily selections are prepared.

Their menu includes items such as soup, sandwiches, burgers, and crab cakes.

If a local pub is more your style, stop in the **Red Horse Tavern** (118 W. Washington St., 540/687-6443, www.redhorsetavern.net, daily 11am-10pm, $9-15). They offer pub fare and a large patio.

ENGLISH

About eight miles west of Middleburg on Route 50 is **Hunter's Head Tavern** (9048 John S. Mosby Hwy. [Rte. 50], Upperville, 540/592-9020, www.huntersheadtavern. com, Mon.-Sat. 11:30am-9:30pm, Sun. 11am-9:30pm, $11-36). This authentic English pub is in a cute, old crooked house right on the road with a red English telephone box out front. Hunter's Head offers local organic farm meat and produce and was the first restaurant in the country to receive a certified humane designation. Original log cabin walls, "settled" floors, and mismatched wooden tables are all part of the charm. Read the extensive menu off the chalkboard and place your order at the window next to the bar (even if you have reservations, which is advised). The menu includes hearty pub fare and fine-dining options, and the offerings change frequently. If the macaroni and cheese is on the menu, it's worth ordering in spite of the calories. The calamari is also good and very tender. Hunter's Head Tavern has good beer on tap as well, and the desserts are fabulous, so save room.

FRENCH

The Conservatory at Goodstone (36205 Snake Hill Rd., 540/687-3333, www. goodstone.com, Wed.-Sun. 5:30pm-9pm, $50-75, prix fixe menu $79 for two courses, $89 for three, chef's tasting menu $115) deserves accolades. This small restaurant, located in the **Goodstone Inn,** serves outstanding "modern American French country cuisine" in a superb country setting. The chef only uses fresh ingredients, and many of them are sourced from the inn's private organic herb and vegetable gardens. Sample menu items include Icelandic cod, beef tenderloin, and lamb loin.

It is a charming place full of simple elegance for a special date or to just get away from it all.

SEAFOOD

Good seafood and a lively atmosphere can be found at the **King Street Oyster Bar** (1 E. Washington St., 540/883-3156, www.kingstreetoysterbar.com, Mon.-Thurs. 11am-9:30pm, Fri.-Sat. 11am-11pm, Sun. 10:30am-9:30pm, $7-59). This small and very popular restaurant is a fun place to grab a drink and eat good oysters. Don't be surprised if you end up making friends with the people seated next to you—it's that kind of place. There's another (original) location in Leesburg (12 S. King St.).

TREATS

Curb your sweet tooth while helping homeless animals. What could be better? Stop in **Scruffy's Ice Cream & Coffee Parlor** (6 W. Washington St., 540/687-3766, Mon.-Sat. 12pm-6pm, Sun. 12pm-5:30pm, under $10) for some delicious ice cream. A portion of the proceeds benefits local homeless animals at the Middleburg Humane Society. Try the chocolate ice cream or the mango sherbet. This is a small place, but there are a few stools inside and some benches outside.

A wonderful local bakery is the **Upper Crust** (4 N. Pendleton St., 540/687-5666, Mon.-Sat. 7am-4pm, under $15, cash only). They serve breakfast and lunch but are known for their pastries and fresh pies. You'll likely smell cookies baking as you approach. They do not take credit cards.

Accommodations

Middleburg is one of the few places in Northern Virginia where you'll have a good selection of private inns and bed-and-breakfasts to choose from. Truly a stay in the country, a night in Middleburg can make you feel light-years away from the city.

$100-200

The stately **Welbourne** (22314 Welbourne Farm Ln., 540/687-3201, www.welbourneinn.com, $170) is an authentic historical treasure in Virginia hunt country. The house was built in the 1700s and has been in the same family ever since. A stay there will take you back to Civil War times (the owners refer to it as "faded elegance"). There are five primary guest rooms with private baths and fireplaces. Relax in a rocking chair on the back porch, or take a hike around the property. Complimentary cocktails (served each evening at 6:30pm) and a wonderful, hearty breakfast are just some of the amenities that make visitors feel like family. Many dogs and horses live at this 520-acre property, so be prepared for four-legged company. The estate is decorated with family heirlooms and antiques. The property is dog friendly.

Another lovely bed-and-breakfast a few miles from town is the **Briar Patch Bed and Breakfast Inn** (23130 Briar Patch Ln., 703/327-5911, www.briarpatchbandb.com, $150-295). This historic home (built in 1805) was damaged during the Civil War and still shows a few scars today. The main house offers eight guest rooms decorated with antiques and colonial quilts. Six of the rooms can be combined into two-bedroom suites. There is also a small cottage and three "chicken coop" rooms. A good buffet breakfast is served daily, and plentiful snacks are available all day. There are resident horses, and the inn is dog friendly.

$200-300

One of the best-known inns in Middleburg is **The Red Fox Inn and Tavern** (2 E. Washington St., 540/687-6301, www.redfox.com, $239-649). This iconic inn and restaurant sits prominently at the center of Middleburg on the corner of East Washington and North Madison Streets. The tavern is famous as a meeting spot for Confederate colonel John Singleton Mosby and his Rangers. The Red Fox Inn is a complex consisting of several buildings with 16 guest rooms and three cottages. The tavern is located in the main building, and there is event space on the first and second floors. Five of the guest rooms are also in the main building on the upper two levels. The rooms are cozy and cleanly appointed in a colonial style, yet not overstuffed. A hunt country breakfast is served each day. The inn is very convenient to shopping and restaurants in the village.

OVER $300

The charming and luxurious ★ **Goodstone Inn & Restaurant** (36205 Snake Hill Rd., 540/687-3333, www.goodstone.com, $325-895) is a wonderful choice for an upscale country getaway. The inn has a highly regarded restaurant with a noted chef, and the service is friendly and genuine. There is also an on-site spa. The property is large (265 acres) and scenic with views of the Blue Ridge Mountains. The 18 tastefully decorated guest rooms and suites are housed in six buildings around the farm (which actually has farm animals). You can hike around the property on a trail that is several miles long and very relaxing. Canoeing is also available.

The **Salamander Resort and Spa** (500 North Pendleton St., 844/303-2723, www.salamanderresort.com, $475-975 plus a $39 per night resort fee) opened in 2013 and was one of the first luxury resorts in the nation to be LEED (Leadership in Energy and Environmental Design) certified. This stately 168-room resort sits on 340 acres in the heart of Virginia's wine and horse country, just outside the historic district of Middleburg. The modern, spacious guest rooms are 545-575 square feet and include sitting areas and a private balcony or terrace. Guests can enjoy a 23,000-square-foot spa, cooking studio, wine bar, billiards room, pool complex, tennis courts, and a two-acre culinary garden that supplies the resort's restaurant. There is also a full-service, 22-stall equestrian center onsite with an arena, riding trails, and instructional classes.

Information and Services

Middleburg's information center, the **Pink Box** (12 N. Madison St., 540/687-8888, daily 11am-3pm) is a good place to pick up brochures. They also offer information on a self-guided walking tour of the town. Downloadable driving maps are also available from the **Mosby Heritage Area Association** (www.mosbyheritagearea.org).

Coastal Virginia

Coastal Virginia sounds like a simple concept:

the place where the Atlantic Ocean meets the land. It's actually much more complicated than that. The Chesapeake Bay is a defining feature along the coast, and the area where it opens into the Atlantic Ocean has developed into one of the world's largest and busiest natural ports. Several large rivers empty into the Chesapeake Bay as well, including the Potomac, Rappahannock, James, and York Rivers.

The coastal region can be divided into five main areas. The first is the Northern Neck, which sits between the Potomac and Rappahannock Rivers, both of which flow into the bay. The Northern Neck is quiet and flat, and farms line the riverbanks. The area is home to several notable historic sites including George Washington's birthplace. The second

Highlights

Look for ★ to find recommended sights, activities, dining, and lodging.

★ **Colonial Williamsburg:** This unmatched living museum takes you back in time. It's one of America's most popular family destinations (page 176).

★ **Historic Jamestowne:** The original site of the Jamestown settlement spans centuries of history. Founded in 1607, it was the first permanent English settlement in the New World (page 186).

★ **Nauticus National Maritime Center:** This nautical-themed science and technology center in Norfolk is also home to the battleship USS *Wisconsin* (page 205).

★ **Virginia Beach Boardwalk:** The most popular beach resort in the state provides access to miles of wonderful sand and surf (page 212).

★ **Virginia Aquarium & Marine Science Center:** Hundreds of exhibits, live animals, and hands-on learning make this amazing aquarium one of the most popular attractions in the state (page 212).

★ **Tangier Island:** This remote island in the middle of the Chesapeake Bay feels like another country. The residents even have their own language (page 223).

★ **Chincoteague National Wildlife**

Refuge: This 14,000-acre wildlife refuge protects a herd of wild ponies and thousands of birds. Enjoy miles of natural beaches and hike or bike through the marsh (page 228).

area is known as the Historic Triangle, which includes the colonial cities of Williamsburg, Jamestown, and Yorktown. These cities sit along the James and York Rivers, which also flow into the Chesapeake Bay. Next is the huge area of Hampton Roads. This is where everything converges. The rivers flow into the bay just to the north, and the Chesapeake Bay flows into the Atlantic Ocean just to the east. The main cities in this area are Newport News, Hampton, and Norfolk. Then we have Virginia Beach. The Virginia Beach resort area is truly on the Atlantic coast. Our final region, Virginia's Eastern Shore, is sandwiched between the Chesapeake Bay on the west and the Atlantic Ocean on the east. It is sparsely populated compared to its mainland neighbors and offers charming historical towns and ample bird-watching and fishing.

PLANNING YOUR TIME

Visiting Coastal Virginia requires some planning, a love of water, and no fear of bridges.

Although there is some public transportation between specific cities, the easiest way to get around is by car. I-64 runs from Richmond down to the Historic Triangle and Hampton Roads areas, while US Route 17 and State Route 3 traverse the Northern Neck. US Route 13 runs the length of the Eastern Shore.

Coastal Virginia is a beautiful region but one that takes days, not hours to explore. If you are limited on time, select one or two key destinations, such as Williamsburg and Virginia Beach, or maybe spend a day or two on the Eastern Shore. Wherever you decide to go, keep in mind that the area is heavily visited in the summer months, so you will likely have a few thousand close friends to share the experience with, especially in the historic towns and the beachfront areas.

If you are looking for a one-of-a-kind experience, spend a day visiting Tangier Island. This isolated sandbar of a town is 12 miles out in the Chesapeake Bay and almost feels like a different country.

Northern Neck

The Northern Neck is a peninsula bordered by the Potomac and Rappahannock Rivers, not far from the Chesapeake Bay and approximately 75 miles from Washington DC. The Northern Neck is laden with history and was explored as early as 1608 by the famed Captain John Smith. George Washington, who was born here, called the region the "Garden of Virginia" for the tidewater landscape and the many forests and creeks that shape this area of the state.

During the steamboat era between 1813 and 1937, the Northern Neck supported a network of approximately 600 steamboats. These mechanical works of art were used to transport both people and goods throughout the Chesapeake Bay area.

In modern times, the Northern Neck is still rural and supports a thriving, generations-old fishing industry. It is also a popular area for recreational boating and water sports. It offers small-town charm, historical sites, colonial architecture, and marinas. Many establishments are only open seasonally, so if you are traveling during the colder months, a quick call ahead could pay off.

SIGHTS
George Washington's Birthplace
Although the father of our country only lived in the Northern Neck until he was three years old, his birthplace on **Pope's Creek Plantation** (1732 Popes Creek Rd., Colonial

---

Previous: crabbing boat in Reedville; carriage in Colonial Williamsburg; in the Jamestown Settlement

Coastal Virginia

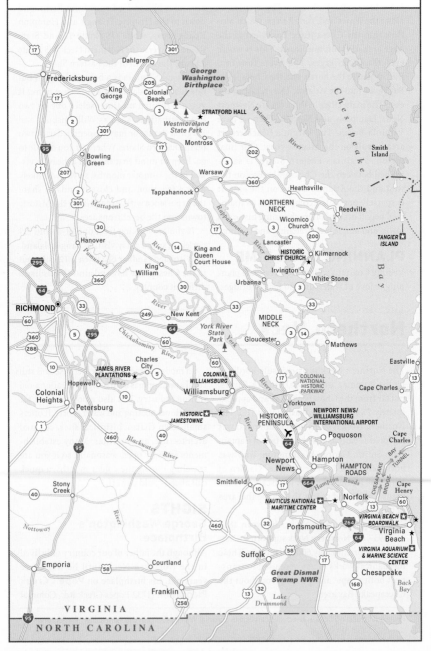

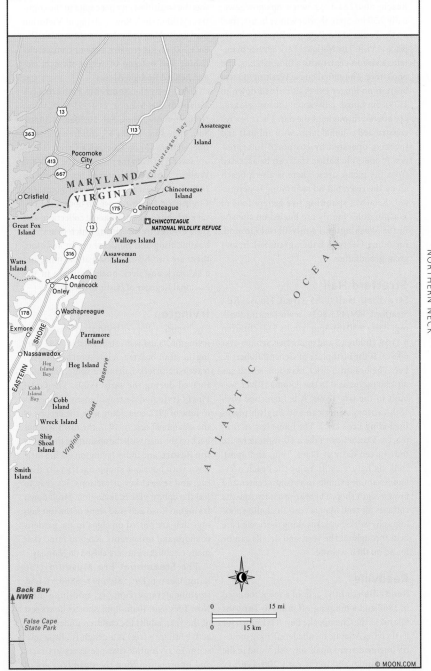

© MOON.COM

Beach, 804/224-1732, www.nps.gov/gewa, daily 9:30am-5pm, shorter winter hours, free) on the banks of the Potomac River is a lovely place to visit. The National Park Service maintains a visitors center with a film, exhibits, and bookstore. The actual house Washington was born in no longer exists (it burned down in 1779), but ranger talks about the historic area are offered throughout the day. There is a reconstructed colonial farm, with animals and tobacco, operated by costumed interpreters. A one-mile nature trail can be accessed from the picnic area. There is also a beach along the river, but no swimming is permitted. Relatives spanning five generations of Washington's family are buried on the site in the Washington Family Burial Ground, including George's father, grandfather, and great-grandfather.

Stratford Hall

Stratford Hall (483 Great House Rd., Stratford, 804/493-8038, www.stratfordhall. org, daily 9:30am-5pm, adults $14, children 6-11 $9, children 5 and under free, seniors over 60 $13) is the birthplace of General Robert E. Lee. The beautiful brick mansion, which sits on 1,900 acres next to the Potomac River, was built in the late 1730s. It is furnished with 18th-century American and English pieces (including Lee's crib). The home has 16 fireplaces. Visitors can take a 60-minute house tour (given daily at 11am, 1pm, and 3pm), walk six nature trails, enjoy the beach overlook, examine exhibits in a visitors center, and browse a gift shop. There are even two on-site cottages for rent. Many events (including photography workshops, kayaking tours, etc.) are held throughout the year, and details can be found on their website.

Reedville

Reedville is a little gem of a town founded in 1867 and a jumping-off point to **Tangier Island** in the Chesapeake Bay. It is known for its thriving Atlantic menhaden-fishing industry (menhaden are small, oily fish found in the mid-Atlantic) and in the early 20th century was the wealthiest city per capita in the country. (Millionaire's Row, a string of Victorian mansions along the water, attests to this affluence.) Reedville remains a major commercial fishing port in terms of weight of catch, second behind Kodiak, Alaska.

Don't miss the **Reedville Fishermen's Museum** (504 Main St., 804/453-6529, www. rfmuseum.org, Tues.-Sat. 10:30am-4:30pm, Sun. 1pm-4pm, adults $5, children under 12 free, seniors $3) on Cockrell's Creek. There are several parts to the museum: the **William Walker House,** a restored home built in 1875 that represents a waterman's home; the **Covington Building,** which houses temporary exhibits and a permanent collection; and the **Pendleton Building,** which contains a boatbuilding and model shop. In addition, there are two historic boats at the museum, a skipjack and deck boat. Both are in the National Register of Historic Places.

Irvington

The historic village of **Irvington** (www.town. irvington.va.us) was established in 1891 during the steamboat era. A busy port on the well-traveled Norfolk-Baltimore route, the town thrived during the early 1900s. The Great Fire of Irvington destroyed many businesses in June of 1917, coinciding with the decline of the steamboat era. In 1947, the town was put back on the map with the opening of the **Tides Inn Resort,** and today Irvington is a hip little town with boutique shopping, friendly dining, and several key attractions. It's easy to feel the upbeat vibe in Irvington. Stroll down Irvington Road and read some of the fun sayings that are posted on signs in the gardens of shops and restaurants. Keep in mind that many establishments are closed on Monday.

The **Steamboat Era Museum** (156 King Carter Dr., 804/438-6888, www. steamboateramuseum.org, mid-June-mid-Nov. Tues.-Sat. 10am-4pm, shorter hours rest of the year, adults $5, children under 12 and active military free) is a delightful little museum in Irvington that preserves artifacts and information from the steamboat era of

The Steamboat Era

the Steamboat Era Museum

Steamboats came on the scene in the Chesapeake Bay in the early 1800s. As their popularity rose, they quickly became as important to the cities along the bay as the railroad was to the rest of the country. By the mid-1800s, steamboats were used to transport passengers, mail, and goods.

By the turn of the 20th century, nearly 600 steamboats cruised the bay, carrying thousands of passengers to the cities of Norfolk, Virginia, and Baltimore, Maryland, and every place in between. Steamboat excursions became extremely popular, and commerce flourished. Farms grew as their potential for distributing goods expanded, and many canneries were built near the shore. At one time, 85 percent of the world's oyster trade came from the Chesapeake Bay, and these little delicacies were shipped via steamboat.

The 20th century brought the development of the automobile and the slow demise of the steamboat. As cars became affordable and more common, passenger traffic on the steamboats began to dwindle. Still, the boats were used for commerce until the 1930s, when a hurricane in 1933 wiped out many of the Chesapeake Bay wharfs.

The final excursion of a popular steamboat named the *Anne Arundel* was made on September 14, 1937. That day is still celebrated in Virginia as "Steamboat Era Day."

Visit the **Steamboat Era Museum** (156 King Carter Dr., 804/438-6888, www.steamboateramuseum.org, Tues.-Sat. 10am-4pm, closed in winter) in Irvington to learn more about the steamboat era of the Chesapeake Bay. Additional information on the era can be found on the museum's website.

the Chesapeake Bay (1813-1937). Steamboats were a vital mode of transportation along the bay for both goods and people and the lifeline of the economy connecting the region to cities such as Norfolk, Virginia, and Baltimore, Maryland. This is the only museum fully dedicated to the steamboats of the Chesapeake Bay, and the docents are very entertaining and knowledgeable.

The most treasured historic structure in the Northern Neck is arguably the **Historic Christ Church and Museum** (420 Christ Church Rd., Weems, 804/438-6855, www.christchurch1735.org, May-Oct. Mon.-Sat. 10am-4pm, Sun. 1pm-4pm, Apr. and Nov. Mon.-Thurs. by appointment only, Fri.-Sat. 10am-4pm, Sun. 1pm-4pm, Dec. by appointment only, $5). Less than two miles north of

Irvington, the church was finished in 1735 and remains one of the few unaltered colonial churches in the United States. It was a center of social and political activity during colonial times, and Sunday service was a big event. In addition to being a place or worship, it was a place to exchange news and the cornerstone of the community. The detailed brickwork in the tall walls and a vaulted ceiling help make it one of the best-crafted Anglican parish churches of its time. Services are still held there, and the interior boasts a triple-decker pulpit, walnut altar, and high-backed pews. **The Carter Reception Center** houses a museum dedicated to the church and its founder, Robert Carter. Guided tours are available from the center, and there is also a gift shop.

RECREATION
Westmoreland State Park
Westmoreland State Park (145 Cliff Rd., Montross, 804/493-8821, www.dcr.virginia. gov, $7-10 per vehicle) along the Potomac River offers riverfront beaches, hiking trails, a public pool, kayak and paddleboat rentals, a pond, and cliffs housing fossils. It became one of Virginia's first state parks in 1936. This 1,300-acre park also provides camping cabins for rent year-round and 133 seasonal campsites. The Potomac River Retreat is a lodge that is available for rent; it holds 15 overnight guests and up to 40 people for meetings. There is a small camp store, but it's best to bring your own food because they stock only limited drinks and snacks. Dogs and cats are allowed in the park and cabins for an additional fee. Take in the great view of the Potomac from **Horsehead Cliffs,** and don't miss a stroll down Fossil Beach, where you might even find some ancient shark's teeth. There is a visitors center that is open daily 8am-4:30pm.

Westmoreland Berry Farm
If picking berries makes you feel connected to colonial times, stop by the **Westmoreland Berry Farm** (1235 Berry Farm Ln., Colonial Beach, 804/224-9171, www.westmorelandberryfarm.com, May-Nov. Wed.-Sat. 9am-5pm, Sun. 10am-5pm). This farm on the banks of the Rappahannock River offers visitors the opportunity to pick their own fruit and berries (depending on what's in season). Or you can browse their country store for fresh produce or have lunch at the country kitchen.

Canoeing and Kayaking
The country's first national water trail, the **Captain John Smith Chesapeake National Historic Trail** (www.nps.gov) includes 3,000 miles of routes through the Chesapeake Bay, Northern Neck, Middle Neck, and their tributaries in Virginia and Maryland. The route was inspired by the regions explored in the 17th century by Captain John Smith.

Kayak rentals are available at **Westmoreland State Park** (www.dcr. virginia.gov, 1 hour $15, 4 hours $45).

Fishing
Captain Billy's Charters (545 Harveys Neck Rd., Heathsville, 804/580-7292, www. captbillyscharters.com) runs boat charters for both fishing and cruising from the **Ingram Bay Marina** into the Chesapeake Bay. **Crabbe Charter Fishing** (51 Railway Dr., Heathsville, 804/761-0908, www. crabbescharterfishing.com, $660 for up to six people) is another charter fishing company in the Northern Neck. They offer outings year-round.

Bird-Watching
Bird-watchers have many opportunities to view songbirds, waterfowl, eagles, and wading birds along the **Northern Neck Loop** birding trail (www.dgif.virginia.gov). This driving trail passes by historical sites and through an area known to have the largest population of bald eagles on the Eastern Seaboard.

1: Pope's Creek Plantation 2: The Local in Irvington
3: Stratford Hall

ENTERTAINMENT AND EVENTS

Many of the events in the Northern Neck revolve around water and nature. The **Blessing of the Fleet** is an annual event in Reedville that opens the fishing season on the first weekend of May. There is a parade of boats and the official blessing service.

Mid-September brings the **Reedville Antique and Traditional Small Boat Show** (www.acbs.org), featuring an antique boat parade, while mid-November is the time for the much-anticipated **Reedville Fishermen's Museum Oyster Roast** (www.rfmuseum.org). Tickets go on sale in September and sell out quickly for this mouth-watering event.

Wine enthusiasts will enjoy the **Taste by the Bay: Wine, Food, Arts & Ale** (www.lancasterva.com) held annually in November. It offers tastings and sales from Virginia wineries including some along the **Chesapeake Bay Wine Trail** (www.chesapeakebaywinetrail.com), Virginia craft brews, local restaurant tastings, live music, and art vendors.

FOOD
Reedville

The Crazy Crab Restaurant (902 Main St., 804/453-6789, www.crazycrabreedville.com, Tues.-Fri. 5pm-9pm, Sat. noon-9pm, Sun. noon-8pm, $17-26), at the Reedville Marina, is a casual joint offering an abundance of local seafood choices and a few land-based options. The waterfront view from the restaurant is nice, the atmosphere is fun, and outdoor seating is available.

Cockrell's Seafood (567 Seaboard Dr., 804/453-6326, www.smithpointseafood.com, seasonal Mon.-Thurs. 11am-3pm, Fri.-Sat. 11am-4pm, $8-10) is a seafood deli on the waterfront. The atmosphere is very casual, with diners sitting at picnic tables. They serve delicious crab dishes.

Satisfy your sweet tooth at **Chitterchats Ice Cream** (846 Main St., 804/453-3335, www.chitterchatsicecream.com, $5-10, closed in the off season). This family-oriented ice-cream shop offers delicious homemade ice cream in roughly 20 flavors.

Irvington

The Office Café (4346 Irvington Rd., 804/438-8032, www.theofficeirvington.com, Tues.-Wed. 11am-3pm, Thurs.-Sat. 11am-9pm, $9-14) is a trendy little find in town. The menu offers tasty flatbreads, sandwiches, salads, seafood baskets, and desserts. Try some of their originals, such as the Pastrami Dog, Crabby Dog, or the Drunken Sausage Flatbread. This place is worth a stop.

The Local (4337 Irvington Rd., 804/438-9356, www.thelocalblend.com, Mon.-Sat. 7am-3:30pm, Sun. 7am-2:30pm, under $10) is a good choice for grabbing breakfast or a sandwich at lunchtime. This friendly little restaurant has cute decor and a good selection of sandwiches (both breakfast and lunch) and salads. They also have a coffee bar and a handful of desserts.

ACCOMMODATIONS
$100-200

Ma Margaret's House (249 Greenfield Rd., Reedville, 804/453-9110, www.mamargaretshouse.com, $75-225) is a cozy, 4,000-square-foot home built in 1914 that belonged to the owner's grandparents. It offers several guest suites, a lot of privacy, and a wonderful staff.

$200-300

★ **The Hope and Glory Inn** (65 Tavern Rd., Irvington, 804/438-6053, www.hopeandglory.com, $245-395) is a boutique inn with six rooms and six cottages. Lavish and romantic, with a little sense of humor, the inn was originally a schoolhouse built in 1890. The school had two front doors, one for girls and one for boys. The building now boasts beautifully appointed rooms, lush gardens, and even a moon garden with flowers that only bloom in the evening. There's a spa, meeting facilities, and a dock for boating, kayaking, or canoeing on-site as well as an outdoor pool and an outdoor bath (that is not a typo, there really is a claw-foot tub in an enclosed area outside). Tennis and three golf courses are a short distance away. The town of Irvington, which sits on the Chesapeake Bay, offers trendy shopping and a fun atmosphere.

Wine lovers won't want to miss visiting **The Dog and Oyster,** the Hope and Glory Inn's vineyard. It's named for the establishment's rescue dogs, who guard the grapes from area wildlife, and also in honor of the local oysters, which pair well with the wines. If the weather is nice, enjoy a bottle of wine on the porch.

The **Tides Inn** (480 King Carter Dr., Irvington, 804/438-5000, www.tidesinn.com, $185-530) is a well-known resort bordered by the Potomac and Rappahannock Rivers and the Chesapeake Bay. This romantic waterfront inn hangs on the banks of Carters Creek as a little oasis of red-roofed buildings offering peace and relaxation to visitors of all ages. It features luxurious waterfront accommodations, golf, a marina, and a spa. There is also a sailing school with many options for lessons and family sailing activities. Packages include some geared toward golf, family vacations, and romance. There are also several good restaurants on-site, and the inn is dog friendly.

CAMPING

Westmoreland State Park (1650 State Park Rd., Montross, 804/493-8821, www.dcr. virginia.gov) offers 133 campsites and a handful of camping cabins. Camping sites feature fire-ring grills or box grills. Forty-two sites offer electric and water hookups for $40 per night; sites without these amenities are $30 per night. There is also one group tent site that can accommodate up to 40 people ($148). Camping cabins have a maximum capacity of four and require a two-night minimum stay. Cabins do not have bathrooms, kitchens, heat, air-conditioning, or linens. Bathhouses are available on-site for all campers.

INFORMATION AND SERVICES

For additional information on the Northern Neck, visit www.northernneck.org.

Williamsburg and the Historic Triangle

The "Historic Triangle," as it is known, consists of Williamsburg, Jamestown, and Yorktown. These three historic towns are just minutes apart and are the sites of some of our country's most important Revolutionary War history.

The **Colonial Parkway,** a scenic, 23-mile-long, three-lane road, connects the points of the Historic Triangle. Millions of travelers drive the road between Williamsburg, Jamestown, and Yorktown each year. The parkway is maintained by the National Park Service and was designed to unify the three culturally distinct sites while preserving the scenery and wildlife along the way. The construction of the parkway took more than 26 years and stretched through the Depression and World War II. It was completed in 1957. The parkway enables motorists to enjoy the surrounding landscape and has a speed limit of 45 miles per hour.

The National Park Service also maintains the **Colonial National Historical Park,** which contains two of the most historically significant sites in the country: the **Historic Jamestowne** National Historic Site (which is jointly administered by Preservation Virginia) and **Yorktown Battlefield.** These sites are connected by the Colonial Parkway.

WILLIAMSBURG

The original capital of the Virginia Colony, Jamestown, was founded in 1607. It was located on the banks of the James River with a deepwater anchorage on a peninsula between the York and James Rivers. By 1638, an area

Colonial Williamsburg

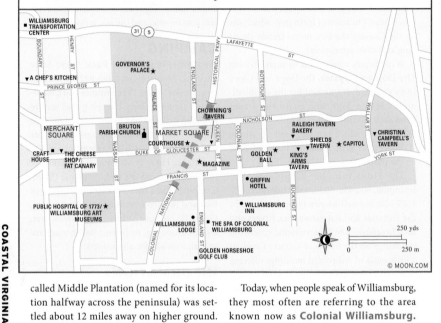

WILLIAMSBURG
■ TRANSPORTATION
CENTER

31 5

LAFAYETTE ST

BOUNDARY ST

HENRY ST

GOVERNOR'S
PALACE ★

▼ A CHEF'S KITCHEN

PRINCE GEORGE ST

ENGLAND ST

HISTORICAL PKWY

BOTETOURT ST

CHOWNING'S
TAVERN

NICHOLSON ST

WALLAR ST

MERCHANT
SQUARE

BRUTON
PARISH CHURCH ⚲

MARKET SQUARE

RALEIGH TAVERN
BAKERY

CHRISTINA
CAMPBELL'S
TAVERN

COURTHOUSE ★

PALACE ST

QUEEN ST

COLONIAL ST

SHIELDS
TAVERN

CAPITOL ★

CRAFT
HOUSE ■

▼ THE CHEESE
SHOP/
FAT CANARY

NASSAU ST

DUKE OF GLOUCESTER ST

GOLDEN
BALL ★

KING'S
ARMS
TAVERN

YORK ST

★ MAGAZINE

FRANCIS ST

● GRIFFIN
HOTEL

BUCKTROT ST

PUBLIC HOSPITAL OF 1773/ ★
WILLIAMSBURG ART
MUSEUMS

COLONIAL NATIONAL

● WILLIAMSBURG
INN

WILLIAMSBURG
LODGE

ENGLAND ST

■ THE SPA OF COLONIAL
WILLIAMSBURG

COLONIAL

GOLDEN HORSESHOE
■ GOLF CLUB

0   250 yds

0   250 m

© MOON.COM

called Middle Plantation (named for its location halfway across the peninsula) was settled about 12 miles away on higher ground. In 1676, Jamestown burned down, and the government seat was temporarily moved to Middle Plantation. The statehouse was rebuilt, but burned down again in 1698. Once again, the capital was relocated to Middle Plantation. Finding the temporary location to be safer and less humid than Jamestown, the House of Burgesses permanently moved the colonial capital there in 1699. A village was planned in the new location, and the name Middle Plantation was changed to Williamsburg in honor of King William III of England.

Williamsburg is one of America's earliest planned cities. It was designed as the capital of the Virginia Colony, which was the most populous of the British colonies in America in 1699. As such, Williamsburg had the oldest legislative assembly in the New World, and a series of elaborate capitol buildings were erected as the city developed into the thriving center of Virginia. Williamsburg remained the capital of Virginia until 1780, when the seat of government was moved to its current location in Richmond.

Today, when people speak of Williamsburg, they most often are referring to the area known now as **Colonial Williamsburg.** This original capital city is the country's prime example of not only the preservation of American colonial history but also its interpretation. However, although Colonial Williamsburg is the best-known attraction in the Williamsburg area, there are many other attractions nearby, including the historic **College of William & Mary** and a number of popular theme parks.

Sights

TOP EXPERIENCE

★ COLONIAL WILLIAMSBURG

Colonial Williamsburg (888/965-7254, www.colonialwilliamsburg.com, adult one-day ticket $44.99, children 6-12 $24.99, adult three-day ticket $54.99, children 6-12 $29.99) is the largest living museum in the country, and it is truly a historical marvel. It is open 365 days a year and run by the private, not-for-profit **Colonial Williamsburg Foundation.**

The museum encompasses the restored 18th-century colonial Virginia capital city, which was the center of politics in Virginia for 80 years, and includes the real city streets and buildings that were erected during that time. There are historical exhibits, taverns, shops featuring original trades, and many other sites within the museum area. Ticketholders gain access to the historical buildings, theatrical performances, more than 20 site tours, 35 exhibitions, and museums. It is free to wander the streets themselves.

Although Colonial Williamsburg is open all year, if you are flexible in choosing when to visit, spring and fall can be the most rewarding. This is when crowds are less dense and the temperatures are the most moderate (plan to do a lot of walking around the city). Summer is the busiest tourist season because school is out of session, and it can also be very hot and humid, especially in August.

It is best to begin your visit at the **Colonial Williamsburg Regional Visitor Center** (101 Visitor Center Dr., 866/691-7063, daily 8:45am-5pm). The staff can help you put together an itinerary for your stay that will allow you to hit the highlights and choose additional sites you are interested in. You can also purchase tickets and learn about events and activities taking place during your time here. The highlights in Colonial Williamsburg can be seen over a weekend, but to really soak in the atmosphere, it can be fun to spend an extra day or two, or to make it your base for exploring other nearby attractions.

Everything within the museum area is neat, clean, well maintained, and historically correct. The staff is dressed in period clothing and plays their roles very seriously. Conversations between staff members and the public are always in character. Visitors become "Residents of the City" and are immersed in history—and can enjoy authentic colonial-era dining and shopping while staying in hotels with all the modern conveniences.

There's a large pedestrian area through the center of the historical enclave along **Duke of Gloucester Street.** President Franklin D. Roosevelt called this road the "most historic avenue in all of America." Horses and horse-drawn carriages are allowed on the street if they are part of the museum.

Market Square, the center of activity in Colonial Williamsburg, straddles Duke of Gloucester Street. Residents went there on a regular basis (if not daily) to purchase goods and socialize. Visitors can experience the same atmosphere along Duke of Gloucester Street, where the official Williamsburg-brand shops are located.

Ticket-holding visitors can explore a variety of historical buildings, such as the reconstructed **Capitol** (daily 9am-5pm), which sits at the east end of Duke of Gloucester Street. The current building is the third capitol to stand on the site, but it is very much the same as the original, completed in 1705. A trip through this tall brick building is like a history lesson on the government in colonial Virginia and the contributions the colony made to the American Revolution. Evening programs in the Capitol include reenactments of political and social events that actually occurred here in the 18th century. One day a year, a naturalization ceremony is carried out at the Capitol for immigrants becoming Americans, carrying on a tradition that began nearly 300 years ago.

The impressive **Governor's Palace,** built between 1706 and 1722 at the end of Palace Green Street off of West Duke of Gloucester Street, was home to seven royal governors, as well as Thomas Jefferson and Patrick Henry. After many decades as a symbol of the power of royal England, the home served as a military headquarters and twice as a wartime hospital (156 soldiers and 2 women are buried in the garden, casualties of the Battle of Yorktown). The original structure burned to the ground in 1781, but the building was reconstructed to its current grandeur in the 1930s. Since then, the home has been furnished with American and British antiques in the colonial revival style. This is perhaps the most popular site in Colonial Williamsburg,

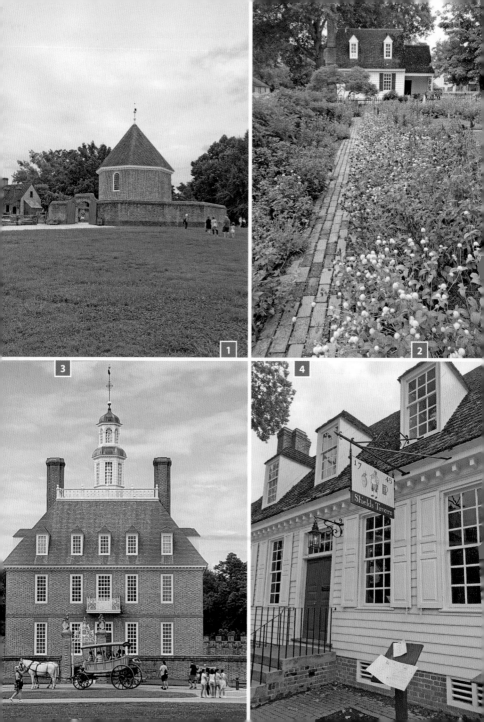

so make it first on your list, early in the day, before the crowds set in.

The **Courthouse** (W. Duke of Gloucester St.) is a focal point of Market Square and one that no doubt struck fear in the hearts of many criminals in its day. Built in 1770, it is one of Williamsburg's original 18th-century buildings, and it housed the municipal and county courts until 1932. The building's T-shaped design is common to many Virginia courthouses, but an octagonal cupola and several other formal design elements (such as a weather vane, arched windows, and a cantilevered pediment) make it distinct in appearance. The signing of the Treaty of Paris (ending the Revolutionary War) was announced at the Courthouse.

A small but fascinating building is the **Magazine** (E. Duke of Gloucester St.). It was constructed in 1715 at the request of Governor Alexander Spotswood, who wanted a solid-brick house in which to store and protect weapons and ammunition. The Magazine is well known for its role in the **Gunpowder Incident** of April 20, 1775, an episode that occurred in the opening days of the Revolutionary War between the royal governor, Lord Dunmore, and the militia (led by Patrick Henry). Lord Dunmore gave orders to remove all the gunpowder from the Magazine and move it to a Royal Navy ship. This led to unrest in Virginia and the movement of Patrick Henry's militia toward Williamsburg to secure the gunpowder for the colonial troops. The matter was resolved peacefully, but Dunmore retreated to a naval ship, thus ending royal governance of the colony. The incident helped move Virginia toward revolution.

Many craftspeople, some of whom have spent years learning the trade, create colonial-era crafts in dozens of shops throughout Colonial Williamsburg. Visitors can watch blacksmiths and armorers shape tools, weapons, and hardware out of iron and steel at **Anderson's Blacksmith Shop & Public Armoury** (E. Duke of Gloucester St.) or visit the **Wigmaker** (E. Duke of Gloucester St.) to learn the importance of 18th-century wigmakers and barbers and how these trades were essential to the social structure of the day. Other crafters include the **Shoemaker** (W. Duke of Gloucester St.), the **Weaver** (W. Duke of Gloucester St.), and the **Bindery** (E. Duke of Gloucester St.).

A number of historic taverns and restaurants are also located in Colonial Williamsburg and serve authentic colonial-style food. Look for the colonial flags out in front of the buildings. If a flag is out, it means the establishment is open.

More than 20 tours, both guided and self-led, are included in a Colonial Williamsburg admission ticket. The visitors center is the best place to find out what tours are offered on the day(s) you are there and what time they leave.

Active U.S. military receive complimentary admission for a single day once a year for themselves and up to three direct dependents (retired military and veterans receive 50 percent off).

WILLIAMSBURG ART MUSEUMS

Two top-notch art museums, the **DeWitt Wallace Decorative Arts Museum** (325 W. Francis St., 855/776-1765, daily 10am-7pm) and the **Abby Aldrich Rockefeller Folk Art Museum** (326 W. Francis St., 877/848-8039, daily 10am-7pm) are located in the same building and can be reached by walking through the **Public Hospital of 1773** (326 W. Francis St., admission is included with the Colonial Williamsburg ticket). The DeWitt Wallace Decorative Arts Museum opened in 1985, funded by a generous donation from DeWitt and Lila Wallace, the founders of *Readers Digest*. It houses a large collection of American and British art and antiques, including the world's most extensive collection of Southern furniture. The Abby Aldrich Rockefeller Folk Art Museum features a colorful variety of paintings, sculptures, and other

1: Magazine in Colonial Williamsburg **2:** garden in Colonial Williamsburg **3:** Governor's Palace **4:** Shields Tavern

art forms. Each work was created by self-taught artists and shows an imaginative array of details and color selections. There is also a kid-friendly animal-themed exhibit called *Down on the Farm*. While you're there, take in the exhibits at the Public Hospital. It was the first facility in North America dedicated to caring for the mentally ill. In this day and age, the hospital is seen as part jail, part infirmary, and the treatments used in the 18th and 19th centuries are thankfully just part of history.

THE COLLEGE OF WILLIAM & MARY

Early on, Williamsburg developed into a hub for learning. **The College of William & Mary** (200 Stadium Dr., www.wm.edu), which is the second-oldest college in the country, was founded in 1693. It is just west of Colonial Williamsburg and an easy walk from the colonial city. William & Mary turned out many famous early political leaders including Thomas Jefferson, John Tyler, and James Monroe. Today, the 1,200-acre campus is bustling with students. Visitors can enjoy a handful of historical attractions right on campus, including the **Sir Christopher Wren Building,** which was built 1695 and is known for being the oldest college building in the country. It was named for a royal architect, although concrete evidence has not been found that Wren actually designed it.

WILLIAMSBURG WINERY

Wine lovers will want to stop in for a tour and tasting at the **Williamsburg Winery** (5800 Wessex Hundred, 757/229-0999, www.williamsburgwinery.com, Mar. 16-Oct. 31, Sun.-Thurs. 11am-5:30pm, Fri.-Sat. 11am-6:30pm, Nov.-Mar. 15, Sun.-Thurs. 11am-4:30pm, Fri.-Sat. 11am-5:30pm, tastings $10-18), about a 10-minute drive from the Colonial Williamsburg visitors center. The winery is one of Virginia's largest and is part of the Wessex Hundred, a beautiful, 300-acre farm that includes two restaurants and an inn.

BUSCH GARDENS WILLIAMSBURG

Busch Gardens Williamsburg (1 Busch Gardens Blvd., 757/229-4386, www.buschgardens.com, hours vary greatly throughout the year but generally open at 10am during the season, $86.99) is a theme park with rides, re-created European villages, shows, exhibits, and tours. The park is less than five miles southeast of Williamsburg and is owned by SeaWorld Parks & Entertainment. Hair-raising roller coasters, water rides, and special attractions for little kids are just part of the fun at this beautiful park. Test your nerves on the Griffon, a 205-foot dive coaster where brave riders free-fall at 75 miles per hour, or the Verbolten, an indoor/outdoor multi-launch coaster set in Germany's Black Forest. The park's classic ride is the Loch Ness Monster, a 13-story, double-loop roller coaster that made Busch Gardens famous in 1978. This popular park also offers an Oktoberfest Village, a high-tech simulator ride that takes passengers over Europe, and animal attractions such as Jack Hanna's Wild Reserve, where visitors can see and learn about endangered and exotic animals. A combined Busch Gardens Williamsburg and Water Country USA ticket can be purchased for $109.99.

WATER COUNTRY USA

Busch Gardens Williamsburg's sister park, **Water Country USA** (176 Water Country Pkwy., 757/229-4386, www.watercountryusa.com, Memorial Day-Labor Day daily 10am-close, $61.99), is the largest water theme park in the mid-Atlantic. It is approximately three miles southeast of Williamsburg, just north of Busch Gardens. The park offers water-slides, pools, Virginia's first water coaster, and more than 30 rides for kids of all ages as well as restaurants and live entertainment. A combined Busch Gardens Williamsburg and Water Country USA ticket can be purchased for $109.99.

Recreation

GOLF

The **Golden Horseshoe Golf Club** (401 S. England St., 757/220-7696, www. colonialwilliamsburg.com, $52-79) is part of Colonial Williamsburg and offers 45 walkable holes. This scenic course is well maintained and has received accolades from publications such as *Golf Magazine* and *Golfweek*.

The **Kingsmill Resort** (1010 Kingsmill Rd., 757/253-1703. www.kingsmill.com, $60-165) offers three championship 18-hole courses that are open to the public (one of which was ranked in the top 10 for women by *Golf Digest*).

The award-winning **Williamsburg National Golf Club** (3700 Centerville Rd., 757/258-9642, www.wngc.com, $69-89) has two 18-hole courses.

SPAS

The **Spa of Colonial Williamsburg** (307 S. England St., 757/220-7720, www. colonialwilliamsburg.com) is behind the Williamsburg Inn. Enjoy treatments made from botanicals used by the early settlers or a variety of soaks and massages. Packages are available.

HORSEBACK RIDING

If horseback riding seems appropriate while visiting Williamsburg, contact **Lakewood Trails** (2116-A Forge Rd., Toano, 575/566-9633, www.lakewoodtrailrides.com, $75) for one-hour guided trail rides.

GO APE TREETOP ADVENTURE

For something completely different, try a **Go Ape** (5537 Centerville Rd., 800/971-8271, www.goape.com, ages 16 and up $59, ages 10-15 $39) Treetop Adventure. This adventure course is appropriate for ages 10 and up (who are taller than 4 feet, 7 inches) and includes high wires, ladders, tunnels, zip lines, and a lot of treetop excitement. A junior course is available for children under 10 who are 3 feet, 3 inches or taller.

Entertainment and Events

Colonial Williamsburg doesn't shut down after dark. A variety of tours are available, including **The Original Ghost Tour** (345 W. Duke of Gloucester St., text questions to 757/342-6599, www.theghosttour.com, Mar.-Nov. daily 8pm, Jan.-Feb. Fri.-Sat. 8pm, $13). This is a family-friendly, candlelit, walking ghost tour of the town and taverns that offers a relaxing end to a day of sightseeing.

The **Kimball Theatre** (428 W. Duke of Gloucester St., 757/221-2674, www. kimball.wm.edu) is a film and stage venue in Merchants Square, right in the middle of Colonial Williamsburg. It offers programming in alliance with the College of William & Mary, including foreign, classic, and documentary films, along with live concerts.

Outside of the historic center—but only minutes away—visitors can play pool and enjoy live music on some nights at **The Corner Pocket** (4805 Courthouse St., 757/220-0808, www.thecornerpocket.us, Mon.-Tues. 11:30am-1am, Wed.-Fri. 11:30am-2:30am, Sat. 11:30am-2am), an upscale pool hall.

Busch Gardens Williamsburg hosts an annual **Howl-O-Scream** (1 Busch Gardens Blvd., www.buschgardens.com) starting in mid-September and running through October. During Howl-O-Scream, the park becomes a horrorfest for brave souls, featuring scary shows, creepy creatures lurking about the park, and fun characters. It is not advisable to take young children.

The holiday season is a very popular time to visit Colonial Williamsburg. The **Grand Illumination** (www.colonialwilliamsburg. com), held on the Sunday of the first full weekend in December, is an eagerly awaited street festival where the entire historic area is decorated with traditional natural adornments for the season, such as pinecones, evergreen branches, and candles. The area flickers at night by candlelight as carols are sung, concerts are held, and fireworks light up the night.

Shopping

Williamsburg offers endless shops. Strip malls and outlet stores can be found in much of the area surrounding Colonial Williamsburg. For unique souvenirs, try stopping in the **Williamsburg Craft House** (420 W. Duke of Gloucester St., 757/220-7747), run by the Colonial Williamsburg Foundation. Pewter and ceramic gifts, jewelry, and folk art are for sale. Other favorite shops in the historic district include **The Prentis Store** (214 E. Duke of Gloucester St., 757/229-1000), which sells handcrafted leather pieces, pottery, furniture, ironware, and baskets; the **Market House** (102 W Duke of Gloucester St., 888/965-7254), an open-air market on Duke of Gloucester Street that sells hats, toys, and other handmade items; and the **Golden Ball** (406 E. Duke of Gloucester St., 757/229-1000), which sells one-of-a-kind jewelry.

Food

AMERICAN

If you just need to grab a quick sandwich or you'd like to enjoy a gourmet cheese platter and a glass of wine, stop in **The Cheese Shop** (410 W. Duke of Gloucester St., 757/220-0298, www.cheeseshopwilliamsburg.com, Mon.-Sat. 10am-8pm, Sun. 11am-6pm, under $15) in Merchants Square. They make custom cheese plates (from 200 varieties of imported and domestic cheese) at their cheese counter (to the left) and deli sandwiches at the back of the store (try their chicken salad; it has just enough bacon to taste wonderful but not enough to feel guilty). The store also carries fresh-baked bread and a variety of snacks and drinks. Their wine cellar has more than 4,000 bottles of wine. There's seating outside (pay before you exit).

The ★ **Fat Canary** (410 W. Duke of Gloucester St., 757/229-3333, www.fatcanarywilliamsburg.com, daily 5pm-10pm, closed Mon. Jan.-Feb., $29-42) in Merchants Square is named for the wine brought to the New World by ships that stopped in the Canary Islands for supplies. The wine was called a "canary," and this wonderful restaurant knows its wine. Widely considered one of the top dining spots in Williamsburg, The Fat Canary is an upscale restaurant that delivers an interesting menu of mouthwatering entrées such as quail, scallops, lamb, and beef tenderloin. They also have delicious desserts. The restaurant has a romantic ambience with soft pendant lighting and friendly service. This is a great place for a date or to relax after a day touring Colonial Williamsburg. Reservations are strongly suggested.

For a unique dining experience, make reservations at **A Chef's Kitchen** (501 Prince George St., 757/564-8500, www.achefskitchen.biz, Tues.-Sat. seating 6:30pm, $105), in the heart of Williamsburg. This food destination allows guests to learn about the fare they are eating and how it's prepared while being entertained by a talented chef. The fixed-price menu is for a multicourse meal in which recipes are prepared, served, and paired with great wines. Diners sit at elegant long tables in tiered rows. The menu changes monthly, but sample dishes include asparagus and sweet pea soup, scallion and lime Gulf shrimp cake, roast rack of lamb, and strawberries sabayon in a lace cup cookie. This small restaurant only seats 26 people, and it only offers one seating per night, so reservations are a must. Plan for 2-3 hours of dining time.

FRENCH

For an expertly prepared, upscale French meal, make a reservation at **Café Provençal** (5810 Wessex Hundred, 757/941-0317, www.williamsburgwinery.com, Tues.-Sun. 5:30pm-9pm, $26-42). This charming restaurant is located on the 300-acre Wessex Hundred farm (home of the Williamsburg Winery). They feature selections made from their own harvest and also support smaller farms that are dedicated to humanely raising animals and practicing environmental stewardship. Their menu changes seasonally but includes selections such as Juniper Chicken Roulade, filet mignon, and Local Farro Cast Iron Porridge.

TREATS

To satisfy a craving or pick up an afternoon snack, stop in the **Raleigh Tavern Bakery** (410 E Duke of Gloucester St., behind the Raleigh Tavern, 888/976-0916, under $10). They offer a selection of fresh cookies, muffins, rolls, sandwiches, drinks, and other treats. Try the sweet potato muffins and the gingerbread cookies, which are done to perfection and are much better than the peanut butter and chocolate chip cookies. Casual seating is available in the courtyard outside. A cookbook with the recipes is available for purchase, and this writer knows firsthand that almost nothing has changed in this historical little bakery in the past 30 years—but then again, that's the idea here.

The **Jamestown Pie Company** (1804 Jamestown Rd., 757/229-7775, www.buyapie. com, Mon.-Sat. 9am-9pm, Sun. 10am-9pm, $15-32) sells everything round including pizza and dessert pie. Pies are also available to go or ship.

COLONIAL TAVERNS

There are four taverns in the historic area of Williamsburg, and dining in one is a great way to get into the spirit of the town. Costumed servers bring authentic dishes from two centuries ago to wooden tables in flickering candlelight. Don't be hesitant to try some 18th-century staples such as spoon bread and peanut soup. There are a few featured items available in all four taverns, but aside from that, each specializes in its own dishes. Make reservations when you book your hotel, as these restaurants are very popular.

Christiana Campbell's Tavern (101 S. Waller St., 855/263-1746, Tues.-Sat. 5pm-7:45pm, $30-50) is noted as George Washington's favorite tavern. It specializes in seafood dishes. The tavern was re-created from artifacts excavated on-site and from a sketch of the building found on an original insurance policy. George and other famous colonial figureheads often met here for business and pleasure, and private rooms could be reserved alongside public chambers where travelers sometimes shared beds with complete strangers when the tavern was full. The crab cakes are a signature dish.

Chowning's Tavern (109 E. Duke of Gloucester St., 855/270-5114, daily 11:30am-9pm, $12-19) is a casual alehouse where lively singing and other reenactments of 18th-century life are common. All-day pub fare includes pork barbecue sandwiches, ribs, and Brunswick stew. Outdoor seating is available behind the tavern in the garden.

The King's Arms Tavern (416 E. Duke of Gloucester St., 855/240-3278, Thurs.-Mon. 11:30am-2:30pm and 5pm-7:45pm, $23-40) is a genteel tavern serving Southern food and decadent desserts. This chophouse-style tavern offers entrées such as game hen, pork chops, and prime rib. The peanut soup is a signature dish. Their lunch menu offers sandwiches, stew, and fried chicken ($14-17).

Shields Tavern (422 E. Duke of Gloucester St., 855/268-7220, Tues.-Sat. 11:30am-2:30pm and 5pm-7:45pm, $27-34) is the largest of the taverns, and it specializes in comfort food such as fried chicken, blackened catfish, and pork shank. Their lunch menu offers less expensive sandwiches, stew, and hamburgers ($8-17).

Accommodations

If Colonial Williamsburg is the focus of your Williamsburg trip, and you'd like to be immersed in the Revolutionary City, book a room in one of the Colonial Williamsburg Foundation hotels or guesthouses. These are conveniently located near the museum sites and have a historical feel to them. Reservations, especially during the peak summer months, should be made well in advance.

COLONIAL WILLIAMSBURG FOUNDATION

The **Colonial Williamsburg Foundation** maintains several hotels/lodges and 24 guesthouses. Each offers a different atmosphere and price range. Hotel guests have access to a terrific fitness facility located behind the Williamsburg Inn that includes a spa, state-of-the-art fitness room, indoor lap pool, and two gorgeous outdoor pools. Hotel guests also receive the best rate on general admission passes and discounts on special events. Reservations for all are handled through the foundation (855/231-7240, www. colonialwilliamsburghotels.com), and all the hotels are dog friendly. The **Colonial Houses** ($189-989) are individual colonial homes and rooms, each with a unique history. The number of rooms per house varies, but all are decorated with authentic reproductions of period pieces such as canopy beds, and all have modern amenities. Look out over Duke of Gloucester Street, or sleep in the home where Thomas Jefferson lived while attending The College of William & Mary. Some homes are original historic buildings and others are replicas.

The luxurious ★ **Williamsburg Inn** (136 E. Francis St., $449-649) was built in 1937 by John D. Rockefeller Jr., and the decor and furnishings in the lobby are still arranged exactly the way his wife, Abby Aldrich Rockefeller, designed it. This stately, upscale hotel has hosted many heads of state, including President Dwight D. Eisenhower, Queen Elizabeth II, and Sir Winston Churchill. In 1983, the inn welcomed the Economic Summit of Industrialized Nations, hosted by President Ronald Reagan. It is listed in the National Register of Historic Places but offers modern first-class accommodations in its 62 guest rooms. The hotel was the first in the United States to have central air-conditioning. Each elegant and spacious room is furnished similar to an English country estate. The setting and decor are charming, and the service is excellent. Mrs. Rockefeller wished for guests to feel at home in the inn and as such instilled a warmth throughout the staff that still radiates today. Every last detail is attended to in the luxurious rooms, from beautifully tiled, temperature-controlled showers to a fresh white rose in the bathroom (the rose is the official inn flower) and little comforts such as vanity mirrors and nightlights. The hotel is centrally located adjacent to Colonial Williamsburg. The Golden Horseshoe Golf Club is behind the inn, and daily participatory events such as lawn bowling are offered to guests. There are two restaurants on-site (one formal dining room and a more casual lounge), and the hotel is very family friendly.

The **Williamsburg Lodge** (310 S. England St., 855/294-5683, $227-389) is owned by the Colonial Williamsburg Foundation but is part of Marriott's Autograph Collection. It is decorated in the classic Virginia style. Colorful fabric, leather, and warm woods give this hotel a lodge feel. This 300-room hotel hosts many conferences, and its unique garden gives it a relaxing focal point. The rooms are spacious, the lodge is conveniently located near Colonial Williamsburg, and it's an easy walk to the attractions.

The **Williamsburg Woodlands Hotel and Suites** (105 Visitor Center Dr., $179-199) is next to the visitors center for Colonial Williamsburg. This 300-room hotel offers contemporary rooms in a wooded setting. It is one of the least expensive options of the Colonial Williamsburg Foundation hotels.

The **Griffin Hotel** (302 E. Francis St., $179-269) is located in a natural setting a short walk from historic Colonial Williamsburg and the visitors center.

OUTSIDE COLONIAL WILLIAMSBURG

There are quite a few choices for accommodations outside Colonial Williamsburg. Many are within an easy drive of the historical area.

The **Marriott's Manor Club at Ford's Colony** (101 St. Andrews Dr., 757/258-1120, www.marriott.com, $161-339) is in the private community of Ford's Colony and offers colonial architecture, deluxe guest rooms, and one- and two-bedroom villas. Each villa has a kitchen, living/dining area, washer and dryer, a balcony or patio, and a fireplace. This is a great place for families or groups who need a bit more space or plan an extended stay. Colonial Williamsburg and the College of William & Mary are about a 15-minute drive away, and Busch Gardens is about 20 minutes. There's a spa and golf course in the community, a fitness center, indoor and outdoor pools, and a sport court. Rooms are nicely appointed, and the buildings are spread out on a well-manicured property.

Wedmore Place (5810 Wessex Hundred, 757/941-0310, www.wedmoreplace.com, $155-700) offers 28 individually decorated rooms and suites in a variety of price ranges. Each room is designed after a European province and a different time in history, including all the furnishings and wall hangings. The 300-acre farm is also the site of the Williamsburg Winery and is about a 10-minute drive to the Colonial Williamsburg visitors center. All rooms include continental breakfast.

If you're looking for a kid-oriented hotel, the **Great Wolf Lodge** (549 E. Rochambeau Dr., 757/229-9700, www.greatwolf.com, $229-549) provides endless amusement for the little ones. This Northwoods-themed lodge offers 405 guest rooms and a huge indoor water park complete with waterslides, a wave pool, and a tree house. It is a four-season resort.

The **Kingsmill Resort and Spa** (1010 Kingsmill Rd., 757/253-1703, www.kingsmill.com, $146-479) offers 425 luxurious rooms and suites (with up to three bedrooms) as well as breathtaking views of the James River. It also has golf, a spa, an indoor pool, and summer children's programs. This is a great place for a romantic getaway or to spend time with friends playing golf or taking a spa day.

Camping

There are several good options for camping in Williamsburg. The **Anvil Campground** (5243 Mooretown Rd., 757/565-2300, www.anvilcampground.com, $55-155) is open year-round and offers 77 campsites and two cottages. It has been in operation since 1954 and is close to Colonial Williamsburg with shuttle service available to attractions, restaurants, and shopping. The **Williamsburg KOA Campground** (4000 Newman Rd., 757/565-2907, www.koa.com, starting at $48) is another good option close to Colonial Williamsburg and the theme parks. They offer 180 acres of wooded sites and patio sites (with more than 100 sites total). They also offer bus service to attractions in the peak season. Two additional campgrounds in Williamsburg are the **Williamsburg RV Resort and Campground** (4301 Rochambeau Dr., 757/566-3021, starting at $57), with 158 sites, and the **American Heritage R.V. Park** (146 Maxton Ln., 757/566-2133, www.americanheritagervpark.com, starting at $38), with 103 sites.

Information and Services

The best information on Colonial Williamsburg can be obtained from the **Colonial Williamsburg Foundation** (888/965-7254, www.colonialwilliamsburg.org and www.colonialwilliamsburg.com) and at the **Colonial Williamsburg Regional Visitor Center** (101 Visitor Center Dr., 866/691-7063, daily 8:45am-5pm). For additional information on Williamsburg, contact the **Greater Williamsburg Chamber and Tourism Alliance** (www.williamsburgcc.com) or visit www.visitwilliamsburg.com.

Getting There

Most people arrive in Williamsburg by car. The city is off I-64 approximately 1 hour from Richmond, 1 hour from Norfolk, and 2.5 hours from Washington DC.

The **Newport News/Williamsburg International Airport** (PHF, 900 Bland Blvd., Newport News, www.flyphf.com) is off I-64 at exit 255B. Williamsburg is a 20-minute drive from the airport.

Amtrak (468 N Boundary St., 800/872-7245, www.amtrak.com) offers train service into Williamsburg.

Getting Around

Getting around Colonial Williamsburg

requires a lot of walking. The pedestrian area, where you'll find many of the attractions, is preserved as it was during Revolutionary times when there were no cars. If you are not staying at one of the Colonial Williamsburg hotels, you will want to arrive early during peak season to park outside the pedestrian area. Parking spaces can be difficult to come by, but designated areas are clearly marked. The important thing to remember is not to park in private lots or at the College of William & Mary (even in the summer). Parking restrictions are strictly enforced.

Williamsburg has a reliable bus system called the **Williamsburg Area Transit (WATA)** (www.gowata.org), which offers bus service seven days a week and stops at many of the local hotels. An all-day pass is $3.

Shuttle service between the Colonial Williamsburg Regional Visitor Center and select hotels is available for free to those who have a Colonial Williamsburg ticket. Shuttle tickets can also be obtained at the visitors center.

JAMESTOWN

Jamestown was the first permanent English settlement in America. It was founded in 1607, more than a decade prior to the Pilgrims' arrival at Plymouth. Three small ships carrying 104 men made landfall at Jamestown (which is actually an island) on May 13, 1607. They moored the ships to trees, came ashore the following day, and never left. The newly formed town served as the capital of Virginia during the 17th century.

★ Historic Jamestowne

Historic Jamestowne (1368 Colonial Pkwy., 757/856-1250, www.historicjamestowne.org, daily 9am-5pm, adults $20, children 15 and under free, $10 with receipt from Yorktown Battlefield, discounts given to active military and National Park Pass holders) occupies the site of the original Jamestown settlement on the banks of the James River. It is run by the National Park Service and Preservation

Virginia. The site was also the location of a military post during the American Revolution where prisoners were exchanged from both sides.

Purchase your admission ticket at the visitors center, which shows an informative 18-minute video that is a good start to orienting yourself with the site. From there, continue to "Old Towne," the original settlement site, and explore it on foot. Highlights include the original Memorial Church tower (the oldest structure still standing in the park), a burial ground (many of the first colonists died here), a reconstructed sample of a "mud-and-stud" cottage, and the foundations of several buildings. Another don't-miss sight is the Jamestown Rediscovery excavation, where remains of the original James Fort built in 1607 are being uncovered at an archaeological dig site open to visitors. History programs and children's events are held in the summer months.

Continue on to "New Towne," where you can explore the part of Jamestown that was developed after 1620. The foundations of many homes were excavated in the 1930s and 1950s, and replicas can be seen throughout the site. Next, take a cruise along the Loop Drive, a five-mile wilderness road. Be sure to stop to read the interpretive signs and view the paintings along the route to learn how inhabitants used the island's natural resources, or visit the **Glasshouse** to see artisans creating glass products as glassblowers did back in the early 1600s.

Jamestown Settlement

The **Jamestown Settlement** (2110 Jamestown Rd., 757/253-4838, www.historyisfun.org, daily 9am-5pm with extended summer hours, adults $17.50, children 6-12 $8.25, under 6 free) is one of the most popular museums in Coastal Virginia. It is

1: participants in period costume in Historic Jamestowne 2: navigation tools at Jamestown Settlement 3: Yorktown Battlefield 4: interactive exhibit at the American Revolution Museum at Yorktown

a living museum that re-creates and honors the first permanent English-speaking settlement in the country and takes visitors back to the 1600s. Costumed guides share facts about a Powhatan Village, and there are replicas of the three ships that sailed from England under the command of Captain Christopher Newport and eventually landed at Jamestown. The ships are a highlight of the museum, and the costumed crew does an excellent job of answering questions and showing off every nook and cranny of the ships. The **James Fort** is another main attraction. There, visitors can see authentic meals being prepared, witness arms demonstrations, and even try on armor. Thanksgiving is a great time to visit because special events are held in the museum. Combination tickets can be purchased to other Historic Triangle sites.

Getting There

Jamestown is nine miles southwest of Colonial Williamsburg along the Colonial Parkway.

YORKTOWN

The quaint waterfront village of Yorktown was established in 1691 and is most famous as the site of the historic victory in the American Revolutionary War. It was also an important tobacco port on the York River, where crops were exported from local plantations. During its peak in the mid-1700s, it had nearly 2,000 residents and several hundred buildings. It was a thriving city of primarily merchants, planters, shopkeepers, and indentured servants.

There are many earthworks surrounding Yorktown. These were first built by British troops in 1781, when nearly 80 percent of the town was damaged or destroyed during the Siege of Yorktown. These earthworks were built over with new fortifications by Confederate troops during the Civil War. During the **Siege of 1862,** the Union army was held back by the Confederates for more than a month in this area. After the Confederates left town, Union troops settled in for the rest of the war.

In addition to learning about history, visitors can enjoy art, shopping, special events, and water sports.

Sights
YORKTOWN BATTLEFIELD AND VISITOR CENTER

The **Yorktown National Battlefield** (757/898-2410, www.nps.gov/york) is a national park that marks where, on October 19, 1781, the British army, led by General Charles Lord Cornwallis, surrendered to General George Washington, ending the Revolutionary War. Visitors can see the battlefield, Washington's Headquarters and tent, and the actual surrender field.

The **Yorktown National Battlefield Visitor Center** (1000 Colonial Pkwy., 757/898-2410, reservations 757/898-2411, daily 9am-4:30pm, adults $10 for 7-day pass, children 15 and under free) is a great place to begin your exploration of the battlefield and town. It is a living-history museum where re-creations are staged by historical interpreters in costume. Two self-guided driving tours allow visitors to learn about the Siege of Yorktown at a relaxed pace. An audio tour is available on CD for the drive for $4.95. Guided group tours are also available for a fee (rates vary depending on the number of participants), and reservations should be made two months in advance.

The entrance fee is paid at the visitor centers, where maps are available as well as an informative 15-minute orientation film that should be your first order of business if you're a first-timer to the site. The admission fee at Yorktown includes entrance into historic houses, entrance to the battlefield, and access to a variety of interpretive programs and is good for seven days. Your pass can be upgraded to visit Jamestown Settlement at the Historic Jamestown Visitor Center for an additional $10.

The 84-foot-tall **Yorktown Victory Monument** and the **Moore House,** where the surrender terms were negotiated, are fascinating sites at the battlefield. The Victory

Monument was not erected until 100 years after the end of the war. Its purpose was to "keep fresh in memory the all decisive successes that had been achieved." The four-sided base has an inscription on each side: one for victory, one for a succinct narrative of the siege, one for the treaty of alliance with France, and one for the resulting peace treaty with England. The pediments over the inscriptions feature emblems of nationality, war, alliance, and peace. The monument's podium is a "symbol of the birth of freedom." The column (coming out of the podium) symbolizes the greatness and prosperity of the United States after a century. On top of the monument's shaft is a sculpture of Liberty, which attests to the existence of a nation governed by the people, for the people.

AMERICAN REVOLUTION MUSEUM AT YORKTOWN

Near the battlefield is the **American Revolution Museum at Yorktown** (200 Water St., 757/253-4838, www.historyisfun. org, daily 9am-5pm with extended summer hours, adults $15, children 6-12 $7.50, under 6 free), an informative museum dedicated to the American Revolution that chronicles the entire era beginning with unrest in the colonies and ending with the creation of a new nation. Visitors can view hundreds of artifacts, enjoy interactive exhibits, and take in *The Siege of Yorktown* film on a 180-degree screen.

Outdoor exhibits include the re-creation of a Continental Army encampment featuring live historical interpreters and daily demonstrations that teach about artillery, cooking, and medical treatment of the time. They also include a reconstructed farm that even has an orchard, crop fields, and tobacco barn.

Summer is the best time to visit since there are outdoor living-history exhibits (you might even be asked to help load a cannon), but the museum is wonderful to visit all year.

If you're lucky enough to be here on the Fourth of July, you can experience the **Liberty Celebration** firsthand. What better location to celebrate American's independence than where it all began? The celebration includes a plethora of reenactments, military drills, and food demonstrations. This event complements the **Yorktown Fourth of July Celebration** that takes place in the evening on July 4.

HISTORIC YORKTOWN

Yorktown still has a sparse population of full-time residents. Its streets are lined with historic homes, some more than two centuries old. There's Yorktown Beach, a pleasant sandy beach along the York River, and overall, Yorktown offers a relaxing place to explore history, shop, and dine.

Riverwalk Landing (425 Water St., 757/890-3500, www.riverwalklanding.com) is a pedestrian walkway along the York River. This quaint area includes retail shops and dining. Take a stroll on the mile-long River View path that runs along the York River from the Yorktown Battlefield to the Yorktown Victory Center. Riverwalk Landing is a great place to take a walk, go shopping, or grab an ice-cream cone on a hot day.

The **Watermen's Museum** (309 Water St., 757/887-2641, www.watermens.org, Apr.-Dec. 22 Tues.-Sat. 10am-5pm, Sun. 1pm-5pm, closed the rest of the year, adults $5, seniors and students $4, children under 6 and military free) highlights the role that watermen on the Chesapeake Bay's rivers and tributaries had in the formation of our country. This is done through displays illustrating the methods of their trade and craft. Visitors learn what it means to earn a living harvesting seafood from the Chesapeake Bay watershed. The museum offers educational programs and a waterfront facility that can be rented for events.

The **Nelson House** (501 Main St., 757/898-2410, www.nps.gov/york, open as staffing permits, $10) is a prominent 18th-century structure on Main Street. It was built in the Georgian manor style by the grandfather of

Thomas Nelson Jr., one of Yorktown's most famous residents. The younger Nelson was the governor of Virginia in 1781 and the commander of the Virginia militia during the siege. He was also a signer of the Declaration of Independence. Damage from the siege is still evident at the Nelson House. Informal tours are available throughout the year. It's best to call for hours because the house is not open continuously.

Recreation

Yorktown is a waterfront town and outdoor recreation haven. The mile-long **Riverwalk** is a great place for a power walk or to stretch your legs after travel. The two-acre beach near the Riverwalk offers a great location for launching a kayak, swimming, and beachcombing.

There are also kayak and canoe launches at nearby **Old Wormley Creek Landing** (1110 Old Wormley Creek Rd.), with access to Wormley Creek and the York River; **Rodgers A. Smith Landing** (707 Tide Mill Rd.), with access to the Poquoson River and the lower Chesapeake Bay; and **New Quarter Park** (1000 Lakeshead Dr., Williamsburg, 757/890-5840, www.yorkcounty.gov), with access to Queens Creek and the York River.

The **Riverwalk Landing Piers** (425 Water St.) is a pleasant place to enjoy a day of fishing, and visitors can dock their boats there.

For bicycle rentals ($7.50 per hour or $25 for four hours), kayak and stand-up paddleboard (SUP) rentals ($30-45 for two hours), or guided Segway tours ($39 for one hour or $65 for two hours), contact **Patriot Tours & Provisions** (757/969-5400, www.patriottoursva.com).

If sailing on a romantic schooner sounds appealing, **Yorktown Sailing Charter** (757/639-1233, www.sailyorktown.com, adults $37, children 12 and under $25 for two hours) docks its beautiful sailing vessel, the schooner *Alliance,* at the pier at Riverwalk Landing April-October. They offer daily sailing trips during the day and at sunset. Daytime trips leave at either 11am or 2pm.

Sunset cruise times vary by month. Its sister schooner, *Serenity,* offers pirate cruises (adults $37, children 12 and under $25), educational trips, and charters for those looking for a bit of adventure.

Entertainment and Events

The **Lighted Boat Parade** (Yorktown Beach) kicks off the holiday season in early December with a festive procession featuring power- and sailboats adorned with holiday lights. Musical performances and caroling are held on the beach by the light of a bonfire, and hot cider is served. The event is free to the public.

The **Yorktown Wine Festival** (425 Water St. at Riverwalk Landing, tastings $30-35) is held in October and features wines from throughout Virginia. Art and food vendors also share their wares at the festival. Another October festival is the **York River Maritime Heritage Festival** (309 Water St., 757/887-2641, www.watermens.org, free). It offers two days of music, vendors, re-enactors, and crafts.

Shopping

Yorktown's Main Street in the Historic Village is lined with unique shops and galleries. There are antiques stores, galleries, and jewelry and glass shops to name a few. Down by the water at Riverwalk Landing are additional shops featuring colonial architecture and offering art, home items, jewelry, quilts, and clothing.

Auntie M's American Cottage (330 Water St., 757/369-8150, Mon.-Sat. 10:30am-6:30pm, Sun. 11am-6:30pm) sells handcrafted work that is made in America.

Viccellio Goldsmith & Fine Jewelry (325 Water St., 757/890-2162, Sun 12pm-4pm, Mon.-Sat. 10am-6pm) sells unique jewelry made by local master goldsmith and precious metals craftsman J. Henry Viccellio.

Food

The **Carrot Tree Kitchen** (323 Water St., 757/988-1999, www.carrottreekitchens.com, daily 10am-4pm, under $10) is a small, casual lunch spot on the waterfront with delightful food. Don't be turned off by the paper plates and plastic utensils; the Carrot Tree offers delicious lunches of sandwiches and comfort food. Save room for the carrot cake—it's their signature dessert.

The **Riverwalk Restaurant** (323 Water St., 757/875-1522, www.riverwalkrestaurant. net, Mon.-Sat. 11am-9pm, Sun. 10am-8pm, $10-42) provides diners with a scenic view of the York River through large glass windows and a cozy fireplace for cool evenings. The fare is primarily seafood and steak, but they also offer a selection of salads. This is a great place to relax after a day of sightseeing.

If fresh seafood and cold beer right on the beach sound like a good ending to a day of exploration in Yorktown, stop in at the **Yorktown Pub** (540 Water St., 757/886-9964, www.yorktownpub.com, Sun.-Thurs. 11am-midnight, Fri.-Sat. 11am-2am, $9-29). The atmosphere is very casual, but the food and service are good. The pub burger, local oysters, and hush puppies are among the best choices. The place is crowded on the weekends, so plan ahead.

Accommodations
UNDER $200

The **Duke of York Hotel** (508 Water St., 757/898-3232, www.dukeofyorkhotelwaterfro ntyorktownva.com, $149-169) is an older hotel with a great location right on the water. This family-run establishment has all river-view rooms (some have balconies and some open to landscaped grounds), an outdoor pool, and an on-site café and restaurant. The Yorktown Trolley stops in front of the hotel.

The **York River Inn Bed & Breakfast** (209 Ambler St., 757/887-8800, www. yorkriverinn.com, $135-165) sits on a bluff overlooking the York River and offers two rooms, a suite with private bathrooms, and all the hospitality you can imagine from its friendly owner (who is also a knockout breakfast chef). This is a wonderful, colonial-style inn with elegant rooms.

The **Marl Inn Bed & Breakfast** (220 Church St., 301/807-0386, www. marlinnbandb.com, $115-145) is two blocks from the Riverwalk. This colonial-style home is a private residence and inn offering four guest rooms; rates can be booked with no breakfast or with full breakfast. The owner is a great-grandson of Thomas Nelson Jr. of Nelson House.

$200-300

The ★ **Hornsby House Inn** (702 Main St., 757/369-0200, www.hornsbyhouseinn.com, $149-238) offers five beautiful guest rooms with private modern bathrooms in an exquisite colonial home. The inn is in the heart of Yorktown and offers a great view of the York River. It is also just a short walk from the Yorktown Battlefield. The inn is run by two friendly brothers who grew up in the house and provide exemplary service, wine and cheese, and a delicious fresh breakfast each morning. The owners take the time to eat breakfast with and get to know their guests as well as share the history of their home. They also make recommendations for attractions in the area and the best strategy for enjoying them. The house is beautifully appointed and is a warm and inviting home away from home. Book the Monument Grand Suite and enjoy a private outdoor terrace overlooking the York River and Yorktown Victory Monument.

Information and Services

For additional information on Yorktown, visit www.visityorktown.org and www.yorkcounty. gov.

Getting There and Around

Yorktown is 13 miles southeast of Williamsburg along the Colonial Parkway. The **Yorktown Trolley** (757/890-3500, www.visityorktown.org, daily 11am-5pm, extended service hours June-Aug., free) is a free seasonal trolley service with stops in nine locations around Yorktown. It runs every 20-25 minutes from the end of March until November.

James River Plantations

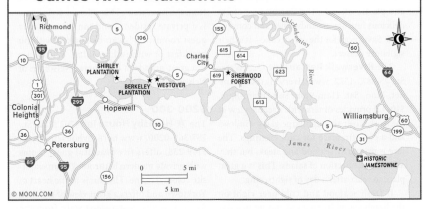

JAMES RIVER PLANTATIONS

Between Richmond and Williamsburg (in Charles City County) along State Route 5 are four stunning plantations that survived the Revolutionary War, War of 1812, and Civil War. These treasures, which span three centuries, are all privately owned National Register properties that are open to the public. For additional information on all four plantations, visit www.jamesriverplantations.org.

Sherwood Forest

Sherwood Forest (State Route 5, 14501 John Tyler Hwy., Charles City, 804/829-5377, www.sherwoodforest.org, grounds open daily 9am-5pm) sounds like a place out of a fairy tale, and it kind of is. This beautiful plantation was the home of President John Tyler for 20 years. The home has been the residence of the Tyler family continuously since he purchased it in 1842.

At more than 300 feet in length—longer than a football field—Sherwood Forest is the longest frame house in the country. The home evolved from a modest 17th-century English-style home (circa 1660) into a substantial 19th-century "Big House" that features a ballroom designed specifically for dancers to engage in the Virginia reel. There is also a resident ghost.

Self-guided walking tours of the grounds are available for $10 per person (children 15 and under free). The tour features 21 numbered stations on 25 acres with information on the 19th-century plantation. The grounds include terraced gardens, quiet woodlands, and lush lawn. A printed guide is available at a kiosk at the main entrance and features descriptions and history information for each station. House tours are only available by appointment and cost $35 for adults and $25 for children.

Westover

Speaking of fairy tales, **Westover** (off State Route 5, 7000 Westover Rd., 804/829-2882, www.westover-plantation.com, grounds open daily 10am-5pm, adults $5, children 7-16 $2, children 6 and under free) could have come straight off the pages of one. William Byrd II, who founded the city of Richmond, built the home in 1730. Westover is known for its architectural details, but kids of all ages will love it for its secret passages and enchanting gardens. The mansion is widely considered to be one of the top examples of Georgian architecture in the country. The house itself is not open to the public, but there are still many interesting things to see on the grounds, which offer wide views of the James River. The icehouse and another small structure to the east of the mansion contain a dry well and passageways leading under the house and down to the river. These were created as an escape route from the house during attacks.

Shirley Plantation

Shirley Plantation (501 Shirley Plantation Rd., 804/829-5121, www.shirleyplantation. com, daily mid-Mar.-Dec. 10am-4pm, house and grounds admission for adults $25, children 7-16 $17.50, seniors 60 and over $22.50, military/veterans $20, children 6 and under free) was the first plantation built in Virginia. It was established in 1613, just six years after Jamestown, and construction was completed in 1738. This property has a legacy of 11 generations of one family (descendants of Edward Hill I) who still own and operate the colonial estate. It has survived attacks, war, and the Great Depression and remains the oldest farm and family-owned business in the United States.

Admission includes a guided house tour that showcases original furnishings, artwork, silver, and hand-carved woodwork. Special architectural features include a "flying staircase" and a Queen Anne forecourt. A self-guided grounds tour features gardens and original outbuildings. Allow at least one hour for your visit. Admission for just the grounds is also available (adults $11, children

7-16 $7.50, seniors and military $9.50, children 6 and under free).

Berkeley Plantation

Berkeley Plantation (12602 Harrison Landing Rd., 804/829-6018, www. berkeleyplantation.com, daily Jan.-Feb. 10:30am-3:30pm, Mar.-Dec. 9:30am-4:30pm, adults $12.50, children 6-16 $7, seniors 60 and over and military $11.50, children 5 and under free) is famous for being the site of the first official Thanksgiving in 1619, although substantiated claims for the first Thanksgiving also belong to locations in Florida, Texas, Maine, and Massachusetts. It is also the birthplace and home of Declaration of Independence signer Benjamin Harrison and President William Henry Harrison. The beautiful Georgian mansion, which was erected in 1726, sits on a hilltop overlooking the James River. The brick used to build the home was fired on the plantation.

Guided tours are conducted in the mansion and feature a nice collection of 18th-century antiques. An audiovisual presentation is included in the tour, as is access to a museum collection of Civil War artifacts and unique paintings by artist Sydney King. Visitors can then tour the grounds on their own and explore five terraces of boxwood and flower gardens. Allow approximately 1.5 hours for the house tour and to roam the gardens.

Hampton Roads

The Hampton Roads region is all about water. In sailors' terms, "Roadstead" means a safe anchorage or sheltered harbor. The word "Hampton" came from an English aristocrat, Henry Wriothesley, who was the third earl of Southampton. Hence, Hampton Roads.

Hampton Roads, which used to be known as Tidewater Virginia, contains one of the largest natural deepwater harbors in the world. The harbor is where the James, Elizabeth, and Nansemond Rivers meet the

Chesapeake Bay. Pioneers first settled the area in 1610, after disease struck nearby Jamestown. The area was a throughway for goods from both the colonies and England and, as such, drew merchants and pirates. One of history's most famous pirates, Blackbeard (Edward Teach), plundered the port and waters of Hampton Roads, which was just a short distance from his base in North Carolina.

The port in Hampton Roads is the country's second largest to New York City and is notable for remaining ice-free year-round. It is also the birthplace of the modern U.S. Navy.

Defining the Hampton Roads area can be a bit confusing. Technically, the Historic Triangle is considered part of Hampton Roads, but the coastal cities from Newport News to Virginia Beach are more commonly thought of as the Hampton Roads area.

NEWPORT NEWS

Newport News is a short drive from Williamsburg, Virginia Beach, and the Atlantic Ocean. There are several versions of whom Newport News was named for, but the most widely accepted is that it was named for Captain Christopher Newport, who was in charge of the three ships that landed in Jamestown in 1607. The "news" part of the name came from the news that was sent back to England on the ships' safe arrival.

Sights
THE MARINERS' MUSEUM AND PARK

The Mariners' Museum and Park (100 Museum Dr., 757/596-2222, www. marinersmuseum.org, Mon.-Sat. 9am-5pm, Sun. 11am-5pm, museum admission $1, children 3 and under free, museum and 3D movie $7, children 3 and under free) is one of the largest maritime history museums in the United States. It has more than 60,000 square feet of gallery space showing maritime paintings, artifacts, figureheads, ship models, and small craft from around the world. Exhibits include vessels for warfare, exploration, pleasure, and fishing. A highlight of the museum is the USS Monitor Center, where a full-scale replica of the Civil War battleship USS *Monitor* is housed. In 1862 the *Monitor* battled the CSS *Virginia* in what went down in history as the first engagement of steam-powered iron warships (aka The Battle of the Ironclads). Visitors can learn about the historic encounter in the Battle Theater. The center is also home to recovered parts of the original battleship, which sank off the coast of Cape Hatteras, North Carolina, in December 1862.

The museum offers countless other collections including the **Crabtree Collection of Miniature Ships.** The museum is very kid friendly and offers numerous events, lectures, and even a concert series (check the website for upcoming events). The park (daily 6am-7pm, free) offers a five-mile trail along Lake Maury. There is also boating and hiking.

THE VIRGINIA LIVING MUSEUM

Endangered red wolves, loggerhead turtles, and moon jellyfish are just some of the amazing animals you can get close to at **The Virginia Living Museum** (524 J. Clyde Morris Blvd., 757/595-1900, www.thevlm. org, daily 9am-5pm, extended summer hours, adults $20, children 3-12 $15). This is a wonderful place to learn about Virginia's natural heritage. Indoor exhibits, outdoor exhibits, four interactive discovery centers, and gardens showcase Virginia's geographical regions and the more than 250 species of plants and animals that live in the state. The 30,000-gallon aquarium is a focal point for kids of all ages. Many hands-on activities are also offered, such as touch tanks and live feedings, and there is even a planetarium.

VIRGINIA WAR MUSEUM

The **Virginia War Museum** (9285 Warwick Blvd., 757/247-8523, www.warmuseum.org, Mon.-Sat. 9am-5pm, Sun. noon-5pm, adults $8, children 7-18 $6, children under 7 free, seniors 62 and over and military $7) explains the development of the U.S. military from 1775 to modern times. Its many exhibits showcase war efforts throughout our country's history. Weapons, artifacts, and uniforms are displayed from the Revolutionary War through the Vietnam War, and exhibits explain the evolution of weaponry, the role of women in the military, and contributions made by African Americans to military history, as well as provide a tribute to prisoners of war.

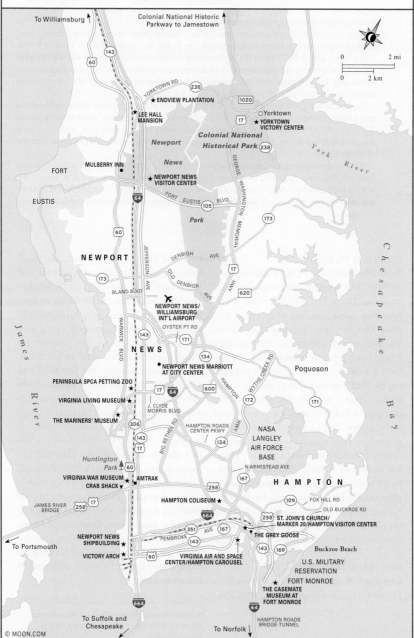

Northern Hampton Roads

Shipbuilding in Newport News

Newport News is home to the largest privately owned shipyard in the country, **Newport News Shipbuilding** (a division of Huntington Ingalls Industries, https://nns.huntingtoningalls.com) on Washington Avenue along the James River. The facility was built in 1886 for a sum of $7 million and was called the Chesapeake Dry Dock and Construction Company. Its 4,000 employees repaired the many vessels that came to use the ever-growing transportation hub in the Hampton Roads area. The yard produced its first tugboat (named *Dorothy*) in 1891. By 1897, the company had produced three additional tugboats for the U.S. Navy.

Business took off with the onset of the Great Naval Race of the early 1900s. At the start of World War I, shipbuilding was in full swing, and the company constructed six dreadnoughts and 25 destroyers for the U.S. Navy. The company has been going full force ever since, with its achievements including building the first nuclear-powered submarine and the famous ocean liner the SS *United States*.

Today, the company is the largest private employer in Hampton Roads. The 20,000 employees (many of whom are third- and fourth-generation shipbuilders) turn raw steel into some of the world's most complex ships. The shipyard is the country's sole designer and builder of nuclear-powered aircraft carriers and also one of only two companies that design and build nuclear submarines.

ENDVIEW PLANTATION

Endview Plantation (362 Yorktown Rd., 757/857-1862, www.endview.org, Apr.-Dec. Mon. and Thurs.-Fri. 10am-4pm, Sat. 10am-5pm, Sun. noon-5pm, Jan.-Mar. Thurs.-Sat. 10am-4pm, Sun. 1pm-5pm, adults $8, children 7-18 $6, seniors 62 and over $7, children under 7 free) was a privately owned estate that was used briefly as a Confederate hospital during the 1862 Peninsula Campaign. The small, white, T-frame Georgian-style home was later occupied by Federal troops. The house sits on top of a knoll, and a spring flows at the base of the hill. This, coupled with the beautiful rolling farmland that surrounds the place, has made it an attractive location for centuries. The city of Newport News purchased the plantation in 1995 and restored it to its original configuration. School programs are held at the plantation, and guided tours of the house and grounds are offered periodically.

LEE HALL MANSION

Lee Hall Mansion (163 Yorktown Rd., 757/888-3371, www.leehall.org, Apr.-Dec. Mon. and Thurs.-Fri. 10am-4pm, Sat. 10am-5pm, Sun. noon-5pm, Jan.-Mar. Thurs.-Sat. 10am-4pm, Sun. 1pm-5pm, adults $8, children 7-18 $6, seniors $7, children under 7 free) is the only remaining large antebellum plantation on the lower Virginia peninsula. The 6,600-square-foot structure is a blend of several architectural styles, including Italianate, Georgian, and Greek Revival. The primary style, however, is Italianate. The redbrick home was built on a rise in the 1850s and was home to wealthy planter Richard Decatur Lee. Due to the mansion's commanding view, the home served as headquarters for Confederate generals John Magruder and Joseph E. Johnston during the 1862 Peninsula Campaign. Visitors can take a step back in time to the mid-Victorian period and view hundreds of artifacts in the mansion's authentically furnished rooms. Combination admission tickets for Lee Hall Mansion, Endview Plantation, and the Virginia War Museum can be purchased for $21 for adults, children $15, and seniors $18.

1: The Mariners' Museum 2: The Virginia Living Museum in Newport News 3: Victory Arch in Newport News

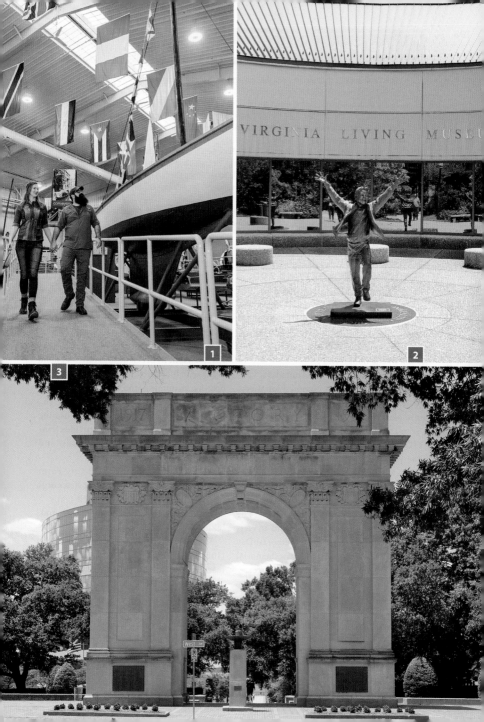

The Peninsula Campaign of 1862

The Peninsula Campaign of 1862 was an aggressive plan designed by Union forces during the Civil War to outsmart Confederate defenses in Northern Virginia by moving 121,000 troops by sea to the Virginia Peninsula between the York and James Rivers. This would place them to the east of Richmond, the Confederate capital. Having bypassed the Northern Virginia forces, the army, led by General George B. McClellan, would be able to advance on Richmond without meeting entrenched opposition.

The failure of this plan remains a highly debated episode in the war. Union troops moved slowly and never made a serious attack on Richmond, despite their strategic placement. Although they were met by small Confederate forces, McClellan blamed the failure on Washington for not providing men and support for the effort, even though his troops outnumbered the Confederates throughout the campaign.

From the Confederate standpoint, the Peninsula Campaign of 1862 resulted in the emergence of two great commanders, Stonewall Jackson and Robert E. Lee, who jointly kept the Union forces out of Richmond.

PENINSULA SPCA PETTING ZOO

The **Peninsula SPCA Petting Zoo** (523 J. Clyde Morris Blvd., 757/595-1399, www. peninsulaspca.org, Mon.-Sat. 11am-5pm, $3) is a fun place to bring the kids for a hands-on experience with barnyard animals. The zoo is run by the nonprofit Peninsula Society for the Prevention of Cruelty to Animals (SPCA). Visitors can enjoy the company of sheep, goats, chickens, ducks, and other friendly animals.

VICTORY ARCH

The **Victory Arch** (25th St. and West Ave., 757/926-1400, www.nnva.gov) was built in 1919. Troops returning from World War I marched through the arch in victory parades after disembarking from their ships. The arch was reconstructed in 1962, and an eternal flame was added to it on Memorial Day in 1969. Today the arch stands as a memorial to all men and women of the armed forces.

Recreation
PARKS

The **Newport News Park** (13560 Jefferson Ave., 757/888-3333, www.newport-news.org) is one of the largest municipal parks in the country, encompassing nearly 8,000 acres. Boat and bike rentals are available in the park, as are hiking and biking trails, picnicking, canoeing, archery, disc golf, fishing, and camping. The park's Discovery Center has many hands-on activities and historical artifacts.

Huntington Park-Beach, Rose Garden & Tennis Center (361 Hornet Cir., 757/886-7912, www.newport-news.org) offers a public beach with lifeguards, a playground, baseball, boating, swimming, and tennis.

King-Lincoln Park (600 Jefferson Ave., 757/888-3333, www.nnva.gov) overlooks the Hampton Roads Harbor and provides fishing, tennis, picnicking, playgrounds, and basketball.

Riverview Farm Park (105 City Farm Rd., 757/886-7912, www.newport-news.org) has two miles of multiuse paved trails, a 30,000-square-foot community playground, biking, hiking, and soccer fields.

The Mariners' Museum Park (100 Museum Dr., 757/596-2222, www. marinersmuseum.org) offers a five-mile trail along Lake Maury. There is also boating and hiking.

GOLF

Golfers can get their fix at two local courses: **Kiln Creek Golf Club and Resort** (1003 Brick Kiln Blvd., 757/874-2600, www.kilncreekgolf.com, $33-59) and **Newport News Golf Club at Deer Run**

(901 Clubhouse Way, 757/886-7925, www. nngolfclub.com, $17-38).

FISHING

Fishing enthusiasts will enjoy the **James River Fishing Pier** (2019 James River Bridge, 757/274-0364, adults $9, children 6-12 and seniors 65 and over $7), which is made entirely of concrete and has LED lights. It is one of the longest fishing piers on the East Coast.

BOATING

Boaters can make the **Leeward Marina** (7499 River Rd., 757/274-2359, www.newport-news. org) a base for exploration of the Hampton Roads Harbor and the Chesapeake Bay.

Entertainment and Events

FERGUSON CENTER FOR THE ARTS

The **Ferguson Center for the Arts** (1 Ave. of the Arts, 757/594-8752, www.fergusoncenter. org) at Christopher Newport University is a performance hall that also houses the university's theater, arts, and music departments. The center contains a 1,725-seat concert hall and a 200-seat studio theater. It offers a wide range of performances. Check the website for upcoming events.

PENINSULA FINE ARTS CENTER

The **Peninsula Fine Arts Center** (101 Museum Dr., 757/596-8175, www.pfac-va.org, Tues.-Sat. 10am-5pm, Sun. 1pm-5pm) is dedicated to the promotion of the fine arts. It offers exhibits, a studio art school, an interactive gallery, educational programs, and hands-on activities for children.

EVENTS

The **Newport News Fall Festival** (www. nnva.gov) is held on the first weekend in October and has been running since 1972. The festival draws 35,000 visitors annually and has more than 150 exhibitors featuring trade demonstrations, crafts, and food.

The **Newport News Children's Festival of Friends** (www.nnva.gov) is held at the beginning of May and offers a variety of themed areas for children. Activities, rides, entertainment, and food are all part of the fun of this popular festival that's been going on since 1990.

Shopping

The **City Center at Oyster Point** (701 Town Center Dr., 757/873-2020, www. citycenteratoysterpoint.com) is an outdoor town center with retail stores, gourmet eateries, spas, and salons.

The **Patrick Henry Mall** (12300 Jefferson Ave., 757/249-4305, www. shoppatrickhenrymall.com) is the largest mall on the peninsula, with more than 120 stores in a single-level, indoor configuration.

Food

AMERICAN

★ **Circa 1918 Kitchen & Bar** (10367 Warwick Blvd., 757/599-1918, Tues.-Sat. 5pm-10pm, $18-32) offers delicious food, a lovely wine list, wonderful specials, seasonal selections, and friendly, professional service. Sample menu items include bison meat loaf, pan roasted sea scallops, and grilled lamb burgers. The restaurant is in the historic, two-block-long Hilton Village neighborhood. The atmosphere is relaxed and comfortable, and separate groups of patrons actually talk to each other. Don't shy away from interacting—you could get a great tip for what to order. This is a small restaurant with only about a dozen tables, so reservations are highly recommended.

Fin Seafood (3150 William Styron Sq., 757/599-5800, www.finseafood.com, daily 11am-10pm, $28-100) is a great choice for a romantic dinner or a large gathering. It is a local favorite for delicious seafood and high-end steaks. They use mostly organic and sustainable produce and proteins, as well as seasonal ingredients.

Second Street American Bistro (115 Arthur Way, 757/234-4448, www.secondst. com, Mon.-Thurs. 11:30am-10pm, Fri.-Sat. 11:30am-11pm, Sun. 11am-10pm, $8-31) is an upscale yet casual restaurant with a wide menu selection, including small plates, pizza, burgers, steak, chicken, ribs, fish, and many desserts. There is also a wonderfully extensive wine list and they offer tasting events.

Brickhouse Tavern (141 Herman Melville Ave., 757/223-9531, www. welcometobrickhouse.com, daily 11am-2am, $8-13) is a casual restaurant serving a variety of pub food, including burgers and pizza. **Chic N Fish** (954 J. Clyde Morris Blvd., 757/223-6517, www.chicnfishva.com, Mon.-Sat. 11am-9pm, $5-25) serves up a little bit of everything including burgers, seafood, and Korean fried chicken.

One of the best views in town is from the **Crab Shack** (7601 River Rd., 757/245-2722, www.crabshackonthejames.com, Sun.-Thurs. 11am-11:30pm, Fri.-Sat. 11am-12:30am, $8-24), on the James River waterfront. This casual seafood restaurant serves sandwiches and entrées in a window-lined dining room or on an outdoor deck.

ITALIAN

For good mid-priced Italian food, try **Al Fresco** (11710 Jefferson Ave., 757/873-0644, www.alfrescoitalianrestaurant.com, Mon.-Fri. 11am-3pm and 5pm-10pm, Sat. 5pm-10pm, $8-27).

Accommodations

UNDER $100

The **Mulberry Inn & Plaza at Fort Eustis** (16890 Warwick Blvd., 757/887-3000, www. mulberryinnva.com, $63-139) is a 101-room hotel offering standard rooms, efficiencies, and studios that can hold up to four people. It is close to I-64 and has amenities such as an outdoor pool, a fitness center, and a business center. Hot breakfast is included, and they are pet friendly.

$100-200

The **Comfort Suites Airport** (12570 Jefferson Ave., 757/947-1333, www. choicehotels.com, $89-170) is the hotel closest to the Newport News/Williamsburg

International Airport. It offers all suite accommodations, a free airport shuttle, an indoor pool, and a spacious workout facility.

The **Hilton Garden Inn Newport News** (180 Regal Way, 757/947-1080, http:// hiltongardeninn3.hilton.com, $119-129) offers 122 guest rooms, an indoor heated pool and spa, an airport shuttle, and easy access to the city center and military bases.

OVER $200

The **Newport News Marriott at City Center** (740 Town Center Dr., 757/873-9299, www.marriott.com, $187-409) is a 256-room hotel near shopping and many restaurants. It offers a pool and workout facility.

Camping

Year-round camping is available in **Newport News Park** (13564 Jefferson Ave., 757/888-3333, www.nnva.gov, $33-40). This is one of the biggest municipal parks on the East Coast, and it has 188 campsites with hot showers and restroom facilities. The 8,000-acre park is a combination of woods, meadows, and lakes (campsites are wooded).

Information and Services

For additional information on Newport News, visit www.newport-news.org or stop by the **Newport News Visitor Center** (13560 Jefferson Ave., 757/886-7777, daily 9am-5pm), off I-64 at exit 250B.

Getting There and Around

Newport News is located along I-64 and US Route 60.

The **Newport News/Williamsburg International Airport** (PHF, 900 Bland Blvd., www.flyphf.com) is off I-64 at exit 255B. Downtown Newport News is a 15-minute drive from the airport.

Amtrak (9304 Warwick Blvd., 757/245-3589, www.amtrak.com) has a station in Newport News at Huntington Park. Consult the website for schedules and fares.

Newport News, Hampton, Norfolk, and Virginia Beach are connected by **Hampton**

Roads Transit (757/222-6100. www.gohrt. com). Consult the website for schedules and fares.

HAMPTON

Hampton is the oldest continuously inhabited English-speaking community in the United States, with a history dating back to 1607. It is also home to Langley Air Force Base. Hampton was partially destroyed during three major wars—the Revolutionary War, the War of 1812, and the Civil War—but was rebuilt each time and continues to undergo renovations even today. The city now offers an attractive waterfront filled with modern sailing and fishing boats and a variety of attractions for visitors and residents.

Sights

VIRGINIA AIR & SPACE CENTER

The **Virginia Air & Space Center** (600 Settlers Landing Rd., 757/727-0900, www. vasc.org, Mon.-Sat. 10am-5pm, Sun. noon-5pm, extended summer hours, adults $20, children 3-18 $16.50, under 3 free, active military $17, seniors $18, includes IMAX) houses more than 100 interactive exhibits that detail the historic achievements of NASA. Topics include space travel, aircraft development, and communications, as well as a hands-on space gallery. Hampton was the birthplace of the space program in the United States and has played an important role in the 100-plus-year history of flight. Displays include more than 30 historic airplanes, the Apollo 12 command module, a passenger jet, moon rocks, and many replicas.

THE HAMPTON CAROUSEL

The **Hampton Carousel** (602 Settlers Landing Rd., Carousel Park, 757/727-1610, www.hampton.gov, Apr.-Dec. Tues.-Sun. 11am-8pm, $1) was originally built for an amusement park at Buckroe Beach, where it resided between 1921 and 1985. It is now on the waterfront in downtown Hampton, fully restored and protected from the elements. The merry-go-round's 48 horses and chariots were hand-carved out of hardwood, and it is adorned with original paintings and mirrors. It also still plays the original organ music.

THE CASEMATE MUSEUM AT FORT MONROE

The **Casemate Museum** (20 Bernard Rd., 757/788-3391, www.fortmonroe.org, Tues.-Sun. 10:30am-4:30pm, daily during the summer, free) on the grounds of Fort Monroe shares many exhibits about the fort, which was built in 1834 to protect the Chesapeake Bay, James River, and Hampton River. This is the largest stone fort in the country. The museum contains the prison cell where Confederate president Jefferson Davis was held and also the living quarters of Robert E. Lee while he was stationed there from 1831 to 1834. Other displays include military uniforms and supplies. The grounds at Fort Monroe are open year-round for walking and other outdoor activities.

ST. JOHN'S EPISCOPAL CHURCH

St. John's Episcopal Church (100 W. Queens Way, 757/722-2567, www. stjohnshampton.org) is the oldest English-speaking parish in the United States. The church was founded in 1610, and the current structure was built in 1728. The church was designed in the shape of a Latin cross and boasts beautiful colonial-style brickwork, two-foot-thick walls, and stained glass windows. The church survived the Revolutionary War, the War of 1812, and the Civil War. The silver used for communion dates back to 1618 and is considered to be the most valuable relic in the American Anglican Church. Services are still held here; consult the website for details.

Recreation

Buckroe Beach (N. 1st St., www.hampton. gov) is a wide, sandy, eight-acre beach on the Chesapeake Bay. There is a playground, picnic shelters, a bike path, and certified lifeguards on duty. Concerts are held in the summer months, as is an outdoor family-movie series.

COASTAL VIRGINIA
HAMPTON ROADS

Grandview Nature Preserve (State Park Dr., www.hampton.gov) is a local secret. This nature preserve and beach at the end of Beach Road in Grandview is great for families and allows dogs in the off-season.

Hampton is located at the entrance to the Chesapeake Bay and is a convenient stopping point for boaters. Those traveling by boat can stop at the **Blue Water Yachting Center** (15 Marina Rd., 757/723-6774, www.bluewateryachtcenter.com), which offers daily dockage.

If you don't have your own boat but wish to take a relaxing sightseeing cruise, board the double-decker *Miss Hampton II* (757/722-9102, www.misshamptoncruises.com, adults $27, children 7-12 $17, active military $13.50, retired military and seniors 65 and over $25, 6 and under free, for 2.5-3 hours), a motorized vessel that offers cruising in Hampton Harbor and on the Chesapeake Bay.

Golf enthusiasts can play at the **Woodlands Golf Course** (9 Woodlands Rd., 757/727-1195, www.hampton.gov, $13-19) or the **Hamptons Golf Course** (320 Butler Farm Rd., 757/766-9148, www.hampton.gov, $14-21).

Entertainment and Events
The **Hampton Coliseum** (1000 Coliseum Dr., 757/838-4203, www.hamptoncoliseum.org) is the premier venue in Hampton for concerts, performances, and sporting events. A list of upcoming events can be found on the website. The Coliseum is convenient to I-64 and offers free parking.

The annual **Hampton Jazz Festival** (www.hamptonjazzfestival.com) has been going on since 1968. It is held for three days at the end of June in the Hampton Coliseum. Information on the lineup and tickets can be found on the website.

The **Hampton Cup Regatta** (www.hamptoncupregatta.com) is billed as the "oldest continually run motorsport event in the

world." It is held for three days in September in Mill Creek, between Fort Monroe and the East Mercury Boulevard Bridge. Another fun water festival is the **Blackbeard Pirate Festival** (www.blackbeardfestival.com), held at the beginning of June each year. The Hampton waterfront is overrun with pirate re-enactors as visitors are taken back to the 18th century. There is live music, children's activities, vendors, fireworks, and arts and crafts.

Food
Surf Rider Bluewater (1 Marina Rd., 757/723-9366, www.surfriderrestaurant.com, opens daily 11am, $7-30) is a family-owned seafood restaurant in the Blue Water Yachting Center off Ivy Home Road. This is a great place for local seafood, which you can tell by the number of local residents eating here. Their crab cakes are famous, as are the oysters, tuna, and hush puppies.

Venture Kitchen and Bar (9 E. Queens Way, 757/325-8868, www.venturekitchenandbar.com, Mon.-Thurs. 11am-10pm, Fri.-Sat. 11am-midnight, Sun. 10am-10pm, $8-15) offers a little bit of everything. Tapas, pizza, sandwiches, seafood, meatballs, pasta, salads, and more are served in a cozy atmosphere (bar and booths) with friendly service. They also have gluten-free and vegan options plus an extensive cocktail menu.

Another local favorite is **Marker 20** (21 E. Queens Way, 757/726-9410, www.marker20.com, Mon.-Fri. 11am-2am, Sat.-Sun. 10am-2am, $8-25). This downtown seafood restaurant has a large, covered, outdoor deck and inside seating. Enjoy a casual menu of soups, salads, sandwiches, and seafood specials, along with dozens of types of beer.

The cute **Grey Goose** (118 Old Hampton Way, 757/723-7978, www.greygooserestaurant.com, Mon. 11am-3pm, Tues.-Thurs. 11am-8pm, Sat. 10am-9pm, Sun. 10am-2pm, $8-14) serves homemade soups, salads, sandwiches, and bakery items made from fresh ingredients.

1: Virginia Air & Space Center in Hampton 2: Blue Water Yachting Center in Hampton

Accommodations

$100-200

The **Candlewood Suites Hampton** (401 Butler Farm Rd., 757/766-8976, www.ihg.com, $105-120) offers 98 reasonably priced, spacious rooms in a quiet location. The hotel is geared toward extended-stay guests and offers per diem rates for members of the armed services. The service is good, and the staff is caring and friendly. The rooms are well stocked, and there are free laundry facilities on-site.

The **Hilton Garden Inn Hampton Coliseum Central** (1999 Power Plant Pkwy., 757/310-6323, www.secure3.hilton.com, $139-169) is another good value. It offers 149 guest rooms, an on-site restaurant, fitness center, and complimentary parking. It is also pet friendly.

OVER $200

The **Embassy Suites by Hilton Hampton Hotel Convention Center & Spa** (1700 Coliseum Dr., 757/827-8200, www.embassysuites3.hilton.com, $259-589) offers 295 suites with kitchenettes. The hotel has warm decor with an attractive atrium, and the staff provides good, reliable service. There's a restaurant and a nicely appointed fitness center. Spa service is also available.

Information and Services

For additional information on Hampton, visit www.hampton.gov and www.visithampton.com or stop in at the **Hampton Visitor Center** (120 Old Hampton Ln., 757/727-1102, daily 9am-5pm).

Getting There and Around

Hampton is approximately 10 miles southeast of Newport News.

The **Newport News/Williamsburg International Airport** (PHF, 900 Bland Blvd., Newport News, www.flyphf.com) is off I-64 at exit 255B. Hampton is a 20-minute drive from the airport.

Greyhound (2 W. Pembroke Ave., 757/722-9861, www.greyhound.com) offers bus service to Hampton.

Hampton Roads Transit (www.gohrt.com) is a public transit service that serves the Hampton Roads area including Hampton. It currently offers transportation by bus, light rail, ferry, and Paratransit (a service for people with disabilities).

NORFOLK

Norfolk is the second-largest city in Virginia and home to the largest naval base in the world. A longtime navy town, the city has an appealing downtown area and a nice waterfront. The city has undergone a rebirth in recent history that is most evident in the delightful restaurants and shops in the trendy Ghent village, located just northwest of downtown, not far from the Elizabeth River. The city also boasts numerous universities, museums, and a host of other attractions including festivals and shopping.

Sights

CHRYSLER MUSEUM OF ART

The **Chrysler Museum of Art** (1 Memorial Pl., 757/664-6200, www.chrysler.org, Tues.-Sat. 10am-5pm, Sun. noon-5pm, free) is one of Virginia's top art museums, with 50 galleries and 30,000 pieces of artwork including paintings, textiles, ceramics, and bronzes. The art on display spans thousands of years and comes from around the world. A highlight is the glass museum (a museum within a museum) that is entirely devoted to glass art and features 10,000 glass pieces (spanning 3,000 years) and a glass-art studio. Other collections include European painting and sculpture, American painting and sculpture, modern art, a gallery of ancient and non-Western art, contemporary art, photography, and decorative arts.

NORFOLK BOTANICAL GARDEN

Something is always in bloom at the **Norfolk Botanical Garden** (6700 Azalea Garden Rd., 757/441-5830, www.norfolkbotanicalgarden.org, daily 9am-5pm, Apr.-Sept. open until 7pm, $12, children 3-17 $10, seniors/military $10, 2 and under free). This 155-acre garden contains more than 60 different themed areas

Norfolk and Vicinity

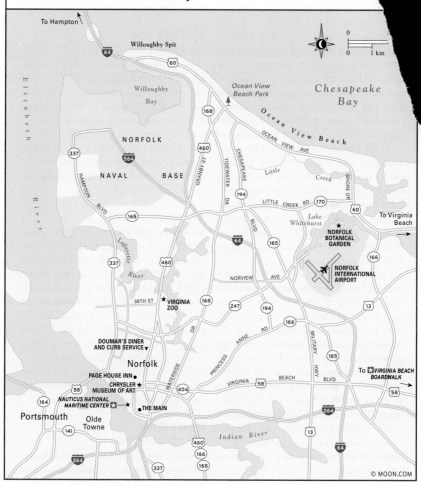

© MOON.COM

and thousands of plants. It is open to visitors year-round. Inside the garden is the three-acre **WOW Children's Garden,** which is geared toward children and families and houses several learning areas.

★ NAUTICUS NATIONAL MARITIME CENTER

The **Nauticus National Maritime Center** (1 Waterside Dr., 757/644-1000, www. nauticus.org, Memorial Day-Labor Day Mon.-Sat. 10am-5pm, Sun. noon-5pm, rest of the year Tues.-Sat. 10am-5pm, Sun. noon-5pm, adults $15.95, children 4-12 $11.50, seniors 55 and over $14.95, military $12.95, 3 and under free) is an incredible interactive science and technology center. They have a great floor plan with a lot of interesting permanent and rotating exhibits including hands-on activities for children (they also offer an escape room). Be sure to catch one of the 3D movies on the third floor.

Battleship *Wisconsin* is one of the on-site attractions, and the center fea- many exhibits related to the ship. It is of the biggest and also one of the last tleships built by the U.S. Navy. The ship ved in World War II, the Korean War, and peration Desert Storm. Admission to the ship is included with admission to Nauticus, and visitors can take a self-guided tour of the deck. For $35.95 (which includes Nauticus admission), guided **Battleship *Wisconsin* Topside Tours** are available. These tours in- clude the administration area, radio room, main deck with enlisted berthing, the cap- tain's cabin and sleeping quarters, the flag bridge, and the combat engagement center. Participants must be at least eight years old and have the ability to climb stairs to four decks and be comfortable in small spaces. They also offer overnight family/adult stays on the ship during the summer.

The **Hampton Roads Naval Museum** (free admission) is also located inside the Nauticus National Maritime Center on the second floor. The museum is run by the U.S. Navy and details the 237-year history of the Hampton Roads region fleet. Exhibits in the museum include an 18-pounder cannon from 1798, artifacts from the cruiser **CSS *Florida*** and the sloop of war **USS *Cumberland,*** a World War II Mark 7 undersea mine, and a torpedo warhead from a German submarine.

Allow at least 2-4 hours to explore the cen- ter and the ship. The facility includes a casual restaurant serving sandwiches, salads, bever- ages, and snacks.

NAVAL STATION NORFOLK

Norfolk offers a unique opportunity to tour the largest naval base in the world. The **Naval Station Norfolk** sits on 4,300 acres on Sewells Point and is home to 75 ships and 134 aircraft. The 45-minute bus tour leaves from the **Naval Tour and Information Center** (9079 Hampton Blvd., 757/444-7955, www. visitnorfolk.com, adults $10, children 3-11 and seniors over 60 $5, cash only) next to gate 5. The tour rides past destroyers, aircraft

carriers, frigates, amphibious assault ships, and the airfield. Tour times change frequently so call for a current schedule.

VIRGINIA ZOO

The **Virginia Zoo** (3500 Granby St., 757/441-2374, www.virginiazoo.org, daily 10am-5pm, ages 12 and over $17.95, 2-11 $14.95, seniors 62 and over $15.95) occupies 53 acres adjacent to Lafayette Park. It opened in 1900 and houses more than 400 animals including elephants, giraffes, orangutans, otters, and birds. The zoo is operated by the City of Norfolk and the Virginia Zoological Society. It offers many ed- ucational and children's programs including behind-the-scenes tours.

ST. PAUL'S CHURCH

St. Paul's Church (201 St. Paul's Blvd., 757/627-4353, www.saintpaulsnorfolk.com) is the oldest building in Norfolk, dating back to 1739. A cannonball that was fired into the church on the night before the Revolutionary War began is still lodged in its southwestern wall. Tombstones in the church's historic cemetery date back to the 17th and 18th cen- turies. Episcopalian services are still held at St. Paul's, and the public is welcome during daylight hours to the churchyard. Self-guided- tour brochures can be found in the vestibule. Guided tours are available upon request.

Recreation
SPECTATOR SPORTS

Harbor Park (150 Park Ave., www.milb.com) is home to the **Norfolk Tides,** the Class AAA affiliate of the Baltimore Orioles. The park is considered one of the best minor league base- ball facilities in the country, boasting a prac- tical design and a terrific view of downtown Norfolk. The park opened in 1993 on the Elizabeth River.

The **Norfolk Admirals** (www. norfolkadmirals.com) take to the ice season- ally at the **Scope Arena** to compete in the

---

1: the Virginia Zoo 2: Nauticus National Maritime Center

ECHL. Consult the website for schedules and tickets.

BEACHES
Beachgoers can enjoy miles of public beach at **Ocean View Beach Park** (100 W. Ocean View Ave., www.oceanviewbeachpark.org). The park offers a boardwalk, bandstand, beach-access ramp for people with disabilities, commercial fishing pier, and open recreation space. There is a bathhouse, and parking is free. Dogs are allowed on leashes in the off-season.

SAILING
A trip with **American Rover Sailing Cruises** (333 Waterside Dr., 757/627-7245, www.americanrover.com, $25-30) is a relaxing way to tour the Hampton Roads Harbor and the Elizabeth River. The *American Rover's* red sails are a distinctive sight in the Hampton Roads area. From April through October, they offer 1.5- and 2-hour narrated cruises. Guests can help out with sailing the ship or just sit back and relax.

Entertainment and Events
Chrysler Hall (215 St. Paul's Blvd., 757/644-6464, www.sevenvenues.com) is the top performing arts venue in the Hampton Roads area. It hosts Broadway shows, concerts, theatrical performances, the **Virginia Symphony** (www.virginiasymphony.org), the **Virginia Arts Festival** (www.vafest.org), and the **Virginia Ballet** (www.vaballet.org).

The **Virginia Opera** (www.vaopera.org, 866/673-7282) performs in three locations throughout Virginia (Norfolk, Richmond, and Fairfax). The Norfolk venue, the **Harrison Opera House** (160 E. Virginia Beach Blvd., 757/627-9545), is a beautifully renovated World War II USO theater that seats just over 1,600 people.

The **Scope Arena** (201 E. Brambleton Ave., 757/644-6464, www.sevenvenues.com) is a 12,000-seat complex that hosts concerts, family shows, and conventions. It is also the home of the **Norfolk Admirals** of the ECHL (East Coast Hockey League).

Norfolk also has a number of quality small venues featuring good nightlife and entertainment. The **NorVa** (317 Monticello Ave., 757/627-4547, www.thenorva.com) is a 1,500-person concert venue that hosts a variety of artists such as Ingrid Michaelson, Citizen Cope, and The Legwarmers. **The Banque** (1849 E. Little Creek Rd., 757/480-3600, www.thebanque.com) is a popular, award-winning country-and-western nightclub and restaurant offering a large dance floor and well-known artists.

Norfolk Festevents (757/441-2345, www.festevents.org) presents 10 months of events annually, including concerts and festivals in **Town Point Park** (on the Elizabeth River in the center of the business district in downtown Norfolk) and **Ocean View Beach Park** (at the end of Granby St. at Ocean View Ave.). One of the most popular events, the **Norfolk Harborfest** is held annually for four days at the beginning of June and attracts more than 100,000 people. This large festival covers more than three miles on the Norfolk waterfront and offers visitors three sailboat parades, tall ships, the largest fireworks display on the East Coast, and seemingly endless entertainment. Another Festevent, the **Norfolk Waterfront Jazz Festival** is a two-day festival held in late August. Tickets are $30-200.

The **Town Point Virginia Fall Wine Festival** is held in Town Point Park for two days in October. More than 200 Virginia wines are featured. Tickets start at $25 and can be purchased online.

Shopping
The **MacArthur Center** (300 Monticello Ave., 757/627-6000, www.shopmacarthur.com) is a large shopping mall with close to 150 retail stores and restaurants. There is also a movie complex.

A trendy shopping area worth checking out is **The Palace Shops and The Palace Station** (301 W. 21st St., 757/622-9999, www.

ghentnorfolk.org) in the historic Ghent neighborhood. This is a trendy, three-block restaurant-and-retail area near downtown Norfolk.

Food

★ **Freemason Abbey Restaurant** (209 W. Freemason St., 757/622-3966, www. freemasonabbey.com, Mon.-Thurs. 11am-9:30pm, Fri.-Sat. 11am-10:30pm, Sun. 9:30am-9:30pm, $8-32) is a local favorite in downtown Norfolk for fresh seafood, steak, and pasta. It is housed in a renovated church built in 1873 and has been a restaurant since 1989. The atmosphere is friendly, elegant, and casual with beautiful decor that retains a church-like feel yet has cozy seating. Try the award-winning she-crab soup. Reservations are highly recommended on the weekends.

Saltine (100 E. Main St., 757/763-6280, www.saltinenorfolk.com, daily 11:30am-3pm and 5pm-close, Sat. 10am-3pm, $8-40) is a terrific seafood restaurant located on the street level in the **Hilton Norfolk The Main** hotel. This hip downtown spot has an inviting atmosphere and exposed brick and tile. They use locally sourced ingredients and offer selections from their raw bar, whole fish, shellfish, and a handful of farm-based entrees.

Seafood lovers can also get their fix at **AW Shucks Raw Bar & Grill** (2200 Colonial Ave., 757/664-9117, www.awshucksrawbar. com, daily 11am-1:30am, $9-25). They seem to be firm believers that any meal can include seafood. Try their burger topped with lump crab, or a po'boy; both are well seasoned, huge, and delicious. Finding the place can be a bit tricky—look on 22nd Street in the plaza rather than along Colonial Avenue. The staff is friendly and attentive, and the atmosphere is social. This is a good choice for reasonably priced, yet tasty food. There are also plenty of nonseafood selections.

Doumar's Barbeque & Curb Service (1919 Monticello Ave., 757/627-4163, www. doumars.com, Mon.-Thurs. 8am-11pm, Fri.-Sat. 8am-12:30am, under $10) is a legendary diner that was featured on the show *Diners,*

Drive-Ins and Dives. Its origin was an ice-cream stand that opened in 1907 in Ocean View Amusement Park. The business moved to its current location in 1934 and is still owned by the same family. Famous for barbecue and ice cream, they bake their own ice-cream cones in the original cone machine. Take a seat inside the diner, or dine from your car and enjoy their carhop service. This is a fun, genuine, old-school diner that is inexpensive and has a great history.

Accommodations
$100-200

There are many chain hotels in Norfolk. A few stand out for above-average accommodations, good service, and proximity to downtown attractions and the airport, such as the **Courtyard Norfolk Downtown** (520 Plume St., 757/963-6000, www.marriott.com, $149-199) and the **Holiday Inn Express Hotel & Suites Norfolk International Airport** (1157 N. Military Hwy., 757/455-5055, www. ihg.com, $108-210).

In addition to the selection of large chain hotels, there are some very nice bed-and-breakfasts and historic hotels in Norfolk. The **Page House Inn** (323 Fairfax Ave., 757/625-5033, www.pagehouseinn.com, $183-253) is a historic bed-and-breakfast (circa 1899) next to the Chrysler Museum of Art in the Ghent Historic District. This stately redbrick mansion has four guest rooms and three guest suites, decorated with 19th-century furniture, antiques, and art. A delicious full breakfast is served each morning, and refreshments are served each afternoon. The innkeepers are warm and welcoming.

OVER $200

The **Hilton Norfolk The Main** (100 E. Main St., 757/763-6200, www3.hilton.com, $289-2,500) is a wonderful upscale hotel choice in an excellent downtown location. They offer 300 guest rooms, 39 meeting rooms (including a conference center), indoor pool, fitness center, and three restaurants that include a roof lounge. Self-parking is $20, valet $26.

Information and Services

For additional information on the Norfolk area, visit www.visitnorfolktoday.com.

Getting There and Around

Norfolk is 16 miles south of Hampton.

The **Norfolk International Airport** (ORF, 2200 Norview Ave., www.norfolkairport.com) is convenient for those traveling by air to the Norfolk area. It is one mile east of I-64 (exit 279) and just minutes from downtown Norfolk.

The city is serviced by **Amtrak** (280 Park Ave., www.amtrak.com) rail service and by **Greyhound** (701 Monticello Ave., 757/625-7500, www.greyhound.com) bus service.

Norfolk Electric Transit (www.virginia. org) is a free commuting service that links many downtown attractions. It is part of **Hampton Roads Transit,** which also offers additional bus routes around Norfolk (www.gohrt.com, $2) and the **Paddlewheel Ferry** (www.gohrt.com, $2) service on three passenger paddle-wheel boats. Each boat holds 150 passengers and runs between downtown Norfolk (at the Waterside) and Portsmouth. The ferry operates every 30 minutes. Extended service kicks in during peak summer weeks. Passengers are allowed to bring bicycles aboard.

Virginia Beach

Virginia Beach is the state's premier beach destination. It is a thriving, year-round city with more than 442,000 full-time residents and an influx of nearly 19 million visitors annually. *King Neptune* (31st St. and the Boardwalk), a 34-foot-tall bronze statue designed by Paul DiPasquale and cast by Zhang Cong, seems to be the official Virginia Beach greeter. He stands on the boardwalk at the entrance to Neptune Park and invites visitors to enjoy the wonders of the ocean responsibly.

The resort area runs along more than 20 miles of beach, which is maintained and replenished on a regular basis. The area is booming with commercialism and has more than its share of touristy gift shops and oversize hotels but also offers a variety of attractions, events, parks, and wildlife refuges. The farther north you travel, the quieter it gets, and the northern reaches are mostly residential.

The three-mile-long boardwalk is the center of activity, and the aquarium, water sports, fishing, and parks keep visitors coming back year after year. Accommodations are plentiful but also book quickly during the peak summer season, especially those right on the beach. The beach is busiest not only in the summer but also during March and April, when thousands of college students arrive for spring break. Keep this in mind when planning your trip since it may be best to avoid these windows unless you are joining in the fun.

Tourism in Virginia Beach began with the opening of the first hotel in 1884. The boardwalk was built just four years later. The strip has been growing ever since, and a few historic landmarks, such as the Cavalier Hotel (circa 1927), still stand today.

A population boom in the 1980s resulted in some bad press for the beach area, which experienced some pains from the onslaught of visitors and the hard partying that came with them. Since then, the municipality has made a concerted effort and spent millions of dollars to revamp the beach's reputation as a family resort. They've succeeded on most levels by encouraging more high-end businesses to come to the beach and by making the main thoroughfares more visually pleasing to visitors with fresh lighting and landscaping. The area is now known for its excellence in environmental health,

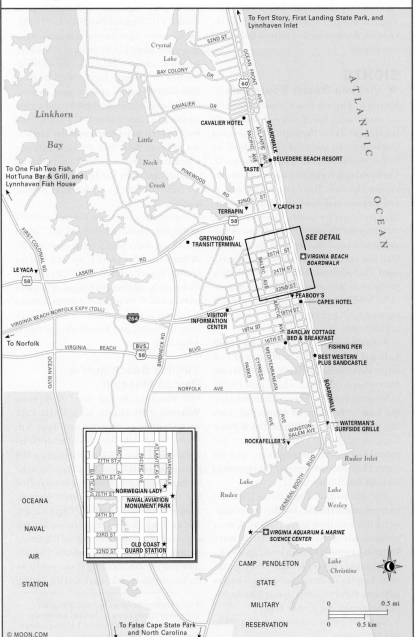

Virginia Beach

To Fort Story, First Landing State Park, and Lynnhaven Inlet

Crystal Lake

52ND ST

BAY COLONY DR

OCEAN FRONT AVE

60

CAVALIER DR

Linkhorn

CAVALIER HOTEL

Bay

Little

PACIFIC AVE

ATLANTIC AVE

BOARDWALK

Neck

BELVEDERE BEACH RESORT

To One Fish Two Fish, Hot Tuna Bar & Grill, and Lynnhaven Fish House

PINEWOOD RD

Creek

TASTE

32ND ST

TERRAPIN

CATCH 31

58

GREYHOUND/ TRANSIT TERMINAL

SEE DETAIL

26TH ST

VIRGINIA BEACH BOARDWALK

RD

BALTIC AVE

24TH ST

FIRST COLONIAL RD

22ND ST

LE YACA

58

LASKIN

RD

ARCTIC AVE

PEABODY'S

CAPES HOTEL

19TH ST

VIRGINIA BEACH-NORFOLK EXPY (TOLL)

264

VISITOR INFORMATION CENTER

18TH ST

To Norfolk

VIRGINIA BEACH

BUS.

58

BIRDNECK RD

BLVD

16TH ST

BARCLAY COTTAGE BED & BREAKFAST

FISHING PIER

BEST WESTERN PLUS SANDCASTLE

OCEAN BLVD

PARKS AVE

CYPRESS AVE

MEDITERRANEAN AVE

BOARDWALK

NORFOLK AVE

WINSTON-SALEM AVE

WATERMAN'S SURFSIDE GRILLE

ROCKAFELLER'S

Rudee Inlet

GENERAL BOOTH BLVD

Lake Rudee

Lake Wesley

OCEANA

27TH ST

ATLANTIC AVE

PACIFIC AVE

BOARDWALK

BALTIC AVE

26TH ST

NAVAL

25TH ST

NORWEGIAN LADY

NAVAL AVIATION MONUMENT PARK

AIR

24TH ST

Lake Christine

STATION

23RD ST

OLD COAST GUARD STATION

22ND ST

Virginia Aquarium & Marine Science Center

CAMP PENDLETON

STATE

MILITARY

0   0.5 mi

RESERVATION

0   0.5 km

To False Cape State Park and North Carolina

ATLANTIC OCEAN

COASTAL VIRGINIA

VIRGINIA BEACH

© MOON.COM

and as more and more sporting events are booked for the beach, it is becoming a destination for the fitness-minded. In a nutshell, Virginia Beach is a modern and affordable vacation destination that offers a little bit of everything.

SIGHTS
★ Virginia Beach Boardwalk

No trip to Virginia Beach is complete without a stroll along the 28-foot-wide boardwalk running parallel to the ocean for three miles (between 1st St. and 42nd St.) on one of the longest recreational beach areas in the world. The boardwalk is perfect for getting some exercise with a view. There are lanes for walkers and bicycles, and many running events utilize a portion of the boardwalk on their route, including the **Shamrock Marathon** (www.shamrockmarathon.com) and the **Rock 'n' Roll Marathon Series** (www.runrocknroll.com). The boardwalk is adorned with benches, grassy areas, play areas, amusement parks, arcades, hotels, restaurants, shops, and other entertainment. There is also a large fishing pier at 15th Street.

A handful of monuments along the boardwalk pay tribute to U.S. military and first responders, including the **Naval Aviation Monument** (25th St.), which pays tribute to Virginia Beach's deep aviation heritage; the **Law Enforcement Memorial** (35th St.), which honors the Virginia Beach Police Department, Sheriff's Office, and state and federal law enforcement agencies; and the **Navy SEAL Monument** (38th St.) honoring Virginia Beach Navy SEALs.

The *Norwegian Lady* statue (16th St.) commemorates the lives lost during the shipwreck of a boat from Moss, Norway. A sister statue stands in Moss. At 13th Street is the **Virginia Legends Walk,** a landscaped walkway that pays tribute to some of Virginia's most famous citizens, including Thomas Jefferson, Robert E. Lee, Captain John Smith, Ella Fitzgerald, and Arthur Ashe.

There are public restrooms at 17th, 24th, and 30th Streets.

★ Virginia Aquarium & Marine Science Center

The **Virginia Aquarium & Marine Science Center** (717 General Booth Blvd., 757/385-3474, www.virginiaaquarium.com, daily 9am-6pm, adults $24.95, children 3-11 $19.95, seniors 62 and over $22.95) is a must-visit attraction in Virginia Beach. With its more than 800,000 gallons of aquariums, live animal habitats, numerous exhibits, and a giant six-story 3-D movie screen ($7.95), you could spend several hours or an entire day here and not get bored. More than 300 species are represented in numerous educational exhibits, and there are many hands-on experiences in the center, including a touch pool of friendly animals.

A great attraction is the **Adventure Park at Virginia Aquarium** (757/385-4947, adults $59, 13 and under $49). It offers adventure for children over five years of age and also for adults. The park is a trail of wooden platforms connected by zip lines and bridges. A play area is also available for younger children. This is a wonderful attraction when you need a break from the beach, and kids of all ages find it compelling.

Virginia Beach Surf & Rescue Museum

The **Virginia Beach Surf & Rescue Museum** (2401 Atlantic Ave., 757/422-1587, www.vbsurfrescuemuseum.org, Tues.-Sat. 10am-5pm, $1, children 6 and under free) houses more than 1,800 artifacts and 1,000 photographs that honor Virginia's maritime heritage. Two galleries relate the history of the U.S. Life-Saving and Coast Guard Services, along with shipwrecks off the Virginia coast. The building itself was constructed in 1903 and is the only one of five original life-saving stations built that year along the Virginia coast that remains standing. It now resides on the boardwalk at 24th Street, and the rooftop

---

1: *King Neptune* designed by Paul DiPasquale and cast by Zhang Cong 2: The Old Cape Henry Lighthouse 3: Virginia Aquarium & Marine Science Center

"Towercam" enables guests to look at ships in the Atlantic.

The Old Cape Henry Lighthouse

The Old Cape Henry Lighthouse (583 Atlantic Ave., Fort Story, 757/422-9421, www.preservationvirginia.org, Jan.-Mar. 15 daily 10am-4pm, Mar. 16-Dec. daily 10am-5pm, adults $10, students $8, senior 60+ and military $9, under 42 inches tall free) is part of the Fort Story military base. It once protected the entryway to the Chesapeake Bay at the northern end of Virginia Beach. Construction of the lighthouse was authorized by George Washington as one of the first acts of the newly organized federal government, and it was the first federal construction project. Alexander Hamilton oversaw its construction. The lighthouse was completed in 1792. This octagonal sandstone edifice remains one of the oldest surviving lighthouses in the country and is a National Historic Landmark. Visitors can climb to the top of the lighthouse and enjoy commanding views of the Chesapeake Bay and the Atlantic Ocean. Guided tours of the grounds are also available, and there's a gift shop. To reach the lighthouse, you must drive through a security gate at Fort Story. Photo identification is required to enter, and car searches are frequently made.

RECREATION
Parks and Wildlife

First Landing State Park (2500 Shore Dr., 757/412-2300, www.first-landing-state-park. org, $7) is the site where the first permanent English settlers landed in 1607. This 2,888-acre park offers 20 miles of hiking trails, biking, fishing, a boat ramp, and camping.

Mount Trashmore Park (310 Edwin Dr., 757/385-2995, www.vbgov.com, free) is a famous land-reuse park that was built on an old landfill. The 165-acre park was created by compressing multiple layers of waste and clean soil. The park includes playgrounds, picnic areas, volleyball courts, and a large skate park.

Back Bay National Wildlife Refuge (4005 Sandpiper Rd., 757/301-7329, www.fws. gov, $5) includes approximately 9,000 acres of beach, marsh, and woods. It is a haven for many migratory birds. There is both fresh- and saltwater fishing, a canoe and kayak launch, biking, and hiking.

False Cape State Park (4001 Sandpiper Rd., 757/426-7128, www.dcr.virginia.gov, $4) is an ocean-to-brackish-water area that is only accessible by boat, bike, or on foot. The land trail leading in is five miles long. A tram from the Back Bay National Wildlife Refuge visitors center is also available (call for a schedule). Primitive camping is allowed.

Boat Ramps

The Owl Creek Boat Ramp (701 General Booth Blvd.) is a free launch facility next to the Virginia Aquarium & Marine Science Center. Other boat ramps include First Landing State Park (2500 Shore Dr., www.first-landing-state-park.org), Bubba's Marina (3323 Shore Dr., www. bubbaseafoodrestaurant.com), and Munden Point Park (2001 Pefley Ln., www.vbgov. com).

Kayaking and Boat Tours

There are many local outfitters in the Virginia Beach area offering seasonal kayak tours, rentals, and ecotours. Chesapean Outdoors (757/961-0447, www.chesapean.com) provides an exciting guided dolphin kayak tour ($60) where guests can paddle with bottlenose dolphins at the north end of Virginia Beach. They also offer guided sunset paddle tours ($60) and rentals (SUP, one hour $20, two hours $30; single kayak, one hour $20, two hours $30; tandem kayak, one hour $30, two hours $40). Kayak Nature Tours (757/480-1999, www.kayaknaturetours.net) also has guided dolphin kayak tours (2.5 hours, $62) and flat-water guided trips (2.5 hours, $53).

Explore the creeks near the Virginia Aquarium & Marine Science Center (www.virginiaaquarium.com) on a guided pontoon boat, or ride along with aquarium

The Great Dismal Swamp

The **Great Dismal Swamp National Wildlife Refuge** (3100 Desert Rd., Suffolk, free) is a 112,000-acre refuge southwest of Virginia Beach. The refuge is primarily forested wetlands and is home to numerous birds and animals. It also encompasses 3,100-acre Lake Drummond, which is the largest natural lake in Virginia. One hundred miles of trails are open daily for hiking, walking, and biking (sunrise to sunset).

Although humans first occupied the swamp as much as 13,000 years ago, there was not much interest in the area until Lake Drummond was discovered by William Drummond (a governor of North Carolina) in 1665. The area was later surveyed, and the state line between Virginia and North Carolina was drawn through it in 1728. The name of the land was recorded as the Great Dismal (dismal was a common term at the time for a swamp). Shortly thereafter, George Washington visited the swamp and developed the Dismal Swamp Land Company, with designs on draining and logging parts of it. The name "great" was likely added to the swamp's name due to its large size. Logging continued in the swamp until 1976, with all parts of the swamp having been logged one or more times.

The dense forests in the swamp have traditionally been a refuge for animals but have also been used by people for a similar reason. The swamp was at one time a haven to people fleeing slavery, and as a result, the swamp was the first National Wildlife Refuge to be recognized officially as part of the Underground Railroad.

Today, more than 200 species of birds live in the refuge either permanently or seasonally. Perhaps an even more impressive fact is that 96 species of butterflies have also been recorded here. More than 47 mammals live in the refuge, including black bears, bobcats, white-tailed deer, river otters, and mink.

For more information, visit www.fws.gov or contact the park headquarters at 757/986-3705.

COASTAL VIRGINIA
VIRGINIA BEACH

staff on a 90-minute seasonal dolphin-watching excursion (adults $22.95, children 3-11 $16.95, under 3 free). The aquarium also offers ocean collections boat trips (for the same price), during which a variety of sea creatures are brought aboard, and several other trips (including a Craft Brews Cruise).

Kayaking and SUP tours are also available through **Back Bay Getaways** (757/589-1069, www.backbaygetaways.com, $40-65), and kayak tours are available through **Ocean Eagle Kayak** (757/589-1766, www.oceaneaglekayak.com, $75).

Fishing

The Virginia Beach coastline and inshore waterways are thoroughfares for many species of fish, including tuna, bluefin, blue marlin, Atlantic mackerel, red drum, and flounder. Private fishing charters are available through a number of companies including **Dockside Seafood and Fishing Center** (3311 Shore Dr., 757/481-4545, www.fishingvabeach.com), **Rudee Tours** (200 Winston Salem Ave., 757/425-3400, www.rudeetours.com), **Virginia Beach Fishing Center** (200 Winston Salem Ave., 757/491-8000, www.virginiafishing.com), and **Fisherman's Wharf Marina** (524 Winston Salem Ave., 757/428-2111, www.vabeach.com).

There are also several fishing piers that are great for dropping a line, including the **Virginia Beach Fishing Pier** (15th St.), the **Little Island Fishing Pier** (3820 S. Sandpiper Rd., www.vbgov.com), and the **Sea Gull Fishing Pier** at the Chesapeake Bay Bridge-Tunnel (www.cbbt.com).

Amusement Park

The **Atlantic Fun Park** (233 15th St., 757/422-0467, www.atlanticfunpark.com) has a yesteryear vibe that is nostalgic for parents and pure fun for the kiddies. The park offers thrill rides, family rides, and kiddie rides, including a 100-foot Ferris wheel. Single-ride tickets ($3.30-5.50) or unlimited-ride armbands ($24.99-39.99) can be purchased.

ENTERTAINMENT AND EVENTS

Endless entertainment can be found on the Virginia Beach boardwalk, including concerts, athletic events, and performances.

Nightlife

Virginia Beach doesn't sleep when the sun goes down. In fact, in the summer it doesn't seem to sleep at all. Live music can be found at the **Hot Tuna Bar & Grill** (2817 Shore Dr., 757/481-2888, www.hottunavb.com). They offer Top 40 dance music daily. Another dance bar is **Peabody's** (209 21st St., 757/422-6212, www.peabodysvirginiabeach.com). They've been around since 1967 and have one of the largest dance floors in the area.

If a game of pool is more your speed, try **Q-Master II Billiards** (5612 Princess Anne Rd., 757/499-8900, www.q-masters.com). They are the premier billiards room in the region and have 70 tables. They also host competitions.

Those wishing to kick back for some live music (country, reggae, folk, etc.) should check out **Elevation 27** (600 Nevan Rd., 757/716-4028, www.elevation27.com). They offer live entertainment and a large menu from **The Jewish Mother** that includes delicious deli sandwiches. If comedy is more up your alley, catch a show at the **Funny Bone Comedy Club & Restaurant** (217 Central Park Ave., 757/213-5555, www.vb.funnybone.com). They host well-known comics and offer tables with a full dinner and bar menu during the show. Shows are for ages 21 and older.

Events

Some popular annual events include the **American Music Festival** (5th St. and Atlantic Ave., www.beachstreetusa.com, starting at $25), one of the largest outdoor music events on the East Coast. It runs for three days over Labor Day weekend and features local and national artists. Sounds of rock, jazz, country, blues, and R&B flow out to the oceanfront from a huge stage on the beach at 5th Street and from stages in many parks along the water. Another favorite is the **Boardwalk Art Show and Festival** (http://virginiamoca.org), held annually for four days in mid-June. This event began in 1956 and is one of the oldest and best outdoor art shows on the East Coast. It is held on the boardwalk between 17th and 24th Streets.

Those looking for a little something different can take in a **sand wrestling** (www.sandwrestling.com) competition. Sand wrestling, which is also known as beach wrestling, is a version of traditional wrestling. Established as an international style of amateur wrestling in 2005, it is quickly gaining popularity and offers competition for males and females of all ages.

Runners won't want to miss the annual **Shamrock Marathon** (www.shamrockmarathon.com) weekend in mid-March. The Shamrock Marathon has been around since 1973 and is now a premier running event and Boston Marathon qualifier.

FOOD
American

Firebrew Bar & Grill (1253 Nimmo Pkwy., Ste. 117, 757/689-2800, www.fire-brew.com, Mon.-Thurs. 11am-10pm, Fri.-Sat. 11am-11pm, Sun. 11am-9pm, $8-26) is a casual bar and grill with a few twists. Most menu items (flatbread, steak, tacos, etc.) are prepared on an open-flame fire deck, and the restaurant proudly states that they do not use microwaves or fryers. Their extensive bar includes local craft brews and a self-service wine station.

Terrapin (3102 Holly Rd., 757/321-6688, www.terrapinvb.com, Sun.-Thurs. 5pm-9pm, Fri.-Sat. 5pm-10pm, $17-35) supports sustainable organic farmers and is committed to using fresh ingredients with no hydrogenated oils or high-fructose corn syrup. Their menu includes homemade pasta (including a delicious lobster and corn ravioli), selections such as ribeye and chicken for the table, salads, seafood, and a cheeseburger. They also offer an extensive wine menu.

If you're looking for a good place to grab a sandwich, stop in **Taste** (36th St. and Pacific Ave., 757/422-3399, www.taste.online, daily 9am-7pm, $4-14). This pleasant sandwich shop and specialty food store, a block from the beach, has ample seating, good variety, and a friendly atmosphere. They also sell wine, cheese, and other gourmet snacks, and at times there's even a little farmers market outside.

French

★ **Le Yaca French Restaurant** (741 First Colonial Rd., Ste. 107, 757/500-4773, www. leyacawilliamsburg.com, Tues.-Thurs. 11:30am-2:30pm and 5pm-9pm, Fri.-Sat. 11:30am-2:30pm and 5pm-10pm, Sun. 11am-2:30pm and 5pm-9pm, $16-80) is an elegant and delicious departure at the beach from traditional seafood and burgers. This contemporary French restaurant is the second U.S. location (the first is in Williamsburg) and offers traditional French and modern selections for brunch, lunch, and dinner. They offer a prix fixe menu, chef's tasting menu and an à la carte menu. Don't let the strip mall location deter you; this is a great place for a date or celebration. Fresh flowers and delightful service add to the wonderful experience.

Seafood

Catch 31 (3001 Atlantic Ave., 757/213-3472, www.catch31.com, Mon.-Fri. 6am-2am, Sat.-Sun. 7am-2am, $14-49) is inside the Hilton Virginia Beach Oceanfront and is one of the finest restaurants along the main strip. They are known for offering at least 15 types of fresh fish, and their signature dish is the seafood towers that include crab legs, mussels, lobster, and shrimp. The restaurant's high ceilings, ocean-blue walls, and indoor/outdoor bar add to the ambience. If the weather is nice, dine outside on their beachfront terrace. They serve breakfast, lunch, and dinner.

A restaurant popular with Virginia Beach residents is **Rockafeller's** (308 Mediterranean Ave., 757/442-5654, www. rockafellers.com, Mon.-Sat. 11am-10pm, Sun. 10am-10pm, $7-33). This dependable local favorite offers seafood, steaks, pasta, and salads in a large three-story home on Rudee Inlet. Double-decker porches provide lovely seating, or you can dine inside. There's a bar and raw bar and nice views from indoors as well.

Waterman's Surfside Grille (5th St. and Atlantic Ave., 757/428-3644, www.watermans. com, Mon.-Sat. 11am-10pm, Sun. 9am-10pm, $8-35) is one of the few freestanding restaurants left on the strip that isn't connected to a hotel. It offers a lively atmosphere, good seafood, and outstanding cocktails.

ACCOMMODATIONS
$200-300

The **Belvedere Beach Resort** (3603 Atlantic Ave., 800/425-0612, www. belvederebeachresort.com, $209-297) is a privately owned hotel on the oceanfront on the northern end of Virginia Beach. The light-filled, wood-paneled rooms offer private balconies with views of the beach. The hotel has adult-size bicycles for guest use and direct access to the boardwalk. Rooms are quiet, and the staff is very friendly and helpful. The **Wave Trolley** stops in front of the hotel for easy access to many places on the beachfront. This is not a luxurious resort, but a very pleasant, comfortable choice in a fantastic location. The hotel is open seasonally, normally April through the beginning of October. Minimum stays may be required. Coffeepots are available upon request.

The **Capes Hotel** (2001 Atlantic Ave., 757/428-5421, www.capeshotel.com, $219-329, closed Oct.-Mar.) is a pleasant oceanfront hotel on the boardwalk. It has an indoor pool with a view of the ocean and nicely kept grounds. The hotel is convenient to all the beach attractions. The 59 oceanfront rooms are cozy rather than large, but all are comfortable with an airy feel and good views. The service is also very dependable. There is a small café on-site with an oceanfront patio. This is not a luxurious resort, but it doesn't attempt to be; it's a good value in a great location, with a friendly staff.

Another good value on the beachfront is the **Best Western Plus Sandcastle Beachfront Hotel** (1307 Atlantic Ave., 757/428-2828, www.bestwestern.com, $212-374). This pleasant oceanfront hotel features a heated indoor pool, free breakfast buffet, free parking, and a fitness center. There is also a restaurant on-site.

Over $300

★ **The Cavalier Hotel** (4200 Atlantic Ave., 757/425-8555, www.cavalierhotel.com, $299 and up during off-season, $499 and up in peak season) is a historic hotel that opened in 1927. A Virginia Beach icon and a National Register of Historic Places property, the grand hotel was built on a hill overlooking the ocean and has welcomed 10 U.S. presidents, celebrities such as Frank Sinatra, Judy Garland, and Bette Davis, and international dignitaries. It was also used as a naval training center during World War II. The hotel completed a $70 million renovation in 2017, at which point it became a member of Marriott International's Autograph Collection. Today the hotel portrays the bygone age of grand hotels as it sits majestically above the hubbub of activity on the oceanfront. The Cavalier Hotel offers 85 guest rooms and suites, three restaurants, a spa, a bourbon distillery and tasting room, a museum, ballroom, meeting space, poolside vistas and loggias, a fitness center, and electric-car-charging stations.

The imposing 21-story **Hilton Virginia Beach Oceanfront** (3001 Atlantic Ave., 757/213-3000, www.hiltonvb.com, $349-459) offers oceanfront luxury with amenities such as a rooftop infinity pool, an indoor pool, the Sky Bar, a fully equipped fitness center, and bicycle rentals. There are 289 modern rooms and suites, outfitted with beach decor and offering a choice of city or ocean views. There are several on-site restaurants and convenient parking ($10 for self-park and $16 for valet per day).

Bed-and-Breakfast

The ★ **Barclay Cottage Bed and Breakfast** (400 16th St., 757/422-1956, www.barclaycottage.com, $179-309) is a beautiful B&B offering five comfortable guest rooms. Three rooms have private bathrooms, and two others share bath facilities. Each room is individually decorated with its own colors and theme (such as nautical or floral). The white, two-story, porch-wrapped cottage (complete

The Cavalier Hotel

with rocking chairs) is within walking distance of many attractions and a few blocks from the beach.

House and Condo Rentals
There are several local real estate offices in Virginia Beach that offer rentals for a week or longer. **Sandbridge Realty** (800/933-4800, www.sandbridge.com) is in southern Virginia Beach and offers a property-search feature on its website, as does **Siebert Realty** (877/422-2200, www.siebert-realty.com), which is also in southern Virginia Beach.

CAMPING
First Landing State Park (2500 Shore Dr., 757/412-2300, www.dcr.virginia.gov, $30-46) on the north end of Virginia Beach offers 200-plus beach campsites near the Chesapeake Bay. There are also 20 cabins for rent ($151-173).

INFORMATION AND SERVICES
For additional information on Virginia Beach, visit www.virginiabeach.com or stop by the **Visitor Information Center** on Parks Avenue (2100 Parks Ave., 800/822-3224, daily 9am-5pm) or in First Landing State Park (2500 Shore Dr., 757/412-2300, daily 9am-4:30pm). There are also two kiosks run by the Visitor Information Center that are available from May to September; they are on the Boardwalk at 17th Street and on Atlantic Avenue at 24th Street.

GETTING THERE
Most people arrive in Virginia Beach by car. I-64 connects with the Virginia Beach-Norfolk Expressway (I-264), which leads to the oceanfront at Virginia Beach.

The **Norfolk International Airport** (ORF, 2200 Norview Ave., Norfolk, www.norfolkairport.com) is approximately 17 miles from Virginia Beach. Daily flights are available through multiple commercial carriers.

Rail service does not run to Virginia Beach, but **Amtrak** (800/872-7245, www.amtrak.com) serves Newport News with connecting bus service to 19th Street and Pacific Avenue in Virginia Beach. Reservations are required. Bus service is also available to Virginia Beach on **Greyhound** (971 Virginia Beach Blvd., 757/422-2998, www.greyhound.com).

GETTING AROUND
There are plenty of paid parking lots in Virginia Beach. The cost per day ranges about $7-10. Municipal parking lots are located at 2nd Street, 4th Street, 9th Street, 19th Street, 25th Street, and 31st Street. **Hampton Roads Transit** (www.gohrt.com, $2-4) operates about a dozen bus routes in Virginia Beach.

Virginia's Eastern Shore

Visiting Virginia's Eastern Shore can be a bit like stepping back in time. The long, narrow, flat peninsula that separates the Chesapeake Bay from the Atlantic Ocean has a feel that's very different from the rest of the state. The pace is more relaxed, the people take time to chat, and much of the cuisine centers on extraordinary seafood fished right out the back door.

Traveling from the Virginia Beach area to the Eastern Shore requires passage over and through one of the great marvels of the East Coast. The **Chesapeake Bay Bridge-Tunnel** (www.cbbt.com) spanning the mouth of the Chesapeake Bay is an engineering masterpiece. The four-lane, 20-mile-long bridge-and-tunnel system is a toll route and part of US Route 13. It takes vehicles over a series of bridges and through two-mile-long tunnels that travel under the shipping channels. Five-acre artificial islands are located at each end of the two tunnels, and a fishing pier and restaurant/gift shop were built on one.

Upon arrival on the Eastern Shore, you are greeted by endless acres of marsh, water, and wildlife refuge areas. Agriculture and fishing are the primary sources of revenue on the peninsula, and tourism in the towns provides a nice supplement.

A handful of charming towns dot the coastline on both bodies of water, and most have roots prior to the Civil War. In fact, many beautiful 19th-century homes have been refurbished, as have the churches, schools, and public buildings.

The first town on the southern end of the Eastern Shore is Cape Charles, and the northernmost is Chincoteague Island. Bus transportation runs between the two via **Star Transit** (757/787-8322, www.vatransit.org, Mon.-Fri.).

CAPE CHARLES

Cape Charles is the southernmost town on Virginia's Eastern Shore, 10 miles from the Chesapeake Bay Bridge-Tunnel. The town was founded in 1884 as the southern terminus of the New York, Philadelphia, & Norfolk Railroad. It was also a popular steamship port for vessels transporting freight and passengers across the Chesapeake Bay to Norfolk.

Today, Cape Charles is primarily a vacation town. It is not large, nor is it particularly well known, but this is part of the charm. It offers a quiet historic district, sandy beaches, golfing, boating, and other outdoor recreation.

Sights

The **Historic District** (757/331-3259) in Cape Charles is approximately seven square blocks and boasts one of the largest groups of turn-of-the-20th-century buildings on the East Coast. The area offers a pleasant atmosphere of shops and eateries near the Chesapeake Bay waterfront. State Route 184 runs right into the historic district and ends at the beach.

Cape Charles Beach (Bay Ave., www. capecharles.org) has a pleasant, uncrowded atmosphere and wonderful sunsets over the Chesapeake Bay. The beach is clean, family oriented, and free to the public. The water is generally shallow with little to no waves.

The **Cape Charles Museum and Welcome Center** (814 Randolph Ave., 757/331-1008, www.smallmuseum.org, mid-Apr.-Nov. Mon.-Fri. 10am-2pm, Sat. 10am-5pm, Sun. 1pm-5pm, free, donations appreciated) is a nice place to begin your visit to Cape Charles. It is located in an old powerhouse and has a large generator embedded in the floor. Visitors can view boat models, pictures, and decoys as they learn about the history of Cape Charles.

Kiptopeke State Park (3540 Kiptopeke Dr., 757/331-2267, www.dcr.virginia.gov, daily 6am-10pm, $7) is approximately 10 miles south of the Historic District in Cape Charles. It encompasses a half mile of sandy beach open to the public during the summer. There are no lifeguards on duty, so swimming is at your own risk. There are also hiking trails, a fishing pier, a boat ramp, and a full-service campground. The park is known for its robust bird population. Many bird studies are conducted here by the U.S. Fish and Wildlife Service. Some of the birds encountered in the park include hawks, kestrels, and ospreys.

Recreation

SouthEast Expeditions (239 Mason Ave., 757/331-6190, www.southeastexpeditions. com, starting at $45) offers kayaking tours in Cape Charles. Trips of different lengths are available, and paddlers of all experience levels are welcome. They also rent kayaks (starting at $20) and SUPs (starting at $20).

Golfers will enjoy the beautiful atmosphere and two challenging courses designed by Arnold Palmer and Jack Nicklaus at the **Bay Creek Golf Club** (1 Clubhouse Way, 757/331-8620, www.baycreek.net, $35-120).

A big annual event in October in the Cape Charles area is the **Eastern Shore Birding & Wildlife Festival** (www. chesapeakenetwork.org). The area is one of the most important East Coast migration stops for millions of birds each year, and festivalgoers can observe the spectacle firsthand in early October.

Food

★ **The Oyster Farm Seafood Eatery** (500 Marina Village Circle, 757/331-8660, www.theoysterfarmatkingscreek.com, Mon.,Wed., Thurs., and Sun. 11:30am-9pm, Fri.-Sat. 11:30am-10pm, $14-36) is the top choice for food and ambience in Cape Charles. The modern beachfront building offers a trendy "water-to-table" eating experience in a comfortable waterfront dining room. The food is delicious, with many creative seafood items and land entrées as well. The scene is semi-upscale with a lively clientele. This is a great place to bring the family or relax with friends for an unrushed and tasty meal. There is a beautiful waterfront patio and lawn games for entertainment.

The Bay Creek Resort's **Coach House Tavern** (1 Clubhouse Way, 757/331-8630, www.baycreek.net, Sun.-Thurs. 7am-8pm, Fri.-Sat. 7am-9pm, winter hours Mon. 8am-8pm, Tues.-Thurs. 8am-5pm, Fri. 8am-9pm, Sat. 7:30am-9pm, Sun. 7:30am-8pm, $6-24) is located at the golf clubhouse and overlooks the golf course. The rustic ambience of the beautifully appointed building is due in part to the use of reclaimed wood and bricks from a farmhouse that once stood on the property. The restaurant offers traditional pub fare with exquisite soups and sandwiches. There is patio seating, and the atmosphere is upscale and inviting.

For a quick and casual breakfast, burger, or seafood meal, stop in **Sting Ray's Restaurant** (26507 Lankford Hwy., 757/331-1541, Sun.-Thurs. 6:30am-8pm, Fri.-Sat. 6:30am-8:30pm, $6-30). This restaurant shares a roof with a gas station and offers a full breakfast menu featuring homemade biscuits and omelets. The lunch menu includes hot dogs, burgers, and barbecue, while the dinner menu offers a large variety of local seafood. Order at the counter, and the server will bring the food to your table.

Accommodations

$100-200

The **King's Creek Inn** (3018 Bowden Landing, 757/678-6355, www.kingscreekinn.com, $150-210) is a beautiful historic plantation home that has offered guest accommodations since 1746. The home has been fully renovated and has four guest rooms with private bathrooms. The inn sits on 2.5 acres and overlooks Kings Creek (with access to the Chesapeake Bay). A private dock is available for guest use. The cozy salon offers great ambience for breakfast, or guests can enjoy meals on their balconies. The home has a long and exciting history and some interesting legends that include stories of the Underground Railroad and a possible resident ghost.

$200-300

The **Fig Street Inn** (711 Tazewell Ave., 757/331-3133, www.figstreetinn.com, $175-250) is a year-round boutique bed-and-breakfast offering four comfortable guest rooms with private bathrooms. All rooms have memory foam mattresses, lush towels, flat-screen televisions, wireless Internet, and a jetted tub or gas fireplace. The house has been renovated and is decorated with antiques. The beach and shops are within walking distance.

OVER $300

★ **Bay Creek Resort** (3335 Stone Rd., 757/331-8750, www.baycreek.net, $400-900) is the premier resort community in Cape Charles. The resort offers rentals of vacation homes, villas, and condos in a well-landscaped waterfront and golf community on more than 1,700 acres. Golf packages are available, and golf condos offer three-bedroom, two-bath units with garages and a balcony or patio. Single-family homes are also available overlooking the golf course. Those who prefer a water view will enjoy the Marina District. Rental options include single-family villas with views of the Chesapeake Bay or the Kings Creek Marina. One- and two-bedroom suites are also available. Nightly and longer-term stays can be accommodated. A beautiful restaurant is located on the golf course. The staff is extremely helpful and friendly.

The Oyster Farm at Kings Creek (500 Marina Village Circle, 757/331-8660, www.theoysterfarmatkingscreek.com, $219-619) offers beautiful villas, suites, and houses for rent on 39 acres of waterfront property on the Chesapeake Bay and Kings Creek. There is a great on-site restaurant and an events center on the property.

Camping

Camping is available at **Kiptopeke State Park** (3540 Kiptopeke Dr., 757/331-2267, www.dcr.virginia.gov). The park has multiple types of facilities including tent sites ($30-47), cabins ($122-194), and a six-bedroom lodge ($382-488). Minimum stays may apply in the summer. There is a $5 reservation fee.

Information and Services

For additional details on Cape Charles, contact the **Northampton County Chamber of Commerce** (757/678-0010, www.northamptoncountychamber.com).

ONANCOCK

Thirty-eight miles north of Cape Charles is the picturesque town of Onancock. The town sits on the shore of Onancock Creek and has a deepwater harbor. Cute, 19th-century homes with gingerbread trim line the streets, and visitors can shop, visit art galleries, partake in water sports, or just relax and enjoy the tranquil atmosphere. The town was founded in 1680 by English explorers, but its name is derived from the native Algonquian word *auwannaku*, which means "foggy place."

Onancock was one of the colonies' 12 original "Royal Ports." Its deepwater access to the Chesapeake Bay made it appealing for ships, and its port provided safety during storms. For more than 250 years, Onancock was the trade center on the Eastern Shore and was closely connected (in terms of commerce) to Norfolk and Baltimore.

The homes along Market Street belonged to sea captains who worked on the Chesapeake Bay. These homes harken back to a time during the steamboat era when Onancock was a stop on the way to bustling Baltimore.

Today, Onancock retains a small working harbor and offers a pretty port of call for recreational boaters. It has modern boats in its harbor, and outdoor enthusiasts paddle colorful kayaks around its waters. Its wharf is also the jumping-off point for a small ferry that goes to and from Tangier Island. The town is a pleasant place to spend a day or two, and about 1,200 people make it their permanent home. There are free parking areas located around town and by the wharf.

Sights

The key sight in Onancock is **Ker Place** (69 Market St., 757/787-8012, www.shorehistory.org, Mar.-Dec. Tues.-Sat. 11am-3pm, admission by donation), one of the finest federal-style manors on the Eastern Shore. John Shepherd Ker was the owner and a renaissance man of his time. He was a successful merchant, lawyer, banker, and farmer. His estate was built in 1799 and originally comprised 1,500 acres. The home is now restored to its original appearance and features period furniture, detailed plasterwork, and rich colors throughout. The headquarters for the **Eastern Shore of Virginia Historical Society** are in the house, and the second floor contains a museum, the society's library, and archives space. A smaller, newer section of the house serves as a welcome center with a museum shop. Visitors can view Eastern Shore artwork throughout the home, and rotating exhibits are displayed regularly. Tours are given on "a loop," and reservations can also be made for private tours.

Recreation

A public boat ramp at the wharf has a launch for canoes and kayaks ($5 launch fee). **SouthEast Expeditions** (209-A Mason Ave., 757/331-6190, www.southeastexpeditions.com) offers kayak and SUP rentals (starting at $20) and tours ($45-125) from the wharf. Guided kayak trips are also offered by two local travel writers and kayak guides through **Burnham Guides** (2 King St., 757/710-5137, www.burnhamink.com). Visitors arriving by boat can dock at the Town Marina but should call the **harbormaster** (757/787-7911) for reservations.

Free self-guided walking tours are a fun way to learn about the town. Pick up a tour brochure at the visitors center (located on the wharf) and learn about Onancock's historic homes and gardens.

Food

Mallards Restaurant (2 Market St., 757/787-8558, www.mallardsvamd.com, Sun.-Mon. 11am-4pm, Tues.-Thurs. 11am-8pm, Fri.-Sat. 11am-9pm, $8-29) is on the wharf. The menu includes fresh seafood, ribs, duck, pasta, and many more delicious entrées. Don't be surprised if chef Johnny Mo comes out of the kitchen with his guitar to play a few tunes. He's a local legend.

The **Blarney Stone Pub** (10 North St., 757/302-0300, www.blarneystonepubonancock.com, Tues.-Thurs. 11am-9pm, Fri.-Sat. 11am-10pm, Sun. 11am-7pm, $11-20) is an Irish pub three blocks from the wharf serving traditional pub fare. It has indoor and outdoor seating and frequent live entertainment.

Accommodations

★ **The Charlotte Hotel and Restaurant** (7 North St., 757/787-7400, www.thecharlotte.com, $140-200) is a boutique hotel with 10 guest rooms. The owners take great pride in this lovely hotel and even made some of the furnishings by hand. There is an award-winning restaurant on-site that can seat more than 30 people, and the American cuisine served is made from products supplied by local watermen and farmers.

The Inn at Onancock (30 North St., 757/787-7711, www.innatonancock.com, $199-239) is a luxurious bed-and-breakfast with five guest rooms, each offering a stylish modern bathroom and feather-top bed. Full-service breakfasts are served in their dining

room, or guests can choose to eat on the porch in nice weather. A wine hour is also hosted every evening. Soda and water are available to guests all day.

The **Colonial Manor Inn** (84 Market St., 757/787-3521, www.colonialmanorinn.com, $109-139) offers six spacious rooms decorated with period furnishings. The home was built in 1882 and is the oldest operating inn on the Eastern Shore in Virginia. A delicious full breakfast is served daily.

Information and Services

Additional information on Onancock can be found at www.onancock.com. There is also a small, seasonal visitors center at the wharf.

★ TANGIER ISLAND

Tangier Island is a small 3.5-mile-long island, 12 miles off the coast of Virginia in the middle of the Chesapeake Bay. It was first named as part of a group of small islands called the Russell Isles in 1608 by Captain John Smith when he sailed upon it during an exploration of the Chesapeake Bay. At the time, the island was the fishing and hunting area of the native Pocomoke people, but it was allegedly purchased from them in 1666 for the sum of two overcoats. Settlers were drawn to the island for the abundant oysters and crabs.

The unofficial history of the island states that John Crockett first settled here with his eight sons in 1686. This appears to be accurate since most of the 700 people who live on Tangier Island today are descendants of the Crockett family, and the majority of the tombstones on the island bear the Crockett name. The island was occupied by British troops during the Revolutionary War, and it has also survived four major epidemics, with the most devastating being the Asian cholera epidemic of 1866. So many people died in such a short period of time that family members buried their dead in their front yards. Cement crypts can still be seen in many yards on the island.

There is a tiny airstrip, used primarily for the transport of supplies, but most visitors come by ferry (without their cars). There are no true roads on the island, and golf carts and bicycles are used to get around (you can rent a golf cart or hire one with a driver). A few residents have cars, but they have to receive permission from local authorities.

Tangier Island is only five feet above sea level, and it is known as the "soft-shell crab capital" for its delectable local crabs. It is also known for the unique dialect the people on Tangier Island speak. They converse in an old form of English and have many euphemisms that are unfamiliar to visitors. It is thought that the island's isolation played a role in preserving the language that was spoken throughout the Tidewater area generations ago.

Tangier Island can be toured in a couple of hours. The ferry schedules are such that they allow enough time to cover the sights on the island, grab lunch, and head back the same day. If you enjoy the slow pace of the island, limited overnight accommodations are available, but be aware there is not much, if any, nightlife, and the island is "dry." Addresses aren't frequently used when describing how to get to a place on Tangier Island. Basically, you can see the whole island from any given point. The ferry drops visitors off in the heart of the small commercial area, and if you can't see the establishment you are looking for immediately, take a short walk or ride down the main path and you'll find it. The island residents are also very friendly, so if in doubt, just ask someone walking by.

There are very limited services on Tangier Island. The island hasn't changed much in the last century, and it looks much as it did 30 or 40 years ago. There is a post office and one school that all local children attend (most go on to college elsewhere in the state). There is spotty cell service on the island, but some establishments do offer wireless Internet. More important, there are no emergency medical facilities on the island; however, there is a 24-hour clinic, **The Tangier Island Health Foundation** (www.tangierclinic.org), where a physician's assistant is available.

Many establishments do not accept credit cards, so it's best to bring cash and checks. There is only one ATM on the island (located by **Four Brothers Crab House**).

Sights
TANGIER HISTORY MUSEUM AND INTERPRETIVE CENTER
The **Tangier History Museum and Interpretive Center** (16215 Main Ridge, 757/891-2374, www.tangierisland-va.com, mid-May-mid-Oct. daily 11am-4pm, other times by appointment, $3) is a small museum down the street from the ferry dock. It doubles as the island's vistors center and is worth a visit and the small fee to learn about life on Tangier Island and its interesting heritage. Watch the short movie to begin with, and then view island artifacts and a five-layered painting of the island that illustrates the erosion it has experienced since 1866. Visitors can also learn about the many sayings that are common on the island but completely foreign to those on the mainland, such as "He's adrift," which means, "He's a hunk," and the term "snapjack," which means "firecracker." A handful of kayaks are available behind the museum for visitors to borrow (for free) for exploring the surrounding waterways. There's also a small gift shop on-site (they don't take credit cards).

TANGIER BEACH
At the south end of Tangier Island is the nice, sandy public **Tangier Beach.** Rent a golf cart from **Four Brothers** and head out of the village on the winding paved path and over the canal bridge. The beach is at the very end of the path on the left side of the island. There's a small parking area for carts and a sandy path to the beach. There is no lifeguard on duty so swimming is at your own risk. Bring plenty of water with you since there are also no services at the beach. Water machines and soda machines can be found along the golf

---

1: golf course at Bay Creek Resort in Cape Charles
2: Ker Place in Onacock **3:** harbor at Tangier Island
4: Chincoteague Pony Centre

cart paths on the island if you need to pick up beverages on your way. There is also a very small grocery store near the ferry dock with a few bare essentials, but it's best to bring provisions with you.

Recreation

Kayaking the waterways of Tangier Island is a wonderful way to explore the marshes. Kayaks can be borrowed from the Tangier History Museum, and a listing of water trail routes can be found at www.tangierisland-va.com. The marshes also offer a terrific opportunity for bird-watching. Black skimmers, great blue herons, common terns, double-crested cormorants, Forster's terns, clapper rails, and ospreys are just some of the birds living on the island.

Since there are no roads on Tangier—only paved paths—the place is very conducive to casual biking. Bikes can be brought over on the ferry on weekdays only (call ahead to schedule), and a fleet of older-model cruising bikes can be rented from **Four Brothers** on the island. Since the island is only 3.5 miles long, it is easy to cover the entire length by bicycle in a short time.

For a unique local experience, take a **Crab Shanty Tour** (757/891-2269, ask for Ookire). This 30- to 45-minute tour is led by a Chesapeake Bay waterman. Other island tours are available outside the ferry dock. Tour guides wait in golf carts for guests when the ferries arrive, and offer guided tours in their vehicles.

Shopping

There are two small gift shops on Tangier Island: **Wanda's Gifts** (16139 Main Ridge Rd., 757/891-2230) and **Sandy's Place** (16227 Main St., 757/891-2367). Both are on the main path not far from the ferry dock. They sell souvenir T-shirts and trinkets.

Food

Visitors arriving by ferry will likely see the **Waterfront Restaurant** (757/891-2248, mid-May-Nov. 1 Mon.-Sat. 10am-4pm, Sun.

1pm-4pm, under $15) as they depart the ferry. This small, seasonal restaurant is right by the dock and offers a variety of casual food including burgers, fried seafood baskets, and crab cakes.

Four Brothers Crab House & Ice Cream Deck (757/891-2999, www.fourbrotherscrabhouse.com, lunch and dinner daily) will likely be the next establishment you see when you take the short path from the dock to the main path in the small commercial area. While this is the place to rent golf carts, crabbing equipment, and bicycles, they also serve a casual menu of seafood and sandwiches on their deck, along with 60 soft-serve ice-cream flavors. Four Brothers also offers free wireless Internet; however, they do not accept credit cards. Another fun place for ice cream is **Spanky's Place,** just down the path.

A short walk from the ferry terminal is **Lorraine's Seafood Restaurant** (4409 Chambers Ln., 757/891-2225, Mon.-Fri. 10am-2pm and 5pm-10pm, Sat. 10am-2pm and 5pm-11pm, Sun. noon-5pm, under $15). Take a right on Main Street, and the restaurant is on the right. They serve snacks, lunch, and dinner. As at all the restaurants on the island, local, fresh seafood is the specialty, and this place is known for its soft-shell crabs. Lorraine's also delivers to any of the inns on the island.

Across from Lorraine's, **Fisherman's Corner Restaurant** (4419 Long Bridge Rd., 757/891-2900, www.fishermanscornerrestaurant.com, daily 11am-7pm, $6-26) has a long menu with steaks and seafood. Sandwiches and a kids' menu are also available. It's no surprise that fresh crab is a highlight, and their crab cakes contain large, succulent blue crab meat with little filler.

The best-known and oldest restaurant on the island is ★ **Hilda Crockett's Chesapeake House** (16243 Main St., 757/891-2331, www.chesapeakehousetangier.com, daily 7am-9am and 11:30am-5pm, $11-25). They offer an all-you-can-eat breakfast with selections such as scrambled eggs, fried bread, and potatoes. They are most famous, however, for the family-style lunch and dinner. For $22, guests can enjoy unlimited homemade crab cakes, clam fritters, ham, potato salad, coleslaw, pickled beets, applesauce, green beans, corn pudding, and rolls. The family-style setting means you may share a table with other guests.

Accommodations

It is difficult to find more friendly innkeepers than those at the **Bay View Inn** (16408 W. Ridge Rd., 757/891-2396, www.tangierisland. net, $125-150). This family-run bed-and-breakfast offers seven motel-style rooms, two cottages, and two guest rooms in the main house. A scrumptious homemade breakfast is included with your stay. The inn is on the west side of the island and has lovely views of the Chesapeake Bay and decks to watch the sunset. The inn is open year-round. They do not take credit cards.

Hilda Crockett's Chesapeake House (16243 Main St., 757/891-2331, www. chesapeakehousetangier.com, $100-165) is the oldest operating bed-and-breakfast on the island and was established in 1939 as a boardinghouse. It is located in the small commercial area not far from the ferry dock. There are eight guest rooms in two separate buildings.

Renovated in 2018, the **Brigadune Beachside Getaway** (16650 Hog Ridge Rd., 757/891-2580, www. brigadunebeachsidegetaway.com, $155-250) overlooks the bay and offers modern bed-and-breakfast accommodations. Their rooms have private bathrooms, and breakfast is delivered to your door daily.

Those arriving by private boat can rent a slip at the **James Parks Marina** (16070 Parks Marina Ln., 757/891-2581). They offer 25 slips and showers, but no pump-outs. Docking fees start at $25.

Information and Services

For additional information, visit www. tangier-island.com.

Getting There

Getting to Tangier Island is half the fun. Three seasonal ferries travel to and from the island May-October. The first is the *Chesapeake Breeze* (804/453-2628, www.tangiercruise. com, one-way adults $20, children 4-12 $10, 3 and under free, round-trip adult $28, children 4-12 $13, 3 and under free), a 150-person passenger boat that leaves at 10am daily from Reedville for the 1.5-hour trip. The ship heads back to Reedville at 2:15pm. The second is the *Steven Thomas* (410/968-2338, www. tangierislandcruises.com, one-way $20, $27 round-trip for same-day service, $35 for overnight, children 7-12 $12, 6 and under free), a 90-foot, 300-passenger boat that leaves from Crisfield, Maryland, daily (May 15-Oct. 15) at 12:30pm and arrives on Tangier at 1:45pm. The return voyage departs Tangier at 4pm. The third ferry is the *Joyce Marie II* (757/891-2505, www.tangierferry.com, one-way $20, $25 round-trip for same-day service, $30 for overnight, children 6-12 $10, 5 and under $5), a small fiberglass lobster boat that holds 25 people and runs from Onancock, Virginia, to Tangier Island daily May-September. The trip takes 65 minutes. Ferry service is offered twice a day with departures from Tangier Island at 7:30am and 3:30pm and departures from Onancock at 10am and 5pm.

Getting Around

There are no cars on Tangier Island. The best way to get around is by renting a golf cart from **Four Brothers Crab House & Ice Cream Deck** (757/891-2999) or a bicycle. They do not take reservations—rentals are first-come, first-served.

CHINCOTEAGUE ISLAND

Chincoteague Island is 7 miles long and just 1.5 miles wide. It is nestled between the Eastern Shore and Assateague Island. Chincoteague is famous for its herd of wild ponies, and many children and adults first became familiar with the island through the popular book *Misty of Chincoteague,* which was published in 1947. Many local residents made appearances in the movie that followed.

The island is in the far northeastern region of the Eastern Shore in Virginia and has a full-time population of 2,900 residents. It attracts more than one million visitors each year to enjoy the pretty town and to visit the Chincoteague National Wildlife Refuge and the beautiful beach on nearby Assateague Island.

Chincoteague is a working fishing village with world-famous oyster beds and clam shoals. It is also a popular destination for bird-watching. During the summer, the town is bustling with tourists, but in the off-season things slow down considerably and many establishments close.

The town of Chincoteague is accessed via State Route 175. A scenic causeway spans the water and marsh and ends on Main Street, which runs along the western shore of the island. Maddox Boulevard meets Main Street and runs east to the visitors center and Chincoteague National Wildlife Refuge.

Sights
★ **CHINCOTEAGUE NATIONAL WILDLIFE REFUGE**

The **Chincoteague National Wildlife Refuge** (8231 Beach Rd., 757/336-6122, www.fws.gov, May-Sept. daily 5am-10pm, Apr. and Oct. daily 6am-8pm, Nov.-Mar. daily 6am-6pm, $20 per car for 7-day pass, pedestrians and cyclists free) is a 14,000-acre refuge consisting of beach, dunes, marsh, and maritime forest on the Virginia end of Assateague Island. It was established in 1943, and the area is a thriving habitat for many species of waterfowl, shorebirds, songbirds, and wading birds. The popular herd of wild ponies that Chincoteague is known for also lives in the refuge.

Assateague Island itself extends south from Ocean City, Maryland, to just south of Chincoteague Island. It is a thin strip of beautiful sand beach, approximately 37 miles long. The entire beach is a National Seashore, and the Virginia side is where the Chincoteague National Wildlife Refuge is located.

One of the main attractions is the **Assateague Island Lighthouse,** which visitors can hike to. The lighthouse is painted with red and white stripes and is 142 feet tall. It was completed in 1867 and is still operational. There are also 15 miles of woodland trails for hiking and biking (the wild ponies can often be seen from the trails). The lighthouse is open for climbing (free) spring-fall, but the days it is open change seasonally and with the weather so call ahead for the current schedule. **Refuge Treks** (adults $14, children 12 and under $7) are also available for wildlife viewing. Transportation is provided on a 7-mile service road with stops at select locations.

To get to the refuge, travel east on State Route 175 onto Chincoteague Island and continue straight at the traffic light onto Maddox Boulevard. Follow the signs to the refuge. The entrance is at the end of Maddox Boulevard. The road ends at the Atlantic Ocean, where there's a large parking area for beachgoers. Parts of the beach are open to swimming, surfing, clamming, and crabbing. A visitors center is situated near the beach and is where information and trail brochures can be obtained.

MUSEUM OF CHINCOTEAGUE ISLAND

The **Museum of Chincoteague Island** (7125 Maddox Blvd., 757/336-6117, Tues.-Sun. 11am-5pm, adults $4, children under 12 free) is on Maddox Boulevard just prior to the entrance to the National Wildlife Refuge. The museum was formerly the Oyster and Maritime Museum and is dedicated to sharing the history of the island and to the preservation of the "material culture that reflects the historical progression of the life on Chincoteague Island." One of the most noteworthy exhibits in the museum is the Fresnel lens that was part of the Assateague Island Lighthouse. This lens helped guide ships as far out to sea as 23 miles for nearly 96 years.

CHINCOTEAGUE PONY CENTRE

For those wishing to see the local ponies up close, the **Chincoteague Pony Centre**

(6417 Carriage Dr., 757/336-2776, www.chincoteague-pony-centre.business.site, Thurs.-Sat. and Mon. 10am-5pm, Sun. 11am-4pm, closed Jan.-Feb.) has a herd of ponies from the island in their stable and a field facility for visitors to enjoy. The center offers pony rides, riding lessons, shows, day camps, and a large gift shop.

Recreation

Kayaks can be launched on the beach on Assateague Island, but not in areas patrolled by lifeguards. Kayak tours are available through **Assateague Explorer** (757/336-5956, www.assateagueexplorer.com, $49-59). **Snug Harbor Resort** (7536 East Side Rd., 757/336-6176, www.chincoteagueaccommodations.com) also offers tours ($49) and rents kayaks (single kayak half day $38, full day $48, tandem kayak half day $48, full day $58).

Jus' Bikes (6527 Maddox Blvd., 757/336-6700, www.jus-bikes.com) rents bicycles ($4 per hour or $12 per day), scooters ($15 per hour or $45 per day), surreys ($20 per hour or $75 per day), tandems ($5 per hour or $25 per day), and three-wheelers ($3 per hour or $18 per day).

Fishing enthusiasts can have all their needs met at several fishing and tackle establishments, including **Capt. Bob's Marina** (2477 Main St., 757/336-6654, www.captbobsmarina.net) and **Capt. Steve's Bait & Tackle** (6527 Maddox Blvd., 757/336-0569, www.stevesbaitandtackle.com).

For an interactive cruise, contact **Captain Barry's Back Bay Cruises** (6262 Marlin St., 757/336-6508, www.captainbarry.net). They offer interactive "Hands on Eco-Expedition" (adults $45, children under 1 $40) and "Champagne Sunset Cruises" (adults-only, $45) leaving from the Chincoteague Inn Restaurant at 6262 Main Street. They do not take credit cards.

Entertainment and Events

The premier event on Chincoteague Island is the annual **Wild Pony Swim** (www.chincoteague.com), which takes place each year in late July. At "slack tide," usually in the morning, the herd of wild ponies is made to swim across the Assateague Channel on the east side of Chincoteague Island (those ponies that are not strong enough or are too small to make the swim are ferried across on barges). The first foal to complete the swim is named "King" or "Queen" Neptune and is given away in a raffle later that day. After the swim, the ponies are given a short rest and are then paraded to the carnival grounds on Main Street. The annual Pony Penning and Auction is then held, in which some foals and yearlings are auctioned off. Benefits from the auction go to support the local fire and ambulance services. The remaining herd then swims back across the channel.

Another big event in town is the **Chincoteague Island Oyster Festival** (8128 Beebe Rd., www.chincoteagueoysterfestival.com, $45, children under 5 free). This well-known event has been happening since 1973 and offers all-you-can-eat oysters prepared every which way imaginable. It is held in early October, and tickets are available online.

Food
AMERICAN

If you like a casual beach environment, eating outside, and lounging in hammocks, then **Woody's Serious Food** (6700 Maddox Blvd., Mon.-Sat. 11am-8pm, Sun. 1pm-8pm, $8-28) is worth checking out. They specialize in barbecue (pulled pork, ribs, chicken, etc.) and offer sides such as corn nuggets. Wash it down with peach tea and you're ready to go. The restaurant is dog friendly, and there are outdoor games for the kids.

For a quick bite to go, stop at the ★ **Sea Star Café** (6429 Maddox Blvd., 757/336-5442, www.seastarcafeci.com, Thurs.-Mon. 11am-6pm, daily July and Aug., $5-10). They have yummy sandwiches and wraps to go (order at the window; be sure to know what you're ordering before going up when there's a crowd). Everything is fresh and made to order, and they have a large vegetarian menu. The café sits back off the road a little and offers a few picnic tables but no restrooms. The menu is handwritten on a chalkboard, and items contain whatever is fresh that day.

SEAFOOD

Seafood is the mainstay on Chincoteague Island, and the local oysters and crabs are especially delicious. Many restaurants are only open seasonally, so finding open eateries in the off-season can pose a bit of a challenge.

AJ's on the Creek (6585 Maddox Blvd., 757/336-5888, www.ajsotc.com, Mar.-Dec. Mon.-Thurs. 11:30am-8:30pm, Fri.-Sat. 11:30am-9:30pm, $15-35) is the longest-operating restaurant on the island under one management. They are one of a few upscale restaurants on the island, and they serve delicious seafood menu items such as crab imperial, shellfish bouillabaisse, crab cakes, and grilled scallops. The restaurant is owned by two spunky sisters originally from Pittsburgh.

Don't let the plain exterior of Bill's Seafood Restaurant (4040 Main St., 757/336-5831, www.billsseafoodrestaurant.com, daily from 6am for breakfast, lunch, and dinner, $15-35) fool you. They offer delightful seafood entrées such as lobster tail, scallops, oysters, and crab cakes, as well as pasta selections. This is one of the few restaurants in town that is open all year.

TREATS

The Island Creamery (6243 Maddox Blvd., 757/336-6236, www.islandcreamery.net, year-round daily 11am-10pm) is "the" place to go for ice cream. The place is large for an ice-cream joint and offers friendly smiles, samples, and dozens of flavors. It's a popular stop, so the line can be long and parking difficult, but it's worth it.

Accommodations
$100-200
If you're looking for a charming bed-and-breakfast, spend a night at ★ Miss Molly's

Inn (4141 Main St., 757/336-6686, www.missmollys-inn.com, $180-240) on Main Street. This beautiful Victorian B&B offers seven delightful guest rooms and five porches with rocking chairs. The home overlooks the bay and has a pretty English garden. Marguerite Henry stayed at the bed-and-breakfast when she wrote the famous book *Misty of Chincoteague,* and the room she stayed in has since been named after her. A full breakfast is included. The sister inn to Miss Molly's is the Island Manor House Bed and Breakfast (4160 Main St., 757/336-5436, www.islandmanor.com, $178-253), which offers eight guest rooms and plenty of common areas. This house was built in the popular Maryland-T style, which borrows from both federal and Georgian architecture. Refreshments are available 24 hours a day. They provide a gourmet breakfast each day and easy access to Main Street attractions.

$200-300
The ★ Hampton Inn & Suites Chincoteague Waterfront (4179 Main St., 757/336-1616, www.hamptoninnchincoteague.com, $222-309) is known as one of the premier Hampton Inns in the country. Its bayfront location offers beautiful views, and it is close to many shops and restaurants in town. The rooms are well appointed with light wood furniture, and everything is oriented toward the water. The landscaping is appealing, the breakfasts are better than standard chain fare, and there is a boat dock next to the hotel. Amenities include a large indoor heated pool, a fitness center, laundry facilities, a waterfront veranda, and wireless Internet. The staff and owner are also very friendly. Ask for a room on the third floor with a balcony looking over the water, and don't be surprised if you spot dolphins swimming by.

Camping
Camping is available on Chincoteague Island at several campgrounds. The Chincoteague

Island KOA (6742 Maddox Blvd., 757/336-3111, www.koa.com, $75) has 550 campsites and 361 utility hookups. **Tom's Cove Campground** (8128 Beebe Rd., 757/336-6498, www.tomscovepark.com, $36-58) has waterfront campsites near the pony swim, three fishing piers, and a pool. They are open March-November. **Pine Grove Campground** (5283 Deep Hole Rd., 757/336-5200, www.pinegrovecampground.com, $35-45) offers campsites on 37 acres April-December. There are six ponds on the property.

Information and Services

For additional information on Chincoteague Island, visit www.chincoteaguechamber.com or stop by the **Chincoteague Island Visitor's Center** (6733 Maddox Blvd., 757/336-6161, Mon.-Sat. 9am-4:30pm).

Getting There

Visitors should arrive on Chincoteague Island by car; the surrounding waters are shallow and difficult to navigate by boat. The closest airport is **Wicomico Regional Airport** (410/548-4827), which is 52 miles away in Salisbury, Maryland.

Shenandoah and Northwestern Virginia

Bounded to the east by the Blue Ridge

Mountains and to the west by the Appalachians, Northwestern Virginia and the Shenandoah Valley make up one of the prettiest regions in the nation.

From the charming town of Winchester, with its historic homes, apple orchards, and inviting pedestrian area, south to Staunton, one of the oldest cities in the Shenandoah Valley, this area is filled with history and charm. Civil War battlefields, forts, and other military-related structures dot the landscape, and ghosts of fallen soldiers are said to haunt many of the towns.

Nature fans can get their fill of outdoor bliss with stunning mountain vistas, intricate caverns, rolling foothills, and lush forests.

Highlights

Look for ★ to find recommended sights, activities, dining, and lodging.

★ **Museum of the Shenandoah Valley:** This impressive complex in Winchester focuses on the art, history, and culture of the Shenandoah Valley (page 234).

★ **Skyline Drive:** This stunning 105-mile road takes travelers from vista to vista through beautiful Shenandoah National Park (page 242).

★ **Old Rag Mountain:** Enjoy the challenging and rewarding nine-mile hike to the summit (page 243).

★ **Luray Caverns:** Enter a subterranean world of mystery that took more than four million centuries to create (page 251).

★ **New Market Battlefield State Historical Park:** This 300-acre park was the site of a historic 1864 battle that forced Union troops out of the Shenandoah Valley (page 254).

★ **Grand Caverns Regional Park:** Grand Caverns is the oldest continuously operating "show" cave in the country (page 258).

Virginia's pride and joy, Shenandoah National Park, makes up a large part of the region, covering more than 200,000 acres. Its highest point is 4,051 feet. The wide and picturesque Shenandoah River winds through the park, nearly 40 percent of which is protected wilderness. This long, narrow park is home to Skyline Drive, one of the most scenic stretches of road in the nation.

The town of Luray is another prime destination. It is home to the world-famous Luray Caverns, the largest caverns in the eastern United States. This landmark has drawn millions of visitors since it was discovered in 1878. It comprises vast chambers up to 10 stories tall that contain natural columns, stalactites, stalagmites, mudflows, and pools.

Other towns in this region include Harrisonburg, home of James Madison University, and the quaint town of New Market, which is the site of the New Market Battlefield, a 300-acre historical park.

PLANNING YOUR TIME

Shenandoah National Park and northwestern Virginia can be covered by car in a long weekend, but nature lovers will want to allot more time to truly explore the region. The park itself deserves a couple of days to fully appreciate by cruising Skyline Drive, taking a hike or two, and staying at one of the park lodges. If you plan to visit the park to see the fall foliage, keep in mind that Skyline Drive can be very crowded, and you may have to wait in a line of traffic to access it. Those wishing to relax in the Hot Springs area may want to plan on a day or two just for that, especially if you book a room at The Omni Homestead Resort. The cities along I-81—Winchester, New Market, Harrisonburg, and Staunton—can be visited in a few hours each, but you should plan on incorporating a bit more time into your schedule for Luray, especially if you plan to go down into the famous Luray Caverns, which can take at least two hours to tour if you also visit the aboveground attractions.

Winchester

Lying in the northwest corner of the state, Winchester is one of the loveliest towns in Virginia. Founded in 1744, Winchester is also the oldest Virginia city west of the Blue Ridge Mountains. It is the county seat of Frederick County and has a population of around 26,500. It is known mostly for its Civil War history (General Stonewall Jackson had his headquarters here during the winter of 1861-1862), its apple blossoms, acres of orchards, and its charming downtown area with many historic buildings and tree-lined streets.

Although industry has developed in Winchester during the past decades with employers such as Rubbermaid, Kraft, and American Woodmark, many people make the daily commute into Washington DC or the Northern Virginia area and then enjoy their little slice of heaven when they get home.

The downtown area has a very pleasant mall lined with shops and restaurants, with a pedestrian section located on Loudoun Street between Piccadilly and Cork. Winchester is also home to Shenandoah University.

SIGHTS
★ Museum of the Shenandoah Valley

The **Museum of the Shenandoah Valley** (901 Amherst St., 540/662-1473, www.themsv.org, Tues.-Sun. 10am-5pm, adults $10, youth 13-18 and seniors $8, 12 and under free, free to individuals and families on Wed.) is a complex that focuses on the art, history, and culture of

---

Previous: view from Stony Man Mountain Hike; Skyline Drive; Luray Caverns

Shenandoah and Northwestern Virginia

the Shenandoah Valley and also features historical information on Winchester. The well-landscaped site includes multiple collections on display in three venues. The first is the 18th-century **Glen Burnie House,** which exhibits paintings, furniture, and decorative items. The second is seven acres of gardens, and the third is a 50,000-square-foot museum made up of four galleries.

The museum itself is reason enough to visit the complex. This is an outstanding facility with comprehensive and well-thought-out exhibits. The **Shenandoah Valley Gallery** is where the history of the valley comes to life through multimedia presentations and dioramas. The **Founders Gallery** features rotating exhibits of fine art and antiques. The **R. Lee Taylor Miniatures Gallery** displays the work of more than 70 artists through fully furnished miniature houses and rooms. The fourth gallery is the **Changing Exhibition Gallery,** where a new exhibit is featured every 3-6 months.

The historic house and gardens welcome the public April to October, but the museum is open all year. The hours of operation are the same year-round. The complex can be explored in a few hours. There is a café and gift store on-site.

Stonewall Jackson's Headquarters Museum

Stonewall Jackson's Headquarters Museum (415 N. Braddock St., 540/667-5505, www.winchesterhistory.org, Apr.-Oct. Mon.-Sat. 10am-4pm, Sun. noon-4pm, adults $5, students K-12 $2.50, seniors $4.50) is nestled in a neighborhood on Braddock Street. It is a lovely little Hudson River Gothic Revival-style home that was used by General Jackson over the winter of 1861-1862. Jackson occupied two rooms in the home, including an office on the lower level. The house features a large collection of authentic Jackson belongings, as well as personal items that belonged to his staff. His office remains much as it looked when he used it. Allow about an hour to tour the home.

Winchester

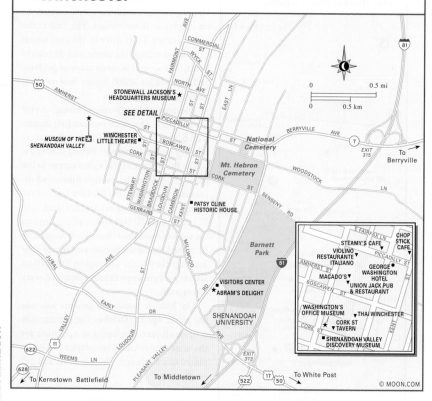

George Washington Office Museum

From September 1755 to December 1756, George Washington used a small log building in Winchester as an office while he supervised the construction of Fort Loudoun on the north side of town. Today, that office is the middle room of the **George Washington Office Museum** (32 W. Cork St. and Braddock St., 540/662-4412, www.winchesterhistory.org, Apr.-Oct. Mon.-Sat. 10am-4pm, Sun. noon-4pm, adults $5, students K-12 $2.50, seniors $4.50). Visitors can see some of Washington's personal items on display, along with surveying equipment and a model of Winchester circa 1755. A cannon that General Edward Braddock left in Alexandria is also displayed on the museum grounds.

Site of Historic Fort Loudoun

During the French and Indian War, Fort Loudoun was George Washington's regimental headquarters. During 1755 and 1756, Washington oversaw the construction of Fort Loudoun from his small office in Winchester. The log fort was considered the "most formidable fort on Virginia's colonial frontier" and was the command center for a series of fortifications. Washington is said to have brought his personal blacksmith from Mount Vernon

---

1: Museum of the Shenandoah Valley **2:** Abram's Delight

to craft the ironwork at the fort, which housed 14 mounted cannons on half an acre. The fort held barracks for 450 men and had its own well, which remains there still. Today, the fort is no longer standing, but the **Site of Historic Fort Loudoun** (419 N. Loudoun St., 540/665-2046, www.frenchandindianwarfoundation.org, daily 8am-5pm, free) can be visited during daylight hours. A marker between the sidewalk and a fenced yard recounts the fort's history.

Shenandoah Valley Civil War Museum

A nice Civil War exhibit can be found in the Historic Frederick County Court House building in the **Shenandoah Valley Civil War Museum** (20 N. Loudoun St., 540/542-1145, www.civilwarmuseum.org, Mon.-Sat. 10am-5pm, Sun. 1pm-5pm, adults $5, children under 16 free, seniors 62 and over $4.50). The Georgian-style building is located on the downtown mall and in a past life served as a prison, hospital, and Civil War barracks for both armies. One of the unique features of the building is the original graffiti from both Union and Confederate soldiers that is still visible. The museum displays more than 3,000 Civil War items.

Patsy Cline Historic House

Patsy Cline fans will enjoy the **Patsy Cline Historic House** (608 S. Kent St., 540/662-5555, www.celebratingpatsycline.org, Apr.-Oct. Mon.-Sat. 10am-4pm, Sun. 1pm-4pm, adults $8, seniors 65 and over $7, active military with ID free). Cline lived in the little house with her family between 1948 and 1953. The house is furnished with some Cline family personal items and is decorated as it was when the singer lived there. The admission price includes a 45-minute guided tour of the house.

Shenandoah Valley Discovery Museum

The **Shenandoah Valley Discovery Museum** (19 W. Cork St., 540/722-2020, www.discoverymuseum.net, Tues.-Sat.

9am-5pm, Sun. 1pm-5pm, $9, children under 2 free) offers many hands-on exhibits for children. This little museum right near the downtown mall is a fun place to go on a rainy day and is particularly interesting for children under 10. Some activities include moving apples around a packing shed, riding in a mock ambulance, stepping into a kaleidoscope, and playing in a sandbox.

Abram's Delight

The oldest home in Winchester, built in the mid-1700s, is **Abram's Delight** (1340 S. Pleasant Valley Rd., 540/662-6519, www.winchesterhistory.org, Apr.-Oct. Mon.-Sat. 10am-4pm, Sun. noon-4pm, adults $5, students K-12 $2.50, seniors $4.50). The stone house was home to five generations of the Hollingsworth family, spanning 200 years. Tours give visitors a great look into life between the colonial period and the Civil War. The antiques furnishing the home include rope beds that had to be tightened each night by crank (which some believe to be the origin of the phrase, "Sleep tight"). The friendly ghost of Abraham Hollingsworth is said to haunt the house.

RECREATION AND EVENTS

If you visit Winchester during apple season, you'll be missing out if you don't sample the local produce. Stop in at a "pick-your-own" orchard before leaving town. A good place to pick and sample these delights is **Marker-Miller Orchards** (3035 Cedar Creek Grade, www.markermillerorchards.com). Pick-your-own apple time begins September 1.

The premier event in Winchester is the spring **Shenandoah Apple Blossom Festival** (www.thebloom.com). This 10-day event takes place in April/May and features music, parades, parties, celebrities, and a lot of tradition. The first festival was held back in 1924. There is even a 10k race and the coronation of the Apple Blossom Queen. Many local businesses close on the first Friday of Apple Blossom weekend.

Patsy Cline: Winchester's Sweetheart

Patsy Cline Historic House

It is hard to make your way around Winchester without bumping into a photo or poster of **Patsy Cline.** Patsy was born as Virginia Patterson Hensley in Winchester Memorial Hospital on September 8, 1932. Her family moved around Virginia many times during her early years, but in 1948, after her parents separated, she returned to Winchester with her mother and siblings. "Ginny," as she was known, dropped out of school to help support the family and went to work in a local poultry plant. She later held a number of different jobs around town and began singing in the evenings and on weekends for additional income.

Over the next few years, Ginny's singing career grew as she won contests, was featured on local radio, and sang with several local bands. In 1952, Ginny was hired by a bandleader named Bill Peer to sing on a regional music circuit. He gave her the stage name Patsy.

In 1953 she married Gerald E. Cline and became Patsy Cline. Her big break came in 1954, when she signed a contract with a record company and produced her first titles in Nashville. Her first songs included "Hidin' Out," "Honky-Tonk Merry-Go-Round," "Turn the Cards Slowly," and "A Church." Cline's first single was released in July 1955. Her most recognizable song, a cover of Willie Nelson's "Crazy," was released in 1961.

Cline died in 1963 and is buried in Winchester.

Local theater fans will thoroughly enjoy the **Winchester Little Theatre** (315 W. Boscawen St., 540/662-3331, www.wltonline. org), which produces several shows throughout the year, including dramas, mysteries, comedies, and even musicals. The cast and staging are professional, and it is clear everyone involved is very passionate about their performance. The stage itself is set in an old train station, which adds to the fun.

FOOD
American

One block west of the downtown mall is the appropriately named **One Block West** (25 S. Indian Alley, 540/662-1455, www. oneblockwest.com, Tues.-Thurs. 11am-2pm and 5pm-8:30pm, Fri.-Sat. 11am-2pm and 5pm-9pm, $21-36), which serves creative American cuisine and is known for using very fresh ingredients and local products in its dishes. The chef/owner is very hands-on and speaks with guests, takes reservations, and does much of the cooking. The menu changes daily based on what is available in local markets, generally split between seafood and meat. Sample items include trout, bison, crab cakes, and shepherd's pie. They also offer a seven-course chef's tasting menu ("menu of the moment") for $75.

Grab a mini-burger and dine where Patsy Cline did at the **Snow White Grill** (159 N. Loudoun St., 540/431-5977, Wed.-Thurs. 11am-5pm, Fri.-Sat. 11am-6pm, under $10). This historic burger joint opened in 1949 and hasn't changed much since. Their famous mini-burger is a small ground beef patty with mustard, a pickle, and grilled onions. It's served on a steamed bun just like Patsy had it when she dined here "daily." They also serve sandwiches and ice cream. Grab a seat at the counter (there are no tables) and enjoy the nostalgia. This is the complete 1950s experience—and probably one of the few restaurants in the country with no bathroom.

For a beer and a burger and cozy ambience, try **Union Jack Pub and Restaurant** (101 N. Loudoun St., 540/722-2055, www.theunionjackpub.com, Mon.-Thurs. 11am-11:30pm, Fri. and Sat. 11am-1am, Sun. 11am-11pm, $7-29). This multilevel restaurant serves good pub food, including gluten-free and vegetarian options. The long wooden bar is a focal point, and the friendly staff helps to create the warm atmosphere.

Those of us who were first introduced to **Macado's** (121 N. Loudoun St., 540/323-7162, www.macados.net, Sun.-Thurs. 8am-11:30pm, Fri.-Sat. 8am-12:30am, under $10) in college will always have a soft spot for their massive sandwich menu, nachos (with a side of onion dip), draft beer, and ice cream. This regional chain is known for their college and small-town locations throughout western Virginia. Personal favorites include the Brooklyn Bridge, Custer's Last Stand, Diamond Jim, and the Turkey Trot. They open at 8am but don't have a breakfast menu.

Good coffee and delicious handmade bagels can be found at **Steamy's Cafe** (38 E. Piccadilly St., 530/392-8372, www.steamyscafe.com, Mon.-Fri. 7am-noon, Sat.-Sun. 8am-noon, under $10).

A good lunch stop is **Bonnie Blue Southern Market and Bakery** (334 W. Boscawen St., 540/686-7490, www.bonniebluebbq.net, Mon.-Thurs. 8am-6pm, Fri. 8am-8pm, Sat. 8am-5pm, Sun. 10am-4pm, $9-15), housed in a former gas station at the corner of Boscawen and Amherst Streets. They offer tasty sandwich selections and also carry locally made goods and excellent homemade bakery items. There is only outdoor seating, but it's a fun place to stop on a sunny day. This is more of a market than a restaurant, but they have good food.

Italian

★ **Violino Restaurant** (181 N. Loudoun St., 540/667-8006, www.violinorestaurant.com, Tues.-Fri. 11:30am-2pm and 5pm-9pm, Sat. noon-2pm and 5pm-9pm, $16-35) is known for its delicious northern Italian dishes and hearty sauces. The staff is friendly, professional, and very good at suggesting wine pairings. The food is downright superb, and it is also consistent. The menu includes many specialty dishes such as lobster *pansotti gondoliera* (Mediterranean lobster ravioli sautéed in a lemon parmesan sauce) and *galletto al limone* (grilled Cornish hen marinated and pressed with rosemary, garlic, and lemon). They also offer a wonderful selection of authentic Italian desserts. The restaurant is on the north end of the downtown mall.

Thai

A great little place to grab some Thai food is the **Chop Stick Café** (207 N. Kent St., 540/450-8691, www.chopstickcafe.biz, Mon.-Thurs. 11am-9pm, Fri. 11am-10pm, Sat. noon-10pm, Sun. noon-8pm, $9-14). They serve traditional Thai food, sushi, and even a few burgers. The place is a little cramped, but don't let that fool you: It's friendly, slightly funky on the inside, and even has good music.

They also specialize in home-baked pies—unusual for a Thai place, but they're delicious.

ACCOMMODATIONS
$100-200

Comfortable lodging choices include the **Holiday Inn SE Historic Gateway** (333 Front Royal Pike, 540/667-3300, www.ihg.com, $97-117), just off I-81. This friendly hotel was built in 2008 and has 130 nicely appointed rooms with comfortable beds. There is an indoor pool, fitness center, Internet, and an on-site restaurant.

Another good option is the **Country Inn & Suites Winchester** (141 Kernstown Commons Blvd., 540/869-7657, www.countryinns.com, $80-157). This pet-friendly hotel (additional $20) offers an indoor pool, fitness room, free wireless Internet, and a complimentary breakfast. The hotel is a 10-minute drive from the historic downtown area.

A third comparable option is the **Candlewood Suites Winchester** (1135 Millwood Pike, 540/667-8323, www.ihg.com, $97-117). This extended-stay hotel is near I-81 and offers 70 guest suites with fully equipped kitchens, 32-inch TVs, workspace, and free high-speed Internet. There are also free laundry facilities, a convenience store, and a 24-hour fitness center on-site.

$200-300

The most historic and luxurious hotel in town is ★ **The George Washington Grand Hotel** (103 E. Piccadilly St., 540/678-4700, www.wyndham.com, $129-439). This downtown treasure was built in 1924 and features 90 guest rooms and a unique indoor swimming pool designed to look like a Roman bath complete with columns and statues. The soaring ceilings, beautiful marble floors, antique front desk (the original), and traditionally decorated rooms help make the atmosphere inviting and elegant. The staff is exceptional, and guests are treated with the utmost respect. The hotel restaurant serves breakfast, lunch, and dinner, and there is a bar in the lobby. There is also a spa, fitness room, business center, and high-speed Internet access. The hotel is within walking distance of most downtown attractions and was originally built near the B&O Railroad depot to accommodate train travelers. Famous guests have included Lucille Ball and Jack Dempsey.

INFORMATION AND SERVICES

For additional information on Winchester, contact the **Winchester-Frederick County Convention and Visitors Bureau** (1400 S. Pleasant Valley Rd., 540/542-1326, www.visitwinchesterva.com, daily 9am-5pm).

GETTING THERE AND AROUND

Winchester is 75 miles northwest of Washington DC off US 50 and I-81. The local **Winchester Transit** (540/667-1815, www.winchesterva.gov, Mon.-Fri. 6am-8pm, Sat. 9am-5pm, $1) provides bus service throughout the city during the day.

Shenandoah National Park

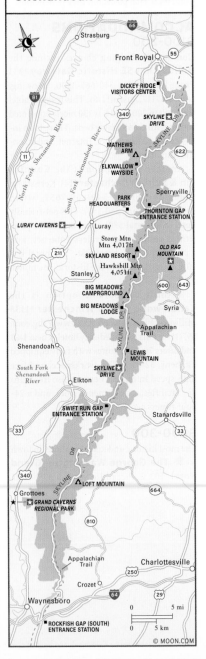

Shenandoah National Park

Seventy-five miles west of Washington DC is 200,000 acres of protected parkland known as **Shenandoah National Park** (540/999-3500, www.nps.gov/shen, $30 per vehicle or $15 per person, admission good for 7 consecutive days). The park is a popular escape for people living in the densely populated areas of Northern Virginia and Maryland, and for good reason: It offers superb outdoor recreation, stunning mountain scenery, and the lovely Shenandoah River.

The park stretches 105 miles from north to south and has four primary entrances: from Front Royal (via I-66 and US 340), at Thornton Gap (via US 211), at Swift Run Gap (via US 33), and at Rockfish Gap (via I-64 and US 250).

Shenandoah National Park is a prime location for hiking. There are more than 500 miles of trails here, mostly through lush forests. Trail maps are available at entrance stations and visitors centers. The park is also a great place to view wildlife. Some of the resident animals include coyote, black bear, bald eagles, and the timber rattlesnake. Dogs are welcome in the park as long as they are leashed.

TOP EXPERIENCE

★ SKYLINE DRIVE

One of the most beautiful stretches of road in the East, **Skyline Drive** (540/999-3500, www.nps.gov/shen, $30 per vehicle) is the most popular attraction in Shenandoah National Park. This 105-mile road takes travelers from vista to vista along a stunning byway that runs the entire length of the park from north to south. It is the only public road that goes through the park. Access to Skyline Drive is from four entry points: from Front Royal at the northern terminus (near I-66 and US 340), at Thornton Gap (US 211), at Swift Run Gap (US 33), and near Waynesboro at Rockfish Gap at I-64 and US 250 (at the southern terminus). Skyline Drive ends where the **Blue Ridge Parkway** begins. It takes approximately three hours to drive the entire road.

The most popular time to visit Skyline Drive is during the fall. Virginia is known for having one of the most beautiful leaf displays in the country, and this route showcases the best of the best. Unfortunately, this can often mean long lines leading into the park when the colors are at their peak, so expect to have a lot of company, especially on a weekend. Inclement weather can also close the road at any time during the year. Call or visit the park's website for a status if the forecast calls for fog, snow, or heavy rain. The road is also closed at night during deer-hunting season (mid-Nov. through early Jan.). Hikers are allowed into the park on foot even if the road is closed.

RVs, camping trailers, and horse trailers are allowed on Skyline Drive but will need to use a low gear. There is also a low tunnel (Marys Rock Tunnel) south of the entrance at Thornton Gap off US 211 that is 12 feet, 8 inches high. The speed limit on Skyline Drive is 35 miles an hour. This is partly because of the curves and steep inclines and partly to protect wildlife in the area.

Mileposts (mp) demarcate the entire length of Skyline Drive on the west side of the road starting with 0.0 in Front Royal. All park maps use these as location references.

There are 75 overlooks along the route. Visitors can see the beautiful Shenandoah Valley to the west and the Piedmont to the east. Wildflowers and other stunning blooms keep the area colorful throughout the warmer months.

HIKING
★ Old Rag Mountain

The most popular hike in Shenandoah National Park is **Old Rag Mountain** (www. nps.gov/shen). It is also the most challenging and dangerous. A day at Old Rag is an experience to remember, as summiting the peak requires a vigorous uphill ascent and many rough areas of scrambling near the top.

The hike is a 9-mile circuit that can take up to seven or eight hours. The route at the top changes periodically but always involves a hefty scramble requiring good upper body strength. Children and shorter adults may need assistance to get through some sections.

Several search-and-rescue missions are required each year at Old Rag, but this shouldn't deter you from the hike. It is a fun way to spend the day, and the views from the top are very rewarding. A safety video on the park website should be viewed prior to your hike. Bring food and water (at least two quarts per person) with you. Arrive early in the morning to ensure you can get a parking space; this is a very popular hike and can be crowded on nice days, especially on weekends.

Most people arrive at Old Rag Mountain from the eastern park boundary near Sperryville. From the intersection of State Route 211 and US 522 in Sperryville, take US 522 south for 0.8 mile. Turn right on State Route 231 and go eight miles. Turn right on State Route 601. Continue three miles, following the signs to the parking lot. Parking can be tough on weekends. Hikers must use the designated parking area at the Old Rag Fee Station and then walk to the trailhead; the small parking lot at the trailhead is not open for public parking. This is not a pet-friendly hike, and pets are not allowed on parts of the trail. A valid Shenandoah National Park entrance pass is required.

White Oak Canyon

At milepost 42.6 on Skyline Drive, just south of Skyland Resort, is the parking lot and trailhead for the popular **White Oak Canyon** hike (www.nps.gov/shen). This moderate hike offers one of the premier waterfall views in the park and treats hikers to spectacular scenery as they walk down a steep gorge past boulders, pools, and six waterfalls (35-85 feet in height). This hike is steep in sections (there is an elevation gain of 1,200 feet), but the trail is well used and maintained. It can also be very

crowded in peak season. Allow four hours for this 4.8-mile up-and-back hike.

Dark Hollow Falls

A scenic, family-friendly hike near Skyline Drive is the 1.5-mile round-trip route to **Dark Hollow Falls.** The trail begins just north of Big Meadows at mile 50.7. The trail follows the Hogcamp Branch stream out of the Big Meadows spring to the falls. The hike to the 70-foot waterfall is downhill, which means it is uphill on the way back. The trail is especially pretty in the spring when the mountain laurel along the path blooms a vibrant pink. The trail is shaded by the tree canopy, keeping it relatively cool in the summer.

FOOD

There are two park-operated dining facilities in Shenandoah National Park. The first is the **Pollock Dining Room** (dinner entrées $9-28) at Skyland Resort. They serve breakfast, lunch, and dinner and offer regional cuisine (such as rainbow trout and beef tenderloin). Be sure to try the Blackberry Ice Cream Pie. The **Mountain Taproom** is also at Skyland Resort and has family-friendly entertainment and adult drinks. Visitors can also purchase boxed lunches to go. Just ask the hostess for a "picnic to go."

The second dining facility is the **Spottswood Dining Room** (dinner entrées $9-29) at Big Meadows Lodge. They are open for breakfast, lunch, and dinner and serve regional cuisine such as roasted turkey and steak. The **New Market Taproom** is also on-site with live music and specialty drinks.

In addition to the two sit-down restaurants, the park operates three **Wayside Food Stops** along Skyline Drive. **Elkwallow Wayside** (mp 24.1, open mid-Apr.-Oct.) has carryout food in addition to groceries, camping supplies, and gasoline. **Big Meadows Wayside** (mp 51.2, open mid-Mar.-mid-Nov.) offers full-service meals (breakfast, lunch, and dinner), groceries, camping supplies, and gasoline. **Loft Mountain Wayside** (mp 79.5, open May-Oct.) provides a snack counter, groceries, camping supplies, and gasoline.

ACCOMMODATIONS

Park-operated lodges and campgrounds in Shenandoah National Park can provide a unique base for exploration. Reservations for prime seasons such as summer and especially during fall foliage (mid-Sept. to mid-Oct.) should be made well in advance. Many places accept reservations up to a year in advance.

Lodges

There are three park-run lodges in Shenandoah National Park. Information on all can be found at www.goshenandoah.com (877/847-1919). **Skyland Resort** (open Apr.-Nov., $135-344) occupies 36 acres at the highest point on Skyline Drive (mp 41.7). The resort sits at an elevation of 3,680 feet and has incredible views of the Shenandoah Valley. It offers 179 rooms, multiunit lodges, rustic cabins, and modern suites for rent in 28 buildings. Skyland Resort is not luxurious; there are no phones or wireless Internet access in the rooms. It is geared toward the enjoyment of the surrounding nature.

Big Meadows Lodge (open mid-May-Oct., $91-197) is near the center of the park at milepost 51.2. This is the largest developed area of the park, and it is named after a beautiful large meadow near the lodge where deer come to graze. The exterior of the main lodge is made of stones cut from Massanutten Mountain back in 1939, while the interior structure was constructed from chestnut trees (now extinct in the area).

The main lodge at Big Meadows has 29 guest rooms. There is a full-service dining room offering breakfast, lunch, and dinner, a taproom with light fare and nightly entertainment, and a gift shop. Five cabins and six multiunit buildings are also near the lodge.

Big Meadows is close to the Shenandoah River and the Shenandoah Valley. There are

1: sun rays on Skyline Drive **2:** Dark Hollow Falls in Shenandoah National Park **3:** view from Old Rag Mountain in Shenandoah National Park

no phones or wireless access in the lodge rooms, but free wireless Internet is available in the Great Room of the main building.

Lewis Mountain (open Apr.-mid-Nov., $138-169) offers cabins for rent in a quiet wooded setting near milepost 57.5. Cabins have electricity, private bathrooms, heat, towels, linens, and an outdoor grill pit. There are no phones or wireless access in the cabins. The Shenandoah River and the town of Luray are nearby.

Camping

Most of Shenandoah National Park is open to backcountry camping (a free permit is required). In addition, there are four seasonal, park-operated campgrounds with a variety of amenities (877/444-6777, www.goshenandoah.com and www.nps.gov/shen) that are open from spring to fall. They are located at milepost 22.1 (**Mathews Arm Campground,** mid-May-Oct., $15), milepost 51.2 (**Big Meadows Campground,** late Apr.-Dec., $20), milepost 57.5 (**Lewis Mountain Campground,** May-Nov., $15), and milepost 79.5 (**Loft Mountain Campground,** mid-May-Oct., $15). Mathews Arm Campground has approximately 178 sites (tent, generator-free, and group sites),

restrooms, water, and a trash and recycle center. Big Meadows Campground has more than 200 sites (tent, generator-free, and group sites), restrooms, showers, and a trash and recycle center. Lewis Mountain Campground has approximately 30 tent sites, restrooms, a camp store, and a trash and recycle center. Loft Mountain Campground has more than 200 sites (tent, generator-free, and group sites), restrooms, showers, and a trash and recycle center. Reservations are taken (and advised) at all the campgrounds except Lewis Mountain Campground, which only operates on a first-come, first-served basis.

INFORMATION AND SERVICES

There are two visitors centers in Shenandoah National Park. **Dickey Ridge Visitor Center** (mp 4.6 on Skyline Dr., 540/999-3500, Apr.-mid-May weekends 9am-5pm, mid-May-Nov. daily 9am-5pm) has an information desk, restrooms, an orientation movie, maps, permits, first aid, and publications. **Harry F. Byrd, Sr. Visitor Center** (mp 51 on Skyline Dr., 540/999-3500, Apr.-mid-May weekends 9am-5pm, mid-May-Nov. daily 9am-5pm) has an information desk, restrooms, publications, maps, permits, and first aid.

Front Royal

The northern gateway to the popular **Skyline Drive** in Shenandoah National Park is **Front Royal** in Warren County. The town has a population of around 15,000.

The Shenandoah River runs through Front Royal, offering opportunities for fishing, canoeing, and tubing. The downtown area is worth a visit in itself, with a **Town Hall** that looks like it came from a movie set, many cute stores, and several first-rate restaurants. The two main roads in downtown Front Royal are Royal Avenue and East Main Street. The Village Commons off of East Main Street house Front Royal's trademark gazebo,

a large red caboose, and the visitors center. Front Royal is also known for a series of elegant murals painted on buildings in the downtown area.

SIGHTS
Warren Rifles Confederate Museum

The **Warren Rifles Confederate Museum** (95 Chester St., 540/636-6982, Apr. 15-Nov. 1 Mon.-Sat. 9am-4pm, Sun. noon-4pm, by

---

1: Gadino Cellars **2:** Luray Singing Tower **3:** gazebo on Main Street in Front Royal

appointment the rest of the year, $5, students and active military free) is in a plain brick home and offers displays of Civil War relics such as weapons, battle flags, uniforms, photos, and rare documents. Memorabilia of famous Civil War players in the Front Royal area (such as Belle Boyd, John S. Mosby, Jefferson Davis, General Robert E. Lee, and General Stonewall Jackson) are also on exhibit. There is a book and gift shop.

Belle Boyd Cottage

Nearly across the street from the Warren Rifles Confederate Museum, in one of the oldest buildings in Front Royal, is the **Belle Boyd Cottage** (101 Chester St., 540/636-1446, www.warrenheritagesociety.org, year-round Mon.-Fri. 10am-4pm, Mar. 30-Nov. 16 also Sat. 11am-4pm, adults $10, children 6-18 $5, 5 and under free). Belle Boyd was a charming female spy who helped Stonewall Jackson capture Front Royal in May 1862. Boyd was well known among Union forces and had been reported no fewer than 30 times, arrested a half-dozen times, and even spent time in jail. For a time during the war, Front Royal was her home base, and she stayed in this cottage owned by her relatives. Visitors can learn more about Boyd's life and her spy adventures.

Skyline Caverns

A wonderful underground experience, **Skyline Caverns** (10334 Stonewall Jackson Hwy., 540/635-4545, www.skylinecaverns. com, June 15-Labor Day daily 9am-6pm, Mar. 15-June 14 and Labor Day-Nov 14. Mon.-Fri. 9am-5pm, Sat.-Sun. 9am-6pm, Nov. 15-Mar. 14 daily 9am-4pm, adults $22, children 7-13 $11, under 6 free) opened to the public in 1939. Visitors are led by professional guides through a maze of living caverns on a one-hour tour. Expect to see magical cave formations, three underground streams, and a 37-foot waterfall. A fun mirror maze is also offered for both children and adults for an additional $6. Skyline Caverns is just southwest of town.

RECREATION

The Shenandoah River is ideal for float trips. A handful of outfitters offer gear and shuttle service for visitors wishing to spend a day on this normally peaceful river. **Front Royal Outdoors** (8567 Stonewall Jackson Hwy., 540/635-5440, www.frontroyaloutdoors.com, open Apr.-Oct.) offers self-guided trips down the river (3-11 miles) in canoes ($50-60), kayaks ($38-60), four-person rafts ($110-120), and six-person rafts ($165-172). They offer three-mile tubing trips (complete with a tube for your cooler) for $25 per person. They also rent stand-up paddleboards and fishing kayaks. **Skyline Canoe Company** (540/305-7695, www.skylinecanoe.com) offers self-guided canoe ($40-55) and kayak ($30-40) trips of 3-12.5 miles. They also offer three-mile tubing trips ($20).

Mountain bikers can challenge themselves on trails that go up to 3,300 feet in elevation, traversing deep valleys and wooded slopes. A popular expert trail is the **Elizabeth Furnace** trail, approximately 11 miles west of Front Royal in **George Washington National Forest** (www. singletracks.com). The 15-mile trail starts with a long uphill climb on a fire road, followed by a long, bumpy ride downhill. It is very challenging and offers many water crossings, outcrops, technical sections, and rock gardens. Another local favorite is the 13-mile network of trails in **Shenandoah River State Park** (350 Daughter of Stars Dr., Bentonville, www.dcr.virginia.gov), 9 miles southwest of Front Royal. The trails are wide and smooth and not nearly as daunting as the Elizabeth Furnace trail, but there are moderate climbs. There are also scenic views of the river.

Equine enthusiasts may enjoy a trail ride with **Royal Horseshoe Farm** (509 Morgan Ford Rd., 540/636-6375, https:// royalhorseshoe.com, starting at $35). They offer trail rides for riders of all levels of experience.

Blue Ridge Whiskey & Wine Loop

The Front Royal and Northern Blue Ridge Mountains area is home to many lovely vineyards and wineries. The Blue Ridge Whiskey Wine Loop is a driving tour through scenic country roads with stops at wineries, a whiskey distillery, and other attractions. A map of the tour and recommended stops can be downloaded at the Discover Shenandoah website (www.discovershenandoah.com). Some popular wineries along the tour include:

- **Chester Gap Cellars** (4615 Remount Rd., Front Royal, 540/636-8086, www.chestergapcellars.com)

- **Desert Rose Winery** (13726 Hume Rd., Hume, 540/635-3200, www.desertrosewinery.com)

- **DuCard Vineyards** (40 Gibson Hollow Ln., Etlan, 540/923-4206, www.ducardvineyards.com)

- **Gadino Cellars** (92 Schoolhouse Rd., Washington, 540/987-9292, www.gadinocellars.com)

- **Quievremont** (162 Gid Brown Hollow Rd. #335, Washington, 540/827-4579, www.quievremont.com)

- **Rappahannock Cellars** (14437 Hume Rd., Huntly, 540/635-9398, www.rappahannockcellars.com)

- **Sharp Rock Vineyards** (5 Sharp Rock Rd., Sperryville, 540/987-8020, www.sharprockvineyards.com)

- **Wisteria Farm and Vineyard** (1126 Marksville Rd., Stanley, 540/742-1489, www.wisteriavineyard.com)

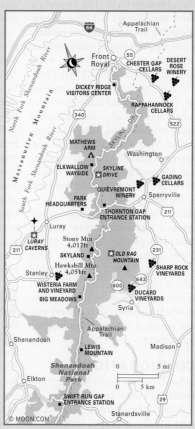

FOOD

A few restaurants in Front Royal have grabbed the attention of weekend visitors. The first is **Blue Wing Frog** (219 Chester St., 540/622-6175, www.bluewingfrog.com, Wed. and Thurs. 11am-9pm, Fri.-Sat. 11am-10pm, Sun. 10am-9pm, $8-32). They are a bit eclectic, in a good way, starting with the setup. Walk in, grab a menu, find a table, and when you're ready, order at the counter. Then, return to your seat and they'll bring out your food. When you're done, pay up front. The menu changes a lot and offers a lot, from salads and burgers to grilled cheese and steak. Even catfish tacos make an appearance. The restaurant is committed to sustainability, buying local and making as much in house as possible, even their own ketchup and peanut butter.

The popular **Element** (317 E. Main St., 540/636-1695, www.elementonmain.com,

Tues.-Sat. 11:30am-2:30pm and 5pm-9pm, $16-32) offers a delectable menu of salads, veggie selections, seafood, beef, pork, and starters. They also serve lunch. The atmosphere is modern, and there is a full bar and handpicked wine list. The menu changes regularly.

Another favorite is **Ben's Family Cuisines** (654 W. 11th St., 540/551-3147, www.bensfamilycuisines.com, Tues.-Thurs. 11am-9pm, Fri.-Sat. 11am-10pm, Sun. noon-8pm, $10-24). This unassuming family restaurant is a bit hidden in a small brick building in a residential neighborhood. They offer Thai, Cambodian, Vietnamese, Korean, Japanese, and American dishes. All meals are made to order, and the staff is warm and delightful. Try the Ben's Family Pancake Wrap; it is unique and scrumptious.

If you're craving a burger and frozen custard, stop in at **Spelunker's Frozen Custard and Cavern Burgers** (116 South St., 540/631-0300, www.spelunkerscustard.com, daily 11am-10-pm, under $10). They offer dine-in and drive-through service with fun custard flavors of the day. One of the sweetest is The Circus, which is cotton candy custard with rainbow sprinkles, marshmallow topping, and sugar cookies.

ACCOMMODATIONS

Several hotels provide rooms in Front Royal for around $100, such as the **Holiday Inn Hotel & Suites Front Royal Blue Ridge Shadows** (111 Hospitality Dr., 540/631-3050, www.ihg.com, $93-208). The hotel is next to the Blue Ridge Shadows Golf Club and offers 124 guest rooms on seven floors, with free high-speed Internet, a heated indoor pool, a 24-hour fitness center, and a 24-hour business center.

Another good option is the **Hampton Inn Front Royal** (9800 Winchester Rd., 540/635-1882, www.hamptoninn3.hilton.com, $123-177). This pleasant, 102-room hotel is located just off I-66 and is a short drive from town. Guests can enjoy a complimentary breakfast, free wireless Internet, and a fitness room.

For those who prefer to stay in a bed-and-breakfast, the lovely **Woodward House on Manor Grade** (413 S. Royal Ave., 540/635-7010, www.acountryhome.com, $120-225) is a cozy spot with a homey feel. This charming home has six guest rooms and two cabins (all with private bathrooms). A delightful breakfast is served daily, and each room comes with snacks, fresh-baked cookies, and water. The house sits on a hill above town and has nice views.

INFORMATION AND SERVICES

For additional information on Front Royal, contact the **Front Royal-Warren County Visitor Center** (414 E. Main St., 540/635-5788, www.discoverfrontroyal.com, daily 9am-5pm).

GETTING THERE

Front Royal is 70 miles west of Washington DC and is easily accessed from I-66.

Luray

The town of Luray is nestled in the scenic Shenandoah Valley in Page County. The town is less than five square miles and has a population of fewer than 5,000 people. Luray is a western gateway to Shenandoah National Park and is a two-hour drive from Washington DC. The charming downtown area along Main Street is the focal point of Luray and offers visitors a choice of restaurants and shops. The streets are decorated with seasonal flowers, and the lovely Shenandoah Valley scenery is everywhere. Luray is a great day or overnight trip from many areas of Virginia and Maryland and offers small-town charm, friendly residents, outdoor recreation, and the world-famous Luray Caverns.

SIGHTS
★ Luray Caverns

There are many cavern attractions in the Blue Ridge Mountains, but the cream of the crop is **Luray Caverns** (970 US 211 West, GPS 101 Cave Hill Rd., 540/743-6551, www.luraycaverns.com, opens daily at 9am with tours beginning every 20 min., closing hours vary by season: Apr.-June 6pm, June 15-Labor Day 7pm, day after Labor Day-Oct. 6pm, Nov.-Mar. weekdays 4pm, weekends 5pm, adults $28, children 6-12 $15, seniors 62 and over $25, children 5 and under free). This incredible natural wonder has been awing visitors since it was first discovered in 1878. Upon entering the caverns, you are transported into a subterranean world of mystery that took more than four million centuries to create. A series of paved walkways guide visitors through massive cavern "rooms" filled with natural stalagmites, stalactites, and, when the two join, columns or pillars. Some of the chambers have ceilings that are 10 stories high.

There are many attractions along the paved route in the caverns, including the famous **Stalacpipe Organ.** It is considered the world's largest musical instrument and is made up of stalactites covering 3.5 acres. The organ produces symphonic-quality sounds when the stalactites are tapped (electronically) by rubber-tipped mallets. It took 36 years to perfect the organ, but visitors can hear its haunting melodies played on every tour.

The general admission rate includes the entrance fee to the caverns, a cavern tour (tours depart every 20 minutes and are one hour), a self-guided tour of the **Car and Carriage Caravan Museum,** which displays restored cars, carriages, and coaches from 1725 to 1941, and entrance to the **Luray Valley Museum,** which interprets early Shenandoah Valley culture from as far back as precontact native people and includes a Swiss Bible (in the German vernacular) from 1536. Visitors can also enjoy displays of thousands of toys and train-related artifacts at **Toy Town Junction.**

Other attractions at the caverns can be enjoyed for an additional fee, including the Rope Adventure Park, a challenging multilevel ropes course with trails consisting of several poles connected by acrobatic elements; the **Stonyman Mining Company Gem Sluice,** a re-created operational mining station; and the **Garden Maze,** a half-mile evergreen-hedge maze.

Another interesting sight opposite Luray Caverns is the **Belle Brown Northcott Memorial,** which is also known as the **Luray Singing Tower.** This beautiful 117-foot-tall bell tower was built in 1937 and contains 47 bells (the largest of which is 7,640 pounds with a diameter of six feet). The tower holds regular recitals from spring through fall.

Luray Zoo

The **Luray Zoo** (1087 US 211, 540/743-4113, www.lurayzoo.com, Apr.-Oct. daily 10am-5pm, Nov.-Feb. Wed.-Sun. 11am-4pm, Mar. daily 11am-4pm until daylight savings time then 10am-5pm, adults $12, children 3-12 $6, seniors age 56 and over $11, children 2 and under free) is a small zoo that rescues exotic animals. The more than 250 animals that live there have all been taken from sad and harmful situations and given a permanent home. The friendly zookeepers interact with both the animals and the visitors and are happy to answer any questions. The zoo's reptile center has one of the largest collections of snakes on the East Coast. There is a petting section of the zoo for children, with animals such as goats, deer, a burro, and a potbellied pig.

RECREATION

Luray is an outdoor town. Tucked in the Shenandoah Valley, Luray offers visitors a wonderful home base for hiking, fishing, canoeing, tubing, and kayaking. **Shenandoah River Outfitters** (6502 S. Page Valley Rd., 540/743-4159, www.shenandoah-river.com) is a great place to rent boats and gear. They rent white-water and flat-water canoes and kayaks ($36-56 per day) and offer 3-4-mile tubing trips ($22). They also rent furnished log cabins ($150-250 per night).

Those wishing to hike can take the **Stony**

Underground Adventures

stalactites, stalagmites, and other formations at Luray Caverns

The mountains of Virginia harbor some of the nation's best caverns. Many are open to the public and can be explored in a couple of hours.

- **Luray Caverns** (page 251) is the granddaddy of all caverns. This awe-inspiring natural wonder in Luray, Virginia, transports visitors into an underground world of mystery and adventure that took more than four million centuries to create (yes, *centuries*).

- **Skyline Caverns** (page 248) near Front Royal, Virginia, offers kids of all ages a magical subterranean experience. With cave formations, three streams, and a 37-foot waterfall, this is another top cavern experience in rural Virginia.

- **Grand Caverns Regional Park** (page 258) near Harrisonburg, Virginia, is the oldest continuously operating "show" cave in the nation. It opened to the public in 1806 and at one time hosted elaborate balls in its 5,000-square-foot "Grand Ballroom."

- **Natural Bridge Caverns,** along the Blue Ridge Parkway, is 34 stories below ground. Visitors can see this natural wonder during a trip to a unique aboveground attraction, **Natural Bridge** (page 313).

Man Mountain Hike (www.hikingupward. com), in Shenandoah National Park. This short (less than four miles) loop hike is pleasant, easy, and offers stunning views of the park. Just under the main peak is a fun rock-climbing area known as **Little Stony Man.** The trailhead is off of Skyland Drive (between mp 41 and 42).

Triathletes can compete in the annual **Luray Triathlon** (luraytriathlon.com), which is held over two days in August and features both international- and sprint-distance races.

FOOD

Moonshadows Restaurant (132 E. Main St., 540/743-1911, www.moonshadowsonmain. com, Thurs.-Mon. 4pm-8:30pm, Sat.-Sun. 10:30am-2:30pm, $12-29) offers an elegant atmosphere (white tablecloths, wood floors, etc.) with delicious food in a beautifully renovated blue house on Main Street. The wonderful food presentation matches flavorful selections such as Brazilian steak, lump crab cakes, jumbo shrimp, and blueberry bread pudding. They also offer a patio/garden dining space. This is a great spot for a date, special occasion, or simply a good meal with friendly service.

Outstanding New York-style pizza, pasta, and delicious cheesesteaks can be found at **Gennaro's Pizza and Italian Restaurant** (402 W. Main St., 540/743-2200, daily 11am-9:30pm, $4-14). The owner is from Napoli, and many of the recipes are family heirlooms.

For a cup of coffee or casual sandwich, stop in the **Gathering Grounds Patisserie and Cafe** (24 E. Main St., 540/743-1121, www.ggrounds.com, Mon.-Thurs. 7am-6pm, Fri. 7am-7pm, Sat. 8am-7pm, Sun. 11am-3pm, $10-15). They serve a variety of egg sandwiches, wraps, quiche, soup, salads, and homemade baked treats (different every day). They also have delicious coffee, frappuccino, chai lattes, smoothies, beer, and wine. The atmosphere is warm and friendly.

A wonderful wine bar and bottle shop right on Main Street is **The Valley Cork** (55 E. Main St., 540/743-1207, www.thevalleycork. com, Thurs.-Fri. 4pm-10pm, Sat. 2pm-10pm, Sun. 2pm-8pm, $6-17). They offer Virginia and international wines (by the glass or bottle), small plates, flatbread, and charcuterie boards. They also feature live music.

ACCOMMODATIONS

There are many cabins for rent in and around Luray. Some overlook the Shenandoah River while others are mountain-view retreats. The **Luray & Page County website** (www. luraypage.com) has an extensive listing of available cabins and is a good resource for private accommodations.

There are also several inns and motels in town. The **Mimslyn Inn** (401 W. Main St., 540/743-5105, www.mimslyninn.com, $150-359) is the premier overnight location in Luray. The colonial-style inn is just a short walk from the historic downtown area and strives to offer "vintage Southern hospitality." Visitors enter the property on a circular driveway leading to a portico lined with columns.

The winding staircase in the lobby is reminiscent of those found in grand homes of the Old South, and each guest is warmly greeted by the attending staff. The inn has 45 guest rooms, each individually decorated. Rooms are available in a variety of sizes in several price ranges. There is a spa, fitness room, and business center on-site as well as a formal dining room and casual tavern.

The **Inn of the Shenandoah** (138 E. Main St., 540/300-9777, www.innoftheshenandoah. com, $140-195) is a nice, three-suite bed-and-breakfast with antique glass windows and European accents. The house has a pretty front porch and second-story balcony. Behind the inn is a renovated farmhouse called the **Cottage of the Inn,** which offers two additional suites.

The **Hotel Laurance** (2 S. Court St., 540/742-7060, www.hotellaurance.com, $185-225) is a boutique hotel offering 12 guest rooms, many with full kitchens. The decor is lovely and modern, and their website has detailed write-ups about each room. This hotel is geared toward hosting small weddings and events.

The very similar **Luray Caverns Motel East** (at the east entrance to Luray Caverns across from the Luray Singing Tower) and **Luray Caverns Motel West** (at the west entrance to Luray Caverns) offer standard accommodations. Both have free wireless Internet and swimming pools. Rates for both range $79-99 per night, and reservations can be made by calling 540/743-6551.

CAMPING

Several local campgrounds are convenient to Luray, including **Yogi Bear's Jellystone Park** (2250 US 211, 540/300-1697, www. campluray.com, camping $76-110, cabins $190-286), which offers camping and cabin rentals three miles east of downtown off US 211 and **Camp Roosevelt** (540/984-4101, www.fs.usda.gov, $10), 8.5 miles northwest of Luray on State Route 675 in the George Washington and Jefferson National Forests.

INFORMATION AND SERVICES

Begin your visit to Luray at the **Luray Train Depot and Visitor Center** (18 Campbell St., 540/743-3915, www.visitluraypage.com, daily 9am-5pm). This lovely building houses knowledgeable staff, brochures, and clean bathrooms amid a parklike setting. It is downtown about a block off Main Street and is within easy walking distance to shops and restaurants.

GETTING THERE

Luray is 93 miles southwest of Washington DC on US 211. US 340 also runs through Luray.

New Market

Fourteen miles west of Luray is the town of New Market. It was established in 1796 and became known for its printing and publishing industry in the early 1800s. During the Civil War, the town was a key thoroughfare in the Shenandoah Valley and witnessed Stonewall Jackson's troops marching through at four different times. The historic Battle of New Market took place in 1864 and is reenacted annually in mid-May.

Visitors to New Market will find a cozy, quiet downtown area on the east side of I-81 and the historic battlefield on the west side of the interstate. Explore the battlefield or take in a show at the **Rouss Center for the Arts** (9357 N. Congress St., 888/341-7313, www. rousscenter.org). They offer theater performances including plays, musicals, and dramatic readings. They also showcase local artists and artwork.

SIGHTS

★ New Market Battlefield State Historical Park

The main attraction in New Market is the **New Market Battlefield State Historical Park** (8895 George R. Collins Pkwy., 866/515-1864, www.vmi.edu, daily 9am-5pm, adults $10, children 6-12 $6, seniors 65 and over $9, children 5 and under free). This 300-acre park occupies the site of a Civil War battle on May 15, 1864, famous for being the only

New Market Battlefield State Historical Park

Destination Dining

Inn at Little Washington

One of the premier dining destinations in Virginia is the famous **Inn at Little Washington Restaurant** (309 Middle St., Washington, 540/675-3800, www.theinnatlittlewashington.com). This extremely high-end restaurant is renowned for its incredible food, scenery, and service. Located in the town of Washington, between Front Royal and Luray and not far off US 211 and US 522, the inn sits on a historic street that hasn't changed much since George Washington himself named the town roads in 1749 (he was only 17 at the time).

The inn was founded in 1978, and the main building (where the restaurant is) occupies the space of a former garage, dance hall, and general store. It has since grown into a campus of sorts, incorporating many additional properties in the village (some dating back to the 1700s) into its accommodations (in addition to nearly a dozen guest rooms and suites located in the main building). There is also a cutting garden (where fresh herbs and vegetables are grown), a walking path, a ballroom, and a gift shop.

The inn describes itself as an "unassuming dark blue building festooned with flags on the corner of Middle and Main Streets." This may be true, but once you step inside and see the crackling fire and tables adorned with silver and crystal, you will know you've entered a very special restaurant that is renowned for its exquisite food. Not only do they purchase food from local farmers, but the inn also has its own gardens and orchards.

Dinner reservations are accepted up to a year in advance. They offer three tasting menus to choose from. Prices vary during holidays and special events, but are generally $238 per person (not including beverages, tax, or gratuity). An optional wine pairing of $170 per person is available. Main course selections can include items such as pan-roasted Maine lobster, juniper-crusted venison loin, and seared rare tuna crusted with mustard seeds, while desserts may include choices such as a Southern butter pecan ice-cream sandwich, lemon-meringue tartlet with toasted pistachios, or cocoa nib napoleon with caramelized bananas.

This is truly a special and memorable dining experience in a beautiful location.

occasion in American history when college cadets were responsible for victory in combat. During the battle, cadets from the Virginia Military Institute in Lexington fought alongside Confederate soldiers to force Union troops out of the Shenandoah Valley.

Today visitors can explore nine structures at the 19th-century **Bushong Farm** that provided shelter to the Bushong family as the battle unfolded around them on their property (primarily in the orchard right behind the house). After the battle, the farmhouse was used as a field hospital for a week (bloodstains can still be seen in the parlor).

Another on-site attraction is the **Virginia Museum of the Civil War.** This museum has information and exhibits on the entire Civil War but focuses on the conflict in Virginia. The museum is housed in the **Hall of Valor,** a monument building dedicated to young people who have served in the military during times of national need. Plan to watch the Emmy Award-winning film *Field of Lost Shoes* during your visit.

The park also offers walking trails, scenic overlooks of the Shenandoah River, and wonderful picnic areas. The park is a National Historic Landmark.

It is important to note that the nearby New Market Battlefield Military Museum, on the way to the battlefield park, is not part of the state-run battlefield facility (despite its official-looking Greek Revival exterior with large white columns). It offers a private collection of relics, many of which are not Civil War related.

FOOD

New Market isn't known as a foodie's paradise, but good comfort food can be found on Congress Street. A local favorite with an old-fashioned ambience is the **Southern Kitchen** (9576 S. Congress St., 540/740-3514, daily 7am-9pm, $5-15). They serve simple, Southern cooking (think country ham, pork barbecue, burgers, and fried chicken) in a friendly atmosphere. Look for the neon sign and crowded parking lot; it is hard to miss in small downtown New Market. They are open for breakfast, lunch, and dinner.

Another popular choice is **Jalisco Mexican Restaurant** (9403 S. Congress St., 540/740-9404, Mon.-Thurs. 11am-10pm, Fri.-Sat. 11am-10:30pm, Sun. 11am-9:30pm, $5-15). This eatery serves traditional Mexican food from an extensive menu. The atmosphere is lively (for New Market), and the place has a friendly vibe. They have good chorizo and a lot of vegetarian options as well as dishes with shrimp.

ACCOMMODATIONS

There aren't many choices for hotels in New Market. There are a few inexpensive chain hotels such as the **Quality Inn Shenandoah Valley** (162 W. Old Cross Rd., 540/740-3141, www.choicehotels.com, $120-125), with 100 rooms and an adjoining restaurant, and the **Days Inn New Market Battlefield** (9360 George Collins Pkwy., 540/740-4100, www.wyndhamhotels.com, $67-84), which has a continental breakfast, free wireless Internet, and a seasonal pool.

Another option is the **Shenvalee Golf Resort** (9660 Fairway Dr., 540/740-3181, www.shenvalee.com, $92). Accommodations here include a guesthouse and motel less than three miles from New Market Battlefield State Historical Park. The 42 rooms are not luxurious, but they offer balconies with golf course or pool views, free Wi-Fi, and minifridges. The guesthouse has four bedrooms, a kitchen, and a mountain view. There is also a restaurant on-site.

The **Rosendale Inn Bed and Breakfast** (17917 Farmhouse Ln., 540/325-4544, www.rosendaleinn.com, $150) is a good choice for a quiet getaway. The historic home was built in 1790 and has two lovely 60-foot verandas (with rocking chairs and benches) and a two-story front porch. Accommodations include four rooms in the main house and a separate cozy cottage that has a fireplace. The owner is an author and has many interesting stories to share about the area. He goes out of his way to make sure each guest has a good experience.

There is a barn on the property that can accommodate guests' horses.

If you'd prefer a bed-and-breakfast that includes the entire house with your stay, the **Jacob Swartz House** (574 Jiggady Rd., 540/740-9208, www.jacobswartz.com, $150) is for you. The house is a lovely historic cottage and renovated cobbler shop that sits on a river bluff. It has a master bedroom and a second loft bedroom as well as a living room (with a woodstove), dining area, and full kitchen (stocked with staples). The house has wireless Internet and is located outside of town on a long country road.

INFORMATION AND SERVICES

Additional information on New Market can be found at www.newmarketvirginia.com and www.shenandoahvalleyweb.com.

GETTING THERE

New Market is 113 miles (approximately two hours) southwest of Washington DC off US 211 and I-81.

Harrisonburg

Harrisonburg, tucked away in the Shenandoah Valley, is part of Rockingham County and has a population of around 50,000. It is best known as the home of **James Madison University.** The historic section of its downtown area includes 10 blocks of locally owned restaurants, galleries, and museums.

Harrisonburg is an active town, due in part to the large population of students that live here much of the year and also to its proximity to the Blue Ridge Mountains. The town was named as a top location for families to "beat nature deficit disorder" by *Backpacker Magazine.*

SIGHTS
James Madison University

James Madison University (JMU) (800 S. Main St., 540/568-6211, www.jmu.edu) is the largest attraction in Harrisonburg. The school was founded in 1908 and offers more than 130 degree programs. With over 21,000 students and 148 buildings on 721 acres, the school dominates the Harrisonburg landscape. JMU has earned many national rankings and recognitions and is considered to be one of the most environmentally responsible colleges.

The beautiful campus is a pleasure to walk around, with the focal point being the large grassy quadrangle on South Main Street, where students can be seen lounging, reading, or playing ball when the weather is nice. This is also the location of the stately **Wilson Hall,** which houses a 1,372-seat auditorium under its red roof and was named after President Woodrow Wilson. It is said that on a clear day, it is possible to see Staunton, Virginia—the birthplace of its namesake—from its cupola.

The campus is split by I-81, with the original buildings on the west side and the newer **College of Integrated Science and Technology** on the east side (along with other academic and resident buildings). A bridge and a tunnel connect the two sides.

A highlight of the campus is the **Edith J. Carrier Arboretum** (540/568-3194, open daily dawn to dusk, free) on University Boulevard. This beautiful, 125-acre landscaped area offers nature trails and guided tours by appointment.

Explore More Discovery Museum

For those traveling with children, the **Explore More Discovery Museum** (150 S. Main St., 540/442-8900, www.iexploremore. com, Tues.-Sat. 9:30am-5pm, open Mon. June 10-Aug. 26, $7.50, children under 1 free) is a great stop that has interactive exhibits geared toward children under 10 on topics such as health, construction, art, science, mechanics, theater, farms, the outdoors, and much more.

Virginia Quilt Museum

The **Virginia Quilt Museum** (301 S. Main St., 540/433-3818, www.vaquiltmuseum.org, mid-Feb.-mid-Dec. Tues.-Sat. 10am-4pm, adults $8, students with ID $5, military, first responders, and seniors over 65 $7, children under 12 free) is a small specialty museum that features a wonderful permanent collection of nearly 300 quilts, antique sewing machines, and a gift store. They also have a handful of rotating exhibits throughout the year. The museum is housed in a pretty home that was built in 1856. Tours are self-guided, but guided group tours can be arranged.

★ Grand Caverns Regional Park

Approximately 15 miles southeast of Harrisonburg is **Grand Caverns Regional Park** (5 Grand Caverns Dr., Grottoes, 540/249-5705, www.grandcaverns.com, Nov.-Mar. daily 10am-4pm, Apr.-Oct. daily 9am-5pm, adults $20, children $11, seniors $18). Discovered in 1804 and opened to the public in 1806, Grand Caverns is the oldest continuously operating "show" cave in the country. The caverns are made up of an impressive network of caves, including Cathedral Hall, one of the most massive underground rooms on the East Coast, as well as the Grand Ballroom, which is 5,000 square feet and literally was the site of balls in the early years after the caverns were discovered. Many famous people have visited the caverns, including Thomas Jefferson and both Confederate and Union soldiers (of which more than 200 signed their names on the cave walls). This is a great attraction for both adults and children. Seventy-minute tours are given on the hour. Admission to the caverns is by guided tour only.

The park also features a pool, minigolf, fitness, cycling and hiking trails, fishing, picnic areas, and **Fountain Cave** (tours offered in May on Sat., June-July Tues., Thurs., and Sat.,

must be at least 12 years old, starting at $50). Fountain Cave was a commercial cave almost 100 years ago and is now open for two-hour tours. There are no lights in the cavern, and guests are given helmets, headlights, kneepads, and gloves. Exploring is via a rough path from the 1800s or the more adventurous way, which includes crawling and strenuous climbing.

RECREATION

The nearby **Massanutten Resort** (1822 Resort Dr., Massanutten, 540/289-9441, www.massresort.com) is a 6,000-acre, four-season family destination that offers lodging, skiing, snowboarding, snow-tubing, golfing, fishing, mountain biking, a water park, a spa, and hiking around Massanutten Peak as well as panoramic views of the Blue Ridge Mountains. Best known as a ski resort, Massanutten has 14 trails (all with lights for night skiing) with 1,110 feet of vertical drop (lift tickets are $44-77). Massanutten is about 15 miles southeast of Harrisonburg.

Cycling is big in Harrisonburg. Both road biking and mountain biking are popular, and many events are scheduled throughout the year. For information on cycling in the area visit the **Shenandoah Valley Bicycle Coalition** website (www.svbcoalition.org). Mountain bike rentals are available at Massanutten Resort (starting at $50).

FOOD

Fresh local ingredients, beautiful exposed brick walls, white tablecloths, and great food are some of the key ingredients to the success of the ★ **Local Chop & Grill House** (56 W. Gay St., 540/801-0505, www.localchops.com, Mon.-Thurs. 5pm-9pm, Fri.-Sat. 5pm-10pm, $16-34). This wonderful restaurant occupies the former building of Harrisonburg's Old City Produce Exchange, which is perfect for this modern establishment whose menu features fresh, handpicked local and seasonal

---

1: stunning view from Massanutten Resort **2:** Joshua Wilton House

foods. They specialize in steak and seafood and have a large selection of savory house-made sauces.

Another local favorite is **Vitos Italian Kitchen** (1047 Port Republic Rd., 540/433-1113, www.vitositaliankitchen.com, Sun.-Thurs. 11am-10pm, Fri.-Sat. 11am-11pm, $8-17). This wonderful Italian restaurant is a great place to bring the family. The atmosphere is warm and inviting, the food is delicious, and the staff is friendly. The menu has traditional Italian items, house specials, and pizza. Their house Italian salad dressing deserves accolades on its own.

ACCOMMODATIONS

The **Hotel Madison and Shenandoah Conference Center** (710 S. Main St., 540/564-0200, www.hotelmadison.com, $167-228) is a 230-room hotel with a restaurant, fitness center, indoor pool, and coffee shop. It is connected to a 21,000-square-foot conference center. The rooms and suites are modern and offer downtown or mountain views. On-site parking is $5.

Charming lodgings can be found at the **Joshua Wilton House** (412 S. Main St., 540/434-4464, www.joshuawilton.com, $150-175). This lovely inn and restaurant has five beautiful guest rooms in an elegant Victorian home. Each offers a feather-top queen-size bed, private bathroom, ceiling fan, antique furniture, robes, and free wireless Internet. A continental breakfast is included with each stay. The inn is also known for its restaurant and wonderful seasonally inspired menu. They offer beer- and wine-tasting dinners and more than 100 bottles of wine on their wine list. The Joshua Wilton House is where actor Richard Dreyfuss spent his honeymoon in 2006.

INFORMATION AND SERVICES

For additional information on Harrisonburg, visit the **Harrisonburg Tourism** website at www.visitharrisonburgva.com or stop by **Harrisonburg Tourism and Visitor Services** (212 S. Main St., 540/432-8935, daily 9am-5pm).

GETTING THERE

Harrisonburg sits right on I-81 and is 132 miles (about a 2.25-hour drive) southwest from Washington DC.

Staunton

Founded in 1747, Staunton is the self-proclaimed "Queen City of the Shenandoah." It sits in Augusta County and has approximately 24,000 residents.

The focal point of Staunton is the charming and compact historic downtown area. Beautiful Victorian architecture, unique restaurants, local galleries, and independent shops lend the area to exploration on foot. Staunton was lucky that it escaped destruction during the Civil War, and many of its original 18th- and 19th-century homes still stand today. The city does a wonderful job preserving the town's heritage and visual appeal by disallowing power lines and cell towers within view in the historic districts.

If you hear someone mention the "Wharf," don't look around for water. The Wharf is the neighborhood surrounding the train station. The name dates back to the 19th century when the warehouses in this historic neighborhood resembled those commonly seen in port towns.

Staunton was President Woodrow Wilson's birthplace. It is also the home of **Mary Baldwin University, Stuart Hall School** (a private prep school), and the **Virginia School for the Deaf and Blind.**

Haunted Staunton

There are many stories of hauntings throughout Virginia and Maryland, a number of which center on towns where Civil War battles were fought. Staunton is no exception, and in fact, seems to have more than its fair share of tales of the paranormal.

The most famous haunting in Staunton is at the train station. This is where a member of an opera troupe, Myrtle Knox, was killed in 1890 when a train carrying her troupe derailed and demolished Staunton's C&O depot. The 18-year-old actress bled to death at the site after multiple injuries. It has been reported many times by eyewitnesses that Knox's spirit now haunts the rail station and was even seen looking through windows at the former Pullman Restaurant (which is now closed). It is interesting to note that the train station has been featured in several movies, including *The Love Letter* in 1998.

Another well-known haunting is at the Thornerose House at Gypsy Hill. The home was built in 1912. Shortly after, the owner's 10-year-old son became very ill. His dedicated nurse, Caroline, spent day and night by the boy's side trying desperately to keep him alive, but he eventually died. It is said that Caroline now roams the house looking for him. The house served as a bed-and-breakfast for many years, and guests reported meeting Caroline in what was called the Canterbury Room (where she had lived), at which point she would introduce herself and then disappear. She was also known to play tricks on people by stealing their keys and bringing them to her room.

The Selma House was built in approximately 1848 and is the site of another famous Staunton haunting. In 1864, when Union troops were stationed in Staunton, they were said to have chased a young Confederate soldier into the house. He stopped in front of the fireplace, turned toward the door, and was shot and killed. The young man's blood flowed onto the wooden floor and caused a rather disturbing bloodstain that became a permanent mark on the floor despite numerous efforts to remove it. In addition to his blood, the soldier's spirit is said to have never left the house, and is described by the many who have seen him as a "polite man in uniform" who listens intently to conversations going on in the home. One hundred years after his death, he is said to have pushed a woman out of her bed in the middle of the night. The Selma House is a private residence, but it is easily spotted at the top of Selma Boulevard near the park.

Many additional ghost sightings have been reported in Staunton locations, including at the Stonewall Jackson Hotel, Emilio's restaurant, the Clock Tower, Mary Baldwin University, the grounds of the Commonwealth Center for Children & Adolescents, and in private homes.

SIGHTS
Frontier Culture Museum

The **Frontier Culture Museum** (1290 Richmond Rd., 540/332-7850, www.frontiermuseum.org, mid-Mar.-Nov. daily 9am-5pm, Dec.-mid-Mar. daily 10am-4pm, adults $12, students $11, children 6-12 $7, seniors $11.50, under 6 free) is a popular family destination that tells the fascinating story of the thousands of immigrants who settled colonial America. The fun and informative museum explores the lives of people from England, Germany, Ireland, and West Africa and how they all contributed to the success of our country. The museum is a collection of original and reproduced buildings that represent the Old World and America. Each features interpretive signage, period furnishings, food, animals, and living-history demonstrations presented by costumed interpreters.

Woodrow Wilson Presidential Library and Museum

The **Woodrow Wilson Presidential Library and Museum** (20 N. Coalter St., Staunton, 540/885-0897, www.woodrowwilson.org, Mon.-Sat. 9am-5pm, Sun. noon-5pm, adults $15, youth 6-15 $8, over 60 $14, active military $12, under 6 free) tells the story of our country's 28th president. Self-guided tours lead visitors through seven galleries depicting different phases of Wilson's life. A highlight is the president's restored

Pierce-Arrow limousine from 1919. He liked it so much his friends bought it for him when he left office. There is also a state-of-the-art World War I trench experience, a research library, gardens, and a hands-on kids' corner.

At the same address is the **Woodrow Wilson Birthplace.** This wonderfully restored Greek Revival home offers guided tours and a window into what life was like back in 1856, the year Wilson was born. The home contains period furniture and artifacts from the Wilson family. Behind the house is a beautiful Victorian-style garden that was created in the 1930s.

ENTERTAINMENT AND RECREATION

The **Blackfriars Playhouse** (10 S. Market St., 540/851-1733, www.americanshakespearecenter.com) is a widely popular local theater in Staunton. Run by **The American Shakespeare Center,** the theater is said to be the only re-creation of Shakespeare's indoor theater in the world. It may sound small, with just 300 seats, but the performances are greatly entertaining and energetic. Balcony seats are sold as general admission, but offer a terrific view. Aim to get there early (they have entertainment before the show) so you can grab a balcony seat in the front row. This is a fun theater with a relaxed atmosphere.

Gypsy Hill Park (600 Churchville Ave.) is a lovely 214-acre public park with an outdoor gym, walking paths, ball fields, playgrounds, a duck pond, tennis courts, a small train, and an outdoor pool. Pets are allowed, but they must remain on a leash.

FOOD

American

★ **Zynodoa** (115 E. Beverley St., 540/885-7775, www.zynodoa.com, Mon.-Tues. 5pm-9:30pm, Wed.-Sat. 5pm-10:30pm, Sun. 10am-2pm and 5pm-9:30pm, $21-30) offers wonderful contemporary Southern cuisine. This farm-to-table restaurant has an ever-changing menu (depending on what fresh ingredients are available). They even have their own 50-acre farm from which they harvest many ingredients for their dishes (including fresh eggs). Examples of menu items include wood-smoked pork, blackened wild blue catfish, and double-cut New York strip steak. The service is outstanding; servers are well versed in the details of the menu and are also helpful with suggestions and wine pairings. This is one of the few restaurants open late on Sunday nights.

For great ribs and delicious steak and burgers, stop in the **Mill Street Grill** (1 Mill St., 540/886-0656, www.millstreetgrill. com, Mon.-Thurs. 4pm-9:30pm, Fri.-Sat. 4pm-10:30pm, Sun. 11am-9pm, $8-30). The restaurant is housed in a former turn-of-the-20th-century flour mill. It has a loyal client base and can be crowded on weekends. The menu also includes seafood, pasta, sandwiches, and vegetarian choices. If you happen to be in town during Mardi Gras, they offer jazz entertainment and go all out with their decorations.

The slightly out-of-the-way **Depot Grille** (42 Middlebrook Ave., 540/885-7332, www. depotgrille.com, Sun.-Thurs. 11am-10pm, Fri.-Sat. 11am-11pm, $9-24) is a unique little restaurant in the historic freight-train station in Staunton. The atmosphere is train oriented, cozy, and fun. The main dining room maintains the original hardwood floors from the station, and the dining booths were once church pews. There is also a 40-foot-long Victorian bar that came from a historic luxury hotel in Albany, New York. They offer a lot of variety on their menu (including ribs, chicken, prime rib, salads, sandwiches, and seafood), and there is an enclosed deck with views of the downtown area.

A downtown restaurant offering a flavorful Southern menu is **Byers Street Bistro** (18 Byers St., 540/887-6100, www. byersstreetbistro.com, Sun.-Thurs. 11am-11pm, Fri.-Sat. 11am-midnight, $10-25). This upbeat favorite has a large patio and live entertainment many nights. The menu includes selections such as shrimp and grits, fish tacos, ribs, steak, and gourmet pizza.

Italian

A large dining establishment with a small-restaurant feel is **Emilio's** (23 E. Beverley St., 540/885-0102, www.emiliositalianrestaurant.com, Tues.-Thurs. 11am-9:30pm, Fri.-Sat. 11am-10:30pm, Sun. 11am-8:30pm, $15-27). This wonderful, friendly Italian eatery has terrific food and great ambience with its downtown location, lounge, four fireplaces, and a rooftop patio. Fresh pasta, wonderful specials, wine tastings, and live entertainment many nights in the lounge help make this a fun place to spend an evening.

ACCOMMODATIONS
$100-200

The **Stonewall Jackson Hotel and Conference Center** (24 S. Market St., 540/885-4848, www.stonewalljacksonhotel.com, $129-199) was built in 1924 and has since been fully restored. It has 124 guest rooms, a heated indoor pool, a fitness center, and a business center. The rooms aren't large, but they are comfortable and well appointed. The public areas are nice also. A big plus for this hotel is its location in downtown Staunton, convenient to attractions and dining. The hotel is also pet friendly ($50). Parking is $7.50.

The ★ **Blackburn Inn** (301 Greenville Ave., 540/712-0601, www.blackburn-inn.com, $135-250) is a welcome recent addition to the hotel scene in Staunton. This fully restored, 49-room boutique hotel was formerly the headquarters of the Western State Hospital (originally named the Western Lunatic Asylum), which was one of two key hospitals in Virginia for those with mental illness. The hotel was named after Thomas Blackburn, the original building architect (circa 1828), who worked as an apprentice for Thomas Jefferson. The hospital relocated in the 1970s, and the building became a medium-security prison in 1981. Abandoned in 2002, the property was purchased in 2006, and the renovated hotel opened in 2019. Today guests enjoy rooms with 27 unique floor plans, modern furnishings, tall ceilings, and an incredible spiral staircase on the fourth floor that leads to a cupola with stunning views of Staunton. There is also a fitness room and bistro on-site. The hotel is dog friendly (no extra fee) with complimentary amenities for your best friend (such as bowls, beds, treats, and waste bags).

$200-300

The ★ **Inn at WestShire Farms** (1329 Commerce Rd., 540/248-4650, www.westshirefarms.com, $199-305) is a cozy bed-and-breakfast just north of town. The inn was built prior to the Civil War and has nine guest rooms in two buildings. The main house contains the common areas including an English-style conservatory, living room (with a fireplace and baby grand piano), meeting room, breakfast room, and outdoor patios. A beautifully renovated barn contains eight guest rooms, a common area living room, and decks overlooking the valley. The house and grounds are elegant and well maintained. A delicious full breakfast is served each morning, or guests can opt for a light breakfast or breakfast to go.

INFORMATION AND SERVICES

For additional information about visiting Staunton, go to www.visitstaunton.com or visit the downtown **Staunton Visitor Center** (35 S. New St., 540/332-3971, daily 9:30am-5:30pm).

GETTING THERE

Staunton is located in the Shenandoah Valley off I-81, 28 miles south of Harrisonburg and 36 miles north of Lexington.

Allegheny Highlands

The western reaches of the state toward the West Virginia border include Highland County, Bath County, and parts of Augusta and Allegheny Counties. The Allegheny Mountains spill into West Virginia, and the area is split by river valleys. This region is scenic and sparsely populated. US 220 from Monterey to Covington is a particularly scenic drive. Part of the enjoyment of a trip to this region can be the drive there and back.

HOT SPRINGS

The village of Hot Springs is in a beautiful area of Bath County that offers visitors a blend of resort atmosphere and natural scenery. Bath County is one of the wealthiest in Virginia, thanks to several resorts that have taken advantage of numerous natural thermal springs. Native tribes originally hailed their healing powers, but wealthy Virginians quickly learned what a wonderful retreat the mountain air and spring waters made. The area became the site of lavish resorts and to this day remains a destination for vacationers.

Hot Springs is quaint and small, and it contains many buildings that have existed for more than 150 years. The population is just over 700 people. During the summer months, Hot Springs hosts a local farmers market, and its **Garth Newel Music Center** (403 Garth Newel Ln., 540/839-5018, www.garthnewel.org) is a popular venue for chamber music, blues, and jazz performances.

Hot Springs is known as home to one of Virginia's premier resorts, ★ **The Omni Homestead Resort** (7696 Sam Snead Hwy., 540/839-1766, www.omnihotels.com, $279-463), off US 220. This enormous, 483-room resort has origins dating back to 1766 and was built around magnificent warm springs. The crystal-clear springs are still a focal point of the resort and maintain a uniform temperature and flow all year long. The mineral content of the springs is also very high, making them easy to float in. The spring pools are named for President Thomas Jefferson, who visited them in 1818.

The resort encompasses 2,000 manicured acres and has impressive stately brick buildings, two premier golf courses, and clay tennis courts. It offers elaborate lodging, dining, and many year-round recreational opportunities. It is also a popular conference site for Virginia businesses.

The resort is nothing short of a self-contained campus, with many restaurants, stores, a first-class European-style spa, and countless guest activities including a trout stream, a shooting club, and a small ski resort.

Additional information on Hot Springs can be found at www.discoverbath.com.

DOUTHAT STATE PARK

About 26 miles southeast of Hot Springs (much less as the crow flies) is one of the oldest state parks in Virginia, **Douthat State Park** (14239 Douthat State Park Rd., Millboro, 540/862-8100, www.dcr.virginia.gov, $7 entrance fee). The park is just under 4,500 acres and offers all of the following: 40 miles of hiking trails; a 50-acre lake for swimming, boating, and fishing; rental cabins ($86-405); camping ($10-40); horseback riding; nature programs; picnic areas; a camp store; laundry facilities; and a restaurant. This is a wonderful park for families and outdoor enthusiasts.

GETTING THERE

The Allegheny Highlands are approximately 200 miles from Washington DC. Much of the trip is on major highways such as I-66 and I-81, but the last 60 miles are in more rural, mountainous areas. This part of the trip is slow going but very scenic.

Central and Southern Virginia

Central and Southern Virginia is teeming with both history and natural beauty. It's a place where breathtaking byways and small country roads lead to state parks and country inns, and Civil War battlefields and presidential homes attest to the land's deep roots and historical importance.

The region encompasses a vast amount of acreage but is much less densely populated than Northern Virginia and Coastal Virginia. This part of the state is home to many colleges and universities, including the University of Virginia and Virginia Tech, and the state capital, Richmond.

From the Civil War battlefields in Fredericksburg to Robert E. Lee and Stonewall Jackson's final resting place in Lexington, Central

Highlights

Look for ★ to find recommended sights, activities, dining, and lodging.

★ **Fredericksburg & Spotsylvania National Military Park:** Hear the story of four important Civil War battles that resulted in more than 100,000 casualties (page 271).

★ **Capitol Square:** This beautifully landscaped 12-acre parcel in the heart of Richmond is home to several state buildings, including the Virginia State Capitol (page 282).

★ **Monticello:** This amazing 5,000-acre plantation was the home of Thomas Jefferson, author of the Declaration of Independence, and the University of Virginia's founder (page 301).

★ **Natural Bridge State Park:** This 20-story solid limestone arch is an impressive natural formation (page 313).

★ **Thomas Jefferson's Poplar Forest:** The president's personal retreat is an architectural masterpiece and the first octagonal house in the country (page 315).

★ **Virginia Military Institute:** The oldest state-supported military college in the country was founded in Lexington, Virginia, in 1839 (page 320).

★ **Taubman Museum of Art:** This popular museum in Roanoke highlights the culture of

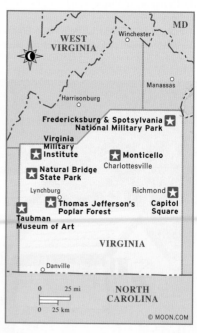

the Roanoke Valley and Southern Virginia (page 334).

Virginia offers visitors many opportunities to learn firsthand about the conflicts fought on the nation's soil and the many soldiers who gave their lives in those wars. Thomas Jefferson also had strong ties to Central Virginia, and his influence can be seen in many places. His home, Monticello, is a popular attraction in Charlottesville and is close to the University of Virginia, which was founded by Jefferson himself.

Southern Virginia is home to the scenic Blue Ridge Parkway and vast tracts of farmland and mountains that provide a deep contrast to the more populated regions of the state. Business suits are traded for fishing waders and limousines for tractors. Visitors can sample a slower pace of life through small towns and historic cities such as Lynchburg and Roanoke and gain an appreciation for the natural beauty of the state.

PLANNING YOUR TIME

You could easily spend weeks exploring Central and Southern Virginia. The drive time alone between Fredericksburg and Abingdon is approximately five hours. Since most of the cities in this region are about an hour away from each other, it is best to focus on a handful of destinations over a few days and to go from one to the next hitting the highlights.

If Civil War history is your passion, then Fredericksburg is a must. If you're fascinated with the accomplishments of Thomas Jefferson, then Charlottesville will be on your list.

If it's beautiful mountain scenery you seek, then a ride down the Blue Ridge Parkway should be on your agenda—especially during the fall. The parkway's Virginia portion stretches 218 miles and can be driven in one day but is best experienced over two days. This allows time to explore the unique sights and towns along the way and take in some of the best scenery the state has to offer.

The best way to move between cities is by car. The highways in Virginia are easy to navigate and are generally in excellent shape. I-95 and I-64 are the primary routes through Central Virginia, while I-81 is the main highway in Southern Virginia.

Fredericksburg

Fredericksburg is a far-reaching suburb of Washington DC and the largest city between Washington and Richmond. It is easily accessed from I-95, and the quaint historic district is a popular day trip from many locations in Virginia and Maryland.

Fredericksburg is known for its extensive history. It was established in 1728 and named after the Prince of Wales and the father of King George III. Fredericksburg was a prominent port during the colonial era and home to George Washington during his boyhood. It also has an extensive Civil War history due in part to its location halfway between the Union and Confederate capitals.

Although the Fredericksburg area is home to many commuters who drive north for work, it is also home to the **University of Mary Washington** (www.umw.edu) and several large employers (such as GEICO). The city sits within the county lines of Spotsylvania but is an independent city with approximately 28,000 residents.

SIGHTS
Old Town Fredericksburg
Old Town Fredericksburg takes visitors

Central and Southern Virginia

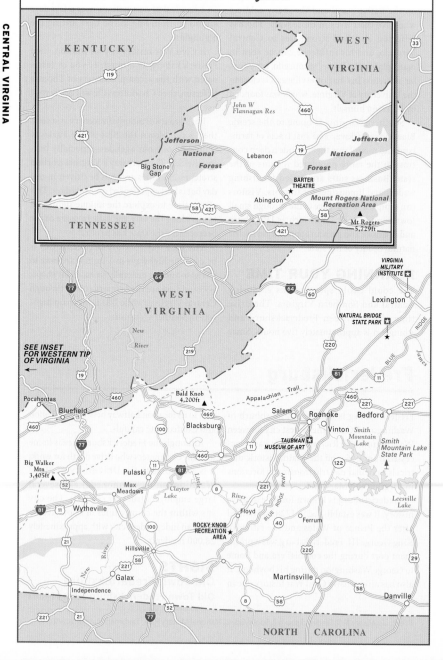

KENTUCKY

WEST VIRGINIA

119

John W Flannagan Res

460

421

Jefferson

National

Forest

Lebanon

19

Jefferson

National

Forest

Big Stone Gap

BARTER THEATRE ★

Abingdon

Mount Rogers National Recreation Area ▲

58 421

58

Mt Rogers 5,729ft

TENNESSEE

421

33

WEST VIRGINIA

64

77

64 60

VIRGINIA MILITARY INSTITUTE ✚

Lexington

NATURAL BRIDGE STATE PARK ✚

★

New River

219

220

BLUE RIDGE

James

SEE INSET FOR WESTERN TIP OF VIRGINIA
←

19

81

11

Appalachian Trail

Bald Knob 4,200ft ▲

460

460

Salem

Roanoke

460

221

221

Bedford

Pocahontas

Bluefield

460

100

Blacksburg

TAUBMAN MUSEUM OF ART ✚

Vinton

Smith Mountain Lake

Smith Mountain Lake State Park

460

11

Big Walker Mtn 3,405ft ▲

52

11

Pulaski

Max Meadows

Claytor Lake

81

8

Little *River*

221

BLUE RIDGE PKWY

122

Leesville Lake

Wytheville

100

Floyd

40

Ferrum

220

21

ROCKY KNOB RECREATION AREA ★

New River

Hillsville

221 58

Galax

Independence

8

58

Martinsville

58

Danville

29

221

21

52

77

NORTH   CAROLINA

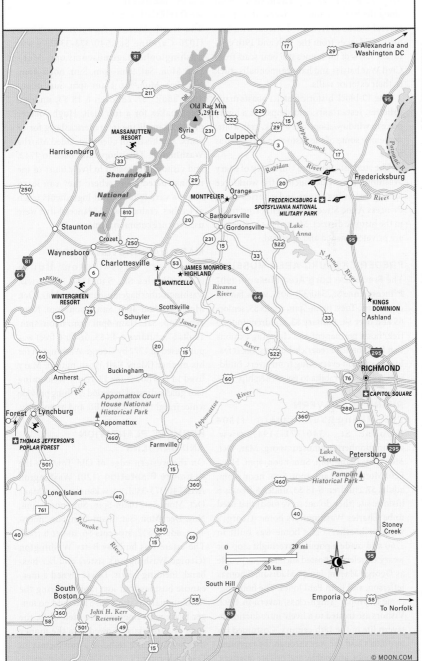

© MOON.COM

back to the Civil War era. The town was built along the Rappahannock River and includes several blocks of tree-lined streets with historic residences from the 18th and 19th centuries. A few of the homes still bear scars from Civil War battles and have cannonballs stuck in their exterior walls.

The 40-block historic district boasts many galleries, restaurants, and shops. It's a lovely place to window-shop, take a walk, grab a bite, and enjoy some of the history in this famous town.

The students from the University of Mary Washington provide much of the workforce for the charming stores and eateries along Princess Anne Street and neighboring roads in the historic district. Most of the businesses are privately owned and operated.

FREDERICKSBURG AREA MUSEUM

The **Fredericksburg Area Museum** (907 Princess Anne St., 540/371-3037, www.famva. org, Thurs.-Tues. 10am-5pm, adults $5, seniors 65 and over $4, military $3, children under 5 free) hosts permanent and changing exhibits that focus on the Fredericksburg region. It features topics on everything from rivers, buildings, and memorabilia to pet ownership.

RISING SUN TAVERN

The **Rising Sun Tavern** (1304 Caroline St., 540/371-1494, www. washingtonheritagemuseums.org, Mar.-Oct. Mon.-Sat. 10am-5pm, Sun. noon-4pm, Nov.-Feb. Mon.-Sat. 11am-4pm, Sun. noon-4pm, adults $7, children 6-18 $3, under 6 free) is a historic site (they do not serve food) that used to be Charles Washington's home (George's younger brother). The home was built in 1760 and made a popular overnight stop for weary travelers. It hosted such famous people as George Mason, James Madison, Thomas Jefferson, and John Paul Jones. The home became a "proper" (high-class) tavern in 1792. Visitors are treated to a lively introduction to tavern life in the 18th century. Costumed interpreters lead the way through the taproom, dining room, and public and private quarters.

HUGH MERCER APOTHECARY SHOP

The **Hugh Mercer Apothecary Shop** (1020 Caroline St., 540/373-3362, www. washingtonheritagemuseums.org, Mar.-Oct. Mon.-Sat. 9am-4pm, Sun. noon-4pm, Nov.-Feb. Mon.-Sat. 11am-4pm, Sun. noon-4pm, adults $7, children 6-18 $3, under 6 free) makes for a fun visit. Hugh Mercer practiced medicine in Fredericksburg for 15 years, and his list of clients included Martha Washington. This shop dates back to 1742, and visitors are treated to lively tours of the reconstructed shop, where they can learn about a variety of natural ingredients (such as leeches, crab claws, and lancets) that were used to cure common ailments.

MARY WASHINGTON HOUSE

The **Mary Washington House** (1200 Charles St., 540/373-1569, www. washingtonheritagemuseums.org, Mar.-Oct. Mon.-Sat. 9am-4pm, Sun. noon-4pm, Nov.-Feb. Mon.-Sat. 11am-4pm, Sun. noon-4pm, adults $7, children 6-18 $3, under 6 free) was purchased in 1772 by George Washington for his mother (Mary Ball Washington). Mary lived in the house for 17 years. Welcoming tour guides dressed in period clothing provide a nice insight into Mary's life and personality.

KENMORE PLANTATION AND GARDENS

On the western edge of Old Town is the **Kenmore Plantation** (1201 Washington Ave., 540/373-3381, www.kenmore.org, Mar.-Oct. Mon.-Sat. 10am-5pm, Sun. noon-5pm, Nov.-Dec. Mon.-Sat. 10am-4pm, Sun. noon-4pm, adults $12, students $6, under 6 free). The estate was built by Betty Washington (George Washington's sister) and her husband, Fielding Lewis. Lewis owned a mercantile business but lost money during the Revolutionary War because he could no longer trade with England. He died while the state of Virginia still owed him the money that he had lent it to build a gun factory in Fredericksburg.

Downtown Fredericksburg

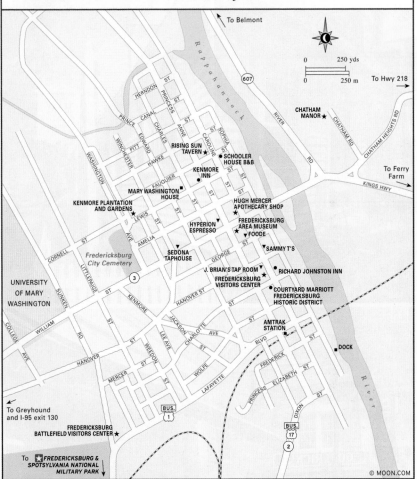

To Belmont

607

CHATHAM
MANOR ★

To Hwy 218 →

0   250 yds
0   250 m

HERNDON ST
PRINCESS ST
CANAL
PRINCE
EDWARD
CHARLES
PITT
WINCHESTER
WASHINGTON ST
HAWKE
FAUQUIER
LEWIS
AVE
AMELIA
CORNELL ST
LITTLEPAGE ST
Fredericksburg
City Cemetery

ANNE ST
CAROLINE
SOPHIA ST
RISING SUN
TAVERN ★
KENMORE
INN
MARY WASHINGTON
HOUSE
KENMORE PLANTATION
AND GARDENS
HYPERION
ESPRESSO
SEDONA
TAPHOUSE

● SCHOOLER
HOUSE B&B

HUGH MERCER
APOTHECARY SHOP
▼ FREDERICKSBURG
AREA MUSEUM
▼ FOODE
▼ SAMMY T'S

GEORGE
J. BRIAN'S TAP ROOM ▼
FREDERICKSBURG
VISITORS CENTER

● RICHARD JOHNSTON INN

● COURTYARD MARRIOTT
FREDERICKSBURG
HISTORIC DISTRICT

UNIVERSITY
OF MARY
WASHINGTON

SUNKEN
KENMORE
HANOVER ST

JACKSON ST
CHARLOTTE
LEE AVE
WEEDON ST
COLLEGE
AVE
WILLIAM
HANOVER
MERCER ST
WOLFE
LAFAYETTE

AMTRAK
STATION

BLVD
FREDERICK
PRINCESS
ELIZABETH
DIXON ST

■ DOCK

To Greyhound
and I-95 exit 130

BUS.
1

FREDERICKSBURG
BATTLEFIELD VISITORS CENTER ★

BUS.
17
2

To ★ FREDERICKSBURG &
SPOTSYLVANIA NATIONAL
MILITARY PARK ▼

Rappahannock River

KINGS HWY

CHATHAM RD
CHATHAM HEIGHTS RD
RD

To Ferry
Farm

River

3

© MOON.COM

The Georgian-style brick home sits on three acres and is open for tours. It is elegant inside and out and noted for having stunning decorative plaster ceilings. Tours begin at the **Crowninshield Museum,** to the left of the front gate. Decorative arts and antique furnishings are on display there. Next, guides lead a 45-minute tour of the mansion's first floor and kitchen. The gardens are then available to explore on your own. Visitors who wish to visit both Kenmore and Ferry Farm can purchase a combination ticket for $19 for adults and $8.50 for students.

★ Fredericksburg & Spotsylvania National Military Park

Between 1862 and 1864, four Civil War battles were fought on the streets of Fredericksburg and in the fields and forests surrounding the city. The result was more than 100,000 casualties. The **Fredericksburg & Spotsylvania**

National Military Park (540/693-3200, www.nps.gov/frsp, free) is the second-largest military park in the world. It can take two days to fully explore, or visitors can choose to see specific sights. There are two visitors centers: the **Fredericksburg Battlefield Visitors Center** (1013 Lafayette Blvd., 540/693-3200, daily 9am-5pm) and the **Chancellorsville Battlefield Visitor Center** (9001 Plank Rd., Spotsylvania, 540/693-3200, daily 9am-5pm). Orientation films are available at both locations (ages 10-61 $2, over 61 $1, under 10 free), as are maps to trails and driving tours.

The most important and well-known battle of the four that occurred here was the **Battle of Fredericksburg**, which took place on December 11-15, 1862. The battle was one of the largest (nearly 200,000 soldiers) and deadliest of the war and is known for being the "first major opposed river crossing in American military history." It was also the first time Union and Confederate troops fought right on city streets and as such is considered the first location of urban combat.

The Union's plan for the battle was for General Burnside's command to defeat General Lee's southern flank at Prospect Hill, while also holding the Confederate First Corps at Marye's Heights. The bloody battle raged for several days, eventually resulting in a Confederate victory and Burnside's troops retreating back across the river. Four generals were killed in the battle (two from each side).

The **Fredericksburg National Cemetery** (1013 Lafayette Blvd., 540/373-6122, daily dawn to dusk) was placed on Marye's Heights as the final resting place of more than 15,000 soldiers. Approximately 20 percent of the soldiers buried there have been identified.

A driving tour can be made of Prospect Hill and Marye's Heights. The route is five miles long. Directions for self-guided walking trails for a 400-yard walk around the Sunken

---

1: Hugh Mercer Apothecary Shop 2: Mary Washington House 3: a sunny day in charming Fredericksburg

Road, a short loop through the Fredericksburg National Cemetery, and several other short walks can be downloaded at the National Park Service website (www.nps.gov/frsp).

Across the Rappahannock from Fredericksburg is **Chatham Manor** (120 Chatham Ln., 540/693-3200, daily 9am-4:30pm), which served as a hospital during the battle. The home was built between 1768 and 1771. Five of the 10 rooms of this 12,000-square-foot Georgian estate are open for touring (free). Interior exhibits provide information on the home's 15 owners and the mansion's role in the Civil War.

Another Civil War battle that took place near Fredericksburg was the **Battle of Chancellorsville** (Apr. 30-May 6, 1863). It is best known as General Lee's "perfect battle," since his risky move of dividing his army against much greater enemy forces ended in a Confederate victory. During this battle Stonewall Jackson was mortally wounded by friendly fire. He died eight days later at age 39.

The third battle that took place here is the **Battle of the Wilderness** (May 5-6, 1864). This engagement marked the start of the Overland Campaign, known as the bloodiest campaign of the war. It was also the first battle between Robert E. Lee and Ulysses S. Grant.

The fourth was a continuation of the Battle of the Wilderness, known as the **Battle of Spotsylvania Court House.** This conflict marked a sea change in the war: The Union army moved forward to Spotsylvania and continued to push forward for the rest of the war.

Ferry Farm

Ferry Farm (268 Kings Hwy., 540/370-0732, www.kenmore.org, Mar.-Oct. Mon.-Sat. 10am-5pm, Sun. noon-5pm, Nov.-Dec. Mon.-Sat. 10am-4pm, Sun. noon-4pm, adults $9, students $4.50, under 6 free) was George Washington's childhood home. The 80-acre park is in Stafford, across the river from Fredericksburg. It is so named because people (including the Washingtons) used to cross the river by ferry from the farm to reach Fredericksburg. Washington lived

The Angel of Marye's Heights

the Kirkland Monument

During the horribly bloody Battle of Fredericksburg, more than 8,000 Union soldiers were wounded or killed in front of Marye's Heights at the Sunken Road on December 13. As dawn came on the morning of the 14th, many wounded soldiers who were not able to walk to the field hospital lay moaning and crying on the battlefield suffering from their wounds and a lack of water. Both armies had ceased fire and were forced to sit and listen to the agony.

A young soldier from the Confederate army, Richard Rowland Kirkland, finally requested permission to help the wounded Union soldiers by giving them water. He was first denied, but later was given permission at his own risk. The young man collected canteens, filled them with water, and risked his own life walking out on the battlefield. Realizing what he was doing, soldiers from both sides watched in silence and not one shot was fired.

Kirkland spent an hour and a half running between his lines and the wounded, bringing them water, blankets, and warm clothing. Wounded soldiers cried out for water as Kirkland performed his task, and he did not stop until he had helped each one that lay on the Confederate side of the field.

Kirkland was killed in battle only a year later. However, he will always be known as the Angel of Marye's Heights. A statue of him by artist Felix de Weldon (who also created the U.S. Marine Corps War Memorial) was erected in front of the stone wall at the Sunken Road and unveiled in 1965.

there between the ages of 6 and 20, and this is where he is rumored to have chopped down the cherry tree and thrown a penny across the Rappahannock River. Not much remains of the original house, but there is a visitors center where colonial and Civil War artifacts that were found on the property are on display (there is an archaeological lab on-site where scientists work on weekdays). There are also gardens to explore featuring plants commonly grown in the 18th century. Visitors who wish to visit both Kenmore and Ferry Farm can purchase a combination ticket for $19 for adults and $8.50 for students.

Gari Melchers Home and Studio at Belmont

The **Gari Melchers Home and Studio at Belmont** (224 Washington St., Falmouth, 540/654-1015, www.garimelchers.org, Apr.-Oct. daily 10am-5pm, Nov.-Mar. daily 10am-4pm, adults $10, 18 and under free with paying parent – limit 2) is the estate of one of the most sought-after painters of the late 1800s and early 1900s, Gari Melchers. It is in Falmouth, two miles north of Fredericksburg, and visitors can tour the home where Melchers and his wife lived between 1916 and 1932 and enjoy the site's beautiful 27-acre grounds. There are four stunning art galleries with 1,677 paintings and drawings by Melchers and approximately 3,000 of his personal furnishings and decorative objects. There are also gardens and trails to enjoy. The home (originally built around 1790) and studio are one of just 30 artists spaces named in the National Trust for Historic Preservation's Historic Artists' Homes and Studios consortium. Tours of the estate, which run throughout the day, take 90 minutes and include a 12-minute film.

TOURS

Trolley Tours of Fredericksburg (540/898-0737, www.fredericksburgtrolley.com, adults $20, children 5-12 $8, military $18) last 75 minutes and depart from the **Fredericksburg Visitor Center** (706 Caroline St.). Reservations are recommended during the summer months.

Old Towne Carriages (540/371-0094, www.oldetownecarriages.com, starting at $20 for adults, children $10) carries visitors around Fredericksburg in horse-drawn carriages. They offer daily tours in the historic district and can arrange private evening tours. Tours depart from the **Fredericksburg Visitor Center** (706 Caroline St.), and tickets can be purchased there.

Another fun tour is the **Flavors of Fredericksburg** (540/656-7272, www.flavorsoffredericksburg.com, starting at $60) food and history tour. This walking tour through the downtown area stops for tastings at restaurants and shops while providing fun details on historical sites, architecture, and famous historical residents.

RECREATION

Fredericksburg sits on the banks of the Rappahannock River. As such, it lends itself to canoeing, kayaking, and boating in a relaxed and mostly pristine environment. At the southern end of Old Town is **City Dock Park** (207 Sophia St.). The historic dock was in place during George Washington's time, and the boat ramp there offers the best access to the Rappahannock River. Follow the river east along Sophia Street; the road dead-ends at the ramp. Fishing is allowed 24/7. There is a nice parking area in which to leave your car. Be aware that water levels fluctuate a lot on the river. Springtime can bring massive floods, while late summer and fall can offer low, slow-moving water. The Chesapeake Bay can be reached via the Rappahannock River. Head downstream if you are in anything other than a kayak or canoe (away from the railroad bridge). Upstream can be very rocky, especially in low water.

Two local outfitters that can arrange outdoor instruction and rentals are the **Virginia Outdoor Center** (3219 Fall Hill Ave., 540/371-5085, www.playva.com) and **Clore Brothers Outfitters** (5927 River Rd., 540/786-7749, www.clorebros.com).

Mountain bikers can learn about local trails and events by visiting the **FredTrails** website (www.fredtrails.org).

SHOPPING

In the past decade or two, the Fredericksburg area has seen tremendous growth as an exurb of Washington DC. As sprawling housing developments sprang up along the I-95 corridor, so did numerous strip malls. Many national chain stores can be found along State Route 3 and farther north into Stafford County.

Old Town Fredericksburg, however, has remained a fun and charming place to shop. Art galleries and independently owned gift shops and boutiques line the historical streets, offering a nice break from the chain stores and the opportunity to buy one-of-a-kind merchandise. Princess Anne Street is the main shopping area and contains several blocks of stores and restaurants. This is a pleasant area to window-shop or to look for a special Civil War-era gift or items made in Virginia.

Beck's Antiques & Books (709 Caroline St., 540/371-1766, www.becksantiques.com, daily 12pm-5pm) is a serious antique dealer with pieces selected mostly from homes and estates in Virginia.

A combination art gallery, store, and classroom, **Ponshop** (712 Caroline St., 540/656-2215, www.ponshopstudio.com, Mon.-Sat. 10am-6pm, Sun. 11am-5pm) offers artwork, clothing, and handmade pieces created by local artists. They also offer art classes.

FOOD
American
Yummy pub fare with a healthy twist is what **Sammy T's** (801 Caroline St., 540/371-2008, www.sammyts.com, Mon.-Thurs. 11:30am-9pm, Fri.-Sat. 11:30am-10pm, Sun. 11:30am-7pm, $5-20) is known for. A local favorite, this friendly place has a lot of atmosphere and a fun vibe. Sit at the bar and chat with new friends, or grab a table and be treated to good service. They serve a wide variety of dishes and have many vegetarian and vegan entrées. There is an indoor beer garden for events and a few outdoor seats right on Caroline Street.

J. Brian's Tap Room (200 Hanover St., 540/373-0738, www.jbrianstaproom.com, Sun.-Thurs. 11am-10pm, Fri.-Sat. 11am-11pm, $8-22) is a great local eatery in the historic district that's been around since 1961. They have delicious food at reasonable prices and offer a friendly atmosphere in an old building that has a lot of character. They have outdoor seating that is dog friendly (they even provide water bowls). The crab bisque is a winner, but their pizza and sandwiches are also good choices. This is a fine place to grab a drink with friends or enjoy a casual meal.

The **Sedona Tap House** (591 William St., 540/940-2294, www.sedonataphouse.com, Mon.-Thurs. 11am-11pm, Fri.-Sat. 11am-midnight, Sun. 10:30am-10:30pm, $14-32) is part of a small chain of restaurants with several locations in Virginia. They serve a menu of Southwest-inspired selections such as Smoky BBQ Beef Short Rib, crab cakes, pasta, steak, and a large salad menu. Sides include Mexican street corn and bacon succotash. This is a very popular restaurant, but they update their waitlist online.

The popular **Foode** (900 Princess Anne St., 540/479-1370, www.foodefredericksburg.com, Tues.-Thurs. 11am-3pm and 4pm-9pm, Fri.-Sat. 11am-3pm and 4pm-10pm, Sun. 9am-3pm, $16-31) is located in the historic National Bank Building downtown. The menu changes seasonally and highlights local products and produce and organic ingredients. The dinner menu includes items such as Rosie's Buttermilk Fried Chicken, burgers, steak, and shrimp and grits. They also offer signature cocktails and desserts.

Treats and Coffee
Hyperion Espresso (301 William St., 540/373-4882, www.hyperionespresso.com, Mon.-Thurs. 7am-8pm, Fri.-Sat. 7am-10pm, Sun. 8am-8pm, under $10) is the local favorite for coffee lovers. It is a comfortable, unpretentious place to grab a good cup of coffee and a light meal or snack. Sit outside (you can bring your pooch) and watch the world go by. This is a hometown coffee place that will please even the pickiest travelers.

No trip to Fredericksburg is complete without a stop at ★ **Carl's** (2200 Princess Anne St., www.carlsfrozencustard.com, mid-Feb.-late Nov. Sun.-Thur. 11am-11pm, Fri.-Sat., 11am-11:30, under $10). Carl's is perhaps the most famous ice-cream stand in the state and is truly a landmark. Don't be scared off if the line of eager patrons is wrapped around the building (which will no doubt include everyone from your grandmother to police officers, small children, and tattoo-clad bikers). The line will move quickly—just have your money and your order ready when it's your turn at the window.

ACCOMMODATIONS
There are many large hotels in the Fredericksburg area, but in the historic district

---

1: Sammy T's 2: Carl's 3: historic Kenmore Inn
4: Foode

visitors can choose from among a handful of lovely and historic bed-and-breakfasts.

$100-200

Comfort Suites Fredericksburg South (4615 Southpoint Pkwy., 540/891-1112, www.choicehotels.com, $85-134) is an all-suite hotel offering 85 guest rooms with two double beds or one king bed. All suites have a parlor with a sofa bed. The hotel is near I-95 and a short drive to the historic district. The hotel lobby welcomes guests with a five-story atrium and a large stone fireplace. A complimentary hot breakfast is included, and there is an indoor pool and fitness room.

The **Hampton Inn & Suites Fredericksburg South** (4800 Market St., 540/898-5000, www.hilton.com, $127-150) offers 121 guest rooms and is a five-minute drive from the historic district. There is an indoor pool, and a hot breakfast is included.

The **Schooler House Bed and Breakfast** (1303 Caroline St., 540/287-5407, www.theschoolerhouse.com, $160-175) is a small, Victorian-style home built in 1891. It offers two guest rooms with private fireplaces and bathrooms. Original pine floors and trim are still in place throughout much of the house, and the four fireplaces have restored antique tile. The home is decorated with many antiques (even the wicker furniture on the front porch is antique). A full breakfast is included, as is Wi-Fi. Pets and children are discouraged.

The historic **Kenmore Inn** (1200 Princess Anne St., 540/371-7622, www.kenmoreinn.com, $130-225) offers nine well-appointed guest rooms with private bathrooms in a historic home on Princess Anne Street. The rooms are not terribly large, but they are beautiful and cozy. Luxury rooms are located in the original portion of the home, which was built in 1793. These rooms have high ceilings, hardwood floors, and wood-burning fireplaces. Deluxe rooms are located in an addition that was put on the home in 1933 and have antique furniture and wall-to-wall carpeting. The inn has a comfortable porch

with chairs and swings. Some street parking is available. Breakfast is served in the main dining room, and evening meals can be taken in the wonderful restaurant downstairs. Ask for a room in the front of the house.

The ★ **Richard Johnston Inn** (711 Caroline St., 540/899-7606, www.therichardjohnstoninn.com, $165-300) was built in 1770 and during the 1800s was home to Richard Johnston, the mayor of Fredericksburg. The inn has seven guest rooms and two suites, all with private bathrooms. A continental breakfast is served during the week, and a full breakfast is served on weekends. The inn has two pet-friendly rooms. It is located three blocks from the train station, and parking is available on-site.

The **Courtyard Marriott Fredericksburg Historic District** (620 Caroline St., 540/373-8300, www.marriott.com, $185-239) offers 94 comfortable, modern rooms in the historic district.

INFORMATION AND SERVICES

The **Fredericksburg Visitor Center** (706 Caroline St., 540/373-1776, www.visitfred.com, Sun.-Thurs. 9am-5pm, Fri.-Sat. 9am-8pm) provides wonderful information on touring the Fredericksburg area. Maps, brochures, parking information, tickets, and lodging information are just some of the things visitors can learn about from the helpful staff. A short orientation film about the city is shown there.

GETTING THERE AND AROUND

Fredericksburg is about 50 miles south of the nation's capital. A **Virginia Railway Express** (800/743-3873, www.vre.org) and **Amtrak** (800/872-7245, www.amtrak.com) station can be found at 200 Lafayette Boulevard. Commuter service runs to Alexandria and Washington DC.

The local bus system, called the **Fredericksburg Regional Transit (FRED)**

(540/372-1222, www.ridefred.com, $1.25), provides local bus transportation on weekdays year-round and on weekends during the University of Mary Washington school year.

Richmond

Richmond is the capital of the Commonwealth of Virginia. The city is independent, but the Richmond area encompasses part of Henrico and Chesterfield Counties.

The city was founded in 1737 and is significant in both Revolutionary and Civil War history. During the Revolutionary War, Richmond was the site of Patrick Henry's famous "Give me liberty or give me death" speech, and it became the capital of Virginia in 1780. During the Civil War, Richmond was the Confederate capital.

Richmond was known in the early 20th century as home to one of the first successful streetcar systems. It was also a center of African American culture.

Today, Richmond is a vibrant, ever-changing city. Many neighborhoods have undergone major revitalizations over the past decades, although some are still waiting for their turn. Outdoor recreation is gaining popularity, even in the shadow of the downtown buildings. This is due in part to the James River flowing through the city limits and the plethora of activities it invites.

The Richmond economy is fueled by the presence of federal, state, and local government agencies, banking firms, and legal agencies. The U.S. Court of Appeals for the Fourth Circuit and the Federal Reserve Bank of Richmond are located in Richmond. Many private companies, large and small, also call Richmond home.

Richmond is a city of colleges and universities. The University of Richmond (UR), Virginia Commonwealth University (VCU) and its Medical College of Virginia branch, Virginia Union University, and the Union Theological Seminary all call the city home.

Safety can be an issue on the downtown streets after dark. It is best to drive through town at night rather than walk. Many hotels offer shuttles around the city, but if yours does not, drive or call a cab or car service.

SIGHTS

Richmond is carved up geographically into five primary sections: Downtown, the East End, West End, North Side, and South Side. It sounds simple at first, but Richmonders like to further distinguish areas of the city by neighborhood names. This becomes confusing to visitors who have no frame of reference for each neighborhood and is further complicated by the loosely defined boundaries. For simplicity's sake, the sights in this guide are broken out by the directional distinctions, and additional information is provided on specific neighborhoods that are either commonly known or have distinct characteristics that might be of interest to visitors.

Downtown

Downtown, like it sounds, is at the heart of Richmond. The area includes the financial district and several popular neighborhoods such as **Court End,** which sits to the north of Capitol Square and East Broad Street. This neighborhood was developed during the federal era, just after the state capital was moved to Richmond. The area is a combination of historic mansions and modern office space.

Jackson Ward is historically the center for African American commerce and entertainment. It is less than a mile from the capitol, west of Court End and north of Broad Street. Many famous people such as Duke Ellington, Ella Fitzgerald, Lena Horne, Billie Holiday, and James Brown frequented the neighborhood.

Monroe Ward is a historic district (east of the Fan District) that is now home to many

Central Richmond

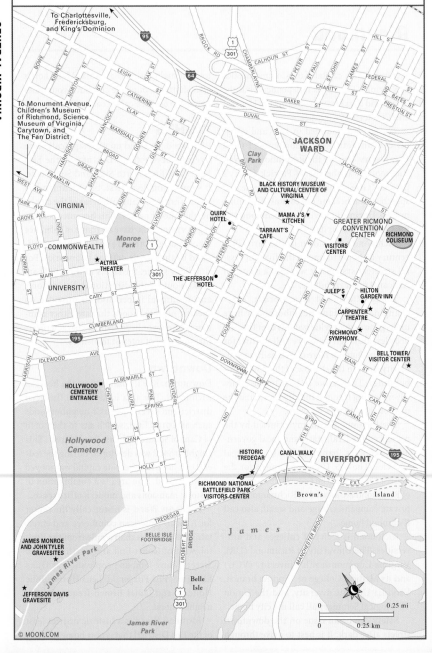

To Charlottesville, Fredericksburg, and King's Dominion

To Monument Avenue, Children's Museum of Richmond, Science Museum of Virginia, Carytown, and The Fan District

JACKSON WARD

BLACK HISTORY MUSEUM AND CULTURAL CENTER OF VIRGINIA

QUIRK HOTEL

MAMA J'S KITCHEN

TARRANT'S CAFE

GREATER RICMOND CONVENTION CENTER

RICHMOND COLISEUM

VISITORS CENTER

ALTRIA THEATER

THE JEFFERSON HOTEL

JULEP'S

HILTON GARDEN INN

CARPENTER THEATRE

RICHMOND SYMPHONY

BELL TOWER/ VISITOR CENTER

HOLLYWOOD CEMETERY ENTRANCE

Hollywood Cemetery

HISTORIC TREDEGAR

CANAL WALK

RIVERFRONT

RICHMOND NATIONAL BATTLEFIELD PARK VISITORS CENTER

Brown's Island

James River Park

JAMES MONROE AND JOHN TYLER GRAVESITES

JEFFERSON DAVIS GRAVESITE

BELLE ISLE FOOTBRIDGE

James

Belle Isle

James River Park

Monroe Park

Clay Park

0   0.25 mi

0   0.25 km

© MOON.COM

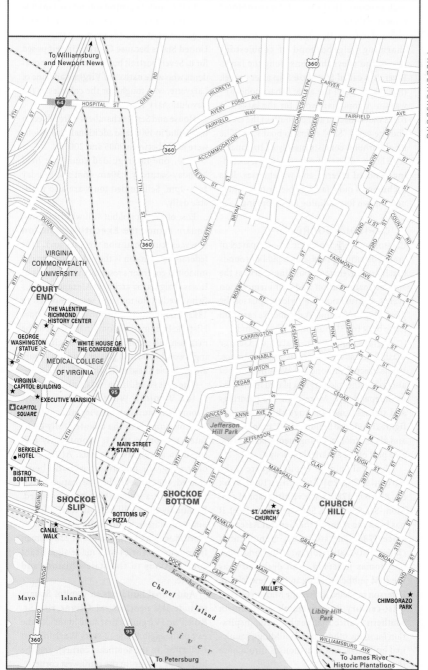

VCU students. The historic **Jefferson Hotel** is located there.

Not far from the financial district is a charming neighborhood of cobblestone streets and alleys that runs along the James River. It is called **Shockoe Slip** after a creek that ran through the area. "Shacquohocan" was an Algonquian word for the large flat rocks that collected at the mouth of the creek, and the word "Slip" refers to boat slips. The neighborhood consists mainly of Italianate-style brick and iron-front structures, including restored taverns and warehouses. It is Richmond's most fashionable district and is now known for its dining and shopping.

★ CAPITOL SQUARE

Capitol Square is a historic 12-acre parcel of grassy, beautifully landscaped public grounds that house government buildings, serve as the site for inauguration and commemoration events, and function as a civic campus for the governing of Virginia. A distinctive cast-iron fence built in 1818 surrounds the grounds.

A giant equestrian statue of George Washington sits at the formal square entrance. It was erected in honor of Washington, but also to hail the role Virginia played in the road to independence. More than 130 paintings and statues honor distinguished American figures inside the buildings in Capitol Square and also outdoors. Living memorial trees are also part of the square's landscape.

The focal point of Capitol Square is the **Virginia Capitol Building** (1000 Bank St., 804/698-1788, www.virginiacapitol.gov, Mon.-Sat. 9am-5pm, Sun. 1pm-5pm, free). It has been the home of the General Assembly since 1788. The stunning, monumental, classical-style structure was the handiwork of Thomas Jefferson, who designed it as the first public building in the New World. Jefferson modeled it after the Maison Carrée, a 1st-century Roman temple at Nîmes in southern France that has been the inspiration for many other capitol buildings, municipal buildings, and courthouses throughout the country.

In the capitol's central rotunda is a marble sculpture of George Washington. It is said to be the most valuable marble statue in the United States because George himself posed for it. Seven portrait busts of other U.S. presidents who were natives of Virginia and one of Lafayette, who fought for the colonies in the Revolutionary War, are also displayed.

House and Senate chambers were added to the capitol in 1904, and additional renovations were made between 2005 and 2007.

Free, one-hour guided tours are held Monday-Saturday 9:30am-4pm and Sunday 1pm-4pm. Self-guided tours are also available daily.

East of the capitol but still within Capitol Square stands the **Executive Mansion** (www.executivemansion.virginia.gov). This federal-era mansion is the oldest continually inhabited governor's residence in the country. It was designed by architect Alexander Parris (who lived in Boston) and was completed in 1813. The home is a Virginia and National Historic Landmark. Rooms in the front of the mansion still retain most of the original ceilings, woodwork, and plaster cornices. Tours are available Tuesday-Thursday.

The latest addition to Capitol Square is the **Virginia Women's Monument** (womensmonumentcom.virginia.gov), the only monument in the country fully dedicated to women that is prominently featured on statehouse grounds. At the time of writing, the monument was still being erected; the fist seven bronze statues of notable Virginia women have been unveiled. Eventually there will be 12 in total. A plaza made of granite features the glass **Wall of Honor,** which has the names of 230 women from four centuries who made significant contributions to the state's history and culture.

Additional buildings in Capitol Square include the neoclassical **Oliver Hill Sr. Building** (Virginia's first state library, to the east of the capitol), the 12-story **Washington Building** (in the southeast corner), and the brick **Bell Tower** (in the southwest corner).

AMERICAN CIVIL WAR MUSEUM

The **American Civil War Museum** (804/649-1861, www.acwm.org) is located on three sites in Richmond and the surrounding region (**Historic Tredegar**, the **White House of the Confederacy**, and the **American Civil War Museum – Appomattox**). It is the result of a merger between the former Museum of the Confederacy and the American Civil War Center at Historic Tredegar. It interprets the American Civil War from the Union, Confederate, and African American viewpoints.

Historic Tredegar (500 Tredegar St., daily 9am-5pm, adults $15, children 6-17 $8, seniors $13, 5 and under free) is located on the James River at the historic Tredegar Iron Works site. A new building contains the museum visitors center, store, exhibits, a theater, and hundreds of artifacts.

The **White House of the Confederacy** (1201 E. Clay St., daily 10am-5pm, adults $12, children 6-17 $6, seniors $10, 5 and under free) was the executive mansion and residence of Confederate President Jefferson Davis between 1861 and 1865. The fully restored home served as the political, social, and military center of the Confederacy. Forty-five-minute guided tours share information on the lives of the people who lived there.

The **American Civil War Museum – Appomattox** (159 Horseshoe Rd., Appomattox, summer daily 10am-6pm, shorter hours the rest of the year, adults $12, 6-17 $6, seniors $10, 5 and under free) interprets both the end of the Civil War and the beginning of a reunified nation. This location features many audiovisual stations and artifacts from the surrender. Parking is free with admission.

A combination admission ticket for the two sites in Richmond (adults $27, 6-17 $14, seniors $23) or all three sites (adults $39, 6-17 $20, seniors $33) is available.

BLACK HISTORY MUSEUM AND CULTURAL CENTER OF VIRGINIA

The **Black History Museum and Cultural Center of Virginia** (122 W. Leigh St., 804/780-9093, www.blackhistorymuseum.org, Tues.-Sat. 10am-5pm, Sun. by appointment, adults $10, students and seniors $8, children 4-12 $6, 3 and under free) is a permanent repository for artifacts as well as visual, oral, and written records that commemorate the accomplishments of African Americans in Virginia. It features detailed exhibits on Richmond's African American history and a gift shop. The museum is housed in the historic Leigh Street Armory.

MAGGIE L. WALKER NATIONAL HISTORIC SITE

The **Maggie L. Walker National Historic Site** (600 N. 2nd St., 804/771-2017, www.nps.gov/mawa, Tues.-Sat. 9am-5pm, free) covers about a quarter of a city block in the Jackson Ward neighborhood. The site is dedicated to Maggie Lena Walker, an inspirational woman who devoted her life to the advancement of civil rights, education, and economic empowerment for African Americans and women. She was the president of a bank, a newspaper editor, and a fraternal leader. Maggie L. Walker's home (which is impeccably preserved) and surrounding buildings are part of the site and make up the exhibit hall and visitor center. Be sure to watch the featured film. Parking can often be found along the surrounding streets.

CANAL WALK

Richmond's **Canal Walk** (14th St. and Dock St., www.rvariverfront.com) was completed in 1999 and stretches for 1.25 miles through downtown Richmond in the Shockoe Slip area along the Haxall Canal and James River and Kanawha Canal. The walk can be accessed from 5th Street, 7th Street, Virginia Street, 14th Street, 15th Street, and 17th Street. Four centuries of history can be explored along the walk as it passes by monuments and exhibits

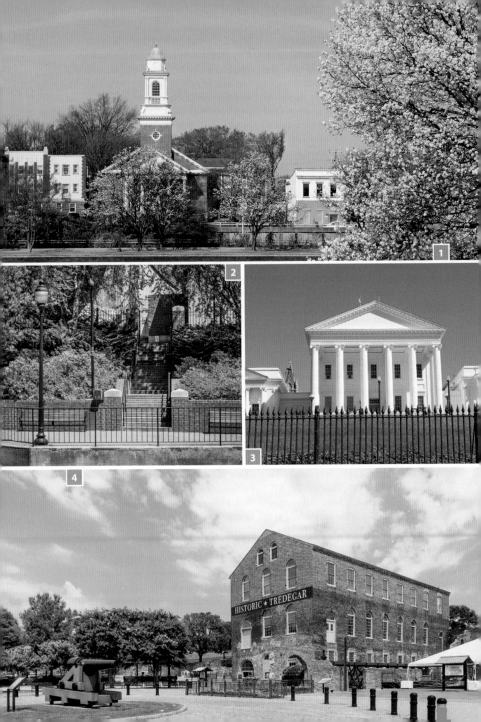

and also the popular **Brown's Island,** a park that hosts festivals, art exhibits, and concerts.

RICHMOND NATIONAL BATTLEFIELD PARK

The **Richmond National Battlefield Park** (www.nps.gov/rich, daily sunrise to sunset, free) is a collection of 13 individual sites that preserve more than 1,900 acres of Civil War history. The sites are located in Hanover, Henrico, and Chesterfield Counties as well as the city of Richmond. The park tells the story of Richmond's involvement in the war between 1861 and 1865.

The **Tredegar Visitor Center** (470 Tredegar St., 804/226-1981, daily 9am-5pm) is the main visitors center for the park. It is housed inside the former Tredegar Ironworks building, which was an important asset to Confederate troops since it produced their cannons and ammunition. The center offers three floors of displays and an orientation film. The **Chimborazo Medical Museum** (3215 E. Broad St., 804/226-1981, Wed.-Sun. 9am-4:30pm) is another visitors center for the park that contains exhibits that focus on Confederate medical equipment and hospitals. This building is also the park headquarters. One additional visitors center is located in the park: **Cold Harbor Battlefield Visitor Center** (5515 Anderson-Wright Dr., 804/226-1981, Wed.-Sun. 9am-4:30pm), which offers a book store, ranger programs in the summer, and electric map programs that provide information on the 1862 Battle of Gaines' Mill and the 1864 Battle of Cold Harbor.

East End

The East End of Richmond is a collection of neighborhoods loosely defined as the area north of the James River and east of the historic Virginia Central Railroad-Chesapeake & Ohio Railway line.

Church Hill, one of the largest existing 19th-century neighborhoods in the country, is located at the end of Broad Street, a primary east-west road through Richmond. It retains numerous examples of period architecture.

Fulton Hill runs roughly from Gillies Creek to the Richmond city limits. This is an urban neighborhood that is finally seeing renovations after years of neglect, which can be credited in part to the dedication of its community in dealing with criminal activity in the area.

Major nightlife can be found in **Shockoe Bottom,** just east of downtown near the James River. This is one of Richmond's oldest neighborhoods, and although it has a history of flooding from the James River, it has become a hot spot for dining, entertainment, and partying. Just east of Shockoe Bottom is **Tobacco Row,** so named for a group of multistory brick tobacco warehouses and factories producing cigarettes. The buildings were vacated in the 1980s, but many of the warehouses have since been converted into loft apartments, condos, retail space, and offices. The neighborhood sits adjacent to the James River and was the site of two famous Confederate prisons, **Libby Prison** and **Castle Thunder.**

One of the most historic neighborhoods in Richmond is **Union Hill,** an area bordered to the south by Jefferson Avenue, to the north by Venable Street, to the east by 25th Street, and to the west by Mosby Street. Union Hill sits high on a bluff above Shockoe Bottom. Its mix of antebellum, Victorian, classical revival, and modern architecture has landed the neighborhood in the National Register of Historic Places and the Virginia Landmarks Register.

SAINT JOHN'S CHURCH

Saint John's Church (2401 E. Broad St., 804/648-5015, www.historicstjohnschurch.org, Mon.-Sat. 10am-4pm, Sun. 1pm-4pm), in Church Hill, was built in 1741 and served as a place of worship but also as a local meeting hall. When the assembly of the Second Virginia Convention moved from Williamsburg to Richmond, Saint John's was

1: Byrd Park **2:** spring color along the Canal Walk **3:** Virginia Capitol Building **4:** historic Tredegar

its meeting place. In March of 1775, as things heated up between Virginia and England, many prominent historical figures, such as George Washington, Thomas Jefferson, and Richard Henry, attended the meeting where Patrick Henry gave his famous "Give me liberty or give me death" speech. Services are still held in Saint John's Church, and visitors are welcome.

CHIMBORAZO PARK

Chimborazo Park (3201 E. Broad St., open sunrise to sunset), in Church Hill, is the former site of the Chimborazo Hospital, the largest American Civil War hospital. The hospital served the Confederate army between 1862 and 1865. During that time, more than 76,000 soldiers were treated there, and it had a 20 percent mortality rate. The National Park Service now owns the site. The 30-acre park offers a 180-degree view of the city and is home to the headquarters of Richmond National Battlefield Park. There is a small house on the east side of the park that is available to rent for events. The **Church Hill Dog Park** is also located on the east side of the park and includes an area for large dogs and one for small dogs.

West End

The boundaries of the West End are most commonly considered to be north of the James River, west of I-195, and south of Broad Street.

Byrd Park is a residential neighborhood north of a park with the same name and south of the Downtown Expressway. The neighborhood contains row homes from the 1920s and bungalows, ranch houses, Cape Cods, and American foursquare homes from the 1930s and 1940s.

Carytown is a thriving and eclectic cluster of 1920s homes, restaurants, antiques stores, clothing stores, and cafés. The 2800-3500 blocks of Cary Street, west of **Arthur Ashe Boulevard** (a historic street that provides entrance to Byrd Park and divides Carytown and the Museum District from the Fan District), are the most active. The neighboring

Museum District is just north of Carytown. This neighborhood (also known as West of the Boulevard) is home to a number of large institutions such as the **Virginia Museum of Fine Arts** and the **Virginia Historical Society.**

On the eastern edge of the West End of town is the **Fan District.** It is named simply for the "fan" formed by the streets that run west from Belvidere Street. The area is bordered to the north by Broad Street and to the south by I-195. The neighborhood is mostly residential and includes late-19th-century and early 20th-century homes. Historic **Monument Avenue** is located there, as are numerous cafés.

South of Cary Street, west of Belvidere Street, and north of the James River is **Oregon Hill,** a neighborhood of affordable housing that is a popular location for students to live. The Cowboy Junkies rock band released a song in 1992 called "Oregon Hill," the lyrics of which describe this neighborhood.

BYRD PARK

Byrd Park (600 South Blvd., www. richmondgov.com, sunrise to sunset) is a 287-acre public park just south of the Byrd Park neighborhood. It has a one-mile trail, an amphitheater, three small lakes, tennis courts, baseball fields, and a playground. Pedal boats are available for rent during the summer (804/646-0761). The park is named after William Byrd II, whose family owned a large portion of the land in Richmond when it was founded in 1737.

★ VIRGINIA MUSEUM OF FINE ARTS

The **Virginia Museum of Fine Arts** (200 N. Arthur Ashe Blvd., 804/340-1400, www. vmfa.museum, Sat.-Wed. 10am-5pm, Thurs.-Fri. 10am-9pm, free) first opened its doors in the middle of the Great Depression in 1936. Its purpose was to become the flagship art

1: Amuse Restaurant at the Virginia Museum of Fine Arts 2: Virginia Museum of Fine Arts

museum in Virginia and to lead an educational network throughout the state to bring the best of world art to Virginia. Today, the museum is state-supported and privately endowed. It has nearly 40,000 items in its permanent collection spanning 6,000 years. The museum is known for its wide range of world art collections and their exceptional aesthetic quality.

The museum building and grounds are lovely, and the exhibits are first-rate. Permanent exhibits cover topics such as African art, American art, ancient art, East Asian art, European art, English silver, Fabergé imperial jewels, and modern and contemporary art. Its holdings include paintings by European masters such as Monet and Goya and American masters such as Winslow Homer.

The Virginia Museum of Fine Arts supplements its collection with stunning temporary exhibitions. Over the years, these have included everything from modernist works from Walter P. Chrysler Jr.'s collection by artists from the School of Paris (a "bold" presentation for its time in the early 1940s) to masterpieces of Chinese art in 1955.

The **Amuse Restaurant** (804/340-1580, Sat.-Wed. 11:30am-4:30pm, Thurs.-Fri. 11:30am-4:30pm and 5pm-8:30pm), located on the upper level of the museum, offers fine dining, a full-service bar, and views of the atrium and sculpture garden. Reservations are available. The museum is located in the Museum District.

VIRGINIA MUSEUM OF HISTORY AND CULTURE

The **Virginia Museum of History and Culture** (428 N. Arthur Ashe Blvd., 804/340-1800, www.virginiahistory.org, daily 10am-5pm, adults $10, children 6-17 $5, seniors 65 and up $8, 5 and under free), in the Museum District, is a research and teaching center for Virginia history as well as a large repository. It offers many award-winning exhibits. Their key exhibition, *The Story of Virginia*, covers 16,000 years of history in the state (prehistoric

to present) and contains over 500 artifacts. The museum has the largest display of artifacts from Virginia.

MONUMENT AVENUE

The most recognized street in Richmond is Monument Avenue. It runs through the northern border of the Fan District and is known as one of the most beautiful boulevards in the world. According to the National Park Service (www.nps.gov) it is "the nation's only grand residential boulevard with monuments of its scale almost unaltered to the present day." The tree-lined street with a large grass median and six grand statues along a 1.5-mile section is a significant example of the "Grand American Avenue"-style of city planning. The first statue was of Robert E. Lee and was erected in 1890. Other famous Americans honored on the street include Civil War figures J. E. B. Stuart, Jefferson Davis, and Stonewall Jackson, as well as Matthew Fontaine Maury (a Richmond native known as the "Father of the Seas") and tennis star Arthur Ashe.

Monument Avenue is lined with beautiful historic homes and churches, and a one-mile segment is still surfaced with original cobblestones. The avenue is listed in the National Register of Historic Places and has been named one of 10 "great" streets in America by the American Planning Association.

HOLLYWOOD CEMETERY

Just west of Oregon Hill is the **Hollywood Cemetery** (412 S. Cherry St., 804/648-8501, www.hollywoodcemetery.org, daily 8am-5pm, free). Jefferson Davis, James Monroe, and John Tyler may be the most famous "residents" in this forever home, but many others, such as J. E. B. Stuart and more than 20 additional Confederate generals, two Supreme Court justices, six Virginia governors, and the very first battle casualty of the Civil War, keep them company. The cemetery sprawls over 135 acres and has stunning views of the James River. Walking, Segway, and private trolley tours are offered April-November.

North Side

The North Side of Richmond has a diversity of residential neighborhoods with a wide mix of architectural styles represented. Portions of Henrico County and Hanover County are broadly regarded as part of the North Side.

The most noted neighborhood on the North Side is **Three Corners,** which sits north of Broad Street and east of Arthur Ashe Boulevard. The triangle-shaped area (hence the name) has notable landmarks situated near each corner. Near the north point is **The Diamond** baseball stadium (3001 N. Arthur Ashe Blvd.), home to the VCU Rams and the Richmond Flying Squirrels (a minor league baseball team). Near the west corner is the **Science Museum of Virginia,** and near the east corner is the **Sauers Vanilla Factory (C.F. Sauer Company),** which displays one of the country's oldest moving lightbulb billboards.

SCIENCE MUSEUM OF VIRGINIA

To the west of Three Corners is the **Science Museum of Virginia** (2500 W. Broad St., 804/864-1400, www.smv.org, daily 9:30am-5pm, exhibits only admission adults $15, youth and seniors $13.50, preschool $10, exhibits and dome show adults $19, youth and seniors $17.50, preschool $14). Housed in the former Broad Street Station (built in 1919) and established in 1970, the museum includes many exciting permanent exhibits on space, electricity, health, and the Earth and also has unique visiting exhibits from around the globe. Some of the things you can expect to see include the world's largest analemmatic sundial (located in the parking lot), the world's first aluminum submarine, the world's first solar airplane, a giant 76-foot-screen movie theater (The Dome), live animals, and the world's largest kugel ball. You can't miss the green copper dome that sits on top of the building. This is a great stop for both children and adults.

South Side

The South Side refers to areas that are south of the James River.

Manchester is both a residential and industrial neighborhood across the James River from the Canal Walk. This is an area of new development where modern homes, loft condos, and businesses are part of the revitalization process.

Westover Hills, an established neighborhood also south of the James River, sits at the intersection of State Route 161 and the Boulevard Bridge. It is home to many restaurants, churches, and businesses.

The **Woodland Heights** neighborhood was built in the early 1900s along the James River. It is listed in the National Register of Historic Places and also in the Virginia Landmarks Register.

RECREATION
Spectator Sports

There are many sporting events throughout the year at the University of Richmond and VCU. A list of events can be obtained through both athletic departments at www.richmondspiders.com and www.vcuathletics.com, respectively.

The **Richmond Coliseum** (601 E. Leigh St., 804/780-4970, www.richmondcoliseum.net) hosts numerous professional and college sporting events such as football, basketball, wrestling, and monster-truck events. A list of events is available on the website.

Five miles north of Richmond, the **Richmond International Raceway** (600 E. Laburnum Ave., 866/455-7223, www.richmondraceway.com) hosts NASCAR racing on weekends in April and September. Additional events are held at the raceway throughout the year.

If horse racing is more your thing, then **Colonial Downs** (10515 Colonial Downs Pkwy., 804/966-7223, www.colonialdowns.com) in New Kent offers a pari-mutuel-betting racecourse with a five-level grandstand and some of the nicest amenities of any track in the country.

Outdoor Recreation

Runners, walkers, climbers, and

The Grand Kugel

kugel ball at the Science Museum of Virginia in Richmond

The word *kugel* is a German term for ball or sphere. A kugel ball is a large, heavy, perfectly spherical sculpture made of granite that is supported by a thin film of water. Although it can weigh thousands of pounds, the ball spins on top of the water due to the lubrication provided by the water.

Kugel balls are found in many parts of the world. One popular kugel ball is at the Science Museum of Virginia in Richmond and is famous for its enormous size. The ball currently on display is actually their second ball; the first, the "Grand Kugel" unveiled in 2003, was carved from South African black granite, was more than eight feet in diameter, and cost approximately $1.5 million. However, shortly after its installation, the Grand Kugel cracked, eventually preventing it from floating. In 2005, a replacement kugel ball was installed. It is recognized as the world's largest floating-ball sculpture by the *Guinness Book of World Records*. The original can be found on display behind the museum.

boaters can enjoy **James River Park** (www.jamesriverpark.org), which includes more than 500 acres of parkland in the city and several islands on the James River. Access to the park is from 22nd Street, 43rd Street, and at Reedy Creek where the park headquarters and a canoe launch are located.

Cyclists will find a lot of company both on and off road in the Richmond area. The **Richmond Area Bicycling Association** (www.raba.org) has information on local group rides for road cyclists, while the **Mid-Atlantic Off Road Enthusiasts** (www.more-mtb.org) has information on local mountain biking.

White-water rafting is a big sport in

Richmond. The James River runs right through the city and offers rapids up to Class IV. Visitors can book a guided raft trip through a handful of outfitters including **Riverside Outfitters** (804/560-0068, www.riversideoutfitters.com, starting at $59).

Hot-air ballooning is popular in Central Virginia. When in Richmond, contact **Balloons Over Virginia, Inc.** (804/798-0080, www.balloonsovervirginia.com, from $275) for piloted balloon rides.

Amusement Parks

A half hour north of Richmond off I-95 is one of the mid-Atlantic's favorite theme parks, **Kings Dominion** (16000 Theme

Park Way, Doswell, 804/876-5000, www.kingsdominion.com, June-Aug. daily, late May and Sept.-Oct. weekends, starting at $45). This 400-acre park first opened in 1975 and offers more than 60 rides. It is known for its large collection of roller coasters (12), including classic wooden coasters such as the Grizzly as well as many new steel coasters. The Intimidator 305 plunges riders 305 feet at more than 90 mph. The park holds special events and a fun Halloween Haunt in October. There is also a 20-acre water park on-site.

ENTERTAINMENT AND EVENTS
Tours
Richmond History Tours are provided through the **Valentine Richmond History Center** (1015 E. Clay St., 804/649-0711, ext. 301, www.thevalentine.org, from $15). They offer hundreds of tours by foot, bus, and even with your dog. Professional guides lead all tours.

Performing Arts
The **Dominion Energy Center** (600 E. Grace St., 804/592-3330, www.dominionenergycenter.com) is a multistage performing arts venue in the downtown area offering a wide array of performances. The primary venue is the **Carpenter Theatre,** a beautifully renovated grand theater built in 1928.

The **Altria Theater** (6 N. Laurel St., 804/592-3368, www.altriatheater.com) first opened in 1927 as a Shriner facility and was called the Mosque Theater. The City of Richmond purchased the theater in 1940. This popular stage on the VCU campus west of downtown hosts concerts, lectures, comedians, commencements, and fashion shows. It has a seating capacity of 3,600.

The **Richmond Symphony** (612 E. Grace St., 804/788-1212, www.richmondsymphony.com) was founded in 1957 and gives more than 200 appearances each year. Consult the website for a list of upcoming performances.

The **Virginia Opera** (866/673-7282, www.vaopera.org) is the premier opera performance company in Virginia. They offer 40 performances in three markets (Richmond, Fairfax, and Norfolk). Consult the website for a schedule of events.

The largest ballet company in town is the **Richmond Ballet** (407 E. Canal St., 804/344-0906, www.richmondballet.com), one of the best ballet companies on the East Coast. The **Concert Ballet of Virginia** (804/798-0945, www.concertballet.com) is another wonderful local ballet company.

Theater
A beautiful historic movie palace called the **Byrd Theater** (2908 W. Cary St., 804/353-9911, www.byrdtheatre.org) in Carytown was built in 1928 at the astronomical cost of $900,000 (which would be more than $11 million today). Movie tickets were 50 cents. It now shows second-run movies for $4 (big-screen classics $5). The original manager of the theater, Robert Coulter, remained there until 1971 and is rumored to now haunt the theater.

Nightlife
Richmond is an active city with a large population of students and twentysomethings. There's no shortage of nightlife, especially around the Shockoe Slip neighborhood. Establishments in Virginia are required by law to serve food if they serve alcohol, so much of the action can be found in local restaurants. As with many cities, it is safer to drive or take a cab or car service after dark in Richmond.

The **Tobacco Company** (1201 E. Cary St., 804/782-9555, www.thetobaccocompany.com, no cover) is a Shockoe Slip restaurant that includes a classy lounge and bar area featuring dancing on the weekends (Thurs.-Sat. 8pm-2am). They have a dress code.

It is difficult to beat the atmosphere at **Havana 59** (16 N. 17th St., 804/780-2822, www.havana59.net, Mon.-Sat. bar opens at 4:30pm) in Shockoe Bottom. They strive to re-create a feeling of Havana in the 1950s and do a great job with strung lights, wood floors, high ceilings, ironwork, and the famous rooftop bar (where you can salsa dance on Thursday nights). Cigars are allowed on the second floor. You can purchase them there or bring your own. The club is known for delicious drinks and friendly service. Business casual attire is expected.

More than 200 types of bottled beers can be ordered at the **Capital Ale House** (623 E. Main St., 804/780-2537, www.capitalalehouse.com, daily 11am-1:30am) in the heart of downtown Richmond. This classic alehouse, housed in a century-old building half a city block long, also has 51 taps, two cask-conditioned ale hand pumps, and a gaming area with pool tables and darts. They also have a beer garden. This is a great place for serious beer lovers to share their passion with other like-minded souls. There is also a music hall by the same name next door.

A small venue with outstanding, reasonably priced drinks and an atmosphere reminiscent of a speakeasy is **The Jasper** (3113 W. Cary St., www.jasperbarrva.com, daily 5pm-2am). Their slogan is "Full Pours and Honest Prices," and they seem to live up to it.

Events

The **State Fair of Virginia** (www.statefairva.org) in nearby Doswell is a 10-day fair full of tradition. There are rides, food, livestock, music, arts, and even a circus. The fair started back in 1854 and is held annually at the end of September and beginning of October.

SHOPPING

Shopping in Richmond offers everything from quaint boutiques, antiques shops, and specialty stores to upscale modern shopping malls. A unique area to shop is **Carytown,** where nine blocks of West Cary Street (between Thompson Street and Arthur Ashe Boulevard) are alive with stores selling clothing, furniture, jewelry, and toys, along with many independent eateries.

The **Shoppes at Bellgrade** (11400 W.

Huguenot Rd.) include clothing stores, specialty shops, and stores selling athletic gear. Two additional shopping areas are **Shockoe Slip** (E. Cary Street) between 11th and Virginia Streets and **Shockoe Bottom** between Broad and Dock Streets from 14th to 21st Streets.

FOOD
American

The stunning Jefferson Hotel in downtown Richmond is the venue of one of the nicest restaurants in town: ★ **Lemaire** (101 W. Franklin St., 804/649-4629, www.lemairerestaurant.com, daily 5pm-10pm, $12-36). This "Virginia Green Certified" restaurant offers not only farm-to-table-influenced menu items, but also exceptional service. The menu isn't extensive but certainly offers a little of everything (including small plates, burgers, and seafood). The wine list, however, has more than 200 selections, including a significant selection of bottles under $30 and wines offered by the glass. They also have a creative list of cocktails and a lovely lounge to enjoy them in. Ask for a table by the window so you can see both the dining room and the view onto Franklin Street. A great time to go is around the holidays, when the hotel is festively decorated.

For some true Southern-style comfort food and a healthy dose of city atmosphere in downtown Richmond, grab a bite at **Mama J's Kitchen** (415 N. 1st St., 804/255-7449, www.mamajskitchen.com, Sun.-Thurs. 11am-9pm, Fri.-Sat. 11am-10pm, $5-12). Between Clay and Marshall Streets, this feel-good restaurant full of food made from family recipes serves wonderful cocktails and gut-warming selections such as fried chicken, catfish, and mac and cheese. They also have cobbler and ice cream for dessert. Their slogan is "welcome home," and it's easy to see why.

Southern-style cooking can also be found downtown at the upscale **Julep's** (420 E. Grace St., 804/377-3968, www.juleps.net, Mon.-Sat. 5pm-10pm, $25-35). Their "New Southern Cuisine" puts a fancy spin on some old favorites such as shrimp and grits, lacquered duck breast, and petite filet mignon. The restaurant is housed in the historic Shields Shoes building on the first floor. The dress is equivalent to business casual, and you'll want to make a reservation.

The former Tarrant Drug Company building at the corner of Foushee and Broad Streets now houses one of Downtown's most popular eateries. **Tarrant's Café** (1 W. Broad St., 804/225-0035, www.tarrantscaferva.com, Mon.-Thurs. 11am-11pm, Fri. 11am-midnight, Sat. 10am-midnight, Sun. 10am-11pm, $10-30) is a quaint restaurant with an upscale feel. It is quite dark inside but has nice paintings, exposed brick walls, and a hip and pleasant atmosphere. It has a long, full-service bar and two dining areas with booths and tables. Reminders of the building's pharmacy past are in the form of signs noting Prescriptions, Soda, Drugs, and Tobacco. The huge menu includes a number of Italian dishes, Southern comforts, seafood, beef, salads, sandwiches, pizza, and wraps. Portions are generous, the service is excellent, and there's a large Sunday brunch menu.

What do you call a deep-fried, bacon-wrapped jumbo beef hot dog topped with hand-pulled pork, barbecue sauce, and coleslaw? At the **HogsHead Café** (9503 W. Broad St., Henrico, 804/308-0281, www.thehogsheadcafe.com, Tues.-Sat. 11:30am-9pm, $7-32), they call it a "Hog Dog." Build-your-own hot dogs, ribs, barbecue, seafood, and beer served in mason jars—it's all part of the fun atmosphere at this Southern restaurant. The food is authentic, the service is friendly and quick, and the patrons are lively. They also offer takeout and catering.

For those wanting the comfort of a diner with more upscale food, visit **Millie's** (2603 E. Main St., 804/643-5512, www.milliesdiner.com, Tues.-Fri. 11am-2pm and 5:30pm-10pm, Sat.-Sun. 9am-3pm, $19-26), on the edge of Shockoe Bottom (look for the black-and-white dog out front). For starters, don't wait to be given a menu—it's on the chalkboard. You'll most likely have to wait for a table, so plan on

having a mimosa and people watching. Their brunch is legendary (example: lobster in a puff pastry with lightly scrambled egg and hollandaise sauce for $14). The 44-seat restaurant serves upwards of 300 brunch customers on Sunday. The lunch and dinner menu is wonderful too. Be sure to take a look at the vintage jukeboxes (they have an impressive collection of 45s).

French

Those yearning for a little French bistro need look no further than **Bistro Bobette** (1209 E. Cary St., 804/225-9116, www.bistrobobette.com, Mon. 5pm-10pm, Tues.-Fri. 11:30am-2:30pm and 5pm-10pm, Sat. 5pm-10pm, $21-36) in trendy Shockoe Slip. They serve Provençal food in a casual yet elegant atmosphere, and the owners do a wonderful job at making guests feel welcome. The menu stands up to the most seasoned foodie and offers a diverse yet creatively prepared choice of entrées and sides. Fresh ingredients are clearly standard in this establishment and contribute to an overall delightful dining experience.

Greek

Everyone feels like family at a hidden gem called ★ **Stella's** (1012 Lafayette St., 804/358-2011, www.stellasrichmond.com, Mon.-Thurs. 11am-3pm and 5pm-10pm, Fri. 11am-3pm and 5pm-11pm, Sat. 5pm-11pm, Sun. 10am-3pm, $10-30). The modern and traditional Greek cuisine is exquisite, and the atmosphere in this neighborhood establishment makes guests feel like they are visiting friends (there's even a communal table). There is a meze menu (the Greek equivalent of tapas), full entrées, and numerous sides to choose from. There are also delicious desserts. Stella's has many loyal customers, so make a reservation if you plan on dining here on a weekend evening. Parking is on the street.

Italian

No city is complete without a favorite pizza joint. **Bottoms Up Pizza** (1700 Dock St.,

804/644-4400, www.bottomsuppizza.com, Mon.-Wed. 11am-10pm, Thurs. and Sun. 11am-11pm, Fri.-Sat. 11am-midnight, large pizza $13-26) may be under the I-95 overpass, but it serves fantastic pizza with a thick sourdough crust. They have great specialty pies with unique toppings (crab, artichoke, spinach, etc.) and two outdoor decks to enjoy when it's nice out. They reimburse parking fees from the Main Street Parking Lot (see details on their website).

ACCOMMODATIONS
Under $100

The **Candlewood Suites Richmond Airport** (5400 Audubon Dr., 804/652-1888, www.candlewoodsuites.com, $79-103) is a good value near the airport. The hotel caters to a business clientele with a business center, free wireless Internet, complimentary laundry service, and a 24-hour fitness center, but vacationers can also enjoy the apartment-style suites and proximity to the downtown area. Candlewood even offers a library of DVDs that guests can borrow.

$100-200

A pretty little European-style hotel in the Shockoe Slip is the **Berkeley Hotel** (1200 E. Cary St., 804/780-1300, www.berkeleyhotel. com, $144-175). This charming boutique hotel has 55 elegant guest rooms with traditional furniture. Many rooms have great views of downtown Richmond. The service is excellent, and rooms come with free wireless Internet, coffeemakers, terry robes, a morning paper, and access to a health club. Laundry and dry cleaning services are available, as is valet parking.

$200-300

The **Hilton Richmond Downtown** (501 E. Broad St., 804/344-4300, www3.hilton.com, $149-302) is a good choice for staying right in the city. They offer 250 modern rooms and suites in a historic downtown building. Each room has a minifridge, microwave, free wireless Internet, and access to an indoor pool, a

modern fitness center, and a business center. There is a restaurant on-site. Valet parking is available for $27 a day (no self-parking), and the hotel is pet friendly ($100 fee).

A good hotel on the far northwest side of Richmond (near where I-64 and I-295 meet) is the **Hyatt House Richmond-West** (11800 W. Broad St., Henrico, 804/360-7021, www. hyatt.com, $193-252). The hotel can accommodate long stays and offers 134 spotless guest rooms and suites. They provide a complimentary hot breakfast, a 24-hour fitness room, and an indoor heated pool. Next door, the Short Pump Town Center is home to many shops and restaurants.

The **Westin Richmond** (6631 W. Broad St., 804/282-8444, www.marriott.com, $152-304) is a modern hotel with 250 rooms just off I-64 on the west side of town. The hotel has comfortable beds and nice bathrooms (most king rooms have a stand-up shower while most double rooms have a bathtub shower). There is an extra charge for Internet access.

Located a few blocks from Virginia Commonwealth University, **Quirk Hotel** (201 W. Broad St., 804/340-6040, www. destinationhotels.com, $179-239) is a fun boutique hotel occupying the former J. B. Mosby Department Store, built in 1916. The hotel offers 74 guest rooms and has an art-driven theme. The 13-foot ceilings and original wood floors reveal the building's roots, but the rest of the hotel's charm is in the details—for one, the rooms are pink. It may sound unusual (and it is), but it works for this hotel. Rooms are decorated with regional and local artwork. Each floor features a unique papier-mâché portrait of an animal or human and the lobby features art made from used coffee lids (they have their own custom blend of coffee). All the beds are made of reclaimed wood and floor joists. The rest of the details you'll need to see for yourself.

Over $300

★ **The Jefferson Hotel** (101 W. Franklin St., 804/649-4750, www.jeffersonhotel.com, $225-445), located near the state capitol, first opened on Halloween in 1895 and has a long and interesting history. This grand hotel has hosted 12 U.S. presidents, numerous actors, musicians, and politicians, and even had alligators living in the marble pools of its Palm Court for a period of time (the last one died in 1948). The hotel has undergone many changes including the addition of an indoor swimming pool in 2000. The most recent update began in 2013 and included the transformation of the hotel's 262 guest rooms into 181 new rooms and suites.

The public areas in the hotel are tremendous. The center attraction is the 36-step polished marble staircase that many believe was the model for the one shown in *Gone with the Wind*. The staircase leads to the Palm Court, which has a beautiful Tiffany stained glass dome and a life-size statue of Thomas Jefferson. The court had, at one time, a grass lawn surrounding marble pools, but both have long since been removed.

The many amenities in the hotel include a large fitness center, massage treatments, a salon, and an extensive business center. All rooms and suites have high ceilings, marble bathrooms, soaking tubs, and plush bathrobes.

There are two restaurants on-site: the upscale Lemaire and the more casual TJ's.

INFORMATION AND SERVICES

There are three **Richmond Region Visitors Centers** (804/783-7450, www. visitrichmondva.com). The main location is in the **Greater Richmond Convention Center** (405 N. 3rd St., 804/783-7300, daily 9am-5pm). A second is found at the **Richmond International Airport** (804/236-3260, Mon.-Fri. 9:30am-4:30pm, Sat.-Sun. noon-5pm), on the lower level near baggage claim, and the third is inside the **Bass Pro Shops** (11550 Lakeridge Pkwy., Ashland, 804/496-4700, daily 10am-9pm). Staff at each can provide local maps and make hotel reservations.

Another visitors center (that has information on the entire state) is located in the southwest corner of **Capitol Square** inside the Bell Tower (9th St. and Franklin St., 804/698-1788, daily 6am-11pm).

The Jefferson Hotel rotunda lobby and grand staircase

GETTING THERE AND AROUND

Richmond is 98 miles south of Washington DC. The city sits at the intersection of I-95 and I-64.

Air service to Richmond is through the **Richmond International Airport** (RIC, 1 Richard E. Byrd Terminal Dr., 804/226-3000, www.flyrichmond.com), approximately nine miles east of downtown. This is the busiest airport in Central Virginia and has seven carriers that operate approximately 170 daily flights to major domestic cities and connections worldwide.

Amtrak (800/872-7245, www.amtrak.com) provides train service to the **Main Street Station** (1500 E. Main St.) in Shockoe Slip and also the **Staples Mill Road Station** (7519 Staples Mill Rd.). There is a **Greyhound** (804/254-5910, www.greyhound.com) bus terminal at 2910 North Arthur Ashe Boulevard.

The **GRTC Transit System** (804/358-4782, www.ridegrtc.com) provides local bus service in the Richmond area. They offer more than 30 routes and operate daily in the city between 5am and 1am.

PETERSBURG

Petersburg, 25 miles south of Richmond, served as an important supply hub for the Confederate capital during the Civil War. It had five railroad lines and several key roads running through it, and General Grant knew that if he could cut off this resource to General Lee's army, the Confederates would be forced out of Richmond.

Petersburg National Battlefield

The Siege of Petersburg was the longest single Civil War military event. It lasted more than nine months and produced 70,000 casualties.

In June 1864, the Union army began using force against Petersburg, thus beginning a long tough fight for control of the city. By February 1865, General Lee had only 60,000 troops against Grant's 110,000, and finally on April 2, Lee's army was forced out of the strategic location.

Today, visitors to the **Petersburg National Battlefield** (804/732-3531, www.nps.gov/pete) can follow a 33-mile route that includes 13 battlefield sites and three visitors centers. It takes an entire day to fully explore the park.

The **Eastern Front** (5001 Siege Rd., 804/732-3531, ext. 200, daily 8am-8pm, free) visitors center is a great place to begin exploration of the battlefield. It has audiovisual programs and standing exhibits that explain the progression of the siege and its overall impact on the Civil War. Be sure to watch the introductory movie.

At **Grant's Headquarters at City Point** (1001 Pecan Ave., Hopewell, 804/458-9504, daily 8am-5pm, free) visitors can learn about the huge Union supply base and field hospital. There is also information on a plantation that sat on the battlefield before the war overtook the area.

The western side of the tour route is where the **Five Forks Battlefield** (9840 Courthouse Rd., Dinwiddie, 804/469-4093, daily 8am-5pm, free) is located. The Union victory here sealed the fate of Petersburg and Richmond.

The park hosts a number of special events throughout the year including tours, lectures, and living-history demonstrations. Downloadable brochures are available on the website.

Pamplin Historical Park & The National Museum of the Civil War Soldier

Pamplin Historical Park & The National Museum of the Civil War Soldier (6125 Boydton Plank Rd., 804/861-2408, www.pamplinpark.org, daily 9am-5pm, weekends only in winter, adults $15, children 6-12 $8, seniors 62 and over, military, teachers, and students $12, under 6 free) is a 424-acre historical campus that features multiple indoor and outdoor exhibits.

A primary attraction in the park is one of

the nation's best-known Civil War museums, the **National Museum of the Civil War Soldier.** This 25,000-square-foot building features a seven-gallery exhibit called *Duty Called Me Here,* which allows visitors to follow the personal experiences of Civil War soldiers through an MP3 audio player, video, interactive computers, original artifacts, dioramas, and a multisensory battlefield simulator. Another popular feature is the Remembrance Wall, which displays the names of people who "responded to the call of duty during the Civil War."

The **Tudor Hall Plantation** is another popular attraction in the park. Just a short walk from the National Museum of the Civil War Soldier, this 1812 house is fully restored and furnished with period antiques. The house was used by Confederate general Samuel McGowan as his headquarters.

Visitors can also tour the **Field Quarter,** the area of the plantation where the agricultural enslaved people lived. Elements common to field quarters of the time have been re-created to give a sense of slave life at the plantation. Guided tours of the plantation are available. To find out specific tour dates, call 804/861-2408.

Be sure to also make time to visit the **Field Fortifications Exhibit.** This unusual exhibit is the only one of its kind and features 60 yards of re-created late-war field fortifications. Other exhibits in the park include a military encampment, a battlefield center with a theater and fiber-optic battle map, a battlefield walk with three loop trails (0.3-1.25 miles long), and the historic **Banks House,** which served as General Grant's headquarters in 1865. Plan for a minimum of 2-4 hours to explore the park.

Charlottesville

Charlottesville (aka C-ville) is an independent city in the foothills of the Blue Ridge Mountains that is surrounded by, but not included in, Albemarle County. Charlottesville was established in 1762 and encompasses 10.4 square miles.

Charlottesville was home to two U.S. presidents: Thomas Jefferson and James Monroe. James Madison also lived nearby in Orange. Monticello, Jefferson's home, hosts nearly 500,000 visitors each year and is one of the top attractions in the area. Ash Lawn-Highland, James Monroe's home, is just down the road from Monticello. Both Jefferson and Monroe also served terms as the governor of Virginia, during which time each traveled the 71-mile historic **Three Notch'd Road,** a popular east-west route across Virginia, back and forth to Richmond.

Despite the city's small size, there are many attractions and historic sites in and near Charlottesville. Right in town on West Main Street between 6th Street East and 2nd Street

East is the **Downtown Mall.** This beautiful outdoor pedestrian section of the city is one of the longest of its type in the nation. It is a pleasant mix of trees, statues, benches, shops, restaurants, and vendors. There is also a movie theater at the west end. At the east end is the **Sprint Pavilion,** where concerts and the popular free "Fridays after Five" concerts featuring local talent are held. A large white tent marks the pavilion.

The **University of Virginia (UVA)** also calls Charlottesville home. The main grounds of UVA along University Avenue are next to a neighborhood known as **The Corner,** which is an eight-block area (between Chancellor St. and 10th St. NW) full of bars, restaurants, and UVA-related stores. Greek life abounds on nearby Rugby Road and adds to the buzz of social life at the local bars. A commercial district that runs from The Corner to the Downtown Mall along West Main Street is home to more restaurants, bars, and private businesses.

Charlottesville

To Barboursville, Orange, and Montpelier

To Hilton Garden Inn, Clifton Inn, and Keswick Hall

To Richmond

KLUGE RUHE ABORIGINAL ART COLLECTION

Riverview Park

MONTICELLO

To James Monroe's Highland

MICHE TAVERN

To Carter Mountain Apple Orchard

VIRGINIA DISCOVERY MUSEUM

DOWNTOWN MALL

THE PARAMOUNT THEATER

PIEDMONT-VIRGINIA COMMUNITY COLLEGE

To The Inn at Monticello and Charlottesville KOA

HAMPTON INN CHARLOTTESVILLE

ENGLISH INN OF CHARLOTTESVILLE

To Airport

BODO'S BAGELS

CONTINENTAL DIVIDE

BODO'S BAGELS

HAMPTON INN AND SUITES

AMTRAK

GREYHOUND

KLOCKNER STADIUM

FRALIN MUSEUM OF ART

UNIVERSITY OF VIRGINIA ART MUSEUM

ROTUNDA

The Lawn

UNIVERSITY OF VIRGINIA

To Foxfield

To Waynesboro

BOAR'S HEAD INN

To Waynesboro

To Waynesboro

0.5 mi

0.5 km

© MOON.COM

Across the train tracks from downtown Charlottesville is the Belmont neighborhood. It is a short walk (about 10 minutes) from the east side of downtown. Belmont used to be a farm but has undergone several transformations over the years. It is now an area of great restaurants and the home of the **Bridge Progressive Arts Initiative** (209 Monticello Rd., 434/218-2060, www.thebridgepai.com), a nonprofit inclusive arts organization that provides space to working artists and community programming.

SIGHTS
University of Virginia

The **University of Virginia** (434/924-0311, www.virginia.edu) is one of the top-rated state universities in the nation, with 11 schools in Charlottesville and one in southwest Virginia. The university, founded by Thomas Jefferson, opened in March 1825 with 123 students. Jefferson was heavily involved with the students and faculty for the first year of operation, but he passed away on July 4, 1826. UVA now adds almost 22,000 students to the local population in Charlottesville during the school year.

The main grounds are situated on the west side of Charlottesville. Thomas Jefferson's Academical Village, also referred to as "The Lawn," is its focal point. The Academical Village reflects Jefferson's vision that daily life at college should be infused with learning. He designed 10 pavilions, each focused on a different subject, that had faculty living quarters upstairs and classrooms downstairs and were attached to rows of student housing. The Lawn is a long esplanade with two premier buildings: the elegant early republic-style **Rotunda** (which Jefferson designed, standing 77 feet tall with a diameter of 77 feet) and the stately **Old Cabell Hall** (which faces the Rotunda and has a pediment sculpture that reads, "Ye shall know the truth, and the truth shall make you free.").

The Rotunda is open daily 9am-5pm, and free, guided tours of the Rotunda and Lawn (www.virginia.edu) are offered daily at 10am, 11am, 2pm, and 3pm during the academic year. They depart from the Rotunda's Lower East Oval Room.

THE FRALIN MUSEUM OF ART AT THE UNIVERSITY OF VIRGINIA

The Fralin Museum of Art at the University of Virginia (155 Rugby Rd., 434/924-3592, www.uvafralinartmuseum. virginia.edu, Tues., Wed., Fri., and Sat. 10am-5pm, Thurs. 10am-7pm, Sun. noon-5pm, free) is one block north of the Rotunda. It houses a permanent collection of more than 14,000 artifacts. Exhibits include (but are not limited to) 15th to 20th-century European and American painting and sculpture, Asian art, American figurative art, and photography. There is a special focus on the "Age of Thomas Jefferson" (1775-1825), and temporary exhibits change often throughout the year.

Kluge-Ruhe Aboriginal Art Collection of the University of Virginia

The **Kluge-Ruhe Aboriginal Art Collection of the University of Virginia** (400 Worrell Dr., 434/244-0234, www.kluge-ruhe.org, Tues., Wed., Fri., and Sat. 10am-4pm, Thurs. 10am-8pm, Sun. 1pm-5pm, free) is the only museum in the nation fully dedicated to Australian indigenous artwork. The museum collaborates with artists, scholars, and art professionals to advance the knowledge of Australia's indigenous people and to provide learning opportunities for the university community. The museum houses one of the premier Aboriginal art collections in the world. It is located approximately three miles east of the UVA campus. Free tours are given on Saturdays at 10:30am.

★ **Monticello**

Monticello (931 Thomas Jefferson Pkwy., 434/984-9880, www.monticello.org, hours change throughout the year, entrance with tour: adults Mar.-Oct. $29.95/$26.95 online, Nov.-Feb. $25/$23 online, youth June-Aug. online only $17, children 5-11 $10, under 5 free), located on a mountaintop approximately four miles southeast of Charlottesville, is one of the most visited historic sites in the region. The 5,000-acre plantation was the home of Thomas Jefferson, our nation's third president, author of the Declaration of Independence, and the University of Virginia's founder.

Jefferson inherited the land Monticello sits on from his father and began building the house at the age of 26. He maintained and lived in Monticello the rest of his life, always working on and expanding the beautiful home.

Jefferson conceived of his home as a functioning plantation house. Although the design was influenced by Italian Renaissance architecture, it included many elements that were fashionable in late 18th-century Europe and even more elements that were entirely Jefferson's own.

Monticello has one of the most recognized exteriors of any home in Virginia. The large brick structure has a facade adorned by columns and a dramatic octagonal dome. Two large rooms anchor the interior: an entrance hall that Jefferson used to display items of science and a music room. The dome, which sits above the west front of the building, had a room beneath it that is perhaps the most famous part of the house. This "dome room" has yellow octagonal walls and a green wooden floor. Each wall contains a circular window. The top of the dome (the oculus) also has a window that is made of brown glass. The room functioned as an apartment but is said to not have been used much. Visitors are prohibited from entering the room today due to fire regulations.

Jefferson never sat idle. He is said to have told his daughter in a letter, "Determine never to be idle . . . It is wonderful how much may be done, if we are always doing." As such, he created many unusual contraptions in his home, and some are still on display today. Fascinated with time, Jefferson put a clock in nearly every room of his mansion. One notable clock is the Great Clock in the entrance hall. He designed the Great Clock to tell both the time and day of the week, and it has both an interior face, which faces the hall, and an exterior face that looks outside over the plantation. The exterior face bears a huge hour hand so enslaved people on the plantation could read it. It also contained a gong that sounded so loudly that the time could be heard three miles away. Another fun invention was Jefferson's clothing rack. Instead of climbing a ladder to reach the top of his tall closet, he created a large spiral rack with 50 arms to hold his clothing. He then turned the rack with a stick to make his outfit selection.

Thomas Jefferson was a terrific gardener and grew many varieties of plants and vegetables. There are three main gardens on the grounds of Monticello for flowers, fruits, and vegetables.

Monticello is the only house in the country included on the UNESCO World Heritage List. Visitors can take a guided, 45-minute tour of the first floor of this beautiful mansion and see original furnishings and personal items that belonged to Jefferson.

Monticello offers tours on a timed-ticketing basis. To ensure you get a tour time that's convenient for you, purchase your ticket online. Be sure to arrive 30 minutes ahead of your ticketed time since it takes 30 minutes to submit tickets and ride the shuttle bus from the ticketing area to the house. Allow two hours for your visit. Tours run throughout the day, and tours of the grounds and gardens are included in the price of the house tour (visitors are welcome to walk the grounds on their own at other times of the year). Interpreters lead these 45-minute walking tours and provide plant identification, stories, and historical insight into the extensive gardens.

1: downtown Charlottesville 2: Monticello, the home of Thomas Jefferson

Several additional tours are offered, such as the "Behind the Scenes" tour ($49-65) visiting the upstairs of the mansion, and the "Hemings Family Tour" ($28-31), which shows Monticello through the eyes of the best-documented enslaved family in the country.

James Monroe's Highland

James Monroe's Highland (2050 James Monroe Pkwy., 434/293-8000, www.highland. org, Apr.-Oct. daily 9am-6pm, Nov.-Mar. daily 11am-5pm, self-guided and augmented reality [AR] tour $13, guided and AR tour adults $19, youth 6-11 $13, under 6 free) sits 2.5 miles south of Monticello and was formerly called Ash Lawn-Highland. Highland is not a grand mansion like Monticello; instead, it is a 535-acre working farm, a performing arts site, and a historic home museum. James Monroe (fifth President of the United States) and his wife, Elizabeth Kortright Monroe, owned the estate from 1793 to 1826 and lived there most of the time. The estate is now open to the public and displays examples of Victorian and early American architecture, features period craft demonstrations, showcases decorative arts, and is the site of special events and a summer music festival. Original period furnishings are on display in the main house, including some the Monroes had while living in the White House. There are even rumors of a resident ghost.

The College of William & Mary (Monroe's alma mater) maintains the estate, and many events and workshops are hosted there throughout the year.

Virginia Discovery Museum

A great place to bring the little ones is the **Virginia Discovery Museum** (524 E. Main St., 434/977-1025, www.vadm.org, Mon.-Sat. 9:30am-5pm, adults and children $8, under 1 year old free). This children-oriented museum at the east end of the Downtown Mall is small compared to other children's museums in large cities, but it is still a wonderful little attraction, especially on a rainy day. The interactive exhibits are excellent for little kids (under 10) and offer crafts, science, and opportunities to run around. Don't miss the beehive in the back of the museum.

Montpelier

Another presidential home, **Montpelier** (11350 Constitution Hwy., Montpelier Station, 540/672-2728, www.montpelier.org, daily 9am-5pm, adults $22, 6-14 $9, under 6 free, 62 and up and military $21) was home to the "Father of the Constitution," James Madison, and the country's first first lady, Dolley Madison. Madison spent six months in the library of the home performing research and designing the principles for a representative democracy. These ideas first became the "Virginia Plan" and were later used to frame the Constitution.

Today the estate features Madison's mansion, a garden, archaeological sites, and other historical buildings. The Madisons frequently hosted guests at the estate, and the central feature of the compound is their stately brick mansion. Admission tickets include a guided tour of the mansion, highlighting the dining room that was used to host dinner parties, the drawing room, and the presidential library. A self-guided tour of additional exhibits on the second floor of the home, the cellars, gardens, and grounds is also covered by admission. Plan on spending at least two hours at the mansion.

Wineries and Vineyards

October is officially "wine month" in Charlottesville, but any of the 35 local vineyards on the local **Monticello Wine Trail** (www.monticellowinetrail.com) can be enjoyed year-round. Part of the reason for the success of vineyards in this part of the state is the topography. The eroded mountains create wonderful growing conditions, which in turn yield beautifully complex wines. Following are a few vineyards in and around Charlottesville that should be included on any wine tour.

Barboursville Vineyards (17655 Winery Rd., Barboursville, 540/832-3824, www.

1: Jefferson Vineyards 2: tree-lined drive at James Monroe's Highland 3: Montpelier, home of James Madison

Jefferson
V I N E Y A R D S™

...ere in 1774, Th. Jefferson and Phillip Mazzei ...anted Virginia's first commercial vineyards, ...tending to export their wine back to Europe. ...he vineyard was abandoned in 1776 with the ...vent of the Revolutionary War.

...ffer... effort to grow grapes on a smaller ... ...ued at Mont...llo one mile N...th. ...he... original vineyard ...tes and others ... ...planted in 1981 by Stanley Woodward.

bbvwine.com, Mon.-Sat. 10am-5pm, Sun. 11am-5pm, $10) is a popular stop on the local wine-tour scene. It's on a beautiful 18th-century estate, less than a half hour from Charlottesville. They were the first in the region to seriously develop European wine varietals and offer daily tastings.

Blenheim Vineyards (31 Blenheim Farm, Charlottesville, 434/293-5366, www.blenheimvineyards.com, daily 11am-5:30pm, $10) was established in 2000 by Dave Matthews, of Dave Matthews Band fame. The vineyard is a family-owned and -operated business 20 minutes southeast of the city. They have two vineyard sites and grow chardonnay, viognier, cabernet franc, petit verdot, and cabernet sauvignon. The timber-frame tasting room has cool glass flooring that allows visitors to look into the tank-and-barrel room below.

Thatch Winery (1650 Harris Creek Rd., Charlottesville, 434/979-7105, www.thatchwinery.com, daily 11am-6pm, $8-15) offers wines that have received state, national, and international awards. They were formerly called First Colony Winery and produce chardonnay, viognier, merlot, cabernet franc, and cabernet sauvignon. They have tastings, a gift shop, a beautiful 2,000-square-foot event room, and picturesque grounds for picnicking.

Jefferson Vineyards (1353 Thomas Jefferson Pkwy., Charlottesville, 434/977-3042, www.jeffersonvineyards.com, daily 11am-6pm, $12) sits on the site between Monticello and James Monroe's Highland where Thomas Jefferson and Filippo Mazzei of Italy first decided to establish a vineyard. The vineyard makes wine entirely from grapes grown in Virginia.

Keswick Vineyards (1575 Keswick Winery Dr., Keswick, 434/244-3341, www.keswickvineyards.com, daily 10am-5pm, $15) specializes in the production of small lots of wine. Their international award winners include viognier, verdejo, chardonnay, cabernet franc, cabernet sauvignon, merlot, petite verdot, syrah, Norton, chambourcin, and touriga.

Their wines are all produced from their own fruit. Tastings are available daily.

Pippin Hill Farm and Vineyard (5022 Plank Rd., North Garden, 434/202-8063, www.pippinhillfarm.com, Tues.-Fri. and Sun. 11am-5pm, Sat. 11am-4:30pm, $13) is a boutique winery and vineyard just outside Charlottesville. It offers a sustainable viticulture program, an exquisite event space, and landscaped gardens. The tasting room features signature wines and food pairings, which can be enjoyed at a beautiful hand-carved bar or out on a stone terrace.

RECREATION
Spectator Sports
There are no professional sports teams in Charlottesville, but a plethora of sporting events take place at **UVA** (434/924-8821, www.virginiasports.com). Whether it's football at **Scott Stadium,** basketball at the **John Paul Jones Arena,** or soccer and lacrosse games at **Klockner Stadium,** you can catch the Wahoo spirit most anytime during the school year.

Spring and fall steeplechases are held annually at **Foxfield** (2215 Foxfield Track, 434/293-9501, www.foxfieldraces.com). A full day of tailgating, people watching, and, of course, horse racing is a tradition on the last Saturday in April and the last Sunday in September. Patrons who drink are encouraged to leave their cars on the property and may do so for up to 48 hours after the race.

Outdoor Recreation
Intermediate and advanced mountain bikers should check out the five-mile single-track trail at **Walnut Creek Park** (4250 Walnut Creek Park Rd., North Garden, www.cambc.org, $4.50), about 10 miles southwest of Charlottesville. This challenging loop runs through a hardwood forest surrounding a 23-acre lake. The trail is twisty, tight, and technical. Less experienced riders may enjoy the easier trail along the water. There are 15 miles of trails in this 525-acre park.

Fishing and boating (electric motors only)

Follow the Brew Ridge Trail

Grapes aren't the only things growing in Charlottesville. Hop vines also love the Central Virginia climate. In fact, once upon a time, Virginia was the hop capital of the world. Albemarle County and nearby Nelson County are home to many small-batch brewhouses that produce a wide variety of handcrafted beers. The Brew Ridge Trail (www.brewridgetrail.com) gives beer lovers a chance to tour a small number of these breweries.

The five breweries along the trail are listed below. Maps of the trail and additional information about upcoming events are available on the trail website.

· **Blue Mountain Barrel House** (495 Cooperative Way, Arrington, 434/263-4002, www. bluemountainbrewery.com)

· **Blue Mountain Brewery** (9519 Critzer's Shop Rd., Afton, 540/456-8020, wwwbluemountainbrewery.com)

· **Devils Backbone Brewing Company** (200 Mosbys Run, Roseland, 434/361-1001, www. dbbrewingcompany.com)

· **Starr Hill Brewing Company** (5391 Three Notched Rd., Crozet, 434/823-5671, www. starrhill.com)

· **Wild Wolf Brewing Company** (2461 Rockfish Valley Hwy., Nellysford, 434/284-5220, www.wildwolfbeer.com)

---

are popular pastimes on **Beaver Creek Lake** (4365 Beaver Creek Park Rd., www.albemarle. org, $4.50). This 104-acre lake is stocked with sunfish, channel catfish, and largemouth bass. A Virginia state fishing license is required.

Mint Springs Valley Park (6659 Mint Springs Park Rd., Crozet, 434/296-5844, www.albemarle.org, $4.50) in nearby Crozet is a 520-acre park with an 8-acre lake. It offers a beach with swimming during the summer, four hiking trails ranging from 0.5 miles to 1.8 miles, fishing (license required), and boating (electric motors only).

Pick your own apples and peaches (depending on the season) April through December at **Carter Mountain Apple Orchard** (1435 Carters Mountain Trail, 434/977-1833, www. chilesfamilyorchards.com), next to Michie Tavern near Monticello.

ENTERTAINMENT AND EVENTS
Live Music

The music scene in Charlottesville is surprisingly active. The best-known local talent is the Dave Matthews Band. Dave was a bartender

at **Miller's Downtown** (109 W. Main St., 434/971-8511, www.millersdowntown.com, daily 11:30am-2am), a local restaurant where they have a full schedule of live music (jazz and otherwise). It is on the Downtown Mall and used to be a hardware store.

The **Southern Café and Music Hall** (103 S. 1st St., 434/977-5590, www. thesoutherncville.com) is another truly local establishment. They feature locally sourced ingredients on their menu, have local artwork on their walls, and host great live music nearly every night. There's not a bad spot in the house. Visitors enter through a brick patio in this nearly belowground establishment.

The **Jefferson Theater** (110 E. Main St., 434/245-4980, www.jeffersontheater.com) is one of the best live venues in Charlottesville and attracts better-known acts such as Eric Hutchinson and Amos Lee. They have a more advanced sensory experience with improved lighting and sound systems.

The **Paramount Theater** (215 E. Main St., 434/979-1333, www.theparamount.net) is a historic theater on Main Street that first opened in 1931. It became an icon and local landmark immediately and flourished during the Great Depression and even as the era of the American movie palace declined. The venue closed in 1974 but was refurbished and reopened in 2004. It now hosts larger acts as well, such as Gladys Knight and Lyle Lovett. The **Sprint Pavilion** (700 E. Main St., 434/245-4910, www.sprintpavilion.com) also hosts nationally known talent such as Elvis Costello, Kacey Musgraves, and Dwight Yoakam in an outdoor concert series from spring until fall.

The largest local venue, the **John Paul Jones Arena** (295 Massie Rd., 434/243-4960, www.johnpauljonesarena.com), is a major concert venue featuring talent such as Willie Nelson, Ariana Grande, and Cardi B.

Performing Arts

Charlottesville's number one performance company is **Live Arts** (123 E. Water St., 434/977-4177, www.livearts.org). They are a volunteer theater offering a rounded schedule of drama, comedy, dance, music, and performance arts.

The **Martin Luther King Jr. Performing Arts Center** (1400 Melbourne Rd, 434/466-3880, www.charlottesvilleschools.org) is a 1,276-seat venue run by the Charlottesville City School Division. It hosts student and commercial performances.

Events

The annual **Dogwood Festival** (www.cvilledogwood.com), held each spring in mid-April, is the largest festival in the city and lasts for two weeks. It is a great celebration of the city itself and features fireworks, a carnival, food, and a parade.

The **Virginia Film Festival** (617 W. Main St., 2nd Fl., 434/982-5277, www.virginiafilmfestival.org) is an annual event hosted by the University of Virginia in late October. The festival features more than 70 films and more than 80 guest artists and presenters at a variety of venues. Free panel discussions take place on topics important to both high- and low-budget film processes.

Featured guests in the past have included big-name actors such as Sandra Bullock, Anthony Hopkins, and Sigourney Weaver.

The **Virginia Festival of the Book** (www.vabook.org) draws over 20,000 writers and readers for five days each March to celebrate reading, books, literacy, and literacy culture.

SHOPPING

The Downtown Mall is Charlottesville's premier browsing district and is considered one of the best urban parks in the nation. There are more than 120 independent shops on or near Main Street, with delightful surprises such as rare-book stores, funky boutiques, galleries featuring local artists, craft stores, wine shops, and many others.

Farm-fresh produce can be found seasonally at the **Charlottesville City Market** (www.charlottesvillecitymarket.com). This market, which started in 1973, is held on Saturdays in the parking lot at 1st and Water Streets.

FOOD

American

The ★ **Ivy Inn** (2244 Old Ivy Rd., 434/977-1222, www.ivyinnrestaurant.com, daily 5pm-9:30pm, $11-32) is an elegant restaurant serving "locally inspired seasonal American cuisine." The restaurant is just one mile from UVA in a beautiful home built in 1816; the business itself was established in 1973. The food is excellent. They offer limited choices, but all are done exceptionally well. Examples of the menu include pan-roasted halibut, beef tenderloin, and spinach and ricotta ravioli. The atmosphere is genteel and refined, but not pretentious. The staff is friendly and very knowledgeable about the food and wine list.

For some colonial charm and old-world atmosphere, the **Michie Tavern** (683 Thomas Jefferson Pkwy., 434/977-1234, www.michietavern.com, Apr.-Oct. daily 11:15am-3:30pm, Nov.-Mar. daily 11:30am-3pm, adult $18.95, ages 12-15 $10.95, ages 6-11 $6.95, one child under 6 eats free with each paying adult, vegan/vegetarians $10.95) offers a bountiful lunch buffet in a tavern that was built in 1784. The tavern is a half mile from Monticello and was a popular lodging option for travelers more than 200 years ago. Today they offer a Southern-style buffet lunch with fried chicken, pork barbecue, baked chicken, black-eyed peas, corn bread, stewed potatoes, and other colonial favorites, served by staff dressed in period clothing. The cider ale is wonderful, and the tavern does beer and wine tastings in the evening. The food is served in five dining rooms known as **The Ordinary.** Meals are eaten on steel/pewter plates to add to the experience. A pescatarian option is available with 24 hours notice. Tours of the tavern are also available.

The Local (824 Hinton Ave., 434/984-9749, www.thelocal-cville.com, Sun.-Thurs. 5:30pm-10pm, Fri.-Sat. 5:30pm-11pm, $8-22) showcases the products of local farmers, artisan cheese makers, distilleries, vineyards, and breweries. They serve trout, chicken, beef, and pasta entrées and offer an extensive wine list and a variety of desserts (try the brownie sundae or blackberry cobbler). The brick and wood building dates back to 1912, when it housed a shoe-repair shop (the proprietor lived upstairs in what is now part of the restaurant). The building has served as a church, general store, furniture store, pool hall, motorcycle shop, and photography studio. Start with the crispy shrimp appetizer; it is a unique and delicious dish.

Good burgers, fries, and beer can be found at the Downtown Mall at **Citizen Burger Bar** (212 E. Main St., 434/979-9944, www.citizenburgerbar.com, Sun.-Thurs. 11:30am-10:30pm, Fri.-Sat. 11am-11:30pm, $8-21). This lively spot is a popular choice when students, visitors, and locals crave a meal on a bun (gluten-free buns are available). The portions are large, the food is locally sourced, the beef is grass-fed, and the cheese is made in Virginia. They also offer vegan burgers. Sides such as cheese fries and sweet potato fries are big enough to share. Their bar is well stocked with interesting cocktails and more than 110 types of beer.

Bodo's Bagels (www.bodosbagels.com) serves top-notch bagels at three locations (1418 Emmet St., 434/977-9598; 505 Preston Ave., 434/293-5224; 1609 University Ave., 434/293-6021; all-day breakfast, lunch, and dinner Mon.-Sat., breakfast and lunch Sun., hours vary by location). Their New York-style "water" bagels are simply delicious, and they have great bagel sandwiches, salads, and soups.

Italian

The rustic **Tavola** (826 Hinton Ave., 434/972-9463, www.tavolavino.com, Mon.-Sat. 5pm-10pm, $21-26) is a cozy little Italian restaurant that is big on taste. This isn't a typical American Italian place; the meals are freshly prepared and full of authentic flavor. The atmosphere is lively and fun (aka noisy), but it is charming at the same time and feels like a European bistro. They don't take reservations, so put your name on the list and go to one of the neighboring bars for a drink while you wait. The restaurant is in the Belmont district.

Tex-Mex

The "Get in Here" sign may be the only clue to the entrance to the **Continental Divide** (811 W. Main St., 434/984-0143, Mon.-Thurs. 5pm-10pm, Fri.-Sat. 5pm-10:30pm, Sun. 5pm-9:30pm, $5-14). This little hole-in-the-wall is known for incredible tuna tostadas and the best margaritas in town. The atmosphere is lively and noisy (and not family friendly), so be ready for a party when you finally find the front door. The food is fantastic and cheap, and there's normally a line out the door on weekends. The restaurant is in Midtown across from the Amtrak station.

Turkish

Excellent kabobs are a staple at **Sultan Kabob** (333 2nd St. SE, 434/981-0090, www.sultankebabcville.com, Sun.-Thurs. 11am-9pm, Fri.-Sat. 11am-9:30pm, $5-18). The atmosphere is comfortable, the prices are reasonable, and the staff is friendly. This is a quiet, relaxing place where the food takes center stage. For something different, try the hummus casserole. They also have vegan and gluten-free options.

Treats

For a tasty Italian treat, stop in **Splendora's Gelato** (317 E. Main St., 434/296-8555, www.splendoras.com, Mon.-Thurs. 7:30am-9pm, Fri. 7:30am-10pm, Sat. 9am-10pm, Sun. noon-9pm, under $10) on the Downtown Mall. They offer between 24 and 36 flavors of delectable gelato every day as well as espresso and other desserts.

ACCOMMODATIONS
$100-200

The **English Inn of Charlottesville** (2000 Morton Dr., 434/971-9900, www.englishinncharlottesville.com, $129-159) is an independent hotel with 106 rooms and suites. Built in the Tudor style, this friendly hotel offers free Internet access, a fitness room, an indoor pool, and a free hot breakfast.

The **200 South Street Inn** (200 W. South St., 434/979-0200, www.southstreetinn.com, $135-219) has 19 rooms and suites just two blocks from the pedestrian mall, one mile from the University of Virginia, and four miles from Monticello. The inn is made up of two restored homes, one built in 1856 and the other in 1890. It is decorated with antiques, and many rooms have fireplaces, whirlpool baths, and canopy beds. Larger suites with living rooms are available. All rooms have private baths. Guests can enjoy a continental breakfast in the library or, in nice weather, on the veranda. Cookies are also available around the clock. Rooms are comfortable but lack some of the modern conveniences of large hotel chains. Still, the personal attention given by the innkeepers, the charming atmosphere, and proximity to the downtown area make this a good choice in Charlottesville.

The **Hampton Inn Charlottesville** (2035 India Rd., 434/978-7888, www.hamptoninn3.hilton.com, $140-159) has 123 guest rooms, an outdoor pool, free breakfast, and wireless Internet. The hotel is a few miles from the downtown area, but there are chain restaurants and stores within walking distance. The staff is exceptionally friendly and helpful.

A second Hampton Inn in Charlottesville is the **Hampton Inn & Suites Charlottesville at the University** (900 W. Main St., 434/923-8600, www.hamptoninn3.hilton.com, $169-259). It has 100 guest rooms and suites near UVA and complimentary breakfast.

Over $200

★ **The Clifton** (1296 Clifton Inn Dr., 434/971-1800, www.the-clifton.com, $150-849), formerly the Clifton Inn, is a luxurious inn with 20 guest rooms in five late-18th- and early 19th-century buildings. This romantic establishment sits on 100 acres, with sweeping Blue Ridge Mountain views, and was built and used by Thomas Jefferson's son-in-law, Thomas Mann Randolph Jr., who was also the governor of Virginia (the estate also offers views of Monticello). During the Civil War, the family of Colonel John Singleton Mosby stayed at Clifton after fleeing their home near Middleburg in Northern Virginia. Mosby had a secret hiding area outside the main house where he is said to have left supplies for his family when Union troops were nearby. Today, guests enjoy first-rate service in the serene environment of this charming estate, which underwent major interior renovations with new ownership in 2018. Guests enjoy many amenities such as an infinity pool, private lake, gardens, walking trails, on-site restaurant, bar, and wine cellar.

Two miles west of town is the highly acclaimed ★ **Boar's Head Resort** (200 Ednam Dr., 434/296-2181, www.boarsheadresort.com, $185-325). The 573-acre estate is a destination in itself, with 175 rooms and suites, a fitness club, a spa, 20 tennis courts, a lap pool, golf course, biking, fishing, hiking, and even hot-air-balloon rides. There are also four restaurants and 20 event spaces. The inn is a certified "Virginia Green" establishment.

1: The Clifton entry 2: Ivy Inn 3: Citizen Burger Bar
4: Keswick Hall

Getaway to Wintergreen Resort

condos at Wintergreen Resort

Forty minutes southwest of Charlottesville is **Wintergreen Resort** (39 Mountain Inn Loop, Wintergreen, 434/325-2200, www.wintergreenresort.com). This beautiful, year-round destination is perched on the eastern side of the Blue Ridge Mountains. Unlike traditional mountain resorts, Wintergreen is built at the top of the mountain ridges instead of at the base of the mountain. The elevation is approximately 4,000 feet.

There is a large full-service spa on-site, 40,000 square feet of meeting space, and 300 choices of condos and homes for rent. There is also an aquatics center with indoor and outdoor pools.

Skiing and snowboarding ($39-89 for lift tickets) are popular on the 26 trails (14 of which are lit for night skiing). There is also a 900-foot tubing trail with 12 lanes and a terrain park. There are five chairlifts, and the resort can make snow on 100 percent of its trails.

During the summer, there are 45 holes of championship golf, tennis, hiking on 30 miles of trails, and many family activities such as minigolf, a climbing tower, and a bungee trampoline.

Rooms are decorated with antique furnishings and have beautiful bathrooms with modern conveniences. Premium bath items, plush bathrobes, and high-quality bedding are standard. The service is top-rate. The inn is close enough to downtown attractions to be convenient, but far enough away that you feel like you're out in the country. Rooms are spread out over several buildings. Ask for one in the main inn building.

The award-winning ★ **Keswick Hall** (701 Club Dr., Keswick, 434/979-3440, www. keswick.com, $310-1,000) at Monticello is a 1912 Italianate villa that was turned into a grand resort by the widower of designer Laura

Ashley. Guests are welcomed into this extravagant home in a comfortable lounge opening onto a patio that overlooks the 600-acre estate grounds. Guests in its 48 rooms can enjoy access to the Keswick Club, where they can play golf or tennis, swim in the saltwater pool, and use the spa. At the time of writing, the resort was closed for major renovations throughout the entire hotel and was scheduled to reopen in 2020.

INFORMATION AND SERVICES

The **Charlottesville-Albemarle Convention and Visitors Bureau**

(610 E. Main St., 434/293-6789, www. visitcharlottesville.org, daily 9am-5pm) provides visitors with maps and brochures about Charlottesville and the surrounding area. They are on the Downtown Mall.

GETTING THERE AND AROUND

Charlottesville is 115 miles southwest of Washington DC. The main highways running through Charlottesville are I-64, US 250, and US 29.

The **Charlottesville-Albemarle Airport** (CHO, 100 Bowen Loop, 434/973-8342, www.gocho.com) is a public airport with commercial service eight miles north of Charlottesville. Three airlines provide service to six cities, and approximately 25 flights are scheduled daily. Rental cars are available on-site.

Amtrak (800/872-7245, www.amtrak.com) provides service to Charlottesville at 810 West Main Street (not far from the UVA campus), and **Greyhound** (800/231-2222, www.greyhound.com) bus service is also available at 310 West Main Street.

Charlottesville Area Transit (CAT) (434/970-3649, www.charlottesville.org, Mon.-Sat. 6am-11:45pm, times vary by route, $0.75) offers 12 bus routes throughout the city. CAT also provides free trolley services daily from the Downtown Transit Station (615 E. Water St.) along Main Street. It also goes through the grounds of UVA.

Blue Ridge Parkway

The **Blue Ridge Parkway** (www.blueridgeparkway.org) is one of the most popular units of the national park system. The parkway is 469 miles long and connects **Great Smoky Mountains National Park** in North Carolina and Tennessee with **Shenandoah National Park** in Virginia. The parkway was designed during the Great Depression, and its creators took advantage of the beautiful terrain and followed the natural contours of the ridgeline. Gorgeous scenery is the key ingredient to this outstanding park, and visitors can enjoy overlooks of the Blue Ridge Mountains, countless vistas, beautiful old meadows, and picturesque farmland.

A 217-mile stretch of the Blue Ridge Parkway is in Virginia, with the prettiest part being the 114 miles between Waynesboro and Roanoke. This section follows the crest of the Blue Ridge Mountains.

Attractions and landmarks along the parkway are announced by mileposts (mp). Milepost 0 is at the northern end of the parkway at Rockfish Gap. This is also the southern end of Shenandoah National Park. Milepost 218 is at the North Carolina border. The speed limit along the entire Blue Ridge Parkway is 45 miles per hour. Visitors should expect slower traffic during peak foliage time in the fall and also during the summer months.

PLANTS AND ANIMALS

Wildflower meadows, colorful leaves, spotted fawns, and black bear cubs can all be seen at times along the Blue Ridge Parkway. There are millions of varieties of flora and fauna that can be found on this famed stretch of road.

There are more than 130 species of trees growing along the parkway (as many as are found in all of Europe). Some of the most popular types include evergreens such as Virginia pine, white pine, spruce, fir, and hemlock. The altitude along the entire parkway varies from just under 650 feet to 6,047 feet. Because of this, the fall foliage season is rather long since the fireworks of colored leaves burst at slightly different times at each altitude. A current **Fall Color Report** can be heard by calling 828/298-0398 (press 3).

Dogwood, sourwood, and black gum leaves change to deep red, while hickory and tulip tree leaves turn bright yellow. Red maples

Blue Ridge Parkway

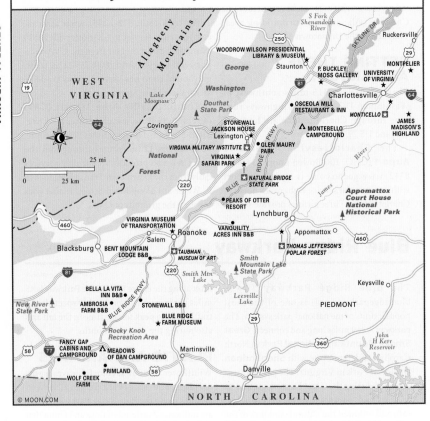

produce multicolored leaves, while sassafras trees add orange leaves to the mix. The fall is an amazing time to explore the parkway. There's nothing quite like the autumn foliage in Virginia, and the Blue Ridge Parkway offers the crème de la crème of this incredible spectacle.

There are many types of flowers along the parkway. The Blue Ridge Parkway website (www.blueridgeparkway.org) has a helpful **Bloom Schedule** that gives tentative blooming periods for many popular flowers. There is also a **Wildflower Report** available on the Parkway Information Line (828/298-0398) during the spring and summer. It should be noted that all plants along

the parkway are protected and should not be picked or destroyed.

Many animals make their home in the wilds along the Blue Ridge Parkway. There are more than 50 species of mammals, 250 species of birds (159 that nest there), 40 species of reptiles, 50 types of salamanders, and 50 species of fish. Many people are interested to know that of the 22 species of snakes living in the region, only two types are venomous: the timber rattlesnake and the copperhead. Both are not aggressive and prefer to avoid contact with people altogether.

Wildlife should be left wild. No matter how friendly they may seem, any animals in the park should not be fed or interacted with.

Picture taking, from a distance, is of course acceptable, but no close contact should be made.

SIGHTS

There are many wonderful attractions along or just off the parkway as it passes close to numerous towns. Locations are best described by their corresponding mileposts. Visitors centers are located at milepoint 5.8 (Humpback Rocks), milepoint 63.6 (James River), milepoint 86 (Peaks of Otter), milepoint 115 (Explore Park), milepoint 169 (Rocky Knob), and milepoint 213 (Blue Ridge Music Center).

Woodrow Wilson Presidential Library and Museum

The **Woodrow Wilson Presidential Library and Museum** (mp 0, 20 N. Coalter St., Staunton, 540/885-0897, www. woodrowwilson.org, Mon.-Sat. 9am-5pm, Sun. noon-5pm, adults $15, youth 6-15 $8, over 60 $14, active military $12, under 6 free) is a historical destination and the former home of Woodrow Wilson. It offers multiple attractions such as the Woodrow Wilson Museum (self-guided tours are available through seven galleries), a state-of-the-art World War I trench experience, a research library, gardens, and a hands-on kids' corner.

Milepost 0 is also where the **P. Buckley Moss Gallery** (329 W. Main St., Waynesboro, 540/949-6473, www.pbuckleymoss.com, Mon.-Sat. 10am-5pm, Sun. noon-4pm, closed Mon. Jan.-Mar.) is located. The gallery is home to the permanent art collection of Virginia artist P. Buckley Moss, who is known for her rural landscape paintings and those depicting life in the Shenandoah Valley. At the museum, visitors can learn about her life and achievements in art.

Stonewall Jackson House

The **Stonewall Jackson House** (mp 45.6, 8 E. Washington St., Lexington, 540/464-7704, www.vmi.edu, daily 9am-5pm, adults $8, youth 6-17 $6, 5 and under free) is the former home of the Civil War general. It has been beautifully restored and contains some original Jackson family furnishings. Guided tours, a garden, and a museum shop are part of the offerings.

★ Natural Bridge State Park

Natural Bridge State Park (mp 61.6, 6477 S. Lee Hwy., Natural Bridge, 540/291-1326, www.naturalbridgestatepark.org and www. dcr.virginia.gov, daily 9am-4pm, extended summer hours, adults $8, children 6-12 $6, under 6 free) is a National Historic Landmark that was once owned by Thomas Jefferson. The 20-story solid limestone rock arch created by nature is an awesome sight and one that has inspired people for generations. A variety of other attractions are also at the Natural Bridge, including the **Caverns at Natural Bridge** (15 Appledore Ln., Natural Bridge, 540/291-2482, daily 9am-4pm, Nov.-mid-Mar. Fri.-Sun. only, adults starting at $18.50, ages 7-17 $12.75, under 7 free), which sit 34 stories below ground. A combo bridge-and-caverns ticket can be purchased for $30 for adults, children 6-12 $19.50.

Virginia Safari Park

Four miles north of the Natural Bridge is the **Virginia Safari Park** (mp 61.6, 229 Safari Ln., Natural Bridge, 540/291-3205, www. virginiasafaripark.com, mid-Mar.-Nov. daily 9am-5pm, extended weekend and summer hours, adults $21.95, children 2-12 $14.95, seniors 65 and over $20.95, under 2 free). This 180-acre drive-through zoo houses more than 1,000 animals that are free to roam in a natural setting. Three miles of roads meander through woods and fields, allowing visitors to see animals such as deer, zebras, elk, antelope, giraffe, camels, and bison. The free-roaming animals literally stick their heads inside your car waiting to be fed. Buckets of feed are available at the entrance to the park. There is also a walk-through area where visitors can feed giraffes, goats, pigs, and baby llamas.

★ Thomas Jefferson's Poplar Forest

Thomas Jefferson's Poplar Forest (mp 86, 1542 Bateman Bridge Rd., Forest, 434/525-1806, www.poplarforest.org, Mar. 15-Dec. 30 daily 10am-5pm, adults $16, teens 12-18 $8, youth 6-11 $4, seniors 65 and over $14, military $14, under 6 free) was Thomas Jefferson's personal retreat. He originally inherited the land from his father-in-law as a working tobacco farm, and it offered him a nice source of income. Ten miles west of Lynchburg, the home is an architectural masterpiece built in 1806 and one of only two that Jefferson designed and constructed for his personal use. It was also the first octagonal house in the country. It was a three-day ride for Jefferson between Monticello and Poplar Forest, but he went there several times a year and stayed from two weeks to two months each visit. Visitors to Poplar Forest learn about life in the early 19th century, the architecture of the home, and its preservation. They also witness ongoing excavation of the property and can see authentic artifacts from the plantation. Admission includes a guided 40-minute tour of the house and a self-guided tour of the grounds.

Virginia Museum of Transportation

Farther south, in Roanoke, is the **Virginia Museum of Transportation** (mp 112.2, 303 Norfolk Ave. SW, Roanoke, 540/342-5670, www.vmt.org, Mon.-Sat. 10am-5pm, Sun. 1pm-5pm, adults $10, youth 13-18, students with ID, and seniors 60 and over $8, children 3-12 $6, under 3 free). This large museum is mostly outdoors and holds more than 50 railway exhibits, road vehicle exhibits, and air exhibits. It is best known for its exhibits on the Norfolk & Western Class J-611 and Class A-1218 modern steam locomotives.

Blue Ridge Farm Museum

For a lesson on farm life, check out the **Blue Ridge Farm Museum** (mp 152, 20 Museum Dr., Ferrum, 540/365-4412, www.ferrum.edu, mid-May-Labor Day Sat. 10am-5pm, Sun. 1pm-5pm, free). The farm takes visitors back to 1800 to experience what life was like on a Virginia German farmstead. Interpreters dressed in period clothing complete numerous farm chores such as cooking, driving oxen, and blacksmith work.

Mabry Mill

The most photographed location on the Blue Ridge Parkway is **Mabry Mill** (mp 176.1). This charming, water-powered mill (built in 1867) is visited by several hundred thousand people each year. The gristmill and sawmill have been restored, and visitors can see a working miller demonstrate the milling process. The mill grounds are lovely and tranquil, although crowded in the summer months, and include interpretive media.

RECREATION

The Blue Ridge Parkway has numerous attractions and recreational opportunities along its winding route. Campgrounds, hiking trails, interpretive centers, and picnic areas are just some of the possibilities for a break when traversing this gorgeous roadway. The famed **Appalachian Trail,** which runs 2,184 miles from Maine to Georgia, meanders along the parkway from Rockfish Gap (at the northern end) down to Roanoke.

Near the northern end of the parkway is a beautiful area known as **Humpback Rocks** (mp 5.8). Visitors can see farm buildings from the 19th century and enjoy numerous hiking trails suitable for all abilities. Interpretive programs in which park rangers demonstrate making local mountain crafts are held during the summer months.

At milepost 64, a section of the **James River** can be explored. Visitors can see one of the restored canal locks from the James River and Kanawha Canal, a prime commercial route in Virginia in the mid-1800s, and

---

1: Blue Ridge Parkway overlook **2:** Stonewall Jackson House in Lexington **3:** Thomas Jefferson's Poplar Forest home **4:** Natural Bridge State Park

also go fishing from a public dock. There are plenty of areas for picnicking.

The popular **Peaks of Otter** area at milepost 86 offers incredible views and an abundance of natural beauty. The area has been a popular tourist attraction since 1834. Ranger programs are offered at the visitors center, and a lovely picnic area along Little Stoney Creek provides tables, grills, and restroom facilities. There are six hiking trails at Peaks of Otter, and Abbott Lake is open to the public for fishing (with a Virginia or North Carolina fishing license).

Virginia's Explore Park (mp 115, Blue Ridge Pkwy., 540/427-1800, www.explorepark. org), located near Roanoke, is a 1,200-acre park with nine miles of mountain bike trails, a one-mile interpretive trail, fishing, canoeing, and kayaking. There is also a Treetop Quest (adults $35, ages 12-17 $29, ages 7-11 $22, ages 4-6 $15) aerial adventure course that has obstacles and zip lines.

The **Smart View Trail** (mp 154.5) is a popular 2.6-mile loop hiking trail around the Smart View Picnic Area. It is a level trail through the woods with nice views.

The beautiful **Rocky Knob** area at milepost 169 offers several great hiking trails of different lengths. The Rock Castle Gorge Trail (blazed in green) is a moderate-to-strenuous 10.8-mile loop with elevation ranges from 1,700 feet to 3,572 feet. Sections are steep and rocky on this National Scenic Trail. The Black Ridge Trail (blazed in blue) is a moderate 3-mile loop hike with good views to the north from the top of Black Ridge. This trail joins the Rock Castle Gorge Trail on the return trip. The Rocky Knob Picnic Area Trail (blazed in yellow) is an easy 1-mile loop walk through mature forest.

ENTERTAINMENT

The **Blue Ridge Music Center** (mp 213, 700 Foothills Rd., Galax, 276/236-5309, www. blueridgemusiccenter.org) is a modern performing arts venue that was constructed for the purpose of promoting historical Blue Ridge music. Old-time and bluegrass music

frequently floods the facility and surrounding area. Visitors can take in a show, explore the visitors center, and check out the views of Fisher Peak.

FOOD

At milepost 27 (halfway between Staunton and Lexington) is the **Osceola Mill** (mp 27, 352 Tye River Turnpike, Steeles Tavern, 540/377-6455, www.osceolamill.com, Fri. and Sat. 5pm-10pm, $26-40). This elegant but casual restaurant serves seafood, steak, and veal. The menu varies weekly depending on what is in season. The Mill Stone dining room has huge chestnut beams, original millworks, and views of the mill's waterwheel.

The **Liberty Station Restaurant** (mp 86, 515 Bedford Ave., Bedford, 540/587-9377, www.oldelibertystation.com, Mon.-Thurs. 11am-9pm, Fri.-Sat. 11am-10pm, $9-21) in Bedford is housed in a former railroad station. It serves traditional American food and is known for its cheesecake.

Seven miles from the parkway at milepost 121 is the **Roanoker Restaurant** (mp 121, 2522 Colonial Ave., Roanoke, 540/344-7746, www.theroanokerrestaurant.com, Tues.-Sat. 7am-9pm, Sun. 8am-9pm, $10-17). They serve American home-style food and are open for breakfast, lunch, and dinner. Their menu includes a variety of seafood, salads, and sandwiches at reasonable prices.

If you're looking for food near milepost 164, the **Blue Ridge Cafe** (mp 164, 113 E. Main St., Floyd, 540/745-2147, www. blueridgecafefloyd.com, Mon.-Wed. 6am-4pm, Thurs.-Fri. 6am-8pm, Sat. 7am-8pm, Sun. 7am-4pm, $4-16) is a good stop for traditional diner food. This no-frills place across from the courthouse in Floyd, six miles from the parkway, will satisfy your appetite in a casual, friendly environment. They are open for breakfast, lunch, and dinner.

The **Mabry Mill Restaurant** (mp 176, 266 Mabry Mill Rd. SE, Meadows of Dan, 276/952-2947, www.mabrymillrestaurant.com, May-Oct. Mon.-Fri. 7:30am-5pm, Sat.-Sun. 7:30am-6pm, under $12) offers home-style cooking and is known for its buckwheat pancakes, country ham, and Virginia barbecue. They serve breakfast all day. The restaurant is located next to the **Mabry Mill.**

Not far from milepost 199.5 is **The Gap Deli at the Parkway** (mp 199.5, 7975 Fancy Gap Hwy., Fancy Gap, 276/728-3881, www.thegapdeli.com, Sun.-Thurs. 10am-4pm, Fri.-Sat. 10am-7pm, under $10). They serve a nice variety of sandwiches, wraps, salads, and dessert.

ACCOMMODATIONS

There are many wonderful independent inns, lodges, and bed-and-breakfasts nestled in the mountains along the Blue Ridge Parkway. Most are family owned and operated and offer reasonable rates. Book early when visiting during peak season.

In a town called Steeles Tavern (between Staunton and Lexington) is the **Osceola Mill** (mp 27, 352 Tye River Turnpike, Steeles Tavern, 540/377-6455, www.osceolamill.com, $105-200). They offer bed-and-breakfast accommodations, cabin rentals, and a restaurant. There are four rooms and one individual cabin for rent in a peaceful, beautiful six-acre compound. Another good option near milepost 27 is the **Sugar Tree Inn** (mp 27, 145 Lodge Trail, Vesuvius, 540/377-2197, www.sugartreeinn.com, closed Jan., $148-248). This peaceful log inn offers accommodations in the main lodge (three rooms) and four additional cabins/houses. There are 13 guest rooms total. It has expansive views and wood-burning fireplaces in all guest rooms. A full breakfast is included with your stay.

A nice bed-and-breakfast in Bedford near milepost 86 is the **Vanquility Acres Inn** (mp 86, 105 Angus Terrace, Bedford, 540/587-9113, www.vanquilityacresinn.com, $115-145). This 10-acre farm has wonderful views of the Blue Ridge Mountains, fishing, fireplaces, wireless Internet, and suites with private bathrooms. There are five guest rooms. The better-known **Peaks of Otter Lodge** (mp 86, 85554 Blue Ridge Pkwy., Bedford, 866/387-9905, www.peaksofotter.com, $112-188) sits between two mountains on the parkway and looks over tranquil Abbott Lake. It offers 63 rooms and has a restaurant on-site.

Unique accommodations can be found at the ★ **Depot Lodge Bed and Breakfast** (mp 112.2, Rte. 311, Paint Bank, 540/897-6000, www.thedepotlodge.com, $149-289), about an hour from Roanoke in the Jefferson National Forest. This restored train depot was built in 1909 as the final stop on the Potts Valley Branch line of the Norfolk & Western Railroad. They offer nine guest rooms in the depot and surrounding historic buildings, including cabins, and a romantic restored caboose. There is also an Airstream trailer and two luxurious "glamping" tents.

The **Bent Mountain Lodge Bed and Breakfast** (mp 136, 9039 Mountain View Dr., Copper Hill, 540/651-2500, www.bentmountainlodgebedandbreakfast.com, $120-150) has 10 guest suites with private bathrooms. This 15,000-square-foot lodge is between Floyd and Roanoke (20 minutes away from each). Room rates include continental breakfast. The lodge is pet friendly.

The **Bella La Vita Inn Bed and Breakfast** (mp 161, 582 New Haven Rd. SE, Floyd, 540/745-2541, www.bellalavitainn.com, $149-160) is less than two miles from the Blue Ridge Parkway and offers four delightful European-style guest rooms and in-house massage therapy.

A good overnight stop near milepost 165 is the **Stonewall Bed and Breakfast** (mp 165.2, 102 Wendi Pate Trail SE, Floyd, 540/745-2861, www.stonewallbed.com, $70-130). They have six guest rooms in the main house and two cabins for rent. This lovely three-level log house is in the woods and has a warm and inviting atmosphere.

The **Ambrosia Farm Bed and Breakfast** (mp 171.5, 271 Cox Store Rd., Floyd, 540/745-6363, www.ambrosiafarm.net, $90-135) is housed in a restored log farmhouse that is 200 years old. It now contains four cozy guest rooms. The home has lovely views, porches to enjoy them from, and an on-site pottery studio.

Getaway to Primland

Primland

Primland (2000 Busted Rock Rd., Meadows of Dan, 866/960-7746, www.primland.com, $300-1,890) might be the best-kept secret in all of Virginia. Nestled in the beautiful Blue Ridge Mountains on more than 12,000 acres, this LEED-certified, upscale resort offers complete relaxation, as well as stunning scenery, plentiful activities, great food, and attention to every last detail.

Unpretentious, yet classy in every respect, this unique four-season property is the perfect getaway for a range of occasions, from family vacations to business conferences and even honeymoons. In addition to its luxurious suites, the main lodge offers a formal dining room, a cozy pub, a conference space, a beautiful spa, an indoor swimming pool, a fitness center, a game room, a common space, and a large deck with a fire pit. The lodge also features an observatory with a Celestron CGE Pro 1400 series telescope, and nightly tours of the universe are offered by a local astronomer. Additional accommodations include stunning secluded tree houses, golf-course-view cottages, pinnacle cottages, and individual homes.

The list of amenities and activities available at Primland includes the highly ranked Highland Golf Course, hiking, sporting clays, fly fishing, RTV rides, hunting, kayaking, horseback riding, disc golf, geocaching, nature walks, tree climbing, mountain biking, and an authentic Virginia moonshine experience. They also offer a Tesla charger, a smoking house, and eco-conscious extras throughout the resort.

Just 200 yards from the Blue Ridge Parkway near milepost 174 is the **Woodberry Inn** (mp 174.1, 182 Woodberry Rd. SW, Meadows of Dan, 540/593-2567, www.woodberryinn.com, $99). They offer 16 simply appointed rooms (each with a private bathroom), free wireless Internet, and a restaurant on-site. They are pet friendly.

For stunning upscale accommodations, treat yourself to a stay at ★ **Primland** (mp 177.7, 2000 Busted Rock Rd., Meadows of Dan,

866/960-7746, www.primland.com, $300-1,890). Primland offers 62 units that include lodge rooms, suites, cottages, treehouses, and mountain homes. There is a mile-long list of amenities and activities offered on the premises, including a spa, fitness center, and golf course. Turn east at milepost 177.7 to take Route 58/Jeb Stuart Highway for 4.5 miles to Busted Rock Road.

The **Wolf Creek Farm** (mp 192, 688 Gid Collins Rd., Ararat, 276/952-8869, www.

wolfcreekfarmva.net, $135-160) offers two guest rooms and one cabin for rent in the town of Ararat. It sits on 102 acres and has a fishing lake and swimming pool.

CAMPING

Camping and fishing can be found three miles from the parkway at milepost 27 and the **Montebello Camping and Fishing Resort** (mp 27, 15072 Crabtree Falls Hwy., Montebello, 540/377-2650, www. montebellova.com, $30-46). This full-service campground accommodates RVs, trailers, and tent camping. There's a four-acre lake and cabins on-site.

The **Glen Maury Park Campground** (mp 45.6, 101 Maury River Dr., Buena Vista, 540/261-7321, www.bvcity.org, $22-30) is five miles from the parkway on 315 acres. They have 52 sites and modern facilities. A few miles down the parkway is the **Lynchburg NW/Blue Ridge Parkway KOA** (mp 61.5, 6252 Elon Rd., Monroe, 434/299-5228, www. koa.com, $30-53), sitting just one mile from the parkway and open all year. They have RV and tent camping.

Visitors can pitch a tent at one of 74 tent sites in the **Roanoke Mountain Campground** (mp 120.4, Blue Ridge Dr., Roanoke, 540/342-3051, www.blueridgecampgrounds.com, $16). Facilities include 30 RV/trailer sites, comfort stations, water, flush toilets, and sinks (no showers).

Near milepost 177.7 is the **Meadows of Dan Campground** (mp 177.7, 2182 Jeb Stuart Hwy., Meadows of Dan, 276/952-2292, www. meadowsofdancampground.com, $30). They have full hookups, a separate tent area, a bath-house, and a dumping station. They also offer log cabin rentals.

The **Fancy Gap Cabins and Campground** (mp 199.5, 202595 Blue Ridge Pkwy., Fancy Gap, 276/730-7154, www. fancygapcabinsandcampground.com, $25-70) is right on the Blue Ridge Parkway in Fancy Gap. They offer tent sites, RV sites, camping cabins ($25-55), and motel rooms ($70) with scenic views. They are pet friendly.

INFORMATION AND SERVICES

For additional information on the Blue Ridge Parkway, visit www.blueridgeparkway.org or stop by one of their visitors centers, located at milepost 5.8 (Humpback Rocks, May-Oct. daily 10am-5pm), milepost 63.6 (James River, June-Oct. Wed.-Sun. 10am-5pm), milepost 86 (Peaks of Otter, May-Oct. daily 10am-5pm), milepost 169 (Rocky Knob, June-Oct. Thurs.-Mon. 10am-5pm), and milepost 213 (Blue Ridge Music Center, June-Oct. daily 10am-5pm).

Lexington

Lexington is a popular tourist stop due to its lovely location in the southern part of the Shenandoah Valley, vibrant military history, and the fact that it is home to **Washington and Lee University** and the **Virginia Military Institute (VMI).** Lexington is part of Rockbridge County. Buena Vista is the closest town (15-minute drive), and Natural Bridge near the Blue Ridge Parkway is about 20 minutes away.

Many historic residences are preserved along the town's tree-lined streets and in the downtown area, making Lexington a charming mix of homes, shops, and restaurants. There are numerous cozy inns and bed-and-breakfasts to choose from, and many are within walking distance of local attractions.

Two of the most famous Confederate heroes, Robert E. Lee and Stonewall Jackson, are buried in Lexington. Both lived and worked in Lexington, and their legacies live on in this somewhat quiet community.

Lexington was founded in 1777 and was destroyed by fire in 1796. It was quickly rebuilt

Lexington

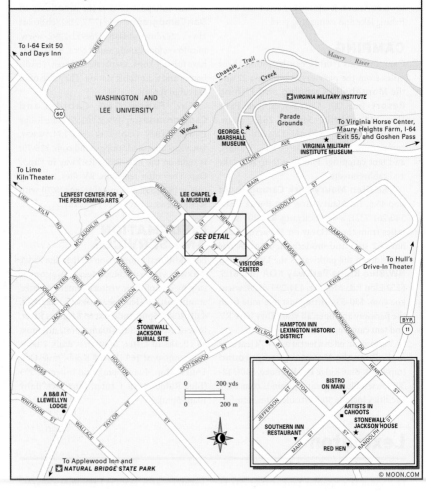

but was again partly destroyed in 1864 by Union gunfire. Today it is a lovely Southern town, steeped in history, where cadets in uniform can be seen strolling down the streets, and tourists enjoy leisurely meals in local eateries.

SIGHTS

★ Virginia Military Institute

The **Virginia Military Institute** (319 Letcher Ave., 540/464-7230, www.vmi.edu) is the oldest state-supported military college in the country (founded in 1839). Many famous leaders have graced its doorstep, including General Stonewall Jackson, who was a professor there prior to the Civil War. Be sure to check the VMI website for the cadet parade schedule. This is a highlight of any trip to the institute. Cadet-led tours of campus are also available.

One of the most interesting sights on campus is the **George C. Marshall Museum** (340 VMI Parade, 540/463-2083, www.

marshallfoundation.org, Tues.-Sat. 11am-4pm, adults $5, students $2, seniors $3), an informative space dedicated to the life of a legendary five-star general who rose to fame during World War II. The museum follows Marshall's career beginning as a young lieutenant. Visitors can get a dose of military history and learn about the evolving role of the United States military during the 20th century. The museum also illustrates how Marshall learned to be such a strong leader. Items featured in the museum include Marshall's Nobel Peace Prize, a narrated World War II map, and a Jeep from 1943. A good place to begin is by watching the video presentation on Marshall's life. Allow 1-2 hours to visit. The museum is in the southwest corner of campus, and there is plenty of parking behind it.

Another VMI museum is **The Virginia Military Institute Museum** (Jackson Memorial Hall, 415 Letcher Ave., 540/464-7334, www.vmi.edu, daily 9am-5pm, $3 suggested donation) in Jackson Memorial Hall. Visitors can learn about the history of VMI and hear stories of its alumni. Special features include a statue of Stonewall Jackson's horse, his field desk, and his uniforms. There is also an antique firearms collection.

Stonewall Jackson House

The **Stonewall Jackson House** (8 E. Washington St., Lexington, 540/464-7704, www.vmi.edu, daily 9am-5pm, adults $8, youth 6-17 $6, 5 and under free) offers an interesting look at life in Lexington prior to the Civil War. Visitors can learn about many aspects of Stonewall Jackson's life including his time as a professor at the Virginia Military Institute (VMI), his role as a leader in his church, his time as a businessman, and his private affairs. The museum first opened in 1954 and was meticulously restored to its original appearance in 1979. Owned by VMI, the museum contains many of Jackson's personal belongings. Guided tours are available on the hour and half hour.

Stonewall Jackson Burial Site

General Stonewall Jackson was laid to rest in Lexington in May 1863 following his death from pneumonia. His remains were moved to their current resting place in 1890, now known as the **Stonewall Jackson Memorial Cemetery** (314 S. Main St., 540/463-2931). A statue marks his tomb on the south end of Main Street, which is surrounded by grave sites of other prominent Civil War soldiers

Virginia Military Institute

Stonewall Jackson

Thomas Jonathan Jackson was born in western Virginia (in Clarksburg, which is now part of West Virginia) in 1824 and was orphaned at the age of seven. Raised by extended family, Jackson was a constable and a teacher prior to his appointment to the U.S. Military Academy at West Point. After graduation, he served in the U.S. Army and fought in the Mexican-American War before being stationed in New York and Florida.

In 1851 Jackson was appointed as a professor at the Virginia Military Institute in Lexington, where he taught natural and experimental philosophy and was an artillery instructor. Some of his methods are still passed on there today. While in Lexington, he married Elinor Junkin in 1853 and joined the Lexington Presbyterian Church. After only one year of marriage, Elinor died in childbirth. The child was stillborn, and Jackson was suddenly alone.

In 1857, Jackson married Mary Anna Morrison, and the couple bought a home on Washington Street. They lived there quietly until 1861, when Jackson went off to fight in the Civil War just weeks after it began.

Stonewall Jackson's burial site in Lexington

Jackson entered the war as an infantry colonel but was soon promoted to brigadier general. During the First Battle of Bull Run on July 21, 1861, Jackson and his brigade provided reinforcements to Confederate lines that were under heavy Union fire. As other Confederate troops began to flee the battle, Jackson and his troops held their ground. Seeing this, General Barnard E. Bee Jr. yelled, "There is Jackson, standing like a stone wall," and thus, Jackson earned the nickname "Stonewall."

Jackson became known for his superb leadership skills and was promoted to major general. His most noted accomplishment was the Valley Campaign of 1862, during which Jackson's army of 17,000 marched 646 miles in 48 days and won five big victories against forces numbering around 60,000. It is thought of as one of the most brilliant campaigns in history.

In May 1863 at Chancellorsville, Virginia, Jackson's troops won a great victory. During the battle, Jackson was accidentally fired on by Confederate troops. The shots killed two of his aides and seriously wounded the general's left arm and right hand. Doctors in a field hospital decided to amputate his left arm. As Jackson lay in bed, Robert E. Lee looked at him and said, "He has lost his left arm, but I have lost my right."

Weakened by the amputation, Jackson contracted pneumonia and died on May 10.

and citizens. The grounds are open dawn to dusk.

Washington and Lee University

Washington and Lee University (204 W. Washington St., 540/458-8400, www.wlu.edu) is the ninth-oldest institution of higher learning in the United States. It was founded in 1749 as the Augusta Academy. The school has undergone four name changes in the past 250 years and is now named for George Washington (who gave the school its first endowment) and Robert E. Lee (who served as president of the school and is now buried there). It is a private liberal arts school that was originally all male. The first women were admitted to the university's top-ranked law school in 1972, but it wasn't until 1985 that they were allowed in undergraduate programs. The charming campus full of Georgian-style buildings with redbrick facades and multistory porticos is right in downtown Lexington.

LEE CHAPEL & MUSEUM

The **Lee Chapel & Museum** (100 N. Jefferson St., Washington and Lee University, 540/458-8768, www.wlu.edu, Apr.-Oct. Mon.-Sat. 9am-5pm, Sun. 1pm-5pm, Nov.-Mar. Mon.-Sat. 9am-4pm, Sun. 1pm-4pm, $5 suggested donation) was built in 1867 at the request of Robert E. Lee. At the time, Lee was the university president of what was then called Washington College. Lee was a regular at weekday services in the chapel and had his office in the lower level of the building. When he died in 1870, he was buried under the chapel, but his remains were moved in 1883 into a family crypt that was added to the lower level of an addition to the building. Other members of Lee's family are also buried in the crypt, and the remains of his horse Traveller were laid to rest just outside the entrance to the museum. Today the chapel hosts concerts, lectures, and other events in an auditorium on the main level. There is seating for 500 people. The lower level houses an informative museum that discusses the contributions both George Washington and Robert E. Lee made to education and features Lee's office. There is also a museum shop. The museum plays a part in many university events, so it is best to call ahead prior to visiting.

Virginia Horse Center

The enormous **Virginia Horse Center** (487 Maury River Rd., 540/464-2950, www.vahorsecenter.org) is a 600-acre equestrian compound three miles north of downtown Lexington. The beautiful grounds house a coliseum that holds 4,000 spectators, eight barns that hold 1,200 horses, 17 outdoor riding rings, two indoor arenas, a cross-country and combined-carriage-driving course, a campground, and food services. The center hosts many horse events throughout the year but also hosts non-horse-related events such as dog shows, agricultural programs, the Rockbridge Regional Fair and Farm Show, and BMX competitions.

RECREATION

Lexington is surrounded by the **George Washington** and **Jefferson National Forests,** which encompass land in the Appalachian Mountains of Virginia, West Virginia, and Kentucky. The two forests are managed jointly by the U.S. Forest Service. Together at 1.8 million acres they form one of the largest public land areas in the eastern part of the country. Easy access to this large wilderness area provides ample possibilities for outdoor recreation near Lexington.

The seven-mile **Chessie Nature Trail** (www.traillink.com) links Lexington with the neighboring town of Buena Vista. The trail begins at State Route 631 in Lexington and follows the north bank of the Maury River along mile markers on the former Chesapeake & Ohio Railroad route. Travelers can expect to see scenic Virginia countryside along the way and a variety of wildlife and farm animals. Be aware that cattle gates are sometimes closed along the trail.

Local streams are teeming with trout. Expert fly-fishing guides and instruction can be found at **Fly Fishing Adventures** (540/463-3235, www.vatrout.com). They offer fishing trips and instruction for beginners and experienced fly fishers.

Lexington is horse country. The pristine Virginia Horse Center is a prime example of this; however, there are also 65 miles of **horse trails** that wind through the George Washington and Jefferson National Forests near Lexington (https://www.fs.usda.gov). Multiple trailheads with room for trailer parking are located in the forest.

Canoeing, kayaking, and float trips on tubes on the James and Maury Rivers can be arranged April-October through **Twin Rivers Outfitters** (653 Lowe St., Buchanan, 540/254-8012, www.canoevirginia.net). They are a full-service livery in Buchanan (about 25 miles from Lexington) and have been in business since 1978.

Take a shot at some sporting clays at **Quail Ridge Sporting Clays** (336 Murat Rd., 540/463-1800, www.quailridgesportingclub.

com). They offer a challenging course with multiple types of targets at different speeds and distances.

ENTERTAINMENT AND EVENTS

Lexington is a charming city to explore. **Doc's Guide Service** (540/463-4501, $20/hour) specializes in personal historic, Civil War, architecture, and scenic tours. They will meet you anywhere in the area and they're available on short notice.

Starting each Memorial Day and running through Halloween, the **Visitor Center of Lexington** (106 E. Washington St., 540/463-3777, www.lexingtonvirginia.com) offers **Haunting Tales** (540/464-2250, ages 13 and up $15, ages 6-12 $7) tours of Historic Lexington. This 90-minute tour by candlelight follows in the footsteps of Generals Lee and Jackson. Costumed guides reveal ghost stories about the city that will likely raise the hair on your neck or at least make you shiver. Reservations are required, and tours begin at the visitors center.

For those who prefer to let a horse do the walking, the **Lexington Carriage Company** (540/463-5647, www.lexcarriage.com, daily 11am-4:30pm, adults $16, children 7-13 $7, children 4-6 $4, seniors 65 and over $14) offers horse-drawn-carriage tours April through October. Tours last 40-45 minutes and are narrated by a professional guide. Tours pass through historic residential streets and go by the Stonewall Jackson House, Lee Chapel, Washington and Lee University, and the Stonewall Jackson Cemetery. Tours meet across the street from the Visitor Center of Lexington (106 E. Washington St.).

Theatergoers will love the unique **Lime Kiln Theater** (607 Borden Rd., 540/463-7088, www.limekilntheater.org). This beautiful outdoor venue was erected out of the ruins of a 19th-century kiln. The theater is set among the vine-covered stones of the ruins and has two stages (one that is open to the stars). The theater hosts classic theater, concerts, and civic celebrations April to October.

Concerts and theater performances can also be found at the **Lenfest Center for the Performing Arts** (100 Glasgow St., 540/458-8000, www.wlu.edu) at Washington and Lee University. The center hosts more than 250 performances a year by both students and professionals.

Moviegoers can take in the action from the comfort of their cars at **Hull's Drive-in Theater** (2367 N. Lee Hwy., 540/463-2621, www.hullsdrivein.com, adults $7, children 5-11 $3, under 5 free), a seasonal drive-in theater that first opened in 1950. Its first showing was of John Wayne's *The Wake of the Red Witch*.

A yearly celebration is held to honor the birthdays of General Robert E. Lee and General Stonewall Jackson on **Lee-Jackson Day** (www.leejacksonday.webs.com) in mid-January. The celebration actually spans two days and features a variety of speakers, an annual memorial service, a parade, a luncheon, and a ball. Free tours of Jackson's home are also given during the celebration.

Another much-anticipated annual event is the **Balloons Over Rockbridge Festival** (www.lexingtonvirginia.com). This free event lasts for three days over the Fourth of July and is a spectacular gathering of brightly colored hot-air balloons. Visitors can purchase piloted balloon rides during the event.

SHOPPING

Lexington is an antiques collector's dream. There seems to be at least one antiques store on every block. The largest is **Duke's Lexington Antique Center** (1495 N. Lee Hwy., 540/463-9511, www.lexingtonvirginia.com). This impressive 20,000-square-foot space features more than 200 antiques dealers and consignments. It is open 365 days a year and has ample parking for cars and RVs.

A wonderful local gallery run by an artist cooperative is **Artists in Cahoots** (21 W. Washington St., 540/464-1147, www.artistsincahoots.com). The cooperative, which is closed January and February, was founded in 1983, and the gallery features paintings, jewelry, pottery, ironwork, woodwork, furniture, bird carvings, decoys, photography, sculpture, printmaking, fabric art, and more.

FOOD

For comfort food with a Southern touch, dine at the ★ **Southern Inn Restaurant** (37 S. Main St., 540/463-3612, www.southerninn. com, Mon.-Sat. 11:30am-10pm, Sun. 10am-9pm, $8-45). They serve contemporary American food (such as pan-seared sea scallops and roasted duck breast) along with classic American dishes such as meat loaf, rainbow trout, and fried chicken. There is also a good wine list and homemade desserts. The restaurant was established in 1932 but has been updated by the current owners cosmetically, functionally, and with a refreshed menu. A seat at the bar invites a casual evening with locals, as this is a popular place with visitors and residents alike.

Another contemporary American restaurant that is well worth a visit is the **Bistro on Main** (8 N. Main St., 540/464-4888, www. bistro-lexington.com, Tues.-Sat. 11:30am-2:30pm and 5pm-9pm, Sun. 11am-2pm, $8-32), which has a great little bar and serves creative dishes with a variety of influences. Try the shrimp and grits, duck breast with blackberry sauce, or jambalaya; each dish is different, yet delicious. Their brunch menu is also good (a personal favorite is the smoked salmon omelet paired with a Bloody Mary). The atmosphere is comfortable, intimate, and has an upscale feel to it, yet the food is reasonably priced. There is a plate charge for split dishes.

A favorite farm-to-table restaurant right in town is the **The Red Hen** (11 E. Washington St., 540/464-4401, www. redhenlex.com, Tues.-Sat. 5pm-9pm, $24-35). This cozy little restaurant in a little red house serves imaginative, well-planned entrées that have great flavor combinations. The menu changes daily depending on what produce and meat are fresh. Whether it is local steak or fresh beet risotto, there is always something new to try. The wine list is also carefully picked to pair well with the current menu, and they focus on serving natural wines that come from vineyards using organic growing methods. At the time of writing, they charged a $45 reservation fee per person. It's credited to your dining bill, but it's a bit odd.

ACCOMMODATIONS

Lexington is known for its lovely bed-and-breakfasts and inns. There are dozens of them in and around the town. Some offer visitors a piece of history, some offer stunning landscape views, and some offer both. Although there are more than 1,500 rooms to rent, these can fill up quickly when there's an event going on in town or at the area's universities. It is best to book a room as early as possible if you know you'll be competing with many other out-of-town guests.

$100-200

While you explore Lexington, **A Bed and Breakfast at Llewellyn Lodge** (603 S. Main St., 540/463-3235, www.llodge.com, $120-259) is a great place to get spoiled. They offer six guest rooms with private bathrooms, high-speed Internet, and air-conditioning in a charming gray-brick colonial home. The lodge is in a residential area of Lexington, just a short walk from shops, restaurants, and attractions. The innkeepers are experts in hospitality and serve a delicious full breakfast (from a menu). They are also experts on the Lexington area and eager to share their knowledge.

An ecofriendly bed-and-breakfast is the **Applewood Inn & Llama Trekking** (242 Tarn Beck Ln., 540/463-1962, www. applewoodbb.com, $169-255). They offer "green" lodging in a three-story passive-solar home built in 1979. The inn is south of town, at the end of a dirt road in a private setting on 37 acres. They have three lovely rooms with wood floors and private bathrooms, as well as a two-bedroom cottage. One room comes with a private hot tub. Guests can use the pool and kitchen. The inn also offers guided llama trekking, which can be arranged at the house. Treks last about two hours.

The **Comfort Inn Virginia Horse Center** (62 Comfort Way, 540/463-7311, www.choicehotels.com, $89-152) offers clean, comfortable rooms at a good value near the Virginia Horse Center. They have 80 guest rooms, a small heated indoor pool, a sundeck, and a picnic area for guest use.

$200-300

The ★ **Brierley Hill Bed and Breakfast** (985 Borden Rd., 540/464-8421, www. brierleyhill.com, $159-425) offers six guest rooms/suites and two cottages, all with private bathrooms. The inn was built in 1993 specifically as a bed-and-breakfast and was named after the antique clock that hangs in the foyer. Located just outside Lexington, the B&B has wonderful views of the Shenandoah Valley landscape, and the house is meticulously maintained. They serve wonderful gourmet breakfasts and afternoon cookies and lemonade, and the staff is very friendly.

The **Hampton Inn Lexington— Historic District** (401 E. Nelson St., 540/463-2223, www.hamptoninn3.hilton.com, $144-269) is an unusual chain hotel that is in part a historic manor house called the Col Alto Mansion. There are 10 rooms in the restored manor house and 76 hotel rooms. The hotel sits on seven acres and is within walking distance of many attractions in downtown Lexington. The grounds are nicely kept, and there are beautiful old trees on the property. There is a fitness center and outdoor pool for guest use, free high-speed Internet, and free breakfast.

CAMPING

Lake Robertson Park (106 Lake Robertson Dr., 540/463-4164, www.co.rockbridge.va.us, $30-35) offers 53 tent and full hookup camping sites. The 581-acre park has a lake, boat rentals, tennis courts, a swimming pool, a picnic pavilion, and hiking trails. Pets are welcome, and there is a laundry facility on-site.

Lee Hi Campground (2516 N. Lee Hwy., 540/463-3478, www.leehi.com, $15-35) has 15 tent sites and 50 full hookup sites, a bathhouse, restaurant, playground, laundry facility, and a dump station. Pets are welcome.

The **Virginia Horse Center** (487 Maury River Rd., 540/464-2950, $25-40) also offers camping. They have more than 90 campsites with hookups and four campgrounds.

INFORMATION AND SERVICES

Lexington has a great **Visitors Center** (106 E. Washington St., 540/463-3777, www.lexingtonvirginia.com, daily 9am-5pm). They provide an information video, a small museum, and very helpful employees.

GETTING THERE AND AROUND

Lexington is in central Virginia off I-81 and I-64, 185 miles southwest of Washington DC, approximately 55 miles east of the West Virginia border, and 50 miles north of Roanoke. There is no direct air or rail service to Lexington.

Lynchburg

Lynchburg is a city of 50 square miles in the foothills of the Blue Ridge Mountains and along the James River. It sits near the geographic center of Virginia.

Lynchburg was settled in 1757 when 17-year-old John Lynch began a ferry service across the James River to a 45-acre parcel of land he owned. In 1786, he was granted a charter for the town, and in 1805 Lynchburg was incorporated.

Early Lynchburg relied on tobacco and iron as its primary sources of revenue. Due in part to Lynch's ferry system, the town became one of the largest tobacco markets in the country. During the Civil War, Lynchburg was a major storage depot and burial spot for soldiers. Many Confederate generals were laid to rest here. Lynchburg was the sole major city in Virginia that was not overtaken by the Union during the Civil War.

Lynchburg is nicknamed the "City of Seven Hills," and each hill has a historical reference behind its name, including Franklin Hill, which was probably named after Ben Franklin, and College Hill, which was named after a military college that existed prior to the Civil War.

Lynchburg is also known as the core of Virginia's conservative religious community and is sometimes referred to as the "Buckle in the Bible Belt." Jerry Falwell's Liberty University is here, as are more than 130 places of worship. As such, many businesses (including restaurants) are closed on Sunday. The city is also considered to have a strong network of safe neighborhoods and good schools, and its residents enjoy a high quality of life.

SIGHTS
Historic Districts

Lynchburg has five historic districts. **Court House Hill** overlooks the James River and downtown Lynchburg. The main street, Court Street, is home to the historic **City Court House,** a Greek Revival building that is the main attraction in this small district. Many churches with distinctive steeples also line the street, which is otherwise a mix of government and private offices. **Daniel's Hill** is a linear district that contains high-traffic Cabell Street. The area was developed for residential use in the 1840s and overlooks the James River and Blackwater Creek.

The most diverse historical district is **Diamond Hill.** This 14-block area contains a large variety of architectural styles including Georgian revival and colonial revival homes. The district is bounded by steep hills and the Lynchburg Expressway. Major streets in the district include Washington Street, Church Street, Harrison Street, and Grace Street. Diamond Hill is the largest historic district and encompasses more than 100 historic structures. Most of the homes were built during the late 19th and early 20th century. The area is well maintained, and extensive renovations are apparent throughout its streets.

Federal Hill offers views toward downtown. The primary street is Federal Street. Many houses in the district were constructed in the 1820s, and the area is known for the fine craftsmanship of its buildings. Many of the homes in the district face maintenance issues but retain most of their original character.

One of the best-preserved neighborhoods in Lynchburg is the historic **Garland Hill** district. The district begins off 5th Street and runs along tree-lined Madison Street to its end overlooking Blackwater Creek and includes Harrison and Clay Streets. The neighborhood was built between the early 19th century and the early 20th century and includes architectural styles such as Gothic Revival, Victorian, and Queen Anne. The area was home to many distinguished residents who worked in the tobacco industry.

Lynchburg

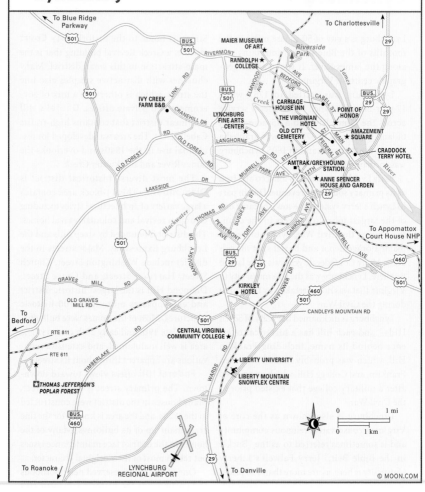

Amazement Square

Amazement Square (27 9th St., 434/845-1888, www.amazementsquare.org, Tues.-Sat. 10am-5pm, Sun. 1pm-5pm, $10.75, seniors 60 and over $7.75) is a hands-on museum for children with a happy atmosphere. It is the first multidisciplinary, interactive children's museum to be established in Central Virginia, and it has set a high standard. Kids make their way through four floors of exciting exhibits where they can climb, slide, and participate in a variety of programs and activities on the topics of art, the humanities, science, and health. Allow at least two hours to explore the museum. The staff is excellent.

Old City Cemetery

A fascinating historical spot in Lynchburg is the **Old City Cemetery** (401 Taylor St., 434/847-1465, www.gravegarden.org, daily dawn to dusk, free). It is the oldest public cemetery in Virginia that is still in use, and it has an estimated 20,000 "residents." Civil War notables, artists, inventors, civil servants—all are buried here, including 2,200 Confederate graves. A stroll through the grounds is a history lesson and a look at a who's who of Lynchburg. There are five small free museums on-site that interpret the history of the area, the city, and the cemetery itself. Four are designed for self-guided tours and can be viewed whenever the cemetery gates are open. The fifth, the **Mourning Museum,** is inside the Cemetery Center, a visitors center for the cemetery (Mon.-Sat. 10am-3pm). A scatter garden for human and pet ashes and a rose garden are also in the cemetery. A looped trail beginning at Taylor and 4th Streets takes visitors around the plots. Guided tours are available for a small fee and are by appointment only.

Point of Honor

Perched on a hill overlooking the James River is **Point of Honor** (112 Cabell St., 434/455-6226, www.pointofhonor.org, Mon.-Sat. 10am-4pm, Sun. noon-4pm, adults $6, children 6-17 $3, college students $4, seniors over 60 $5, under 6 free), a gorgeous Federal-style mansion. The home was built in 1815 and has been meticulously restored. It is not certain how it got its name, but there are two theories.

The first is that duels were fought here for honor, as was the custom in centuries past; the second theorizes that the name refers to the prominent point of land the home sits on looking out on the James River. The **Diggs Gallery** inside the home provides an orientation video and rotating exhibits. House tours are given daily and last 45 minutes.

Maier Museum of Art

A few blocks away from Point of Honor is the **Maier Museum of Art** (1 Quinlan St., 434/947-8136, www.maiermuseum.org, academic year schedule Tues.-Sun. 1pm-5pm, May-Aug. Wed.-Sun. 1pm-5pm, free, donations appreciated). This nationally recognized art museum at Randolph College features works by 19th to 21st-century American artists. The museum's permanent collection includes thousands of paintings, photographs, and drawings, with a focus on American impressionism and early 20th-century realism. They have a large collection of works by visionary modernist Arthur B. Davies and painter, printmaker, and photographer Ben Shahn. Special exhibits and programs are offered year-round as well as internships and class visits. The museum is located on campus, behind the athletic fields, and offers a

Point of Honor

great opportunity to see an amazing collection of artwork without the crowds.

Anne Spencer House and Garden

The **Anne Spencer House and Garden** (1313 Pierce St., 434/845-1313, www.annespencermuseum.com, adult tours $15, college students $5, children under 12 $3, seniors $10) is a two-story Queen Anne-style home that once belonged to poet Anne Spencer (1882-1975). Spencer's work is considered to be part of the Harlem Renaissance, and she wrote of love and beauty. While living in the home, the author entertained many famous guests, such as Martin Luther King Jr., Thurgood Marshall, and George Washington Carver. The gardens are open daily from dawn to dusk, and visitors can pick up a brochure at the garden cottage. There is no fee to visit the garden. Tours of the house are by appointment only and must be scheduled at least two weeks in advance. The house is closed November-March.

Lynchburg Museum

The **Lynchburg Museum** (901 Court St., 434/455-6226, www.lynchburgmuseum.org, Mon.-Sat. 10am-4pm, Sun. noon-4pm, free) is located in the old courthouse downtown. It relays a historical timeline of the people of Lynchburg in the main Court Room Gallery, more than 10,000 photos, an exhibit on African American education in Lynchburg, an exhibit on the courthouse itself, and two rotating exhibits.

Appomattox Court House National Historical Park

Twenty-two miles east of Lynchburg is **Appomattox Court House National Historical Park** (113 National Park Dr., 434/352-8987, ext. 226, www.nps.gov/apco, daily 9am-5pm, free). The park is the site of General Lee's surrender at the close of the Civil War on April 9, 1865. The park consists of numerous historic structures in the village of Appomattox and sits on 1,700 acres.

Begin your exploration at the visitors center, a reconstructed courthouse building that also serves as a museum offering exhibits that include artifacts from the surrender (including surrender documents and a pencil used by General Lee). The three-story **McLean House-Surrender Site** is the reconstructed house where the actual surrender took place approximately 150 yards west of the visitors center. The parlor inside the house, where the surrender meeting occurred, is furnished with both original and reproduced items. Park ranger interpretation is offered daily at the house, and tours are offered seasonally on the hour. Several outbuildings are also open to visitors, including the kitchen, outhouse, and slave quarters. Living-history programs are offered daily during the summer and feature historical interpretations from the 1860s.

Walton's Mountain Museum

Die-hard fans of *The Waltons* television series will enjoy the **Walton's Mountain Museum** (6484 Rockfish River Rd., Schuyler, 434/831-2000, www.walton-mountain.org, daily 10am-3:30pm, $10, under 5 free), 50 miles northeast of Lynchburg in Schuyler. See the childhood home of Earl Hamner (creator of *The Waltons*) and replicas of John Boy's bedroom, Ike Godsey's Store, the Waltons' kitchen, and the Waltons' living room. There's a good 30-minute video featuring Earl Hamner and stars of the television show.

RECREATION

Ski enthusiasts can indulge year-round at the **Liberty Mountain Snowflex Center** (4000 Candlers Mountain Rd., 434/582-3539, www.liberty.edu, skiing and snowboarding $8 per hour, tubing $13 per hour). This unusual ski complex opened on the campus of Liberty University six miles south of Lynchburg in 2009 as the first facility in the United States to offer skiing and snowboarding on simulated snow. The 5,000-acre mountain has a bunny slope, intermediate and advanced slopes, and even a freestyle park. A tubing chute and ski lodge complete the simulated ski experience.

Rental equipment is available ($14). They also offer an Olympic trampoline ($5).

Liberty Mountain also offers 50 miles of trails for mountain biking, hiking, and running. Trails are open to the public daily dawn to dusk. Visit www.liberty.edu for trail maps. Another popular, well-marked trail is the **James River Heritage Trail,** a 9.5-mile trail combining two smaller trails, the **Blackwater Creek Trail & Bikeway** and the **RiverWalk Trail** (www.lynchburgparksandrec.com). The trail passes through downtown Lynchburg and also lush forest areas. The RiverWalk section is one of the most popular. Its 3.5 miles of paved trail begin on Jefferson Street and run east along the waterfront. To reach the Blackwater Creek Bikeway trailhead, take US 501 north from the Lynchburg Expressway. Turn right onto Old Langthore Road. The trailhead is on the right.

A favorite park in Lynchburg, **Riverside Park** (2238 Rivermont Ave., 434/455-5858, www.lynchburgparksandrec.com) offers more than 49 acres of recreation area with views of the James River. Walking trails, tennis, basketball, a large playground, and a seasonal "sprayground" are some of the main attractions. There is also a transportation exhibit that features a train locomotive, tender, and caboose.

The **James River Canoe Ramp** (7th St.) is a good place to launch hand-carried watercraft on the James River. It is located at the end of the 7th Street.

Running and cycling are popular in Lynchburg, and there are many local races and events throughout the year. For a rundown, visit www.localraces.com.

ENTERTAINMENT AND EVENTS

Options for live entertainment are less than abundant in Lynchburg. The **Academy of Fine Arts** (600 Main St., 434/846-8499, www.academycenter.org) offers live music, classes, and theatrical events. They have a list of their venues and upcoming events on their website. Live music can be found on most weekends

at **Phase 2 Dining & Entertainment** (4009 Murray Pl., 434/846-3206, www.phase2club.com). They offer a restaurant, concert hall, and banquet facilities. Concerts feature mostly country and rock. At the time of writing, the venue was for sale. The **Lynchburg Symphony Orchestra** (621 Court St., 434/845-6604, www.lynchburgsymphony.org) offers performances in a variety of locations in Lynchburg.

FOOD
American

You may not associate shoes with food, but at ★ **Shoemakers American Grille** (1312 Commerce St., 434/455-1510, www.shoemakersdining.com, Mon.-Sat. 5pm-9:30pm, $9-37) shoes are part of the history. The restaurant is housed in a building that used to be home to the largest shoe manufacturer in the country. The exposed brick is a nod to the building's factory roots, while the interior decor is modern and welcoming. The taste-bud-pleasing menu includes a wide variety of salads, steak, seafood, yummy sides (such as smoked gouda mac & cheese) and scrumptious desserts (try the Shoemaker's Candy Bar). They also have an extensive wine list. The restaurant is the perfect place for a date or to relax with friends. The atmosphere is lively and comfortable, and the service is some of the best in town. There's an outdoor patio that is perfect when the weather is nice.

The **Main Street Eatery & Catering Co.** (907 Main St., 434/847-2526, www.mainsteatery.com, Mon.-Sat. 4:30pm-9:30pm, $9-28) serves a delicious menu of seafood, pasta, beef, veal, and poultry. The menu isn't large, but they rotate offerings seasonally so there's always something new. In addition, each item is uniquely prepared with flavorful touches, and the wine and drink menus are extensive. Don't skip the dessert tray; it will tempt you even if you think you're full. Exposed brick and hardwood floors make a cozy atmosphere, and the owner frequently visits tables to check on his customers.

The sister eatery to the Texas Tavern

in Roanoke, the **Texas Inn** (422 Main St., 434/846-3823, www.texasinn.com, Mon.-Wed. 5am-midnight, Thurs.-Sat. 24 hours, Sun. closed, $1-8), also called "The T Room," is the oldest dining establishment in Virginia. It opened in 1935 and is a local icon that stays open late, is cheap, and serves greasy food. Grab a spot at the counter (it's your only choice for seating) and order the Cheesy Western. This signature dish is a hamburger with cheese and a fried egg topped with a delicious secret mustard relish. The chili is also legendary. Not a date place, not a business place, but a sacred institution nonetheless. There's a second location in Lynchburg at 110 Cornerstone Street.

Asian

Kings Island Restaurant (2804 Old Forest Rd., 434/384-0066, www.kingsislandrestaurant.com, Mon.-Thurs. 11:15am-10pm, Fri. 11:15am-10:45pm, Sat. 4:15pm-10:45pm, Sun. 11:15am-10pm, $8-28) is your best bet for Chinese and Japanese food in Lynchburg. It is also the oldest Chinese restaurant in town, first serving customers in 1977. The food is good, with the typical menu items for American Chinese restaurants, and the sushi is a step above. They earn extra points for the atmosphere, which is quiet and cozy without being dark and drab. The food is reasonably priced, and the service is excellent.

Italian

A great choice for pizza is **Waterstone Fire Roasted Pizza** (1309 Jefferson St., 434/455-1515, www.waterstonepizza.com, Mon.-Thurs. 11am-10pm, Fri.-Sat. 11am-11pm, Sun. 11am-9pm, $8-17). This popular pizza joint opened in 2010 and has a loyal following. Natural ingredients and wonderful flavor are the keys to their mouthwatering pizzas. They also have a brewery on-site. If you're lucky to go on a nice day or evening, grab a seat on the patio. The neighboring historic buildings offer a pleasant backdrop and make for an inviting atmosphere.

Mexican

Good Mexican food can be found at **La Carreta** (www.lacarretaonline.com, $7-14), a local chain that has seven locations within a 10-mile radius of Lynchburg. They serve flavorful, authentic fare at a very reasonable price. The salsa is fresh and delicious, and the beer is served in frosted mugs. This is a great place to bring a group, and it has a loyal local following. Consult their website for the most convenient location and hours.

ACCOMMODATIONS
$100-200

The ★ **Craddock Terry Hotel** (1312 Commerce St., 434/455-1500, www.craddockterryhotel.com, $138-197) may well be a first: This trendy boutique hotel is a converted turn-of-the-20th-century shoe factory. The large red lady's shoe out in front of the brick building might give that away, but the interior is far from its factory roots. The renovated space now offers 44 large modern rooms and suites with high ceilings, large windows, comfortable beds, luxurious bathrooms, and ecofriendly bath products. Views from the rooms include downtown, the James River, and the Blue Ridge Mountains. The decor is contemporary, with many historical artifacts from the Craddock-Terry Shoe Corporation and modern shoe-themed accents. They offer complimentary amenities such as parking, overnight shoeshine service, sedan service to the airport and Amtrak station, and high-speed Internet. Complimentary continental breakfast also arrives at your room each morning in a wooden shoeshine box. There are two restaurants, a fitness room, Tesla charging station, and business center on-site. The resident hotel dog, a wirehaired fox terrier, is named Penny Loafer, and guest pets are also welcome ($50).

The **Kirkley Hotel** (2900 Candlers Mountain Rd., 434/237-6333, www.kirkleyhotel.com, $102-149) is a reasonably priced hotel with many recent renovations. They have 168 rooms and suites with free wireless Internet, free parking and airport shuttle, comfortable beds, complimentary hot breakfast, indoor pool, fitness center, and business center. Suites have dining rooms, wet bars, and living rooms. This is a Wyndham hotel.

$200-300

A lovely bed-and-breakfast is the **Carriage House Inn** (404 Cabell St., 434/846-1388, www.thecarriagehouseinnbandb.com, $189-209) in the Daniel's Hill Historic District. This six-guest-room bed-and-breakfast offers comfortable accommodations in a beautifully renovated 1878 Italianate mansion featuring a grand spiral staircase and many original details such as molding, woodwork, and fixtures. The Carriage House Inn was the first lodging facility in Lynchburg to earn a "green" certification. Rooms are spacious with high ceilings, and the house has a nice porch with rocking chairs. Hiking and biking trails are just six blocks away. The entrance to the bed-and-breakfast is easy to miss from the road, so look carefully for the sign.

★ **The Virginian Lynchburg** (712 Church St., 434/329-3200, www.curiocollection3.hilton.com, $184-675) is an upscale and stately downtown hotel that is part of Hilton's Curio Collection. The building was erected in 1913 and has been beautifully restored. The hotel offers 115 large, modern, comfortable rooms/suites with free wireless Internet and a fitness center. The staff is friendly and helpful throughout. The hotel features a coffee shop and a rooftop restaurant and bar with great views. Self-parking and valet parking are available for $10. This is an excellent choice with a great location downtown.

INFORMATION AND SERVICES

The **Lynchburg Visitors Information Center** (216 12th St., 434/485-7290, www.discoverlynchburg.org, Mon.-Sat. 10am-4pm, Sun. noon-4pm) is a great additional resource for information and services in the city.

GETTING THERE

Lynchburg is 180 miles from Washington DC. **Lynchburg Regional Airport** (LYH) (350 Terminal Dr., no. 100, 434/455-6090, www.lynchburgva.gov) is a small, city-owned airport located about five miles southwest of downtown Lynchburg. The airport has a dozen arriving and departing flights a day through the regional carrier American Eagle.

Carriage House Inn

Rental cars are available on-site, and there is free wireless Internet.

Train service runs to the **Amtrak** station (825 Kemper St., 800/872-7245, www.amtrak. com). **Greyhound** (800/231-2222, www. greyhound.com) bus service is also available in the same location.

Local bus service is provided by the **Greater Lynchburg Transit Company** (434/455-5080, www.gltconline.com, $2), with 37 buses traveling 14 routes Monday-Saturday.

Roanoke

Roanoke is the largest city in southwest Virginia. It sits in the picturesque Roanoke Valley and is bisected by the Roanoke River. The history of Roanoke dates back to the 1740s, when the area near natural salt marshes in the center of the valley was first settled. The marshes were called "licks" and served as gathering places for deer, elk, and buffalo. The first village was known as Big Lick.

When the Shenandoah Valley Railroad came to the area, Big Lick was renamed Roanoke, and in the late 1800s Roanoke became a crossroads for the railroad. This spurred the city's growth. A market opened not long after and remains the cornerstone of downtown commerce. Roanoke is now southwest Virginia's thriving center for transportation, manufacturing, trade, and entertainment.

Roanoke is known to offer residents a good quality of life. It is metropolitan, yet has a less stressful pace than many other cities. There is a vibrant downtown area with culture and business, and Roanoke has the largest airport in southwestern Virginia. Roanoke is also easily accessible via I-81.

SIGHTS

★ Taubman Museum of Art
The **Taubman Museum of Art** (110 Salem Ave. SE, 540/342-5760, www. taubmanmuseum.org, Wed.-Sat. 10am-5pm, Sun. noon-5pm, first Fri. of each month 10am-9pm, free) attracts visitors with its shiny, modern building that opened in 2008 on Salem Avenue. Between 100,000 and 130,000 people visit the museum each year to take in exhibits on subjects such as art, crafts, dance, sculpture, graphic arts, photography, poetry, and film. The museum has 2,400 items in its permanent collection. Exhibits reflect cultural traditions throughout America as well as of a global nature, but also feature local culture from the Roanoke Valley and southern Virginia. There is an arts center at the museum called **Art Venture** ($5), where children and their families can create their own art and learn different artistic techniques. This hands-on gallery offers painting, drawing, theater, sculpture, music, and more. Exhibits change at the museum every six to eight weeks, so there is always something new to experience. The museum houses a store that showcases merchandise related to current exhibits and regional crafts and gifts from around the globe.

Virginia Museum of Transportation
The **Virginia Museum of Transportation** (303 Norfolk Ave. SW, Roanoke, 540/342-5670, www.vmt.org, Mon.-Sat. 10am-5pm, Sun. 1pm-5pm, adults $10, youth 13-18, students with ID, and seniors 60 and over $8, children 3-12 $6, under 3 free) is a unique, mostly outdoor museum featuring more than 50 exhibits. It provides a wonderful overview of the extensive railway heritage in Virginia and is best known for its exhibits on the Norfolk & Western Class J-611 and Class A-1218 modern steam locomotives. The museum's road exhibits take visitors through the history of road transportation starting

Downtown Roanoke

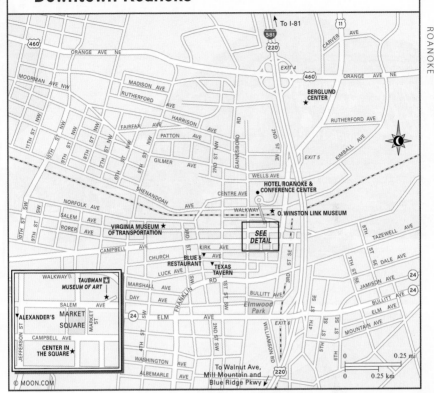

© MOON.COM

with the horse and buggy and ending with modern-day cars and trucks. Air exhibits discuss early aviation, commercial aviation, military aviation, and airports. The museum also features model trains and a gift shop.

Mill Mountain Star and Park

The **Mill Mountain Star and Park** (210 Reserve Ave., 540/853-2236) is famous for its huge illuminated star that sits on top of Mill Mountain. Roanoke is nicknamed "the Star City of the South," which was the inspiration for the construction of the massive star erected in 1949. It is the largest man-made illuminated star in the world. It is 88.5 feet tall and lit by 2,000 feet of neon tubes channeling 17,500 watts of power. The star is lit each evening, but is turned off at midnight.

O. Winston Link Museum

The **O. Winston Link Museum** (101 Shenandoah Ave., 540/982-5465, www.roanokehistory.org, Tues.-Sat. 10am-5pm, adults $6, children $5, seniors, students, and military $5.50) houses the largest exhibit of O. Winston Link's famous photographs depicting life in the 1950s along the railroad in Virginia. Even people who don't know anything about railroads can appreciate the talent of this photographer and the era that is represented in the museum. Each photograph captures a story, and many are accompanied by articles that appeared in a large variety of magazines and textbooks. The museum is housed in a restored historic passenger train station and shares space with the **Museum**

of Western Virginia, which features exhibits that share the history of western Virginia.

Center in the Square

In the southwest corner of Market Square (a historic market at the intersection of Campbell Avenue and Market Street) is a five-story cultural center called **Center in the Square** (1 Market Sq., 540/342-5700, www.centerinthesquare.org). The center opened in 1983 as the cornerstone of a redevelopment program in an urban area that was once facing economic decline. Several organizations focused on arts and science now call the center home: the **Science Museum of Western Virginia** (540/342-5710, www. smwv.org), **Harrison Museum of African American Culture** (540/857-4395, www. harrisonmuseum.com), **Mill Mountain Theatre** (540/342-5740, www.millmountain. org), and the **Roanoke Pinball Museum** (540/342-5746, www.roanokepinball.org). Visitors can now enjoy a thriving cultural community in the square and also visit private stores and restaurants. The most famous, perhaps, is the **Roanoke Weiner Stand,** which opened just after the original Center in the Square building (first called the McGuire Building) opened in 1915 and is a city landmark. As the name suggests, they serve outrageously good hot dogs and have a huge local following.

RECREATION

Outdoor recreation is a favorite pastime in Roanoke. Whether your preferred mode of transport is by mountain bike or foot, the Roanoke area has more than 600 miles of trails to explore. **Virginia's Explore Park** (mp 115, Blue Ridge Pkwy., 540/427-1800, www.explorepark.org) is about a 10-minute drive from downtown Roanoke on the Blue Ridge Parkway. This 1,200-acre park has nine miles of mountain bike trails, a one-mile interpretive trail, fishing, canoeing, and kayaking.

Hikers can enjoy numerous trails near Roanoke and even explore parts of the **Appalachian Trail.** One of the most famous trails, the **McAfee Knob Hike** (www. visitroanokeva.com), is a challenging 8.8-mile round-trip hike that offers stunning views of the Catawba Valley and more than 1,700 feet of climbing (allow four hours). McAfee Knob itself, a large rocky outcrop, is one of the most photographed areas on the Appalachian Trail. To access the trail, take I-81 south from Roanoke to exit 141. Turn left at the light onto State Route 419 (Electric Rd.) and continue for less than a mile. Take State Route 311 north for 5.6 miles up the mountain. The trailhead parking lot is at the top of the mountain on the left. A great ending to this hike includes a stop at **The Homeplace Restaurant** (4968 Catawba Valley Dr., 540/384-7252) for dinner. To get there, continue north on State Route 311 for one mile to a large white farmhouse.

Another well-known local trail is **Dragon's Tooth** (www.roanokeoutside. com). This difficult, 4.5-mile out-and-back hike travels to its namesake geological feature, a collection of large Tuscarora quartzite spires that jut out of the top of Cove Mountain, the tallest being 35 feet. The Dragon's Tooth summit rewards hikers with great views year-round. The parking lot is about 20 minutes south of downtown Roanoke. Take I-81 south to exit 141. Turn left on State Route 419 (Electric Rd.) and then turn right on State Route 311. Continue for 10 miles to the Dragon's Tooth parking lot on the left.

Baseball fans will want to take in a **Salem Red Sox** (1004 Texas St., Salem, 540/389-3333, www.milb.com) home game in nearby Salem. This minor league baseball team is a Class A farm team for the Boston Red Sox. Virginia Tech fans can cheer on the Hokies just 45 minutes south of Roanoke in Blacksburg.

ENTERTAINMENT AND EVENTS

There's always something going on at the **Berglund Center** (710 Williamson Rd., 540/853-2241, www.theberglundcenter.com),

1: Roanoke 2: Taubman Museum of Art

Getaway to Smith Mountain Lake

Smith Mountain Lake is the perfect mountain lake retreat and a favorite among Virginians. This is where the movie *What About Bob?* starring Richard Dreyfuss and Bill Murray was filmed, and it was also featured in the independent film *Lake Effects* in 2012.

Smith Mountain Lake is the largest artificial lake in Virginia; it covers 32 square miles and has 500 miles of shoreline. The average depth of the lake is 55 feet. The lake itself was created in the early 1960s when the Roanoke River was dammed at Smith Mountain Gap. It is equidistant from Lynchburg and Roanoke (about an hour's drive) and is a four-hour drive from Washington DC.

The community of Smith Mountain Lake has approximately 22,000 residents, but the area is a popular destination for vacationers. Residential growth was slow during the initial decades after the lake was created but has been increasing steadily since the mid-1980s. Upscale residences, condominiums, and golf course communities are the norm now, and commuters from Roanoke and Lynchburg also make their homes in the community. Retirees from Northern Virginia are part of the latest growth trend at Smith Mountain Lake, and the influx of new residents has contributed to recent retail and commercial development in the community.

State Route 122 is the only highway that crosses the lake. The area is accessed by State Routes 24, 116, and 40.

Smith Mountain Lake State Park (1235 State Park Rd., Huddleston, 540/297-6066, www.dcr.virginia.gov, daily 8:15am-dusk, $7/vehicle) provides a beach and public swimming on the lake, and there are a handful of public golf courses.

In addition to beautiful scenery and endless opportunities for outdoor recreation in the form of boating, biking, hiking, swimming, and fishing, Smith Mountain Lake offers shopping, antiquing, art, entertainment, and wonderful dining.

There are several marinas on Smith Mountain Lake, including **Parkway Marina** (16918 Smith Mountain Lake Pkwy., 540/297-4412, www.parkwaymarina.com), **Bridgewater Marina** (16410 BT Washington Hwy., 540/721-1639, www.bwmarina.com), and **Mitchells Point Marina** (3553 Trading Post Rd., 540/484-3980, www.mitchellspoint.com).

Vacation rentals can be booked through **Smith Mountain Lake Vacation Rentals** (877/773-2452, www.smithmountainlakerentals.com) and **Smith Mountain Lake Properties** (540/797-0477, www.smithmountainlakeproperties.org). For additional information on Smith Mountain Lake, visit www.smithmountainlake.com.

---

formerly known as the Roanoke Civic Center. This is the premier venue for concerts, ice hockey, expos, and even public ice-skating. For a more intimate setting, take in a performance at the **Jefferson Center** (541 Luck Ave., 540/345-2550, www.jeffcenter.org), a historic venue that hosts classical and contemporary performances.

The **Roanoke Festival in the Park** (www.roanokefestival.com) is the premier festival in Roanoke. It takes place annually over Memorial Day weekend and spans four days of art, music, and nightly concerts. Daytime events are free, but tickets are required for nighttime concerts ($15).

The **Salem Fair** (www.salemfair.com), in nearby Salem, is the largest fair in Virginia

and features 10 days of rides, demos, and events that draw around 350,000 people. It takes place in early July. There is no admission fee.

The **Anthem GO Outside Festival** (www.roanokegofest.com) is a free festival that takes place over three days in October at the **Rivers Edge Sports Complex** (210 Reserve Ave.) and features approximately 125 outdoor events and activities with camping, music, competitions, and demos.

SHOPPING

The heart of downtown Roanoke is **Market Square** (213 Market St., 540/342-2028), where the **Historic Roanoke Street Market** first opened in 1882. It is the oldest continuously running open-air market in Virginia. It now has 40 permanent tables displaying an incredible selection of local fruits, vegetables, plants, meat, and handcrafted merchandise. The market is open year-round, its tables covered in festive white and yellow awnings. One vendor, Martin's Farm, has been a part of the market since 1905.

FOOD
American

For a special occasion, a celebration at ★ **The Regency Room** in the Hotel Roanoke & Conference Center (110 Shenandoah Ave., 540/985-5900, www.hotelroanoke.com, Mon.-Fri. 6:30am-10:30am, 11:30am-2pm, and 6pm-9pm, Sat.-Sun. 7am-10:30am, 11:30am-2pm, and 6pm-9pm, $22-45) can help make the evening memorable. This first-class restaurant first opened in 1938 and offers the same candlelit ambience as it did so many decades ago. White tablecloths, heavy drapery, and a baby grand piano give the dining room a cozy, upscale feel. The menu is simple and elegant, offering classics such as steak and lobster for entrées, but traditional Virginia menu items such as peanut soup, spoon bread, and bread pudding are also featured. They also offer a sensational crab cake with a Virginia twist: It is served with a corn-and-leek puree. The restaurant holds 150 people comfortably, and the tables are nicely spaced so you don't hear the conversation next door. Reservations are recommended.

The cosmopolitan atmosphere at **Alexander's** (105 S. Jefferson St., 540/982-6983, www.alexandersva.com, Wed. 11am-2pm, Tues.-Thurs. 5pm-9pm, Fri.-Sat. 5pm-10pm, $31-50) is unique in Roanoke, and the contemporary menu will impress most die-hard foodies. This intimate restaurant uses many ingredients from its own farm and gradually changes the menu with the growing season. Their seafood, steak, lamb, duck, and other entrées are masterfully prepared, and the staff is polite and knowledgeable. The wine list is impressive. Even the vases on their tables are filled with flowers and herbs from their own garden. Small plates, wine, and cocktails are served Tuesday-Saturday at 4pm.

This author first discovered ★ **The Homeplace Restaurant** (4968 Catawba Valley Dr., Catawba, 540/384-7252, Thurs.-Fri. 4pm-8pm, Sat. 3pm-8pm, Sun. 11am-6pm, $15 for two meats, $16 for three, $3 extra for dessert) as a poor student at Virginia Tech. Groups of students would make a pilgrimage of sorts to seek out home-cooked meals sorely missed while living in student housing. The Homeplace is just as it sounds: a great place to dine on wonderful food like you would expect to be served at grandma's house and for a very reasonable price. The restaurant is even inside a beautiful old house on a large property. A set menu of classic Virginia fare is brought out to the entire table, family-style. There is roast beef or country ham, fried chicken, mashed potatoes, gravy, green beans, fresh biscuits, coleslaw, and cobbler for dessert. The best part is, the food keeps coming until you swear your pants will split. This place is an institution in the Roanoke area, but not just for students; friends, family, and even hikers detouring from the Appalachian Trail come together at this comfortable restaurant to share an old-fashioned home-cooked meal. The Homeplace is 16 miles northwest of Roanoke.

The **Blue 5 Restaurant** (312 2nd St., 540/904-5338, www.blue5restaurant.com, Tues.-Thurs. 11:30am-midnight, Fri. 11:30am-1am, Sat. 4pm-1am, $17-29) offers good food, craft beer, and live music. It's hard to argue with those offerings, and they do all three well. They serve Southern cuisine (the shrimp creole and grits is over-the-top delicious) and have 46 beers on tap. They offer live music four nights a week.

Pubs and Diners
The **Texas Tavern** (114 W. Church Ave., 540/342-4825, www.texastavern-inc.com, open 24/7, under $5) is the definition of a dive. This tiny tavern opened on Friday, February 13, 1930, and stays that way 24 hours a day every day of the year except for Christmas. This family business serves breakfast, lunch,

and dinner and can seat a handful of people at the bar (there are also shelves by the window if you want to stand). If everyone is very familiar with each other, it might hold 15 people, but more than that would be pretty cozy. One of their slogans is "We seat 1,000 people, 10 at a time."

For a casual sandwich, salad, or burger, visit **Hollywood's Restaurant and Bakery** (7770 Williamson Rd., 540/362-1812, www.hollywoodsrestaurant.com, Mon.-Sat. 11am-10pm, $5-13). They offer a dine-in menu with a large variety of delicious salads and sandwiches served on freshly made bread. They have many vegetarian options and will also prepare tailgate packages when reserved the day before.

ACCOMMODATIONS
$100-200

The **SpringHill Suites Roanoke** (301 Reserve Ave., 540/400-6226, www.marriott.com, $179-239) is less than a mile from downtown Roanoke and has 127 nonsmoking suites. The rooms are large and have flat-screen LCD televisions, refrigerators, microwaves, and wireless Internet. There is a lovely indoor pool and fitness center at the hotel, and they offer complimentary shuttle

service to the airport and to attractions within a 10-mile radius. There is an on-site bar. Breakfast is included.

For a good night's sleep in a historic bed-and-breakfast, book a room at the **King George Inn** (315 King George Ave. SW, 757/657-4034, www.kinggeorgeinnbandb.com, $145-160), a 1900s colonial revival home fully restored and within walking distance of downtown Roanoke. There are four spacious guest suites with private bathrooms, relaxing common areas, and a library. There are no televisions in the rooms. A gourmet breakfast as well as afternoon refreshments are included with all stays. The innkeepers are warm, helpful, and eager to make recommendations for things to do in the area. This establishment does not allow children.

$200-300

The ★ **Hotel Roanoke & Conference Center** (110 Shenandoah Ave., 540/985-5900, www.hotelroanoke.com, $175-408) is the most famous hotel in Roanoke and has been a prime destination since it was built in 1882. The restored historic Tudor hotel was originally supported by the railroad industry as a stop for rail travelers (it was owned by Norfolk and Western), but its popularity as a vacation

Hotel Roanoke & Conference Center

destination has kept it going long after the railroad heyday. As you stroll past the stunning facade, you will walk where numerous celebrities and presidents have trod, including Amelia Earhart and the King himself, Elvis Presley. The hotel is decorated with artifacts that showcase its long history and also American history. Portraits of two famous Virginians, George Washington and Robert E. Lee, adorn the lobby walls. Rooms are traditionally decorated but have modern amenities, and a business center is available to guests. The hotel is listed in the National Register of Historic Places and is part of the International Association of Conference Centers with its 34 meeting rooms and two ballrooms. There are 330 guest rooms and suites, which include many types of accommodations to choose from in a variety of price ranges. They also offer allergy-friendly guest rooms. Self-parking ($10) and valet parking ($16) are available.

The Hotel Roanoke is part of Hilton's Curio Collection. It's convenient to the Roanoke Regional Airport (with a free shuttle) and many local attractions. A walkway connects the hotel to Market Square. There are two restaurants on-site: **The Regency Room** and **The Pine Room.** There's a seasonal outdoor pool on the property and a fitness center. Spa services are also available in your room. The staff is exceptional at this hotel, and there are many fun little touches, such as the weekday-specific carpets in the elevators that say things like "Have a pleasant Friday!"

CAMPING

Visitors can pitch a tent at one of 74 tent sites in the **Roanoke Mountain Campground** (mp 120.4, Blue Ridge Dr., Roanoke, 540/342-3051, www.blueridgecampgrounds.com, $16). Facilities include 30 RV/trailer sites, comfort stations, water, flush toilets, and sinks (no showers).

INFORMATION AND SERVICES

For more information on the Roanoke area, visit www.visitroanokeva.com or stop by the

Roanoke Valley Convention and Visitors Bureau (101 Shenandoah Ave., 540/342-6025, daily 9am-5pm).

GETTING THERE AND AROUND

Roanoke is 56 miles southwest of Lynchburg and 240 miles southwest of Washington DC. The **Roanoke-Blacksburg Regional Airport** (5202 Aviation Dr. NW, 540/362-1999, www.flyroa.com) is the primary regional airport in southwest Virginia. It is 5 miles north of downtown Roanoke. The airport has more than 40 scheduled daily flights and is served by commercial airlines such as American, Delta, and United. Car rentals are available at the airport.

The **Valley Metro** bus service (540/982-2222, www.valleymetro.com, Mon.-Sat. 6am-8:45pm, $1.75) provides bus transportation throughout Roanoke. Its main terminal is at Campbell Court (17 W. Campbell Ave.).

BLACKSBURG

Forty miles southwest of Roanoke near I-81 is Blacksburg, home of **Virginia Polytechnic Institute and State University, or Virginia Tech.** Blacksburg has a population of around 45,000, with approximately 34,000 students in attendance at Virginia Tech. Blacksburg is a cross between a charming mountain town and a technology-driven city. It offers endless outdoor recreation, beautiful scenery, diversity, culture, and opportunity while maintaining a small-town feel.

Blacksburg is known for the Blacksburg Electronic Village (BEV), a Virginia Tech project with the goal of linking the entire town through an online community. The project officially launched in 1993 and was the "first" in many aspects of networking.

Virginia Tech

Virginia Tech (210 Burruss Hall, 540/231-6000, www.vt.edu) was founded in 1872 as an agricultural and mechanical land-grant college and has long had a thriving cadet program. Today, the school is Virginia's leading research institution, with approximately 280 degree programs (both undergraduate and graduate) and a research portfolio over $531 million. One of the powerhouse universities in the state, its campus includes more than 2,600 beautiful acres, 125 buildings, and the enormous Lane Stadium (which seats

more than 65,000). Most of the buildings are neo-Gothic limestone edifices. A large grassy drill field leads up to stately Burruss Hall, the main administration building on campus, which houses a 3,000-plus-seat auditorium where major events and concerts are held.

Danville

Danville was settled in 1793 and sits just a half hour's drive from the North Carolina border. It has a population of around 42,000 and was formerly one of the most important tobacco-auction centers in the country. It also had a thriving textile industry. Glimpses of its economic heyday are evident in several historic districts, including **The Danville Historic District,** where the popular **Millionaires' Row,** on River Park Drive, is located. Millionaires' Row is where those who were prosperous in the tobacco and textile industries resided in the late 19th century, and it has one of the premier collections of both Victorian and Edwardian architecture in the South. Five architecturally significant churches grace its streets and helped Danville earn the nickname "City of Churches."

The **Danville Tobacco Warehouse District** is the prime area for new development. Former tobacco warehouses are now home to new businesses, housing, and nanotechnology research. The focal point of the district is the **Crossing of the Dan** complex, which is a restored railroad station that now houses exhibits for the **Danville Science Center** and a community marketplace. The **Carrington Pavilion** is also there and features summer concerts.

The Dan River is a prominent feature in the city, and along both sides runs the **Dan River Historic District.** A historic canal, original textile factories from the 1880s, and several beautiful arch bridges can be found in the area.

SIGHTS
Danville Museum of Fine Arts & History
The **Danville Museum of Fine Arts & History** (975 Main St., 434/793-5644, www.danvillemuseum.org, Tues.-Sat. 10am-5pm, Sun. 2pm-5pm, adults $10, students age 7-college $4, seniors 62 and over $8, under 7 free) showcases nationally acclaimed and emerging artists, national traveling exhibits, and local and regional artists. The museum is housed in the Italianate Sutherlin Mansion in Millionaires' Row. The home served as the last capitol of the Confederacy for just nine days in April 1865, several weeks before the end of the Civil War. The museum has an impressive collection of Civil War memorabilia, and the history of the mansion itself will be of interest to Civil War buffs.

AAF Tank Museum
Take a trip back in time through the largest private collection of international tank and cavalry artifacts in the world. The **Tank Museum** (3401 US 29 N., 434/836-5323, www.aaftankmuseum.com, Jan.-Mar. Sat. 10am-4pm, Apr.-Dec. Fri.-Sat. 10am-4pm, adults $15, children 5-12 $10, seniors $12, veterans $10, under 4 free) has over 30,000 artifacts and 120 tanks and artillery pieces displayed spanning several hundred years. The museum is housed in a large warehouse, and the tanks are displayed on mini sets, complete with sand, woods, rice paddies, and plastic human figures. Additional items on display include helmets, guns, uniforms, and many

Danville

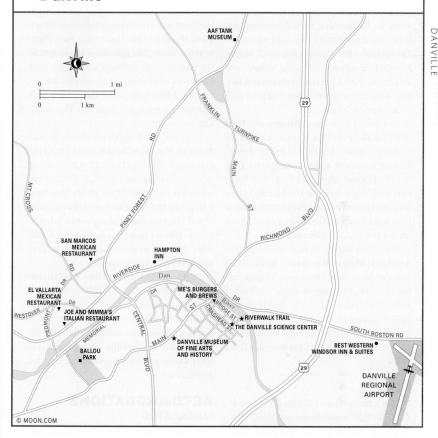

AAF TANK
MUSEUM

29

FRANKLIN RD

TURNPIKE

MAIN ST

RICHMOND BLVD

MT CROSS RD

PINEY FOREST RD

SAN MARCOS
MEXICAN
RESTAURANT

HAMPTON
INN

RIVERSIDE DR

Dan

EL VALLARTA
MEXICAN
RESTAURANT

PIEDMONT DR

WESTOVER

JOE AND MIMMA'S
ITALIAN RESTAURANT

MEMORIAL DR

CENTRAL BLVD

MAIN ST

BALLOU
PARK

ME'S BURGERS
AND BREWS

CRAGHEAD ST

BRIDGE ST

River Dr

RIVERWALK TRAIL
THE DANVILLE SCIENCE CENTER

DANVILLE MUSEUM
OF FINE ARTS
AND HISTORY

SOUTH BOSTON RD

BEST WESTERN
WINDSOR INN & SUITES

29

DANVILLE
REGIONAL
AIRPORT

0   1 mi
0   1 km

© MOON.COM

personal items. This is an interesting, one-of-a-kind museum.

The Danville Science Center

The Danville Science Center (677 Craghead St., 434/791-5160, www.dsc.smv.org, Mon.-Sat. 9:30am-5pm, Sun. 11:30am-5pm, admission and exhibits adults $7, youth and seniors $6, exhibits and digital dome adults $10, youth and seniors $9) is in the Danville Tobacco Warehouse District in the Crossing of the Dan complex. The center is part of the Science Museums of Virginia network, whose facilities aim to make science fun for kids of all ages by offering interactive exhibits and special programs. A butterfly station and garden are open between April and October.

A special collection at the Science Center is the **Estelle H. Womack Natural History Collection.** This exhibit is located in the Science Station (where the local Amtrak station is) and features artifacts donated by local residents of Danville over the years. The museum also features a **Digital Dome Theater** that takes viewers on a journey through the night sky and shows giant-screen films.

EVENTS AND RECREATION

Danville's **Festival in the Park** (760 W. Main St., Ballou Park, www.danvilleva.gov) is an annual event that's been held since 1974. The three-day festival takes place each May in historic Ballou Park. The festival includes arts and crafts, food, entertainment, a health fair, kids' activities, vendors, rides, and a 5K run/walk/wheelchair race.

The paved eight-mile **Riverwalk Trail** that runs along the Dan River is designed for walkers, runners, bikers, and inline skaters. Parking is available at the Crossing at the Dan, the Dan Daniel Memorial Park (302 River Park Dr.), Main Street at the Martin Luther King Bridge, and Anglers Park (350 Northside Dr.). A trail map and brochure can be downloaded at www.danvilleva.gov.

Mountain bikers should check out the **Anglers Ridge Mountain Bike Trail System** (www.danville-va.gov). This incredible network of 25 miles of single-track offers a technically challenging ride on sections such as Hot Tamale and Witchback, while novice riders will likely enjoy the more moderate terrain on Anglers Ridge and the Riverside Drive trails.

FOOD

★ **Me's Burgers and Brews** (215 Main St., 434/792-0123, www.mesburgers.com, Tues.-Thurs. 4pm-10pm, Fri.-Sat. 4pm-11pm, $9-16) is a trendy little surprise located downtown at the south end of the Main Street bridge. The mother-daughter owner duo artfully pulled together every little detail to make this beer-and-burger joint a step above the norm. They offer an ever-changing draft brew selection from local Virginia and North Carolina breweries, alongside a scrumptious menu of high-quality burgers named for classic authors. Burgers are served on potato rolls created by a Mennonite bakery with a sourdough starter. The mouthwatering sweet potato salad is made from a secret family recipe. Be sure to finish off the evening with their glazed doughnut bread pudding.

Tasty Mexican food can be found at **El Vallarta Mexican Restaurant** (418 Westover Dr., 434/799-0506, www.elvallartamexicanrestaurant.net, Mon.-Thurs. 11am-10pm, Fri.-Sat. 11am-11pm, Sun. 11am-9:30pm, $8-16). The cozy decor is upstaged by the friendly staff and delicious menu. With hundreds of choices for lunch and dinner, making a selection can be the hardest part. If you're stumped, try the fajitas, cheese dip, and a margarita.

Another good Mexican choice is **San Marcos Mexican Restaurant** (165 Holt Garrison Pkwy., 434/792-4202, www.sanmarcosrestaurant.com, Sun.-Thur. 11am-10pm, Fri.-Sat. 11am-11pm, $9-18). They have a large dining room and offer many traditional Mexican dishes along with a few surprises. This is a nice place to bring the family since there are so many menu options. They also make a decent margarita.

Joe and Mimma's Italian Restaurant (3336 Riverside Dr., 434/799-5763, www.joeandmimmasdanville.com, Mon.-Thurs. 11am-9:30pm, Fri.-Sat. 11am-10pm, $7-23) is a local favorite for delicious Italian food. They advertise "healthy" ingredients and serve a variety of entrées, pizzas, subs, pastas, and seafood.

ACCOMMODATIONS

Under $100

Fall Creek Farm (2556 Green Farm Rd., 434/791-3297, www.fall-creek-farm.com, $80-100) offers a unique bed-and-breakfast experience. Guests stay in individual log cabins, complete with fireplaces, period antiques, and continental breakfast delivered to their doorstep. The farm sits on 50 acres and offers a heated pool, hiking trails, and stream and pond fishing. There are also miniature donkeys at the farm.

$100-200

The **Courtyard Danville Marriott** (2136 Riverside Dr., 434/791-2661, www.marriott.com, $136-169) has 89 modern rooms, a fitness room, and an outdoor pool. The staff is

That Old-Time Bluegrass

The second week in August marks a very special time in the southern Virginia town of Galax. This town, 104 miles west of Danville and 90 miles east of Abingdon, near the North Carolina border, is the home of the largest old-time bluegrass fiddlers' convention in the country.

Galax is famous for a long history of "old-timey" music, and that tradition remains strong even with the younger crowd. The **Annual Old Fiddlers' Convention** (276/236-8541, www. oldfiddlersconvention.com) has been a main event in town since 1935. Hundreds of people from all over the country come with their instruments to compete for prize money totaling more than $10,000. Thousands more fans converge on the town to witness the contest and to hear up-and-coming bluegrass musicians.

The goal of the convention hasn't changed over time. It is dedicated to "Keeping alive the memories and sentiments of days gone by and make it possible for people of today to hear and enjoy the tunes of yesterday." Instruments featured in the competition include everything from mouth harps to bull fiddles. Some competitors have attended nearly every convention since 1935.

Tickets to the event are only sold at the gate and cost $7-13 per day. Attendees are advised to bring rain gear and boots since rain is common at that time of year and the fields where the performance stages are can get muddy.

Camping is available for $100, but spaces are only sold at the gate. Recordings of the highlights of each year's events are produced by Heritage Records and can be purchased by calling 276/236-9249.

exceptionally pleasant and helpful. This is one of the nicest hotels in the area and is good for business and leisure travel.

For a clean, quite stay, the **Best Western Windsor Inn & Suites** (1292 S. Boston Rd., 434/483-5000, www.bestwestern.com, $93-140) is a centrally located all-suite hotel. They offer 74 guest suites with refrigerators, microwaves, work desks, and sitting areas. The rooms are spacious, and there's a whirlpool, indoor pool, and fitness room on-site. Breakfast is included with your stay, and fresh-baked complimentary cookies are available in the evening.

Another good option is the 58-room **Hampton Inn Danville** (2130 Riverside Dr., 434/793-1111, www.hamptoninn3.hilton.

com, $112-142). It offers free breakfast, a fitness room, business center, and outdoor pool.

INFORMATION

Additional information on Danville can be found at the **Welcome Center** (645 River Park Dr., www.danville-va.gov, Mon.-Fri. 8:30am-5pm, Sat.-Sun. 9am-5pm).

GETTING THERE

Danville is 80 miles southeast of Roanoke and 248 miles southwest of Washington DC. Most visitors arrive by car, but train service through **Amtrak** (677 Craghead St., 800/872-7245) and bus service through **Greyhound** (515 Spring St., 434/792-4722) are available.

Abingdon

Abingdon (named for Martha Washington's home parish in England) was incorporated in 1778 and is the oldest English-speaking town west of the Blue Ridge Mountains. It is hard to believe the town is still in Virginia, as it is a six-hour drive from Washington DC and is as far west as Cleveland. Abingdon, however, is a Virginia Historic Landmark and offers a 20-block historic district with beautiful tree-lined streets, brick sidewalks, and quaint 19th-century homes. The town is also known for its performing and visual arts.

Main Street in Abingdon is a collection of historic treasures. There are galleries, museums, inns, eateries, and a theater. The land the town occupies was originally surveyed in the mid-1700s. Daniel Boone named the area "Wolf Hill" after his hunting dogs were attacked by a pack of wolves nearby. The location of the attack is known as **Courthouse Hill.** In past years, 27 wolf sculptures could be seen around the town, but most have been sold and moved.

SIGHTS
The Arts Depot
One of the most popular sights in Abingdon is **The Arts Depot** (314 Depot St., 276/628-9091, www.abingdonartsdepot.org, Wed.-Sat. 10am-4pm and by appointment, free). Visitors can watch artists at work, walk through galleries, attend workshops, and listen to lectures in this former railroad freight station that is now dedicated to the arts.

William King Museum of Art
The **William King Museum of Art** (415 Academy Dr. NW, 276/628-5005, www.williamkingmuseum.org, Mon.-Sat. 10am-5pm, Sun. 1pm-5pm, first Thurs. of each month until 8pm, free) is a delightful visual arts museum and center that is located in a historic school building (from 1913). It offers fine world art, regional works, and exhibits on cultural heritage. The exhibits change frequently. In addition to three main galleries (housing nine primary exhibits), the museum features a gallery with pieces from area school and college students and exhibits from local artists.

White's Mill
A short drive north of town brings you to **White's Mill** (12291 White's Mill Rd., 276/628-2960, www.whitesmill.org, Wed.-Thurs. 10am-3pm, Fri.-Sun. 10am-5pm, free), the only remaining water-powered gristmill in southwest Virginia. The mill was built in the late 18th century and provided flour and meal for the community. It was also a gathering place for local residents. The mercantile (store) at the mill sold goods to residents and now offers handmade arts and crafts, local books, and regional music.

Abingdon Vineyards
Wine enthusiasts can visit **Abingdon Vineyards** (20530 Alvarado Rd., 276/623-1255, www.abingdonvineyards.com, Wed.-Sun. 11am-6pm) to sample local wine in a welcoming, rustic atmosphere.

RECREATION
The **Virginia Creeper Trail** (www.vacreepertrail.org) is a 34-mile recreation trail that starts in Abingdon (off Pecan St. across the train tracks), runs through Damascus, Virginia, and ends at the North Carolina border. The trail is a former railroad bed and is now a shared-use trail, which means mountain bikers, hikers, and horses can all partake in the trail. There is a welcome center at the trailhead in Abingdon (300 Green Spring Rd.) and three visitors centers on the trail (Damascus Caboose, the Old Greene Cove Station, and the Whitetop Station) that are open on weekends May-October. Restrooms are provided in Damascus, the Straight

Abingdon

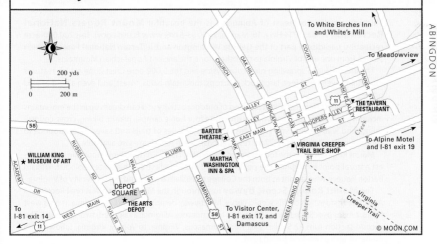

To White Birches Inn
and White's Mill

To Meadowview

THE TAVERN
RESTAURANT

To Alpine Motel
and I-81 exit 19

BARTER
THEATRE

VIRGINIA CREEPER
TRAIL BIKE SHOP

WILLIAM KING
MUSEUM OF ART

MARTHA
WASHINGTON
INN & SPA

DEPOT
SQUARE

THE ARTS
DEPOT

To
I-81 exit 14

To Visitor Center,
I-81 exit 17, and
Damascus

Virginia
Creeper Trail

© MOON.COM

Branch parking lot, Creek Junction parking lot, Green Cove train station, Whitetop train station, and at the trail welcome center in Abingdon. The **Virginia Creeper Trail Bike Shop** (201 Pecan St. SE, 276/676-2552, www.vacreepertrailbikeshop.com, $17-27) is one shop that offers bike rentals. Several others offer rentals and shuttles and can be found on the trail website.

Twenty-four miles southwest of Abingdon, across the Tennessee state line in Bristol, is the **Bristol Motor Speedway** (151 Speedway Blvd., Bristol, 423/989-6900, www.bristolmotorspeedway.com), a NASCAR short-track venue and a highly popular one at that. The track is known for its steep banking as well as for being one of the loudest venues.

ENTERTAINMENT AND EVENTS

The **Barter Theatre** (127 W. Main St., 276/628-3991, www.bartertheatre.com) was opened in 1933 by a young actor named Robert Porterfield. Porterfield came up with a unique idea during the Depression to barter produce from local farms in exchange for a ticket to the theater. It opened under the slogan, "With vegetables you cannot sell, you can buy a good laugh." The price of a ticket was 40 cents or the equal in produce. Most patrons gained entrance in this manner and also bartered with dairy products and livestock. The town jail was beneath the stage and is now used for dressing rooms. Today, the theater hosts drama, comedy, musicals, and mystery performances much as it has done for more than 70 years, only it no longer accepts produce as payment.

Abingdon hosts one of the top 100 annual tourist events in the country. The **Virginia Highlands Festival** (www.vahighlandsfestival.org) is a 10-day event held in August that showcases music, art, crafts, and writing indigenous to the Appalachians. The festival began in 1948 and was founded by the same man who set up the Barter Theatre, Robert Porterfield. It started as a weeklong festival geared toward Appalachian arts and crafts and evolved into 10 days of festivities in a variety of venues. A large antiques market is also featured at the festival, and there is wine-tasting, gardening instruction, and even a hot-air-balloon rally.

Those who like ghost stories won't want to miss taking an **Abingdon Spirit Tour** (276/706-6093, www.visitabingdonvirginia.

Getaway to Mount Rogers

Thirty-five miles northeast of Abingdon is the beautiful **Mount Rogers National Recreation Area** (3714 Hwy. 16, Marion, 276/783-5196, www.fs.usda.gov). This 200,000-acre recreation paradise is part of the George Washington and Jefferson National Forests, which stretch from one end of Virginia to the other along the ancient Appalachian Mountains.

The area includes sprawling rural countryside and the 5,000-acre Crest Zone, which features mountains over 4,000 feet, large rock outcrops, mountain balds, forest, and even a herd of wild ponies.

The area also offers just about any kind of outdoor activity you can dream up in the mountains including camping, horseback riding (there are four horse camps), hiking, biking, cross-country skiing, and wildlife viewing. There are hundreds of miles of trails and seven campgrounds to choose from (call 877/444-6777 for reservations). Cabin rentals are also available.

Mount Rogers itself is the focal point of the region. This 5,729-foot-high mountain is the highest natural point in Virginia. The peak is named after the first Virginia state geologist, William Barton Rogers, who taught at both the College of William & Mary and the University of Virginia.

The **Mount Rogers Scenic Byway** runs through the Mount Rogers National Recreation Area. The first section of this scenic, curvy, hilly byway begins in Troutdale, Virginia. It runs west for 13.2 miles over State Route 603 and on to Konnarock, Virginia, as a paved, two-lane road. The second section runs 32.5 miles east from Damascus, Virginia, to Volney, Virginia, following US Route 58, also a two-lane paved road.

com). Since 1998, this popular two-hour walking tour has sent chills down visitors' spines as they learn Abingdon history including where skeletons are buried and local ghost lore. Tours are animated and fun and depart from many different locations (check website for more information).

SHOPPING

One of the oldest crafts cooperatives in the nation, **Holston Mountain Artisans** (214 Park St., 276/628-7721, www.holstonmtnarts.com) offers a large assortment of traditional arts and crafts from the region including home decor items, gifts, musical instruments, art, books, and photographs. The cooperative began in 1971 and represents more than 130 local artists. They are located in the historic jailhouse on Park Street.

A unique shopping stop on Main Street is the **Abingdon Olive Oil Company** (152 E. Main St., 276/525-1524). This fun tasting gallery and shop features a large variety of organic, extra-virgin, and naturally infused oils and balsamic vinegars. The friendly staff gives free tours and tastings.

FOOD
American

The **Rain Restaurant and Bar** (283 E. Main St., 276/739-2331, www.rainabingdon.com, Tues.-Sat. 11am-2pm and 5pm-9pm, the bar is open later with a limited menu, $22-29) is a wonderful place to spend an evening. This modern, colorful restaurant has good food, friendly and attentive staff, and lovely cocktails (try the cucumber martini). The menu includes steak, pasta, seafood, and chicken with an interesting and delicious assortment of soups and starters (try the buffalo crawfish).

Sisters at the Martha (150 W. Main St., 276/628-3161, www.themartha.com, daily 5pm-9pm, $18-40), within the Martha Washington Inn and Spa, has a lovely menu of Southern-style seafood, steaks, and poultry. This is a classy but casual setting, perfect for a quiet or romantic evening out. Reservations are recommended.

To sample local beer, go to **Wolf Hills**

1: Barter Theatre 2: Martha Washington Inn & Spa in Abingdon

Brewery (350 Park St., 276/451-5470, www. wolfhillsbrewing.com, Mon.-Fri. 5pm-9pm, Sat. 1pm-9pm, Sun. 1pm-6pm) in the old ice house near the Virginia Creeper Trail and the train tracks. They do not have a restaurant, but they hold special beer events.

Intercontinental

★ **The Tavern Restaurant** (222 E. Main St., 276/628-1118, www.abingdontavern.com, Mon.-Sat. 5pm-9pm, $16-44), housed in the oldest building in Abingdon, was originally a tavern and inn for stagecoach travelers. The doors and wood floors of this 1779 building lean a little, but that adds to the charm of this landmark. The delicious menu includes seafood, steak, and poultry with German, Austrian, and Swiss influences (the owner's background is German). There's a cozy bar on the first floor and nice dining areas upstairs. The beer menu is inspiring, as is the wine menu. This is a great place for families and a good place for a date, and the atmosphere is warm and inviting.

ACCOMMODATIONS
Under $100

For a classic, no-frills motel experience, the **Alpine Motel** (882 E. Main St., 276/628-3178, www.alpinemotelabingdon.com, $59-89) is a good choice. This well-maintained, clean motel sits against a hillside overlooking woods and farmland. It is comfortable and offers 19 spacious rooms.

A good-quality chain hotel near I-81 is the **Quality Inn & Suites** (930 E. Main St., 276/676-9090, www.choicehotels.com, $80-129). They offer 75 clean rooms with refrigerators, ironing boards, coffeemakers, hair dryers, and cable television. A free hot breakfast, a fitness center, and a seasonal outdoor pool are also available to guests.

$100-200

The five-guest-room **White Birches Inn** (268 White's Mill Rd., 276/676-2140, www.whitebirchesinn.com, $159-179) was Abingdon's first green bed-and-breakfast. It is a lovely and reasonably priced choice for accommodations in Abingdon. All guest rooms are named after famous playwrights who bartered their work at Abingdon's Barter Theatre. There is a lovely porch out back and a small pond. Breakfast is included with your stay.

The **Hampton Inn Abingdon** (340 Commerce Dr., 276/619-4600, www. secure3hilton.com, $135-153) is another solid choice for a chain hotel in Abingdon. It is off I-81, within walking distance of the historic district. The property is nice, and the staff is warm and friendly. There are 68 guest rooms, and breakfast is included. The hotel offers walking trails, a fitness center, and an outdoor pool.

$200-300

The **Cooper Lantern Boutique Inn** (133 E. Valley St., 276/525-1919, www. copperlanterninn.com, $225-250) was built in 1873 and is conveniently located within walking distance of many attractions in Abingdon. Warm Southern hospitality comes with your room in this cozy bed-and-breakfast. The Georgian colonial-style home has a beautiful stained glass front door and offers eight individually named and furnished rooms, all with their own special history. Rooms are outfitted with Egyptian combed-cotton towels and fine bed linens with comfortable mattresses. Relax on the front porch or swing in the love seat in this friendly, comfortable setting. The food is also wonderful and homemade.

Over $300

The ★ **Martha Washington Inn & Spa** (150 W. Main St., 276/628-3161, www. themartha.com, $340-550) is a beautiful historic hotel with a lot of charm. Guests are drawn in by the attractive, sprawling front porch and the friendly staff, but they stay because of the relaxing atmosphere. The hotel has 55 rooms and eight suites and is decorated with some antiques but offers comfortable furnishings throughout. All rooms are fully renovated and have flat-screen TVs and wireless Internet. The hotel was once a private residence, then a women's college. It is across from the Barter Theatre on Main Street and convenient to many attractions. The rooms are nicely decorated and plenty large, and there is a spa, fitness room, heated saltwater pool, bikes, and tennis courts on-site. You can also schedule a carriage ride. A full hot breakfast is included, as is a glass of port wine each evening. The hotel offers bike rides on the Virginia Creeper Trail, where they will drive you out 17 miles, drop you off with a box lunch, and then let you ride downhill back to the inn. There is free valet parking for guests, a Tesla charging station, and free wireless Internet throughout the inn.

CAMPING

Scenic camping can be found approximately 10 miles south of Abingdon on the shores of South Holston Lake and in the surrounding area.

The **Lakeshore Campground** (19417 County Park Rd., 276/628-5394, www. virginia.org, Apr.-Nov., $30-45) on South Holston Lake offers 200 campsites, a sanitation facility, swimming, boating, boat storage, fishing, a game room, and telephones. Most of their sites are rented for a full season rather than nightly.

Seven miles north of Abingdon is **Riverside Campground** (18496 N. Fork River Rd., 276/623-0340, www. riversidecampground.org, Apr.-Oct., $29-42). They have more than 100 tent and RV sites along the North Fork of the Holston River. The campground is family oriented.

Washington County Park (19482 County Park Rd., 276/628-9677, Apr.-Sept., $25) is another campground on South Holston Lake. They offer 132 campsites with electric hookups, water, and sanitation facilities. They also offer 10 tent sites. They have a playground, picnic shelters, boating, fishing, and telephone access.

INFORMATION AND SERVICES

For additional information on Abingdon, stop by the **visitors center** (335 Cummings St., 276/676-2282, Mon.-Sat. 9am-5pm, Sun. 11am-5pm) or visit www.abingdon.com.

GETTING THERE

Most people arrive in Abingdon by car. It is just off I-81 in the southwestern corner of Virginia. The public **Tri-Cities Regional Airport** (2525 Hwy. 75, Blountville, TN, 423/325-6000, www.triflight.com) in Sullivan County, Tennessee, is 33 miles southwest of Abingdon. Carriers such as American and Delta offer service to the airport.

Maryland's Capital Region

Bordering Washington DC to the north,

Montgomery County is trendy and urban, with cultural and historical sights and attractions. To the east of DC is Prince George's County,
more suburban and rich in natural beauty.

Montgomery County has easy access to Washington DC via road
and the Metrorail service. It is one of the most affluent counties in the
country, with trendy city centers and a variety of restaurants, shopping areas, and hotels.

Prince George's County is a hub for federal government agencies.
It includes the National Harbor, an area along the Potomac River that
has become a hot spot for tourism, dining, and nightlife. It's also home

Look for ★ to find recommended sights, activities, dining, and lodging.

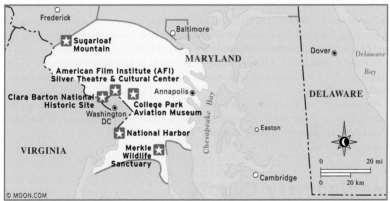

★ **Clara Barton National Historic Site:** This beautiful home was the residence of the pioneering woman who founded the American Red Cross (page 357).

★ **American Film Institute (AFI) Silver Theatre & Cultural Center:** This state-of-the-art film center grew out of the restored art deco Silver Theatre, built in 1938 (page 368).

★ **Sugarloaf Mountain:** This popular recreation area offers hiking, picnicking, and rock climbing (page 371).

★ **National Harbor:** Enjoy restaurants, shops, and entertainment options for both adults and kids right on the Potomac River (page 373).

★ **Merkle Wildlife Sanctuary:** Birders can explore the wintering ground for thousands of Canada geese (page 377).

★ **College Park Aviation Museum:** This great little museum set in a historic airport focuses on the earliest days of mechanical flight (page 381).

to the stadium for the Washington Redskins and one of the best fossil parks in the eastern United States.

PLANNING YOUR TIME

Cities in Maryland's Capital Region are relatively close together, so it is advantageous to select the sights you are most interested in seeing to determine where and how long you will stay. Many sites can be visited as a half- or full-day trip when staying in Washington DC, or the Capital Region can be your home base while exploring DC. Accommodations in Montgomery and Prince George's Counties are generally less expensive than those in DC, yet are still convenient to the major downtown sites.

Commercial air service to Maryland's Capital Region is provided at **Ronald Reagan Washington National Airport (DCA)** (703/417-8000, www.mwaa.com) in Arlington, Virginia; **Washington Dulles International Airport (IAD)** (703/572-2700, www.mwaa.com) in Dulles, Virginia; and **Baltimore Washington International Thurgood Marshall Airport (BWI)** (410/859-7111, www.bwiairport.com) near Baltimore, Maryland.

Train service is available on **Amtrak** (www.amtrak.com) to Rockville in Montgomery County and to Landover in Prince George's County.

The **Washington Metropolitan Area Transit Authority (WMATA)** (www.wmata.com) provides **Metrorail** and **Metrobus** service to both counties. Montgomery County is serviced by Metrorail's Red Line, while Prince George's County is serviced by the Green, Blue, and Orange Lines.

Montgomery County has a public bus transit system called **Ride On** (www.montgomerycountymd.gov), and Prince George's County has a public bus system called **TheBus** (www.princegeorgescountymd.gov).

The Maryland Transit Administration's **Maryland Area Rail Commuter (MARC)** (http://mta.maryland.gov) rail runs train service to both Montgomery County and Prince George's County.

Travel by car around the Capital Region is easy if you are prepared to deal with traffic. I-270 is a primary northwest-southeast roadway that connects to the Capital Beltway (I-495). Montgomery County, in particular, is known for its use of automated speed cameras and red-light cameras, especially on secondary roads, so keep this in mind when traveling by car. Rush hour throughout the Capital Region is spread out over many hours. For the best chance of missing traffic during the week, travel between the hours of 10am and 2pm.

Montgomery County

Montgomery County is named after Revolutionary War general Richard Montgomery and was the first county in Maryland not named after royalty. As a densely populated metropolitan area, the boundaries between cities and towns in Montgomery County are blurred at best. There are a few clearly defined city centers, such as in Bethesda and Rockville, but in many other parts of the county one neighborhood runs into the next.

Just north of Washington DC is the bustling business hub of Silver Spring. Its once-tired downtown area recently realized a grand rebirth and now offers a vibrant city center for entertainment and shopping.

The I-270 Technology Corridor runs through Rockville, Bethesda, and

Previous: rural Montgomery County, Maryland; College Park Aviation Museum; *The Awakening* sculpture, created by J. Seward Johnson, in National Harbor

The Capital Region

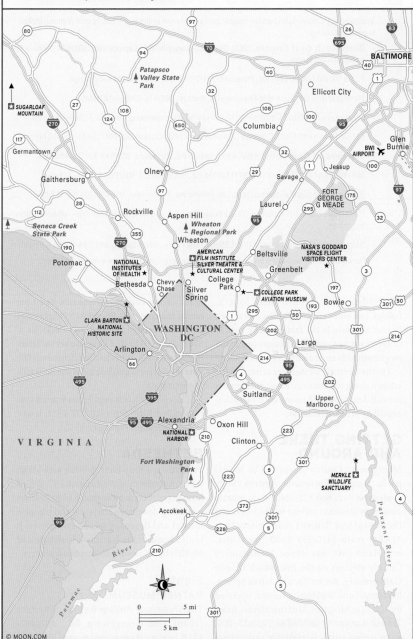

Golf-Crazy Montgomery County

Montgomery County is known for its golf, and visitors can enjoy many public golf courses, including the following:

- **Blue Mash Golf Course** (5821 Olney-Laytonsville Rd., Laytonsville, 301/670-1966)—18 holes/driving range

- **Falls Road** (10800 Falls Rd., Potomac, 301/299-5156)—18 holes/driving range

- **Hampshire Greens** (616 Firestone Dr., Ashton, 301/476-7999)—18 holes

- **Laytonsville Golf Course** (7130 Dorsey Rd., Gaithersburg, 301/948-5288)—18 holes

- **Little Bennett Golf Course** (25900 Prescott Rd., Clarksburg, 301/253-1515)—18 holes

- **Needwood Golf Course** (6724 Needwood Rd., Derwood, 301/948-1075)—18 holes

- **Northwest Golf Course** (15711 Layhill Rd., Silver Spring, 301/598-6100)—27 holes

- **Poolesville Golf Course** (16601 W. Willard Rd., Poolesville, 301/428-8143)—18 holes

- **Rattlewood Golf Course** (13501 Penn Shop Rd., Mt. Airy, 301/607-9000)—18 holes/driving range

- **Sligo Creek Golf Course** (9701 Sligo Creek Pkwy., Silver Spring, 301/585-6006)—9 holes

For additional information on golfing in Montgomery County, visit www.mcggolf.com.

Gaithersburg and is home to many biotechnology and software companies. Northwest of Gaithersburg is the fast-growing suburb of Germantown, which encompasses many neighborhoods and suburban communities.

In the farther western reaches of the county, along the Potomac River, rural routes are still detectable, and towns are loosely connected by private farmland.

GETTING THERE AND AROUND

Montgomery County is serviced by several public transportation systems. **Amtrak** (307 S. Stonestreet Ave., 800/872-7245, www.amtrak.com) provides train service to Rockville, and the **Maryland Transit Administration** MARC train (410/539-5000, www.mta.maryland.gov) has three Montgomery County stations on the Brunswick Line in Gaithersburg, Rockville, and Silver Spring. **Metrorail** and **Metrobus** service, operated by the **Washington Metropolitan Area Transit Authority (WMATA)** (202/637-7000, www.wmata.com), is available throughout much of the county. Metrorail's Red Line enters the county at Friendship Heights and continues through Bethesda past Rockville to Shady Grove. The Red Line also serves Silver Spring through Wheaton to Glenmont. The Amtrak station is also housed at the Rockville Metro station.

The county has a public bus transit system called **Ride On** (240/777-0311, www.montgomerycountymd.gov, $1.75).

BETHESDA

Bethesda is a busy metropolitan area about seven miles north of Washington DC. With a local population of more than 63,000, it offers a bustling downtown shopping and business district and dozens of restaurant choices. It is also home to the **National Institutes of Health (NIH)** (www.nih.gov) headquarters.

Sights
RATNER MUSEUM
The **Dennis & Phillip Ratner Museum** (10001 Old Georgetown Rd., 301/897-1518, www.ratnermuseum.org, open by

appointment only for 10 or more people, free) is a lovely and unique art museum with both permanent and traveling exhibits. The upper level of the museum features a permanent collection of artwork by contemporary artist Phillip Ratner that depicts stories from the Bible through sculpture, drawings, paintings, and other graphics. Visitors can literally take a walk through the Bible by looking at the displays. The lower level, where exhibits change monthly, features work from both established and upcoming local artists. Mediums include painting, photography, glass, wood, and silk panels.

Other traveling exhibits are also featured. A children's art and literature museum is housed in another building called the Resource Center. Additional activities held at the museum complex include lectures, concerts, and readings. Phillip Ratner is perhaps best known for being the artist of five sculptures at the Statue of Liberty and 40 sculptures at Ellis Island. Dennis Ratner is Phillip's second cousin and owner of the nation's largest privately owned salon chain, the Hair Cuttery. The two established the museum together.

BE WITH ME CHILDREN'S PLAYSEUM

The **Be With Me Children's Playseum** (7000 Wisconsin Ave., 301/807-8028, www. playseum.com, Mon.-Fri. 10am-5pm, Sat. 10am-7pm, Sun. 2pm-7pm, $9) is a great play space for young kids, offering many rooms with individual themes such as a grocery store, kitchen, and princess dress-up, all of which kids can enjoy at their leisure. There is also an arts and crafts room (some projects cost extra) and an open play area with a stage and musical instruments. This is a fun and entertaining place to spend an afternoon.

MCCRILLIS GARDENS

A little-known treasure in a quiet residential neighborhood near downtown Bethesda is **McCrillis Gardens** (6910 Greentree Rd., 301/962-1455, www.montgomeryparks.org, daily 10am-sunset, free). This lovely garden and the home that sits on the grounds were donated to the Maryland National Capital Park and Planning Commission in 1978 by its former owners. The gardens are considered a premier shade garden and offer beautiful ornamental trees, shrubs (including many azalea bushes), annuals, ground covers, perennials, and other flowers. There is a pavilion and benches on the grounds. There is no parking on the grounds, but some street parking is available during the week. On weekends (and after 4pm on weekdays), parking is available across the street at the Woods Academy.

AUDUBON NATURALIST SOCIETY

The **Audubon Naturalist Society's Woodend Sanctuary** (8940 Jones Mill Rd., Chevy Chase, 301/652-9188, www. audubonnaturalist.org, trails open daily dawn to dusk, free) in nearby Chevy Chase is the headquarters for the Audubon Naturalist Society. The sanctuary is one of the few grand old estates remaining in the area and sits on 40 acres. The Woodend Mansion, which was designed in the 1920s and bequeathed to the Audubon Naturalist Society in 1968, is a beautiful example of Georgian revival architecture. Visitors can enjoy self-guided nature trails, a wildflower meadow, and a pond on the grounds. No pets are allowed in the sanctuary. On the first Saturday of every month, a free family nature walk is hosted by a naturalist from 9am to 10am. Topics such as trees, insects, birds, and animals are covered. An on-site bookshop sells nature and birding books and gifts.

★ CLARA BARTON NATIONAL HISTORIC SITE

Just southwest of Bethesda in Glen Echo is the **Clara Barton National Historic Site** (5801 Oxford Rd., Glen Echo, 301/320-1410, www. nps.gov/clba, guided house tours Fri.-Sat. on the hour 1pm-4pm, free). Clara Barton was a pioneer among American women and is credited with founding the American Red Cross. The historical site was established at the home where Barton spent the last 15 years of her life

Clara Barton: Angel of the Battlefield

Clara Barton National Historic Site

Clara Barton was born on Christmas Day in 1821 in Massachusetts. She is known as a pioneer for her work as a teacher, patent clerk, nurse, and humanitarian, all during a time when very few women held jobs outside the home.

Barton was dedicated to helping others and always held a passion for nursing. At a young age she nursed her injured dog back to health when he hurt his leg, and later saved her brother's life by nursing him back to health after he fell off their family's barn roof.

Barton first became a schoolteacher and later opened a free school in New Jersey. Although attendance at her school rapidly grew to more than 600 students, the school's board hired a man to head the operation instead of Barton. After this insult, Barton moved to Washington DC and became a clerk at the U.S. Patent Office. She was the first woman to receive a salary equal to a man in a substantial clerkship position in the federal government.

During the Civil War, Barton was put in charge of the hospitals at the front of the Army of the James (a Union army that included units from Virginia and North Carolina). She soon became known as the "Angel of the Battlefield."

After the war, Barton led the Office of the Missing Soldiers in Washington DC and gained wide recognition for giving lectures across the country on her experiences during the war. During this time, she began a long association with the women's suffrage movement and also became an activist for African American civil rights.

During a trip to Geneva, Switzerland, Barton became acquainted with the Red Cross and provided the society assistance during the Franco-Prussian War. Barton also engaged in additional humanitarian work throughout Europe for a couple of years. Upon returning to the United States, Barton started a movement for recognition by the U.S. government of the International Committee of the Red Cross. After much effort, Barton succeeded by arguing that the American Red Cross could assist with crisis situations other than just war. She became the president of the American branch of the Red Cross and held the first branch meeting in her home in Washington DC in 1881.

Clara Barton died at her home in Maryland on April 12, 1912. She was buried in Massachusetts.

(1897-1912). This National Park Service site is a tribute to her accomplishments and one of the first National Historic Sites dedicated to a woman. The home also shares the early history of the American Red Cross and was the first headquarters for the organization. The restored home can be visited by guided tour only and offers visitors the chance to see 11 of the original 30 rooms, including Barton's bedroom, the parlors, and the Red Cross offices. Tours last approximately one hour. The site is seven miles northwest of Washington DC on a bluff looking over the Potomac River.

Entertainment and Events

The **Strathmore** (5301 Tuckerman Ln., North Bethesda, 301/581-5100, www.strathmore.org) is a beautiful concert venue in North Bethesda. The hall itself is a work of art, with contemporary styling, light woodwork, wonderful acoustics, and comfortable seats. World-class performers and international artists make up a full schedule of offerings including folk, rock, blues, pop, R&B, jazz, and classical music. Friendly and professional staff and volunteers make the experience at the Strathmore even better, and parking is free.

The **Imagination Stage** (4908 Auburn Ave., 301/280-1660, www.imaginationstage.org) is a theater arts center for young people in downtown Bethesda. Its shows are professionally prepared, entertaining, and offer a nice break for kids from museums and playgrounds. The theater is open year-round. Pay attention to the target age for each performance.

Live stand-up comedy can be found at the **Laugh Riot** at Positano Italian Restaurant in Bethesda (4948 Fairmont Ave., http://standupcomedytogo.com, Sat. 8pm-9:30pm, $15) on Saturday nights. The shows are R rated, and seating is on a first-come, first-served basis. Full bar service is available during the show. Admission is cash only.

The **Round House Theatre** (4545 East-West Hwy., 240/644-1100, www.roundhousetheatre.org) is a professional theater company that produces just under 200 performances a year.

A great weekend-long event held annually in mid-May is the **Bethesda Fine Arts Festival** (www.bethesda.org, free). Visitors can enjoy artwork created by 130 national artists, entertainment, and local food in the Woodmont Triangle neighborhood, along Norfolk, Auburn, and Del Ray Avenues.

Shopping

Downtown Bethesda is home to almost 700 retail stores and businesses. Most any shopping need or desire can be met in this destination. Fashion boutiques, art galleries, home furnishings stores, and salons are just a few examples of the types of retailers available. For a searchable list of stores visit www.bethesda.org.

Sports and Recreation

A great place to bring the little ones (including the four-footed kind) is **Cabin John Regional Park** (7400 Tuckerman Ln., 301/495-2595, www.montgomeryparks.org). This great park has just about everything, including playgrounds, trails, a little train (spring-fall), picnic tables, an amphitheater, and a dog park (10900 Westlake Dr.). The dog park is split into two areas: one for dogs 20 pounds and over and one for dogs less than 20 pounds. The park is very popular but also has plenty of room.

Just west of Bethesda on the Potomac River is **Carderock Recreation Area** (off Clara Barton Pkwy., Carderock), a 100-acre park that is part of the **Chesapeake & Ohio Canal National Historical Park** and one of the premier rock-climbing destinations in the Washington DC area, with more than 100 established climbing routes and plentiful bouldering. Climbers can enjoy friction slabs, cracks, and overhangs. Most routes are best with a toprope. Climbs range 30-50 feet and have seen such notable climbers as Chris Sharma.

Carderock also offers hiking, biking, and picnicking. A section of the **Billy Goat Trail**

Hike the Billy Goat Trail

Billy Goat Trail at Great Falls Park

Hikers of all abilities can enjoy the popular Billy Goat Trail, running between the C&O Canal and the Potomac River in Montgomery County near Great Falls. The trail is 4.7 miles long and has three sections.

The northern section (Section A) is 1.7 miles long and the most heavily traveled. It runs through rocky terrain on Bear Island. There is a steep climb along a cliff face bordering the Potomac River in Mather Gorge that requires scrambling in parts. Pets are not allowed on Bear Island. Section A is accessible from the **Great Falls Tavern Visitor Center** (11710 MacArthur Blvd., Potomac, 301/767-3714).

Section B is less strenuous and has only one short segment where scrambling is required. It is 1.4 miles long. Section C is the easiest, with no scrambling. It is 1.6 miles long. Sections B and C can be accessed from **Carderock Recreation Area** (off Clara Barton Pkwy., Carderock). Leashed dogs are allowed on these two sections.

The three sections of the trail are not contiguous but are connected by the C&O Canal Towpath. The Billy Goat Trail is marked with light-blue blazes. Access to the trail is free, although a small parking fee is charged by the visitors center. There is no fee at Carderock.

passes through the park, and the **C&O Canal Towpath** can be accessed via a short wooded trail across the parking lot from the restrooms in the northernmost parking lot. The park is near the Carderock Division of the Naval Surface Warfare Center. Access to the park is free.

Food

There is no shortage of wonderful restaurant choices in Bethesda. In fact, this area is known for its great variety of international cuisine.

A stroll through the eight-block "restaurant row" between Rockville Pike/Wisconsin Avenue and Old Georgetown Road will give you a taste of what is available. If you're in the mood for something different, you won't be disappointed.

AMERICAN

Upscale American cuisine that includes burgers, seafood, and steak can be found at ★ **Woodmont Grill** (7715 Woodmont Ave., 301/656-9755, www.woodmontgrill.com,

Mon.-Sat. 11:30am-10pm, Sun. 11:30am-9pm, $18-48). Their prices may seem high for what sounds like casual fare ($18 for a cheeseburger, $37 for barbecue ribs, etc.), but the quality of the food is excellent, the atmosphere is relaxing, and their bread is made fresh in house. This is a great choice for business, family, and romantic occasions. There is live jazz nightly and free parking on-site. Be sure to make a reservation; the restaurant is very popular. There is also a dress code.

Barrel and Crow (4867 Cordell Ave., 240/800-3253, www.barrelandcrow.com, Mon.-Thurs. 11:30am-2:30pm and 5pm-10pm, Fri. 11:30am-2:30pm and 5pm-11pm, Sat. 11am-2:30pm and 5pm-11pm, Sun. 11am-2:30pm and 5pm-9pm, $21-29) is a comfortable, regional restaurant with friendly service. Their menu is modern and not overwhelming in size, but offers a nice mix of entrées such as pan-roasted trout, fried Amish chicken and waffles, and grilled hanger steak. They also offer an extensive beer, wine, and cocktail menu.

ASIAN

A good consistent go-to restaurant for sushi is **Raku Asian Dining, Sushi and Sake** (7240 Woodmont Ave., 301/718-8680, www.rakuasiandining.com, lunch Mon.-Fri. 11:30am-2:30pm, Sat.-Sun. noon-3pm, dinner Mon.-Thurs. 5pm-10pm, Fri.-Sat. 5pm-10:30pm, Sun. 5pm-9:30pm, $8-34). This is a favorite lunch restaurant among the local business crowd, and that is no accident. They serve great sashimi, sushi, and rolls for all tastes, along with scrumptious soup and bento boxes. They offer modern, Asian decor and friendly service. The food is freshly prepared and nicely presented. They have been in business for many years and have quite a following.

ITALIAN

For good, reasonably priced Italian food, dine at **Olazzo** (7921 Norfolk Ave., 301/654-9496, www.olazzo.com, Sun.-Thurs. 11:30am-10pm, Fri.-Sat. 11:30am-11pm, $9-25). This is a very popular restaurant that doesn't take reservations, so plan on a wait during prime time. The food is delicious and consistent, with warm, fresh bread, wonderful martinis, and scrumptious entrées. The rose sauce is delectable. The atmosphere is cozy and rustic with dim lighting and candles on the tables. This is a good value for the quality of the food.

MEDITERRANEAN

Seafood lovers will go wild for the Mediterranean dishes at the family-owned and -operated ★ **Chef Tony's** (4926 St. Elmo Ave., 301/654-3737, www.cheftonysbethesda.com, brunch Sun. 11am-3pm, lunch Wed.-Fri. 11:30am-2:30pm, dinner Tues.-Sat. 5pm-10pm, Sun. 3pm-8pm, $8-35). The ambience is simple and the food is simply excellent. Sample menu items include pan-roasted PEI mussels, Turkish branzino, lobster pasta, and grilled surf and turf. Save room for dessert—they have a sizable selection of delicious sweets, including cheesecake, tiramisu, and caramelized sweet potato pie. Chef Tony partners with local farmers whenever possible.

Accommodations

A good extended-stay hotel is the **Bethesda Marriott Suites** (6711 Democracy Blvd., 301/897-5600, www.marriott.com, $149-273), which is 30 minutes from downtown Washington DC by car and popular for business travel. It offers 272 suites on 11 floors and has 10 meeting rooms. The facility includes a fitness center, an indoor heated pool, and a seasonal outdoor pool.

The **Residence Inn Bethesda Downtown** (7335 Wisconsin Ave., 301/718-0200, www.marriott.com, $119-246) is a modern, friendly facility in a central location near the Metrorail and dining. They offer 188 suites on 13 floors with well-equipped kitchens, wireless Internet, and free breakfast. A seasonal, outdoor, rooftop pool and year-round fitness center are also available to guests. There is a $27 valet parking fee (no self-parking) and a $175 fee for pets.

A short walk from the Bethesda

Metro station is the **Hilton Garden Inn Washington DC/Bethesda** (7301 Waverly St., 301/654-8111, www.hiltongardeninn3. hilton.com, $121-180). They offer 216 large, comfortable rooms with high-speed Internet and good beds. A fitness center and pool are on-site. Parking is $16.50.

Information and Services

For additional information on Bethesda, visit www.bethesda.org.

Getting Around

There is garage parking in many parts of Bethesda, and it is mostly free on the weekends. The Bethesda Metrorail station (in the center of the downtown area) moves more than 9,000 passengers on a normal weekday. Taxi service is also readily available on most streets.

ROCKVILLE

Rockville is the fourth-largest city in Maryland and encompasses a little more than 13 square miles in central Montgomery County. It is approximately 12 miles north of Washington DC and has always had close connections to the nation's capital. In 1873, the first public transportation between Rockville and Washington was established with the arrival of the Baltimore & Ohio Railroad. Not too long after, trolley service began between Georgetown and Rockville, which continued until the automobile became the preferred mode of transportation.

During the Cold War, Rockville was considered a safe place for evacuation during a nuclear attack, and as such, many bomb shelters were built and I-270 was designated as an emergency landing runway for aircraft. Two Nike missile sites were also located in Rockville until the mid-1970s. The Nuclear Regulatory Commission headquarters is just south of Rockville's corporate limits.

Rockville's downtown area has had ups and downs since the 1960s but in recent years has enjoyed a rebirth with boutique stores, trendy restaurants, and upscale condominiums. It was even featured in REM's popular song released in 1984 titled "(Don't Go Back To) Rockville," written by Mike Mills.

Sights

BEALL-DAWSON HOUSE

The **Beall-Dawson House** (103 W. Montgomery Ave., 301/762-1492, www. montgomeryhistory.org, Sat.-Sun. noon-4pm, adults $7, seniors and military $5, under 6 free) was built in 1815 for the county's clerk of the court, Upton Beall. The large, federal-style brick house is impressive both inside and out and remained a private home until the 1960s. At that time, it was purchased by the city as the headquarters for the Montgomery County Historical Society. The home is now a furnished museum that depicts life in the early 19th century, reflecting the lifestyle of both the upper-class homeowners and the enslaved African Americans who lived there.

Rotating gallery exhibits are displayed in two rooms and feature collections owned by the historical society. Tours of the home also include a tour of the **Stonestreet Museum of 19th Century Medicine,** a historic one-room doctor's office located on the property. Tours last 45 minutes to an hour.

GLENVIEW MANSION

Glenview Mansion (603 Edmonston Dr., 240/314-8660, www.rockvillemd.gov, Mon.-Fri. 8:30am-4:30pm, free) is a beautiful 19th-century home that sits on the grounds of the 153-acre Rockville Civic Center Park. Visitors can take a guided tour (docents are available during business hours) or walk through the pillared, neoclassical mansion that dates back to 1836 on their own. The home can be rented for private events and also features an art gallery on the second floor that showcases local artwork. The mansion grounds offer walking trails and a formal garden.

F. SCOTT AND ZELDA FITZGERALD GRAVE

It may seem odd that F. Scott Fitzgerald and his wife, Zelda, are buried near a busy thoroughfare in Rockville, but Fitzgerald's father's family was from the area, and he visited here many times. Many members of his family are buried in **St. Mary's Catholic Cemetery** (520 Viers Mill Rd.), the oldest cemetery in Rockville. After attending his father's funeral in 1931, Fitzgerald decided that he and his wife would also be buried there. The quote on their joint tombstone is the final line of *The Great Gatsby,* "So we beat on, boats against the current, borne back ceaselessly into the past."

ASPIN HILL PET CEMETERY

One of the oldest pet cemeteries in the country is the **Aspin Hill Pet Cemetery,** also known as the **Aspen Hill Memorial Park & Animal Sanctuary** (13630 Georgia Ave., 240/252-2555, www.mchumane.org). The cemetery was established in 1921 and is owned by the Montgomery County Humane Society. The memorial park is the final resting place of General Grant, or Jiggs, whom you might know better as Petey from *The Little Rascals.* This cute dog with the circle around one eye lived from 1928 to 1938. He is kept company by J. Edgar Hoover's dogs and a few dozen humans who are buried with their pets. The cemetery is also the site of a memorial to medical rats. It was originally named after a kennel in England, which explains why the name is sometimes spelled with an "i" rather than an "e" in Aspen.

GLENSTONE MUSEUM

Just west of Rockville in Potomac is the **Glenstone Museum** (12100 Glen Rd., 301/983-5001, www.glenstone.org, Thurs.-Sun. 10am-5pm, free), a beautiful contemporary art museum in a gorgeous natural setting. This gem features changing art installations indoors and out that can be explored on a self-guided basis (there are friendly docents to answer questions). The grounds and architecture were created in harmony with both the art and landscape and are part of the experience. Admission is by reservation only (scheduled on the half hour until 3pm) and can be reserved online (although it is sometimes difficult to obtain), but this keeps the crowds down and the experience extremely enjoyable. Come prepared to walk (cart transportation is available for people with disabilities). They have complimentary umbrellas to borrow for sun and rain and there is a café on-site.

Entertainment and Events

The **F. Scott Fitzgerald Theatre** (603 Edmonston Dr., 240/314-8690, www.rockvillemd.gov) is a 446-seat performing arts venue in Rockville Civic Center Park. Both local and professional touring companies offer stage performances at the theater.

One of the most popular annual events in Rockville is the **Rockville Antique and Classic Car Show** (603 Edmonston Dr., www.rockvillemd.gov) at the end of October. It features more than 500 classic automobiles from 25 local car clubs. Live music, food, and a flea market are also part of the festivities.

Shopping

Rockville Town Center (200 E. Middle Ln., www.rockvilletownsquare.com) is a pedestrian-friendly town square with locally owned and operated shops and restaurants. It is also a thriving neighborhood with ice-skating in the winter and year-round programs. Shopping is a favorite pastime in the square, with more than 20 stores to choose from. Clothing boutiques, jewelry stores, home furnishing shops, and specialty athletic stores can all be found here, as well as salon and spa services.

There are also plenty of neighborhood shopping areas in Rockville. **Congressional Plaza** (1683 Rockville Pike, www.congressionalplaza.com) has more than 50 stores and restaurants, including national chains, local boutiques, and a gourmet grocery store. **Falls Grove Village Center** (14955 Shady Grove Rd., www.fallsgrovevillagectr.com) offers retail, restaurants, and a grocery store. The **King Farm Village Center** (403 Redland Blvd., www.kingfarmvillagecenter.com) is a charming local shopping area with retail stores, a grocery store, and restaurants.

Montrose Crossing (12055 Rockville Pike) is home to mostly chain retail stores that specialize in home furnishings, sports, and clothing. The **Traville Village Center** (9700 Traville Gateway Dr.), which is accessible from Darnestown Road and Shady Grove Road, is a neighborhood shopping area that offers a mix of boutique stores, a grocery store, and restaurants. **Wintergreen Plaza** (815-895 Rockville Pike, www.wintergreenplaza. com), on Rockville Pike, is home to many specialty stores, restaurants, food providers, and services.

A popular seasonal **farmers market** is held at the Rockville Town Center on the corner of Route 28 and Monroe Street on Saturday mid-May to mid-November.

Sports and Recreation

Rock Creek Regional Park (6700 Needwood Rd., Derwood, 301/948-5053, www.montgomeryparks.org) is an 1,800-acre park with two lakes (Lake Needwood and Lake Frank), 13 miles of wooded trails, picnic facilities, a playground, archery range, and nature center. Boat rentals are available on-site ($14 per hour and $50 per day for kayaks, canoes, and rowboats, $12 per half hour for pedal boats), and 30-minute pontoon boat tours are offered on weekends for $4.

The **Chesapeake & Ohio Canal National Historical Park** (301/739-4200, www.nps.gov/choh), a 184.5-mile path that stretches from Georgetown in Washington DC to Cumberland, Maryland, runs along the Potomac River near Rockville. A lovely stretch in Montgomery County is located between Rileys Lock (0.2 miles before mp 23) and Swains Lock (0.4 miles before mp 17). The terrain is mostly hard-packed dirt or pebble dirt, and the scenery is woodlands with river and canal views. The path is ideal for mountain biking, horseback riding, walking, and running.

Wanna feel like Tarzan? Then an afternoon at **Go Ape** (6129 Needwood Lake Dr., 800/971-8271, www.goape.com, ages 10-15 $49, 16 and up $59) is a must. This incredible treetop adventure is a big obstacle course in the trees that is designed for most age groups. Test your climbing skills and fear of heights on ladders, bridges, walkways, ropes, zip lines, and even tunnels. Safety instruction and all equipment are included.

For something a little different, catch a **Free State Roller Derby** (www. freestaterollerderby.com) competition. This flat-track roller derby league is based in Rockville.

Food

When it comes to food, neighborhood gems are scattered throughout Rockville, mostly camouflaged in drab-looking strip malls. International cuisine is some of the best in the region, if you know where to look.

ECLECTIC

Have you ever tried a waffle sandwich? If not, the place to have your first is ★ **Mosaic** (186 Halpine Rd., 301/468-0682, www. mosaiccuisine.com, Sun.-Thurs. 8am-9pm, Fri.-Sat. 8am-10pm, $11-30), near the Twinbrook Metro station. Mosaic is an eclectic, internationally inspired restaurant with a passion for waffles. Their food is loosely based on French cuisine with influences from all over the globe. You'll find French onion soup, Peking duck rolls, crab quesadilla—you get the picture. Now back to the waffles. The chefs at Mosaic searched for a good alternative to using bread or tortillas for their sandwiches. Out of this creative desire to differentiate themselves with a healthy alternative, the waffle sandwich was born. They then spent time perfecting a unique light and crispy waffle recipe suitable for sandwiches, with fewer carbs and more protein. The result is a menu of waffles served all day. Breakfast is by far their most popular meal. They offer traditional favorites such as eggs Benedict and French toast but also have an entire

1: Glenview Mansion in Rockville **2:** The Strathmore in Bethesda **3:** *Hand of NOAA* bronze sculpture designed by Ray Kaskey **4:** boardwalk at the Glenstone Museum in Potomac

menu section devoted to their beloved waffles. With lunch come salads and a variety of hot and cold sandwiches, available on a choice of breads including their waffles. Dinner is an unusual mix of steak, seafood, pasta, and again, a menu of waffle sandwiches.

LATIN

A plain exterior and average interior atmosphere don't detract from the draw of **La Brasa** (12401 Parklawn Dr., 301/468-8850, www.labrasarockville.com, Mon.-Thurs. 11am-9pm, Fri.-Sat. 11am-10pm, $11-30), which serves great Latin food in an out-of-the-way location. Customers are greeted with warm smiles and fantastic South American dishes. Try the carne asada and the pupusas. They also have great plantains. The dining room is small, but there are a few additional patio seats during the warmer months. This restaurant is family-owned and -operated, and they offer takeout service.

MEDITERRANEAN

Scrumptious Greek food can be found at **Cava Mezze** (9713 Traville Gateway Dr., 301/309-9090, www.cavamezze.com, Mon.-Fri. 11:30am-2:30pm and 5pm-10pm, Sat. 5pm-10pm, Sun. 5pm-9pm, $11-18). They serve traditional Mediterranean food in a small-plates format. The restaurant was started by two energetic friends and a chef on a shoestring budget, and their endeavor has blossomed into a five-restaurant success story. The *saganaki* (flamed cheese) is delightful, as are the scallop risotto, lamb sliders, and grilled octopus. The atmosphere is energetic yet with a cozy, inviting ambience. Although the service isn't overly friendly, it is prompt. If you're in the mood for very flavorful food, this is a good choice.

MEXICAN

Villa Maya (5532 Norbeck Rd., 301/460-1247, www.villamayarestaurant.com, Mon.-Thurs. 11am-10pm, Fri. 11am-11pm, Sat. 10am-11pm, Sun. 10am-9pm, $9-18) is a great Mexican restaurant hidden behind a plain exterior in a local strip mall. The food is a step above traditional Mexican, the service is good, and the drinks will make you not care about either. This is a fun place with a large menu of both zesty Mexican fare and mild dishes. The seafood burritos are a favorite, as is the fresh guacamole made at your table. If you're looking for a different appetizer to share, try the Yuca con Chicharron (tender pork in a savory juice). The place is packed on weekends, so be prepared for a wait. The staff does an excellent job of taking care of the patrons and is particularly accommodating to seniors.

PERUVIAN

★ **La Limena** (765-B Rockville Pike, 301/424-2733, www.lalimenarestaurant.com, Sun.-Thurs. 11am-9pm, Fri.-Sat. 11am-10pm, Sun. 10am-9pm, $8-21) is one of a growing number of Peruvian restaurants that are sprouting up throughout the Washington DC suburbs. As the Peruvian culture spreads, wonderful, soul-soothing Peruvian food is making its way into many people's go-to restaurant rotation. At first glance, La Limena appears to be a hole-in-the-wall eatery in a strip mall. Once you step inside, it's clear this little bistro is a blend of sophisticated cuisine and a casual, family atmosphere. The food is simply delicious and features dishes such as ceviche with soft sweet potatoes, fried trout with sliced garlic, and a strip steak topped with a fried egg. They also serve Cuban dishes. Reservations are accepted on weekdays but not weekends.

Accommodations

Accommodations in Rockville are primarily chain hotels. There is a big variety, so it is best to select a hotel based on location. If you do not need to be near the Metrorail or the center of town, cheaper rates can be found on the outskirts of the city.

The **Sheraton Rockville Hotel** (920 King Farm Blvd., 240/912-8200, www.marriott.com, $84-160) is in the King Farm development near I-270. It has 152 guest rooms with comfortable beds, 32-inch flat-screen televisions, high-speed Internet, and work desks. Amenities include a fitness center, indoor lap pool, whirlpool, on-site restaurant, and gift shop. The hotel is about eight miles north of downtown Rockville, but it is reasonably priced for the quality of the facility.

Another solid choice in this price range is the **Best Western Plus Rockville Hotel and Suites** (1251 W. Montgomery Ave., 301/424-4940, www.bestwestern.com, $92-139). They have 164 guest rooms and are close to I-270. They offer a complimentary breakfast, a fitness center, a seasonal outdoor pool, free high-speed Internet, and free shuttle to the Metro.

The **Homewood Suites by Hilton Rockville-Gaithersburg** (14975 Shady Grove Rd., 240/507-1900, www.homewoodsuites3.hilton.com, $108-287) is a good choice for extended stays or those who want a fully equipped kitchen. Located in the business district, this is a popular hotel for business travel. Complimentary shuttle service to the Shady Grove Metrorail station and other locations within a three-mile radius of the hotel is offered. Each of the 87 suites has a full kitchen, large living area, and free wireless Internet. A full complimentary breakfast is also included. Hotel amenities such as an indoor heated pool, 24-hour fitness center, whirlpool, and kids' entertainment room with books, DVDs, foosball, and air hockey allow guests several options for relaxation outside their studio, one-bedroom, or two-bedroom suite.

The Homewood Suites is joined at the lobby to the **Hilton Garden Inn Rockville Gaithersburg** (14975 Shady Grove Rd., 240/507-1800, www.hiltongardeninn3.hilton.com, $79-225). Both hotels are relatively new and have excellent staff. They also share some amenities.

Information and Services

For additional information on Rockville, visit www.rockvillemd.gov.

SILVER SPRING

Silver Spring is just north of Washington DC and is a prime business hub with numerous office buildings and a dense population. The city is said to be named after a spring that was discovered by Francis Preston Blair, an American journalist and politician, in 1840 when he was thrown from his horse while riding through the countryside looking for an area to build his personal retreat from Washington. As legend goes, the mica and sand around the spring glimmered like silver, and thus the name.

In recent years, the original downtown area, which had paled compared to some of the region's trendy city centers, began a rebirth of sorts. New businesses moved in to stake their claim, including major retail outlets, restaurants, and residential and office developments. Downtown Silver Spring is now a vibrant city center with entertainment, shopping, and other conveniences.

Sights

NATIONAL MUSEUM OF HEALTH AND MEDICINE

The **National Museum of Health and Medicine** (2500 Linden Ln., 301/319-3300, www.medicalmuseum.mil, daily 10am-5:30pm, free) is one of the few museums where visitors can see the impact of disease on the human body. The museum is a National Historic Landmark that was established during the Civil War and dates back to 1862. It offers unique exhibits and educational programs and engages in ongoing medical research.

Instruments used to diagnose and treat disease can be seen as well as the case histories of patients with the diseases (some exhibits may be a bit graphic for young children). The goal of the museum is to promote the understanding of both historic and modern-day medicine. Special attention is given to military medicine. Fascinating artifacts on display include the bullet that killed Abraham Lincoln and bone fragments from Lincoln's skull.

In the museum's initial years, the first curator collected artifacts from doctors treating soldiers in the Union army. Photos of wounded soldiers were also collected that showed the impact of gunshot wounds and the resulting amputations and surgical procedures. Since then much research has been conducted at the museum, and a sophisticated method of cataloging was established, which formed the framework for the National Library of Medicine.

At the onset of World War II, the museum began to focus primarily on pathology and became a division of the new Army Institute of Pathology. After several name changes, the museum became known under its current title in 1989.

Adult visitors should be prepared to present photo identification at the entrance, and personal belongings may be subject to search for security purposes.

NATIONAL CAPITAL TROLLEY MUSEUM

In the northern reaches of the Silver Spring area is the popular **National Capital Trolley Museum** (1313 Bonifant Rd., Colesville, 301/384-6088, www.dctrolley.org, Sat.-Sun. noon-5pm, adults $10, children 2-17 and seniors over 65 $8). This unusual museum strives to preserve artifacts from electric street railways and to help understand their effect on community development in the Washington DC area. There is a visitors center and several exhibit halls, and guests can enjoy authentic streetcar rides through Northwest Branch Park. Many historic trolleys are on display, and educational programs are also offered.

THE *HAND OF NOAA* SCULPTURE

An interesting piece of public art is located outside the National Oceanic and Atmospheric Administration (NOAA) headquarters (1325 East-West Hwy.). Known as the *Hand of NOAA*, the sculpture depicts a large bronze hand releasing seagulls to the ocean. The seagulls are part of the agency's logo, and the sculpture symbolizes NOAA's commitment to protecting the environment.

★ AMERICAN FILM INSTITUTE (AFI) SILVER THEATRE & CULTURAL CENTER

The **American Film Institute (AFI) Silver Theatre & Cultural Center** (8633 Colesville Rd., 301/495-6700, www.afi.com) is a state-of-the-art exhibition, education, and cultural center that grew out of the restored 1938 art deco Silver Theatre. It offers multiple stadium-seating theaters in 32,000 square feet of space, along with a reception area, exhibit space, offices, and meeting space. They feature retrospectives, new releases, and tribute shows. A full schedule of films is shown there, and memberships are available. Each June, the center hosts the premier seven-day documentary film festival called **AFI DOCS.** It is considered one of the world's best documentary festivals.

Entertainment and Events

The historic **Fillmore Theater** (8656 Colesville Rd., 301/960-9999, www.fillmoresilverspring.com) has brought entertainment to Silver Spring for more than 40 years. With a capacity of 2,000, it offers first-class music and entertainment in the center of the downtown area. A schedule of events can be found on their website.

Shopping

The center of activity in Silver Spring is the **Silver Spring Town Center** (1 Veterans Place, 240/595-8818, www.silverspringtowncenter.com). Located on Georgia Avenue, it comprises retailers, restaurants, a movie theater, and a Whole Foods grocery store. The town center is the anchor to the newly revitalized downtown area. Year-round activities are held at the center, including craft fairs, festivals, and concerts. There is also a seasonal farmers market. A splash fountain is open May-September.

Recreation

The **Capital Crescent Trail** (www.cctrail.org) is an 11-mile off-road rail trail that is designated for shared use by walkers, runners, bikers, and inline skaters. The trail was created in an old railbed of the Georgetown Branch of the B&O Railroad. It runs from Georgetown in Washington DC through Bethesda and ends in west Silver Spring (in Lyttonsville). The trail is heavily used by commuters and recreational users and passes through wooded areas and parks, over four historic bridges, and through two tunnels. Parts of the trail have scenic views of the Potomac River.

Food

The **Sergio Ristorante Italiano** (8727 Colesville Rd., 301/585-1040, Mon.-Fri. 11:30am-9:30pm, Sat. 5pm-9:30pm, $11-30) is underappreciated. This cozy little establishment serves authentic Italian fare with a personal touch. The food is consistently delicious, and the owner is very involved in making sure each guest has a good experience.

For a classic diner experience, the **Tastee Diner** (8601 Cameron St., 301/589-8171, www.tasteediner.com, open 24/7, under $10) is hard to beat. This landmark diner originally opened in 1946 on Georgia Avenue and was moved to its current location in 2000. It remains one of two original diners with a vintage railroad car design in Montgomery County. They are known for their BLTs but have a wide variety of breakfast, lunch, and dinner menu items.

The historic **Mrs. K's Toll House** (9201 Colesville Rd., 301/589-3500, www.mrsks. com, brunch Sun. 10:30am-2:30pm, lunch Tues.-Fri. 11:30am-2pm, dinner Tues.-Thurs. 5pm-9pm, Fri.-Sat. 4:30pm-9:30pm, Sun. 5pm-8pm, $18-38) offers a quaint country-house atmosphere in one of the last existing tollhouses in the county. Built in the early 1900s, the home was a working tollhouse with living quarters for the keeper and his family. The home was turned into a restaurant in 1930 offering a charming ambience, beautiful gardens, and a variety of interior antiques. The menu offers filet, seafood, venison, lamb, and vegetarian dishes. The menu is not oriented towards children. There is a lovely wine bar in the basement.

For delicious Indian cuisine stop in **Jewel of India** (10151 New Hampshire Ave., 301/408-2200, www.jewelofindiamd.com, Sun.-Thurs. 11:30am-3pm and 5pm-10pm, Fri.-Sat. 11:30am-3pm and 5pm-10:30pm, $12-22). This little gem primarily serves dishes from northern India with some Indochinese entrées. The atmosphere is sophisticated and somewhat contemporary. They serve a very tasty and high-quality lunch buffet, and the dinner menu has plenty of variety and vegetarian selections.

A good seafood house that takes pride in its food is **Crisfield Seafood Restaurant** (8012 Georgia Ave., 301/589-1306, www. crisfieldseafood.com, Tues.-Thurs. 11am-9pm, Fri.-Sat. 11am-10pm, Sun. noon-9pm, $15-28). This traditional restaurant has an old-time counter, tiled walls, and a truly retro feel (not a trendy, hip feel—this is the real deal). They serve delicious seafood and some of the best crab cakes in the county. The decor isn't fancy, but the food is simple and fresh.

Accommodations

Silver Spring offers mostly chain hotel accommodations such as the **Hilton Garden Inn Silver Spring North** (2200 Broadbirch Dr., 301/622-3333, www.hiltongardeninn3. hilton.com, $128-153), the **Sheraton Silver Spring** (8777 Georgia Ave., 301/589-0800, www.marriott.com, $139-199), and the **Courtyard by Marriott Silver Spring Downtown** (8506 Fenton St., 301/589-4899, www.marriott.com, $205-699) in downtown Silver Spring.

Getting There and Around

Downtown Silver Spring can be reached from Washington DC by car in less than 20 minutes (using Georgia Avenue or 16th Street). Metrobus service is available in Silver Spring, as are Montgomery County's Ride On buses (www.montgomerycountymd.gov).

GAITHERSBURG

Gaithersburg is located in central Montgomery County, five miles north of Rockville, and was incorporated in 1878. It has a population of around 69,000 and is the third-largest incorporated city in Maryland. I-270 runs through Gaithersburg, dividing it into east and west sections of the city.

Eastern Gaithersburg is home to a historic business district that is sometimes referred to as "Olde Town" Gaithersburg. The Montgomery County Fair Grounds are also on the eastern side of the city.

The west side of Gaithersburg is primarily neighborhoods, although several major employers are located there, such as the National Institute of Standards and Technology (NIST) and several information-systems and global services corporations.

Sights

RIO WASHINGTONIAN CENTER

The main center of activity in Gaithersburg is the **Rio Washingtonian Center** (9841 Washingtonian Blvd., 301/203-4159, www.riolakefront.com). This premier shopping area is in the heart of the city in combination with the **Waterfront and Rio Entertainment Center.** Together they offer 760,000 square feet of retail space, restaurants, and entertainment venues. The center is set on a lake, and there is a walkway around the lake, a carousel ($6), playground, and paddleboats for rent ($15-25) on the water. Outdoor dining is plentiful, and the area is generally safe and clean. Parking can be a little tough on the weekends.

INTERNATIONAL LATITUDE OBSERVATORY

The only National Historic Landmark in Gaithersburg is the **International Latitude Observatory** (100 DeSellum Ave., 301/258-6350, www.gaithersburgmd.gov, call ahead for tours). This small, 13-square-foot building was constructed in 1899 as part of an international effort to record the earth's wobble on its polar axis. The observatory is one of six in the world (in the United States, Japan, Russia, and

Italy) that gathered information still used by today's scientists. The station was in operation until 1982, when its functions were replaced by computers. The original Zenith telescope that was used in the observatory is now on display at the **Gaithersburg Community Museum** (9 S. Summit Ave., 301/258-6160, www.gaithersburgmd.gov, Tues.-Sat. 10am-3pm, free), which is in the historic 1884 B&O Railroad Station complex and offers exhibits on the city's history.

Recreation

East of Gaithersburg, on the border with neighboring Howard County, are two wonderful recreational lakes: the **Triadelphia Reservoir** and the **Rocky Gorge Reservoir.** They share an information center (2 Brighton Dam Rd., Brookeville, 301/206-7485, www.wsscwater.com) where boat launch permits ($6) and maps can be obtained. The lakes are both dammed portions of the Patuxent River and provide water to Montgomery and Prince George's Counties. There are no natural lakes in Maryland, so without the creation of reservoirs, it would have been difficult to provide water to the many homes and businesses in the state. The Washington Suburban Sanitary Commission, which is more than 100 years old, created both Triadelphia Reservoir and Rocky Gorge Reservoir and is still responsible for maintaining them. Both are wonderful locations for kayaking and fishing. No gasoline-powered engines are allowed on either lake.

The **Metropolitan Ballet Theatre and Academy** (220 Perry Pkwy., no. 8, 301/762-1757, www.mbtdance.org) provides training in ballet, jazz, tap, hip-hop, and modern dance. Students perform with the company in professional performances (sometimes with professional artists).

Food

Il Porto (245 Muddy Branch Rd., 301/590-0735, www.ilportorestaurant.com, Mon.-Sat. 11:30am-10pm, Sun. 11:30am-9pm, $10-20) is a reasonably priced Italian restaurant serving delicious food. They feature traditional Italian dishes and fresh seafood. All food is made to order. The service is outstanding, and this popular restaurant doesn't seem to rest on its laurels despite its excellent reputation. Expect a crowd on weekend evenings.

Good Mediterranean food can be found in the Kentlands area at **Vasilis Kitchen** (705 Center Point Way, 301/977-1011, www.vasiliskitchen.com, lunch Mon.-Fri. 11am-3pm, brunch Sat.-Sun 11am-3pm, dinner Sun.-Thurs. 4pm-10pm, Fri.-Sat. 4pm-11pm, $17-30). They serve a traditional Greek menu with succulent fresh vegetable side dishes. The lamb is especially savory, meaty, and cooked to perfection. This is a popular restaurant, but they do not take reservations so plan accordingly.

Great beer and upscale pub food can be found at **Dogfish Head Alehouse** (800 W. Diamond Ave., 301/963-4847, www.dogfishalehouse.com, Mon.-Thurs. 11am-11pm, Fri.-Sat. 11am-midnight, Sun. 11am-10pm, $10-20). The restaurant is a little off the beaten path (west of downtown) but is still convenient to many businesses and neighborhoods. They serve sandwiches, pizza, fish, and other pub food, plus a great selection of standard and seasonal beers.

Accommodations

Accommodations in Gaithersburg include many popular chain hotels. The **Comfort Inn Shady Grove** (16216 S. Frederick Rd., 301/330-0023, www.choicehotels.com, $101-123) is one of the nicest Comfort Inns in the area and offers 127 comfortable rooms, good service, and reasonable rates. The **Hampton Inn & Suites Washington DC/ North Gaithersburg** (960 N Frederick Ave., 301/990-4300, www.hilton.com, $197-249) offers 125 guest rooms, free parking, and complimentary breakfast.

The **Courtyard by Marriott Gaithersburg Washingtonian Center** (204 Boardwalk Pl., 301/527-9000, www.marriott.com, $196-269) is a lovely hotel on the lake at the Washingtonian Center. It is very convenient to shopping and restaurants and has 203 rooms and seven suites.

GERMANTOWN

Germantown sits 6.5 miles northwest of Gaithersburg along I-270 with a population of around 90,000. It is one of Montgomery County's fastest-growing areas and has seen a large increase in the number of neighborhoods, communities, and schools in recent years. Germantown is approximately 25 miles from Washington DC.

Black Rock Center for the Arts

The center of Germantown is along Middlebrook Road. This is where the **Black Rock Center for the Arts** (12901 Town Commons Dr., 301/528-2260, www.blackrockcenter.org), a cultural center offering shows, classes, camps, and an art gallery, is located, as well as the **Germantown Commons** (13060 Middlebrook Rd.) shopping area.

Black Hill Regional Park

Just north of Germantown and west of I-270 is **Black Hill Regional Park** (20930 Lake Ridge Dr., Boyds, 301/528-3490, www.montgomeryparks.org, daily sunrise-sunset, free). This lovely 1,843-acre park is home to a scenic recreational lake called **Little Seneca Lake,** a great place to kayak and fish with 505 acres of water and 15 miles of shoreline. The park also features hiking trails and the **Black Hill Visitors Center** (20926 Lake Ridge Dr., 301/528-3488, Wed.-Fri. 11am-5pm, Sat.-Sun. 11am-6pm). Kayak, canoe, and rowboat rentals are available May-September for $14 per hour or $50 per day.

★ Sugarloaf Mountain

North of Germantown in nearby Frederick County is **Sugarloaf Mountain** (7901 Comus Rd., Dickerson, 301/874-2024, www.sugarloafmd.com, daily 8am-one hour prior to sunset, free). Sugarloaf Mountain is a popular recreational area for people in Maryland's Capital Region. It is a small mountain (1,282 feet) that is a designated National Natural Landmark.

Sugarloaf Mountain is a monadnock, which is an isolated mountain that rises sharply from the surrounding ground. Because of this, the mountain can be seen for miles away and is an easily recognizable landmark.

The mountain is a public park that is accessible for recreation at no charge. Activities in the park include hiking, picnicking, and rock climbing. It is also known for its scenic views of the Monocacy Valley.

Sugarloaf Mountain is 15 miles northwest of Germantown and 10 miles south of Frederick. From I-270 take the Hyattstown exit to State Route 109 to Comus. Turn right on Comus Road. This will lead to the Sugarloaf Mountain entrance.

White's Ferry

Sixteen miles west of Germantown on the Potomac River in Dickerson is **White's Ferry** (24801 Whites Ferry Rd., Dickerson, 301/349-5200, daily 5am-11pm, $5 one-way or $8 round-trip, cash only), the only one of about 100 ferries that used to be in business on the Potomac River that is still in operation. It is the only crossing on the river between the American Legion Bridge on I-495 and the bridge at Point of Rocks in Frederick County, Maryland. Commuters rely on the small ferry for daily transportation, and the ferry is heavily used by recreational travelers on weekends. The ferry runs on a wire cable every 20 minutes year-round 5am-11pm daily unless the river is flooded or there is bad weather. Bicycles ($2) and pedestrians ($1) are welcome aboard.

Prince George's County

Prince George's County was named after Prince George of Denmark (1653-1708), who was married to Queen Anne of Great Britain. Today the county is a hub for federal government agencies.

Part of the Atlantic coastal plain, Prince George's County has a combination of gently rolling hills and valleys. The county borders the Patuxent River on its east side and has some lovely wildlife habitat.

Prince George's County is more city suburb than tourist destination and faces more crime issues and economic challenges than neighboring Montgomery County. However, there are some gems worth visiting while in the area, including National Harbor, the home stadium for the Washington Redskins, and a well-known site for dinosaur fossils.

GETTING THERE AND AROUND

Amtrak (4300 Garden City Dr., 800/872-7245, www.amtrak.com) provides train service to Landover at the New Carrollton station. The **Maryland Transit Administration** MARC train (410/539-5000, http://mta.maryland.gov) provides weekday-only service to five stations in Prince George's County on the Camden Line (College Park, Greenbelt, Muirkirk, Laurel, and Riverdale) and three stations on the Penn Line (New Carrollton, Seabrook, and Bowie).

The **Washington Metropolitan Area Transit Authority (WMATA)** (202/637-7000, www.wmata.com) provides **Metrorail** and **Metrobus** service to Prince George's County. The county is serviced by Metrorail's Green Line in College Park and Greenbelt, the Blue Line to Largo, and the Orange Line to New Carrollton.

A local bus system in Prince George's County is **TheBus** (301/324-2877, www.princegeorgescountymd.gov, 5:30am-8pm, adults $1.25, under 18, seniors, and disabled ride free), which operates on weekdays only and has 28 routes.

★ NATIONAL HARBOR

Twelve miles south of downtown Washington DC, National Harbor sits across the Potomac River from Old Town Alexandria. This trendy addition to the Washington DC metro area is a little oasis in Prince George's County, offering world-class dining, accommodations, and activities. The area was previously a forgotten 350-acre parcel of land on the Potomac River banks that was the site of an abandoned plantation. Then a large local development firm embarked on a seven-year project to create a new hot spot of local and tourist activity. The first phase of the project opened in 2008, and since then, the site has become the location of a convention center, multiple hotels, restaurants, retail space, and condominiums. The area continues to undergo development. Festivals and other outdoor events are also held at National Harbor.

Sights

CAPITAL WHEEL

The **Capital Wheel** (116 Waterfront St., 301/842-8650, www.thecapitalwheel.com, hours vary daily, adults $15, children 3-11 $11.25, 60 and over $13.50, under 2 free) is a prime attraction at National Harbor. This 180-foot-tall modern Ferris wheel sits on a pier on the Potomac River. The ride offers terrific views of the river and harbor. Each climate-controlled gondola seats up to eight people, with the exception of the VIP gondola, which holds four. The VIP gondola has leather bucket seats and a glass floor ($50). All rides are 12-15 minutes.

CAROUSEL AT NATIONAL HARBOR

The **Carousel at National Harbor** (137 National Plaza, 301/842-8650, www. nationalharbor.com, Memorial Day-Labor Day Sun.-Thurs. noon-8pm, Fri.-Sat. noon-10pm, shorter hours the rest of the year, children $7, adults ride free with a paid child) is an Americana-themed carousel located at the north end of National Harbor on the waterfront. Kids of all ages can enjoy its whimsical animals. There is a playground near the carousel.

THE AWAKENING SCULPTURE

The Awakening is a five-part, 72-foot, cast-iron sculpture that depicts a bearded giant waking up and rising out of the earth. The pieces include the giant's head, hand, outstretched arm, knee, and foot. This impressive artwork by J. Seward Johnson was originally part of a public art exhibition in Washington DC in 1980, when it was installed at Hains Point near the Jefferson Memorial. After the exhibition, the sculpture remained on loan to the National Park Service. *The Awakening* was purchased by the Peterson Companies (which developed National Harbor) in 2008 and moved to the beach at the harbor.

Entertainment and Events

A big draw at National Harbor is the **MGM National Harbor Casino** (101 MGM National Ave., Oxon Hill, 301/971-5000, www.mgmnationalharbor.mgmresorts.com, 24 hours). It contains 125,000 square feet of gaming space with slot machines, blackjack, poker, and other table games.

The Theater (101 MGM National Ave., Oxon Hill, 844/346-4664, www. mgmnationalharbor.mgmresorts.com) at the MGM National Harbor hotel is a prime entertainment venue in the DC area. It is a high-tech theater with 3,000 seats and state-of-the-art sound, lighting, and video. The theater hosts big-name entertainers such as Aerosmith, Avril Lavigne, Britney Spears, Patti LaBelle, and Chris Tucker. VIP suites are available.

If a dueling piano bar sounds like fun, make a reservation at **Bobby McKey's** (172 Fleet St., 301/602-2209, www.bobbymckeys. com, $7-20). This two-story venue holds up to 450 people and hosts regular shows and private parties. Reservations can be made online for standing room or a reserved seat. Due to the popularity of this place as the only live music venue in National Harbor and the only dueling piano bar in the Washington DC area,

it's best to reserve a seat. This is a loud but unique show and can be a lot of fun if you're in the mood for it. Tips are expected for requests.

ICE! (www.gaylordhotels.com) is an annual ice-sculpture event held at the Gaylord National Resort & Convention Center. Visitors walk through a huge winter wonderland carved from 5,000 blocks of ice shipped in from a factory in Ohio. More than 40 international sculptors work for 30 days prior to the event to produce a themed ice "land" where people can see, touch, and walk inside the amazing works of art. The event has a different theme each year and runs mid-November through early January. Tickets are around $30.

Shopping

National Harbor offers a large variety of retail stores including outlet stores, boutiques, jewelry stores, and other specialty shops. For more information visit www.nationalharbor.com.

A Touch of Fancy (164 Waterfront St., 240/319-3163, Mon.-Thur. 11am-8pm, Fri.-Sat. 11am-9pm, Sun. 11am-7pm) offers hand-selected seasonal home décor items with an ever-changing inventory.

America! (177 Waterfront St., 301/686-0413, Mon.-Fri. 9am-9pm, Sat. 8am-10pm, Sun. 10am-7pm) is a popular souvenir shop that sells items such as Official White House Ornaments, mugs, hats, and Washington team clothing.

Sports and Recreation

National Harbor offers a first-class marina with large floating docks and easy water access to many attractions in the Washington DC area via the Potomac River. Kayak, paddleboard, and pedal boat rentals are available right at the dock through **Boating in DC** (165 Waterfront St., www.boatingindc.com, from $16 per hour). Guided bass fishing is also available through **National Bass Guide**

Service (703/380-7119, www.nationalbass.com, from $300 for four hours).

The harbor is also the site of many annual athletic events. Whether you are looking to do a short fun run, a half marathon, a triathlon, a competitive open-water swimming event, or you simply want to do yoga on the beach, National Harbor is the place. A list of events is available on the website (www.nationalharbor.com).

A nice beachfront walking path along the Potomac connects National Harbor to a bike trail on the Woodrow Wilson Bridge. This allows walking and cycling into Alexandria across the river.

Food

Upscale dining at the **Old Hickory Steakhouse Restaurant** (201 Waterfront St., 301/965-4000, www.marriott.com, daily 5:30pm-9:30pm, $28-52) in the Gaylord Hotel is hard to beat. The atmosphere is first-rate, with views of the harbor, and the food is dependable and delicious. This sophisticated restaurant serves high-quality steak and delicious seafood. They also have an award-winning wine list.

Upscale Mexican food can be found at **Rosa Mexicano** (153 Waterfront St., 301/567-1005, www.rosamexicano.com, brunch Sat.-Sun. 11am-3pm, lunch Mon.-Fri. 11:30am-4pm, dinner Mon.-Thurs. 4pm-10pm, Fri. 4pm-11pm, Sat. 3pm-11pm, Sun. 3pm-10pm, $17-29) on the waterfront. They offer indoor and outdoor seating (weather permitting) and lively decor. The menu consists of fresh Mexican dishes featuring seafood, steak, and other delicious ingredients. The signature Guacamole en Mocajete is made tableside and a great choice for a starter. They have an extensive bar menu (not cheap, but good), and the service is wonderful.

For surprisingly good counter-service crab cakes made with lump crabmeat, stop in the **Crab Cake Café** (140 National Plaza, 240/766-2063, daily 11am-10pm, $6-27). This is a low-key-order-at-the-counter-and-grab-a-table-inside-or-on-the-sidewalk-type of

1: *The Awakening* sculpture at National Harbor
2: MGM National Harbor Casino

establishment. They offer soup, salad, sandwiches and entrées. All crab cakes are gluten free. It's a good option for a quick lunch with local flare.

Southern cuisine with inviting brick-and-wrought-iron decor can be found at **Succotash** (186 Waterfront St., 301/567-8900, www.succotashrestaurant.com, lunch Mon.-Fri. 11:30am-4pm, brunch Sat.-Sun. 10am-3pm, dinner Mon.-Thurs. 4pm-10pm, Sat. 3pm-11pm, Sun. 3pm-10pm, $11-39). Delicious and comforting entrées such as fried chicken and waffles, shrimp and grits, and cast-iron trout are staples on the menu, as are snacks such as hushpuppies with green-tomato jam and crispy okra.

Accommodations

The ★ **Gaylord National Resort and Convention Center** (201 Waterfront St., 301/965-4000, www.marriott.com, $199-519) is a Marriott-owned hotel that anchors the National Harbor. This massive 18-floor hotel has 1,890 guest rooms, an impressive 19-story glass atrium, indoor gardens, and panoramic views of the Potomac River. A conference center with 89 meeting rooms, the hotel is always bustling, but the staff is friendly and the rooms are very comfortable. There is a fitness center, indoor pool, spa, 94 event rooms, and seven restaurants on-site. Self-parking is available for $30 a day and valet for $49.

The ★ **MGM National Harbor** (101 MGM National Ave., 301/971-5000, www.mgmnationalharbor.mgmresorts.com, $199-469) is a luxury 23-story, 308-room hotel and entertainment venue. It features a 3,000-seat concert venue, a 125,000-square-foot casino, shops, a spa/salon, multiple restaurants from acclaimed chefs, and a sports bar with 90 televisions. Rooms and suites are available with views of the Potomac River, and the Presidential Suite is 2,462 square feet. Self-parking at the time of writing was complimentary for guests, but the hotel aims to move to pay parking. Valet parking is available for $25 for 12 hours and $45 for 12-24 hours. Discounts throughout the resort are given to active and retired military and their spouses.

The **Residence Inn National Harbor** (192 Waterfront St., 301/749-4755, www.marriott.com, $254-319) has 162 suites on seven floors, some with great views of the water. This Marriott hotel offers roomy suites with full kitchens and separate sitting areas. There is a small pool, a small fitness room, a complimentary breakfast buffet, and a manager's reception Monday-Thursday. The hotel is within walking distance of attractions and restaurants in National Harbor, and there is a parking lot near the rear hotel entrance (a discount on parking is offered to hotel guests).

Another good option for accommodations in National Harbor is the **Hampton Inn & Suites National Harbor** (250 Waterfront St., 301/567-3531, www.hamptoninn3.hilton.com, $171-289). This 151-room hotel is welcoming and convenient to the National Harbor attractions. Guests can enjoy a complimentary breakfast buffet, wireless Internet, a pool, and a fitness center. Parking is available for $20.

Information and Services

For additional information on National Harbor, visit www.nationalharbor.com or stop by the **Potomac River Heritage Visitors Center** (6800 Oxon Hill Rd., Mon.-Sat. 9am-9pm, Sun. 10am-7pm).

Getting There

National Harbor is a 20-minute drive south of Washington DC. The closest major highway is the Beltway (I-495), but from DC, I-295 is the primary route. **Water taxi** service is also available from Old Town Alexandria in Virginia (www.potomacriverboatco.com, adults from $10, kids from $7).

GREATER UPPER MARLBORO

Greater Upper Marlboro is a suburb of Washington DC with approximately 19,000 residents. It is 18 miles west of DC in south-central Prince George's County off US 301 and State Route 4. The area encompasses approximately 77 square miles and is primarily residential with many neighborhoods and housing developments. The Patuxent River runs near Upper Marlboro and with it brings protected land for wildlife and recreation near the city.

Sights

★ MERKLE WILDLIFE SANCTUARY

The **Merkle Wildlife Sanctuary** (11704 Fenno Rd., 301/888-1377, www.dnr.maryland. gov, daily sunrise to sunset, free) is the only wildlife sanctuary run by the Maryland Department of Natural Resources. It is best known as the wintering ground for the largest concentration of Canada geese on the western shore of the Chesapeake Bay. The sanctuary offers visitors a one-way, self-guided 4.3-mile Critical Area Driving Tour (CADT), open to cars on Sunday 10am-3pm year-round. The CADT is available to hikers, bikers, and horseback riders daily January 1 through September 30, but closed to these users the rest of the year in order to provide a peaceful area for the migrating geese and other waterfowl.

The **Frank Oslislo Visitors Center** (weekends 10am-4pm) sits on a hill overlooking several ponds. This beautiful building has a two-story wall of windows, balconies for viewing the surrounding area, and a large bird-feeder-viewing area. The center features exhibits on Canada geese and other wildlife and environmental topics. A live-animal exhibit with turtles, snakes, and toads is also offered for children.

Four hiking trails at the sanctuary provide access to upland forests and marsh areas. The trails are only open to hikers, and weekly nature hikes are available.

Five fishing ponds are open to the public between April 1 and October 1 for largemouth bass, bluegill, and other types of fishing. Those planning to fish should sign in outside the visitors center.

PATUXENT RURAL LIFE MUSEUMS

The **Patuxent Rural Life Museums** (16000 Croom Airport Rd., 301/627-6074, www. pgparks.com, Apr.-Oct. Sat.-Sun. 1pm-4pm, free) comprises several museums and farm buildings that preserve the heritage of southern Prince George's County. The buildings are in the 7,000-acre **Patuxent River Park** and include a tool museum, a blacksmith shop, a tobacco farming museum, a log cabin (with a smokehouse), a 1923 Sears catalog house, and a hunting, fishing, and trapping museum.

Merkle Wildlife Sanctuary

Exhibits are on display in the museums, and living-history demonstrations are featured. Guided tours of the museums are available all year by appointment (301/627-6074, $4). Guided nature hikes ($4) and river ecology boat tours ($4) are also available and take 45-60 minutes. Kayaking/canoeing tours can be scheduled for small groups ($33 per boat).

DARNALL'S CHANCE HOUSE MUSEUM

Darnall's Chance House Museum (14800 Governor Oden Bowie Dr., 301/952-8010, www.pgparks.com, guided house tours by appointment Tues.-Thurs. 10am-4pm, tours by walk-in Fri. and Sun. noon-4pm, adults $5, children 5-8 $2, seniors $4) interprets the history and culture of Prince George's County women in the 18th century. The focus is on a longtime resident of the house, Lettice Lee, who lived there prior to the American Revolution. The home is listed in the National Register of Historic Places, the National Underground Railroad: Network to Freedom Trail, and the Star-Spangled Banner National Historic Trail. The home and grounds are portrayed as they were in 1760 when Lee's first husband passed away and the contents of the house were documented room by room. The museum also portrays the lives of the enslaved African American women who worked in the home, and tours address the similarities and differences between their lives and that of Lee. Interactive children's programs and events are held throughout the year.

A rare 17-foot-long burial vault was discovered at the museum in 1987. It contained household garbage from the 18th and 19th century as well as the remains of nine people (three adults and six children).

Recreation and Events

The **Prince George's Equestrian Center** (14900 Pennsylvania Ave., 301/952-7900, www.showplacearena.com) is the primary event venue in Upper Marlboro and includes numerous tracks, a schooling ring, and stables for more than 200 horses. The center hosts the annual **Prince George's County Fair** (www.countyfair.org) each September. The fair began in 1842 and is the longest-running fair in Maryland. Other popular events that take place at the center include antiques shows and concerts. The center is also the site of the **Show Place Arena** (www.showplacearena.com), which hosts circuses, rodeos, hockey games, conventions, and trade shows.

Six Flags America (13710 Central Ave., 301/249-1500, www.sixflags.com, mid-May-Aug. daily, early May and Sept.-Oct. select weekends, tickets start at $42.49) is located between Upper Marlboro and Bowie (near Largo). This large theme park is the only one of its kind in Maryland and features more than 100 rides, a water park (Hurricane Harbor), shows, and other attractions. This is a fun place to bring the kids, but the park is a bit aged, and it is not uncommon for some of the rides to be closed due to malfunctions. The park has nine roller coasters and new rides open seemingly every season. They also have specific rides for small kids. The park opens at 10:30am but closing times vary a lot throughout the season; check the website or call ahead for more information.

Watkins Regional Park (301 Watkins Park Dr., 301/218-6700, www.pgparks.com, daily dawn-dusk, free) is a great regional park with an antique carousel, train, nature center, tennis, camping, and miniature golf. The **Old Maryland Farm** (Tues.-Fri. 9am-4pm, Sat. 9am-4:30pm, Sun. 11:30am-4:30pm) is within the park (a short walk from the train station) and features agricultural exhibits, gardens, and live animals.

Food

Jasper's (9640 Lottsford Ct., Largo, 301/883-9500, www.jaspersrestaurants.com, Mon.-Thurs. 11am-1am, Fri.-Sat. 11am-2am, Sun. 10am-midnight, $7-27) offers seafood, steak, burgers, and sandwiches in an upscale and casual environment. This is a popular restaurant with good food. They are open late and are often very busy on weekends. The entire menu is available to go.

Greenbelt: A Planned City

Greenbelt was conceived as a New Deal housing project and will be forever known as the first planned community in the country to be built by the federal government. It was designed in 1935 as a complete city, including housing, businesses, schools, roads, government facilities, and recreational facilities. The city was an experiment in social and physical planning modeled after 19th-century English garden cities. It included one of the first mall shopping centers.

The name came from the area of green forests that surround the city and from the "belts" of natural areas between its neighborhoods that keep residents in contact with nature. Greenbelt is a National Historic Landmark.

If you're in the mood for good Caribbean food, stop by **Caribbean Flava** (5050 Brown Station Rd., 301/574-2003, Mon.-Thurs. noon-9pm, Fri.-Sat. noon-10pm, $6-20). They offer dishes such as seafood soups, curry goat, oxtail, jerk chicken, and curry vegetables. They even make homemade drinks such as ginger beer and carrot mango juice. Order before you get there since everything is made when ordered. There is limited seating but they offer takeout and delivery.

Accommodations

Upper Marlboro isn't known for its selection of good accommodations. Visitors may prefer to spend the night in neighboring Largo, northwest of Upper Marlboro, where there are a few choices such as the **Holiday Inn Express I-95 Beltway Largo** (9101 Basil Ct., 301/636-6090, www.ihg.com, $136-200), which has 89 rooms, an indoor pool, and a fitness center; or the **Residence Inn Largo Capital Beltway** (1330 Caraway Ct., 301/925-7806, www.marriott.com, $170-311), located within walking distance of the Largo Towne Center DC Metrorail station. They offer a free hot breakfast and free parking.

LANDOVER

Landover is a suburban area northwest of Upper Marlboro and Largo. It is 11 miles northeast of Washington DC and is best known as the home of the **Washington Redskins** professional football team. Their home field, **FedExField** (1600 FedEx Way, 301/276-6000, www.redskins.com) was built in 1994 and originally called Jack Kent Cooke Stadium after the former owner of the team. When the team was purchased by Daniel Snyder, FedEx Corporation purchased the naming rights. Although FedExField is one of the largest football stadiums in terms of seating capacity in the NFL (with seating for 85,000), it sells out all nonpremium tickets every year and has a season-ticket waiting list of more than 30 years.

FedExField has its own exit from I-495 (the Beltway): 16 (Arena Drive).

GREENBELT

Greenbelt, seven miles north of Landover and 30 minutes from Washington DC, is home to **NASA's Goddard Space Flight Visitor Center** (8800 Greenbelt Rd., 301/286-8981, www.nasa.gov, Sept.-June Tues.-Fri. 10am-3pm, Sat.-Sun. noon-4pm, July-Aug. Tues.-Fri. 10am-5pm, Sat.-Sun. noon-4pm, free). The center is a wonderful place to learn about NASA's work in earth science, astrophysics, planetary science, technology development, and other projects. Unique interactive exhibits teach people of all ages about topics such as climate change and space exploration. Exhibits include *Decade of Light,* which explores how humans will maintain contact with Earth as they venture further into the Solar System; *Goddard Rocket Garden,* a collection of artifacts from space; and *Solarium,* a large-scale sun-focused digital art installation featuring footage that scientists use. This is a fun place for kids who are interested in space travel.

BOWIE

Ten miles northeast of Landover is the city of Bowie. With a population of nearly 59,000, the city has blossomed from its beginnings as a small rail stop on the Baltimore & Potomac Railroad to the biggest municipality in the county.

Bowie was originally called Huntington City when it was founded in 1870. The original downtown area is now referred to as "Old Bowie," but some landmarks still bear the Huntington name.

Sights

BELAIR MANSION

The **Belair Mansion** (12207 Tulip Grove Dr., 301/809-3089, www.cityofbowie.org, Tues.-Sun. noon-4pm, free) is a Georgian plantation home that was built in 1745 for the provincial governor of Maryland, Samuel Ogle. In the early 1900s, the mansion became the residence of a noted Thoroughbred horse breeder named William Woodward. The home is listed in the National Register of Historic Places, and the museum interprets the lives of the people who lived there between 1747 and 1950. Visitors can see items such as family silver, a stunning colonial revival card table, paintings, and other artwork.

The mansion's stables now operate as the **Belair Stable Museum** (2835 Belair Dr., 301/809-3089, www.cityofbowie.org, Tues.-Sun. noon-4pm, free). Although horse breeding began on the property in the 1740s, the current barn that houses the museum was built in 1907 as part of the Belair Stud Stable, one of the top breeding stables in the country from the 1920s to 1960. The only father/son horses to win the Triple Crown race series (Gallant Fox in 1930 and Omaha in 1935) were raised in the stable. The museum highlights the 200-year Thoroughbred-racing legacy of the Belair's bloodstock and explains other agricultural uses of the property. Both museums are operated by the city of Bowie.

BOWIE RAILROAD MUSEUM

The **Bowie Railroad Museum** (8614 Chestnut Ave., 301/809-3089, www. cityofbowie.org, Tues.-Sun. 10am-4pm, free) sits next to active train tracks at the no-longer-in-service Bowie Railroad Station. The museum features displays on the history of the railroad in Bowie and includes photographs and artifacts in three structures: a switch tower, a passenger waiting shed, and a freight depot. A caboose that dates back to 1922 and was part of the Norfolk and Western Railroad is on the museum grounds.

NATIONAL CAPITAL RADIO AND TELEVISION MUSEUM

Radio and television buffs will enjoy the **National Capital Radio and Television Museum** (2608 Mitchellville Rd., 301/390-1020, www.ncrtv.org, Fri. 9am-4pm, Sat.-Sun. noon-4pm, free). This small, two-story museum offers a tour back in time through the evolution of radio and television. There are displays of memorabilia and a large collection of antique receivers. Visitors can hear authentic radio broadcasts and view early television shows on vintage televisions.

Sports and Recreation

A great minor league baseball park (home of the Class AA Bowie Baysox) is **Prince George's Stadium** (4101 Crain Hwy., 301/805-6000, www.milb.com). This clean, friendly ballpark offers reasonably priced seats, free parking, and the opportunity to see up-and-coming Baltimore Orioles players.

A pleasant 85-acre, family-oriented park is **Allen Pond Park** (3330 Northview Dr., 301/809-3011, www.cityofbowie.org, daily sunrise to sunset). It has a pond, walking path, playground, skateboard ramp, indoor ice rink (Bowie Ice Arena), amphitheater, basketball courts, fields for baseball, lacrosse, and soccer, and more. The park hosts a great fireworks display each July 4th.

Food

"Fresh, Casual, and Friendly" is the slogan of the **Chesapeake Grille & Deli** (6786 Race Track Rd., 301/262-4441, www.eatchesapeake. com, Sun.-Thurs. 11am-9pm, Fri.-Sat. 11am-10pm, $10-23), and they deliver with flavorful sandwiches, seafood, and steak. This is not a fancy place, but the family-owned restaurant offers good food and dependable service. They are open daily for lunch and dinner.

The only place to find the original Crab Bomb is **Jerry's Seafood** (15211 Major Lansdale Blvd., 301/805-2284, www.jerrysseafood.com, Mon.-Sat. 11:30am-10pm, Sun. noon-8pm, $12-39). This family-owned seafood house is known for its crab dishes (the trademarked Crab Bomb includes 10 ounces of jumbo lump crabmeat), but they also offer other types of seafood and several nonseafood dishes. This restaurant is also known for good service.

Accommodations

For short and extended stays, the **Towne Place Suites Bowie Town Center** (3700 Town Center Blvd., 301/262-8045, www.marriott.com, $119-309) is hard to beat. This Marriott hotel offers 119 suites on four floors, complimentary breakfast, a fitness center, pool, and free on-site parking. The rooms are amply sized and clean. Pets are allowed for an additional fee. It is near shopping and restaurants.

The **Comfort Inn Conference Center** (4500 Crain Hwy., 301/464-0089, www.choicehotels.com, $109-159) offers mini fridges, microwaves, and coffeemakers in each room, complimentary breakfast, and wireless Internet. On-site parking is available, and there is a restaurant and bar at the hotel. This is a good hotel for business travelers, and the breakfast food is above average for a chain hotel.

Information and Services

For additional information on Bowie, visit www.cityofbowie.org or stop by the **Old Town Bowie Welcome Center** (8606 Chestnut Ave., 301/575-2488, Tues.-Sun. 10am-4pm).

COLLEGE PARK

College Park is 13 miles west of Bowie in the northwestern part of Prince George's County. The city has a population of around 32,000 and is best known as the location of the **University of Maryland, College Park.** The U.S. National Archives and Records Administration also has a facility in College Park known as Archives II.

Sights
UNIVERSITY OF MARYLAND, COLLEGE PARK
The **University of Maryland, College Park** (301/405-1000, www.umd.edu) was founded in 1856 as a public research university. It is the largest university in Maryland, with more than 40,000 students, and it offers more than 90 undergraduate majors in 12 colleges and 230 graduate programs. On campus is a 150-acre research park that was honored as an Outstanding Research Park in 2015. The campus also features the Physical Sciences Complex, which encompasses more than 160,000 square feet and is a space for collaborative efforts with nearby federal agencies, such as NASA.

★ COLLEGE PARK AVIATION MUSEUM
The **College Park Aviation Museum** (1985 Corporal Frank Scott Dr., 301/864-6029, www.collegeparkaviationmuseum.com, daily 10am-5pm, adults $5, children $2, seniors $4) is a nice little museum that is affiliated with the Smithsonian Institution and focuses on the earliest days of mechanical flight. Many of the exhibits in the 27,000-square-foot space are geared toward children and offer a hands-on experience with coloring, video games, puzzles, a flight simulator, and a plane to climb on. There is also information on the Wright Brothers, who made a flight attempt nearby.

The museum is in an open 1.5-story exhibit space on the site of the world's oldest continuously operating airport. The airport opened in 1909 when Wilbur Wright gave flight instruction there to the inaugural group of military aviators in the first army aviation school. The airport has numerous other notable "firsts" in the aviation field, such as the first mile-high

flight, the first bomb-dropping test, the first female passenger in the United States, and many more. Visitors can watch planes on the runway from the glass windows inside the museum.

This is a nice family museum, and the volunteers are friendly and informative. There are no food services at the museum, but visitors can picnic outside in nice weather.

Entertainment and Events

The **Clarice Smith Performing Arts Center** (8270 Alumni Dr., 301/405-2787, www.theclarice.umd.edu) is part of the University of Maryland, College Park, and offers many free and reasonably priced events such as musical and theatrical performances, lectures, and workshops.

Food

Get the traditional diner experience at the **College Park Diner** (9206 Baltimore Ave., 301/441-8888, open 24/7, under $10). This great little place runs like a well-oiled machine. The breakfast food is the best choice (served all day), but the country-fried steak is also a winner. Patrons can watch their meal being cooked since the kitchen is at the front of the building. This is a good place to come when looking for a local establishment or a late-night eatery. The tables turn over quickly, the servers are friendly and helpful, and you may even be called "Hon."

Good, inexpensive pho can be found at **Pho D'Lite** (8147 Baltimore Ave., 301/982-5599, www.phodlite.com, daily 10:30am-9:30pm, $8-11). They offer good specials on weekday afternoons. Try their Thai iced tea.

Accommodations

There are a handful of national hotels in College Park. For the most part, they are fairly comparable with standard accommodations and conveniences. Three hotels that

are convenient to the University of Maryland campus are the **Holiday Inn Washington College Park** (10000 Baltimore Ave., 301/345-6700, www.ihg.com, $91-125), which has 220 guest rooms on five floors and free wireless Internet; the **Hampton Inn College Park** (9670 Baltimore Ave., 301/345-2200, www.hamptoninn3.hilton.com, $94-140), with 80 guest rooms, free breakfast, free high-speed Internet, and a fitness room; and the **Best Western Plus College Park** (8419 Baltimore Ave., 301/220-0505, www.bestwestern.com, $101-209), with 40 guest rooms, complimentary full breakfast, a fitness center, and free Wi-Fi.

Information and Services

Additional information on College Park can be found at www.collegeparkmd.gov.

LAUREL

Laurel is 10 miles north of College Park in northern Prince George's County and also spills into Anne Arundel and Howard Counties. It was originally developed as a mill town, its cotton mills utilizing the power of the Patuxent River. It has a population of around 25,000.

Sights

DINOSAUR PARK

You may be surprised to learn that one of the most important dinosaur sites east of the Mississippi River is in Laurel. Most people rush past the site on Route 1 and never have a clue what lies nearby. At **Dinosaur Park** (13100 Mid-Atlantic Blvd., 301/627-1286, www.pgparks.com, daily dawn-dusk, free), rare fossil deposits from the Early Cretaceous period include those from several types of dinosaurs (including *Astrodon johnstoni*), early mammals, and early plants and trees. What makes this location special is that it is part of an exposed layer of the Muirkirk Deposit, a rare fossil-bearing clay found on the East Coast. The park was created to preserve and protect the rare fossil deposits, to provide a natural laboratory for scientists to discover

1: bronze statue on the University of Maryland, College Park campus of Kermit the Frog with alumnus Jim Henson, created by artist Jay Hall Carpenter 2: College Park Aviation Museum

Maryland's State Dinosaur

Dinosaur bones were found in Maryland as early as the late 1800s. The first dinosaur remains discovered in Maryland were that of a long-necked plant-eater named *Astrodon johnstoni* (think "veggiesaur" from the movie *Jurassic Park*). Astrodon was gigantic (at least 60 feet long) and weighed several tons. One femur was found in the 1990s that weighed 220 pounds and was six feet long. The name Astrodon came from a starburst pattern found in a cross section of the dinosaur's teeth. The species name *johnstoni* was added later in honor of a Maryland Academy of Sciences dentist, Christopher Johnson, who played a significant role in its identification.

In 1998, the Maryland State Assembly officially designated *Astrodon johnstoni* the official state dinosaur. Only six states (Maryland, Colorado, Wyoming, Missouri, New Jersey, and Texas) and the District of Columbia have official dinosaurs.

new fossils, and to allow the public the opportunity to work with paleontologists to uncover new findings. The public is welcome to explore an interpretive garden that is open daily and features descriptions of the prehistoric landscape in Maryland and the dinosaurs that lived there. A fenced-in fossil area is only accessible during featured programs and during open houses held on the first and third Saturday of each month noon-4pm.

NATIONAL WILDLIFE VISITOR CENTER

The **National Wildlife Visitor Center** (10901 Scarlet Tanager Loop, 301/497-5770, www.fws.gov, Fri.-Wed. 9am-4:30pm, free) is a U.S. Fish and Wildlife Service facility that sits on more than 12,000 acres in the **Patuxent Research Refuge.** The center is the largest science and environmental education center within the U.S. Department of the Interior. The center features interactive exhibits that teach the value of wildlife research and also focus on worldwide environmental issues. They also explore migratory bird routes, wildlife habitat, and recovery efforts for endangered species. There are countless opportunities for recreation in the surrounding forests, lakes, and trails.

MONTPELIER MANSION

The **Montpelier Mansion** (9650 Muirkirk Rd., 301/377-7817, www.pgparks.com, Mon., Tues., Thurs., and Fri. 9am-5pm, Sat.-Sun. 11am-4pm, $5) is a Georgian-style mansion that was built in the 1780s for Major Thomas Snowden and his wife. Many noteworthy guests were entertained in the home, including George Washington. The home sits on 70 acres and is a National Historic Landmark. Several rooms in the mansion were refurbished to appear as they did at the close of the 18th century. Both guided and self-guided tours of the home are available. Montpelier Mansion hosts many concerts, festivals, and seminars.

Entertainment and Events

The **Venus Theatre** (21 C St., 202/236-4078, venustheatre.org) is a regional theater with the largest production company in Maryland. Their focus is on the adaptation of classics.

The **Laurel Mill Playhouse** (508 Main St., 301/617-9906, www.laurelmillplayhouse. org) is a local playhouse that is home to the Burtonsville Players, a community theater group that has been around for more than 35 years.

Sports and Recreation

The **Laurel Park Racecourse** (Route 198 and Racetrack Rd., 301/725-0400, www. laurelpark.com) is a Thoroughbred racetrack that opened in 1911. The track has hosted legendary horses such as War Admiral and Secretariat. Races are still held there regularly, and a schedule can be found on the website.

The **Fairland Sports and Aquatics**

Complex (13820 and 13950 Old Gunpowder Rd., 301/362-6060, www.pgparks.com) is part of **Fairland Regional Park.** The complex includes facilities for swimming, tennis, racquetball, gymnastics, weightlifting, and massage therapy. The **Gardens Ice House** (www.thegardensicehouse.com) is also within the park and offers three ice rinks for skating, hockey, curling, and speed skating.

Food

The **Dutch Country Farmers Market** (9701 Fort Meade Rd., 301/421-1454, www. laureldutchmarket.com, Thurs. 9am-6pm, Fri. 9am-7pm, Sat. 8am-3pm) is a wonderful market that's open three days a week. Stop in and enjoy the smell of fresh-baked pies and other delectables. There is a wide variety of food to purchase including meat, fresh produce, homemade soup, smoothies, and bread. A restaurant on-site serves simple but tasty food and has good service.

Accommodations

Like much of Prince George's County, Laurel primarily offers national chain hotel accommodations. One worth considering is the **Hampton Inn Laurel** (7900 Braygreen Rd., 240/456-0234, www.hamptoninn3.hilton. com, $123-175). It provides 80 guest rooms with strong, free wireless Internet service and complimentary breakfast.

The **Double Tree by Hilton Laurel** (15101 Sweitzer Ln., 301/776-5300, www. doubletree3hilton.com, $98-155) has 208 guest rooms on six floors, a fitness center, and wireless Internet. There's a restaurant on-site. They are pet friendly.

The **Holiday Inn Express Laurel** (14402 Laurel Pl., 301/206-2600, www.ihg.com, $108-140) has 117 suites, offers complimentary breakfast, is pet friendly, and has free high-speed Internet access, an indoor pool, and a fitness center. Guest laundry services are also available.

Information and Services

For additional information on Laurel, visit www.cityoflaurel.org.

Baltimore

Baltimore has been a major port city since the 1700s. This hardworking city is the birthplace of many industries: the first sugar refinery in the country (1796), the first gaslight company (1819), and the first railroad for commercial transportation (1828). Having spent much of its history as a rough industrial seaport, Baltimore managed to keep its treasures to itself. In the 1970s, outsiders started to recognize the city's hidden charm, and the working-class town was nicknamed "Charm City." Today, after a series of successful urban renewal projects, Baltimore has blossomed into a major mid-Atlantic tourist destination. It flaunts world-class museums, state-of-the-art sports venues, fine dining, and luxury hotels—all while retaining its fierce spirit and authenticity.

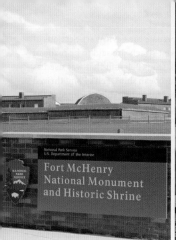

Highlights

Look for ★ to find recommended sights, activities, dining, and lodging.

★ **National Aquarium, Baltimore:** The gem of the Inner Harbor offers close encounters with sharks, dolphins, and many other sea creatures. Catch a show or sign up for a special slumber party (page 391).

★ **Historic Ships:** This unique collection on display in the Inner Harbor features four military ships and one lighthouse within easy walking distance (page 393).

★ **Port Discovery Children's Museum:** One of the top children's museums in the country, this educational playground offers three floors of interactive exhibits (page 394).

★ **B&O Railroad Museum:** See the birthplace of the American railroad system. Vintage engines and cars are part of the fun (page 396).

★ **Baltimore Museum of Industry:** This fascinating museum shares the history of many everyday conveniences (page 403).

★ **Fort McHenry National Monument and Historic Shrine:** This 1802 fort inspired the poem written by Francis Scott Key that became the U.S. national anthem (page 403).

★ **The Walters Art Museum:** This remarkable collection spans 5,000 years and includes a mummy from 1000 BC and two imperial eggs (page 405).

★ **Carroll County Farm Museum:** Glimpse rural life in the mid-19th century on a 142-acre farm (page 437).

ORIENTATION

For simplicity's sake, we're going to focus on six primary sections of Baltimore. They are key areas where popular sights are located, as well as trendy neighborhoods where you can find a delightful selection of food, nightlife, and activities.

Downtown and the Inner Harbor

Most of the beauty shots of Baltimore are taken downtown and at the Inner Harbor. The harbor has long been the center of activity in this port city and was once a thriving destination for visitors and supplies arriving by steamship. Although most people think that Baltimore sits on the Chesapeake Bay, the harbor is actually the mouth of the Patapsco River. The river flows into the bay east of the city, which is why this deepwater yet protected harbor has been popular for centuries. After the collapse of the steamship era, the port still saw industrial action, but lapsed into a state of neglect as the city fell off the radar as a vacation destination.

In the 1970s interest in the city was revived as Baltimore underwent extensive, innovative redevelopment. The Inner Harbor benefited greatly from the rejuvenation and became home to many attractions, museums, restaurants, upscale hotels, and a beautiful waterfront promenade. The surrounding downtown area received a boost as well and offers a blend of businesses, historic buildings, and museums.

Fell's Point and Little Italy

On the harbor, Fell's Point is about a five-minute drive east from the Inner Harbor or can be reached by water taxi. It is one of the oldest neighborhoods in Baltimore, with many historic buildings and trendy eateries. Fell's Point was first settled by the English Quaker William Fell in 1726, and many of the 350 historic buildings were constructed before 1800 (200 predate the Civil War). Sections of the waterfront streets are said to be made of blond block from Belgium that was used as ballast in European ships. Fell's Point thrived until the need for sailing ships declined in the early 1900s, after which the neighborhood entered a steep decline. The waterfront became a collection of rough saloons, and in the mid-1960s plans for the building of I-95 had it running right through the neighborhood. The community was able to stop the highway, and instead the neighborhood became the first National Historic District in Maryland.

Nearby Little Italy (www.littleitalymd.com) was settled in the mid-1800s by Italian immigrants, who opened businesses and restaurants in the cozy little area between the Inner Harbor and Fell's Point. The area now boasts almost 30 restaurants and also offers visitors vibrant festivals and a bit of old-world Italy.

Canton

East of Fell's Point on the waterfront is the historic community of Canton, which dates back to the late 19th century. Modern condos and old row houses fuse Baltimore's past and present, and lively **Canton Square** on O'Donnell Street offers bars, restaurants, and endless nightlife for the local partying crowd. The Canton waterfront includes views of navy ships as they dock nearby.

Federal Hill

Opposite the Inner Harbor on the south side of the harbor, Federal Hill is named after an imposing rise that boasts a fantastic vantage point for viewing the Inner Harbor and downtown Baltimore. Federal Hill has great shopping, bars, restaurants, and entertainment as well as a thriving residential area. It is home to the famed 120-by-70-foot neon Domino Sugar sign, which casts a glow over the city from its 160-foot-high perch. A Baltimore icon, the sign has been a fixture on the harbor since 1951.

Previous: Fell's Point waterfront; Fort McHenry National Monument and Historic Shrine; National Aquarium, Baltimore

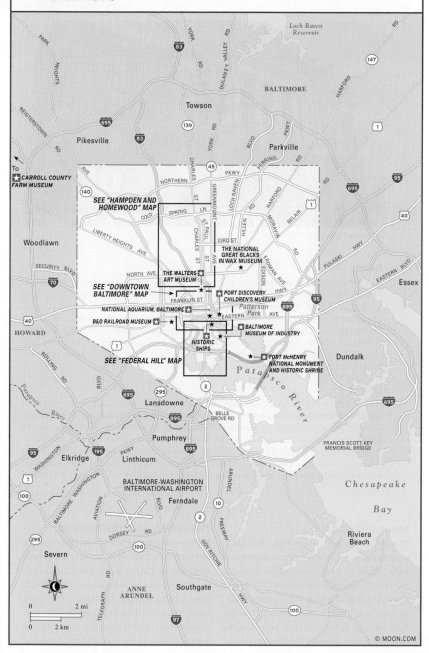

Baltimore

BALTIMORE

© MOON.COM

Best of Baltimore

Sagamore Pendry Baltimore hotel

DAY 1

Start in the popular **Inner Harbor,** where you can get around on foot and visit the **National Aquarium** and the **Historic Ships** collection. Choose one of the restaurants in the busy harbor area for lunch before driving or taking the water taxi to the **Fort McHenry National Monument,** where Baltimore fended off a British attack during the War of 1812 and Francis Scott Key penned "The Star-Spangled Banner." Jump back on the water taxi or drive over to **Fell's Point** to explore its charming waterfront streets before having dinner at **Bar Vasquez.** End your evening at the cozy **Cat's Eye Pub** for some blues, jazz, or folk music, and then turn in for the night at the **Sagamore Pendry Baltimore.**

DAY 2

Start your day with breakfast at the popular **Blue Moon Café.** After breakfast, drive or take a cab to the Mount Vernon neighborhood and visit the **Walters Art Museum,** then climb the 228 stairs of the **Washington Monument** for a great view of the city. Grab some pizza at **Joe Squared,** then continue your cultural tour at the **Baltimore Museum of Art** in Homewood. Have dinner at **Woodberry Kitchen** just west of Hampden, and finish in time to take in a performance at **Centerstage** in Mount Vernon. Finish up your two-day tour with a drink and a wonderful view of the city at the classy **Owl Bar** in the historic Belvedere Hotel building.

Mount Vernon

Mount Vernon, north of downtown Baltimore, is the cultural center of the city. Museums and halls provide endless opportunities to take in a show or listen to the symphony. The neighborhood is full of grand 19th-century architecture, and marble-clad homes originally built for wealthy sea captains surround the first monument to honor our first president.

Hampden and Homewood

Northwest of Mount Vernon is the settlement of Hampden. This 19th-century neighborhood was originally a mill town but is now an eclectic mix of bars, restaurants, thrift stores, galleries, and boutiques. The local residents are both hardworking families and young adults, which gives the area a hip yet grounded feel. To the east of Hampden is the neighborhood of Homewood. Best known as the home of **Johns Hopkins University,** it also has nice parks and museums.

PLANNING YOUR TIME

You could easily spend a couple of weeks in Baltimore to really see all the city has to offer, but most people pick and choose sights of particular interest to them and explore the city in a long weekend.

People traveling with children may wish to stay at the Inner Harbor so they can visit the **National Aquarium,** the **Maryland Science Center,** and the **Port Discovery Children's Museum** and see the **Historic Ships** in the harbor. A visit to **Fort McHenry** is another fun option to pique the little ones' interest in history.

History buffs can pick almost any location in the city as their base and from there take in the **Baltimore Civil War Museum,** the **Star-Spangled Banner Flag House and Museum,** the **Washington Monument,** **Fort McHenry,** and Edgar Allan Poe's grave site at **Westminster Hall Burying Ground and Catacombs.**

Others come to sample the many restaurants and bars in the busy Fell's Point area or to take in a ball game at Camden Yards. No matter what your interests, there is no shortage of exciting itineraries to create. Baltimore is easy to get around and offers many appealing sights and activities regardless of how long you have to spend there.

If you have time for a full- or half-day excursion from Baltimore, consider putting Westminster or Havre de Grace on your list of places to visit. Westminster, 45 minutes northwest of Baltimore by car, sits in a rural part of the state and has a history of Civil War battles, spies, and ghosts. An hour car ride north on I-95 will take you to the bayside town of Havre de Grace. Its charming seaside atmosphere at the head of the Chesapeake Bay makes the town a rewarding destination for touring and outdoor recreation.

Sights

DOWNTOWN AND THE INNER HARBOR

TOP EXPERIENCE

★ National Aquarium, Baltimore

The **National Aquarium, Baltimore** (501 E. Pratt St., 410/576-3800, www.aqua. org, Sun.-Thurs. 9am-5pm, Fri. 9am-8pm, Sat. 9am-6pm, adults $39.95, children 3-11 $29.95, seniors 65 and over $34.95) is perhaps the most treasured sight in Baltimore's Inner Harbor. Opened in 1981, it was the anchor to the redevelopment plan of the Inner Harbor. The aquarium was one of the first large aquariums in the country and remained independent until it joined with the National Aquarium in Washington DC under the blanket name "National Aquarium" in 2003.

Close to 20,000 animals live at the National Aquarium, representing more than 660 species of fish, amphibians, reptiles, birds, and mammals. See the brilliant coral-filled Blacktip Reef exhibit, which mimics Indo-Pacific reefs and offers stunning floor-to-ceiling "pop-out" viewing windows so visitors can get personal with 65 species of animals. Then watch fearsome sharks swim by in their 225,000-gallon ring-shaped tank in Shark Alley, or see divers feed brightly colored fish as you descend the winding ramp through the 13-foot-deep tropical reef tank in the Atlantic Coral Reef exhibit. Another breathtaking experience can be found in the Tropical Rain Forest. This world-renowned exhibit expertly mimics a real rain forest with live tropical birds, sloths, Tamarin monkeys, and even poison dart frogs. A diverse

Downtown Baltimore and the Inner Harbor

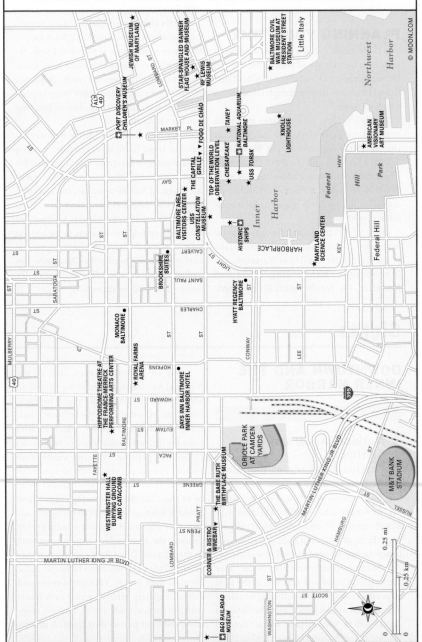

© MOON.COM

Harbor Pass

Many of the popular sights in Baltimore can be accessed with a single ticket that offers discounted entry over individual admission prices. A four-day **Harbor Pass** (877/225-8466, www.baltimore.org, adults age 13 and up $74.95, ages 3-12 $56.95) includes admission over four consecutive days into five top attractions. Different options are available for the pass, but all include the National Aquarium, Top of the World (Observation Level), Maryland Science Center, plus two additional museums such as the Port Discovery Children's Museum, the American Visionary Art Museum, the Reginald F. Lewis Museum of Maryland African American History & Culture, and the Babe Ruth Birthplace Museum.

selection of authentic rain forest plant life is also part of this habitat.

The aquarium's award-winning habitats are expertly designed and instantly engage visitors by drawing them into the world of the animals they feature. They also offer demonstrations such as the Dolphin Discovery, where visitors can see dolphins feeding, training, and enjoying playtime.

4-D Immersion films ($5) are shown at the aquarium, and behind-the-scenes tours ($15-195) are available. Overnight dolphin and shark sleepovers, in which guests can spend the night at the aquarium ($125), are two of the more popular activities. Reservations for all the behind-the-scenes activities should be made well in advance. Tickets to the aquarium are issued on a timed-entry system (allow at least three hours for your visit), so you can purchase tickets online for the time you'd like to visit. The aquarium is a popular attraction year-round but can be especially crowded during the hot summer days when school is out of session. Try to avoid this time if your schedule allows for it, or visit late in the day after the crowds have thinned out.

★ Historic Ships

The **Historic Ships** (Inner Harbor Piers, 301 E. Pratt St., 410/539-1797, www.historicships.org, June-Aug. Sun.-Thurs. 10am-5pm, Fri.-Sat. 10am-6pm, shorter hours rest of year, adults up to two ships $15, four ships $18, students/teens 15-20 and seniors over 60 up to two ships $13, four ships $16, youth 6-14 up to two ships $7, four ships $9, children 5 and under free, lighthouse included in all passes) in the Inner Harbor form one of the most impressive military-ship collections in the world. Visitors can tour four ships and a lighthouse (all within easy walking distance of one another) and view 50,000 photographs, documents, and personal items that relate to the ships.

The first, the **USS *Constellation*** (Pier 1), was a sloop of war from 1854 to 1955. The USS *Constellation* was the last all-sail ship built by the U.S. Navy, and it was the flagship of the U.S. African Squadron from 1859 to 1861. Visitors can begin their tour in the museum gallery at the pier to learn about the ship's history through artifacts and personal items that once belonged to the crew. From there, grab a complimentary audio tour wand and go aboard. The "Plan of the Day" will be posted with a list of activities taking place on the day of your visit. If you're lucky, you may get to witness the live firing of the Parrott rifle. Uniformed crew members are on board to answer questions as you explore the ship's four decks.

The second, the submarine **USS *Torsk*** (Pier 3), is the most exciting to visit. Commissioned in 1944, it was one of just 10 Tench-class submarines to serve in World War II. Visitors can tour the entire boat, including the torpedo rooms, operation station, engine room, crew quarters, and navigation station. It is difficult to believe that more than 80 navy personnel lived aboard the sub at one time.

The third ship is the lightship *Chesapeake* (Pier 3), built in 1930. Used as a navigational aid, a lightship is moored on a permanent or semipermanent basis and has beacons mounted to it. Lightship duty meant long days sitting in place on the water and scary times riding out storms. Visitors can see a unique exhibit on sailors' canine companions.

The fourth ship is the USCG cutter *Taney* (Pier 5), built in 1935. A cutter is defined as a Coast Guard ship that is over 65 feet in length and has accommodations for a crew to live aboard. Visitors can tour this authentic cutter that was decommissioned in 1986 and remains pretty much the same as it was when in use.

Standing 40 feet tall, the **Knoll Lighthouse** (Pier 5) is one of the oldest Chesapeake Bay-area lighthouses and was erected at the mouth of the Patapsco River on a shallow shoal known as Seven Foot Knoll. It offers a detailed exhibit on how the lighthouse was built back in 1856.

Guided walking tours of the USS *Constellation* (adults 21-59 $12-15, seniors 60+ $9-12, teen/student 15-20 or with valid ID $9-12, youth 6-14 $5-6, children 5 and under free) are available for groups of 10 or more people over age six. Tours include museum admission, presentations, hands-on activities, and a Civil War-era sailor as your guide through the ship. Powder Monkey Tours are offered to children ages six and over. These interactive tours teach little ones about the young boys (ages 11-18) who served on fighting ships during the Civil War and were responsible for moving gunpowder from the powder magazine of the ship to the artillery pieces. Powder Monkey Tours are available every Saturday and Sunday at 1pm.

The Babe Ruth Birthplace Museum

The Babe Ruth Birthplace Museum (216 Emory St., 410/727-1539, www. baberuthmuseum.com, Apr.-Sept. daily 10am-5pm, Oct.-Mar. Tues.-Sun. 10am-5pm, adults $10, children 5-16 $5, seniors/military $8), three blocks west of Oriole Park at Camden Yards, is located inside the home where Babe Ruth was born in 1895 (you can

even visit the bedroom where he first entered the world). From the west side of the stadium, look down and follow the 60 painted baseballs on the sidewalk to the museum. Babe Ruth memorabilia are on display in the museum, and visitors can learn little-known information on this legend's private life. The museum also screens a film entitled *"The Star-Spangled Banner" in Sports* and has a courtyard for events.

★ Port Discovery Children's Museum

The **Port Discovery Children's Museum** (35 Market Pl., 410/727-8120, www. portdiscovery.org, Memorial Day-Labor Day Mon.-Sat. 10am-5pm, Sun. noon-5pm, shorter hours the rest of the year, $17.95, children under one year free), one of the top five children's museums in the country, is geared toward children up to age 10. The museum offers three floors of interactive exhibits with the goal of connecting learning and play. Exhibits focus on art, science, and health.

Interactive exhibits draw children into a learning adventure. The *Adventure Expeditions* area is "part physical adventure and part mental obstacle course," in which children decipher hieroglyphics, look for clues, and are eventually led to a lost pharaoh's tomb in Egypt. Another fully interactive exhibit is *Kick It Up*, an indoor soccer and games stadium. Here children either play soccer or get involved in interactive, electronic games during which they can compete in a dance competition, ride a bike, and sharpen their balance. Toddlers (ages 2 and up) can "cook" and serve their parents food in Tiny's Diner, a realistic, 1950s-style diner.

The museum is geared completely toward children, so adults can take pleasure in the joy on their little ones' faces but shouldn't expect a lot of exhibits that will capture their own interests. Also, children are free to run through

---

1: Baltimore skyline **2:** USS *Constellation*, one of the historic ships docked in the Inner Harbor **3:** Port Discovery Children's Museum **4:** the B&O Railroad Museum

the halls and explore the many fun and entertaining exhibits, so things can get a bit chaotic on busy days. Socks and sneakers are the recommended footwear in order to participate in all the activities. The museum is just north of the Inner Harbor. It gets crowded in the summertime, so going early or late in the day is a good option.

Maryland Science Center

The **Maryland Science Center** (601 Light St., 410/685-2370, www.mdsci.org, Apr.-June Mon.-Fri. 10am-5pm, Sat. 10am-6pm, Sun. 11am-5pm, July-Aug. daily 10am-6pm, shorter hours in winter, adults $24.95, children 3-12 $18.95, seniors 62 and over $23.95) is a great place to bring the kids for a hands-on learning experience. The *Dinosaur Mysteries* exhibit is a must-see that will amaze the little ones with life-size models of prehistoric creatures. *Your Body: The Inside Story* takes kids on an adventure to learn what happens inside a human body in a 24-hour period. In this unique exhibit, visitors can go inside a heart and lungs and feel the heart beat and the lungs breathe. They can also hear a loud concert of digestive noises and interact with germs. Other exhibits cover topics such as life on other planets, everything electric, and a kids' room for children under eight. Additional features in the center include *Science Encounters*, where visitors can see animated data projected on a sphere or look at the night sky through a telescope in the on-site observatory. The museum also has a planetarium and an IMAX theater.

Top of the World

For the best view of Baltimore, visit the **Top of the World** (401 E. Pratt St., 410/837-8439, www.viewbaltimore.org, June-Sept. Mon.-Thurs. 10am-6pm, Fri.-Sat. 10am-9pm, Sun. 11am-6pm, reduced hours the rest of the year, adults $6, children 3-12 $4, seniors 60 and over and military $5), on the 27th floor of **Baltimore's World Trade Center.** The Top of the World is a 360-degree observation area with a spectacular view of the city skyline, the harbor, and surrounding areas through expansive windows. Stationary binoculars and photo map guides are available. Visitors are subject to manual searches of personal belongings.

★ B&O Railroad Museum

The **B&O Railroad Museum** (901 W. Pratt St., 410/752-2490, www.borail.org, Mon.-Sat. 10am-4pm, Sun. 11am-4pm, adults $20, children 2-12 $12, seniors over 60 $17) is a National Historic Landmark and the birthplace of the American railroad system. The Baltimore & Ohio Railroad (yes, the one on the Monopoly game board) originated on Pratt Street in Baltimore in 1828. The facility was a station and repair shop on 100 acres. Visitors can go inside the 123-foot-tall roundhouse built in the early 1870s that was the turn-around area for large steam engines (they rolled onto a large turntable to reposition). The roundhouse is now a museum for historic train cars. Museumgoers can look at the cars and also take a short ride on the original rail tracks. The Alex Brown & Sons Exhibition Gallery displays railroad-related artifacts from the museum's collection and those of other institutions such as the Smithsonian. Displays on the B&O Railroad's critical role in the Civil War show how the railroad changed the tactics for war and tell personal stories of the people who kept the railroad running during the conflict.

Westminster Hall Burying Ground and Catacombs

What came first, the church or the cemetery? In the case of the **Westminster Hall Burying Ground and Catacombs** (519 W. Fayette St., 410/706-2072, daily during daylight hours, free), the answer is the cemetery by more than 65 years. The cemetery was first used in 1786. Many famous Baltimore residents are interred in the burying ground, including Edgar Allan Poe (who was actually buried there twice—his coffin was relocated from his family plot to its current spot near the cemetery gate), General James McHenry,

The Edgar Allan Poe Toaster

Edgar Allan Poe was one of Baltimore's most famous and mysterious citizens. He led a life of tragedy plagued by poverty, illness, and death. Poe was born in 1809 in Boston. The grandson of a Revolutionary War patriot, David Poe Sr., Edgar Allan Poe was orphaned at the age of three. Although he went to live with the Allan family in Richmond, he was never legally adopted and never really accepted fully into the family.

Poe enlisted in the army and after his discharge came to Baltimore to live with his widowed aunt in the neighborhood now known as Little Italy. He left for a brief time to attend West Point, but returned to live with his aunt and a few other family members again, although this time in West Baltimore on Amity Street. It was here that Poe began writing short stories (prior to this time he had focused primarily on poetry).

Poe was awarded a $50 prize by a Baltimore newspaper for his short story "MS Found in a Bottle." Many short stories followed, including "Berenice," which caused a stir for being too gruesome. In 1835 Poe returned to Richmond. The following year, he married his 13-year-old cousin, Virginia, in Richmond.

Edgar Allan Poe's grave at Westminster Hall Burying Ground and Catacombs

In 1847, Virginia died of tuberculosis. Poe only lived another two years before he died mysteriously back in Baltimore and was buried with his wife and aunt in **Westminster Hall Burying Ground and Catacombs** (519 W. Fayette St., 410/706-2072, daily during daylight hours, free).

The author is still shrouded in mystery, even after death: For 60 years (1949-2009), an unidentified visitor made a yearly trip to Poe's grave in the early hours on his birthday. The visitor was called the "Poe Toaster" because he made a toast of cognac to the grave and left three roses. Although he ended his visits in 2009 for reasons unknown, the Toaster had such an influence that the tradition was resurrected in 2016 with a new Toaster as part of a staged daytime event.

The **Edgar Allan Poe House & Museum** (203 N. Amity St., 410/462-1763, www.poeinbaltimore.org, Thurs.-Sun. 11am-4pm, adults $8, students/military/seniors $6, 12 and under free) is the house Poe lived in for a short time in West Baltimore. The house itself, which is a 2.5-story, five-room brick duplex (now part of a line of row houses) is the primary attraction of the museum and displays a few of Poe's personal items including a telescope. The immediate surrounding area is not recommended for sightseeing for safety reasons.

and Francis Scott Key's son, Philip Barton Key. Westminster Hall was built in 1852, at the intersection of Fayette and Greene Streets. The church was constructed above some of the graves on top of brick piers. The result was the creation of catacombs under the church, which visitors can tour. The outside burying ground, where Poe's grave is, is free to tour. There is a fee (adults $5, children $3) to tour Westminster Hall and the Catacombs; public tours are offered on the first and third consecutive Friday (at 6:30pm) and Saturday (at 10am) of the month from April to November. At least 15 people are required for a tour.

Baltimore Visitors Center

The **Baltimore Visitors Center** (401 Light St., 877/225-8466, www.baltimore.org, daily 10am-5pm) is on the waterfront on the Inner Harbor. This 8,000-square-foot facility offers information on sights, events, harbor cruises, and other activities to do in Baltimore. Visitors can even purchase tickets here for local attractions. There's a walk-in fountain

The Johns Hopkins Hospital: Pioneering Modern Medicine

The Johns Hopkins Hospital

The Johns Hopkins Hospital (1800 Orleans St.) is known as one of the best hospitals in the world. In the heart of Baltimore, north of Fell's Point and east of Mount Vernon, this teaching hospital and biomedical research facility for the Johns Hopkins University School of Medicine forms with that institution a $5 billion system of physicians, scientists, and students.

Funding for the hospital and school originally came from a wealthy Baltimore banker and merchant, Johns Hopkins, who willed $7 million in 1873 for their founding.

Both the university and hospital set the standard for many modern American medical practices. Numerous specialties were developed here, including endocrinology and neurosurgery. From the beginning, the goal was to combine research, teaching, and patient care. This concept developed into the first model of its kind and led to unmatched success and an international reputation for excellence.

The Johns Hopkins Hospital is currently ranked third in the nation overall out of more than 4,700 hospitals. For additional information, visit its website at www.hopkinsmedicine.org.

next to the center where kids of all ages can cool off on hot days.

FELL'S POINT AND LITTLE ITALY
Fell's Point Visitors Center

A good place to begin exploring Fell's Point and Little Italy is at the **Fell's Point Visitors Center** (1724 Thames St., 410/675-6750, Tues.-Thurs. 10am-5pm, Fri.-Sat. 10am-8pm, Sun. 10am-5pm). They offer a great brochure for a walking tour of the neighborhood as well as information on the sights in the area.

Seasonal guided historic walking tours also leave from the center, and there is a gift shop.

Frederick Douglass-Isaac Myers Maritime Park

The **Frederick Douglass-Isaac Myers Maritime Park** (1417 Thames St., 410/685-0295, www.douglassmyers.org, Mon.-Fri. 10am-4pm, Sat.-Sun. noon-4pm, adults $5, children 6-17 $2, under 6 free, seniors $4) is a national heritage site/museum dedicated to African American maritime history. A series of exhibits chronicle the lives of Frederick

Fell's Point and Little Italy

0.25 mi

0.25 km

WASHINGTON

WOLFE ST

ST

ST

ST

ST

PETER'S INN

ANN

ROBERT LONG HOUSE

THAMES STREET OYSTER HOUSE

FELL ST

BROADWAY

MAX'S TAPHOUSE

SAGAMORE PENDRY BALTIMORE

BLUE MOON CAFE

FELL'S POINT VISITORS CENTER

KOOPER'S TAVERN

THAMES

PRATT ST

ST

EASTERN

FLEET

BOND

ALICEANNA

ONE-EYED MIKE'S

LANCASTER

ADMIRAL FELL INN

THE HORSE YOU CAME IN ON SALOON

LOMBARD ST

ST

CAROLINE

EDEN

BAR VASQUEZ

Fell's Point

BALTIMORE ST

ST

CENTRAL

CHARLESTON RESTAURANT

EXETER

JEWISH MUSEUM OF MARYLAND ★

STAR-SPANGLED BANNER FLAG HOUSE AND MUSEUM ★

AMICCI'S ▾

ANGELI'S PIZZERIA ▾

HIGH ST

ALBEMARLE ST

ST

Little Italy

COURTYARD MARRIOTT BALTIMORE DOWNTOWN/INNER HARBOR ★

ALT 40

PHOENIX (OLD BALTIMORE) SHOT TOWER ★

RF LEWIS MUSEUM ★

VACCARO'S ITALIAN PASTRY SHOP ★

PRESIDENT

BALTIMORE CIVIL WAR MUSEUM AT PRESIDENT STREET STATION ★

BALTIMORE MARRIOTT WATERFRONT HOTEL ●

Northwest Harbor

FAYETTE ST

BALTIMORE ST

ST

GAY ST

MARKET PL

PORT DISCOVERY CHILDREN'S MUSEUM ✚ ★

NATIONAL AQUARIUM, BALTIMORE ✚

TOP OF THE WORLD OBSERVATION LEVEL ★

HISTORIC SHIPS ★

Inner Harbor

AMERICAN VISIONARY ART MUSEUM ★

Federal HWY

Hill

Park

CALVERT

USS CONSTELLATION MUSEUM ★ ✚

HARBORPLACE

KEY

Federal Hill

© MOON.COM

Douglass and Isaac Myers. Douglass was a leader in the abolitionist movement, a former enslaved person, and a successful statesman and orator. He lived and worked on the docks in Baltimore. Myers was a mason and labor leader who created a first-of-its-kind union for African American caulkers just after the Civil War. Union members ultimately formed a cooperative, and that cooperative purchased a shipyard and railroad in Baltimore called the Chesapeake Marine Railway and Dry Dock Company. The park encompasses 5,000 square feet of gallery space and features interactive exhibits, maps, photos, and artifacts that share the history of the African American community and how it influenced Baltimore in the 1800s.

Robert Long House and Colonial Garden

The **Robert Long House and Colonial Garden** (812 S. Ann St., 410/675-6750, www.preservationsociety.com, guided tours of the first floor by reservation Jan.-Mar. Tues.-Sat. 1pm-2:30pm, Apr.-Dec. Mon.-Sat. 1pm-2:30pm) is the oldest city row house in Baltimore, having been built in 1765. It is a Georgian-style brick row house with a pent roof and now serves as the headquarters for the Preservation Society of Fell's Point and Federal Hill. The home belonged to Robert Long, who was a quartermaster for the Continental Navy. Visitors can see the garden and restored building, its interior furnished as it would have been during the Revolutionary War period.

Baltimore Civil War Museum at the President Street Station

The **Baltimore Civil War Museum** (601 President St., 443/220-0290, www. baltimorecivilwarmuseum.com, Fri.-Mon. 10am-4pm, adults $3, children 13-19 $2, 12 and under free) is a great stop for Civil War buffs. The museum is housed in a restored freight- and passenger-train depot that was known as the **President Street Station.**

Built in 1850, the depot is the oldest surviving city railroad terminal in the country. It was an important rail stop during the Civil War and the location of a famous riot that took place in April 1861 when the first Union troops stopped there on the way to Washington. The altercation marked the first bloodshed of the Civil War, and more than a dozen people (both soldiers and civilians) died in the riot. The museum displays artifacts and pictures that detail Baltimore's involvement in the Civil War. Tours are available by appointment.

Star-Spangled Banner Flag House and Museum

The **Star-Spangled Banner Flag House and Museum** (844 E. Pratt St., 410/837-1793, www.flaghouse.org, Tues.-Sat. 10am-4pm, adults $9, students $7, under 6 free, seniors/military $8) was the home of Mary Pickersgill, the woman who made the enormous and famous flag that flew over Fort McHenry on September 14, 1814, during the War of 1812 and inspired the poem written by Francis Scott Key that eventually became the U.S. national anthem. The house was built in 1793, and visitors can see what it looked like back when Mary lived there. The museum depicts the daily life in the home (that was also used as a business) around 1812, and living-history staff portray members of the Pickersgill family.

Jewish Museum of Maryland

The **Jewish Museum of Maryland** (15 Lloyd St., 410/732-6400, www.jewishmuseummd. org, Sun.-Thurs. 10am-5pm, adults $10, students 13 and over $6, children 4-12 $4, seniors 65 and over $8) offers visitors the opportunity to learn about regional Jewish history, culture, and community. One of the country's leading museums on regional Jewish history, it displays photographs, papers, and artifacts that are rotated regularly. The museum does a wonderful job of relating Jewish life in early

---

1: the pagoda in Patterson Park 2: Phoenix Shot Tower 3: Fell's Point

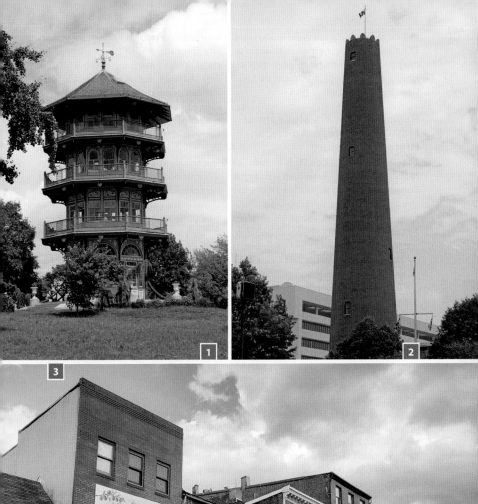

Baltimore and other small towns in Maryland. The museum oversees a modern museum facility and two historic synagogues: the B'nai Israel Synagogue, built in 1876, and the Lloyd Street Synagogue, built in 1845.

Reginald F. Lewis Museum of Maryland African American History & Culture

The **Reginald F. Lewis Museum of Maryland African American History & Culture** (830 E. Pratt St., 443/263-1800, www.africanamericanculture.org, Wed.-Sat. 10am-5pm, Sun. noon-5pm, adults $8, children 7-17, students with ID, seniors 65 and over, and veterans $6, children 6 and under free) is the largest museum on the East Coast dedicated to African American culture. Visitors can learn about the contributions of African Americans in Maryland throughout the state's history. The museum includes galleries, a genealogy center, recording studio, theater, café, and gift shop.

Phoenix Shot Tower

The **Phoenix Shot Tower** (801 E. Fayette St., 410/605-2964, adults $5, students, military, and seniors 65 and over $4, under 6 free), which is also known as the **Old Baltimore Shot Tower,** stands nearly 235 feet tall near the entrance to Little Italy. It was built in 1828 out of one million bricks and, at the time, was the tallest structure in the country. From 1828 to 1892, it was used to produce lead shot, done by dropping molten lead from a platform at the top of the tower. The lead ran through a sieve and landed in cold water. It is a National Historic Landmark. Tours of the Shot Tower are offered Saturday and Sunday at 4pm.

CANTON
Patterson Park

One of the oldest parks in Baltimore, **Patterson Park** (27 S. Patterson Park Ave., 410/276-3676, free) encompasses 134 acres and has a great view of the harbor. On **Hampstead Hill** inside the park, a pagoda designed in 1890 stands at the site where local residents rallied in 1814 to protect their city from the British. British troops had come up the Patapsco River and attacked Fort McHenry, and on land, they had forces just east of the city at North Point. As they entered Baltimore, the British saw 20,000 troops and a hundred cannons facing them on Hampstead Hill. This caused them to retreat from Baltimore and go back to their ships. The area became a park in 1853 but saw more military activity during the Civil War, when a military camp and war hospital were built there.

Today the park offers recreation trails, a lake, pavilions, playgrounds, an ice-skating rink, a public swimming pool, a recreation center, a stadium, and an adult day-care center.

Captain John O'Donnell Monument

The **Captain John O'Donnell Monument** (O'Donnell St. and S. Curley St.) is in the center of Canton Square. John O'Donnell was an Irish sea captain who purchased 1,981 acres in the 1780s in the area that is now Canton. He allegedly named it after the cargo from his ship, which contained goods from Canton, China. Captain O'Donnell's land included a house near current-day Boston Street and all the waterfront land east of the northwest branch of the Patapsco River between Colgate Creek and Fell's Point.

SS *John W. Brown*

The **SS *John W. Brown*** (Pier C, 2220 S. Clinton St., 410/558-0646, www.ssjohnwbrown.org, Wed. and Sat. 9am-2pm, free, donations appreciated) is one of two remaining Liberty ships out of the 2,700 that were produced by the Emergency Shipbuilding Program during World War II. They were designed for swift construction, and the SS *John W. Brown* was built in just 56 days. The ships were used for sealifts of troops, arms, and gear to all war locations.

The SS *John W. Brown* made 13 voyages and was awarded several honors during the war. Oddly, after the war, the ship served as a vocational high school in New York City from 1946 to 1982. It was acquired in 1988 by the current owner, Project Liberty Ship, and fully restored as a museum and memorial. As the only Liberty ship in operation on the East Coast, the boat hosts six-hour Living History Cruises several times a year. During these cruises, it visits other ports on the East Coast. The ship is part of the National Register of Historic Places and also a recipient of the World Ship Trust's Maritime Heritage Award.

FEDERAL HILL
American Visionary Art Museum

The **American Visionary Art Museum** (800 Key Hwy., 410/244-1900, www.avam.org, Tues.-Sun. 10am-6pm, adults $15.95, students/children $9.95, 6 and under free, seniors 60 and over $13.95) holds a collection of visionary art—slightly different from folk art in nature, but which to the untrained eye can look similar. The museum defines it as "art produced by self-taught individuals, usually without formal training, whose works arise from an innate personal vision that revels foremost in the creative act itself." In a nutshell, it seems like anything goes in this funky, interesting, and inspiring museum. It has art in all mediums—oil, mosaic, watercolor, toothpicks, and even bras.

★ Baltimore Museum of Industry

The **Baltimore Museum of Industry** (1415 Key Hwy., 410/727-4808, www.thebmi.org, Tues.-Sun. 10am-4pm, adults $12, students with ID and youth 7-18 $7, 6 and under free, seniors 62 and over $9) is housed in the original 1865 Platt Oyster Cannery building, the only remaining cannery structure in the city, and has exhibits on the history of industry and manufacturing in the Baltimore area. Traditionally a key industrial center, Baltimore was home to the first passenger train, the world's biggest copper refinery, the first traffic light, and the first gas company. Collections include 100,000 artifacts relating to small business, factory workers, and other citizens whose hard work helped shape the country. Featured fields include the garment, automobile, pharmaceutical, newspaper, and food industries and the Maryland Lottery. Many of the exhibits are interactive for both adults and children.

The museum is easy to find—just look for the large red crane out front. Be sure to watch the short introductory video near the museum entrance; it provides good insight into the background of the museum. Exhibits aren't limited to the indoors; visitors can also see the coal-fired SS *Baltimore,* a restored and operational steam tugboat from 1906, just outside the museum. Group tours of the museum are available. This is an interesting place for both adults and children over age 10. Plan on spending approximately two hours.

Federal Hill Park

Federal Hill Park (300 Warren Ave., 410/396-5828) is a lovely spot right off the harbor that offers great views of the Inner Harbor and downtown from atop Federal Hill. The park is on the south side of the harbor, and the terrain rises steeply. During the colonial era, the grassy hill was a mine for paint pigment, and the drooping hillside and footpaths indicate where old tunnels remain underground. The area has been a park since the late 1700s and remains a nice recreation and picnic area. There is also a playground on-site. On the northern side of the park are cannons from the Civil War that are symbols of those positioned by Union troops to face the city as a warning to Confederate sympathizers.

★ Fort McHenry National Monument and Historic Shrine

The **Fort McHenry National Monument and Historic Shrine** (2400 E. Fort Ave., 410/962-4290, www.nps.gov/fomc, daily 9am-5pm, extended summer hours, free admission to park, seven-day permit for Star Fort/historical area adults $15, children 15 and under free) is a 43-acre national park with

Federal Hill

CAMDEN YARDS

CONWAY ST

RUSSELL ST

S SHARP ST

FLEET ST

ALICEANNA ST

LANCASTER ST

MARTIN LUTHER KING, JR BLVD

395

LEE ST

KEY HWY

Federal

Inner Harbor

Fell's Point

BLOCK ST

W HILL ST

CHARLES ST

E MONTGOMERY ST

Hill Park

AMERICAN VISIONARY ART MUSEUM

295

W HAMBURG ST

E CHURCHILL ST

WARREN AVE

PSI NET STADIUM

E HAMBURG ST

RYLEIGH'S OYSTER BAR

ABBEY BURGER BISTRO

E CROSS ST

W CROSS ST

RACE ST

W WEST ST

CROSS STREET MARKET

COVINGTON ST

HARBORVIEW DR

W OSTEND ST

E WEST ST

E OSTEND ST

LIGHT ST

WILLIAM ST

BATTERY AVE

BALTIMORE MUSEUM OF INDUSTRY

WEBSTER ST

BOYLE ST

395

MARSHALL ST

E FORT AVE

HENRY ST

JACKSON ST

KEY HWY

E FORT AVE

LEADENHALL ST

RACE ST

2

E RANDALL ST

W HEATH ST

OLIVE ST

HARDEN CT

E HEATH ST

Riverside Park

E BARNEY ST

E BARNEY ST

E WELLS ST

95

95

Swan Park

To FORT McHENRY NATIONAL MONUMENT AND HISTORIC SHRINE

W DICKMAN ST

E CROMWELL ST

Patapsco River

S HANOVER ST

Middle Branch

Middle Branch Park

WATERVIEW AVE

SEAMON AVE

POFFE ST

0   0.25 mi

0   0.25 km

© MOON.COM

a historical area that houses Fort McHenry. It is east of Federal Hill and juts out into the harbor. Built between 1799 and 1802, the fort was named after James McHenry, secretary of war between 1796 and 1800, and constructed in the shape of a star with five points (aka the Star Fort). The star-shaped design was popular at the time since each point was within view of others to the left and right and the entire fort and surrounding area could be guarded with only five sentries.

Fort McHenry is known as the inspiration for "The Star-Spangled Banner." Francis Scott Key wrote the words to the anthem during the War of 1812 when he was held on a truce ship during the British attack on Baltimore. As the battle went on, Key watched from the water and through a smoke-filled landscape, and at "dawn's early light" on September 14, 1814, he could see the huge 30-by-42-foot American flag still flying above Fort McHenry as a symbol that Baltimore had not surrendered.

Begin your exploration at the visitor center and view the 10-minute video on the fort's history (shown every half hour starting at 9:05am). Exhibits on the fort, a gift shop, and restrooms are at the center. Then take a self-guided tour (approximately one hour) of the fort. Inside the fort is a large grassy area, and the rooms of the fort feature displays and authentic artifacts. Continue into the barracks (which include exhibits such as the enlisted men's quarters, weapons, uniforms, junior officer's quarters, the powder magazine, commanding officer's quarters, and the 1814 guard house). Children can participate in the Flag Change Program daily at 10am and 5pm, when they can assist rangers in raising and lowering a reproduced "Star-Spangled Banner" flag. On summer weekends, living-history interpreters tell stories about the fort and the people who lived in Baltimore while the facility was active. Allow 1.5-2 hours for your visit. There is no charge to visit the grounds.

MOUNT VERNON
★ The Walters Art Museum

The Walters Art Museum (600 N. Charles St., 410/547-9000, www.thewalters.org, Wed.-Sun. 10am-5pm, Thurs. until 9pm, free) showcases the personal art collection of two men: William Thompson Walters, an American industrialist and art collector, and his son, Henry Walters. Both collected paintings, antiques, and sculptures. Upon Henry Walters's death, their joint collection of more than 22,000 works of art was left to the city of Baltimore for the benefit of the public.

The Walters Art Museum houses fascinating permanent and temporary collections that span 5,000 years and five continents. It includes pieces from ancient Egypt, Roman sarcophagi, Renaissance bronzes, Chinese bronzes, and art nouveau jewelry. Two must-see items are an ancient Egyptian mummy from 1000 BC and one of the best collections of armor in the country (including a child's set of armor).

Be sure to visit the Chamber of Wonders, where the museum has brought to life an intricate scene from a 1620 painting that came from the area that is now Belgium. The scene

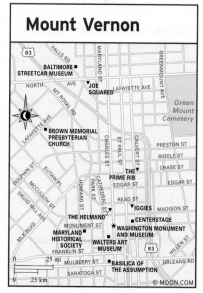

replicates the painting in detail and is a re-creation of a chamber of natural history wonders that taps into human ingenuity from all over the globe. A highlight of the room is a 12-foot-long stuffed alligator. Although general admission to the museum is free, purchased tickets are required for special exhibits.

Washington Monument and Museum at Mount Vernon Place

The **Washington Monument and Museum at Mount Vernon Place** (699 N. Charles St., 410/962-5070, www.mvpconservancy.org, Wed.-Sun. 10am-5pm, free) is the site of the first monument planned to honor George Washington. Completed in 1829, the white marble monument stands 178 feet tall and has a rectangular base, a relatively plain column, and a statue of Washington on the top. The monument looks even more imposing than its 178 feet because it sits on a hill. It was a landmark for boats making their way up the river from the Chesapeake Bay. Today, visitors can climb 228 narrow stone stairs to the top and enjoy a great view of Baltimore (adults $6, children under 13 $4). There is a little museum at the base of the monument.

Baltimore Streetcar Museum

The **Baltimore Streetcar Museum** (1901 Falls Rd., 410/547-0264, www.baltimorestreetcarmuseum.org, Sat.-Sun. noon-5pm, adults $10, children 4-11 $8) details the history of streetcars in the city and their evolution from horse-drawn transportation to an electricity-driven system. The fun part of this interesting little museum is that a number of original historic streetcars have been salvaged, and visitors can actually ride in them (accompanied by volunteer conductors) down the old tracks. Unlimited rides are included with the admission fee.

Basilica of the Assumption

The **Basilica of the Assumption** (409 Cathedral St., 410/727-3565, ext. 220, www.baltimorebasilica.org, Mon.-Fri. 8:30am-8pm,

Sat.-Sun. 8:30am-5:30pm, except during mass, $5 requested donation for tours) was the first Catholic cathedral built in the United States after the Constitution was ratified, and the building quickly became a symbol of the new country's religious freedom. It was constructed between 1806 and 1821, and the design and architecture were overseen by John Carroll, the first bishop in the country (and later archbishop of Baltimore), and Benjamin Henry Latrobe, who designed the U.S. Capitol. The basilica sits on a hill above the harbor and features a grand dome and what was considered cutting-edge neoclassical architecture to match that of the new federal city of Washington DC. Great effort went into creating an architectural symbol of America rather than using a European Gothic design. At the time the cathedral was built, its only architectural rival in terms of scale and size was the U.S. Capitol, and the basilica was considered the most architecturally advanced structure in the country.

The full name of the cathedral is the Basilica of the National Shrine of the Assumption of the Blessed Virgin Mary. It is ranked as a minor basilica but is also a national shrine. The basilica is a cultural institution in Baltimore and offers services, tours, concerts, and lectures. It also has a prayer garden nearby on the corner of Franklin and North Charles Streets. Saturday tours are sometimes not possible due to weddings and special services. Tours are not required for visitation, but sightseeing is not permitted during mass.

Brown Memorial Presbyterian Church

The **Brown Memorial Presbyterian Church** (1316 Park Ave., 410/523-1542, www.browndowntown.org, daily 9am-6pm, free) is a historic Gothic Revival-style Presbyterian church that was built in 1870. A unique

---

1: Baltimore Museum of Industry 2: Fort McHenry National Monument and Historic Shrine 3: Druid Hill Park 4: Howard Peters Rawlings Conservatory and Botanic Gardens

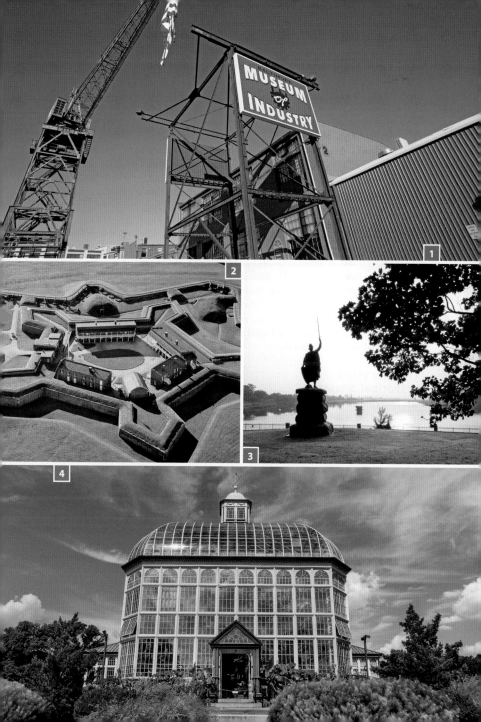

feature is its 11 Tiffany stained glass windows representing scenes from the Bible, several of which are nearly three stories tall. The windows were added in the early 1900s, which made the church a local art treasure.

The National Great Blacks in Wax Museum

The National Great Blacks in Wax Museum (1601 E. North Ave., 410/563-3404, www.greatblacksinwax.org, hours vary throughout season, adults $15, children 12-17, college students with ID, and seniors over 55 $14, children 3-11 $12, under 3 free) is the first wax museum in Baltimore and the first African American-oriented wax museum in the country. It was established in 1983 and displays more than 100 figures. The museum does a nice job of telling the history behind each figure through audio and text displays. Several famous Baltimore residents are depicted in the museum, including Frederick Douglass and singer Billie Holiday.

The Maryland Historical Society

The Maryland Historical Society (201 W. Monument St., 410/685-3750, www.mdhs. org., Wed.-Sat. 10am-5pm, Sun. noon-5pm, museum only with no library hours on Sun., adults $9, children 3-18 and students with ID $6, seniors $7, under 3 free) is a great starting point for discovering Baltimore. You can view more than one million objects on display in two museum buildings, including photographs, paintings, manuscripts, and lithographs. It also includes a huge library with more than seven million items, including the most treasured: the historical manuscript to "The Star-Spangled Banner." Exhibits cover a diversity of topics including the War of 1812, African American history, women's history, maritime history, the history of Fell's Point, immigration, furniture, and mining. The Historical Society is easy to spot—the 1,700-pound, 14-foot-tall statue of Nipper the RCA Dog sits on its rooftop facing Park Street.

HAMPDEN AND HOMEWOOD
Druid Hill Park

Druid Hill Park (2600 Madison Ave., 443/281-3538, www.druidhillpark.org, daily dawn to dusk, free) is a 745-acre park developed in 1860. Approximately two miles from Hampden, it is one of the country's oldest landscaped public parks, along with Central Park in New York City and Fairmount Park in Philadelphia. Druid Park has something else in common with Central Park: It was formed at the northern edges of the city at the time it was established. To this day, the northern end of the park features forest that is some of the oldest in Maryland. The southern end of the park, however, has always been a popular area for those living in the city. Druid Hill Lake was built in 1863 and is one of the biggest earthen dammed lakes in the nation. Many fountains and artificial ponds that were original features in the park have been drained and reclaimed by nature, although their remains can still be found. The park also features tennis courts, a pool, disc golf, and workout equipment. There is also a zoo in the middle of the park, accessible only through the official zoo entrance. Safety can be a concern in the park at any time, but mostly after dark. Be aware of your surroundings, and if you feel uncomfortable, cut your visit short.

THE MARYLAND ZOO IN BALTIMORE

The Maryland Zoo in Baltimore (Druid Park Lake Dr., 410/396-7102, www. marylandzoo.org, Mar.-Dec. daily 10am-4pm, shorter hours Jan.-Feb., adult $21.99, children 2-11 $17.99, under 2 free, seniors 65 and over $18.99), inside the large Druid Hill Park to the west of Hampden, opened in 1876 and is one of the oldest zoos in the country. It houses more than 1,500 animals. One of the premier exhibits is the Polar Bear Watch, where visitors can take a large viewing buggy (like they use on the tundra) to watch three polar bears in their habitat. The

The Dog Who Found His Way Home

Nipper gracing the Maryland Historical Society

The 14-foot-tall, 1,700-pound RCA Dog, known as Nipper, which sits atop the Maryland Historical Society roof, has a long history of adventure. The original Nipper was a stray terrier adopted in the 1880s by a man named Mark Barraud. He named the little black-and-white dog Nipper because he nipped at people's legs. When Barraud passed away, his brother, Francis, who was a painter, adopted the dog.

At the time, the phonograph was the latest technology. Nipper was captivated by the sound of the machine and would sit with his head tilted near its trumpet, listening. Francis thought this would make a great advertisement, and he painted a picture of Nipper and sold it to the Gramophone Company (which made phonographs). A United States patent was issued for the trademark of the image, and after two sales of the company, RCA ended up with the image in 1929.

In 1954, The Triangle Sign Company of Baltimore made the statue of Nipper, and it was placed on top of the D&H Distributing building. D&H Distributing was an RCA distributor. But when the company moved in 1976, they left the statue behind.

A collector from Fairfax, Virginia, wanted the statue, and after he spent six years trying to convince D&H Distributing to let him buy it, they finally sold it to him for $1. Baltimore residents and officials were outraged. They felt Nipper was a Baltimore landmark, but a sale is a sale, and Nipper left Baltimore and was moved to Virginia, where he sat on the collector's front lawn for 20 years.

In 1996, the collector decided to move, and he sold Nipper to the Baltimore City Life Museum for $25,000. Two years later, the museum closed, and the Maryland Historical Society took over its collections and, in turn, inherited Nipper and placed him on the roof. Today visitors can still enjoy the 1,700-pound pooch, who found his way home to Baltimore and seems to be here to stay.

zoo also offers other hands-on experiences such as camel rides and a Children's Zoo, where the little ones can pet certain animals. Family sleepovers at the zoo called "Snooze at the Zoo!" are available.

HOWARD PETERS RAWLINGS CONSERVATORY AND BOTANIC GARDENS

The **Howard Peters Rawlings Conservatory and Botanic Gardens** (3100 Swan Dr., 410/396-0008, www. rawlingsconservatory.org, Wed.-Sun.

Hampden and Homewood

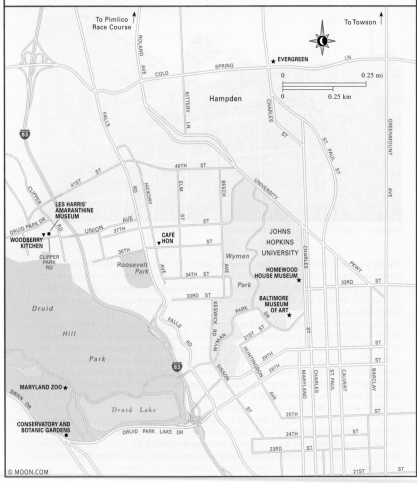

© MOON.COM

10am-4pm, free, $5 donation encouraged), within Druid Hill Park, is the only remaining public conservatory in Baltimore. The complex dates back to 1888 and consists of two buildings from the Victorian era. There are also three newer buildings. Five different climates are represented in the buildings, and there are also beautiful outdoor gardens. The Palm House is one of the most interesting buildings. The Palm House was built in 1888 and was designed by George Frederick (who also designed Baltimore's City Hall). Towering palms reach the upper windows of the impressive five-story house and block some of the natural sunlight in the conservatory.

Les Harris' Amaranthine Museum

It would be a challenge to find another museum comparable to **Les Harris' Amaranthine Museum** (2010 Clipper Park Rd., 410/456-1343, www.

amaranthinemuseum.org, Sept.-June Sun. 1pm-3pm and by appointment, $5). This unusual museum, which is open during very limited hours, takes visitors through a maze of the late Baltimore artist Les Harris's work while telling the history of art in chronological order, starting with prehistoric times and going out into the future. The museum is a labyrinth of art history and the creative process, made up of rooms, chambers, and passages and decorated from floor to ceiling with Harris's art. The Amaranthine Museum itself (the word *amaranthine* means eternally beautiful) is a unique art form and a fun deviation from traditional museums.

Baltimore Museum of Art

The **Baltimore Museum of Art** (10 Museum Dr., 443/573-1700, www.artbma.org, Wed.-Sun. 10am-5pm, free) is a cultural destination in Baltimore and one of two great art museums in the city (the other is the Walters Art Museum in Mount Vernon). The museum is adjacent to the Homewood campus of Johns Hopkins University.

The museum was founded in 1914 and grew from housing one single painting to offering 90,000 pieces on display. Its collection of 19th-century, modern, and contemporary art is internationally known and includes the famous Cone Collection of more than 3,000 pieces by world-famous artists donated by wealthy socialite sisters Claribel and Etta Cone. Worth approximately $1 billion, the Cone Collection includes the largest single collection of works by Henri Matisse in the world (500 total); 42 oil paintings, 18 sculptures, and 36 drawings are among the Matisse pieces. It also displays work by Cézanne, Picasso, Degas, Manet, Van Gogh, and Gauguin.

In addition to the Cone Collection (housed in the Cone Wing), the museum features many other galleries. The West Wing for Contemporary Art contains 16 galleries with 20th- and 21st-century art including abstract expressionism, minimalism, conceptual art, and works by Andy Warhol. American galleries feature paintings, sculptures, decorative arts, and works on paper. There is also an African art collection of more than 2,000 pieces with works spanning from ancient Egypt to contemporary Zimbabwe.

The museum also offers visitors two lovely outdoor gardens with 20th-century sculptures.

Johns Hopkins University

Johns Hopkins University (410/516-8000, www.jhu.edu) is a private not-for-profit research university that was founded in 1876 and named for philanthropist Johns Hopkins, its benefactor. The university maintains two main campuses in Baltimore: the Homewood Campus (3400 N. Charles St.) and the Medical Institution Campus (600 N. Wolfe St.). There are secondary campuses in Washington DC, Italy, Singapore, and China. Johns Hopkins developed the concept of a modern research university in the United States and is known throughout the world as one of the best. At least 37 Nobel Prize winners are affiliated with Johns Hopkins.

The Homewood Campus has a parklike setting even though it is located in a large city, with lovely old trees, large grassy areas, stately brick academic buildings, and red-brick residence halls. The Medical Institution Campus is located north of Fell's Point in east Baltimore.

HOMEWOOD HOUSE

The **Homewood House** (3400 N. Charles St., 410/516-5589, www.museums.jhu.edu, Tues.-Fri. 11am-4pm, Sat.-Sun. noon-4pm, adults $8, youth 6-17, students with ID, and Johns Hopkins alumni and retirees $5, seniors 65 and over $7) on the eastern side of Johns Hopkins University is a wonderful example of federal architecture. Completed in 1808, the house is decorated with well-researched colors, patterns, and furniture from the period, much of it original. The country home was owned by wealthy Baltimore residents during the colonial era and then by the son of Charles Carroll, a signer of the Declaration of Independence.

EVERGREEN MUSEUM & LIBRARY
The **Evergreen Museum & Library** (4545 N. Charles St., 410/516-0341, www.museums. jhu.edu, Tues.-Fri. 11am-4pm, Sat.-Sun. noon-4pm, adults $8, youth 6-17, students with ID, and Johns Hopkins alumni and retirees $5, seniors 65 and over $7) is a beautiful mansion that was built in the mid-19th century and purchased by the president of the B&O Railroad, John W. Garrett, in 1878. This wonderful exemplar of the Gilded Age sits surrounded by Italian-style gardens on 26 acres. The museum and library hold a collection of rare books, manuscripts, and artwork. The estate's 48 rooms, housing more than 50,000 items from the Garrett family (including a 24K gold-leafed toilet), can be viewed by the public only on guided tours. Tours begin every hour on the hour with the last tour starting at 3pm. Concerts and lectures are also given on the property. The museum is 4.5 miles north of the Inner Harbor.

WALKING TOURS

Historic walking tours around Baltimore are given by the **Society for the Preservation of Federal Hill and Fell's Point** (410/675-6750, www.preservationsociety.com).

Recreation

SPECTATOR SPORTS

Oriole Park at Camden Yards

Oriole Park at Camden Yards (333 W. Camden St., 888/848-2473, www.mlb. com/orioles) is the home of Major League Baseball's **Baltimore Orioles.** The park opened in 1992 in downtown Baltimore, just a short walk from the Inner Harbor. Camden Yards is consistently rated one of the top professional baseball parks in the country. The train station at the intersection of Howard and Camden Streets services the stadium for the Baltimore Light Rail.

M&T Bank Stadium

A stone's throw from Camden Yards is **M&T Bank Stadium** (1101 Russell St., 410/261-7283, www.baltimoreravens.com), home to the **Baltimore Ravens** of the National Football League. The multipurpose venue opened in 1998. The Hamburg Street Station of the Baltimore Light Rail services the stadium.

Royal Farms Arena

The **Royal Farms Arena** (201 W. Baltimore St., www.royalfarmsarena.com) is the location for the **Baltimore Blast** (www. baltimoreblast.com) professional indoor soccer team's home games. The team was founded in 1992 and is part of the Major Indoor Soccer League.

BIKING

Baltimore has a large biking community that is working hard to make the city more bike-friendly. More than 40 on-street bike-lane miles and nearly as many miles of off-road trails have been created in and around the city since 2006, and the Downtown Bicycle Network includes 10 miles in the downtown area alone.

The **BWI Bike Trail** (www.bikewashington. org) is an 11-mile, asphalt surface, loop trail that circles Baltimore Washington International (BWI) Airport. It has short sections on city streets and is mostly level with a few bridge hills and one tougher hill. A bike rack is located on a spur of the trail near the international terminal close to a light-rail station (a drinking fountain, restrooms, and vending machines are accessible at the station). Parking is available in several spots including the **Dixon Aircraft Observation Area** (Route 176 on Dorsey Road) and at the

1: Oriole Park at Camden Yards 2: "Chessie" paddleboats in the Inner Harbor

light-rail station (on the west side of Route 648).

The **Baltimore and Annapolis Trail** (www.traillink.com) is a 13-mile paved trail that runs along a railroad route from Dorsey Road (near BWI Airport) to Jonas Green Park near the Annapolis waterfront. At the north end of the trail is a short connector to the BWI Bike Trail.

The **Gwynns Falls Trail** (www.gwynnsfallstrail.org) covers 15 miles between the I-70 Park and Ride trailhead and the Inner Harbor. The trail connects 30 neighborhoods in west and southwest Baltimore.

Bikes can be rented in the Federal Hill neighborhood at **Race Pace Bicycles** (1414 Key Hwy., 410/986-0001, www.racepacebicycles.com, Mon.-Fri. 10am-8pm, Sat. 10am-6pm, Sun. 11am-5pm, hybrids $45 per day, mountain bikes, road bikes and electric bikes $75 per day).

PADDLEBOATS

Most kids get wide-eyed when they see the lineup of brightly colored "Chessie" the sea monster paddleboats at **Paddleboats**

Team Chessie (301 E. Pratt St., https://livingclassrooms.org, Memorial Day-Labor Day daily 11am-10pm, mid-Apr.-day before Memorial Day and day after Labor Day-mid-Nov. daily 11am-6pm, $20 per half hour) on the waterfront. Renting a paddleboat for a half hour or an hour is a fun way to get a new perspective on the harbor. Electric pirate ships are also available for rent (starting at $25 per half hour).

CRUISES
Urban Pirates

Bring the family on a unique, 1.5-hour adventure in the harbor. **Urban Pirates** (Ann St. Pier, Fell's Point, 410/327-8378, www.urbanpirates.com, ages 3 and over $22 plus 10 percent tax, 2 and under free) offers pirate cruises out of Fell's Point. Three pirates lead an interactive adventure where guests can dress up, have their faces painted, get a tattoo, and then depart on a cruise complete with songs, games, water cannons, and treasure. Adult cruises are also offered ($25 plus 10 percent tax).

Entertainment and Events

NIGHTLIFE

Whether you're looking for delicious cocktails, a large wine selection, or a wild night of dancing, Baltimore has it all.

One block from the Inner Harbor is a great collection of bars and clubs in an entertainment complex called **Power Plant Live!** (34 Market Pl., www.powerplantlive.com), named for a neighboring former power plant on Pier 4 that faces the Inner Harbor. Restaurants, bars, and nightclubs line an outdoor plaza where free music is offered May-October on the plaza stage. A popular venue in the complex is **Rams Head Live** (20 Market Pl., 410/244-1131, www.ramsheadlive.com). This general-admission, standing-room-only venue features five full-service bars and two food

kiosks. A wide variety of groups have played here, including Patti Smith, Big Head Todd and the Monsters, They Might Be Giants, Citizen Cope, and Cody Johnson.

To test your luck, stop by the **Horseshoe Casino Baltimore** (1525 Russell St., 844/777-7463, www.caesars.com/horseshoe-baltimore, 24 hours). They have a 122,000-square-foot gaming floor and offer slots, table games, poker, four restaurants, and a Topgolf Swing Suite.

Those looking for a terrific place to catch live jazz won't be disappointed by **An Die Musik Live** (409 N. Charles St., 2nd Fl., 410/385-2638, www.andiemusiklive.com), downtown on the second floor of a town house. This intimate concert venue is for true music lovers. The cool, renovated building offers great acoustics, comfortable seating, and a high caliber of artists. There is no elevator, so be prepared to climb some stairs.

Not far away is a popular, old-school drinking establishment called **Club Charles** (1724 N. Charles St., 410/727-8815, www. clubcharles.us, daily 6pm-2am). This art deco bar is dark and crowded, but the bartenders are fantastic and the drinks are strong. There's even a resident ghost that plays pranks at the bar.

A classy place to linger over a drink is the **Owl Bar** (1 E. Chase St., 410/347-0880, www. theowlbar.com, Mon,-Thurs. 11am-midnight, Fri. 11am-2am, Sat. 10am-2am, Sun. 10am-10pm). This Mount Vernon establishment is housed in the historic Belvedere Hotel building, which was known during the early part of the 20th century as the premier hotel in the city; it hosted U.S. presidents, foreign dignitaries, and movie stars.

Mount Vernon's **Sangria Patio Bar** (930 N. Charles St., 443/708-2279, www. sangriabaltimore.com, Tues.-Thurs. 5pm-midnight, Fri.-Sat. 5pm-1am) serves signature sangria cocktails and tapas. The place has a hip vibe, modern DJ, nice decor, and a patio. The drinks are a bit pricey.

A local landmark in Fell's Point, the **Cat's Eye Pub** (1730 Thames St., 410/276-9866, www.catseyepub.com, Mon. 4pm-2am, Tues.-Thurs. 2pm-2am, Fri.-Sun. noon-2am) is known for nightly live music despite the close and often crowded space. Music at this cozy pub includes blues, jazz, and folk.

A charming little wine bar on the waterfront in Fell's Point is **V-NO** (905 S. Ann St., 410/342-8466, www.v-no.com, Mon.-Tues. 4pm-9pm, Wed. noon-9pm, Thurs. noon-10pm, Fri.-Sat. noon-midnight, Sun. noon-9pm). They offer indoor and outdoor seating and a lovely wine list with enough of a selection to keep things interesting. This is a great place to unwind away from the crowds.

The Horse You Came In On Saloon (1626 Thames St., 410/327-8111, www. thehorsebaltimore.com, daily 11am-1:30am) is America's oldest continuously operated saloon (it operated before, during, and after Prohibition). It first opened in 1775 and is allegedly the last place Edgar Allan Poe was seen alive. It may be where Poe had his last drink, and it's been rumored that his ghost haunts the saloon. The saloon originally had hitching posts out back to park horses. Menu items include traditional bar food, and there's nightly live entertainment (rock and roll). The saloon's slogan is "Where no one's ugly at 2am." It also has Maryland's only Old No. 7 club, where members purchase their own bottles of Jack Daniel's and the saloon stores them in a coveted space in their custom Jack Daniel's case. The saloon sells more Jack Daniel's than any other bar in Maryland.

PERFORMING ARTS

Hippodrome Theatre at France-Merrick Performing Arts Center

The **Hippodrome Theatre at France-Merrick Performing Arts Center** (12 N. Eutaw St., 410/837-7400, www.france-merrickpac.com) is a well-known, circa 1914 theater on the west side of Baltimore. In the 1940s, this part of town had a flourishing arts scene and saw big-time acts such as Frank Sinatra, Bob Hope, and Benny Goodman, but the neighborhood declined in the following decades. This performing arts center is part of the rebirth of the area, and the Hippodrome Theatre was beautifully restored as part of that project. The center now offers musicals, holiday performances, and many other types of performances.

Centerstage

Centerstage (700 N. Calvert St., 410/332-0033, www.centerstage.org) in Mount Vernon is a historic venue with two intimate performance spaces, two rehearsal halls, and three lobbies. The six-story building is a local landmark that has roots as the former Loyola College and High School. It offers a close-up theater experience for classical and contemporary performances and lends itself well to audience interaction. There are no bad seats in the house.

Royal Farms Arena

The **Royal Farms Arena** (201 W. Baltimore St., 410/347-2020, www.royalfarmsarena. com) is showing its age a bit (it was built in the 1960s) but still hosts musical artists such as Carrie Underwood, well-known shows such as Cirque du Soleil and Disney on Ice, and sporting events.

Patricia & Arthur Modell Performing Arts Center at the Lyric

The **Patricia & Arthur Modell Performing Arts Center at the Lyric** (140 W. Mount Royal Ave., 410/900-1150, www.modell-lyric. com) is a music hall that originally opened in 1894. Today it plays host to a wide variety of talent from kids' shows to top musical artists.

Arena Players

The longest continuously running African American community theater in the country is the **Arena Players** (801 McCulloh St., 410/728-6500, www.arenaplayersinc.com). Founded in 1953, this respected theater supports local actors and writers.

Joseph Meyerhoff Symphony Hall

Joseph Meyerhoff Symphony Hall (1212 Cathedral St., 410/783-8000, www.bsomusic. org) is a 2,443-seat music venue in the Mount Vernon neighborhood. The venue is named for a former president of the Baltimore Symphony, Joseph Meyerhoff, who made a sizable donation for the construction of the hall. The venue is currently home to the **Baltimore Symphony Orchestra.**

EVENTS

The **Visit Baltimore** website (www. baltimore.org) is a great online resource that lists local events throughout the city.

Hundreds of boats (both power and sail) can be found at the **Baltimore Convention Center** (1 W. Pratt St., 410/649-7000, www. bccenter.org) for four days in mid- to late January during the **Baltimore Boat Show** (www.baltimoreboatshow.com, adults $14, 12 and under free). The show features exhibits and activities for all ages.

For something completely different, attend the American Visionary Art Museum's annual **Kinetic Sculpture Race** (www.avam. org), which takes place on a Saturday in early May. This race showcases human-powered

artist creating a street mural during Honfest

Pimlico Race Course

The second leg of the famed Triple Crown horse races, the **Preakness Stakes,** is held on the third Saturday in May at **Pimlico Race Course** (5201 Park Heights Ave., 410/542-9400, www. pimlico.com), northwest of Hampden. The historic racecourse is the second-oldest in the country, having opened in 1870. The course was built after the governor of Maryland, Oden Bowie, made a proposition over dinner in 1868 to racing gurus in Saratoga, New York. The proposition included a race, to be held two years after the dinner, between horses that were yearlings at the time of the dinner. The American Jockey Club wanted to host the race, but Bowie pledged to build a state-of-the-art racetrack in Baltimore if the race was held there. After the pledge was made, plans were put in place for the birth of Pimlico.

Pimlico (originally spelled "Pemblicoe") was a name given to the area west of the Jones Falls, an 18-mile-long stream that runs through the city of Baltimore and into the Inner Harbor, during the colonial era. The Maryland Jockey Club bought 70 acres in the area for $23,500 and constructed the racetrack for $25,000. Race day was always a big event at Pimlico, and horse-drawn carriages made their way through Druid Hill Park toward the course before additional roads were built directly to the track.

Pimlico quickly became an institution. It has survived wars, recession, the Great Depression, fire, and storms. The first Preakness Stakes was held here in 1873 and the race remains a time-honored tradition.

works of art that can travel on the land, water, and through mud. These "machines" are often made of old bicycle parts, gears, etc. and can be "driven" by one person or a team. Fun awards are given out such as the "Grand Mediocre East Coast Champion Award (to the vehicle finishing in the middle of the pack)," the "Next to Last Award," and the "Best Bribe" award.

A more serious race that also takes place in May is the **Preakness Stakes** (www. preakness.com). With a history of more than 140 years, this second leg of the Triple Crown of Thoroughbred Racing (which consists of the Kentucky Derby, the Preakness Stakes, and the Belmont Stakes) is a big deal in Baltimore and in horse racing overall.

Honfest (www.honfest.net) in Hampden is a major city festival that started out as a neighborhood celebration and blossomed into an event with an international following that attracts more than 35,000 attendees. The festival takes place in mid-June along 36th Street. The "Hon" is short for "honey" ("hon" is a commonly used term of endearment in Baltimore) and refers to a ladies' fashion that evolved in the 1960s. The style included large, brightly

colored horn-rim glasses, loud prints, spandex and leopard-print pants, thick makeup, and beehive hairdos. The festival features many Hons in full attire, and one is crowned "Miss Hon." There is also the running of the Hons. Hair and makeup can be done by vendors right in the street.

Baltimore's **Fourth of July** celebration (www.baltimore.org) is an annual favorite in the Inner Harbor. It features live music and a fireworks display. The fireworks celebration can be viewed from many vantage points around the city, including Federal Hill, Fell's Point, and Canton.

America's largest free arts festival, **Artscape** (Mount Royal Ave., www.artscape. org) is held for three days each July and attracts more than 350,000 people. The festival is a rare opportunity for visitors and people from all neighborhoods in Baltimore to interact. More than 150 artists display their craft at this well-known event that began in the early 1980s.

Miracle on 34th Street (www. christmasstreet.com) is the premier holiday extravaganza in Hampden. Throughout December, one block of 34th Street becomes a magical (although somewhat over-the-top) display of lights, reindeer, and really any type of decoration you can think of. It's quite the spectacle, but also quite festive, and definitely worth checking out if you don't mind sitting in traffic with the other spectators.

The **Night of 100 Elvises** (www. nightof100elvises.com) is actually a three-day event downtown held in the beginning of December that benefits the Johns Hopkins Children's Center and the Guardian Angels. This ticketed party features a dozen bands and multiple Elvis tribute performances.

Shopping

DOWNTOWN AND THE INNER HARBOR

Harborplace

Harborplace (201 E. Pratt St., www. harborplace.com, Mon.-Sat. 10am-9pm, Sun. noon-6pm) is the premier shopping market in downtown Baltimore. It was created in 1980 as a main attraction during the rebirth of the Inner Harbor. The market consists of two pavilions: the **Pratt Street Pavilion** and the **Light Street Pavilion.** National stores and restaurants are abundant at Harborplace, but specialty shops such as **Life in Charm City** (Pratt Street Pavilion, 410/230-2652, Mon.-Sat. 10am-9pm, Sun. noon-6pm), which sells Baltimore-related merchandise, can also be found.

The Gallery

The Gallery (200 E. Pratt St., www. thegalleryatharborplace.com, Mon.-Sat. 10am-9pm, Sun. noon-6pm) opened a few years after Harborplace in a glass building across Pratt Street (attached to the Renaissance Hotel). The two shopping areas are connected by a skywalk. Many upscale national stores and restaurants are located in the four-story structure, but local merchants running Maryland-themed shops can also be found there.

Lexington Market

The iconic **Lexington Market** (400 W. Lexington St., www.lexingtonmarket.com, Mon.-Sat. 6am-6pm) was established back in 1782 and is an extensive indoor market with more than 100 vendors. It is primarily a food market with a wide variety of seafood, meat, and produce.

FELL'S POINT

Some of the most charming shops in Baltimore can be found in Fell's Point. Whether you're in the market for jewelry, home items, music, or clothing, you should turn up plenty to keep you interested if you poke around the historic streets and venture up some side alleys. **B'More Betty** (1500 Thames St., 443/869-6379, www.onlybetty. com, by appointment only) is a trendy buyer and seller of designer handbags, shoes, and accessories. If shoes are your thing, pop into **Poppy & Stella** (728 S. Broadway, 410/522-1970, www.poppyandstella.com, Mon.-Fri. 11am-8pm, Sat. 10am-8pm, Sun. 11am-6pm). Their goal is to "bring cute women's shoes to Baltimore." For all types of hats, visit **Hats in the Belfry** (813 S. Broadway, 667/239-3655, www.hatsinthebelfry.com, Mon.-Thurs. 10am-8pm, Fri.-Sat. 10am-9pm, Sun. 10am-7pm).

FEDERAL HILL

Charles Street and Light Street are the best areas in Federal Hill to do some window browsing. Small boutiques and shops selling clothes and home goods are scattered through the charming neighborhood. Favorites include **Phina's for the Home** (919 S. Charles St., 410/685-0911, www.phinas.com, Wed.-Sat. noon-6pm, Sun. noon-4pm), a boutique linen store selling home and spa items and gifts;

and **Brightside Boutique & Art Studio** (1133 S. Charles St., 410/244-1133, www.shopbrightside.com, Mon.-Thurs. 11am-8pm, Fri.-Sat. 10am-8pm, Sun. 10am-6pm), selling clothes, accessories, and home items.

HAMPDEN

The happening place in Hampden is 36th Street, known locally as "The Avenue." This is especially true for shoppers, since there are four blocks of retail stores offering clothing, furniture, antiques, beauty supplies, and some funkier items. The stores are locally owned, and the merchants are helpful if you're looking for a specific item. For starters, visit **Atomic Books** (3620 Falls Rd., 410/662-4444, www.atomicbooks.com, Sun.-Tues. 11:30am-7pm, Wed.-Thurs. 11:30am-9pm, Fri. 11:30am-10pm, Sat. 11:30am-9pm) to find unique titles and comics, or visit **Ma Petite Shoe** (832 W. 36th St., 410/235-3442, www.mapetiteshoe.com, Mon.-Sat. 11am-7pm, Sun. noon-5pm) for designer shoes and artisan chocolate.

Food

DOWNTOWN AND THE INNER HARBOR
American
The Capital Grille (500 E. Pratt St., 443/703-4064, www.thecapitalgrille.com, Mon.-Thurs. 11:30am-10pm, Fri. 11:30am-11pm, Sat. 5pm-11pm, Sun. 4pm-9pm, $30-85) on Pratt Street is part of a national chain of restaurants, but still offers a superb dining experience in a great location on the Inner Harbor. Steak and seafood make up the bulk of the menu in this traditional steak house, but the good service and pleasant atmosphere add to its overall appeal.

The **Corner & Bistro Winebar** (213 Penn St., 410/727-1155, www.cbwinebar.com, lunch Tues.-Sat. 11am-2pm, Sun. 11am-3pm, dinner Tues.-Thurs. 5pm-10pm, Fri.-Sat. 5pm-11pm, Sun. 5pm-9pm, $8-26) is a casual little bistro and wine bar that serves a bar menu of tasty appetizers and a small lunch and dinner menu of salads, burgers, and sandwiches. Try the Chesapeake, a grilled marinated chicken breast sandwich with crab dip and grilled tomatoes. The bistro is easy to walk to from attractions such as the Babe Ruth Birthplace Museum and is about a half block off Pratt Street.

Brazilian
For die-hard carnivores, it's hard to beat the Brazilian steak house **Fogo de Chão** (600 E. Pratt St., 410/528-9292, www.fogodechao.com, lunch Mon.-Fri. 11:30am-2pm, dinner Mon.-Thurs. 5pm-10pm, Fri. 5pm-10:30pm, Sat. 2pm-10:30pm, Sun. 2pm-9pm, Brazilian Brunch Sat.-Sun. 11:30am-2pm, $34.50-144.95). This dining experience includes a large salad bar with more than 30 items, then an onslaught of 15 cuts of fire-roasted meats brought tableside. Each guest has a card to turn to green when you'd like more meat offered or red when you are taking a break or have had enough. This is a fun place to bring business guests and a good place for groups.

Turkish
Cazbar (316 N. Charles St., 410/528-1222, www.cazbar.pro, Mon.-Sat. 11am-11pm, Sun. 3pm-11pm, $11-30), Baltimore's first authentic Turkish restaurant, offers consistently good food, a warm and pleasant atmosphere, and friendly staff. As one person sitting close by commented, "I will eat here until my mouth burns like the fires of hell. It's that good." Although the food isn't generally that spicy, it's always good to know someone will take one for the team. The servers know the menu well and can help with tough decisions. Try their hummus or Mohamra walnut dip for a starter. They also have Turkish beer and sangria. On Friday and Saturday nights there are

free belly dancing shows—not many places can say that.

FELL'S POINT AND LITTLE ITALY
American

Peter's Inn (504 S. Ann St., 410/675-7313, www.petersinn.com, Tues.-Sat. 6pm-11pm, $11-30) is a casual contemporary eatery that is known for its innovative dishes and fresh ingredients. The building dates back to 1850 and was mainly known as a biker bar throughout the 1980s and early 1990s, but it has since transformed into a great food-focused restaurant. The menu changes weekly (look for the chalkboard) with the exception of salad, steaks, and garlic bread, which are staples. The restaurant is crowded on weekends so expect a wait (perhaps at their bar). They take limited reservations.

Beer lovers will think they've won the lottery after stepping inside ★ **Max's Taphouse** (737 S. Broadway, 410/675-6297, www.maxs.com, daily 11am-2am $9-16). With 140 rotating drafts, 102 taps, five casks, and 1,200 bottles in stock, you could spend a lifetime here searching for your favorite beer. This beer lover's institution is Baltimore's premier beer pub and has been featured in countless magazines and "best of" lists. The friendly owner, expert "beertenders" (many of whom have been here for years), and delicious pub menu make this well-known establishment in the heart of Fell's Point not just a great drinking spot, but also a great place to eat and hang out with new and old friends. For the sports minded, they offer numerous televisions, pool tables, foosball, and dartboards. Private rooms are available with large-screen TVs, custom beer lists, and great sound systems. Weekday specials such as "Monday sucks happy hour" and "Friday big ass draft happy hour" occur weekly in addition to great annual events such as Max's Annual German Beer Fest and the Hopfest.

If you are looking for a classy restaurant with a lovely atmosphere and delicious food, and you don't mind paying for it, then make a reservation at the acclaimed ★ **Charleston Restaurant** (1000 Lancaster St., 410/332-7373, www.charlestonrestaurant.com, Mon.-Sat. 5pm-10pm, $79-222). They offer an extensive prix fixe tasting menu with three to six courses and an award-winning wine list of more than 800 labels. Chef Cindy Wolf has been a James Beard Award finalist for best chef, mid-Atlantic, on multiple occasions, and is one of the best-known chefs in the city. Wolf's cooking is a blend of French fundamentals and South Carolina's Low Country cuisine. The restaurant is in Harbor East near Fell's Point. A jacket and tie are recommended but not required.

Named for the owners' yellow lab, **Kooper's Tavern** (1702 Thames St., 410/563-5423, www.kooperstavern.com, Mon.-Fri. 11am-2am, Sat.-Sun. 10am-2am, $7-29) is a great stop for a beer and a bite across from the waterfront and the Sagamore Pendry Baltimore Hotel. This friendly tavern sources their food locally and is known for their burgers, but their extensive menu offers seafood, flatbread, salads, and sandwiches. Their Bavarian pretzel with crab dip is out of this world and will likely be larger than your head.

The **Blue Moon Café** (1621 Aliceanna St., 410/522-3940, www.bluemoonbaltimore.com, daily 7am-3pm, weekends 24 hours, $5-16) is a well-known breakfast café that was featured on Guy Fieri's show *Diners, Drive-Ins and Dives*. Open 24 hours on weekends, this small eatery inside a converted row house has a line out the door on the average Saturday or Sunday. The reason couldn't be that they're serving Cap'n Crunch—or could it? Cap'n Crunch french toast is one of their most popular dishes, but Maryland Eggs Benedict and delightful homemade biscuits and gravy are other very convincing reasons.

A unique find is **One-Eyed Mike's** (708 S. Bond St., 410/327-0445, www.oneeyedmikes.com, Mon.-Thurs. noon-2am, Fri.-Sun. 11am-2am, $7-35). This little treasure is one of the

---

1: pretzel at Kooper's Tavern 2: Café Hon, a local institution in Hampden 3: Bar Vasquez

oldest operating taverns in Baltimore. It's housed in a tiny space on the edge of Fell's Point in an off-the-beaten-path row house. Walk through the bar and to the lovely little restaurant in the back, where they serve salads, sandwiches, and entrées such as crab cakes and steak. The staff is fun, the atmosphere is comfortable, and the food is good. The back bar was hand carved, and they still have the original tin ceiling, both of which were put in during the 1860s. There is courtyard seating in nice weather. Ask about their Grand Marnier Club.

Argentinean

Don't let the plain exterior of a former machine factory deter you from stepping through the doors of **Bar Vasquez** (1425 Alicaenna St., 410/534-7296, www.barvasquez.com, Mon.-Thurs. 5pm-10pm, Fri.-Sat. 5pm-midnight, $17-85). This elegant, upscale restaurant retains a rustic feel with decor of white lights, dark wood, palm fronds, and vast open space. The menu will satisfy even the staunchest carnivore with a plentiful selection of steak but also has delightful seafood selections such as salmon, shrimp, and octopus. A bar menu exudes Argentinean flair with smaller plates ($7-18) of flavorful empanadas, cheeses, cured meats, and chorizo. The lounge is known for an extensive whiskey menu, and the upper-level bar boasts a certified bourbon master to help personalize your experience. There is live music nightly.

British Pub

The **Wharf Rat** (801 S. Ann St., 410/276-8304, www.thewharfrat.com, daily 11am-2am, $7-28) harkens back to a day when old seaport taverns were filled with visiting sailors. The name itself is a term used in the 18th century for seafarers and pirates when they came ashore. This is a fun place for great beer and pub food (their specialty is crab-dip pizza and fish-and-chips). The bartenders are also the cooks, so be patient with your food. The atmosphere is friendly and inviting, and the pub is allegedly haunted.

Seafood

Thames Street Oyster House (1728 Thames St., 443/449-7726, www. thamesstreetoysterhouse.com, lunch Wed.-Sun. 11:30am-2:30pm, dinner Sun.-Thurs. 5pm-9:30pm, Fri.-Sat. 5pm-10:30pm, raw bar open until 11:30pm, $9-36) is a slightly upscale gem amid the bar scene in Fell's Point. They offer a fun staff and a lively nighttime atmosphere but can also be a great place for a romantic seafood dinner if you reserve a table early in the evening. This is a classic oyster house with a great raw bar. There's a large bar area and a water view from the upstairs.

Italian

There is no shortage of great Italian restaurants in Little Italy and the surrounding area. ★ **Amiccis** (231 S. High St., 410/528-1096, https://amiccis.com, daily 11am-11pm, $14-19) has been a tradition in Baltimore since 1991. It's a self-proclaimed "very" casual eatery whose mission is to provide great homemade Italian comfort food in a relaxed environment. All the menu items are wonderful, but first-timers should try the signature appetizer, the Pane' Rotundo. People in the know call it "that great shrimp and bread thing," and you'll see why after you try it. The atmosphere is lively, and the patrons are a mix of locals and visitors.

★ **Vaccaro's Italian Pastry Shop** (222 Albemarle St., 410/685-4905, www. vaccarospastry.com, Sun.-Thurs. 9am-10pm, Fri.-Sat. 9am-midnight, pastries and cookies $3-11, sandwiches and salads $6-12) is *the* place to go in Baltimore for Italian pastries. Widely known for their incredible cannoli filling, they also offer many other delectable baked goods such as rum cake, biscotti, and cheesecake, a café menu of salads and sandwiches, and cakes, cookie trays, and other items such as tiramisu for parties and other occasions. There are three additional locations throughout the Baltimore area (2919 O'Donnell St., 118 Shawan Rd., and 696 Baltimore Pike).

A recent addition to the pizza scene in

Little Italy is **Angeli's Pizzeria** (413 S. High St., 443/708-7556, www.angelispizzeria.com, Sun.-Thurs. 11am-10pm, Fri.-Sat. 11am-11pm, $3-21). This casual but highly regarded restaurant had a long history in New Orleans before Hurricane Katrina forced its closure. Its revival in Little Italy was a labor of love for owners who now work with local farms and products imported from Italy to create an authentic Italian menu of pizza, salads, sandwiches, pasta, and a handful of Italian desserts. Their motto is "Ain't Nothing a Pizza Can't Fix," and they aim to please with a welcoming interior, friendly staff, and delightfully crisp pizza crust topped with a choice of four sauces, seven cheeses, 10 meats, and numerous veggies.

CANTON
American
The raven handrails are just one of many "Poe" details at **Annabel Lee Tavern** (601 S. Clinton St., 410/522-2929, www.annabelleetavern.com, Mon.-Sat. 4pm-1am, Sun. 3pm-midnight, $11-30). Baltimore is a natural setting for a restaurant and bar done in "Edgar Allan Poe," and this unique little restaurant is a warm, funky place to have a good meal or a house cocktail off the Poe-themed drink list. The walls are inscribed with Poe's work. The tavern serves affordable upscale comfort food from an interesting but not over-the-top menu (try the rosemary beef tenderloin gyro or the roasted orange roughy tacos). They offer many daily specials and nice vegetarian options but are known for their duck-fat fries, which are worth a try if you've never had them.

The **Blue Hill Tavern** (938 S. Conkling St., 443/388-9363, www.bluehilltavern.com, Mon.-Thurs. 11:30am-9pm, Fri. 11:30am-10pm, Sat. 4pm-10pm, Sun. 3pm-9pm, $9-32) is a great little modern tavern a few blocks off O'Donnell Street in Canton. Presentation is key in this trendy restaurant, and the food tastes as good as it looks. The menu includes a variety of American food with a heavy lean toward seafood. Try the mushroom Wellington,

crab cakes, or diver scallops. They also offer pizza, a hearty burger, and salads. There's a rooftop patio for summertime dining that is one of the best in the city, even though it isn't on the water.

Greek
The **Sip and Bite Restaurant** (2200 Boston St., 410/675-7077, www.sipandbite.com, open 24/7, $5-30) is a Baltimore landmark that was featured on *Diners, Drive-Ins and Dives*. This 1948 original between Fell's Point and Canton is owned by a husband-and-wife team that are the third generation in one family to run this diner. They offer a huge menu of breakfast, lunch, and dinner with a slant toward Greek dishes. They serve classic Greek specialties such as gyros, but also have killer crab cakes made from a 60-year-old family recipe.

Seafood
Mama's on the Half Shell (2901 O'Donnell St., 410/276-3160, www.mamasmd.com, Mon.-Fri. 11am-2am, Sat.-Sun. 9am-2pm, $28-42) is a Canton tradition. This classic seafood house sits on the corner of O'Donnell Street and South Linwood Avenue in the heart of the neighborhood. They specialize in large, succulent oyster dishes (oyster stew, fried oysters, grilled oysters—you get the picture) but also have wonderful crab dishes, other seafood favorites, and a filet mignon selection. The two-story restaurant has a dark wood interior, a long bar on the first floor, and patio seating. The staff is warm and friendly, and they offer daily specials.

Italian
Baltimore's first pizzeria, **Matthew's Pizza** (3131 Eastern Ave., 410/276-8755, Mon.-Thurs. 11am-10pm, Fri.-Sat. 11am-11pm, Sun. noon-9pm, $5-13), was established in 1943 and continues to have a strong following. This small but brightly decorated restaurant is comfortable and inviting, with wicker and wood chairs, painted murals, and friendly staff. The pizza is pan style (thick and puffy crust) with ample cheese, and they've been

Natty Boh: Baltimore's Iconic Brew

The one-eyed, handlebar-mustached Mr. Boh pictured on a gold-and-white National Bohemian Beer can is not just the symbol for **National Bohemian Beer** (aka "Natty Boh"), but also a treasured icon in Baltimore. National Bohemian Beer was first brewed in Baltimore in 1885 by the National Brewing Company. After Prohibition, National Bohemian introduced Mr. Boh, who wears a distinctive smile that has delighted the people of Baltimore for decades.

Now make no mistake; Natty Boh is a cheap, domestic beer (think Pabst Blue Ribbon and Miller High Life); in fact, the brand is now owned by Pabst Brewing Company. The beer's slogan is "From the Land of Pleasant Living," which refers to the Chesapeake Bay.

In 1965, Natty Boh became the Baltimore Orioles' official sponsor, and the beer was served at their former home, Memorial Stadium, as "the official beer of Baltimore."

The brand has been sold several times (the first in 1979 to Heileman Brewing Company), and in 1996 its production was moved out of the state. The beer was no longer available on tap in Baltimore. Disappointed fans went for years without their favorite beer being offered fresh from the keg (almost 90 percent of Natty Boh sales are in Baltimore), but in 2011, good news came. Pabst Blue Ribbon announced the return of the famous brew to Baltimore and the rest of Maryland on tap.

Nacho Mama's in Canton was one of the first to tap the newly available kegs, and did so on February 3, 2011. A packed house welcomed Natty Boh back. A total of eight official keg-tapping parties were held throughout the area, and it looks like the people of Baltimore can enjoy their beer on tap for the foreseeable future.

voted Best Pizza in Baltimore City numerous times. Try their legendary crab pie: Its jumbo lump-crab meat, two cheeses, and chopped-onion filling will bring you back for more.

Mexican

If you like good Mexican food and you can put up with a few house rules, such as "Report any Elvis sightings to server," "Be nice or leave," and "Don't feed kitchen staff," then take a table at **Nacho Mama's** (2907 O'Donnell St., 410/675-0898, www.nachomamascanton. com, daily 11am-2am, $9-22) in the heart of Canton. Nacho Mama's has been a hot spot in Baltimore since it opened on Elvis's birthday in 1994. The decor is a mix of the King, Natty Boh, the Orioles, the Baltimore Colts, and everything else Baltimore. The food is delicious, the portions are large, and they have more than a dozen kinds of margaritas. This is a great place to bring visitors to share some Baltimore tradition.

FEDERAL HILL
American

Peanut butter burgers, waffle fry nachos,

pretzel roll buns, and homemade chips are just some of the items to try at **The Abbey Burger Bistro** (1041 Marshall St., 443/453-9698, www.abbeyburgerbistro.com, Mon. 5pm-1am, Tues.-Thurs. 11am-1am, Fri.-Sat. 11am-1:30am, Sun. 11am-1am, $10-26). This burger-and-beer-focused eatery has a great menu for both, including a build-your-own burger section and a rotating beer list (they even take requests online). This is a great place to stir your creativity, fill your burger appetite, and wash it all down with a cold brew.

Hull Street Blues Cafe (1222 Hull St., 410/727-7476, Mon.-Sat. 11am-2am, Sun. 10am-2am, $7-28) has a long history. It got its start as a saloon back in 1889 and is now a lovely neighborhood café. Nestled amid the blocks of row houses in Locust Point, the café is named for its side street address on Hull Street (which was named after a naval hero of the War of 1812, Isaac Hull). The restaurant has two sides: One is a casual barroom (where bar fare is served) with a 40-foot-long bar, and the other is the nautical-themed Commodore Room, where guests can enjoy gourmet meals with linens and stemware in front of the fireplace. Seafood, beef, and poultry are at the heart of the menu, but other options such as the chipotle-lime barbecue pork loin are local favorites.

Seafood

A great seafood restaurant is **Ryleigh's Oyster Bar** (36 E. Cross St., 410/539-2093, www.ryleighs.com, Mon.-Sat. 11am-10pm, Sun. 11am-9pm, $8-30). The atmosphere is more upscale than a bar scene, and they offer really fresh oysters on their old slate oyster bar. There is a gourmet seafood menu with items such as crab cakes, tuna, and shrimp and grits. The crab pretzels are a great way to start, and they also offer salads and sandwiches and other items that aren't seafood.

MOUNT VERNON
Afghan

The Helmand (806 N. Charles St., 410/752-0311, www.helmand.com, Sun.-Thurs. 5pm-10pm, Fri.-Sat. 5pm-11pm, $11-30) looks like a simple restaurant but has been serving incredible Afghan food since 1989. It is one of a handful of eateries owned by a prominent Afghan family that helped bring the cuisine to the United States. Considered by many to be a local treasure, the *kaddo borawni,* a pumpkin appetizer, is a must-try before making the difficult entrée decision.

American

The tuxedoed servers, stuffed leather seats, live piano music, and stiff drinks haven't changed a bit at ★ **The Prime Rib** (1101 N. Calvert St., 410/539-1804, www.theprimerib.com, Mon.-Thurs. 5pm-10pm, Fri.-Sat. 5pm-11pm, Sun. 4pm-9pm, $26-56) since its opening in 1965. Jackets are required, and the place looks like an establishment Sinatra would have frequented. The best part, however, is the food. The Prime Rib has been named one of the best in the country by *Esquire* magazine for its steaks, and it is easy to believe. This is a place to come when you want first-class food and service to match, and you don't mind paying for it.

The funky little pizza shop **Joe Squared** (33 W. North Ave., 410/545-0444, www.joesquared.com, Mon.-Wed. 11am-10pm, Thurs. 11am-11pm, Fri.-Sat. 11am-midnight, Sun. noon-9pm, $8-19) offers coal-fired square pizza, seven varieties of risotto, an extensive rum list, good beer, and free live music (funk, soul, jazz, old time, etc.). Featured on *Diners, Drive-Ins and Dives,* the restaurant is family-owned, and the food is delicious. The clientele is mainly college-aged, and the area isn't ideal after dark.

Italian

A great choice for pizza in Mount Vernon is **Iggies** (818 N. Calvert St., Ste. 1, 410/528-0818, www.iggiespizza.com, Tues.-Thurs. 11:30am-9pm, Fri.-Sat. 11:30am-10pm, Sun. 11:30am-8pm, $10-18). The pizza has a thin, crispy crust and a multitude of interesting topping options (think peaches, gorgonzola, rosemary, etc.). The place is very casual, and you must BYOB if you'd like to drink. When you enter, wait to be seated. Once seated, leave your plate on the table and get in line to order. When your food is ready, the staff will call your name and order number. The pizza is excellent, and the crowd is young and lively. It's a great place to grab a bite before heading to Centerstage.

HAMPDEN AND HOMEWOOD
American

★ **Woodberry Kitchen** (2010 Clipper Park Rd., 410/464-8000, www.woodberrykitchen.com, brunch Sat.-Sun. 10am-2pm, dinner Tues.-Thurs. 5pm-9pm, Fri.-Sat. 5pm-10pm, Sun. 5pm-9pm, $19-38) is a hip little restaurant in the historic Clipper Mill west of Hampden. They serve local meats and seafood and use fresh organic ingredients. The menu is based on what is seasonal and includes many regional dishes (think brined pork chops and oysters roasted in a wood-burning oven). The atmosphere is contemporary in design, and the space, a renovated 19th-century industrial mill, offers the warm ambience of exposed brick, wood, and soft lighting. On nice evenings, diners can also enjoy patio seating under market umbrellas and white lights. Reservations are a must on weekends and should be made weeks in advance if possible.

It's hard to find a more local dining institution in Hampden than **Café Hon** (1002 W. 36th St., 410/243-1230, www.cafehon.com, Mon.-Thurs. 11am-9pm, Fri. 11am-10pm, Sat. 9am-10pm, Sun. 9am-8pm, $7-25), and

it's hard to miss the two-story pink flamingo that stands over its front door. The café name is a tribute to the "hon" culture in Hampden (see Honfest in the *Events* section of this chapter), and the café serves a mix of comfort food and seafood. Over the years the restaurant has had its share of press, both good and bad, and was even featured on an episode of *Kitchen Nightmares* back in 2012. The adjoining Hon Bar offers live music and oyster shucking.

Accommodations

$100-200

The **Courtyard Marriott Baltimore Downtown/Inner Harbor** (1000 Aliceanna St., 443/923-4000, www.marriott.com, $144-220) has 195 rooms and 10 suites not far from the waterfront. The staff at this hotel is exceptionally friendly and helpful. They also offer great packages for family members of patients at Johns Hopkins Hospital, which include a discounted room rate, breakfast, and cab vouchers to and from the hospital. There is a small indoor swimming pool, a small fitness room, and an on-site restaurant and bar serving breakfast, lunch, and dinner. High-speed Internet is included. Ask for an upper-floor room on the harbor side of the hotel, where limited water views are available.

For a less expensive stay that is still convenient to the Inner Harbor, the **Days Inn by Wyndham Baltimore Inner Harbor** (100 Hopkins Pl., 410/576-1000, www. wyndhamhotels.com, $169-199) is the ticket. Just a few blocks from the stadiums and Inner Harbor, the 250 rooms are clean and convenient. Although the rooms aren't large, this is a well-located hotel with an affordable price tag.

Budget-conscious travelers can also have a great stay at the **Brookshire Suites** (120 E. Lombard St., 410/625-1300, www. brookshiresuites.com, $157-201) just a block away from the Inner Harbor on Lombard

Street. The 11-story, 97-room hotel has a distinct exterior with a large black-and-white geometric pattern that can't be missed. The interior is contemporary with traditional-style rooms. This is a Modus Hotel, and if you book directly through their website, your stay includes free breakfast and you can bring a pet with no extra fee. This hotel caters to business travelers and offers a nice business center and laundry facilities, but its central location makes it a good choice for pleasure travel as well.

Travelers looking for a charming boutique hotel near bustling O'Donnell Street in Canton will be thrilled with the **Inn at 2920** (2920 Elliott St., 410/342-4450, www. theinnat2920.com, $145-165). This five-room inn is inside a rather regular-looking row house on Elliott Street. Look for the pale-green door on the corner. Once inside, the rooms are lovely, unique, and contemporary, with exposed brick walls and modern furnishings. This hip little hotel is definitely something special, and you'll feel like a local stepping out onto the street. The water is within walking distance, but Fell's Point is a good 15-20 minutes by foot.

$200-300

The ★ **Hyatt Regency Baltimore** (300 Light St., 410/528-1234, www.hyatt.com, $161-411) offers one of the best locations in the Inner Harbor. Situated right across Light Street from Harborplace and connected to it by two skywalks, the hotel offers tremendous harbor views. The rooms are modern and comfortable with large bathrooms and contemporary furniture. The building's lit-up, glass-enclosed elevators seem to shoot through the lobby roof and along the outside of the hotel. They are beautiful to look at and afford incredible views to the people inside. The hotel staff is also extremely helpful and pleasant. Bistro 300 on the third floor serves breakfast, lunch, and dinner (and has a nice bar). There is a small gift shop on-site, a fitness room, and pool. Ask for a harbor-view room on an upper floor; the corner rooms offer spectacular floor-to-ceiling windows overlooking the water.

The **Kimpton Hotel Monaco Baltimore Inner Harbor** (2 N. Charles St., 443/692-6170, www.monaco-baltimore.com, $163-246) is consistent with other Kimpton Hotels as a top-notch choice for accommodations. This warm and friendly hotel is housed in the restored B&O Railroad building on Charles Street a few blocks northwest of the Inner Harbor. The personal service and attention to detail they offer is hard to beat. The hotel has Tiffany stained glass windows, a marble staircase, and vaulted ceilings. The rooms are large and modern with high ceilings and a hint of funky styling that's unique to Kimpton. The staff is wonderful, and the location is convenient to many restaurants and attractions even though it's not right on the water. They offer bikes and bike route maps to guests and a hosted wine hour in the evenings. They have 24-hour valet parking with in-and-out services for $38. The hotel is pet friendly.

A good choice on the waterfront in the Harbor East area of Baltimore between Fell's Point and the Inner Harbor is the **Baltimore Marriott Waterfront Hotel** (700 Aliceanna St., 410/385-3000, www.marriott.com, $218-329). This towering 31-story hotel is on the water's edge and offers stunning harbor views and great access to many of the best attractions. It also has a heated indoor pool and fitness center. There are 733 modern rooms and 21 suites. Harbor-view rooms and city-view rooms are available.

A lovely boutique hotel directly on the water on the eastern side of Fell's Point, the ★ **Inn at Hendersons Wharf** (1000 Fell St., 410/522-7777, www.hendersonswharf.com, $244-289) is located in an 1893 brick building, which it shares with condos and a conference center. The inn's 38 cozy rooms have exposed-brick walls, colonial decor, feather beds, and 30-inch televisions with satellite service. There's a pretty interior courtyard. Rooms include a continental breakfast, access to a fitness center, and high-speed Internet. Self-parking is available for around $10 per night. The hotel is close to restaurants and shops in Fell's Point but far enough away to filter the noise. Ask for a harbor view.

If you want to be where the action is in Fell's Point, book a room at the **Admiral Fell Inn** (888 S. Broadway, 410/522-7380, www.admiralfell.com, $169-249). This historical, European-style hotel includes seven buildings, some of which date back to the 1770s. Many stories surround the inn, as the building has served many purposes, such as a ship chandlery, boardinghouse, theater, and YMCA. No two rooms are alike at the inn, but each is decorated in modern furnishings with cozy decor. Two specialty rooms are available, one with two levels and the other with a balcony overlooking the waterfront. The Tavern at the Admiral Fell Inn is open Wednesday-Saturday evenings to serve beer, wine, cocktails, and traditional spirits.

OVER $300

A luxurious addition to the Fell's Point waterfront is the ★ **Sagamore Pendry Baltimore** (1715 Thames St., 443/552-1400, www.pendryhotels.com, $361-935). This upscale boutique hotel opened in 2017 in the historic Recreation Pier building (circa 1914). Meticulously restored and beautifully appointed, this sophisticated and trendy hotel offers 128 guest rooms, a fine Italian chophouse, whiskey bar, and seasonal poolside bar and grill. Their comfortable, warmly decorated rooms have courtyard or harbor views, and some feature balconies. Architectural features such as floor-to-ceiling windows, an infinity pool overlooking the harbor, and views of the city complement a host of personal touches such as a choice of stuffed animals for the kids, late-afternoon macaroons, and a Moët & Chandon vending machine. The property is dog friendly (up to two pets for an extra $150 fee per pet per stay).

Right near the Baltimore Marriott Waterfront Hotel is the **Four Seasons Hotel Baltimore** (200 International Dr., 410/576-5800, www.fourseasons.com, $1,100-4,000+), which offers great views of the harbor and an elegant interior. There are 256 rooms and suites with views including the harbor, city, and marina. The rooms offer generous space, and the impressive Presidential Suite is more than 2,800 square feet. The corner suites offer stunning views. The service is on par with other Four Seasons hotels, which is to say much above average.

Information and Services

Helpful tourist information on Baltimore can be found on the **Baltimore Area Convention and Visitors Association** website at www.baltimore.org. The website has details on events and attractions throughout the city and answers many common questions. Special offers are also available through the website. The **Baltimore Area Visitor Center** (401 Light St., 877/225-8466, daily 10am-5pm) in the Inner Harbor is a great place to begin any trip to Baltimore. The 8,000-square-foot center offers information on nearly everything the city has to offer.

The most widely read paper in the city is the *Baltimore Sun* (www.baltimoresun.com). It is also Maryland's largest daily newspaper and covers local and regional news.

There are many hospitals in the metropolitan area of Baltimore. Top-ranking facilities include **Johns Hopkins Hospital** (1800 Orleans St., 410/955-5000, www.hopkinsmedicine.org) and the **University of Maryland Medical Center** (22 S. Greene St., 410/328-8667, www.umm.edu).

Getting There

AIR

The **Baltimore Washington International Thurgood Marshall Airport (BWI)** (410/859-7111, www.bwiairport.com) is just 10 miles south of Baltimore and a short 15-minute car ride from downtown Baltimore. This busy regional airport is a hub for Southwest Airlines and offers some of the best fares in the Washington DC/Baltimore area. Most other major airlines offer flight service to BWI as well. Parking is available at the airport by the hour or day, and there is a free cell phone lot for those who are picking up arriving passengers.

Car rentals are available at the airport from numerous national car rental companies, and courtesy shuttles run between the airport and major downtown hotels. The **SuperShuttle** (www.supershuttle.com, approximately $20 for a shared van) runs 24-hour service from the airport to locations throughout Baltimore and has a reservation counter on the lower level of the airport near baggage claims 1 and 10.

Uber and Lyft services are allowed to and

Bring Fido

Baltimore is surprisingly pet friendly for such a large and industrial city. Many hotels throughout the city allow your best friend to accompany you in your room. Additional fees and rules may apply to your four-legged friend, so ask when you make a reservation. Some hotels that allow dogs include:

- **Admiral Fell Inn** (888 S. Broadway, 410/522-7380)
- **Biltmore Suites** (205 W. Madison St., 410/728-6550)
- **Brookshire Suites** (120 E. Lombard St., 410/625-1300)
- **Crowne Plaza Baltimore—Inner Harbor** (105 West Fayette St., 410/347-5707)
- **Days Inn by Wyndham Baltimore Inner Harbor** (100 Hopkins Pl., 410/576-1000)
- **Four Seasons Hotel Baltimore** (200 International Dr., 410/576-5800)
- **Hilton Baltimore Convention Center Hotel** (401 W. Pratt St., 443/573-8700)
- **Holiday Inn Express Baltimore—Downtown** (221 N. Gay St., 410/400-8045)
- **Kimpton Hotel Monaco Baltimore Inner Harbor** (2 N. Charles St., 443/692-6170)
- **Lord Baltimore Hotel** (20 W. Baltimore St., 410/539-8400)
- **Pier 5 Hotel** (711 Eastern Ave., 410/539-2000)
- **Residence Inn Downtown Baltimore/Inner Harbor** (17 Light St., 410/962-1220)
- **Sagamore Pendry Baltimore** (1715 Thames St., 443/552-1400)
- **Sheraton Inner Harbor Hotel** (300 S. Charles St., 410/962-8300)
- **Sleep Inn & Suites Downtown Inner Harbor** (301 Fallsway, 410/779-6166)

from the airport and cost roughly $25-35 to downtown Baltimore. Cab service is also available from the airport, but this can be a costly option with fares running upward of $45 to downtown Baltimore.

Train service is available from the airport to downtown Baltimore through the Maryland Transit Administration (MTA) on their **Light Rail** (410/539-5000, www.mta.maryland.gov, Mon.-Fri. 4:45am-12:40am, Sat. 5:05am-12:45am, Sun. 10:35am-8:40pm, $1.90). The BWI Marshall Light Rail station can be found outside the lower lever of the terminal near Concourse E.

CAR

Baltimore is a very accessible city. Strategically located right on I-95, it can be reached easily by car from both the north and south. The drive from major cities such as New York (3.5 hours, 188 miles), Philadelphia (2 hours, 100 miles), Washington DC (1 hour, 39 miles), and Richmond (2.75 hours, 152 miles) is a straight shot and takes between one and four hours. I-83 also runs into the city from the north.

TRAIN

Pennsylvania Station (1500 N. Charles St., 800/872-7245, www.amtrak.com) is centrally located on Charles Street near Mount Vernon and is less than two miles from the Inner Harbor. The stately 1911 building is nicely restored, and the station is one of the busiest in the country. Amtrak runs dozens of trains through Penn Station daily from all corners of the country. They offer ticket discounts for seniors, children, students, veterans, and conference groups.

A commuter rail service called **Maryland Area Rail Commuter (MARC)** (410/539-5000, www.mta.maryland.gov) operates trains on weekdays between Washington DC and Baltimore ($4-16 one way). This is another option for visitors traveling during the week.

BUS

Just south of downtown Baltimore in an industrial section of the city is the **Greyhound** bus station (2110 Haines St., 410/752-7682, www.greyhound.com). Bus service runs daily from multiple destinations. It is advisable to take a cab from the station to points around Baltimore. Walking near the station is not advisable after dark.

A number of private bus lines provide service between cities in the mid-Atlantic and offer reasonable fares from cities such as Washington DC, Philadelphia, and New York City. An example is **Peter Pan Bus Lines** (800/343-9999, www.peterpanbus.com, $10 one-way from DC). Additional service can be found on www.gotobus.com.

Getting Around

Although walking is a viable option for getting to many of the sights in Baltimore, depending on where you are staying, it is often easiest (and safest at night) to move around the city by car. Public transportation does provide other alternatives; however, most public transportation is geared toward commuters and isn't the most convenient for visitors wishing to explore major attractions.

The exception to this is the **Charm City Circulator** (www.charmcitycirculator.com, year-round Mon.-Thurs. 7am-8pm, Fri. 7am-midnight, Sat. 9am-midnight, Sun. 9am-8pm). This free, ecofriendly shuttle service has a fleet of 30 Hybrid electric shuttles that serve four routes in Baltimore City. The Green Route offers transportation from City Hall to Fell's Point and to Johns Hopkins. The Purple Route serves locations from 33rd Street to Federal Hill. The Orange Route runs between Hollins Market and Harbor East, and the Banner Route goes from the Inner Harbor to Fort McHenry. Shuttles stop every 10-15 minutes at each designated stop.

CAR

Downtown Baltimore is divided by two main streets. Baltimore Street runs east to west, and Charles Street runs north to south. All streets north of Baltimore Street (or above Baltimore Street if you're looking at a map) have the "north" designation (such as N. Highland Street). Likewise, those south (or below) Baltimore Street have a "south" designation. The same is true for the streets east and west of Charles Street (which is a one-way street running north downtown). Those streets to the east of Charles Street (or to the right) have "east" designations. Those to the west (left) have "west" designations.

When driving, it is very important to be aware that there are many one-way streets in Baltimore. Parking isn't too difficult in most parts of the city on weekends; however, garages right around the Inner Harbor can be expensive. Parking during the week is more of a challenge, when commuters are in town and spaces are in short supply. There is on-street parking in many areas, and pay lots are scattered throughout town. Be sure to read parking signs carefully, as many neighborhoods have resident-only parking and time restrictions.

Overall, driving in Baltimore is much as it is in other big cities. Drive with purpose and have a plan as to where you are headed. Sightseeing out the window in the middle of traffic can result in some less-than-friendly gestures from those in cars around you. When in doubt, or if you miss a turn, just drive

All Aboard the Water Taxi

a water taxi docked at Inner Harbor

For decades residents and visitors to Baltimore have enjoyed an alternative form of public transportation around the city. The **Baltimore Water Taxi** (410/563-3900, www.baltimorewatertaxi.com) is a fun, easy way to travel between some of the best attractions, shopping areas, and restaurants in town. The famed blue-and-white boats can be seen zipping between 10 well-placed landings along the waterfront. The taxi service shuttles thousands of commuters and visitors alike on a daily basis, and local businesses rely on the service to bring their customers.

The taxi runs Monday-Thursday 11am-10pm and Friday-Sunday 10am-10pm. All-day passes are $16 for adults, $9 ages 3-12, and $14 for seniors 65 and over, and trip times range from 10 to 20 minutes. Private charters are also available. Tickets can be purchased online or onboard with a major credit card. Landing areas are as follows:

- Landing 1: Aquarium

- Landing 2: Harborplace

- Landing 4: Federal Hill

- Landing 5: Pier Five

- Landing 7: Harbor East

- Landing 8: Maritime Park

- Landing 10: Locust Point

- Landing 11: Fell's Point

- Landing 16: Canton

- Landing 17: Fort McHenry

around the block; it's difficult to get too lost if you keep an eye on the harbor.

BUS

Bus service provided by the **Maryland Transit Administration (MTA)** (410/539-5000, www.mta.maryland.com, $1.90) includes more than 70 routes in Baltimore. Forty-seven of these routes are local routes inside the city. Bus routes primarily serve commuters on weekdays and are more limited on weekends, but it pays to check out the latest schedule online.

RAIL

Two public rail systems serve Baltimore, although each only has one rail line. The first, called **Light Rail** (410/539-5000, www.mta.maryland.gov, Mon.-Fri. 4:45am-12:40am, Sat. 5:05am-12:45am, Sun. 10:35am-8:40pm, $1.90) runs from BWI Airport north to Hunt Valley Mall (in northern Baltimore County). This is only a good option if you are traveling between two specific points on the line, such as Camden Yards to Mount Vernon (there are no east-west stops). The second is the **Metro Subway** (410/539-5000, www.mta.maryland.gov, Mon.-Fri. 5am-midnight, Sat.-Sun. 6am-midnight, $1.80), which runs from the suburbs northwest of town and into downtown and Johns Hopkins. The line is 15.5 miles long and has 14 stations. Trains run every 8-10 minutes during rush hour, every 11 minutes on weekday evenings, and every 15 minutes on weekends. Again, this line is geared toward commuters and isn't too helpful for visitors wishing to move around town between sights.

CAR SERVICE AND TAXI

Uber and Lyft are available throughout the Baltimore area. Taxi service is also available through several providers including **Yellow Cab** (410/685-1212) and **Diamond** (410/947-3333). Hailing a cab on the street can be an impossible feat on busy nights in the city, so it's best to bring their phone numbers and try calling from your cell phone. Metered rates in Baltimore are $1.80 for the first one-eleventh of a mile or fraction thereof. Each additional one-eleventh of a mile is $0.20; $0.20 is also charged for each 30 seconds of wait time.

WATER TAXI

Water taxi service (410/563-3900, www.baltimorewatertaxi.com, seasonal Mon.-Fri. 6am-11am, 2:30pm-8pm) is available around the harbor between many of the popular sights. This is a great service for visitors. The little boats with the blue awnings that can be seen scooting around the harbor are the taxi boats. They move between 10 stops that include all the prime waterfront destinations (including Fell's Point, Canton, and Fort McHenry in the summer). The boat captains are often chatting and make excellent tour guides.

The **Harbor Connector** (410/563-3900, www.charmcitycirculator.com, Mon.-Fri. 6am-11am and 2:30pm-8pm) is a free boat-shuttle service that runs weekdays between Maritime Park, Tide Point, Canton Waterfront Park, Harbor View, and Harbor East.

BIKE

Biking in Baltimore as a mode of transportation is becoming more popular. Many attractions have iron bike racks that look like bicycles stationed out front, so cyclists have a convenient place to lock up their bikes (yes, lock your bike). New bike lanes are being added around the city to encourage biking, although narrow roads and hills will always be a factor, and riding in traffic can be risky when the streets are crowded.

Excursions

Havre de Grace

If you have extra time and want to venture outside of Baltimore for a half- or full-day excursion, Havre de Grace and Westminster are two very different, yet equally alluring towns to visit. Havre de Grace provides the attractions of a historic bayside community, while Westminster offers Civil War history and a wonderful farm museum.

HAVRE DE GRACE

Havre de Grace is a beautiful little town in Harford County that sits at the head of the Chesapeake Bay and the mouth of the mighty Susquehanna River. Its name in French means "Harbor of Beauty" or "Harbor of Grace."

The city was once seriously considered for the location of the nation's capital. Havre de Grace was incorporated in 1785 and has a population of around 13,000. Its seaside-like atmosphere makes it a popular tourist and outdoor recreation destination.

Havre de Grace is halfway between Baltimore and Philadelphia. It was, at one time, a popular stop for stagecoaches traveling between the two cities. Between 1912 and 1950, it was home to the Havre de Grace Racetrack, a popular horse-racing track. Famous horses such as Man o' War, his son War Admiral, Seabiscuit, and Challedon raced here during its heyday. For years, the Havre de Grace Handicap was one of the most highly regarded races in the Northeast. The track was sold in 1951 to the owners of two other Maryland racetracks (Pimlico Race Course and Laurel Park Racecourse). The new owners closed the Havre de Grace course and moved the track's racing allotment dates to their own facilities.

Havre de Grace shelters well over 100 historic structures, and the town is designated a National Historic District. The town was first mapped in 1799, and the structures that remain today are of many different ages and architectural designs. Simple Victorian duplexes

stand side by side with single-family homes and Queen Anne estates built by wealthy residents.

Sights

HAVRE DE GRACE MARITIME MUSEUM

The **Havre de Grace Maritime Museum** (100 Lafayette St., 410/939-4800, www. hdgmaritimemuseum.org, Apr.-Oct. 14

Wed.-Sat. 10am-5pm, Sun. 1pm-5pm, Oct. 15-Mar. Sat. 10am-5pm, Sun. 1pm-5pm, individual $4, family $9) is a small window into the history of the upper Chesapeake Bay and lower Susquehanna River. Exhibits explore topics such as fishing, waterfowl hunting, lighthouses, navigation, the Native Americans who lived in the region, European settlers, and wooden boat building.

CONCORD POINT LIGHTHOUSE

The **Concord Point Lighthouse** (corner of Concord St. and Lafayette St., 410/939-3213, www.concordpointlighthouse.org, Apr.-Oct. Sat.-Sun. 1pm-5pm, free, donations appreciated) is a pretty little piece of history on the waterfront in Havre de Grace. The lighthouse was built in 1827 out of local granite and is one of the oldest lighthouses on the East Coast that has operated continuously. Now fully restored, it stands on a scenic stretch of the promenade. The climb up the 30-foot lighthouse tower is fairly short (as lighthouses go), so it's a fun activity to do with children (but they must be at least 42 inches tall). The lighthouse offers terrific views of the Susquehanna River and the Chesapeake Bay. There are a few informative exhibits at the Keeper's House (which used to be a bar) that give details on the lighthouse's first keeper, John O'Neil, and the history of the lighthouse. There is also a gift shop.

HAVRE DE GRACE DECOY MUSEUM

The **Havre de Grace Decoy Museum** (215 Giles St., 410/939-3739, www.decoymuseum. com, Mon.-Sat. 10:30am-4:30pm, Sun. noon-4pm, adults $6, children 9-18 $2, 8 and under free, seniors 60 and over $5) is more than a showcase for wooden birds. Decoys have been part of the culture on the Chesapeake Bay for centuries. Originally, they were not considered art but were made purely to lure waterfowl within hunting range. Today decoys are an art form. Carvers create sophisticated reproductions of birds using centuries-old skills. This pretty little museum is home to one of the best collections of functional and decorative Chesapeake Bay decoys in existence. Visitors can learn the history of waterfowling on the upper Chesapeake Bay and also how decoys are made through exhibits, lectures, tours, and demonstrations. More than 1,200 decoys are on display. Annual festivals are held at the museum, and there is a nice little gift shop with decoys, books, and other waterfowl-related items. Group tours for more than 10 people are available (adult tours $4 per person, youth tours $3 per person).

TYDINGS PARK

Tydings Park (350 Commerce St., at the southern end of Union Ave., 410/939-1800, daily 5am-11pm) is a 22-acre park on the waterfront in Havre de Grace. It is situated at the head of the Chesapeake Bay and is the site of several annual festivals and concerts. The park facilities include a fishing pier, boat ramp, picnic area, tennis courts, gazebos, and a playground. It is also the starting point of the half-mile **Havre de Grace Promenade,** a waterfront walkway that goes past the Maritime Museum and continues to the Concord Point Lighthouse. The park is also known as the **Millard E. Tydings Memorial Park.**

THE SUSQUEHANNA MUSEUM AT THE LOCK HOUSE

The **Susquehanna Museum at the Lock House** (817 Conesteo St., 410/939-5780, www. thelockhousemuseum.org, mid-Apr.-Oct. Fri.-Sun. 1pm-5pm, free) is a museum inside a historic house, which was built in 1840 and was home to one of the lock tenders for the Susquehanna and Tidewater Canal (which ran 45 miles between Havre de Grace and Wrightsville, Pennsylvania). It also served as the office for the toll collector. The two-story brick building was almost twice the size of other lock houses on the canal (there were 29 locks total). Exhibits in the museum recreate life along the canal and provide details on Havre de Grace's role in the growth of the country.

Recreation

There are several **boat-launch sites** in Havre de Grace. The first two are at the mouth of the Susquehanna River. One is north of the train bridge at the intersection of Otsego and Union Streets (on Water Street at Jean Roberts Memorial Park). The second is just downstream, off of Franklin Street by the Tidewater Grille (this is just for cartop boats since there is no ramp). A third launch site is at Tydings Park off Commerce Street, on the south side of town. This site is right on the Chesapeake Bay. It is important to know that boating near the Aberdeen Proving Ground south of the city is strictly forbidden. In addition to getting a fine for trespassing, landing anywhere on the proving grounds can be very dangerous because there are live munitions. Obey all signage in the area and respect the buoy markers.

Three miles northwest of Havre de Grace is the beautiful **Susquehanna State Park** (4118 Wilkinson Rd., 410/557-7994, www.dnr. maryland.gov, daily 9am-sunset, $4). The park offers boating ($12 launch fee), hiking, mountain biking, kayaking, fishing, a playground, and picnicking. There are also several historic buildings on-site, such as a 200-year-old gristmill (visitors can tour its four floors), a stone mansion, a barn, a tollhouse, and a miller's house. All buildings are open on weekends between Memorial Day and Labor Day 10am-4pm. A section of the former **Susquehanna and Tidewater Canal** can be seen in the park. This canal was built in 1836 and connected Havre de Grace with Wrightsville, Pennsylvania. Mule-drawn barges made this an important commercial route for more than 50 years. To reach the park, take I-95 to exit 89, and then proceed west on Route 155 to Route 161. Turn right on Route 161 and then right again on Rock Run Road.

The Black-Eyed Susan (723 Water St., 410/939-2161, www.blackeyedsusanhdg.com, from $33) is an authentic paddle wheeler that is docked in the marina in Havre de Grace. It is designed for entertainment and offers daily cruises and charters.

Food

★ **The Vineyard Wine Bar** (142 N. Washington St., 443/502-2551, www. vineyardwinebar.com, Mon., Wed., and Thurs. 11:30am-10pm, Fri.-Sat. 11:30am-11pm, Sun. noon-8pm, $9-22) offers a menu of small plates that includes salads, flatbreads, cheeses, and assorted pâtés designed to complement their extensive wine menu. They also offer "light, medium, and full bodied" selections such as seafood, shrimp and grits, steak, pasta, and delicious rarities such as Salmon Wellington. They only offer one seating per evening (diners must be over 12 years of age), and diners have a reserved table for the entire evening. They have received the Wine Spectator Award for "one of the most outstanding restaurant wine lists in world" multiple times. Their retail wine shop offers more than 300 wines from around the globe.

French- and Creole-style seafood can be found at **Backfin Blues Creole de Graw** (400 N. Union Ave., 443/502-8191, www. backfinbluesgroup.com, Wed. 11am-9pm, Thur.-Sat. 11am-10pm, Sun. 10am-8pm, $18-33). They offer casual selections such as crab cakes, gumbo, and shrimp and grits and accompaniments such as sweet-potato tots. There is live entertainment on Thursday nights.

Cold beer, good pub food, and friendly service can be found at **Coakley's Pub** (406 St. John St., 410/939-8888, www.coakleyspub. com, Mon.-Sat. 11am-10pm, Sun. 11am-9pm, $6-35) on St. John Street. This cozy spot offers quality fare with Chesapeake Bay flair (try the crab pretzel or coconut shrimp). The food and service are consistent, and the atmosphere is casual and inviting.

A popular waterfront restaurant is the **Tidewater Grille** (300 Franklin St., 410/939-3313, www.tidewatergrille.com, Mon.-Thurs. 11am-8pm, Fri.-Sat. 11am-9pm, Sun. 9am-noon, $11-55). They offer a traditional seafood menu with a great view of the Susquehanna and Chesapeake headwaters. Ask for a seat by the window, or sit on the patio when it's nice out. Free docking is available for those coming by boat.

Accommodations

The elegant **Vandiver Inn** (301 S. Union Ave., 410/939-5200, www.vandiverinn.com, $150-169) offers 18 guest rooms in three beautifully restored Victorian homes. Eight are in the Vandiver Inn mansion (built in 1886), and an additional 10 are in the adjacent Kent & Murphy Guest Houses. All have private bathrooms. Each guest is treated to a lovely breakfast, free in-room wireless access, and in-room cable television. The inn is within blocks of the Chesapeake Bay and within the city of Havre de Grace. Many special events are held at the inn, so if you are looking for a quiet stay with little activity, ask about events during your stay when you make a reservation.

The only Victorian mansion built of stone in Havre de Grace is the **Spencer Silver Mansion** (200 Union Ave., 410/939-1485, www.spencersilvermansion.com, $89-174). This nicely restored 1896 home offers four guest rooms and a lovely carriage house for rent. A full breakfast is served each morning until 10:30am. The mansion is a short walk from the Chesapeake Bay and is near the attractions in downtown Havre de Grace. It is also pet friendly.

Five miles south of Havre de Grace is the **Hilton Garden Inn Aberdeen** (1050 Beards Hill Rd., 410/272-1777, www.hiltongardeninn3.hilton.com, $155-163) in Aberdeen, Maryland. This modern hotel offers a fitness center and indoor pool. All rooms have 32-inch HD flat-screen televisions, microwaves, refrigerators, and complimentary wireless Internet.

Camping

Camping is available at **Susquehanna State Park** (4122 Wilkinson Rd., 888/432-2267, www.dnr.maryland.gov, Apr.-Oct., $21.49-50.49 plus $4 park fee). They have 69 sites (6 have electric and 6 have camper cabins). There are two comfort stations with hot showers.

Information and Services

For additional information on Havre de Grace, stop by the **Havre de Grace Office of Tourism & Visitor Center** (450 Pennington Ave., 410/939-2100, Mon.-Fri. 9am-5pm, Sat. 11am-4pm) or visit www.explorehavredegrace.com.

Getting There

Havre de Grace is approximately one hour by car (37 miles) north of Baltimore. It is off I-95, on the southern side of the M. E. Tydings Memorial Bridge. Exit onto MD 155 and follow that road past the Susquehanna Museum and into the historic district of Havre de Grace.

WESTMINSTER

Westminster, founded in 1764 and incorporated in 1838, is the seat of Carroll County and has a population of around 18,500. This picturesque town primarily surrounded by farmland and rolling terrain saw a cavalry battle known as Corbit's Charge fought right on the downtown streets during the Civil War. It was also the first locale in the country to offer rural mail delivery.

Westminster is also the home of the late Whittaker Chambers's farm. He hid the "pumpkin papers," which were the key to a controversial case concerning espionage during the Cold War, in a hollowed-out gourd here. The papers resulted in the 1950 conviction of former State Department official Alger Hiss. This evidence confirmed Hiss's perjury in front of Congress when he denied being a Soviet spy.

Westminster is also known for its above-average number of tornadoes, including several major storms that have resulted in varying degrees of destruction.

Today, Westminster is a lovely little city with many artists and art galleries. It is also home to **McDaniel College** (2 College Hill, 410/848-7000, www.mcdaniel.edu), a private liberal arts and sciences college founded in 1867 with just over 1,500 undergraduate students.

Sights
DOWNTOWN WESTMINSTER

Downtown Westminster offers a pleasant historic district along Main Street with many old buildings and stories to surround them. The pedestrian-friendly area shelters many independent shops, galleries, and restaurants. Large trees line the streets, and there is plenty of parking in two parking decks and outdoor lots.

Many buildings on Main Street in Westminster have a long history, but none as varied as **Odd Fellows Hall** (140 E. Main St.). This plain, three-story brick building was erected in 1858 for $9,000 by the Salem Lodge No. 60 of the Independent Order of Odd Fellows. It was a central location for gatherings in Westminster.

Prior to the Civil War, the building was used by a local militia with Southern sympathies. Not long after the war, a comedian from Alabama performed at the hall and made jokes about President Grant and other officials in the government. As legend has it, the patrons did not appreciate the jokes and threw rocks at him. After being hit in the neck, the performer became upset and left the stage. The local sheriff offered him protection for the night, but the performer refused and went out back to saddle his horse. He was found dead behind the hall shortly after, having had his throat slit. Shortly after that day, and from then on, reports of people seeing a ghost behind the hall of a man engaged in monologue have been common. The building later became a town library, a saloon, a concert hall, and a newspaper office.

In 1912, the building was known as the Opera House, when the Odd Fellows created an opera room that became the first movie theater in town. In recent years it was home to the Opera House Printing Company, but at the time of writing, it was empty.

HISTORICAL SOCIETY OF CARROLL COUNTY

The **Historical Society of Carroll County** (210 E. Main St., 410/848-6494, www.hsccmd. org), on the east end of Westminster's downtown area, has exhibits on the heritage of Carroll County and the surrounding Piedmont area.

★ CARROLL COUNTY FARM MUSEUM

The **Carroll County Farm Museum** (500 S. Center St., 410/386-3880, www. carrollcountyfarmmuseum.org, Mon.-Sat. 9am-4pm, Sun. noon-4pm, adults $5, family $10, seniors over 60 $4) offers visitors a unique opportunity to see what rural life in the mid-19th century was like. Part of a 142-acre complex, the museum demonstrates how families had to be self-sufficient by producing everything they needed (food, household items, soap, yarn, etc.) right on their own land.

The museum features a three-story brick farmhouse and authentic farm buildings built in the 1850s, including a log barn, smokehouse, saddlery, broom shop, springhouse, and wagon shed. A guided tour conducted by costumed interpreters of the farmhouse's seven rooms is included with admission, as is a self-guided walking tour of the various exhibit buildings. The wagon shed houses the buggy that was used for the first rural mail-delivery route, which ran between Westminster and Uniontown. Although the route signaled the development of a sophisticated mail-delivery system, many residents were not happy about it because they felt cut off from the rest of the community when they were no longer forced to take regular trips into town to get news and socialize.

There are also public buildings on-site such as a firehouse, schoolhouse, and general store. Artifacts and antiques from the period (many of which were donated by local families) are also on display. There are many live animals at the museum such as sheep, geese, pigs, goats, and horses, which make this a great place to bring children. There is also a gift store.

ART GALLERIES

At the west end of the downtown area, the **Carroll Arts Center** (91 W. Main St.,

410/848-7272, Mon., Wed., Fri., and Sat. 10am-4pm, Tues. and Thurs. 10am-7pm) houses several free art galleries, the **Tevis Gallery, Director's Hall Gallery,** and the **Community Gallery.** It also has a 263-seat theater where it hosts concerts, plays, lectures, recitals, and films year-round. In addition, there are a handful of independent galleries along Main Street and Liberty Street.

The **Esther Prangley Rice Gallery** (410/857-2595, Mon.-Fri. 12pm-4pm, Sat. 12pm-5pm, free), in Peterson Hall at McDaniel College, features work by students and local artists.

WALKING TOURS

Walking tours are popular in Westminster, and brochures with self-guided tours are available at www.westminstermd.gov. One of the most popular is the Ghost Walk brochure that tells tales of local hauntings.

Shopping

Many national stores and chain restaurants can be found along Route 140, but the historic downtown area offers a mix of locally owned retail shops and restaurants. Westminster blends cultural experiences with the atmosphere of a small town.

The **Downtown Westminster Farmers Market** (Conaway Parking Lot, Railroad Ave. and Emerald Hill Ln., www.downtownwestminsterfarmersmarket.com) is held on Saturdays from the week after Mother's Day through the week before Thanksgiving 8am-noon. It is a "producers-only" market and offers fresh produce, baked goods, flowers, and local honey.

Food
AMERICAN

A nice and cozy casual neighborhood restaurant, **Rafael's** (32 W. Main St., 410/840-1919, www.rafaelsrestaurant.com, Mon.-Thurs. 11am-9:30pm, Fri. 11am-10:30pm, Sat. 8am-10:30pm, Sun. 8am-9pm, $5-21) has good food and reasonable prices and is especially known for its hamburgers. They serve lunch and dinner daily and breakfast on weekends. The staff is friendly, and the food is consistent.

A popular local eatery with home-brewed beer is **Johansson's Dining House** (4 W. Main St., 410/876-0101, www.johanssonsdininghouse.com, Mon.-Thurs. 11am-10pm, Fri.-Sat. 11am-11pm, Sun. 10am-10pm, $9-31). This casual restaurant serves a varied menu (filet mignon, seafood, pizza, and sandwiches) and homemade desserts. The place has a lot of character, good decor, and is in the heart of Westminster. The 1913 building opened as a restaurant in 1994.

IRISH

O'Lordans Irish Pub (14 Liberty St., 410/876-0000, www.olordansirishpub.com, Sun. and Tues.-Thurs. 11am-10pm, Fri.-Sat. 11am-11pm, $9-30) is a lively spot on Liberty Street. The pub has a traditional Irish pub feel with a fireplace, murals, dark wood, plank floors, and a stone facade. The bartenders are witty, and the food portions are ginormous and delicious. The pub offers a great happy hour menu and has developed a loyal fan base.

MEXICAN

Papa Joe's Mexican Restaurant (250 Englar Rd., 410/871-2505, www.papajoeswestminstermd.com, Mon.-Sat. 11am-10pm, $8-16) is the local favorite for Mexican food. They offer traditional Mexican dishes in a friendly, colorful atmosphere. The restaurant is family owned and operated, and they have fun specials such as a salsa bar night on Monday. The fajitas are a signature dish and come smothered in a wonderful cream sauce, which is a little different from traditional fajitas. Seating is limited, but there is outdoor seating when the weather is nice.

TEAROOM

The best tearoom in Westminster (okay, maybe it's the only tearoom in Westminster, but it's a good one) is **The Kate Pearl Tea Room** (111 Stoner Ave., 410/857-0058, www.thekatepearltearoom.com, Tues.-Sat. 10am-4pm, $10-34), located in the town's oldest home (the Historic William Winchester House), which was built by town founder William Winchester. This English-style tearoom serves everything from Mid-Morning Tea with scones, fruits, and spreads to Royal Tea with soup, salad, sandwiches, and dessert. They also offer catering for special occasions. The tearoom is located in a rural setting near town. It also has a gift shop. Proper attire is suggested (no jeans, halter tops, or shorts).

Accommodations

Accommodations right in Westminster are mainly limited to chain hotels such as the **Westminster Days Inn** (25 S. Cranberry Rd., 410/857-0500, www.daysinn.com, $102-130) and the **Best Western Westminster Catering and Conference Center** (451 WMC Dr., 410/857-1900, www.book. bestwestern.com, $113-145).

Ten minutes from downtown Westminster is **Solace, the Bed and Breakfast** (1705 Bachmans Valley Rd., 443/952-1290, www. solacebandb.com, $125-150). This lovely bed-and-breakfast offers four guest rooms in a modern farmhouse and one in a vintage log home. They advertise a quiet, peaceful setting on farmland along Big Pipe Creek.

Information and Services

Additional information on Westminster can be found at the **Carroll County Visitor Center** (1838 Emerald Hill Ln., 410/848-1388, Mon.-Sat. 9am-4pm).

Getting There

Westminster is 35 miles northwest of Baltimore and 56 miles north of Washington DC. MD 140 runs through Westminster from east to west, and MD 97 runs north to south.

Annapolis and Southern Maryland

Capital city Annapolis has been the crown jewel of Maryland throughout its rich history. The city is known as the sailing capital of the world, as the birthplace of American horse racing, and for having more 18th-century buildings than any other city in the United States. Annapolis has remained extremely well preserved as a colonial-era town despite its popularity with tourists and businesses. It is a fun place to visit, a great place to people watch, and a fantastic place to eat seafood.

Southern Maryland offers a relaxed atmosphere compared to the bustle of Annapolis. The cities along the western shore of the Chesapeake Bay vary from sleepy seaside towns to active sailing communities. Crisscrossed with scenic roadways and state and

Highlights

Look for ★ to find recommended sights, activities, dining, and lodging.

★ **Annapolis City Dock:** This public waterfront boasts beautiful scenery, impressive yachts, and many shops and restaurants (page 445).

★ **U.S. Naval Academy:** More than 85,000 men and women have graduated from this prestigious school and gone on to serve in the U.S. Navy and Marine Corps (page 445).

★ **Calvert Marine Museum:** This wonderful museum shares the whole history of the Chesapeake Bay, focusing on prehistoric times, the natural environment, and the bay's unique maritime heritage (page 458).

★ **Calvert Cliffs State Park:** More than just a beautiful sandy beach with stunning cliffs, this park offers superb fossil hunting (page 459).

★ **Historic St. Mary's City:** This living outdoor museum teaches visitors about life in Maryland's original capital city during colonial times (page 461).

national parks, this area makes for a lovely excursion.

PLANNING YOUR TIME

Annapolis and Southern Maryland can be explored in a long weekend or over several day trips from Baltimore. The distance between Annapolis and Point Lookout is approximately 82 miles (about two hours by car). Annapolis and Solomons Island are good choices for overnight stays or for boating on the Chesapeake Bay.

The closest airport to Annapolis is **Baltimore Washington International Thurgood Marshall Airport (BWI)** (410/859-7040, www.bwiairport.com), but parts of Southern Maryland are actually closer to **Ronald Reagan Washington National Airport (DCA)** (703/417-8000, www.metwashairports.com), just outside Washington DC in Arlington, Virginia (Point Lookout is 79 miles from DCA and 99 miles from BWI). Normally, the lowest airfares can be obtained by flying into BWI, so it pays to explore both options. Once you arrive in the region, it is best to explore by car. Parking is plentiful except for right in downtown Annapolis, but even there, most hotels have parking available, and public garages can be found.

Annapolis

Maryland's capital city of Annapolis is a picturesque and historic seaport on the Chesapeake Bay. It is widely known as the Sailing Capital of the World due to its popularity as a sailing port for both resident and international vessels. Literally hundreds of sailboats cruise the surrounding waters year-round, with regular races being held several times a week during the summer.

In 1649, a settlement named Providence was founded on the northern shore of the Severn River by Puritans exiled from Virginia. The settlement was later moved to the southern shore and renamed several times before finally becoming Annapolis, a tribute to Princess Anne of Denmark and Norway, who was in line to be the queen of Great Britain. The city was incorporated in 1708. Annapolis prospered as a port and grew substantially during the 18th century. It even served as the temporary capital of the United States in 1783.

From its earliest days more than 300 years ago, Annapolis was known as a center for wealth, social activities, and a thriving cultural scene. It was also known for its cozy pubs and abundant seafood restaurants, which welcomed prosperous visitors from all over the globe. Annapolis was also the birthplace of American horse racing—several of the original stock of the American Thoroughbred line entered through its port, and people came from all over the colonies to watch and bet on horse races. George Washington is even said to have lost a few shillings at the local track.

Annapolis is a great place to visit and explore. It has a vibrant waterfront with many shops and restaurants and is quaint and historical, yet welcomes an international crowd. The city was designed more like the capital cities in Europe with a baroque plan, rather than the grid layout customary to U.S. cities. Circles with radiating streets highlight specific buildings, such as St. Anne's Episcopal Church (one of the first churches in the city) and the State House. Numerous magnificent homes were built in the city's early days and hosted many of the founders of our country for lavish social events. Today Annapolis is home to the U.S. Naval Academy and St. John's College.

Annapolis and Southern Maryland

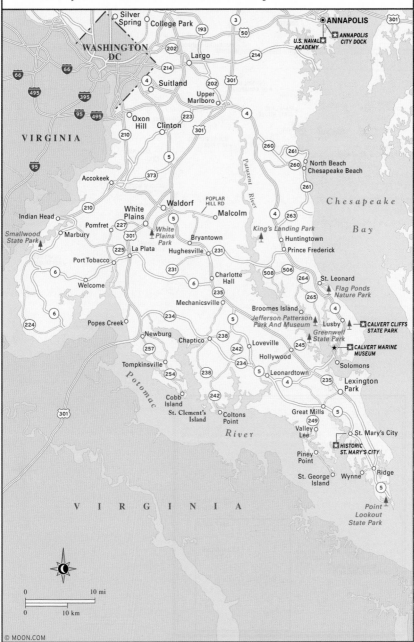

© MOON.COM

Annapolis

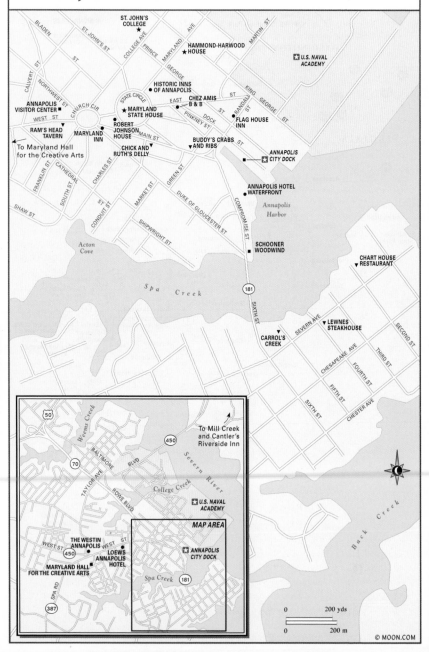

ST. JOHN'S COLLEGE ★

HAMMOND-HARWOOD ★ HOUSE

★ U.S. NAVAL ACADEMY

HISTORIC INNS ● OF ANNAPOLIS

CHEZ AMIS ● B & B

ANNAPOLIS VISITOR CENTER ■

★ MARYLAND STATE HOUSE

● FLAG HOUSE INN

RAM'S HEAD TAVERN ▼

MARYLAND INN ●

ROBERT JOHNSON HOUSE ●

To Maryland Hall for the Creative Arts

CHICK AND RUTH'S DELLY ●

BUDDY'S CRABS ▼ AND RIBS

ANNAPOLIS ★ CITY DOCK ■

ANNAPOLIS HOTEL ■ WATERFRONT

Annapolis Harbor

SCHOONER ■ WOODWIND

Acton Cove

Spa Creek

CHART HOUSE ▼ RESTAURANT

181

Carrol's Creek

SIXTH ST

▼ LEWNES STEAKHOUSE

CARROL'S ▼ CREEK

To Mill Creek and Cantler's Riverside Inn

50

450

Weems Creek

70

BALTIMORE BLVD

TAYLOR AVE

ROWE BLVD

Severn River

College Creek

★ U.S. NAVAL ACADEMY

THE WESTIN ANNAPOLIS ●

WEST ST

450

WEST ST

LOEWS ANNAPOLIS HOTEL ●

MARYLAND HALL ■ FOR THE CREATIVE ARTS

SPA RD

387

MAP AREA

★ ANNAPOLIS CITY DOCK

Spa Creek

181

Back Creek

0   200 yds

0   200 m

© MOON.COM

The most popular neighborhood for visitors is the Historic Downtown area. This is where the scenic waterfront and City Dock are located, as well as charming boutiques, fabulous restaurants, and historic homes. Another popular tourist area is Eastport, just south of Historic Downtown. This area is home to "Restaurant Row" and offers sweeping Chesapeake Bay views and a fun-loving, slightly funky atmosphere.

SIGHTS

★ Annapolis City Dock

The **Annapolis City Dock** (Dock St. on the waterfront) is the heart of the downtown area. Annapolis boasts more 18th-century buildings than any other American city, and many of these charming structures line the dock area. Locally owned shops, boutiques, and souvenir stands beckoning shoppers off the busy streets and waterfront restaurants help fuel the energy of this hot spot. The public waterfront is where visitors can take in the beautiful scenery while getting a good look at many expensive yachts. The waterfront area is also known as **Ego Alley,** since a steady parade of high-end sailing and motor vessels can be seen going by on nearly every weekend and evening.

TOP EXPERIENCE

★ U.S. Naval Academy

The **U.S. Naval Academy** (121 Blake Rd., 410/293-1000, www.usna.edu) was founded in 1845 by the secretary of the navy. Since that time, more than 85,000 men and women have graduated from this prestigious school and gone on to serve in the U.S. Navy or the U.S. Marine Corps. The student body is referred to as the "Brigade of Midshipmen." The academy is directly northeast of downtown Annapolis at the confluence of the Severn River and the Chesapeake Bay. Guided walking tours of the 300-plus-acre campus led by professional guides are offered to visitors through the **Armel-Leftwich Visitor Center** (52 King George St., 410/293-8687, www.usnabsd.com,

Mar.-Dec. daily 9am-5pm, Jan. and Feb. daily 9am-4pm, $12). Tours are 1.25 hours and are offered throughout most of the day while the visitors center is open; they cannot be booked in advance. Tours provide a close-up look at the imposing marble buildings and monuments on campus and cover topics such as history, architecture, traditions, and life as a midshipman.

Access to the Naval Academy grounds is limited. Government-issued photo identification is required for admission. Parking is available at the stadium on Rowe Boulevard inside the Noah Hillman Parking Garage (enter from Duke of Gloucester or Main St.). There are also parking meters around City Dock.

Maryland State House

The **Maryland State House** (100 State Circle, 410/260-6445, www.msa.maryland. gov, daily 9am-5pm, free) is the oldest legislative house in the country that has been in continual use. It is also the oldest peacetime capitol. The State House was built in the 1770s, and the first Maryland legislature meeting was held here in 1779. The building is architecturally significant—its dome is the largest wooden dome constructed without nails in the United States.

During 1783 and 1784, when Annapolis served as the U.S. capital, the State House was home to the U.S. government. It was there that two significant events took place. The first was that George Washington resigned his commission before the Continental Congress on December 23, 1783, and the second was that the Treaty of Paris ending the Revolutionary War was ratified here on January 14, 1784. Self-guided-tour information is available on the first floor of the State House.

St. John's College

St. John's College (60 College Ave., 410/263-2371, www.sjca.edu) is the oldest college in town, despite the misconception that this distinction belongs to the U.S. Naval Academy. The school was founded in 1696 as

King William's School. It is the third-oldest college in the country behind Harvard and William & Mary. One block from the State House (across King George Street from the Naval Academy), the school sits on 32 scenic acres adorned with stately brick buildings, tree-lined paths, and sprawling lawn. It is also a National Historic Landmark with several 18th-century buildings.

St. John's College offers a liberal arts curriculum. Because of its location at the confluence of the Chesapeake Bay and the Severn River, the school offers strong sailing, crew, and rowing opportunities. Each April, St. John's College and the Naval Academy play each other in a highly anticipated croquet match on the front lawn of the St. John's campus. Both teams dress for the event, which has become a spirited spectacle.

St. John's College adopted the "Great Books" program of study in 1937. This mandatory four-year program requires students to read Western civilization's prominent authors in philosophy, theology, math, science, poetry, music, and literature. Classes are then discussion based. The school uses a series of manuals in place of textbooks, lectures, and exams. Grades are only released at the student's request and are based on papers and class participation.

Hammond-Harwood House

There are many historic homes in Annapolis. If you can only choose one to visit, the **Hammond-Harwood House** (19 Maryland Ave., 410/263-4683, www. hammondharwoodhouse.org, Apr.-Dec. Wed.-Mon. 9am-5pm, Jan.-Mar. by appointment only, $10) should be it. It is one of the most superb British colonial homes in the country and the most impressive in Annapolis. Designed in the Anglo-Palladian style (a variation of the classical Roman revival style), construction began on the house

---

1: Ego Alley view of the Chesapeake Bay Foundation's Skipjack 2: U.S. Naval Academy sailing

in 1774. It was completed sometime after 1776, but the exact year is unknown. The home is special because it offers perfectly preserved architecture and one of the best collections of furniture and decorative art from the 18th century in Maryland. It is a National Historic Landmark.

Fifty-minute walk-in tours begin at the top of each hour and provide insight into the history of the house, information on its architect and the people who lived in the home, and the opportunity to learn about the collections, such as a large collection of the works of Charles Willson Peale, a painter well known for his Revolutionary War-period portraits. Visitors can also tour the garden at no extra cost. In-depth, two-hour architectural tours of the home are offered by appointment for $20.

St. Anne's Episcopal Church

St. Anne's Episcopal Church (1 Church Circle, 410/267-9333, www.stannes-annapolis. org, free) was the first church in Annapolis. The original structure was established in 1692 and completed in 1704 and was one of 30 original Anglican parishes in Maryland. Its bell was donated by Queen Anne. The original 65-foot-by-30-foot structure was razed in 1775 to make way for reconstruction of the second St. Anne's Episcopal Church on the same grounds. Building of the new church was delayed due to the Revolutionary War but was finally finished in 1792. The new church was larger and more structurally sound, but burned down on Valentine's Day in 1858 due to a furnace fire. The church that stands in Church Circle today was built in 1858 (although the steeple was finished in 1866). Its design incorporated part of the old tower. The clock in the church steeple actually belongs to the city due to a special agreement it made with the church when a city clock was needed. Visitors to St. Anne's can examine the church's Romanesque revival architecture with its original archways, pews, and stained glass windows. They can also visit the first cemetery in the city, which is located on

The Chesapeake Bay

The Chesapeake Bay is the largest estuary in the country. Its drainage basin includes more than 64,000 square miles with more than 150 tributaries. The bay is approximately 200 miles long, starting at the mouth of the Susquehanna River on the northern end and the Atlantic Ocean on the southern end. At its widest point it is 30 miles across, and at its narrowest point it is 2.8 miles.

The Chesapeake Bay is part of the Intracoastal Waterway, a 3,000-mile navigable inland water route that runs along the Atlantic and Gulf coasts. The bay links the Delaware River with the Albemarle Sound in North Carolina.

More than 300 species of fish and countless shellfish live in the Chesapeake Bay. Maryland is known for its abundant local seafood, especially the famed blue crab, which can be found on nearly every menu in the region.

Many shorebirds live all or part of their lives on the Chesapeake Bay or in the bordering wetlands, including bald eagles, great blue herons, ospreys, peregrine falcons, and piping plovers.

The Chesapeake Bay is a prominent feature in Maryland. During the second half of the 19th century and the first half of the 20th, the bay was a vital link between major cities in Maryland and Virginia, such as Baltimore and Norfolk, and was home to passenger steamships and packet boats (boats that kept regular schedules and were originally designed to transport mail, passengers, and freight). When road crossings were built in the late 20th century, making the steamboat industry obsolete, the bay became known for its seafood production, with a focus on the blue crab and oyster industries. By the mid-20th century, nearly 9,000 full-time watermen worked on the bay. Plentiful oyster harvests were the inspiration for Maryland's state boat, the skipjack, which remains the only type of working boat in the country that operates under sail.

Today, the Chesapeake Bay produces less seafood than it did in the last century due to runoff from many mainland areas, overharvesting, and the invasion of foreign marine species. The Chesapeake Bay Foundation (www.cbf.org), headquartered in Annapolis, is the largest conservation organization dedicated to the well-being of the Chesapeake Bay watershed.

the grounds. Four Sunday worship services are held weekly at 8am, 9:30am, 11:15am, and 5:30pm.

RECREATION

Two-hour sailing cruises can be booked on two beautiful, 74-foot wooden schooners through Schooner *Woodwind* Annapolis Sailing Cruises (410/263-7837, www. schoonerwoodwind.com, rates start at $45 for adults, $31 for children under 12, and $43 for seniors over 60). Cruises depart mid-April to late October from the Annapolis Waterfront Hotel (across from the City Dock) and sail by the U.S. Naval Academy and into the Chesapeake Bay. Private cruises can also be booked.

Pirate Adventures on the Chesapeake (311 3rd St., 410/263-0002, www. chesapeakepirates.com, $22, under age 2 $12) is a children's adventure aboard a pirate ship. Kids quickly become part of a pirate tale with face painting, costumes, and a lot of imagination. Once aboard, they learn the rules of the ship, read treasure maps, and find a message in a bottle. They even engage in battle using water cannons. Cruises leave from the company's office in Annapolis year-round. Face painting and dress-up begin 30 minutes prior to departure; sailing time is 75 minutes.

The Baltimore & Annapolis Trail (www. traillink.com) is a 13-mile paved rail trail that is part of the former route of the Baltimore & Annapolis Railroad. It opened in 1990 and runs from Boulters Way in Annapolis to Dorsey Road in Glen Burnie. The southern part of the trail is primarily residential and winds through pleasant suburban neighborhoods. The northern part of the trail is much more urban.

An extremely popular nearby park right on the Chesapeake Bay is **Sandy Point State Park** (1100 E. College Pkwy., 410/974-2149, www.dnr.state.md.us, $7). This lovely 786-acre park, 10 miles northeast of Annapolis at the western terminus of the Chesapeake Bay Bridge, used to be the site of a ferry that shuttled people and cars between the mainland and the Eastern Shore prior to completion of the bridge. Today it offers a wide sandy beach, swimming area, bathhouse, boat landing, picnic areas, and stunning views of the Chesapeake Bay. It is also a great place for bird-watching. The park is off US 50 at exit 32.

ENTERTAINMENT AND EVENTS
Nightlife

Annapolis harbors one of the best little venues in the mid-Atlantic for intimate concerts with big-name artists. **Rams Head on Stage** (33 West St., 410/268-4545, www. ramsheadonstage.com) is the performance venue at the popular **Rams Head Tavern** (www.ramsheadtavern.com), which has been a fixture in Annapolis since 1988. Rams Head on Stage is a reserved-seating venue with food and drink service during the shows. Nearly all shows at this venue are 21 and older. There are no bad seats in the house, and the bands play right in front of the tables. Samples of recent performances include David Crosby, Brett Dennen, Amy Grant, and the Marshall Tucker Band.

The **49 West Coffeehouse, Winebar & Gallery** (49 West St., 410/626-9796, www.49westcoffeehouse.com) is a great place to kick back and enjoy coffee or a great martini (depending on the time of day) and listen to jazz. They host live music most nights and jazz for brunch on Sunday. The establishment is also an art gallery and features different artists monthly. They offer a neighborhood feel near the downtown area and serve breakfast, lunch, and dinner daily.

Performing Arts

The **Maryland Hall for the Creative Arts** (801 Chase St., 410/263-5544, www. marylandhall.org) is an active center for the performing arts. Resident companies include a symphony, opera, ballet, and chorale, offering performances throughout the year in the 800-seat theater.

Events

The **Maryland Renaissance Festival** (1821 Crownsville Rd., Crownsville, 410/266-7304, www.rennfest.com) is a long-standing tradition in Maryland. After passing through the entry gates to the festival, visitors become part of a wooded, 25-acre 16th-century English village named Revel Grove. There are plenty of activities to keep the entire family busy, with shows on 10 major stages, a jousting arena, games, crafts, five pubs, and of course, tons of delicious food. The festival is open on Saturday, Sunday, and Labor Day Monday from the end of August through late October. The festival is held in Crownsville, eight miles northwest of Annapolis.

Many events are scheduled throughout the year in Annapolis, including several footraces such as the **Annapolis Ten Miler** (www. annapolisstriders.org), festivals, food celebrations, and art shows. For a list of events, visit www.downtownannapolis.org.

SHOPPING

There are many boutiques and locally owned shops in downtown Annapolis. Maryland Avenue, Main Street, and West Street are great places to start a shopping adventure. Some examples of the types of stores you can browse include jewelry stores, maritime stores, home furnishings shops, women's boutiques, antiques stores, glass shops, and fine-art galleries.

Blanca Flor Silver Jewelry (34 Market Space, 410/268-7666, Mon.-Sat. 10am-6pm, Sun 11am-6pm) is located at the City Dock and offers a terrific selection of silver jewelry, artwork and Mexican crafts.

Haunted Pub Crawl

Sometimes referred to as "a drinking town with a sailing problem," Annapolis has long known how to get its drink on. The city is filled with all kinds of history, including tales of hair-raising hauntings at local watering holes. **Annapolis Tours and Crawls** (443/534-0043, www. toursandcrawls.com, $22) offers a great two-hour haunted-pub crawl through the downtown area. They take guests through some of the most haunted taverns, pubs, and bars while telling stories that are sure to give you goose bumps. Each stop is about 30 minutes and can be different each time. This drinking tour is a great way to learn the history of some of the best taverns in town, with an added twist. Tours meet at the top of Main Street and are for people 21 and over.

FOOD
American

The premier steak house in Annapolis is ★ **Lewnes Steakhouse** (401 4th St., 410/263-1617, www.lewnessteakhouse.com, Sun.-Mon. 4pm-9pm, Tues.-Thurs. 4pm-10pm, Fri.-Sat. 4pm-10:30pm, $19-45). This independent restaurant opened in 1921 and is still owned by the same local family. They serve prime steak that is properly prepared to sear in the flavorful juice while browning the exterior. Their menu includes filet, prime rib, porterhouse, New York strip, rib eye, and some nonbeef selections such as tuna steak and lobster. They also have an extensive, well-selected wine list. The food and wonderful staff are the lure of this restaurant, and the atmosphere is well suited for a romantic evening. This is a restaurant that really cares whether the guests are satisfied.

A local institution, the **Rams Head Tavern** (33 West St., 410/268-4545, www. ramsheadtavern.com, Mon.-Sat. 11am-2am, Sun. 10am-2am, $12-25) has been serving tasty pub food since 1989. This friendly, multiroom tavern (including the original space in the cozy downstairs) serves sandwiches, burgers, and pub favorites such as shepherd's pie, brats and mash, chicken stuffed with crab imperial, and shrimp and grits. They have a terrific brunch menu on Sunday with a wonderful variety of entrées that are beautifully presented. They also serve beer from the Fordham Brewing Company, which used to be on-site. The atmosphere is classically "pub" with warm, friendly service and convivial patrons. This can be a busy place on concert nights at the adjoining Rams Head on Stage.

Quarter-pound crab cakes with no filler, seasoned to perfection, are the calling card of a local favorite named ★ **Chick & Ruth's Delly** (165 Main St., 410/269-6737, www. chickandruths.com, Sun.-Thurs. 6:30am-11:30pm, Fri.-Sat. 6:30am-12:30am, $6-29). Just a block from the State House, the sandwich shop was opened by Chick and Ruth Levitt in 1965, and it has been growing ever since. Specialty sandwiches named after politicians augment the traditional Jewish deli fare, along with seafood, pizza, wraps, burgers, and tasty ice-cream treats. This is a touch of New York with an Annapolis flair.

Vin 909 Winecafe (909 Bay Ridge Ave., 410/990-1846, www.vin909.com, Tues. 5:30pm-10pm, Wed.-Thurs. noon-3pm and 5:30pm-10pm, Fri. noon-3pm and 5:30pm-11pm, Sat. noon-3pm and 5pm-11pm, Sun. 5pm-10pm, $14-21) is a wine-tasting café. They offer more than 35 types of wine by the glass and an extensive selection of beer. The café is in what once was a private residence, a bit off the beaten path south of the historic area of Annapolis (across Spa Creek). Prices for wine and food are reasonable, and there is frequently a wait for a table (they do not accept reservations). They specialize in pizza, panini, and plates to share. The ambience is cozy and modern with wooden floors and low lighting. There is an outdoor patio with seating when the weather is nice.

1: the docks at Sandy Point State Park **2:** flowers on Church Circle **3:** Chick & Ruth's Delly **4:** jousting at the Maryland Renaissance Festival

Feeling Crabby?

Maryland is known for its blue crabs, and the full "crab" experience can be enjoyed at a number of traditional crab houses throughout the bay region. For those new to the authentic crab experience, be prepared for a casual event, but not necessarily a cheap one. Traditional crab houses will often have long tables spread with brown paper and equipped with wooden mallets, claw crackers, and picks. Cold beer can accompany the appetizer, main course, and dessert. Patrons bring a lot of time, good cheer, and their appetites. Eating crabs is a social and messy event, but it is also one of the best experiences on the Chesapeake Bay.

Where to crack a claw:

- **Abner's Crab House** (3748 Harbor Rd., Chesapeake Beach, 410/257-3689, www. abnerscrabhouse.com)

- **Bo Brooks Crab House** (2780 Lighthouse Point, Baltimore, 410/558-0202, www.bobrooks. com)

- **Buddy's Crabs and Ribs** (100 Main St., Annapolis, 410/626-1100, www.buddysonline.com)

- **Cantler's Riverside Inn** (458 Forest Beach Rd., Annapolis, 410/757-1311, www.cantlers. com)

- **Captain James Crab House** (2127 Boston St., Baltimore, 410/327-8600, www. captainjameslanding.com)

- **Mike's Restaurant and Crab House** (3030 Riva Rd., Riva, 410/956-2784, www. mikescrabhouse.com)

Crab Houses

If you like seafood, you can't visit Annapolis without eating local blue crabs. *The* place to go for the authentic crab house experience is ★ **Cantler's Riverside Inn** (458 Forest Beach Rd., 410/757-1311, www.cantlers.com, Sun.-Thurs. 11am-10pm, Fri.-Sat. 11am-11pm, $11-32), a short distance from the downtown area and accessible by both car and boat. It is situated on a cove right on the water in a mostly residential neighborhood and sells local steamed crabs by the dozen (in all sizes) as well as offering other fresh seafood such as crab cakes, shrimp, and oysters. They also serve pizza and sandwiches for nonseafood eaters. This is not a fancy place; it is a place to relax, get messy picking crabs, and meet new friends. They have indoor seating, a covered deck, and outdoor picnic tables. This used to be where the locals went, but in recent years it has become a popular tourist restaurant also. They also have a large bar inside the dining room. Word of warning: Don't rub your eyes with Old Bay seasoning on your hands.

Another popular crab house right in the historic downtown area is **Buddy's Crabs and Ribs** (100 Main St., 410/626-1100, www. buddysonline.com, Mon.-Thurs. 11am-9:30pm, Fri.-Sat. 11am-10pm, Sun. 9am-9pm, $10-39). This lively icon on Main Street is a family-owned restaurant and also the largest restaurant in Annapolis. They specialize in serving large groups and also give special pricing to kids. Steamed crabs are the entrée of choice at Buddy's, but the homemade crab cakes are also a front-runner. Buddy's has a wide menu for both the seafood lover and the nonseafood eater and offers three all-you-can-eat buffets.

Italian

If you're looking for good pizza in a family atmosphere and want to get away from the crowds of the downtown area, go to **Squisito Pizza and Pasta** (2625 Riva Rd., 410/266-1474, www.squisitopizzaandpasta.com, Sun.-Thurs. 11am-9:30pm, Fri.-Sat. 11am-10pm, $5-18). This casual restaurant serves delicious pizza, pasta, and sandwiches at very reasonable prices. They are a small franchised chain with a handful of locations in Maryland and Virginia. Order at the main counter and then take a seat. A server will bring you your meal. This is a very casual restaurant that is popular with families with children.

Seafood

A great place for local seafood and waterfront dining is **Carrol's Creek** (410 Severn Ave., 410/263-8102, www.carrolscreek.com, Mon.-Thurs. 11:30am-9pm, Fri.-Sat. 11:30am-10pm, Sun. 10am-8:30pm, $21-36). A short walk from the historic area across the Spa Creek Bridge, the bright-red building is easy to spot along Restaurant Row in Eastport. The menu offers local seafood, fresh fish, steak, chicken, and vegetarian dishes. Their scallops are to die for. They also have a large wine list. The restaurant is locally owned and run, and much of the staff has been there for decades. There is plenty of free parking. Reservations are recommended (ask for a seat by the windows). They are nut-free certified.

The **Chart House Restaurant** (300 2nd St., 410/268-7166, www.chart-house.com, Mon.-Thurs. 4:30pm-10pm, Fri.-Sat. 4:30pm-11pm, Sun. 10am-9pm, $25-45) offers fantastic waterfront views of the City Dock and is within walking distance of the historic district. The restaurant is part of an upscale national chain and is housed in a historic building with soaring ceilings and huge picture windows overlooking Spa Creek. The menu is heavily weighted toward seafood and steak, with fresh fish, crab, lobster, filet, and surf and turf. They also offer chicken and salads. The food and decor are above average, which is reflected in the prices, but the restaurant has a great location and the service is excellent. Reservations are recommended.

Another lovely waterfront restaurant is the **Severn Inn** (1993 Baltimore Annapolis Blvd., 410/349-4000, www.severninn.com, Mon.-Sat. 11:30am-2:30pm and 5pm-close, Sun. 10am-2pm and 5pm-close, $16-47), situated on the east side of the Naval Academy Bridge, overlooking Annapolis and the Severn River. They describe themselves as a "modern American seafood house" and serve local and nonlocal seafood and other dishes such as a wonderful filet mignon. They have pleasant decor inside with white tablecloths and a comfortable yet airy feel to the dining room, as well as a large waterfront deck with pretty blue market umbrellas (open after April). Sunset is especially scenic, and if you're an oyster lover, grabbing a drink and a few oysters while watching the sun go down is a combination that's hard to beat.

ACCOMMODATIONS
$100-200

A good option for an economical stay is the **Hampton Inn & Suites Annapolis** (124 Womack Dr., 410/571-0200, www.hamptoninn3.hilton.com, $164-189). The hotel is in a business park four miles from the historic area of Annapolis. The 117 rooms are comfortable and come with complimentary wireless Internet, a minifridge, 37-inch television, and free breakfast. The hotel is pet friendly.

$200-300

If you are looking for charming accommodations in a historic property, **Historic Inns of Annapolis** (58 State Circle, 410/263-2641, www.historicinnsofannapolis.com, $194-389) offers three boutique hotels housed in 17th- and 18th- century buildings. The **Maryland Inn** (16 Church Circle) has 44 guest rooms within view of the State House, Main Street, and the waterfront. The inn was built in the late 1700s and has hosted presidents, statesmen, and political dignitaries. The decor includes Victorian-era furnishings. It has a fitness center, a restaurant, and a Starbucks on-site. The **Governor Calvert House** (58 State Circle) is across the street from the Maryland State House and is one of the oldest buildings in Annapolis (built in 1695). It has 51 guest rooms, a colonial garden, meeting space, Internet, cable television, and views of the State House. Rooms are small, but this was originally a private home and was even the residence of two former Maryland governors. This property is where guests of all three historic properties check in. The **Robert Johnson House** (23 State Circle) is a smaller hotel with 29 guest rooms. This brick home was built in 1773 and has views of the Governor's Mansion and the State House. The house has Georgian-style architecture and is furnished with 19th-century furniture.

For a comfy bed-and-breakfast stay, the lovely ★ **Chez Amis Bed and Breakfast** (85 East St., 410/263-6631, www.chezamis. com, $219-247) offers four beautiful rooms and wonderful service. Each room in this 1890s home has a private bathroom, a television, and free wireless Internet. A delicious three-course breakfast is served each day at 9am, and cookies and refreshments are available all day. The bed-and-breakfast is within walking distance of downtown Annapolis, but a complimentary shuttle is offered to restaurants. The owners live on the bottom floor of the home.

The **Flag House Inn** (26 Randall St., 410/280-2721, www.flaghouseinn.com, $199-269) is a wonderful bed-and-breakfast with off-street parking in historic Annapolis. Just a half block from the City Dock, this comfortable, friendly inn is a great home base for exploring Annapolis. They offer four guest rooms and a two-room suite with private bathrooms and a full hot breakfast each morning.

The Hotel Annapolis (126 West St., 410/263-7777, www.thehotelannapolis.com, $144-365) is a lovely hotel in downtown Annapolis within walking distance of many attractions (10 minutes to the City Dock). The bright, nautical decor is perfect for the hotel's location, and the 198 guest rooms are luxurious and large (there are also 17 suites). Parking is available on-site for an additional fee ($23 for self-parking and $26 for valet). Amenities include a fitness room and spa (no pool) for hotel guests, and free wireless Internet service. There is also a restaurant on-site. The hotel is pet friendly ($50 per stay).

The **Westin Annapolis** (100 Westgate Circle, 410/972-4300, www.marriott.com, $189-259) is an immaculate, top-notch hotel a short distance from all the action in downtown Annapolis. The 225 guest rooms are spacious and modern, and there's a lovely, well-stocked bar in the lobby. Free shuttle service is available to the downtown area, and there is parking on-site. It has an indoor pool and fitness center, and the hotel is pet friendly.

Governor Calvert House

Over $300

Fabulous waterfront views can be found at the **Annapolis Waterfront Hotel** (80 Compromise St., 410/268-7555, www. annapoliswaterfront.com, $341-530). This Marriott hotel is the only waterfront hotel in Annapolis; many of the rooms overlook the Chesapeake Bay, and some have balconies (other rooms view Annapolis Harbor and the downtown area). The hotel is walking distance to historic attractions, shopping, restaurants, and the Naval Academy. Allergen-free rooms are available. The hotel offers standard amenities such as a fitness center and meeting facilities. Valet parking and Internet service are available for an additional fee. Their waterfront restaurant, **Pusser's Caribbean Grille,** is a popular dining spot for seafood and also offers great views. This premium location doesn't come cheap, but if you are after a room with a view, it delivers.

INFORMATION AND SERVICES

For additional information on Annapolis, stop in the **Annapolis & Anne Arundel County Conference and Visitors Bureau** (26 West St., 410/280-0445, daily 9am-5pm) or visit www.visitannapolis.org.

GETTING THERE

Most people arrive in Annapolis by car. The city is a quick 45-minute drive east from Washington DC (32 miles) via US 50 and about 30 minutes (26 miles) south of the Inner Harbor in Baltimore (via State Route 97).

Annapolis is 22 miles from **Baltimore Washington International Thurgood**

Marshall Airport (BWI) (410/859-7040, www.bwiairport.com).

GETTING AROUND

Parking can be challenging in the downtown area, but **The Circulator** (410/216-9436, www.parkannapolis.com, every 10 minutes Mon.-Sat. 7:30am-11pm, Sun. 8am-8pm) is a great way to move around Annapolis. It is a trolley service that provides free transportation around the central business district and stops at four downtown parking garages (www.annapolisparking.com). The four garages are **Gotts Court Garage** (25 Northwest St., first hour $2, $15 maximum), the **Noah Hillman Garage** (150 Gorman St., $2 an hour, $20 maximum), the **Knighton Garage** (corner of Colonial Ave. and West St., $1 first hour, $10 maximum), and the **Park Place Garage** (5 Park Pl., $1 an hour, $10 maximum). Stops are located along the trolley's loop route from Westgate Circle to Memorial Circle and start at the Westin Annapolis Hotel at Park Place. Trolleys also stop at popular areas such as Church Circle and City Dock. If you aren't at a stop but want to get on the trolley, simply raise your hand when one drives by and it will pull over to pick you up.

There is also metered parking at City Dock near Spa Creek, and there is a parking lot at Navy-Marine Corps Memorial Stadium (Taylor Ave. off Rowe Blvd.). Trolley rides from the stadium lot cost $2 since it is not within the central business district.

The free **State Shuttle** operates on a loop between the stadium and the Central Business District. It leaves the stadium every 20 minutes Monday-Friday 6:30am-8pm.

Southern Maryland

Southern Maryland contains a thousand miles of shoreline on the Chesapeake Bay and the Patuxent River. The region includes Calvert, Charles, and St. Mary's Counties and is a boater's playground, a bird-watcher's paradise, and

a seafood lover's dream. Traditionally a rural agricultural area connected by steamboat routes, today Southern Maryland is traversed by scenic byways that connect charming towns and parks. The communities in the region have grown tremendously in recent decades and welcome tourists and those seeking outdoor recreation such as boating, fishing, crabbing, hiking, and biking.

CHESAPEAKE BEACH

Chesapeake Beach is on the mainland in Calvert County about 45 minutes south of Annapolis (29 miles). The town was founded in 1894 by the Chesapeake Bay Railway Company and was intended to be a vacation destination for Washingtonians. The town thrived as such during the early 1900s when visitors arrived by train. Today, long after the railroad days, visitors can still enjoy nice views of the Chesapeake Bay, beach access, and charter fishing.

Sights

A nice little museum that does a good job of presenting local history is the **Chesapeake Beach Railway Museum** (4155 Mears Ave., 410/257-3892, www. chesapeakebeachrailwaymuseum.com, hours vary by season, free). The small, three-room museum is housed in a restored train depot and provides information on the train that once ran between Chesapeake Beach and Washington DC. Artifacts, photos, maps, equipment, and postcards are on exhibit, and the volunteers are very friendly and helpful. The museum hosts many family events throughout the year.

If you're looking for summer fun and a break from the heat, bring the kids to the **Chesapeake Beach Water Park** (4079 Gordon Stinnett Blvd., 410/257-1404, www. chesapeakebeachwaterpark.com, mid-June-mid-Aug. Mon. 11am-6pm, Tues.-Sun. 11am-7pm, $27-34). It features eight waterslides, pools, fountains, waterfalls, and giant floating sea creatures to climb on. There are even "adult" swim times.

Surfing enthusiasts will enjoy spending an hour or two at **Bruce "Snake" Gabrielson's Surf Art Gallery and Museum** (Rte. 261, three miles south of Chesapeake Beach, 240/464-3301, www.hbsnakesurf.com, open

evenings by appointment on Mon., Wed., and Thurs., free). Maryland's only surfing museum opened in 2012 and showcases the personal treasures collected by its founder, surfing legend Bruce Gabrielson, over the course of 60 years. Featured items include antique surfboards, photographs, and posters signed by various surfing legends. It is a little off the beaten path in the offices of the National Surf Schools and Instructors Association.

Food

The two restaurants within the **Chesapeake Beach Hotel and Spa** (4165 Mears Ave., 410/257-5596, www. chesapeakebeachresortspa.com) are a couple of the best dining options in Chesapeake Beach. The **Rod 'N' Reel** (410/257-2735, Sun.-Thurs. 8am-1am, Fri.-Sat. 8am-2am, $10-35) serves breakfast, lunch, and dinner. They have a nice selection of sandwiches and seafood entrées and items from the land. They also have an extensive wine list. **Boardwalk Cafe** (Sun.-Thurs. 11am-8pm, Fri.-Sat. 11am-11pm, $9-24) is a casual restaurant on the resort boardwalk. They serve soup, salads, and casual seafood. It is a great spot to grab a drink and enjoy the scenery.

Another choice in Chesapeake Beach is the family-owned **Trader's Seafood Steak and Ale** (8132 Bayside Rd., 301/855-0766, www. traders-eagle.com, Mon.-Sat. 7am-10pm, Sun. 7am-9pm, $8-24), offering seafood, burgers, and other entrées for lunch and dinner and many traditional options for breakfast. The atmosphere is friendly and casual and they have a deck bar. They also have a breakfast buffet on Sunday (7am-1pm).

Accommodations and Camping

The **Chesapeake Beach Resort and Spa** (4165 Mears Ave., 410/257-5596, www. chesapeakebeachresortspa.com, $134-197) is a well-maintained property with 72 guest rooms. The hotel is on the Chesapeake Bay waterfront, and some rooms have balconies

Pirates of the Chesapeake

Although Blackbeard the pirate was best known for his ruthless handiwork in the Caribbean and his eventual beheading in Ocracoke, North Carolina, he often retreated to the Chesapeake Bay to repair his ship and prepare her for sea. He was not alone on the bay. The tobacco industry thrived along its shores for nearly 200 years (between roughly 1600 and 1800), bringing with it explorers from all parts of Europe as well as large populations of pirates.

Initially pirates settled in the southern part of the bay, but later they spread through most of the area. Although they often attacked colonial ships, the outlaws were tolerated by the colonies and in some ways helped them become independent from England. Privateers often sold goods to colonists that they could not purchase from England.

Despite their success, pirate life was very difficult, and most died young. Entire crews could be wiped out by disease, as living conditions were filthy aboard their ships. Many also suffered fatal wounds during battle. Although some did go on to enjoy the riches they stole, this was the minority.

overlooking the water. A full-service spa is on-site, and there is also a marina. There are two waterfront restaurants at the hotel, a fitness room, sauna, game room, and an indoor swimming pool. Complimentary continental breakfast is served on weekdays. Fishing charters can be arranged through the hotel.

Breezy Point Beach and Campground (5300 Breezy Point Rd., 410/535-0259, www.co.cal.md.us, May-Oct., $55 per night) is a public beach and campground six miles south of Chesapeake Beach at **Breezy Point Beach** (410/535-0259, May-Oct. daily 6am-dusk, adults $10, children 3-11 and seniors over 60 $6). The half-mile beach has a swimming area, bathhouse, picnic area, playground, and a 300-foot fishing pier. Camping includes water and sewage. Multiple-night minimums may be required on certain days. No pets are allowed on the beach or in the campground.

Information and Services

For additional information on Chesapeake Beach visit www.chesapeake-beach.md.us.

SOLOMONS ISLAND

Solomons Island sits at the southern tip of Calvert County at the confluence of the Chesapeake Bay and the Patuxent River. It is about a 1.5-hour drive southeast from Washington DC (61 miles), a 1.75-hour drive south of Baltimore (81 miles), and an 80-minute drive (58 miles) south from Annapolis. It is connected to St. Mary's County by the **Governor Thomas Johnson Bridge,** a 1.5-mile bridge over the Patuxent River on State Route 4.

Solomons was first settled by tobacco farmers, but a surge in the oyster industry following the Civil War led it into the oyster-processing and boatbuilding trades. The town quickly became a shipbuilding, ship-repair, and seafood-harvesting stronghold. In the 1880s, the local fishing fleet counted more than 500 boats, and many of them were built right in Solomons. Among these were "bug-eyes," which were large, decked-over sailing canoes, mostly built from shaped logs. The city soon became the dominant commercial center in Calvert County.

By the late 1920s, oyster harvests had begun to decline. This was followed by the Great Depression and the worst storm to ever hit the island (in 1933), which left the lower half of it under water. World War II brought better times, when the island became a staging area for training troops readying for amphibious invasions.

Today, tourism, boating, and outdoor recreation play an important role in Solomons' economy. It houses countless marinas, boat suppliers, charter boat companies, a pilot station, and other types of water-related business such as kayak outfitters. Many restaurants

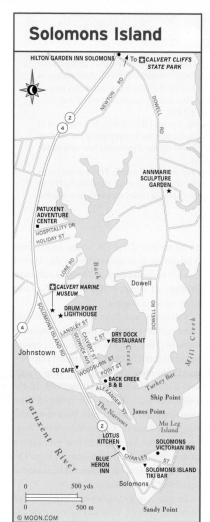

Solomons Island

HILTON GARDEN INN SOLOMONS
To ✚ CALVERT CLIFFS STATE PARK
NEWTON RD
DOWELL RD
2
4
ANNMARIE SCULPTURE GARDEN ★
PATUXENT ADVENTURE CENTER
HOSPITALITY DR
HOLIDAY ST
LORE RD
Back Creek
✚ CALVERT MARINE MUSEUM
Dowell
DRUM POINT LIGHTHOUSE ★
4
SOLOMONS ISLAND RD
LANGLEY ST
CALVERT ST
SEDWICK AVE
C ST
DRY DOCK RESTAURANT
Johnstown
WOODBURN ST
POINT ST
CD CAFE
Creek
DOWELL RD
Mill Creek
BACK CREEK B & B
ALEXANDER ST
Turkey Bar
Patuxent River
The Narrows
Ship Point
Janes Point
Ma Leg Island
2
LOTUS KITCHEN
SOLOMONS VICTORIAN INN
BLUE HERON INN
CHARLES ST
SOLOMONS ISLAND TIKI BAR
Solomons
Sandy Point
0   500 yds
0   500 m
© MOON.COM

prehistoric times, the natural environment, and the bay's unique maritime heritage. There are three exhibit galleries totaling 29,000 square feet, including a discovery room with fossils, live animals (such as otters, fish, and rays), and a paleontology exhibit.

Behind the museum is a marsh walk that enables visitors to stroll over the salt marsh flats. Wildlife is abundant in the marsh, and you can expect to see signs of inhabitants such as raccoons, opossums, water snakes, crabs, herons, and ducks. This great natural exhibit is a living study of the local plant and animal life.

On the museum's waterfront is the iconic **Drum Point Lighthouse,** a "screwpile," cottage-style lighthouse that is one of only 3 that still stand out of an original 45 on the bay. The lighthouse is fully restored and houses early 20th-century furniture. Guided tours are available.

The museum's small-craft collection is housed in a 6,000-square-foot building that is open toward the boat basin. The collection has 20 boats in a range of sizes. Some boats are displayed on land, and others are in the water.

Sightseeing sailing cruises on the river leave from the museum dock weather permitting. They are one hour long and go through the inner harbor, underneath the Governor Thomas Johnson Bridge, and turn around at the Naval Recreation Center. The cost is $7 for adults and $4 for children 5-12 (under 5 free). Trips can accommodate 40 passengers and leave the dock at 2pm Wednesday-Sunday (May-Oct.). On Saturday and Sunday in July and August, additional 12:30pm and 3:10pm cruises are offered. Call 410/326-2042, ext. 15. Tickets can be purchased at the museum the day of the cruise.

The museum also has a woodworking shop and a reference library.

ANNMARIE SCULPTURE GARDEN AND ARTS CENTER

The **Annmarie Sculpture Garden and Arts Center** (13480 Dowell Rd., 410/326-4640, www.annmariegarden.org, sculpture

and inns serve the influx of tourists to this beautiful waterside town.

Sights
★ CALVERT MARINE MUSEUM

The **Calvert Marine Museum** (14200 Solomons Island Rd., 410/326-2042, www.calvertmarinemuseum.com, daily 10am-5pm, adults $9, children 5-12 $4, seniors over 55 $7) does a wonderful job of sharing the story of the Chesapeake Bay, with exhibits on

garden daily 9am-5pm, arts building daily 10am-5pm, adults $5, children 6-17 $3, seniors 65 and up $4) features a lovely sculpture garden accessed by a quarter-mile walking path. The path goes through a wooded garden where sculptures both on loan and part of the center's permanent collection can be viewed. More than 30 sculptures are on loan from the Smithsonian Institution and National Gallery of Art. The arts building features a rotating exhibit space and a gift shop. The center offers many family activities throughout the year and also hosts annual festivals. This is a peaceful place to walk or bring the kids.

★ CALVERT CLIFFS STATE PARK

One of the prime recreation attractions in Calvert County is **Calvert Cliffs State Park** (10540 H. G. Trueman Rd., Lusby, 443/510-9920, www.dnr.maryland.gov, daily sunrise to sunset, $7 per vehicle). This day-use park is about 7 miles north of Solomons Island, right on the Chesapeake Bay, and offers a sandy beach, playground, fishing, marshland, and 13 miles of hiking trails. The main attraction in this park, however, is fossil hunting along the beach. At the end of the Red Trail (1.8 miles from the parking lot), the open beach area gives rise to the dramatic Calvert Cliffs.

More than 600 species of fossils have been identified in the cliff area, dating back 10 to 20 million years. The most common types of fossils found include oyster shells from the Miocene era and sharks teeth. Visitors can use sieves and shovels to look through the sand, but it is illegal to hunt fossils beneath the cliffs for safety reasons (dangerous landslides can occur). Swimming off the beach is allowed at your own risk, as there are no lifeguards on duty.

Recreation

Those wishing to rent a kayak or paddleboard (starting at $35 for three hours) or take a guided kayak tour (starting at $50 per person) can do so from **Patuxent Adventure Center** (13860C Solomons Island Rd., 410/394-2770, www.paxadventure.com, Tues.-Fri. 8am-7pm, Sat.-Sun. 8am-5pm). They also sell bikes and kayaks and other outdoor gear and accessories.

Nightlife

The **Solomons Island Tiki Bar** (85 Charles St., 410/326-4075, www.tikibarsolomons.com, mid-Apr.-mid-Oct., daily 11am-2am) is a local institution in Solomons. This well-known shack/tiki village near the harbor makes a

Calvert Marine Museum sailing cruise

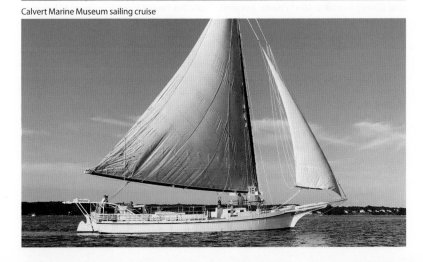

killer mai tai and caters to pretty much anyone over 21 looking for a good time, good drink, and a fun island atmosphere. Visitors come by land and sea for this "adventure." Just be sure to decide ahead of time who is driving or sailing you home.

Food

Relaxed waterfront dining can be found at **The Dry Dock Restaurant** (251 C St., 410/326-4817, www.zahnisers.com, Mon.-Thurs. 4:30pm-9pm, Fri.-Sat. 4:30pm-9:30pm, Sun. 10am-2pm and 4:30pm-9pm, $10-38). This harborfront restaurant specializes in steaks and seafood and prides itself on using as much local produce and sustainable seafood as possible. Large windows overlook the harbor, and there is outside deck seating in the warmer months. This is a small, intimate establishment that has been part of a marina for many years. There is an interesting collection of antique wooden decoys around the bar that were part of a private collection.

The ★ **CD Café** (14350 Solomons Island Rd., 410/326-3877, www.thecdcafe.com, Mon.-Sat. 11am-3:30pm and 5:30pm-9:30pm, Sun. 11am-3:30pm and 5:30pm-9pm, $12-32) is a small, 11-table restaurant with a large menu of simply delicious food. They are open daily and serve lunch (pasta, burgers, salad) and dinner (seafood, steak, pasta, burgers). This is a popular restaurant, so expect to wait at prime times (there is a nice bar and waiting area), but the atmosphere is warm and inviting, the staff is genuinely helpful and friendly, and the food keeps residents and tourists coming back. Try the hummus, the cheesecake appetizer, and the salmon.

The **Lotus Kitchen** (14618 Solomons Island Rd., 410/326-8469, www. lotuskitchensolomons.com, Mon. 9am-5pm, Wed.-Thurs. 9am-8pm, Fri. 9am-9pm, Sat.-Sun. 9am-6pm, under $10) offers healthy food and a scenic view in a charming converted house right in town. The offering includes breakfast sandwiches, deli sandwiches, quiche, soup, meat and cheese boards, beer, wine, and coffee drinks. With menu items

with names such as the Good Karma, Give Peas a Chance, and Crepe Expectations, half the fun is picking out your order. They are also known for their famous Kim's Key Lime Pie.

Accommodations

There is no shortage of wonderful bed-and-breakfasts in Solomons Island. The ★ **Back Creek Inn Bed and Breakfast** (210 Alexander Ln., 410/326-2022, www. backcreekinnbnb.com, $120-235) is a beautiful waterfront inn with seven clean and spacious guest rooms. They have two deepwater boat slips on their 70-foot pier (at mile marker 5 on Back Creek) and two bicycles for guest use. The inn is in a quiet part of town and can accommodate small business groups with indoor and outdoor meeting space. They also have free wireless Internet throughout the property. A full hot breakfast is served daily at 8:30am. Coffee and continental breakfast are available starting at 8am.

Another lovely waterfront bed-and-breakfast is the ★ **Blue Heron Inn** (14614 Solomons Island Rd., 410/326-2707, www. blueheronbandb.com, $179-249). Their two suites have king-size beds, and the two guest rooms have queens. All rooms have private bathrooms and a water view (with either a private balcony or access to a common balcony). Wireless Internet and cable are included with all rooms.

Guests are treated to a gourmet breakfast each morning in a sunny breakfast room with access to the balcony (where breakfast can be served on nice days). A complimentary glass of wine is available each evening. Docking is available for those arriving by boat.

Solomons Victorian Inn (125 Charles St., 410/326-4811, www. solomonsvictorianinn.com, $145-250) offers great harbor views and a lush garden and is within a short walk of shops and restaurants. At the southern tip of Solomons Island, on the western Chesapeake Bay shore, this gracious inn was built in 1906 and was the home of a renowned yacht builder. Several of the rooms are named after his boats. Six guest rooms and one carriage house with a separate entrance are available to rent, and each includes a private bathroom, television, wireless Internet, and a full breakfast. Most rooms have a harbor view.

A good option for hotel accommodations in Solomons Island is the **Hilton Garden Inn Solomons** (13100 Dowell Rd., 410/326-0303, www.hiltongardeninn3.hilton.com, $129-159), which is a half mile from the downtown attractions. They have clean, comfortable rooms, a fitness center, indoor pool, seasonal outdoor pool, business center, and complimentary wireless Internet.

Information and Services

For additional information on Solomons Island, visit www.solomonsmaryland.com or stop by the **Solomons Island Visitor Center** (14175 Solomons Island Rd., 410/326-6027, May-Sept. Thurs.-Fri. 12:30pm-5pm, Sat.-Sun. 11am-5pm, shorter hours Oct.-Apr.).

ST. MARY'S CITY

St. Mary's City is a small community an hour and 45 minutes south of Annapolis (73 miles) and two hours south of Baltimore (96 miles) in extreme Southern Maryland. It sits on the western shore of the Chesapeake Bay and the eastern shore of the St. Mary's River (a Potomac River tributary). Established in 1634, the area is the fourth-oldest permanent settlement in the country and is widely known as the "birthplace of religious tolerance."

St. Mary's City is in St. Mary's County, a beautiful rural area with abundant farmland and water access. St. Mary's County has many Amish and Mennonite communities, and motorists are warned to be alert for horse-drawn carriages along the highways. Amish farms dot the landscape and are recognizable by their windmills and the lack of power lines running along their properties.

St. Mary's was Maryland's capital for 60 years. Roman Catholics founded the city in their quest for religious freedom. When the state capital moved to Annapolis, St. Mary's went into a steep decline and had dropped out of existence by 1720. In 1840, St. Mary's College was developed by Maryland legislature to celebrate the state's founding site. In 1966, the state of Maryland started the process of preserving the site and created the Historic St. Mary's City Commission. Today the city is still home to **St. Mary's College of Maryland** (State Route 5, www.smcm.edu) and **Historic St. Mary's City.**

Sights
★ **HISTORIC ST. MARY'S CITY**
Maryland's premier outdoor living-history museum, **Historic St. Mary's City** (18751 Hogaboom Ln., 240/895-4990, www.hsmcdigshistory.org, hours change by season, adults $10, children 6-18 $6, seniors over 60 $9, under 5 free) is a re-creation of colonial St. Mary's City. The complex includes more than 40 points of interest, including the *Dove* ship that first brought settlers to the area, an early tobacco plantation, the State House of 1676 (47418 Old State House Rd.), and a woodland Native American hamlet.

Although visitors should not expect the living museum to be on the same scale as Williamsburg, Virginia, the park is still a wonderful place to visit and has costumed interpreters, archaeological discoveries, a visitors center (18751 Hogaboom Ln.), outdoor living-history exhibits (where you can watch new buildings being erected in the town center, learn about Native American culture, and see the people and livestock at a tobacco plantation), reconstructed colonial buildings, the St. John's site museum, and a working 17th-century farm.

Visitors to St. Mary's City can participate in many hands-on activities and special events during the open season, such as a workshop on dinner preparation at the plantation and a hands-on pirate experience. Professional archaeologists are actively working to rediscover the city's past, and excavation sites can be seen throughout this National Historic Landmark.

POINT LOOKOUT

Point Lookout State Park (11175 Point Lookout Rd., Scotland, 301/872-5688, www. dnr.maryland.gov, daily 6am-sunset, $7) encompasses 1,042 acres at the southern tip of St. Mary's County near Scotland, Maryland. The park is two hours (82 miles) south of Annapolis on a beautiful peninsula at the confluence of the Chesapeake Bay and the Potomac River. It is managed by the Maryland Department of Natural Resources.

Captain John Smith was the first to explore the peninsula in 1612, but the park is best known as the location of a prison camp during the Civil War. In the years leading up to the war, the area was a thriving summer resort thanks to its sandy beaches and stunning location. The coming of the war brought financial hardship, and the area was leased by the Union army as the site of a hospital facility, and then later the largest Confederate prison camp.

Conditions were horrible at the camp, which was primarily for enlisted men, and many of the prisoners froze to death during the winter months. Those who survived were plagued by filth. It is said that more than 52,000 Confederate soldiers were held at the camp during the war, and between 3,000 and 8,000 died there. Two monuments and an on-site museum recall this part of the park's past.

Whether or not you believe in ghosts, the park boasts countless incidents of unexplained phenomena and firsthand encounters with "ghosts" of soldiers. The most haunted location is said to be the lighthouse, which is no longer in use.

Today the park is primarily known as a wonderful recreation spot. It has several boat launch locations ($12), canoe rentals, a camp store, fishing, hiking trails, picnic areas, a playground, beaches, swimming, and a nature center. The park is also pet friendly.

In addition to being surrounded by water, there is a large lake in the center of the park (Lake Conoy), which is a perfect spot for boating and fishing. A water trail guide for the park is available for purchase at the park headquarters.

Camping is offered in the park April-October on 143 wooded sites ($21.49). Twenty-six have full hookups ($38.49) and 33 provide electricity ($33.49). There are also a half dozen four-person camper cabins for rent ($50.49) on a nightly basis. Off-season camping is available with limited services. Call 888/432-2267 for reservations.

Maryland's Eastern Shore and Atlantic Beaches

Maryland is blessed with thousands of miles of shoreline along the Chesapeake Bay and Atlantic Ocean. One of the most scenic areas in the state, the Eastern Shore is made up of a series of bayside towns that retain the charm of yesteryear and are still partly supported by the local fishing industry.

Most travelers are welcomed to the Eastern Shore in the seafood haven of Kent Island after crossing the Chesapeake Bay Bridge. From there they head north to historic towns such as Chestertown and Rock Hall, or south to upscale St. Michaels or the quaint towns of Tilghman Island and Oxford. Easton and Cambridge offer their own special charm with bustling downtown areas and ample sports and recreation.

Maryland and Delaware share a thin strip of barrier island along

Highlights

Look for ★ to find recommended sights, activities, dining, and lodging.

★ **Schooner** *Sultana:* This amazing replica of a British Royal Navy ship serves as an educational center and the site of the annual Chestertown Tea Party (page 468).

★ **Historic District in St. Michaels:** Beautiful churches, colonial homes, interesting shops, and great restaurants charm in this elegant downtown area (page 474).

★ **Chesapeake Bay Maritime Museum:** This wonderful museum in St. Michaels fills 18 acres with all things Chesapeake Bay (page 474).

★ **Pickering Creek Audubon Center:** This 400-acre working farm in Easton includes forest, meadow, wetlands, and more than a mile of shoreline (page 479).

★ **Blackwater National Wildlife Refuge:** This beautiful waterfowl sanctuary features 27,000 acres of protected freshwater, brackish tidal wetlands, meadows, and forest (page 485).

★ **Assateague Island National Seashore:** This protected coastline is a haven for wild ponies and migrating birds (page 488).

★ **Ocean City Boardwalk:** Along three miles of wood-planked boardwalk sit dozens of restaurants, shops, and amusement parks (page 491).

★ **Ocean City Life-Saving Station Museum:** Learn the history of rescues at sea along the Maryland coast (page 491).

★ **Rehoboth Beach Boardwalk:** This mile-long walkway offers stunning views of the Atlantic and enough activity and food to keep a family busy for days (page 504).

★ **Historic Lewes:** Victorian homes, upscale restaurants, and cozy inns are the trademark of this relaxing little coastal town (page 508).

the Atlantic coast, offering beachgoers many choices for a sun-filled vacation. On the very southern end, the Assateague Island National Seashore, which is shared with Virginia, is a quiet place to calm your spirits, view wildlife, and enjoy a long, pristine beach. Its northern neighbor is the bustling beachfront community of Ocean City. With its exciting boardwalk, active nightlife, and plentiful activities, Ocean City never sleeps. Three popular Delaware beaches—Bethany, Rehoboth, and Lewes—stretch to the north.

PLANNING YOUR TIME

The Eastern Shore of the Chesapeake Bay can be explored in a day or two, but many people choose to go there for extended relaxation and to spend a little downtime. Getting around by car is the best option, as public transportation is sparse. US 301 is the major north-south route in the northern part of the Eastern Shore, while US 50 is the major route in the middle and southern regions.

A good plan of action is to choose one or two towns to explore and spend a weekend enjoying them and learning about the Chesapeake Bay. The distance between Chestertown and Cambridge is about 52 miles, so the distances are not too cumbersome when traveling by car. Be aware, however, if you are traveling during the busy summer months, especially on a weekend, that traffic can back up on US 50. Friday evening drives over the Bay Bridge (toll $4) can mean long wait times and bumper-to-bumper traffic.

The Atlantic beaches in Maryland and Delaware can be explored individually over a weekend, but people often spend a week at a time here over the summer months for a relaxing vacation. In the high season—generally, mid-June until Labor Day—many accommodations have minimum stays. The off-season is a great time to go if you don't have school constraints. Spring and fall offer cooler temperatures and fewer crowds at the beaches, and generally, prices for accommodations are reduced.

If you plan to visit just one of the beaches, keep in mind they all have unique characteristics. If you seek excitement, activity, and the bustling hubbub of a busy boardwalk, then Ocean City is a good choice. If you prefer the charm of a quaint, harborside historic town with close access to the beach, then Lewes, Delaware, may be a better option. If it's something in between that you are looking for, perhaps a more family-oriented beach scene with fewer hotels and more beach house rentals, then Bethany Beach is a good choice. Finally, if you seek the activity of a boardwalk, but a scaled-down version is more your style, then Rehoboth Beach may suit you.

Regardless of where you end up, you will find good seafood and many excellent choices for restaurants at all the beaches. Keep in mind, "Maryland is for Crabs," and delicious blue crab dishes are available in many places. This is *the* place to eat them.

The vast majority of visitors to the Maryland and Delaware beaches drive there. Once you arrive, it's difficult to get too lost as long as you know where the beach is. One main road, the Coastal Highway, runs along the coast; it goes by Route 528 in Maryland and DE 1 in Delaware.

The **Ocean City Municipal Airport** (12724 Airport Rd., Berlin, 410/213-2471) is three miles west of the downtown area of Ocean City and can accommodate general aviation and charter aircraft. Commercial air service is provided at the **Salisbury-Ocean City Wicomico Regional Airport** (5485 Airport Terminal Rd., Salisbury, 410/548-4827), five miles from downtown Salisbury on Maryland's Eastern Shore.

The Eastern Shore and Atlantic Beaches

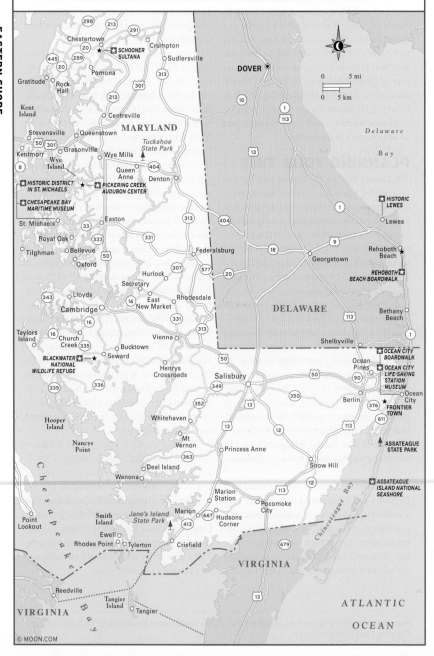

© MOON.COM

The Eastern Shore

The Eastern Shore holds a special place in many Marylanders' hearts. The wide peninsula between the Chesapeake Bay and the Atlantic Ocean contains endless miles of shoreline, beachfront resorts, nature preserves, and small seaside towns. Water is everywhere on the Eastern Shore and so are the culinary delights fished right from the bay. Amazing restaurants with million-dollar views, cozy inns, and plentiful outdoor activities welcome visitors nearly year-round.

KENT ISLAND AND KENT NARROWS

The Chesapeake Bay Bridge stretches from Sandy Point near Annapolis on the mainland to Kent Island. Kent Island is the largest island in the Chesapeake Bay and the gateway to the Eastern Shore. The island is bordered on the east by a narrow channel called the Kent Narrows.

Kent Island welcomes Bay Bridge drivers to a gathering of easily accessible waterfront restaurants. Visitors traveling US 50 are immediately thrown into a seaside atmosphere, and the urge to stop and sample some of the local cuisine is hard to resist.

Food

The ★ **Fisherman's Inn & Crab Deck** (3116 Main St., Grasonville, 410/827-8807, www.fishermansinn.com, daily 11am-10pm, $9-40) serves a large selection of local seafood and has a seafood market so you can take some with you. There is extensive waterfront seating and an open-air interior and bar (weather permitting). You can also dock your boat. Try the crab salad (a recommendation from a friendly server that was much appreciated!). It features a large portion of fresh lump crabmeat with just a bit of dressing. Their shrimp salad and hushpuppies are also winners.

The **Narrows Restaurant** (3023 Kent Narrows Way South, Grasonville, 410/827-8113, www.thenarrowsrestaurant.com, Mon.-Sat. 11am-close, Sun. 11am-close, $18-36) is one of the most popular seafood restaurants on the island. It has a nice atmosphere and a great view. Patio seating is available.

Another local favorite is **Harris Crab**

Fisherman's Inn & Crab Deck

House (433 Kent Narrows Way, Grasonville, 410/827-9500, www.harriscrabhouse.com, daily lunch and dinner from 11am, $10-110). They have two levels of waterfront dining and outdoor seating. The views are great, and the seafood is plentiful. This is a casual place with a crab house atmosphere.

CHESTERTOWN

Chestertown is a pretty waterfront colonial town with fewer than 5,000 residents. It is 40 minutes (29 miles) northeast of Kent Island on the Chester River, a tributary of the Chesapeake Bay. It is about 35 miles northeast of the Chesapeake Bay Bridge.

The town's history dates back to 1706, and it was known as one of Maryland's six "Royal Ports of Entry" (second only to Annapolis as a leading port). The town was a spot for the wealthy in its heyday, which is reflected in the numerous brick mansions and row houses that line the waterfront. The port is still a popular location for sailing ships and tourists. It is also home to **Washington College** (www.washcoll.edu), a private liberal arts college of which George Washington was a founding patron. The school was established in 1782, making it the 10th-oldest college in the country.

Sights
HISTORIC CHESTERTOWN

Chestertown is worth exploring on foot. The state's second-highest concentration of colonial homes (after Annapolis) can be found in Chestertown, and there is a scenic waterfront promenade. Tours of the historic waterfront and the **Custom House** (101 S. Water St., 410/810-7161, www.washcoll.edu, Fri. noon-4pm and Sat. 11am-4pm, free) are provided by Washington College's C. B. Starr Center for the Study of the American Experience. They begin at the Custom House and continue along the waterfront. The Custom House was built in 1746 and was the residence of Thomas Ringgold, a local Sons of Liberty leader. At times it was also a warehouse, store, and living quarters for British redcoats during the

French and Indian War. Group tours can be scheduled by appointment.

★ SCHOONER *SULTANA*

The schooner *Sultana* (located on the waterfront, 410/778-5954, www.sultanaeducation. org) is a replica of a British Royal Navy ship that sailed during the 18th century and patrolled the North American coastline just before the Revolutionary War. The ship lives in the Chestertown Harbor and is used to teach students about the Chesapeake Bay history and environment. Two-hour public sails are held on weekends from the end of April to the beginning of November (adults $30, children under 12 $15). Many events are offered throughout the season on the ship; a list is available on the website.

Events

The biggest annual event in Chestertown is the **Chestertown Tea Party** (www. chestertownteaparty.org), held at the end of May. In May 1774, five months after the famous Boston Tea Party when the British closed the port of Boston, residents of Chestertown resolved to prohibit the purchase, sale, or drinking of tea. Legend has it that they then held their own version of the Boston Tea Party staged on the schooner *Sultana* on the Chester River to show their colonial defiance. The annual festival celebrates this heritage through a reenactment of the tea party and a weekend of family events.

Aviation enthusiasts won't want to miss the annual **Potomac Antique Aero Squadron's Antique Fly-In** (www.fly-ins. com, free but donations appreciated). This wonderful one-day antique aircraft show is held in June at the **Massey Aerodrome** (33541 Maryland Line Rd., Massey, www. masseyaero.org), approximately 17 miles northeast of Chestertown. It is sponsored by the Potomac Antique Air Squadron. More than 200 antique and rare aircraft make up this impressive show. Visitors can see the airplanes up close, speak with the owners, and enjoy delicious food.

William Preston Lane Jr. Memorial Bay Bridge

William Preston Lane Jr. Memorial Bay Bridge

Once upon a time, Marylanders had to depend on boats to cross the Chesapeake Bay. The first plan to connect the mainland to the Eastern Shore came in 1927 but was abandoned first until 1938 and then again until 1947. Finally, under the leadership of Governor William Preston Lane Jr. the State Roads Commission began building the "Bay Bridge" in 1949.

The original span of the bridge, which is used for eastbound traffic today, cost $45 million and became the longest continuous overwater steel structure in the world at 4.3 miles. It first opened to traffic on July 30, 1952. The bridge is part of US 50 and US 301 and quickly became an important connection to the Baltimore/Washington DC area from the Eastern Shore and Ocean City, Maryland.

The second span, which currently carries westbound traffic, was started in 1969 at a cost of $148 million. This span opened in 1973. This architectural marvel has a vertical clearance of 186 feet, and the suspension bridge towers are 354 and 379 feet tall. The bridge starts on the mainland next to Sandy Point State Park and stretches to Kent Island. The bridge can accommodate 1,500 vehicles per lane per hour.

Shopping

A dozen or so art galleries, studios, and shops feature the work of local, regional, and international artists in the historic waterfront district of Chestertown.

From late March to late December a local farmers market is held on Saturday mornings in the heart of the downtown area in Fountain Park (High St. and Cross St.). It features fresh bakery items, produce, plants, herbs, and local artwork.

Food

The most well-known eatery in town is **The Kitchen at the Imperial** (208 High St., 410/778-5000, www.imperialchestertown. com, Mon.-Sat. 11:30am-9pm, Sun. 10am-3pm and 5pm-9pm, $9-34). This wonderful restaurant is located in the Imperial Hotel, which first opened in 1903 and still offers three rooms for rent. The restaurant is open for lunch and dinner and offers a Bloody Mary brunch on Sunday. Their fresh menu varies

seasonally, but they usually have terrific local seafood dishes and meat from local farms.

An ample menu of wood-fired pizza, seafood, pasta, salad, and other tasty dishes made from locally grown ingredients can be found at **Luisa's Cucina Italiana** (849 Washington Ave., 410/778-5360, www.luisasrestaurant. com, Mon.-Sat. 11am-9pm, Sun. 11am-8pm, $10-23). The restaurant offers a warm, welcoming, family-friendly atmosphere where quality is paramount. They offer a nice selection of vegetarian dishes and a gluten-free menu.

A wonderful local restaurant is **Uncle Charlie's Bistro** (834B High St., 410/778-3663, www.unclecharliesbistro.com, Mon.-Thurs. 11am-8pm, Fri. 11am-9pm, Sat. noon-9pm, $10-28). This comfortable, casual eatery features chowder, sandwiches, burgers, steak, seafood, and homemade desserts. It's a bit hard to find, located behind a Subway shop, but it's well worth the hunt. Charlie himself (aka Chuck) is on-site most of the time, making sure his customers are taken care of and happy. Reservations are recommended.

A great place to grab a drink in the summer and watch the sun set is **The Sandbar at Rolph's Wharf** (1008 Rolph's Wharf Rd., 410/778-6389, www.rolphswharfmarina.com, Wed.-Thur. 5pm-close, Fri.-Sun. 11am-close). This is a small outdoor bar that is primarily open on weekends. It offers wonderful views of the Chester River, cold beer, and snacks.

The **Chestertown Farmers Market** is held every Saturday (late Mar.-late Dec.) from 8am to noon at **Fountain Park** (220 High St.).

Accommodations

A pre-Revolutionary War landmark, the **White Swan Tavern** (231 High St., 410/778-2300, www.whiteswantavern.com, $150-280) is a cozy bed-and-breakfast in the historic district of Chestertown. The inn was built in 1733 and has been used for a number of purposes throughout its history, including as a private home and a tavern. A special room in the inn houses many artifacts that were found when the building was restored in 1978. There are six guest rooms, one of which was the original one-room dwelling that housed shoemaker John Lovegrove prior to 1733. The rooms are large and comfortable, and the location of this inn couldn't be any better if you are looking to explore the downtown area and waterfront. A continental breakfast and afternoon tea are served to guests. The bed-and-breakfast can accommodate small weddings and conferences. Two additional apartments are available for long- or short-term stays near the inn.

A cute home away from home very convenient to Washington College (it's 100 yards from campus) and within a 15-minute walk of the riverfront is **Simply Bed and Bread** (208 Mount Vernon Ave., 410/778-4359, www. simplybedandbread.com, $129-149). They offer two allergy-friendly guest rooms in a 1947 Cape Cod-style home. One room has a queen bed, and the other has a king. Each clean, cozy room has ample space. The innkeepers do a great job of making guests feel welcome. A continental breakfast is served each morning, and guests are treated to welcome sweets upon arrival.

One mile outside of Chestertown is the lovely **Brampton Bed and Breakfast Inn** (25227 Chestertown Rd., 410/778-1860, www. bramptoninn.com, $175-395), a restored plantation house built in 1860. It has 13 guest rooms, suites, and cottages available to visitors. All accommodations have private bathrooms, sitting areas, fireplaces, flat-screen televisions with DVD players (no cable), bathrobes, and bath amenities. The estate is well cared for with beautiful gardens and a large front porch. A full à la carte breakfast is served in the dining area daily between 8:30am and 10am, although guests may opt to have breakfast delivered to their rooms. One cottage on the property is pet friendly.

A few chain hotels are options near the historic district in Chestertown. The **Holiday Inn Express Hotel & Suites Chestertown** (150 Scheeler Rd., 410/778-0778, www.ihg.

1: The Waterman's Museum in Rock Hall
2: Schooner *Sultana*

com, $163-183) has 81 guest rooms, complimentary breakfast, and free wireless Internet, and the adjacent **Comfort Suites** (160 Scheeler Rd., 410/810-0555, www.choicehotels.com, $136-166) has 53 guest rooms, complimentary continental breakfast, and an indoor pool.

Information and Services

For additional information on Chestertown visit www.townofchestertown.com or stop by the **Kent County Visitor Center** (122 N. Cross St., 410/778-5841, Mon.-Fri. 9am-5pm, Sat.-Sun. 10am-2pm).

ROCK HALL

Fourteen miles southwest of Chestertown is the small waterfront town of Rock Hall. Rock Hall sits directly on the Chesapeake Bay and has a population of fewer than 1,500 people. Sometimes referred to as the Pearl of the Chesapeake, this quaint maritime town has a history of fishing and boating and during the colonial era was a stop for passenger boats and shipping boats transporting tobacco and seafood. Today Rock Hall still has a working harbor and a fleet of professional watermen and -women.

Sights

There are three small museums in Rock Hall. **The Rock Hall Museum** (at the Municipal Building on S. Main St., 410/639-7611, www.rockhallmd.com, Mon.-Fri. 8:30am-4:30pm, free, donations appreciated) is a two-room facility a short walk from the town center housing artifacts from the town's history and focusing on the lifestyle, economy, and traditions of the community. **The Waterman's Museum** (Haven Harbour Marina, 20880 Rock Hall Ave., 410/778-6697, www.havenharbour.com, daily 10am-4pm, free) features a unique collection of vintage photographs taken during the watermen era, as well as boats and local carvings. The third museum, **Tolchester Beach Revisited** (Main St. behind the Shoppes at Oyster Court, 410/639-7611, www.rockhallmd.com, by

Tiki Bar Boat Stop

If you are exploring the Chesapeake Bay by boat and could use a taste of the islands and a party-hardy atmosphere, stop in **Jellyfish Joel's Tiki Bar** (22170 Great Oak Landing Rd., Chestertown, 410/778-5007, www.mearsgreatoaklanding.com, in-season Fri. starting 2pm and Sat.-Sun. starting 11am). This waterside bar sits on a peninsula by the beach on Fairlee Creek nine miles west of Chestertown and is a favorite boating stop. It offers a sandy beach, palm trees, and sunset beach parties every Friday during the summer. Boats can anchor or tie up on the floating docks. The bar is the main attraction, with cold beer and colder tropical drinks with names such as Painkillers and Pain n'de Ass. They have live entertainment on the weekends and sell snacks and sandwiches.

appointment), is a unique little place with artifacts and memorabilia from a former amusement park that was at a nearby steamboat landing. In its prime, it included 155 acres of amusement space and brought in as many as 20,000 visitors during a weekend by six steamships and one ferry. The park included a dance hall, bowling alley, bingo parlor, roller coaster, pony carts, a roller-skating rink, and numerous vendors. The park closed for good in 1962.

A warm and friendly local theater, **The Mainstay** (5753 Main St., 410/639-9133, www.mainstayrockhall.org) is a cultural and arts center in Rock Hall. It occupies a building that was constructed more than a century ago. With just 120 seats, this is an intimate theater that offers more than 50 blues, folk, classical, and jazz concerts every year. They sell beer, wine, soft drinks, and home-baked treats during performances.

Food

The **Osprey Point Inn Restaurant** (20786 Rock Hall Ave., 410/639-2194, www.ospreypoint.com, year-round Wed.-Sun. starting at 5pm, also Sun. May-Sept.

10:30am-2pm, $12-34) features great water views from the Osprey Point Inn. The setting is comfortable and relaxing, and the young but highly skilled chef is truly passionate about his work. They have a fresh, seasonal menu with seafood and land-based choices.

A casual, waterfront option in Rock Hall is the **Harbor Shack** (20895 Bayside Ave., 410/639-9996, www.harborshack.net, Sun.-Mon. and Wed.-Thurs. 11:30am-8pm, Fri.-Sat. 11:30am-9pm, $10-33). They offer sandwiches, salads, chicken, ribs, Mexican, and many seafood entrées. They often feature local bands.

Accommodations

The serene waterfront setting of the ★ **Inn at Huntingfield Creek** (4928 Eastern Neck Rd., 410/639-7779, www.huntingfield.com, $210-345) is hard to beat. Guests can literally swim, kayak, and bike right from the front door of this beautiful farm estate that was once a high-end hunting club and horse racing track. Five guest rooms in the manor house and seven private cottages allow for a variety of accommodations (pets are allowed in the cottages). The estate is a blend of old-world charm and modern conveniences. It has lovely grounds, a view of the Chesapeake Bay, a saltwater pool, wireless Internet, and a library. Gourmet breakfasts are served daily in the gorgeous manor house.

The **Osprey Point Inn** (20786 Rock Hall Ave., 410/639-2194, www.ospreypoint.com, $180-1,250) offers luxurious accommodations in three settings. There are seven guest rooms in the main inn, four rooms in the farmhouse, and seven rooms at the marina annex. Guests in all three locations can enjoy the amenities at the inn, including a pool and daily continental breakfast. A marina provides boat access, docks, and a bathhouse. There is also a lovely on-site restaurant that features delicious food in a waterfront setting (dinner Wed.-Sun. starting at 5pm).

Information and Services

Additional information on Rock Hall can be found at www.rockhallmd.com.

ST. MICHAELS

The historic waterfront town of St. Michaels is approximately one hour (51 miles) from Annapolis (from US 50, exit on Route 322 and follow the signs for Route 33 to St. Michaels). This charming vintage port is a popular tourist destination and features manicured colonial, federal, and Victorian homes, stunning churches, and a scenic shopping area with specialty stores, restaurants, exclusive inns, and bed-and-breakfasts. Seafood lovers can eat their fill of local crab, fish, and oysters, and those looking to go out on the water can take a cruise or launch a kayak.

St. Michaels was founded in the mid-1600s as a trading stop for the tobacco and trapper industries. The town's name came from the Christ Episcopal Church of St. Michael Archangel parish that was founded in 1677. The historic center of St. Michaels, known as St. Mary's Square (between Mulberry St. and E. Chestnut St.), was created in 1778 when a wealthy land agent from England purchased 20 acres and created 58 town lots. Many of the homes in St. Michaels that were built in the late 1700s and 1800s still stand today.

St. Michaels earned the nickname "the town that fooled the British" during the War of 1812, when residents protected their town from British gunfire using trickery as their defense. Warned of a nighttime attack from British barges positioned in their waters, the townspeople strung burning lanterns in the treetops above the town to fool the attackers into overshooting their targets. The plan worked, and only one house, still known today as the "cannonball house," was hit in the attack.

In the late 1800s and early 1900s, St. Michaels's economy was primarily supported by seafood processing and shipbuilding. Slowly, toward the end of the 20th century, the town became a popular tourist destination and a weekend getaway spot for Washingtonians and other regional residents.

Sights

★ HISTORIC DISTRICT IN ST. MICHAELS

The charming and historic downtown area of St. Michaels is a cornucopia of churches, colonial homes, shops, restaurants, and galleries. This elegant district was added to the National Register of Historic places in 1986 and is a destination for many tourists and area residents. The area includes a scenic harbor on the Miles River. South Talbot Street (Route 33) is the main artery through town, just a few blocks from the waterfront.

★ CHESAPEAKE BAY MARITIME MUSEUM

The **Chesapeake Bay Maritime Museum** (213 N. Talbot St., 410/745-2916, www.cbmm.org, May-Oct. daily 9am-5pm, Nov.-Apr. daily 10am-4pm, adults $15, children 6-17 $6, seniors $12) is an 18-acre waterfront learning center for all things Chesapeake Bay. There are 12 exhibit buildings, a large floating display of traditional bay boats, and the Hooper Strait Lighthouse, built in 1879.

The museum is a wealth of information on Chesapeake Bay history and the people who live there. Instead of relying on tour guides or reenactors to teach visitors about the bay, the Chesapeake Bay Maritime Museum employs real people of the Chesapeake who live and work on the bay and share their actual experiences. Examples include master decoy carvers, retired crab pickers, and ship captains. Visitors can also witness a boat restoration in progress in the museum's working boatyard or climb a lighthouse.

The museum offers scenic 45-minute cruises on the Miles River on a replica buyboat (June-Oct. Wed.-Mon. at noon, 1pm, 2pm, and 3pm). Buyboats were used to buy catches off watermen's boats and take them directly to market. Cruises depart from the lighthouse (tickets are sold in the Admissions Building, adults $10, children 6-17 $3, under 5 free).

Both self-guided tours (by map) and guided tours are available with admission to view the museum's many exhibits, including art and maritime displays.

Recreation

St. Michaels is all about water. Those looking for an upscale sailing adventure can charter the *Selina II,* a vintage catboat, through **Sail Selina** (101 N. Harbor Rd., 410/726-9400, www.sailselina.com, May-Sept.). Passengers are limited to just six per two-hour outing and are offered a personal sailing experience/tour through the harbor and on the Miles River. Guests are invited to help sail the vessel or to just sit back and relax. The boat is docked at the Harbor Inn and Marina. Outings start at $65 per person.

Narrated cruises up the Miles River are also available through **Patriot Cruises** (410/745-3100, www.patriotcruises.com, early spring-late fall, adults $26.50, children 12-17 $12.50, children 3-11 $5, seniors 65 and over $24, under 3 free). This two-level, 49-passenger cruising boat is climate-controlled and offers 60- to 70-minute tours. It leaves from 301 North Talbot Street.

If you long to sail aboard an authentic skipjack, the **Skipjack H. M. Krentz** (410/745-6080, www.oystercatcher.com, Apr.-Oct. daily, $48) offers two-hour narrated cruises aboard a 70-foot working skipjack from the 1950s. Sailing cruises leave from the Chesapeake Bay Maritime Museum.

Kayaks ($35 per hour), stand-up paddleboards ($35 per hour), and bikes (starting at $30) can be rented from **Shore Pedal & Paddle** (store: 500 S. Talbot St., dock: 125 Mulberry St., 410/745-2320, www.shorepedalandpaddle.com). They also offer guided two-hour kayak tours in St. Michaels Harbor on weekends and by appointment during the week. Bikes can also be rented from **TriCycle & Run** (929 S. Talbot St., 410/745-2836, www.tricycleandrun.com, starting at $10 for 2 hours).

Shopping

Talbot Street is the place to start your shopping adventure in St. Michaels. For unique gifts, stop by **The Preppy Redneck** (213A S. Talbot St., 410/745-8072, www. thepreppyredneck.com), a fun gift shop; **NE Time Designs** (404 S. Talbot St.,) for home decor, gifts, and jewelry; and **Ophiuroidea** (100 S. Talbot St., 410/745-8057) for coastal-inspired furnishings and gifts.

Food

AMERICAN

Good food with a romantic atmosphere and modern ambience can be found at **Theo's Steaks, Sides, and Spirits** (409 S. Talbot St., 410/745-2106, www.theossteakhouse. com, Wed.-Sun. for dinner at 4:30pm, $31-60) on Talbot Street. This popular eatery offers a small but diverse menu of pub fare and steaks, expertly prepared and presented.

Another good date-night spot is **208 Talbot** (208 N. Talbot St., 410/745-3838, www.208talbot.com, Wed.-Sun. for dinner at 5pm, tavern menu $12-24, dining room menu $30-36). They offer delicious steak and seafood dishes such as pan-seared grouper, grilled rib eye, and seared sea scallops in the dining room and a casual menu with items such as pizza, burgers, and shrimp and grits in their tavern. Reservations are recommended.

"Creative American cuisine" with a hint of French flavor can be found at **Bistro St. Michaels** (403 S. Talbot St., 410/745-9111, www.bistrostmichaels.com, Mon.-Thurs. 5pm-8:30pm, Fri.-Sat. 5pm-9pm, brunch Sat.-Sun. starting at 10am, $21-30). This charming bistro offers a modest but varied menu of seafood, steak, lamb, and salads, with the option to add sides such as cheddar grits and crispy mushrooms.

ITALIAN

Theo's sister restaurant, **Ava's Pizzeria and Wine Bar** (409 S. Talbot St., 410/745-3081, www.avaspizzeria.com, open daily at 11:30am, $11-30) serves exceptional pizza, pasta, and sandwiches. They also have an extensive wine and beer menu. The atmosphere is fun and inviting with an outdoor patio, fireplaces, and even a waterfall. They do not take reservations, although they do have a call-ahead list. They are known for pizza, but the meatballs are out of this world.

MEXICAN

Feeling funky? Then try **Gina's Cafe** (601 S. Talbot St., 410/745-6400, Wed.-Sun. noon-10pm, $11-30). This tiny, 1,000-square-foot Southwestern eatery on the corner of Talbot Street and East Chew is barely large enough to be termed a restaurant, but they serve up interesting, south-of-the-border goodness with a nod to fresh seafood. They offer fish tacos, drinks, and house-made tortilla chips, in addition to a host of other unique favorites. This is the place to come when your taste buds need a break from the usual restaurant fare. People either love it for its uniqueness or dislike it for its quirkiness. Try the soft-shell tacos with crab and guacamole or the crab nachos.

SEAFOOD

A good waterfront seafood house is the **St. Michaels Crab and Steakhouse** (305 Mulberry St., 410/745-3737, www. stmichaelscrabhouse.com, Thurs.-Mon. at 11am for lunch and dinner, $10-31). They offer a large menu of seafood favorites along with sandwiches, steak, pasta, and salad. All meals are made to order, and they pride themselves on being flexible in accommodating requests. The atmosphere is fun and lively. This is a good place to grab a drink and enjoy the local food and a good view.

Many people familiar with East Coast beaches associate the name Awful Arthur's with the Outer Banks of North Carolina. Their latest restaurant (and first in Maryland) is located in a beautiful spot right in the historic district. **Awful Arthur's Seafood Company** (402 S. Talbot St., 410/745-3474, www.awfularthursusa.com, Sun.-Thurs. 11am-9pm, Fri.-Sat. 11am-10pm, $9-28) features an authentic oyster bar with more than nine oyster varieties, shrimp, clams, crab legs, mussels, etc. They also have a large seafood and land-based menu. They offer indoor seating and a gorgeous outdoor patio.

ICE CREAM

Mouthwatering ice cream in a friendly atmosphere can be found at **Justine's Ice Cream Parlour** (106 N. Talbot St., 410/745-0404, Mon.-Fri. 1pm-9pm, Sat.-Sun. noon-9pm, under $10) on North Talbot Street. They have been a staple in St. Michaels for decades. They serve ice cream, floats, shakes, and malts.

Accommodations

$200-300

Bring your kayak or fishing rod to the **Point Breeze Bed and Breakfast** (704 Riverview Ter., 410/745-9563, www.pointbreezebandb.com, $235-415, minimum stays may apply). This lovely home has 400 feet of waterfront on the harbor, a pier, and complimentary kayaks, canoes, and bicycles for guest use. There are several guest rooms, all decorated with family heirlooms from five generations. Breakfast is included with each stay.

There are several beautiful bed-and-breakfasts located on Cherry Street (between the harbor and N. Talbot St., the main street through the historic district). A great choice is **Aida's Victoriana Inn** (205 Cherry St., 410/745-3368, www.victorianainn.com, $249-329). This lovely bed-and-breakfast is also located on the harbor and sits on almost an acre. It offers seven guest rooms.

For a phenomenal view, book a room at the lovely **Wades Point Inn** (10090 Wades Point Rd., McDaniel, 410/745-2500, www.wadespoint.com, $199-289), in nearby McDaniel. This waterfront bed-and-breakfast offers 26 rooms in four buildings, including several in the Georgian-style main house, which was built in 1819. They serve a daily breakfast buffet.

OVER $300

Just across Cherry Street from Aida's Victoriana Inn is the ★ **Hambleton Inn Bed & Breakfast** (202 Cherry St., 410/745-3350, www.hambletoninn.com, $220-805). It arguably has the best location in town, with wonderful waterfront views right in the historic district. With private parking off the

street, you can leave your car and walk everywhere during your stay. This elegant home offers seven rooms and one suite with private bathrooms and is tastefully decorated with antiques and upscale artwork. It was originally a shipbuilder's home (circa 1850). The home's two large porches are a focal point and have inviting rocking chairs that look out to the harbor. Reservations include a fantastic and plentiful gourmet breakfast, evening wine, and gracious hosts.

The lavish **Inn at Perry Cabin** (308 Watkins Ln., 410/745-2200, www.innatperrycabin.com, $626-1,070) is a grand old resort and spa formerly owned by Sir Bernard and Lady Laura Ashley. It sits on the Miles River and has lovely views of the water. The hotel was built around 1816 and is surrounded by antique gardens from the same period. Docking facilities (free for guest use), a fitness center, heated outdoor pool, and complimentary bicycles are some of the property amenities. There are 78 guest rooms, and the resort is pet friendly. Ask for a room on an upper floor with a view of the water.

The Harbour Inn Marina & Spa (101 N. Harbor Rd., 410/745-9001, www.harbourinn.com, $309-739) is also located on the Miles River and offers 52 guest rooms and suites and a full-service marina. This is a lovely property in a good location. They allow dogs with no size restrictions ($50 for the first dog, $25 for the second).

Information and Services

For additional information on St. Michaels, visit www.stmichaelsmd.org.

TILGHMAN ISLAND

Tilghman Island is one of the few remaining working watermen's villages in the mid-Atlantic. It provides an unvarnished look at life on the Chesapeake Bay. Tilghman Island is home to the last commercial fishing sailing fleet in North America. The fleet is known

1: 1879 Hooper Strait Lighthouse at Chesapeake Bay Maritime Museum 2: Hambleton Inn Bed & Breakfast

as the Skipjacks in honor of the classic oyster boat (and Maryland's state boat), which visitors can see at **Dogwood Harbor,** on the east side of the island. Tilghman Island is in the middle Chesapeake Bay region and is separated from the Eastern Shore by Napps Narrows, but is easily accessed by driving over a drawbridge. Tilghman Island is three miles long and reachable via MD 33, 11 miles west of St. Michaels. It has a population of fewer than 900 people.

Sights

The **Phillips Wharf Environmental Center** (6129 Tilghman Island Rd., 410/886-9200, www.phillipswharf.org, summer Thurs.-Mon. 10am-4pm, winter Sat.-Sun. 10am-4pm, free, donations appreciated) is a wonderful place for children and adults to learn about creatures living in the Chesapeake Bay. The center gives visitors the opportunity to see, touch, and learn about wildlife such as horseshoe crabs, turtles, and oysters. They also sponsor a number of events throughout the year including lectures, triathlons, and social events.

Tilghman's Watermen's Museum (6031 Tilghman Island Rd., 410/886-1025, www.tilghmanmuseum.org, Sat.-Sun. 10am-3pm, free) features exhibits on the heritage of the local watermen. It houses a collection of artifacts, boat models, and artwork by local artists.

Recreation

Lady Patty Classic Yacht Charters (6176 Tilghman Island Rd., 410/886-1127, www.ladypatty.com, adults $45, children under 12 $25) offers seasonal two-hour charters in the waters surrounding Tilghman Island. Beer, wine, and cocktail service are available on all charters. Private charters can be arranged.

Charters aboard the oldest working skipjack on the Chesapeake Bay can be arranged on the **Skipjack *Rebecca T. Ruark*** (410/829-3976, www.skipjack.org, adults $30, children under 12 $15). This beautiful boat was built in 1886, and the wonderful captain helps make this a great two-hour sail. Sailing charters leave from **Dogwood Harbor** (21308 Phillips Rd.).

Tilghman Island Marina (6140 Mariners Ct., 410/886-2500, www.tilghmanmarina.com) also offers charter fishing boats ($500-1,200/day) and rents fishing boats, pontoon boats, WaveRunners, Jet-Skis, and kayaks.

Several **Tilghman Island Water Trails** (410/770-8000, www.dnr.maryland.gov) are available for kayaking. The **East Tilghman Island Trail** is 10.2 miles and explores the eastern portion of the island, while the **Tilghman Island Trail** tours the entire island. Maps can be downloaded at the trail website.

Food

Two If By Sea Restaurant (5776 Tilghman Island Rd., 410/886-2447, www.twoifbysearestaurant.com, Mon.-Tues. and Thurs. 8am-11am, Wed. and Sun. 8am-2pm, Fri.-Sat. 8am-2pm and 6pm-9pm, $15-25) is a cozy little restaurant serving breakfast, lunch, and dinner. They have wonderful traditional breakfasts, sandwiches, salads, fresh seafood, and homemade pastries. This is a delightful choice for a casual meal at a reasonable price.

The **Marker Five Restaurant** (6178 Tilghman Island Rd., 410/886-1122, www.markerfive.com, summer hours Wed.-Thurs. noon-10pm, Fri.-Sat. noon-9pm, Sun. noon-8pm, $9-28) offers a casual waterfront dining experience. They serve soup, sandwiches, local seafood, and other items such as barbecue and house-smoked ribs. They have an outdoor bar with more than 30 beers on tap.

If you're looking for a great view and a laid-back atmosphere, grab a seat on the deck at the **Characters Bridge Restaurant** (6136 Tilghman Island Rd., 410/886-1060, www.charactersbridgerestaurant.com, Wed.-Sun. 11am-10pm, $10-29). The menu offers staples such as local seafood, burgers, and steak. This is a great place to watch the boats on Knapps Narrows and the activity at the drawbridge.

Accommodations

There is no shortage of waterfront accommodations on Tilghman Island. For peace, serenity, and perhaps the best view on the island, stay a few nights at the **Black Walnut Point Inn** (4417 Black Walnut Point Rd., 410/886-2452, www.blackwalnutpointinn.com, $225-350). This charming bed-and-breakfast sits on six acres at the southern point of Tilghman Island and is bounded by water on three sides. The main house offers four rooms with private baths. Two nicely appointed cabins right on the Choptank River provide a larger, more private space, and one is wheelchair accessible. The innkeepers are extremely friendly and knowledgeable about the long history of the property. Full breakfast is served each morning in the dining room, and the beautiful grounds offer a swimming pool, hot tub, pier, bird-watching trails, and unrivaled views of the Chesapeake Bay.

A vintage property re-invented in 2018 is the **Wylder Hotel** (21551 Chesapeake House Dr., 877/818-1922, www.wylderhoteltilghmanisland.com, $208-455). Built as a boarding house in 1898, this nine-acre private resort offers 54 rooms, an on-site restaurant and bar, salt-water pool, private marina (with 25 boat slips), lawn games, bicycles, and water activities. The rooms are simple but nicely renovated and the staff is outstanding. This is a great place to enjoy the water, make new friends around a fire, and relax. The property is dog friendly.

The **Knapps Narrows Marina and Inn** (6176 Tilghman Island Rd., 410/886-2720, www.knappsnarrowsmarina.com, $125-260) is a wonderful little waterfront inn, restaurant, and tiki bar that offers 20 guest rooms and great views of the Chesapeake Bay. Each room has a private waterfront patio or balcony. The inn is three stories, and each room is nicely furnished but not overstuffed. The staff is truly accommodating and friendly. The inn is adjacent to the Knapps Narrows Bridge (the entrance to the island). There is an outdoor pool on-site.

Information and Services

For additional information on Tilghman Island, visit www.tilghmanisland.com.

EASTON

Easton is a wonderful small town on the Eastern Shore that was founded in 1710. It is an hour's drive (42 miles) southeast of Annapolis. Easton is the largest town in Talbot County, with a population of around 16,500. It offers residents and visitors a beautiful downtown area with colonial and Victorian architecture, casual and fine restaurants, shopping, antiques, and galleries, while also providing ample opportunities for recreation such as golf and water sports on the Chesapeake Bay.

Sights
ACADEMY ART MUSEUM

The **Academy Art Museum** (106 South St., 410/822-2787, www.academyartmuseum.org, Fri.-Mon. 10am-4pm, Tues.-Thurs. 10am-8pm, $3, children under 12 free, free admission on Wed.) is a little museum near downtown Easton that has five studios. It is housed in a charming building that was finished in 1820 and was the location of the first chartered school in Easton. It is now a historic landmark. The museum offers both regional and national exhibits; hosts concerts, lectures, and educational programs; and offers performing arts education for adults and children. More than 50,000 visitors come to the museum each year. Past exhibits have included works by Ansel Adams, Roy Lichtenstein, and N. C. Wyeth.

★ PICKERING CREEK AUDUBON CENTER

The **Pickering Creek Audubon Center** (11450 Audubon Ln., 410/822-4903, www.pickeringcreek.audubon.org, trails and viewing areas daily dawn-dusk, free) is a 400-acre working farm next to Pickering Creek in Talbot County. The property is a natural habitat of forest, marsh, meadow, a freshwater pond, wetlands, more than a mile of shoreline, and farmland. More than four miles of

Easton

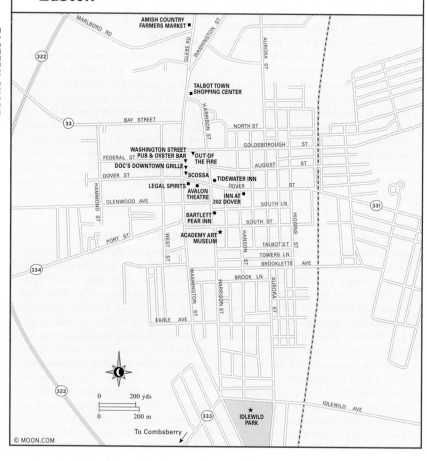

walking trails are available as well as gardens, a canoe and kayak launch, and 100 acres of hardwood forest. Trails and viewing areas are open to the public from dawn until dusk every day, and there is no admission fee. The center is great for bird-watching and features viewing platforms, a bluebird trail, and 90 acres of wetlands. Office hours at Pickering Creek are Monday-Friday 9am-5pm. The center is north of Easton: Take Route 662 north past the airport. Turn left on Sharp Road (west) and go right at the Y. Turn right (north) on Presquille Road and then right again on Audubon Lane.

THE AMISH COUNTRY FARMERS MARKET

The Amish Country Farmers Market (101 Marlboro Ave., 410/822-8989, www.amishcountryfarmersmarket.com, Thurs. 9am-6pm, Fri. 9am-7pm, Sat. 9am-3pm) is a tradition on the Eastern Shore. The market features numerous authentic Amish vendors from Pennsylvania selling a great variety of produce, dairy products, baked goods, meats, candy, furniture, and crafts. Many locals do their regular grocery shopping at the market, but it is a popular stop for tourists wishing to purchase fresh foods and handmade products.

IDLEWILD PARK
Idlewild Park (115 Idlewild Ave., 410/822-2525, www.eastonmd.gov, dawn to dusk, free) is a great place to take the little ones to burn some energy. This 15-acre park features a large play structure with swings, forts, and slides that is big enough to inspire unlimited imagination. The park also offers ball fields, a quarter-mile track, tennis courts (on a rubberized surface), picnic areas, and flower gardens. There is plenty of parking and restroom facilities spring-fall.

Recreation and Entertainment
Easton is home to the popular **Hog Neck Golf Course** (10142 Old Cordova Rd., 800/280-1790, www.hogneck.com, starting at $17/50 9-hole/18-hole, seniors $15/45). The facility offers an 18-hole championship course and a 9-hole executive course.

Visitors can catch a show at the **Avalon Theatre** (40 E. Dover St., 410/822-7299, www.avalonfoundation.org). This cozy little theater has a full schedule of entertainment including theatrical performances, symphonies, bluegrass, jazz, comedians, and art festivals.

The largest annual event in Easton, and one of the best known on the Eastern Shore, is the **Waterfowl Festival** (www.waterfowlfestival.org, $20 for three days, children under 10 free). Taking place over three days in November, this event began in the early 1970s and now hosts 18,000-plus visitors, 1,500 volunteers, and 300 of the best wildlife artists, craftspeople, and vendors. This is a citywide event that closes several streets and prompts businesses to decorate their buildings with natural greens. The festival is a leader in promoting conservation of waterfowl and natural habitat.

Shopping
Downtown Easton is a shopper's delight, with many gift stores, antiques shops, crafts, clothing, and shops with collectibles. Two of the prime streets to include on your shopping journey are Harrison and Washington, although many lovely stores may be found on various side streets. The **Talbot Town Shopping Center** on North Washington Street offers national retail chains.

Vintage Books and Fine Art (4 North Washington St., 410/562-3403, www.vintagebooksmd.com, Wed.-Sat. 10am-5pm, Sun. 11am-2pm) sells used and rare books, as well as antique maps, historic newspapers, and fine art from local artists.

Food
Good Northern Italian food is served at **Scossa** (8 N. Washington St., 410/822-2202, www.scossarestaurant.com, Thurs.-Sun. 11:30am-3pm, dinner daily starting at 4pm, $8-40) in the heart of the downtown area on North Washington Street. The owner/chef was born in northern Italy and has an impressive culinary résumé. The modern dining room is the perfect place to meet with friends, business associates, and family. The dinner menu is a step above traditional Italian with creative combinations, fresh ingredients, and daily specials that offer something new each visit. They also offer a prix fixe menu for $40. Lunch is a completely different experience and features wonderful salads and sandwiches. The bar area is very inviting and serves top-shelf wine and liquor. They have a large specialty drink menu. Sunday brunch is also served.

Another excellent choice for Italian food is **Out of the Fire** (22 Goldsborough St., 410/770-4777, www.outofthefire.com, Tues.-Thurs. 11:30am-2pm and 5pm-9pm, Fri.-Sat. 11:30am-2pm and 5pm-10pm, $9-28) on Goldsborough Street. They serve gourmet pizza and other creative entrées made from high-quality ingredients procured from mostly local farmers and vendors (try the mussels). The wraps and sandwiches are delicious, and they offer organic and gluten-free choices. The atmosphere is very warm and relaxing with tile floors and soft lighting.

For a good pub-style meal in Easton, go to the **Washington Street Pub & Oyster Bar**

(20 N. Washington St., 410/822-1112, www. washingtonstreetpub.com, daily 11am-2am, $9-25). The trendy decor and lively atmosphere rival the food at this cozy pub and raw bar. They also have a good selection of beer on tap. Try the Chesapeake chicken sandwich (crab imperial and cheese on top of chicken); it is decadent to say the least.

For a fun atmosphere or to watch your favorite sports event, dine at **Doc's Downtown Grille** (14 N. Washington St., 410/822-7700, daily 11am-2am, $9-25). They serve traditional pub food and delicious local seafood (crab cakes, shrimp po'boys, fried oysters, etc.). The restaurant is family owned and operated, and their passion for their business is evident in the friendly service.

Accommodations

The ★ **Bartlett Pear Inn** (28 S. Harrison St., 410/770-3300, www.bartlettpearinn. com, $232-289) is a beautiful property on South Harrison Street in downtown Easton. This lovely inn dates back to the late 1700s and offers seven individually decorated guest rooms named for different types of pears. The handsome brick building with white covered porches is on a quiet street within walking distance of shopping and restaurants. The husband-and-wife owners are very gracious hosts, and they pay attention to the small details that make their guests feel welcome. The inn is pet friendly and can even accommodate large dogs. Ask for a room on the upper floor; this will provide the most quiet and privacy.

The gracious **Tidewater Inn** (101 E. Dover St., 410/822-1300, www.tidewaterinn. com, $189-252) is the landmark lodging property in Easton. This elegant downtown hotel opened in 1949 and is known as a romantic getaway. The inn has 89 guest rooms with yesterday's charm and some modern conveniences such as wireless Internet and flat-screen televisions. The hotel does not have some of the amenities many travelers are used to such as a fitness room and on-site pool, but many of the rooms were renovated in 2016 and 2018. If you are looking for a comfortable

manor-house atmosphere with good service, this is a lovely choice. There is a good restaurant (the Hunter's Tavern) on-site and many more within walking distance.

The **Hummingbird Inn** (14 N. Aurora St., 410/376-5632, www.hummingbirdinneaston. com, $195-239) is a beautiful Victorian-style home with a 1,000-square-foot wraparound porch and six welcoming guest rooms. They serve a multicourse hot breakfast with a choice of entrées. The inn's host is charming and attentive, and not only is the property dog friendly, but they offer dog sitting/care for guests.

Information and Services

For additional information on Easton, visit www.eastonmd.org or stop by the **Talbot County Visitors' Center** (11 S. Harrison St., 410/770-8000, Mon.-Fri. 8:30am-5pm, Sat. 10am-2pm).

Getting There and Around

Most people arrive in Easton by car. There is a small public airport, the **Easton Airport** (29137 Newnam Rd., 410/770-8055, www. eastonairport.com), two miles north of Easton.

OXFORD

The small waterfront town of Oxford, 10 miles southwest of Easton, is a fun day-trip destination. Oxford was settled in the mid-1660s on just 30 acres and is one of the oldest towns in Maryland. It was selected shortly after its settlement to be one of only two ports of entry for the Maryland Province (the other was Anne Arundel, which later became Annapolis). What followed was a period of prominence for the little town, and it became known as an international shipping center and home to many thriving tobacco plantations. After the Revolutionary War, when British ships stopped visiting its waters for trade, the town

1: downtown Easton 2: the Oxford Inn 3: Cambridge waterfront 4: kayaking at Blackwater National Wildlife Refuge

declined. Today, Oxford has a population of fewer than 700 people, but it remains a scenic and inviting place.

Oxford-Bellevue Ferry

The **Oxford-Bellevue Ferry** (27456 Oxford Rd., 410/745-9023, www.oxfordferry.com, mid-Apr.-mid-Nov. daily, one-way/round-trip $12/20 car and driver, $6/9 motorcycle, $4/7 bike, $3/5 pedestrian) is one of the oldest privately run ferries in the country, dating back to 1683. It runs between Oxford and Bellevue, Maryland, across the Tred Avon River. The trip is less than a mile and takes approximately 10 minutes. The ferry accommodates cars, motorcycles, bikes, and pedestrians and has a capacity of nine vehicles. The ferry starts running at 9am from Oxford and has continuous crossings every 15-20 minutes. This is a popular connection for cyclists biking a circular route from St. Michaels.

Food and Accommodations

Overnight visitors to Oxford can enjoy a stay at the **Oxford Inn** (504 S. Morris St., 410/226-5220, www.oxfordinn.net, $145-375). This lovely bed-and-breakfast is on a charming street across from a small marina. The exterior of the building is white with a green roof, covered porches, and seven dormer windows. The seven guest rooms are quaintly decorated in a country style, and the inn has a wonderful European bistro, **Pope's Tavern** ($8-18), that offers elegant dinner space for 40 guests. They serve entrées such as flatbread, crab cakes, steak, and seared tuna. There is also a cozy teak bar with seating for 12. A note at the bottom of their menu states "unattended children will be given a double espresso and a puppy."

The ★ **Robert Morris Inn** (314 N. Morris St., 410/226-5111, www.robertmorrisinn.com, $190-265), near the ferry landing, is the oldest full-service inn in the country. This historic building with a yellow exterior and large patio dates back to 1710 and was once the home of a prosperous merchant and famous financier of the American Revolution, Robert Morris. A close friend of George Washington, Morris

entertained Washington at his home on multiple occasions. In later years, author James Michener spent time at the inn while working on his novel *Chesapeake*. The rooms offer a choice of cozy period furniture and canopy beds or more-modern furnishings, but there is no elevator (and some stairs are steep). Breakfast is included.

The inn contains a great restaurant, **Salter's Tavern and Tap Room,** that serves breakfast ($4-14), lunch ($10-24), and dinner ($12-34). The ambience is warm and inviting, with redbrick walls, slate floors, and timber beams. The casual menu is centered on the local seafood treasures found in the bay, such as crab, oysters, and fresh fish, but also features land-based menu items such as burgers and salads. The restaurant is overseen by Mark Salter, a well-known British master chef.

Information and Services

For additional information on Oxford, visit www.oxfordmd.net.

CAMBRIDGE

Cambridge is 17 miles south of Easton off US 50. It is the largest town in Dorchester County and one of the oldest colonial cities in Maryland, having been settled in 1684. It sits directly on the Choptank River (which was the setting for James Michener's book *Chesapeake*) near the Chesapeake Bay. The town was originally a trading center for tobacco.

In the late 19th century, Cambridge opened food-processing businesses that canned foods such as oysters, tomatoes, and sweet potatoes. At its peak, the primary packing concern, Phillips Packing Company, employed 10,000 people. By the 1960s the decline in the canning industry had led to the closure of the company and left behind a struggling city that is still fighting to prosper.

Today Cambridge offers a pretty downtown area with historic 18th- and 19th-century homes and scenic waterfront parks and marinas.

Sights

RICHARDSON MARITIME MUSEUM

Visitors can learn about the lost tradition of wooden boatbuilding at the **Richardson Maritime Museum** (401 High St., 410/221-1871, www.richardsonmuseum.org, Sat. 10am-4pm, Sun. 1pm-4pm, $3). This historic brick building on the corner of High and Locust Streets housed a bank for almost a hundred years. One step into the museum takes visitors into the world of wooden sailing vessels and their role on the Chesapeake Bay. Boat models, building tools, and original artifacts are just some of the items on display. The rich wooden-boat history includes everything from crabbing skiffs to dovetails to clipper ships and even schooners.

CHOPTANK RIVER LIGHTHOUSE

The **Choptank River Lighthouse** (100 High St., 410/463-2653, www.choosecambridge.com, May-Oct. daily 9am-6pm, by appointment Nov.-Apr., free) is an icon on the Choptank River at Long Wharf Park (Water St. and High St.). It is a replica of a six-sided screw-pile lighthouse, a style of lighthouse that was common on the Chesapeake Bay. The original lighthouse was built in 1871 and was the only manned lighthouse on the river to guide vessels to Cambridge. The lighthouse is located on Pier A. Visitors can take a self-guided tour, enjoy great views of the river, and visit a small maritime museum on-site.

HARRIET TUBMAN MUSEUM & EDUCATIONAL CENTER

The **Harriet Tubman Museum & Educational Center** (424 Race St., 410/228-0401, www.visitdorchester.org, Tues.-Fri. noon-3pm, Sat. noon-4pm, tours by appointment only, free) is a tribute to Harriet Ross Tubman (1822-1913), a freedom fighter and former enslaved person who was known for leading many people to freedom through the Underground Railroad. This small museum is dedicated to telling stories of this heroine's life and features exhibits on her work helping dozens of enslaved people. It is also part of the

Harriet Tubman Underground Railroad Byway (www.harriettubmanbyway.org), a scenic, self-guided driving route with more than 30 sites related to freedom seekers from the 1800s. Tubman was a Dorchester County native.

J. M. CLAYTON COMPANY

Pay a visit to the market at the world's oldest working crab house, **J. M. Clayton Company** (108 Commerce St., 410/228-1661, www.jmclayton.com, Mon.-Fri. 8am-5pm) on Commerce Street. This historic crab house is still operated by the same family that started it back in 1890. They even have an 80-year-old canning machine. Their market is open daily and visitors can purchase local crabmeat and crab-related items. Plant tours are available for $5 per person.

★ BLACKWATER NATIONAL WILDLIFE REFUGE

Blackwater National Wildlife Refuge (2145 Key Wallace Dr., 410/228-2677, www.friendsofblackwater.org, daily dawn-dusk, vehicles $3, pedestrians $1, cyclists $1) was established in 1933 as a sanctuary for waterfowl migrating along the **Atlantic Flyway** (a migration route along the Atlantic coast). The refuge is located 12 miles south of Cambridge and encompasses 27,000 acres including freshwater, brackish tidal wetlands, meadows, and forest. It is open year-round.

More than 250 species of birds live in the refuge, and it is home to the largest breeding population of bald eagles on the East Coast north of Florida. The eagle population swells in the winter months, when many birds migrate here from northern areas. During the winter, the refuge is also home to more than 35,000 geese and 15,000 ducks. Fall (Sept.-Nov.) is the best time to see migrating waterfowl and songbirds.

A wide variety of mammals also live in the refuge. Delmarva fox squirrels, southern flying squirrels, voles, shrews, nutria, gray foxes, red foxes, river otters, mink, skunks, deer, and beavers all call the refuge home.

There is a wonderful visitors center on Key Wallace Drive (year-round Mon.-Fri. 8am-4pm, Sat.-Sun. 9am-5pm) with wildlife exhibits, nature books, birding guides, a butterfly garden, maps, restrooms, and a gift shop. The prime attraction in the refuge is Wildlife Drive, a four-mile paved road where visitors can drive, bike, and walk through the refuge to view wildlife. There is also a great viewing platform over the marsh. In addition to Wildlife Drive, the refuge has four land trails and three paddling trails. Visitors can also hunt, fish, and crab. Environmental education programs are also offered for young people.

Recreation and Events

One-hour **Historic High Street Walking Tours** (410/228-1000, adults $8, children under 12 free) are offered by the West End Citizens Association. Reservations are not required but they are recommended. Tours meet at 11am on Saturday April-October at Long Wharf (High St. and Water St.).

Two-hour cruises on the skipjack **Nathan of Dorchester** (Long Wharf on High St., 410/228-7141, www.skipjack-nathan.org, most Saturdays May-Oct. 1pm-3pm, adults $35, children 6-12 $10, call for reservations) offer an authentic Chesapeake Bay experience. Tours go out on the Choptank River and teach the history of oystering.

Two lovely parks in Cambridge offer nice views of the Choptank River. **Great Marsh Park** (at the end of Somerset Ave. on the Choptank River, www.choosecambridge. com) has a boat launch, fishing pier, playground, and picnic tables. **Sailwinds Park East** (2 Rose Hill Pl., 410/228-1000, www. visitdorchester.org) is next to the Dorchester County Visitor Center (daily 8:30am-5pm). There is a playground, and the park is known as a good spot to fly kites.

Cambridge is the site of many endurance events including the **Ironman 70.3 Eagleman Triathlon** (www.ironman.com) in June, **Ironman Maryland** (www.ironman. com) in early October, and the **Six Pillars** **Century** bike ride (www.6pillarscentury. org) in early May.

Blackwater Paddle & Pedal (2524 Key Wallace Dr., 410/901-9255, www. blackwaterpaddleandpedal.com) offers guided three-hour bike tours and two-hour kayak tours. Bike tours depart from the Hyatt Regency, and kayak tours leave from the Hyatt Beach. They also offer rentals for bikes, kayaks, and paddleboards (call for pricing).

Food

An unexpected French treat in Cambridge is the ★ **Bistro Poplar** (535 Poplar St., 410/228-4884, www.bistropoplar.com, Thurs.-Mon. starting at 5pm, tapas $6-21). They serve a tapas menu of traditional French cuisine infused with local seafood flavors such as scallops and flounder. The restaurant is housed in a historic building constructed in 1895. The interior is unmistakably French with ornate floor tiles, dim lighting, a dark-framed bar, and red velvet cushions. The food is artfully presented by servers well versed in the menu. This is a special find in Cambridge and has won many awards.

Don't let the modest exterior deter you from trying **Carmela's Cucina** (400 Academy St., 410/221-8082, www.carmelascucina1.com, Mon.-Wed. 10am-9pm, Thurs.-Sat. 10am-10pm, $7-25). This friendly Cambridge staple has been in business for decades and offers Italian dishes such as pizza, pasta, chicken, seafood, and subs.

For scrumptious breakfast and "lunch-ish" stop by **Black Water** (429 Race St., 443/225-5948, www.black-water-bakery.com, daily 7am-4pm, under $15). This delightful restaurant, bakery, and coffee house is known for its breakfast and home-baked goods, but they have equally delicious lunch. The menu includes omelets, quiche, sandwiches, pancakes, and waffles.

The **Blue Point Provision Company** (100 Heron Blvd., at Rte. 50, 410/901-6410, www. chesapeakebay.hyatt.com, Wed.-Sun. 5:30pm-9pm, $12-48) at the Hyatt Regency is a waterfront restaurant with a great seafood menu and a wonderful deck overlooking the Choptank River. The restaurant is at the far end of the resort, a short walk down the beach from the main complex. The interior is inviting, with nautical touches and soaring ceilings, beautiful ceiling fans, parquet floors, and wooden furniture. There is also a large bar area. The menu offers goodies such as Maryland crab dip, Asian barbecued salmon, fried oysters, and the famous Drunkin' Dancin' Jumbo Shrimp. They also have fresh fish selections daily based on the local catch at area fish markets. For landlubbers, they offer steak and chicken.

For good beer and pub fare, stop in **RaR Brewing** (504 Poplar St., 443/225-5664, www.rarbrewing.com, Mon. noon-9pm, Tues.-Thurs.noon-10pm, Fri.-Sat. 11am-midnight, Sun. 11am-9pm, under $15). Located inside a former billiards hall, this friendly brewery is a local favorite. They serve a casual menu with pizza, crab dip, hummus, hot dogs, sandwiches, and more than a dozen delicious beers.

Good diner food at a reasonable price can be found at the **Cambridge Diner and Restaurant** (2924 Old Rte. 50, 410/228-8898, www.dinercambridge.com, daily 6am-10pm, $11-24). They serve traditional comfort food in large portions.

Accommodations

At first glance, ★ **The Hyatt Regency Chesapeake Bay Golf Resort, Spa & Marina** (100 Heron Blvd., at Rte. 50, 410/901-1234, www.chesapeakebay.hyatt.com, $288-499) seems a bit "glam" for the quiet town of Cambridge, but it does quite well in providing a self-contained oasis of luxury for both golfing and nongolfing visitors. One of the premier hotels on the Eastern Shore, it sits on 400 acres along the Choptank River and has beautiful views of the water and surrounding marsh. The resort offers elegant rooms and enough activities that visitors can easily park their car and never leave the compound during their stay. The resort is known for its golf course, the River Marsh Golf Club, but is also family friendly, with planned children's activities and many amenities (two pools, hot tub,

minigolf, game room, fitness center, spa, water sports, etc.). The first floor is dog friendly.

Guests can grab a drink or a bottle of wine and relax in one of the big rocking chairs that line the patio. The centerpiece is a large open fireplace where guests can toast marshmallows or gather for happy hour. There are several dining options at the hotel that are nice but not as exquisite as might be expected. Book a room with a view and/or balcony; it costs more but makes a big difference. Opening your curtains in the morning to look out at the water is worth the added expense. Rooms are clean and spacious, and the beds are comfortable. The staff does a good job of making guests feel welcome, and the hotel can also make arrangements for activities both on and off the property.

A lovely historic district bed-and-breakfast is the **Cambridge House Bed and Breakfast** (112 High St., 410/221-7700, www.cambridgehousebandb.com, $170-275). This pretty red home with a large front porch was built in 1847 as a sea captain's manor. It is located just one block from Long Wharf Park on the Choptank River and is also within walking distance of restaurants and shops. They offer six large, traditionally furnished rooms with private bathrooms. Most have electric fireplaces. A full breakfast is served as well as afternoon refreshments.

Another lovely inn is **The Albanus Phillips Inn** (314 Mill St., 410/228-2990, www.albanusphillipsinn.com, $199-350). This private Queen Anne Victorian-style manor was completed in 1903 and owned by Colonel Albanus Phillips Jr. (from the Phillips Packing Company). The beautiful home boasts Italian Renaissance and Edwardian features including Italian marble throughout (there are three types on the front porch alone). It has 10 bedrooms and has welcomed famous guests such as President Teddy Roosevelt and President Taft.

Additional accommodations in Cambridge include large chain hotels such as the **Holiday Inn Express Cambridge** (2715 Ocean Gateway, 410/221-9900, www.ihg.com,

$109-184), which is clean, quiet, and well located on US 50. This hotel has 85 guest rooms, an indoor pool, wireless Internet, and a fitness room. Each room comes with a refrigerator. Another similar option is the **Comfort Inn and Suites** (2936 Ocean Gateway, 410/901-0926, www.choicehotels.com, $180-229). This hotel is also on US 50 and has 65 guest rooms. It also offers an indoor pool, fitness room, free breakfast, and free wireless Internet.

Information and Services

Additional information on Cambridge can be found at the **Visitors Center at Sailwinds Park East** (2 Rose Hill Pl., daily 8:30am-5pm) or online at www.visitdorchester.org.

Getting There

Most travelers arrive in Cambridge on US 50. This east-west route runs from Ocean City, Maryland, to Sacramento, California. The road is known locally as the Ocean Gateway.

The **Cambridge-Dorchester Airport** (5263 Bucktown Rd.) is southeast of Cambridge. It is a general aviation airport with one runway.

Assateague Island

Assateague Island sits opposite Ocean City across the Ocean City Inlet. It is considered part of both Virginia and Maryland. The inlet didn't always exist: It was formed during the Chesapeake-Potomac Hurricane in 1933, which created a nice inlet at the south end of Ocean City, and the Army Corps of Engineers decided to make it permanent.

In its southern reaches, Assateague Island borders Chincoteague Island. Both Assateague and Chincoteague are known for their resident herds of wild ponies and the famous **Wild Pony Swim** (www.chincoteaguechamber.com) that takes place each year in late July, when the herd is taken for a swim from Assateague Island across the channel to Chincoteague Island.

SIGHTS
★ Assateague Island National Seashore

Assateague Island National Seashore (www.nps.gov, year-round in Maryland, 24 hours, 7-day pass $20 per vehicle, annual senior pass $20) was established in 1962. It is managed by three agencies: the National Park Service, US Fish & Wildlife Service, and the Maryland Department of Natural Resources. The island includes a beautiful 37-mile beach, dunes, wetlands, and marsh. The island is protected as a natural environment, and many opportunities exist for wildlife viewing. Assateague Island is a stopover for migrating shorebirds and provides important areas for feeding and resting. More than 320 bird species can be viewed here during the year, including piping plovers, great egrets, and northern harriers.

Assateague Island is also known for its wild ponies. It is widely believed that the ponies originally came to the island years ago when a Spanish cargo ship loaded with horses sank off the coast and the ponies swam to shore. In 1997, a Spanish shipwreck was discovered off the island, which supports this theory.

Other mammals in Assateague include rodents as small as the meadow jumping mouse, along with red foxes, river otters, and deer. Several species of whales feed off the island's shore, along with bottlenose dolphins.

There are two entrances to the national seashore. One is eight miles south of Ocean City at the end of Route 611. The second is at the southern end of the island at the end of Route 175, two miles from Chincoteague, Virginia. Visitors to Assateague Island mostly stay in Chincoteague or Ocean City since there are no hotel accommodations on the island, but camping is allowed and quite popular.

Park hours and fees are different in Virginia and Maryland and also vary by month in

Virginia. Consult www.assateagueisland.com for specific information for the time of year and location you wish to visit.

The **Assateague Island Visitor Center** (Maryland District of Assateague Island, 11800 Marsh View Ln., Berlin, 410/641-1441, Jan.-Feb. Thurs.-Mon. 9am-5pm, Mar.-Dec. daily 9am-5pm) offers a film on the wild ponies, brochures, aquariums, a touch tank, maps, and other exhibits.

The **Maryland District Ranger Station** (6633 Bayberry Dr., Berlin, 410/641-3030, open year-round, hours change seasonally) offers entrance passes, information on campgrounds and hunting, and permits for backcountry camping and over-sand vehicle use.

Assateague Island Lighthouse

The red-and-white-striped **Assateague Island Lighthouse** (www.assateagueisland. com, a half mile from Chincoteague Island and accessible from Chincoteague by car in approximately five minutes and from Maryland in an hour, 757/336-3696, Apr.-Nov. weekends 9am-3pm, free but donations encouraged) is on the Virginia side of Assateague Island. A trail connects Chincoteague with Assateague Island that can be walked or accessed by bicycle. The original lighthouse was built in 1833 but was replaced by a taller, more powerful lighthouse in 1867. The lighthouse is still in operation and features twin rotating lights that sit 154 feet above sea level. The US Coast Guard maintains the light as a working navigational aid, but the Chincoteague National Wildlife Refuge is responsible for the lighthouse preservation efforts. The top of the lighthouse can be visited by the public.

RECREATION

Due in part to its relative isolation, Assateague Island has one of the nicest beaches on the East Coast. Visitors can enjoy the area by kayaking, beach walking, swimming, fishing, biking, and bird-watching.

The **Maryland Coastal Bays Program** (www.mdcoastalbays.org) rents kayaks ($15 per hour), canoes ($22 per hour), paddleboards ($20 per hour), and bikes ($6 per hour) at a stand on Assateague Island National Seashore (13002 Bayside Dr., Berlin, 410/656-9453) daily in summer and weekends the rest of the year. To find the stand, take the second right after the park tollbooth. A 3.5-mile paved bike path leads from Route 611 through the parks.

wild pony, Assateague Island

CAMPING

Camping is allowed on the Maryland side of the national seashore through the **National Park Service** (877/444-6777, $30). Oceanside and bayside campsites are available all year. Sites do not have hookups but can accommodate tents, trailers, and RVs. There are also horse sites ($50) and group tent sites ($50). Cold showers and chemical toilets are available on-site. Camping is also permitted in **Assateague State Park** (7307 Stephen Decatur Hwy., 410/641-2918, late Apr.-Oct., $28, with electric $39), also on the Maryland side of the island. There are 342 campsites here. Each site has a picnic table, fire ring, room for one car, and access to a bathhouse with warm showers. Backpackers and kayakers can also take advantage of back-country camping. Camping information can be found at www.assateagueisland.com.

GETTING THERE

There are two entrances to Assateague Island National Seashore. One is eight miles south of Ocean City at the end of Route 611. From Ocean City, cross the bridge on US 50 heading west. Turn left at the third traffic light onto Route 611. Follow the brown signs to the park. The second is at the southern end of the island at the end of Route 175, two miles from Chincoteague, Virginia. There are no hotel accommodations on the island; visitors to Assateague Island can stay in Chincoteague or Ocean City.

Ocean City

For many people, the quintessential summer vacation is a trip to the beach. Ocean City, the most popular destination in Worcester County, stretches for 10 miles along the Atlantic Ocean between Delaware and the Ocean City Inlet. It offers enough stimulation to keep kids of all ages entertained for days. The three-mile wooden boardwalk is packed with shopping, restaurants, games, and amusements and is open all year. Seemingly every inch of real estate is claimed along the strip, and more than 10,000 hotel rooms and 25,000 condominiums provide endless choices for accommodations.

Ocean City's history dates back to the 1500s, when Giovanni da Verrazano came through the area while surveying the East Coast in service of the King of France. By the 17th century, British colonists had settled the area, after moving north out of Virginia. Ocean City took off as a beach community in 1900 when the first boardwalk was built. Back then, the boardwalk was a seasonal amenity that was taken apart each winter, plank by plank, and stored until the following season.

Today, Ocean City is bustling, to say the least. It is a major East Coast destination for people who enjoy the beach, company, entertainment, and a lot of activity. Visitors can get a good taste for the town in a weekend, but many people stay for a week or more. Approximately eight million people visit Ocean City each year.

Ocean City is a family town but also a party town. Unlike its northern neighbor, Atlantic City, it lacks casinos and has limited development options and, as such, is able to keep the beach as its main focus. Although the city refers to itself as "The East Coast's Number One Family Resort," it is also a popular area for high school seniors letting off steam after graduation at what is traditionally known as "Senior Week" or "Beach Week." Keep this in mind if you plan to visit in June. You will have a lot of young, unchaperoned company (the average number of graduating seniors visiting in June is 100,000). Some rental complexes even cater specifically to high school and college groups.

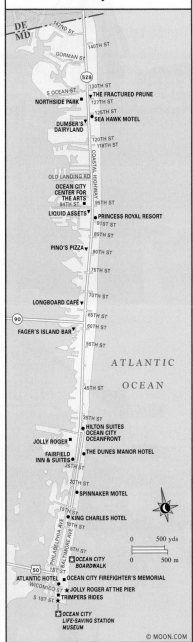

Ocean City

TOP EXPERIENCE

★ Ocean City Boardwalk

The primary attraction in Ocean City is the three-mile-long boardwalk. It begins at the south end of the beach at the Ocean City Inlet. The boardwalk is lined with dozens of hotels, motels, condos, shops, restaurants, and entertainment venues. There is 24-hour activity on the boardwalk, and many attractions and establishments orient visitors by their proximity to this popular landmark. During the summer season the boardwalk is very crowded, so if you like hearing the ocean, smelling french fries, and listening to the sounds of vacationers enjoying themselves, then this is the place to go.

Ocean City Beach

The beach in Ocean City is wide and sandy. Brightly colored umbrellas are lined up like soldiers in the sand in front of most hotels and are available for rent. Lifeguards are on duty throughout the season and go through a vigorous training program. The beach is swept every night so it remains in fairly clean condition. It is also patrolled regularly by the local police force. In peak season, the beach and water can get very crowded, so visitors should be prepared for a lot of company.

★ Ocean City Life-Saving Station Museum

The **Ocean City Life-Saving Station Museum** (813 S. Atlantic Ave., 410/289-4991, www.ocmuseum.org, May-Oct. daily 10am-5pm, Nov.-Apr. Sat.-Sun. 10am-4pm, adult $5, children, seniors, and military $3) preserves the history of Ocean City and the US Life-Saving Service (a predecessor of the coast guard that conducted marine rescues). Several fascinating exhibits are on permanent display, including one of the best historic life-saving equipment collections in the U.S., the history of local sport surfing, and aquariums housing local marine life. The museum is located in a beautifully renovated historic building at

the extreme southern end of the Ocean City Boardwalk. Visitors can learn about the history of the boardwalk and its lifeguards, how sailors were rescued at sea, and see examples of old-fashioned bathing suits. This well-maintained, one-of-a-kind museum offers an inexpensive learning experience, powerful exhibits, and great views of the beach. There is a gift store on-site and parking in the municipal lot next door. They often offer a buy-one-get-one-free admission coupon on their website.

Ocean City Center for the Arts

A tranquil and modern place to enjoy local artwork is the **Ocean City Center for the Arts** (502 94th St., 410/524-9433, www.artleagueofoceancity.org, Mon.-Fri. 9am-4pm, Sat.-Sun. 11am-4pm, free). This beautiful art oasis showcases the work of local artists, houses individual studios, and offers art classes and events. There's even a small gift shop on-site.

The Fenwick Island Lighthouse

The **Fenwick Island Lighthouse** (103 146th St., www.fenwickislandlighthouse.org, end of May-June, Fri.-Sun. 9am-noon, July-Aug. Thurs.-Mon. 9am-noon, Sept. Fri.-Sat. 9am-noon, free) is located just over the Delaware border and stands 87 feet above Fenwick Island. It was built in 1859 after an increase in shipwrecks near the Fenwick Shoals (a shallow area six miles offshore). The operational lighthouse tower is closed to visitors, but there is a small museum at its entrance that is run by the New Friends of the Fenwick Island Lighthouse. Admission is free but donations are appreciated.

Northside Park

Northside Park (125th-127th Streets on the bay, 410/250-0125, www.ococean.com, open 24 hours) is a beautiful, 58-acre park at the end of 125th Street. It is Ocean City's largest

park and has ball fields, a fishing lagoon, paths for walking or biking, a playground, two piers, a picnic shelter, an indoor gym, conference facilities, and a 21,000-square-foot sports arena. Regular events such as Sundaes in the Park (entertainment and make-your-own sundaes) are held regularly.

Amusement Parks

There are two famous amusement parks on the boardwalk in Ocean City. **Trimpers Rides** (S. 1st St. and the boardwalk, 410/289-8617, www.trimpersrides.com, unlimited rides during the day $26) is a historical icon in Ocean City. This amusement park was built in 1893 at the southern point of the board-walk near the inlet. There are three outdoor amusement lots (summer Mon.-Fri. from 3pm, Sat.-Sun. from 12pm) and an indoor facility (summer Mon.-Fri. from 1pm, Sat.-Sun. from 12pm). A historic carousel, the Herschel-Spellman merry-go-round, dating back to 1902, is also at Trimpers Rides.

The **Jolly Roger at the Pier** (at the pier at the south end of the Boardwalk, 410/289-3031, www.jollyrogerpieroc.com, operating days and hours change with the weather, call 410/289-4902 for information) is home to the tallest Ferris wheel in town, a double-decker carousel, a coaster called Crazy Dance, and many other amusements. The view from the Ferris wheel is phenomenal. A second Jolly Roger Park is at 30th Street. There is no admission fee to the parks; the rides are pay-as-you-go, and costs vary between rides. Unlimited-ride passes are also available for both parks for $24.99 during the day and $28.99 at night.

There are several other amusement parks in Ocean City including the **Frontier Town Western Theme Park** (8428 Stephen Decatur Hwy., Berlin, 800/228-5590, www.frontiertown.com, June-Aug.) and **Baja Amusements** (12639 Ocean Gateway/Rte. 50, www.bajaoc.com, June-Aug. 9am-midnight, shorter hours Apr.-May and Sept.).

1: Ocean City Center for the Arts **2:** Ocean City Firefighter's Memorial **3:** Ocean City Boardwalk

Ocean City Firefighter's Memorial

The **Ocean City Firefighter's Memorial** (Boardwalk and N. Division St., www.ocvfc.com) is a six-foot-tall bronze statue of a firefighter that stands on a black granite base. The memorial honors firefighters of the world, the Ocean City firefighters of the past, present, and future, as well as the 343 FDNY firefighters lost on 9/11. The memorial stands in a 2,500-square-foot plaza, surrounded by engraved brick pavers. A recovered piece of twisted steel from the World Trade Center also stands as a memorial to the firefighters who lost their lives on 9/11. A memorial event is held at the site each year on September 11.

RECREATION
Fishing

Ocean City is known as the "White Marlin Capital of the World." A large fishing tournament called the **White Marlin Open** (www.whitemarlinopen.com) is held there each year at the beginning of August.

Anglers of all abilities will find plenty of places to cast a line, whether it be off a boat, pier, or in the surf. For starters, try the public fishing piers at **Inlet Park** (S. 2nd St. on the bay), the **Third Street Pier** (bayside), **Ninth Street Pier** (bayside), and **Northside Park** (125th Street, bayside). Fishing charter companies include **Ocean City Girl** (311 Talbot St., 302/381-4255, www.ocgirl.com, starting at $625) and **Saltwater Adventures** (445/235-9696, www.ocsaltwater.com, starting at $375).

Boating

There are several public boat ramps in Ocean City including ones at **Assateague Island Park** (Route 611 at the Assateague Island Bridge), **Gum Point Road** (off Route 589), and **Ocean City Commercial Harbor** (Sunset Ave. in West Ocean City).

Kayaking, Paddleboarding, and Windsurfing

For some hands-on action on the water, rent a kayak or paddleboard from **48th Street Watersports** (4701 Coastal Hwy., 410/524-9150, www.48thstreetwatersports.com, starting at $15). This bayfront facility has a wonderful beach and is a great location to try out a number of water sports. Learn to sail, try out sailboarding—they have just about every type of water toy you can dream of. They will even deliver kayaks to your location and pick them up at no extra charge. Kayak rentals and tours are also available from **Ayers Creek Adventures** (8628 Grey Fox Ln., Berlin, 443/513-0889, www.ayerscreekadventures.com, starting at $15) in nearby Berlin.

Boat Tours

Take a nature excursion with **The Angler** (312 Talbot St., bayside, 410/289-7424, www.angleroc.net, adults $18, children $9) aboard a 65-foot boat to explore the shores of Assateague Island and catch a glimpse of the resident ponies on land and dolphins at sea. Tours originate at the Ocean City Inlet. The Angler also offers deep-sea fishing (adults $68, children $36) and 45-minute scenic evening cruises (starting at $16).

Surfing

If surfing like a local is more your style, rent a board from **Chauncey's Surf Shop** (2908 Coastal Hwy., 410/289-7405, www.chaunceyssurfshop.com, $25). They also rent stand-up paddleboards ($50).

Biking

Bike rentals are available from **Dandy Don's Bike Rentals** (1109 Atlantic Ave., 410/289-2289, www.ocmdbikerentals.com, from $7). They rent beach cruisers, "Boardwalk Cars," banana bikes, and surreys. **Bike World** (6 Caroline St., 410/289-2587, www.bikeworldoc.com, from $8/hour) also rents bikes and surreys near the boardwalk.

Miniature Golf

Ocean City boasts a wide selection of miniature golf courses. Try one or two or a new one every day. **Old Pro Golf** (outdoor locations

23rd St., 28th St., 68th St., and 136th St., indoor locations 68th St. and 136th St., 410/524-2645, www.oldprogolf.com, $10) has four locations in Ocean City. The indoor golf courses and arcades on 68th Street and 136th Street are open all year. **Lost Treasure Golf** (13903 Coastal Hwy., 410/250-5678, www.losttreasuregolf.com, open Mar.-Nov.) offers 18 holes dedicated to noted explorer Professor Duffer A. Hacker.

ENTERTAINMENT
Nightlife

There's no shortage of nightlife in Ocean City. One of the premier hot spots is **Seacrets** (117 W. 49th St., 410/524-4900, www.seacrets.com), a Jamaican-themed entertainment complex featuring 14 bars and a dance club with nightly music (DJ and live). It is open all year and has an artificial beach and real palm trees. It is one place where people of different ages can mingle together. There is a dress code, so consult the website if you think your attire might be questionable. They also have a distillery on the same street (111 49th St., 410/524-2669).

The Purple Moose Saloon (on the boardwalk between Talbot St. and Caroline St., 410/289-6953, www.purplemoose.com) is a nightclub on the boardwalk that offers nightly live rock and roll mid-May-August. It is one of the few places on the boardwalk where you can walk in and just have a drink.

Fager's Island Bar (201 60th St., on the bay, 410/524-5500, www.fagers.com) is a good place to have a drink on the bay. They offer nightly entertainment with dancing, live music, and DJs. Jazz and bluegrass music is featured early with pop and dance music taking over after 9pm. The establishment has a bit of a split personality. The restaurant side has an upscale feel to it, while the nightclub side caters to the younger dance crowd.

FOOD
American

Longboard Café (6701 Coastal Hwy., 443/664-5639, www.longboardcafe.net,

Mon.-Thurs. 11am-9pm, Fri.-Sat. 11am-10pm, Sun. 10am-9pm, $12-35) is a beautiful modern restaurant with a surfing motif. It's on Coastal Highway near 67th Street. Sit inside under a high ceiling of exposed beams or outside on their inviting deck. They offer pub fare served all day, lunch, dinner, and Sunday brunch. The menu is American (wings, burgers, steak, pasta, etc.) with local fresh seafood. They also have Mexican selections, a hot-sauce bar, and 10 different margaritas. They offer beer flights and a great cocktail menu that includes a decadent chocolate martini. Gluten-free items are noted on the menu. You'll find people of all ages enjoying the contemporary menu. Reservations are highly recommended in season.

Liquid Assets (9301 Coastal Hwy., 410/524-7037, www.la94.com, Sun.-Thurs. 11:30am-11pm, Fri.-Sat. 11:30am-midnight, $12-32) is a surprisingly trendy little restaurant hidden within a strip mall, inside a liquor store. Guests pick their wine right off the shelf with or without the help of the staff and pay a corking fee to drink it with dinner. The menu is wide-ranging, the food is delicious, and the presentation is appealing. This unusual little gem is geared toward adults and does not serve a children's menu. The bar area is rustic with oak barrels, and the bistro has couches and tables that are well spaced so you aren't sitting on top of your neighbor. There's normally a long wait for seating, but they do not take reservations.

Italian

For good pizza, try **Pino's Pizza** (8101 Coastal Hwy., 410/723-4000, www.pinosoc.com, open daily in summer season, hours vary by month, $7-39). This joint has terrific pizza with a zesty sauce and is open until 4am. They offer pickup and delivery only—no dining in. They are very generous with their cheese (both mozzarella and white cheddar) and toppings, and the slices are delicious and filling. They have reliable, friendly service and often offer coupons on their website. Be aware when ordering the really large pizzas that sometimes the price of two smaller ones is much cheaper.

Seafood

★ **The Shark on the Harbor** (12924 Sunset Ave., 410/213-0924, www.ocshark.com, Mon.-Thurs. 11:30am-4pm and 4:15pm-9pm, Fri.-Sat. 11:30am-4pm and 4:15pm-10pm, Sun. 10:30am-4pm and 4:15pm-9pm, $7-35) offers an ever-changing menu of fresh seafood, dictated by what is available and fresh on that day. They serve lunch and dinner daily and have a happy hour and a kids' menu. The restaurant is on a commercial fishing harbor and is known for having great views of the harbor and Assateague Island. The owners describe the style of food offered as "globally influenced seasonal cuisine," which allows them to be creative in their daily menu offerings. Local seafood is prominently featured on the menu, and they also serve organic produce and natural dairy and meat products. Don't let the plain exterior fool you; the inside of this restaurant is hip and comfortable and has large windows. The large bar is the primary internal feature, with seating on three sides. The full menu can be ordered at the bar, at pub-style tables, or at regular dining tables. The clientele is a good mix of vacationers and locals, and the owners are extremely friendly.

For great local crab cakes visit the **Crabcake Factory** (12000 Coastal Hwy., 410/250-4900, www.crabcakefactoryonline.com, Mon.-Fri. 11:30am-close, Sat.-Sun. 9am-close). They specialize in local seafood, including their signature crab cakes, peel-and-eat shrimp, and crab pizza. They are also known for their breakfasts and Bloody Marys. Breakfast is served weekends at the original Ocean City location, and a second location in Fenwick Island (37314 Lighthouse Rd., 302/988-5000, Sun.-Thur. 9am-9pm, Fri.-Sat. 9am-10pm) serves breakfast daily and has great views of the bay. There is also a third location (11805 Coastal Hwy., 410/874-0101, Fri. 3pm-close, Sat.-Sun. 11am-close). If you are interested in taking some "vacation"

home with you, they will gladly ship their crab cakes.

Doughnuts

The Fractured Prune (127th St. and Coastal Hwy., 410/250-4400, www.fracturedprune.com) is a well-known doughnut shop that was featured on the Food Network's *Unwrapped*. It is hidden in the North Bay Shopping Center near Ledo Pizza. The specialty is hot-dipped, made-to-order doughnuts, and they encourage you to create your own. Guests can select from multiple glazes and toppings to create their dream doughnut. Standard Fractured Prune flavors include interesting names such as "Black Forest" and "Sand." This small shop turns out 840 yummy cake doughnuts each hour and has become an icon at the beach. The shop doesn't offer prune toppings; it was named after a lady named Prunella, who lived in Ocean City in the early 1900s and traveled around competing against men in different sports. She was always on crutches from getting hurt, so the shop is named the Fractured Prune after her. There are seven additional locations, including two on the boardwalk.

Classic Beach Food

The beach and ice cream go hand in hand. Family owned and run **Dumser's Dairyland** (www.dumsersdairyland.com) is an Ocean City icon for ice cream. Established in 1939, the shop makes fresh ice cream daily and now has seven locations. Their main location on 123rd Street (12305 Coastal Hwy., 410/250-5543, open daily at 8am, closing time varies, $4-15) serves a full breakfast menu, lunch, and dinner. Their 49th Street location (4901 Coastal Hwy., 410/524-1588, open daily at 11am, closing time varies by season) serves lunch and dinner. Their menu is everything you'd expect at this classic beach venue: seafood baskets, french fries, wings, fried chicken, and a few salads. Five additional locations serve only ice

1: lobster roll at The Shark on the Harbor in Ocean City **2:** Dumser's Dairyland

cream and typically offer around 15 flavors, sundaes, milkshakes, and floats. Three are stands on the boardwalk (2 S. Atlantic Ave., 410/289-3449; boardwalk and Wicomico St.; 410/289-3236, and 601 S. Atlantic Ave., 410/289-0934) with hours that vary by season but are generally open until around 11:30pm in the summer with shorter hours in the off-season. Two additional locations (501 S. Philadelphia Ave., 410/289-1192, and 12702 Ocean Gateway, 410/213-7106) are stands with a few outdoor benches/tables.

Another longtime favorite is **Thrasher's French Fries** (410/289-7232, www. thrashersfries.com, under $5). They've been making french fries on the boardwalk since 1929. With three locations in Ocean City—at the pier, 2nd Street and the boardwalk, and 8th Street and the boardwalk—the aroma of Thrasher's is one of the defining smells of the boardwalk.

Dolle's (500 S. Boardwalk at Wicomico St., 410/289-6000, www.dolles.com, Sun.-Thurs. 10am-6pm, Fri.-Sat. 10am-8pm) has been a staple on the boardwalk since 1910. They make mouthwatering saltwater taffy, fudge, popcorn, and other candy. They have three additional locations (6701 Coastal Hwy., 443/664-2909; 120th St. and Coastal Hwy., 410/524-0040; and 12720 Ocean Gateway, 443/664-7951).

Fisher's Popcorn (200 S. Boardwalk, 888/395-0335, www.fisherspopcorn.com, late May-Sept. daily 9am-11pm, Oct.-May hours vary) is another Ocean City icon. This family-owned and -operated business opened in 1937 and offers many flavors of mouthwatering popcorn. They are especially known for their caramel popcorn.

ACCOMMODATIONS
$100-200

A good value is the **Sea Hawk Motel** (12410 Coastal Hwy., 410/250-3191, www. seahawkmotel.com, $178-210). This older motel is a half block from the beach and offers 60 motel rooms and efficiencies with kitchens. Sleeping areas are separated from living areas.

The rooms are spacious and clean, and there's an outdoor pool.

The **King Charles Hotel** (1209 N. Baltimore Ave., 410/289-6141, www. kingcharleshotel.com, $119-209) is a small hotel a half block from the boardwalk. The 21 rooms are modest but competitively priced and clean. They are available with one queen bed or two double beds. There are small refrigerators and microwaves in the rooms. The hotel owners are very friendly and make it feel more like a bed-and-breakfast (minus the breakfast) than a hotel.

The **Atlantic Hotel** (401 S. Baltimore Ave., 410/289-9111, www.atlantichotelocmd. com, $160-270) was the first boardwalk hotel in Ocean City. It was built in 1875 and was considered one of the finest hotels on the East Coast. It burned down in a devastating fire in 1925 but was rebuilt the following year. Today, the hotel is still going strong and offers guests a central location on the boardwalk and a rooftop deck overlooking all the action and the ocean. They offer 100 rooms with one or two queen beds, and there are also two apartments for rent on a weekly basis. The rooms are small and cozy but clean. They feature dark wood furniture and small private bathrooms. There is an outdoor pool for guests. The staff is very friendly, and the location is ideal for those wanting to stay on the boardwalk.

$200-300

The ★ **Atlantic House Bed and Breakfast** (501 N. Baltimore Ave., 410/289-2333, www. atlantichouse.com, $190-270) is a diamond in the rough in a town packed with imposing hotels and motels. This little Victorian-style treasure built in the 1920s sits right on North Baltimore Street and is conspicuously different from the surrounding accommodations. The nine guest rooms (seven with private baths and two with semiprivate) are small since the home was originally a boardinghouse, but they are immaculate and tidy. Second-story room decor is mostly floral and wicker, while the third-floor rooms have paneling. The grounds are nicely maintained, and there is a wonderful front porch where guests can watch the bustle of activity on the busy street. The location is central to Ocean City attractions, just one street back from the boardwalk. The innkeepers are extremely warm and helpful and are a great asset to the establishment. Breakfast is delicious and plentiful with egg dishes, meats, fruit, and waffles. Snacks are also offered each afternoon. This bed-and-breakfast gets a lot of repeat business.

A modern, attractive hotel just a short walk from the boardwalk is the **Fairfield Inn & Suites Ocean City** (2501 Philadelphia Ave., 410/289-5000, www.marriott.com, $245-298). Amenities include free wireless Internet, minifridges, an indoor pool, fitness center, and a complimentary breakfast buffet. This is a good choice if you don't need to be oceanfront.

The **Spinnaker Motel** (18th St. and Baltimore Ave., 410/289-5444, www.ocmotels. com, $205-350) offers 100 clean guest units with kitchenettes within a short walk of the boardwalk (about a half block). Although not fancy, the rooms are reasonably priced and many have good views of the ocean. There is free parking on-site, an outdoor pool, and free wireless Internet. This hotel is a good value for families on a budget.

Over $300
The ★ **Hilton Ocean City Oceanfront Suites** (3200 N. Baltimore Ave., 410/289-6444, www.oceancityhilton.com, $611-731) is one of the nicest hotels in Ocean City. All 225 modern rooms are oversize, luxurious suites on the oceanfront and offer nicely sized balconies. Each suite has a kitchen. The hotel has both an indoor pool and a lovely outdoor pool overlooking the ocean with a swim-up bar. There is also a children's pool with a waterslide and a lazy river. The hotel is about five blocks from the boardwalk (10-minute walk). The hotel offers live music, movie nights, and children's activities. It is very family oriented. Parking right at the hotel is limited, but there

is additional parking across the street. This is a beautiful hotel with nice amenities, as it should be for the price.

The **Princess Royale Resort** (9100 Coast Hwy., 410/524-7777, www.princessroyale. com, $240-645) is an oceanfront hotel with 310 two-room suites and 30 condos. They offer pleasant rooms with kitchenettes, comfortable beds, and great views. Ask for a room with a good view; the staff will often do their best to accommodate the request. The hotel has a large indoor pool and scheduled activities such as movie night on the beach and live music by the outdoor bar. They offer free, convenient parking and an on-site restaurant (**Schooners**) that serves breakfast, lunch, and dinner.

Condos
There are many condos for rent in Ocean City. **Summer Beach Condominium** (410/289-0727, www.summerbeachoc.com), **Holiday Real Estate** (800/638-2102, www.holidayoc. com), and **Coldwell Banker** (800/633-1000, www.cbvacations.com) are management companies that offer weekly rentals.

Camping
Frontier Town (8428 Stephen Decatur Hwy., Berlin, 800/228-5590, www.frontiertown.com, Apr.-Nov., starting at $37) in nearby Berlin offers tent and RV facilities. They are open seasonally and only five minutes from Ocean City.

INFORMATION AND SERVICES
For additional information on Ocean City, visit www.ococean.com or stop by the **Ocean City Visitor Information Center** (12320 Ocean Gateway, 410/213-0144, daily 8:30am-4:30pm).

GETTING THERE
Ocean City is a 2.5-hour drive from Annapolis (109 miles). Most people arrive by car via US 50 or US 113 (the two primary routes to the area). **Greyhound** (12848 Ocean Gateway,

410/289-9307, www.greyhound.com) bus service is also available to Ocean City.

GETTING AROUND

Route 528 is the only major road running north-south in Ocean City. It is called Philadelphia Avenue at the southern end and the Coastal Highway everywhere else. Streets running east-west in Ocean City are numbered beginning in the south and run up to 146th before the Delaware border. Locations are normally explained by the terms "oceanside" (east of the Coastal Highway) or "bayside" (west of the Coastal Highway).

The **Boardwalk Tram** (410/289-5311, June-Aug. daily 11am-midnight, shorter hours spring and fall, $3 per ride or $6 unlimited daily pass) is a seasonal tram that runs the entire length of the boardwalk from the inlet to 27th Street. The tram stops at most locations along the boardwalk. It takes 30 minutes to ride the entire length of the boardwalk.

The **Ocean City Beach Bus** (410/723-2174, www.oceancitymd.gov, June-mid-Sept. 6am-3am, all-day pass adults $3, 65 and over $1.50, children 42 inches and under free) is a municipal bus service that runs 24/7 along the Coastal Highway. Free parking is available at the two bus transit centers: the South Division Street Transit Station and the 144th Street Transit Station.

Delaware Beaches

Just north of Ocean City, along the Coastal Highway, is the Delaware state line and some of the nicest beach resort areas in the mid-Atlantic. Three main areas—Bethany Beach, Rehoboth Beach, and Lewes—attract visitors year-round. They offer first-class restaurants, historic beach charm, and lovely accommodations in all price ranges. Although not as busy as their southern neighbor, they each offer their own attractions and have sights of historical interest.

BETHANY BEACH

Bethany Beach is located in southeastern Delaware, 15 miles north of Ocean City, Maryland. It is part of a 7-mile stretch of beach referred to as the "Quiet Resorts," along with South Bethany Beach and Fenwick Island. Bethany Beach is small and much lower-key than nearby Ocean City and Rehoboth Beach. It is mostly residential, and there is a small shopping area at its heart.

Since 1976, visitors to Bethany Beach have been greeted by **Chief Little Owl**, a 24-foot-tall totem pole that was donated to the town as part of a project by sculptor Peter Wolf Toth, who carved more than 50 wooden works of art in honor of famous Native Americans and gave one to every state. The current totem is actually the third version of the sculpture to stand in Bethany Beach. The first two were destroyed by decay. The current version was created in 2002 of red cedar and is expected to last 50-150 years.

Sights
BETHANY BEACH
The beach at **Bethany Beach** is wide, sandy, and family oriented. Although it would be a stretch to say it's empty during the season, it is mostly quiet at night and offers a relaxing atmosphere during the day. Visitors will need to pay to park May 15-September 15 (there are meters near the beach entrance on Garfield Pkwy.).

BETHANY BEACH BOARDWALK
The **Bethany Beach Boardwalk** is a pleasant family area with less fanfare than the boardwalk in nearby Ocean City. It is basically a nice walkway made of wooden planks. The boardwalk entrance is at the end of Garfield Parkway, and the boardwalk itself stretches between 2nd and Parkwood Streets. There is

plenty to do and see with shops, restaurants, and free concerts at the bandstand on weekends during the summer.

BETHANY BEACH NATURE CENTER

The **Bethany Beach Nature Center** (807 Garfield Pkwy., Rte. 26, 302/537-7680, www.inlandbays.org, Tues.-Fri. 10am-3pm, Sat. 10am-2pm, free, donations appreciated) offers interactive exhibits that enable visitors to explore the Inland Bays watershed and learn about local flora and fauna. It is housed in a beautiful cottage built around 1901. Nature trails on the 26-acre grounds take visitors through wetlands and forest. There is also a play area for children.

DISCOVERSEA SHIPWRECK MUSEUM

The **DiscoverSea Shipwreck Museum** (708 Coastal Hwy., Fenwick Island, 302/539-9366, www.discoversea.com, June-Aug. daily 11am-8pm, free, donations appreciated) is a dynamic museum that recovers and preserves the area's maritime history. Exhibits are centered on shipwreck artifacts dating back to the colonial era (gold, coins, cannons, personal items, even old rum). The museum is run by public donations and owner contributions. Exhibits change with the discovery and acquisition of new artifacts, but the average number of items on display is 10,000. Many additional items are rotated through exhibits around the world. Check the website for hours during the off-season. The museum is located above Sea Shell City.

Recreation and Entertainment

Delaware Seashore State Park (DE 1 between Bethany Beach and Dewey Beach, 302/227-2800, www.destateparks.com, $10) is to the north of Bethany Beach along the coast. The park of more than 2,800 acres covers a thin strip of land between the Atlantic and Rehoboth Bay. The primary attraction in the park is the beach itself—a six-mile-long beach lover's paradise—where visitors can swim and relax along the shore. There

are modern bathhouses with showers and changing rooms, and lifeguards are on duty during the day in the summer. There are also snack vendors and beach equipment rentals such as chairs, rafts, and umbrellas. Fishing is popular in the park and can be done in the surf in designated locations or from the banks of the Indian River Inlet. There is also a special-access pier for the elderly or people with disabilities.

Just north of the inlet on the beach in Delaware Seashore State Park is a designated surfing area. The shallow bays are also good areas for sailboarding and sailing. A boat ramp for nonmotorized craft is also available.

Holt's Landing State Park (Holt's Landing Rd., 302/227-2800, www.destateparks.com, $10) is on the southern shore of the Indian River Bay; take Route 26 West from Bethany Beach and turn right on County Road 346 to the park entrance. Clamming, fishing, and crabbing are possible in the park, along with facilities such as a picnic pavilion, playground, horseshoe pit, and ball fields. Two great kayaking trails start in the park. The first is a 10-mile paddle to the **Assawoman Wildlife Area** (allow five hours), and the second is to Millsboro, which is just under 10 miles.

Minigolf is a staple at the beach, and **Captain Jack's Pirate Golf** (21 N. Pennsylvania Ave., 302/539-1122, www.captainjackspirategolf.com, $8.50) is the place to go in Bethany Beach. It has eye-catching features such as a large skeleton pirate and pirate's ship, rock and water features, and palm trees. The course is well maintained and a fun place for the entire family. There's a small gift shop on-site.

If you're visiting the Saturday after Labor Day, check out the one-day **Annual Bethany Beach Boardwalk Arts Festival** (Bethany Beach Boardwalk, 302/539-2100, www.bethanybeachartsfestival.com). More than 100 artists exhibit their work on the boardwalk and surrounding streets. Local and national artists partake in this anticipated

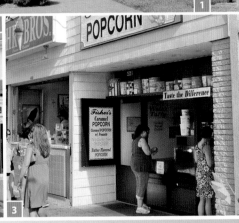

event that draws more than 7,500 visitors. Admission is free.

Food

★ **Off the Hook** (769 Garfield Pkwy., 302/829-1424, www.offthehookbethany. com, daily 11:30am-10pm, $9-35) offers excellent seafood in an off-the-beaten-path location. The seafood and the atmosphere are both fresh, with creative dishes and specials. They are known for their cioppino. The restaurant prides itself on supporting local farmers and anglers. They do not take reservations, so there can be a long wait time.

Delicious waterside dining can be found at ★ **Bluecoast Seafood Grill and Raw Bar** (30904 Coastal Hwy., 302/539-7111, www. bluecoastseafoodgrill.com, daily 5pm-10pm, $21-38). This popular restaurant serves beautifully prepared upscale local seafood. Their menu is carefully crafted and changes seasonally. They also offer an extensive wine list and terrific cocktails. If you're up for a calorie splurge, order the truffle-pecorino tots. They have indoor and outdoor seating.

A local favorite is the **Cottage Café Restaurant** (33034 Coastal Hwy., 302/539-8710, www.cottagecafe.com, Mon.-Thur. 11am-11pm, Fri.-Sat. 11am-12am, Sun. 9am-11pm, $10-29). This is a good family restaurant serving local seafood. The staff is kind and patient, and the menu is wide enough to satisfy most tastes. Menu selections include crab cakes, fried oysters, stuffed flounder, pot roast, and meat loaf. The food is not fancy, but it is consistent and reasonably priced.

Mexican food and trains may seem like an odd combination for the beach, but at **Salted Rim** (27 Atlantic Ave., 302/537-7373, www. saltedrimde.com, Sun.-Thurs. 11am-11pm, Fri.-Sat. 11am-1am, $7-23) you can get both—you can eat Mexican food on one of two train cars (or in their main restaurant). Although a little drive from the oceanfront, this lively restaurant offers good drinks and plentiful dishes with a smile. They also host movie-themed nights in their authentic train cars.

A fun place to bring your dog is **Fin's Ale House and Raw Bar** (33544 Market Pl., 302/539-3467, www.finsrawbar.com, Mon.-Thurs. 11am-9:30pm, Fri.-Sat. 11am-10pm, Sun. 10am-9:30pm, $8-31). They are part of a local chain and feature a large, pet-friendly patio (water bowls included) in addition to a modern yet beachy interior dining space. They have a large oyster menu plus soup, salads, sandwiches, and entrées of primarily seafood with a few other choices (burgers, chicken, and steak).

For fresh crepes, visit **Sunshine Crepes** (100 Garfield Pkwy., 302/537-1765, www. sunshinecrepes.com, summer daily 8am-2pm, under $10). This casual and affordable breakfast stop in downtown Bethany Beach by the boardwalk makes fresh savory and sweet crepes with a nice selection of fillings. You can even watch the kitchen staff at work. The atmosphere is not fancy, but the portions are large and the food is tasty. This is a nice alternative to regular bacon and eggs. If you like bananas, try the banana crepe. This is a wonderful local business offering something a little different coupled with friendly service.

Accommodations

Meris Gardens Bed & Breakfast (33309 Kent Ave., 302/752-4962, www. merisgardensbethany.com, $199-639) is a small bed-and-breakfast that used to be a motel. They offer 14 comfortable rooms and are located in a quiet area of Bethany Beach. All rooms have private bathrooms and they are dog friendly ($20 per dog per night). It is convenient to the beach (four blocks), and downtown Bethany Beach is within walking distance. Breakfast is included. This property offers simple, friendly accommodations with personal service.

The **Addy Sea** (99 Ocean View Pkwy., 302/539-3707, www.addysea.com, $240-420) is a renovated oceanfront Victorian home and guesthouse that is now an adults-only bed-and-breakfast. The home offers 13 guest

---

1: Bethany Beach Nature Center **2:** Off the Hook restaurant in Bethany Beach **3:** Fisher's Popcorn in Rehoboth Beach **4:** Rehoboth Beach Boardwalk

rooms and is furnished with antiques, tin ceilings, and original woodwork. The rooms are comfortable, the staff is friendly, and the location is wonderful. The breakfasts are also plentiful with good choices. Book a room with an ocean view for the best experience. Not all rooms have private baths, and Room 12 is the only one with a television.

The **Sea Colony Resort** (DE 1 and Westway Dr., 888/500-4261, www.seacolony.com, from $130) is a large and well-known resort just south of Bethany Beach with 2,200 condos, town houses, and single-family homes. Rentals are available through a number of management companies. Amenities include 24-hour security, tennis courts, fitness centers, a small shopping area, 12 pools (including 2 indoor), trails, picnic areas, and a playground. The beaches around Sea Colony are some of the busiest in Bethany Beach due to the large number of condos in the complex; however, the half-mile stretch of beach is for guests and visitors of the resort only, which does make it somewhat private. Units of different sizes are available for rent. Additional information can be obtained at www.wyndhamvacationrentals.com.

Information and Services

For additional information on Bethany Beach, visit www.townofbethanybeach.com or stop by the **Bethany-Fenwick area visitor information center** (302/539-2100, daily in season Mon.-Fri. 9am-5pm, Sat. 9am-3pm) on the Coastal Highway between Fenwick Island State Park and Lewes Street.

TOP EXPERIENCE

REHOBOTH BEACH

Rehoboth Beach is 14 miles north of Bethany Beach. It is the happy medium among the Maryland and Delaware beaches. It is larger and more commercial than Bethany Beach, yet smaller and less commercial than Ocean City.

Rehoboth Beach was founded in 1873 as a Methodist Episcopal Church beach camp. Today, the town is known as "the Nation's Summer Capital," since so many visitors come from Washington DC each year. The town is also noted for its eclectic shops, wonderful eateries, artistic appeal, and the large number of LGBT-owned businesses. Downtown Rehoboth Beach is one square mile and has more than 200 shops, galleries, and spas, 40 hotels and bed-and-breakfasts, and more than 100 restaurants.

Just south of Rehoboth is **Dewey Beach,** which is known as a party town for young adults during the summer months. The two towns share a beautiful strand of sandy white beach that continues to be the main attraction despite all the built-up distractions.

Dogs are not permitted to run loose on the beach in Rehoboth. They are prohibited from the beach and boardwalk 24 hours a day between May 1 and September 30, but they are allowed on the beach in Dewey prior to 9:30am and after 5:30pm (although they still must be leashed and have a Dewey Beach license). There is a strict leash law, and owners must pick up after their dogs.

Sights
★ REHOBOTH BEACH
    BOARDWALK

The easiest public access to the mile-long boardwalk in Rehoboth Beach is from Rehoboth Avenue. Less crowded than Ocean City, yet more lively than Bethany Beach, the boardwalk offers all the action you could want at the beach, including terrific views of the ocean, french fries, T-shirt shops, games, candy stores, and entertainment. The boardwalk is wide and clean and stretches from Penn Street at the south end to Virginia Avenue at the north end. Parking is available on Rehoboth Avenue, and parking meters are enforced during the summer months 10am-10pm. The meters take quarters, credit cards, and the Parkmobile app (www.parkmobile.com). Change machines are available at the bandstand on Rehoboth Avenue.

Rehoboth Beach

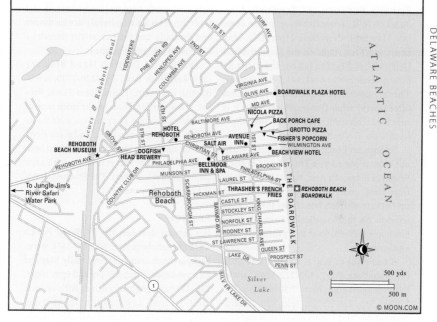

© MOON.COM

REHOBOTH BEACH MUSEUM

The **Rehoboth Beach Museum** (511 Rehoboth Ave., 302/227-7310, www.rehobothbeachmuseum.org, Labor Day-Memorial Day Mon.-Fri. 10am-4pm, Sat.-Sun. 11am-3pm, free, donations appreciated) is a small museum with displays portraying the history of Rehoboth Beach. Visitors can see vintage bathing suits, postcards, and classic boardwalk rides and games and learn about the early beach hotels in town.

Recreation

Jungle Jim's River Safari Water Park (36944 Country Club Rd., 302/227-8444, www.funatjunglejims.com, $38) is Delaware's largest water park and also offers minigolf, batting cages, and bumper boats. **Funland at Rehoboth Beach** (6 Delaware Ave., 302/227-1921, www.funlandrehoboth.com) is a tradition on the boardwalk dating back to the early 1960s. It offers 21 rides and operates on a ticketed basis ($0.40 per ticket).

Entertainment and Events

The **Clear Space Theatre Company** (20 Baltimore Ave., 302/227-2270, www.clearspacetheatre.org) is a year-round professional theatrical company that presents musical and dramatic productions.

The **Rehoboth Beach Jazz Festival** (www.rehobothjazz.com) is an annual event that takes place for four days in October. There are three stages throughout the town for performances as well as additional venues in local establishments.

Shopping

The first thing shoppers should know is that there is no sales tax in Delaware. The second thing is that every outlet store you can think of may be found in a large shopping area on Route 1 between Rehoboth and Lewes, at **Tanger Outlets** (36470 Seaside Outlet Dr., 302/226-9223, www.tangeroutlet.com).

Food

CLASSIC BEACH FOOD

Fisher's Popcorn (48 Rehoboth Ave., 302/227-2691, www.fishers-popcorn.com, late May-Sept. daily 9am-11pm, Oct.-May hours vary) is a staple on the Maryland and Delaware beaches. You can buy the addicting little morsels by the bucket (0.5-6.5 gallons). They are known for the caramel popcorn but offer several other flavors. Please note: It is easy to eat this until you feel sick. Stopping is hard to do. You've been warned.

Perhaps no beach trip is complete without at least one stop at **Thrasher's French Fries** (26 Rehoboth Ave., 302/227-7366, daily from 11am, under $10). This local icon serves up buckets of fresh fries from the walk-up window on the boardwalk. Even die-hard ketchup lovers will want to try them with salt and vinegar.

A fun place to stop is **Kaisy's Delights** (70 Rehoboth Ave., 302/212-5360, www.kaisysdelights.com, Mon. 7:30am-3pm, Fri. 7:30am-5pm, Sat. 7:30am-6pm, Sun. 7:30am-5pm, under $10) for an Austrian Kaisy (actually *Kaiserschmarrn*, a treat made of sweet custardy dough with your choice of toppings such as ice cream or fruit sauce). Their delicious samples may lure you into a sweet Kaisy or even a breakfast Kaisy (they are available with eggs, sausage, and bacon). The coffee is also good. They're open all year.

AMERICAN

★ **Salt Air** (50 Wilmington Ave., 302/227-3744, www.saltairrestaurant.com, Sun. and Wed.-Thurs. 5pm-9pm, Fri.-Sat. 5pm-10pm, $16-35) is a busy, upscale farm-to-fork restaurant with a good vibe. Patrons can watch the skilled kitchen at work and get a text message when their table is ready. The cuisine is American, and there are a lot of creative seafood dishes. Start with the crab deviled eggs; a plate of four can be a bite each for a small group. The menu is full of little surprises (but changes often) such as boardwalk fries, oven-roasted honey sriracha wings, and seafood stew. They also serve incredible salads. The

kids' menu is worth mentioning, because it strays from the usual chicken tenders to provide small portions of real food, like steak and fresh fish. This is a wonderful place for dinner and cocktails, and their creativity includes a long list of delightful martinis.

The original **Dogfish Head Brewery** (320 Rehoboth Ave., 302/226-2739, www.dogfish.com, Sun.-Thurs. 11am-11pm, Fri.-Sat. 11am-1am, $6-26) is on the main strip of Rehoboth Avenue. They serve a wide menu of fish, burgers, sandwiches, and pizza along with an ample selection of their delicious beer. Seasonal beers are always rotating, with a few staples available all year. The SeaQuench Ale is a personal favorite.

FRENCH

For several decades, the ★ **Back Porch Café** (59 Rehoboth Ave., 302/227-3674, www.backporchcafe.com, June-Sept. daily, May and Oct. weekends, 11am-5:30pm and 6pm-10pm, $36-47) has delighted visitors with upscale creations from its award-winning chef and owner. The cuisine is unmistakably French, with many wonderful sauces, root veggies, and some entrées such as rabbit, but they also look to seasonal ingredients for inspiration. Start with the seafood ravioli, a sure crowd-pleaser, and then choose carefully from the interesting array of main courses. If the wild king salmon is on the menu, it is one outstanding choice. The interior is cozy with a bar and some outdoor seating. This restaurant is open for lunch, brunch, and dinner in the summer but is closed in the off-season. Reservations are encouraged. There is no kids' menu.

ITALIAN

Lupo Italian Kitchen (247 Rehoboth Ave., 302/226-2240, www.lupoitaliankitchen.com, Sun.-Thurs. 5pm-9pm, Fri.-Sat. 5pm-10pm, $18-27) is a beautiful little restaurant on the first floor of the Hotel Rehoboth on Rehoboth Avenue. It is light and airy inside and offers a menu of salads, homemade pasta, seafood, and delightful house classics such as chicken parmesan. Their fried calamari is perhaps the best in the area. They have shorter hours in the off-season and different off-season specials each night of the week. They also have a kids' menu.

Touch of Italy (19724 Coastal Hwy., 302/227-3900, www.touchofitaly.com, Sun.-Thurs. 10am-9pm, Fri.-Sat. 10am-10pm, $10-28) is a dine-in and carryout Italian deli focused on specialty meats, cheeses, and Italian pastries. They have a huge menu, and all sandwiches are made to order.

It would be almost negligent not to mention the classic Rehoboth Beach pizza joint, **Nicola Pizza** (8 N. 1st St., 302/227-6211, www.nicolapizza.com, daily 11am-midnight, $6-28). This pizzeria has been a staple in town since 1971, and for many it is *the* beachy place to bring the family. The wood floors and booths are a reminder of the restaurant's long history. Wait times in the summer can easily be an hour or more. The most popular dish is the "Nic-o-Boli," which is their name for *stromboli* (a kind of rolled turnover)—they can sell up to 2,000 in one night. This is worth a try if you've never had one, although the regular pizza is also a good choice. There's a second location at 71 Rehoboth Avenue.

Another classic pizza place in Rehoboth is **Grotto Pizza** (36 Rehoboth Ave., 302/227-3278, www.grottopizza.com, Sun.-Thurs. 11am-9pm, Fri.-Sat. 11am-11pm, under $15). This well-recognized restaurant has been around since 1960 and has three locations in Rehoboth Beach. The other two locations are on the boardwalk at 15 Boardwalk and Baltimore Avenue and at 17 Surf Avenue. They offer dine-in, carryout, and walk-up pizza.

Accommodations

The **Avenue Inn & Spa** (33 Wilmington Ave., 302/226-2900, www.avenueinn.com, $309-444) is an independently owned hotel one block from the beach. There are 60 guest rooms with many amenities, such as full breakfast, complimentary wine and cheese, evening cookies, a day spa, indoor heated pool, fitness room, sauna, beach chairs, beach shuttle, and free parking.

The **Bellmoor Inn and Spa** (6 Christian St., 302/227-5800, www.thebellmoor.com, $419-679) is a comfortable inn about three blocks from the beach. They offer 56 guest rooms and 22 suites. There are two pools on-site and an enclosed hot tub. Breakfast is served daily (with omelets on the weekends), and the staff is friendly and helpful.

The ★ **Boardwalk Plaza Hotel** (2 Olive Ave., 302/227-7169, www.boardwalkplaza. com, $329-632) is an elegant, Victorian-style oceanfront hotel right on the boardwalk. The hotel is furnished with antiques and antique-style furniture and offers oceanfront rooms with deluxe amenities. The hotel is friendly to children (and even offers special events for them such as craft time) but also has special amenities and areas for adults only (including a rooftop hot tub). The 84 guest rooms are comfortable, clean, and warmly decorated. The staff is friendly and goes out of its way to make visitors feel at home. There's also a restaurant on-site that offers water-view dining, a cozy bar, and a boardwalk patio.

A great choice for a clean, affordable, welcoming stay near the boardwalk is the **Beach View Hotel** (6 Wilmington Ave., 302/227-2999, www.rehobothbeachview.com, $288-329). This small hotel offers ocean-view rooms with private balconies and poolside rooms with no balconies. Breakfast and evening cookies are included. This hotel is a good value in a convenient location.

Information and Services

For additional information on Rehoboth Beach, visit www.cityofrehoboth.com and www.rehobothboardwalk.com, or stop by the **Rehoboth Beach-Dewey Beach Chamber of Commerce and Visitors Center** (501 Rehoboth Ave., 302/227-2233, year-round Mon.-Fri. 9am-5pm, Sat.-Sun. 9am-1pm).

LEWES

Lewes is seven miles north of Rehoboth and can be summed up in one word: charming. This quaint little town near the beach is a relaxing alternative to the busier beaches along the Delaware and Maryland shore. Lewes is also known as the "first town in the first state," since it was the site of the first European settlement in Delaware, founded in 1631. The town has an upscale beach feel to it and draws visitors of many age groups who come to relax, drink wine, eat good food, and shop.

Sights

★ HISTORIC LEWES

The historic downtown area of Lewes is on the harbor, just a short distance from the Atlantic. The town's main thoroughfare, 2nd Street, offers wonderful dining and shopping with a cozy, friendly feel. The downtown area is lovely all year round. It truly is one of the prettiest spots on the mid-Atlantic coast, with its historic homes (some dating back to the 17th century), friendly atmosphere, and tidy, well-kept streets. Boutique stores and independently owned restaurants line the sidewalks, and the local residents are friendly and welcoming to tourists.

Shipcarpenter Square (www. shipcarpentersquare.com) is a community of delicately and accurately preserved and restored 18th- and 19th-century homes in the historic district. The homes in Shipcarpenter Square are mostly colonial farmhouses built in the late 1700s-late 1800s in other parts of Sussex County and moved to the site in the early 1980s. Other relocated buildings include three barns, a schoolhouse, an inn, a log home, a lifesaving station, a lighthouse, a market, and two Victorian houses.

The Shipcarpenter Square community stretches from 3rd and 4th Streets on the east and west side to Burton and Park Streets on the north and south sides, respectively. Parking access is provided to homeowners in this area. Pedestrians can enter a foot-traffic-only area from Park Street and two areas on the north and south edges of the common greens that are located in the heart of the community.

ZWAANENDAEL MUSEUM

The **Zwaanendael Museum** (102 Kings Hwy., 302/645-1148, http://history.delaware. gov, Apr.-Oct. Tues.-Sat. 10am-4:30pm, Sun. 1:30pm-4:30pm, Nov.-Mar. Wed.-Sat. 10am-4:30pm, free, donations appreciated) is an interesting-looking building (a replica of the Town Hall of Hoorn in the Netherlands) that features Dutch elements from the 17th century such as terra-cotta roof tiles, decorated shutters, a stepped facade gable, and stonework. The museum takes visitors through the history of Lewes as the state's first European settlement (by the Dutch) in 1631 and offers exhibits on the attack on Lewes by the British during the War of 1812, the Delaware coastline, and the Cape Henlopen Lighthouse. The museum also includes a maritime and military history of the town.

CAPE MAY-LEWES FERRY

The **Cape May-Lewes Ferry** (43 Cape Henlopen Dr., 800/643-3779, www. capemaylewesferry.com, car and driver one-way $35, round-trip $65, extra passenger or pedestrian one-way $10, children 6-13 $5, seniors $8, military $8, children under 6 free) docks on Cape Henelopen Drive and makes daily 17-mile, 85-minute trips across Delaware Bay to Cape May, New Jersey. Auto and foot passengers are welcome and bicycles pay the foot-passenger fee. Ferry schedules vary throughout the season so check their website for current departures.

Recreation

Cape Henlopen State Park (15099 Cape Henlopen Dr., 302/645-8983, www.

1: Zwaanendael Museum 2: apple and moon cheese guacamole at Agave Mexican Restaurant and Tequila Bar 3: the wharf in Lewes

destateparks.com, $10) covers five miles of shoreline at the mouth of Delaware Bay where it meets the Atlantic. It has a long military and shipping history. A storm in 1920 took out the lighthouse that used to guide ships through the bay, but breakwater barriers still provide a safe harbor during storms and rough water.

A military base was established at the cape in 1941, and bunkers were hidden among the dunes for protection. Observation towers built of cement, which are still standing, were also put in place along the shore to search for enemy ships. The park was created in 1964. Today the park provides many acres of seaside habitat. There's a nature center, hiking, fishing, swimming, a picnic pavilion, fishing pier, and camping in the park. The two swimming beaches are watched over by lifeguards in the summer.

There are several companies offering fishing supplies and charters in Lewes, including **Katydid Charters** (499 Anglers Rd., 302/858-7783 or 302/645-8688, www.katydidsportfishing.com, starting at $400 for 10 people), **Angler's Fishing Center** (213 Anglers Rd., 302/644-4533, www.anglersfishingcenter.com, starting at $35), and **First Light Charters** (907 Pilottown Rd., 302/853-5717, www.firstlightcharters.net, starting at $275).

Sightseeing cruises are also available at the **Fisherman's Wharf** (107 Anglers Rd., 302/645-8862, www.fishlewes.com, $34-40). They offer two- and three-hour dolphin-watching cruises and a sunset cruise each evening during the summer from the wharf docks. The trip goes down the canal and out to the ocean and then turns around near the ferry terminal.

Dogfish Head Brewery (302/745-2925, www.dogfish.com, $65) offers a 3-hour "Pints and Paddles" tour with **Quest Kayak** (www.questkayak.com) May-October. This kayaking outing for beer enthusiasts is a unique out-and-back paddle on the Broadkill River in the McCabe Nature Preserve (a Nature Conservancy area), followed by a tour of the Dogfish Head Brewery (including samples for those over 21).

Shopping

The primary shopping district in historic Lewes is on 2nd Street, off Savannah Street. Upscale boutiques, houseware shops, and even a wonderful store for dogs (**P.U.P.S. of Lewes**, 117 2nd St.) line the manicured street. Ice-cream shops and other snack shops offer a nice break from sightseeing or shopping.

Food

The ★ **Agave Mexican Restaurant and Tequila Bar** (137 2nd St., 302/645-1232, www.agavelewes.com, Sun.-Thurs. noon-8:45pm, Fri.-Sat. noon-9:45pm, $7-26) is a funky, upscale, sought-after Mexican dining spot that Laura Bush even stopped in one evening unannounced to sample the authentic cuisine. All the food is delicious, but they do a particularly good job with their mole, shrimp and garlic guacamole, and fish tacos. For something a little different, try the apple and moon cheese guacamole. Brightly painted glasses adorn patrons' tables and hold three sizes of margaritas (they have more than 100 types of tequila). The atmosphere is warm, the service is attentive and friendly, and the clientele is lively. The only downside to this fabulous little gem is the long wait time for a table (sometimes as much as two hours or more). Plan a late lunch or early dinner to get a jump on the competition. A second location is rumored to be opening in Rehoboth Beach in 2020.

For a great view, **Gilligan's Restaurant and Bar** (134 Market St., 302/644-7230, www.gilliganslewes.com, Wed.-Sat. 11am-9pm, Sun. 11am-8pm, $9-32) is the place to go. Enjoy alfresco dining on their canal front deck or order one of their specialty drinks in their lively bar. They are known for their large (nearly tennis-ball-size), flash-fried crab cakes, with virtually no detectable filler, but their menu includes other good seafood choices (scallops, salmon, and shrimp), rib eye, sandwiches, salads, and great daily specials. The staff is friendly, the decor is modern, and the wine pours are generous.

Pizza, wine, beer, and dessert: That's what **Half Full** (125 2nd St., 302/645-8877, www.halffulllewes.com, Wed.-Fri. opens at 4pm, Sat.-Sun. opens at noon, $7-15) serves up in outstanding style. Their 8-by-12-inch rectangular pizza can be ordered from standard selections or a mix and match of specialty toppings such as apples, pine nuts, brisket, and *soppressata* (Italian dried salami). They also serve soup and salads.

For good seafood in a lively pub atmosphere, dine at **Striper Bites** (107 Savannah Rd., 302/645-4657, www.striperbites.com, Mon.-Sat. from 11:30am, $10-32). They offer casual dining indoors or on a patio. The seafood choices are excellent, and the service is friendly and usually prompt. The decor is wood furnishings and things from the sea. This is a go-to place for many locals. They don't take reservations, and on a busy night it can be quite loud indoors, but for the most part it offers a pleasant dining experience and delicious food.

Crooked Hammock Brewery (36707 Crooked Hammock Way, 302/644-7837, www.crookedhammockbrewery.com, Sun.-Thurs. 11am-11pm, Fri.-Sat. 11am-1am, $8-22) is a fun brewery that offers an energetic atmosphere and a large outdoor space. They have a good selection of craft beers and a menu of casual appetizers, salads, sandwiches, and main dishes such as sweet-tea fried chicken, ribs, crab cakes, and salmon.

Accommodations

INNS AND HOTELS

★ **The Inn at Canal Square** (122 Market St., 302/644-3377, www.theinnatcanalsquare.com, $250-625) is a pretty, canal-front inn in the heart of Lewes. The inn has 22 rooms and three VIP suites and can accommodate short- or long-term stays. Many of the rooms have water views and balconies, and the suites offer two bedrooms, full kitchens, washers and dryers, fireplaces, screened porches, and decks. The grounds are adorned with lavish plantings, and fresh flowers are brought into the common areas weekly. Special packages that include birding and biking are available. Breakfast is included with your stay, and the friendly staff can assist with recommending the perfect restaurant for lunch and dinner. The inn is convenient to all the shops and dining options on 2nd Street, and it provides free parking and wireless Internet.

The **Hotel Blue** (110 Anglers Rd.,

The Inn at Canal Square

302/645-4880, www.hotelblue.info, $264-349) is a comfortable, adults-only boutique hotel with individually decorated rooms. Each has unique features such as a lighted koi pond and curved windows. Fireplaces, private balconies, and pillow-top mattresses are standard. There is also a beautiful rooftop pool and lounge area and a fitness room.

BED-AND-BREAKFASTS

There are several wonderful bed-and-breakfasts in Lewes near the historic district. Most have minimum night stays during the season, some do not allow small children, and some do not take credit cards, so be sure to ask about these things when you make your reservation if they are important to you.

The **Savannah Inn** (330 Savannah Rd., 302/645-0330, www.savannahinnlewes.com, $245-340) is a lovely, turn-of-the-20th-century brick home that was remodeled and now offers six contemporary guest rooms with modern bathrooms. The owners are very personable and take pride in their establishment, which goes a long way in making guests feel welcome. The inn is very clean, and the decor is airy and inviting. It is an easy walk to the historic downtown area and the waterfront. The inn is a family-run business, from the reservations to the kitchen. It is an adults-only inn.

The **John Penrose Virden House** (217 2nd St., 302/644-0217, www.virdenhouse.com, $230-260) is a charming, green-colored 19th-century Victorian bed-and-breakfast centrally located on 2nd Street. The three guest rooms are well appointed with antiques and offer beach equipment such as towels and chairs. The hosts do a lovely job of making visitors feel welcome and greet guests with fresh fruit and flowers in their rooms. They also serve a scrumptious homemade breakfast to remember and hold a cocktail hour with snacks and beverages. Bicycles are also available for guests. They do not accept credit cards, only cash or checks. This is also an adults-only establishment.

The **Blue Water House** (407 E. Market St., 302/645-7832, www.lewes-beach.com, $185-220) is a bed-and-breakfast a short walk from the beach and geared toward sandy fun. It offers slightly funky decor with bright colors. There are nine guest rooms, each with a private bathroom. The owner pays attention to every last detail and goes above and beyond to make guests feel welcome and to keep the house immaculate. Guests are offered many beach amenities, such as towels, beach chairs, sunscreen, umbrellas, cold water, and bicycles. Children are welcome, and the house is equipped with games and books.

Information and Services

For additional information on Lewes, visit www.lewes.com or stop by the **Lewes Visitors Center** (120 Kings Hwy., 302/645-8073, www.leweschamber.com, Mon.-Fri. 10am-4pm). It is housed in the historic Fisher-Martin House, a preserved 1730s home.

Frederick and Western Maryland

Settled by German immigrants in 1745, Frederick was founded as a trading outpost and a crossroads for goods making their way to outlying settlements and farms. Today, the city's wonderful boutiques, antiques shops, and nearby Civil War attractions provide plenty of options for visitors to explore. Although the surrounding area has seen an explosion of suburban housing, the historic city center has maintained its colonial-era charm.

Beyond Frederick is Western Maryland, the "mountain side" of the state, where the biggest decision of the day can be whether to go fishing or hiking. Deep Creek Lake in Garrett County offers beautiful private homes, inns, restaurants, and parks providing year-round recreation.

Western Maryland also hosted several well-known Civil War

Highlights

Look for ★ to find recommended sights, activities, dining, and lodging.

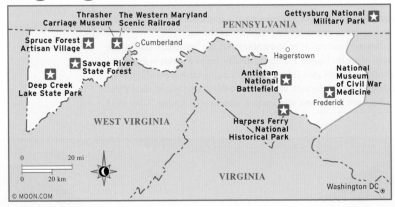

Thrasher Carriage Museum ★
The Western Maryland Scenic Railroad ★
○ Cumberland
Gettysburg National Military Park ★
PENNSYLVANIA
Spruce Forest Artisan Village ★
Savage River State Forest ★
○ Hagerstown
Deep Creek Lake State Park ★
Antietam National Battlefield ★
National Museum of Civil War Medicine ★
Frederick
WEST VIRGINIA
Harpers Ferry National Historical Park ★
0 20 mi
0 20 km
VIRGINIA
Washington DC ®
© MOON.COM

★ **National Museum of Civil War Medicine:** Learn little-known facts about medical practices during the Civil War (page 515).

★ **Gettysburg National Military Park:** Commemorate the historic three-day Battle of Gettysburg that took place on July 1-3, 1863 (page 524).

★ **Harpers Ferry National Historical Park:** Explore more than 25 historic buildings and 3,700 acres of protected land (page 529).

★ **Antietam National Battlefield:** The Battle of Antietam was the bloodiest single-day confrontation in American history. The battlefield serves as a reminder of the 23,000 casualties (page 535).

★ **The Western Maryland Scenic Railroad:** This fun 32-mile excursion offers passengers a tour of the beautiful countryside between Cumberland and Frostburg (page 538).

★ **Thrasher Carriage Museum:** This great little museum houses one of the country's best collections of horse-powered carriages (page 543).

★ **Spruce Forest Artisan Village:** A dozen cabins house working art studios where visitors can watch fine craftsmanship in progress (page 544).

★ **Savage River State Forest:** This 54,000-acre forest offers a wealth of outdoor recreation year-round (page 545).

★ **Deep Creek Lake State Park:** This beautiful park boasts one mile of shoreline and endless recreation (page 547).

battles, including the Battle of Antietam, and the Battle of Gettysburg was just over the Pennsylvania state line. Even just one day spent exploring these sites will give you a sense of the depth of history throughout this region. The historic town of Harpers Ferry, just over the West Virginia state line, is also included with this region. It was the location of abolitionist John Brown's 1859 raid on a national arsenal, an event that helped trigger the Civil War.

PLANNING YOUR TIME

How big a history buff you are will dictate how long it will take to explore Frederick and Western Maryland. Geographically, the area can be explored in 2-3 days, but the battlefields themselves can warrant a half day or even a full day of exploration for those with a keen interest in Civil War history. Major travel routes in the region include I-70 and Route 68.

If your time is limited, select a couple of key towns to explore, such as Frederick, Gettysburg, or Harpers Ferry. Gettysburg is a must-see from a historical perspective; Harpers Ferry is both historic and an outdoor-recreation haven; and Frederick offers a wonderful downtown and dining experience. All can be visited as day trips from Baltimore and Washington DC, although to thoroughly explore Gettysburg an overnight trip is recommended unless you have a lot of energy.

The far western reaches of the state are best traveled by car and can be explored in a long weekend. Many people make the popular Deep Creek Lake area their destination for a longer vacation, which allows time to enjoy lake activities and visit the many parks along and near its shores. Those traveling in winter can enjoy skiing and other cold-weather activities but should be advised to check weather conditions prior to their trip. Driving through the mountains can offer challenges in inclement weather.

Frederick

The city of Frederick was founded by German settlers in 1745. It was an important crossroads during the Civil War, and several major battles, including those at Antietam and Gettysburg, were fought nearby. Frederick was spared from burning during the Civil War when a hefty ransom ($200,000) was paid by the townspeople to the Confederates. It served as a hospital town for those wounded in the battles fought around the region.

By the turn of the 20th century, Frederick had begun making its living off of canning, knitting, and tanning while utilizing the railroad to deliver its goods to Baltimore.

Today, downtown Frederick is a lovely collection of shops, galleries, restaurants, and antiques stores. It is less than an hour's drive from Washington DC and is a popular spot for a day trip of antiques hunting. There is a 40-block historic district, and the town is the hub of arts, culture, and commerce in Frederick County.

Many of Frederick's attractions and restaurants are near the center of town. Park your car on one of the side streets and make your way around on foot. The layout of the town is a simple grid, so it's hard to get lost. The central intersection is Market Street and Patrick Street.

SIGHTS
★ National Museum of Civil War Medicine
The **National Museum of Civil War**

Frederick and Western Maryland

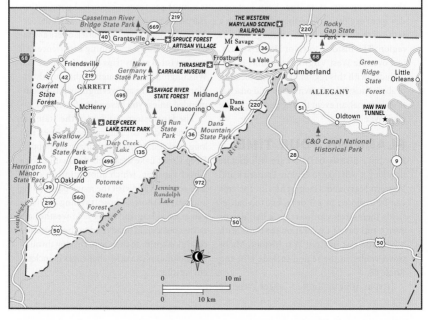

Medicine (48 E. Patrick St., 301/695-1864, www.civilwarmed.org, Mon.-Sat. 10am-5pm, Sun. 11am-5pm, adults $9.50, seniors over 60 $8.50, children under 9 free) is tucked away on Patrick Street in the historic area of Frederick. This interesting little museum started as a private collection. Exhibits cover many little-known facts about medicine and disease during the war (such as, two-thirds of the soldiers who died during the war succumbed to disease, not wounds, and doctors at the time had no knowledge of antiseptic practices or germ theory). It even explains the process used to embalm dead soldiers on the battlefield so they could be transported home. In fact, the historic building that the museum is housed in served as an embalming station following the Battle of Antietam in 1862. Information on veterinary medicine during the war and the development of large-animal infirmaries is also featured, as the armies were dependent on horses and mules. There are also many original artifacts such as medical tools

and even an operating table. The museum is not appropriate for small children, and kids under age 16 must be accompanied by an adult. Allow 1-2 hours to see the museum.

Schifferstadt Architectural Museum
The **Schifferstadt Architectural Museum** (1110 Rosemont Ave., 301/663-3885, www.fredericklandmarks.org, Sat.-Sun. 1pm-4pm, $5) is in one of the oldest homes in Frederick, dating back to 1758, and one of the best examples of early colonial German architecture in the nation. The simple stone home was built during the French and Indian War at a time when many settlers were forced to leave their farms due to raids. It is thought that Schifferstadt may have provided a safe refuge for entire families. The museum provides wonderful insight into the French and Indian War era and also shares information on early German settlers. The grounds also feature an award-winning garden.

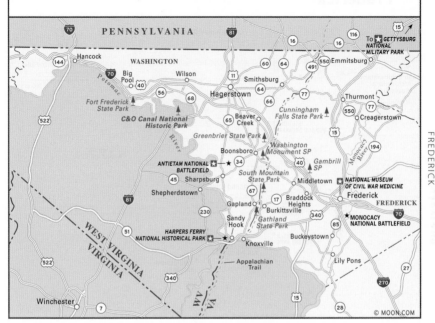

© MOON.COM

Monocacy National Battlefield

Southwest of the city is the **Monocacy National Battlefield** (5201 Urbana Pike, 301/662-3515, www.nps.gov/mono, daily sunrise-sunset, visitor center daily 9am-5pm, free), site of the "Battle That Saved Washington." The Civil War conflict that took place here in July 1864 is formally known as the **Battle of the Monocacy Junction,** so named since the fighting occurred on the banks of Monocacy River. It is often credited with saving the Federal capital because it was one of the last battles fought in Union territory as a Confederate army approached Washington DC and threatened to capture it.

Visitors should begin their exploration at the visitors center, which features interactive multimedia exhibits and maps of the battle. There is also a bookstore at the center. Information on driving and walking tours to five monuments located on the grounds can be picked up at the center.

Roads and Rails Museum

Children and train enthusiasts will likely enjoy the **Roads and Rails Museum** (200 N. East St., 301/624-5524, www.roadsnrails. com, Mon., Fri., and Sat. 10am-5pm, Sun. noon-5pm, adults $10, children $5, under 3 free), home to one of the largest interactive miniature model train exhibits in the United States.

RECREATION

A 15-minute drive north of Frederick on US 15 will take you to **Cunningham Falls State Park** (14039 Catoctin Hollow Rd., Thurmont, 301/271-7574, www.dnr.maryland. gov, $5). This wonderful, 6,000-acre park sits on Catoctin Mountain and offers swimming, hiking, a 43-acre lake, fishing, a boat launch ($5), canoeing, and a remarkable 78-foot waterfall. The park is made up of two primary areas. The Manor Area off US 15 (three miles south of Thurmont) includes an aviary, camping, and the historic Catoctin Iron Furnace,

Frederick

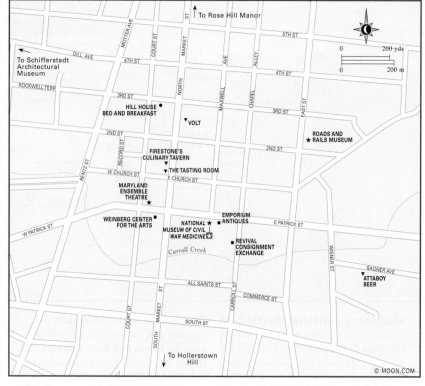

© MOON.COM

where iron was made for more than 100 years. The second section, the William Houck Area, is three miles west of Thurmont on Route 77 and encompasses the lake, falls, and a camping area.

Adjacent to Cunningham Falls State Park is a unit of the National Park Service called **Catoctin Mountain Park** (14707 Park Central Rd., Thurmont, 301/663-9388). The park has 25 miles of hiking trails, rental cabins, camping, and live demonstrations. The park is best known as the site of Camp David.

Northwest of Frederick is **Gambrill State Park** (8602 Gambrill Park Rd., 301/271-7574, www.dnr.maryland.gov, $5). This beautiful park off Route 40 in the Catoctin Mountains in Frederick County is known for its 16 miles

of trails suitable for hiking, mountain biking, and horseback riding. There are two primary areas in the park: Rock Run and High Knob, the latter with several stunning overlooks from its namesake 1,600-foot knob. The park offers camping, picnic areas, and a small fishing pond.

Frederick is home to the **Frederick Keys** minor league baseball team. This Class A affiliate of the Baltimore Orioles plays at **Harry Grove Stadium** (21 Stadium Dr., 301/662-0018, www.milb.com), which is a great family venue. Ticket prices are reasonable, and there's not a bad seat in the house. There are also many nice choices for food vendors.

1: Schifferstadt Architectural Museum in Frederick
2: National Museum of Civil War Medicine

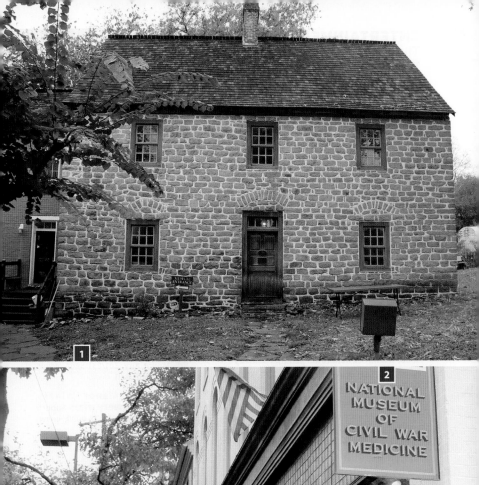

ENTERTAINMENT
Theater

Three downtown theaters can be found on Patrick Street. The **Maryland Ensemble Theatre (MET)** (31 W. Patrick St., 301/694-4744, www.marylandensemble.org) is a 100-seat black-box theater that puts on an eclectic schedule of thought-provoking plays. The **Weinberg Center for the Arts** (20 W. Patrick St., 301/600-2828, www.weinbergcenter.org) is a historic performing arts venue with a full schedule of performances throughout the year, including music, theater, dance, film, a speaker series, and other visual arts. **New Spire Arts** (15 W. Patrick St., 301/620-4458, www.newspirearts.org) offers a variety of performing arts experiences.

Brewery Tours

Brewery tours in Frederick include **Flying Dog Brewery** (4607 Wedgewood Blvd., 301/694-7899, www.flyingdog.com), **Rockwell Brewery** (880 N. East St., 301/732-4880, www.rockwellbrewery.com), **Attaboy Beer** (400 Sagner Ave., 301/338-8229, www.attaboybeer.com), and **Monocacy Brewing Co.** (1781 N. Market St., 240/457-4232, www.monocacybrewing.com). Tour times vary.

SHOPPING

Shopping is what brings many visitors to the historic district in Frederick. Many antiques shops line the streets, making the town a popular destination for treasure hunters. Some shops are even dog friendly (look for paw prints in store windows), including **Emporium Antiques** (112 E. Patrick St., 301/662-7099, www.emporiumantiques.com), which offers more than 100 dealers and is known for vintage furnishings and home decor items; and **Revival Consignment Exchange** (21 S. Carroll St., 301/662-8899, www.consignfrederick.com), a large home decor consignment store.

FOOD
American

Firestone's Culinary Tavern (105 N. Market St., 301/663-0330, www.firestonesrestaurant.com, Tues.-Sat. 11am-1:30am, Sun. 10am-1am, $10-44) is a fun place to meet friends or have a romantic dinner. The mix of wood, white tablecloths, and delicious gourmet menu items makes this a comfortable restaurant with an upscale feel. The dinner entrées include many steak and seafood choices such as pan-seared scallops, hanger steak, cowboy steak, and salmon. Their tavern menu offers a burger, sandwiches, and salads. Sunday brunch is lovely and includes traditional favorites such as eggs Benedict, as well as a great list of appetizers that can be combined into a meal.

★ **Volt** (228 N. Market St., 301/696-8658, www.voltrestaurant.com, Tues.-Fri.

The Frederick Wine Trail

Travel historic roads around Frederick County to sample wine, tour vineyards, and enjoy many events.

- **Catoctin Breeze Vineyard** (15010 Roddy Rd., Thurmont, 240/578-3831, www.catoctinbreeze.com)
- **Elk Run Vineyards** (15113 Liberty Rd., Mount Airy, 410/775-2513, www.elkrun.com)
- **Hidden Hills Farm and Vineyard** (7550 Green Valley Rd., Frederick, 301/660-8735, www.hiddenhillsfarmandvineyard.com)
- **Linganore Winecellars** (13601 Glissans Mill Rd., Mount Airy, 301/831-5889, www.linganorewines.com)
- **Links Bridge Vineyards** (8830 Old Links Bridge Rd., Thurmont, 301/466-8413, www.linksbridgevineyards.com)
- **Loew Vineyards** (14001 Liberty Rd., Mount Airy, 301/831-5464, www.loewvineyards.net)
- **Springfield Manor Winery Distillery Brewery** (11836 Auburn Rd., Thurmont, 301/271-0099, www.springfieldmanor.com)

5:30pm-9:30pm, Sat.-Sun. 11:30am-2pm and 5:30pm-9:30pm, $45-150) may be in a league of its own for Frederick dining. This creative, upscale, American-style restaurant is perhaps the crown jewel of the town. Volt is co-owned by celebrity chef Bryan Voltaggio. The menu changes frequently and includes seafood, pasta, meat, and game. The restaurant itself is a masterpiece, housed in a 19th-century brownstone mansion. The elegant yet contemporary dining room reflects the original Gilded Era building construction, while a glass-enclosed conservatory shows off the walled garden outside. In addition to their regular menu, they offer a 15-course tasting menu at the chef's counter (Table 21) for $150. Their dress code is business casual.

A popular modern American restaurant and wine bar is **The Tasting Room** (101 N. Market St., 240/379-7772, www.trrestaurant. com, Mon.-Thurs. 11am-10pm, Fri.-Sat. 11am-11pm, Sun. 11am-8pm, $30-60). This upscale establishment offers, as they say, a "cosmopolitan atmosphere" in the heart of downtown Frederick. The interior is nicely done with floor-to-ceiling windows that provide a view of the historic district. The food is consistently good, and the dishes are prepared with many local ingredients. Whether you have one of several delicious seafood selections, the rack of lamb, or a center cut of beef tenderloin, each is presented well and tastes equally remarkable. The service is highly professional, and the specialty drinks are imaginative. They also have a great wine list.

Scrumptious handcrafted sandwiches are the sought-after items at **a.k.a. Friscos** (4632 Wedgewood Blvd., 301/698-0018, www.akafriscos.com, Mon.-Thurs. 11am-7pm, Fri.-Sat. 11am-9pm, Sun. 11am-4pm, $4-12). This lively, friendly place is a little hard to find (it's located in an industrial park), but it's still the best place in town for a sandwich. Try the "exploded" potatoes, a house special. Portions are generous, so arrive hungry.

Irish

The **Shamrock** (7701 Fitzgerald Rd., Thurmont, 301/271-2912, www. shamrockrestaurant.com, Mon. 11am-9pm, Wed.-Thurs. 11am-9pm, Fri.-Sat. 11am-10pm, Sun. noon-9pm, $9-27), in nearby Thurmont, is one of those places you pass by again and again (it's right next to US 15) and think, "why is it always so crowded, even in the middle of the day?" This local landmark offers casual dining and a friendly atmosphere. They are known for their excellent fried shad roe, but also offer other traditional Irish fare. The restaurant is 15 miles north of Frederick and 15 miles south of Gettysburg, but is convenient if you're spending the afternoon at **Cunningham Falls State Park.**

ACCOMMODATIONS
$100-200

The **Fairfield Inn & Suites by Marriott** (5220 Westview Dr., 301/631-2000, www. marriott.com, $153-175) is a modern hotel with three floors and 105 guest rooms. The rooms are clean, the beds are comfortable, and a hot breakfast is included with your stay. They have a swimming pool and fitness center on-site as well as free wireless Internet. Ask for a room on one of the upper floors.

Hollerstown Hill (4 Clarke Pl., 301/228-3630, www.hollerstownhill.com, $139-149) is a quaint bed-and-breakfast with four cozy guest rooms. This late Victorian home was built around 1900. The house is amply decorated and showcases the owners' collectibles and antiques. It is located in a quiet neighborhood outside of the downtown area. Wireless Internet access is included.

Hill House Bed and Breakfast (12 W. 3rd St., 301/682-4111, www.hillhousefrederick. com, $145-195) is in a three-story Victorian town house in downtown Frederick. The location is perfect for easy access to shopping and restaurants (it is around the corner from Volt). The house was built in 1870 and offers four pleasant guest rooms. This is not a luxurious bed-and-breakfast, but if you are looking for convenience while visiting Frederick, the address is ideal.

$200-300

The perfect location for a relaxing weekend or romantic getaway is **The Inn at Stone Manor** (5820 Carroll Boyer Rd., Middletown, 301/271-0099, www.innatstonemanor.com, $200-225). The inn is on a 100-acre estate eight miles from downtown Frederick in Middletown, Maryland. The manor house is a beautifully maintained 18th-century stone mansion with a sprawling stone terrace and manicured grounds. The house was built in three sections, the oldest dating to 1750. Each of the six guest suites is unique and individually appointed with appropriate period antiques. The innkeepers are well known for being warm, helpful, and making each guest feel welcome and comfortable. Since each suite is different, guests can select the specific amenities they want including a private porch, fireplace, whirlpool tub, or a separate sitting room. All suites have private, modern bathrooms, and your stay includes a hearty, homemade breakfast served with fresh fruit.

CAMPING

Camping is available in **Cunningham Falls State Park** (14039 Catoctin Hollow Rd., Thurmont, 301/271-7574, www.dnr. maryland.gov) from April through October in the William Houck Area (three miles west of Thurmont on Route 77) and Manor Area (off US 15). They offer standard tent sites, campsites with electricity, camper cabins, four-person cabins, and six-person cabins. Reservations start at $27.49 per night plus reservation fee ($6.25) and daily use fee ($5). There are 180 sites total.

Camping is also available at **Gambrill State Park** (8602 Gambrill Park Rd., Frederick, 301/293-4170, www.dnr.maryland. gov) from June through August. They offer standard campsites, campsites with electricity, and camper cabins. Reservations start at $27.49 per night plus reservation fee ($6.25) and daily use fee ($5). There are 31 sites.

INFORMATION AND SERVICES

For additional information on Frederick, visit www.visitfrederick.org or stop by the **Frederick Visitor Center** (151 S. East St., 301/600-4047, daily 9am-5:30pm).

GETTING THERE

Most people travel to Frederick by car. Frederick is about an hour's drive northwest of Washington DC (49 miles) via I-270 and an hour's drive west of Baltimore (49 miles) via I-70. Bus service is available on **Greyhound** (100 S. East St., 301/663-3311, www.greyhound.com).

The **Frederick Municipal Airport (FDK)** (310 Aviation Way, 301/600-2201) is just east of the city. It is a general aviation airport with two runways.

Gettysburg, Pennsylvania

Gettysburg (10 miles from the Maryland state line) was the site of the famous Battle of Gettysburg. The town was founded in 1761 with a single tavern, but by 1860 it was home to 2,400 people and had a thriving community of tanneries, carriage manufacturing, shoemaking, and other industries. The town was etched into American history in July 1863, when the Confederate Army of Northern Virginia (consisting of 75,000 men led by General Robert E. Lee) and the Union's Army of the Potomac (consisting of 95,000 men led by Major General George G. Meade) converged there for a bloody three-day battle. The Battle of Gettysburg is considered the great conflict of the Civil War. With 51,000

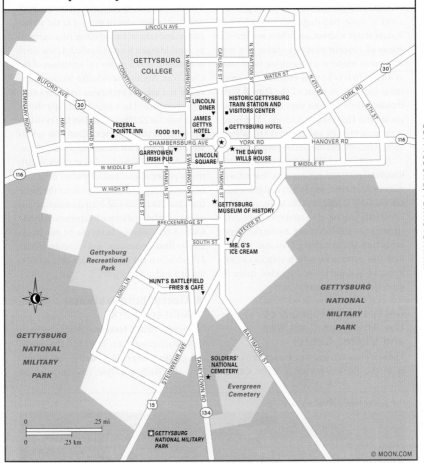

Gettysburg

casualties, more men fought, died, and were wounded in this battle than in any other land engagement in American history. The battle also signaled a turning point in the war when the North's eventual victory became clear.

Several months after the battle, on November 19 of the same year, President Abraham Lincoln gave his famous Gettysburg Address here at the dedication ceremony of the Soldiers' National Cemetery, established as a final resting place for Union soldiers killed in the battle.

SIGHTS

When visiting Gettysburg, you feel the history all around. Since the town itself was part of the battlefield, many homes and businesses standing during the battle still bear the scars of bullet holes and other artillery fire, such as the famous **Jennie Wade House** (548 Baltimore St., 717/334-4100, www.gettysburgbattlefieldtours.com, hours vary by season, adults $9, children 6-12 $6.75, under 5 free), which was the site of the only civilian death during the Battle of Gettysburg (the house is now a museum and gift shop). **Lincoln Square** is a focal point of the town, where several primary roads come together at a traffic circle. Buildings here have a Lincoln Square street address, and there is a life-size statue of Lincoln next to a statue of a man dressed in modern-day clothing (so it looks as if Lincoln is talking to a tourist) in a prominent location in front of the **David Wills House,** where Lincoln slept the night before giving the Gettysburg Address. The house is open to visitors and features six galleries about Lincoln and the Gettysburg Address.

The citizens of Gettysburg embrace their historical past and are eager to share it with visitors. Many historical tours and ghost tours are available throughout the town, and actors in period clothing are a common sight in the streets and establishments. By far the biggest attraction is Gettysburg National Military Park (the battlefield), which visitors can tour by car or foot, guided or unguided, to see the battlefield and cemetery.

Gettysburg Museum of the American Civil War and Visitor Center

The best place to begin your tour of Gettysburg is at the **Park Service Visitor Center** (1195 Baltimore Pike, 717/338-1243, www.gettysburgfoundation.org, daily 8am-6pm). Visitors can obtain information on the park and Gettysburg area in general at the visitor center, and take in a compelling film narrated by actor Morgan Freeman called *A New Birth of Freedom,* which covers the key issues of the Civil War. Another wonderful feature in the center is a massive cyclorama (circular painting accompanied by a sound-and-light show). Then tour the 22,000-square-foot **Gettysburg Museum of the American Civil War** (adults $9, children $7). This wonderfully detailed museum offers exhibits, Civil War relics, multimedia presentations, and interactive programs on Gettysburg. The museum covers the battle from start to finish and even provides details on the horrifying aftermath experienced by the town. A combination ticket can be purchased for the film, cyclorama, and museum (adults $15, children 6-12 $10, seniors over 65 $14, under 5 and military free).

★ Gettysburg National Military Park

The **Gettysburg National Military Park** (1195 Baltimore Pike, 717/334-1124, www.nps.gov/gett, Apr.-Oct. daily 6am-10pm, Nov.-Mar. daily 6am-7pm, free) is the site of

Gettysburg National Military Park

the three-day Battle of Gettysburg that took place July 1-3, 1863. Visitors can see nearly 1,400 monuments and historic markers on the 6,000-acre battlefield. Allow a minimum of four hours to explore the park. A self-guided auto tour (by map, no cost) and a self-guided audio tour (available for purchase at the visitors center bookstore, 717/334-2288) are great ways to tour the park. Field exhibits also help interpret significant sights throughout the battlefield.

Visitors are welcome to hike or bike through the park (dogs are welcome in outdoor areas on a leash), and designated trails are marked for this purpose. Park brochures are available at the visitor center with trail maps. Biking is allowed on paved paths only.

For those wanting a more personal tour experience, licensed tour guides are available to drive you in your car as you explore the battlefield. Tours are about two hours in duration. Reservations are required at least three days in advance. Personal tour fees start at $75 and go up depending on the number of people in your group. Bus tours are available during peak summer months (two hours, adults $35, children 6-12 $21, under 5 free). Reservations can be made ahead of time by calling 877/874-2478.

A unique way to see the park is on horseback. Tours are offered through **Hickory Hollow Farm** (717/253-6300, www.hickoryhollowfarm.com, starting at $75) in groups of up to 14 riders. Tours last a minimum of two hours.

The **Gettysburg Heritage Center** (297 Steinwehr Ave., 717/334-6245, www.gettysburgmuseum.com) features 3D photographs and displays that tell the story of the Battle of Gettysburg from the perspectives of civilians and soldiers. They also offer a 20-minute orientation movie.

Gettysburg National Cemetery

The historic **Gettysburg National Cemetery** (97 Taneytown Rd., 717/334-1124, www.nps.gov, Apr.-Oct. daily 6am-10pm, Nov.-Mar. daily 6am-7pm, free) is located in Gettysburg National Military Park. It is the burial site for thousands of Union soldiers who lost their lives in the Battle of Gettysburg. The cemetery was dedicated when President Lincoln gave his famous Gettysburg Address on November 19, 1863. Graves marked by plain rectangular slabs of gray granite are arranged by state. Each marker extends nine inches above the lawn. Officers and enlisted men are buried next to each other in an effort to reinforce the egalitarian practices of the Union army. Additional war veterans have been buried here since the late 1880s. Visitors can park in a lot across Taneytown Road from the cemetery. A walking tour brochure is available at the visitors center (within walking distance of the cemetery).

David Wills House

The **David Wills House** (8 Lincoln Sq., 717/334-2499, www.nps.gov/gett, hours vary by season, adults $7, children 6-12 $4, seniors over 65 and military $6, under 5 free) sits on the corner in Lincoln Square in downtown Gettysburg. The home weathered the famous battle in Gettysburg and soon after became the center of recovery efforts for the town. It is best known as the home where President Abraham Lincoln stayed the night before delivering the Gettysburg Address and the location where he finished writing the famous speech. The house is open to the public as a museum and contains exhibits on Gettysburg, the battle, and the creation of the Gettysburg National Cemetery. A life-size statue of Lincoln stands on the street just in front of the house.

Engraved bricks are fixed in the historic pathway in front of the house as a way for people to honor veterans, family, and friends. The bricks cost $125 each and become the property of the Borough of Gettysburg. Visit www.mainstreetgettysburg.org for details.

Gettysburg Lincoln Railroad Station

The **Gettysburg Lincoln Railroad Station** (35 Carlisle St., 717/338-1243, www. destinationgettysburg.com, Memorial Day-Labor Day daily 10am-5pm, shorter hours rest of year, free) was built in 1859 and was the western terminus of the Gettysburg Railroad line. It also served as a field hospital after the Battle of Gettysburg, processing some 15,000 wounded soldiers. During that time the station served as a symbol of hope, as it was the exit point for escaping the horror of the battle. President Lincoln arrived at the station on November 18, 1863, prior to delivering the Gettysburg Address. Visitors can see special exhibits throughout the year at this historic station, which is also available for event rentals. The station is listed in the National Register of Historic Places.

Gettysburg Museum of History

The **Gettysburg Museum of History** (219 Baltimore St., 717/337-2035, www. gettysburgmuseumofhistory.com, Sun. and Tues.-Wed. 11am-5pm, Thurs.-Sat. 11am-8pm, shorter hours in off-season, free, donations appreciated) is a great little museum stuffed full of interesting artifacts (4,000 of them). Easy to understand, easy to view, and covering history beyond the Civil War, this is a gem of a museum right on Baltimore Street. Exhibits include artifacts from the Civil War, World War I, World War II, presidencies, and pop culture (including Elvis Presley's X-rays, books, and personal toiletries).

Lincoln Train Museum

Near the site of Lincoln's Gettysburg Address is the **Lincoln Train Museum** (425 Steinwehr Ave., 717/334-5678, www.lincolntrain.com, Apr.-Oct. Sun.-Thurs. 10am-5pm, Fri.-Sat. 10am-7pm, shorter hours the rest of the year, adults $7, children 6-12 $4, military and seniors $5). This museum features a simulated interactive journey through American history with Abraham Lincoln. It also welcomes visitors aboard the full-size Lincoln Funeral Train Car and offers displays of working model trains.

Walking Tours

One of the most popular visitor activities in Gettysburg is taking a ghost walking tour. Several tour operators offer guided tours led by costumed interpreters/storytellers including **Gettysburg Ghost Tours** (47 Steinwehr Ave., 717/338-1818, www. gettysburgghosttours.com, starting at $10) and **Miss Betty's Ghosts** (443/789-9602, www.missbettysghostsingettysburg.com, $20).

Historical walking tours (not ghost related) are another great way to see the town. The **Gettysburg Convention and Visitors Bureau** (717/334-6274, www. destinationgettysburg.com) offers a free, self-guided walking tour that can be mailed out on request, downloaded from the website, or downloaded as a free app. The tour helps visitors understand life in the town prior to the Civil War, as well as during and after the war.

Gettysburg Wine & Fruit Trail

Wine and food enthusiasts may enjoy the **Gettysburg Wine & Fruit Trail** (www. gettysburgwineandfruittrail.com). This agritourism trail showcases farms, orchards, vineyards, cafés, and accommodations in the South Mountain region of Pennsylvania. Information on the trail and each location featured can be found on the trail website.

ENTERTAINMENT AND EVENTS

Ten miles northwest of Gettysburg is the South Mountain Fairgrounds and the site of the annual **National Apple Harvest Festival** (615 Narrows Rd., Biglerville, www. appleharvest.com, $10, seniors $9). This annual event features more than 300 arts and crafts vendors and is held over the first two weekends in October. There is also live entertainment, food, hayrides, and other activities. If the weather is nice, the crowds can be large, so expect to be sitting in traffic on your way in.

Civil War buffs won't want to miss the annual **Gettysburg National Civil War Battle Reenactment** (965 Pumping Station Rd., 717/338-1525, www.gettysburgreenactment. com, adults $29, children $16 for one day, adults $49, children $24 for two days, and adults $69, children $29 for three days), held in July in Gettysburg near Gettysburg National Military Park. This three-day event includes seven exciting battles, field demonstrations, live mortar-fire demonstrations, and living-history programs.

FOOD
American

The **Lincoln Diner** (32 Carlisle St., 717/334-3900, open 24 hours, $4-20) is everything you'd expect from a small-town diner. The breakfast is all-American with eggs, pancakes, omelets, and french toast (okay, almost all American). The food is homemade (even the pies), dependable, and fresh, and they accommodate special orders. They somehow manage to cook eggs perfectly every time. They also have a lunch/dinner menu. If you're lucky, you'll witness the exchange of a few friendly insults between the regulars and staff. Their milk shakes are a favorite.

A must for cheesesteak lovers is ★ **Hunt's Battlefield Fries & Café** (61 Steinwehr Ave., 717/334-4787, daily 8am-8pm in season, under $10). This family-owned café is a true diamond in the rough. Walking in, you'd never expect to eat one of the best cheesesteaks of your life. Seat yourself, order a cheesesteak, and then amuse yourself by reading the vintage posters tacked on every wall. The friendly owners may come chat with you (they are longtime residents of the area). Be careful when ordering the fries, as a large bucket will feed a town. This restaurant is small, so expect a wait in peak tourist season or opt for takeout.

Another good option for outstanding casual fare is **Food 101** (101 Chambersburg St., 717/334-6080, www.food101gettysburg. com, Sun.-Thurs. 11am-8pm, Fri.-Sat. 11am-9pm, $8-18). They serve a little of everything, including pizza, salads, sandwiches, and entrées such as pasta, chicken, salmon, and steak. Their pizza is a winner, as is their mac and cheese. This is a BYOB establishment.

Irish

Guinness and a Reuben: That's all you need to know about the **Garryowen Irish Pub** (126 Chambersburg St., 717/337-2719, www. garryowenirishpub.net, daily 11am-2am, $9-22). The most authentic Irish pub in town, Garryowen (aka "The GO") serves up great traditional Irish fare and equally impressive beer and whiskey selections. The prices are reasonable too. The staff and Irish owners are friendly, and the ambience is authentic and cozy. It's a great choice for celebrating St. Patrick's Day, but get there early! Beware if you order the fish-and-chips—it's gigantic.

Italian

Deliso Pizza (829 Biglerville Rd., 717/337-9500, Tues.-Thurs. 10:30am-9:30pm, Fri.-Sat. 10:30am-10:30pm, Sun. 11am-9pm, under $15) is a wonderful casual Italian restaurant with great pizza. The homemade sauce and bread are worth the short drive just north of town. The atmosphere inside is very casual, and they offer pizza by the slice and takeout. Place your order at the counter and find a table if you're eating in. Their pastas and subs are good too. Entrées come with a fresh salad and bread.

Snacks

Curb your sweet tooth at **Mr. G's Ice Cream** (404 Baltimore St., 717/334-7600, Sun.-Thurs. noon-9pm, Fri.-Sat. noon-10pm, under $5). They serve yummy homemade ice cream and also soft serve. There are many interesting flavors to choose from, and the building has a lot of character.

ACCOMMODATIONS

There are charming and historic hotels in Gettysburg that complement the historical nature of the town.

The **Gettysburg Hotel** (1 Lincoln Sq., 717/337-2000, www.hotelgettysburg.com, $170-369) is a charming historic property dating back to 1797. The hotel is a public landmark in Lincoln Square in downtown Gettysburg. It withstood the battle at Gettysburg and, nearly a century later, became the site of President Dwight D. Eisenhower's national operations center while he recovered from a heart attack suffered at his nearby farm. The hotel has undergone extensive renovations over the years and currently offers 119 guest rooms and suites. It is also a popular choice for wedding receptions and offers a banquet room, fitness room, restaurant, pub, rooftop swimming pool, business center, and high-speed Internet. The rooms are comfortable and charming, but not extravagant. Parking is available in a public garage just behind the hotel. The hotel is centrally located within walking distance of the battlefield, museums, shops, and restaurants. Make your last stop before bedtime the bar at One Lincoln, just off the reception area. They offer a large variety of pints and have a friendly staff, and a quick drink will help make the beds a little more comfortable.

The **James Gettys Hotel** (27 Chambersburg St., 717/337-1334, www. jamesgettyshotel.com, $159-259) offers 12 guest suites in a historic downtown hotel. This glorified bed-and-breakfast has individually decorated rooms with a sitting room, kitchenette, and private bathroom. A continental breakfast basket is provided daily. Each suite has free wireless Internet. The interior is comfortable but a bit dated and is decorated with European touches. The staff is friendly and helpful, and the hotel is within walking distance of many attractions. There is free parking and no extra charge for the "ghosts" that may live there.

A beautiful and interesting hotel is the **Federal Pointe Inn** (75 Springs Ave., 717/334-7800, www.federalpointeinn.com, $189-220). This elegant boutique hotel is in a historic 1897 schoolhouse in downtown Gettysburg. It has 18 guest rooms and suites with modern amenities. The rooms are tasteful yet not overstuffed and have high ceilings and granite bathrooms. The innkeepers are professional and friendly.

GETTING THERE AND AROUND

Gettysburg is about 10 miles from the Pennsylvania-Maryland border off US 15. It is a 45-minute drive (35 miles) north of Frederick. Most people arrive by car, but the **Gettysburg Regional Airport (GTY)**, two miles west of Gettysburg, is a general aviation airport with one runway.

Harpers Ferry, West Virginia

Harpers Ferry is a beautiful historic town at the confluence of the Shenandoah and Potomac Rivers in West Virginia. It is well known as the location of **John Brown's Raid,** when in 1859, famous abolitionist John Brown led 20 men in a raid on a national arsenal. His plan was to use the weapons in the arsenal to start a slave uprising in the South. Five of the men in the raid were African Americans (three free African Americans, one freed enslaved person, and one fugitive). At the time, it was illegal to assist a fugitive slave, which further compounded the severity of the raid. The raid resulted in a force of 86 marines coming to the town, led by Robert E. Lee. The raiders were captured but not without casualties.

Harpers Ferry is also known for its hard times during the Civil War, when the town changed hands eight times. It also was the site

Harpers Ferry

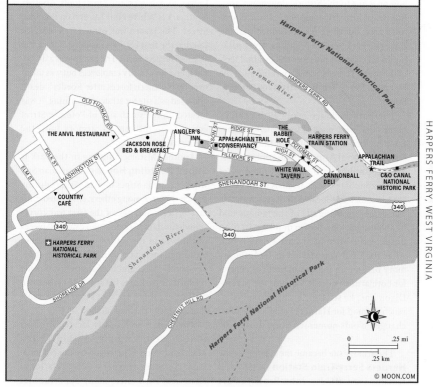

THE ANVIL RESTAURANT

OLD FURNACE RD

RIDGE ST

ANGLER'S INN

RIDGE ST

JACKSON ROSE BED & BREAKFAST

JACKSON ST

APPALACHIAN TRAIL CONSERVANCY

FILLMORE ST

THE RABBIT HOLE

HARPERS FERRY TRAIN STATION

POTOMAC ST

HIGH ST

APPALACHIAN TRAIL

Potomac River

Harpers Ferry National Historical Park

HARPERS FERRY RD

POLK ST

ELM ST

WASHINGTON ST

UNION ST

WHITE WALL TAVERN

SHENANDOAH ST

CANNONBALL DELI

C&O CANAL NATIONAL HISTORIC PARK

340

COUNTRY CAFÉ

340

340

HARPERS FERRY NATIONAL HISTORICAL PARK

Shenandoah River

340

SHORELINE DR

CHESTNUT HILL RD

Harpers Ferry National Historical Park

0   .25 mi

0   .25 km

© MOON.COM

of the largest surrender of Federal troops during the war when, in 1862, General Stonewall Jackson captured a 12,500-soldier Union garrison.

Harpers Ferry is also the site of **Storer College,** one of the first integrated schools in the United States. It operated from 1865 to 1955. The school's former campus is now part of Harpers Ferry National Historical Park.

Harpers Ferry is about a 1.5-hour drive from both Washington DC and Baltimore, Maryland. The town is known as an outdoor recreation destination and offers adventures in hiking, white-water rafting, tubing, canoeing and kayaking, mountain biking, and fishing.

Parking in the lower part of town is difficult. Strict parking restrictions were put in place to maintain the historic appearance of the town.

SIGHTS
★ Harpers Ferry National Historical Park
Harpers Ferry National Historical Park (304/535-6029, www.nps.gov/hafe, daily 9am-5pm, $15 by car, $7 on foot, $10 by motorcycle) is made up of 3,700 acres of parkland and the lower portion of the town of Harpers Ferry. It features more than 25 historic buildings in the Shenandoah Street, High Street, and Potomac Street areas. The town sits at the confluence of the Potomac and Shenandoah Rivers (which makes it prone to flooding during high water).

The best way to begin exploration is to park at the **Visitors Center** (171 Shoreline

Dr., 304/535-6298, daily 9am-5pm), tour the center, pick up a map of the town, and then hop on a bus to the historic downtown area. It is possible to drive into the historic downtown area, but there is very limited parking since the Park Service prohibits street parking in an effort to preserve the original look of the town. There is a small parking lot at the **Harpers Ferry Train Station** on Potomac Street.

The park includes many 19th-century homes that were erected by the federal government for people working for the **Harpers Ferry National Armory.** The armory mass-produced military arms for the United States and was one of two such arsenals in the country (the other was located in Massachusetts). The armory was the site of the famous raid by abolitionist John Brown in 1859, part of an unsuccessful attempt to start a slave revolt. After the Civil War started in 1861, the armory became an important point of control for both armies since it was near the Mason-Dixon line. Its strategic location resulted in much turmoil for Harpers Ferry, as the town changed hands numerous times during the war.

The armory site became the location of the **Harpers Ferry Train Station** in 1889 and remains as such today. **John Brown's Fort** (which was the armory's guardhouse) is the only surviving building from the Civil War. It was moved several times and now sits approximately 150 feet east of its original location (the original site is now covered by the railroad).

Victorian and federal-style homes in the town entertained well-known guests such as Woodrow Wilson, Mark Twain, and Alexander Graham Bell. General Stonewall Jackson also spent time in Harpers Ferry during the Civil War when he used the town as a command base.

There are many museums and historic landmarks in town, including a museum on **Meriwether Lewis,** who came to Harpers Ferry in 1803 to purchase weapons from the U.S. National Arsenal for his transcontinental

expedition. Among the items he bought were 15 rifles, 15 powder horns, 30 bullet molds, knives, tomahawks, and repair tools. Another landmark is **White Hall Tavern** on Potomac Street. The tavern was owned by Frederick Roeder, the first civilian casualty of the Civil War in Harpers Ferry. The tavern was a drinking house for armory employees but was taken over by Northern forces after Roeder's death and used as a site for strategic planning. It was located on the south side of Potomac Street across from the original armory (now the train station).

Another historic building in the park is **Stipes' Boarding House** (Shenandoah St.), where Cornelia Stipes took in visitors during the Civil War. Among others, she hosted military officers and one of the first war correspondents, James Taylor, who captured pieces of the war in his military sketches. Other buildings include a mill, blacksmith shop, dry-goods store, and bookshop. Just outside the historic park area but still within the town of Harpers Ferry are shops and restaurants that are easily reached on foot.

The park is technically located in three states—West Virginia, Virginia, and Maryland—and is managed by the National Park Service. Harpers Ferry National Historical Park offers many opportunities for outdoor adventure including trail hiking, boating, biking, and guided ranger tours. Visitors can get a lovely view of the water gap where the Potomac and Shenandoah Rivers meet by hiking up to the spot visited by Thomas Jefferson on October 25, 1783, now called **Jefferson Rock.** From the lower part of town, make your way to High Street and the stone steps that lead up to St. Peter's Church. The steps continue past the church and turn into a steep five-minute climb. The view is spectacular, and you will find out why Jefferson said it was "worth a voyage across the Atlantic." Much of the area is tree covered,

---

1: Harpers Ferry **2:** museum on Meriwether Lewis and White Hall Tavern in Harpers Ferry **3:** Harpers Ferry Train Station **4:** Appalachian Trail Conservancy Headquarters and Visitors Center

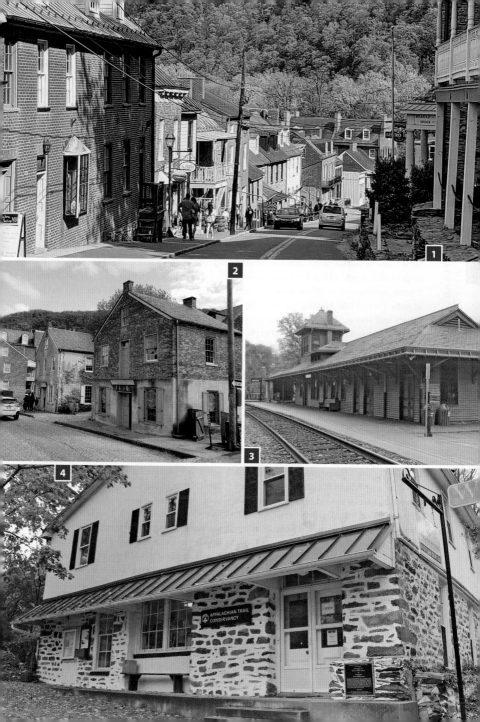

and more than 170 bird species and 30 mammal species are found in the park.

Appalachian Trail Conservancy Headquarters and Visitors Center

Harpers Ferry is one of the few towns that the **Appalachian Trail (AT)** passes directly through. The **Appalachian Trail Conservancy Headquarters** (799 Washington St., 304/535-6331, www.appalachiantrail.org, daily 9am-5pm) is just a quarter mile off the trail. They offer maps, membership services, books, and other merchandise for sale. They can also answer all types of questions regarding the AT. The center is home to an enormous raised-relief map of the entire Appalachian Trail. It is one-of-a-kind and more than 10 feet long. Pictures of more than 15,000 Appalachian Trail thru-hikers and section-hikers who have passed through the town since 1979 are kept in photo albums in the headquarters building.

The **Harpers Ferry AT Visitor Center** is in the same building as the Appalachian Trail Conservancy headquarters and shares the same address, phone number, and hours. It offers great information on the town and is a starting point for many beautiful day hikes.

RECREATION

The **C&O Canal National Historical Park** (www.nps.gov/choh) is a great place to ride a mountain bike or hybrid bike just across the Potomac River from Harpers Ferry. Access to the park's towpath is from a walkway along the railroad bridge that crosses the Potomac River at the end of Shenandoah and Potomac Streets. Access to the **Appalachian Trail** is from the same footbridge and offers great hiking along the famous 2,180-mile trail.

If you're feeling adventurous, take a Zip Line Canopy Tour from **River Riders Family Adventure Resort** (408 Alstadts Hill Rd., 304/535-2663, www.riverriders.com, Memorial Day-Labor Day daily 8am-6pm, shorter hours in the off season with limited services, $64-109). A guide will take you high above the ground through the trees on eight lines up to 800 feet high. There are also ladders to climb and bridges to cross. Tours last 2-3 hours.

River Riders also offers white-water rafting trips on the Shenandoah and Potomac Rivers. Trips are 2-3 hours and are available guided or self-guided (starting at $54). They also offer 45-90-minute flat-water tubing trips on the Shenandoah (starting at $29), 1-3-hour white-water tubing trips on the Potomac River (starting at $29), and an Aerial Adventure Park (2 hours, starting at $44 for adults and $34 for children).

The **Harpers Ferry Adventure Center** (540/668-9007, www.harpersferryadventurecenter.com) is another outdoor outfitter in Harpers Ferry that offers guided white-water rafting on the Shenandoah and Potomac Rivers (daily Mar.-Oct., starting at $50), flat-water tubing on the Shenandoah River (May-Oct., starting at $24), white-water tubing trips on the Potomac River (May-Oct., starting at $24), ropes courses, and zip-line adventures.

Bike rentals are also available through **River & Trail Outfitters** (301/834-9950, www.rivertrail.com, $31 for a half day).

ENTERTAINMENT

For a great history lesson and a pleasant walk, join **Ghost Tours of Harpers Ferry** (304/725-8019, www.harpersferryghost.20m.com, adults $14, children 8-12 $10, under 8 free, cash or check only). This is a wonderful and entertaining way to learn about the buildings in town and the stories behind them. The tour is family and dog friendly and sometimes draws a large crowd. Tours are given year-round and meet at the Piazza (front patio) of St. Peter's Catholic Church (100 Church St.). Tours are around two hours and cover 14 blocks.

FOOD

A good place to grab a sandwich is the **Cannonball Deli** (148 High St., 304/535-1762, Mon.-Fri. 11am-5pm, Sat.-Sun.

Following the Appalachian Trail

The Appalachian Trail passes through 14 states on the East Coast and is approximately 2,180 miles long. It is one of the longest continuously marked trails in the world. The trail's northern terminus is in Katahdin, Maine, and the southern terminus is at Springer Mountain in Georgia.

Each year, between 2 and 3 million people hike on the Appalachian Trail, and more than 2,500 people attempt to hike the entire trail in one season. These people are called "thru-hikers." About 25 percent who start hiking with the intent of completing the trail in one season finish each year. For those who hike it end to end, it normally takes between five and seven months. Thru-hikers normally adopt a "trail name" or are given one by other hikers they meet along the way. The names are often funny or descriptive, such as "Iron Toothpick," "Thunder Chicken," or "Mr. Optimist."

The Appalachian Trail was completed in 1937 and is part of the national park system, although it is managed by a combination of public and private entities. Although Harpers Ferry is home to the trail headquarters, only about four miles of the trail pass through West Virginia. Virginia claims the most miles along the trail at approximately 550.

There are literally hundreds of entrances to the Appalachian Trail, making it accessible to millions of people. Some people called "section-hikers" also hike the entire length of the trail, but do so in segments over several years. The total elevation gain on the Appalachian Trail equals the elevation gain of climbing Mt. Everest 16 times.

Additional information can be found on the Appalachian Trail Conservancy website at www.appalachiantrail.org.

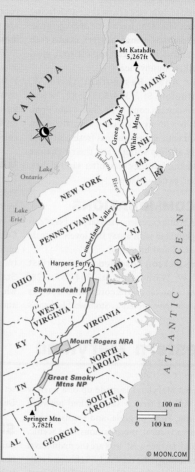

© MOON.COM

10:30am-6:30pm, under $10). They offer quick service, a pleasant staff, good food, and a nice patio. The menu has a variety of casual items such as sandwiches, gyros, and hot dogs. This is a popular stop with Appalachian Trail hikers.

If you're yearning for a mom-and-pop restaurant with a friendly atmosphere and good food, stop in the **Country Café** (1723 W. Washington St., 304/535-2327, www.country-cafe.com, Tues.-Sun. 7:30am-3pm, under $10). They serve breakfast and lunch in a cozy atmosphere and have been doing so since 1989.

Don't let the partially hidden entrance to **The Rabbit Hole** (186 High St., 304/535-8818, daily 11am-6pm, $8-17) deter you from trying this 2019 addition to the Harper's Ferry food scene. Once through the door, you'll find a cheery staff, a cozy tavern atmosphere inside, and terrific views from their deck facing the river. The menu has a little of everything: salads, pierogis, wings, burgers, even a crab cake sandwich. You can top off your meal with a Beer Bunny Float.

The Anvil Restaurant (1290 W. Washington St., 304/535-2582, www.anvilrestaurant.com, Wed.-Sun. 11am-9pm, $9-28) is a lovely restaurant specializing in seafood with entrées such as fresh Maryland oysters, shrimp scampi, and their signature crab cakes, but they also offer sandwiches, chicken, pasta, and beef.

ACCOMMODATIONS

An authentic experience in Harpers Ferry can be highlighted with a stay in a lovely historic inn or bed-and-breakfast.

The Jackson Rose Bed and Breakfast (1167 W. Washington St., 304/535-1528, www.thejacksonrose.com, $135-150) is known to have served as Stonewall Jackson's headquarters for a short time near the start of the Civil War. This beautiful bed-and-breakfast offers four nicely appointed guest rooms and welcoming innkeepers. They are also known for serving scrumptious breakfasts.

The Angler's Inn (867 W. Washington St., 304/535-1239, www.theanglersinn.com, $165-175) is another nice option in a good location on Washington Street. They offer four comfortable guest rooms with private bathrooms. Professional fishing guide services are available through the inn.

GETTING THERE

Harpers Ferry is 21 miles southwest of Frederick via US Route 340 west. It is serviced by **Amtrak** (112 Potomac St., 800/872-7245, www.amtrak.com) and **Maryland Area Rail Commuter (MARC)** (410/539-5000, http://mta.maryland.gov, weekdays only). Both offer trains to the historic **Harpers Ferry Train Station** (Potomac St. and Shenandoah St.), which was originally built by the Baltimore and Ohio Railroad and dates back to 1889.

Western Maryland

Western Maryland is made up of a narrow strip of land that is sandwiched between Virginia, West Virginia, and Pennsylvania. The area is rural, mountainous, and scenic. I-70 and, farther west, I-68 are the main travel routes through the region. I-68 ebbs and rolls just under the Pennsylvania border. Winter can come early in this part of the state due to its high elevation, and windy conditions often prevail. On average, the region receives about 100 inches of snow per year. Key towns to visit in Western Maryland are Sharpsburg, famous for Antietam National Battlefield; Cumberland, a historic railroad town; Frostburg, a small university town tucked in the mountains; Grantsville, originally founded as a small Amish and Mennonite settlement; and the popular vacation area of Deep Creek Lake.

SHARPSBURG

Sharpsburg is a small town about 70 miles northwest of Washington DC. It has a population of around 650 people and was founded circa 1740. It is best known as the location of the Battle of Antietam, the bloodiest single-day confrontation to ever take place on US soil. Sharpsburg is the ending point on the 126-mile **Antietam Campaign Scenic Byway,** which begins in White's Ferry, Maryland. This byway follows the events of Robert E. Lee's army as they crossed the Potomac River into Maryland and then retreated back into West Virginia after the Battle of Antietam.

Antietam and the Evolution of Photography

In the spring of 1861, thousands of young soldiers came to Washington DC to defend the capital. In their wake were many photographers, eager to capture camp scenes and confident young greenhorns wearing uniforms for the first time.

Photographer Alexander Gardner, who owned a studio in DC, was eager to increase his business and take advantage of the happenings around him. To that point, nobody had taken photographs on the battlefield as photography was still new, having originated in 1839. In September 1862, Gardner ventured to Antietam two times, once just two days after the battle, and the second time two weeks later when President Lincoln visited the battlefield. Gardner was the first to capture the horror of the battlefield before the dead were buried. This was merely a novelty at first, but it ultimately transformed photography into an incredible medium for communication and signaled the true beginning of photojournalism.

Sights

★ ANTIETAM NATIONAL BATTLEFIELD

The **Battle of Antietam** was the first Civil War battle held on Union ground. It was also the bloodiest battle to ever take place in a single day in US history, with approximately 23,000 casualties (from both the North and the South). During the battle on September 17, 1862, the Union Army of the Potomac launched several assaults against the Confederates, who, for the first time, had invaded the North. Vicious counterattacks went back and forth between both armies in areas near Sharpsburg known as **Miller's Cornfield** and the **West Woods.** The day ended in a draw, but the Confederates were checked of any advancement into Northern territory. This tactical victory spurred Abraham Lincoln to issue the Emancipation Proclamation.

Antietam National Battlefield is a National Park Service unit that encompasses more than 3,200 acres in the foothills of the Appalachian Mountains. This park is a small treasure for historians and anyone wishing to visit a non-commercialized yet very relevant battlefield. Visitors should begin at the **Visitor Center** (5831 Dunker Church Rd., 301/432-5124, www.nps.gov/anti, daily 9am-5pm, three-day pass $7 per person and $15 per vehicle) to learn about that fated day in 1862 before heading out to the battlefield. The all-inclusive park entrance fee can also be paid there.

The visitors center offers exhibits on the battle and the Civil War, an observation room, ranger-led interpretive talks, and a museum store. A 26-minute orientation film narrated by James Earl Jones is shown every half hour.

The battlefield itself has an 8.5-mile paved road that visitors are welcome to drive, bike, or walk (a tour map can be downloaded from the park website or picked up at the visitors center). It is designed as a self-guided tour that takes approximately 1.5 hours. The route is well marked with informative signs and designated areas where you can get out of the car and tour on foot. Sights along the route include the famous Miller's Cornfield, where much of the early fighting took place; the West Woods, where 2,200 men were killed or wounded in under half an hour; and "Bloody Lane," a sunken road where 5,000 casualties occurred. A self-guided audio driving tour with 11 stops can be purchased at the Visitor Center museum shop. Private tours of the battlefield are also available through **R. C. M. History Tours** (301/491-0002, www.rcmhistorytours.com, starting at $20), during which expert guides ride along with you in your car, or they can provide transportation.

The battlefield features 96 monuments. Most are dedicated to Union forces since the former Confederacy was not able to pay for monuments after the war. The monuments were erected mostly by veterans of the battle to commemorate the sacrifices made by their fellow soldiers. Six generals fell during the Battle of Antietam, and each is honored at the spot where he was killed or mortally wounded by a mortuary cannon (a cannon barrel that is inverted inside a block of stone).

The battlefield park grounds are beautifully maintained and noncommercialized. It is easy to envision what happened during the battle since the site looks much the same as it did in 1862. During the summer months, frequent ranger talks are offered. A schedule is available daily in the visitor center. Allow a minimum of three hours for your visit.

ANTIETAM NATIONAL CEMETERY

A key attraction near the battlefield is the **Antietam National Cemetery** (E. Main St., www.nps.gov, daily dawn-dusk, free). The site is maintained by Antietam National Battlefield and is part of the National Cemetery System.

After the Battle of Antietam, Sharpsburg became a sprawling hospital and burial ground. Soldiers who died during the fight were buried by the hundreds in shallow graves on property extending miles in all directions. After the end of the war, an effort was made to relocate the bodies to proper cemeteries, and the Antietam National Cemetery was formed. Due to a lack of funds from the South and hard feelings over the war in general, the cemetery became a Union cemetery and only contains the remains of Union soldiers from the Civil War (the remains of Confederate soldiers were moved to three other cemeteries in other towns). In later years the cemetery also became a site for graves of veterans and family from the Spanish-American War, World War I, World War II, and the Korean War. Like the battlefield, the cemetery is run by the National Park Service. It is 11 acres and contains more than 5,000 graves.

TOLSON'S CHAPEL

Tolson's Chapel (111 E. High St., www.tolsonschapel.org, tours available by appointment) is a historic African American church in downtown Sharpsburg. The small 1866 wooden church was a key spiritual and educational center for African Americans after the Civil War. The church no longer holds services, but local residents are working to preserve the building and its cemetery. The chapel is listed in the National Register of Historic Places. The chapel is open the first Saturday of the month April-October 10am-4pm. Tours can be scheduled by emailing tolsons.chapel@gmail.com.

Food

There aren't many choices for food in Sharpsburg, but **Captain Benders Tavern** (111 E. Main St., 301/432-5813, www.captainbenders.com, Mon.-Thurs. 11am-midnight, Fri.-Sat. 11am-2am, Sun. noon-midnight, $9-29) offers a good selection of sandwiches, wraps, salads, and casual entrées. If you're up for the challenge, their Monument Tower of Death, which includes three 8-ounce Black Angus burger patties with all the fixings (including cheese fries), is free if you eat it in 30 minutes. They also have a good bar and live music some nights. The tavern has been serving food since 1936 and is named after a C&O Canal boatman.

For a great scoop of ice cream, visit **Nutter's Ice Cream** (100 E. Main St., 301/432-5809, www.nuttersicecream.com, daily 1pm-9pm, under $5). They serve generous portions of delicious ice cream at a great price. The line can be out the door and they only take cash, but you won't be disappointed. Order a Lollipop—it is the specialty. Their door faces South Mechanic Street.

Accommodations

The **Jacob Rohrbach Inn** (138 W. Main

1: Captain Benders Tavern in Sharpsburg
2: Nutter's Ice Cream in Sharpsburg **3:** the Sunken Road on the Antietam National Battlefield

St., 301/432-5079, www.jacob-rohrbach-inn.com, $165-225) offers five beautiful guest rooms with private bathrooms. Guests are treated to a lovely country-style, multicourse breakfast, fresh-baked cookies, coffee, and beverages. The inn's garden provides many herbs, fruits, and flowers. The home was built in 1804 and is conveniently located in town near the battlefield. Gracious hosts add to the charm of this historic bed-and-breakfast.

Another choice is the **Inn at Antietam** (220 E. Main St., 301/432-6601, www.innatantietam.com, $160-175). This charming inn is next to the Antietam National Cemetery and offers five guest rooms. The rooms are comfortable but do not have televisions or Internet access. The inn serves a delightful breakfast and afternoon refreshments. They have a super charger available for electric vehicles, and they are dog friendly.

Getting There

Sharpsburg is near the West Virginia border along Route 34. It is approximately 70 miles northwest of Washington DC and 22 miles west of Frederick.

CUMBERLAND

Cumberland is the largest city in Allegany County, with nearly 20,000 people. It was founded in 1787. Although it is the regional center for business, it is also one of the more economically challenged areas in the country based on per capita income.

Cumberland is going through a renaissance of sorts, with a focus on the revitalization of the downtown area with new stores, restaurants, and galleries. Downtown Cumberland is quaint and charming, with its trademark church steeples, pleasant cobblestoned pedestrian area on Baltimore Street, and extensive railway history. Outdoor enthusiasts will enjoy the Great Allegheny Passage trail and the C&O Canal trail and the sights at Canal Place.

Sights

CANAL PLACE

Canal Place (13 Canal St., 301/724-3655, www.canalplace.org) is a 58-acre park off Canal Street by the Western Maryland Railway Station. The park is home to the **Cumberland Visitor Center** (301/722-8226, daily 9am-5pm) for the **Chesapeake & Ohio Canal National Historical Park** and marks the end of the C&O Canal Towpath. It also offers a picnic area, a replica of a canal boat, shops, and the jumping-off point to the Western Maryland Scenic Railroad. Exhibits at the visitors center explain how the canal was constructed and how cargo was transported on the canal, and also provide information on the locks and crew that kept the canal in operation.

The canal boat replica (called *The Cumberland*) is located in the Trestle Walk at Canal Place, a brick promenade that connects the train station and canal. Visitors can view the captain's cabin, the mule shed, and the hay house.

★ THE WESTERN MARYLAND SCENIC RAILROAD

Western Maryland is railroad country. Many historic railroad milestones occurred in the Cumberland area, including the use of the first iron rail made in the United States and the production of unique steam engines by the Cumberland & Pennsylvania Railroad. **The Western Maryland Scenic Railroad** (13 Canal St., 301/759-4400, www.wmsr.com, 11:30am General Excursion departure, days vary by season, $42-165) provides fun round-trip excursions from downtown Cumberland to nearby Frostburg on tracks that used to belong to the Western Maryland Railway. The trip is made by diesel locomotive and is 32 miles round-trip. The excursion takes 3 hours. There is a 1-hour stop in Frostburg where passengers can have lunch, sightsee, and watch the train rotate on a giant

1: downtown Cumberland **2:** an old-fashioned steam locomotive—part of The Western Maryland Scenic Railway

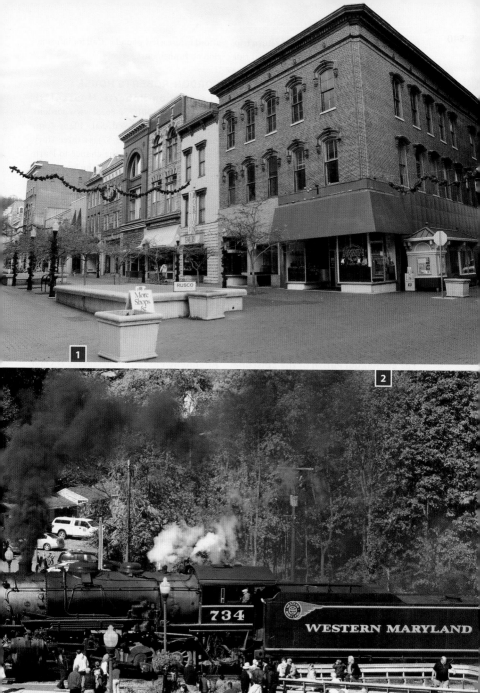

turntable to position itself for the return trip. This is an entertaining and educational ride through a scenic Appalachian landscape. The train even passes through the Narrows, a cut in the mountains that was considered at one time to be the gateway to the West. October is the busiest month, so make a reservation early. Dinner and other specialty trips are available.

ALLEGANY MUSEUM

The **Allegany Museum** (3 Pershing St., 301/777-7200, www.alleganymuseum.org, mid-Mar.-Dec. Tues.-Sat. 10am-4pm, Sun. 1pm-4pm, free) is a small gem. It is located on two floors of a restored neoclassical revival building from the 1930s and shares exhibits that celebrate local heritage. Topics include the C&O Canal, Native American artifacts, folk art, glassmaking, and breweries.

EMMANUEL PARISH OF THE EPISCOPAL CHURCH

The **Emmanuel Parish of the Episcopal Church** (16 Washington St., 301/777-3364, www.emmanuelparishofmd.org, free) is on the former site of Fort Cumberland, the place where George Washington started his military career. Earthwork tunnels built in 1755 from the original fort remain under the church and can be visited. The tunnels were created for several purposes: to keep perishable food fresh, to store gunpowder, and to provide British soldiers a safe route to reach their defenses during the French and Indian War. A hundred years later, the same tunnels were used by the Underground Railroad to harbor escaping enslaved people seeking safety. The Gothic Revival-style church was originally built in 1803, and the current structure was completed in 1851. It contains beautiful stained glass windows from three distinct periods. Services are still held regularly, and the public is welcome, as the church makes clear: "We extend a special welcome to those who are single, married, divorced, gay, filthy rich, dirt poor, yo no habla Ingles…those who are crying new-borns, skinny as a rail or could

afford to lose a few pounds." Call for information on tunnel tours.

GORDON-ROBERTS HOUSE

The **Gordon-Roberts House** (218 Washington St., 301/777-8678, www.gordonrobertshouse.com, Wed.-Sat. 10am-4pm, guided tours on the hour, $7) is a three-story home offering visitors the chance to learn about life in Cumberland in the late 1800s. The Second Empire-style home is one of a handful in that style located in the historic district of Washington Street. The home is constructed from handmade bricks. It was owned by an upper-middle-class family and displays furnishings, textiles, art, toys, clothing, and other artifacts. The home is owned and run by the Allegany Historical Society.

Recreation

Two highly regarded trails meet in Cumberland: **Chesapeake & Ohio Canal National Historical Park** and the **Great Allegheny Passage.** Chesapeake & Ohio Canal National Historical Park runs 184.5 miles between Cumberland and Georgetown in Washington DC, and the Great Allegheny Passage runs 141 miles between Cumberland and Pittsburgh, Pennsylvania.

Rocky Gap State Park (12900 Lakeshore Dr., Flintstone, 301/722-1480, www.dnr.maryland.gov, free) is seven miles northeast of Cumberland in Allegany County. This picturesque, 3,400-acre park is surrounded by mountains and has a beautiful 243-acre lake, Lake Habeeb, with white-sand beaches. The complex includes a snack bar, ranger station, bathhouse, and nature center. There are forested trails for hiking, mountain biking, and trail running, and the park is home to the **Rocky Gap Casino and Resort** (16701 Lakeview Rd., 301/784-8400, www.rockygapcasino.com), which features an 18-hole golf course.

Food

Ristorante Ottaviani (25 N. Centre St., 301/722-0052, www.ottavianis.com, Mon.-Sat.

Side Trip: The Chesapeake & Ohio Canal National Historical Park

Great Falls Tavern Visitor Center at Chesapeake & Ohio Canal National Historical Park

Chesapeake & Ohio Canal National Historical Park (301/722-8226, www.nps.gov/choh) is a 184.5-mile-long park covering 12,000 acres that runs parallel to the Potomac River. The park is a linear towpath (7-12 feet wide) along the old canal that extends from Cumberland, Maryland, to Georgetown in Washington DC.

The original canal was in operation between 1831 and 1924 and served many communities along the Potomac River by providing a transport system for coal, lumber, and agricultural products. The canal boats were pulled by mules that walked alongside the canal on the towpath. At one time there could be as many as 2,000 mules working on the canal (operating in six-hour shifts).

The 605-foot elevation change and many stream crossings along the canal were accommodated by 74 locks, more than 150 culverts, and 11 aqueducts. There is also a 3,118-foot tunnel—the Paw Paw Tunnel—that the canal went through.

Cumberland was not planned as the western terminus of the canal, but when the canal reached Cumberland, the project ran out of money. The end of the C&O Canal is marked in Cumberland, and a statue of a mule stands nearby at Chesapeake & Ohio Canal National Historical Park.

The park is a beautiful and popular multistate trail for biking, running, walking, and boating. It passes near several popular towns, such as Harpers Ferry, West Virginia, and Sharpsburg, Maryland. Two reproduced canal boats (pulled by mules) offer historical rides in the park (301/739-4200, June-Sept. Fri.-Sun. 11am, 1:30pm, and 3pm, shorter hours rest of the year, adults $8, children 4-15 $5, seniors 62 and over $6).

Bike and boat rentals are available through two National Park Service partners at the downstream portion of the canal in Washington DC: **The Boathouse at Fletchers Cove** (mp 3.2, 4940 Canal Rd. NW, Washington DC, 202/244-0461, www.boatingindc.com, kayak $16 per hour, canoe $25 per hour, rowboat $16 per hour, paddleboard $22 per hour, bike $11 per hour) and **Thompson Boat Center** (mp 0, 2900 Virginia Ave. NW, Washington DC, 202/333-9543, www.boatingindc.com, kayak $16 per hour, canoe $25 per hour, paddleboard $22 per hour).

542

5pm-10pm, Sun. 5pm-9pm, $19-38) offers top-notch Italian food in a romantic atmosphere (white tablecloths, dim lighting). This family-owned restaurant is a favorite in downtown Cumberland, despite its somewhat bland exterior. The menu is imaginative and contains recipes passed down for generations. The staff is extremely accommodating and goes out of its way on special occasions. The wine list is well planned and reasonably priced.

The **Baltimore Street Grill** (82 Baltimore St., 301/724-1711, Mon.-Sat. 11am-midnight, $11-30) is a great local place with lively conversation, friendly patrons (and staff), and good food. This is the happening spot in Cumberland, and in the summer the outdoor seating makes it even better. They have good pub food—think crab cakes, Cajun food, spicy wings, salads, and more.

The **M and M Bake Shop** (80 Baltimore St., 301/722-2660, Mon.-Sat. 5:30am-2pm) is an old-style bakery in downtown Cumberland. They sell all sorts of sweet delights, such as cookies, brownies, doughnuts, pies, and cakes, as well as bread. All items are made on-site.

For a good quick lunch and some local flair, stop by **Curtis Famous Weiners** (35 N. Liberty St., 301/759-9707, Mon.-Sat. 9am-9pm, under $10). This old-time hot dog shop has been a Cumberland fixture since the early 1900s. Generations of local families have memories of eating yummy hot dogs and fries and drinking root beer here. These are hands down the best hot dogs in town, and patrons have been known to drive several hours for them.

Accommodations

Several chain hotels have representation in Cumberland including the **Fairfield Inn & Suites Cumberland** (21 N. Wineow St., 301/722-0340, www.marriott.com, $179-199), which has 96 rooms in downtown Cumberland, and the **Ramada Cumberland Downtown** (100 S. George St., 301/724-8800, www.ramada.com, $129-139), which offers 130 rooms and is also downtown.

The Inn on Decatur (108 Decatur St., 301/722-4887, www.theinnondecatur.net, $145-160) has two immaculate rooms, delicious full breakfast, and a wonderful innkeeper. This Federal-style bed-and-breakfast (circa 1870) offers a relaxing atmosphere with modern amenities and a location just two blocks from the downtown pedestrian area. The knowledgeable host is also a tour operator and provides complimentary tours of Cumberland to her guests. There are no televisions in the rooms, but there is high-speed Internet.

Rocky Gap Casino and Resort (16701 Lakeview Rd., Flintstone, 301/784-8400, www.rockygapcasino.com, $159-219) is on Lake Habeeb in **Rocky Gap State Park,** in nearby Flintstone. There are 220 guest rooms, a casino, an 18-hole golf course, a spa, restaurants, and meeting facilities. The exterior and grounds of the lodge are lovely, and the location right in Rocky Gap State Park is hard to beat. Rooms have a lake or golf course view, and there are many hiking and biking trails in the park. The lodge is a bit isolated but extremely convenient to I-68.

Information and Services

Additional information on Cumberland can be found at www.visitmaryland.org or by stopping by the visitors center in the **Western Maryland Railway Station** (13 Canal St., Rm. 100, 301/722-8226, daily 9am-5pm).

Getting There

Cumberland is best reached by car and is located off I-68. It is 90 miles west of Frederick (1.5-hour drive) and 138 miles from Washington DC.

FROSTBURG

Frostburg is eight miles west of Cumberland on I-68 and US 40. It is a small city with a population of just under 8,000 and home to Frostburg State University. Frostburg has a small downtown area with local shops, pizza parlors, and other casual restaurants that are patronized mostly by students from the university.

Sights

★ THRASHER CARRIAGE MUSEUM

The **Thrasher Carriage Museum** (19 Depot St., 301/689-3380, www.thethrashercarriagemuseum.com, May and Sept. Fri.-Sun. 12:30pm-2:30pm, June-Aug. Thurs.-Sun. 12:30pm-2:30pm, Nov.-Dec. Sat.-Sun 12:30pm-2:30pm, $2) is a fantastic little museum next to the railroad station on Depot Street (at the bottom of the big hill). The museum has one of the best collections of horse-powered carriages in the country (more than 50 vehicles) and features everything from milk carriages to funeral wagons. Visitors can learn from interpretive guides about carriages used for pleasure, work, and even sleighs in their renovated 19th-century warehouse. The museum offers a rare glimpse into the everyday lives of Victorian Americans and represents vehicles from all economic segments of the local community. It is a great site to visit when taking the Western Maryland Scenic Railroad.

OLD DEPOT

Across Depot Street from the carriage museum is the **Old Depot.** This historic station was built in 1891 by the Cumberland & Pennsylvania Railroad Company, a local railway. It was originally a passenger and freight depot, but service subsided in 1942 when car travel became more popular. The station was renovated in 1989 and is now the turnaround point for the Western Maryland Scenic Railroad. A restaurant and shops are located in the depot, as is the large turntable used to turn around the steam engine for its return trip to Cumberland.

Food

The **Hen House Restaurant** (18072 National Pike, 301/689-5001, www.henhouserestaurant.com, Wed.-Fri. 5pm-9pm, Sat. noon-9pm, Sun. noon-7pm, $10-29) located seven miles west of downtown Frostburg off Alternate US Route 40 is known for seafood (especially crab), even though it is named after the staple of the first menu back in 1961, chicken. They are, in fact, the largest seafood restaurant in Maryland west of Frederick. The menu includes crab dip, crab cakes, salmon, and other nonseafood items such as burgers. The business has been owned and operated by the same family from the very beginning.

Good Italian food can be found just off Main Street in an old brick building. **Guiseppe's** (11 Bowery St., 301/689-2220, www.giuseppes.net, Tues.-Thurs.

Thrasher Carriage Museum

4:30pm-11pm, Fri.-Sat. 3pm-11pm, Sun. 4:30pm-9pm, $11-33) serves traditional Italian dishes, a number of good house specials, and pizza. The ambience is warm and inviting, and they have a nice bar area.

Among the multiple choices for pizza in Frostburg, one place stands out. **Fat Boy's Pizza Shack** (116 E. Main St., 301/689-2727, Sun.-Thurs. 11am-10pm, Fri.-Sat. 11am-11pm, under $15), although unremarkable in ambience and decor, makes a great pizza. They also offer a nice pizza buffet for under $10.

Accommodations

The **Trail Inn Lodging & Campground** (20 Depot St., 301/689-6466, www. trailinnatfrostburg.com, rooms $70-189, camping $15) offers basic accommodations in 12 rooms next to the Old Depot and near the Great Allegheny Passage. Queen rooms and bunk rooms are available. There is also a campground on-site. The Trail Inn is a pleasant, no-frills kind of place with reasonable prices. There is a café on-site. Downtown Frostburg is a steep hike up Depot Street (or five flights of stairs).

The guest cabins are stunning two-story log structures with beautifully appointed interiors. Each has a sleeping loft with a queen or king bed, a luxurious bathroom, a downstairs living area, a gas fireplace, and a kitchenette. Eight luxury yurts are also available for rent. The lodge is pet friendly.

The ★ **Savage River Lodge** (1600 Mt. Aetna Rd., 301/689-3200, www. savageriverlodge.com, $280-300) is 10 miles from downtown Frostburg, or about a 30-minute drive. Tucked into the 750-acre Savage River State Forest, the lodge is constructed of spruce and fir. Its 18 luxurious and private white pine cabins offer rustic but comfortable accommodations with upscale amenities. The beautiful lodge sits on 45 private acres and has a three-story multiuse area with 10,000 square feet of space. It also houses a library and meeting space. An on-site restaurant serves breakfast, lunch, and dinner. It has seating for 75 people and serves American

Great Allegheny Passage

Where the C&O Canal Towpath ends, the Great Allegheny Passage (GAP) begins. This 141-mile rail trail connects Cumberland with Pittsburgh, Pennsylvania, and is known as a great biking trail (although it is a multiuse trail and excellent for hiking also). Travelers can enjoy a fairly flat trail that meanders along rivers, through valleys, and through scenic small towns.

The Great Allegheny Passage is part of the Potomac Heritage National Scenic Trail, which is one of only eight scenic trails that is nationally designated. For additional information on the GAP, call 888/282-2453 or visit www.gaptrail.org.

cuisine. They provide a splendid, carefully selected wine list. There is a gift shop and ski shop at the lodge.

Additional lodging in Frostburg includes the **Hampton Inn Frostburg** (11200 New Georges Creek Rd., 301/689-1998, www. hamptoninn3.hilton.com, $112-124), with 72 guest rooms and an indoor pool.

Information and Services

For additional information on Frostburg visit www.frostburgcity.com.

GRANTSVILLE

Grantsville is a very small town in northern Garrett County with a population of fewer than 1,000. It is 14 miles west of Frostburg on US 40. It was founded as a Mennonite and Amish settlement and was originally located in the middle of a tract of land owned by Daniel Grant (circa 1796).

Sights
★ **SPRUCE FOREST ARTISAN VILLAGE**

As you approach Grantsville from the east on US 40, you will pass the **Spruce Forest Artisan Village** (177 Casselman Rd., 301/895-3332, www.spruceforest.org, hours vary by artisan, free). It is a half mile before Grantsville near the **Casselman Bridge,** a 354-foot-long stone arch bridge beside US 40 that dates back to 1811. The artisan village was founded in 1957 and now has a dozen log and frame cabins. Many of the structures are historic and were relocated to the artisan village from other sites (some even date back to the Revolutionary War). The cabins house artist studios that sell items such as carvings, stained glass, handloom weaving products, baskets, teddy bears, and pottery. Visitors can stroll through the village and see the artists at work. This place is very cute and feels like a Bavarian village. It is worth a stop, especially when combined with a meal at the Penn Alps Restaurant.

★ SAVAGE RIVER STATE FOREST

The **Savage River State Forest** (127 Headquarters Ln., 301/895-5759, www.dnr. maryland.gov, daily 24 hours, free day use) protects the watershed in Garrett County and encompasses more than 54,000 acres. The forest is part of the Appalachian Plateau, the western section of the Appalachian Mountains, and contains the 360-acre Savage River Reservoir, a boat launch, 100 miles of multiuse trails (hiking, biking, cross-country skiing, horseback riding, etc.), picnicking facilities, and a shooting range ($5 permit required). Trail maps are available at the forest office. Pets are allowed in the forest but must be under control at all times.

There are two state parks within the boundaries of Savage River State Forest. The 455-acre **New Germany State Park** (349 Headquarters Ln., 301/895-5453, www.dnr. maryland.gov, daily 8am-sunset, free day use) is five miles from downtown Grantsville. It has a 13-acre lake with swimming and fishing and also offers 10 miles of multiuse trails for hiking, running, biking, and cross-country skiing. There is no cell phone service in the park. **Big Run State Park** (10368 Savage River Rd., 301/895-5453, www.dnr.maryland. gov, daily 8am-sunset, free day use), at the mouth of the Savage River Reservoir, also offers access to the reservoir for boating and other recreation as well as trails and picnic areas.

Food

The **Penn Alps Restaurant** (125 Casselman Rd., 301/895-5985, www.pennalps.com, Mon.-Thurs. 11am-7pm, Fri. 11am-8pm, Sat. 8am-8pm, Sun. 8am-6pm, $10-21) is next to the Spruce Forest Artisan Village, housed in the "last log hospitality house on the National Pike." It offers a variety of menu items but is best known for its soup and salad bar and weekend buffet. They serve salads, sandwiches, and entrées with a German flair, such as roast pork and sauerkraut. There is a craft shop on-site that sells some items from the artisan village as well as from other local crafters. It is a great place to find one-of-a-kind gifts.

The **Casselman Inn** (113 E. Main St., 301/895-5055, www.thecasselman.com, Mon.-Sat. 7am-8pm, $9-14) has a charming restaurant serving breakfast, lunch, and dinner. The menu contains simple country food influenced by the Pennsylvania Dutch and the Amish. Sample dinner entrées include honey-dipped chicken, Grandma's pot roast, and chargrilled sirloin. Homemade baked goods are prepared in the in-house bakery, and visitors are welcome to watch the bakers in action. There are two dining rooms: one in the original historic inn, and one in an addition that was built in the early 1970s. Both are cozy and comfortable.

Accommodations

The **Casselman Inn** (113 E. Main St., 301/895-5055, www.thecasselman.com, $84-199) is right on Alternate US Route 40, the main road through Grantsville. Guests can be accommodated in the historic inn (which has one suite and two guest rooms, all with private bathrooms) or in the **Casselman Motor Inn** ($63-83), which is also on the property and offers 40 guest rooms. The inn was built in the mid-1840s to serve travelers passing through the area. It is a pretty,

three-story, Federal-style brick home with a fireplace in each room. Many original features remain in the house today, including a stunning cherry railing on the third-floor staircase. A charming restaurant services both the inn and motel as well as visitors not lodging at the Casselman.

The **Comfort Inn** (2541 Chestnut Ridge Rd., 301/895-5993, www.choicehotels.com, $115-125) is right off I-68. It has 96 standard, clean rooms and efficient service. Guests get a free hot breakfast with a room, and there is a fitness room and indoor pool at the hotel.

Camping

There are 70 primitive camping sites in **Savage River State Forest** (127 Headquarters Ln., 301/895-5759, www.dnr. maryland.gov, open all year, $10 per night). Guests can self-register for the sites at the Headquarters Office (127 Headquarters Ln.) or at one of six self-registration sites (a map is available on the website) within one hour of occupying the site. No more than six people are allowed at one site and no more than two tents or camping units (RVs, campers, etc.). No more than two vehicles are allowed at each site. Backpacking is allowed throughout the forest. Backcountry campers must also self-register ($10 per night).

New Germany State Park (349 Headquarters Ln., 301/895-5453, www.dnr. maryland.gov, Apr.-Oct., starting at $18.49 per night for tent sites, cabins $76.75-116.75 per night) features 48 campsites and 11 cabins (2-8 people), as well as a bathhouse with restrooms and showers. Pets are permitted in 9 sites.

Big Run State Park (10368 Savage River Rd., 301/895-5453, www.dnr.maryland.gov, open all year) offers 29 primitive campsites ($10 per night), one large group campsite ($55.49 per night), one large youth group site ($11.75 per night with MD Youth Group pass), and one picnic shelter for rent ($76.75). Each

site has a picnic bench and fire ring. Leashed pets are permitted.

Information and Services

For additional information on Grantsville, visit www.visitgrantsville.com.

Getting There

Grantsville is best reached by car. It is off I-68 on US 40.

DEEP CREEK LAKE

Deep Creek Lake forms the heart of Garrett County. It is 18 miles southwest of Grantsville (via Route 495) in the Appalachian Mountains and is 161 miles from Washington DC and 178 miles from Baltimore. Deep Creek Lake is a former logging and coal-mining area turned all-season vacation area, with mild summer temperatures and low humidity, and enough snowfall for winter sports.

Deep Creek Lake is a hydroelectric project that was constructed on Deep Creek in the 1920s. It was developed by the Youghiogheny Hydroelectric Company. The lake covers almost 4,000 acres and is the largest artificial lake in Maryland. In recent decades it has become *the* spot for vacation homes for many people from the busy Washington DC area.

Several small towns dot the shoreline of Deep Creek Lake, including **McHenry, Oakland,** and **Swanton.**

Sights

TOP EXPERIENCE

★ **DEEP CREEK LAKE STATE PARK**

Deep Creek Lake State Park (898 State Park Rd., Swanton, 301/387-5563, www.dnr. maryland.gov, daily 8am-sunset, $5) sits along one mile of shoreline on beautiful Deep Creek Lake. It is 10 miles northeast of Oakland on the east side of the lake. It is also west of the Eastern Continental Divide and inside the Mississippi River watershed. The land was part of the historic Brant coal mine.

Wildlife is abundant in the park. Some

1: Spruce Forest Artisan Village 2: Casselman Inn in Grantsville of its residents include black bears, bobcats, white-tailed deer, wild turkeys, raccoons, skunks, red-tailed hawks, and great horned owls.

Public access is available for launching motorized and cartop boats (additional fees apply), beach swimming, fishing, canoeing, hiking, picnicking, and snowmobiling. There are trails in the park on Meadow Mountain that are open to hiking, mountain biking, horseback riding, wildlife viewing, hunting, snowmobiling, and snowshoeing. More than 100 campsites can also be reserved at the **Meadow Mountain Campground** April 15-December 15.

The park is home to the **Deep Creek Discovery Center** (898 State Park Rd., Swanton, 301/387-7067, www. discoverycenterdcl.com, May-Labor Day daily 10am-5pm, rest of year Fri.-Sun. 10am-4pm, included with park admission). The center is an interpretive resource for people of all ages and offers hands-on exhibits focusing on local flora and fauna and the area's historical heritage.

The Deep Creek Lake State Park headquarters is located at the intersection of Brant and State Park Roads.

WISP RESORT

Wisp Resort (296 Marsh Hill Rd., McHenry, 301/859-3159, www.wispresort.com, year-round) is a popular all-season recreation resort at the northern end of Deep Creek Lake. It is the only ski resort in Maryland (peak-season lift tickets adults $29-59, junior $24-49). They offer 34 slopes on 172 acres of terrain with an elevation of 3,115 feet. The vertical drop is 700 feet. There is night skiing on 90 percent of the slopes. Other winter activities include snowboarding, tubing, snowshoeing, and cross-country skiing.

Wisp also offers activities at all other times of the year. They have an 18-hole golf course and a partnership with a summer sports center that includes white-water rafting and kayaking, pontoon boat tours, paddleboarding, and bike rentals. The resort also has a canopy

tour, mountain bike trails, hiking, and disc golf. A mountain coaster is also available for kids of all ages. This hybrid coaster is a mix of a roller coaster and a mountain slide. It is 3,500 feet long and glides downhill for more than 350 vertical feet.

SWALLOW FALLS STATE PARK

Swallow Falls State Park (2470 Maple Glade Rd., Oakland, 301/387-6938, www. dnr.maryland.gov, 8am-sunset, $5) is a very popular recreation area a few miles west of Deep Creek Lake and nine miles northwest of Oakland. The Youghiogheny River passes along the border of the park through stunning rock gorges. The park has fantastic scenery and wonderful waterfalls, including **Muddy Creek Falls,** which is the highest waterfall in Maryland at 53 feet tall. A choice of pleasant, well-marked hiking trails can be found in the park, including a short, 1.5-mile hike that takes nature lovers past four waterfalls. Visitors can hike, mountain bike, and picnic in this gem of a park that features woods, rivers, and some of the most breathtaking scenery in Western Maryland. Camping is also available.

Recreation

Outdoor recreation is what Deep Creek Lake is all about. Bike, stand-up paddleboard, and kayak rentals are available from **High Mountain Sports** (21327 Garrett Hwy., Oakland, 301/387-4199, www. highmountainsports.com, kayaks $16 per hour, stand-up paddleboards $15 per hour, bikes $16 for two hours).

If the lake, area parks, and Wisp Resort don't satisfy your recreational itch, try participating in one of the many athletic events held in the area, such as the **SavageMan Triathlon Festival** (https:// kineticmultisports.com) in September or the **Garrett County Gran Fondo** (www. garrettcountygranfondo.org) bike ride, which comprises five rides of varying distances in June.

Those interested in horseback riding can

take a trail ride at **Circle R Ranch** (4151 Sand Flat Rd., Oakland, 301/387-6890, www. deepcreeklakestable.com, $30-55). They offer relaxing trail rides on well-cared-for and well-behaved horses. Trail rides are available for 30 minutes, 60 minutes, or 90 minutes. The minimum age is seven.

Food
MCHENRY

The **Mountain State Brewing Company** (6690 Sang Run Rd., McHenry, 301/387-3360, www.mountainstatebrewing.com, Mon.-Thurs. noon-10pm, Fri.-Sat. noon-11pm, Sun. noon-10pm, $7-15) sits alone off Sang Run Road across from a cornfield. Don't let the drab exterior fool you—this is a fun place to eat with good food and even better brew. The rustic interior with wooden tables and chairs is the perfect setting for delicious homemade brick-oven pizza and craft-brewed beer. There are nice mountain views, and the patio is dog friendly.

Canoe on the Run (2622 Deep Creek Dr., McHenry, 301/387-5933, Mon.-Fri. 8am-2:30pm, Sat.-Sun. 8am-3:30pm, under $10) serves breakfast, lunch, and espresso and coffee drinks. Breakfast is 8am-noon and includes sandwiches, cereal, breakfast burritos, and scones. Lunch is sandwich-oriented with wraps and original specialty sandwiches. Carryout is available.

No vacation spot is complete without a local ice-cream shop, and in Deep Creek the **Lakeside Creamery** (20282 Garrett Hwy., McHenry, 301/387-2580, www.lakesidecreamery.com, mid-Apr.-fall Sun.-Thurs. 11am-11pm, Fri.-Sat. 11am-midnight, under $10) fits the bill. This old-time ice-cream parlor makes more than 90 flavors of homemade ice cream and sherbet using milk from local dairy farmers. Arrive by car on Garrett Highway or by boat (it's about a mile south of the Route 219 bridge).

OAKLAND

The place for pizza at Deep Creek Lake is **Brenda's Pizzeria** (21311 Garrett Hwy., Oakland, 301/387-1007, www.brendaspizzeria. com, opens daily at 11am, $8-20). They are easy to find in a little shopping strip on Garrett Highway and dish out delicious and large pizzas. A great place for a group and also for kids, they offer a friendly atmosphere and tasty food made with fresh ingredients.

Good coffee and breakfast are served each morning downstairs from Brenda's Pizzeria at **Trader's Coffee House** (21311

cascading rapids in Swallow Falls State Park

Garrett Hwy., Oakland, 301/387-9246, www. traderscoffeehouse.com, opens daily at 7am, under $10). They have fresh baked goods and some interesting breakfast options, such as a protein wrap with bananas, peanut butter, granola, and honey, as well as traditional breakfast sandwiches and waffles.

Dutch's at Silver Tree (567 Glendale Rd., 301/387-0525, www.dutchsatsilvertree. com, Wed.-Thurs. 4pm-9pm, Fri. 3pm-10pm, Sat. 11:30am-10pm, Sun. 11:30am-9pm, $25-100) serves delicious steak and seafood with a fabulous view of the lake. It offers a cozy yet sophisticated atmosphere with attentive wait staff. Dinner entrées include several combinations of surf and turf, scrumptious blackened salmon, and stuffed jumbo shrimp. Their lunch menu offers soup, salad, and sandwiches. This is an equally good choice for a romantic dinner or a family outing.

Another waterfront dining option is **Ace's Run Restaurant & Pub** at the **Will O' the Wisp Condominiums** (20160 Garrett Hwy., Oakland, 301/387-6688, www.acesrun.com, Sun.-Thurs. 11am-9pm, Fri.-Sat. 11am-10pm, $9-28). They serve an American menu of burgers, salads, and entrées such as shepherd's pie, wild mushroom ravioli, and steak. Large windows provide a view of the lake, and there is a dock for visitors coming by boat.

Accommodations

There are many private homes for rent in the Deep Creek Lake area. A good starting place to find the perfect rental is at www.deepcreek. com.

MCHENRY

★ **The Lodges at Sunset Village** (23900 Garrett Hwy., McHenry, 301/387-2227, www. dclfun.com, $246-395) provide a delightful stay in one of 27 individual log cabins for a reasonable price. The property is located close to skiing options and in the heart of the Deep Creek Lake area. There are six floor plans (for one and two levels) to choose from, all nicely appointed with cozy yet modern log furnishings. Each cabin has lake access, free Wi-Fi, a flat-screen TV, a kitchen or kitchenette, and a fireplace. Hot tub cabins are also available. The staff is very helpful and accommodating, and the cabins are pet friendly.

Lake Star Lodge (2001 Deep Creek Dr., McHenry, 301/387-5596, www.lakestarlodge. com $184-299) offers 20 guest rooms and one three-bedroom suite on the north side of Deep Creek Lake in McHenry. The lodge is lakefront, and all rooms have a lake or mountain view. The lodge is near Wisp Resort and Deep Creek Lake State Park, so winter and summer activities are close at hand.

Wisp Resort (296 Marsh Hill Rd., McHenry, 301/859-3159, www.wispresort. com, $164-264) is a popular destination in the Deep Creek Lake area. It is a four-season resort with a ski area, mountain coaster (a hybrid mountain slide and roller coaster), summer adventure park, canopy tour, and golf course. The hotel offers traditional guest rooms close to the activities. Although the facility is a bit dated, it has nice amenities such as an indoor lap pool, fitness room (accessed at the far end of the pool), and restaurants. The resort also operates a beach area at Deep Creek Lake State Park. The staff is very friendly, and the lovely lobby is the perfect place to relax in front of the gas fireplace. The hotel is dog friendly.

SWANTON

Carmel Cove Inn (105 Monastery Way, Swanton, 301/387-0067, www.carmelcoveinn. com, $175-195) in Swanton is a renovated monastery with 10 individually decorated guest rooms. This pretty little inn is lakeside on Deep Creek in a very pleasant, private setting. It is away from the main highway but close to restaurants and activities. Each guest room has a private bathroom, wireless Internet, and a flat-screen television with DirecTV and HBO. The inn provides fishing poles, canoes, inner tubes, paddleboats, mountain bikes, and snowshoes. There is also a tennis court on-site.

OAKLAND

The **Inn at Deep Creek Lake** (19638 Garrett Hwy., Oakland, 301/387-5534, www. innatdeepcreek.com, $189-209) has five types of spacious guest rooms with queen or king beds. The inn is right on Garrett Highway but sits back from the road for privacy. It is well maintained and has warm and inviting decor. Rooms offer flat-screen televisions and free wireless Internet. Some rooms have fireplaces.

Camping

Camping is available in **Deep Creek Lake State Park** (898 State Park Rd., Swanton, 301/387-5563, www.dnr.maryland.gov, spring-fall) at the **Meadow Mountain Campground.** There are 112 campsites, and the complex includes heated restrooms with hot-water shower facilities. They offer primitive sites ($21.49), sites with electrical hookups ($27.49), a three-sided camping unit ($36.75), a yurt ($46.75), and camper cabins ($65.49). Pets are allowed in designated sites.

Swallow Falls State Park (2470 Maple Glade Rd., Oakland, 301/387-6938, www.dnr. maryland.gov, mid-Apr.-mid-Dec.) offers 65 wooded campsites ($21.49) and modern bathhouses with hot water. Each site has a fire ring, lantern post, and a picnic table. Three sites are available with electric, water, and sewer ($32.49), and there are mini cabins ($50.49). Call 888/432-2267 for reservations. There is a two-night minimum on weekends and a three-night minimum on holiday weekends. Up to six people are allowed at one site.

Information and Services

Additional information on Deep Creek Lake can be found at www.deepcreek.com.

Getting There and Around

It is best to travel to Deep Creek Lake by car, as there is no public bus or train route to the area. Deep Creek Lake is on Route 219 (Garrett Highway). It is a three-hour drive from Baltimore and Washington DC; follow I-70 to I-68, and then take exit 14 onto Route 219 south. Follow Route 219 approximately 13 miles.

There is also no local public transportation system in the Deep Creek Lake area, so once you arrive, you will need a car to get around.

Background

The Landscape

GEOGRAPHY

Together, Virginia and Maryland encompass more than 55,000 square miles and stretch from the Atlantic Ocean to the Appalachian Mountains.

Virginia and Maryland are divided into five geographic regions. The Atlantic coastal plain (also called the Tidewater) is the easternmost portion of both states, bounded on the west by Washington DC and Richmond. It includes salt marshes, coastal areas, the Eastern Shore, and the Atlantic beaches. The Piedmont is the low, rolling, fertile

central region of both states and sits just west of the Atlantic coastal plain. It is the largest geographic region, extending from Richmond west to the Blue Ridge Mountains.

The Blue Ridge region is a narrow band that is mostly mountainous (over 1,000 feet). The highest peak in Virginia, Mount Rogers (5,729 feet), is in this region at the southernmost part of the state near the North Carolina border. West of the Blue Ridge is the Appalachian Ridge and Valley Region, which is a series of valleys divided by mountains. This region includes the Shenandoah Valley in Virginia, the Great Valley in Maryland, and a slice of the Allegheny Mountains. The far southwestern corner of Virginia and the westernmost reaches of Maryland are part of the Appalachian Plateau. This area is known for its forests, rivers, and streams. Maryland's highest peak, Backbone Mountain (3,360 feet) in Garrett County, is located in this region.

CLIMATE

Virginia and Maryland have what many residents feel is the perfect climate. There are four distinct seasons, and the weather is seldom extreme. Having said this, most of the region—eastern and central Virginia and Maryland—is considered subtropical, which is defined by hot, humid summers and mild, cool winters. The western portions of both states have a humid continental climate, which is defined by large seasonal temperature fluctuations with warm to hot summers and cold to severely cold winters.

The abundance of water to the east of both states, which includes the Atlantic Ocean, the Chesapeake Bay, and many large rivers and their tributaries, helps fuel the humidity commonly associated with the region. It's no surprise that the humidity is much higher in the coastal regions of both states, whereas the western mountain regions are typically 10 degrees cooler throughout the year and considerably less "sticky."

Springtime in Virginia and Maryland is fragrant and colorful. There are flowering fruit trees, blooming dogwoods, spring bulbs, and wildflowers throughout both states. Rivers swollen from melted winter snow rush by blankets of blooming bluebells, and azaleas explode throughout suburban neighborhoods. Temperatures in the spring can vary greatly but overall offer comfortable, warm days with chilly nights.

Summer brings ample sunshine with frequent afternoon thunderstorms. The humidity can be far more uncomfortable than the heat, but there are days, especially in August, where both seem unbearable and the air is so thick you'll think you can swim through it. The good news is, there are rare washout days in the summer when it rains continuously, and when it does, it's a welcome break from the heat. The shore areas offer refuge during the summer as do the mountains, but neither is a close second to the comfort of modern air-conditioning.

Fall is brilliant in Virginia and Maryland. Temperatures are cool, the humidity recedes, and the landscape explodes from exhausted greens to vibrant reds and yellows. The autumn foliage is some of the best in the country, especially in the mountainous areas to the west. Peak foliage is normally in mid-October but varies year to year. The local news broadcasts usually keep tabs on the foliage and let people know the best days for leaf peeping. This spectacular natural display, coupled with crisp sunny days and chilly nights, makes fall the best time to visit the region.

When the leaves finally fall and the pumpkins are ripe on the vine, winter is approaching. For most of Virginia and Maryland, winter temperatures usually set in sometime in December and don't thaw until early March. Even so, the area receives minimal snowfall, normally a handful of snow events each season. Although it is possible to get a large snowstorm, it does not happen every year. Likewise, temperatures can dip into the single digits, but that is not the norm. The thermometer normally rests somewhere between 25 and 40 degrees during the day in winter, but cold spells and also warm spells aren't unheard of. The exception to all of this is western Maryland, which can receive more than 100 inches of snow annually and has temperatures on average of about 10 degrees cooler than the central and eastern parts of the state. Virginia's mountains can also see more snow than their neighbors in the Piedmont, but snow totals average about 25 inches a year.

ENVIRONMENTAL ISSUES

One of the biggest environmental issues in Virginia and Maryland is the health of the Chesapeake Bay. The bay faces many problems including nutrient and sediment pollution from agriculture, storm water runoff, wastewater treatment plants, and air pollution; contamination from chemicals; overharvesting; invasive species; and the effects of development on its shores and tributaries. All of these threats impact the health of the bay and its ability to maintain a viable aquatic ecosystem.

Excess nutrients are the primary pollutant in the Chesapeake Bay. They increase algae bloom growth, which blocks vital sunlight to aquatic grasses. These grasses are crucial to the bay's ecosystem since they provide food and habitat to aquatic animals, reduce erosion, and produce oxygen. In addition, when the algae die and decompose, it depletes the water of the oxygen that all aquatic animals need.

The issues facing the bay are not localized problems. The Chesapeake Bay's watershed covers 64,000 square miles through six states and DC. There are 17 million residents living in this area.

Mass media attention in recent years has led to a greater awareness of the issues facing the bay and its tributaries, but there is still a very long way to go before the problems are solved.

The **Chesapeake Bay Foundation** (www.cbf.org), headquartered in Annapolis, Maryland, is the largest conservation organization dedicated to the well-being of the Chesapeake Bay watershed. Its famous "Save the Bay" slogan defines the continued quest to protect and restore the bay's natural resources.

Another environmental issue that is common to both Virginia and Maryland is the need for healthy farming. Unsustainable farming practices have contributed to water and air pollution throughout both states and have also resulted in soil erosion, animal abuse, and poor human health. Organizations such as **Environment Virginia** (www.environmentvirginia.org) and **Environment Maryland** (www.environmentmaryland.org) are looking for ways to expand opportunities for sustainable farmers that grow food in ways that don't pollute the environment.

PLANTS

The state of Virginia published a book titled *Flora of Virginia,* which is the only existing guide to nearly 3,200 species of trees, grasses, shrubs, flowers, and cacti that currently grow in the state. This huge book (weighing nearly seven pounds) took 11 years and $1.7 million to put together. It is a testament to the wide variety of plant life that has taken root in this region over the centuries. Maryland shares much of the same flora as Virginia, although both have been cultivated since settlers first arrived.

Virginia and Maryland's central location on the East Coast allows them to boast both southern and northern flora. Visitors can see northern tree species such as spruce and fir in the western mountain areas and then drive east to visit cypress swamps in the coastal regions.

Trees

Forest covers roughly two-thirds of Virginia and one-third of Maryland. Much of the mountainous region in the western portion of both states is heavily forested and contains dozens of species of trees such as the eastern white pine (which can grow to 200 feet), Virginia pine, pond pine, eastern hemlock, and even red spruce. Forested areas can also be found in the Piedmont and coastal regions of the states. In fact, the loblolly pine, which is the most important commercial timber tree in Virginia, grows near the coast in both states. Maryland is the northern reach of the loblolly pine's territory, and the same is true for the bald cypress.

Other common trees found throughout the region include the eastern red cedar, black willow, black walnut, bitternut hickory (swamp hickory), American beech, American elm, yellow poplar, sycamore, northern red oak, and white oak (which is the Maryland state tree).

Many ornamental trees are also native to the region, such as holly, red maple, magnolia, and the flowering dogwood (which is both the state tree and the state flower of Virginia).

Plants, Shrubs, and Flowers

Because of the mild climate, there are many flowering shrubs and 85 species of ferns in Virginia and Maryland. Nothing announces the arrival of spring like the bright yellow blooms of the forsythia. This sprawling bush is a favorite of homeowners since it provides pretty blooms in the spring and a good screen in the summer. Several varieties of azaleas are native to the region, and in May residential neighborhoods are painted in their vibrant red, pink, purple, and white blooms. Rhododendrons are also native to the region, as are the butterfly bush (sometimes referred to as summer lilac) and the stunning hydrangea.

Spring and summer yield thousands of wildflowers across both states. Shenandoah National Park alone has 862 species, providing a breathtaking display from early spring through summer. Species include hepatica, violets, trillium, wild geraniums, mountain laurel, columbine, and wild sunflowers. In the coastal areas, wildflowers grow among marsh grasses and over sand dunes.

Although many native flowers grow quite well across both states, such as the woodland sunflower, hibiscus, lupine, lobelia, and phlox, some species are partial to either the eastern or western side of the states since the geography is so varied between the two. At least two types of asters are found primarily in the mountain regions: the smooth blue aster and the New England aster. The American lily of the valley is also partial to the mountainous region. The coastal region has its own share of plant species that exclusively call the area home, such as the New York aster and seaside goldenrod.

ANIMALS

Virginia and Maryland are full of wildlife, and their mild climate and varied geography allow many types of animals to flourish. Since the mountainous areas are heavily forested and less populated, they are home to the most animals. Although most are shy, there are often sightings of foxes, skunks, raccoons, rabbits, chipmunks, squirrels, and white-tailed deer. In some of the park areas, the deer have become too friendly with humans and will literally walk right up to you. Under no circumstances should you feed the wildlife, no matter how cute and convincing they are. Other animals that live in the western regions include the coyote, bobcat, and black bear.

The central regions of both states (dominated by the large Piedmont region) provide shelter for many species of animals that have learned to coexist well with nearby human populations. Raccoons, opossums, squirrels, chipmunks, beavers, and, more recently, coyotes, can be found throughout the region.

The coastal regions' wetlands, marshes, and rivers entice populations of lizards, muskrats, butterflies, and snakes. Animals from the Piedmont can also be found in coastal areas, but less forest means fewer places to hide from predators and the harsh summer sunshine.

There are three types of venomous snakes in Virginia and Maryland and 31 nonvenomous. The most common type of venomous snake, found across both states, is the

More Than Tasty Bivalves

Oyster lovers flock to the Chesapeake Bay region to feast on the famous eastern oyster. For more than 100 years, this delectable yet peculiar-looking creature flourished in the bay and was one of the most valuable commercial fishing commodities. However, in recent decades, overharvesting, disease, and pollution have severely reduced its numbers. This is more than just a bummer for oyster eaters; oysters are a vital piece of the Chesapeake Bay's ecosystem.

Oysters provide habitat for many aquatic animals. Their hard shells with many nooks and crannies act as much-needed reefs and are relied on by hundreds of underwater animals such as sponges, crabs, and fish. Oysters and their larvae are also an important food source for many aquatic residents and some shorebirds. In addition, oysters are filter feeders, which means they pump large amounts of water through their gills when they eat. This filters the water, removing chemical contaminants, nutrients, and sediments, which helps keep the water clean. One oyster can filter more than 50 gallons of water in a single day.

northern copperhead, which has dark-colored cross bands shaped like an hourglass. Next comes the timber rattlesnake, which is found in all the mountainous regions of both states and in the southeastern corner of Virginia. It also has a patterned back with wavy cross bands. The eastern cottonmouth snake is only found in southeastern Virginia south of Newport News. It can be yellowish olive to black in color and has approximately 13 black cross bands that are wide at the sides and narrow at the backbone.

Birds

A huge variety of birds live in Virginia and Maryland, from migratory shorebirds to tiny songbirds—and even bald eagles. Virginia has 340 native bird species and Maryland 222, but these numbers are much greater if you include seasonal birds that do not actually nest in the states. In spring and early summer, the woods are alive with the happy calls of songbirds, but during winter, many migrate south. On the flip side, some northern birds, such as snow geese, come down from Canada because the winters are milder here.

Many hawks live throughout the region, and the red-tailed variety can often be spotted (although they will surely see you before you see them). Another impressive and frequently seen bird is the turkey vulture, also known as a buzzard. They are huge and can have a wingspan up to six feet. Wild turkeys are also prevalent and look like they walked out of a children's Thanksgiving story. Game birds such as the grouse are residents of the area and sometimes startle hikers by launching themselves in the air when they see someone approach.

Migratory birds such as warblers frequent the mountain regions during the winter, and the Piedmont region offers sightings of bald eagles, pileated woodpeckers, great blue herons, cormorants, and bufflehead ducks. The coastal areas are prime for bird-watching. More than 40 types of ducks, geese, and swans alone have been documented in water-rich areas. This area is also home to ospreys, oystercatchers, plovers, peregrine falcons, black skimmers, and dozens of other shorebirds.

History

IN THE BEGINNING

It is believed that the first humans arrived in the Virginia and Maryland region approximately 18,000 years ago. They were hunter-gatherers most likely organized into seminomadic bands. As time went on, hunting tools became more efficient, and delicacies from the Chesapeake Bay, such as oysters, became an important food source. With new developments came the first Native American villages and the formation of social structures. Successive Native American cultures continued for thousands of years prior to the arrival of Europeans.

THE COLONIAL PERIOD

After many failed attempts at establishing a permanent settlement, in 1607 the first English settlers arrived at the mouth of the Chesapeake Bay in three ships and traveled 30 miles up the James River under the guidance of Captain John Smith. The settlers disembarked and promptly began to build a settlement at what later became Jamestown.

They found the coastal area inhabited by Algonquian natives (called the Powhatan Confederacy) who controlled land stretching from what is now North Carolina to the Potomac River. These native settlements included approximately 10,000 people who relied on hunting, fishing, and farming for survival. Another native group controlled what is now Maryland and the mountain regions of both states stretching west into the Allegheny Mountains.

The settlers were met with rich lands, many game animals, and initially friendly natives. Even so, they were not prepared for the physical labor and inevitable problems that came with starting a new settlement, and the colony nearly failed in the first few years. Around 1612, a colonist named John Rolfe brought in the first tobacco seeds, which he had gathered from an earlier voyage to Trinidad. The first tobacco crops were planted and were soon in high demand back in England. This provided an instant boost to the New World's economy.

Put mildly, life was very difficult for the early settlers. Disease, famine, and attacks from Native Americans wiped out much of the early population. Although the Native Americans were initially friendly, it didn't take long for their feelings to change when they realized the settlers intended to stay permanently. In just a couple of years, most of the Native American settlements had been seized, and it became unsafe for the settlers to venture past their settlement fences. A temporary truce resulted in 1614 from the marriage of the 13-year-old daughter of Chief Powhatan, named Pocahontas (who had earlier saved Captain John Smith's life when her father tried to kill him), to John Rolfe. The truce ended quickly with a surprise Powhatan attack that killed 400 settlers.

Meanwhile, in 1609, an Englishman named Henry Hudson arrived in the Delaware Bay. Working on behalf of the Dutch West India Company, Hudson was pleased with the wonderful conditions he found in the region. As a result, in 1631, a group of Dutch West India traders established a small whaling port and tobacco-growing center in what is now Lewes, Delaware. At the same time, Maryland's first European settler, William Claiborne, came to that region and established a fur-trading post on Kent Island.

In 1632, Charles I of England granted approximately 12 million acres north of the Potomac River and Virginia to Cecilius Calvert, second Baron Baltimore. The area was substantially larger than today's Maryland, and Maryland later lost some of the land to Pennsylvania. The first full settlement was established in 1634 on St. Clement's Island.

Maryland was established as a refuge for religious freedom for Catholics, although many Protestants moved there also. This caused religious feuds for years in the colony. At the same time, its economy relied on tobacco fueled by African slave labor and indentured servants. Farming, tobacco, and the abundance of land slowly brought prosperity to the early colonies.

As land along the coast filled up, pioneers began to move farther inland toward the mountains. New immigrants continued to arrive, including people from places such as Germany and Scotland.

In 1649 a settlement called Providence was founded on the north shore of the Severn River and was later moved to a more protected harbor on the south shore. It was then called Town at Proctor's, which changed to Town at the Severn, and later Anne Arundel's Towne. The city became very wealthy as a slave trade center. In 1694, the town became the capital of the royal colony and was renamed Annapolis for the future queen of Great Britain, Princess Anne of Denmark and Norway. Annapolis was incorporated in 1708 and flourished until the Revolutionary War.

By the early 1700s, many colonists in Virginia were enjoying generous fortunes earned through growing tobacco. The Church of England was the official church in Virginia, which differentiated it from Maryland and the New England colonies. But the church became a secondary interest since there was a short supply of clergy and houses of worship. In 1705, Virginia's capital was moved from Jamestown to nearby Williamsburg.

Virginia and Maryland were regions of large plantations and minimal urban development. Since much of the plantation labor was supplied by indentured servants, few women came to the area. This, combined with a high rate of disease, made for the slow growth of the local population.

By 1700, most Native Americans had been driven out of Virginia and Maryland. At the same time, the number of enslaved African people had grown rapidly in the region as the number of indentured servants declined. Throughout the first half of the century, tensions between the colonies and their European motherland grew as England tried to squeeze as much money as possible out of the colonists through taxes while extending them far fewer rights than held by those living in the home country. One of the final straws came in 1763 with the passing of a law prohibiting westward expansion of the colonies, which angered many colonists. A passionate and heated speech delivered by Patrick Henry in Williamsburg in 1765 implied publicly that the colonies might be better off without King George III. Tension between England and the colonies continued to grow, and rebellious outbreaks such as the Boston Tea Party in 1773 began to grow more frequent. Maryland had its own tea party in Chestertown in 1774, when colonists burned the tea-carrying ship *Geddes* in the town's harbor.

In 1775 Henry delivered his famous speech at St. John's Church in Richmond where he was quoted as saying, "I know not what course others may take; but as for me, give me liberty or give me death."

THE REVOLUTIONARY WAR

Although no major Revolutionary War battles were fought in Maryland, it was the first colony to adopt a state constitution. Virginia became a primary center of war activity since it was the largest and most populated colony. Virginia experienced fighting from the earliest days of the war, although it managed to escape much of the destruction for the first three years. Virginia's capital was moved to a safer location at Richmond in 1780 after British ships sailed into the Hampton Roads area, and the capital has remained there ever since.

Major Virginia confrontations included the Battle of Great Bridge, where British authorities were removed from the colony, and the Yorktown Campaign. The Yorktown Campaign moved through Petersburg when British forces landed along the James River in 1781 in order to support Lord Cornwallis's army based in North Carolina. Twenty-five hundred British troops moved against Petersburg, and a clash with 1,200 militia occurred in what is now the neighborhood of Blanford.

The most well-known battle took place in Yorktown, where 18,000 members of the Continental and French armies defeated British forces, causing their surrender in 1781. This battle was the final victory that secured America's independence.

EXPANSION

In 1788, Virginia became the 10th state in the new nation. One year later, Virginia-born George Washington became the first U.S. president. Many of the country's founding fathers came from Virginia, including Thomas Jefferson, James Madison, and George Mason. At the time, the state was home to 20 percent of the country's population and more than 30 percent of its commerce. A new law that enabled owners to free their enslaved people was also passed, and by 1790, there were more than 12,000 free African Americans in Virginia.

The city of Baltimore incorporated in 1797 and experienced rapid growth as a shipbuilding and industrial center. By 1800, its population outnumbered that of Boston, and the development of Maryland's resources became a priority. Virginia fell behind in this aspect of development, and the port in Hampton Roads paled in comparison to that in Baltimore.

Baltimore was spared seizure during the War of 1812 but suffered a 25-hour attack at Fort McHenry (during which Francis Scott Key wrote "The Star-Spangled Banner"). British troops went on to burn the young capital city of Washington DC.

After the war, steam locomotives and clipper ships were developed, greatly expanding trade possibilities. A series of canals was built, including the Chesapeake & Ohio Canal along the Potomac River, and railroads such as the Baltimore & Ohio Railroad were constructed. This greatly increased access between East Coast ports and land west of the Appalachians. By the mid-1800s, railroad lines ran through both Virginia and Maryland, bringing wealth and prosperity to many agricultural-based businesses, although it was not until after the Civil War that railroads connected all primary population centers in Virginia.

THE AMERICAN CIVIL WAR

Thomas Jefferson predicted a conflict regarding the issue of slavery. He felt that "God is just: that his justice cannot sleep forever" and a change in the current situation was very possible. Soon, calls for emancipation spread through the North, and scattered revolts against slavery gained momentum. In 1859, a raid on the federal arsenal in Harpers Ferry led by an American abolitionist named John Brown resulted in the death of 21 people—both free African Americans and whites—and the realization by the country that slavery opponents were willing to kill and die themselves for their cause.

In 1860, Abraham Lincoln was elected president and pledged to keep slavery out of the territories. In December that same year, South Carolina seceded from the Union and was followed shortly thereafter by Mississippi, Alabama, Georgia, Florida, Louisiana, and Texas.

Although technically still a slave state in 1860, Maryland was one of the border states that stayed with the Union during the Civil War, but Maryland soldiers fought on both sides. Virginia, however, joined its southern neighbors and seceded from the nation in 1861, after which it became a prominent Confederate state.

Four years of bloody fighting took place on soil passionately defended less than a century before in the Revolutionary War. More than 600,000 Americans lost their lives in the war, more than those lost in both World Wars combined. Virginia suffered more casualties and witnessed more major battles than any other state. In just four years, the state was left in ruins. Some of the major battles fought in Virginia include the First and Second Battles of Bull Run (Manassas), Battle of the Ironclads, Seven Days' Battles, Battle of Fredericksburg, and Battle of Chancellorsville. Maryland also hosted several well-known battles, including the famous Battle of Antietam, the Battle of South Mountain, and the Battle of the Monocacy.

Richmond was burned on April 3, 1865. Six days later, General Robert E. Lee asked General Ulysses S. Grant for a meeting. Terms of the surrender were drafted and signed at Appomattox Court House, and the Confederate army turned over arms in a formal ceremony on April 12.

MODERN TIMES

The 1900s brought a diversification of industry to both Virginia and Maryland. Baltimore suffered a devastating fire in 1904, but recovered quickly. World War I gave a boost to Maryland by increasing the demand for industrial products, while Virginia benefited from enormous expansion to the Newport News shipyard. The Great Depression slowed growth in some markets, but overall, both Virginia and Maryland fared well through that difficult time.

By the middle of the 20th century, Virginia had evolved from a rural state into an urban one. World War II had again given a boost to the Hampton Roads area in support of the Norfolk Naval Base and shipyard. In contrast, as American industry diminished, Maryland turned to agriculture and U.S. government-related research and services.

RECENT HISTORY

In recent decades, the Washington DC area has experienced an economic and technological boom, resulting in an increase in population, housing, and jobs in both Northern Virginia and the capital region of Maryland. By the early 1990s, Virginia had a population of more than 6 million while Maryland had 4.7 million.

The early part of the new millennium was scarred for both states by the terrorist attacks on 9/11 and by the sniper shootings in the DC area in 2002 that left 10 people dead. A resilient community that was actually united by these events, Maryland and Virginia are today more closely bound as the two states face common issues such as rapid suburban development, economic fluctuations, and environmental preservation.

Government and Economy

VIRGINIA GOVERNMENT

Virginia is traditionally a conservative state. It is governed by the Constitution of Virginia, which was adopted in 1971 and is the seventh constitution. There are three branches of government in Virginia: the legislative, executive, and judicial branches. The executive branch has three elected officials: the governor, lieutenant governor, and attorney general, which are elected individually statewide to four-year terms.

Virginia's governor is the chief executive officer of the Commonwealth and the commander in chief of the state militia. Governors can serve multiple terms, but they must be nonconsecutive. The lieutenant governor is the president of the Senate of Virginia and first in the line of succession to the governor. A lieutenant governor can run for reelection. The attorney general is second in the line of succession to the governor and the chief legal advisor to both the governor and the General Assembly. He or she is also the chief lawyer of the state and heads the Department of Law.

The legislative branch in Virginia is the General Assembly made up of 40 senators (serving four-year terms) and 100 delegates (serving two-year terms). The General Assembly claims to be the "oldest continuous law-making body in the New World" and traces its roots back to the House of Burgesses in Jamestown.

The Virginia judiciary is made up of the Supreme Court of Virginia and subordinate courts such as the Court of Appeals, the Circuit Courts, and the General District Courts. The judiciary is led by the chief justice of the Supreme Court, the Judicial Council, the Committee on District Courts, and Judicial Conferences.

Thomas Jefferson designed the State Capitol Building in Richmond, and Governor Patrick Henry laid the cornerstone in 1785.

MARYLAND GOVERNMENT

Maryland is traditionally a liberal state. Like Virginia, Maryland has a state constitution and three branches of government. Maryland is unique in the sense that it allows each of its counties to have significant autonomy.

There are five principal executive branch officers in Maryland: the governor, lieutenant governor, attorney general, comptroller, and treasurer. With the exception of the treasurer, all are elected statewide, with the governor and lieutenant governor running on one ticket. The treasurer is elected by both houses of the General Assembly on a joint ballot.

The legislative branch is a General Assembly made up of two houses with 47 senators and 141 delegates. Members of both houses are elected to four-year terms. Each house establishes its own rules of conduct and elects its own officers.

Maryland's judiciary branch consists of four courts. Two are trial courts (the District Court and Circuit Courts), and two are Appellate Courts (the Court of Special Appeals and the Court of Appeals). The Court of Appeals is the highest court.

VIRGINIA'S ECONOMY

Virginia is traditionally a wealthy state and typically has the most counties and independent cities in the top 100 wealthiest jurisdictions in the country. Perhaps the wealthiest Southern state prior to the Civil War, Virginia recovered quickly from its Civil War scars and also weathered the Great Depression much better than the rest of the South. Much of the wealth is concentrated in the northern part of the state near Washington DC, where housing prices are sky-high. Loudoun and Fairfax Counties have two of the highest median household incomes out of all the counties in the nation. Virginia is one of 24 right-to-work states where union security agreements are prohibited.

Virginia's economy includes a balance of income from federal government-supported jobs, technology industries, military installations, and agriculture. The military plays a prominent role in the state's financial picture with facilities such as the Pentagon in Arlington, Marine Corps Base Quantico, and the privately owned shipyards in Newport News.

High-tech firms and government contractors have replaced dairy farms and now dominate Northern Virginia, which is home to 10 Fortune 500 companies and is the planned site of Amazon's East Coast headquarters. Richmond has an additional 7 Fortune 500 companies.

Although modern farming techniques have put many small farmers out of business and sent them to metropolitan areas in search of new careers, agriculture still plays a role in much of the state, with crops such as tobacco, sweet potatoes, peanuts, tomatoes, apples, grains, hay, and soy. True to its roots, Virginia is still the third-largest tobacco producer in the country. Livestock is also a thriving commodity, and cattle fields can be seen along much of I-81 in the western part of the state. Despite the natural resources of the Chesapeake Bay, Virginia makes only a small portion of its revenue from the fishing industry.

The number of wineries is on the rise in Virginia, with acres of vineyards in the Northern Neck, Charlottesville, and near the Blue Ridge Mountains. Predictions are that in decades to come, Virginia will rise through the ranks of the great wine-producing states.

MARYLAND'S ECONOMY

Maryland is a small but wealthy state whose economy has traditionally been heavily weighted toward manufacturing. Two Maryland counties, Howard and Montgomery, are consistently listed in the nation's top 15 richest counties.

In recent years, Maryland's economic activity has included a strong focus on the tertiary service sector, which is largely influenced by its proximity to Washington DC. Technical administration for the defense and aerospace industry and bioresearch laboratories is also key in its economy. In addition, many government agencies have satellite headquarters in Maryland for which they need staffing.

Transportation is another major revenue generator for Maryland, thanks to the Port of Baltimore. The port is one of the largest automobile ports in the country but also accommodates a large variety of other goods including bulk commodities such as petroleum, sugar, iron ore, and fertilizers. These goods are distributed on land in trucks and by rail, further adding to the transportation influence.

A third major contributor to the state's economy is educational and medical research. Several key institutions are located in the state, the largest being Johns Hopkins University. Johns Hopkins is currently the largest single employer in the Baltimore area.

Maryland is also known for its food production, thanks mostly to commercial fishing in the Chesapeake Bay and offshore in the Atlantic Ocean. Prime catches include blue crab, striped bass, menhaden, and oysters. Dairy farming in the Piedmont region also contributes to the economy.

People and Culture

PEOPLE AND CULTURE IN VIRGINIA

Traditionally, the people in Virginia were hardworking farmers, political pioneers, and sailors. The early colonists came mostly from rural England but were soon joined by French, Irish, German, and Scots-Irish who immigrated from abroad and also came to the Shenandoah Valley through Pennsylvania and Maryland. African Americans were a large part of early culture in Virginia; many initially arrived as indentured servants, followed by larger numbers through the African slave trade. Native American populations were devastated by European disease to the point that just a very small population survived to see modern times.

Today Virginia is largely diversified, with 85 percent of its residents living in metropolitan areas. Northern Virginia especially is a highly transient area with residents from all over the globe. Many households speak a language other than English at home, and many fabulous restaurants serving authentic international cuisine can be found.

African Americans make up the largest minority in Virginia, totaling nearly 20 percent. The African American population is heavily concentrated in the eastern portion of the state, with the largest populations being in Richmond and Norfolk. Second is the Latino population, which comprises approximately 10 percent of the population (located primarily in Northern Virginia), followed by an Asian population of approximately 7 percent (also primarily in Northern Virginia).

Many parts of southern and western Virginia embrace the culture of the southern United States. It is there you can find authentic Southern cuisine and Virginia-specific food such as Virginia ham (country ham produced in Virginia), Virginia barbecue (pork with a vinegar-based sauce, similar to North Carolina barbecue), marble cake, shoofly pie, Brunswick stew, and peanut soup.

The first colonists came to Virginia motivated primarily by material wealth rather than religious freedom. This is not to say that the colonists weren't religious; they just assumed religion and government went together and that the Anglican Church would be the designated church. There was some rivalry between Virginia and Catholic-established Maryland, although to attract settlers, the Anglicans of Virginia were flexible to newcomers. As such, they encouraged groups such as the Pennsylvania Dutch to move south into the Shenandoah Valley in part so they could alert eastern settlements of attacks by the French or Native Americans coming from bases in the Ohio River Valley. To this day, the German Mennonite heritage is still evident west of the Blue Ridge.

Thomas Jefferson and James Madison led first Virginia and then the nation to end government involvement in religion. This spread tolerance of religious freedom throughout the state and resulted in a permanent acceptance throughout the Commonwealth of various forms of religion and the option to follow no religion at all.

It's almost impossible to summarize the attitudes of Virginians across the board because the state is so diverse. But in the smaller towns and rural areas, everyone waves, people ask strangers for directions, and you might get slipped a free piece of apple pie at a local diner for no apparent reason. Many areas in Virginia still offer a secure sense of community, although in some cities crime is unfortunately an issue.

PEOPLE AND CULTURE IN MARYLAND

Historically, Marylanders were fishers and farmers. Although southern and western Maryland are still mostly rural, the rest of the state is now primarily urban with dense populations, especially in Baltimore and near Washington DC. This makes for a unique blend of both southern and northern American culture and a melding of ideals from both regions.

Unlike Virginia, Maryland was founded as a place for Roman Catholics to escape religious persecution, since the Catholic religion was repressed in England following the founding of the Anglican Church.

During colonial times, groups of Quakers moved into Maryland from Pennsylvania, and in the mid-17th century a group of conservative Protestants called Puritans settled south of Baltimore. Although Puritans are not defined as such today, another conservative Protestant group, the Old Order Amish, is still strong in some areas of southern Maryland and the Eastern Shore. Their horse-drawn wagons can be seen on many roads throughout those areas.

Other religions quickly made their way into Maryland, with the first Lutheran church being built around 1729 and the first Baptist church in 1742. Methodists came to the state as well, and a large Jewish population settled in Baltimore in the early part of the 1800s.

Today Maryland is widely accepting of religious diversity, and people from all faiths (and of no faith) can be found within its borders.

Maryland has always had a large African American population. During the time of slavery, Maryland had the largest population of free African Americans of the northeastern slave states. Today, African Americans make up approximately 31 percent of Maryland's population.

Unfortunately, race relations have traditionally been strained in Maryland, and many neighborhoods are strictly delineated by race. Baltimore is the most diverse area of the state, while western Maryland (Garrett County) is the least.

THE ARTS

Virginia and Maryland offer numerous opportunities for residents and visitors to not only enjoy the arts but to become part of them. In fact, the arts are an important part of many people's lives in this region, whether they realize it or not. Access to top-rated performances, historic architecture, quality handicrafts, and literature is often taken for granted by the people who live here. A recent survey in Maryland, for instance, showed that 70 percent of the state's residents engage in art in some form or another, whether by attending a musical performance, taking part in a festival, or visiting a museum or gallery. Another example is the **Virginians for The Arts** organization, which lists more than 4,500 state organizations and individual advocates for the arts in Virginia alone.

These states' long histories, diversified populations, proximity to the nation's capital, and relative tolerance for religious and social beliefs open the region to many traditional and forward-thinking expressions of artistic community to everyone who passes through the area.

Countless theatrical venues throughout the region, including world-renowned venues in Washington DC, invite the highest-quality performances to the doorstep of many local communities, and specialized venues provide access to cutting-edge artistic advances.

Essentials

Transportation

Due in part to their proximity to Washington DC, Virginia and Maryland are easily accessible from many parts of the United States and from other countries.

AIR

Most major airlines serve the three primary airports in Virginia and Maryland. The first is **Ronald Reagan Washington National Airport (DCA)** (703/417-8000, www.flyreagan.com), just outside Washington DC in Arlington, Virginia. It is a 15-minute drive from

the airport to downtown Washington DC. The airport is serviced by the Blue and Yellow Metrorail Lines. Taxi service is available at the Arrivals curb outside the baggage claim area of each terminal. Rental cars are available on the first floor in parking garage A. A shuttle to the rental car counter is available outside each baggage claim area. Rideshare services such as Uber and Lyft are also available.

The second is **Washington Dulles International Airport (IAD)** (703/572-2700, www.flydulles.com), 27 miles west of Washington DC in Dulles, Virginia. It is a 35-minute drive to downtown Washington DC from Dulles. Bus service between Dulles Airport and Metrorail at the Wiehle Avenue Station in Reston (Silver Line) is available through **Washington Flyer Coach Service** (703/572-7661, www.flydulles.com, $5 one way, under 2 free). Tickets can be purchased at the ticket counter in the Main Terminal at Arrivals door 4 or at the Metrorail station at Wiehle Avenue. Buses depart approximately every 15-20 minutes. Passengers going from the Wiehle Avenue Metrorail station should follow signs for the Washington Flyer bus stop. **Metrobus** (202/637-7000, www.wmata.com) operates an express bus (Route 5A) between Dulles Airport and the L'Enfant Plaza Metrorail station in Washington DC. Passengers can board the bus at the airport at the Ground Transportation Curb (on the Arrivals level) at curb location 2E. Metrobus has proposed the elimination of this route several times since the opening of the Metrorail Silver Line, so check their website before relying on this route. Rideshare services such as Uber and Lyft are also available.

The third is **Baltimore Washington International Thurgood Marshall Airport (BWI)** (410/859-7040, www.bwiairport.com), 32 miles from Washington DC near Baltimore, Maryland. It is approximately 50 minutes by car from BWI to Washington DC and 15 minutes to downtown

Baltimore. BWI is serviced on weekdays by Maryland Area Rail Commuter (MARC) trains at the BWI Marshall Rail Station. Free shuttles are available from the station to the airport terminal. Shuttle stops can be found on the lower-level terminal road. Metrobus service is available between BWI and the Greenbelt Metrorail station (Green Line) on the **BWI Express Metro** (202/637-7000). Bus service is available Monday-Friday 6:30am-9:33pm with buses running every 60 minutes. Rideshare services such as Uber and Lyft are also available.

Washington Dulles Taxi and Sedan (703/554-3509, www.washingtondullestaxisedan.com) provides taxi and sedan service for passengers at all three airports. Shuttle service is also available from all three airports through **SuperShuttle** (800/258-3826, www.supershuttle.com).

The **BayRunner Shuttle** (www.bayrunnershuttle.com) provides daily, scheduled shuttle service between the Eastern Shore of Maryland and BWI and Western Maryland and BWI. Areas serviced on the Eastern Shore include Kent Island, Cambridge, Easton, and Ocean City. Areas serviced in Western Maryland include Frederick, Cumberland, Frostburg, and Grantsville. Shuttle service is also available to the Baltimore Bus Terminal.

There are also major airports near Richmond, Norfolk, Newport News/Williamsburg, Charlottesville, and Roanoke in Virginia and near Salisbury and Hagerstown in Maryland.

Flying between locations in Virginia and Maryland is possible but usually cost-prohibitive and less convenient compared to other travel options.

CAR

Virginia and Maryland, like most regions of the United States, are easiest to explore by car. The two states together encompass a large amount of land. It can take six hours to drive from Washington DC to the southern end of Virginia and nearly four hours to drive from Western Maryland to the Eastern Shore. Thankfully, a large network of interstate highways provides access throughout the entire area, even in the more rural areas on the western sides of the states.

I-95 is the main north-south travel route along the East Coast and connects Baltimore, Washington DC, and Richmond. This highway is a toll road in Maryland. I-81 is the main north-south travel route in the western portions of the states and connects Roanoke, Harrisonburg, and Winchester in Virginia and cuts through a narrow portion of Maryland at Hagerstown before continuing into Pennsylvania.

In Virginia, I-66 is a primary east-west route in the northern part of the state, starting at the Washington DC border in Arlington and ending past Front Royal at I-81. I-66 has High Occupancy Vehicle (HOV) restrictions and Express toll lanes during rush hour on weekdays. The other primary east-west route is I-64, which connects Norfolk, Richmond, and Charlottesville and ends near Staunton at I-81.

In Maryland, I-70 is the primary east-west route and links Baltimore to Frederick and runs out to Western Maryland before swinging north into Pennsylvania, at which point I-68 becomes the primary highway running east-west in the western corner of the state. I-270 is another primary route that runs north-south between Bethesda and Frederick. US 50 is the major route through the Eastern Shore in Maryland. It starts in Ocean City, runs west to Salisbury, then turns north to Cambridge, across the Bay Bridge (where there is a toll), past Annapolis, and continues west into Washington DC. It then continues into Virginia as a minor route.

Washington DC is circled by I-495, also called the Beltway, which runs through both Virginia and Maryland as part of I-95. This massive highway has access points to many of the Virginia and Maryland suburbs and can have extreme rush hour traffic. Baltimore has a similar beltway, I-695, which is not part of I-95 but has a toll at Key Bridge.

Speed limits are posted throughout Virginia and Maryland. The maximum allowable speed limit in Virginia is 70 miles per hour, while in Maryland it is 65 miles per hour, although most roads in both states have speed limits posted much below their maximums. Keep in mind that state-maintained roads can have both a name and a route number.

In Virginia, all drivers are banned by law from text messaging, and drivers under the age of 18 are prohibited from using cell phones and text messaging. In Maryland and DC, text messaging and handheld cell phone usage are banned for all drivers. Drivers under 18 are prohibited from all cell phone use. Seatbelt laws are enforced throughout both states.

The Washington area is not known for its efficiency at clearing snow off the roads in winter, but for the most part, state-maintained roads are plowed fairly quickly. The biggest hazard in both states is ice, specifically black ice, especially when above-freezing temperatures during the day melt ice and snow and then below-freezing temperatures at night cause a refreeze. Fog can sometimes be an issue when driving in the mountains, especially along Skyline Drive and in Western Maryland.

Both states' departments of transportation are good resources for maps, toll rates, webcams, road conditions, and details on HOV restrictions. Visit www.virginiadot.org and www.mdot.maryland.gov.

TRAIN

Amtrak (800/872-7245, www.amtrak.com) offers rail service to 21 stations in Virginia and 8 stations in Maryland. There is also 1 station in Washington DC—Union Station. Although a train ticket can rival the cost of airfare, it can also be more convenient and more comfortable to travel by train.

Amtrak connects to the **Virginia Railway Express (VRE)** (703/684-1001, www.vre.org)

in Virginia. VRE runs commuter train service between the Northern Virginia suburbs along the I-66 and I-95 corridors, to Alexandria, Crystal City, and Washington DC. They have 19 stations and 16 trains. Amtrak also connects to the **Maryland Area Rail Commuter (MARC)** (410/539-5000, www.mta.maryland. gov) train in Maryland. MARC operates on weekdays only and provides service to areas such as Harford County, Baltimore, Brunswick, Frederick, and Washington DC.

BUS

Many cities in Virginia and Maryland can be reached by **Greyhound** (800/231-2222, www. greyhound.com). Tickets are less expensive when purchased in advance, and discounts are often available to students, seniors, and military personnel.

Local bus service is available in many cities, with the most extensive being the **Metrobus** (202/637-7000, www.wmata.com/bus) service in and around Washington DC and its suburbs. Metrobus has an incredible 11,500 bus stops on 325 routes throughout Washington DC, Virginia, and Maryland and is the sixth-busiest bus service provider in the nation. They have more than 1,500 buses.

Tourist-friendly bus systems exist in both Washington DC with the **DC Circulator** (www.dccirculator.com, free) and Baltimore with the **Charm City Circulator** (www. charmcitycirculator.com, free).

SUBWAY

Washington DC and the surrounding area has a clean, reliable, and generally safe subway system called **Metrorail** (202/637-7000, www.wmata.com/rail) that is run by the **Washington Metropolitan Area Transit Authority (WMATA).** The Metrorail system is commonly known as the Metro and provides service to more than 600,000 customers a day. The system is number two in the country in terms of ticket sales and serves more than 91 stations throughout DC, Virginia, and Maryland.

There are six color-coded rail lines: the Red, Orange, Blue, Yellow, Green, and Silver. The system layout is easy to understand, as most stations are named for the neighborhood they serve, and getting from one station to another normally requires no more than a single transfer. Metrorail stations are marked with large "M" signs at the entrance that have colored stripes around them to show which line they serve. A complete list of fares and a map of each train line can be found on the website. Metrorail opens at 5am on weekdays, 7am on Saturday, and 8am on Sunday. It closes at 11:30pm Monday-Thursday, 1am Friday-Saturday, and 11pm Sunday. Bicycles are permitted during nonpeak hours.

WATER

If you're lucky enough to cruise into Virginia or Maryland on a private boat, you'll have options for docking in marinas along the Chesapeake Bay, the Intracoastal Waterway, and the Potomac River. Most towns on the water offer marina slips, but making plans ahead of time is advised, especially during the prime summer months and in popular areas such as Annapolis.

Recreation

If you can dream it, you can do it in Virginia and Maryland. Well, almost anyway. People in this region are crazy about getting outside, and with the mountains and seashore just a few hours apart, the opportunities are endless.

HIKING

Thousands of hiking trails are available throughout Virginia and Maryland, including a large portion of the **Appalachian Trail.** The best part is, you only need a good pair of trail shoes or hiking boots and you're on your way. **Shenandoah National Park** alone has more than 500 miles of trails, but other favorites include the C&O Canal Towpath, the Washington & Old Dominion Trail, and the Virginia Creeper Trail.

The **Potomac Appalachian Trail Club** (www.potomacappalachian.org) is a wonderful resource for hikers throughout the area and offers maps, books, and trip information.

BIKING

Whether you like to road bike, mountain bike, or just toddle along on a cruiser enjoying the scenery, Virginia and Maryland are the places to do it. From the flat Eastern Shore to the challenging mountains of the Shenandoah and Western Maryland, there are endless choices for getting out and pedaling.

For those who are competitive, the racing scene is thriving in the region, and road races are held most weekends April through October. Mountain bike races are also very popular and run even later in the year.

Road Cycling

Many organized rides take place in Virginia and Maryland, including the famous **Seagull Century** (www.seagullcentury.org), held each October on the Eastern Shore of Maryland. Wide, flat roads with little traffic make the Eastern Shore a favorite place to bike almost any time of the year. The terrain is nearly pancake flat, although there is often a headwind. **Bike Virginia** (www.bikevirginia. org) is a six-day bike tour that goes through a different part of Virginia each year in June. Riders can choose from a variety of distances to pedal each day.

More-challenging rides include the fierce **Mountains of Misery** (www. mountainsofmisery.com) ride in southern Virginia and the **Garrett County Gran Fondo** (www.garrettcountygranfondo.org) in Western Maryland.

Not all roads are conducive to road cycling, given the extreme traffic conditions in many urban areas. Be wise about choosing a biking route; accidents do happen, and usually the bike is on the worse end of it.

Mountain Biking

Mountain biking is big in the mid-Atlantic, and Virginia and Maryland are no exception. Charlottesville, Virginia, was even rated the eighth-best dream town in the country for mountain bikers by *Mountain Bike* magazine. Mountain bike trails can be found near the cities, in the rural areas, and throughout the mountains. Fat-tire races are also held throughout the year. **MTB Project** (www. mtbproject.com) and **Singletracks** (www. singletracks.com) are good resources for mountain biking in the region.

CANOEING AND KAYAKING

Canoeing is one of the most popular ways to enjoy the multitude of rivers, creeks, and lakes throughout Virginia and Maryland. Dozens of outfitters and liveries rent canoes, and many offer guided trips.

Flat-water kayaking has become extremely popular in Virginia and Maryland. Kayak tours and instruction are available on many eastern rivers, lakes, the Chesapeake Bay, and at the beaches.

White-water kayaking is a much more specialized sport enjoyed throughout the region on rivers such as the Potomac and James. A training center for racing is located on the Potomac River. Additional information can be obtained from the **Potomac Whitewater Racing Center** (www.potomacwhitewater.org).

BOATING AND SAILING

Saltwater, lakes, marinas, dock-and-dine restaurants—Virginia and Maryland have them all. The Chesapeake Bay alone has 11,684 miles of shoreline, which is more than the West Coast of the United States. Every town on the bay has a marina, and access can also be gained from public boat ramps in many locations. Many visitors even arrive from other regions by water. Take a look at the boats in Annapolis Harbor and where they're from; there's a good reason Annapolis is called the "Sailing Capital of the World." It's a sailor's dream.

Commercial and recreational powerboats must be registered in Virginia or Maryland if that is where they are primarily used.

FISHING

Fishing is a favorite activity in Virginia and Maryland. There are more than 2,800 miles of trout waters in the Blue Ridge alone. Whether you prefer fishing in a quiet lake, fly-fishing in a mountain stream, surf fishing, or taking a deep-sea fishing charter, you can do it all in this region. Most state parks offer fishing, and some areas are stocked through breeding programs.

Some favorite fishing spots in Virginia include Smith Mountain Lake (striped bass), the South Fork of the Shenandoah River (redbreast sunfish), the New River (yellow perch), the Chesapeake Bay (bluefish, flounder, and drum), and off the shore of Virginia Beach (marlin, sea bass, and sailfish). Favorite spots in Maryland include Sandy Point State Park (striper, white perch, and rockfish), Deep Creek Lake (bass), Point Lookout State Park (rockfish, bluefish, and hardhead), and Assateague Island (surf fishing for stripers).

Licenses are required in both states and Washington DC. Virginia fishing licenses can be purchased online from the **Virginia Department of Game and Inland Fisheries** (www.dgif.virginia.gov). Both freshwater licenses (resident $23, nonresident $47) and freshwater-and-saltwater licenses (resident $40, nonresident $71) are available. If you wish to fish in designated trout-stocked waters, an additional trout license (resident $23, nonresident $47) is required. Licenses are good for one year from the date of purchase.

Maryland fishing licenses can be purchased online from the **Department of Natural Resources** (www.dnr.maryland.gov) or by calling 855/855-3906. Nontidal licenses are $20.50 for residents and $30.50 for nonresidents. Chesapeake Bay and coastal sport-fishing licenses are $15 for residents and $22.50 for nonresidents. Licenses are valid from January 1 to December 31 of the same year.

Fishing licenses in Washington DC can be purchased from the **Department of Energy and the Environment** (www.doee.dc.gov). Licenses are $10 for residents and $13 for nonresidents and are valid from January 1 to December 31 of the same calendar year.

CRABBING AND CLAMMING

Getting dirty in the mud and risking losing a finger are free in Virginia and Maryland if you are doing so to crab or clam for personal use only. Public access to beaches and marsh areas is prevalent in both states, but keep in mind that limits and regulations apply. Current Virginia regulations can be found at http://mrc.virginia.gov and those for Maryland at http://dnr.maryland.gov.

GOLF

Hundreds of public golf courses are located in Virginia and Maryland. A listing of courses in Virginia can be found at www.virginiagolf.

com, and a listing of Maryland courses can be found at www.golfmaryland.com.

WINTER SPORTS

It's no surprise that winter sporting opportunities are concentrated in the western regions of Virginia and Maryland. A handful of ski resorts, such as **Massanutten Resort** (www. massresort.com) near Harrisonburg, Virginia, and **Wisp Resort** (www.wispresort.com) in the Deep Creek Lake area of Maryland, are open during the winter months. The **Liberty Mountain Snowflex Center** (www.liberty. edu) in Lynchburg, Virginia, offers year-round skiing on fabricated snow.

Cross-country skiing and snowmobiling are available on a limited basis when the weather cooperates on designated trails. Ice-skating and hockey, however, are available throughout both states in indoor and seasonal outdoor facilities.

Travel Tips

FOREIGN TRAVELERS

Visitors from other countries must present a valid passport and visa issued by a U.S. consular official unless they are a citizen of a country eligible for the Visa Waiver Program (such as Canada) in order to enter the United States. A foreign national entering the country by air that is a citizen of a country eligible for the Visa Waiver Program must present an approved Electronic System for Travel Authorization and a valid passport. A list of exceptions (38 total) can be found on the Department of Homeland Security website at www.cbp.gov.

ACCESS FOR TRAVELERS WITH DISABILITIES

Accessibility is in the eye of the beholder. Despite the Americans with Disabilities Act, it is unfortunate that universal access in public places is still not a reality in most parts of the country. Virginia and Maryland are no exceptions. Although many restaurants, theaters, hotels, and museums offer ramps or elevators, some smaller, privately owned establishments (such as bed-and-breakfasts) do not always provide these necessities. Many historic properties are also not up to ADA standards because they are prevented from updating by law or by architecture. It is best to call ahead and verify the type of access that is available.

Accessible Virginia (www. accessiblevirginia.org) is a great resource for information on access throughout Virginia. A list of state and public lands in Maryland that offer accessible amenities can be found on Maryland's **Department of Natural Resources** website at www.dnr.maryland. gov.

GAY AND LESBIAN TRAVELERS

Virginia as a whole tends to be on the conservative side, but especially so south of the Washington DC suburbs. Some of the more densely populated areas such as Richmond, Charlottesville, Norfolk, and Virginia Beach have LGBTQ-friendly communities and businesses, but these are rarer in rural areas. Washington DC, Baltimore, and Rehoboth Beach have large LGBTQ populations and readily accept same-sex couples and families. Most other parts of Maryland welcome business from everyone, so unless you need specialized accommodations, travel shouldn't be a concern. The **Gay and Lesbian Travel Center** (www.gayjourney.com) is a great resource for travel.

TRAVELING WITH CHILDREN

Although most places don't make specific accommodations for children, in general, most tourist attractions throughout Virginia and Maryland are family friendly (except for obvious exceptions where noted). Some cities, such as Baltimore and Charlottesville, offer museums devoted specifically to children, but many other sights have a children's component to them. For a list of kid-oriented attractions in Virginia, visit the "Cool Places for Kids" section of the Virginia Is for Lovers website at www.virginia.org.

TRAVELING WITH PETS

In recent years more and more pet-friendly establishments have been popping up in the Virginia and Maryland region. Many higher-end hotels (such as the Kimpton hotel chain) allow four-legged family members, and some establishments even host doggie happy hours. It's not uncommon for attractions, stores, historical sites, campgrounds, outdoor shopping malls, parks, beaches, and even the patios at some restaurants to welcome dogs with open arms. It is always best to call ahead before assuming an establishment is pet friendly.

Service and guide dogs are welcome nearly everywhere with their human companions.

DISCOUNTS

Numerous hotels, venues, and attractions offer discounts to **seniors**; all you have to do is ask when making your reservations or purchasing your tickets. The **American Association of Retired Persons (AARP)** (www.aarp.org) is the largest organization in the nation for seniors. They offer discounts to their members on hotels, tours, rental cars, airfare, and many other services. Membership in AARP is just $16 a year, so it's worth joining.

Many places also offer discounts to active **military** and/or veterans (and sometimes family members). Some require identification, so ask when making your reservations. **Students** often get discounts as well. Some attractions require a student ID, so it's best to check the website before heading out.

TIPPING

A 15-20 percent tip is standard throughout Virginia and Maryland on restaurant bills. Other service providers, such as taxi drivers and hairstylists, typically also receive 15-20 percent. Bellhops and airport personnel normally receive $1-2 per bag.

Information and Services

TOURIST INFORMATION

For information on tourism in Virginia, visit the **Virginia Is for Lovers site** (www.virginia.org) or the official **Virginia state site** (www.virginia.gov). For information on tourism in Maryland, visit the **Maryland Office of Tourism site** (www.visitmaryland.org). For information on tourism in Washington DC, visit the official **DC tourism site** (www.washington.org).

COMMUNICATIONS AND MEDIA

Cell Phone Coverage

Cell phone coverage is generally available in most parts of Virginia and Maryland. As with any state, there are scattered pockets of spotty coverage even near large cities, but overall, coverage is reliable. As a rule, the more rural the region you are traveling through (such as Central and Southern Virginia and Western Maryland), the less coverage is available, but for the most part, the major highways have fairly consistent coverage. Once you leave the major highways, coverage can be a concern.

Large parks, such as Shenandoah National Park, do not have reliable coverage, especially once you leave the main roads (such as Skyline Drive). Any time you head into the backcountry, be sure to bring supplies in case of an emergency instead of relying on your cell phone.

Internet Access

Internet access is readily available in hotels throughout Virginia and Maryland and is very commonly included with the price of a room, but sometimes as an add-on. A few cities even offer wireless Internet access throughout their downtown areas, such as Roanoke and Charlottesville (on the pedestrian mall). A list of free Wi-Fi hotspots in both states can be found at www. openwifispots.com.

Media

Major city newspapers and magazines are available throughout Virginia and Maryland.

The most widely circulated daily newspaper in the Washington DC area (including Northern Virginia and the Capital Region of Maryland) is the *Washington Post* (www. washingtonpost.com). The paper features world news and local news and places an emphasis on national politics. The *Washington Times* (www.washingtontimes.com) is another daily newspaper that is widely circulated. Weekly and specialty newspapers include the *Washington City Paper* (www. washingtoncitypaper.com), an alternative weekly newspaper, and the *Washington Informer* (www.washingtoninformer.com), a weekly newspaper serving the DC area's African American population.

The most widely read paper in Baltimore is the *Baltimore Sun* (www.baltimoresun.com). It is Maryland's largest daily newspaper and covers local and regional news.

Many smaller cities offer daily local papers. They are typically found in convenience stores, grocery stores, and on newsstands.

Health and Safety

For emergencies anywhere in Virginia and Maryland, dial 911 from any telephone at no charge. From a cell phone, the state police can be reached by pressing #77. Generally speaking, hospitals in both states are very good, and excellent in the larger cities. Emergency room treatment is always costlier than a scheduled appointment, but emergency care facilities can also be found in most areas to treat minor conditions.

LYME DISEASE

Virginia and Maryland are in prime tick area, so **Lyme disease,** which is transmitted through the bites of deer ticks, is a risk. Use insect repellent, and check yourself thoroughly after spending time in the woods or walking through tall grass. If you are bitten or find a red circular rash (similar to a

bull's-eye), consult a physician. Lyme disease can be life-threatening if it goes untreated.

INSECTS

Mosquitoes are common throughout Virginia and Maryland and aside from being annoying can carry diseases. Damp, low areas can harbor large populations of these little vampires, so use insect repellent and steer clear of stagnant water. **Bees, wasps, yellow jackets,** and **hornets** are all permanent residents of the region and are particularly active (and aggressive) in the fall.

Female **black widow spiders** are also found in the region and can be identified by a small red hourglass shape on their black abdomens. They live in dark places such as rotting logs and under patio furniture. Symptoms of their bite include severe abdominal pain and should be treated. The males are harmless.

The **brown recluse spider,** contrary to common belief, is not native to this region. They can on occasion be found here, but only as a transplant.

ANIMALS

There are three types of **venomous snakes** in Virginia and Maryland. The most common is the northern copperhead. This snake can be found across both states and has dark-colored cross bands shaped like an hourglass. The second type is the timber rattlesnake, which is found in all the mountainous regions of both states and in the southeastern corner of Virginia. It also has a patterned back with wavy cross bands. The eastern cottonmouth snake is only found in southeastern Virginia (south of Newport News). It can be yellowish olive to black in color and has approximately 13 black cross bands that are wide at the sides and narrow at the backbone.

Swimming in the Atlantic Ocean or the Chesapeake Bay could put you in contact with stinging **jellyfish** or **sea nettles** (especially in the Chesapeake Bay). **Sharks** are also found occasionally in both bodies of water and have even been spotted in the Potomac River near Point Lookout.

PLANTS

Poison ivy, poison oak, and **poison sumac** are all native to the region and should be avoided even if you have never had a prior allergic reaction (you can develop one anytime). As the saying goes, "Leaves of three, let it be." Local mushrooms and berries can also be poisonous, so don't eat them unless you are 100 percent sure of their identification.

WEATHER

In addition to the obvious presence or prediction of a tornado, tropical storm, hurricane, or snowstorm (all of which are possible but rare in the region), be aware that **lightning** is a greater danger on exposed ridges, in fields, on golf courses, on the beach, or anywhere near water. Thunderstorms can pop up quickly, especially during the summer months, so check the weather before venturing out and be prepared with a plan B. Hypothermia can also be an issue. Being wet, tired, and cold is a dangerous combination. Symptoms include slurred speech, uncontrollable shivering, and loss of coordination.

CRIME

As in many states, downtown areas of larger cities such as Richmond, Baltimore, parts of Washington DC (including neighboring Prince George's County), and Norfolk can be unsafe, especially at night. Ask hotel staff about the safety of the area you're staying in, lock your doors, take a cab or ride-hailing service instead of walking, and don't leave valuables in your car.

Resources

Suggested Reading

HISTORY
General History

Barbour, Philip, and Thad Tate, eds. *The Complete Works of Captain John Smith, 1580-1631.* Chapel Hill: University of North Carolina Press, 1986. Three volumes of Captain John Smith's work.

Dabney, Virginius. *Richmond: Story of a City.* Charlottesville: University of Virginia Press, 1990. Tells the story of Virginia's state capital.

Doak, Robin. *Voices from Colonial America: Maryland 1634-1776.* Washington DC: National Geographic, 2007. First-person accounts, historical maps, and illustrations tell Maryland's history.

Jefferson, Thomas. *Notes on the State of Virginia.* Chapel Hill: University of North Carolina Press, 1996. This classic shows Jefferson's personality and discusses life in the 18th century.

Kelly, C. Brian. *Best Little Stories from Virginia.* Nashville, TN: Cumberland House Publishing, 2003. A collection of more than 100 stories since Jamestown's founding.

McWilliams, Jane W. *Annapolis, City on the Severn.* Baltimore: The Johns Hopkins University Press, 2011. The story of Annapolis.

Civil War History

Catton, Bruce. *America Goes to War: The Civil War and Its Meaning in American Culture.* Middletown, CT: Wesleyan University Press, 1992. An interesting study on the Civil War.

McPherson, James. *Battle Cry of Freedom: The Civil War Era.* New York: Ballantine Books, 1988. Perhaps the best single-volume history of the war.

SCIENCE AND NATURE

Duda, Mark Damian. *Virginia Wildlife Viewing Guide.* Helena, MT: Falcon Press, 1994. Provides information on 80 of Virginia's best wildlife-viewing areas.

Fergus, Charles. *Wildlife of Virginia and Maryland and Washington, D.C.* Mechanicsburg, PA: Stackpole Books, 2003. Provides details on the animals in the diverse habitats throughout Virginia and Maryland.

Frye, Keith. *Roadside Geology of Virginia.* Missoula, MT: Mountain Press, 2003. Provides general information on the state's geology.

Gupton, Oscar. *Wildflowers of the Shenandoah Valley and Blue Ridge Mountains.* Charlottesville: University of Virginia Press, 2002. A unique guide dedicated to wildflowers.

RECREATION

General Outdoor

Carrol, Steven, and Mark Miller. *Wild Virginia*. Helena, MT: Falcon Press, 2002. A guide to wilderness and special-management areas throughout Virginia with a focus on the western and southern areas.

High, Mike. *The C&O Canal Companion*. Baltimore: Johns Hopkins University Press, 2015. A well-written guide to C&O Canal National Historical Park.

Hiking

Adkins, Leonard. *Explorer's Guide 50 Hikes in Maryland*. Woodstock, VT: The Countryman Press, 2007. A good resource for hiking in Maryland.

Adkins, Leonard. *50 Hikes in Northern Virginia*. Woodstock, VT: The Countryman Press, 2015. A good resource for hiking in Northern Virginia.

Blackinton, Theresa Dowell. *Moon Take a Hike Washington DC: 80 Hikes within Two Hours of the City*. 2nd edition. Berkeley, CA: Avalon Travel, 2013. A terrific resource for hiking the Washington DC area, including hikes in metropolitan DC, the Shenandoah, Western Maryland, Eastern Maryland, and Virginia's Piedmont and Coastal Plains.

Burnham, Bill, and Mary Burnham. *Hiking Virginia*. 4th Edition. Guilford, CT: Falcon Guides, 2018. A lively and award-winning guide to hiking in Virginia.

de Hart, Allen. *The Trails of Virginia: Hiking the Old Dominion*. Chapel Hill: University of North Carolina Press, 2003. A very comprehensive resource for hiking in Virginia.

Bicycling

Adams, Scott. *Mountain Bike America: Virginia*. Guilford, CT: Globe Pequot, 2000.

Scott Adams is one of the best guidebook writers for mountain biking, and this is a great and informative read.

Adams, Scott, and Martin Fernandez. *Mountain Biking the Washington, D.C./ Baltimore Area*. 5th edition. Guilford, CT: Falcon Guides, 2015. A great guide to mountain biking around Washington DC and Baltimore.

Eltringham, Scott, and Jim Wade. *Scott & Jim's Favorite Bike Rides*. Arlington, VA: S&J Cycling, 2006. A fun guide to biking in Northern Virginia and central Maryland.

Homerosky, Jim. *Road Biking Virginia*. Guilford, CT: Falcon Guides, 2002. Wonderful resource for road bikers in Virginia.

Fishing

Beasley, Beau. *Fly Fishing Virginia: A No Nonsense Guide to Top Waters*. Tucson, AZ: No Nonsense Fly Fishing Guidebooks, 2007. An award-winning guide to fly-fishing spots in Virginia.

Gooch, Bob. *Virginia Fishing Guide*. 2nd edition. Charlottesville: University of Virginia Press, 2011. A wonderful guide to fishing in Virginia.

Moore, Steve. *Maryland Trout Fishing: The Stocked and Wild Rivers, Streams, Lakes and Ponds*. Calibrated Consulting, 2011. An informative guide to trout fishing in Maryland.

Kayaking

Gaaserud, Michaela Riva. *AMC's Best Sea Kayaking in the Mid-Atlantic*. Boston: Appalachian Mountain Club Books, 2016. A great resource for coastal kayaking in Virginia and Maryland.

Rock Climbing

Horst, Eric, and Stewart M. Green. *Rock Climbing Virginia, West Virginia, and Maryland.* Helena, MT: Falcon Press, 2013. Detailed information on climbs in Shenandoah National Park, Great Falls, and Carderock.

Internet Resources

STATE RESOURCES

Virginia

www.virginia.gov
The official Commonwealth of Virginia website
www.virginia.com
General travel information within Virginia.
www.virginia.org
The official visitor website for the Commonwealth of Virginia.

Maryland

www.maryland.gov
The official Maryland website.
www.visitmaryland.org
The official tourism website for Maryland.

WASHINGTON DC

www.washington.org
Visitor information on Washington DC.
www.si.edu
Information on the Smithsonian Institution.
www.wmata.com
Information on Metrorail and Metrobus service.

RECREATION

www.nps.gov
The National Park Service website, a comprehensive guide to national parks throughout the country.

www.dcr.virginia.gov
Information on the Virginia Department of Conservation and Recreation.
www.dnr.maryland.gov
Information on the Maryland Department of Natural Resources.
www.hikingupward.com
Contains a wonderful interactive map of Virginia hikes.
www.baydreaming.com
Offers an excellent list of marinas and boating facilities in the Chesapeake Bay area.
www.findyourchesapeake.com
The Chesapeake Bay Gateways Network website provides information on public access parks around the bay.

LOCAL RESOURCES

www.mtnlaurel.com
A nice resource for life in Virginia's Blue Ridge.
www.virginialiving.com
Virginia Living Magazine has many fascinating articles on Virginia.
www.chesapeakebaymagazine.com
Chesapeake Bay Magazine is full of interesting articles on the bay area.
www.baydreaming.com
A guide to Chesapeake Bay events.

Index

XYZ

List of Maps

Photo Credits

All interior photos © Michaela Riva Gaaserud except: page 2 © NPS/Neal Lewis; page 8 © (top left) Harperdrewart | Dreamstime.com; (top right) Visit Annapolis; (bottom) Mark Vandyke | Dreamstime. com; (bottom left) Zrf| Dreamstime.com; (bottom right) Virginia Museum of Fine Arts; page 10 © Visit Annapolis; page 12 © (top) NPS/Neal Lewis; page 13 © George Washington's Mount Vernon; page 14 © (top) Virginia Museum of the Civil War; (bottom) National Aquarium; (middle) Jsumner | Dreamstime.com; page 16 © (bottom) Smithsonian Institution, National Museum of African American History and Culture Architectural Photography; page 18 © (top) NPS/Neal Lewis; page 20 © (top) Steven Roncin | Dreamstime. com; page 22 © (top) Rafael Vilches | Dreamstime.com; page 25 © (bottom) Joe Sohm | Dreamstime.com; page 30 © (bottom) World War II Observation Tower at Cape Henlopen State Park; page 33 © (top right) Stitched Panorama; (top right) Kevin Tietz | Dreamstime.com; (bottom) Mariagroth | Dreamstime.com; (top right) Alan Karchmer/NMAAHC; (bottom right) Eric Long, National Air and Space Museum, Smithsonian Institution; (bottom) Dreamstime.com; page 63 © (top right) Faina Gurevich | Dreamstime.com; (bottom) Erik Lattwein | Dreamstime.com; (bottom) Amy Nicolai | Dreamstime.com; page 71 © (top) David Tulchinsky | Dreamstime.com; page 80 © (top) Richard Gunion | Dreamstime.com; (bottom) Cvandyke | Dreamstime. com; page 84 © Askoldsb | Dreamstime.com; page 91 © (bottom) Joe Sohm | Dreamstime.com; page 98 © George Washington's Mount Vernon; (top right) Jon Bilous | Dreamstime.com; page 129 © (top) Marybeth Charles | Dreamstime.com; (left middle) Diane Penland, National Air and Space Museum, Smithsonian Institution; page 156 © (top left) Christian Delbert | Dreamstime.com; (top right) Jamestown-Yorktown Foundation; page 187 © (top) Joe Sohm | Dreamstime.com; (left middle) Jamestown-Yorktown Foundation; page 197 © (top left) The Mariners' Museum and Park; page 207 © (bottom) Wangkun Jia | Dreamstime.com; page 232 © NPS/Katy Cain; page 233 © (top left) NPS/Neal Lewis; (top right) Zrf| Dreamstime.com; (bottom) Teresa Kenney | Dreamstime.com; page 239 © Winchester-Frederick County CVB; page 244 © (top left) NPS/ Neal Lewis; (top right) NPS/Neal Lewis; page 252 © Jgorzynik | Dreamstime.com; Randall Stout/Taubman Museum of Art; (bottom) James Kirkikis | Dreamstime.com; page 274 © James Kirkikis | Dreamstime. com; page 284 © (top) Type01 | Dreamstime.com; (left middle) Jon Bilous | Dreamstime.com; (bottom) Liudmila Arsenteva Dreamstime.com; page 287 © (top) Virginia Museum of Fine Arts; (bottom) Virginia Museum of Fine Arts; page 309 © (top) Bethany Snyder; page 310 © Wintergreen Resort; (right middle) Jill Lang | Dreamstime.com; (bottom) Larry Metayer | Dreamstime.com; (bottom) Tim Hursley/Taubman Museum of Art; page 352 © Xavier Ascanio | Dreamstime.com; page 360 © Avmedved | Dreamstime.com; (bottom) Ritu Jethani | Dreamstime.com; page 382 © (top) Luckydoor | Dreamstime.com; (bottom) Michael Stewart/College Park Aviation Museum; page 387 © (top right) National Aquarium; page 395 © (left middle) Jacqueline Nix | Dreamstime.com; (bottom) B&O Railroad Museum; page 398 © Jon Bilous | Dreamstime. com; page 407 © (left middle)Ken Stanek Photography; (right middle) Visit Baltimore; (bottom) Justin Tsucalas; page 416 © Visit Baltimore; page 431 © Lei Xu | Dreamstime.com; page 440 © Visit Annapolis; page 441 © (top left) Visit Annapolis; (top right) Calvert Marine Musuem; page 446 © (top) Visit Annapolis; (bottom) Visit Annapolis; page 459 © Calvert Marine Musuem; page 464 © (top left) Chesapeake Bay Maritime Museum; page 477 © (top) Chesapeake Bay Maritime Museum; page 483 © (top) Jon Bilous | Dreamstime.com; page 489 © Izanbar | Dreamstime.com; page 513 © Jon Bilous | Dreamstime.com; page 514 © (top left) Daniel Thornberg | Dreamstime.com; page 524 © Zrf| Dreamstime.com; (bottom) Ken Cole | Dreamstime.com; page 541 © Jon Bilous | Dreamstime.com; page 552 © Ken Stanek Photography; page 565 © NPS/Neal Lewis

ROAD TRIPS AND DRIVE & HIKE GUIDES

MOON

Drive & Hike
APPALACHIAN TRAIL

THE BEST TRAIL TOWNS, DAY HIKES,
AND ROAD TRIPS IN BETWEEN

TIMOTHY MALCOLM

MOON

BLUE RIDGE PARKWAY
Road Trip

INCLUDING SHENANDOAH & GREAT SMOKY
MOUNTAINS NATIONAL PARKS

JASON FRYE

MOON

CALIFORNIA
Road Trip

SAN FRANCISCO, YOSEMITE, LAS VEGAS,
GRAND CANYON, LOS ANGELES,
& THE PACIFIC COAST HIGHWAY

STUART THORNTON

MOON

NASHVILLE TO NEW ORLEANS
Road Trip

NATCHEZ TRACE PARKWAY • MEMPHIS •
TUPELO • MISSISSIPPI BLUES TRAIL

MARGARET LITTMAN

MOON

NEW ENGLAND
Road Trip

BOSTON, ACADIA NATIONAL PARK, WHITE
MOUNTAINS, BERKSHIRES, NEWPORT, AND CAPE COD

JEN ROSE SMITH

MOON

NORTHERN CALIFORNIA
Road Trip

SAN FRANCISCO, WINE COUNTRY, SONOMA, REDWOODS,
LAKE TAHOE, SHASTA, LASSEN, YOSEMITE, BIG SUR

STUART THORNTON & KAYLA ANDERSON

MOON

PACIFIC COAST HIGHWAY
Road Trip

CALIFORNIA,
OREGON & WASHINGTON

IAN ANDERSON

MOON

Drive & Hike
PACIFIC CREST TRAIL

THE BEST TRAIL TOWNS, DAY HIKES,
AND ROAD TRIPS IN BETWEEN

CAROLINE HINCHLIFF

MOON

PACIFIC NORTHWEST
Road Trip

SEATTLE, VANCOUVER, VICTORIA,
THE OLYMPIC PENINSULA, PORTLAND,
THE OREGON COAST & MOUNT RAINIER

ALLISON WILLIAMS

MOON.COM | ROADTRIPUSA.COM

MOON
ROUTE 66
Road Trip

JESSICA DUNHAM

MOON
SOUTH FLORIDA & THE KEYS
Road Trip

WITH MIAMI, WALT DISNEY WORLD, TAMPA & THE EVERGLADES

JASON FERGUSON

MOON
SOUTHERN CALIFORNIA
Road Trips

DRIVES ALONG THE BEACHES, MOUNTAINS, AND DESERTS WITH THE BEST STOPS ALONG THE WAY

IAN ANDERSON

MOON
SOUTHWEST
Road Trip

LAS VEGAS, ZION & BRYCE, MONUMENT VALLEY, SANTA FE & TAOS, AND THE GRAND CANYON

TIM HULL

MOON
VANCOUVER & CANADIAN ROCKIES
Road Trip

VICTORIA, BANFF, JASPER, CALGARY, THE OKANAGAN, WHISTLER & THE SEA-TO-SKY HIGHWAY

CAROLYN B. HELLER

MOON
YELLOWSTONE TO GLACIER NATIONAL PARK
Road Trip

JACKSON HOLE, CODY, THE GRAND TETONS & THE ROCKY MOUNTAIN FRONT

CARTER G. WALKER

Road Trip USA

Covering more than 35,000 miles of blacktop stretching from east to west and north to south, *Road Trip USA* takes you deep into the heart of America.

This colorful guide covers the top road trips including historic Route 66 and is packed with maps, photos, illustrations, mile-by-mile highlights, and more!

Craft a personalized journey through the top national parks in the U.S. and Canada with Moon Travel Guides.

MOON

USA NATIONAL PARKS

THE COMPLETE GUIDE TO ALL
59 PARKS

BECKY LOMAX

MOON

ACADIA
NATIONAL PARK

HILARY NANGLE

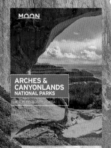

MOON

**ARCHES &
CANYONLANDS**
NATIONAL PARKS

MOON

**BANFF
NATIONAL PARK**

HIKE · CAMP · KAYAK

ANDREW HEMPSTEAD

MOON

**DEATH VALLEY
NATIONAL PARK**

MOON

GLACIER
NATIONAL PARK

MOON

**GRAND
CANYON**

HIKE · CAMP
RAFT THE
COLORADO RIVER

TIM HULL

MOON

**GREAT SMOKY
MOUNTAINS**
NATIONAL PARK

HIKE · BIKE · CAMP

JASON FRYE

**MOUNT RUSHMORE
& THE BLACK HILLS**

LAURA L. & HOWELL

MOON

**ROCKY
MOUNTAIN**
NATIONAL PARK

HIKE · CAMP
SEE WILDLIFE

MOON

**SEQUOIA &
KINGS CANYON**

HIKE · CAMP
SEE REDWOODS

LEIGH BERNACCHI

MOON

**YELLOWSTONE
& GRAND TETON**

HIKE · CAMP
SEE WILDLIFE

BECKY LOMAX

MOON

YOSEMITE
SEQUOIA &
KINGS CANYON

ANN MARIE BROWN

MOON

**ZION &
BRYCE**

W. C. McRAE JUDY JEWELL

MAP SYMBOLS

≡≡≡	Expressway	○	City/Town	✈	Airport	⚐	Golf Course
━━━	Primary Road	◉	State Capital	✈	Airfield	🅿	Parking Area
━━━	Secondary Road	⊛	National Capital	▲	Mountain	▰	Archaeological Site
- - -	Unpaved Road	★	Point of Interest	✦	Unique Natural Feature	⛪	Church
━━━	Feature Trail	•	Accommodation			⛽	Gas Station
------	Other Trail	▾	Restaurant/Bar	🅰	Waterfall		
·········	Ferry	■	Other Location	▲	Park		Glacier
≡≡≡	Pedestrian Walkway	∧	Campground	▯	Trailhead		Mangrove
▥▥▥	Stairs			⛷	Skiing Area		Reef
							Swamp

CONVERSION TABLES

°C = (°F – 32) / 1.8
°F = (°C x 1.8) + 32
1 inch = 2.54 centimeters (cm)
1 foot = 0.304 meters (m)
1 yard = 0.914 meters
1 mile = 1.6093 kilometers (km)
1 km = 0.6214 miles
1 fathom = 1.8288 m
1 chain = 20.1168 m
1 furlong = 201.168 m
1 acre = 0.4047 hectares
1 sq km = 100 hectares
1 sq mile = 2.59 square km
1 ounce = 28.35 grams
1 pound = 0.4536 kilograms
1 short ton = 0.90718 metric ton
1 short ton = 2,000 pounds
1 long ton = 1.016 metric tons
1 long ton = 2,240 pounds
1 metric ton = 1,000 kilograms
1 quart = 0.94635 liters
1 US gallon = 3.7854 liters
1 Imperial gallon = 4.5459 liters
1 nautical mile = 1.852 km

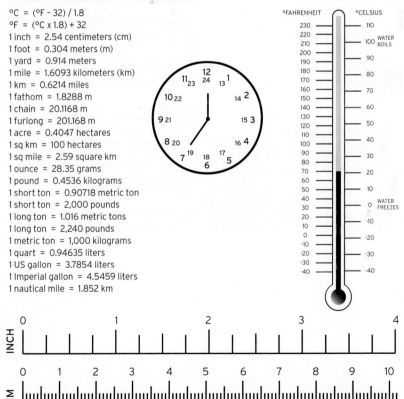

MOON VIRGINIA & MARYLAND

Avalon Travel
Hachette Book Group
1700 Fourth Street
Berkeley, CA 94710, USA
www.moon.com

Editor: Rachael Sablik
Acquiring Editor: Nikki Ioakimedes
Series Manager: Kathryn Ettinger
Copy Editor: Denise Leto
Graphics Coordinator: Lisi Baldwin
Production Coordinator: Lisi Baldwin
Cover Design: Faceout Studios, Charles Brock
Interior Design: Domini Dragoone
Moon Logo: Tim McGrath
Map Editor: Mike Morgenfeld
Cartographers: Austin Ehrhardt and Mike Morgenfeld
Proofreader: Deana Shields
Indexer: Greg Jewett

ISBN-13: 978-1-64049-870-9

Printing History
1st Edition — 2014
3rd Edition — July 2020
5 4 3 2 1

Text © 2020 by Michaela Riva Gaaserud.
Maps © 2020 by Avalon Travel.
Some photos and illustrations are used by permission and are the property of the original copyright owners.

Front cover photo: Doyles River Falls, Shenandoah National Park, Virginia © Sam Spicer/Getty Images
Back cover photo: fall foliage on Monument Avenue in Richmond, Virginia © Sky Noir Photography by Bill Dickinson/Getty Images

Printed in China by RR Donnelley

As a New Mother, Do You Suffer From . . .

- Moderate to severe anxiety or panic attacks?
- Lack of interest in caring for your child?
- Aversion to touching your baby?
- Unexplained weight loss or gain, constipation, thinning of hair?
- Frequent crying?
- Fear of harming your infant or yourself?
- Feelings of personal worthlessness or despair?
- Loss of interest in sex?

If you answered "yes" to any of these questions, you could be experiencing postpartum depression. *THE NEW MOTHER SYNDROME* "offers real help for new mothers . . . firm you-are-not-alone support, and some practical suggestions on avoiding or ameliorating the problem."

—Kirkus Reviews

"There is no doubt that physicians as well as patients will benefit from this book—indeed, that it will be required reading. With this impetus to understanding, postpartum illness should be as rare as smallpox by the end of the century."

—Dr. James Hamilton, from the Introduction

Carol Dix is a medical journalist and co-author, with Dr. Jonathan Scher, of *Everything You Need to Know about Pregnancy in the 1980's*. Her articles have appeared in such publications as *Glamour*, *Redbook*, *Working Woman*, *Mothers Today*, *Mademoiselle*, and *Working Parents*. In *THE NEW MOTHER SYNDROME*, Ms. Dix draws on the latest research, interviews and case histories of over 300 women (including her own postpartum experience).

The New Mother Syndrome

Coping with Postpartum Stress and Depression

By Carol Dix

POCKET BOOKS

New York   London   Toronto   Sydney   Tokyo

To Alice and Yasmin Eady

Article on pages 65–70 used with permission
of LADIES' HOME JOURNAL. All rights reserved.

POCKET BOOKS, a division of Simon & Schuster Inc.
1230 Avenue of the Americas, New York, N.Y. 10020

Published by arrangement with Doubleday & Company, Inc.
Library of Congress Catalog Card Number: 85-1638

ISBN: 0-671-64485-8

First Pocket Books printing January 1988

10 9 8 7 6 5 4 3 2

POCKET and colophon are trademarks of
Simon & Schuster Inc.

Printed in the U.S.A.

"If Rhett had understood the changes we mothers go through after having a baby, perhaps he would not have left Scarlett."

—*a mother from Ohio, 1984*

CONTENTS

PREFACE

There was a sharp ring at my doorbell. Not expecting anyone other than the mailman, I called out to leave the package there, but the insistent ringing brought me to the door. A slender, frail young woman with deep, brooding eyes stood framed for a few seconds in the empty doorway. At first I did not even see the stroller and the perhaps five-month-old little boy in a jolly red snowsuit waiting behind her. The woman asked for me by name and I nodded. She had read my query about the "baby blues," or PPD (postpartum depression), she said, and seeing my address was so close to hers, she decided to come see me in person.

Anne-Marie was her name, and her little boy was Clayton. "I've been suffering from PPD terribly ever since he was born. I just don't know what to do," she told me. Anne-Marie had turned against food since the birth (an atypical but possible symptom of depression). She was seeing a doctor and was on some medication, but nothing seemed to shift the depression. Her husband, Ralph, was by now desperate for her to get better help. "I was so relieved to read that letter, so pleased to think postpartum depression is being taken seriously at last," she said gently.

When I finally returned to my typewriter, disturbed by

the very real evidence of PPD at my door, I found myself shaking my head again at the ridiculous situation we have let ourselves slide into. We promote the attitude that all the care and information about pregnancy and birth should be packed into the nine months *before* the baby arrives, and that no information or support should be given to mothers (or fathers) once the baby has arrived, other than tips on diapering, burping, and promoting baby's sleep.

During pregnancy, the push is toward educating the mother in the correct approach to her health and well-being while she carries the child. For labor, most of us these days attend some form of preparation class, learning about nonmedical techniques for alleviating pain and ensuring the baby's healthy and safe passage. After labor, we swaddle the baby in pink or blue, are heaped with flowers, and then are forgotten about.

As a former journalist, a ten-year veteran of freelance magazine and book writing, and then a mother, I came to the research on this book after a much milder bout with PPD than Anne-Marie was suffering. Working in London during my first pregnancy (in 1978), I had at least been made aware of PPD (in England they call it postnatal depression, PND) by an excellent television documentary that featured the famous British TV personality, Esther Rantzen.

Esther had decided to discuss openly her own terrible experience of PPD, completely to the surprise of the British public. Her honesty was striking enough to really catch the public eye, and I know she received a tremendous amount of mail from that program. Esther Rantzen at the time had her own television program, a sort of "Real People": upbeat, sharp, and witty, it was delivered on her strong personality. Esther's love for and eventual marriage to another TV personality had been covered in detail by the popular press, as it had led to a much-publicized divorce. Then, when Esther became pregnant, the news was greeted with great excitement. I remember that the day the baby was born, the tabloids ran it as a front-page headline: ESTHER'S BABY. She must have been the *last* person anyone imagined suffering depression at any time, let alone after the birth of this special baby.

Esther described an alarming array of symptoms that terrified her: she feared for her sanity. Her PPD eventually vanished of its own accord, she maintained, with the love, understanding, and support of her husband, doctor, and friends. She was able to talk about her feelings and was grateful to have discovered a doctor who not only recognized the symptoms but was able to explain their cause, which helped make recovery a swifter process.

My own mysterious bout with depression did not bring me so close to the borders of insanity, but I know now from the women I have spoken to or corresponded with that that sensation is not even unusual in the first year after childbirth. My experience was marked more by a dull feeling of joylessness, of a downward sliding, this-is-it depression. The PPD came after the birth not of my first but of my second child. Then settled in New York, I turned, like any new mother might do, to the bookstores and libraries for some explanation of this mood, only to find at most a paragraph or two in a pregnancy book, and certainly no book for the general reader that could make sense of the problem.

Obviously there should be a book for new mothers to read, one that was not laced with platitudes or determined to shift the blame back on the woman herself. Halfway through the research I was still left wondering if I should really be taking this subject so seriously; perhaps I had invented a category of illness to defend or explain my own unacceptable behavior. I was left doubting and isolated until responses to the questionnaire I had sent out came pouring in. Then I knew my fears were unfounded. Other women did need information, did need to understand what was happening or had happened to them when, instead of greeting a much-antici- pated motherhood with delight, they found themselves locked in a mood of despair.

So, before going any further, I want to offer my thanks to all the mothers who have helped me on this book. With the women I personally contacted and those who wrote to me, some three hundred mothers contributed to this book. They helped broaden the base of my approach and gave me ideas I never would have come to on my own. The letters came from all over the country: from a woman who had been eighteen on first giving birth, to a grandmother now in her fifties remembering her own suffering all too clearly.

Then there were all those women who gave me their time in personal interviews, or lengthier correspondence and phone calls: some were actually suffering depression, rocking their babies, as we talked. Understandably, no one wanted her real name printed, so I have used fictional names throughout to protect their privacy.

I am happy for the opportunity to revise and update this new edition of the book, so that it now includes information about the support groups that are being started up specifically for PPD. Also, I am happy to tell you about the growing campaign, for wider education and understanding of PPD, that is right now being nurtured by all those determined people involved.

During the very exciting eighteen months since the book's original publication in the fall of 1985, the term PPD has become nationally recognized; women have been able to come together out of their isolation; and doctors are opening up to the possibility that yes, there can be emotional and mental disorder following childbirth, and it does merit their attention!

I would particularly like to thank these people for their generosity: Cheryl, Lucy, Monica, Sarah, Elaine, Pat, Lynne, Janine, Andrea, Lee, Jane, Suzanne, Nancy, Carol, Sue, Janet, Deidre, Alison, Linda, Robin, Laura, Jane, Nancy B., Susan H., Karen, Glenn, Rick, Sharon, Angela, and Danuta.

My gratitude extends particularly to Dr. James Hamilton of San Francisco, then secretary of the Marcé Society (an international association of doctors and scientists interested in PPD), for all his help, encouragement, and support during the research and writing of this book; and to the other Marcé members who have so inspired me with their enthusiasm for the promotion of the diagnosis and treatment of PPD.

Jane Honikman, of PEP (Postpartum Education for Parents) in Santa Barbara, has become a friend and colleague through our shared concern and belief in this topic, although our collaborative efforts between East and West Coast were at the mercy of time lapses and the seemingly impossible stricture of finding times, in both houses, when children were quiet or asleep and neither of us was too exhausted for a lengthy phone conversation.

Nancy Berchtold, of Depression After Delivery (DAD), became the most important person in helping the campaign for wider understanding and education of PPD grow. Nancy, her husband John, and their daughter Allison all became good friends through our non-stop work together.

Glenn Comitz, who courageously campaigned for his wife Sharon's release from prison (for infanticide), also joined the campaign with incredible strength and energy, and is now actively seeking to form a national organization.

My thanks, too, to Linda Lipton of the Family Resource Coalition (FRC) of Chicago, and especially to Lynne Pooley, for the work involved in compiling the remarkable and up-to-date list of parent support groups nationwide. I am grateful to Janet Spencer King and Lyn Roessler of *Mothers Today,* Vivian Cadden and Laura Mosedale of *Working Mother,* the editor of the New York *Times Book Review,* and the editor of *Birthwrites,* a publication of the Houston parent education group, all of whom printed my articles or queries seeking responses from women who felt they had undergone PPD.

There were those doctors who willingly gave of their time to talk to me about their own studies and work with the PPD or with depression. My thanks go especially to Dr. Elisabeth Herz of the George Washington University School of Medicine; Dr. Anthony Labrum of the University of Rochester Medical School; Dr. Peter Whybrow of Dartmouth Medical School; Dr. Katharina Dalton of London; Judith Klein and the Women's Psychotherapy Referral Service in Manhattan; and Dr. Adam Lewenberg of Manhattan.

The other doctor who offered me inestimable help is obstetrician Jonathan Scher, with whom I was coauthor of *Everything You Need to Know About Pregnancy in the '80s* (Dial/Doubleday 1985). And most certainly thanks to my editors, Joyce Johnson, Frances McCullough, and Anne Sweeney for the Pocket Books edition, the helpful advice and support of executive editor Sydny Miner, who was herself just about to give birth as the revisions were being put in place; also to my agent, Jane Gelfman—as women or mothers, we have been able to share many laughs on the relative "joys of motherhood," although Deborah Schneider, assistant to Jane Gelfman, was happily pregnant at the time this book was being much talked about, and all she could say was, "I don't want to know about *that!*"

On the home front—and what book by a woman with a family can ever be written without the home being right there in the front of the picture?—I want to thank Juana Vincent and especially Jane Guenther. Their unflagging care and support of both me and the children as the baby-sitters, if that word can ever begin to describe the work of a substitute mother, gave me the time, space, and peace of mind in which to write. I want to thank Marjorie Dix for enduring the emotional crises of mothering me, and my sister, Margaret Groves, who welcomes the children into her home with much more capable arms than I can manage. Above all, I have to thank Allan Eady, my husband, without whom none of this would have been possible, and who seems to enjoy his fathering with far less conflict than I approach my mothering. Last, if never least, I must thank Alice and Yasmin Eady, without whom I would never have needed to write this book!

CAROL DIX

INTRODUCTION

Here is the rather amazing story of a well-known malady that twentieth-century medicine buried. Psychiatric illness following childbearing was acknowledged by the ancient world: Hippocrates described it in the fourth century B.C. During the nineteenth century scores of very able physicians, led by L. V. Marcé in France, described postpartum symptoms and illness with great accuracy. Marcé ascribed this malady to unknown "connexions" between the organs of generation and the brain. These "connexions" were discovered in the early twentieth century—the influence of blood-borne chemicals, the hormones, on many bodily and mental activities. Further clinical studies of postpartum illness revealed unmistakable clues to its hormonal origin, and by 1935 the outlines of the endocrine system were well known. Continuing clinical studies revealed clues of the hormonal origin of these psychiatric syndromes which stuck out like quills on a porcupine. The stage was set for a breakthrough in understanding the causes of postpartum illness.

At precisely this moment, a catastrophe occurred: the medical establishment turned their backs on the historical record of postpartum illness and ignored the evidence that pointed to the endocrine system's role in "motherhood blues." Indeed, the leaders of American psychiatry mandated that the word *postpartum* and its synonyms be expunged from the nomenclature of illness. Patients with symptoms of psychiatric distress after childbearing were from that time on to be classified in hospital records as having chronic mental illnesses such as schizophrenia, "manic-depressive insanity," or "toxic-exhaustive psychosis." The assumption was that the event of childbearing had merely uncovered a latent condition. Research stood still for almost a half-century.

What caused this extraordinary denial? Malevolent intent? Antifeminism? Probably not. A curious set of circumstances led to a major error of institutional judgment—perhaps the term institutional stupidity is appropriate—and then this error was perpetuated through inertia and ignorance. The very existence of postpartum illness was denied, because no one could classify it according to the system of the day.

At the turn of the century, advances in pathology and bacteriology had led to the positive identification of the causes of many diseases. Diseases were named and classified according to the organism or agency that caused them. Several Nobel Prizes fell to the physicians who developed the new understanding and nomenclature. Psychiatrists, eager to follow suit, sought better ways to name and classify mental illness. At first they looked for a system based on *causes*, but the causes of mental illness resisted classification. Giving up, they turned to a new system based on similarity of symptoms. In the early 1930s it appeared that this might be a successful system, and enthusiasm was high. Then a "flaw" in the system was discovered: the word *postpartum* implied that the cause of the illness was some aspect of parturition.

A very distinguished psychiatrist, E. A. Strecker, who was a leader of organized psychiatry and a coauthor of the leading textbook, contrived a solution. In a paper he published with his associate, F. G. Ebaugh, he excoriated the word *postpartum* as archaic and proposed that all psychiatric illness that developed in the months after giving birth be named and classified without reference to the act of childbearing. Soon afterward, official classifications of mental illness began to emerge with *postpartum* deleted, and this is still the official position of American psychiatry.

The deed was done. The professors of psychiatry were content. Virtually no progress was made in research or treatment until the late 1970s. Then a few British psychiatrists found themselves associated with hospitals in which women with illness following childbirth were assigned to wards that treated only these patients. This specialization of care is partly a reflection of the way the British health system works and partly the result of a British predisposition to hospitalize nursing babies with their mothers when the latter are ill. First the British psychiatrists and then many physicians on the continent of Europe and in Japan began to see that they were dealing with a phenomenon that was unique, a set of syndromes that were distinct entities related to childbearing.

Professor Ian Brockington, then at Manchester, called a conference to discuss these observations, which generated worldwide enthusiasm except in the United States. An international scientific society, The Marcé Society, was organized, and it has facilitated communication between research workers all over the world. The renaissance of research on postpartum illness is underway: with new studies clarifying the complex hormonal mechanisms that are almost certainly related to postpartum psychiatric problems, and the development of two promising preventative regimes, it is likely that rational treatment for postpartum psychiatric illness is imminent.

Carol Dix has made an enormous contribution in writing *The New Mother Syndrome*. In this book, she describes the magnitude and diversity of psychiatric problems that may follow childbearing. She explores their probable causes and new possibilities for treatment. There is no doubt that physicians as well as patients will benefit from this book—indeed, that it will be required reading. With this impetus to understanding, postpartum illness should be as rare as smallpox by the end of this century.

JAMES A. HAMILTON, M.D., PH.D.
San Francisco, California

PART ONE

◆

The Problem
with No Name

◆

1

BECOMING AWARE

The mood set in after my second child was born, at about the third month. Our first baby was not yet two years old, my husband had narrowly escaped dying in an accident, my mother had just gone home, and I sat in our neighborhood playground with my adorable children feeling utterly depressed. Outsiders might have pinned the mood on my near scrape with widowhood, or on my mother's departure, but I sensed that neither was the real cause. One phrase summed it up in my mind: How had my life come to this?

I couldn't make sense of my feelings. I had wanted children, had been delighted and thrilled to meet a man I not only loved but who also wanted children. We were leading a good life. I still had vestiges of my former life as a writer (though at that point my career was suffering severe strains from the second pregnancy and my general immobility). Crazy to be feeling this way now, I said. Why didn't I feel it after our first child?

Then, I had many more reasons. New to New York, I had just left home, career, and a lifetime of friends behind in England to begin my new life in this city. I had lived through new motherhood knowing scarcely a soul, let alone having the support of close women friends, mother, or sister. Our first child, moreover, had been no dream for a new mother. She had been born screaming and seemed to continue doing so until she was nearly three years old, when finally language came to her aid and she could put her grievances into words. I hadn't been depressed then. Overwhelmed, suffering extreme culture shock from the abrupt change in lifestyle, I most certainly was, but not depressed. I had even rationalized that uprooting myself just before giving birth had been a protective device; with no former life to miss in the new land, I had been able to surge forward full of hope, optimism, enthusiasm, and a determination to be a wonderful example of new motherhood.

What I couldn't see at the time was that having the second baby had disproportionately curtailed my freedom, ruined that self-styled image of new motherhood, and consequently my whole self-image had gone awry. What I failed to see then was that I was suffering an acute identity crisis, and that was the root of this depression.

With just one baby in a Snugli (I had even refused to purchase a carriage or stroller until the baby was seven months old and her feet were dangling down by my knees, so determined was I not to feel hampered or tied down by having a baby), I had been able to cling to my sense of freedom, cling too to my former identity as a struggling writer and newly married woman who enjoyed her independence and spontaneity. It had been fun for the two of us to pack the baby in the car and go, at a moment's notice, for evening drives. It had been easy to rush into town to meet my husband after work: squeezing baby in Snugli I could still follow my whims. Having one *small* baby did not seem to have caused too many drastic changes to our life or style. But all that slid away very quickly once the second baby was with us. Then I felt well and truly saddled, as the verb so accurately describes the feeling a horse must suffer when it is tamed, harnessed, and forced to carry a burden. I had a twenty-two-month-old terrible "terrible two" and a newborn. I was no longer a free agent.

Worse than that, I felt I had been unfairly cast in a role I knew belonged to my mother and her generation, not to me. I love my mother dearly, yet I had spent most of my teenage and young adult years in a not-so-secret battle endeavoring *not* to turn into her. But here I was, after all the attempts at revolution and radical lifestyles, in effect just like her. My former identity had been a sham. I had no identity. I was a nobody.

"Oh, I'm all right," I confided to one friend who could not begin to understand what I was talking about, "but I just don't seem able to feel any *joy* in life, when I know I should."

Looking back, I can see that I had grossly underestimated the recent events in my life. My husband had barely escaped death, and I had gone through a twenty-four-hour period not knowing if he would survive, waking at 4 A.M. to feed the baby and phone the hospital. My mother had been staying with me, and although I appreciated her help, which gave me time to visit the hospital every day, she was another concern on my mind. How could I be putting her through this? Then there was the exhausting routine of feeding the baby, dashing an hour each way to the hospital, spending an hour with my husband, racing home in time to feed her again. I was breast-feeding; everyone needed me; there was nothing, but nothing, to restore my energy and spiritual levels. I felt like Samson, holding up the fragile walls of our lives.

But the crisis had passed. My husband had made a quick and miraculous recovery. We had pushed the event out of our minds. I should not have been feeling depressed.

Yet I had also overlooked another personal crisis that led to the empty "I'm a nobody" feeling. It had never occurred to me to question how my self-confidence would hold up, when my own work, so precious to me over all my adult years, had just about disappeared over the past few months. From school days on I had been a driven, success-oriented, highly determined person, and my career as a writer, choppy though such careers necessarily are, had always been very important to my sanity and self-esteem.

A dear friend, a male colleague, called me just after the birth of this second baby with his own wonderful news—his novel had been sold for one of those mammoth advances we're always hearing about. It feels so petty now, but I remember saying, "How great," in a low voice. He had achieved success, fame, and fortune overnight. I'd had a baby.

So there I was, self-esteem negligible ("My only use in this world is to feed and diaper the baby, chase and scold the two-year-old"); identity crushed ("I used to be a visible writer, now I'm an invisible mother"); feeling trapped, despondent, and consequently lethargic. I was very lucky in having a sensitive husband. I don't know to this day if he appreciated the extent of my mood, but he did make two suggestions: (1) why not give up the breast-feeding, as I was obviously exhausted, and he could take on a greater share of the nightly feedings if we bottle-fed the baby; (2) if I bottle-fed her, it would be a good idea for me to get away on my own, go back to London for a few days, while he would look after both children.

More selfless mothers out there might have said, "No, I couldn't do that to the baby." It took me only a day to think it over; by then some feeling of exhilaration was seeping back into my bloodstream. The baby took to her bottle so contentedly I felt almost guilty for keeping her on a forced ration of my own depleted milk stock.

To my mind it was an image you find in the movies: woman without sense of identity returns to former life and rediscovers who she was and is. Obviously it was simpler for me than for most mothers, as I had a convenient location where I had acted my former part. Back in London, visiting family and friends, I was "free" again. I was someone people knew and maybe even respected. What no one seemed to comprehend was who was looking after the children. What husband ever voluntarily takes on a two-year-old and a four-month-old, they seemed to be saying. Well, mine did.

The real rescue of my self came from a visit to the newspaper office in which I had worked for many years. My male colleagues had always been fun, loved to tease, and tended to refer to me by my last name—I assume because they found it amusing. That day, I had convinced myself that no one in the old department (the women I had previously worked with having moved on to other jobs by now) would remember me. I had gone first to the editor's office and begged him to take me along and introduce me. A kind, fascinating man, he looked at me strangely but agreed to escort me. I'm sure he was shier than me, for he soon vanished as the cry went up, "It's Dix!"

We all had lunch together, talking and laughing. I certainly felt like *me* again. Whether it wrought overnight change, I very much doubt. I was still elated on the plane journey home, looking forward to seeing my children and newly fired with a determination to get my career going again. It meant my husband agreeing that we would find a playgroup for the toddler and a baby-sitter for some part of the week to give me time to find work. It meant forcing myself to a strict discipline and preparing to tap into those deep wells of seemingly bottomless self-confidence the free-lancer needs to face rejection and disappointment. The career did not recover magically. But just under a year later, I had work and a new book contract. I was back on the road again.

WHY WOMEN SUFFER IN SILENCE

I never told a soul I had suffered postpartum depression. Far too embarrassed, I just allowed those few months of heavy going to blend into history, as the smile returned to my face and the vigor to my step. I know I am not alone in remaining silent. Most women suffering any form of PPD not only suffer in isolation but continue to ignore or deny its existence. But that, surprisingly, is not the real reason why PPD, until very recently, has been a problem with no name.

Mothers having emotional problems? The very idea is anathema to our way of thinking. Most mothers-to-be won't even consider the possibility. Mother is "apple pie" in our society; she is security, she is steadfast when others fail; she may have a hard time juggling her many roles but she is elated at being a mother, eager to read any and every book or magazine available that will encourage, support, and improve her. Content with that "joy of motherhood" image, along with her husband, mother, and other children, she does not want to conceive of such a negative picture. Mothers cannot be depressed by motherhood, we think. They must have been prone to depression, or vulnerable to psychological disorders, before the birth.

We are in the midst of a baby boom. Everywhere we

read something about mothering, pregnancy, labor, delivery, or childcare. Having delayed their own turn for parenting, today's new mothers and fathers are coming to their task with renewed vigor, determined enthusiasm, and sometimes overpowering gratitude that they have been able to bear a child and become a family. How can they begin to accept that becoming parents might not be the fun-filled, all-inspiring event they had let themselves believe? They *know* that older mothers and fathers become parents just as well, if not better, than their younger colleagues. They *know* that working mothers can juggle roles with sufficient ease to please the child psychologists and education professionals.

The pressure is most definitely on us all. Mothers are supposed to be happy people. They are meant to adore and be adored by their children. They may be superwomen, superwives, supermoms. No one is forcing them to stay home, or to work. Yes, today's women have it all—so don't complain!

There's another side to the story. Child abuse statistics, and their accompanying sensational news stories, increase daily. Violence in the home is becoming one of the most urgent social issues. Divorce rates are catastrophic, especially among couples with children. Infanticide can and does happen, and mothers in America are more likely than in any other Western civilization to receive harsh and punitive sentencing for the crime, with no consideration or sympathy given to the effects of PPD (in its most severe and rarest form of postpartum psychosis). Maternal suicide statistics are startlingly high, though never talked about.

PPD is no respecter of persons. It does not affect only the poor, the disadvantaged, the educationally or emotionally deprived. It does not care about our income level, or social class, or happiness in marriage, number of cars or homes owned. Even if we have a happy history with one or two babies, it can strike us with a new one. We are all vulnerable.

Perhaps the most unfortunate aspect of the problem is that the majority of obstetricians, psychiatrists, pediatricians, family doctors, and social workers appear to know little or nothing about this condition that can so devastate a woman's life, her family's welfare, and her children's future. Since it is not supposed to exist, women either deny its presence or suffer alone in shame and guilt.

PPD is the hormonally and biochemically induced reaction to the body's upheaval in giving birth. Research, documentation, discovery, methods of treatment, and suggested support are all available. Yet this knowledge is so widely scattered and unevenly shared among doctors at large that women still tend to blame themselves for their condition. "She is weak, dependent, unable to deal with change or lack of control, hates her mother, hates children, was obviously the depressive type or a latent schizophrenic anyway" are all common arguments used to explain mothering reactions that are viewed as not normal.

To aggravate the situation even more, there is no professional expert to deal with women after childbirth. There is no one type of doctor to turn to if you are suffering PPD. The pediatrician is the baby's doctor; once the birth is accomplished the obstetrician's job is finished. Unless suffering serious mental distress, a mother is unlikely to take herself to a psychiatrist or mental health clinic for diagnosis. This is the most crushing problem these women are faced with. There is no one to turn to.

PPD: DEFINITIONS

The PPD you might be experiencing in the quietness of your home very likely is neither catastrophic nor sensational. Your PPD may be characterized by a general depression, dullness, lethargy, and lack of joy or zest for life that has unexpectedly overtaken you since the birth of a child. Its onset could have been at any time in the first year after you gave birth.

Our biochemical makeup undergoes massive change and stress after childbirth and can, if subjected to other overloading factors—whether they are internally formed stresses of the mind or externally formed stresses of changes in lifestyle (relationships, expectations of ourselves as mothers)—lead to a temporary breakdown in the normal flow of brain chemicals that creates our natural state of mental balance. The person we used to be seems to have vanished, almost overnight. Even if we have not experienced emotional swings or depression before, we may be subject to them once we become mothers.

The two principal syndromes of PPD are determined by time of onset (number of days after childbearing) and severity. The early syndrome starts during the first three weeks and ranges from mild or moderate blues to severe psychosis. The late syndrome begins after three weeks, is mainly depressive in mood, and also ranges in severity from mild or moderate to severe. Severe cases in both syndromes, statistically about two to three in 1,000 births, usually require hospitalization.

After birth, a latent period of about three days occurs, during which there is rarely any psychological disturbance. From the third day to the fifteenth, two conditions may emerge: (1) the blues, which is a mild, short-lived syndrome; and (2) puerperal psychosis, which is very severe. Both of these share the characteristic anxiety and agitation. The blues is a temporary disturbance of mood that, apart from anxiety, will also be evidenced as restlessness, tearfulness, insomnia, and sometimes confusion. It occurs in 25 to 50 percent of mothers and often clears up in a few hours or at most a few days. It is seen as a normal sequel to childbirth.

Puerperal psychosis has the same time frame of onset, many of the same symptoms, but in addition it manifests itself as hallucinations, delusions, great agitation, marked deviation in moods, wild, crazy thoughts, fears of harming yourself or your baby, and either severe depression, mania, or changes from one to the other. The severe symptoms may necessitate hospital care within the first three weeks after birth; or, if not so extreme and urgent, the condition can merge into the depressed condition of PPD as weeks pass by.

The late-onset subsyndromes, which also come under the umbrella PPD, begin from the twentieth to the fortieth day postpartum. The predominant mood of this form of PPD is depression. The onset is usually slow and insidious. Symptoms may include a feeling of sadness, lack of energy, feelings of futility, plus a number of physical symptoms such as chronic tiredness, delayed return of menstruation, peripheral edema usually evidenced by ankle swelling or a weight increase that is not dietary, loss of hair, severe insomnia, and a marked loss in sexual responsiveness. (These same physical symptoms can also be found when an early puerperal psychosis merges with a later depression.)

Again, there are mild and moderate examples of these late-onset depressions; there are also severe cases where mothers might be feeling suicidal or fear they will harm their babies. Although rare, PPD can come on at very late stages following weaning from breast-feeding. Although little research has yet been done to identify the link, some women have noticed severe mood changes (even psychosis) when weaning their babies. Parents are advised to watch out for symptoms at this particular time.

Although statistics are hard to come by, particularly in the U.S. where no such data have yet been kept, at a conservative estimate nearly 40,000 women per year will undergo serious psychiatric illnesses requiring hospitalization in this country alone. And if we take into consideration the ten percent of new mothers who will suffer mild to moderate PPD, we are talking about something like 400,000 women each year.

PIECES OF THE PUZZLE

Why am I saying the problem has no name when I contentedly refer to it as PPD? Let me go back a few steps to the beginning of my research. Fired by a determination to discover all I could about PPD, I began by talking to obstetricians who had made some relevant comments in the past about women after childbirth. I was introduced to one of the psychosomatic obstetrician/gynecologists in the United States, Dr. Elisabeth Herz, in Washington, D.C., who is very much involved with the problem and has been of invaluable help.[1] I also talked to psychiatrists and clinical psychologists about depression and treatments available.

But the pieces would not fit together. Something was missing. I was gathering disparate threads of information that did not add up to a whole. I seemed to be chasing two leads: it was either the hormonal argument or the psychological argument. Library catalogues did not list "postpartum depression" as a subject.

Then, in London, I interviewed pioneer gynecologist Dr. Katharina Dalton, who had previously revolutionized our knowledge of premenstrual syndrome (PMS) and who, I knew, was making a similar study of PPD.[2] Dr. Dalton suggested I contact other experts in the United States, particularly Dr. James Hamilton of San Francisco.[3] In passing, Dalton mentioned that Hamilton was secretary of the Marcé Society. I had stumbled on the very thing I had been looking for: the missing link. The Marcé Society is an international organization of obstetricians, psychiatrists, endocrinologists, scientific researchers, nurses, and social workers, all involved in work on PPD. Begun in 1980, it has produced the most encouraging work, worldwide, on causes, symptoms, and treatments of PPD.

Dr. James Hamilton, now retired (formerly associate clinical professor of psychiatry at Stanford School of Medicine), has never been one to defer his own views to the traditional or accepted attitudes of the profession; he greeted my initial telephone call with delight. "There was a flurry of interest in PPD about twenty years ago," he told me. "But since then it has died down." I went to see him in his San Francisco office and we talked away a whole day. He was as excited to meet a writer interested in a book on postpartum women as I was to meet this unique man who has for years led a campaign to get PPD on the medical and psychological maps.

WHY SO LITTLE IS KNOWN

"We formed the Marcé Society after a conference in Manchester, England, called by Professor Ian Brockington, that brought together doctors from different disciplines, for the very first time, in an effort to rectify the situation," explained Hamilton. "But it is incredible how time has stood still. Louis Victor Marcé, after whom we named the society, was a physician in mid-nineteenth-century France who knew as much about PPD as we do today."

Over a century ago, terms such as postpartum depression (and psychosis) were used by the medical profession. But, in 1926, when psychiatry was a relatively new branch of medicine and labels were being hastily sought to consolidate diseases and knowledge, a much-honored psychiatrist, E. A. Strecker, wrote that there was no such thing as postpartum depression (or psychosis), that women suffering such symptoms were really showing easily recognizable disorders such as schizophrenia, mania, depression, or other affective disorders, and that they should be treated accordingly.[4]

Such was Strecker's influence that the terms were deleted from the textbooks and from official classification. PPD is not coded for computer classification in the United States' 1980 revised DSM-III (Diagnostic and Statistical Manual of Mental Disorders) sponsored by the American Psychiatric Association, although Dr. James Hamilton reports that the new DSM-IV, due out in 1993, will list postpartum psychosis as one of the psychiatric conditions that are related to physical states, such as sleep and premenstrual disorders. Finally, PPD is going to see some official recognition. Nor is it yet listed in Britain's ICD (International Classification of Diseases). In April 1984, *JAMA,* the *Journal of the American Medical Association,* reported this omission.[5]

For the scientist intent on research on PPD, the hunt for cases becomes an endless job. All psychiatric hospital admission records of women in childbearing years have to be read through to confirm that their condition followed the birth of a child. Medical and psychiatric students are not taught about PPD. They learn, instead, the official accepted wisdom: that women—even if severely affected after childbirth—who have had no previous mental disorders are showing a latent mental disorder, and their treatment should follow the same course as any other mental patient's.

Is it any wonder women have remained silent? Not only are they ashamed, guilty, and isolated, but they are downright afraid of being classified as insane.

The nameless problem deepens that sense of isolation. Working my own way through libraries, searching for material, I concentrated my efforts at the American Medical Association's (AMA) excellent Manhattan library, looking up anything remotely relevant: "motherhood," "postpartum," "puerperal," "depression." As I came upon papers and articles, I noted their bibliographies and so tracked down much of the available material. One woman who wrote to me had similarly tried to research PPD for a graduate paper. She worked for a major pharmaceutical company and had access to their well-stocked library. She asked the librarian to run a computer search on PPD. It came up with only *one* reference, and that was a small paragraph in a medical book.

At the most recent conference of the Marcé Society, one of the leading topics of discussion was the classification problem and the desperate need for the condition, disorder, or syndrome to be categorized.[6] I have adopted the term postpartum depression and the easy-to-remember PPD. Although it is used by other writers and doctors as well, it is not yet official terminology.

THE UNITED STATES LAGS IN RESEARCH

At this first conference held in the United States, it was rather embarrassing that the Americans constituted perhaps one quarter of the attendance and an even smaller percentage of the scientific papers that were presented.

A few double specialists, in obstetrics and psychiatry, represented the handful of such well-qualified people in the United States, notably Dr. Raphael Good of the University of Texas, Galveston. The National Institute of Mental Health was represented by psychiatrist Dr. Barbara Parry. Good news was announced at the conference: Dr. Michael O'Hara, of the department of psychology at the University of Iowa, had just been awarded a major three-year grant from the NIMH to study the psychiatric and biochemical causes of PPD.

By far the strongest contingent was from Britain, whose National Health Service has been most efficient in detecting PPD in women and in treating them. Doctors from Manchester described mother and baby units attached to some psychiatric hospitals, so mothers do not have to be separated from the newborn (or its siblings) at this crucial time, and Dr. Margaret Oates described a unique experiment in Nottingham, where at-home care is provided, even for the most serious cases, by an intensive team of psychiatric nurses and doctors.

Norway, Sweden, Holland, France, Germany, Italy, and Canada were all represented at the meeting, as were doctors from Australia and New Zealand. The Japanese also were far ahead of the United States in this field. Professor Yutaka Honda, from the department of neuropsychiatry at the University of Tokyo, headed their team. Professors Bernhard Pauleikhoff from Universitats Nervenklinik, in Münster, West Germany; Ian Brockington, from Queen Elizabeth Hospital's department of psychiatry, in Birmingham, England; Merton Sandler from Queen Charlotte's Maternity Hospital, London; and noted epidemiologist Professor Ralph Paffenbarger, of Stanford University Medical Center, added weight to the scientific register.

WOMEN DOCTORS BREAK THE SILENCE

One of the most fascinating aspects of that conference, for me, was meeting a group of women psychiatrists who had originally trained as obstetricians or family doctors. I was intrigued by the success with which they had managed—as wives and mothers—to juggle the various parts of their lives to accommodate large families and careers. Three of the women had four children each, and one had six. Drs. Christine Dean, Diana Riley, and Margaret Oates from England, Dr. Judith Treadwell from New Zealand, and Dr. Ione Railton from the United States all knew the problems women encounter after childbirth, not only as professionals, but as mothers.

"I can remember only too well wanting to throw my first baby out of the window," one of them confessed. "What we have to consider is just what degree of abnormal behavior is really *normal* after birth. Every woman fantasizes and goes through some sort of unacceptable emotional changes, once she becomes a mother. I'm sure most of us have had PPD to some degree. But if you are poor, or come before a psychiatrist or social worker, those types of comments are written down as significant and as part of your diagnosis. We need to draw up some limits for what is 'normally abnormal' for new mothers."

Another said, "When I was starting in practice as a gynecologist, I was pregnant with my fourth and had three young ones at home. I'd ask the new mothers how they were doing at home. If the answer was a bland 'fine,' I'd say, 'You're lucky, mine are driving me bloody crazy!' That usually broke the ice, and then we could talk more honestly."

FUTURE OF THE PROBLEM

Although PPD occurs mainly in women who have never suffered depression before, if left untreated many of these women will continue to experience psychological problems up to four years after childbirth—and some never recover properly. Of course these cases swell the numbers of women considered mentally unwell in our society. Yet, as we will see, PPD is rapidly becoming understood, treatable, and curable by rational and effective methods.

Now is the time for public attention to turn to PPD, for research to gather momentum, for doctors of all disciplines to take the problem seriously, rather than just dismissing it as the "crazy lady" syndrome. A different generation is having babies now, a generation of women with greater expectations for themselves, with less invested in the traditional myths of motherhood. Their social role is not circumscribed by marriage and mothering. These women discuss and analyze every other aspect of their lives. If they find themselves confused when the pieces of their mothering puzzle don't fit, they will push for answers. We must stand together and attempt to shatter the myths surrounding one of society's last taboos. Motherhood is not always easy. But then neither is life.

2

◆

UNDERSTANDING PPD

Visiting San Francisco the first time in over a year, I phoned an old friend in great excitement——her first baby had been born on Christmas Eve and was now just six weeks old. Looking forward to seeing them both, I overlooked, even with my own understanding of what state she might be in, the reality of the situation: first-time mother with six-week-old in her arms.

Anne P. is thirty-six and an accomplished book editor. A beautiful woman who met and married her husband while both were still students, she has been married for seventeen years.

Her tired voice answered the ringing. "I'm sorry," I instantly apologized. "I should have realized you might be sleeping late."

"It's all right." Anne's voice lacked its usual depth and richness. "The baby woke at 2 A.M. She's usually very good. But the pattern seems to be changing."

"How are you doing?" I said hesitantly. Anne and her husband had had seventeen years of childless married life: a calm, uncluttered routine, nice jobs, two dogs to be walked, and a cabin in the country for weekends. Hardly domestic souls, she and Peter seldom cooked much at home. But she

17

must have known, I thought defensively. She must have guessed what it would be like. She'd had us to stay on our travels, seen the struggle with my two. Surely she knew it wouldn't be easy?

Skirting the issue, as women over the centuries have done, we chatted for a while. Then I sneaked in a small laugh before saying, "Have you begun to realize yet that all you wanted was to see what it would be like to have a baby, play the game a bit? But you never appreciated the twenty-four-hour-a-day, seven-day-a-week commitment?"

"Don't worry. I've thought it already," Anne responded quickly. "There are times I wish I could send her back. Yet I don't. You know what I mean."

I most certainly did. Is there really a woman out there who has not felt some degree of the devastating change of emotions and mental outlook that follows a birth? Ambivalence is a large part of the game. Anne, in fact, was not depressed. She seemed to be coping well with the ambivalence. (A year later, I am sad to report, she and Peter were on the verge of separating.) But we can all be caught by surprise, shocked by our own reactions.

"Surely the misery I am feeling right now is a symptom of my own failure and inadequacy as woman and mother, not a definable condition experienced by many new mothers," we think.

In case you are wondering if the term postpartum depression applies to you, the after-birth blues come in all shapes, forms, and degrees. As we sit in our lonely kitchens or nurseries, we really are not alone. We are all in the same situation. It has just taken until now for us to open up and understand that these unexpected feelings are not strange.

EARLY, OR BABY, BLUES

The term "baby blues" tends to be used for a specific, temporary experience that the majority of women go through in the first few days after giving birth and that is supposedly self-limiting to the first ten days postpartum. Known throughout history as the "maternity blues," or the "three-day blues," the "weepies," and sometimes still as "milk fever" (it was associated with milk coming into the breasts on the third day), its most common aspect is uncontrollable crying. It is so common that doctors and nurses treat it as a normal part of birthing and no one gets upset—except you and your husband.

We tend to feel foolish when it takes over, for we know that we have everything to feel grateful for: we should be radiantly happy, glowing with pride and new maternal joy. And there we are crying, sometimes inconsolably. As one research paper on the early blues has shown, it can be set off by feelings of rejection; the doctor not showing proper attention, one's husband coming late to visit at the hospital, a nurse or orderly being offhand or rude; by good news, such as another birth in the family; or by a sense of inadequacy, if the milk doesn't come in properly or we have problems with breast-feeding.[7]

How common is it? Professionals agree that 80 percent of all new mothers experience some form of the symptoms: these may be the rapid fits of crying, or they can extend to sleeplessness, feeling irritable and angry, feeling hostile to the doctor, hospital, husband, and, very often, feeling confused. Up to 50 percent of new mothers have episodes of crying from the fifth to the tenth day after birth.

Most pregnancy books make some reference to the blues, with the advice that it passes very quickly and we should not be unduly concerned. "Everything will be fine when you get home," they promise us. From the women I have talked to or corresponded with, I know that most new mothers are aware of this classic early blues syndrome: indeed, they are waiting for it to happen while in the hospital.

Few of us know why it happens. Certainly even fewer know that it can attack very severely, destroying our personal vision of how we will react to being a new mother, or that even if the blues leaves us alone in the first few postpartum days, it may come on much more slowly and affect us later.

Most doctors feel that the classic early blues has a basic hormonal cause. Katharina Dalton explained that during pregnancy there is exaggerated hormonal output to hold the fetus in the uterus, create its nest, and nurture its survival. By the time a woman goes into labor, the levels of her estrogen and progesterone, for example, are fifty times higher than before a pregnancy.

The most acute hormonal change happens on the first day after delivery, when progesterone and estrogen levels plunge dramatically. Within twenty-four to thirty-six hours after childbirth the estrogen and progesterone fall from these high levels to levels that are below prepregnancy levels.

This drop in hormones can affect us in a way similar to drug withdrawal, with related symptoms. In Katharina Dalton's view, the normal adjustment a mother makes to these body changes is in fact not so much normal as *heroic*.

But many of us adjust less well. The early blues can be more disturbing than mere bouts of heavy crying for a day or two. It can leave us anxious, confused, worried about our maternal instincts. Most of the women who wrote to me had experienced something beyond a temporary, easy-to-accept weepiness.

Jenny T., 25, a secretary and a single mother, went through a euphoric pregnancy, with an incredibly successful four-hour natural delivery of a beautiful, healthy girl. She was so happy. Then, "Something got me. That 'something' was soon to be labeled the baby blues by all the hospital staff, my family, and finally, my roommate.

"My baby blues included (a) uncontrollable crying, (b) no sense of reality, (c) severe depression to the point of believing my daughter didn't need me as a mother, (d) lack of concern for the baby, (e) inability to sleep anytime, (f) lack of appetite, both sexual and for food. A male doctor said that everything I was feeling was normal. If this was normal, I wanted to be abnormal!"

Jenny was fortunate that her mother, a surgical nurse, was sympathetic and took her home to care for her. Around eight to nine months later, after her daughter started walking, Jenny began to feel all right again.

Jenny's was a typical experience. What she had gone through was not just a touch of the blues, the sort we are allowed and expected to have, but a sign of something much deeper going on.

We can begin to comprehend what Jenny was experiencing by understanding that hormonal changes are irrevocably tied to major biochemical changes within the body during pregnancy and after birth.

THE PSYCHOENDOCRINE CONNECTION

The biochemical changes may cause agitation, inability to sleep, mental confusion, or hours of uncontrollable crying not necessarily linked to a cause. The biochemistry of the body affects the nervous system: there is a more complete mind-body connection than we probably realize.

As an umbrella term, the *psychoendocrine* functioning of the body captures a complex idea. Endocrine means the hormonal system, and of course psycho refers to the mind. The words are linked to mirror the indelible tie between the two sides of our existence. We cannot have a hormonal change without a change in biochemistry and without some mental change. In our search for the root cause of the bodily and psychic upheaval, we must turn to the relatively new science of endocrinology and ongoing studies attempting to associate hormonal changes and depression.[8]

"The presentation of PPD has always been that it is a psychiatric disease," commented Katharina Dalton. "They say the woman is mentally disturbed because she has to share herself with the baby and husband. But really it is a hormonally induced state. One day we will recognize that all depressions are caused by chemical disorders and imbalances."

Hormones take their name from the Greek word meaning "to set in motion." They are the chemical messengers of the body to the brain, produced by tissues and organs. Some produce internal adjustments to the different systems of the body, some respond to external events and provoke behavioral reactions. Hormonal effects on mood and behavior have long been recognized, and current research is concentrating on how and why they work.

The hormones are secreted by the body's main glands: thyroid, parathyroid, adrenals, pancreas, and gonads. They move directly into the bloodstream to target the organs they regulate. For example, estrogen and progesterone are increased soon after a conception takes place, to protect the embryonic development in the uterus.

The brain has its own set of hormones, produced by neurons, which act as transmitters. Located in the hypothalamus, these neurohormones are directed to travel along special pathways in the brain. They, in turn, affect the output of the body's endocrine hormones. In effect, brain and body are entwined in a never-ending dance.[9]

Psychosomatic ob/gyn Dr. Elisabeth Herz helped with her own interpretation of the complex events that can lead from hormonal change to depression or mental distress in new mothers.

"In our brains we have the hypothalamus, one of the deep brain centers where physical and psychological equilibrium is constantly monitored. It regulates many involuntary functions, including sleep, body rhythms, and appetites. In the hypothalamus, neurotransmitters, which control our moods, interact with important neural hormones that stimulate all the other hormones, maintaining our systems and, usually, equilibrium.

"The hypothalamus receives constant internal input from various parts of the body via the hormones and metabolism; it also gets messages from the higher brain centers that have been exposed to external stimuli. The hypothalamus's job—influenced by a person's genetic makeup—is to balance it all out. However, if the system is overloaded—an imbalance of hormones, for example—the hypothalamus gets into a state of disequilibrium. Disorganization all around can result.

"This is why, in addition to mood changes, we also find sleep disturbances, changes in appetite, and decreased sexual desire. The regulatory system can't cope. It is a multifactoral picture, but explains why stresses that a woman could cope with at other times, when exacerbated by the internal changes, just become too much."

NATURE'S OWN TRANQUILIZERS

One main area of research today is into the actual effect of the neurohormones on the endocrine system, and vice versa.

The neurohormones—dopamine, serotonin, and norepinephrine being the most common—travel along prescribed pathways in the brain, through the millions of tiny threadlike branches of brain tissue, rather like electric current moves along wires. Scientists want to discover why the current is sometimes faster and sometimes slower, how the brain hormones affect our moods, and whether medical intervention can help in cases of depression.

After childbirth, we experience major endocrine changes: the rapid drop in estrogen and progesterone, the two main hormones of pregnancy, comes within hours of delivery. There are also falls in thyroid levels (to a point lower than the prepregnant state), and a decrease in pituitary function. At the same time, we undergo massive blood loss and drop in body fluids; prolactin is increased for breast-feeding; there is sleep disturbance; and we experience other, more technical, changes, such as altered levels of adrenal steroids, free and binding corticosteroids, and gonadotrophins.

If our levels of thyroid, progesterone, estrogen, and adrenal corticoids, for example, are shooting down, the flow of norepinephrine, serotonin, and dopamine will also be reduced. The link between progesterone and mood can easily be seen, for the hormone can be used as a sedative in high doses, dulling anxiety and the agitated moods of the manic. The thyroid, too, has an obvious effect: at its highest level it makes us speedy and overanxious, and at its lowest level we become sluggish. Estrogen at peak levels makes for well-being; in decline, as at the menopause, it can lead to distress and depression.

The neural pathways along which the neuroendocrine transmitters travel, the fine branches of brain tissue, have spaces between them, which are called *synapses*. The vigor and quantity of the neurohormones at the synapses, their ability to cross the spaces, is known to be the key to mood stabilization. When the neurohormones are vigorous, we are happy and relaxed. When they are sluggish, we are dull and depressed.

Taking the neurotransmitter argument further, it is known that one vital pathway of norepinephrine crosses alongside the hypothalamus, close to what has been located as the "pleasure centers" of the brain; i.e., those areas where our relaxed, most pleasant moods are located. The norepinephrine pathway, therefore, seems to bear a direct relationship to regulating our level of euphoria or depression. The latest of the neurohormones to be singled out for such research has an even closer link with these pleasure centers. Known collectively as *endorphins* (a contraction of the words "endogenous morphinelike substances"), they are internally produced opiates that bind themselves to special receptors in the brain. If we are low on levels of endorphins we will be low on the natural opiates that make us feel good. Moreover, endorphin levels are linked to levels of all other neurohormones. Don't you wish you could go out and buy a vial of endorphins?

The idea that we can intervene with the production of the neurohormones to rebalance the basic brain chemistry if depression takes over is one of the more revolutionary and exciting new concepts. Some scientists enjoy provoking their colleagues in the psychiatric professions by saying, "In the future we will not need psychiatrists once we understand brain chemistry better." For now, however, we wait, and in waiting hope for better treatment, cures, understanding, and sympathetic doctors and other professionals. We especially hope for more discussion of PPD and how it may affect our lives.

Theories about neuroendocrinological change may not impress the women who are undergoing a surprising and unexpected bout with PPD. Examples of the early kind of blues reactions that are not covered by the "everything will be fine" comments of the pregnancy books are found in the following stories from Dianne and Kathy. Both women underwent violent reactions that left them questioning their own sanity. Both were confused and perplexed, left to grapple for reasons within their own psyches. Neither sought outside help or support. In many ways, therefore, their stories are typical and relevant to many new mothers.

Dianne and Kathy: Early Intense Reactions

I had been told of a woman going through a heavy early blues reaction. She had begun crying in the hospital and could not stop. I was nervous about meeting her, frightened of making her feel worse. But Dianne McL. was a thoughtful, reflective person. As a commercial artist and weekend painter, thirty years old, she was newly and happily married and had been thrilled to become pregnant. She had always wanted a baby and now she had a good home to offer her new family. Dianne was mature and wise. Her baby girl was beautiful, but, she said, "It all started about three days after the birth. During the pregnancy I had read several books but skimmed the few lines on the blues, never imagining it would happen to me. The books devoted so little time to the subject I was sure it was unimportant. After all, I wanted this baby so badly, I could be nothing but happy and filled with joy."

Dianne had a surprise C-section. The first few days after this, things were complicated. However, at one point she began to have hallucinations, was fearful, felt paranoid and crazy, and couldn't stop shaking.

"I remember feeling that the flowers in my room were somehow there to get me and that I didn't deserve them. They were rising up to mock me. My paranoia became so severe I was afraid that the orderlies in the hall were going to rape me in the middle of the night.

"Everything I thought caused me to cry, and all I did was cry. In the morning the friendly nurses came in, and I tried to fight back my tears. I was ashamed. I had a beautiful baby girl, just what I wanted, and she was perfect. I was able to breast-feed her, as I had wanted. Everything was perfect, but every time I looked at my baby tears would roll again down my face. Every time I looked at anything, tears would well."

Dianne later thought she found an emotional explanation for the crying within herself—she recognized a sense of loss, or separation, from her own mother (she was adopted at eighteen months). Maybe the crying was a release for all those years of pent-up feelings about losing her mother, she reasoned.

The excitement I discovered in my own research, the breakthrough I was so determined to open up, was to explain the lie, or maybe negligence would be nearer the truth, that has so affected our lives. The one thing we should all be reciting along with our Lamaze mantras is: *after birth the body undergoes hormonal and biochemical upheaval, not experienced at other times in our lives, and these changes may affect us profoundly both physically and mentally.*

The trigger that will compound these hormonal imbalances, to set off a serious emotional response, may well be found in our response to the outside world: to the enormous lifestyle changes and awareness of responsibility not held before.

Kathy S., a twenty-nine-year-old office manager with a pharmaceutical company, suffered an extreme and unexpected early PPD crisis after the birth of her son; not in the usual crying form, but with a much stronger signal. She had wanted to walk out of the hospital alone.

"I had a C-section. I came around from the operation and it began right there in the recovery room. I remember freezing with fear. I didn't want this baby! It was all a mistake. It got steadily worse. I felt so depressed and I'd lie there in bed deliberately thinking of depressing things, willfully determined to make myself feel worse."

Back at home things did not improve. "I was the worst mother you could imagine. I still wanted to run away. I fantasized taking my clothes and leaving them, my husband and son. The only strength I had in those days was not to do that."

Yet Kathy had always seen herself as a strong person. After seven years of marriage, she very much wanted and planned for a baby. She was well established in her work, and knew she would go back after a couple of months' leave. The pregnancy had been perfect. She had even carried well.

"You can imagine how horrified I was to have those feelings I least expected toward the baby. But at least I admit it. I sometimes wonder if women who crack up later in life do so because they've repressed these feelings early on, and it festers. People tried to tell me it was because of the C-section. I thought about it a great deal, but I knew otherwise. The depression miraculously lifted when Joe was six months old. I had been back at work for three months by then. I was happy to be at work. *Being a mother was the thing that really scared me.*"

LATER ONSET OF PPD

One woman had a late attack of PPD beginning eight months after the birth of her child, another at ten months. Others report onset of depression at two or maybe four months. My own case came about the third month. Until then I had been suffering the usual tiredness, the anxiety of dealing with a new baby and a toddler, and the adaptation problems of disappointment in being tied down again and wondering vaguely what I had done. The depression itself, the dark mood that I could not shift or explain, the deep questioning about my life and future, descended as if by magic at this point.

From the available pregnancy books, we learn that PPD is transitory and will soon pass. It should begin on the third day, they say, and be gone in a few days; or at worst within eight or ten weeks. That does little to help the person who begins to suffer at about the eighth or tenth week.

A PPD coming on after the second month might, we assume, be caused mostly by the social and emotional aspects of motherhood, rather than by the biochemical or hormonal forces. But there is evidence to the contrary from the description of symptoms given by women themselves. Rosie J., for example, became a single mother shortly after graduating from college and starting a career when she was twenty-two years old. Her baby was twenty-two months old when Rosie contacted me. Two months after the baby's birth, Rosie began to suffer periods of insecurity, paranoia, crying, and shaking.

"I thought I was going crazy, and so did everyone else," she said. Fortunately she read an article on PPD and realized that the symptoms were related. Rosie was prescribed a mild sedative to keep the shaking at bay. She felt it was the responsibility of her voluntarily assumed single motherhood that had so frightened her. The idealistic vision of single parenthood did not fit the reality of being young, needing to start a career, and feeling very much alone.

The blues has been defined as the agitated, distressed type of reaction, whereas the symptoms that are likely to emerge after six or seven weeks will be those of depression and inertia—the woman will be fearful, withdrawn, backward in relating to others; she will have no energy, may be constipated, and will probably find sex anathema.

The two types of symptoms, for early and late PPD, are so different from each other that doctors have traditionally viewed them as separate diseases. Yet there is an integral relationship between the two. What might begin as a mild attack of early blues may develop into the dragging form of depression, though a woman need not have had any symptoms of early blues to later develop PPD.

The hormonal imbalance that occurs in the first few days after birth may, later in the first postpartum year, lead to what Dr. Herz described as the overloaded regulatory system if the stresses and strains of adjusting to motherhood (or parenting) are so great that the individual cannot recover from the original imbalance. A late-onset PPD may well have a biochemical component, just like the traditional early blues.

TEMPORARY OR SERIOUS?

Crying her eyes out shortly after the birth of her son, a friend of mine was cautioned by her mother, "You'd better stop crying or you'll really go crazy." There is an old, and widely held, view that if we give way to the crying fits of early blues the condition will worsen rather than go away of its own accord. How can we tell if our symptoms are temporary or the beginnings of something serious that might require treatment?

Kelly M., a nurse who assumed she was quite prepared for becoming a mother, was happily married, twenty-eight years old, with a career that she felt had taught her all there was to know about pregnancy, labor, and postpartum care. Kelly's symptoms of PPD became so severe she had to receive outpatient psychiatric care and was on antidepressant medication for five months. Although cured, she still could recall the guilt and loneliness of that time, which had made her suffering harder.

Mary Ann A. had been happily married to husband David for five years, had worked as a legal secretary for ten years, and was ready and willing to have a baby at the age of twenty-nine. A good pregnancy, easy delivery, and healthy baby son were all picture perfect. Mary Ann even had a nurse's help for the first three and a half weeks back home, but still she could not sleep, could not stop crying, and began to feel she was cracking up. "At times I wanted to kill myself or the baby," she said.

Her family doctor, a psychiatrist, and a gynecologist all recognized PPD but said it was normal and would soon pass. Finally, Mary Ann's mother-in-law put her in touch with another doctor. Within hours she was referred to a different psychiatrist, who recommended that if antidepressants did not clear up her suicidal feelings within four to five days, she should be hospitalized.

Mary Ann's condition was not temporary. It needed prompt, good treatment. Back home, she took the first tablets and, maybe because the initial effects of antidepressants can be to make you *more* depressed or utterly confused, she completely broke down. At Mary Ann's request she was hospitalized that same night.

Very often, the swiftest therapy may be found in good or sympathetic care. Mary Ann's recovery began in the hospital. "I think it was the relief of knowing that someone was finally going to help," she said. Mary Ann spent ten weeks on a psychiatric ward. Her son was a year old when she was able to reduce the level of medication. Back at work, she finally realized that getting out of the house and back to her former lifestyle had helped a lot. She was one of the many victims of the ignorance surrounding postpartum women, though thankfully she found help in time.

What can we learn from her experience about the turning point from temporary to serious form of PPD? The most obvious symptoms to watch out for are suicidal feelings, a desire to hurt or kill the child, or a total inability to function, to care for yourself or the baby. Mary Ann admitted that she had been battling alone against the stronger forces of her metabolism, trying in vain to pull inner strength, positive thinking, and social pressures to the foreground, so she would appear to be the good mother she so desperately wanted to be. Now she hopes her story can help other women, by telling them not to be afraid: "You can be treated. It will get better."

As women with more serious levels of PPD are unlikely to be reading a book of this kind, I extend my words to the husbands, mothers, or close friends of a new mother who talks of killing herself or who threatens to abuse her child. *Help her.* Do your best to find a doctor who understands and who will treat her condition sympathetically. Her negative feelings are not her fault. She is most likely incapable of helping herself. No amount of telling her to pull herself together will improve the situation; just the opposite. The new mother is undergoing, for whatever complex reasons, an extreme version of the psychoendocrine reaction. The overloaded hypothalamus has radically altered her mood.

PPD in this serious form is an acute condition that can be treated and cured, as we cure any other specific disease. In Britain and Scandinavia, where there is greater understanding of PPD and its treatment, there are now mother and baby units attached to some major psychiatric hospitals. Mothers who need admission for PPD may come with their babies, and sometimes young children, for sympathetic, nonalarmist care. These women are not filled with the fear that they are joining the ranks of the chronically insane, which tragically is so often the case in the United States.

"PPD can be very frightening if you don't know what is happening and why. I would like to help anyone who is going through it by reassuring them that it will pass, they won't be insane," said Kim S., a model housewife and mother with three children who had undergone PPD three times. The first two times Kim felt were mild, but in retrospect she could see they were becoming progressively worse. After her third baby, Kim was hospitalized, still with no understanding of what was going on.

"I really thought I was losing my sanity. I was crying all the time, panicking over nothing, my stomach would be tied up in knots, and I had acute anxiety attacks. I was just falling to pieces and why, I didn't know. It didn't make sense. I had no history of mental problems." Kim was successfully treated with antidepressants when it was finally explained to her that the tablets would rebalance her body's metabolism.

As there is very little help to judge in advance who will be affected by such a serious attack, my advice would be: rather than worry that their crying bouts are going to lead to

What about [?] without husbands?

the psychiatric wards, mothers should concentrate on making sure they understand the syndrome, what can happen and why. If they do begin to feel out of control, then together with their husbands they will have a better chance of knowing where help can be found and of how to seek proper professional care.

PMS, PPD, AND MIGRAINE

Is a PMS (premenstrual syndrome) sufferer more or less likely to become a victim of PPD? There is no direct correlation, but a woman who before giving birth has had no problem with premenstrual mood swings may discover that a case of PPD, without her realizing it, slowly develops into a characteristic PMS.

Dr. Katharina Dalton, probably the world's leading pioneer on research into premenstrual syndrome, related both PPD and PMS to progesterone deficiency. When I visited her in her London office, she explained the connection: "In the last two weeks of any menstrual cycle, after ovulation, the hormone progesterone is present in our nonpregnant bodies to help the ovulated egg nest in the uterus. Ironically, it is in those same two weeks that we might experience progesterone deficiency, if we do not naturally produce a high enough quantity. It is this deficiency that leads to the mood and physical changes associated with PMS."

As Dr. Penny Budoff mentioned in her book on menstrual cramps, traditionally women going through PMS were seen as crazies with problems relating to their own femininity.[10] But medical and psychological ideas have been forced to change.

How and why did Katharina Dalton link progesterone with PMS? "Thirty years ago, I was about to qualify in medicine, but I was suffering terrible PMS and migraine headaches. I saw a colleague, who said to me, 'Think about your progesterone levels.' I did. I gave myself an injection of naturally synthesized progesterone and it did the trick."

Dr. Dalton runs a revolutionary practice in London, where she treats women for PMS or PPD with injections or suppositories of the naturally synthesized hormone. In the United States, progesterone therapy is not used by obstetricians or psychiatrists for the relief of PPD, although progesterone clinics do exist here for the treatment of PMS alone. These clinics are not recognized by the AMA and are private, for-profit agencies, so any reader should be cautious in using their services.

The American medical profession is very reluctant to lend credence to Dalton's theories, since she has not yet conducted conclusive double blind tests. As one gynecologist put it, Katharina Dalton is a charismatic woman. It might be that the women who become her patients feel so much confidence in her and are so well looked after that their symptoms vanish.

However, the link between PMS and PPD has been recognized by many women without professional help, and is certainly worthy of more research, as possible treatment for PPD sufferers could follow PMS lines. Sharon W., a full-time mother in her early twenties with two young children, seems to be typical of a certain type of PMS and PPD sufferer: trapped in a cycle of depressions.

"When I was a child, people thought I was moody and, I suppose, I've grown up to accept that I must be the moody type. I did have a peculiar early life, but even so a lot has to do with hormones. I would say 80 percent of my problem is hormonal, the other 20 percent I'll put down to me.

"I never realized I had PMS at all until my first daughter was born. Then, because PPD was so bad, I went to the gynecologist. He felt I should be able to deal with this, as an adult, and in fact I'm seeing his wife for psychotherapy. He's right, I don't want to be taking drugs all the time. But I have migraine headaches too, and I just wish there was a way I could handle it all. My husband gets crazy: it's either one thing or the other with me. I know the difference in myself if it's PMS or PPD. The PMS mood is more angry and frustrated; the PPD is crying and down."

Extending the link to migraine as well, a connection that many women will recognize as an obvious chain in our hormonal responses, Lynne S., a full-time housewife and mother for thirteen years, now holding a job as a bookkeeper, helped fit more of the pieces together. As Lynne put it, "For some reason I never connected the depressions and crying spells with PPD, until I looked back at the whole of my married life. I've spent more than half my thirteen years of marriage as a crazy woman!"

When she was twenty-one, after her first child was born, a depression began that did not go away for twelve years, until finally Lynne received treatment for the headaches that had begun when she was eleven and first menstruating. For Lynne that experience with PPD spelled complete failure as a woman. She had been the eldest of seven siblings, had helped her mother raise them, and had been the neighborhood's best baby-sitter from the time she was twelve. How could one little boy, her own son, so ruin the perfect picture?

A second child in three years did not lead to a repeat episode with PPD. Another year later, however, with two toddlers, Lynne became very depressed and nearly suicidal. She finally changed doctors, and Lynne's new gynecologist agreed to her sterilization and began to treat her for PMS.

"I still had not connected PMS and PPD with my life, until I saw a neurologist for the migraine headaches. I had begun a full-time job and could no longer afford the three or four days off work a month, caused by the migraines. But when I started to study migraine and PMS it was incredible. I was reading *my life*. There was such a sense of relief, to know that someone understood what I had been going through."

The neurologist put Lynne on an antidepressant and a vascular constrictor for the headaches. She has been on a daily 75-mg dosage of the antidepressant for two years, and unfortunately finds it impossible to lower the dose or the headaches become frequent again. With the relief of those migraine symptoms, Lynne feels in control of her life once more. She wishes doctors had understood both conditions many years before. "PMS and PPD are not just figments of women's imaginations," she wrote, "but very real ailments."

Sleep Deprivation: Barbara

It is perhaps strange that no major study has been done yet on the effect on new mothers of sleep deprivation, of broken sleep cycles that are such an obvious and intrinsic part of the postpartum period. In a recent book on psychosomatic medicine, sleep deprivation is listed as causing irritability, paranoid thinking, visual hallucinations, and episodic rages, which most of us who have been up in the night with one or more children know only too well.[11]

Broken sleep affects the rapid eye movement and deep sleep cycles, our dreaming, and our ability to store information, relax nerves, process the emotions of the day, and generally bring ourselves back together for the morning.

Broken sleep also affects the neuroendocrine system by disturbing the circadian rhythms. The term "circadian," first used in 1954, means "about a day" and refers to the day-night, light-dark, wake-sleep cycles shared by all animals. The control of our biological rhythms is involuntary and an important adaptive device enabling us to synchronize internal, biological, and behavioral processes vital to normal functioning.

Whether disturbed sleep helps create or set up the situation for depression we can only guess. Barbara B., an intelligent, educated woman who suffered an extreme case of PPD, felt that it must have been a major cause. Barbara had had a long and difficult natural childbirth, but she and husband Phil greeted the birth of their son, Nathan, with joy. During the labor Barbara had pulled leg and back muscles, so, for a long time, she was unable to sit up or walk without pain. Barbara was twenty-nine years old, happily married, living in a major city; she had enjoyed an interesting career in advertising and planned to go back to it when she was settled with the baby. She had family around her, and they were financially comfortable. Barbara was the last person she or anyone else would expect to suffer from PPD.

The exhaustion of sleeplessness, her muscle pain, the baby's needing to be fed every three hours, plus a stomach virus that she contracted, led to a chronic form of fatigue and soon to depression. She had had no real sleep for fifteen nights when symptoms began to worsen.

"At first, when I closed my eyes at night, I felt the bed whirl and saw psychedelic lights, moving geometric patterns, and the amputated heads, arms, and legs of babies. Later, when I tried to sleep, my thoughts moved so rapidly that I could not control them enough to relax. Vivid memories from my childhood flashed across as if I was watching a fast movie. I became so excited I could not lie still.

"A bizarre sense of humor exerted itself and each new problem seemed somehow astonishingly funny. I prayed, screamed, giggled, and cried. My speech became frantic and rapid. Once I started talking, I couldn't stop. Words and sentences ran together."

The mood swings were getting more pronounced, from hysteria to silent exhaustion, then crying and giggling. Once Barbara came terrifyingly close to putting Nathan down their apartment building's incinerator. Fortunately, Phil was on hand, and she thrust Nathan into his arms and asked him to take the baby away and leave her alone. Then she went into a zombielike stupor. Aware she was cracking up, Barbara herself called a psychologist for help. The psychologist, her doctor, husband, and Barbara conferred. She was put on an antipsychotic medication (Thorazine) immediately (or she would have had to be hospitalized). A live-in nurse was hired to stay with her twenty-four hours a day. Twice a week she was to see the psychologist.

Barbara began her medication, and at first progress was good, for at least she was sleeping. But she was still manic, often overdemanding, and bossy, wrote copious diary entries, and spoke for hours on the phone. At Phil's suggestion, she changed to a psychiatrist and was given a combined antidepressant-antipsychotic medication, which in her case proved very effective.

"The results were astonishing," Barbara said. "My mind stopped racing, and I found myself beginning to relax. I slept each night for ten hours, waking in the morning refreshed and hopeful. After two weeks, my basically happy personality returned." Barbara discovered Nathan waiting for her, wanting to be cuddled and loved. The psychiatrist announced that she no longer needed to be a patient and could stop taking the medication, warning her that she must get enough sleep and not tire herself out. Barbara couldn't believe it all happened to her, which is why she was intrigued by the question of sleep deprivation and its effects on new mothers.

In trying to understand the complex picture of PPD, we have first to overcome years, if not centuries, of misinformation, negligence, and psychological dumping on women of what is now obviously a biochemically induced syndrome (or syndromes because there is more than one manifestation of

PPD). But you will still find doctors, psychiatrists, and scientists arguing over the relative importance of the biochemical or psychogenic makeup of the emotional condition the new mother finds herself in. So let us turn to a closer examination of how PPD has been regarded in history and the major breakthroughs in research and treatment that are currently underway.

3

◆

PPD: PAST, PRESENT, AND FUTURE

The first description of postpartum mental illness comes from the fourth century B.C., by Hippocrates, in the *Third Book of Epidemics*.[12] Hippocrates cited the case of a woman who gave birth to twins, experienced severe insomnia and restlessness on the sixth day postpartum, became delirious on the eleventh day and then comatose, and she died on the seventeenth day. Hippocrates offered two hypotheses for the cause of her postpartum mental illness: (1) that lochial discharge, when suppressed, could be carried toward the head and result in agitation (the *lochia* being the blood discharge following delivery); and (2) that "when blood collects at the breasts of a woman, it indicates madness." His hypotheses became the medical dogma for the condition for the next two thousand years.

The nineteenth century saw a revival of interest in postpartum mental disorders. The French doctor Esquirol published a two-volume *Des Maladies Mentales* in 1838, with a forty-three-page discussion of postpartum women. He based his discussion on the ninety-two cases he had observed, noting that postpartum illness could occur in a variety of syndromes and suggesting that several causal factors might be responsible: heredity, "extreme susceptibility," previous attacks after childbirth, emotional instability, and traumatic events.

The methods of treatment recommended by Esquirol included careful nursing, tepid baths, and purgatives. He also believed that the incidence of such disorders was greater than statistics indicated because a large number of mild to moderate cases were cared for at home by relatives and were never recorded (a situation that continues today).

Early in the nineteenth century it became customary to separate events and diseases that occurred after childbirth into two categories: (1) "puerperal" if it happened within six weeks of childbirth, and (2) "lactational" if it came on after six weeks. For decades, psychiatrists used to separate the two groups rigidly on this six-week baseline.

Treatment for postpartum women in nineteenth-century America used to be baths at a temperature of 94 to 98°F and large doses of opium. In England, at the same time, postpartum women were being treated by bloodletting, restraint (they were tied to the bed), or with opium and Indian hemp.

A courtroom battle at the Lent assizes in Essex, England, in 1848 stimulated much public and medical interest in postpartum problems and led to sensationalized news stories of infanticide and postpartum conditions for many years. The case was of a woman accused of murdering her child by slitting its throat. Her doctor testified that she had been suffering from puerperal mania and was not guilty on grounds of insanity. The lord chief justice criticized the doctor's testimony as rash and carelessly given, but the jury disregarded his directives and returned a verdict of not guilty because of insanity. The lord chief justice then came in for widespread criticism, as his own *father* had been a famous obstetrician who had written on the hazards of suicide and infanticide after childbirth.

The most outstanding contribution to the literature of such problems was Marcé's book, *Traité de la Folie des Femmes Enceintes*, published in 1858. It is still the *only* comprehensive book in the world literature on this subject. The Marcé Society took its name in memory of this brilliant young French doctor. Louis Victor Marcé was born in 1828 and, as a medical student in Nantes, soon built up a brilliant reputation in the psychiatric field of medicine. In need of money to support a new wife, after completing his medical training he accepted a post in the mental hospital at Ivry-sur-Seine, which had been founded by the famous Esquirol. Marcé was encouraged to continue the observations on mental illness after childbirth that had been begun by Esquirol. The young doctor was thirty years old when his book was published.

Four years later he published a 672-page book, *Traité Pratique des Maladies Mentales*. Just two years later, at the age of thirty-six, he was dead. Since his death, medical science has lagged behind those Victorian pioneers in research and interest, due largely to internal squabbles between the professions of obstetrics and psychiatry.

Marcé had been struck by the tandem march of psychological syndromes and physical changes that follows childbirth. He had believed in a connection between reproduction and the brain, suspecting there was a connection between abnormal psychology and abnormal behavior. He used the term *sympathie morbide*. Marcé's conclusions foresaw the birth of the science of endocrinology.

Since the nineteenth-century spurt of interest, however, progress has been decidedly slow. When I met Dr. Hamilton in his busy San Francisco office he apologized for acting like a television evangelist who gets his audience by the sleeve and won't let go till they are also believers. But this remarkable man has carried out a campaign for the past twenty years to have PPD accepted as a disease, to have the classification changed.

Hamilton's *Postpartum Psychiatric Problems*, written more than twenty years ago, dealt with many cases in his own practice. He genuinely had hoped that the impact of the book would result in PPD's reclassification. "But by 1975, when I realized that I had not dented the establishment one iota, I embarked on an eighteen-month campaign to reclassify the condition. I cajoled, cried, threatened, worked on committees, and still made no progress." Since the formation of the Marcé Society, however, Hamilton has joined with several other internationally renowned doctors and psychiatrists, and the results are at last encouraging.

The conference held in Manchester, England, in June 1980 brought together a disparate group of people who were impressed over the course of 48 hours, by the evidence of an explosive growth of information that was developing in many professional areas besides psychiatry: obstetrics, endocrinology, nursing, social services, and others. At the end of the conference, a group of doctors came together and agreed to work toward better communication. The founding members of the Marcé Society were Professor Ian Brockington, now of Queen Elizabeth Hospital, Birmingham, England; Professor R. E. Kendell, of the Department of Psychiatry, Edinburgh Hospital, Edinburgh, Scotland; Dr. Channi Kumar, of the Institute of Psychiatry, London, England; Professor Ralph Paffenbarger, of the Department of Epidemiology, Stanford School of Medicine, Stanford, California; Dr. James Hamilton, of San Francisco, California; and Professor George Winokur, of the Department of Psychiatry, University of Iowa.

Nancy: Problems of Misdiagnosis

At the 1984 conference of the Marcé Society, it was agreed: "Step one is to acknowledge the unique features of postpartum illness by stopping its enforced classification with chronic psychiatric illness and by giving it the identity of its own name, or names. This is a primary goal of the Marcé Society."

In the Diagnostic and Statistical Manual (DSM-III) (published by the American Psychiatric Association), the reference for postpartum mental disorders reads: "Postpartum psychosis. See Schizophrenic disorder, Brief reactive psychosis, Major affective disorders, Organic brain syndrome."

While we are considering the effects of this lack of classification of PPD as a mental disorder related specifically to childbirth, we should look at a case and appreciate just how the lack of understanding affects the individual and the family.

Like any woman's story, if we dig deep enough, Nancy E.'s example has much of an individual nature that led to her own overloaded circuits. A former elementary school teacher turned administrative assistant in her husband's business, mother to an eight-year-old, stepmother to four other children, and new mother to a four-month-old baby, Nancy's swift decline into severe PPD began a couple of months after her triumphant return home from the hospital with baby Val, who, she dreamed, would finally complete the family she loved and intended to keep so happy.

But this second baby was not the angel her elder sister had been. Colic, screaming, sleepless night after sleepless night, and lack of support from her pediatrician, friends, or family finally led Nancy to collapse on the bedroom floor at six in the morning, begging her husband to help her.

She was rushed to the hospital where she was sedated, and sleep did, indeed, seem to offer the magic cure. (For Val, too, who took a bottle and fell gratefully to sleep.) The symptoms of PPD proper had not even then begun to appear. Only after she returned home, maintained Val on a routine, and seemingly was getting herself back to normal life did Nancy show the disturbing symptoms. "I began to have severe anxiety attacks. I really thought I was losing my mind. I would sit talking to friends feeling completely distanced from them, and from the baby, wondering if they could see I was crazy."

The danger signals that Nancy overlooked were her fleeting thoughts of suicide, her chronic guilt for being this way, and her complete lack of self-worth.

Her husband, David, took Nancy to see a psychiatrist. Now feeling ashamed as well as guilty, at first she was relieved to learn that her condition was depression. On antidepressant medication Nancy began to feel more like her old self in a week or two. But the psychiatrist's diagnosis of her condition as melancholia—in itself an archaic misnomer—which might last for several years (with periods of remission), burdened her with guilt, shame, and revulsion at the thought of her change in mental well-being. How had this come to pass when she had been such a happy, contented woman?

When Nancy and David later had to change their medical coverage, she found that one company refused to offer her benefits because of this history of "mental disease." As far as the psychological profession and the insurance companies were concerned, Nancy had joined the ranks of the chronically insane.

When Nancy first contacted me it was with great relief that she had finally read something about PPD. "Until I saw your article, by accident, I had never heard of PPD. I had vaguely heard of the baby blues, but I had no idea that there was a condition, quite common, that can be treated with short-term therapy and that does not mean we are permanently ill. I'm the type who reads everything on childcare possible. Without your article, I would still be worrying that I was seriously mentally ill."

Nancy had to continue with antidepressant medication until slowly her mood lifted. Val turned into an angel, and Nancy returned to part-time work with her husband, two days a week. She found that getting back into work, freeing herself from the house and childcare routine, helped restore that vulnerable balance we call mental well-being. Like many women, she has had to learn a more realistic view of motherhood, to adapt some of her childlike fantasies of herself as a mother to herself as an adult in today's world.

CURRENT DIRECTIONS

The three main arguments in today's attitudes toward PPD remain that (1) it is not linked at all with childbirth but merely is symptomatic of latent psychological vulnerability in the woman; (2) the psychological stress of becoming a mother is the sole cause of PPD; (3) the act of childbirth sets off neuroendocrinological changes not otherwise experienced in daily life.

The psychological aspects of mothering that might help trigger onset of PPD are discussed in Part Two. For now, I want to concentrate on the various avenues of thought that scientists and doctors are currently pursuing in their search for the biochemical cause and treatment of PPD.

Let us look at the effect of one important pregnancy hormone: *thyroid*. Both the thyroid gland and the pituitary increase and enlarge during pregnancy. After childbirth, the level of thyroid slowly decreases in the following weeks to a level lower than before pregnancy, and it remains low for a year or more. The effects of a low thyroid level do not show up in those cases of agitated early blues, but in the PPDs that begin two to four weeks after birth, that often continue for the whole of the first year of the child's life. Although thyroid deprivation (hypothyroidism) has not been proven as a cause of mental disorder after childbirth, symptoms certainly seem related. Hypothyroidism leaves a victim mentally slow, lethargic, melancholy, having headaches, and feeling the cold. A mother so affected also feels no joy or happiness, has difficulty in thinking, has a poor memory and slow speech, and is highly emotional. She might even suffer amenorrhea (no periods) or find that her hair is falling out. All are symptoms of the late type of PPD that characteristically develops four weeks or so after childbirth.

Dr. Hamilton came to the thyroid connection when a woman was referred to him who had been given electric shock treatments (ECT) at a nearby hospital, deemed cured, and allowed to go home. She had previously been released from the prestigious Mayo Clinic after treatment for severe PPD. Within days of discharge she had fallen to pieces and tried to commit suicide. Her desperate family turned to Hamilton for help.

Hamilton ran every possible test on the woman. He found only a thyroid deficiency, so he treated her with thyroxine. The cure was striking in its speed and thoroughness. As Hamilton said, "You see a woman whose feet are swollen, who has slowness of speech, is very fatigued, her hair is falling out, and she has no interest in sex; then you find a thyroid deficiency, give her thyroxine, and she feels good; it does not take a genius to realize the thyroid medication was good not only for the swollen feet, but for her mood. Many doctors have noticed and connected it. But as yet it has not been accepted as a valid treatment for PPD."

Thyroid has been connected with mental disorders, even in the public mind, since the 1937 publication of A. J. Cronin's novel *The Citadel*. Watching the recent dramatization of the novel on PBS, I was struck by the appalling circumstances that had led victims of "myxedema" to be straight-jacketed and committed for life to insane asylums, when a short course of thyroid medication cured them completely.

THE DRAMATIC EFFECTS OF
THYROID

Pamela D., a woman in her mid-thirties, described her own particular experience of thyroid irregularity, which she became aware of after surgery for a benign cyst on the thyroid gland. The symptoms were not directly related to giving birth (though she had had two children in the past four years), but serve to show the dramatic effect thyroid imbalance can have on the body and the mind.

"I had been suffering anxiety, insomnia, loss of weight, huge appetite, nervous hands and general speediness, and had almost taken myself to a psychiatrist, when I discovered the lump in my neck myself. The effect of the cyst was obviously to increase thyroid production, although according to the blood tests my thyroid was not hyperactive. However, the most dramatic effects of thyroid changes came when I returned home following surgery to remove the cyst and one lobe of the thyroid gland. I had been assured that tests showed my thyroid function had immediately returned to normal and I was showing no ill-effects of the surgery (and the lump had been benign so I had no cause for fear). But that first night home, I experienced the most awful wakeful nightmares that filled me with terror.

"I was convinced the room was filled with an electrical charge, that I was an evil spirit, that the furniture was hostile to me. I fled downstairs, shaking, and tried to pull myself together. I had never experienced hallucinations or been delirious at any time in my life, and was consequently horrified by the strength of those feelings. I now understand and sympathize more with people who go through mental illness. The feelings are out of your control. It was as though something was taking me over from within."

Marsha H., a TV producer, was also able to point the finger at thyroid. Apart from early problems with breastfeeding, and her age (she was over thirty-five and that made her feel inadequate as a new mother), Marsha adjusted quickly to the sheer delight and joy in baby Jason, whom both she and her journalist husband, Bob, adored. Everything should have been fine. Marsha was working just one or two days a week, easing herself back into her career. Even that proved too much. Fatigue, despair, uncontrollable agitation, and mood swings drove her to stagger to the family doctor, when Jason was just five weeks old. She collapsed in floods of tears and rage. Marsha had no strength left. "I had become impossible to live with, full of tension, generally unable to cope with my stress. I was snapping and shouting at Bob, which is not really my nature, and certainly not something I was used to doing with him; he is such a kind and supportive man. Consequently I was getting more and more depressed—at myself."

At first the doctor gave Marsha tranquilizers to control her mood, but they only made her more tired and less able to cope. When she turned to another doctor, who ran some blood tests, it was discovered by accident that Marsha had an almost nonfunctioning thyroid. Marsha had told the doctor that hypothyroidism ran in her family, as it had affected both her mother and sister, but the doctor did not think there was anything in it until he ran the tests. Marsha was then treated with thyroxine. Although she had no overnight cure, her progress was slow and sure. Her case was unusual in that her thyroid deficit was so low as to be glaringly obvious. Unfortunately for research into thyroid deficiency and PPD, convincing results are hard to come by. Hamilton reacted severely to the prospect of running double blind tests on postpartum women, especially if they were suicidal or severely depressed, because offering a placebo instead of the thyroxine to these women would be downright cruel.

Further complicating the matter, as psychiatrist Junich Nomura and thyroidologist Nobuyuki Amino, both of Japan, have reported, an early agitated case of severe PPD may result from abnormally *high* levels of thyroxine in the blood.[13] As research at this level is very new, psychiatrists would have to work in tandem with good endocrinologists when treating women with thyroid therapy.

ADRENAL CORTICOIDS: AN ANSWER?

The 1984 conference of the Marcé Society revealed many new and striking developments in the field of PPD. Probably the most remarkable of these was a report by Ione Railton,

M.D., Associate Clinical Professor of Medicine at the University of California School of Medicine in San Francisco.[14] Dr. Railton reported on observations and studies that began in the late 1950s and that were reported in a medical journal in 1961. The reports suggested that a curious aberration of the adrenal glands may be related to severe early PPD (puerperal psychosis), and that this condition may be amenable to rational hormonal treatment. As with many other important findings in the field of PPD, Railton's have gone unnoticed by psychiatrists, and were never verified or disproved by others.

Doctor Railton completed her senior residency in internal medicine in the mid-1950s. She became interested in possible relationships between psychiatric symptoms and medical illnesses, and was granted a fellowship to study these matters at Langley Porter Clinic, the psychiatric service of the University Hospital in San Francisco. At Langley Porter, her attention was attracted by several patients with early, agitated postpartum illness.

As Railton observed, these patients showed marked restlessness, severe insomnia, peculiar trancelike appearance, rapid changes from manic to normal behavior, depression with great anxiety, and fleeting hallucinations and delusions. She was struck by a similarity to a number of patients she had seen on the medical wards, who had been overmedicated with cortisone and then rapidly withdrawn.

In the late 1940s, cortisone, a hormone of the adrenal cortex, was found to be very effective in treating a number of diseases, including painful and disabling conditions such as rheumatoid arthritis. The relief of symptoms was almost magical, and the drug was widely used. Then it was discovered that cortisone could have serious side effects, such as stomach ulcers, diabetes, hypertension, and sometimes undesirable psychiatric symptoms. When the side effects appeared, cortisone was discontinued. A considerable number of patients developed restlessness, severe insomnia, vague trancelike behavior, manic episodes, depression, and transitory episodes of apparent normality.

In the Department of Medicine at UCSF it had been found that the cortisone-deprived patients could be helped by small doses of prednisolone, a substance related to cortisone. Railton consulted with a distinguished endo-crinologist on the staff at UC, Dr. Peter Forsham, secured his guidance and encouragement, and persuaded the chief of the psychiatric service to let her try small doses of prednisolone on early, agitated postpartum patients. The results were very gratifying, and she published a paper in 1961 on sixteen postpartum cases, comparing them with sixteen controls treated only with tranquilizers and sedatives.

Conservative physicians are aware of the fact that no single study constitutes full proof. However, the usual re-sponse to an important discovery is that it is tested by others, and gradually established or disproved.

Some physicians at the conference reacted to her report with amazement. Others recognized that if prednisolone was indeed effective, a rational explanation was ready: during pregnancy, total adrenal corticoids are high, up to three times the normal range. However, most of the corticoids are phys-iologically inactive, bound by an enormous protein molecule. The active free cortisol, possibly representing current pro-duction, is a "floater" that comprises roughly 10 percent of the total corticoids. This current production could be low, in response to the sluggish postpartum pituitary. The normal sensor of low cortisol is located in the hypothalamus. If cortisol is very low, and the pituitary adrenals unresponsive to signals from the hypothalamus, the hypothalamus might "explode" and generate many of the symptoms observed in postpartum depression.

A very careful psychiatrist, under the watchful eye of an endocrinologist, might produce remarkable and favorable re-sults with prednisolone. But psychiatrists unskilled in the use of the adrenal steroids and unaware of their hazards could easily administer too-high doses of prednisolone or administer the drug over too long a time and suppress the patient's adrenal glands. There is great concern lest Railton's finding, possibly a major medical discovery, be abused by overeager psychiatrists. Railton's observations must be tested by other researchers. Efforts are being made to en-courage this, with her enthusiastic support.

* * *

THE PHENOMENON OF HYPOTHALAMIC-PITUITARY COLLAPSE

There is an intriguing postchildbirth drama called *hypothalamic-pituitary collapse*, with short-term and long-term implications. Let us say that the order has gone out from the hypothalamus to the pituitary for more cortisol. The pituitary, having been very active, productive, and with an increased blood supply in pregnancy, has suddenly fallen into a state of relative inactivity, its secretory cells in a resting phase and its circulation greatly diminished since birth. The postpartum pituitary is sluggish. It fails to produce ACTH, which, in turn, would activate the adrenal cortex, thereby generating more cortisol. The level of free *active* cortisol gets lower and lower, the sensor in the hypothalamus responds again, to no avail.

But further external stimuli are hitting the hypothalamus (the center of the body's autonomic nervous system): for example, the mother may be reacting with extreme joy to her newborn, with extreme stress to the nursing and hospital staff, with anger because her husband is late to visit her, with concern for her other children back home—any number of stresses and stimuli that blast the hypothalamus, forcing it to continue its call for cortisol, still with no effect. The victim of this hormonal imbalance begins to have symptoms of emergency reactions: insomnia, fear, palpitations, panic attacks (similar to those brought on by a rush of adrenaline).

Then a catastrophic neurophysiological event occurs: the hypothalamus overreacts, wtih nerve impulses spreading to areas at some distance from the cortisol sensor, affecting sleep, and the autonomic nervous system. Strange sensations and uncomfortable psychological experiences are activated.

PREVENTION OF PPD

Currently, there are two methods of PPD prevention. One is Katharina Dalton's administration of progesterone, beginning with an injection immediately after delivery and for several days thereafter, followed by progesterone pills for several weeks. She has reported a recurrence rate of 9 percent among seventy-seven women who received progesterone prophylaxis after moderate to severe PPD, against an expected rate of 68 percent among control cases. The results suggest that the administration of progesterone may cushion the normal precipitous fall in progesterone level, thereby forestalling events that could lead to a recurrence.

"I know that progesterone works and that it is safe," Dr. Dalton has said. "Given my way, I would let any woman take it in low doses throughout her reproductive life—I mean for thirty-five years, from the ages of fifteen to fifty—and that way she would never have PMS or PPD. The progesterone we give is natural and has been synthesized from yams. It is not the same as the artificial formula of progestogen used in the Pill [which only helps to reduce levels of the natural progesterone, hence bringing on depression in many women who take the Pill]. No association has been made between this natural hormone and cancer or any other medical problem."

If PPD symptoms develop in the week or two following birth, progesterone cannot be used because the body by then has gone into what Dalton calls the refractory stage (pituitary collapse), and progesterone alone will not trigger the system back into action.

Dalton is a very able and impressive physician. However, some believe that her results might be hard to duplicate with rigid experimental controls. Dalton is the first to suggest that her preventive program should be checked by others.

Certain pioneering doctors in the United States have now begun to use progesterone as a preventive medication for women who have undergone a previous severe postpartum psychosis or depression, so far with excellent results. To obtain the information, the doctors have contacted Dalton in London. The women who have subjected themselves to the so-called experiment all express their relief to be able to contemplate having a second child—which otherwise they most likely would never have considered.

Another natural substance that may alleviate PPD is the vitamin *pyridoxine,* or B_6, which of course can be purchased from health food stores. The medical and psychiatric professions are following studies of it with keen interest. Dr. Diana

Riley, a psychiatrist from Aylesbury, Buckinghamshire, England, presented documented evidence at the 1982 and 1984 Marcé Society conferences. Her most recent study was with a group of fifty-one women who were likely to have a recurrence of PPD and a similar group of controls. They were administered 100 mg of pyridoxine daily for twenty-eight days after delivery. The controls were given a placebo for the twenty-eight-day trial.

Riley's results were convincing enough to make even traditional eyebrows raise. The symptoms of depression in the control group were considerably higher than in the group thought likely to suffer PPD.

Dr. Elisabeth Herz believes there is good reason to think B_6 might be helpful because the vitamin is essential for the synthesis of the neurotransmitters. Riley put forward the notion that the vitamin works directly to correct a deficiency in serotonin uptake (one of the neurotransmitters). Pyridoxine is already in use in Britain and the United States for PMS treatment. As long as the dose does not reach toxic levels—no higher than 200 mg daily, suggested Dr. Herz—the substance is harmless and is likely to be beneficial.

So far, neither of these lines of research has reached standards required of experimental excellence, by which they might be taken on by the remainder of the medical and psychiatric professions. The debate continues over the advisability of running experiments on severely depressed postpartum patients or on those whose conditions might be considered life-threatening. In the meantime, we wait for more funding, more research, and greater interest in the findings. I hope the wait won't take us into the twenty-first century.

ANTIDEPRESSANT MEDICATION

The one area of treatment for PPD that *must* be looked at most carefully, the method of choice for most doctors today (for moderate cases), is *antidepressant medication*. Many women I have spoken with had successfully taken a course of the medication; others had felt no better taking the pills and had given them up; still others had refused to try them, either not wishing to take a drug in this sensitive period after birth, particularly if they were breast-feeding, or from a deep objection to the possibility that they would become dependent on the pills.

Antidepressants are not to be confused with tranquilizers.[15] They are a successful method of treatment for depression and specifically for PPD. Tranquilizers are *not* a good method of treatment for PPD because they increase fatigue and confused thoughts. Tranquilizers sedate and dull anxiety attacks, but they mask the other symptoms of PPD rather than curing them. Antidepressants, however, are used specifically to *reverse* abnormal brain chemistry, to speed up the flow of those neurotransmitters.

In severe cases of postpartum psychosis, when the patient may be very agitated or a danger to herself, a small dose (such as 25 mg) of Thorazine, three times daily, can take the edge off the violence and severe anxiety.

Anti-psychotic medication such as Thorazine or Navane might seem alarming to the patient or her family, but women who have experienced postpartum psychosis and have emerged to tell their tales with a newfound self-confidence and wry humor, emphasize that the medication is life-saving and should never be rejected. Generally, breast-feeding will have to be discontinued once the patient is taking the anti-psychotics, but treatment should be short, as long as the physician truly understands the biochemical nature of the psychotic episode.

Dr. Ricardo Fernandez, consulting psychiatrist at the Robert Wood Johnson University Hospital, part of Rutgers University in New Brunswick, New Jersey, who has been involved in the treatment of many women in the past eighteen months for PPD, said: "The difference between women going through postpartum psychosis and the patient who has symptoms of schizophrenia or manic depression, is that they need anti-psychotic medication but can be taken off much more quickly. Yet women with PPD come to me who have been on the anti-psychotics for six months to one year.

"They look terrible: the side-effects of the medication make their faces appear very stiff, with no expression, their thinking is slowed, and they look 'abnormal.' Their families imagine it is all part of the disorder, which then becomes severe in their minds."

Tranquilizers are sometimes given to women with PPD, but, as with all medications, they should be used sparingly and with caution. Dr. Herz explained that, in one sense, antidepressants actually resemble vitamin supplements; they, too, make up for a deficiency in our natural systems. In this case, however, the deficiency is in the neurotransmitters themselves. There are three major groups of antidepressants: those commmonly known as the tricyclic or tetracyclics (they have three or four chemical rings); the MAOIs (mono-amine oxidase inhibitors); and lithium carbonate. The tricyclics are most often used in the United States for PPD, while MAOIs are more common in Europe. Lithium is generally used for recurring depression or mania.

MAOIs appear, logically, to be the perfect course of treatment for PPD, as they work specifically to block an enzyme that renders norepinephrine and serotonin inactive. Dr. Fernandez remarked, "Again, the doctor should be aware of the difference with PPD patients, who often respond to certain antidepressants they may not usually use. The key point is the serotonin changes, and medication that increases levels of serotonin should be the method of choice." Dr. Herz explained that MAOIs are used with caution in the United States because doctors fear that the patient may not adhere to strict dietary rules; even minor deviations could lead to hypertensive crisis and ultimately death. The dietary rules are to prevent elevated blood pressure as a reaction to foods containing tyramine: cheese, pickled herring, sausage or other cured meats, and red wine or sherry. MAOIs work quickly, however, taking only ten days to two weeks to reach their full effect.

Prof. George Winokur, of the department of psychiatry at University of Iowa, on the founding committee of the Marcé Society and author of one of the best books on depression for the general public, *Depression: The Facts*, explains that the tricyclics work by blocking the re-uptake of the neurotransmitters serotonin and norepinephrine at the synapses, thereby allowing a greater amount of the neurohormones, so vital to our moods, to be in those all-important spaces between the nerve cells. Some formulas have a more sedating action than others, and doctors will very likely have to experiment with different doses and different brands.[16]

Tricyclic antidepressants may lead to a confused state of mind, dizziness, constipation, fogginess, or skin rash. They take up to three weeks to reach their full effect, and they will reverse the biological abnormality. Ideally, a patient should stay on treatment for several months to prevent a relapse.

Lithium, a naturally occurring substance in the same chemical group as sodium and potassium (one of the salts), has been used successfully for mania for over thirty years. It sedates the hyperactive and may lead to lethargy, but it is not usually prescribed for PPD.

FUTURE TRENDS

So often, serious PPD symptoms have been treated as classical mental illness, from the initial diagnosis right through treatment, and new mothers and their husbands have been left wondering whether these symptoms mean the rest of their lives are going to be affected by PPD; whether any fantasy they may have shared of happy family life will have been crushed. The one main area of change, therefore, that psychiatrists, obstetricians, and scientists would like to see right now is in the treatment of postpartum mothers once they reach the psychiatric wards.

As we have seen with stories like those of Nancy and Barbara, severe symptoms usually get emergency action. The mother is rushed to a psychiatrist or to the hospital, where she will immediately be admitted for treatment and tests; leaving the new father to struggle and cope with the baby, at home.

However, women who have been hospitalized recently for short two- to three-week periods, which is ample if medication is used correctly, testify that the hospital experience does not have to be something out of the Dark Ages. American hospitals are no doubt a long way from allowing mothers and infants to be there at the same time, with all the problems of insurance to deal with, but postpartum mothers can be treated with sympathy and understanding; and the family should receive full explanation of the disease and its prognosis.

The most pressing problem, in the mother's mind, however, will always be "Where is my baby? Who is looking after her? Why am I such a failure that I cannot be home with her?" These are issues of which hospital staff must be aware.

In Britain, the situation has been different for the past ten years or so. In many major towns and cities there are mother and baby units attached to psychiatric hospitals for admission of the infant with the PPD mother. The first such wing to be tested in the United States is at the Massachusetts Mental Health Center, and more will surely follow in the next few years.[17]

One of Dr. Hamilton's main criticisms of the psychiatric profession and its current handling of PPD is the appalling circumstances that surround the new mother's admission to the hospital. "The ritual admission interrogation, often conducted by an eager staff assistant, involves questions about sexual aberrations and feelings of personal inadequacy. This provides fuel for the fires of hallucination and delusion, and advances the fear of mental breakdown and failure."

Traditionally, mothers were not allowed to bring their infants into the hospital with them because of the archaic assumptions about PPD: (1) the mother's psychiatric problems might lead to an inability to deal with her own hostility toward the child—recovery depended on their separation; (2) the mother was a potential physical and psychological danger to the child; (3) the disturbed behavior of other patients would be harmful to the child; and (4) the presence of young children would be disruptive to the other patients' therapy.[18]

In 1948, Dr. T. F. Main, in Surrey, England, first admitted a mother suffering from PPD into a hospital with her infant. At the time, some hospitals were allowing mothers to stay with infants or young children, because current opinion was concerned with the effects on a *child* of early separation from its mother. But what about the effects on the *mother* of separation from the infant? When that became a focus of interest in the last ten years, units were set up and many interesting studies have emerged.[19]

Ideally, a mother and baby unit would be attached to a

psychiatric hospital or in a separate building: it should be a pleasant place, with nursery, playroom, and provision for toddlers as well as infants. There would be outpatient hospital provision, with day care, for those better served by treatment during the day and going home at night. It has been recognized that separation of a mother from her infant, because of PPD, leads to a "gradual slackening in the longing and concern for her child, and precipitates guilt feelings which make resuming motherhood harder."[20]

Better treatment for the most severe cases of PPD (known as postpartum psychosis) has perhaps understandably received the most concentrated effort. Yet even women with these severe cases will still be sent home in a muddle of confused emotions and thoughts if they are not helped to a fuller understanding of their situation.

As the stories in the next chapter illustrate, too many women have received peremptory treatment, often unsympathetic care, and have emerged from their experience of PPD somewhat battle-scarred. It may seem incredible that, in today's sophisticated world, women have been receiving such short shrift from the medical and psychiatric professions, when their problems follow childbirth. These stories must be heard, for the situation has not much improved. As the members of the Marcé Society are quick to emphasize, the scientific community is only at the very beginning of necessary, vital research, and all of its work is still hampered by a general reluctance to accept PPD as a real problem, affecting real women and their families, with a real and urgent need to be studied and more widely understood.

For all the Marcé Society's recent conferences, mailings, support for one another, and occasional encouragement in the form of government grants for new research, they are self-described as a handful of determined men and women trying to keep in touch with one another across the world, when the walls between their separate professions make such communication an enormous obstacle.

4

◆

"AM I REALLY CRAZY?"

Severe symptoms of PPD are a pattern of not being able to eat or sleep; high anxiety level or panic attacks; a feeling of being utterly unable to cope; a sluggish depression so deep you cannot get yourself out of bed let alone look after the baby; not being able to bear to touch the baby; constant crying that in itself is disruptive to family life; fear about harming the baby; talk of taking your own life; and a feeling that you are worthless and all would be better off if you were dead.

The severity of such symptoms has led women to describe the effect in words like these: "I thought I was losing my mind," "I cried constantly, screamed at my husband, barely ate or slept, and wanted to die," "I was ashamed, embarrassed, and disgusted with myself. I thought I was going crazy and no one cared," "I felt like I was hanging onto my sanity with my fingernails."

One twenty-eight-year-old mother with a one-month-old baby experienced an extreme case of the "distorted crazy" feelings. Helen E. admitted that events had piled up at home, leading to some form of emotional crisis. She had given up work to have the baby, and she missed her job and its financial security. Her husband had used up all their savings to open a new business. There were demands from him to help out, conflicting demands from the baby to be home and be a "real mother," and other demands from family and friends. Helen felt as though she was desperately struggling to keep up a front for everyone. Eventually she could neither eat nor sleep, and she became paranoid.

"One very hot night, I dreamed about the devil. I really believed a demon was trying to get my child," Helen said. Sweating, she had awoken feeling constrained, as though she had a heavy weight on her chest, and there was a buzzing in her head. Helen immediately phoned the family doctor and was referred to the mental health clinic. The psychiatrist there was a rare gem who gave Helen good, reassuring advice. "You are not crazy. You are suffering from PPD." He put her in touch with other women with similar symptoms, offered some therapeutic group sessions, and advised her to avoid all caffeine.

Three stories emerged from my research that, to me, were most frustrating indications of the inadequacy of treatment and type of attitude that so often prevails with new mothers. Linda S. was viewed as a potential child abuser, and her unsympathetic treatment followed the classic lines of the psychological approach. Adele M. realized long after the event that her depression may not have been totally avoidable, given her personal ambivalence toward having a baby at that time of her life, but still her treatment made it much worse. And Jane L. received what was considered proper treatment, but was left confused and unsure of what had happened, so that, even fifteen years later, she suffers from chronic guilt about her PPD.

Linda: Hormone Imbalance, Not Suicidal Neurosis

Linda's doctors diagnosed her condition, after the birth of her second baby, on strictly psychological grounds. In the words of Gregory Zilboorg, one of the founding fathers of psychiatry, in a paper published in 1957 that is often still quoted, what we supposedly see in women such as Linda is "frigidity and potential homosexuality. . . . We deal here with a castration complex of the revenge type . . . with an unresolved Oedipus situation . . . or with father identification."[21]

Linda and her husband, Tommy, were young and inexperienced parents of two babies eleven months apart. The second child was born shortly before Tommy's departure on a Navy cruise, and Linda knew he would be away for several months; she also knew she just would not be able to cope alone. They had been using contraception and she had not wanted a second baby so quickly. But an IUD failure led to the second baby's conception, delivery was by C-section, and Linda named the infant girl Stephanie, which she remembers thinking was the prettiest name in the world. On recovering from the operation she was overcome by a terrible sadness.

Back home, as the days wore on Linda didn't want to touch Stephanie, or be near her. She could barely manage to feed and clothe her. Linda went to see the Navy chaplain, who reported to Tommy that his wife was unbalanced. Things grew worse, and Linda wanted to put the baby up for adoption. The Navy mental health clinic said they could do nothing to help unless Linda had actually abused her baby. But she wanted help *before* she hurt her. Although they signed adoption papers at one point, the couple panicked and Stephanie was eventually put into foster care along with her year-old brother, Sam.

Linda continued to be treated by the mental health clinic—sometimes with as many as ten pills a day, uppers for daytime and downers to sleep. Her psychiatrist first decided she had lesbian tendencies and then that she hated her mother and father. Even her gynecologist dismissed her feelings that the depression might be due to hormonal imbalance after the birth. But Linda was lucid enough to argue, why would she suddenly start to hate her mother and father now, with the second child? "Why could nobody understand me?" she cried out. The diagnosis on her finally read "neurotic with suicidal tendencies," and she spent fourteen months in and out of that clinic.

About a year later Linda and Tommy were allowed to visit Stephanie in the foster home and sometimes have her to their house as long as Tommy was there to supervise. By then Linda had begun to feel like herself again, and at ease as a mother. "Not from the pills, not from the therapy, but because my body was changing, a feeling of strength was returning," she says. "Yet everyone just assumed I had lost my mind."

Eventually the parents retrieved their children and tried to set up family life again, after a year and a half of torment. Linda reports she has weathered other storms since. She and Tommy were divorced five years later, when she was thirty years old and she had a partial hysterectomy in 1982; she bounced back from both those traumatic events without depression. Linda lost a year of her life and a lot of happiness through poor treatment of PPD. "I sometimes wonder how much simpler it would all have been if I had not just been shrugged off as some neurotic attention-seeking broad."

Linda's overload factor was strong and emphatic: closely spaced children, a husband absent for long periods through his work, few family resources, her age, a youthful, ill-thought-out marriage, a terrifying sense of inadequacy leading to inertia. Her diagnosis as a neurotic with suicidal tendencies failed to make any connection with the psychoendocrine upheaval of birth.

Adele: A Mistaken Psychiatric Diagnosis

Adele M. was a very young, newly married woman, still in college, when she accidentally became pregnant. Horror-struck at first at the thought that she would have to give up college and interrupt her career plans, when she talked it over with Stephen they both came around to the idea of having the baby. They became active in the midwife movement and attended the preparation classes with enthusiasm. Adele and Stephen were both, therefore, disappointed in her emergency c-section delivery but they greeted baby Teddy with joy. All too soon, twenty-three-year-old Adele found her elation disappearing. Nothing had prepared her for the reality of motherhood: she was now out of school and living miles away from parents or friends, surrounded by what she felt were hostile neighbors, and coping with Teddy, who was a difficult baby. She said, "Boredom and loneliness soon set in with the guilt and feelings of inadequacy."

Adele saw a family doctor, who reassured her that the

problem was hormonal, the baby blues, and that things would soon get better. But within a week Adele was hardly functioning. Desperate, Stephen took her to a psychiatrist. Adele was drugged senseless and admitted immediately to a hospital. On reflection, Adele has realized that her depression might not have been totally avoidable, given her degree of ambivalence toward motherhood in the first place, but it need not have been so severe or as badly handled. She was hospitalized for nine months, a long time for PPD, leaving Stephen and her mother, who had to come live in their house, to deal with Teddy.

The hospital psychiatrist asked her over and over again about her childhood and any sexual problems. "Finally my mother convinced Stephen that this was not brought on by some childhood trauma, that nothing had happened to me sexually, and that maybe we should try a different doctor because she felt I should be home with Teddy. We saw a new doctor and, you know, his attitude was so different. He just said, 'How soon did the problem come on after the birth?' Then he took me off all medications and sent me home with a list of phone numbers of women in similar circumstances in the area. Part of my problem had been the isolation. I had had no car and felt cut off from anyone like myself."

Stephen understood more about his wife's condition, and they decided together to borrow the money to buy a car so that Adele could return to college, meet with these other mothers, and not suffer the trapped, isolated feelings of new motherhood. It was a family approach to psychotherapy. Care, concern, and an understanding doctor achieved what nine months of heavy psychoanalysis and medication had not even touched.

A year later, Adele had adjusted but was aware enough to recognize that motherhood could still be hard for her; that mealtimes, bedtimes, and potty training were stresses she did not find easy. But at least she could now admit to this supposed failure. "Being a good mother and wife, I learned, meant taking care of *me*, too."

She had joined the cesarean-section prevention movement, was busy with her school work, enjoyed an aerobics class, and was happier with Teddy. Adele felt she could even imagine having another baby, knowing that if things grew bad again she had somewhere to turn for support. Adele's final plea was, why can't there be local PPD groups for new mothers to belong to? Why not indeed?

Jane: A Case of Fatigue and Hopelessness

Jane L.'s symptoms of PPD came after the birth of her second baby. She was a working sculptor who had continued to be productive through her first child's early years. Her husband, Jim, was a specialist in an international field and could be called away from home at one week's notice for three-month intervals. What is interesting is that neither Jane nor the considerate Jim had thought to look into the implications of his being away when she had young children to look after.

With the first child, Kim, Jane had gone to Hong Kong to join Jim, and they had lived there for nearly a year. Jane kept up with her work. When they returned to the States, a much-wanted second pregnancy had begun. It was an easy pregnancy and even easier birth, which, to their delight, they were able to have at home. But the new baby, Jesse, was not the dream baby his sister, Kim, had been. Jesse was born crying and screaming, and although Jane determined to breast-feed him, he never seemed satisfied. "Maybe it was the three-and-a-half-year gap, but I just didn't feel I could cope with it all, this time. I was soon overwrought and overfatigued, and I slumped into a typical type of PPD lethargy, dullness, and mild despair."

Jane was given antidepressants by a family doctor, but then Jim was called away to work in the Caribbean. They arranged that she would fly out with the children, in a couple of months' time, to join him for Christmas. This left Jane with the two young children in a rented house (an "idyllic country cottage"—remote, isolated, and lonely) where supposedly she would paint and revel in the joys of motherhood, miles away from family or any friends.

Endeavoring to pack for their departure, dealing with the isolation, fatigue, and despair, less able to cope because the antidepressants were making her drowsy and confused, Jane decided in late October to put the kids in the car and drive a hundred miles to visit her family. Her mother was ill and she wanted to see her; she also had a married sister and brother in the vicinity. (Jane's father had been a manic depressive all his life, but Jane and her siblings had been continually advised it was not hereditary. Indeed, only now can Jane see that maybe she shared some personality traits with this man she had scarcely known.)

It was not easy staying with relatives with six-month-old Jesse, who was teething, and screaming loudly. The visit turned into a major stressor, as Jane argued with her sister and then felt fear for her mother. The fatigue and feeling of not being able to cope grew worse and worse. She was getting little sleep and was very overwrought. So Jane put the kids back in the car and began the drive home to their rented house.

It was pouring rain and the car broke down on the highway, but she handled that emergency even though Jesse was screaming in his car seat behind her. Wracked with exhaustion, Jane just said to herself, "Plough on, we'll be there soon." But she began to find it harder to peer through the gloom, half-blinded by the other car headlights. Suddenly she knew she could not go on. Jane pulled into a service station and begged for help. The local police were called in, and they tried to contact her family, but neither brother nor sister could come out to help her just then. The police suggested she check into a motel for the night and get some sleep, and they arranged for her brother to pick her up the next morning.

"Why am I being such a bother? Why can't I look after myself?" she was angrily thinking to herself.

That night in the motel room, trying to get the children to sleep by reading them a story, she knew she was cracking up. "My thoughts and thought processes were in turmoil. The wires were jumbled up. I was in a state of panic. I started to fantasize reading the story and it was becoming real to me."

Her brother drove them back to their mother's home. A family doctor gave Jane a sedative to make her sleep all night. But she woke still confused, delirious, helplessly crying. Jane was admitted to the nearby psychiatric hospital. Jesse was sent to stay with his paternal grandparents (in their seventies) and Kim stayed on with the sick maternal grandmother. In her wildest dreams Jane could not have envisioned a worse situation for her children, or for her family. But everything had been taken out of her hands. The body and the mind had given up, knowing they could not cope.

Jane was in a psychiatric hospital for nearly two months. She does not remember much, apart from the four electric shock (ECT) treatments. Heavily sedated, she could hardly think most of the time. Her mother made perhaps the worst mistake, telephoning Jim in the Caribbean and telling him, "Oh no, don't rush home, everything's fine." Jane remained confused, distorted, deeply guilty, and embarrassed throughout her hospital stay. In January, when Jim returned, she recalls, "He walked into the hospital, was patient, kind, concerned, and very sweet to me. Within ten days I was out of there."

Jane's treatment worked, maybe by default. Properly given, ECT may be very effective and not the disturbing treatment for depression of the old days. But Jane may not have needed even the ECT had her real condition been understood earlier. During her stay in a psychiatric hospital, she had received no psychotherapy. No one ever sat down with her and talked about motherhood, about her responsibilities; about how she felt coping alone with her husband away, how she felt about being a mother. As Jane put it, "I never sorted out what it might be. It was such a dramatic thing to happen yet I never understood it. My husband and I never talked about it. It just came and went, like in a vacuum. It has taken me years to get over the guilt."

Jane's story should at least remind fathers of young children that they *must* play a strong, supportive, and near-equal role in the care of their family. It is really cruel to expect a wife to be able to cope just because that's what women have always done. The truth has only recently been emerging: that most women *cannot* cope alone, especially if they are isolated from family and friends, with little money, other resources, or outside activities.

Jane's was a classic case of lack of sleep, of feeling

unable to cope, overwrought, inadequate as a mother, and helplessly alone. The overload factors for her would be obvious to an enlightened observer. Because those around her could not, or would not, see it, her biochemistry finally took over in a complete physical and mental collapse.

POSTPARTUM PSYCHOSIS: THE UNKNOWN TERROR BECOMES UNDERSTOOD

When I first began my research into PPD, I tended to skirt around the topic of postpartum psychosis, feeling in my own uneducated way that the term "psychosis" was too terrifying, or too strong, to describe the reactions many women went through after a birth. But since the original publication of the book, I have met and become friends with so many really wonderful and very normal women who have described to me their psychotic episodes and subsequent hospitalizations, that I have been able to dispel my own fears.

Psychosis is a powerful disease, when the mind completely cuts off from reality. But it can be diagnosed and treated if symptoms are caught in time. Generally speaking, with the lack of awareness of PPD in this country, the mother finds professional help only when she is rushed to hospital by a family that is horrified, alarmed, and determined to hush up the incident.

Nancy Berchtold[21a] has given me permission to print the whole of her story, which was a classic case of postpartum psychosis followed by an equally severe postpartum depression. Determined to help other women understand what might be happening to them, Nancy's main message is for women to understand it is *not your fault*.

Nancy was twenty-nine years old when she and her husband John decided they wanted to start a family. Happily married, they shared housework and a close companionship. Nancy was an art teacher, they owned their own home in Pennsylvania, close to Trenton, New Jersey; no couple seemed more ideally suited to parenthood. Indeed, they are wonderful parents to their now three-year-old daughter Allie. But first they had some tough times to survive. Those experiences led to the formation of the first-ever self-help support group in the nation, Depression After Delivery (DAD). Nancy tells her own story:

"The due date was December twenty-third and no one could have felt more blessed. The pregnancy went well, and we attended Lamaze classes together.

"Labor began two weeks early and lasted twenty-two hours: eighteen hours of Lamaze breathing, followed by two and a half hours of pushing. I hemorrhaged from the episiotomy and lost a dangerous amount of blood. My obstetrician decided against transfusing me, because of the new fear that the blood might be AIDS contaminated. At this time, it could not be checked. After the birth I felt faint: with the blood loss I was highly anemic, and my pulse was racing at 120 bpm, even at rest. At first they would not bring the baby to me, because my blood pressure was so low.

"All evening I lay in that hospital bed worrying that something must be wrong with the baby; and I was equally concerned about my own condition because every two hours they would take my pulse. Eventually they brought Allison in around midnight. The night nurse apologized: there was a baby boom on and they hadn't seen I was upset. But the baby was so beautiful, I was in heaven. She was sleeping, and I lay there wide awake just staring at her with so much love in my heart I could burst. This euphoric happiness, mixed with anxiety, was the beginning of my problem.

"The third day after birth I had a typical 'baby blues,' the kind most mothers experience: weeping at an unknown sense of loss, fearful of taking the baby home, and at the same time overjoyed at our good fortune in this lovely healthy daughter. John came to take us home and, maybe like any new mother, I was convinced we'd have an accident during the car ride. The responsibility for this new life is so overpowering.

"I had been warned to take it easy, but it was the week before Christmas and everyone in our two families came to visit the baby. Overnight I'd also turned into Supermom. I'd never been the ultimate housewife before, but now I was running around cleaning the house, ironing John's shirts, cooking, organizing the Christmas tree, shopping for gifts. This was going to be the best Christmas ever. I wouldn't let

John get up in the night to help with the baby. He had to go to work and, as I was breast-feeding, naturally I assumed all the responsibility. Besides, I was going to be the great breast-feeding Earth Mother too. I didn't even have a plastic bottle in the house. This was my baby and I would cope.

"My mood continued euphoric, indeed everything seemed rose-colored, and I wrote copiously in my journal about my feelings. For the first five or seven days back home, I managed to sleep fitfully between her feeds, not realizing that I was becoming hyperactive, or manic. By the eighth day, my sleep patterns had gone totally haywire. I would doze off for an hour in the night after I'd settled Allison down, only to wake up again long before she cried. I'd sit up in bed writing my journal. On December twenty-third, her due date, when Allison was eight days old, I wrote, 'I should be sleeping, what is wrong with me? Baby is sleeping.' My pulse was still racing and I was so hyped up that, although a normal person would simply fall off to sleep with exhaustion, by now my energy level was so high I was beyond sleep.

"I couldn't stop thinking either, my mind constantly working overtime. I began to make connections with Allison and anything else in my life or memory. My doctor has told me that psychosis drags up fears or nightmares and turns them into living dreams. For example, in recent years I had converted from Catholicism to Quakerism, and my mind was now full of Jesus Christ and his relationship to me and my baby. We lived at the time on the flight path to Newark airport; and childhood fears of the bomb were reliving themselves in this fear of planes carrying nuclear weapons. It was the Christmas season and my family is very sociable, so I imagined all cars were full of people coming to a party.

"Christmas itself came and went in a blur of relatives. I'd just be dozing off when someone else would call or visit. Two days later I began calling old friends on the phone, sometimes for as long as three hours at a stretch. Poor John did not know what to do about me. Of course he yelled at me about the phone bill. At one point he took the phone, and my book of numbers, away from me, saying, 'No more.' But although I don't usually have a photographic memory, in my psychotic state I could remember old numbers! He'd tell me to come to bed, warning me I had to sleep. One night he woke up saying, 'What on earth are you doing?' I was taking photographs of him, Allison, even the dog, all asleep. John is so kind and supportive, he just tried to coax me back to normal behavior. We really had no idea of the danger of the symptoms because on one level I was functioning fine, still breast-feeding and caring for the baby with no problem.

"But my mother called because she was worried. I didn't realize she'd seen a family member go through what looked like similar crises, and was afraid I might be turning manic-depressive. Naturally I wondered what was happening to me, but any books referred only to the 'baby blues' and advised that all would be back to normal in a few days. I asked a social worker friend if she thought it was postpartum depression, that I had read briefly about, but she brushed the suggestion off. I was a friend, not a client, and like everyone else she assumed the 'craziness' would soon pass. Then my father called John at work to suggest he take me to a doctor. Instead, John called me at home and asked if I was all right. Of course, I snapped back, I was fine. I was a mom, how could anything be wrong with me?

"Just before New Year's, I went through a forty-eight-hour period without any sleep. My journal is a picture of the weird thoughts that can take over a mind. Odd comments and drawings are all over the pages. I tell John and Allison how much I love them. I worry about me. There was a puzzle and I was missing the vital piece. My phone calls to old friends were now to other mothers who, I hoped, would tell me how to find that missing piece. I rambled on the phone saying the craziest things; I called one man in the Midwest to tell him his girlfriend was finally pregnant—even though she was having terrible infertility problems. Thank goodness my friends were kind enough to forgive me afterwards.

"The night before New Year's Eve, John came home from work as usual and I made dinner. He couldn't understand why I wouldn't eat with him, but I lied about not being hungry. By then I'd also completely lost my appetite. He went to bed and I talked for hours to my father-in-law who lives on the West Coast, at three in the morning, about the baby and how sad he must be not seeing her.

"Just before dawn, I went into the bedroom and tried to wake John, but he wouldn't stir, so I sat watching the sun come up, desperate for the long night to come to an end. At six in the morning I phoned my neighbor, babbling incoherently. I asked if her husband could come by as we needed help. They must have been shocked at my request because no one came.

"Finally I called my brother-in-law. 'Edward, you have to come over. John needs help,' I said. Thank heavens Edward sensed something was very wrong. When he walked in the door at seven A.M., I finally gave up the battle of trying to appear okay. Ranting and raving, I was screaming that I was dying, because I still had this fear about the hemorrhage. I called out to Christ maybe fifty times and began tearing off my clothes, feeling I was burning up. There were fruit flies over a bowl of apples, and I was obsessed that the swarms were taking us over. The DC9s on short local flights were packed with nuclear weapons.

"Now frantic, John called our obstetrician. That early in the morning he had to wait for the doctor to call back. My husband walked with the phone into the living room so the doctor could hear me. My obstetrician immediately said: 'It sounds like severe postpartum psychosis. Get her to the hospital.'

"The psychotic state is like amnesia, so I remember nothing about my first two days in hospital. Over the holiday, because I was a breast-feeding mother, the doctor on call decided to wait and see if I would come out of the psychosis without medication. They pumped my milk for two or three days, until Jack Ward, the psychiatrist, came in and said I would have to go on Thorazine and to forget the breast-feeding.

"Unfortunately Thorazine, the usual anti-psychotic medication, made me more manic. I had everyone laughing at my jokes, but I was not an easy patient. I kept pulling out the IV in my arm, and for two days I was strapped to the bed in arm restraints. Then, when my milk was drying up, the real horror set in: I had the discomfort of my sore breasts and the nightmare of not knowing what had happened to my baby. I was no longer breast-feeding, so I assumed either she was dead or I was dying.

"Jack Ward changed the medication to Navane and my recovery from the psychosis was surprisingly quick. He knew I was out of it once the planes flying overhead no longer carried bombs. Patiently, the psychiatrist alleviated my parents' fears. Postpartum psychosis can affect women particularly with a family history of manic-depression. But I was old for permanent onset of the disease (the average age is the early twenties); this was an isolated incident related to the biochemical changes of childbirth.

"My psychiatrist did not expect that with the psychosis gone, severe postpartum depression would take its place. The depression was more long-term and just as devastating for me and my family.

"After only two weeks I able to be discharged from hospital into my parents' care. I went back to their home not to assume responsibility for the baby, but rather had to concentrate on rest, sleeping through the night, and eating well. But how could I sleep? I would hear Allison crying in the middle of the night, listen to her screams grow louder as my mother went down to the kitchen to heat up the bottle, all the time developing a powerful lack of self-worth and despair.

"The bottle was a replacement for me. If I wasn't breast-feeding, then I must be totally worthless. My baby didn't know or need me. Here I was in my parents' home being protected from my real role as a mother. In many ways the postpartum depression was harder to deal with than the psychosis, as I battled with all those preconceived notions of the type of mom I'd be.

"After a couple of days I was anxiously pacing the house, unable to concentrate, lacking the motivation to even wash my hair or dress properly, in the depths of depression. I'm an art teacher and have always been an expert on needlework, but I couldn't bring myself to sew or knit. By now I didn't want to take care of the baby, or even to hold her. My mother tried to get me doing things for Allison, but deep down I was afraid of the baby.

"How had all our dreams of happy family life come to this?

"Our married life was shattered, too. John was very strong throughout, always supportive, and never once gave in to impatience by telling me to 'snap out of it,' which he must have felt at times. He would come to my parents' house on Friday evenings to take me and the baby home. But even there I withdrew under the covers in bed and left him to care for her. At that point, I certainly contemplated suicide, and everyone in the family was afraid I'd be hospitalized again.

"When the psychiatrist learned the severity of my depression, immediately he started me on a course of the tricyclic antidepressant, Pertafren, together with a shot of megavitamins, advising me the medication would need two to three weeks to take effect. He was right; slowly my sense of joy and humor in life began to creep back.

"Allison was eight weeks old when I was allowed back home full time, my mother-in-law helping out on a day-to-day basis. Keeping as busy as possible, signing up for classes at a parenting center, filling up my calendar with friends, playgroups, anything not to be alone and left with my thoughts, over the course of six months on the medication I rose up out of postpartum depression. I first said, 'I'm well, I feel myself again,' when Allison was nine months old."

POSTPARTUM TRAGEDIES

Psychosis: when the mind shatters like broken glass. Can a woman be held responsible for her actions at this time? In Britain there has been a law since 1938 which states that in the first twelve months after she gives birth, a woman cannot be charged with the murder of her infant. (She *can* be charged with the lesser offense of manslaughter.) The Infanticide Act reads: "The balance of the mother's mind was disturbed by reason of her not having fully recovered from the effect of giving birth." Untreated, postpartum psychosis can lead to the mother's taking either her child's life or her own.

The stories that follow are true: the names are not changed as those involved have already appeared on television or have been given write-ups in major newspapers. Naturally we are all disturbed by such stories. Nothing galvanizes our instinctive fears more than the thought of a mother killing her own child. What is heartwarming about these cases is the caliber of women involved, the strength of the couples involved to fight society's ignorance and denial which led to the tragedy taking place.

The story of Angela Thompson[21b] really began when their first child Allyson was born. Angela, 31, a registered nurse, and Jeff, 33, a lobbyist for the California Correctional Peace Officers' Association, are an attractive, educated and very supportive, loving couple.

Allyson was only a few months old when their problems started. Early on Angela began to have trouble sleeping. Soon she was getting by on brief naps during the day. Feeling manic, she realized she could get by without sleep. But then hallucinations with a religious theme began that were quite frightening. However, neither she nor Jeff could make sense of what was happening to her. And so they let the symptoms continue.

But as Angela became increasingly agitated, their doctor finally had to advise them to call an ambulance and Angela was taken to a psychiatric hospital where she was kept on a seventy-two-hour hold. One psychiatrist said breezily that such things can happen to women in childbirth, but that was the only allusion to postpartum psychosis.

One day, after her release from the hospital, Angela jumped out of their car and jumped over the side of a bridge, thirty feet into the river below. It was a suicide attempt, under the influence of psychosis, but again they received little help, other than another period of hospitalization. Once she was released again, both Angela and Jeff decided to put this horrifying episode behind them. They did not mention it again.

When Angela became pregnant a second time, two years later, she told her nurse-midwife that she had jumped off a bridge after the first birth and she was worried what would happen this time. The midwife and Angela both cried, but the nurse told her not to worry, it wouldn't happen again.

When their son Michael was born, at first things were fine, until Michael was nine months old and Angela weaned him from the breast. Within forty-eight hours of weaning him, the delusions and fantasies returned. Again the hallucinations were rife with religious imagery, as Angela believed the baby was the devil and that Jeff was God's messenger, like

Jesus. She believed that by killing the devil Jeff would have the opportunity to raise the baby to life again in three days, and the world would know he was Jesus Christ.

Quite calmly, apparently performing most household and motherly duties normally, she gave Allyson lunch and read to her before a nap. Then, while bathing Michael in the bathtub, she drowned him. She carried his body outside to bury him in the yard, leaving him wrapped in a blanket. Then she took Allyson out for an afternoon walk. When Jeff returned home from work at 6 P.M., she told him Michael was dead. Fortunately, when Jeff Thompson called the police, he had the sense to caution them that his wife was mentally ill and should not be charged with murder. Still the Thompsons knew nothing about postpartum psychosis.

In the months after Michael died, Angela was held in two different mental hospitals. She was then released to spend six months at her parents' house in Salinas. She was eventually charged with manslaughter and felony child abuse, but was acquitted of murder by reason of insanity. She underwent inpatient treatment at a halfway house for ninety days, then was allowed home as long as she met the conditions of the court. For six years, she will meet regularly with a psychiatrist.

Both Angela and Jeff Thompson are determinedly working to alert new parents and health professionals that postpartum psychosis must be recognized and treated to help avoid future tragedies. Currently Angela is studying for a master's degree in nursing education.

At the time of writing, they are courageously facing a third baby's birth. This time their approach is wise and cautious. They have taken advice from Dr. James Hamilton, who has recommended preventive medication to her obstetrician—a combination of estrogen, progesterone, and vitamin B_6—and Angela will be under daily psychiatric supervision. They feel they know the symptoms to watch out for, and will do their best to avoid denial or cover-up.

Angela received fairly liberal and sympathetic care from the courts in California. There are other mothers currently serving long prison sentences for infanticide, who have been separated from their elder children, and left to deal with their guilt alone in prison. One such mother is Sharon Comitz, whose story spearheaded the movement for making PPD more widely understood, when her husband Glenn, suffering the loss of his son Garrett, and his wife to prison for eight to twenty years, decided to take action.

Sharon Comitz is a twenty-nine-year-old mother from Osceola Mills, Pennsylvania, who also went through a postpartum psychosis following the birth of the couple's first child, Nicole, who is now six years old. Sharon's symptoms were also neither recognized nor treated. Living in rural Pennsylvania, they were not exposed to any forward thinking. The only advice they received about Sharon's disturbed state of mind following Nicole's birth was to wait five years before having another baby. Glenn Comitz, a design drafter for the DuPont Corp., said, "We would have thought twice about having a second child if we'd known the consequences."

Sharon, in fact, showed symptoms even before their first baby was born: being afraid and agitated as to how she would perform as a mother. Once the baby was back home, she was often very tearful and severely depressed, not wanting to care for the infant, hating herself for her own failure as a woman.

With the birth of their second baby, they both determined she would not go through the experience again. In retrospect, said Glenn, if he'd only understood PPD better, he should have talked more with Sharon about her true feelings, tried more to help, persuaded her to see a mental health professional. But who was to know? They were a normal young couple, living in a very conservative rural area. Mothers didn't go through anything other than the usual stresses of caring for young children, did they?

Sharon's story has been featured on several television programs that have emphasized the horror of the events. Unknown to her family, she was again suffering badly from severe depression with psychotic undertones. Taking Nicole and baby Garrett in the car, she drove to a shopping mall. There she put the baby in a stroller and walked to a bridge over a small stream. It was midwinter when Sharon dropped the baby into the icy water and left him to die. Then she returned with Nicole to the shopping mall, where she walked around with the empty stroller, acting hysterical that her baby had been kidnapped. Police only later decided she was the perpetrator of the crime.

Glenn Comitz described how the drama of events completely overtook them. "You may know a top doctor to see in a crisis, but who knows of a good defense attorney?" Suddenly the police were asking questions and making accusations. Sharon finally confessed under hypnosis. The local district attorney and judge both felt she was responsible for her crime, and Sharon had little or no defense at the hearing. She was found "guilty, but mentally ill, of third degree murder," and was sentenced to eight to twenty years in Muncie State Correctional Institute in Pennsylvania. Glenn Comitz only heard the term "postpartum psychosis" six months after the death of their baby, when Sharon was already in prison. Since that time, he has devoted his life to the campaign, firstly to bring postpartum psychosis within legal status, and secondly, to work for Sharon's immediate release from prison.

For some women the experience of postpartum psychosis seems to be almost purely the body's severe biochemical reaction. However, all human bodies, male or female, are carefully balanced frameworks of the body and mind. The hormonal changes of childbirth can and will lead to mental and emotional changes if there are heavy or unexpected stresses on our psyches. In Part Two, I explore more fully just what those pressures might be. We all have within us the vulnerability to crack under great strain. Unfortunately, that vulnerability may not become evident until after the birth.

PART TWO

◆

Why Do I Feel Like This When I Should Be So Happy?

◆

5

◆

YOUR CHANGING SENSE OF SELF

We come to parenting from very different backgrounds than any of our female predecessors. It is unlikely we were raised solely to be housewives and mothers; very likely that we held a job for several years. Whether this was the beginning of a career or merely a means of awaiting marriage and motherhood, it gave us independence, our own money, a sense of self, and the use of our own time.

In our childless days we led busy lives: long hours out of the home at work, maybe exercise classes or evening classes, running at dawn or dusk, time to spend with friends and with lovers or new husbands. There was probably travel, and self-indulgent shopping for furniture and clothes. Our marriages were formed with time for each other, with neatly revolving lives as two adults went about their business.

Traditionally, women have sacrificed anything and everything on becoming a mother. But that tradition is weakening. Women are voicing discomfort at the lack of freedom they discover with motherhood, at their inability to fit into the role of mother as even they had perceived it. The psychological stress derived from a poor connection between preconceived notions of how we will be as a mother and the rather different reality will lead to that other cause of PPD:

the conflicts of postparenthood adaptation. Like caged animals used to roaming free in the forest, new parents must learn to function and move in more limited space. They must learn to suppress the ego, the desire to do as they please, the self-indulgence, and learn to blend their whole being and psyche with another's. That is not easy.

Child- and baby-care books tend to gloss over this all-too-vital adaptation by the new parents. It is not an adjustment, for that would imply something temporary until the former self could return. Some books indeed offer ideal images of very sane, mature, conscientious parents adjusting to each other's needs, adapting marital, personal, social, and sexual demands to the new stresses and strains of parenting. In reality the two people are probably fighting their way out of a deep pit that threatens to engulf them. The struggle that many go through at this crucial time is for survival of the self, for identity, for a new motivation to carry them through life.

What surprises me is not that we adults find this adaptive process difficult but that, as sensible adults, we expect it to be easy. Do any of us view adolescence or middle age as simple journeys from one life stage to another? Why, I wonder, has it remained an acceptable view that crossing into parenthood is a nontraumatic step? Some recognition of the major risks involved should definitely be part of our new parenthood manifesto, so we can say, with the bumper sticker I saw the other day, "Being a parent is not easy!"

We must bear in mind that the growth stages from single to parent are complex, divisive, potentially destructive, and as deep as any we will have traversed in our own lives since puberty or the early teens.

Unfortunately, I have no magic diets or exercise regimes that will banish overnight the blues or depression; instead, I want to confront the psychological stressors that are an integral part of PPD, working on the neuroendocrinological system. It is the body's overload factor, the final blackout of the system, that will plunge a mother into PPD. But the trigger may well have come from subconscious or conscious stresses loading extra work and energy on the postpartum vulnerable metabolic balance. These demands come at just the wrong time, when the mother does not have the strength or emotional support to meet the new needs.

AMBIVALENCE

Let us look at a very tricky concept, the natural ambivalence everyone feels on becoming a parent. In theory, pregnancy gives mothers at least nine long months of mental time not only to buy baby clothes and furnish the nursery but to work out her relationship and attitude to having a child. But there are so many conflicting emotions and thoughts to work through, I doubt many give it that much conscious thought.

One of the paradoxes of ambivalence is that when a pregnancy is *chosen,* we tend to turn around full circle and in place of arguments against having babies, we can only think of arguments *for.* I know I had been quite antichildren: in the mid- to late 1960s it was from fear of the bomb—who would ever bring up children in such a dangerous world? In the early 1970s, there was zero population growth to work for as an ideal, and people who had babies were seen as selfishly destroying the world. By the mid-1970s, feminism emerged with its own brand of arguments, that women would not have babies until men learned to help them care for them, until men would take time off work for childcare. I had written magazine articles citing reasons why women did not have to have children, and why they should fight the cultural pressures to become mothers.

Then my own biological cravings overcame all that logic. From my late twenties until I finally had my first baby at age thirty-one, I was often reduced to a crying mass of confusion: did I really want to have a baby; could I possibly cope with raising a child; would I ever meet a man I felt would offer the protection and support necessary; if not, would I have a baby on my own? Those questions must afflict many women today. But then I met the man, and he too wanted to start a family. A thunderbolt had struck me, and in so doing managed to block out those anxious, warning, overcautious brain cells; I forgot all my arguments against, and desperately looked forward to having a baby. When ambivalence is so firmly pushed to the back of the mind, it lurks, deceivingly, waiting to creep back up front when there is a gap in the mind's protective devices, to feed disquiet again at a later date. The truth is that ambivalence felt before, even if forgotten during the optimism of pregnancy, is obviously a part of our *whole* self. It can and does return.

Book editor Anne P., having her baby in her late thirties, finally made the decision with her husband that they would try to conceive. Imagining she would have some problem, they expected at least a year of trying to conceive and time to get used to the idea of being parents. She became pregnant the first month. Her instant reaction was total elation, that she had passed the test of fertility and femininity. The elation was followed shortly by panic: "How am I ever going to be a mother when I can't even look after myself?" That was followed by ambivalence: "Of course I want a baby, but I don't want to give up my former life."

We learn to live with the ambivalence, accept it as part of our lives. Some of us with a strong sense of self and humor hide the feelings in a kind of cynical humor. But, if the ambivalence is too heavy, for whatever reason, it can easily lead to a deep-rooted despair that we are not good mothers because we are not living up to our own fantasized image of the sort of mother we should be.

THE FEELING OF ENTRAPMENT

I was moved by the confessional outpourings in the letters I received. Many women expressed openly some of the shock they had experienced on becoming mothers. Sometimes having had a baby made them feel they were trapped, tied down, enslaved again, as though the freedoms of the modern world had vanished overnight, leaving them in that traditional situation of women, mothers, of the past. They were mourning that "free" self of their own pasts; but rather than mourning that past with simple grief, these mothers were confused by a terrible guilt that good mothers would never, ever, feel such emotions.

Admitting to feeling trapped by motherhood seems to take a lot of courage and strength in the face of social judgments that mothers should not complain. Indeed, other mothers may frown to hear such comments; pediatricians or obstetricians might suggest, subtly or overtly, that the mother has no right to such feelings. The new mother who might be suffering mild early warning signs of PPD will withdraw into her protective shell, stay silent, and believe the problems are hers alone, caused only by her inadequacy. Entrapment, however, is a normal, obvious, common experience after childbirth. It's a physical sensation as well as mental or emotional. After the birth of my second child, I felt as though I had literally grown another limb; a limb that was dead-weight and had to be dragged around behind me every waking minute. I could not run to the store, go to an exercise class, or choose to meet a friend without arranging, planning, negotiating my time. I cannot imagine the new mother who would not be affected by the strictures on her self and her freedom.

As Nancy E. put it, "Motherhood does take away a lot of your freedom. It is a lot of work, and a lot of responsibility, and if any woman says that isn't frightening and a sobering thought, I don't think she is being honest."

When Nancy E. first wrote to me, she had to enclose a covering note. She had poured her heart out to me in seven typewritten pages and now she said that doing so had made her break down again. Just to read what she had written reminded her of the pain. Several days had now passed, and she had been able to read it without falling apart. This, she felt, was progress!

Nancy had grown up in a large family, in a rural setting, always knowing she wanted to be a housewife and mother. With her first daughter she had gone back to teaching, but had gladly given that up when her husband began his own business and she could work a couple of days a week for him. Finally, she was able to fulfill her idealized picture of herself—a real mother, baking cookies and all the rest of it.

It was obviously a shock to have to admit she felt trapped by her new life once her second baby was born. Recently she had gone back to helping in her husband's business two days a week, which got her out of the house and back to a semblance of herself again.

"It has helped alleviate the feeling of being trapped and the panic attacks which followed. I still have bad days when I'm overcome with a sensation of panic, and then guilt. I have to remind myself that I still do have a life of my own, that it really won't be that long before the baby is old enough to be truly portable."

Few experts have really understood that mothers genuinely suffer this trapped feeling. In one of Dr. Benjamin Spock's books, *Problems of Parents*, in a section called "Mothers Need a Break Too," Spock endeavored to explain why mothers complain to their doctors about feeling confined and lonely.[22]

In this book, which was originally published in 1962, his view was that women who worked before marriage did so without a sense of commitment and always with an escape hatch. If they were bored at work, they would leave one day when the right man came along. Therefore, unlike men, they had an "illusory sense of freedom." When they had their first baby, the escape hatch seemed to bang shut, and he obviously felt their complaints were the reaction of someone who was spoiled. He pointed out that no one had forced these women into marriage and childbearing; most of them had spent their youthful years dreaming and wanting such a future.

In the most up-to-date Spock (with Dr. Michael Rothenberg), *Baby and Child Care*, which new mothers still turn to for reassurance and guidance, Spock's section called "Parents" has subtitles such as "Parents Are Human" and "Parental Doubts Are Normal." In "Mixed Feelings About Pregnancy," he certainly updates that archaic notion about women and their right to a sense of freedom. "We have an ideal about motherhood that says that a woman is overjoyed when she finds that she is going to have a baby. When it arrives she slips into the maternal role with ease and delight. This is all true to a degree—more in one case, less in another. But it is of course only one side of the picture. Medical studies have brought out (what wise women have known all along) that there are normal negative feelings connected with a pregnancy, too, especially the first one.

"To some degree, the first pregnancy spells the end of carefree youth—very important to Americans. The maidenly figure goes gradually into eclipse, and with it goes sprightly grace. . . . The woman realizes that after the baby comes there will be distinct limitations of social life and other outside pleasures. No more hopping into the car on the spur of the moment, going anywhere the heart desires, and coming home at any old hour. . . ."[23]

There are two pages in *Baby and Child Care* on feeling blue. Spock believes that it is common for mothers to feel discouraged, weep easily, and feel bad about certain things after the birth. "There are all the physical and glandular changes at the time of birth, which probably upset the spirits to some degree." Then he adds, "The majority of mothers don't get discouraged enough in this period even to call it depression."[24] Dr. Spock, I must send you some of the letters I received!

Dr. Guttmacher, in devoting one paragraph to the blues in *Pregnancy, Birth and Family Planning,* maintains that periods of crying and depression are common to new mothers and he advises a woman to discuss it frankly with her doctor, who can "reassure you that he has met postpartum blues many times in stable, well-adjusted, fundamentally happy people, whose depression cleared up in a few days without aftermath or treatment."[25]

More contemporary pregnancy books have devoted some space to women's emotional and psychological adjustment after birth.[26] Many, however, offer advice that really lacks depth of information. The most they offer is the belief that positive thinking will banish the blues or we can work our way out of that mythical "learned helplessness."

It was that type of comment, available in pregnancy and childcare books, that had so offended many of my correspondents who, once PPD really hit them, were anxiously seeking guidance or reassurance in the books that had helped them with all the other problems of pregnancy and the first few months of baby care.

LOSS OF IDENTITY

There is a strange sinking feeling that your ego has been submerged in the baby's, that you have been completely taken over and possessed. Pediatric authors Klaus and Kennell, in their book *Maternal-Infant Bonding,* coined the term "enlargement" to describe the baby's image in our minds becoming huge, grand, larger than life, as though he or she were a giant and we were a mere speck.[27] The authors feel it is possibly a necessary part of bonding. I wonder if it might also be a subconscious expression of the fear that our ego has been swamped.

Many women complain after a birth that their bodies have changed, seemingly irrevocably. At the simplest level, their misery may be over weight gain and an inability to fit into clothes from a former lifestyle. Gaining too many extra pounds does lead to a very real problem in losing that weight. It leads, too, to a confused self-image, and fear they are no longer sexual beings. It can mean they literally lose sight of themselves.

Dianne McL. weighed 220 pounds when she gave birth to her daughter at age thirty. Part of her crying in the hospital was the embarrassment at being unable to look after her baby properly and at her body size. "When you're pregnant," she said, "you are magical and holy. Then all of a sudden you're a big lump of pain and anxiety, and you have a baby with a mouth open to satisfy. You have no identity. You don't look or feel what you were before."

Another young, very active woman Gaynor T. described feeling no longer herself: "My firm breasts were replaced with sagging flabby ones which were much smaller. My thin waist and flat tummy were bigger and flabby. My narrow hips were wider," said Gaynor. At twenty-four, a teacher, she had always been busy with dancing, aerobics, working out at the gym, and jogging. "Yet these disturbing changes to my body didn't go away no matter how hard I worked out."

Many women experience a period after birth when they don't know what to wear anymore. Their sense of clothes, of personal style, seems to have vanished. They really don't know who they are and what clothes would reflect that image. Many new mothers complain they live in jeans and T-shirts. *After all, babies are messy and who am I dressing for anyway?* Are these silly, vain, purely female, responses? I don't believe so. All women experience them to some degree. It is the reality behind the psychological jargon. It takes time, not to adjust but to transmute: to emerge from the chrysalis into a new person.

Another sense of loss we go through is for the child in us, the little girl we once were; the little girl we suddenly know can never come back. It is not easy to grow up, incontrovertibly, overnight. Something must be left inside us crying, "But who will look after me?" We are saddened because of the loss; we feel scared, panic-stricken. When her mother finally went home after staying a few days to help out with the baby, one new mother left all on her own wept just as though it was her first day at kindergarten and her mother had left her.

Dianne McL. wrote of this emotionally vulnerable time in a journal, "I remember before I had the baby, taking a walk with my small dog. It seems when I look back that is when my depression started. I walked up the street leading to my house, a fully ripened piece of fruit, but still one person, independent, carefree at nine months pregnant.

"I remember thinking this may well be the last time I can leave the house alone and enjoy a walk on a summer's evening without a care, with no one else to consider. I remember trying to savor the moment. It brings tears to my eyes now to think of that moment, of that freedom. Somehow your carefree days of youth are over, once you have a child."

Losing the little girl can also make us feel much older. Kathy S. was twenty-six when she had baby Joe. Although she knew she was not old, becoming a mother suddenly represented feeling like her own mother. "She was thirty-three when she had me, so it was not even as though we were the same age." But for Kathy, being like her mother meant being tied down with responsibilities, being unhappy, being middle-aged.

Nancy E. also felt that having her second baby at thirty-one forced her to feel old. At twenty-five, with her first baby, she said, "I knew I'd still be young when she grew up a bit. But with Val I felt I'd never be young again. I felt life passing me by. It seems like more of a sacrifice once you're in your thirties. By the time Val is in school I'll be nearly forty. When you're younger, you're content to sit around with other mothers over coffee. But I don't want to waste my life like that anymore."

MYTHS OF MOTHERHOOD

The biggest myth we have let ourselves believe, the hardest fairy tale to banish from our collective mythology, is that motherhood comes to every woman by instinct and that our very chromosomes programmed us to be good mothers. This naturally nurturing self-image we project is our most vulnerable point after childbirth.

The fantasized self-image of how we will look, be, and act as a mother has dangerous consequences. A girl grows up believing that one day she will be a mother. If she does become one, every aspect of her self-worth, gender identification, and sense of identity, whether she is chairman of the board at IBM or an avid homemaker, can be crushed in seconds if she feels she does not fit that fantasized image. Her fear then leads to the complex assumption she is not a good mother and therefore that she is a failure as a woman.

Dr. Herz emphasized, "Mothering is a learning process, which we have to repeat with each child. The saddest part is that in our attempt to overcome what may be a wrong notion, we usually end up thinking there is something wrong with *ourselves.*" Self-confidence, she pointed out, crashes quickly and easily under stress, and it is hard to rebuild. A diminished self-image contributes to many a case of PPD.

It is certainly incredible that very few hospitals offer women actual courses in basic baby care and handling. The lecture given to the crowd of new mothers, when I had my first baby, on how to bathe your newborn was performed on a plastic doll (whose head did not act as though it would fall off). Diapering cannot be learned from a diagram. Breastfeeding can easily become a nightmare if the mother is tense and feels inadequate, with nurses pushing and pulling and the baby screaming. And who teaches us how to get proper sleep with a baby who cries all the time?

That sense of inadequacy as a mother is perhaps the most common trigger for PPD. For example, Laura S. had suffered a bad attack of "not being a good or a real mother." She says, "I had read up all about infertility, imagining it would take me up to six months to get pregnant, because I was so much the tense working woman. But I got pregnant the first time. I realize now I didn't know the *first thing* about babies or mothering.

"But I approached my pregnancy right. I was the model pregnant person, going to exercise classes, to the right maternity dress shops for pregnant-executive clothes. Nick and I attended Lamaze classes. I thought I looked great. I carried no extra weight and worked right up to the day before delivery. I'd read everything I could on pregnancy, labor, and breast-feeding, and was determined I'd do it right. I even arranged with the nurse at work that I'd go downstairs and pump my breasts during the work day.

"I had a great delivery. We had a boy, which both of us wanted. And then I saw this kid. And I didn't know what to do with it. I panicked. I'm not a selfish person. I'm Italian, from a large extended family, but still I have never been the type to hang around other people's babies. My mind was still focused on work and what I had to do before I went back in. (I had planned to attend some business meetings the very next week!) I didn't know what it was but I started crying right there in the hospital and I couldn't stop."

BREAST-FEEDING PROBLEMS

Laura had problems with breast-feeding. Before Bobby was born she had read everything on breast-feeding and was sure that's what she would do. "I never felt the milk come in. There I was, expecting so much of myself and I had no milk. It just created more tension in me. All the other women in the hospital were heavier than me. I was slim. But I had no milk, while they were flowing everywhere. I felt like such a failure.

"It became an obsession with me to make it work. I had equipment at home—breast pumps and all. The doctor said to relax. I tried everything. I gave up after two weeks. He was feeding every hour and a half, always hungry, crying, quite miserable.

"Because I was going back to work early, the depression worsened. I had invested everything in being able to nurse my child. In six weeks, I thought, I'll walk out of here and leave him with a caretaker. I'm not even breast-feeding, so what am I to this baby? I'm not really his mother."

Laura continued to have problems with her self-image well into the first year of Bobby's life. Was she a real mother? She could not nurse the baby. She went out to work all day and left him with a caretaker. She had no desire to stay home with him in place of work. Who and what was she? Just a receptacle who had carried him into life?

Bobby cried a lot when they got him home. He was never a contented baby. Other women were strolling around, fat and flowing with milk, with fat, happy babies. Laura had lost the weight she gained with no problem. She was thin and elegant. But she had no milk, and her baby screamed. "I felt a complete failure as a mother," she said.

Failure with breast-feeding seems to be devastating to many women. Marsha H. described the horror of turning baby Jason's head to her breast, stroking his cheek as she had been taught, only to find him turning away. There had been chaos in the couple of days after her C-section delivery, with more surgery needed, but nothing was as bad as this experience.

"He cried desperately and the more he cried the more uptight I became. The nurses said things like, 'You've got to get the better of him,' and I felt awful. I was thirty-five years old, I'd been a working woman all my life. It just felt like I was not made to be a mother. My emotions were pulled apart. I'd been so looking forward to it all. I was the laughing stock of the hospital. I'm sure they saw me as a middle-age, bossy woman who was too old to be starting it all.

"The feeding did settle down, but the pressure and anxiety over the battle must have had an impact on my psyche. When you're used to being competent in the working world it's even worse to feel like such a *failure* at something that should be so easy."

It was clear to me that even before pregnancy Marsha saw herself as a working woman, as an older mother, and therefore not as a real mother. I'm not suggesting that those inner feelings caused the feeding problem, but combined they triggered a depression.

I know that feeling well—the "I'm not feminine enough to breast-feed my baby" syndrome. When my first was born, I suffered a similar alienation from myself. After a c-section I was running a temperature, and I was not allowed to hold or nurse my baby for nearly a week. She was bottle-fed in the nursery or by my husband. (My hospital roommate made sure I used the electric pump.)

When I was handed my baby six days later I was terrified of her. Of course she wouldn't want my breast milk, I felt. What had I got to offer her—I wasn't a real mother. But my roommate said gently, "Don't be afraid, she's yours, no one else's. All she wants to do in the world is suckle the breast. There's no competition involved, it's natural to her. She's just a little animal." If one person had looked at me critically, if one nurse had hovered, trying to give instructions, I would have given my daughter a bottle rather than face the humiliation.

We have given ourselves new pressures these days: on top of the fear of failure if we do not give birth naturally, without pain, there is also the fear of not being an earth-mother, flowing with milk. Some of us do find breast-feeding exhausting, limiting, a strain. Our babies cry all the time, we get no sleep, our nerves are frayed, we do not make enough milk, everyone in the house is irritable, and yet we feel we must persevere. To my mind, we should not make breast-feeding into a battle to succeed. If the baby would be happier on the bottle, we would be happier too. If our husbands prefer us to bottle-feed so they can truly share some of the duties, both of us would be happier. We are not in the birthing business to be tested, compete, score points off one another. Babies cannot be given *all* the priorities. They are going to be grown-ups themselves one day.

The Colic Crisis: Nancy

Could any of us ever be mentally or emotionally prepared for the worst forms of colic, or screaming babies? The childcare books try to give advice, that soothing, calming, or keeping the baby stimulated will help. But if colic hits your home for three months or more, devastation will be the name of the game: an exhausted mother and a strained marital relationship bear the brunt of the crisis.

Nancy E.'s story of the crying baby trauma, her desperate attempts to continue breast-feeding, and her ultimate breakdown should be a lesson to us all. The former elementary school teacher had an overload on her emotions even before the birth of Val. Nancy's marriage to her husband meant taking on his four children (at the time of their marriage, a boy of ten, six-year-old twins, and a two-year-old). Nancy's own first baby, Annie, had been a model child and, after putting her on the bottle, she went quickly back to teaching because they then needed the money.

Eight years later, the second baby was due, with the disapproval of Nancy's mother-in-law, who was extremely critical of this plan to further drain her son's finances. Around the same time the elder boy had begun to be a difficult teenager. But the pregnancy went fine and the delivery was easy. When they brought Val home, eight-year-old Annie adored her. Nancy felt she had the whole world by the tail.

Val cried through the first two nights and had to be hospitalized again for jaundice. Nancy was soon exhausted. She caught the flu, became dehydrated, and worried that her milk was drying up. Back home from the hospital, Val continued to cry constantly. The more Nancy tried to nurse her, the more the baby cried.

In the middle of this tense situation, her husband, David, was rushed to hospital for minor surgery. Her stepson flunked out of college and left them a note saying it was all their fault. The mother-in-law felt justified in her criticisms. Nancy began to blame the chaos on herself. Even without the colic and consequent lack of sleep, Nancy's overload factors were probably already causing an undue strain on her precarious metabolic balance after the birth.

Through it all, Val continued screaming. "I knew I didn't have enough milk," said Nancy. "Sometimes she would nurse for one and a half hours and would still be crying with frustration. I tried watching everything I ate, drinking beer, eating brewer's yeast. We even drove hours one night to a hospital so I could sniff oxytocin to help let the milk down. By the time Val was ten weeks old, our home had become unbearable. Every day was pure hell, with the baby screaming, and me trying to nurse, and blaming myself for ruining our happy family.

"I stopped being able to eat. I stopped being able to sleep. One morning, at 6 A.M., after being up all night pumping my breasts, I fell apart. When I begged my husband to help me, he responded, 'For heaven's sake, stop this.' But by then even he could see it was serious. He called the obstetrician, who put me on Seconal, and I slept. They had to bottle-feed Val. Within twenty-four hours she was a different baby. She fed and napped, and slept all night."

What help had Nancy received from advisers on her breast-feeding problem? She felt afterward that she would like to strangle the local La Lèche League, who made her feel guilty enough to continue with the struggle at all costs. Her friends gave her grief, telling her how awful bottle-feeding is. Her pediatrician took it upon himself to pressure her into continuing despite her exhaustion.

"My pediatrician's opinion was I had a tense baby, and I should let her cry. He advised me to hold her, to make eye contact. He actually said if I stopped breast-feeding, I'd have *nothing* to comfort her with, that things would be *worse*. He arranged for a counselor to come visit me and the baby, to help me handle the crying. She would hold the baby until the screaming had stopped, and then say, 'There, that's all she needed. See, the tension has gone.' But I couldn't hold my baby for hours like that, while she screamed. And as soon as the counselor left, the screaming would start up again."

Nancy collapsed from exhaustion, frustration, anxiety, lack of sleep, and emotional devastation. Unfortunately, this was only the beginning of a long, deep depression for her, triggered as we now know by her body's inability to restore enough hormones to deal with the extreme anxiety, tension, and fears of her personal inadequacy in a crisis situation. Was it the baby's colic that was at fault? Or was Nancy's tension partly a cause of the colic? There are so many different arguments and theories about the cause of colic, often offered not only by relatives and friends but by pediatricians too, that a sensitive and vulnerable mother can easily be deeply offended by some of the comments.

Another mother, whose child is now a teenager, recalled that when this baby boy was suffering from colic she read an article in a major magazine saying that extensive research with monkeys had proven that colic resulted from inadequate mothering from a tense, nervous, unconfident mother. A lot of people, including doctors, seem to believe this still: it is hard to shift from our deep subconscious, along with those other myths of motherhood, the idea that a good mother naturally and instinctively knows what is best for her baby. As this woman admits, she was devastated by the article and happily let her aunt, who had come to help her care for the infant, take over. The aunt used old-fashioned wisdom, bottle-fed the baby on a four-hour schedule, and cured him rapidly. She claimed that colicky babies had poor digestion and could not deal with the demand schedules that are popularly believed to be best for babies. The baby did in fact have lots of gas and a belly that was absolutely rigid during an attack. No doubt members of the La Lèche League and similar advocates of total breast-feeding would disagree. Many parents who have bottle-fed their babies have also suffered through colic.

The best advice for mothers undergoing problems, either with breast-feeding or with a colicky baby, is that they must focus on their own anguish, their own loss of self-esteem and fears that they are a failure as a mother, rather than worry about the baby. Lack of sleep, lack of self-confidence, lack of any private time or sense of oneself are all major triggers for PPD, as the body and the brain struggle to cope with the overload of demands placed upon them.

In a very helpful book, *Crybabies: Coping with Colic, What to Do When Baby Won't Stop Crying,* Dr. Marc Weissbluth, director of the sleep disorders center at the Children's Memorial Hospital in Chicago, tries to explain that parents really should be doing less rather than more to overcome colic or extreme crying in newborns.[28] He now believes, after extensive research, that some babies cry more than others mainly because of a confused sleep pattern. Their crying, therefore, does not mean that they are suffering acute indigestion, reacting to your diet, responding to your inadequacy or tension, or a multitude of other reasons that have been proffered over the centuries. They are really crying because they cannot get to sleep. The parents' best form of help might indeed be to let the baby alone, try not to let the crying bother them, and wait till sleep finally takes over. How strange that after decades of theories and controversy, the newest expert opinion should go back to the oldest wives' tale. I remember my mother telling me how, when I was a baby, I was left down at the end of the garden in a carriage (on fine days, no doubt) to cry it out. Nobody picked babies up, caressed them, or made eye-to-eye contact with them to defeat tension. We survived.

Dr. Weissbluth ends his book with the following advice, under the heading What Should I Do?

"Dear parents, when your baby is crying, do nothing. But do nothing deliberately, quietly, gently, confidently and *firmly*. In other words, please try to develop an attitude of:

Purposeful inattention
Studied inattentiveness
Gentle firmness
Constructive resignation
Expectant observation
Watchful waiting

Be attentive to your baby's behavior at night, but try to cultivate a detached and relaxed attitude. As you have read, it does work!"[29]

6

◆

BEFORE AND AFTER LAMAZE

CHILDBIRTH EXPERIENCES

We have become thoroughly involved, in recent years, with the perfection of pregnancy, the birth experience, and motherhood; yet we tend to overlook the crushing effect this drive toward perfection can have on us. Attending childbirth education classes, learning breathing and relaxation techniques, insisting to our doctors that we have a drug-free labor, taking special care with our diets and behavior during pregnancy, taking every precaution for the health and safety of the unborn child, we expect and demand pain-free labor and delivery. I don't quite see how women can stop this urge to perfection in the birth experience. How can we change our attitude so the resulting anticlimax when a C-section is ordered (for good medical reasons) will be accepted as a simple disappointment, without the concurrent hostility and resentment directed at the doctor and anger at ourselves?

Expectations of perfect natural childbirth, and the ensuing disappointment, are major triggers, in many women, of PPD. A sense of personal failure emerges that is so huge and long-lasting, so irrational and emotional, that the resulting depression may last for up to a year. Self-help groups for

94

C-section mothers have proved useful, enabling women to get together and vent their feelings, to discuss and share their mourning for the natural birth experience they so looked forward to and expected of themselves. More emphasis in childbirth preparation classes would also be helpful in explaining just why c-sections may be necessary, what they entail, and why the mother should prepare herself for the eventuality, so she will *not* see herself as a failure should her baby be so delivered.

My own personal experience has been of c-section births. My first baby was delivered by emergency c-section after I had begun to lose blood (from a partial separation of the placenta), my waters had broken, and I had been in transitional labor for four hours. Doctors were staring at the monitor, orders were given, and I was hurried away to the operating room. Afterward, I think I can honestly say I felt no sense of loss at not delivering "naturally"; no sense of failure as a woman. All I felt was thanks and gratitude to be alive and well.

Lying there, through the pains of labor, my heart had gone out to women in the past, to all those women who had travailed in agony, often for days, only to die in childbirth. My baby had become trapped in the uterus, the doctor later informed me. Very likely she would never have emerged naturally through the birth canal. I am perhaps unusual these days, but I have a healthy respect for technology in medicine, for intervention that saves lives of both mothers and babies. My own level of success or failure did not even come into question. When it was time for the second birth, and the same doctor advised an elective c-section, as there was only a twenty-two-month gap, I accepted his decision. The second time, we know what the surgery entails; we also know what the risks and chances of labor entail.

Still, disappointment after a c-section is very common. Judy R. was in her late twenties, an executive secretary who was already back at work with a year-old baby when we talked. Judy's postpartum problems had been compounded by difficulties nursing her son because it hurt her breasts unbearably. She could see, looking back, that the two things worked together against her. "These days an inability to nurse is seen as a lack of real desire. And the fact I had a c-section also made me look a failure, in my own eyes. My mother came to help after the birth but she only contributed further to my lack of confidence and depression. It was getting back to work that finally cleared the PPD. I was so happy to be doing something I knew I *could* do!"

Carol and Derek C. had also both attended natural child-birth classes. They had planned for Derek to be at the delivery, so the emergency c-section came as a great disappointment to the twenty-five-year-old couple. "I just felt a complete failure since I couldn't deliver naturally. I was angry at my body for letting me down," recalled Carol. PPD in the first months after her baby's birth was worsened by the shock of that enormous lifestyle change to Derek and her. "To say the least, I was overwhelmed by parenthood!" she exclaimed.

Kathy S. noted that comments other people make to C-section mothers may intensify the sense of failure, imposing those pressures of perfection on them. A friend had said to her, confidingly, "You poor thing, you'll never know what it's like to have a baby"; a night nurse had breezed through the ward, where two thirds of the women had just had C-sections, muttering, "Can't you mothers remember how to have babies anymore?"

DEPRESSION IN PREGNANCY

Depression felt after a birth may in fact have begun during the pregnancy itself. The first trimester (one to twelve weeks) is noted for the metabolic changes that leave us with nausea, tiredness, and very often feeling down or mildly depressed. Less and less are accidental and unwanted pregnancies a cause of depression, as the majority of births these days are very much wanted. Nevertheless, the timing can sometimes be wrong in our lives. Pregnancy might come too soon in a marriage disrupting the ecstasy of a new relationship, or we may conceive sooner than we imagined and feel we had no time to prepare ourselves emotionally for the change of life.

Prepartum depression is not discussed professionally because obstetricians are used to the mood swings of the nine months. Dr. Katharina Dalton, however, has some significant comments on this period. She points out that some women do not receive enough progesterone late in their pregnancies, and experience depression similar to that of PMS or PPD. Instead of the elation and euphoria commonly experienced in the middle months, they feel terrible, suffering headaches and general malaise. She would prescribe progesterone in such cases, even in pregnancy (see pp. 48–50).

Doctors are quick to assume that women who have psychosomatic complaints and lack of energy and enthusiasm during pregnancy may be the ones to suffer PPD when, in fact, they may be the ones *not* to. Current research is looking into the relationship between mood and emotional changes in pregnancy and mood shifts after birth.

Previous abortions or several miscarriages before a healthy birth might also help contribute to PPD, either because the woman's self-image is loaded with a vision of these previous "failures," or because she is carrying too great an emotional investment in motherhood (implicitly in its "perfection"). Drs. R. Kumar and K. Robson, of the Institute of Psychiatry in London, have related symptoms of PPD to suppressed mourning, or guilt, over a voluntarily lost fetus.[30] The way we cope with therapeutic abortions these days, they emphasized, accentuates the ambivalence women might feel toward motherhood.

It is not easy to decide to abort. It is not easy to be a mother. Women's emotions are complex on both subjects. Perhaps some form of group counseling or therapy in abortion clinics might help women come to terms with their ambivalence and fears about motherhood *before* they finally take the plunge and become mothers.[31]

Some pregnancies are so difficult that we hardly feel surprised when the mother becomes depressed. Just think what she had to go through to have this baby, we say to ourselves. Jackie P. had been married eight years to Ben, and they were financially secure enough for her to give up working when, at age twenty-nine, she decided it was time for them to begin a family. After four years of trying to conceive and four miscarriages, Jackie conceived again and once again appeared to miscarry. An ultrasound scan, however, showed she had lost one of fraternal twins and the pregnancy continued. But not without more drama.

At seven months, Jackie developed preeclampsia and was ordered total bedrest. At eight and a half months high blood pressure was diagnosed and an emergency c-section advised. Her son was delivered healthy, but she learned later that both only narrowly survived. Jackie then spent thirty-six hours in intensive care on anticonvulsive drugs.

Because the couple's new home was not yet finished, Jackie went back to her mother's house, and a nurse was hired to help out. Jackie fired the nurse after three weeks because of their conflicting views on baby care. There was some crying, some exhaustion, she noted, but PPD itself did not set in until she and Ben were ready to move into their new home. A considerate and thoughtful man, Ben had bought all the groceries and even, Jackie remarked, put toilet paper in the new bathrooms. Proudly he carried Jackie and the baby over the threshold to start their new life.

"What did I have to be depressed about? After all this time I had a healthy son, a loving husband, a good marriage, and we even had our dream home. I was the woman who had it *all*. But for the next three months I was in the pits of depression. I saw no one and asked no one's help. How could I?"

Slowly the clouds of depression lifted. Jackie came to some conclusions about the cause of her PPD. Previously she had had a fallopian tube and an ovary removed, and the resulting depression reminded her of PPD. She felt her condition was partly hormonal but, as she expressed it, mainly due to exhaustion, the emotional upheaval of the previous nine months, and lack of sleep. Many women, in fact, have guessed at the cause of their PPD, but have been unable to validate their instincts because of the lack of knowledge about the condition.

PREMATURITY OR DISABILITY

Any mother can identify with the parents of a baby born prematurely or with some disability. Whatever feelings are experienced by the parents of a normal or healthy newborn can only be exaggerated by the very real stress of coming to terms with fear for the child's life, emotional deprivation if they cannot hold the baby, or anxiety about their family's future.

When she was seven months pregnant, bleeding heavily, twenty-three-year-old Sarah J. was ordered bedrest, but the bleeding continued and she had to be rushed to the hospital. The delivery was frightening, with a crowd of doctors waiting in the corridor who raced out of the room with her infant son, the moment he was born, to give him oxygen. One of his lungs had not inflated and he was moved to a downtown hospital with a neonatal intensive care unit. Sarah begged to be allowed home after thirty-six hours, finding it too miserable being with all the happy mothers.

When Sarah visited her son she was totally unprepared for the emotional shock. He was wired to tubes and machines, lying pathetically in a plastic box with portholes, pads on his eyes to protect him from the bright lights. There was further panic when a neurosurgeon was called in. But Peter was fine and recovered fast. After ten days he was moved back to their local hospital, where he was kept for six more days.

"It was the sixteenth day and my birthday," said Sarah. "I really hoped to take him home, but they insisted on keeping him one more day. That's when my blues set in. My husband was working nights, so I was home alone in the house. My father had died some twelve months beforehand. My husband and I went to the restaurant by the hospital to order a sandwich and the waitress got mine wrong. All this and now a dumb sandwich! I started crying and crying. She must never have had such a reaction to a sandwich before!"

For Sarah, the birth of Peter had been the most difficult experience of her life. She felt a relief now on expressing all those complex emotions. "How can you forget the pain, the joy, and the love involved in the birth of a child? The baby blues to me was just part of the *whole*." Sarah was lucky. The blues for her was transitory, Peter recovered quickly, the nightmare was short-lived.

This letter came from a mother of two brain-injured

sons. Shirley B., now in her late thirties, wrote, "I hope you will not neglect the topic, as so many do, of postpartum depression that occurs upon learning your child is handicapped. PPD is not only a normal reaction to a normal child."

Shirley's eldest son, now sixteen, was born severely retarded with autistic symptoms. The problem was not noticed at birth, but Shirley suspected something was wrong when, at five weeks, she felt he was hypersensitive. Left alone to deal with his handicap and her own disappointment, fatigue, and sense of failure, Shirley once begged a doctor to help her. "What can I do?" she cried. "Get rid of what is bothering you," the not so well-meaning doctor replied. Only years later did she dare go back and confront this man with what he had said in that time of grief. "I only meant you should get rid of the problems your son causes," was his flippant reply. Shirley sighed, "Oh, if only it were so simple. Wouldn't we be wealthy if we knew how to do that?"

Three years later, Shirley gave birth to another son. The family now knows that he has a milder form of the same autism, but thankfully he is bright and a reasonably normal child. Shirley has been told that the autism is caused by chromosomal damage that, in her case, is hereditary, for her brother was also born retarded. If she were going through pregnancy today, the obstetrician should take that history of retardation in her family as an indication for genetic counseling before she ever began a family.

Shirley's story highlights so much that is missing in our society: mainly, perhaps, the lack of any one professional to deal with the postpartum period, to help mothers cope with even the *normal* problems of parenting—fear, isolation, sense of inadequacy, responsibility—let alone the extra burdens imposed on the parent of a handicapped child.

Guilt and feelings of failure, which might normally lead to PPD for these parents, are added to the very real emotional, social, and even financial pressures of dealing with any handicap. These parents experience a sense of mourning for the perfect child they had dreamed of, for the perfect mother, or parent, they had fantasized. Shirley's experience was sixteen years ago. Today's parents discovering a handicap or mental impairment would, I hope, be offered basic societal help, would be able to turn to a group of parents with similar circumstances for support and guidance. Certainly no one should be left to the total despair and humiliation of begging a disinterested doctor for help and being told to get rid of the problem.

AFTER LAMAZE

What about society's views of mothers *after* the birth? "The baby-care books tell you when to bathe and burp, but not what to do when you're sitting there nursing, tears rolling down your face, or putting your child in its crib to cry it out because you can't handle it anymore, or wishing you'd never had a child. They don't tell you what to do when you get home—after Lamaze," said Sharon W.

Is there really a way we can extend our knowledge of PPD, so we improve not only care and treatment at professional levels, but also the general information taught or available to pregnant women and new mothers? We take our pregnancies so seriously these days. We approach labor and delivery, and hospital and doctor management, like educated consumers. Lamaze, or some other childbirth education class, is seen as part of a normal premotherhood experience. We expect and demand the best of our bodies, of our professional health-care team, and of our ultimate relationship with the baby. Yet we are chronically guilty of the new myths of motherhood prevalent in our society. We never for a minute expect anything *should* follow after Lamaze.

We love the image of ourselves, as seen in the commercials and magazines: either the ethereal, beautiful, tender, nurturing mother, cradling her beautiful baby; or that other popular image today of the striding, smiling, self-confident, competent mother, skiing, running, cheerfully encountering the world, her baby in a Snugli or backpack. Being a mother can make for such pretty pictures.

Of course we like to think of ourselves that way: the fantasized image of ourselves as mothers is an integral part of the PPD perspective.

"I think it is a crime that all this emphasis and education

is placed on childbirth and nothing is done to help a woman cope postpartum," said Jenny T. vehemently. A recent correspondent told me that the nurse in her hospital-run preparation class maintained that "no one gets the baby blues anymore—it's a thing of the past." There would appear to be deep layers in the national psyche effectively blocking any move for change beyond the myths of motherhood.

Nancy E. telephoned me, as the result of several long talks, to relate the latest in the chain of events regarding her own PPD. Living in a small rural town, Nancy had not met anyone in the community who had also suffered. But she was willing to help others by talking, listening, or running groups and was anxious to start something going along those lines. First Nancy had broached the idea of setting up a postpartum group to her obstetrician and pediatrician. Neither felt there was a need, as no woman had ever asked for such meetings. She insisted, however, that both doctors put her name on file and that they put my magazine article in the same file, in case any depressed woman should ever come to them in the future.

Then she tackled her local childbirth education group, which was run by a social worker and a nurse. The social worker liked the idea of mentioning PPD, its causes and treatments, in the Lamaze classes. But the nurse, who had suffered some mild PPD herself, felt it would unduly worry or frighten the pregnant women and was not suitable for prenatal classes.

"Surely," said Nancy, "they could say that this might happen, and why, and that if it does this is someone to phone?" I agree with Nancy that such simple measures are a must. As one woman who had had severe PPD put it to me, "My baby was actually in danger from me. Yet I had no idea what was going on, that I could turn to anyone, or what to do. That sort of situation must stop."

Many pregnant women would rather *not* know about PPD, would prefer not to focus on any negative image of their future role. There is a fundamental optimism about a chosen pregnancy, a wonder in the magic and mystery of life, an overflowing excitement in the thrill of creating a life, of blending ourselves with a loved partner in one harmonious being. Maybe, biologically, we are tuned toward optimism, away from any negative thoughts. Perhaps, indeed, the pregnant woman can never be the target of education on PPD.

The question remains, who can the new mother turn to for help? If her obstetrician or pediatrician seems unwilling to deal with her personal problems, does that leave her with only the choice of mental health clinic, psychotherapist, or psychiatrist? Very often, one of the main problems experienced by a new mother is lack of anyone to confide in, someone to offer advice and maybe some reassurance. Very often, when women have turned to well-meaning advisers for help, maybe to their mother, family doctor, obstetrician, or even a priest, they have been fended off with a cheery "It's just one of those things," "no one dies of it," "you'll be fine, it's quite normal," or "get yourself out of the house and snap out of it."

We should not even expect help from the usual sources. Our own mothers might appear downright hostile to any mention of PPD if their history included denial of symptoms. Husbands may be scared and no doubt undergoing their own form of depression, leaving them with scant emotional resources to cope with a wife's moods, too. One woman's family priest told her she should battle against her selfishness.

HOW WE CAN HELP OTHER MOTHERS

Psychological or emotional disorders are among the least understood problems in society, despite their prevalence. Very few of us know how to deal with someone who is depressed, nor do we even want to. We have probably all been guilty of bad listening. If a new mother does try to unload her fears on our shoulders, what, if anything, should we do to help her?

The first piece of advice is that to deny the problem or try to cheer her up, which often seems the best course of action, will probably make her feel worse. Psychotherapist Judith Klein, who has a New York practice and a particular interest in women going through PPD (she is in her mid-thirties and the mother of a toddler and baby herself), explained that the implication behind saying "look on the bright side" is that the problem is within her, or that she is in the wrong.[32]

Laura S. experienced that kind of approach and it certainly made her feel worse. "It's such a difficult thing to talk about. I mentioned my depression casually once to my mother, but she never opened up about it. My grandmother and mother, all they lived for was children, how could she ever talk about such a *terrible* thing, was the impression I got." The only colleague Laura knew who was also having a baby seemed to be coping wonderfully and had a fat contented baby to show for it. Neighbors all were smiling and cheerful. It was obvious to Laura that the only person not happy as a mother was *Laura*.

Nancy E. finally saw a psychiatrist when her PPD became so disruptive to family life that her husband made the appointment. The psychiatrist gave her a course of antidepressant medication and offered support in educating her family about the biochemical causes of depression, which were not, he emphasized, Nancy's fault. But he said nothing to Nancy about any postpartum link.

Nancy also commented that her pediatrician, who was so closely involved with them in this period because of her problems with lack of milk supply and struggle to continue breast-feeding, showed total lack of sympathy with her problems. He disapproved of her taking the antidepressant medication and said frankly he would be pleased when she came off it. "I wasn't living up to his expectations of *me*. I was a mother and I shouldn't be on medication. My husband didn't like the fact I was taking antidepressants either, nor did my parents. My friends were critical, or caustic, or changed the subject whenever I brought it up. If they were embarrassed then I felt embarrassed. I used to feel I was a drug addict taking the pills."

Women friends, usually such a source of solace and support in our times of crisis, may react, seemingly out of character, with hostility toward a PPD mother. Presumably the new mother's emotional response contradicts some notion that the friend had about perfect motherhood; the friend may have undergone miscarriages or abortions; have experienced problems finding a man to marry and father her own children; or suffered infertility for months or years.

There are many reasons why women friends can resent a mother's depression. But an understanding of our friends' hostility is hardly what *we* want to be feeling at this critical time. Somehow the lines of communication even between women have to be opened, certain old-fashioned barricades have to be broken down. A new mother may find a male friend more supportive in her crisis than a female friend.

Most women retire into their shells when they discover no one knows or cares to hear what they are talking about. "Thirteen years ago, I had my only child and suffered a terrible PPD. I have never discussed this with anyone at all," wrote a forty-three-year-old woman. Another correspondent, grateful to get her guilty secret off her chest, said, "Unknown to friends or family I've been in therapy since my son was five months old."

Parent support groups and mothers' discussion groups, which are flourishing in many towns and cities across the nation, are perhaps going to be the single most beneficial area of growth in helping mothers find other mothers to talk to, helping them through PPD. The groups of mothers with similar-age children (often evening groups are available for working mothers) meet to discuss problems of childcare and baby management and to explore the emotional and social changes of motherhood . . . the journey all must take to find that lost self.

7

◆

WHEN LOVERS BECOME PARENTS

When a couple become parents they are setting out on a totally different voyage from that of their prechild relationship. They are going to suffer not the pangs of the narcissist, but the very real pain of facing heavy and seemingly overwhelming responsibility; of strain and separation in their own love or erotic relationship; changes in their sexuality and libido; new awareness of what being female or male actually means.

Recently I was talking to Eleanor C., an as yet childless married friend in her early thirties, who whispered to me she felt the time was close when she and her husband would take the plunge. When I asked Eleanor whether she would continue working once she became a mother, and how would they pay for childcare, she became irritated and remonstrated, "Oh, come on. I just wanted a little baby."

We all "just wanted a little baby," didn't we? What we did not necessarily want was the person we became as a mother. An insurance office manager, 29-year-old Juliet T., said, "Nothing in the world could have prepared me for parenthood. I was euphoric about having the baby until I came home, and then I was overtaken by fear, anxiety, and deep sadness about my new responsibilities, by the enormity of what had just occurred, and by my passage into a new role."

Nina S. was even more explicit on this point. At thirty, a secretary for many years, single and living with Colin, who is the father of their child, Nina did not plan the pregnancy, but when it happened she realized she wanted a child. Colin agreed that the time was right, and quickly they became wrapped up in preparing for their new lives. Nina found the ensuing PPD an unwelcome shock, but she was able to see some of the disturbing forces in her life. "I had been used to doing exactly as I pleased for the first thirty years of my life. Now, suddenly, I didn't have as much as five minutes to myself, to take a long luxurious bath, to go out for a ride, even the simple pleasure of reading an article in a magazine had become something of the past."

Nina found herself wondering whether having the baby had all been a terrible mistake. Another mother put it even more bluntly: "I think many of us don't really enjoy being parents. We feel incompetent, we feel guilty, we feel trapped by it. Yet we can't admit it to ourselves."

The life stress scale of the social psychologists, which assigns scores to life crises (death of a loved one ranks highest and marriage often is next highest), has for some reason overlooked childbirth as a major stressor. George Brown and Tirril Harris, in their book *The Social Origins of Depression,* have analyzed the effect of social events on our ability to cope, adapt, or ultimately fall victim to depression. The authors conclude that our ability to adapt to stresses is mostly affected by "recent provoking factors" and "current vulnerability factors": if you lost your mother by the age of eleven, or if you have recently lost someone very close, your provoking, or vulnerability, factors would be very strong.[33]

My feeling is that childbirth is an enormous life stress, when linked to the desires, dreams, and expectations that brought us to want a baby in the first place. The craving to have a baby comes from a deep biological fountain of good-will, a desire to nurture, sexual longings not consciously felt, and a genetically programmed need for the human race to reproduce. These motivations often bear little relation to our ability to perform as wonderful mothers (or fathers), to deal with an infant, raise a toddler, or cope with an adolescent. "I just want a little baby," we say.

FINDING TIME FOR A CHANGING MARRIAGE

The baby-care books tend to trivialize the strains having a child can put on a marriage: they advise patience, understanding, supportive behavior, and an attempt to appreciate what the other partner is going through. This good advice may make us feel that if it's that simple, surely only *our* marriage is suffering. Everyone else out there is sharing baby care, having meaningful conversations in the evenings, smiling benignly over the sleeping infant in the crib, and then going off to bed to have erotic, romantic sex.

Jane Honikman, a mother from Santa Barbara, California, several years ago helped form PEP (Postpartum Education for Parents), one of the many invaluable parent support groups now available across the nation. Also coauthor of PEP's *A Volunteer's Reference Guide,* she is adamant that many new parents end up divorcing simply because they cannot cope with the overwhelming changes.[34] "The intimacy goes from their marriage, they lose interest in each other, all the energy goes into the children and there is no focus on the couple. At some point we have to stop and say, 'Why do we exist as a family?' and hope to save that marriage before it dissolves beyond repair."

Many marriages that were founded on unwritten principles of equality and sharing often relapse, once there is a baby, into traditional role-playing unions. Despite rhetoric on what men or women should or should not do in the house, I believe it is very difficult for husband and wife (with a baby) to dissociate themselves from those traditional roles. The woman sees herself as mother and housewife and her husband as "breadwinner." The man sees himself as father and money earner and his wife as "mother"; she is resentful that the whole burden of domestic duties and baby care is suddenly dumped on her. He is resentful that the whole burden of supporting this family falls on him.

Heather D. was a former teacher and part-time painter

when she and her husband Eric changed from being a couple in their early thirties with few cares or concerns, other than the maximum enjoyment of their lives and each other, to being parents. Heather gave up her teaching job, believing she would now fulfill her creative ambitions while being at home with her family. But disenchantment quickly crept into the marriage.

"Eric would come home and find me watching TV a lot, or talking on the phone. The baby would be screaming. He'd yell at me for not cleaning the house and for doing nothing all day! I resented him fiercely for not helping out. I can tell you I threw dishes at the walls I was so mad. He never ever thought to criticize me for not cleaning the house *before* we had a baby. Why did it suddenly become my chore? You get to know a different side of your husband you don't necessarily like."

On both sides resentment can rear its ugly head. The man and woman withdraw into separate corners. It may take a lot of patience, hard work, and determination to keep a marriage afloat. Julia F., for example, was the kind of traditional woman who was happily married, content in her work and in their lovely home that she enjoyed keeping tidy. When their baby was due, twenty-nine-year-old Julia imagined she would give birth and then slip right back into her work and old routines. She certainly never imagined a marriage problem. At first Julia was proud to be up early cleaning the house, putting in the laundry, preparing the evening meal in her Crockpot, so her husband, Neil, could still have those delicious meals he was used to. She was energetic, enthusiastic, and glowing with pride in her ability to "have it all."

Then depression set in. For the first time in her life, she could not discuss her feelings with Neil. "Sometimes I felt like my whole life, physical and emotional, had changed, yet here he was still going to work in the morning, and coming home in the evening. It didn't seem fair that his adjustment to all this was minimal compared to mine."

Julia finally had to accept the fact that she was overwhelmed. She saw a doctor, who prescribed antidepressants, but they did not make her feel any better, just more tired and confused. She and Neil began to see a marriage counselor "because we don't want to lose our special relationship and we feel that talking to someone about the adjustment would be a help. We've been married three years and knew each other for seven years before that. We've had time to play, travel, and work; we know each other quite well, and hopefully we'll get through this." If only we could all be as wise and far-seeing.

A maternity nurse wrote to me about a near disaster in her marriage, with an eleventh-hour rescue. For Patty and Ted D. the problem was compounded by his work problems. Ted, who also was a nurse, doing many double shifts because of hospital understaffing and their own financial needs, felt trapped in a job he did not like. Patty, twenty-five years old, with two babies twenty-three months apart, missed her job and envied him for at least getting out of the house and being with other people. She had loved her job, but she felt she also loved babies. Now she was suffering a sense of desertion with Ted out of the house so much. "I was lonely, drained, and oppressed. I missed associating with friends at work. Ted had no idea how hard it was to be home with two little kids and what felt like no purpose in life. He thought it was a vacation for me!"

From his side, there was the desire to escape and have time to himself. When he came home he would want to go out hiking or fishing. Patty wanted him home to help her do the dishes, change diapers, take the kids out, wash the clothes. "I was so sunk in frustration and self-pity I could not hear my husband trying to tell me how frustrated he was in the job, which didn't pay what he deserved. He was feeling so sorry for himself that he had to support and maintain a family instead of being able to go out and play in the mountains, that he couldn't bear my unhappiness either."

Patty and Ted separated for one week. She says the split-up led to their mutual discovery "that we loved each other more than our respective miseries." After much talking, they agreed to move closer to their families, cooperate, and make time for each other.

We've all read the advice, countless times, in books and magazines: to talk with our partners, communicate, air our grievances, negotiate rather than fight, make space for adult loving. But when you're sunk in the pits of despair, hopeless and frustrated, it can be hard to find the energy or motivation even to talk.

Nina S. reminisced nostalgically: "I was used to spending unlimited time with Colin on weekends and evenings, just lying in bed, enjoying each other's conversation and bodies. The baby suddenly took up even the closeness we once had. Now it was all baby time, so when I went to bed, I more or less collapsed from fatigue. Colin was having many of the same feelings, I could tell, even though he didn't speak about it often."

A baby too soon in the marriage can lead to disappointment in the loss of romance and that early all-consuming form of love. The adaptation then is twofold: to a different form of marriage and to life as a threesome. Ginny W., at age twenty-seven, had been married only six weeks when she conceived. Ginny said that after the baby came, "I would end up crying to Rob that I wanted it to be like it was before. Just the two of us. I felt the baby was an intruder. My husband's stomach was in knots too. I was not the only one affected by this change."

In *Parenthood: Its Psychology and Psychopathology,* Therese Benedek asks why psychoanalysts have failed to study the developmental situation of parents.[35] Why have they focused all their studies on the development of children? She maintains that they failed to take an objective overview of the various stages parents go through for the simple reason that they are parents themselves and never thought about it![36]

The struggle for growth, the change from being a single unit, from being a child-adult without responsibilities, to becoming a parent with ultimate responsibilities, limitations, and conflicting emotions is a vital part of growing up.

WILL SEX AFTER CHILDBIRTH EVER BE THE SAME?

In the meantime, some of us are left wondering whether our sex lives will ever return to the excitement, romance, and eroticism of before parenthood. In baby-care books, sex after birth receives scant mention. Perhaps parents are not really supposed to be erotic people, for the implication is that the sexual urge is one we should *gladly* repress in our delight over becoming parents. What references are made tend either to be upbeat and blindly optimistic (everything should be back to normal in a few weeks, so just hang in there) or detailed. A Masters and Johnson study, for example, has discovered a lower level of sexuality even at three months postpartum and that achieving orgasm after birth can be more difficult because of fatigue or tension, because of breast tenderness, soreness after an episiotomy, exhaustion from C-section delivery, or fears that sexual organs have changed and that vaginal muscles are either tighter or looser.

One detail that has been overlooked is that a very real symptom of PPD is loss of libido. When that normal postpartum fall in thyroid occurs, it drops below the prepregnancy level and stays there for many months. Loss of thyroid seems to affect the female sexual response in a very direct way. For example, those on thyroid medication usually find a return to normal sexual response in two to three weeks.

Very little is said about deeper psychological strains from changing marital relationships, altered sense of identity, and variable moods. Such is the pressure on us to be having healthy (that is, continuous and frequent) sex lives that we dare not own up to abstinence. Where once we might have been ashamed to mention *having* sex, now we are ashamed to mention *not having* sex![37] What if we are experiencing no sexual desire after the six-week checkup with our obstetrician? Or, as one woman described, what can we make of no feeling in the vaginal area for up to eight months? What if our husbands seem to have turned off sexually? We are left floundering in fear about our own sexual viability.

Sex, as is always the case, is likely to be an indicator of other changes taking place within our psyches and within our relationships. Think again about the resentment a woman may feel toward her husband when he appears to have all the freedom, compared to her sense of entrapment, after the birth of their much-wanted child. She is feeling that her life has radically changed, while his remains pretty much the same in her eyes. Add to that the conflicts taking place at the core of their partnership and there are grounds for discontent on both sides.

Marital tension shoots to the surface; at best, this period of silence and withdrawal may give both parties time to absorb the impact of parenthood on their lives.

The after-birth relationship between a man and a woman undergoes many shifts. The woman very likely mothered her husband to some degree before the baby's advent. Without a child she enjoyed nurturing and caring for her man. He thrived on being pampered and catered to, being number one to the woman who, in return, he adored, as he once adored his mother. But now, with a baby, his wife does not want to mother him. Worse, she even feels contempt for his need to be mothered, when she so obviously feels her own need to be cared for. To her mind, this man she married and so loved has regressed into a self-centered child.

We should consider too what makes a woman, or a man, feel sexy. Certainly not fatigue, loss of identity, feelings of entrapment, or loss of self-esteem. As has often been shown in recent literature, both men and women need fantasies—of idealized partners, idealized situations, or an idealized self—to feel sexual. Without a strong identity how can we fantasize?[38]

Our sexuality, up until motherhood, had been based on a number of variables. How we related to men in general, how we felt about how we looked and dressed, had all been important. None of these variables remained the same after we left our childless lifestyle.

Dianne McL. felt the decline in her sexuality even while she was pregnant. When her baby was nearly two months old, she wrote in her journal, "I haven't had sex for six months already, and really I feel I've lost all interest." Just getting big and fat to begin with had altered her self-image. "I was used to being a size nine, wearing tight clothes. That was part of my identity. I could turn men on in skin-tight jeans, and I knew it and liked it. But now I wouldn't even know what to do to *feel* sexy."

Let us go one step further. Dianne admitted to me that she loved having her baby daughter in bed with her. She did not mind that her husband, Randy, had taken to sleeping on the couch. "One night recently he came back to the bedroom. But I didn't want him. I was happy in bed with my daughter. I was breast-feeding, and it felt so close, just me and her."

What new mother hasn't felt that twisting conflict of loyalties? The baby has become her lover, the husband is the intruder. If not, the baby would be the intruder. The new mother is caught either way. Naturally, cast in this role of outsider, many men feel hurt and withdraw either angrily or in silence.

Unfortunately, the sexual impasse set up by the new parents deepens as the husband, the victim of this particular scenario so out of his control, suffers a chronic sense of rejection, which, coupled with his own changing sense of himself on becoming a father, becomes just too much for him to deal with. His reaction may be intensified by a reawakening of the jealous resentment he felt as a boy at his mother's rejection. The new father may respond in denial or anger. Often his reaction is to leave the house for longer periods during the day. He might find solace in work, where society implies he should be devoting more of his energies now that their need for money is greater. He might find refuge in exercise, sports, after-office drinking, or, of course, as has so often been the case, in the arms of another woman.

The sexual withdrawal a woman experiences on becoming a mother should certainly be the focus of our interest, and not the center of denial. For some women even being caressed or the very thought of sexual penetration is like an invasion. At this very sensitive, vulnerable time, their sexual needs have transferred into a deep cry to be nurtured. That their husbands need them, are demanding of them, can just lead to their greater withdrawal. The new mother feels she is giving on all levels, all at once: emotionally, physically, spiritually; to the baby, to her other children, to her husband. Sex seems like the least pressing need at this time.

Psychotherapist Judith Klein offered some insights into why we might undergo this unexpected response to new motherhood. One of the reasons we mothers feel so sexually attached to our babies is that the experience of giving birth has reawakened the memory of our own birth and those infantile longings for our mother. We want to relive that cuddly, warm, perfect security; the joyous skin contact; the giving sort of sexuality, rather than the give and take of adult heterosexuality. Klein explained more about this relationship with our mother and how it can affect our marriage.

"One of the things therapists often have to deal with is a woman's apparent loss of interest in sex, or her marriage, when she becomes a parent. On the surface it may look as though the relationship is at fault, or that she is rejecting motherhood, but really this all goes much deeper.

"At age five or six she would have gone through the Oedipal stage, when as a little girl she fantasized having a baby with daddy. These fantasies made her feel tremendous guilt about the strong feelings she had for the parent of the opposite sex, and she learned to be afraid of her mother's retaliation: that she would be angry, resentful, jealous, or punishing. If her parents divorced at this time, that would have made things far worse, for it would have been as though mommy had said, 'Here, have daddy.'

"The Oedipal fantasy is repressed over the years, but is often reactivated by the birth of her own child. The undesired fantasy is so anxiety-provoking that she tends to retreat into a masochistic defense and turn against her husband, not allowing herself any pleasure from the relationship—by withdrawing sexually, or maybe having affairs, or deliberately provoking the breakup of the marriage."

Sexuality is linked generally to feelings of energy, psychological balance, and normal mental and biological functioning. It is not encouraged by a situation in which we are overloaded by emotional demands, feeling drained, empty, that there is not enough of us to go around. For some of us, marriage counseling may be the answer; for others, a weekend or evening away together, or simply setting aside time to talk. Somewhere, somehow, we have to find our sexuality again. We have to work at who needs nurturing (the answer probably is both partners), who has what to give.

Julia F., for example, feeling that her marriage to Neil had fallen into decay since the baby had come, decided to book a hotel room on Valentine's Day, fill it with champagne and candles, and take her husband there for dinner. "If I didn't make some kind of effort soon, I knew I would lose him. Even holding hands those days seemed like such an effort. There just wasn't enough of me to go around," she said.

WHEN SEPARATION SEEMS THE EASIER OPTION

Resentment, mutually felt, can reach such a climax that the marriage may begin to look irretrievable. Divorce then appears the much easier option. We don't really have to look at the statistics to know that parenthood drives many a couple finally apart. Maybe the couple has begun to see in each other a new, less flattering, image. Maybe the battle for power and control in the relationship has taken on such shifting demarcation lines that neither feels at ease with the situation. Being a mother may have given the woman a newfound sense of power, which could disturb the sensitive balance of power that kept the couple at peace. Maybe her sexual withdrawal (or his) has been the final wedge that sets them truly asunder. A lot of work needs to be done in a lot of marriages to right this situation. I wish more sympathy and understanding would be extended to the *couple* at such a crucial time.

Cheryl J. had a full-time job as an executive secretary. At twenty-eight, she found herself living alone with her year-old son, separated from her husband, Scott, who walked out on them when Billy was just four and a half months old. Theirs was not an uncommon scenario in today's world. Cheryl had become aware, after Billy arrived, that Scott wanted to be mothered and that she did not want to mother him. She resented his not helping her in the house, and she resented that she *had* to work because of their family's financial situation, and consequently could not be the kind of mother she had always imagined herself.

"I would raise hell with Scott, that I could not do everything. I was back at work, coming home to household chores and mothering. Scott would leave the house for four and a half hours a night while I tried to catch up. I'd be asleep with the baby next to my bed and he wanted to know why I was always sleeping when he came home. I ended up trying to explain, crying, that I couldn't do it all. I needed help, if I was to continue working. Really, I wanted to stay home and raise my children. I wanted to be a good wife."

Cheryl believed her PPD was brought on far less by the separation than by her husband's bad adjustment to becoming a father. She could not, of course, see his side of the picture. Cheryl was resenting not being able to live out her ideal image of herself as a mother. She resented playing both mother and father (breadwinner and household domestic). She felt her depression ease when Scott left them. This way, at least, she regained all the control. "I ended up better off without him. In fact, my PPD ended when my husband left me."

Many women have suggested that men need sensitizing to the effects of PPD; that they should learn what is expected from them in the year after a baby's birth. These women want their men to know that a new mother needs mothering by her husband. They say a new mother would respond better to a man who is nurturing, supportive, patient, and undemanding. Men could understandably respond, "What about us? We need understanding too. What about our needs?"

Indeed, the suffering men may undergo in the process of becoming a parent is grossly overlooked. Maybe this is not surprising in a society that has only just begun to consider what women are undergoing. Nevertheless, when we consider the complex effects of the changes in men's lives brought on by childbirth, we should focus on them as much for the women's sake as for theirs.

8

◆

ON FATHERS AND SOME SPECIAL-CASE MOTHERS

If PPD is induced by a biochemical reaction to the act of childbirth, how, you might ask, can it be experienced by fathers, adoptive mothers, or stepmothers? (The other two sections in this chapter, on older mothers and single mothers, fit more easily into the accepted formula.) Yet new fathers, adoptive mothers, and stepmothers do, by their own description, suffer PPD.

Although I have tried hard to shift the blame from women themselves for the depressions they may suffer, my intention throughout Part Two has been to draw a much-magnified artist's impression of the feelings and emotions we may never recognize consciously but which, nonetheless, can affect us crucially on becoming parents. Taking the case first of fathers, the psychological impact of parenting may be just as overwhelming to them as to their wives.

The majority of men will not go into severe PPD, as would be experienced by a mother, because of the lack of the biochemical quotient. But the resulting confusion in the new father's mind, especially as he may be receiving little or no sympathy for his feelings, can lead to a chronic form of stress or depression that will not be resolved until years later and may be expressed in the abuse of alcohol or drugs, breaking up the marriage, or suffering a stress-related illness, such as a heart attack.

Paradoxically, though fathers are unlikely to receive much sympathy from society as a whole (it is still not seen as manly to be concerned about one's fathering), we are in the midst of a huge "joy of fatherhood" cultural media blitz. The ultimate effect of this emphasis may be to increase levels of PPD in men as they too scramble to achieve a preconceived view of perfection. A current bestseller on fathering, *Good Morning, Merry Sunshine,* by Bob Greene, may bring a smile of recognition and delight to those fathers who have already adopted some of the myths of the new man to their lives, who happily parade their newborns in Snuglis or backpacks around the parks or supermarkets.[39]

We are still left with far too many unanswered questions. There are the millions more men who have not taken on the mantle of new man, who do not wish to consider myths of new fatherhood. There are men who wish they could be "new fathers" but feel they fail before even beginning. There are men whose wives have seen in their spouses just that sort of image and, once they become parents, the wives are disappointed in their husbands' behavior.

We have not yet had time or distance to judge the impact on men of their new fathering, or its impact on our children, or on *ourselves,* now that we women have new levels of expectation with which to assess our husbands as partners. Major questions of control and power come into play between men and women when they become parents. Many women find it harder than they imagined to adjust to life with a new father, when that entails handing over many of the decisions about the child's life to the husband which, traditionally, had all been the woman's domain. The tired wife, complaining that her husband won't make up the bottles, get up in the night, or find a new baby-sitter when their regular help calls in sick, is the same wife who will not give her husband the space or the time to fulfill his part of the bargain.

The woman subtly takes the reins of control out of his hands because, in honesty, she feels insecure without that control. It is never easy to delegate; it is certainly hard to give up one area of dominance in the home and out of it, an area women have clung to for centuries. Many marriages are broken by just this pressure. The man is usually blamed ("He deserted her when they had a newborn—he just wasn't prepared to take on his responsibilities," we say in criticism), yet sometimes I wonder if such men are instead victims of ill-defined new roles.

Unable to comprehend what his place should be in this new family setup; not allowed his traditional role of provider, voice of authority, and backup supporter; not allowed, in place of that, the new role of equal, sharing partner; finding himself undermined on all levels, he leaves. "At least divorced, with a reasonable custody arrangement, I get to see my son on my own terms. I get to make decisions and form my *own* relationship with him," commented Frank M., divorced father of a three-and-a-half-year-old. "She really took over the whole thing, and I was left out, pushed out, like a nobody." Frank left the family home when his son was four months old. Looking back, he realized that his desertion was a way of keeping some of that control he had so needed and wanted.

Nick, Laura S.'s husband, on talking about her still-current PPD five months after the birth of Bobby, said of course it was putting a terrible strain on their marriage, though they had been married for ten years. "You need an awful lot of money in the emotional bank when you decide to have a child," he added quietly, not wishing to get more deeply involved in the discussion.

When men become fathers they can become prey to the same psychological and emotional upheavals as their wives. The father may find old childhood conflicts reactivated, relive his own demands on his mother, or pass through unresolved conflicts with his father, which can be manifested in sexual withdrawal from his wife. If a man had problems relating to, identifying with, or feeling loved by his father, the passage into fatherhood may make him fear confrontation with these sides of himself.

A new father may suffer sibling rivalry with the baby over his wife's attention and love. The rivalry will emerge in an unwelcome resentment toward the baby, who, he feels, does not love him. Or the baby's crying, and obvious preference for its mother, can bring back fears of not being loved in his own infancy.

Sexually, the new father may have begun to discover confused signals in himself once his wife became pregnant. Whether her libido was directly affected or not, his might have been. Oedipal longings for his mother reemerge in a form of terror or revulsion toward his wife in the pregnant state.

Then, too, if his wife suffers PPD, the new father may be called on to play a much stronger and more supportive role than he ever expected, as Kathy S.'s husband, Bill, had to. Bill coped wonderfully, but this unexpected demand on a new father can lead to his own breakdown, as, confused, he is left wondering what happened to his wife, to his fantasies of her as a mother, to his fantasy of family life. Suffering his own identity crisis, fearing his life has gone out of control forever, feeling just as trapped as she is, the father may react in a similarly depressed fashion, or his response may be to withdraw more obviously from the home and bury himself in work.

As Judith Klein points out, we have always attributed men's moods to other stresses: pressure at work, desire to make more money to support their family, fear that their wife's devotion to the baby is leaving them out in the cold. Men are just learning to open up and talk about their feelings, so perhaps in the near future we will begin to hear a lot more about fatherhood and its impact on men.[40]

The pioneer men, who have reversed roles with their wives and acted as househusbands, or really shared equally in the childcare, could have important messages from the front. Simon S. was twenty-eight years old when he and Dana had their daughter, Estelle. Dana already had a good job as a magazine editor, a seemingly flourishing career that could easily support them both. Simon was not as strongly attached to his job, and, as he had always wanted more time to develop his writing and musical pursuits, he agreed to stay home with the baby, at least for the first year.

Such are society's pressures and needs for the image of happy "new fathers" that Simon has often been quoted in upbeat magazine articles and on television as an exemplar. I have known Simon and Dana for many years. Although I did not really understand what was happening to them at the time, I used to sum up Simon's depression and black moods as "housewife's blues" in those early years of his retreat into the home.

They had moved to a pleasant leafy suburb, an easy commute for Dana from the city. Simon enjoyed the peace and the quiet routine, but inevitably he became isolated and withdrawn. He would chat with mothers in the park and at the supermarket, but no real friendships developed. "How could they?" Simon joked. "I'd have all those husbands banging on my door." Simon was busy projecting his own self-image of the new myth. Of course he was happy, he was out of the rat race, he didn't have to commute, and Estelle was a charmer. But his writing did not progress and his moods became very black.

To make matters worse, Dana's career took a sudden upward leap. She changed jobs twice, was recruited by a television network, and ended up as a minor celebrity, with appearances on television talk shows and a magazine column under her own name. To ease Simon's despair, she hired a part-time housekeeper, giving him more freedom. Simon was hospitalized for depression before he received a foreign assignment to write a long article, and with relish he took his pen and notebook and vanished for six weeks.

Simon reemerged sane and wise. He did not want to return to the working world, and that was a major problem he had to work out for himself. He needed time and self-confidence to push himself as a writer, and that meant his earning power was limited, to say the least. What happened to Simon is what happens to so many women once they become mothers. Torn from their former lifestyle, they suffer a sudden identity crisis, loss of self-esteem, and loss of freedom. For Simon the deep questions must have been: Was he man or woman? Was he nurturer or provider? What did masculinity mean to him and to the outside world? Dana confessed that she finally came to the realization that she had to pay a housekeeper, as Simon would never do all the work of a housewife. He would not clean the house, cook the meals, and do the laundry each day. Intent on keeping her own motherhood image intact, Dana worked herself to the bone, cooking for the family every evening, and even preparing Simon's lunch for the next day. What working husband ever does that for his wife?

Dana also noted that they have sought help from marriage counseling at least three times in the last eight years. They have both taken the time and made the effort to work at what has proved to be a very successful marriage and an interesting supportive partnership.

When roles are reversed, we are more sensitive to the vulnerable and precarious balance that keeps a relationship alive and both partners sexually and emotionally content. We do not offer such sensitivity to the average traditional relationship, where the wife assumes those roles that were so burdensome to Simon.

One way to alleviate ther problems, Dana discovered, was to make sure their finances were more equal. The fact that the house was repaired, the new car bought, the vacation taken when Dana's bank account was large enough, only worsened Simon's low self-image. In a classic image of real role reversal, Dana decided to support Simon more completely. She channels monthly income into *his* bank account, balancing their equity. "We have a lot to learn yet, but I believe we have both been happier this way. And Estelle certainly has loved having her father around all these years," Dana commented.

There is a price we pay for motherhood or fatherhood, and that price is painfully clear when father plays mother. Still we refuse to see the strain and stress we expect women to live with when they become mothers. When a thirty-five-year-old father of a newborn was recently forced to give up working because his wife suffered a postpartum stroke and was left in a coma, medical insurance paid for nursing help to come to his house for part of the day so he could get to work or visit his wife in the hospital. A tragic situation and a caring insurance system. But would anyone think to offer that help to a new mother if her husband were hospitalized? No, women are expected to struggle on alone, without help or support. We just expect her to go about her business and not complain. "You wanted the baby, didn't you?" is said with a critical tone and resentful expression if a new mother dares to voice her exhaustion or inability to cope.

OLDER MOTHERS

Many people come to their parenting with a bagful of emotional investment in their ability to do it *better* than previous generations, friends, or colleagues, and they are convinced they can have it all. One group that has particular difficulties are the older mothers.

When I had my first baby, I was thirty-one years old and imagined I was part of the new "older mother" generation. Now I realize I was relatively young.

These mothers have invested much of their lives into their work, and, having a baby somewhere near the age of forty, they are determined to prove, along with their partners, that they are certainly as good, if not better, than the traditional or younger mother. Aware that they somehow offend society's beliefs that women past thirty or thirty-five are too old, that they run an increased risk of bearing a Down's syndrome baby, that they might be set in their ways, inflexible, or too tired, they have a *fierce* determination to succeed, to prove they are in fact little short of perfect. Their expectations may be even further removed from reality than younger mothers'.

Let us look at some of the deeper psychological difficulties inherent in late motherhood, or implicit in the delaying process, for these women have delayed having a baby for the major part of their reproductive lives. In her essay "Psychotherapy with Pregnant Women," therapist Joan Raphael-Leff notes that when a woman comes to motherhood later, pregnancy has been consciously set aside, avoided, ignored, maybe terminated, possibly ambivalently pursued, and denied throughout the preceding years. The conflicting emotions from those earlier years will still be in the subconscious even if consciously overcome.

Maybe the woman's delaying tactics were used until she met the right man or achieved a certain status at work. Maybe the ticking of the biological clock finally forced a decision. The excitement that can come with this abrupt change in viewpoint, with the welcome release of a long-repressed mothering instinct, with the overcoming of fear and denial, can be so heady, so all-consuming, that never for a minute will the older mother let a small negative voice whisper in her ear, "Watch out for reality!"

What is reality for older mothers? Biological clocks cannot be denied, and although having a baby can in some ways be rejuvenating (you feel the age of the traditional mother, somewhere in her twenties), there is no denying that tiredness, fatigue, and exhaustion are very much complements of this form of parenting.

Mary S., for example, is an exciting woman. A smart, breezy newspaper reporter with a string of books to her name, she has an enviable life with an attractive husband and an adorable fifteen-month-old son. Mary had just turned forty when we met. When I asked Mary if she suffered any PPD since Noah's birth, as I had noticed she never finished a sentence and often appeared totally distracted, she laughed easily. "When he was an infant, no. It's now that he is a toddler I cannot manage it. I really feel I'm on a treadmill, with work, and my writing projects, and looking after Noah.

"Bruce and I both really wanted this child. Now I'm forty and here I am with a lovely little boy. I'm remarkably grateful for the opportunity to have had him. I never imagined it would be possible for me. But I have been shocked to discover my own limitations as a parent. I just don't have the patience. There are times I feel I'm about to crack up. I wonder 'where's *me?*' "

Older mothers, and fathers, do tend to be more grateful to have had their children. They know how much a child has enriched their lives, perhaps improved their marriage, that not to have had a child would have been a terrible loss. They feel more guilt than the average parent in suggesting anything might be wrong. The efforts to deny impatience, fatigue, depression, are stronger than for most of us. ("We told you it would be hard having a baby at forty," they hear tongues wagging in the background.)

When I talked to Mary, she refused to say anything at first that would affect the rosy picture she liked to promote. But once she trusted me, she talked more honestly. When I suggested to her, for example, that she might stop writing the books, if running her career with the newspaper, managing husband and child, plus having a social life was all proving too much, she stared at me, nonplussed. "I have to do the books. That's my only creative outlet. The newspaper job is mostly for our income. We couldn't get by on just one salary now, and anyway I like the structure it imposes on my life. But the books, writing, is my greatest love. And so is Noah. I can't cut either of them out of my life."

Then, sighing, she admitted, "I am just not the type to find it cute and funny when I'm trying to do a layout of pictures for a deadline the next day, on the dining room table, when Noah comes in for the third time and messes it all up. You know what I've been doing on Saturdays? While Noah naps, which is for about an hour and a half these days, I jump in a cab and race for the office, where I can snatch an hour or so of peace and quiet to get on with my work. It's worth the ten-dollar cab fare for my sanity!"

Many an older, or a working, mother understands why men escape into their work once they have a family. Given half a chance the women would do the same. Anything for peace, tranquility, and a feeling of being in control of one's life again.

Even if older mothers are not set in their ways, they are likely to be used to certain degrees of competence, control, independence, freedom, and to expect or demand areas of privacy and tranquility in their daily routine. The screaming bedlam of a house full of young children may be harder on their equilibrium than on a younger woman's. Broken sleep may affect them physically more strongly. It may be difficult to tolerate mess, chaos, and crisis, to be patient with a young child's interruptions and constant needs, which conflict with their own needs as a woman, wife, or worker. Whether that is an argument in favor of having children at a younger age, I very much doubt. It is something they should be aware of and accept.

Lily P., now in her early forties and back part-time at her job with a city housing program, had three boys when she was thirty-three, thirty-five, and thirty-seven. There were definite pluses on the side of being an older mother, she maintained, but the minuses should be watched out for. Basically Lily can see a need for one thing when dealing with young children—*energy*.

"By the time I was thirty-nine, with a two-year-old and two others under five, I was exhausted. It nearly drove my husband and me apart. I went weeping to a doctor several times and he gave me tranquilizers, which helped momentarily [she reported regaining sexual energy and fantasizing about younger men in the streets!]. But at one point I really just about cracked up.

"I have always expected, indeed demanded, to have help with the housework and to look after the children when they were little. I had to give up my job completely for two years, as I just couldn't cope. Even now I have only gone back two days a week—I'm lucky I can do that—because any more just puts me under a tremendous strain. The way of life has put a drain on our finances, but my husband has had to agree to it. It was a sacrifice we had to make as a couple, because I really do not have the energy necessary."

SINGLE MOTHERS

Single mothers may also fall into the trap of investing too much myth and optimism into their ability to cope, and consequently overlook some of the unconscious motivating forces that might lead them to distress and PPD. The single mother who chooses to become a parent without a partner, or husband, is almost bound to expect the best of herself and to deny many emotional problems she faces along the way. Other single mothers, who came to their position by default, because of an unwanted separation from the baby's father or his refusal to marry her at the last minute, may fail to connect their mood with the birth of the baby, imputing all their depression to the sense of desertion and betrayal. The baby is seen by these mothers as the one being who brings them happiness, who makes them feel loved and worthwhile, that their life is not altogether hopeless.

A single mother's anxiety and PPD therefore may not show itself in despair, but rather will emerge in her overprotectiveness. Not having anyone around to support her, she may find it hard to leave her baby with a sitter or in day care. As one single mother put it, "We chain ourselves to the source of our duress, like madwomen."

Overprotectiveness; chronic fear that the baby might die, from crib death, for example; inability to move the baby out of her bedroom or, in some cases, her bed; all tend to reflect the mother's own feelings of loneliness and being unloved and *her* fear of rejection, rather than the baby's.

Single mothers are expected to continue working and run up against little criticism for doing so. They are treated like fathers by our society and may be offered more help and support than would be offered to a traditional mother. The single mother's situation may be viewed by the outside world more accurately than that of other mothers.

Dr. Jessie Bernard noted that any woman, once a mother, knew what single motherhood was all about.[41] However helpful her husband, however supportive and financially sound, ultimately the responsibility for that child is hers. Eight or nine times out of ten it is she who is the one to get up at 3 A.M., bathe, feed, wipe the floor, arrange for the baby-sitter, hug, or take the day off work when the child is sick or needs to go to a birthday party.

ADOPTIVE MOTHERS

Adoptive mothers have not given birth. They cannot argue that hormonal shifts might have brought on the biochemical changes leading to depression. Yet women who adopt babies or small children are also subject to depression once the baby has joined their family.[42] There have been few statistics on the incidence of adoptive mothers suffering PPD, but statistics can only reflect the numbers of mothers who report such unwelcome feelings to a doctor or psychiatrist. How many adoptive mothers would report feeling depressed once they have the baby—the same baby they have fought long and hard to be given, with the subsequent fear that the agency might take the baby away again—when they and their husbands have spent months, or maybe years, convincing the social workers what normal, stable, secure people they are?

Adoptive mothers are subject to all the same frustrations and emotional overcharges as natural mothers, fathers, or any parents. They too will be shocked by the reality of motherhood, compared with their dreams and fantasized version. They will endure that sense of entrapment, the loss of identity, submersion of ego, and possibly feeling of despair that their decision has not been the right one. When an adoptive mother experiences such feelings, her guilt, shame, and anger at herself are likely to be even stronger than that of a natural mother because she has convinced herself, as well as the agency, that the one thing she wanted in the world was to be a mother.

Heavy emotional investment in the ideal of being a mother is therefore the adoptive mother's most immediate trigger for psychological distress, which can lead to depression. Her own negative self-image as a woman, which will have been cultivated over the years of her infertility or recurrent miscarriages, will also be playing its part. It is unlikely that any woman who has tried unsuccessfully, and with increasing desperation, over the years to conceive her own child, who has suffered the indignities and humiliations of infertility testing, who has had to accept that she and her husband will not be able to make their *own* baby (i.e., be normal parents) and that their only option is to adopt will avoid all the unconscious negative feelings about her femaleness and worthiness as a mother once she has a real child to look after.[43]

Perhaps the most typical kind of PPD (though, as PPD means postpartum depression, it can only be linked as a related syndrome, due to similar causes of psychological stress) experienced by an adoptive mother is that described by Georgette F. Her reaction was little different from that of many a natural mother, only her case was exaggerated by the speed with which she suddenly, in a matter of minutes, was thrown into motherhood, with no time for rehearsal or real preparedness.

There was building excitement beforehand, then the phone call to say they could bring the baby back home, and then *wham,* the reality—being a perfect mother was nothing like she had fantasized. At twenty-seven, a former data processing supervisor who had been in her job for nine years,

Georgette received the phone call on a Wednesday evening that she and her husband, Bill, could pick up their adoptive baby in the middle of the next week. Georgette and Bill had been married for seven years, and had been trying to adopt a baby for the last three years. Now their dreams were about to come true.

Friday was her last day at work, and Georgette had it all planned that Monday through Wednesday would be spent cleaning the house, preparing herself to welcome little Zoe. On Monday, however, calling the caseworker to see if Zoe was well, she was told to come pick her up that day. Georgette went into a panic. Later that day, the house was full of party guests to greet Zoe into their lives. Then the door closed on an empty house, and Georgette began to learn what motherhood was really like. PPD set in as the last guest closed the door to the empty house, she recalled.

"Before the baby, Bill and I were used to being out of the house a lot. Of course I had always spent my days with other adults at work, holding adult conversations. All of a sudden it was so different! I couldn't take Zoe out because of the cold weather. I was imprisoned in my home with an eight-pound warden. I'd beg Bill in the evenings just to take the three of us to the grocery stores, never one of my favorite chores, but now it seemed like a wild excitement. Anything just to go for a ride in the car."

Georgette suffered enormous PPD and guilt for these feelings. After all that time convincing the agency they would be the best parents in the world, she wondered if they had misjudged themselves. That time rests vividly in her memory, but it did pass. Georgette and Bill now have two beautiful adopted daughters, and they escaped *none* of the psychological and situational side effects of becoming parents.

SECOND-HAND MOTHERHOOD

Becoming a stepmother means you take on parenting second-hand. The stepmother learns everything about parenting, with the negative aspects presented first. She is not in control, is often ill-regarded, and is an object of jealousy or resentment. The consequent guilt and anger may be a heavy burden. The psychological upheaval tends to be accentuated when the stepmother brings home her own baby, and the other children feel ousted from the nest.

Twenty-eight-year-old Lee G. maintained that the many ups and downs of her life, even the trauma of her own divorce, were never as bad as the PPD she experienced when, believing herself blissfully married to a second husband who also very much wanted to start a new family, she brought the baby home to her five-year-old stepson, Dan. Lee was elated that day. But because she had worked for eleven years as a legal assistant, the day her husband, Jeff, left her home with Dan and baby Louise, her world shattered. She was faced with a withdrawn, resentful, five-year-old who would not offer any love to Louise, and she had to deal with her own conflicting emotions over having wanted this baby and how she felt about being a real mother. "I felt cheated, frustrated, hurt, and most of all scared. Inadequate with my own baby, stupid, out of control, and dreadfully alone." As Lee pointed out, "The problems of delivery were nothing compared to the emotional stress in the weeks that followed."

A thirty-five-year-old nurse, who had a fifteen-year-old son from a previous marriage plus a two-year-old and new baby from her second marriage, really believed all her dreams had come true. Said Sheila A., "I had wanted it all—husband, baby, home—so badly. Yet, when I gave up full-time work with the first baby, by the fourth month I had gone into a deep tailspin of despair. Then the second baby came along twenty months later, and I was floundering under stress, with too much to do and not enough outside stimulation."

For Sheila, the result of her emotional overload was total sexual withdrawal. She reported no vaginal feelings for over eight months. Sheila had, like so many special-case mothers, invested far too much in motherhood. Her first marriage, her first attempt at mothering (the now teenage son) were far from wonderful experiences. Now she had a second chance, and, feeling so grateful, she was doubly determined to live up to her ideals.

The reality of motherhood for Sheila, who was used to hospital life, was oppressive. Depressed, guilty, tied to the house, fatigued, Sheila finally admitted some truths to herself and returned to work. Getting away from motherhood, she confessed, had been her cure. With an active working life, an exercise class to help alleviate the stress, and her new, loving family, she learned to approach her mothering role more sensitively, more realistically, and less idealistically. Once the pressures were off, Sheila was able to feel happy again and her sexual feelings for the husband she loved so much returned.

9

◆

MY MOTHER, MY BABY, MYSELF

I wasn't prepared to accept the idea that our previous relationship with our mothers could have much relevance to postpartum mood until midway through my research. The whole idea sounded too involved, too critical of women, too redolent of stereotyped images of how women should be. "She's depressed because she rejected her mother"; "she has a hard time relating to her femininity"; "a tomboy with masculine identification, aggressive in work, controlling, refusing to accept her female role." I think we have a right to feel irritated by the assumption that there is only *one* type of normal behavior and that to react otherwise makes us abnormal or deviant.

Researching the book, meeting other women, talking to them, reading their letters, I became more confident myself, grateful to understand that PPD can affect any woman. The people I was in contact with were individuals. Some loved baking cookies and staying home, others had struggled up the corporate ladder and enjoyed a successful working life, most were somewhere in between. Seeing that PPD was no respecter of persons, I felt more willing to dig deeper into the complex tie of mother, daughter, and child.

Because research into PPD has for years been the domain of the psychiatric profession (if you recall, the view that PPD might have strong links with the physiological changes of childbirth, although first arrived at in the nineteenth century, disappeared from the professional eye until recently), by far the largest amount of literature available in professional journals is from the psychoanalysts. Without being frivolous, I recommend some of this literature as bizarre reading material and a perfect indicator of the state of public opinion on women over the past few decades.

The reason I had objected so strongly to comments in these academic articles that PPD no doubt related to a woman's relationship with her mother, or repudiation of her mother, had let me to scribble a message in the margin of one of my notebooks: "Surely we must all have a problem with the image we hold of our own mothers these days? If that's the case, do we now have a generation of PPD sufferers?"[44] I had in mind the revolution in thinking about women, and in the reality of women's lives, since the 1960s, and our current marked turn away from values of the past. Was this transitional crisis in the role of women then playing a larger part in our own acceptance of motherhood?

My research began, as so much does, in myself. I had to think long and hard about the image I held of my mother, the one that had so upset me when I felt associated with it in my own mind.

With my two babies, I was utterly depressed to realize that my lifestyle was not so revolutionary and different from my parents' and specifically my mother's life pattern. Even though part of me wanted to be a loving, caring, kind mother to my children, as she had been to my sister and me, the sense of becoming like her was terrifying and had dragged me down.

Over the years I have grown to understand that my rebellion against my mother was an attempt to break away from my desperate *need* for her, my dependence and dependent love. My mother and I are good friends, as adults, with a sympathy for our differences. It is through our mothers that we learn to judge, forecast, and assess ourselves as women in the world. The very act of becoming a mother seems to narrow our sense of choices, of ourselves as women, almost overnight, to a vision of ourselves in her light, as though a net had been mysteriously cast over us, reducing us all to *mother*.

Daughters do have to separate from their mothers, we now know. Failure to separate is an unhealthy psychological sign. Our own daughters will have to enact a similar rebellion even if, right now, we like to imagine they will be so inspired by our brilliant, struggling example that they will accept us just as we are without moments of rebellion. The emotional distress the psychological separation from our mothers induces may often contribute to PPD.

CONFLICT WITH THE MOTHERING ROLE

The deeper feelings of loss of a separate identity, independence, and self-esteem are all most likely linked to this new self-image, and we are exposed, as the psychiatrists say, to a conflict with the mothering role. Their interpretation of this conflict is what I object to.

Frederick Melges, then of the department of psychosomatic medicine at the University of Rochester School of Medicine and Dentistry, wrote an article in 1968 that, because it is now some twenty years old, is somewhat archaic in its views.[45] Melges let himself be trapped in traditional male views of what a woman's role or place in society should be. Thirty-five percent of the one hundred postpartum patients (he was looking for incidence of PPD) questioned had "played with dolls slightly if not at all," and "had not worked as baby-sitters" (thereby casting a future generation of sexually and socially liberated young girls into heavy PPD). Melges's respondents expressed a preference to be men, said they related more to their fathers, and had been tomboys as young girls. In the late 1960s, maybe these women were trying to express to the psychiatrists some latent feelings about women's roles that had not even emerged yet under the banner of women's liberation.

Two types of mother personalities were pinned down as models to be rejected: either the controlling, rejecting mother or, by contrast, the passive, downtrodden mother.

From that point on, deciding that I would not be able to rely solely on these psychoanalytic opinions, I returned to my own form of research and added a question to those interviews I felt were deep enough—I asked the women about their relationship with their mothers. Half expecting them to say it was none of my business, or that their mother was the dearest person to their hearts, I was often surprised to hear every woman I asked express her own deep feelings about the rejection of this significant woman in her life.

We would comment on our shared vehemence, and tried to examine together why this should be. The answers were not easy to find, nor were they altogether welcome. Jeanne N., a thirty-five-year-old book editor, for example, whose own mother had worked all her young life, leaving Jeanne to be brought up by nannies, would appear to have had a very different background from my own (my mother was a traditional housewife).

OUR MOTHERS' EXPERIENCE OF PPD

We must not forget that our mothers may also have gone through PPD and, not knowing what it was, probably refused to admit to it. Denial is a common reaction even today. In past generations, however, it must have been hard, if not impossible, to reject the mothering role, the only one freely given to women; to say they had found unhappiness in motherhood, when nothing else was permitted them.

I received several retrospective comments from women, such as this: "I will never forget that dreadful year after my son was born, and that was twenty-one years ago. It was the loneliest time of my life, and I did not know it was PPD, or that it was anything that had a name."

Confronted by her daughter's PPD, Nancy E.'s mother at first snapped, "Get on with dealing with your two children and pull yourself together." But she did open up after the psychiatrist lent the family a pamphlet on depression. Nancy now believes her mother experienced a heavy PPD, too, but still has not really owned up to it.

"When my sister was born, my mother nearly died from toxemia. That was her second child in three years. For a year afterward, she never saw a doctor, or talked about it to anyone, but she feared she was losing her mind. She was very depressed, had anxiety attacks, and would be sitting talking to friends wondering if they could see she was going insane. She had three children in six years, never worked, never got out of the house much, and never complained. I think that's why I really used to believe women were supposed to be utterly self-sacrificing when they were mothers."

When Kathy S. tried to be honest about her feelings with her mother, she was told sharply, "Why have a child if you feel like that?" Kathy's mother continued to reject her daughter, as she had all her life. When I asked Kathy directly about this relationship with her mother, she said sadly, "We never got on, we were never close. One of my first reactions to having my baby, because of the image I carried still of her—always unhappy, tied down, complaining—was, 'Oh no, I'm going to be old and stuck like my mother.' I didn't even want Joe to call me mommy. I hated the sound of the word!

"From the time I was seven," explained Kathy, "until I was nineteen and left home to get married, I knew my mother was unhappy. She told me her problems and made me feel I had to look after her.

"To this day I'm the dominant woman in the family, the one who holds it all together. My mother lives on the same street, won't drive a car, is dependent on me and still critical. I had been married six years to Bill before getting pregnant. Somehow I hoped it might bring me and my mother closer together. She is a strict Catholic, and from the age of twelve she had warned me not to get pregnant out of marriage or she would throw me out of the house. Here I was at twenty-five, married six years, coming to tell her I was pregnant, and I was shivering with nervousness in case she was angry. She wasn't exactly thrilled or elated, but passed it off without much comment."

Kathy grew up with an image of her mother as a down-trodden, passive woman. "If only she'd had some money of her own, she might have been happier; I knew that even as a child." It should have been no surprise to Kathy, therefore, that she was determined to go back to work after having her baby, that she openly expressed fear of staying home all the time with her child. Yet the conflicts within herself clouded that reality. Kathy wanted to be a real mother; but in her mind being a real mother meant being unhappy.

If a woman's mother was cold or rejecting, when she has her own baby, she wants to give that child all the love she was denied. For Sharon W., with two daughters under four, the rejection by her mother was specific and awful. Her stepfather had sexually abused her over several years. Sharon's mother never knew about it, or pretended not to know. "She never had time for me. My sister was born ten months later, and there were three of us before she was twenty-one. I was raised by my grandparents much of the time." In therapy, Sharon began to learn something of herself and her behavior with her own daughters. "I started to see I was trying to break my elder daughter's spirit, just like my mother had broken mine." In an effort to draw closer to her mother after all these years, Sharon tried to explain over the telephone just what had gone on with her stepfather. But confronting her mother with the truth left Sharon feeling even more rejected, for her mother refused to believe the story.

Women have unfortunately been guilty of furthering PPD through the generations in this desire to cover up or deny their real feelings after childbirth. By staying silent, handing on the burden to their daughters with comments like "This is how life is, so just grow up and get on with it," they have helped perpetuate various myths rather than deal with the reality, which might alleviate much of the guilt and shame for what are genuine, acceptable, feelings.

Maybe if we are able to be open, less guilty, more comfortable with the ambivalence and negative feelings, we will begin to improve the situation for our daughters. Just as we intend to be open about menstruation and about sex and female sexuality, to discuss our own emotions and theirs in human, loving, honest ways, maybe we should prepare ourselves to discuss with our sons and daughters our response to motherhood, not in a negative way, but with honesty.

I believe some of our sadness after birth is part of a greater genetic endowment; that we carry within us the misery of women in the past, some of the despair of being trapped that our mothers and grandmothers might have experienced. Culturally, we associate becoming a mother with turning from independent, autonomous people—a victory so recently won—to passive, oppressed, overextended, and underappreciated less-than-human beings.

Even though up to conception, and during pregnancy, we were inspired with the greatest optimism that *we would be doing it differently,* once that baby was in our arms, we suddenly understood and appreciated our forebears more vividly than ever before: we suddenly identified *too* fully with them. Many women have said that only on becoming a mother did they feel real sympathy with their own mothers. As one of my correspondents put it, "A mother's guilt is something that binds all mothers together."

MOTHER LONGING

Therese Benedek takes us to a deeper analytical root of PPD. When we give birth, we regress to the oral phase, which, she says, is the main psychogenic condition for depression, involving the "female child's identification with its mother."[46]

When we give birth, all our own infantile instincts and reactions are reactivated. For some women that might mean reliving ambivalence about our mothers that we experienced as infants: the desire to be separate and the need to merge with her. When we hear our own baby crying, it might stimulate our own feelings of being newborn, our desire to be loved and nourished. Most of us feel a strong urge to be mothered during pregnancy and just after the birth, which is symbolic of the confusion deep within us.

In a long article about the reconstruction of the life of a woman suffering a difficult PPD, psychoanalyst Harold Blum concluded, "How could she be the mother of a separate, living, unique individual when she *wanted* and *dreaded* to be fused with her mother, clinging and separating, regressively eating rather than feeding and caring for her own infant?"[47]

Thirty-year-old Dianne McL. experienced just this type of reactivation when crying heavily in the first few days after her baby's birth. "I stumbled on the reason for it myself. Although I had been in therapy for years, I had never touched on this. I was reexperiencing the pain of separation from my real mother, and this was why I had wanted a child so much, to experience that sense of bonding I had missed out on."

Dianne openly admitted to being a recovering alcoholic who had also had drug problems, and a member of Alcoholics Anonymous for three years (the last two of which she had been sober). The alcohol problem was connected with this oral longing for her mother's love, and yet, after years of intensive psychotherapy and AA, she had not touched on this very real need in her.

Dianne and her brother had been adopted by their aunt and her husband when Dianne was eighteen months old. Their mother, deemed unfit to care for them, was admitted to a mental institution shortly afterward. Tragically for Dianne's mother, no one was much concerned about the cause of her mental problem and, as Dianne put it, "If she was not insane when she went in there, she certainly would be by now, twenty-five years later."[48]

Dianne had said something very important, and it resonated in me. She was crying for the pain of separation from her own mother. She was crying for the ambivalence, for the love she never received enough of, for the bonding she yearned for and missed. She was crying for her mother's sad fate, with which she was now forced to identify. For most of her young adult life Dianne had not given much thought to the woman in the asylum, knowing only her adoptive mother and devoting more energy to thinking about that dynamic and often difficult relationship.

Mother and daughter is a complex relationship, and our responses cannot be passed off glibly as "problems with the feminine role" or "a mothering conflict."

SECOND OR THIRD CHILD

A fascinating aspect of rejecting our mothers comes in the explanation of why we may not suffer PPD with a first baby, but with a second or third child. If our mother had more than one child, we may have successfully avoided identifying ourselves in her image until we suddenly found ourselves with the *same number* of children. Judith Klein explains further:

"The female child, in the Oedipal stage, had to turn from loving her mother to having strong sexual feelings for the parent of the opposite sex. In rejecting her mother, and desiring ultimately to have sex with her father, and bear *his* child, she invoked the image of her mother's retaliation and anger, which led to the child's own anxiety and guilt. Oedipal problems may be compounded and not resolved if the child's father was especially close to her and, to some degree, seductive. I am not even referring to sexual abuse or incest, but to a handsome, adoring daddy who seduces his own daughter into continuing her Oedipal desire for him beyond the normal stage.

"One way a young adult woman may react, to keep such fear and anxieties at bay, is in avoiding having a baby, or avoiding getting married. If married she may deliberately have affairs, try to destroy the marriage, or refuse to play the traditional female role. Another way of avoidance is to have *one less child* than her mother did. While she has one less she is conscious of being different and of not being in direct competition with her."

PPD after the birth of a second, or third, child may be the result of reactivated unresolved Oedipal conflicts, early anxiety, depression, or guilt, a sense of competition with the mother, or perhaps contempt for her ("Daddy prefers me to you"), and, concurrently, fear of identifying with the mother's apparent "female" role.

This brings me back to the generational theory. If a woman today has, to one degree or another, rejected her mother's lifestyle; felt contempt for her version of housewife-mother; felt pity for her lack of independence, money of her own, or ability to act a part in the greater world; or felt pity for her lack of sexual power and freedom, is this woman then more likely to suffer from the psychological causes of PPD? I cannot answer that. But we are living through transitional times and it is unlikely that we will all sail through unscathed.

THE "WELL-ADJUSTED" WOMAN

There is a popular image that a well-adjusted woman does not suffer from PPD; that certain personality types are more likely to make a good mother and adjust better to mothering. Other types, in the same vision, are on a disaster course even before they have conceived.

Women likely to get PPD are variously seen as those who are narcissistic, obsessional, compliant, conformist, oversensitive, have a controlling personality, are defensive against the primitive in life, married to a passive/dominant husband, or in a marriage where both husband and wife are mutually dependent. Certain traits are seen as proof that the woman had a defective personality before becoming a mother: the fault cannot possibly lie with motherhood so it *must* lie with these foolish women.

Such PPD mothers would have predisposing neurotic tendencies; for example, as a child, they would have displayed nail biting, excessive fear of the dark, shyness, night terrors, sleepwalking, temper tantrums, stammering.[49]

PPD women are commonly viewed as being overdependent on their husbands or seeking a mother in their spouses. It has even been suggested that a woman whose husband does housework has a defective personality, presumably because she allows him to do such female work![50] However, these theories were propounded twenty or thirty years ago, and who would have guessed men would turn in droves to doing the housework! Psychiatrist Gregory Zilboorg wrote in 1957 that women who reject their children by spending all day at their own pursuits, hiring a nanny or governess to care for the children, show a basic hostility toward mothering and are classic candidates for PPD.[51] Maybe we cannot expect to learn too much about ourselves from such psychoanalytic pronouncements.

I doubt there is a personality type that predisposes any of us to PPD. We all undergo the same hormonal changes. For some of us, intensive external pressures, whether from responsibilities, relationship and role fluctuations, loss of identity, or confusion over ourselves as women and now mothers, will place undue burden on the hypothalamic-pituitary network, leading to a crisis among the neurohormones—and consequent symptoms of PPD. The cheerful, idealistic, optimistic woman who sees herself as the strong member of the family is just as likely to experience PPD as is the neurotic, sad type of woman.

"I'm not a schizophrenic, I'm strong," cried Kathy S. on first learning of that diagnosis of her PPD symptoms. But now, with much greater understanding and awareness, she can admit and accept its roots and causes in her own life. "Out of my entire life, having my son has been the most significant and shattering event. It wasn't getting married, or going back to college, that affected me so totally. But just becoming a mother."

Laura S. commented, "When you are in a successful career the idea of depression seems ridiculous. I was used to knowing what I wanted to do, going for it, and succeeding. But dealing with my child was something so unpredictable, I couldn't put him or motherhood in any category, it was not like anything I'd read or done before."

Becoming a parent may shock and surprise us when it brings back angry childhood feelings to people or relationships. Conflicts with mother or father, siblings, or authority figures, depressions from the past, fear of separation or of being submerged, fear of being trapped, may all float dangerously near the surface after long being buried.

For myself, being a parent, not so much of babies but of young preschoolers, brought back depressive feelings I had experienced as a child and adolescent: of entrapment, boredom, a fear that I would never get anywhere or do anything significant in my life. Old anger at my parents' control over me became a repressed anger at the control my children were now exerting over me and my life.

When I was newly and so proudly pregnant for the first time, I remember going to see an editor who had given me a break with my first book. Feeling flushed with my triumph, for the book was to be published in the same year my baby would be born (it felt like a double birth), expecting the usual congratulatory platitudes with which we greet pregnant women socially, I was floored by the rather dour comment, "What on earth do you want a baby for? What's wrong with your life now?" He was a father himself, so I could not put his comment down totally to that male selfishness of not wanting children to clutter up their lives.

I laughed off the question at the time, yet it has stayed with me, lingering to be reawakened while I was writing this book. What an interesting question it was. I like the second part best. "What's wrong with your life now?" I can recall thinking petulantly, "Nothing, of course. This baby will be an extension of my life with my husband, not a narrowing." The idealism, the romantic fantasies, that fuel our drive to reproduce; that image of ourselves as mothers and fathers. But his question had a point. A baby will change the life we have now, whether we accept or deny that change. We should be aware of and prepared for the change. We do not really have to come up with good reasons for wanting babies other than a deep desire, or love for our partners, or wish to perpetuate the species. We will be forced, however, by subconscious or conscious pressures to think out our new lives, alter habits, relearn new life patterns, new psychological survival instincts, before we can move on as parents. PPD is a time of mourning; for saying goodbye to childless freedom and identity. Hello to . . . we are not quite sure what.

PART THREE

◆

Working Mothers

◆

10

◆

DEALING WITH THE CHOICES

When we consider mothers who work either full time or part time out of the home or are self-employed in the home, and when we consider mothers who have given up work to be home full time with their children, we are tackling one enormously complex subject of image, identity, role expectations, and personal energy levels. In this section of the book we will look in depth at these problems and concerns. Time and again women asked me to treat the problems of working mothers seriously; nor would I want to underestimate the position of the nonworking mothers. Both come to their motherhood with hopes, desires, fantasies, and an expectation that their chosen path will lead to happiness. No less than those issues brought up in the last section, the whole topic of work or not to work leads women to the particular stresses and strains of PPD. The "why do I feel like this when I should be so happy?" question is a common complaint of women led to believe they have been offered choices, have accepted the offer, and expect roses all the way.

Just as with any other form of stress or psychological confusion, the biochemical disruption can be extensive for a new mother dealing not only with becoming a mother but with that very real bewildering muddle of just what her image is, as woman, worker, and a mother.

Think of the dreams we harbored as small girls, teen-agers, and young women, of what we would be like as moth-ers. No doubt most of us fondly imagined giving up work—if work was in our fantasies at all—to stay home and be perfect mothers. Think of the expectations fostered by our own mothers, husbands, mothers-in-law, friends, and colleagues, that no real mother ever works. Pit those images against our own complex self-assessment. On the one hand, we know we have an interesting job, perhaps even a passionate commit-ment to a career, we enjoy the companionship of working, and we appreciate the financial independence and the extra income for the family. On the other hand, we are not sure if those are valid justifications for continuing to work after the baby is born. We fear society's condemnation of us as self-indulgent, as cold, rejecting mothers; we fear our inadequacy as women and failure as mothers.

Take that particular psychological stew, add to it com-plications from unavailable, expensive, frightening, or un-known childcare options, criticism from relatives, col-leagues, and friends, and you have a deep pot of potential trouble that can all too easily lead to PPD.

This is a very gender-oriented concern. Few men ever face the question of whether becoming a parent may mean the loss of their work life. How do women make their choice? Unfortunately for most of us, the road to decision is haphaz-ard, wavering, and often arrived at by default. One reason for the sometimes chronic indecisiveness is that we underesti-mate ourselves.

We are not just *one* person, straight as a die, sticking resolutely to one set of beliefs and ideas. When Freud asked, "What do women really want?" no one could give an answer. We are all mixtures of possibilities, limitations, genetic pre-disposition, and environmental supports and pressures. I know one part of me sees an intellectual bohemian, a Vita Sackville-West type, who should have been born to greater wealth and status to indulge in writing and the grand life, leaving others to deal with the domestic, mundane, daily maternal duties. Another side of me longs to be a mother like my own mother: devoted, caring, concerned, involved, al-ways there, seemingly content to lead that proscribed life of husband, home, and children. Yet another side would like to live somewhere exotic, with a husband who did not have to work all day, surrounded by a brood of children, devoting my life to a social, carefree existence, forgetting all worldly pursuits.

Just because we have become mothers does not mean that we all have the same needs and desires. Some of us suffer guilt from returning to work because secretly we prefer to *work* than to mother. Some of us resent working because secretly we would prefer to be *mothering*. Others are just plain confused and conflicted, unable to put a finger on what we would rather be doing, on what would make us happiest. Some of us resent that we need to work for money, and deep down feel that our husbands should be able to provide. Some of us resent the implication that we are selfish because we want to work. These confusions over what we think we should, or would really like to, be doing are easy stimuli of PPD.

GOING BACK TO WORK, NOT REALLY WANTING TO

We cannot guess during pregnancy how we will feel once the baby is born. While pregnant, many of us make conscious decisions that we will have our babies and continue to work, knowing full well we enjoy our jobs, need the money, and are convinced we would not be happy staying home as a housewife. Yet, when the real baby is in our arms, a different vision shades our eyes.

Some find it very hard to leave a new baby in those early weeks, even with a husband, mother, or trusted baby-sitter. The thought of going back to work begins to prey on our minds, growing out of all proportion as an enormous threat. We panic. We are consumed by guilt and anxiety, and depression sets in.

Two women, at different ends of the career spectrum, found out just how unexpected these maternal feelings can be. Gina C. was a twenty-five-year-old analyst for an insurance firm in her hometown, and had been married only a year when her son was born. She had always planned to go back to work. As her firm promised to hold the job open for six weeks, she had to commit herself to that small amount of time off. Gina feared that a lengthier leave of absence might jeopardize her job.

But tiredness and the strangeness of becoming a mother, compounded by worries about money, possible loss of the job, and leaving the baby, left her so badly depressed and given to uncontrollable crying spells that she was in no fit state to return to work once the six weeks were up.

Gina had become phobic about leaving her child, even with her own mother. She never went out with her husband, and their relationship slid quickly into decline. "I couldn't understand the way I was feeling. I was aggressively hostile toward my husband, as well as suffering the depression. I just knew I was an awful person who had wanted for years to settle down and have children. Now all I could do was cry and act hateful."

In the end, Gina extended her leave of absence to two and a half months. Finally the day came when she had to return to the office, desperate with fear, anxiety, and guilt. Her depression was such that "it felt like a conspiracy to keep my child away from me. I resented everyone at work as if it were their fault."

Gina's resentment was a symptom of severe PPD. Knowing nothing about it, she struggled on with work and her conflicting emotions. To make matters worse, she had a new boss who seemed to hate women in general. "His view was that women were just a burden to the work force. If they weren't having babies they were having hysterectomies, and he would do everything he could to get rid of them. I'm sure he thought I'd quit when he put me in a new position I hated."

Still burdened by an uncontrollable desire to cry, Gina would hide in the bathroom, to avoid seeming weak. Slowly her personality returned to normal as she reconciled being a mother and being out of the house all day, and her hormonal system had time to settle down along with her psyche.

Marsha H. had planned to return to her work because, as a television producer, she had struggled to gain her position for years. The birth of a first child, at age thirty-five, did not seem reason enough to give it all up. The money she and Bob were bringing in afforded them a comfortable lifestyle with household help, to which both were adjusted and loath to lose.

Once Jason was born, however, the self-assured Marsha was no longer certain that she even liked her work or wanted to stay on.

"Work is no simple solution for women. I went back full time at first, but had to take a downward drop in position, and a salary cut, just to be able to cope. I used to think about Jason all the time. He was constantly on my mind. I was useless at work." She finally opted to work a four-day week on three-quarters salary, and said ironically, "Then I was busy trying to get into a *more* boring job than that, so I could work just a six-day fortnight."

Marsha moved down from producer's level to what she called a hack job, something she could do with only half her mind. She was fortunate to be able to make such a decision. But Marsha was already afflicted with a very strong case of PPD before she even returned to work. She opted contentedly for the compromise of a less significant position at work, on lower pay, which allowed her more time at home with her baby. Marsha had discovered she did not want the full-time professional career if it prevented her from mothering effectively.

The experience of PPD for many women does seem to offer a time for reassessment of values and priorities in life. The crisis brought about by uncontrollable ·emotions and psychological warfare forces theories and judgments into the open—even if they are only argued about at least they are voiced.

GIVING UP WORK, NOT REALLY HAPPY

"I was used to feeling busy, useful, and independent, then all of a sudden everything changed" wrote Pamela B. about her experience after the birth of her first child. At age thirty-two, with a job in an advertising agency, she left work, giving no commitment on when she would return, imagining she would love being home with her baby. By the fifth month, Pamela knew she had to get back to work or she would go out of her mind. Being at home with her child was not the dream she had imagined.

Pamela was perhaps typical of a lot of women today. Go-getting, not necessarily aggressive or ambitious at work, but determined to have a good, full, and interesting life, before becoming a mother she had held down a full-time job, worked out at the gym, practiced karate, enjoyed aerobics, took music lessons, traveled, got enough sleep, and even had time for her husband and to socialize. Pamela kept up the busy pace to the day of delivery.

"And then what?" she exclaimed. Suffering PPD for four months, she felt dragged out and lethargic, trapped by the daily routine of caring for a baby. She had lost blood until the ninth week postpartum, which accentuated her feeling of fatigue. She resented her husband's freedom and was anxious about money. "All through the pregnancy, I was well supported and looked forward to being a mother. But this felt like being put out to pasture to fend for myself alone at a very crucial time."

For Pamela, PPD had come on about a month after the baby's birth, when she had time and energy enough to realize that her whole previous way of life had changed and that the fantasized image of herself at home with her baby was not coming true. Pamela ran the gamut of typical PPD emotions. "That dragged-out, lethargic, trapped" feeling was earlier described as the later-onset type of PPD (compared to the anxious, agitated, often hallucinatory type of PPD that begins in the first week or two after birth).

Pamela's case was not bad enough to send her to a doctor. But she did return to work, and she forced herself back into a routine of exercise. Slowly, her hormonal system returned to normal, and she began to feel more like her old self.

EAGER TO RETURN TO WORK

Kathy S. accepted early on that she was happiest back at work. "I was *glad* to be back there. I couldn't wait to get away from the house," she said. Kathy knew that being at home all day would make her feel trapped, financially dependent, and unhappy—as her mother had been. She adjusted to her role of working mother more easily than to her role of mother. Yet she came in for plenty of social criticism. Other women at work made sure Kathy heard their comments: "Your child is suffering and you don't need the second paycheck." But Kathy had inner strength from the conviction that being at home with her child would *not* be the best possible solution for either of them.

As we have seen earlier from Kathy's story, the eagerness to get back to work and out of the house was her open admission that full-time motherhood was too hard for her to handle. Kathy had woken up from her C-section delivery wishing she could walk out of the hospital alone. She had not wanted to be associated with her mother. She had not wanted her son to call her mommy. How could the PPD have come upon her so quickly? As far as medical opinion is concerned, PPD symptoms cannot show themselves before the third day postpartum, when the initial hormonal shifts have taken place and sown the seeds for distress. In Kathy's case, the psychological confusion was there in her mind from the minute she gave birth. Her mind had begun working in this negative and distressing way even before the hormonal upheaval. Kathy has described herself as nonfunctional as a mother for at least six months from the time she and her husband took Joe home. Eventually, although they never sought any outside help, as the baby developed happily, as she picked up her working life and outside interests, Kathy's body resettled and she was emotionally able to accept Joe as her son, and herself as his mother.

FLOUNDERING IN INDECISION

Other women flounder in confusion. Aileen B. was just such a case. She was twenty-five when she had her daughter, and had worked until that time as a teacher. Aileen and her husband, John, were not planning a family, for she had had an ovary removed and had been told a number of times that she could never conceive. Baby Jennifer's birth was therefore an utter delight. As the couple had a huge mortgage to feed, Aileen returned to teaching soon after the birth. Aileen described going into such a period of gloom after her return to work that it was the most difficult and disturbing time of her life, because being a working mother went against her deepest wishes and dreams.

"The rest of the world believed it was my responsibility to stay home with the baby and I tended to agree. Finally I gave in to popular demand and compromised by getting a part-time job, doing some teaching in the evenings. My husband worked days and we felt it would be the best of all worlds as we would be with the baby twenty-four hours a day." But then things grew worse. For one thing, they had very little money, and this made Aileen feel trapped. She and her husband had no time together; all their time was for the baby. Aileen felt totally inadequate dealing with Jennifer, and that sense of inadequacy was made worse by everyone telling her to pull herself together and get on with being a wife and mother.

"The depression finally ended when I took control of the situation and went back to work full time," she said. Their marriage survived the stress and, with her return to work for a few years, they managed to clear up some of their financial mess. Then Aileen left work again. "I felt motherhood was my real job, and the one I was happiest with," she commented on her final decision.

Confusion, conflict, weighing the pros and cons . . . one twenty-seven-year-old mother who felt she was forced back to work realized two or three months later that she was really feeling tremendous relief, and consequent guilt, at not being home with her baby. When she confessed to a colleague one day, "It feels good to be back at work," the friend replied wryly, "You mean you almost feel bad about feeling good."

PPD, in these cases of chronic confusion, will only lift when somehow the mother is able to confront the conflicting forces battling it out within her and make a compromise that is right for *her*, not for society.

COMPROMISES

Many working women have found compromises in three- or four-day weeks, or perhaps have arranged to finish their day by 4 P.M. so the child is not in alternative care all day. The choice means putting their career on hold, but, ideally, positions will be there when they resume at full speed a few years later, or the compromise will have shown them that their part-time status suits them.

Even a shortened working week will not magically overcome all the exhaustion and confusion of the dual-role conflict. Married to a successful international businessman, Jeanne N., the thirty-five-year-old book editor, had achieved a certain status in her career before she had her two children. Because she had a live-in baby-sitter who stayed with the family three days and nights a week (and alternate weekends), anyone might assume that she was privileged enough to make an easy and successful blend of career and motherhood. Jeanne did not really want to put her career on hold, but she did want to be able to spend time with her children, so she arranged to work a three-day week in the office and be paid for a four-day week, making up the time at home. Surely someone like Jeanne would not suffer PPD.

The situation has worked out fine for her company, but maybe not so fine for Jeanne. Admittedly compulsive about her work, every evening she would rush out of the office to be home by six-thirty. She had her children in bed by seven-thirty or eight, and then would continue her office work. "My husband traveled a lot and worked late hours too, so it was possible to be still working till ten or eleven—but it was exhausting!" she said.

"I really should have had full-time help. I don't believe now you can do part-time work with part-time help. How can you edit an author's book, or talk with another publisher, when you have a screaming toddler and a four-year-old boy who hates to see you work? I had worked the housekeeping arrangement out that she was there when I was not. That meant the days I was not in the office, I also had to spend time with, or take care of, the children.

"My own mother was amazed I chose this option, because I had hated that she worked when I was a child. Once when she asked me what I wanted for Christmas, I had said, 'A mommy who stays home'! My son does the same to me. He sounds like an orphan sometimes. He'll catch me dressing for work in the morning and wail, 'Who's going to take care of me today?' Then, when I do stay home, he's so excited it's very touching. It isn't easy, is it?"

Jeanne was talking about the experience of trying to be good at both—profession and mothering—with a sinking feeling that she had failed at both. "You want to present a competent image—say to an author—of a working woman and a mother. Then, when they call you, your child is screaming and you feel like a bad mother for not heeding her, or, like a lousy professional for saying to the author, 'I'm sorry I can't do this now, my son hasn't seen me all day.'"

Jeanne was also talking about the kind of PPD that becomes a permanent fixture in our lives: born of the fatigue women obviously feel juggling two or more roles, it is fed by anxiety, tension, the stresses of keeping up with different lives, with pleasing different people—and very often, that ultimate stress of having nothing left over for you.

Jeanne, the woman who had everything, also had an underlying, constant, nagging level of PPD—things were just not quite right.

THE TRIPLE WHAMMY

Women in clerical positions, secretaries, nurses, teachers, or those in the service industries may find their bosses very unsympathetic to the needs or concerns of new mothers. It may not be possible for them to work flex-time hours, or a three- to four-day week, or to finish early in the afternoon. The employer may begin from a position of suspicion that the new mother will be exploiting him or her in taking sick days to look after her child. These women may also find themselves returning to work earlier than women with more flexible jobs, fearing loss of pay, loss of their job, or criticism from within the workplace.

All working mothers are vulnerable to the triple whammy: being pulled apart by loyalties to baby, husband, and job; feeling guilt at not giving any of the triad enough of their time and energy; being exhausted from trying. Ideally, no working woman should have to return to work until at least three months after a baby is born, and preferably nearer five months. By the fifth month the baby should be sleeping longer at night, freeing the mother to cope with a working day. Also, the five-month-old infant will be beginning to show signs of independence, so that leaving him or her is not as wrenching an experience for either mother or child.

If coming home from work proves to be little joy for the harried new mother: if it means struggling to prepare an evening meal, make up bottles, put the baby down, clean the house, and shortly thereafter fall asleep herself, depression may not be far behind. Julia F. was seriously depressed when, after returning to her customer service job eight weeks after the c-section delivery of her baby, total exhaustion had almost literally drained the life out of her. Her doctor suggested antidepressant medication but was unsympathetic to her condition and would not sign a statement for sick leave. Julia described the feeling of the triple whammy: "There just wasn't enough of me to go around."

Fatigue that is experienced by any woman after giving birth will be felt acutely by a mother who has returned to work and who tries to cram too much into one short day.

RESPECTING FATIGUE AS A WARNING SIGNAL

Exhaustion, fatigue, call it what you will, must be the single most common warning of potential collapse of the hormonal system. Trying to do everything, assuming we can handle all our new roles at once, can lead us down the fast track to total disintegration. Dr. Elisabeth Herz put it this way: "Modern women think they can have it all, and I don't blame them. They want both career and motherhood, and why not? But they fail to understand that they must compromise somewhere along the line. They may try everything—but they cannot do it all to perfection."

When the feelings of fatigue and being overstretched just won't go away, something has to give. It may be the hours put in at work, the amount of domestic work done after work hours, the time we can give the baby and other children, or time for our husband. If something doesn't give, the giving-out will come from the new mother.

Liz H. was thirty-three and the mother of a third child, just six weeks old, when she returned to work as an administrative assistant at a local college. Not having worked during the other two children's young years, she was eager to be back with adult company and away from the house.

With classes beginning, work was very heavy in those early weeks of fall, and Liz put in ten- to twelve-hour days, six days a week, for a whole month. "I was so mentally and physically exhausted that at home I screamed at my elder daughters and was unresponsive to my husband. I did not know what was happening to me. But I knew I was on the verge of cracking up. I seriously considered suicide, which is why, looking back, the whole thing was so frightening. I didn't even know I was depressed until my doctor referred me to a psychiatrist, who suggested it. I hadn't seen any of the warning signals because I'd never suffered a severe depression before.

"All I know is I didn't care about anything. I cried frequently and was absolutely miserable. I just thought I was a terrible person. I really wish more was known about PPD. It would make it so much easier if we felt we were not the only ones going through this. The joke is I went back to my obstetrician to tell him about it, and to say it seems I had PPD. He didn't agree with me!"

Liz had never been depressed before, she knew nothing about PPD, and she failed to connect her warning signals. Liz had never given her system time to settle down with the heavy responsibilities found at work. More than that, because she had stayed home when her other daughters were babies, she no doubt felt confused about her new role as working mother. The overload on her body and mind was evident.

QUALITY TIME OR QUANTITY TIME?

"Quality time" has become the watchword from the battle lines of the beleaguered working mother camp. Indeed, the plethora of playgroups, nursery schools, and day camp activities that are available in most cities and many towns for children whose mothers do *not* go to work is evidence that society has caught up. Many mothers now accept that a young child may be happier *not* spending all his or her time with the mother alone. Even experts like Dr. Spock have grudgingly admitted that it is good for mothers to have time to themselves, for babies and toddlers to learn to mix with others, to play in groups.[52]

As Dr. Herz comments, however, "quality time" should not be used by working mothers to justify too little time with their children. A young child does need a lot of both the mother's and father's time, since some *quantity* of time is necessary to make it quality time. All our interactions with our children need not be happy, cuddly, or adventurous. There is space in our lives for argument, irritation, and boredom as well. A child who grows up feeling comfortable with these emotions from his or her own parents will find dealing with the outside world less bewildering.

A very busy working mother, with a full-time career that demands long hours away from home, with maybe a commute there and back adding to those hours, and additional "homework" hours, may find herself with little time on a *daily* basis with her baby or young child and can suffer consequent acute guilt that she may be depriving her child of some fundamental nurturing care that should be offered by the mother. And she may be right.

What if you cannot see your child every morning and every evening, at least; or what if whole days go by without him or her catching sight of you in your smart work clothes or even nightclothes? Guilt is one of the strongest emotions felt by new mothers. Forget love, happiness, or warm nurturing feelings, most women probably know guilt better than they do love! Very often the mother who has such a hectic schedule has already come to a compromise with her husband that he will be able to take some of the childcare shifts. Maybe she has a close relative who is able to be around the home for stretches at a time: certainly the constant love of a grandparent is highly beneficial to a young child.

Before any of us looks accusingly at a new mother, we should bear in mind that for generations, wealthy families in Britain and Europe, and many in the United States, hired outsiders—nannies, governesses, au pairs—and that the mothers and fathers were conspicuously absent in the day-to-day raising of the children. For centuries, even further back in history, women of high birth used wet nurses to breast-feed their children, and those new mothers probably had little contact with their children until they were at least on their feet and able to mouth polite endearments to their mothers.

It is only very recently, in the twentieth century, that society or women themselves have deemed it necessary for the mother to be with her child at all times—up to whatever age the expert of the moment says it is healthy for her to do so—or maintained that only the mother can offer good nurturing care for her child. I cannot accept that all those children from past centuries grew up emotionally deprived if their mothers did not personally devote their undivided attention to their infancy.

In an article on the subject, called "The Working Mother as Role Model," Anita Shreve reported that experts had found many positive side effects to the current increase in mothers working out of the house for long hours of the day. Dr. Samuel Ritvo and Dr. Kyle Pruett, professors of psychiatry at Yale University, presented evidence that seeing mother and father as nurturer and achiever had been good for children of either sex. Shreve wrote, "Child specialists suggest that the next generation of women may be less troubled about pursuing both 'masculine' and 'feminine' endeavors. Women may be able more easily to combine career and family life—a juggling act that stymies many women today and often leads to feelings of inadequacy, stress and guilt."[53]

Shreve quotes Betty Friedan as saying, "The daughters of women today are more assertive and have a clearer sense of themselves. They will have both their careers and their children without guilt." Boys too are seen to gain from having working mothers, as they may grow into men more sensitive to the needs of women. "The next generation of lawmakers, both men and women, will have had mothers who are working women," said Friedan.

I know from the women I have met that busy professional working mothers, or those working awkward shifts, go to great lengths to give time to their children—often to the detriment of their personal lives.

Having a child does mean taking time out of our own lives. A child does feed off some part of us, devours some portion of our former selves. No relationship can grow without long stretches of time together. Relations between husband and wife wither and die if they spend too much time apart. But children can feel mothering tangibly in her care and concern, in a warm, happy, secure, interesting home—not only in her daily physical presence and ability to bake cookies.

Of course there have always been parents who have been negligent of their children, in their absence or in the lack of love or life in their homes. One new mother, Mary S., was very much aware of that kind of negligence while, ironically, ensnaring herself in a way of life that very nearly carried on the sins of her parents to her own child.

Mary: On the Treadmill

Newspaper reporter Mary S. had in some ways condemned herself to exhaustion, because the housekeeper who took care of fifteen-month-old Noah was employed to be there only when Mary or her husband, Bruce, were out of the apartment. This meant that Mary had no time to herself. There was not a minute of the day, she explained, that was not preordained to some duty. The minute Mary or Bruce returned home, the housekeeper left for the day. Mary had no time for creative projects, for putting away her winter clothes, or for paying bills. In the end, even Mary saw she had to devise a different plan for all their sakes. One of her new resources was to take *more* time from her daily newspaper job to be with Noah. Somehow by giving him more time, she felt less that she was being robbed of her own. So, instead of lunch one day she took Noah to a birthday party. One morning a week, she arranged to go in to work later so she could take him, herself, to a neighborhood playgroup with other mothers.

Mary was perhaps made aware of the dangers of not being with a child for enough time, from her own childhood experience. Her mother had never worked, yet she and her brother were brought up by housekeepers (her father died when she was two). "I don't even remember going on vacation with my mother, and my brother and I had a very unhappy childhood. I was always separated from my parents, which is probably why I have found leaving Noah so traumatic.

"I have tried to give him a stable routine. I don't leave for work until nearly eleven, and one of us is home by six-thirty or seven-thirty. We spend time with Noah and he goes to bed quite happily before eight. He really seems content, which is why I hope we are doing something right."

We met Mary previously in the section on older mothers. Having just turned forty, juggling to keep up a working life on the newspaper, her personal creative life as a writer of art history books, some semblance of a social life with her husband (and a professional social life too), and be a mother to Noah, she confessed then that she felt so racked by a mental rather than physical exhaustion that she had become very absentminded and anxiety-ridden. She was perpetually rushing to be places, get projects finished, with a sense of always failing. Mary was suffering a mild version of PPD that emerges as a chronic condition—it may go on throughout the child's early life and continue through the birth of the next baby. The fatigue, confusion, juggling of roles, guilt induced by her own mother's negligence, and fears that she herself would not be a good mother to Noah had all contrived to create this state of just-barely-ticking-by exhaustion so common in many working mothers today.

CHILDCARE WITHOUT GUILT

Childcare that helps the mother as much as it helps the child may be the most important investment we make in our working-mother lives. Childcare is big business. More than 62 percent of families (in the United States) have both parents out in the workplace (an increase from 40 percent in 1960). In a survey of 5 million mothers with at least one child of preschool age, taken in June 1982, 14.8 percent placed their child in a nursery school or day care center, and 22 percent left their child for some part of the day in the home of a nonrelative.

Despite occasional scares about the safety and reliability of day care centers, or the qualifications of nursery schools, the vast majority operate responsibly. There is as yet in the United States no government protection of these private institutions, and even little checking in the states on how they are run. It is left to the parents to judge the institution, whether the fees are appropriate, whether the childcare is good, and whether they are happy with the care givers.

The flare-ups that reach our eyes about badly run or abusive centers always give ammunition to the anti-working-mother brigade. But, if we can assume that women work for reasonable and realistic choices, that children would not necessarily be any happier if we all stayed home full time, after we have checked out the particular institution we should look at how the form of childcare is working for *us*. Stressful childcare arrangements will aggravate PPD.

For a newborn's care, the ideal situation would be the child's grandmother, aunt, or other close relative. Many mothers use a day care center or shared baby-sitter. If we can afford it, an exclusive baby-sitter or nanny who comes to our home might be the best solution. We have to feel confident that the baby-sitter will provide love as well as sanitary care, but we also have to feel confident that the baby-sitter is not usurping our child's affection for mommy right there under our own roof.

Judith Klein commented that it is not unusual for the mother to be jealous of the loving relationship being developed between her baby and the sitter. If this does happen, one antidote would be to encourage the baby-sitter to attend a mother-infant playgroup, so her time together with the child is not so exclusive. The kind of personality we choose for a full-time baby-sitter is also very important. The *fit* has to be right for the mother. Some mothers prefer a grandmotherly type, who they feel will dote on the baby and yet not substitute for mommy. Others prefer a motherly woman, who in effect mothers and supports the working mother herself. Others prefer to work with a younger girl, with whom they have the sense of being in control.

Marsha H. finally opted for a younger girl as her nanny. She hired a college-trained nursery nurse, who knew that this was her *job*. "She is not a substitute for me. I told her from the beginning, 'I don't work because I don't want to be with Jason, but for other reasons. You have to fit in with my routine, and my wishes.' She talks to Jason about me a lot during the day, and they come to the window to watch me come home in the car. I feel pretty comfortable about it now."

Whether we have childcare in the home or out will depend on how much we can afford, space at home, and on our own schedule. Childcare out of the home demands a regular work routine and ease of transportation to and fro. If childcare is giving us too much stress, we will always be rushing: watching the clock, hurrying from work, worrying that the bus or subway or traffic conditions will make us late, feeling exhausted as we trek home with the baby or pre-schooler to face the prospect of cooking an evening meal and getting the child to bed before collapsing ourselves. We make ourselves vulnerable to PPD.

We should also watch out for demands the child may make, indicating that a change in the care situation might be necessary. By eighteen months to two years, if we are using a baby-sitter in the home, a toddler may be feeling bored and lacking company. The baby-sitter may not like to get out and about as much as we would, may not sit in the park or join playgroups with stimulating activities. If we find ourselves worrying that a toddler is bored, it will be time for a change. A sitter's hours or routine can be changed. A playgroup or, if the child is two and a half to three years old, a morning nursery school can alleviate the boredom and break up the routine, so the sitter is only picking the child up for the afternoons.

A child's crying may be more than manipulative behavior designed to induce *more* guilt in the working mother. It can also be a warning that he or she has outgrown the situation, is feeling the stress we are under. Maybe the child is being understimulated or overtired, is not getting individual attention, or is feeling lonely or rejected. We don't have to give up working but we may have to rethink and reform the schedule.

We will have guilt about leaving a child with an alternate

care giver, that goes without saying, but we can check, and double-check, that everything is being done for the best. Childcare is going to cost us up to a half of our salary (if not more). Yet the answer might even be to spend a little more. If it eases our stress and makes the child more comfortable, it will be worth it in the end.

11
♦

PROFESSIONAL AND EXECUTIVE WOMEN

Surely successful women are not special cases for suffering PPD? You may believe, as do so many of the women in question *before* they become mothers, that these women are all set to be the new superwomen of our society. They are used to achievement, organizing, and dealing with people and situations. They have status in the working world, probably can negotiate for time off or easier working hours more successfully than a woman with a less flexible job; even better, they have money and can afford good childcare, thereby alleviating some of the guilt. What could they possibly have to complain about?

"We think we can handle anything because we're older and have advanced in our careers. Yet when we take home a tiny infant and realize the baby is totally dependent on us for everything, it's just overwhelming," marveled Suzette S., who, at thirty-six, had a fine career in banking, and was by now the mother of two small daughters. Suzette had been married for eight years before having a child and felt she was ready for anything. "But I was sure wrong!"

Some of those very qualities I have enumerated can make the transition from professional or executive woman into working mother much harder than anyone would have imagined.

Dr. Elisabeth Herz has seen a lot of professionals in her practice. Just as Suzette disarmingly admitted, career women do not always find the path to motherhood and career as primrose-lined as they had fondly imagined. As Dr. Herz sees it, the professional or executive woman has left behind much of the conventional role of women just to get where she is. Becoming a mother pulls her back to a more traditional role: "They have learned to see themselves as different kinds of women; yet once they have been pregnant, given birth, and nursed a baby, they know they are just like other women—and yet they are *not*." The career woman often has no role model for her type of work, the long hours, the dedication and loyalty demanded by her job or company. She has no role model for this new kind of motherhood either. The result may be a woman caught between opposing demands.

Inadequacy, often felt by new mothers, can hit the successful, organized, career woman hard. Used to being in control, meeting deadlines, working under pressure, pleasing her boss, she is not accustomed to dealing with a baby who will not sleep or will not be satisfied, or to dealing with the encroaching fears about her own identity or sanity. Isolated from other women, she seems to be neither a real professional nor a real mother.

Judith Klein commented: "Career women have long identified their work as a major source of gratification. Once they are mothers they no longer feel that same gratification toward the job itself; something else is pulling at their attention. Also, the gratification they are used to feeling at work is not so easily found in caring for an infant. There are no thank-you's, no good reports, no salary increases, no boss popping his or her head around the door to say, 'Well done.' "

Laura: Career Woman, Mommy, or Neither?

By the age of thirty-three, Laura S. was so used to her career in management with an industrial firm that she approached her pregnancy and impending motherhood just as she would a management project. She handled her pregnancy well, buying the right executive pregnancy clothes, attending exercise and Lamaze classes, not putting on too much weight. She obviously had not a clue what having a baby would really be like.

"I worked to the day before delivery, everything went fine. I thought I'd covered my tracks well as a corporate woman. I even scheduled to go in for a couple of meetings a week after the birth, imagining I'd be able to leave the baby with my mother—after all, what's a kid? I had no idea. Nobody anywhere, in Lamaze classes or any of the books, told me, 'Hey, wait a minute. I don't mean to be scary but there's no way you'll be able to go in to the office the first week after giving birth.' It was a nightmare for me.

"I'm a career woman. Yet I started thinking of myself as a mommy. I'm with a very male-oriented company and no one expected me to come back. Those middle-management guys have wives back home in the suburbs and feel a woman's place is at home with the kids. It's even been depressing for me at work, because I find I'm more 'female' now. I get upset and confused, want to cry. I think about Bobby when I should be thinking about work. Being at home and depressed would be helplessness, but this is hopelessness, because I can't do anything right. Bobby is up at nights, and I have a business meeting in the morning. I've never been this emotional before."

One of Laura's problems had been the lack of support she found from other women. Having moved to the suburbs before they started their family, Laura discovered herself isolated in that community, surrounded by stay-at-home mothers. She hunted for a support group either in the suburban area or in the city where she worked, anything that would bring together a group of women *after office hours*. When we met, Laura had been unable to find any such group.

The books on childcare, she pointed out, aim at stay-at-home mothers. "They tell you what to expect each month of your child's development. 'This is the month the child finally falls in love with you, you're the number-one person,' they read. I have a live-in baby-sitter, and I read this section and thought, 'Great, now Bobby is going to fall in love with Lynn. He spends most of his time with her.'" Laura's identity problem was acute.

Perhaps this was the real clue to her mental distress. The

mere fact that she went back to the office for some meetings the week after childbirth would not in itself create a problem. (Laura returned to full-time work after six weeks.) Many women have found getting straight back into office life, if only for one or two days a week, of great help in adjusting to motherhood, and to working motherhood—it has meant not losing touch with their work and their colleagues, thus avoiding being cast in the role of outsider, which women necessarily worry about in today's competitive world.

As we learned in the section on breast-feeding, Laura had first had a problem with the image of herself as a mother. She had quickly lost excess weight after childbirth but had been unable to breast-feed. She had serious doubts about her femininity, which emerged in the acute sense of isolation she felt living in the suburbs, surrounded by stay-at-home mothers, commuting to the city for work, where she was surrounded by male colleagues at her level.

Laura's PPD was evident to herself and to her husband, Nick. But, at the time we met, she had found no help from doctors or books and continued to feel mild despair. She could get by, she said. Her work was not suffering, but her marriage was showing the strains, and her relationship with five-month-old Bobby was still tense. Physically, Laura's PPD could have been evident to doctors too, from the first few days after birth when the milk did not come into her breasts. The hormone prolactin was not being released in sufficient quantities. Her endocrinological system was not flourishing or functioning as it should. One other physical symptom was that even at five months after childbirth, and without breast-feeding, Laura's hair was falling out. If only more were generally understood about PPD, this rather sad young woman would not have had to undergo such a long, lonely time of distress.

THE DRIVE FOR PERFECTION

Executive women put heavy demands on themselves to be perfect. But if they expect to be perfect as professionals and as mothers, they will not succeed at either. Worse, the dissatisfaction with themselves if they fail the "perfect" test can lead to breakdown. Dr. Herz emphasized three main realities executive women should bear in mind to ease this destructive drive:

1. They may fall behind in their careers in the early years of their children's lives. They may not be as good at work nor be able to earn promotions or raises, because drive and ambition will likely decline due to simple exhaustion, primary satisfaction in mothering, or other factors.
2. They will have to hire help, probably full time, unless they happen to have a husband whose hours are flexible enough to take a major role in childcare.
3. They will not be available to their children as and when they might wish they could be.

These realities, if ignored, may result in an unwarranted sense of guilt when a woman faces her lack of energy for coping with husband, child, and career.

TOO SELF-CRITICAL

The more high-powered, the more successful a woman is in her career, the harder she may find adjustment to mothering. Dr. Herz pinpointed another cause of distress that may lead to serious PPD, which any professional mother should consider.

Professional women tend to be compulsive and overly conscientious. They need this personality trait to have achieved their position. Used to striving for perfection and generally quite self-critical, they are—Dr. Herz perceives— too negative and unrealistic in their self-evaluations.

"The gap between a woman's unrealistically idealized image of mother and career woman and her overcritical assessment of what she is may be very great. The wider the gap the worse she feels. What may follow is a total loss of self-confidence with a quick slide into depression. It's one of the dynamics we see over and over again."

Sara G., a thirty-six-year-old lawyer, had been delighted to have her first baby, although in retrospect she suffered a slight depression that had been camouflaged by returning immediately to work, with full-time help, continuing to lead a very active life, and becoming pregnant again shortly after. The second baby was born eighteen months later.

After this second birth, Sara's depression was overwhelming. It was not picked up by her doctor or obstetrician. It was quite a while before she was referred to one of the small band of psychosomatic ob/gyns available. By this time, although still at work, Sara was almost nonfunctional, with a severe sleep disorder, and her work had reached a nonproductive end. Her sense of self-worth was practically nonexistent. She had begun to overeat, and the weight problem was only worsening her low self-esteem.

Sara was started on a course of antidepressants while working closely with a psychiatrist for three months to deal with the lowered self-esteem and confused identity. Discussing a case like this, Dr. Herz explained, "Sadly, some psychiatrists are not really tuned into PPD. They delve too far into the past. I believe we need to know something about a woman's background and her responses and defenses to previous crises, but not necessarily to explore childhood conflicts and relationships.

"The mixture of antidepressants and short-term therapy can be very successful. I will talk to a woman, and when she begins to berate herself, I say, 'Well, tell me what you did yesterday.' When she lists all the things she has accomplished, I point out that she has been doing a lot, and an awful lot very well. But she cannot see it. We discuss in detail what sort of compromises she might be able to make in her own life, either with work or mothering, that would ease the burden."

The professional or executive woman is especially vulnerable to PPD. Because she is used to success and keeping her life in control, a sense of failure or of emotional extremes can be too hard to deal with. In the past, she might have sought a solution in handing the child over to a full-time nanny, returning to the safe security of her own work, and escaping the problems. But today, with more enlightened and concerned care available to her, she can resolve her problems with greater insight.

BUSINESS TRIPS OR TIME AWAY ON YOUR OWN

Can the professional woman safely, or justifiably, take time away from her child—anything from three days to two weeks—to go on a business trip, attend a sales conference, go on a brief vacation, or simply have some time to think and be alone? Women's views on this question will vary, depending on the amount of guilt already felt about leaving the child during the work day, the amount of support received from the husband or other close family, and the mother's own feelings of separation from her child. Another variable will be the level of her ambition or concern about competition within her company.

In my own life, if possible, I travel without my children for a four- to ten-day period each year to give myself some free time in which to pursue business, meet with friends, make necessary contacts, and let that old childless identity breathe again. I doubt I would go for any longer than that brief interlude, during which, I hope, the children have scarcely had time to accept that I am gone before I am back again. Sometimes I find myself imagining, however, that the high-powered career woman who dashes off to three-day conferences or takes important sales trips finds it easier to leave her child with her full-time housekeeper, easier to justify that she must go for her work; easier at least than being forced to admit, "*I am doing this for myself. Time away from motherhood is good for me; helps me put my new life in perspective.*"

The question begs other ones: how do we blend ambition and career with the pressures and concerns of motherhood? Or, *Who is going to sacrifice whose life to whom?* Does motherhood have to equal self-sacrifice?

I have in mind a young actress, married to another actor. While their baby, Ben, was an infant, Carrie D. tended to stay home, but she never forgot her desire to succeed in the theater, which had been as strong as her husband's. They lived in a major city near potential work. But, as luck would have it, her husband, Don, landed a great part in a repertory company five hundred miles away. He took the job, and Carrie was left on her own bringing up Ben for stretches as long as three months at a time. There was not enough money to pay airfares back and forth any more often than perhaps once during the three-month separations.

Ben went to nursery school, and I used to see Carrie looking not exactly depressed but not elated, either. She was hunting for work but finding it hard going. Then I didn't see her for a while. Ben was being picked up from school by a baby-sitter. Eventually I heard that Carrie had landed work—as luck would have it, just like her husband—outside of the city. It was not as far away as Don's company, but in a small town an hour's ride away. Carrie had to stay out of town three nights a week, rushing home the other four. "Who looks after Ben?" was my first thought. They had a baby-sitter sleep over those three nights. "Does he mind?" I asked my source. She laughed. "Ben's an independent, feisty little boy. I have him over to play sometimes after school. It strikes me now that all this stuff about staying home with your kids is non-sense. Carrie brought Ben up to be independent. He's used to dealing with both his parents' absences. He knows she'll be back. Acting is important to Carrie and I think she was right not to turn that work down, even though her husband is out of town too. It's not easy getting acting jobs!"

We make our own decisions based on our blend of ambition, guilt, fear of harming the child, desire to raise an independent child who respects his or her mother's work, and availability of the father or perhaps a grandmother to help out in our absence. We no doubt take the advice of pediatricians and child psychologists and digest the material we wish or are prepared to hear on whether they feel it is safe to leave an infant, a toddler, a two-year-old, three-year-old, etc.

The infant is the easiest to leave for short periods, as long as you are not breast-feeding. Good loving alternative care can be given without the child even knowing mother is not there. Toddlers from a year to two years can be very difficult to leave behind: their emotions are so outward and so passionate that it may be heart-wrenching to witness the pain of their separation. Even three-year-olds who speak well may be quick to pierce the heart with pleas not to be abandoned. But the decision, ultimately, must lie with the individual rather than with what society feels is best. Her work, her need to make that particular trip, her personal development and need for space and time, are all as important considerations as is the welfare of the child. Mother counts too.

If you have a grandparent or another close relative nearby, the best solution to your absence would probably be to pay for outside help in the home (so you are not expecting granny to do all the work) and then invite the relative to your house as a *treat* for the child and as a buffer zone of stability and security in your place.

WEEKEND MOTHERING

One of our much-loved images of working mothers is that they miss their children so badly all day and all week, they long for weekends so they can spend precious time with them. That notion may be the stuff of fairy tales and tends to negate the very real personal needs of mothers and fathers. If we have worked five days, if we have lived by the clock and schedule, come the weekend we crave some time to ourselves. Time to catch up on laundry and household work, buy clothes or birthday presents or groceries; do some cooking for the week ahead, take exercise classes or play tennis, or simply get together with friends or relatives. How do we find that time?

Weekends are also for marriages, for spending time together as husband and wife, for love and socializing, and even for sex! As parents we yearn for those lazy weekends devoted to self-indulgent pursuits. So why not admit it? Now that we are parents thoughts about weekends tend to be, "How can we best entertain the child, get some time to ourselves together, and allow time off individually?"

Even Jeanne N., with her live-in help on alternate weekends, furrowed her brow at the question of weekends. I imagined her life must be a dream compared to most. "Oh, no, they're really hard on us as a couple," she said. "There is no rest or peace. I see my husband very little during the week, with our busy schedules, and although the housekeeper might take the children out to the park for an hour or so, basically we're there with the kids.

"I usually have a lot of reading to catch up on, maybe manuscripts to be worked on, authors to talk to. My husband wants to relax, play tennis. I plead with him that I have work to do. I see that look of frustration in his eyes."

We can all think of one or two women who seem to combine successfully a position as corporate vice president with a happy marriage, one or two children, and the roles of stunning cook, hostess, and interior decorator as well. But a normal human being does not have the energy, emotional strength, or intellectual tenacity to cope perfectly with career, deal lovingly with her husband, give to her children the amount of love and time they, or she, would like, and spend time on domestic duties that suit her self-image as a woman.

We have to accept our own limitations, and some unwelcome compromises. If we don't, we will be leaving ourselves vulnerable to PPD brought on by exhaustion and an overcritical judgment of ourselves that everything we do is a failure. The psychological and the physiological march in tandem for the professional and executive woman as they do for any other mother. Believing she can do everything, refusing to see the need for compromise, and denying the real psychological impact of the lack of role models for her type of mothering can all too quickly lead a driven woman to total collapse and severe PPD.

12

◆

WORKING AT HOME

COMPROMISE OR CHOSEN PATH?

A woman's self-image helps program her for this kind of compromise. In my own life, fantasies had never included myself as a housewife and mother or as a high-powered executive mother. The road to my compromise was plotted long before I had a baby, following some preconceived blueprint of acceptable female behavior that was less consciously worked out than achieved by instinct. I gave up a well-paid, interesting newspaper job in my late twenties to become a freelance home-based writer. Maintaining to the outside world that I had made the bold move because I needed to force myself into insecurity to become a real writer, I also had secret reasons I did not brag about to colleagues or friends.

In the not-so-distant future, though I was not yet married and showed little sign of ever being so, I wanted to be a mother. When I had a child, I would want to be at home, as my mother had always been, to greet my young family coming in from school. Unlike my mother, I knew I would want to keep up my work and felt I should get started now, to be ready when the day came. I was, in effect, feathering the nest.

In my fantasies, you notice, I had conveniently omitted the first five or six years before a child even goes to school to be so warmly greeted home again by the smell of freshly baked cookies. So much for fantasies. Nor had I sat down with a calculator and forecast the cost of childcare and the possibility of my work as a writer being able to fund such a luxurious way of life. Ultimately, however, it has been a good compromise for me.

I can feel like a real mother, yet I am not totally stuck at home. I know that I would hate spending all day, every day, with my children. I am not God's gift to motherhood, have little patience, get easily bored, and do not want to spend my days helping my daughters cut and paste. On the good days, I work contentedly at home, and when the baby-sitter brings my youngest one home from nursery school, we stop to chat before going on with our separate functions.

When the children were younger I had no formal baby-sitting routine, as I was not earning enough to justify the cost. Determinedly I enforced a nap routine and *stole* two or more hours a day in which to work. I craved that time, needed to impose the regimen. My mind needed the freedom and liberty of concentration and focused thought. Any work acts as a tremendous release from the strains of motherhood. Just two hours of concentrated thought on some project of my own, on adult concepts, seemed to be enough to repair the ravages left by dealing with young children.

There is more to it than that. My freelance work gets me out of the house. I meet other adults (not necessarily mothers) and get to talk about things dear to my heart (other than toilet training). Some days are great fun, racing around researching a topic and coming home to my children. Other days are a plain hard grind, working all day at the typewriter, not daring to take time to read the newspaper, or talk to a friend, or indulge myself at all, then having to make dinner and deal with the children. At the end of my working day, the farthest I have to walk is from study to kitchen, there to meet two cranky children, who have to be fed, bathed, listened to, loved, played with, and argued with, and finally put to bed.

And then, oh joy, I get to baby-sit for them and maybe snatch a few hours' more work in the evening. Those are the bad days.

Is working at home really a compromise between the working world and the mothering world? Those women who have taken the option feel they are getting some of the best of both worlds. They are perhaps instinctively, as I can see in myself, avoiding various levels of potential threats of PPD: avoiding the role and identity confusion of the full-time or executive working mother, her exhaustion and inability to find time for all the priorities in her life; and avoiding the traps of loss of identity, loss of financial independence, and the gradual mental vegetation of many stay-at-home mothers who have little outlet for release or escape.

I am not implying that all working mothers should make such a compromise. As the New York *Times Magazine* article "The Working Mother as Role Model," referred to earlier, has shown, babies and young children of full-time working mothers seem to be more than usually alert and contented, either in day care or with an alternative care giver, and they are socially active and perform well on adaptive-skills tests. Perhaps this is so because they have *two* stimulating parents. (Though I beg to differ with the implication that stay-at-home mothers, by definition, are nurturing, warm, and *non*-stimulating!) In my daughter's nursery school, this conversation between two four-year-old girls was reported: discussing what they wanted to be as grown-ups, one replied, "Oh, I don't want to be a lawyer. All mommies do that. It's boring."

WHY THE COMPROMISE SOMETIMES FAILS

Working at home notoriously does not pay well; there are no benefits, no sick pay, no holiday pay, and precious little in the way of status or prestige (unless you get lucky). For the ambitious or career-minded it is therefore often very much a compromise, taken in an effort to fit more mothering and less daily work into their lives. Unfortunately, the situation many women find themselves in, once they become mothers, is not really being sure what they want out of the working world and what they feel they should put in. Then the compromise seems to fail, for these women will not feel adequately rewarded either financially or in terms of status. I doubt their choice of work by itself leads to PPD; their confusion was already strong enough to set off depression.

Ellen C. is such a woman. A former lawyer, now turned forty, with two nearly school-age children, she told me she only gave up work because she could not make up her mind whether she really wanted to continue in a full-time lawyer's position or whether she wanted to be home with her new baby. When her first child was six months old, she quit her job, anxious and paranoid that the sitter she had hired was mistreating her baby. The second baby came within the next year, and suddenly Ellen found that a free decision had become cemented as a way of life. "But I certainly was not made to be a housewife. So I drifted into part-time legal work that I could do from home. I cannot say I am happy, no. I don't any longer know what would make me happy. Going back full-time into a prosecutor's office would not be the answer. But then neither is this stateless, nameless sort of position I hold right now."

Ellen admits that her depression is a chronic but mild one that has become the predominant feature of her life. Whatever germ of PPD set in, in those first few weeks after the baby's birth, has never lifted. Ellen feels out of control of her life. She resents her husband's earning power. Even the fact that they can afford to pay for private schools and Ellen contributes nothing toward that expense makes her feel she accomplishes nothing. "My husband is as good at dealing with the children as I am. He doesn't do more because he has to be out of the house. So where does that leave me? I'm pretty much a nobody these days."

As for Ellen's freelance legal work, for which she has been able to convert a basement into an office, she finds it unsatisfactory because of the long hours spent for little compensation, when she is fully aware how much lawyers can demand in the outside world.

"Also, I don't have a decompression chamber like my

husband does. I may cut myself off from the children, who are brought home by the sitter, to be entertained by her until I'm finished for the day. But it means I walk straight from the office, up the stairs, to deal with arguing, crying, hungry kids. I get angry at my husband again at those times, wondering why he never gets home early enough to take over those duties. But then how many husbands do?"

13

$\blacklozenge$

STAY-AT-HOME MOTHERS

Why do some mothers choose to stay home with their children? That may be a strange question in a world where society is still pushing the importance of that very option, still critical of women who do work once they are mothers. For many women that is the only choice. Maybe as little girls, teenagers, young adult women seeking love and partnership, they saw themselves in the image of full-time nurturing mother. They promised themselves that when they had a baby they would give up working, if only for five years or so.

Once they are mothers, they know a child needs them around, just as their mothers were around for them (or, if not, as they dreamed their mothers would be). They intend to give their child the best possible start in life. They do not trust leaving their baby with a stranger. They would never use day care centers because they believe it is the parents' duty to raise their own children. Who else could possibly give the love needed to their child? Husband, mother, close friends, all expected them to give up working and to do the right thing by the child.

There may be financial reasons for this choice as well. The sort of work many women are involved in does not cover the cost of baby-sitting or alternative care, or does not interest them sufficiently to offer an alternative to mothering as a way of life.

Thankfully, fewer and fewer women are feeling out of control over the decision. Somehow they blend the various forces at work into a valid credo for living. In my own urban neighborhood, the majority of women seem to have opted for full-time motherhood. These are not young girls in their early twenties, with not a clue as to what they are doing or why. For the most part they are women in their late twenties and early to late thirties.

I see them as the "class of '68." There they are, chatting with one another in the playground, content to pass their days entertaining one or two muddied preschool children. Their days are domestically oriented, organized around the child's program rather than theirs. Yet they are not complaining; they are not characters from Marilyn French's *The Women's Room;* they don't feel they are suffering from insensitive husbands who have no idea what their day or routine is like. They don't feel they have sacrificed their career for their husband's, nor do they feel unduly exploited. Content and at ease with the decision to drop the joys of working for the joys of motherhood, they feel perhaps an extra layer of contentment in a deeply rooted aura of self-righteousness.

Stay-at-home mothers as a cultural group tend to be on the defensive about their image and lifestyle choice. One of the saddest outcomes of this flight behind the barriers of self-defense is that full-time mothers have little understanding of or sympathy for working mothers, and vice versa. The two sides appear to be so firmly entrenched in their own dogma that they might be at war. "If you go to work, why have a child in the first place? You never get to see your child during the day, so why become a mother?" argue the stay-at-homes. "They have no identity, they'll be stuck in a few years' time with no work, no money, and their husbands will leave them. What's so great about staying home, when all I see in the supermarkets is these women yelling at their kids or hitting them?" argue the working mothers.

SOME JUST AREN'T SUITED TO STAYING HOME

Stay-at-home mothers have a lot of emotional investment in their mothering, and denial that anything might be wrong is strong in their psyches. PPD can strike stay-at-home mothers as fiercely, if not more so, than any other woman. Worse, their symptoms are more likely to go unchecked as, culturally, they are expected to suffer or react this way and, financially, have not the wherewithal to seek professional help.

Many women who make the choice to be full-time mothers may, along the way, realize it was not the right decision for them. This change of self-image can be hard to reconcile with that self-righteousness. Such mothers may find themselves locked in a resentful, hostile battle with their husbands, expressed either in sexual jealousy or envy of his advancement at work and his comparatively glamorous life. Others may sink into swift decline, finding the cabbage-patch mentality taking them over like an invader from outer space.

When Nancy E., for example, was twenty-five years old and had her first daughter, she had been ecstatic at being a full-time mother. "I just wasn't cut out to be a working mother. At first I had to go back to teaching, for the money, but every moment of my baby's development was too precious to share with someone else. So I gave up teaching and, to take in extra money, I started baby-sitting for friends. I loved taking care of infants, and never had any problems."

When Nancy had the second baby, at age thirty-one, she discovered she had changed in the intervening years in ways she did not recognize. She no longer wanted to be a full-time mother and housewife. This reversal contradicted everything she had ever believed about herself, from the days of playing with dolls and waiting to grow up to be a mommy.

"I had always seen myself as a typical housewife, baking bread, cleaning the house, making cookies. But then it dawned on me, after the second child, that I *hate* housework. I just didn't want to go back to all that."

Immediately after the baby, she felt confined to the

house again, after years of working with her husband in their own business. Nancy said, "I still believed women were supposed to be home with their children, so my picture of myself just didn't fit any more. Yet I also knew I needed something more. I needed my work." Nancy, as we saw earlier, suffered a severe PPD. Her road out of that crisis was partly smoothed by a shared decision with her husband that she would go back into the business two days a week. The treatment she received from the psychiatrist, antidepressant medication, alone would not have shifted the PPD. It took time and honest talking with her husband before she began to fit the pieces together and learn that some of the strain on her psyche had been imposed by her own idealized fantasy of herself as a full-time mother, which just did not fit the reality of her life nearly a decade later.

A MOVE BEYOND TOTAL MOTHERHOOD

PPD may be a sign for some women that they need to branch out in a wider direction, away from total motherhood. Lucy C. was another example of just those forces of change. At twenty-six, after the birth of her second child, following just fifteen months after the first, Lucy expected some weepiness and was prepared for it. She was content with her decision to be home with the children, yet she fell into a severe depression. She was unable to get out of bed in the morning; just getting through the day was hard. Fortunately for her, an eighty-year-old aunt came to stay, and it was the aunt who suggested that, first, Lucy should see a doctor about her depression, and second, maybe she should consider doing something more with her life.

Lucy felt foolish and weak after seeing the doctor, because he implied that her depression was symptomatic of a more severe psychiatric disorder. Lucy dismissed out of hand the idea of seeing a psychotherapist. Finally, however, at her aunt's insistence, she did begin seeing a therapist *and* she went back to school to get her master's degree. The aunt offered to stay for a few weeks, to baby-sit, until Lucy got herself sorted out. Oh, that we could all have such wise and supportive relatives!

"If anyone had told me it would take ten months to shift the PPD after the birth of my son, I would have laughed in their face," Lucy later commented. She had imagined motherhood would be easy. But the full-time commitment had dragged her down, to a status she hardly recognized in herself.

SICKNESS AND SNOWY DAYS: PRISONER TO THE HOME

Whether we are stay-at-home or working mothers, the advent of a heavy snow or a child's sickness, meaning we have to stay home for a day or more, may renew in any of us the entrapment feeling of early PPD. No amount of logic ("It's only a day or so out of a lifetime") seems to banish that fear of being a prisoner in our own homes. The sheer pressure of the huge responsibility can suffocate us, and any notion of freedom or "I've got it all sorted out now" may vanish once the snow or sickness sets in.

Often sick as a child, I hated to discover in myself as a mother a total intolerance and impatience with my elder daughter, who seemed to have inherited my feeble genes almost deliberately to punish me.

Yet my own memories of childhood illnesses are pleasant. I would lie in bed surrounded by toys and coloring books my father would bring home as a special treat in the evenings; my mother would carry carefully thought-out meals to my sickbed and sit with me through the afternoons, reading stories.

Why couldn't I be like that? What had happened to that image of myself as the nurturing-caring-giving mother? There I was again, sliding away from my image of perfect mother.

I am thirty-eight years old and, until recently, it had never occurred to me that my mother might also have resented my sick days. How did she manage something as simple as getting out to buy food? How did her identity hold up under house arrest? I finally asked her and, yes, she hated it, too. She had longed for weekends, when my father would be home and she could leave me, if only to go shopping, anything to get out of the house.

Nancy E. also described complete mood reversals once she was snowed in.

"When I was a child, there were three of us, and my mother often had us all sick at home. My father did nothing to help her. I remember my mother looking like she would drop. On those days she never went out of the house, she dedicated everything to us. I'm not sure if our mothers didn't do us an injustice. I don't think it was good for us to see such self-sacrifice to children, being so totally selfless. When we try and become a mother in that image, that's when we come unstuck," she explained.

We do feel resentment when our sick child needs us most, and we can't help but feel guilty about that. As a self-employed worker, I fear the encroachment of my work time. Will I ever get the project finished? Will my career ever get anywhere? Will I justify the cost of childcare by making enough money?

Part-time working mothers are vulnerable to instant firing if they take too many days off because a child is sick. Full-time working mothers have enormous problems if they rely on a day care center and their child is often out sick or if they rely on a baby-sitter who is herself off sick too many times. Huge rows flare up between husbands and wives; moral debates over who is going to take the day off; who is going to incur the wrath of the boss, risk losing a promotion, risk loss of pay, make the sacrifice.

There is no way around it. Sick days and snow days reemphasize some of the negative aspects of mothering, or the negative aspects of ourselves as mothers. Where is the saint we imagined we would be? And hello again guilt and recrimination, which might set off another bout of PPD, once we felt clear of the despondency.

THERE IS NO SUCH THING AS A FREE LUNCH

For me the involvement of motherhood can best be summed up in that phrase.

It came from a lunch date I had organized with a fellow (childless) writer. Both self-employed and working in our separate homes, we used to meet once a month to gossip, trade notes, and bitch about late payments and rejected manuscripts. But now I had two small children, and to get out for lunch meant arranging a baby-sitter.

Hold on, I said to myself, it is going to cost as much for the sitter as for the lunch, and add to that the transport, plus the fact that it will eat up three hours of my day, and they would be the only "free" hours (paid for and free of children), which would be better served by my working, not lunching.

Now was the time to schedule my available money, who my friends would be, and how I would make ultimate use of the energy levels—and material resources—that realistically I knew existed, not the ones I dreamed of having.

When a woman has a child, unless she has a very helpful husband, mother, or neighbor, any free time will be paid, negotiated for, or traded off against. To go to the hairdresser, dentist, doctor, health club, swimming pool, department store, church, or to do some work—even if the time is just to be alone and think—she will have to pay for it in some fashion.

PART FOUR

◆

Helping Ourselves,
Helping Each Other

◆

14

♦

A GAME PLAN FOR SURVIVAL

Most new mothers would prefer to think they could avoid PPD altogether, with some carefully prepared plan of survival; or that if signs of depression begin to set in that they would know what steps are best taken to prevent it worsening. We have to go right back to basics for any such plan and really think out how we are going to prevent biochemical upheaval from taking over our lives. If the body's and the brain's hormones find the way of life just too overwhelming, they will tell us—in no uncertain manner (even if we had not already got the intensity of the message ourselves)—that it is time for a change.

The self-help techniques I am going to discuss can, advisably, help only those women whose symptoms of PPD are mild or moderate and that come on slowly, with no exaggerated danger signals involved. Any woman who is undergoing suicidal fantasies or fears she might harm her baby should not waste her time trying to pull herself together but must seek good professional help immediately. Unfortunately, the extreme variety of PPD, which usually comes on within the first two weeks after childbirth, symptoms of which are intense and frightening, tends to be completely out of our control and should not be dealt with lightly.

MILD TO MODERATE PPD

Let us look first at the best approach to PPD for the 10 percent of new mothers statistically reported to suffer what we would ourselves describe as mild to moderate symptoms. (In my view the figure is much higher, as very few in this group actually seek professional help.)

The best and most immediate help might come in the form of someone genuinely sympathetic to talk to. That listener may be our husband, a friend who has been there and will admit it, or a counselor or psychotherapist whom we seek out or to whom we have been referred by a concerned obstetrician or family doctor. Parents' or mothers' support groups are of great help for those with mild to moderate PPD, offering us a chance to compare notes, put all the new stresses and burdens in perspective, and share a few laughs.

WHERE ARE YOU FINDING YOUR BASIC RESOURCES?

Any new mother should sit down, preferably with her husband, and begin to discuss where she (or he) is finding her resources and energy levels now that they have a baby. You need to be aware of (a) sleep and adequate rest; (b) time for yourself (and himself) and for yourselves as a couple; (c) money; and (d) stimulating interests outside your new life as parents.

Ideally, a lot of this work would have been done before the baby was born. But it is still a fantasy to imagine couples really facing seriously the problems they might have to overcome once they are parents. However, a prenatal plan can be followed if you have previously suffered PPD and are determined to avoid it this time. For those couples, I would say, forget the buying of crib and diapers, forget the lessons on breathing and relaxation for labor and delivery, and concern yourselves right now with the fundamental life changes and the effects they might have on both of you.

THE PRENATAL PLAN

1. Accept that PPD can easily follow the birth of any child and adopt a nonjudgmental attitude toward yourself. The basis of PPD is hormonal and neurohormonal; it is not an indication of your failure. You should not feel guilt, shame, or fear at unexpected emotional reactions to yourself as a mother or to your baby. You should expect to go through some ambivalence about becoming a mother and toward your baby.

2. Talk to your husband about the possibility of PPD and what you will do in the event; i.e., think of alternate sources of help, face the question of who will look after the baby if you have to get twenty-four hours of sleep or enter a hospital for care. Encourage your husband to appreciate his role as a partner and make sure he understands that you cannot be *expected* to cope with everything.

3. Discuss your attitude to breast-feeding and whether you feel capable of the very real emotional, psychological, and physical drain of full-time nursing. Discuss the idea with your husband of giving your baby one bottle a day so he can share in some of the duties and give you a chance to catch up on sleep, or take time out alone from the baby.

4. Discuss how you are both going to get time to yourselves. Check out baby-sitting arrangements in your area. Would your husband give up one evening a week regularly so you could go out? Would your mother or mother-in-law help? If not, how will you pay for the time? Discuss the costs of childcare and baby-sitting now, and *save*.

5. Try and summarize your lifestyle by writing a list of what you would really miss if it were to be changed. Run through your own index of

independence, desire for freedom, sociability, the significance of hobbies or exercise to you, the need for privacy, and the amount of time you are used to spending alone, with friends, and with other adults.

Imagine yourself under house arrest and underline what you would miss most. Get your husband to do the same. Work together on how you would fit those needs into a new life. If you were used to working all day, exercising after work, meeting friends one evening a week, and your husband was used to going out one evening and sports on a weekend day, what can you *both* give up? Could you trade off two evenings for you against a weekend day for him?

6. If you plan to return to full-time work, don't think only about childcare arrangements, think about *you*. Try to listen very carefully to your heart and head, to your personal contentment level, right now, not only in the job itself but in being out and about in the day, in deriving pleasure from colleagues and in earning your own salary. It is difficult to know whether you should plan to return to work immediately, perhaps for one or two days a week, plan for a minimum of three months' leave, or six months' (taking leave without pay to spend more time with your newborn). But it is a vital decision to your ultimate ease in adjusting to working motherhood.

Keep your options open if you are unsure (and even if you aren't). Don't brag too much about how you are going to hate going back to work, knowing you'll be so happy at home with the baby. Many women have found they returned to work earlier than they had planned because they could not deal with encroaching PPD symptoms and feeling tied down in the house.

Try and talk to some other women at work who have recently had babies, and see if they would be interested in setting up a working mothers' group. Suggest you could meet once every three to four weeks for lunch and to compare complaints, tips, or problems with child-care.

7. Talk to your husband about the change in salary if you are taking a leave of absence. What will one salary mean to both of you? What about the cost of childcare? Could you manage domestic help when you return to work, someone to help out with shopping, laundry, cleaning? Would a baby-sitter who would come to the house and do light chores be easier than day care for you?

8. *Keep your options open* if you are planning not to return to work. You'll never know what you will feel about full-time motherhood until you try it first-hand. Keep some contact with the workplace because you may feel like going back, even half a day a week, or mornings only; or you might change your mind altogether and want to return full time. If you are going to work at home, check out childcare arrangements now and talk to your husband about the need to have some alternate care system worked out, even if you are not fully earning to cover those costs. Accept that you will not be as productive nor able to keep your income at the same level with a child as you were alone, however much you fantasize being skillful at both.

9. Don't get too carried away on the romance and joy of motherhood. Maybe it will come, maybe it won't.

10. What sort of support system will you have? Be honest about this. If your husband is a traditionalist and your family lives miles away, your friends are all single and devoted to wild late-

night parties, is there anyone around who might feel sympathetic? Do you have anyone—close friend, husband, doctor—who is a real confidante? Someone who is not shocked by any disclosure? Has any friend with a baby ever hinted to you that everything is not all roses? She is the one to call after the birth.

One way of trying to ensure you have support resources in the bank would be to baby-sit for a friend's new baby or young children while you are still child-free. You will accustom yourself to some of the inequities of childcare that way, and will then feel less as though you are imposing when you turn to that same friend for help, advice, reassurance—and baby-sitting—once you have your own baby.

11. Do you have overloading factors before giving birth? Spend some time thinking about your life—your desires, personal goals, and attitudes to mothering *now*. You might be able to work out some strategies that would help you achieve all your goals beforehand. Areas you should give thought to: did you delay childbirth because of ambivalence; did you have more than one therapeutic abortion; have you had several miscarriages; are there stepchildren in the household; did you have an infertility problem before this pregnancy; have you recently moved; how well is your work going; do you have a career that you consider important; how do your self-image and confidence survive under stress or attack; have you recently lost someone you loved dearly; did your mother die when you were a child; are you used to spending a lot of time out of the house, either alone or with your husband; is your marriage new and in what experts call the erotic stage.

If you feel that any of these overloading factors might bother you later, get in touch with a counselor or therapist now and talk over some of the difficulties you might have in adjusting to motherhood.

POSTPARTUM PLAN

To avoid biochemical upheaval or psychological distress after childbirth, you will need to give time and thought to the following factors.

STRESS AND TENSION

It is too easy to be flip or patronizing with advice on avoiding stress and tension for new mothers, when the very fact of becoming a new mother provides stress and tension. You may feel zombielike most of the time, so overwhelming will be the changes to your life and life patterns, the intense emotional involvement, and the fatigue of caring for a newborn.

The worst provocation of stress, however, will not be found in the obvious strain and tiredness of infant care. Rather it will be found in the previous section, in the list of overloading factors. Any or all of these factors could be placing an undue burden on your psyche and emotional well-being, and should not be overlooked. During this period, it is advisable to talk over with your husband, or with a very close friend, any of these secret anxieties. Try not to keep up a stoic facade of "I'm coping" because you imagine that's what good mothers do. Try to rid your mind of those preconceived fantasies about what you will be like as a mother. If you don't feel warm and nurturing, but instead tense, aggravated, and resentful, confront those feelings with *someone*. That will help release stress or tension. Accepting that you are not perfect may help you relax more into your new role.

Try to focus on what the stress is doing to *you*, rather than always worrying about its effect on the baby. The likelihood is the baby will breeze through its early months not noticing whether you are the earth-mother type or a neurotic nut-case! The baby only wants to feed and sleep and feel secure—it really does not care about your particular personality makeup at this time. As was discussed in the section on colic, your tension will not be the cause of crying in the newborn. Your inadequacy as a mother will not be the reason your baby fails to sleep through the night or seems to be fussy or cranky.

We have to learn to off-load much of the guilt we have accepted as our own in this motherhood business.

Practically, there are several ways of avoiding stress buildup, or depleting its stock once it has risen to dangerous levels. They are obvious, but often need spelling out to anxious new mothers.

SLEEP

You need sleep just as your baby needs it. Adequate sleep and rest will help prevent mental or physical exhaustion. Broken sleep cycles make the most saintly of us cranky, irritable, nervous, and unable to concentrate and can lead to depression. Broken sleep cycles have been used as an effective form of torture. An accumulation of consecutive nights without sleep may lead you to a total collapse.

Some women have found that after seven or more nights without proper sleep, they drop off on the sofa and, forgetting about the baby, sleep for eight to ten hours. The husband, mother, or friend who is in the home is forced to take over, usually with a bottle of formula. Babies survive the emergency action, even if they are used to total breastfeeding. Mothers who can give in to their physical needs that way usually survive better, too. Women have described to me the point when they knew they could not take the sleeplessness anymore. One woman told her husband he had to take over, and she checked into a local motel for the night. If such actions seem selfish to you, I suggest the opposite. It is too much self-sacrifice that leads to much distress these days. The push for total breast-feeding, on-demand schedules, has forced women to see themselves as the unimportant person in the picture. Their needs have to be denied for the baby's superior needs. That kind of attitude can lead to PPD, since we deny ourselves and in so doing obviously lose touch with our own identity and self-esteem. A little bit of selfishness is very important.

The stress and tension of a second baby, or third, when your children are close-spaced, are obviously much worse.

You must pay attention to your own energy reserves—the supply is not inexhaustible. You *will* need help, to give you time to be with the infant and time to spend with the siblings, about whom you will be suffering acute guilt and anxiety at your betrayal of their needs. Accept your need for help. Make plans for friends, neighbors, family, or, failing any of those resources, talk to your husband about paying for a sitter or some form of household help. Just because women in the past always seemed able to cope does not mean you will be able to. Point out that women in the past usually lived in an extended family and therefore did have help.

If you find yourself cracking under the pressure, and your husband feels you cannot afford to pay for help, maybe you should call on your mother or mother-in-law to come and stay for a while, even if you preferred to go it alone. A few family squabbles might be worth it, if in return you were allowed a little more time to rest, and to yourself. Failing all such measures, I strongly advise that you emulate the woman mentioned on the previous page. Walk out of the house and check into a motel for twenty-four hours, leaving your husband to cope. That way he might see what you mean.

BREAST-FEEDING

Try and evolve a realistic attitude to breast-feeding. Certainly breast milk is best for the baby, and the warm, nurturing relationship between mother and infant can't be bought in a can, but don't sacrifice yourself entirely to the notion of demand feeding. To my mind, we have gone too far in a reaction against the rigid four-hour feeding schedule of our mothers' day, letting ourselves be slave and martyr to the baby. Unless you genuinely enjoy having the baby with you at all hours of the day and night, derive total pleasure from letting the infant suckle at your breasts anytime over a twenty-four-hour period, and are unconcerned by your own lack of sleep and revival periods, I advise you to keep those feedings to a certain limit: every three hours at a maximum.

Having watched women feed on demand, I have to say I do not believe their babies are hungry every hour or half hour. The babies want to suckle, but they can use a pacifier. The babies don't learn to fill their stomachs at one feeding, preferring the ease and comfort of round-the-clock snacks. But they are learning, very early on, to impose on your life, to take over and demand your total attention, instead of blending and fitting in with *your* routine.

If you insist on only giving your baby breast milk, you can express some to refrigerate so your husband can give the baby a bottle of your milk during the night, allowing you precious time to catch up on sleep. If your milk supply begins to wane, it no doubt means you are suffering from lack of sleep and the fatigue of new motherhood that comes from giving away all your resources while not concentrating on restocking the supply. No amount of advice seems to help women once this cycle has set in: whether it be to change her diet, drink more fluids, take brewer's yeast, sip wine to relax her—whatever the latest tips involve. You could try a supplemental bottle of formula given to the baby by someone else during the day or night, so you can sleep. Or, if your doctor will allow it, and the baby is not too young, try a supplement of cereal, which will satisfy the baby's hunger and take some of the pressure off you.

Total breast-feeding does not suit every woman, just as we differ in the types of food we eat, our sex lives, and our choice of just about everything. Just because your friend or sister has fed her baby a particular way does not mean you have to. Always try and keep a perspective on things. You do count, just as much as your baby. If you are overtired, overwrought, and underslept, your baby will not be getting enough milk, and ultimately your crack-up or collapse from exhaustion will be of no use to the baby anyway.

TIME OUT FROM MOTHERHOOD

Stay-at-home mothers and working mothers find themselves equally vulnerable to the permanent-mother trap. All the components of psychological stress we have been discussing in this book, the potential triggers of PPD, are linked to the concept that being a mother can take over your whole life and can overtake you in the process. Whether you feel a resulting loss of self-esteem, confused self-image, or lack of identity and feeling of entrapment, the antidote to the problem is the same: you must find ways of relocating yourself, best achieved by taking some time out for yourself.

Ideally you should be able to work this time out with your husband, for he will be wanting his own private time too, and trade-offs should be possible. You are bound to run into problems with devising time out. One of the running problems of losing your sense of identity is not knowing what you want to do, or could do, on your own. Try and keep in touch with some aspects of your former life: whether that means an exercise class, regular running or swimming, dance lessons, or evening classes in the pursuit of photography or macramé; meeting a friend for dinner or an evening at her home; going to a movie with your husband or by yourself; going to a museum; or just blissful time to yourself to browse in the department stores (even if you can't afford to buy anything).

The important part is that this should not be time you guiltily arrange with a sitter and then dash in and out for a frenzied hour or less. You should be able to leave your baby, or children, with someone you trust and take the time you deserve and need.

The problem of not knowing who you are anymore, or what you could do that would really free you from motherhood, was faced by Regina V. Although her answer included nothing startling or exotic, the way she reached that conclusion is interesting for any new mother. Robin S. faced a different problem: how to manage time to herself with the stress of full-time work and not enough time anyway.

Regina and Robin: Getting Out on Their Own

Regina and her husband Ronnie had moved to a new neighborhood before having their baby Lesley, and as Regina was back at work three days a week, she had had no time to build up any friendships near their home. Lesley had been sick, and she had had to take days off work to stay with her. It was midwinter, and Regina was cooped up and resentful at being stuck in the house all day and at her husband's relative freedom.

Too much work and responsibility, plus resentment and hostility, led Regina into depression. Three weeks of this mood and Ronnie begged her to find some personal outlet. He was feeling guilty about always being the one to ask for time to go play basketball or do something at the weekend, leaving Regina with all the responsibility, increasingly depressed because she was so trapped. But Regina panicked. What could she do? Her sense of self had gone. Her old formulas didn't apply anymore.

Regina finally went to the local library one evening, where she spent two hours away from the baby, the house, and her misery. It may not have seemed wildly exciting, but it was *her* time. "I had a wonderful time doing just as I pleased, and even a year later I still go to the library once a week. Now I get books and toys for Lesley, and read for my own pleasure, and I write in my diary." Regina knew she could rely on those two hours every Wednesday. The time alone helped bring her frazzled nerves together, in what had been a frightening and lonely time.

Robin S., who was back at work full time with a six-month-old baby, also found herself sliding into depression from the lack of time to herself, rest, and recreation. After a year of this routine the crisis came for Robin. "My husband finally yelled at me that I had to see a psychiatrist. I was so angry that I stormed out of the house. As far as I could see it was *his* fault, not mine. But somehow that argument between us helped bring my mind around to a different way of thinking. I realized I had become martyrish. So I arranged to take a week off work and instead of staying home with the baby, I took her to the sitter's and I just spent every day doing what I wanted: long glorious days doing nothing, browsing in stores, going to galleries. I felt guilty, of course, particularly when a male colleague said, 'Are you going to take another week off to spend with your baby? That must have been so nice for you.'"

Finding time to ourselves that is our own, *without guilt,* will be a valuable way of reducing stress and tension and of restoring some of the shattered identity and lowered self-esteem that can be such strong triggers for PPD. It's a question of learning to relax into this new role of motherhood, rather than rushing headlong into its intensity.

DIET AND EXERCISE

So much is written these days on the efficacy of diet and exercise for overcoming virtually every problem that many women assume there must be a particular diet or exercise regimen to avoid or combat PPD. For those with mild depression and a good diet, strenuous exercise will help shift mood and bring about a more cheerful frame of mind in which to review the rest of the picture. If moderate-to-severe depression has set in, it is unlikely to be shifted by these means alone.

There are some tips for developing a diet that can help guard against PPD. First, make sure you eat a good healthy diet. Even if you are trying to lose pregnancy weight, do not go on a crash diet after childbirth, as that will only encourage the onset of depression (from the lack of nutrition that helps stabilize the metabolism under all circumstances). If you are breast-feeding, remember you need to build up your calorie intake, over that of a normal diet, to ensure there is enough caloric energy left over for *you* after the baby has devoured his or hers.

It is advisable to eat little and often in the months after childbirth, every two or three hours, as your body will feel most comfortable with the optimum blood sugar levels. If your starch level becomes low, sugar is removed from the bloodstream by a spurt of adrenalin, and the buildup of adrenalin helps create tension and irritability.

The premenstruum and the postpartum period, according to Katharina Dalton, share a curious factor: in both, the gap between normal and low blood sugar levels narrows. In both crucial times we are more than normally subject to depression.

OTHER DIETARY TIPS INCLUDE:

1. Take multivitamin tablets containing folic acid and vitamin B_6 (pyridoxine). Iron suppplement is also helpful.
2. Do not go back on the Pill, even if you are afraid of another pregnancy, for the artificial hormone progestogen will induce depression.
3. Give up caffeine in coffee or sodas, as it increases anxiety and irritability and could help the onset of PPD.
4. Do not take tranquilizers, as they will make you

feel sleepier and mask the real symptoms of PPD.
5. Eat foods containing potassium, such as bananas, tomatoes, and oranges, to counter potential potassium loss after birth.

If you are feeling sluggish, with no particular joy in life, you may wonder how anyone could suggest strenuous exercise as a way out of PPD. If only you knew how to find the energy, you think to yourself, that would be half the problem solved. However, if there is any way to make yourself begin running, swimming, or exercising as in aerobic classes, the results may well be very encouraging. Expending energy helps restore depleted energy. And the resulting happy feelings induced by the hormonal changes caused by the exercising will begin to trigger your biochemical system back into balance.

Do not expect any overnight cures. Eventually the advantages of exercise will begin to pay off in more ways than one: first, it will have gotten you out of the house; second, the exercise in itself is a good way of leaving motherhood concerns behind; and third, exercise works on the neuroendocrine balance and releases the neurotransmitters we know are necessary for a happy mood. Exercise, it is believed, releases the endorphins, which are the brain's natural opiates and mood enhancers. Hence the natural high exercisers experience, and the way they become addicted, too.

IS STRENUOUS EXERCISE SAFE AFTER BIRTH?

Can you partake in such active exercise shortly after childbirth? Kate B. had been very involved in sports before having her baby. A karate fanatic, Kate sent me the following information, which, as the material was aimed at women in professional football or softball, would be good advice for any form of exercise.

"Since it takes a lengthy time, roughly six months after delivery, for the muscles and soft tissues of the female body to readjust themselves to the prepregnant state, women should avoid being hit during this time. The muscles are unable to withstand a blow, and so there is a risk of injuring the internal organs. It would appear logical to me that this advice could be expanded to any contact sports; specifically, I am thinking of karate. It seems that physically a woman does not have the needed ability to harden her muscles to protect her inner organs from a blow in the first six months.

"My physical therapist, who was working with me for a broken hand after delivery, cautioned me not to do any ballistic exercises or sports until at least two months after I terminated nursing. He explained that it takes that long for relaxin (the hormone) to leave the body, that if ballistic exercises were persisted in, I would run risk of injuring joints or ligaments, which were still quite loose. So I decided against jogging or jumping rope until that time."

KEEPING YOUR MARRIAGE ALIVE

Marriage has to be worked at harder now than perhaps at any time in the couple's relationship. It is so easy to let that affection, passion, companionship you both shared dissipate, given the all-devouring work and demands of dealing with a new baby or a growing family. As women have so often noted, missing out on that one stable, solid, supportive form of love has quickened their descent into PPD. If you find yourself devoting all your energies and time to the baby; if you realize you are riddled with resentment at your husband's relative freedom and lack of entrapment in his new fatherhood; if you see that your lack of sexuality is caused by the changes in your relationship to him and the growing relationship with the baby; then do stop, take note, talk it over with him, and make some real efforts to stop the downward progress.

However tied you feel to the baby, you must take time for you as a couple. Baby-sitters can be hired to give you both evening time to get out of the house together. Even if socializing seems too much of an effort, going out together for dinner, to the theater, or to a movie can relieve you of some of that permanent-mother trap that so easily overpowers, even if this is a second or third baby (each new child changes the rules of the preceding game).

Women have described, in desperation, booking a hotel room for the night and inviting their husbands to join them, leaving the baby, if they were lucky, with a grandmother or some other relative. Others have turned to marriage counseling or family therapy in an effort to restore those bonds that once had been so strong and suddenly appear withered and lifeless. One very good method of rejuvenating a marriage—that my husband and I try to fit in once a year—is to go off on a minivacation together, a sort of second honeymoon, without baby or children, and simply enjoy being lazy, relaxed, and loving together again as we once used to be. Some couples will find it harder than others to leave young children behind, even for four days or a long weekend. To them, I offer this advice: think hard about the effects on the children of being so abandoned, by all means, but think too about the effects on your marriage of no time to yourselves, no chance to be lovers again. The children's peace of mind has to be balanced against your relationship with each other. Being divorced, in the end, is certainly not going to help the children.

AVOIDING ISOLATION

Isolation is a dangerous condition during this time of change and transition. It is also a very frequent complaint of new mothers, whether they have decided to stay home with the baby or have returned to work. The stay-at-home mother obviously has to carve out a whole new life; maybe she has left old friends behind in the workplace and knows no one in the neighborhood home during working hours. The working mother may find herself the only person in her workplace, or at her level, with a new baby; maybe she feels alienated from other mothers, who, she imagines, are all real stay-at-home types.

When we become parents, we naturally tend to drift away from or lose touch with old friends, as our needs, demands, and amount of time and energy available all change. Until we have sorted out our new self-image it can be hard to make new friends. What if you don't see yourself as a mother yet? You may struggle to avoid befriending other mothers. What if you fear your own inadequacy as a mother, blaming yourself if your baby is colicky and stressful, and believing that you are a failure? You will likely avoid other mothers' company for fear that they will judge you as harshly as you are judging yourself.

Isolation encourages depression to take root if we bottle up feelings and channel all our emotions onto the baby. Talk on the phone if you cannot find anyone nearby. If you don't believe that any other new mothers or any of your former friends would be sympathetic, seek some form of professional or supportive help.

Very often friends will be found among those very women we have decided are hostile and not sympathetic, like the other new mothers in our neighborhood, who, we are convinced, are going about their transition with not a drop of difficulty. Just look at all those contented smiles, we torment ourselves. If there is an organized group of new mothers, or of both parents, in the area I highly recommend joining one. In a group with regular meetings, the talk just flows, and those together-looking, organized mothers will be admitting just how afraid and lonely they have been. Strong, lasting friendships are often formed and sealed in these very early days of new mothering.

One level of isolation we may not have considered, before becoming a mother, is whether we have a strong supportive background of female friends. Many young women, in loving relationships with their husbands, lost the friendships of school and college days in turning their loyalty over to their husbands. Many women these days work in male-dominated professions or industries and find they meet few women during the work day and have little need of female companionship in the evenings. When they become mothers they may find few women they can turn to for support.

Vicky: No Communication with Mother

One woman you may rediscover as a friend, despite the complexities of the relationship, will be your mother. Vicky M. really had not wanted to have a baby, certainly not at the time of conception. Newly married, happy being a wife, working in the same company as her husband, able to travel with him on his business trips, she was content with life the way it was. When she became pregnant in her late twenties, however, neither Vicky nor Don felt they could abort their child, and so they eagerly awaited the birth. Vicky gave up her job—another woman determined to act out her image of a real mother.

Within weeks of Sarah's birth, Vicky found she resented the baby and her new life with a terrible anger. "I lived each day as if I were in mourning for my previous life." Loneliness had set in, with her lost freedom, lost job, lost opportunities to meet with women friends, who were all colleagues in the place of work; lost opportunity to travel with her husband, and a lost closeness with him. Vicky felt very much alone, deserted, and, of course, depressed.

When Don was away on a business trip, Vicky was left at home with the baby for three weeks. She knew she was on the verge of cracking up. Finally, she phoned her mother, who lived about an hour and a half's drive away, and with whom, she admitted, she had never been close. Her mother insisted she come to stay while Don was absent. Her younger sister would be home from college and they would be able to help her with Sarah. Vicky had never been the type to open up to her mother or sister, never been one to admit she was in need or that they could help. She was ill at ease discussing her depression, isolation, and resentment. "But," she said, "it was during those two weeks I spent at my mother's house that I began to adapt to my new role a little better. My mother, father, and sister were very helpful with the baby, giving me time to get more rest than I had been used to, baby-sitting so I could go shopping. I spent a lot of time talking with my mother and sister, and although I didn't go as far as to tell them of my feelings of *regret* about having the baby, the conversations and their company were very therapeutic. I suppose my depression began to shift then, though I still don't find it easy."

CHANGING ATTITUDES

Talking to people, finding new friends, working on the relationship with our husbands—all such basic, normal parts of everyday life, yet ironically sometimes so difficult to keep up with once we become parents, and once PPD has begun to set in, depriving us of the energy levels, drive, and commitment we used to hold with confidence and ease. I want to talk now about changing our attitudes toward mothering. This may not come easily without some professional (counseling, psychiatric, or medical) help. But if we can swing our mind round to a new, positive, way of looking at parenting, that can be an enormous help in breaking depression.

We have to turn our mind away from the traditional and socially acceptable standards that have induced in us guilt, fear of inadequacy and failure, and a confused self-image. Try reminding yourself of the following facts in the mornings on waking.

1. We are not alone in our unacceptable feelings. Probably the majority of women are going through similar changes in mood and behavior, and are equally unprepared to meet its challenges.

2. We will feel guilt. Dr. Spock tells us we shouldn't, but it is nearly impossible to rid motherhood of guilt.

3. Help or support is available in different forms, but it may take a lot of digging out. Doctors you are used to relying on may offer not only no help, but no sympathy. It may take strength and courage to find decent professional care, and that is unfair when we have so little strength or courage at this time.

4. We can own up that being a mother is not as easy as we had expected or fantasized, that we don't like it as much as we had imagined, that we are not perfect mothers or perfect parents, but we're not so bad, either.

5. Losing our independence, freedom, and sense of self, particularly if we have been used to a career, active working life, regular exercise routine, or hobbies, will be difficult whether we stay home full time and yearn for our past varied life or

continue working and yearn for past moments of peace and time to ourselves.

Robin: Not Perfect, but a Good Mother and Wife

"I forced myself to repeat every day, especially in the mornings, 'I am not perfect, but I am a good mother and wife.' This eventually led to an attitudinal change, an acceptance of the imperfections of motherhood. I also learned to predict the onset of depression and divert it. I would either warn my husband and we'd talk, or I would permit myself a 'primal scream' if I was alone. Then I'd spend the rest of the day problem solving or accepting the unsolvable," explained Robin S.

Robin came to that change in attitude during her own particular crisis. After nearly a year of depression following the birth of their daughter, Robin's husband suddenly lost all patience. He had tried to persuade her to seek psychiatric help, but Robin had refused. Now he warned her to straighten up or else. His threat made her focus exactly on what was going on. Time had run out, and if she was to continue refusing any outside help she would have to solve her own problems or she would lose husband, dreams, and everything she had always wanted.

Kate: Short-circuiting PPD a Second Time

Some women have sought psychotherapeutic help in a desire to talk over their problems and inner conflicts with a sympathetic, objective person. Kate B. decided to see a women's counselor after her six-month PPD in the hope of finding a solution to this problem should she want a second baby. Kate was a very busy, active woman before motherhood and had suffered from entrapment, resentment of her husband, and other typical PPD symptoms. The counselor gave the following advice, which Kate felt helped change her own attitude.

1. There is no simple solution—women are as individual as their feelings.

2. Feelings are going to come whether they are wanted or not.
3. It helps greatly to ventilate—any way you can do it—whether through yelling, or physical exercise, or talking with someone.
4. There is an element of grieving in every crisis: job loss, PPD, surgery, illness, disease, death. It helps to read up on the subject of loss.
5. Talk. Find a good listener, someone in your same situation or who has been through it.
6. After you figure out how you are feeling, accept those feelings as normal, OK, fine, and not selfish. Then think about what you need to feel better and take some action.
7. Find support groups ahead of time.
8. Don't advise someone else that everything will be fine and let it go at that. That is ignoring the hurt. You need someone to whom you can say, "I hurt," who will acknowledge it and sympathize. You need solutions, rather than denial of the situation.

GETTING THE FEELINGS OUT ON PAPER

As talking is evidently one of the best means of defusing emotional tension, if there is no one to turn to who will listen, if you cannot afford, resent, or feel threatened by the idea of seeking professional help, then keeping a journal, pouring out those shameful thoughts on paper, can be an invaluable process. Many women have instinctively tried this device and found that it did help to release the emotions; even better, in a couple of months they could read it back and gain support from the realization that they had changed and developed in that time.

Sharon W. was seeing a therapist for her PPD, but had refused to take a course of antidepressants, wanting to control or come to terms with her moods without drug help.

"I have learned to control PPD to some degree," she said. "When I feel it coming on, instead of getting mad at my elder daughter, I put her in bed and I write in my journal. It's my private book. I write that I can't stand my husband, that I wish I'd never met him. That's not what I really feel, but I need to express my anger and disappointment. Later I comment on those entries when I'm feeling better. I reread it every couple of months."

Regina: Beside Herself with Anger

Regina V., whom we met before, describing how her release from entrapment and the ties of motherhood had finally been discovered in the library, commented that the feelings of resentment and anger she had been bottling up inside her—with no close friend to talk to, with work, baby-sitters, a child's illness, winter claustrophobia, and a host of other problems—found great release when she wrote about them. She kept a diary that was of great help to her. One part of it, during those winter months of crisis, read like this:

"Feb. 18th. Due to this stressful week with Lesley being sick; *me* being sole caretaker; *me* having to miss work and to call in sick to say I wouldn't be in; *me* having to arrange and rearrange a baby-sitter for Lesley so I could work; *me* having to feed her supper and eat alone because Ronnie was working late and playing basketball or racquetball, *me-me-me!!!* By the time Ronnie got home this evening I was beside myself with anger. I talked with him about my feelings later in the evening after Lesley was in bed.

"I feel bad; I feel defeated; I feel worthless; I feel stagnant; I am depressed; I am resentful; I am unhappy with my body; I am unhappy with my eating habits; I have many problems. I was reaching my breaking point this evening when I even felt Ronnie was *not* my partner anymore. That scares me. I felt alone and overburdened. I feel unchallenged and overchallenged with Lesley and housekeeping. I want to earn money, I want to be with Lesley and care for her, I want Ronnie not to have to work so much, I want him to have Lesley to care for alone—me NOT around. I feel isolated being home with Lesley so much. But I *don't* want her with a sitter more. I can't win. . . . I feel defeated. I wish I had more confidence in myself. I wish I had more respect for myself. I am quickly losing any I had. . . ."

That particular entry led to the confrontation with Ronnie and his plea that she find some outlet for *herself;* that he would look after Lesley one evening a week, on a regular basis. Eventually, by taking the time out, Regina said, "Suddenly I regained a sense of self-worth. It was several weeks before I felt in control of my life again but it did return. It is painful to remember this period of time in my life."

FILLING OUT A QUESTIONNAIRE

Many women who received one of my questionnaires when I was researching this book commented that they didn't mind if I never used their material, it had been such a therapeutic exercise to write about what they had felt. So, for anyone with a secret desire to get a whole load off her chest, I reprint the questionnaire here—for your own personal, private use or to share with a close friend or your husband.

I would like to discuss the following topics:

1. When did you suffer the depression, after a first child, second, or subsequent? After each birth, or only once?
2. Had you heard of PPD, or just of the three-day blues? Were you surprised or shocked to be so depressed?
3. Did you seek any help? From a friend, partner, your husband, ob/gyn, pediatrician, a GP, social worker, priest, preschool teacher, therapist, or hospital emergency room? Or no one?
4. Did you come to your own awareness, or was it pointed out by your husband, a partner, friend, your mother or sister?
5. Do you feel guilty about having such a depression, or at your unacceptable and unexpected feelings?
6. Do you find it hard to speak about it to others in general, to a group of other mothers, to your family?
7. Have you felt any of the following: loss of your own identity; loss of self-esteem; fear that your

life is over (or wish that it was); trapped; confused over how you relate to motherhood (or fatherhood); new sympathy or contempt for your own mother; despair; disillusionment; anger at your husband, partner, other women, doctors, the baby, its siblings, your mother or sister, society in general; mourning that you can never be the little girl (or boy) again; emotional emptiness; wondering if it was a terrible mistake?

8. Do you believe other mothers feel this way?
9. Are you an adoptive mother, a stepmother, a single mother (or father)?
10. How has your husband or partner responded? With anger or hostility? With sympathy? By withdrawing from you and the baby?
11. Do you think working mothers suffer PPD more or less than full-time mothers?

As an example of the way some women wrote to me, and so you can share in their frankness and honesty, I am reprinting the following reply from Joan R. She is articulate and typical of the women who are becoming mothers today—facing new concerns, new ambivalence, new demands on their lives as mothers. Joan's reply especially moved me.

1. I suffered PPD after experiencing a miscarriage with my first pregnancy and again (a much more severe bout) after the birth of my second child. There was really no time for PPD after the second birth (third pregnancy)! Also, I had "exorcised my demons" by that time. Any crying I did was from sheer fatigue.
2. I had heard of the blues but I was very surprised to have such a violent case after the first birth. The depression after the miscarriage seemed, to me, to be normal under the circumstances.
3. After the miscarriage, I called my ob-gyn. He was very unsympathetic to me and suggested

that I seek psychiatric help, as my depression was not normal. Therefore, after the birth of my next child, I *wouldn't* call him. The only reason I had stayed with him was because his office was near my job. My mother and a friend, both of whom had experienced PPD, tried to help but I couldn't talk about it with them.

4. My husband was the one to let me know just how much the PPD was affecting me—and him. He was very worried but sympathetic. My depression went on for about three months before he spoke to me about it. It was as if a dam broke loose within me. All the insecurities in me came out. For instance, my father walked out on my mother when I was four months old. Therefore, in my confused and depressed state, I was trying to figure out how I was going to support this child when my husband left me! I'm sure this sounded crazy but my husband was great about it. He reassured me of his love—for me and our son.

   Motherhood, I believe, is a shock at any age and in any circumstance. I was twenty-nine years old when my son (the first birth) arrived. He couldn't have been more wanted. Yet I felt really trapped and frightened about my ability to take care of this child.

5. I felt guilty about the feelings because I should have been so happy, but instead I was on the brink of despair!

6. I did find it hard to verbalize my feelings until my husband brought them out. I'm active in the Childbirth Education Association and when I'm assisting in a class for expectant parents, I always insist that the group be warned of the possibility of PPD. If it should happen to any of them, they at least know that they are not alone. I encourage anyone who needs a listener to call me.

7. I felt a loss of identity. Instead of being just Joan

R., I was somebody's *mother*. I thought my life was over because I couldn't see beyond the endless fatigue. There seemed to be no future. I felt so trapped. I thought that I would never be "free" from the responsibilities that went with motherhood. Also, my son was born in January so I couldn't get out of the house much. I didn't think I was cut out to be a mother (a little late for that!) and I *was* afraid that I had made a terrible mistake.

One good thing that came of all this was that I gained a new respect for my mother. I really think that having a child makes you appreciate your mother.

I was relieved to see the word "despair" in the questionnaire. For me, PPD does not mean "postpartum depression" but "postpartum *despair*." That had to be one of the lowest points of my life. At times, I questioned my sanity, the futility of my life, even my marriage.

I would like to add that after the birth of my second child, I did change ob-gyns. What a difference! When I became pregnant with my daughter, I spoke with the doctor regarding my previous PPD experiences. He was very sympathetic and promised me that if I needed help, he would be there to offer advice and help.

8. Yes, I believe more mothers have PPD—in varying degrees—than are willing to admit it. Having a baby is supposed to be one of the happiest times of your life. Many women don't want to admit that for some of us—as much as we love our babies—it is anything but happy. Instead it is a time for confusion, despair, feeling unloved and unwanted, not to mention feeling like a giant milk bottle if you are nursing.

9. I am a happily married woman (soon to celebrate my fourteenth wedding anniversary) with a really terrific husband.

10. My husband was bewildered and worried but

sympathetic. He never withdrew from the baby or me.

11. I don't think there are any differences between working mothers and full-time mothers when it comes to postpartum depression. The severity may be more or less due to knowing you have to go back to work. The prospect of going back to work helped me to see that there was life after baby!

Good luck with your book. I hope that I helped in some small way. Thank you for letting me share my experiences with you. Sometimes it helps just to talk about it.

Joan

P.S. I am the mother of James (age eight) and Carol (age five). I can truthfully say that, if I had it to do over again, I would. My children are two of the greatest things that have ever happened to me.

FINDING A SYMPATHETIC DOCTOR

So often women have complained about the lack of sensitivity, understanding, or sympathy they have received from family doctors, obstetricians, or even psychiatrists to whom they were referred with PPD, that the question is left hanging: how are we to find a good, aware, sympathetic doctor?

In most cases, a woman goes through pregnancy without giving potential PPD a thought. But after childbirth, with the unexplained and unrecognizable feelings swamping her, she begins a desperate search, or perhaps she tries the one doctor she imagines will help, only to be rebuffed, and is left to deal with the problem herself.

Because there is no national or centralized method in the United States of recognizing or diagnosing cases of PPD, there are many gaps in the services new mothers are offered.

Former secretary Nina P., 31, for example, describes a twelve-month saga of hunting for a doctor who would understand what she was going through. "I told my obstetrician about the terrible problems with insomnia that began a couple of months after the birth. He said, 'Don't worry,' and gave me sleeping pills. But I became increasingly nervous. Next I saw a nutritionist, who put me on a special diet that made me worse.

"Then I tried a psychotherapist who told me I hated my father and resented my husband, and that I should learn to express aggression. Then I went to an ortho-molecular psychiatrist, who did not believe in drugs, but put me on megavitamin therapy." Finally, Nina contacted DAD after seeing a TV program featuring PPD, and was helped to find a psychiatrist who did understand her condition. She was immediately admitted to hospital for a week, to get some sleep that had eluded her for months.

Nina's problems began in October and she was not properly treated until January. "The misdiagnosis and people telling you different things is very damaging. I just wish in Lamaze they'd have said something. Frankly, I'm disgusted with the doctors and the ignorance I have come across."

MILD SYMPTOMS

Contact a local mothers' support group (see Chapter 15) or call a warm line (see p. 228) for details of a self-help group for new mothers. Either the meetings themselves, with other women, will be sufficient to dispel some of the symptoms, or they might be able to put you in touch with doctors, counselors, or therapists in your area who are most suitable.

MODERATE SYMPTOMS

If PPD has become heavy, if your depression has persisted for more than a few weeks and nothing you have tried will shift it, you might need some professional care, for therapy and treatment with antidepressant medication. Where to find that help will be the same for you as for women with severe symptoms.

SEVERE SYMPTOMS

Symptoms such as the following require good, prompt treatment: a pattern of not being able to sleep or eat; high anxiety level or panic attacks; a feeling of being utterly unable to cope; a sluggish depression that is so deep you cannot get out of bed let alone look after the baby; not being able to bear touching the baby; constant crying that in itself is disruptive to family life; fear about harming the baby; talk of taking your own life; hallucinations, a feeling that you are worthless and all would be better off without you (see Chapter 4).

SEEKING GOOD HELP FOR MODERATE TO SEVERE SYMPTOMS

If your own family doctor or obstetrician seems unsympathetic, you should call your nearest large teaching hospital and find out if their department of obstetrics/gynecology has a psychiatrist attached. Many departments do team up with a psychiatrist who will have experience with PPD. Or, through the resources list in the Appendix of this book, you may discover a highly trained psychosomatic ob/gyn within your area.

You can contact a local mental health clinic for immediate psychiatric care or ask your family doctor to recommend a psychiatrist. As in the cases described earlier, if you feel you are getting nowhere with a particular psychiatrist, do get a second opinion. You deserve good treatment. Unfortunately, with the lack of knowledge even at the professional level, it may be hard to come by.

WHAT IS GOOD CARE FOR PPD?

A sensitive obstetrician should be able to help with incipient PPD by talking honestly with the woman before childbirth and finding time to meet with her and her husband after the baby has been born. Dr. Elisabeth Herz points out that appropriate training for young obstetricians now includes special seminars in PPD. Such enlightened training is by no means regulation, but at this Washington, D.C., hospital she feels they are making the right moves. "I am trying to get across to the young doctors that they should be aware of certain risk factors in pregnant women and that certain women should be watched more closely."

To Dr. Herz, the risk factors include the mother being older than average and expecting her first baby or having a lengthy interval since her last baby. Her hormonal profile might show that she had menstruated early, had had irregular and painful periods, and was a PMS sufferer. If her pregnancy was unplanned she would be at high risk, and talking with her might reveal ambivalence about motherhood. If she had been infertile for several years; if there is marital tension at home, or she is feeling unloved or unsupported by her husband; if she is separated or single; if she is lacking in support from family or friends, these would also increase the risk of PPD.

Dr. Herz believes that a conflicted relationship with her mother might be reflected in the woman's higher education or professional level; the career woman may have unconsciously rejected the traditional female role because she experiences it as a threat to her identity. She recommends watching for overanxious or very hostile women and those who feel out of control of their lives. Recent stressful life events should be taken into consideration. At very high risk is a woman with a previous PPD, as the recurrence rate given by some authorities is as high as 20 to 30 percent, and Dalton, after a ten-year follow-up study, found the alarming rate of 68 percent.

An aware obstetrician working with pregnant women would be prepared to meet with the high-risk new mother at least two extra times after childbirth: perhaps asking a nurse to call the mother at home about three weeks after she returned home just to chat and see how the mother feels she is getting along. "The sooner we handle incipient problems the better," Herz has said.

If the obstetrician felt the mother needed referral to a psychiatrist, that could be arranged in conjunction with special PPD professionals in the field. Dr. Herz is trained in both obstetrics and psychiatry, and is thus admirably suited to coping with new-mother problems in her postpartum office care. Unfortunately, there are only ten or twelve such professionals in the country.

At the first signs of PPD, after the new mother has talked about her adaptation and problems at home and assessed her mood and personality, Dr. Herz can intervene with individual therapy or she may decide the mother needs some form of medication (probably antidepressants) as well.

The sad truth, however, is that most medical and psychiatric training does not carry specific information about PPD. The level of material available, as witnessed by one of the leading textbooks on ob/gyn, is pathetic and most likely to encourage doctors to see these new mothers as crazy ladies.[54]

"Mental illness complicates about 1 in 400–1000 pregnancies. Traditionally, the causes of postpartum psychosis are infectious, toxic, and idiopathic, although it is now apparent that the condition is not a distinct clinical entity and that the underlying problem is the disintegration of personality structure, usually associated with sexual maladjustment, fear, anxiety, and rejection of the pregnancy. A careful inquiry into the patient's history often shows long-standing problems in making social adjustments and in accommodating to the female role."[55]

SCREENING PREGNANT PATIENTS

For the most part, women with mild to moderate cases of PPD do not seek help, in this country. Their recovery comes from waiting the depression out or they might find help in the parent support groups currently flourishing nationwide.

I must put in a word of reluctance about the trend toward psychological screening of pregnant women to detect high-risk cases. There is one article in the PPD literature, by two Canadian doctors, Braverman and Roux, in which a list of nineteen questions is given to pregnant women in their prenatal clinics or doctors' waiting rooms for them to fill out.[56] The questions are as follows:

1. Did you become very depressed or extremely nervous in the period following the birth of your last child?
2. Are you single or separated?

3. Do you have a mother, father, brother, or sister who has been hospitalized for a mental disorder?

4. Do you have a grandmother, grandfather, uncle or aunt who has been hospitalized for a mental disorder?

5. Did you have an unhappy childhood?

6. Do you have marital problems?

7. Was your pregnancy unplanned (accidental)?

8. Can you honestly say at this time that you really do not desire to have a child?

9. Do you have a bad relationship with your mother?

10. Do you have a bad relationship with your father?

11. Do you have serious problems which worry you at present (financial, personal, or other—underline)?

12. Do you feel that your mother was not a good mother?

13. Do you lack confidence in yourself?

14. Is your general health poor in your opinion?

15. Do you more or less regret that you are pregnant?

16. Do you feel that your mother does not love you?

17. Do you see yourself as an immature, dependent individual?

18. Do you often feel that your husband (boyfriend) does not love you?

19. Did your mother, sister, or grandmother tell you that one can be very sick when pregnant?

The results, they felt, showed the value of preventive psychiatry in spotting certain traits as predictors of PPD: personality factors, immaturity, female role rejection, hostility toward the mother and family, past history of mental illness, and heredity.

My own response on reading those questions was first to wonder how valuable a woman's self-assessment would be to such probing questions, and second to imagine the type of replies I would write sitting in my doctor's office. How many women would admit feeling that their husband or boyfriend did not love them? How many would write down, for the doctor to read, that they regret being pregnant? Third, what if you answered no to all the questions, emerging with a healthy score, and later suffered PPD?

THE POSTPARTUM CLINIC

To my mind, the best form of care for reasonably healthy women who might find themselves sufferers of some form of PPD would be provided by the maternity wings of the hospitals where we deliver our babies. A postpartum clinic, within which we would receive some instruction on baby care in the days immediately after delivery, would also offer advice on potential emotional problems once back at home.

The postpartum clinic would be a bright, airy, friendly, cheerful part of the maternity wing, offering playroom or day care facilities for those mothers who need to return for advice or help, bringing older children with them. Attached to the clinic would be a mother and baby unit for those women who have to be readmitted in the year after childbirth for intensive psychiatric treatment.

Women in the maternity wards need not be aware of the psychiatric admissions. Their concerns will revolve around how to care for their baby and what will happen when they are back home. The talks, or discussions, would be in groups of ten new mothers with a nurse, social worker, psychiatrist, and recent mother who can talk about her own experiences. Hormonal shifts and biochemical upheavals would be explained, so all new mothers would know what might happen and, if it did, what they should do to help themselves.

The meetings would offer basic advice and send the mother away with a kit including telephone numbers of people to contact if in doubt, distress, or depression.[57] The telephone numbers would include parent support groups in the community, the hospital social worker, and psychiatrists and therapists who work with PPD mothers. Women might also exchange home numbers for moral support. Finally, they would be advised that they will be welcome back at the postpartum clinic for pediatric advice or motherhood advice anytime they want to drop in for coffee and someone to talk to.

Lacking such hospital-provided services, women have been banding together in an effort to help one another through the crises of parenting (as the crises obviously continue beyond the first year of a baby's life), and the results are found in the burgeoning movement of parent support groups.

15

◆

SHARING AND SUPPORT

"Why has it taken so long for a really very simple idea to catch on; that parents should get together for support and help on how to deal with their kids; that they don't have to operate in isolation, fear, and guilt?" said Sandra Rodman Mann, who has set up a masters' program in teaching parent skills at Fordham University in New York. She was speaking at a conference in New York (May 1984) on "Parent Support Groups: Coming of Age in the '80s." The conference was widely attended by staff of many such groups that are opening around the country, by members of family service and mental health agencies, by politicians, activists, and mothers. Workshops were offered, ideas aired and debated, questions raised, contacts made and shared.

After years of the isolation we all experience to some degree with the nuclear family, one of the best ways out of the depths of despair and depression and the gnawing attacks of anxiety is to help one another and ourselves by meeting in organized, nonjudgmental groups of fellow mothers (or parents). Together we can learn about infant- and childcare, family skills and management; together we can act as forceful pressure groups in the community and among the professions.

"Somewhere out there in the midwest," said Sandra Rodman Mann, "the Family Resource Coalition has flourished. There is a kind of magic about such great organizations, which are volunteerism at its best." The FRC, the national organization that coalesces these support groups, came into being after a conference in May 1981 and has proved to be a highly successful, determined, outward-reaching body with headquarters in Chicago.

At the first-ever national conference of the Family Resource Coalition held in Chicago, October 1986, Jane Honikman and I were invited to deliver a seminar on PPD. We addressed a group of parent support and childbirth educators, social workers, and group coordinators, all of whom were fascinated—and yet astonished—to hear our evidence. A letter I received following the conference, from GeorgeAnn Samuels, coordinator of Bright Beginnings at the Magee-Women's Hospital in Pittsburgh, underlines the new enthusiasm:

"We are in the planning stages of a postpartum support group here in Pittsburgh and so far the response is tremendous. There is very little of this kind of support in our area, and we are very excited about the possibilities. Your book will be used for training and referral. . . ."

The comments Ann Adalist-Estrin, a psychotherapist with the Parent Resource Association, in Wyncote, Pennsylvania, made at the conference are also very important:

"We should all be looking now in a different way at parent support. Postpartum adjustment problems, and postpartum depression, should be seen as *normal* parts of the development into parenthood, not as pathological or abnormal. We have been scared to admit that many, perhaps the majority of, women find the first year after a birth (at least) a time of major change and inward growth.

"Parent education has focused restrictively on 'infant development' and the significance of the maternal-infant relationship in the child's favor. Why have we ignored the mother's development as though obsessively afraid this might be seen as negative?"

Bernice Weissbourd, president of the coalition and founder of a parent support group in Evanston, Illinois, said very firmly, "We no longer view parents as vehicles for the care of children. We recognize the need for healthy 'parent development' too. Parenthood must be a creative period of self-growth, not a guilt-laden duty."

There were many different types of support groups under discussion at the conference. Family Resource Coalition has put together the most up-to-date list of their organizations and affiliates across the country for this book, which you will find in the resources list in the Appendix. Perhaps this will be the most valuable information for any of us to have at our fingertips: a direct line into sharing and support with other mothers.

BIRTH RESOURCE CENTER AND PEP: SANTA BARBARA

As was mentioned in Chapter 7, Jane Honikman, of Santa Barbara, California, founded Postpartum Education for Parents (PEP) with three women friends. These women had no example to follow in the early 1970s, when instinct told them they could not be the only young mothers sitting around in the park wondering what had happened to their lives, their marriages, and their sanity, and wondering how they were going to get through this daunting period of life called parenthood. Their belief in the importance of what they were doing led them on through problems of organization, confirmation, support, and funding to become a successful voluntary self-help agency.

"The reality of caring for a totally dependent infant twenty-four hours a day shattered our expectations," Jane explained. "We were learning about our infants and how to care for them through trial and error. (Somehow our babies did not fit the descriptions of the babies in the books.) We had many questions about our feelings and concerns, and believed there had to be someone who knew how to make parenting this precious new being as purely satisfying as we had expected it to be. We felt confused, inadequate, and overwhelmed. In order to maintain the expected aura of joy that new parents 'should' feel, however, we bottled up our continuing sense of panic and kept on smiling."

They intended to set up a parent support group that would offer discussion groups with a format for sharing common concerns and at the same time solve some typical problems. They wanted to offer a twenty-four-hour telephone service—which they called a warm line to offset the negative connotations of hot or help line—for those mothers who may not have had the courage or energy to go out to a meeting at that point in their lives, but who needed to talk to someone, anyone, in moments of despair, panic, or fear.

The women began their operation by contacting various professionals in the area, from the local ob/gyn doctors and hospitals, pediatricians, county mental health services, and the AAUW (American Association of University Women) to whose Goleta Valley branch they applied for a research and project grant that helped with printing costs.

They agreed to work with mothers who volunteered to be facilitators for their group meetings. The volunteers would be trained as active listeners and would also take shifts on the warm line.

PEP is now a wide-ranging service that sends a speaker to each childbirth preparation class to distribute PEP brochures and to talk about their services. They ask parents to sign a Childbirth Class Summary and Postpartum Call Sheet if they wish to have a volunteer contact them after the birth of their baby. Brochures are distributed to local physicians' offices and family centers.

The Santa Barbara PEP is perhaps rare in its outreach efforts. They follow up the childbirth class talk with a postpartum call made when an announcement of the birth appears in a local paper or they learn of a birth from the Lamaze teacher.

The telephone caller informs the mother where and when PEP groups meet in her area (they have evening groups for working mothers or fathers) and asks a simple, concerned question, such as "How has it been going?" Groups endeavor to match the babies' ages as closely as possible, and the facilitators encourage discussion. Usually, talk at first centers on some problem of childcare, then moves on to the mothers' concerns about themselves. The groups of about eight members meet every two to three weeks for two hours or so. Sometimes the women become such good friends they decide to continue meeting as their babies grow older, without the facilitator.

Since her growing involvement in the campaign for PPD, Jane Honikman has become director of Santa Barbara's Birth Resource Center, from whose base she has been able to make great moves on behalf of all women suffering PPD. Jane's incredible energy and determination led to a major campaign within that community: they sent out questionnaires, and followed up with phone calls, to all physicians, psychiatrists, and obstetricians to determine who had *any* knowledge of PPD, its diagnosis and/or methods of treatment. Jane now has a file of all qualified doctors in that region.

It is a sample of the kind of work that must be performed across the nation. One of the main problems, any leader of support groups finds, is they are hard-pressed to suggest doctors for referral.

Santa Barbara's BRC has now formed its own special PPD group, with good response. Jane has also printed a short brochure on postpartum adjustment problems, called "The Emotional You." It is available for purchase. (Send check or money order, ten for $3.00 or 100 for $20, to Santa Barbara Birth Resource Center, 2255 Modoc Rd., Santa Barbara, California 93101, or call 805/682-7529.)

DEPRESSION AFTER DELIVERY (DAD): MORRISVILLE, PENNSYLVANIA

Nancy Berchtold's own story appears in the chapter "Am I Really Crazy?" Nancy was led to form the group DAD when she hunted around for a support group herself, and found nothing. She contacted the New Jersey Self-Help Clearing House and was offered advice and instruction on setting up such a group. In a recent copy of the newsletter which DAD sends to its many members and friends, Nancy wrote:

"Out of an affirmed determination to find other women suffering from PPD, Depression After Delivery was organized in July 1985. A small announcement in a local paper brought the first phone calls. The first meeting was held at the local YWCA in September with six women in attendance. In less than a year DAD has grown from a few isolated women to a network that reaches across the country. The message rings clearly: *You are not alone!*

"PPD affects ten percent of postpartum women. Sadly, only a few ever learn that this is a hormonally based psychological disorder. It can be treated successfully with medication and/or therapy. One of the most important aspects of recovery is caring support for the postpartum woman affected by this disorder. This is why DAD was founded.

"Our members come from all walks of life, and from all areas of the country. At last count our membership was over 300 women.

"We all have one thing in common: we understand each other's pain. And through our group we can share feelings and our tears. We can share ideas about what helps and what doesn't. And sometimes we can share our laughter."

DAD members have been in the foreground of recent television coverage on PPD. Within seven months the group appeared on nine television shows, two radio talk shows, and numerous print media articles.

DAD members have also become active in the campaign for the release of Sharon Comitz from her eight- to twenty-year prison sentence for infanticide. They appeared on the nationally televised NBC program "1986" which reported the case. The DAD members were quoted as saying that if they had not experienced PPD themselves, they might have suspected Sharon's motives. But, knowing from their more moderate bouts with PPD just how the mind can distort reality, they now felt nothing but sympathy for her. "Judge Charles Brown's sentencing was unfair and extreme. It is our feeling that Sharon should have received psychiatric treatment, not prison." (Sharon receives a total of one half-hour of treatment every two weeks.)

"Glenn Comitz has asked us to voice our feelings to the lieutenant governor of Pennsylvania, and to the Board of Pardons. If you are interested in helping with this effort, contact Nancy Berchtold at DAD."

Write to Depression After Delivery at P.O. Box 1282, Morrisville, Pennsylvania 19067, or call 215/295-3994. Any contributions to the mutual-aid self-help support group to cover costs of telephone and postage will be most welcome.

DAD members run this nationwide lifeline for women as yet without any funding.

PARENTS ADJUSTING TO PARENTHOOD (PAP): SAN DIEGO

Organized by Susan Host, who experienced a severe PPD, and psychologist and therapist Dr. Susan Hickman, Parents Adjusting to Parenthood (PAP) is another major group specifically set up for PPD mothers. "Pregnant with my first child, I thought I was prepared for childbirth," said Susan Host, the mother now of an eight-year-old and three-year-old. "But a sudden unexpected chain of events led to my requiring a c-section delivery. Five days later, on the day I was to go home, I was told my baby was running a temperature and could not accompany me. By nighttime I had become so agitated that I was placed in a psychiatric hospital where I spent a total of six months.

"Years later, with the help of a parent support group facilitated by Drs. Robert and Susan Hickman, I felt the encouragement I needed to have my second child. Being in the group made me more aware of the effectiveness of self-help support systems. I still have a strong desire to help other parents minimize the crippling effects of PPD by increasing awareness of its possibility and providing support for those suffering from its effects."

PAP meetings are held one evening a week in the home of Susan and Tony Host. Parents share day-to-day experiences and present and past feelings. The focus enables them to feel less isolated. Susan Hickman, the group's facilitator, is herself a mother of five, a psychologist, and a family therapist specializing in parenting problems.

Contact: Parents Adjusting to Parenthood (PAP), 5911 Lana Drive, San Diego, California 92117, or call 619/560-6890.

MELD: MINNEAPOLIS

Another such organization is in Minneapolis. Called MELD, it was set up by Ann Ellwood in 1973, in her effort to answer the question of how families can be strengthened. Ellwood felt that parents can learn much from each other, they can give each other support, and they should be free to make informed choices. MELD is also a nonprofit organization, providing group meetings with facilitators and comprehensive material within five subject areas: health, child development, child guidance, family management, and personal growth. There is a MELD for new parents, teenage mothers, parents of preschool or school-age children, and bicultural, military, or religious families. The groups meet about eight times, weekly or biweekly.

MELD has been widely expanded over the last fourteen years, and their programs are now in many different locations across the country. They have replication packages that include training material for the agency, a site coordinator, and volunteer facilitators, and material for parents.

THE MOTHERS' CENTER: NEW YORK

In Nassau County, Long Island, New York, the Mothers' Center Development Project was set up in 1981, run by Lorraine Slepian and Marge Milch. They intend their Mothers' Centers to be as valuable to the community as schools and hospitals—and they wish every community had one. The aim is to provide research and services on mothering, pregnancy, childbirth, and health care. Again, members meet in peer groups, by age of their children, and a separate room is provided for childcare (but one part of their philosophy is that mothers should not mind their child wandering in and out during the group meeting), with two trained facilitators, for a limited number of sessions. Very often, after finishing a ten-week session, the mothers sign up again for another session or perhaps take a break and then return.

The Mothers' Center aims to work with parents throughout the children's stages of development. As Lorraine Slepian says, "Most communities are similar to Nassau County in the inadequate provision of services to pregnant women and mothers. What services there are focus only on the physical aspects of pregnancy. There is little opportunity for women to discuss their deep personal concerns and to find out how to obtain other services they may require." At present there are over twenty Mothers' Centers in other locations.

If you are interested in joining such a group or in helping to set one up, you should contact the Family Resource Coalition in Chicago or any of the local and regional groups in your area (see the resources list in the Appendix). The bigger agencies, such as PEP, MELD, and the Mothers' Center, have manuals and guides that explain how to set up such an organization in your community.

There may also be less formal groups of women meeting that you could track down by contacting one of the national or regional self-help clearing houses (see Appendix). Very often the YWCA, your hospital, or a pediatrician's office will help in getting interested mothers together.

WORKING MOTHERS' GROUPS

Although many of these groups do offer evening sessions for working mothers (or fathers), working women may find such groups scarce out of office hours. Many working mothers are too exhausted even to imagine taking in a parenting group in their spare hours.

One new line of approach is for such groups to be held in the workplace. Before you get too excited about this idea, the only one I know of in existence has been set up by the Financial Women's Association (FWA), which has a Working Mothers Group. Its chairperson, Nan Foster Rubin, is an assistant vice president with Citibank in New York.

When Nan was six months pregnant, a few other women at her level were also pregnant or had young children, and so the idea of a support group was devised. They were all serious professionals who had to cope with problems of childcare, juggling personal and professional lives, and the basic concern of how to be a successful working mother.

The group began in 1979 and has been formally recognized by the FWA. They have a monthly luncheon (in midtown or downtown) to which they invite a visiting speaker or just talk about what is on their minds. It provides support for mothering as well as networking for professional concerns. As Nan notes, "We do talk outside those meetings, too."

The FWA's Working Mothers Group is no doubt the best way to beat that special form of isolation of being the only woman in your company with these concerns. Other professional or union agencies should set up similar groups that are not limited to one company or workplace. However, if you don't have anyone to talk to about your mothering or parenting problems, you might have to be the person who starts a group going. Someone, somewhere, is going to have to find the energy and drive necessary.

EPILOGUE

When I set about writing this book, I thought that most women would be reluctant to discuss the subject of PPD, that I would be forcing my ideas on unwilling listeners. I was surprised and overwhelmed by the abundance of replies that poured in to my request for experiences of the blues or postpartum depression, by the ease with which women spoke, and by the gratitude they expressed at being able to talk, and that someone was finally researching and addressing the issue. PPD is as important and valid a consideration, as much a part of pregnancy and childbirth, as those other topics traditionally discussed in childbirth preparation or Lamaze classes. Yet it is the one area of having a child that we have largely ignored because it is unwelcome, taboo, and certainly does not fit with the generally rosy view we have of motherhood.

For this new edition of the book, I am delighted to report on the response that welcomed publication of *The New Mother Syndrome;* and the overwhelming sense, for all of us now involved in the campaign for PPD awareness, of the need for such a book and the growing network of support available. Many of you may have seen some of the women who have come forward to talk about their experiences with PPD on a television program. This breakthrough to national attention has been invaluable and very exciting.

But these things do not come about by magic, so let me explain just how PPD became a household name. At first on its publication, there was a feeling among booksellers that this was not the type of book new mothers wanted to read. After all, wouldn't a new mother prefer the typical book showing the joy and downright "holiness" of mother and baby? These salesmen were afraid women would be put off by the word "depression" in conjunction with motherhood.

In my own heart I knew, from all the letters I had received, just how many woman out there did *need* such a book and would be far from insulted by such a realistic approach, bringing important information out of the closet.

Nancy Berchtold had already started up her Depression After Delivery support group, convinced there was still *no* reading material available on the subject, when she received a call from a woman in New Jersey who had tracked her down from a book called *The New Mother Syndrome*. "What?" came the urgent cry.

Searching for a support group herself, this woman had come across my book, and she put in a call to the New Jersey Self-Help Clearinghouse, who in turn put her in touch with Nancy. The new DAD members were thrilled to discover a book about *them*. Nancy contacted me by writing care of the publishers.

We talked at length on the phone. Nancy sent me material and local newspaper articles on the group. Echoing so many people's feelings she said, "We really should get PPD on the Donahue Show." I laughed. "Of course, it's easy to say that. But how do we do it?"

Slowly, it was becoming clear in my mind that the topic had to be taken onto television; there were so many women with such gripping stories to tell. A friend gave me the name of a producer on the "Phil Donahue Show." I made the first phone call. The response was a resounding negative. "That's far too depressing for our viewers." I explained why it would not be depressing, when they would in fact be helping so many women.

I sent in a batch of material, and a memo on how the

program could be structured. Nancy bombarded them with her material. Glenn Comitz had newly embarked on his own campaign. He had been on a Philadelphia TV talk show with Sharon's story, and had sent the videotape along, himself, also to a Donahue producer.

That was how Glenn Comitz, Nancy Berchtold, and I came together and how, in May 1986, we all appeared on the "Phil Donahue Show," which brought the message into people's homes in the most effective way possible. Following the success of the Donahue program we were able to contact other television programs and, by spring 1987, we had appeared on the following:

May '86: "Phil Donahue Show"
May '86: "AM Philadelphia"
Jul. '86: "Pittsburgh"/KDKA
Aug. '86: "WOR Straight Talk"/NJ
Aug. '86: "Oprah Winfrey Show"/Chicago
Sep. '86: "Good Day TV"/Boston
Sep. '86: "Hour Magazine"/national syndication
Oct. '86: "Kelly & Co"/Detroit
Dec. '86: "Phil Donahue Show"/rerun nationally
Dec. '86: "Oprah Winfrey Show"/rerun nationally
Dec. '86: NBC's "1986"
Jan. '87: "People Are Talking"/Philadelphia
Mar. '87: "Ira Joe Fisher"/Cincinnati
Mar. '87: "People Are Talking"/Boston

Following each TV show, the phone number of Depression After Delivery (DAD), based in Philadelphia and New Jersey, was given out. Nancy Berchtold has offered advice and support, or sent out information, to the many hundreds of women who have called, sometimes in crisis, or who have written. DAD has handled as many as 180 calls in a forty-eight-hour period, all performed by Nancy and other group members voluntarily—until we find a source of funding for this campaign. And they said women didn't want to hear about PPD!

Glenn Comitz, Jane Honikman, and I have also given lectures and held seminars—part of the next phase of our campaign which is to reach out to the professionals. We need to encourage more understanding of the syndrome among health-care workers who are in contact with pregnant women and new parents. In March 1987, Glenn Comitz and I spoke to a packed hall at the March of Dimes Perinatal Nursing Conference, in Chicago. We explained about PPD, its symptoms and effects. Glenn showed the videotape of the disturbing NBC program "1986," with its full report on Sharon's case. The highly educated and professional nurses were stunned at their own lack of knowledge. We wish to take this opportunity to thank the March of Dimes Chicago Chapter for having the foresight to bring this important topic to nursing professionals, and for the interest they have already shown in our campaign.

I am convinced that honesty, awareness, and understanding of PPD's symptoms, why it happens, and how it can be handled will be as great a liberating force in contemporary women's lives as the struggle to gain the vote, equal rights at work, or sexual emancipation were in the past. We do not have to be tied to the yoke of accepting our mothering in the traditional way it has always been promoted. We do not have to believe that PPD symptoms are evidence of an abnormal reaction. We are complex, rounded, weird, wise; above all we are human, individual women, with needs and desires that have to be satisfied in a variety of ways.

I want to see a different future for my daughters, one in which they not only accept that work is an integral and important part of their lives, but also one in which they view motherhood as an exciting, challenging step into another stage of life, which will help them grow and develop as fully realized people and which, like any stage of growth, won't be a breeze.

If we accept the physical and psychological upheavals women undergo in becoming mothers, I believe we will truly be viewing women as the fascinating, boundlessly creative people they really are.

APPENDIX

RESOURCES

WHOM CAN YOU GO TO FOR HELP?

If you feel you are in need of a doctor with some specialized knowledge of PPD, whether an obstetrician, psychiatrist, or family doctor, the following list includes those doctors known to have more than average interest or information on PPD's causes and best methods of treatment. (It is an ad hoc compilation from literature and other sources and not verification of the doctor's ability.)

Psychiatrists/Psychologists

ANTON, RAYMOND F., JR., M.D., Dept. of Psychiatry and Behavioral Sciences, Medical University of South Carolina, 170 Ashley Ave., Charleston, S.C. 29401

AUCHINCLOSS, ELIZABETH, M.D., Payne Whitney Clinic, The New York Hospital, 525 E. 68th St., New York, N.Y. 10021

BLACKMAN, LIONEL H., M.D., 2001 Embassy Dr., West Palm Beach, Fla. 33401

BLIX, SUSANNE, M.D., Dept. of Psychiatry, Indiana University School of Medicine, 1100 West Michigan St., Indianapolis, Ind. 46223

BRESSLER, BERNARD, M.D., 104 Berrington Court, Richmond, Va. 23221

BROWN, W.A., M.D., Dept. of Psychiatry, Brown University, Prospect, Providence, R.I. 02904

CAMPBELL, JAN L., M.D., Dept. of Psychiatry, VA Medical Center, 4801 Lynwood, Kansas City, Kan. 64128

CARRANZA, JOSE, M.D., Dept. of Psychiatry, Baylor College of Medicine, Texas Medical Center, Houston, Tex. 77030

EATON, MERRILL T., M.D., 602 S. 45th St., Omaha, Neb. 68106

FERNANDEZ, RICARDO, M.D., 35 Tamarack Circle, Skillman, N.J. 08558

GERNER, ROBERT H., M.D., UCLA-NPI, 760 Westwood Plaza, Los Angeles, Cal. 90024

GORODETSKY, GALINA, M.D., 3608 Sacramento St., San Francisco, Cal. 94118

HAMILTON, JAMES A., M.D., Ph.D., 2643 Union St., San Francisco, Cal. 94123

HENDRIE, HUGH C., M.D., Albert E. Stern Prof. and Chairman, Dept. of Psychiatry, Indiana University School of Medicine, 1100 West Michigan St., Indianapolis, Ind. 46223

HERZOG, ALFRED, M.D., Suite 815, 85 Jefferson St., Hartford, Conn. 06106

HICKMAN, SUSAN, Ph.D., 6635 Crawford St., San Diego, Cal. 92120 (psychologist)

HITTELMAN, DR. JOAN, Box 12-3, Dept. of Psychiatry, Downstate Medical Center, 450 Clarkson Ave., Brooklyn, N.Y. 11203

JAMISON, DR. KAY R., Affective Disorders Clinic, Dept. of Psychiatry, UCLA School of Medicine, Los Angeles, Cal. 90024

KLEIN, JUDITH, 100 W. 12th St., Apt. 6K, New York, N.Y. 10011 (psychotherapist)

LABRUM, ANTHONY H., M.D., 601 Elmwood Ave. (Box 668), Rochester, N.Y. 14642

LEVIN, MOLLY HALL, M.D., Payne Whitney Clinic, The New York Hospital, 525 E. 68th St., New York, N.Y. 10021

MCCURDY, LAYTON, M.D., Prof. and Chairman, Dept. of Psychiatry and Behavioral Sciences, Medical University of South Carolina, 171 Ashley Ave., Charleston, S.C. 29401

MELGES, FREDERICK T., M.D., 506 E. Forest Hills Blvd., Durham, N.C. 27707

O'HARA, MICHAEL W., Ph.D., Dept. of Psychology, University of Iowa, Iowa City, Iowa 52242

PARRY, BARBARA, M.D., Assoc. Dir. of Psychiatry, University of California San Diego Medical Center, 225 Dickinson St., San Diego, Cal. 92103-1990

PASNAU, ROBERT O., M.D., UCLA School of Medicine, 760 Westwood Plaza, Los Angeles, Cal. 90024

RAY, LEWIS, M.D., 2429 Ocean Ave., San Francisco, Cal. 94127

Ross, L., M.D., 3809 W. St. NW, Washington, D.C. 20007

Saks, Bonnie, M.D., 195 Colony Road, New Haven, Conn. 06511

Schachter, Meri, M.D., 124 Woodvale Rd., Glen Rock, N.J. 07452

Schneidman, Barbara, M.D., M.P.H., 3846 Cascadia Ave. South, Seattle, Wash. 98118

Sebastian, Simon, M.D., Dept. of Psychiatry, Louisiana State University Medical Center, Box 33932, Shreveport, La. 71130

Shill, J., M.D., 1330 New Hampshire Ave., Washington, D.C. 20036

Sholiton, Marilyn, M.D., University of Cincinnati College of Medicine, Dept. of Psychiatry, 231 Bethesda Ave., Cincinnati, Ohio 45267

Shrivastrva, Ram, 51 Newport Ave., Tappan, N.Y. 10983

Steiner, Meir, M.D., Ph.D., Assoc. Prof. McMaster Psychiatric Unit, St. Joseph's Hospital, 50 Charlton Ave. E., Hamilton, Ontario, Canada L8N 1Y4

Stotland, Nadia, M.D., Liaison Psychiatrist to Dept. of Ob/Gyn, Michael Reese Medical Center, Lake Shore Drive at 31st St., Chicago, Ill. 60616

Targum, Steven, M.D., 2033 K St. NW, Washington, D.C. 20006

Terzian, Edward, M.D., Philadelphia Medical Institute, 1015 Chestnut St., Suite 1303, Philadelphia, Penn. 19107

Trapnell, Richard H., M.D., 909 Hyde St., San Francisco, Cal. 94109

Von Der Mosel, Valentina, M.D., 241 Central Park W., New York. N.Y.; and 75 Columbia Ave., Cliffside Park, N.J. 07010

Williams, Lynne H., M.D., East Twelve Fifth, Suite 203, Spokane, Wash. 99202

Winokur, Prof. George, Dept. of Psychiatry, University of Iowa, 500 Newton Road, Iowa City, Iowa 52242

Wisner, K., M.D., Western Psychiatric Institute, 3811 O'Hara St., Pittsburgh, Penn. 15213

Woodle, Joanne, M.D., Dept. of Psychiatry, University Hospital, SUNY at Stonybrook, N.Y. 11794

Women's Psychotherapy Referral Service, Inc., 25 Perry St., New York, N.Y. 10014

Psychiatric Obstetricians and Gynecologists

Good, Raphael S., M.D., Clinical Prof. of Obstetrics and Psychiatry, University of Texas, University Blvd., Galveston, Tex. 77550

Herz, Elisabeth K., M.D., Assoc. Prof. for Ob/Gyn and Psychiatry and Behavioral Sciences, Dept. of Ob/Gyn, George Washington University, 2150 Pennsylvania Ave. NW, Washington, D.C. 20037

ROSENTHAL, MIRIAM B., M.D., Asst. Prof. of Psychiatry, Asst. Prof.
of Reproductive Biology, Dept. of Obstetrics, Case Western
Reserve Medical School, University Circle, Cleveland, Ohio
44106

SMALL, ELIZABETH CHAN, M.D., Assoc. Clinical Prof. of Obstetrics/
Gynecology and Psychiatry, Tufts University School of Medicine, Boston, Mass. 02111

Obstetricians

ENGELDINGER, J., M.D., Dept. of Obstetrics, University of Iowa,
Iowa City, Iowa 52242

FEINSTEIN, THEODORE A., M.D., 255 S. 17 St., Philadelphia, Pa.
19103

GRAHAM, DAVID, M.D., Dept. of Gynecology/Obstetrics, Johns
Hopkins University School of Medicine, 108 Marvey, Baltimore,
Md. 21205

LAFERLA, JOHN, M.D., University of Michigan, K2026 Holden, Ann
Arbor, Mich. 48109

MOZLEY, PAUL B., M.D., Prof. and Chair of Ob/Gyn, University of
Alabama College of Community Health Sciences, P.O. Box
1408, Tuscaloosa, Ala. 35486

SCHULMAN, HAROLD, M.D., Chairman, Dept. of Obstetrics and
Gynecology, Albert Einstein College of Medicine of Yeshiva
University, 1300 Morris Park Ave., New York, N.Y. 10461

SMITH, DENNIS, M.D., Dept. of Obstetrics, Case Western Reserve
Medical School, University Circle, Cleveland, Ohio 44106

All Other Doctors and Researchers

BLISS-HOLTZ, V. JANE, 343 Third Ave., Lindenwold, N.J. 08021
(Researcher)

BRADLEY, CHRISTINE, Ph.D., 4775 Chancellor Blvd., Vancouver,
B.C., Canada V6T 1C8 (Researcher)

BRAUNSTEIN, GLENN, M.D., Director, Div. of Endocrinology,
Cedars-Sinai Medical Center, Schuman Bldg., Room 516, Los
Angeles, Cal. 90048 (Endocrinologist)

CENTER FOR WOMEN'S HEALTH AND FAMILY BIRTH, 210 S. Palisades, Santa Maria, Cal. 93456

COBLE, P. A., Western Psychiatric Institute and Clinic, 3811 O'Hara
St., Pittsburgh, Penn. 15213

EZRIN, CALVIN, M.D., 18372 Clark St., Suite 226, Tarzana, Cal.
91356 (Endocrinologist)

HONIKMAN, JANE, 927 N. Kellogg, Santa Barbara, Cal. 93111

KANE, FRANCIS, M.D., 700 Fannin St., Houston, Tex. 77030 (Researcher)

KLAUS, MARSHALL, M.D., Prof. of Pediatrics, Michigan State University, B240, Life Sciences, East Lunig, Mich. 48824

MIDWIFERY SERVICES INC., 135 W. 70th St., New York, N.Y. 10023

PAFFENBARGER, RALPH, M.D., Dept. of Epidemiology, Stanford University School of Medicine, Stanford, Cal. 94305 (Epidemiology)

PARRY, BARBARA, M.D., Clinical Psychobiology Branch, National Institute of Mental Health, Bethesda, Md. 20857 (Psychobiology)

RASMUSSEN, HOWARD, M.D., Dept. of Internal Medicine, Yale University School of Medicine, 333 Cedar St., New Haven, Conn. 06510 (Medicine)

WEHR, THOMAS, M.D., Clinical Psychobiology Branch, National Institute of Mental Health, Bethesda, Md. 20857 (Psychobiology)

Nursing

AFFONSO, DR. DYANNE, UCSF School of Nursing, Parnassus Ave., San Francisco, Cal. 94122

BOYER, DIANE, R.N., C.N.M., Ph.D., Asst. Prof. and Dir. Graduate Nursing-Midwifery Programs, College of Nursing, University of Illinois at Chicago, 845 South Damen Ave., Box 6998, Chicago, Ill. 60680

FAWCETT, JACQUELINE, Ph.D., F.A.A.N., University of Pennsylvania School of Nursing, 420 Service Drive/S2, Philadelphia, Pa. 19104

GERDS, ROBERTA, R.N., M.N., UCLA School of Nursing, Center for Health Sciences, Los Angeles, Cal. 90024

KONIAK, DEBORAH, M.D., UCLA School of Nursing, Center for Health Sciences, Factor Bldg 5-266, Los Angeles, Cal. 90024

REEDER, SHARON, R.N., Assoc. Prof. UCLA School of Nursing, Center for Health Sciences, Los Angeles, Cal. 90024

YORK, RUTH, Ph.D., B.S.H., University of Pennsylvania School of Nursing, 420 Service Drive/S2, Philadelphia, Pa. 19104

Professional Organizations

Contact either:

Channi Kumar, M.D.
Institute of Psychiatry
De Crespigny Park
London SE5 8AF
England

Frank Margison, M.D.
Dept. of Psychotherapy
Manchester Royal Infirmary, Gaskell House
Swinton Grove, Manchester M13 OEU
England

American Society of Psychosomatic Obstetricians and Gynecologists. The secretary/treasurer at present is

Dennis H. Smith, M.D.
University Hospitals
2105 Adelbert Road
Cleveland, Ohio 44106

PARENT SUPPORT GROUPS

Another line of action in seeking help for PPD is to join a parent support group (or a mothers' group) in your neighborhood. The wonderful organization *Family Resource Coalition* has coordinated all the groups nationwide that are well-organized and members of FRC. If one of the groups mentioned below is in your area, do get in touch. They are all voluntarily run.

Alabama

FAMILY COUNSELING
  CENTER
6 South Florida St.
Mobile, Ala. 36606
205/471-3466

FAMILY SERVICE
  DIVISION
FAMILY & CHILD
  SERVICES
3600 8th Ave., S.
Birmingham, Ala. 35222
205/324-3411

Alaska

FAMILY CONNECTION
1836 W. Northern Lights Blvd.
Anchorage, Alaska 99503
907/279-0551

CENTER FOR CHILDREN &
  PARENTS
808 East St.
Anchorage, Alaska 99501
907/276-4994

JUNEAU WOMEN'S
  RESOURCE CENTER
110 Seward St., Room 6
Juneau, Alaska 99801
907/586-2977

Arizona

COMMUNITY
  INFORMATION &
  REFERRAL SERVICES,
  INC.
1515 East Osborne
Phoenix, Ariz. 85014
602/263-8856; 1-800-352-3792

ENRICHMENT FOR
  PARENTS
655 North Craycroft
Tucson, Ariz. 85711
602/881-0935

NEW PARENT PROGRAM
JEWISH FAMILY SERVICE
102 North Plumer Ave.
Tucson, Ariz. 85719
602/792-3641

Arkansas

THE PARENT CENTER
1501 Maryland
Little Rock, Ark. 72202
501/372-6890

California

APPLE PARENTING
  CENTER
70 Skyview Terrace
San Rafael, Cal. 94903
415/492-0720

CALIFORNIA PARENTING
  INSTITUTE
1030 Second St.
Santa Rosa, Cal. 95129

CHILDREN'S HEALTH
  COUNCIL
CHILD REARING
  EDUCATION AND
  COUNSELING PROGRAM
100 Willow Road
Palo Alto, Cal. 94304
415/326-5530

DEPARTMENT OF CHILD
  DEV./PARENT
  EDUCATION
LONG BEACH CITY
  COLLEGE
4901 East Carson St.
Long Beach, Cal. 90808
213/420-4454

FAMILY RESOURCES
P.O. Box 963
Bolinas, Cal. 94924
415/868-0616

PARENT EDUCATION
  PROGRAMS
SAN FRANCISCO
  COMMUNITY COLLEGE
1860 Hayes St.
San Francisco, Cal. 94117
415/346-2246

PARENTS PLACE
3272 California St.
San Francisco, Cal. 94118
415/563-1041

HEALTHY MOTHERS,
  HEALTHY BABIES
2131 University Ave., Suite 218
Berkeley, Cal. 94704

PARENT SUPPORT CENTER
  NETWORK
FAMILY SERVICE AGENCY
817 de la Vina
Santa Barbara, Cal. 93101
805/965-1001

PRESCHOOL AND INFANT
  PARENTING SERVICE
  (PIPS)
THALIANS MENTAL
  HEALTH CENTER
8730 Alden Dr.
Los Angeles, Cal. 90048
213/855-3500

A PLACE FOR PARENTS,
INC.
2019 14th St.
Santa Monica, Cal. 90405
213/452-3823

SANTA BARBARA BIRTH
RESOURCE CENTER
2255 Modoc Rd.
Santa Barbara, Cal. 93101
805/682-7529

STEPHEN S. WISE
PARENTING CENTER
15500 Stephen S. Wise Dr.
Los Angeles, Cal. 90024
213/476-8561

Colorado

FAMILY SUPPORT
SERVICES
601 South Irving
Denver, Colo. 80219
303/935-9510

JEWISH FAMILY &
CHILDREN'S SERVICES
300 South Dahlia, #101
Denver, Colo. 80220
303/399-2660

METROPOLITAN STATE
COLLEGE
PARENT EDUCATION
RESOURCE CENTER
1006 11th St.
Denver, Colo. 80204
303/629-8362

PARENTS PLUS
P.O. Box 7515
Colorado Springs, Colo. 80933
303/471-3238

Connecticut

CHILD CARE COUNCIL OF
WESTPORT-WESTON
90 Hillspoint Road
Westport, Conn. 06880
203/226-7007

MOTHERING CENTER,
INC.
235 Cognewaugh Road
Cos Cob, Conn. 06807
203/661-1413

PARENTS TOGETHER
48 Maple Ave.
Greenwich, Conn. 06830
203/869-1979

Delaware

FAMILY SERVICE OF
DELAWARE
809 Washington St.
Wilmington, Del. 19801
302/654-5303

District of Columbia

FAMILIES & CHILDREN IN
TROUBLE (FACT)
FAMILY STRESS SERVICES
OF D.C.
1690 36th St., NW
Washington, D.C. 20007
202/965-1900

THE FAMILY PLACE
1848 Columbia Road, NW
Washington, D.C. 20009
202/265-0149

Florida

FAMILY CENTER OF NOVA
    UNIVERSITY
3301 College Ave.
Fort Lauderdale, Fla. 33314
305/475-7471

PARENT EDUCATION
    PROJECT
VALENCIA COMMUNITY
    COLLEGE
P.O. Box 3028
Orlando, Fla. 32802
305/299-5000

PARENTING PROJECT
PEACE RIVER CENTER
1745 U.S. Highway 17 South
Bartow, Fla. 33830
813/533-3141

PARENT RESOURCE
    CENTER
42 East Jackson St.
Orlando, Fla. 32802
305/425-3663

Georgia

THE MOTHERS' CENTER
    OF ATHENS
190 Lavender Rd.
Athens, Ga. 30606
404/549-4640

THE MOTHERS' CENTER
    OF ROME
Route 1, 313 Haywood Valley
Armuchee, Ga. 30105
404/291-9914

CHILD SERVICE & FAMILY
    COUNSELING CENTER
1105 West Peachtree, NE
Atlanta, Ga. 30357

Hawaii

HAWAII FAMILY STRESS
    CENTER
KAPIOLANI CHILDREN'S
    MEDICAL CENTER
1317 Punahou St.
Honolulu, Hawaii 96826
808/947-8634

Illinois

BEVERLY FAMILY
    CENTER
9300 S. Pleasant St.
Chicago, Ill. 60620
312/779-1230

EARLY YEARS PROGRAM
ORCHARD MENTAL
    HEALTH CENTER
8600 Gross Point Road
Skokie, Ill. 60077
312/967-7300

FAMILY CENTER
229 South Bench St.
Galena, Ill. 61036
815/777-1560, 777-2348

FAMILY FOCUS
2300 Green Bay Road
Evanston, Ill. 60201
312/869-4700

PARENT/CHILD NETWORK
P.O. Box 784
Tinley Park, Ill. 60477
312/795-1949

MOMS, INC.
P.O. Box 59229
Chicago, Ill. 60659
312/583-7997

PARENTS & CHILDBIRTH
 EDUCATION SOCIETY
 (PACES)
P.O. Box 213
Western Springs, Ill. 60558
312/964-2048

NORTHSIDE PARENTS'
 NETWORK
P.O. Box 10584
Chicago, Ill. 60610
312/871-0453, 477-2839

PARENTS & CHILDREN
 TOGETHER (PACT)
405 Wagner Road
Northfield, Ill. 60093
312/446-5370, 251-4451

PARENTAL STRESS
 SERVICES
59 East Van Buren, #1618
Chicago, Ill. 60605
312/427-1161

PARENTHESIS
405 South Euclid
Oak Park, Ill. 60302
312/848-2227

PARENT SUPPORT
 NETWORK
5600 South Woodlawn
Chicago, Ill. 60637
312/288-2353, 241-5164

ROGERS PARK FAMILY
 NETWORK
1545 West Morse
Chicago, Ill. 60626
312/743-2818

VIRGINIA FRANK CHILD
 DEVELOPMENT CENTER
3033 West Touhy
Chicago, Ill. 60645
312/761-4550

FAMILY SERVICE CENTER
 OF SANGAMON COUNTY
1308 S. 7th St.
Springfield, Ill. 62703
217/528-8406

Indiana

CATHOLIC CHARITIES
 BUREAU
603 Court Building
Evansville, Ind. 47708
812/423-5456

FAMILY HOUSE, INC.
203 Franklin
Valparaiso, Ind. 46383
219/464-4160

PARENTS HELPING
 PARENTS
3410 West Virginia St.
Evansville, Ind. 47712
812/479-8423, 425-5525

PARENTS TOGETHER
PORTER COUNTY FAMILY
 SERVICES
2588-P Portage Mall
Portage, Ind. 46386
219/762-7181

PARENT–YOUNG CHILD
 PROGRAM
Family & Child Studies
Dept. of Home Economics
Ball State University
Muncie, Ind. 47306
317/896-5018

FAMILY FOCUS OF
 WHITLEY COUNTY
P.O. Box 497
Columbia City, Ind. 46725
219/691-2297

Iowa

THE PEOPLE PLACE
120 South Hazel
Ames, Iowa 50010
515/233-1677

**FAMILY RESOURCE
   CENTER**
2530 University Ave.
Waterloo, Iowa 50701
319/235-6271

**FAMILY & CHILDREN'S
   SERVICE OF DAVENPORT**
115 W. 6th St.
Davenport, Iowa 52803
319/323-1852

Kansas

**McPHERSON FAMILY LIFE
   CENTER**
Box 1252
McPherson, Kans. 67460
316/241-6603

**FAMILY & CHILDEN'S
   SERVICE**
5424 State St.
Kansas City, Kans. 66102
913/287-1300

Kentucky

PARENTS' PLACE
201 Mechanic St.
Lexington, Ky. 40507
606/233-0444

**FAMILY & CHILDREN'S
   AGENCY**
1115 Garvin Place
Louisville, Ky. 40201
502/583-1741

Louisiana

**FAMILY TREE PARENTING
   CENTER**
P.O. Box 31233
Lafayette, La. 70503
318/988-1136

PARENTING CENTER
7343-C Florida Blvd.
Baton Rouge, La. 70806
504/924-0123

PARENTING CENTER
200 Henry Clay Ave.
New Orleans, La. 70018
504/895-3574

Maine

**LINCOLN COUNTY
   PARENT RESOURCE
   CENTER**
P.O. Box 966
Damariscotta, Maine 04543
207/563-1938

**COMMUNITY
   COUNSELING CENTER**
622 Congress St.
Portland, Maine 04101
207/774-5727

Maryland

PARENT CONNECTION
4701 Sangamore Road
Bethesda, Md. 20816
301/320-2321

**PARENT EDUCATION
   RESOURCE CENTER**
12518 Greenly Dr.
Silver Springs, Md. 20906
301/871-3873

FAMILY LIFE CENTER,
INC.
10451 Twin Rivers Road
Columbia, Md. 21044
301/997-3557

Massachusetts

THE PARENT
CONNECTION
700 Grove St.
Worcester, Mass. 01605
617/852-5658

COPING WITH THE
OVERALL PREGNANCY
& PARENTING
EXPERIENCE (COPE)
37 Clarendon St.
Boston, Mass. 02116
617/357-5588

THE PARENT
CONNECTION
1210 Massachusetts Ave.
Arlington, Mass. 02174
617/641-2229

THE MOTHER
CONNECTION
P.O. Box 59
Andover, Mass. 01810
617/470-0539

THE PARENTS CENTER OF
HOPKINTON
ST. PAUL'S EPISCOPAL
CHURCH
Wood Street
Hopkinton, Mass. 01748
617/435-3062

Michigan

THE CHILD & FAMILY
NEIGHBORHOOD
PROGRAM
33577 Berville Court
Westland, Mich. 48184
313/729-2610

FAMILY SERVICE ASSN.
OF DETROIT & WAYNE
COUNTIES
51 West Warren
Detroit, Mich. 48201
313/833-3733

FAMILY GROWTH CENTER
215 North Capitol
Lansing, Mich. 48933
517/371-4350

MOTHER HAVEN
Haslett Professional Building
5681 Shaw St.
Lansing, Mich. 48909
517/339-8691

PARENTS SUPPORTING
PARENTS
700 Fuller N.E.
Grand Rapids, Mich. 49503
616/247-1373

NEIGHBORHOOD FAMILY
RESOURCE CENTER OF
THE CENTER FOR
URBAN STUDIES
WAYNE STATE
UNIVERSITY
5229 Cass Ave.
Detroit, Mich. 48202
313/577-2208

Minnesota

MINNESOTA EARLY
  LEARNING DESIGN
  (MELD)
123 East Grant St.
Minneapolis, Minn. 55403
612/870-4478

PARENTING RESOURCE
  CENTER
P.O. Box 505
Austin, Minn. 55912
507/437-7746

RURAL FAMILY
  DEVELOPMENT
STAPLES PUBLIC
  SCHOOLS
422 2nd St.
Staples, Minn. 56479
218/894-2430

Mississippi

FAMILY SERVICE ASSN.
  OF GREATER JACKSON
1510 N. State St.
Jackson, Miss. 39202
601/353-3891

Missouri

THE FAMILY CENTER—A
  GROWING PLACE
7423 Wellington
Clayton, Mo. 63105
314/726-1666

FAMILY & CHILDREN
  SERVICES OF KANSAS
  CITY
THE LIVING CENTER FOR
  FAMILY ENRICHMENT
3515 Broadway
Kansas City, Mo. 64111
816/753-5325

JEWISH COMMUNITY
  CENTERS ASSN.
PRIME TIME PROGRAM
2 Millstone Dr.
St. Louis, Mo. 63146
314/432-5700

EARLY EDUCATION
  PROGRAMS
FERGUSON-FLORISSANT
  SCHOOLS
655 January Ave.
Ferguson, Mo. 63135
314/595-2355

LADUE EARLY
  CHILDHOOD CENTER
10601 Clayton Road
St. Louis, Mo. 63131
314/993-5724

THE MOTHERS' CENTER
  OF ST. LOUIS
516 Loughborough
St. Louis, Mo. 63111
314/353-1558

PATHWAY—PARENTS AS
  TEACHERS
1441 Greenlace Drive
Maryland Heights, Mo. 63043

Nebraska

FAMILY SERVICE ASSN.
  OF LINCOLN
1133 H St.
Lincoln, Nebr. 68508
402/476-3327

FAMILY SERVICE
2240 Landon Court
Omaha, Nebr. 68102
402/345-9118

NEWBORN AND PARENT
  SUPPORT GROUP
421 N. Lincoln
Hastings, Nebr. 68901
402/462-5515

New Hampshire

THE CHILDREN'S PLACE—
  A FAMILY RESOURCE
  CENTER
P.O. Box 576
Concord, N.H. 03301
603/224-9920

New Jersey

NEW JERSEY SELF-HELP
  CLEARINGHOUSE
ST. CLARE'S HOSPITAL
Pocono Road
Denville, N.J. 07834
1-800/452-9790

FAMILY COUNSELING
  SERVICES
10 Banta Place
Hackensack, N.J. 07601
201/342-9200

THE TEANECK PARENTS
  CENTER
61 Church St.
Teaneck, N.J. 07666
201/836-8271

FAMILY LIFE RESOURCES
203 2nd St.
Fanwood, N.J. 07023
201/889-4270

New Mexico

THE PARENTCRAFT
  PROGRAM
P.O. Box 6852
Albuquerque, N.M. 87197
505/256-1191

New York

COMMUNITY OF CARING
  CONSORTIUM
144 Bleecker St.
Brooklyn, N.Y. 11221

FAMILIES FIRST
250 Baltic St.
Brooklyn, N.Y. 11201
718/855-3131

FAMILY DYNAMICS, INC.
225 Park Avenue South, #734
New York, N.Y. 10003
212/260-4344

THE MOTHERS' CENTER
  DEVELOPMENT PROJECT
129 Jackson St.
Hempstead, N.Y. 11550
516/486-6614; toll free from
  outside N.Y. 1-800-645-3828
  (call for location of ten
  Mothers' Centers in New York)

THE PARENT CENTER
MT. KISCO ELEMENTARY
  SCHOOL
West Hyatt Ave.
Mt. Kisco, N.Y. 10549
914/666-8215

PARENTING CENTER
92nd STREET YM-YWHA
1395 Lexington Ave.
New York, N.Y. 10028
212/427-6000, x206

PARENTING EDUCATION
  PROGRAM (PEP) OF
  BROOKLYN
P.O. Box 49, Downstate
  Medical Center
450 Clarkson Ave.
Brooklyn, N.Y. 11203
718/270-2176

THE PARENTING PLACE
METROPOLITAN HOSPITAL
  CENTER
Pediatrics Dept.
1901 1st Ave.
New York, N.Y. 10029
212/360-7329

PARENT RESOURCE
  CENTER
FLOWER HILL SCHOOL
Campus Dr.
Port Washington, N.Y. 11050
516/883-4000, x230, 231

PARENTS' PLACE, INC.
3 Carhart Ave.
White Plains, N.Y. 10605
914/948-5187

WEBSTER AVENUE
  FAMILY RESOURCE
  CENTER
134 Webster Ave.
Rochester, N.Y. 14609
716/654-8673

North Carolina

FAMILY & CHILDREN'S
  SERVICE
301 S. Brevard St.
Charlotte, N.C. 28202
704/332-9034

FAMILY SERVICE OF
  WAKE COUNTY
3803 Computer Dr.
Raleigh, N.C. 27609
919/781-9317

Ohio

THE FAMILY PLACE
JEWISH COMMUNITY
  CENTER
3505 Mayfield Road
Cleveland Heights, Ohio 44118
216/382-4000, x218, 282

FOCUS ON MOTHERS
NORTHEASTERN YWCA
5257 Montgomery Road
Cincinnati, Ohio 45212
513/351-6550

MOTHERS' CENTER OF
  CINCINNATI
776 Hanson Dr.
Cincinnati, Ohio 45240
513/851-5963

HEIGHTS PARENT CENTER
13263 Cedar Road
Cleveland Heights, Ohio 44118
216/321-0079

UNITED SERVICES FOR
  EFFECTIVE PARENTING
194 Blenheim Rd.
Columbus, Ohio 43214

WHOLE PARENT/WHOLE
  CHILD
76 Bell St.
Chagrin Falls, Ohio 44022
216/247-6920

Oklahoma

PARENTS' ASSISTANCE
  CENTER
707 N.W. 8th
Oklahoma City, Okla. 73102
405/232-8227 or 8226

TULSA COALITION FOR
  PARENTING
1430 South Boulder
Tulsa, Okla. 74119
918/585-5551

Oregon

BIRTH-TO-THREE
1432 Orchard, #4
Eugene, Oreg. 97407
503/484-4401

METROPOLITAN FAMILY
  SERVICE
2281 N.W. Everett St.
Portland, Oreg. 97210
503/228-7238

Pennsylvania

BRIGHT BEGINNINGS
  WARM LINE
MAGEE WOMEN'S
  HOSPITAL
Forbes Halket
Pittsburgh, Pa. 15213
412/647-4546

FAMILY SUPPORT CENTER
2 Baily Road
Yeadon, Pa. 19050
215/622-5660

PARENT RESOURCE ASSN.
Kent & Fernbrook Roads
Wyncote, Pa. 19095
215/576-7961

PARENTING DEPARTMENT
BOOTH MATERNITY
  CENTER
6051 Overbrook Ave.
Philadelphia, Pa. 19131
215/878-7800, x651

Rhode Island

WOONSOCKET FAMILY
  CENTER
460 S. Main St.
Woonsocket, R.I. 02895
401/766-0900

South Carolina

FAMILY SERVICE OF
  CHARLESTON COUNTY
Community Services Building
30 Lockwood Blvd.
Charleston, S.C. 29401
803/723-4566

South Dakota

FAMILY SERVICE
1728 South Cliff Ave.
Sioux Falls, S.D. 57105
605/336-1974

POSITIVE PARENT
  NETWORK
P.O. Box 2792
Rapid City, S.D. 57709
605/348-9276

Tennessee

FAMILY SERVICE OF
  MEMPHIS
2400 Poplar Bldg.
Memphis, Tenn. 38112
901/324-3637

Texas

AVANCE
1226 N.W. 18th St.
San Antonio, Tex. 78207
512/734-7924

CHILD & FAMILY SERVICE
2001 Chicon
Houston, Tex. 78722

CONFIDENT PARENTING
4034 Leeshire Dr.
Houston, Tex. 77025

**DALLAS ASSN. FOR
PARENT EDUCATION**
13551 N. Central Exp. #12
Dallas, Tex. 75243
214/699-0420

FAMILY SERVICE CENTER
2128 Avenue P
Galveston, Tex. 77550
409/762-8636

**FAMILY RESOURCE
CENTER**
3203 Nacogdoches Road
San Antonio, Tex. 78217
512/657-3094

**HOUSTON ORGANIZATION
FOR PARENT
EDUCATION**
3311 Richmond, #330
Houston, Tex. 77098
713/524-3089

Utah

FAMILY SUPPORT CENTER
2020 Lake St.
Salt Lake City, Utah 84105
801/487-7778

**DAVIS COUNTY SCHOOL
DISTRICT
PARENT EDUCATION
RESOURCE CENTER**
100 South 200 East
Monte Vista Center
Farmington, Utah 84025
801/451-5071

Vermont

**FRANKLIN COUNTY
FAMILY CENTER**
86 North Main
St. Albans, Vt. 05478

**LAMOILLE FAMILY
CENTER**
Box 274
Morrisville, Vt. 05661
802/888-5229

Virginia

FAMILY SERVICE, INC.
116 West Jefferson St.
Charlottesville, Va. 22901
804/296-4118

Washington

**FAMILY LIFE EDUCATION
PROGRAMS
PENINSULA COMMUNITY
COLLEGE**
1502 East Lauridsen Blvd.
Port Angeles, Wash. 98362
206/452-9277

**FAMILY SERVICES OF
KING COUNTY**
107 Cherry St., #500
Seattle, Wash. 98104
206/447-3883

THE PARENT PLACE
1608 N.E. 150th St.
Seattle, Wash. 98155
206/364-9933, 364-7274

PARENT COOPERATIVE
  FAMILY EDUCATION
  PROGRAM
COMMUNITY COLLEGE OF
  SPOKANE
Institute of Extended Learning
W. 3305 Ft. Wright Dr., MS
  3090
Spokane, Wash. 99204
509/459-3737

PEPS
8619 N.E. 24th
Bellevue, Wash. 98024

Wisconsin

FAMILY SERVICE OF
  MILWAUKEE
2819 W. Highland Blvd.
Milwaukee, Wis. 53208
414/342-4558

FAMILY SERVICE OF
  BELOIT
423 Bluff
Beloit, Wis. 53571
608/365-1244

FAMILY ENHANCEMENT
605 Spruce St.
Madison, Wis. 53715
608/256-3890

MILWAUKEE AREA
  TECHNICAL COLLEGE
FAMILY LIVING
  EDUCATION
1015 N. 6th St.
Milwaukee, Wis. 53203
414/278-6835, 278-6219

MILWAUKEE MELD
4385 Green Bay Ave.
Milwaukee, Wis. 53209
414/263-2044

FRC itself can be contacted for any further information; to join the coalition as a member and receive its three-times-a-year *Report*, dues are $15 a year for an individual and $30 a year for an organization. Write to Family Resource Coalition, 230 N. Michigan Ave., Suite 1625, Chicago, Ill. 60601 (312-726-4750).

For any mother wishing to take her interest in parent support groups or parent education further, you might be interested in a degree specialization that has been set up (in 1984) at Fordham University in parent education. Chairperson, Division of Curriculum and Teaching, Room 1102A, Fordham University Graduate School of Education at Lincoln Center, 113 W. 62nd St., New York, N.Y. 10023.

SELF-HELP CLEARINGHOUSES

If you still have a problem finding a group of parents or mothers in your area, you could try these self-help clearinghouses. The list is furnished by the FRC *Report* (October–December 1983).

SAN FRANCISCO SELF-
  HELP CLEARINGHOUSE
Mental Health Assn. of San
  Francisco
2398 Pine St.
San Francisco, Cal. 94115
415-921-4401
Sharon George, Director

CALIFORNIA SELF-HELP
  RESOURCE CENTER
University of California
Psychology Dept.
405 Hilgard Ave.
Los Angeles, Cal. 90024
213-825-3552
Dr. Douglas Anglin

SAN DIEGO SELF-HELP
  CLEARINGHOUSE
P.O. Box 86246
San Diego, Cal. 92138
619-275-2344
Ellen Murphy, Director

CONNECTICUT SELF-HELP
  MUTUAL SUPPORT
  NETWORK
19 Howe St.
New Haven, Conn. 16511
800-842-1501 or 203-789-7645
Vicki Smith

HILLSBOROUGH COUNTY
  SELF-HELP
  CLEARINGHOUSE
Florida Mental Health Institute
13301 N. 30th St.

Tampa, Fla. 33612
813-974-4672
Michelle Kunkel, Coordinator

SELF-HELP CENTER
1600 Dodge Ave., S112
Evanston, Ill. 60201
312-328-0470
Leonard Borman, Director

BERRIEN COUNTY SELF-
  HELP CLEARINGHOUSE
Riverwood Community Mental
  Health Center
2681 Morton Ave.
St. Joseph, Mich. 49085
616-983-7781
Rob Hess/Charles Livingston

MINNESOTA MUTUAL
  HELP RESOURCE
  CENTER
Wilder Foundation Community
  Care Unit
919 Lafond Ave.
St. Paul, Minn. 55104
612-642-4060
Thomas Duke, Director

SELF-HELP INFORMATION
  SERVICES
1601 Euclid Ave.
Lincoln, Nebr. 68502
402-476-9668
Barbara Fox, Director

NEW JERSEY SELF-HELP
CLEARINGHOUSE
St. Clare's Hospital CMHC
Denville, N.J. 07834
201-625-6395
Edward J. Madara, Director

BROOKLYN SELF-HELP
CLEARINGHOUSE
Heights Hills Mental Health
Service
30 Third Ave.
Brooklyn, N.Y. 11217
718-834-7341
Carol Berkvist, Director

LONG ISLAND SELF-HELP
CLEARINGHOUSE
New York Institute of
Technology
Commack College Center
6350 Jericho Turnpike
Commack, N.Y. 11725
516-499-8800
Robert Slotnick/Abe Jaeger, Co-
Directors

NEW YORK CITY SELF-
HELP CLEARINGHOUSE
City University of New York
Graduate Center, 1225
33 W. 42nd St.
New York, N.Y. 10036
212-852-4290
Carol Eisman/Fran Dory, Co-
Directors

WESTCHESTER SELF-HELP
CLEARINGHOUSE
Westchester Community
College
Academic Arts Building
75 Grasslands Road
Valhalla, N.Y. 10595
914-347-3620
Leslie Borck, Director

INFORMATION AND
REFERRAL SERVICES
United Way of The Columbia
Wilamette
718 W. Burnside
Portland, Oreg. 97209
503-222-5555
Nancy Webb-Ranken

PHILADELPHIA SELF-
HELP CLEARINGHOUSE
John F. Kennedy CMHC
112 N. Broad St.
Philadelphia, Pa. 19102
215-568-0860, x276
Jared Hermalin, Director

SELF-HELP INFORMATION
& NETWORKING
EXCHANGE
Voluntary Action Center of NE
Pennsylvania
200 Adams St.
Scranton, Pa. 18503
717-347-5616
Arlene Hopkins, Director

DALLAS SELF-HELP
CLEARINGHOUSE
Mental Health Assn. of Dallas
County
2500 Maple Ave.
Dallas, Tex. 75201-1998
214-748-1998
Carol Madison, Director

GREATER WASHINGTON
SELF-HELP COALITION
(Washington, D.C., N. Va., and
S. Md.)
Mental Health Assn. of
Northern Virginia
100 N. Washington St.
Falls Church, Va. 22046
703-536-4100
Linda Figuerosa, Coord.

National

NATIONAL SELF-HELP
  CLEARINGHOUSE
CUNY Graduate Center, 1206A
33 W. 42nd St.
New York, N.Y. 10036
212-840-1259
Frank Riessman/Alan Gartner,
  Co-Directors

MISCELLANEOUS

Working Mothers

Catalyst, 14 E. 60th St., New York, N.Y. 10022 (212-759-9700) is a national organization that tries to help communication between corporations and women in an attempt to resolve career and family issues. They have a book list that might be of help or interest, and a library that is open to the public, full of resources on women, work, and family.

The Conference Board (New York only) is a clearinghouse of information on work and family. The Financial Women's Association Working Mothers Group: contact Nan Foster Rubin through the FWA of New York, 35 E. 72nd St., New York, N.Y. 10021.

Adoptive Children

Center of Adoptive Families, 67 Irving Place, New York, N.Y. 10003 (212-420-8811) offers family therapy, advice, support, and help with adoption agencies.

Single Parents

Single Parent Resource Center, 225 Park Ave. S., New York, N.Y. 10003 (212-475-4401) is a clearinghouse for groups of single parents, publishes its newsletter *Speak Out,* and offers advice, support, help with housing, and contact with other single parents.

Parents Without Partners, 7910 Woodmont Ave., Washington, D.C. 20014.

Multiples

Mothers of Twins Club, 5402 Amberwood Lane, Rockville, Md. 20853 (301-460-9108).

Publications

Birthwrites, published by the Houston Organization for Parent Education, Inc., 3311 Richmond Ave., Suite 330, Houston, Tex. 77098. The newsletter of HOPE reaches 4,000 couples in the area.

Practical Parenting, ed. Vicki Lansky. Write for her newsletter to 18326B Minnetonka Blvd., Deephaven, Minn. 55391 (612-475-1505).

Working Parents' Forum, an eight-page bimonthly national newsletter designed to put working parents in touch with the latest information on balancing family and career. It is edited by Pattie Carroll Kearns, R.N., a childbirth and parent educator. Write to Center for Family and Community Education, Inc., P.O. Box 4505, New Windsor, N.Y. 12550 (allow six to eight weeks for delivery).

ICEA Review, a publication of the International Childbirth Education Association, P.O. Box 20048, Minneapolis, Minn. 55420-0048.

NOTES

1. Dr. Elisabeth Herz, Associate Professor for Gynecology and Obstetrics and Psychiatry, Director of Psychosomatic Ob/Gyn Program at George Washington University Medical Center, 2150 Pennsylvania Ave., NW, Washington, D.C. 20037. For information about other psychosomatic ob/gyns in the country, contact the ASPOG, Secretary-Treasurer, Dr. Dennis H. Smith, University Hospitals, 2105 Adelbert Road, Cleveland, Ohio 44106.

2. Dr. Katharina Dalton, of London, has published widely on PMS, oral contraceptives, migraine, and puerperal disorders. A list of her articles may be obtained from her office, 100 Harley St., London W.1. The most recent and interesting of her books are *Premenstrual Syndrome and Progesterone Therapy*, 2nd ed. (Chicago: Year Book, 1983); *Once a Month*, 2nd ed. (Claremont, Calif.: Hunter House, 1983); and *Depression After Childbirth* (London: Oxford University Press, 1980).

3. Dr. James Hamilton, formerly a clinical psychiatrist at Stanford University, California, has been involved in work on PPD for more years than perhaps any other doctor in the United States. For many years he has run a sort of mail-order service as distraught new parents have somehow come across his name, in library catalogues or occasional articles that have reached the public eye, and consequently sought his advice. For two years he acted as secretary of the Marcé Society, retiring from that position in 1984, though he will no doubt continue to remain active in Marcé's cause.

4. Dr. E. A. Strecker was a well-known practicing psychiatrist

261

in the 1940s, chairman of the psychiatry department at the University of Pennsylvania, consultant to the Surgeons General of the Army and Navy, and adviser to the Secretary of War. In his Foreword to the book *Their Mothers' Sons* (New York: Longmans, 1946), with the subtitle *The Psychiatrist Examines an American Problem*, Eugene Meyer, Chairman of the National Committee on Mental Hygiene, commented that to Strecker the cold hard facts were that 1,825,000 men were rejected for military service because of psychiatric disorders.

On April 27, 1945, Strecker delivered a lecture before several hundred medical students and physicians at Bellevue Hospital in New York. The lecture has since been controversially titled "the moms lecture" and was influential as the first in a memorial lectureship at the bequest of Dr. Menas Gregory, professor of psychiatry at New York University and head of the psychiatric division at Bellevue. Strecker called his lecture "Psychiatry Speaks to Democracy," but, writes Meyer, it could have been called "Psychiatry Speaks to the Neurotic Moms of Psychoneurotics," for the darts of his comments were directed at the apron-stringing mothers of America and at their indirect effect on democracy. Strecker indicted the doting mother for her sins of commission and omission against her children and, therefore, the nation.

5. Terra Ziporyn, "Rip van Winkle Period Ends for Puerperal Psychiatric Problems," Medical News, *JAMA* 251 (April 1984).

6. The first Marcé Society conference was held in London. This biennial meeting was hosted in San Francisco in 1984. The American conference was sadly underrepresented by U.S. doctors and psychiatrists, but everyone is hoping that situation will be rectified.

7. I. Yalom, D. Lunde, R. Moos, and D. Hamburg, "Postpartum Blues Syndrome," *Archives of General Psychiatry* 18 (1968): 16–27.

8. Two articles so far report unsuccessful attempts to associate specific hormonal changes with mental disorders: P. N. Nott, M. Franklin, C. Armitage, and M. G. Gelder, "Hormonal Changes and Mood in the Puerperium," *British Journal of Psychiatry* 128 (1976): 379–83, and R. Treadway, F. Kane, A. Jarrahi-Zadeh, and M. Lipton, "A Psychoendocrine Study of Pregnancy and the Puerperium," *American Journal of Psychiatry* 125 (1968–69): 1380–86. Very little research has been completed in this fascinating field.

9. I refer readers to two volumes for further help in understanding the psychoendocrine factor: Maggie Scarf's splendid book that so lucidly explains science to the layperson—*Unfinished Business: Pressure Points in the Lives of Women* (Garden City, N.Y.:

Doubleday, 1980); and the NIMH booklet, *Depression, Manic-Depressive Illness and Biological Rhythms,* by Eunice Corfman, Science Reports 1 (ADM) 79-889, 1982.

10. Penny Budoff, *No More Menstrual Cramps and Other Good News* (New York: Putnam, 1980).

11. Dane Prugh, *The Psychosocial Aspects of Pediatrics* (Philadelphia: Lea & Febiger, 1982).

12. James Hamilton, M.D., *Postpartum Psychiatric Problems* (St. Louis: Mosby, 1962).

13. "Postpartum Psychiatric Problems and Thyroid Dysfunctions," by Nobuyuki Amino, Osaka University Medical School, Osaka; and "Clinicoendocrine Studies of Postpartum Psychoses," by Nomura, Okano, Harada, Kitayama, Inoue, Yamaguchi, and Hatotani, Mie University School of Medicine, Tsu, Mie. See Proceedings of the Marcé Society Conference, San Francisco, 1984 (for details apply to the Marcé Society secretary).

14. "The Use of Corticoids in Postpartum Psychiatric Illness." See Proceedings of the San Francisco Conference, ibid.

15. The following information about tranquilizers and antidepressants is taken from *Ms* magazine, May 1984.

"Drugs that calm without impairing consciousness are called tranquilizers. The major ones, used to treat serious cases, such as mania or schizophrenia, are called anti-psychotics (Thorazine, Stelazine, Mellaril, Navane, Prolixin). Minor ones used to treat anxiety and tension are called anti-anxiety drugs such as Valium and Librium. Drugs used to treat depression are anti-depressants, such as Nardil and Elavil" (from *The Doctors and Patients Handbook of Medicines and Drugs* [New York: Knopf, 1984]).

16. George Winokur, *Depression: The Facts* (New York: Oxford University Press, 1981).

17. The mother and baby unit at the Massachusetts Mental Health Center is described by Ian Brockington and Frank Margison, "Psychiatric Mother and Baby Units," in *Motherhood and Mental Illness,* ed. Ian Brockington and R. Kumar (New York: Grune & Stratton, 1982). American experience of admitting babies with their mentally sick mothers is described at length in a book by H. Grunebaum, J. Weiss, B. Cohler, C. Hartman, and D. Galland entitled *Mentally Ill Mothers and Their Children* (Chicago: University of Chicago Press, 1975), pp. 223–38.

18. Ibid.

19. Mother-baby relationships in psychiatric disorder, as witnessed in the mother and baby unit at the Royal Infirmary, Swinton Grove, Manchester, England, were described by Dr. Frank Margison of the department of psychiatry, a very concerned doctor who has been working with the unit for many years now, at the Marcé Con-

ferences of 1982 and 1984 (see Proceedings of both conferences). Margison is now secretary and bulletin editor of the Marcé Society.

20. Brockington and Margison, "Psychiatric Mother and Baby Units."

21. Gregory Zilboorg, "Clinical Issues of Postpartum Psychopathological Reactions," *American Journal of Obstetrics and Gynecology* 73 (1957): 305.

21a. Most of the following story was first written by me for the *Ladies Home Journal*. (At the time this edition of *The New Mother Syndrome* went to press, it had not yet been published.) We are most grateful to the editors of the magazine for this opportunity.

21b. Much of this story about Angela Thompson was first printed in the *Los Angeles Times*, in a groundbreaking article written by Ann Japenga, that appeared on February 1, 1987. Although I have personally spoken to Angela and Jeff Thompson myself many times, I want to thank Ann Japenga for the depth of research in that article.

22. Benjamin Spock, *The Problems of Parents* (Boston: Houghton Mifflin, 1978), pp. 32–38.

23. Benjamin Spock and Michael Rothenberg, *Dr. Spock's Baby and Child Care* (New York: Pocket Books, 1985), pp. 21–33.

24. Ibid., p. 29.

25. Alan Guttmacher, *Pregnancy, Birth and Family Planning* (originally published 1937, revised and updated in 1973 by Viking), p. 272.

26. Boston Women's Health Book Collective, *Our Bodies, Our Selves* (New York: Simon & Schuster, 1984), and Elizabeth Bing and Libby Colman, *Having a Baby After 30* (New York: Bantam, 1980).

27. M. Klaus and J. Kennell, *Maternal-Infant Bonding* (St. Louis: Mosby, 1976). This book has now become a classic on the bonding issue, and has proven very helpful in making obstetricians and pediatricians more aware of mothers' and infants' mutual need for early bonding.

28. Marc Weissbluth, *Crybabies* (New York: Arbor House, 1984) is a convenient paperback that deals thoroughly with the subject of colic in a down-to-earth and sensible fashion.

29. Ibid., p. 168.

30. R. Kumar and K. Robson, "Previous Induced Abortion and Ante-natal Depression in Primiparae: Preliminary Report of a Survey of Mental Health in Pregnancy," *Psychological Medicine* 8 (1978): 711–15.

31. My comments on abortions and their relevance to PPD are my own feelings and should not be imputed to Drs. Kumar and Robson. I would further hate to give the implication that I do not believe in the liberal administration of therapeutic abortions. Given my own feelings about the difficulties of parenting a much-wanted

baby, I would never, ever, try to force women to go through with carrying an unwanted pregnancy to term. I do, however, feel we have become too flippant in our use of the procedure and that most women would be grateful for the opportunity to talk about their confused feelings at such a time.

32. The Women's Psychotherapy Referral Service, 25 Perry St., New York, N.Y. 10014 (212-242-8597), founded in 1972 to provide professional psychotherapists for men and women, comprises over fifty nonsexist therapists in private practice throughout New York City. The service offers to match the client with a therapist who best meets her needs. The initial phone call to the service helps them assess whom to refer you to for an immediate consultation. The initial interview helps the placement process. The New York office may be able to put out-of-town women in search of a good therapist in contact with someone in their area. Judith Klein, who helped with much of the material for this book, was referred to me for this research by the service, as she is known to specialize in women with young children.

33. George Brown and Tirril Harris, *The Social Origins of Depression: A Study of Psychiatric Disorder in Women* (New York: Free Press, 1978).

34. PEP has produced three books that may be of interest to mothers, or to those interested in setting up a parents' group (or mothers' discussion group). They also describe the operation of warm lines and the various outreach services that they provide. The books, published in 1978, are *A Guide for Establishing a Parent Support Program in Your Community, A Leader's Guide for Training Volunteers in Parent Support Services*, and *A Volunteer's Reference Guide*. For details of cost, etc., contact PEP (Postpartum Education for Parents), 5049 University Drive, Santa Barbara, Calif. 93111 (805-964-2009).

35. E. James Anthony and Therese Benedek, eds., *Parenthood: Its Psychology and Psychopathology* (Boston: Little, Brown, 1970). Therese Benedek was a renowned analyst from the Chicago Institute for Psychoanalysis, whose writings on mothering, fathering, the family, and parenthood are well worth reading.

36. For books on parenting today, I recommend the following: Ellen Galinsky, *Between Generations: The Six Stages of Parenthood* (New York: Times Books, 1981), in which she explores our development as parents through the years of a child's life; S. Jaffe and J. Viertel, *Becoming Parents: Preparing for the Emotional Changes of First-Time Parenthood* (New York: Atheneum, 1980); R. Friedland and C. Kort, *The Mother's Book* (Boston: Houghton Mifflin, 1981); Howard Osofsky and Joy Osofsky, *Answers for New Parents* (New York: Walker, 1980); R. Plutzik and M. Laghi, *The*

Private Life of Parents (New York: Dodd, Mead, 1983); R. Wolfson and V. DeLuca, *Couples with Children: What Happens to Your Marriage After Baby Comes Home?* (New York: December, 1981); and J. Procaccini and M. Kiefaber, *Parent BurnOut* (Garden City, N.Y.: Doubleday, 1983).

37. Germaine Greer's book, *Sex and Destiny: The Politics of Human Fertility* (New York: Harper & Row, 1984), has a fascinating argument about abstinence and the pressure we come under in the Western world for continuous sexual activity.

38. "Psychotherapy with Pregnant Women," by Joan Raphael-Leff, in B. Blum, ed., *Psychological Aspects of Pregnancy, Birthing and Bonding* (New York: Human Sciences Press, 1980).

39. Bob Greene, *Good Morning, Merry Sunshine* (New York: Atheneum, 1984): a father's account of his reactions to the first year of his baby's life.

40. There are many interesting fatherhood projects being offered these days: for updated information contact the Family Resources Coalition, 230 North Michigan Avenue, Suite 1625, Chicago, Ill. 60601, for information about *Fatherhood USA,* the first national guide to programs, services, and resources for and about fathers (348 pages, $14.95). Started in 1981, with support from several foundations, the Fatherhood Project of Bank Street College, New York, is a national research and demonstration endeavor designed to encourage wider options for men's involvement in child-rearing. The Project was also preparing another book, *The Future of Fatherhood,* a "state of the nation" report on fatherhood and social change, and two manuals based on its demonstration programs: "How to Start a Father-Child Group" and "How to Start a Baby Care Program for Boys and Girls."

41. Jessie Bernard, *The Future of Marriage* (New York: World, 1972); *The Future of Motherhood* (New York: Dial Press, 1975); *Women, Wives, Mothers: Values and Options* (Chicago: Aldine, 1975).

42. Lois Gilman, *The Adoption Resource Book* (New York: Harper & Row, 1984).

43. For articles on adoption, see V. Bental, "Psychic Mechanisms of the Adoptive Mother in Connection with Adoption," *The Israel Annals of Psychiatry* (1965): 24–34; M. Schechter, "About Adoptive Parents," in E. Anthony and T. Benedek, eds., *Parenthood: Its Psychology and Psychopathology* (Boston: Little, Brown, 1970).

44. J. Selby, L. Calhoun, A. Vogel, and H. E. King, *Psychology and Human Reproduction* (New York: Free Press, 1980). Essays on psychological changes in pregnancy, psychological factors in postpartum reactions, psychological dimensions in controlling con-

ception, and the psychology of the menopause; see particularly pages 87–112 for the section on postpartum reactions.

45. Frederick Melges, "Postpartum psychiatric syndromes," *Psychosomatic Medicine* 30 (1968): 95–108.

46. T. Benedek, "Mothering and Nurturing," in Anthony and Benedek, *Parenthood*, pp. 153–66.

47. H. Blum, "Reconstruction in a Case of Postpartum Depression," *The Psychoanalytic Study of the Child* 33 (1978): 335–61.

48. To comprehend the seriousness of past treatment of women with mental problems, read Gloria Steinem's very moving account of her mother's mental illness in "Ruth's Song (for She Could Not Sing It)," which is a chapter in her book *Outrageous Acts and Everyday Rebellions* (New York: Holt, Rinehart & Winston, 1983), pp. 129–46.

49. C. Tetlow, "Psychosis of Childbearing," *Journal of Mental Science* 101 (1955): 629–39.

50. See Anna Freud, "The Concept of the Rejecting Mother," in Anthony and Benedek, *Parenthood*, pp. 376–86.

51. Gregory Zilboorg, "The clinical issues of postpartum psychopathological reactions," *American Journal of Obstetrics and Gynecology* 73 (1957): 305.

52. Spock and Rothenberg, *Dr. Spock's Baby and Child Care;* see "The Parent's Part," pp. 21–33.

53. Anita Shreve, "The Working Mother as Role Model," New York *Times Magazine,* September 9, 1984, Section 6, pp. 39–45.

54. David Danforth, ed., *Obstetrics and Gynecology* (New York: Harper & Row 1977): this is the major ob/gyn textbook for medical students.

55. Danforth, "Psychiatric Disorder," in *Obstetrics and Gynecology,* pp. 449–50.

56. J. Braverman and J. F. Roux, "Screening for Patients at Risk for Postpartum Depression," *Obstetrics and Gynecology* 52 (1978): 731–36.

57. Shirley Dick, a clinical social worker at the Memorial Hospital, South Bend, Indiana, has developed a presentation on postpartum emotional adjustments that is used in the hospital's maternity ward. She talks to the new mothers about their unrealistic expectations of handling it all and how the superwoman trap can lead to exhaustion and depression. See her article "New Parenthood Initiation," *Mothers Today,* January–February 1983, p. 12.

BIBLIOGRAPHY

BOOKS

BING, E., and COLMAN, L. *Having a Baby After 30*. New York: Bantam, 1980.

Boston Women's Health Book Collective. *The New Our Bodies, Ourselves*. New York: Simon & Schuster, 1984.

Boston Women's Health Book Collective. *Ourselves and Our Children*. New York: Random House, 1978.

BOUKYDIS, Z., ed. *Support for Parents and Infants: A Manual for Parenting Organizations and Professionals*. New York: Methuen, 1987.

BROCKINGTON, I. F., and KUMAR, R., eds. *Motherhood and Mental Illness*. New York: Grune & Stratton, 1982.

BROWN, G., and HARRIS, T. *The Social Origins of Depression: A Study of Psychiatric Disorders in Women*. New York: Free Press, 1978.

BUDOFF, PENNY. *No More Menstrual Cramps and Other Good News*. New York: Putnam, 1980.

CHODOROW, NANCY. *The Reproduction of Mothering: Psychoanalysis and the Sociology of Gender*. Berkeley: University of California Press, 1978.

COLE, K. C. *What Only a Mother Can Tell You About Having a Baby*. Garden City, N.Y.: Doubleday, 1980.

DALTON, KATHARINA. *Depression After Childbirth: How to Recognize and Treat Postnatal Illness*. London: Oxford University Press, 1980.

DANFORTH, DAVID, ed. *Obstetrics and Gynecology.* New York: Harper & Row, 1977.

FRIEDLAND, R., and KORT, C. *The Mother's Book: Shared Experiences.* Boston: Houghton Mifflin, 1981.

GALINSKY, ELLEN. *Between Generations: The Six Stages of Parenthood.* New York: Times Books, 1981.

GREENE, BOB. *Good Morning, Merry Sunshine.* New York: Atheneum, 1984.

HAMILTON, JAMES. *Postpartum Psychiatric Problems.* St. Louis: Mosby, 1962.

INWOOD, D. G., ed. *Recent Advances in Postpartum Psychiatric Disorders.* Washington, D.C.: American Psychiatric Press, 1985.

JAFFE, S., and VIERTEL, J. *Becoming Parents: Preparing for the Emotional Changes of First-Time Parenthood.* New York: Atheneum, 1980.

KITZINGER, SHEILA. *Women as Mothers: How They See Themselves in Different Cultures.* New York: Random House, 1980.

KLAUS, M., and KENNELL, J. *Maternal-Infant Bonding.* St. Louis: Mosby, 1976.

LICHTENDORF, SUSAN. *Eve's Journey: The Physical Experience of Being Female.* New York: Berkley, 1983.

LYNCH-FRASER, DIANE. *The Complete Postpartum Guide.* New York: Harper & Row, 1983.

MARCÉ, LOUIS VICTOR. *Traité de la Folie des Femmes Enceintes, des Nouvelles Accouchées et des Nourrices.* Paris: J. B. Baillière et Fils, 1858.

NOTMAN, M., and NADELSON, C., eds. *The Woman Patient: Medical and Psychological Interfaces.* Vol. 1. *Sexual and Reproductive Aspects of Women's Health Care.* New York: Plenum Press, 1978, pp. 73–86 and 107–22.

OAKLEY, ANN. *Becoming a Mother.* New York: Schocken, 1980.

OAKLEY, ANN. *Women Confined: Towards a Sociology of Childbirth.* New York: Schocken, 1980.

OSOFSKY, HOWARD, and OSOFSKY, JOY. *Answers for New Parents.* New York: Walker, 1980.

PASKOWICZ, PATRICIA. *Absentee Mothers.* New York: Universe, 1982.

PLUTZIK, R., and LAGHI, M. *The Private Life of Parents.* New York: Dodd, Mead, 1983.

PROCACCINI, J., and KIEFABER, M. *Parent Burnout.* Garden City, N.Y.: Doubleday, 1983.

PRUGH, DANE. *The Psychosocial Aspects of Pediatrics.* Philadelphia: Lea & Febiger, 1982.

SANDLER, MERTON. *Mental Illness in Pregnancy and the Puerperium.* London: Oxford University Press, 1978.

SCARF, MAGGIE. *Unfinished Business: Pressure Points in the Lives of Women.* Garden City, N.Y.: Doubleday, 1980.

SELBY, J., CALHOUN, L., VOGEL, A., and KING, H. E. *Psychology and Human Reproduction.* New York: Free Press, 1980.

SHEEHY, GAIL. *Passages.* New York: Bantam, 1977.

SPOCK, BENJAMIN. *The Problems of Parents.* Boston: Houghton Mifflin, 1978.

SPOCK, BENJAMIN, and ROTHENBERG, MICHAEL. *Dr. Spock's Baby and Child Care.* New York: Pocket Books, 1985.

WEISSBLUTH, MARC. *Crybabies: Coping with Colic, What to Do When Baby Won't Stop Crying.* New York: Arbor House, 1984.

WELBURN, VIVIENNE. *Post-Natal Depression.* London: Fontana, 1980.

WINOKUR, GEORGE. *Depression: The Facts.* New York: Oxford University Press, 1981.

WOLFSON, R. M., and DeLUCA, V. *Couples with Children: What Happens to Your Marriage After Baby Comes Home?* New York: Dembner, 1981.

ARTICLES

ASCH, S., and RUBIN, L. "Postpartum Reactions: Some Unrecognized Variations." *American Journal of Psychiatry* 131 (1974): 870–74.

BARGLOW, P. "Postpartum Mental Illness: Detection and Treatment." In Davis, ed., *Gynecology and Obstetrics,* Vol. 1, Part 2, Chap. 57, pp. 1–11 (1977).

BENEDEK, T. "The Psychobiology of Pregnancy," "Motherhood and Nurturing," and "Parenthood and the Life Cycle." In E. Anthony and T. Benedek, eds., *Parenthood: Its Psychology and Psychopathology.* Boston: Little, Brown, 1970, pp. 137–54, 153–66, 185–208.

BENTAL, V. "Psychic Mechanisms of the Adoptive Mother in Connection with Adoption." *The Israel Annals of Psychiatry* 3 (1965): 24–34.

BLUM, B. "Psychological Aspects of Pregnancy, Birthing, and Bonding." In Barbara Blum, ed., *New Directions in Psychotherapy Series,* Vol. 4. New York: Human Sciences Press, 1980.

BLUM, H. "Reconstruction in a Case of Postpartum Depression." *The Psychoanalytic Study of the Child* 33 (1978): 335–61.

BRAVERMAN, J., and ROUX, J. F. "Screening for Patients at Risk for Postpartum Depression." *Obstetrics and Gynecology* 52 (1978): 731–36.

COGAN, R., ed. "Postpartum Depression," *ICEA Review,* 4 (August 1980): 1–8; from International Childbirth Association, Inc., P.O.

Box 20048, Minneapolis, Minn. 55420 (available at a cost of $1.50 per back issue, plus $1 postage and handling).

CORMAN, E. "Depression, Manic-Depressive Illness, and Biological Rhythms." NIMH publication, Science Reports 1, (ADM) 79-889, 1982.

DANIELS, R., and LESSOW, H. "Severe Postpartum Reactions." *Psychosomatics* 5 (1964): 21–26.

FREUD, ANNA. "The Concept of the Rejecting Mother." In E. J. Anthony and T. Benedek, eds., *Parenthood: Its Psychology and Psychopathology.* Boston: Little, Brown, 1970, pp. 376–86.

GARVEY, M., and TOLLEFSON, G. "Postpartum Depression." *Journal of Reproductive Medicine* 39 (February 1984): 113–16.

GORDON, R., KAPOSTINS, E., and GORDON, K. "Factors in Postpartum Emotional Adjustment." *Obstetrics and Gynecology* 25 (1965): 158–66.

HAMILTON, JAMES A. "Puerperal Psychoses." In Davis, ed., *Gynecology and Obstetrics*, Vol. 2, Part 2, Chap. 24n., pp. 1–11 (1970).

HANDFORD, P. "Postpartum Depression: What Is It, What Helps." *Canadian Nurse,* 81: 30–33.

HONIKMAN, J. "How to Start a Parents' Organization." In Boukydis, Z., ed., *Support for Parents and Infants: A Manual for Parenting Organizations and Professionals.* New York: Methuen, 1987.

KUMAR, R., and ROBSON, K. "Previous Induced Abortion and Antenatal Depression in Primiparae: Preliminary Report of a Survey of Mental Health in Pregnancy." *Psychological Medicine* 8 (1978): 711–15.

McKAY, S., ed. "Maternal Stress and Pregnancy Outcome." *ICEA Review* 4 (April 1980): 1–8.

MELGES, F. "Postpartum Psychiatric Syndromes." *Psychosomatic Medicine* 30 (1968): 95–108.

NOTT, P. N., FRANKLIN, M., ARMITAGE, C., and GELDER, M. G. "Hormonal Changes and Mood in the Puerperium." *British Journal of Psychiatry* 128 (1976): 379–83.

PAYKEL, E. S., EMMS, E., FLETCHER, J., and RASSABY, E. S. "Life Events and Social Support in Puerperal Depression." *British Journal of Psychiatry* 136 (1980): 339–46.

RAPHAEL-LEFF, JOAN. "Psychotherapy with Pregnant Women." In B. Blum, ed., *Psychological Aspects of Pregnancy, Birthing and Bonding.* New York: Human Sciences Press, 1980.

ROSENWALD, G., and STONEHILL, M. "Early and Late Postpartum Illness." *Psychosomatic Medicine* 34 (1972): 129–38.

ROTH, N. "The Mental Content of Puerperal Psychoses." *American Journal of Psychotherapy* 29 (1975): 204–11.

SCHECHTER, M. "About Adoptive Parents." In E. J. Anthony and T. Benedek, eds., *Parenthood: Its Psychology and Psychopathology.* Boston: Little, Brown, 1970.

SHREVE, ANITA. "The Working Mother as Role Model." New York *Times Magazine,* September 9, 1984, Section 6, pp. 39–45.

TETLOW, C. "Psychosis of Childbearing." *Journal of Mental Science* 101 (1955): 629–39.

TOWNE, R., and AFTERMAN, J. "Psychosis in Males Related to Parenthood." *Bulletin of the Menninger Foundation* 19 (1954): 19–26.

TREADWAY, R., KANE, F., JARRAHI-ZADEH, A., and LIPTON, M. "A Psychoendocrine Study of Pregnancy and the Puerperium." *American Journal of Psychiatry* 125 (1968–69): 1380–86.

WAINWRIGHT, W. "Fatherhood as a Precipitant of Mental Illness." *American Journal of Psychiatry* 123 (1966): 4044.

YALOM, I., LUNDE, D., MOOS, R., and HAMBURG, D. "Postpartum Blues Syndrome." *Archives of General Psychiatry* 18 (1968): 16–27.

ZILBOORG, GREGORY. "Clinical Issues of Postpartum Psychopathological Reactions." *American Journal of Obstetrics and Gynecology* 73 (1957): 305.

INDEX

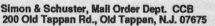